THE ECONOMIC AND SOCIAL HISTORY OF AN ENGLISH VILLAGE

THE VILLAGE POND

A photograph

THE ECONOMIC AND SOCIAL HISTORY OF AN ENGLISH VILLAGE

(CRAWLEY, HAMPSHIRE)

A.D. 909–1928

BY

NORMAN SCOTT BRIEN GRAS

STRAUS PROFESSOR OF BUSINESS HISTORY,
HARVARD UNIVERSITY

AND

ETHEL CULBERT GRAS

NEW YORK / RUSSELL & RUSSELL

HARVARD ECONOMIC STUDIES

PUBLISHED UNDER THE DIRECTION OF
THE DEPARTMENT OF ECONOMICS

VOL. XXXIV

To

CHARLES HOMER HASKINS

Scholar and Teacher

REISSUED, 1969, BY RUSSELL & RUSSELL
A DIVISION OF ATHENEUM PUBLISHERS, INC.
BY ARRANGEMENT WITH HARVARD UNIVERSITY PRESS
L. C. CATALOG CARD NO: 68-27061
PRINTED IN THE UNITED STATES OF AMERICA

PREFACE

Because of the fact that all thought and study, as it seems to us, arise from experience, it is appropriate to present the personal background of the writing of this *History*. The very beginning of the work goes back to an effort to obtain from detailed study an intimate picture of agricultural methods in a single medieval village. Later the study was pushed both backward and forward in answer to a growing desire to get the outline of the whole story of the past and present of a single community, as far as this could be unearthed. Current historical methods are largely comparative and selective, in which scholars pick and choose evidence and facts in support of generalizations which are often formed without an adequate basis of reality. It is out of a high regard for time and place that we have undertaken this detailed investigation, only part of which, of course, appears in this book. We had hoped that the result would lead to a mastery of facts and situations, which we hasten to assert, however, has not been realized. Indeed, our village has proved to be a microcosm of the great world of men and affairs, in no way simple because small, nor yet obvious because rural.

Crawley was chosen for the purpose in hand because it possessed, or seemed to possess, certain characteristics. It is in an older and long settled part of England and therefore has a long history, as a knowledge of the records of the lords of Crawley (bishops of Winchester) clearly indicated. It is located near enough to a town (the City of Winchester) to have come very early under urban influence. Moreover, it appeared, at least at first, to present a case of organic simplicity. Originally an impersonal choice, the little village has become an object of sympathetic regard. After studying its records for several years, we visited it in person and found it fair.

The presentation is chiefly documentary, because we hold that in the long run it is more important to give the evidence for views than to urge the views themselves. Documentary evidence is the very source of historical knowledge which each person may use according as changing interests dictate and as prevailing interpretations suggest. Much of the rewriting of history, so costly in labor and goods, is necessitated by the historian's insistence upon covering up his own trail. We have felt, to be sure, that, in some cases at least, we were also calling the attention of students to material of general value.

In the editing of the documents many difficulties have been encountered. Most of these have been solved (as we hope) by means of comparison of one manuscript with another. Almost everywhere preference has been given to medieval Latin, as against classical Latin, forms. We have generally used the nominative absolute in place of the ablative absolute. The gerund in the ablative is found frequently instead of the present participle. The ablative of time and the dative of place (to which) occur occasionally. Marginal notes have generally been omitted, except where they provide additional information. Capitals in the middle of a word have been ignored. We have italicized letters supplied in the extension of abbreviated words; brackets have been used only when no other manuscript gave the key to the abbreviation. The dating is in the new style.

What could be done by way of a documentary study and presentation very definitely waits upon the discovery of the documents themselves. What has been used, is found in the body of the book. Other kinds of records were sought in vain. We could find no thirteenth- or fourteenth-century survey. No inventory or detailed valuation of Crawley property, sequestered in the Commonwealth period, has yet come to light. Only part of the enclosure award has been discovered. No enclosure map was found, though several of a slightly later date, preserved at Crawley Court, were examined, and some of them studied. It was a great disappointment to fail to unearth the accounts of the yeoman farmers. No diaries setting forth village life could be traced, though there are at least two that are detailed personal revelations.

Besides documentary shortcomings, we have felt the lack of

that intimate knowledge and subtle insight that come only from long residence. Visits in the year 1924–25 were helpful. And correspondence has proved the source of both suggestion and critical revision. The friendly encouragement of the owner, Colonel George Philippi, of the Crawley Court estate, made possible inquiries and researches both at the Court and in the village. Mr. J. O. Robertson, the agent of the Crawley Court estate, Mr. F. W. Pledge, resident tutor and author of an excellent general history of the village, and Professor Thomas Wibberley, agricultural expert and farm manager, were of invaluable assistance. The way in which they gave of their time and knowledge is a good example of the generosity of the British people. Miss Lilian J. Redstone spent some time in Crawley, the village of her ancestors, seeking information and copying certain documents not before adequately studied. To Miss C. M. Calthrop and Miss M. K. Dale we are also indebted for copying manuscripts in various archives. To officials in the Public Record Office and the British Museum, and particularly of the Ecclesiastical Commission, we owe much for courteous and prolonged assistance. Miss A. E. Levett of King's College, London, has been generous in pointing out one valuable manuscript source and in allowing us to draw upon her intimate knowledge of the Winchester manors.

To Dean Guy Stanton Ford, of the University of Minnesota, we are indebted for encouragement and to the University of Minnesota for financial assistance in rotographing some hundreds of records which could not be adequately studied within a year's residence in England. To Mrs. H. P. Mudgett, of the University of Minnesota, we also owe a great deal for an early critical examination of reeves' accounts, particularly with reference to field arrangements. In deciphering and translating parts of the documents Professor Frederick Klaeber and Professor Joseph B. Pike were most helpful. In England both Dr. Hubert Hall and Sir William Beveridge placed at our disposal much of the critical knowledge that they possess of the records we were studying. By means of aid from the Milton Fund of Harvard University we were able to enlist assistance in verifying texts and making additional searches not otherwise possible.

PREFACE

Professor Edwin F. Gay has read the general introduction and the special introductions to the documents themselves. His aid in the later stages of the work, indeed, has been indispensable, especially when it became clear that the study would be documentary. Dr. Henrietta Larson, of the Harvard School of Business, has read critically the manuscript of the general introduction. In facilitating the publication of this book, Professor F. W. Taussig has once again been a friendly patron of economic historical work. In the final stages of putting this book through the press we have had invaluable philological help from Professor Leo Wiener and splendid coöperation on the part of the Harvard University Press.

To Professor Charles H. Haskins, to whom this volume is dedicated, the work owes much that goes back to general study and documentary interpretation begun years ago.

N. S. B. G.
E. C. G.

November, 1928

CONTENTS

PART I

GENERAL INTRODUCTION

PART II

DOCUMENTS AND STATISTICS

CONTENTS

ILLUSTRATIONS

PART I

GENERAL INTRODUCTION

GENERAL INTRODUCTION

§ 1. *Form and Topography of Crawley.* There are six aspects to Crawley's existence as a community. It was first and foremost a group, or village, of cultivators seeking a living from the woods and fields round about. As such, it probably experienced several radical changes, but these occurred in early times. Secondly, it was a manor belonging to the bishopric of Winchester, and as a manor it included the village, village lands, and outlying estates. Thirdly, it was an ecclesiastical parish with a subordinate chapelry at Hunton located in an adjoining parish. Fourthly, it was the senior partner in a public tithing which also included Hunton. Fifthly, it was a private tithing and hundred for legal purposes. And sixthly, in modern times it is a civil and rural parish.

As a village group, Crawley may be classified as nucleated. As we know it, in later times at least, and there is no reason to suspect any change since the early thirteenth century, Crawley village was a cluster of homesteads, or messuages and crofts, as they were called, located on both sides of the street. Or we may put it another way: Crawley was a short winding street of houses and outbuildings running up the hill from the pond to the church. The church may have been more important for the next world, but the pond was more necessary for this life. At this small mere, animals with four legs and with two could get the most precious thing in Crawley — water.

Meitzen associated the form of village with racial or national considerations. Following this explanation we should have to put Crawley down as a hybrid. It is a fairly compact central group of farmsteads, and as such might be Saxon; but it is also a (short) street village, and as a street village might be Celtic. But recent investigations have shown that, generally speaking, topographical conditions constitute a more likely explanation of the form of villages. It is probably the scarcity of water [1] in a chalk-down

[1] See below, § 12, p. 40; § 38, p. 140.

country that explains why the houses were close together rather than strung out along miles of roadway. Either the village pond or the later deep wells, or both combined, were enough to keep the people together, though of course other forces were also at work, such as mutual defence in earliest times and coöperative agriculture prevailing down through the Middle Ages.

There was no river and no considerable stream in Crawley. The subsoil is a deep chalk into which water sinks as into a bottomless pit. In time of great rain — and there is a lot of it in Hampshire — the chalk helps the cultivator; but in seasons of drought, only the deity can be of assistance. The ground becomes hard and unworkable, and there is no water for stock or grain. But at the same time there are no marshes or sloughs in Crawley, no nasty sinks or mired lanes.

Almost the whole of the land is made up of undulating hills providing a moderate form of beauty but no splendor or magnificence. The slopes are not difficult to cultivate, but they do tend to carry off the surface soil to the valleys, leaving thin or barren spots on the crests of the hills. It is from the first field or clearance made in the woods, that Crawley got its name. It is the clearance, or lea, of the crows.

Nature had not put a river through Crawley and man never constructed a main highway through it. But nearby a Roman road had been driven straight from Winchester to Andover, providing an important boundary line for the parish. The other boundaries were very irregular. And other important roads in the district never touched Crawley. The road from Winchester to Salisbury avoided the village, and the later railroads ignored it. While there were roads leading to similar villages on all sides of it, there was freedom from through traffic. And yet Winchester was less than five miles away, to the southeast; and roads leading to all parts of England were within easy walking or riding distance.

§ 2. *Prehistoric Crawley.* There is no strong or conclusive evidence that paleolithic, neolithic, or bronze-age peoples had ever occupied the area of Crawley. Nor, on the contrary, is there any indication that they had not been on the ground. Whether the

TABLE SHOWING LOCAL ADMINISTRATIVE UNITS[1]

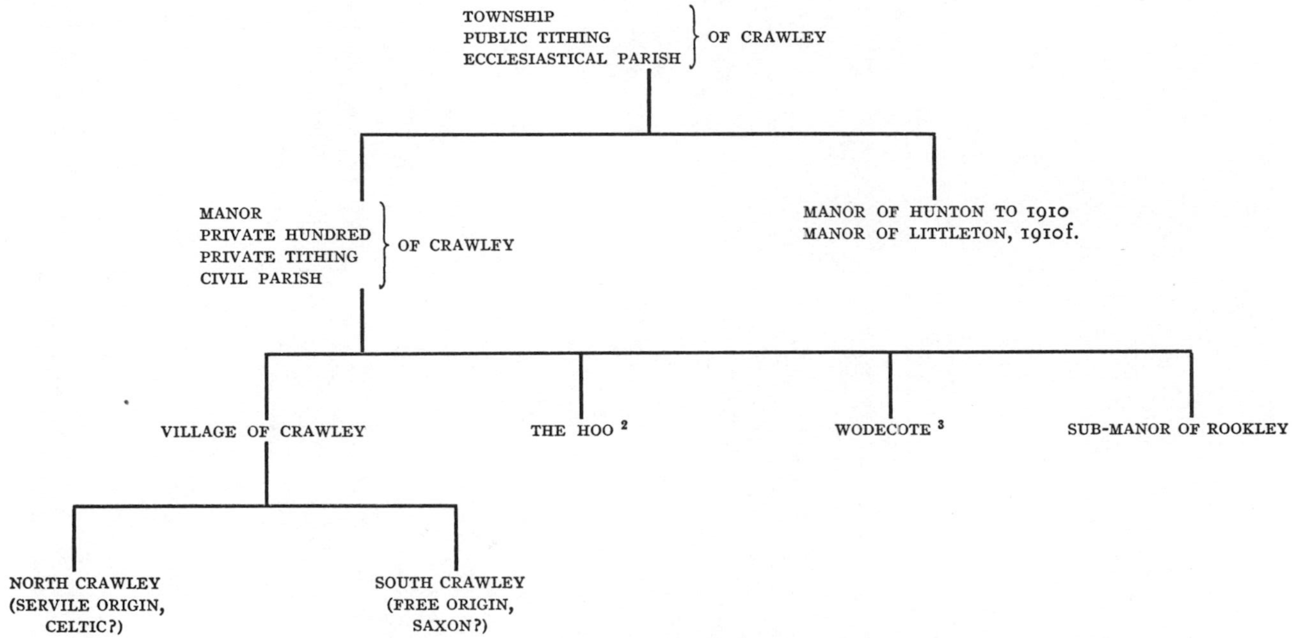

[1] This table is analytic, not chronological.

[2] Hoo close, probably a very old freehold in Crawley.

[3] The modern Northwood Park.

AËRIAL PHOTOGRAPH OF POSSIBLE CELTIC FIELDS

semi-circular mound near the Roman road is Celtic or pre-Celtic, we have no means of deciding.

There are three kinds of evidence for a Celtic, or at least a pre-Saxon, settlement, which are worthy of consideration. First, there are the lynchets, or terraces, which are apparently depicted on the aërial photographs taken by Captain O. G. S. Crawford.[1] These appear to be rectilinear plots more nearly square than the long Saxon strips. In the photographs they seem to be bounded by parallel light and dark lines, the light indicating the cutting into the chalk subsoil and the dark the piling up of the surface humus. On the sloping ground, a terrace could be formed only by eating into the bank and levelling off as far along as the terrace below would admit. The small strips of mountainous countries in widely scattered parts of the world indicate an immensely laborious process of levelling off by hand work, in some cases, as in Japan, for irrigated rice cultivation and in others, as in central and southern France, for non-irrigated cultivation. Of these terraces on the chalk downs of southern England various explanations have been given. It has been surmised that they were caused by the action of the waves; but a slight examination of the configuration of the land disproves this. It has been thought that they were prehistoric cattle pens; but they were too numerous and, moreover, there could have been no great need for level ground for such a purpose. A more challenging explanation is that they were caused by the prolonged use of the Celtic plow, which is said to have turned the furrow only one way, and which was carried back idle to the end of the field to begin all over again. In this case the assumption must be that the plowing was not up and down hill but around the hill. Such an assumption is hardly justified by what we know of the plowing done by the descendants of the Celts elsewhere, and yet there is probably no real evidence against this view. Professor E. F. Gay has suggested that the levelling off came about, not through the plowing but through the breaking of the clods after plowing. These clods would be thrown about in all

[1] See the accompanying Aërial Photograph of Possible Celtic Fields, following this page; see also O. G. S. Crawford, *Air Survey and Archæology*, H. M. Stationery Office (Southampton, 1924), pp. 3–11.

directions, and in the course of time would form a level terrace. And he suggests that the almost square shape of the plots may be due to cross plowing. Of course in a chalk country, with only a shallow surface humus, the terracing may have been done primarily to prevent the washing of the soil into the valleys. To Captain Crawford, scholars should be grateful for having applied to English agrarian history the method of aërial photography already used on the deserts of Egypt to disclose the location of buried tombs. It is interesting to note that the parish of Crawley was completely photographed and was apparently about the first to be photographed from the air in connection with this particular work.

The second kind of evidence in favor of a Celtic settlement in Crawley is to be found in the names of fields, or, more accurately, of furlongs. Most of these names are obviously Saxon, but there may be a few that are adaptations of older Celtic names. Combefurlong seems to be a case in point, combe probably being a form of the Celtic cwm, a hollow between hills.[1] Before much could be done along such lines of explanation, however, an intensive study of the local topography would have to be made to see whether the term in question would fit in more closely with a possible Celtic or a possible Saxon word.

The third kind of evidence is the survival in Crawley, as in Hampshire generally, of a darker type of physique than the Saxon.[2] Whether this would be a Celtic or a pre-Celtic strain is not clear. And, of course, this kind of evidence is very difficult to handle in any but a highly speculative fashion, at least until physical anthropologists have paved a smoother way for us.

§ 3. *Saxon Manorialization.* We can be fairly certain about three happenings in Crawley's history during the Anglo-Saxon period. Crawley was not granted by the king before A.D. 643.[3] It had been granted, however, before 909, probably long before that date, when its ownership by the bishop of Winchester was con-

[1] See T. W. Shore, *A History of Hampshire including the Isle of Wight* (1892), p. 35.

[2] Cf. W. H. Hudson, *Hampshire Days* (1923), pp. 236–237.

[3] See below, §§ 1, pp. 167 ff.

firmed.[1] And thirdly, it had been manorialized long before 1086, when the Domesday inquiry was made.[2]

The site of Crawley was occupied by Celts until about 519, when the Saxon conquest of the district took place. Thereafter Crawley was probably a free Saxon village, at least that part of Crawley later identified with South Crawley, the tenants of which had very favorable terms of occupancy in the thirteenth century.

Crawley became a Church manor very early in its history. In the year 643 a wide circuit around the City of Winchester was granted by the king to the bishop of the West Saxons. This circuit came right up to Crawley, but in the Crawley segment it had very irregular boundaries. There stood an obvious thing to do — to include Crawley in the grant to the bishopric. Just why the line had not been drawn to include Crawley in 643 is an interesting speculation. Certainly it was a well marked off estate at that time, the boundaries being about as numerous and irregular as could well be imagined. At any rate the grant took place some time between 643 and 909, probably nearer the former date. Doubtless there would have been a suitable occasion for the grant when the bishop of the West Saxons moved his see from Dorchester to Winchester about 676.

We are not only uncertain about the exact date of the grant but also about the precise meaning of it. Just what did the king mean to bestow upon the bishop? Just what did the bishop expect to obtain? It is a plausible inference that the bishop requested from Crawley timbers for his building and swine and grain for his household use. Whether it was the sweet compulsion of religious fear or the harsher arm of the secular power that made the people of Crawley bow to the new conditions, is quite unknown. Probably the process of begging and coercion went on gradually until something like a regular practice of yearly donations or tribute ensued. The old village assembly, if such had indeed existed in any formal fashion, became a regular court for deciding questions of cultivation and of justice. Such a village moot would mean convenience to the suitors and income to the lord bishop. Crime or

[1] See below, §§ 3, pp. 177 ff.
[2] See below, §§ 4, pp. 183 ff.

any breach of custom would henceforth be unprofitable to the inhabitants, profitable to the lord.

So far there is no manor in sight, but simply a lordship created by the king of the West Saxons in favor of the local bishop. This lordship was the price paid for religion. Not even Roman missionaries nor their Saxon novices could live without material aid. The administrative degredation of the village was a sacrifice made to facilitate the diffusion of Roman culture, the function of which was to soften the rudeness of Teutonic paganism.

Just how the lordship with its system of tribute became the manor with its system of customary services is a matter of surmise in Crawley as elsewhere. It is a plausible inference, however, that the bishop became dissatisfied with the uncertainty of his tribute as crops failed or animals died of disease. It was at least worth the trial to require services as more dependable than crops and stock under an ineffective system of agriculture. These services could be utilized by putting them to work on a special piece of ground set aside for the purpose in the village itself. In the case of the neighboring Chilcomb, in 909, this was spoken of as land which was plowed for the bishop.[1] The home farm, the nucleus of the lord's demesne, would be managed by the village reeve to whom could be given ideas and orders as to the best methods of getting results. In Crawley the reeve was the agricultural manager down to the early fifteenth century.[2]

But at this point we have to take into account a situation that is not simple and not certain. In the later history of Crawley there was a marked duality[3] which seems to have had its counterpart in the Anglo-Saxon period.[4] In short, South Crawley seems to have been made up originally of freemen while North Crawley appears to have been unfree. It is a likely surmise that North Crawley was an old Celtic village or hamlet which was amalgamated with the chief Saxon free nucleus. And at what more likely time could this have taken place than at manorialization, at the time when

[1] See below, §§ 2, p. 172. Of course it must remain a matter of uncertainty whether this particular passage occurred in the charter as originally granted.

[2] See below, § 8, pp. 22 ff.; § 23, pp. 80 ff.

[3] See below, § 13, pp. 47 ff.

[4] See below, §§ 3, pp. 177 ff.

labor services were in great demand? The North Crawley group of unfree people were given the menial tasks and week-work, while the South Crawley group of freemen were asked to do the more honorable work of helping with harvesting and carting and riding on errands.[1] At any rate, when the Village of Crawley came to possess a demesne with a home farm worked by the people of the village, it had become the Manor of Crawley, at least on the economic side.

§ 4. *The Group of Manors.* The manorial group is quite different from the group of manors. The manorial group is the single manor made up of a group of persons, classes, and officials held together as a social unit. The group of manors, on the other hand, is an aggregation of such units to form a larger whole. In the case of the group of manors belonging to the bishop of Winchester there was an ever increasing number of units from the seventh to the fourteenth century. The *Annales Monasterii de Wintonia* list the early acquisition of estates with great fullness but without completeness, omitting, for instance, Crawley.

ESTATES OF THE BISHOP OF WINCHESTER

Date	Approximate Number
About 643	12 [1]
About 984	34 [1]
About 1086	54 [2]
About 1208	42 [3]
About 1335	61 [4]
About 1503	79 [5]
About 1869	— [6]

[1] J. M. Kemble, *Codex Diplomaticus*, vol. III (1845), p. 203.
[2] Of these, 24 were held by the bishop for his own use and 30 by the bishop as abbot of St. Swithun's. Clearly the figure 54 is too large. See W. Benham, *Winchester*, Diocesan Histories (1884), p. 248.
[3] See Hubert Hall, *Pipe Roll of the Bishopric of Winchester, 1208–1209* (1903), pp. xliv, 66, 67.
[4] See MS., P. R. O., Ecclesiastical Commission, Various, 159347.
[5] MS., Millbank, Ecclesiastical Commission, 155648. This large number arises from a separation of some old items into several smaller ones, e. g., Meon Church becomes Meon Church, parsonage, and fair.
[6] The Ecclesiastical Commissioners refuse to divulge the results of their survey on taking over the manors in 1869.

These estates were of various kinds — manors, boroughs, farms, fairs, mills, and jurisdictions. Manors, however, were the

[1] See below, §§ 4, pp. 183 ff.; §§ 11, pp. 229 ff.

most numerous and the most typical. The group extended from the borough of Taunton in Somerset to the manor of Southwark in Surrey. Although some manors slipped in and out of the group without indicating how or why, still there was but little change through the centuries except for growth and accretion. Perhaps those that left the group can be accounted for in one of three ways. Some, such as Hunton, were sold outright and permanently. Some were alienated to the king, or other powerful layman. And some were apparently exchanged with the Church of St. Swithun's, that is, with the Cathedral organization.

Groups of manors were common in the Middle Ages. The king had an enormous group. Lay lords, archbishops, and bishops had aggregations which varied greatly in size and importance. Conventual bodies of both men and women obtained their supplies from similar groups of manors. The Cathedral Church of St. Swithun at Winchester had its prior and Benedictine monks [1] up to 1539, whose needs were met by a group of manors very much like that belonging to the bishop of Winchester. The latter was, of course, but a single person, but he had a retinue of servants and officials and a number of friends and guests who were in constant need of assistance. And often he was himself a great national official, most commonly treasurer or chancellor.

To meet the household needs of the episcopal organization, manorial products were sent in great number and variety, whether the bishop was living at the palace in Winchester or in Farnham. But more and more did money become a consideration, the products being sold at the most convenient market [2] and returns sent to the bishop's treasury in the palace of Wolvesey in Winchester, the ruins of which are still eloquent of earlier massiveness and strength. There, in Winchester, lived the seneschal who made the round twice a year, holding the lord's court.[3]

In so far as the group of manors had a central organization, it was clearly a big business, buying manufactured wares, wines, spices, and the like and selling such agricultural products as wool,

[1] Except for the period 868–963, when the monks were replaced by secular canons.

[2] See below, § 7, pp. 18 ff.

[3] For further account of the bishop's officials, see below, § 8, pp. 22 ff.

hides, and grain. The chief products that Crawley sent to Wolvesey for sale were grain and wool.[1] But Crawley had other connections and relations within the episcopal group of manors, particularly with the manor of Mardon, about as far to the southwest of Winchester as Crawley was to the northwest. To Mardon and other manors within the group, Crawley sent sheep[2] and grain[3] and from them it received sheep,[4] rams,[5] and grain.[6]

From time immemorial, certainly by 909,[7] Crawley had possessed a sub-manor called Hunton which was maintained as such until sold in or before the thirteenth century.[8] Just what economic connection there had been between the two can only be surmised. It is a plausible guess that to Hunton, situated on a tributary of the River Test, were driven the sheep of Crawley in years of dearth. There were deep wells in Crawley in the thirteenth century, however, and the possession of these may have suggested the sale of Hunton.

Crawley was operated in the later Middle Ages as a small unit within a larger unit. From the standpoint of organization we have only admiration for the system that was evolved. And in this connection we cannot help alluding to the commercial and financial organizations of Italian mercantile families such as the Bardi, Peruzzi, and Medici, or of the later German Welsers, Baumgartners, and Fuggers. Why did not large business organizations become more common in the Middle Ages? The chief reason was the local character of the market, though the market might have been broadened in time, was, in fact, gradually broadened. Another factor was the lack of such an organization as the joint-stock company which entered the field of commerce only in the sixteenth century. A further drawback was the ecclesiastical prohibition of

[1] See below, §§ 20, pp. 338–372, 420–434.
[2] See below, §§ 20, pp. 399, 405, 406.
[3] See below, §§ 5, p. 190; §§ 6, p. 198.
[4] See below, §§ 5, p. 191; §§ 20, pp. 404, 414.
[5] MS., P. R. O., Ecclesiastical Commission, Various, 159277 (1220–21). Rams (40) from Fareham.
[6] See below, §§ 5, p. 190; §§ 12, p. 243; §§ 14, p. 261.
[7] See below, §§ 3, pp. 177 ff.
[8] *Victoria History of the Counties of England, Hampshire and the Isle of Wight*, vol. III (1908), p. 409.

usury, or loaning at what we call interest. Without the chance of borrowing, individual traders could not increase their business, and, without the chance of loaning, individual persons would not save much money. The Church set an example for big business in its manorial organizations, as also, we may add, in its monastic workshops; but it made effective imitation difficult because of its stand on the subject of usury. As has been seen, however, this was not the sole factor in the situation.

§ 5. *Crawley at its Height as a Manor.* Both the manorial group and the group of manors had grown up gradually, the development of the former apparently leading the way. Now comes the question as to when we are to consider the manor at its height. The answer depends in part upon our conception of the essentials of the manor.

A manor was a lordship having a demesne worked by laborers who also possessed holdings of their own. Before the demesne came into existence, there was only a lordship. After the demesne had been leased to a tenant farmer, we may say, only a semi-manorial system survived. But just now we raise the question of the time and circumstances of the highest point of demesne exploitation by unfree labor.

So far as the existing records go the height of the manor was about 1208–1226, or possibly stretching back somewhat into the twelfth century. During that period we find the number of sheep kept by the lord and the area of the arable land which he cultivated at its height.[1] This occurred at a time when there was little or no commutation of labor. Quantitatively, manorial demesne exploitation was at its height. Of course, it is obvious that we are drawing the lines a little too closely about a complicated social organization. But otherwise there can be no answer to so precise a question as the one we have put.

Not only was the gross exploitation of land and labor at its height but the net results were low, not (possibly) when compared with what had gone before but when compared with what came later. About the sheep we cannot say because of the impossibility

[1] See below, § 9, p. 28.

of measurement. But the average net yield of wheat per acre was clearly less than at any time in the history of the demesne for which we have clear evidence. With the methods of cultivation in use and with a reeve who was one of themselves, the laborers (tenants) could probably do no better.

On the side of its relation to the group of manors, we may say that Crawley had reached its height probably a little later in the thirteenth century, when the interdependence of the bishop's manors was slightly greater than it had been before. Had this interdependence proceeded much farther, there would have come into play forces that would have undermined the manor as a unit. The carrying of grain and the driving of sheep from manor to manor would have almost as much effect upon the tenants as the selling of produce in the town market. There was a limit to the development of the manor, as to all social institutions. It is axiomatic that no sooner do institutions reach their height than they begin to decline. Or we may use the metaphor of mountain climbing. There comes a time, at the top, when progress leads downward. It is progress to go down the mountain, but the height of the mountain has been reached. Society goes on but the individual institution has been passed, left behind.

AVERAGE NET YIELD PER ACRE — HOME FARM

(in qrs. of 8 bushels)

Period	Wheat	Spring Barley	Oats	All 3 grains
1208–1226	.473	.956	.546	.658
1231–1314	.585	.849	.487	.640
1315–1383	.704	1.073	.712	.830
1384–1448	.608	1.335	1.159	1.034

§ 6. *Manorial Accounting.* When or where manorial accounts began, is difficult to determine. The earliest account (1208–09) that we have seen is the one printed below.[1] There can be no doubt that accounts were regularly kept for the manors of the bishopric of Winchester in the twelfth century. Beyond that we

[1] See below, §§ 5, pp. 186 ff.

cannot go. It is a likely surmise that these accounts originated in the practices of the Church on the Continent and from there spread both to England and to secular estates. Whether they arose afresh to meet the needs of the Church or were modelled upon more ancient Roman accounts is not known.

The manorial account, as exemplified by the documents here printed, combined a statement of cash receipts and cash disbursements with a physical statistical inventory of stock, grain, products, and occasionally, implements, and utensils. It was put together once a year in October or November for the previous agricultural year, that is, for the period from Michaelmas to Michaelmas. Just how it was compiled we are not told. Probably the reeve, using such tallies, writs, and parts of account as he possessed, some of the last named being obtained from the shepherd, had the rector or other person write out a summary statement of the whole. Then this statement would be checked up by the auditor. It would then be presented to the lord's treasury at Wolvesey, for acceptance, where the bailiff's statement of his own expenses and the seneschal's, along with the receipts from the courts, would be put together with the reeve's account to make a single yearly statement for the Manor of Crawley.

Obviously this made a complicated statement of items of divers kinds. But it was a document of great importance both to the parties concerned and to the student of economic and social history. It is to be studied along with the charter, the survey, the custumal, and the court roll. In its statement of specific happenings it resembles the court roll rather than the others.

Following are some of the most important terms occurring in the manorial accounts: [1]

Reddere compotum de — to render account for
Respondere de — to account for
Liberatio — yield, render, or payment of something due to somebody (money to lord, grain to special workers)
Redditus assisus (gabulum assisum) — fixed rent
Acquietancia — acquittance, or allowance, or credit for a money due, when some special service has been performed in lieu of the money

[1] For other terms, see the Latin text below, §§ 5, pp. 188–192, and its translation, pp. 192–195.

Defectus — default or defect in rent arising through the lack of a tenant or the withdrawal of the tenement
Exitus — yield or income from things or privileges sold
Finis — payment made in the courts on the settlement of an issue
Amerciamentum — penalty for the infraction of a custom or law
Perquisitum — income from amercements
Allocatio — money allowance to some official, either through a writ or without one
Disallocatio — disallowance
Onerare — to charge or enter against
Disonerare — to discharge
Onerare super compotum — 'to enter on account' (of petty items not separately listed) [1]
Respondere cum onere — to answer for with a charge. The reeve answered for so much more grain than was produced.
Vendere super compotum — 'to sell on account.' The reeve was sometimes charged with so much grain, lactage, etc., whether actually produced (or received) by him or not. That is, something not actually received was charged to him. Sales may have been (*a*) made to the reeve, that is, charged to him whether actually made or not. They may have been entered on the back of the account as originally handed in by the reeve and bailiff. Also they may have been (*b*) too small to be separately listed, or (*c*) made after the general account had been closed.
Ut respond*et* se*paratim* [? se*men*] iiii^to — as he [the reeve] answers separately (?) for a fourth. The reeve was held responsible for a crop four times the seed planted. The amount varied from one and a half to five or six. See below, §§25, p. 481.
Vendere super dorsum — same as vendere super compotum (?)

There is not a little about the Crawley accounts that we would like to hasten to admit we are not sure about, for instance, the expression ut r' se iiij^to listed above. Several guesses are possible, but none seem to be entirely satisfactory. Only a study of occurrences in many other accounts than those of Crawley would probably give the solution. Another difficulty, of larger import, but possibly not unconnected, is the relation of the 'yield' to the other items pertaining to the same commodity, as set forth in our tables below.[2] We take it that the yield of any particular account was actually the product of the previous year, which was threshed only in the year of the account by the slow process of hand flailing.

In the course of the thirteenth and fourteenth centuries we can

[1] See below, §§ 15, p. 277; §§ 16, p. 285. Cf. §§ 12, p. 247, n. 2.
[2] See below, §§ 20, pp. 338 ff.

observe minor changes in the accounts. The practice developed of setting down in great detail the sowing of the different grains, even the names of the furlongs being indicated.[1] This particular change may have been due to certain rearrangements of holdings of which we know all too little. There also developed gradually a more detailed analysis of items, particularly expenses,[2] which may have been due to a desire to check up the work of the reeve. And we find the practice coming into being of selling on account (vendicio super compotum).[3] This does not seem to mean sale on credit, but sale that is recorded on the account, or on the back of the account (compotus super dorsum), as it is called later.[4] It would seem that this was the record of late sales put in separately after the main accounts had been closed. In some statements [5] these items on account were separately summarized. In the year 1264–65 a new accounting practice was followed, as noted in the statistical tables below.[6] The grain which had formerly been put down as a total yield became the 'total yield of the grange' or 'of the grange in the granary,' while the grain (oats, etc.) fed in the sheaf or unthreshed was separately entered. That is, there was apparently adopted a stricter method of reckoning than had hitherto been practised.

Sale on credit was apparently rare. One case of it seems to have occurred in 1409–10, when 10 quarters of wheat were sold at 10s. a quarter, whilst other amounts went at 8s. and 8s. 8d. Eight quarters were sold as a loan (per mutuum).[7] It would appear that the high price was due to the deferred payment.

It is of some interest to consider the method of manorial bookkeeping from the standpoint of modern accounting. First of all the manorial account was kept in single, not double, entry. There is therefore no accounting check on error or dishonesty. Error we

[1] See below, §§ 7, pp. 203, 204; §§ 8, p. 210; §§ 9, pp. 218; §§ 14, pp. 260, 264; §§ 16, pp. 279, 282.

[2] See below, §§ 9, pp. 213 ff.; §§ 18, pp. 295 ff.; §§ 19, pp. 304 ff.

[3] See below, §§ 12, p. 242; §§ 13, pp. 252, 257, 258; §§ 19, p. 307.

[4] See below, §§ 28, pp. 500, 503.

[5] See below, §§ 12, p. 242; §§ 13, p. 252.

[6] See below, §§ 20 (oats), pp. 355 ff.

[7] See below, §§ 18, pp. 294, 279. Cf. also, §§ 20, pp. 351, 359.

find frequently [1] and dishonesty occasionally. One case of the latter, though it involves a small amount, is significant. For eighteen years an item of 6d. had not been accounted for. The offence was pardoned by the bishop on the payment of the total amount in question, without usury or interest.[2]

The manorial accounts provide us with no evaluation of capital assets such as land, improvements, implements, and stock, grain, and other produce. For the land and improvements (improvements such as houses, outbuildings, lanes, hedges, sheep folds, ditches, and the like), this would have been very difficult, if not impossible, because of the fact that the assets of the bishop were mixed up with those of the tenants.

The omission of a true balance sheet prevented the bishop from knowing whether he was actually gaining or losing. Of course, it is highly significant that the bishop was not concerned with going ahead. He was chiefly interested, with a few exceptions, in getting as much this year as he had in past years. The point of view was static and customary, not dynamic and progressive.

Expenditures should be allocated to the sources from which they arise, so as to show profit or loss in each case. The cost of a cow is put down much the same as the cost of the hay purchased to feed it. Many items are lumped together, thereby obscuring facts of importance for the modern accountant. Dates and sequence of transactions are omitted. Many other minor criticisms might be made.

On the whole, however, this clumsy annual statement made for Crawley and recorded with two or three scores of accounts from other manors and estates, served its purpose of telling whether anything due and collected last year was not received this year. If the auditing of the original accounts of the reeve and the bailiff had been carefully done, then these general statements, compiled to form the big annual pipe roll of the bishopric would have been sufficient, at least under usual circumstances. We can criticize the

[1] See below, §§ 5, p. 194; §§ 11, p. 233, nn. 1, 2; §§ 17, pp. 289, 291, 292; §§ 18, p. 301, n. 1.

[2] Id*em* re*ddunt* com*potum* de ix s. de vj d. *con*cell*atis* p*er* xviij anno*s* *et* *con*do-nant*ur* p*er* ep*iscop*um. Ecclesiastical Commission, Various, 159278. The date is 1223–24.

accounting, but it is of little avail, given the times and circumstances. The manorial account, in the form known to us, had grown up gradually as a combination of a cash and a physical statement of the manor's condition.

§ 7. *Manorial Marketing.* In the manorial accounts there is a good deal of information about marketing, some of it specific but most of it general. Since the accounts deal with the lord's property and with his income and outgo, the marketing information concerns only his sales and his purchases. Some of the demesne products such as grain, hides, and chickens were sold on the market (in foro),[1] doubtless on the Winchester market. Probably some of the lord's wool was purchased by the wool dealers of Winchester.[2] But most of it was sold in bulk to foreign merchants, for instance about 1326 to a merchant or merchants of Perugia,[3] or to London merchants.[4] From 1208 to 1336 the ordinary sheep's wool was sold by the reeve; but from 1337 to at least 1454, it was sent to Wolvesey, doubtless there to be marketed through a central selling agency, the wool often being sent to London.[5] Lamb's wool was sold by the Wolvesey organization from about 1327 to about 1394, after which it was again sold by the reeve. The reeve seems always to have disposed of the broken and refuse wool.

That the prices given in the accounts represent genuine sales (or purchases) is indicated by the references to sales on the market and to merchants and by the great variation in the prices themselves. For instance, two plow horses were sold for 9s., while a sick

[1] See below, §§ 25, pp. 478, 484.

[2] In 1340 there was a Thomas Palmere of Winchester, king's merchant, who was a wool dealer, that is, probably an exporter. *Calendar of Close Rolls, 1339–1341* (1901), p. 555.

[3] In missione usq*ue* Wolues*eiam et* vend*icione* ib*ide*m p*er* diuu(?) M*er*cator' de Perouche DC j vell*era* pond*erantia* ij sacc*os* xxv clau*os*. Ecclesiastical Commission, Various, 159331.

[4] In allocat*ione* p*re*posit*o* sine br*evi* xxxix li. vij s. ij d. q. de xi ponder*ibus* xxj clau*is* lane gross*e et* Agn*ine* vend*ite* Bernard*o* de P*er*uch*e* M*er*cator*i* London' quos den*arios* d*omi*nus Recepit p*er* man*us* eiusdem. Ecclesiastical Commission, Various, 159331.

[5] A special carter had to be hired (1336–37) for carrying timber, because the carter of Wolvesey with two horses was at London (Carectari*us* de Wolues*eia* cu*m* ij equis fuit apud London*ium*). Ecclesiastical Commission, Various, 159348.

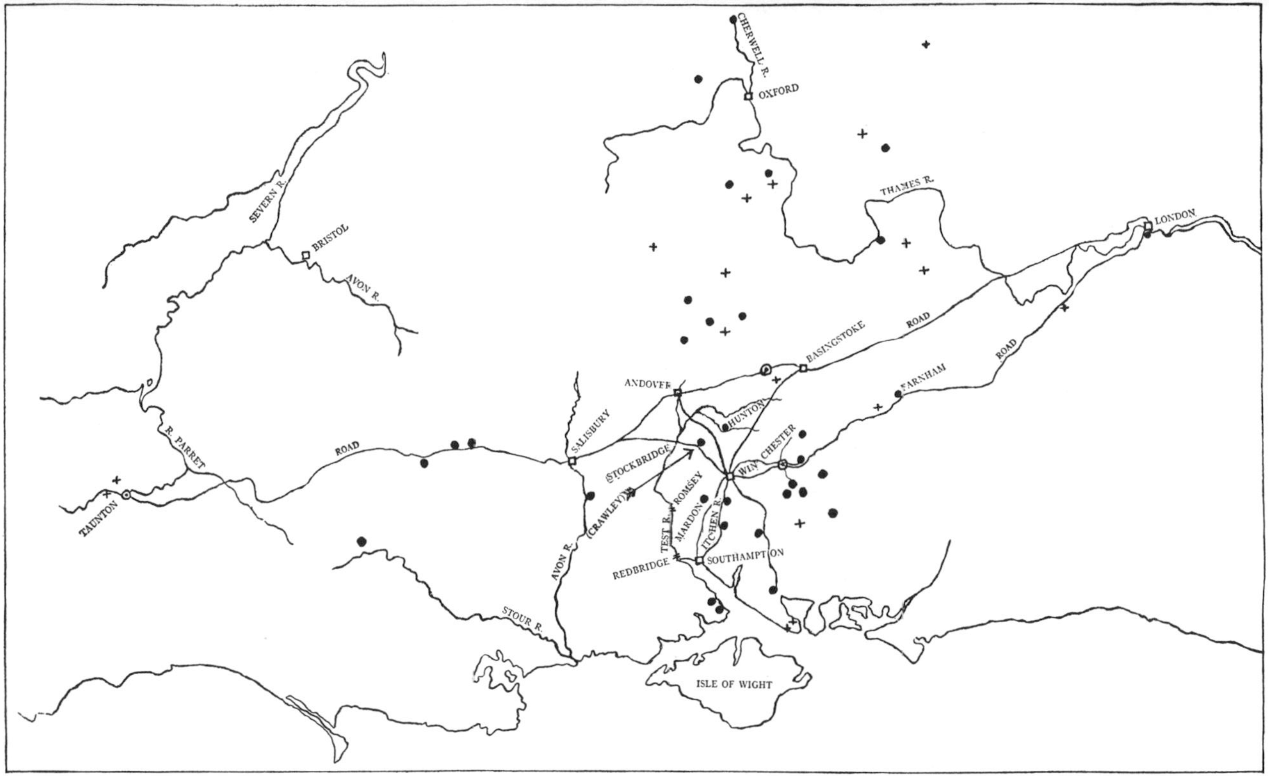

MAP SHOWING CRAWLEY AND OTHER COMMUNITIES (IN THE MIDDLE AGES) BELONGING TO THE BISHOPRIC OF WINCHESTER

● Manors in 1208. + Additional manors found in 1335.

⊙ Towns not belonging to the bishopric of Winchester. □ Towns. = Bridge villages on the River Test.

one brought only 14d.[1] Then we find such variation in the sale of grain in one year, as follows.[2]

PRICES OF WHEAT SOLD, 1272–73

Qrs.	s.	d.	Qrs.	s.	d.
14	5	6	$5\frac{3}{8}$	5	3
8	5	4	11	5	8
4	5	1	10	6	0

Actual money was, of course, required for purchases and general expenses. Moreover, the accounting practices followed, required either cash or a credit instrument, when price was set down. Where credit was given, the same was indicated by a tally, duly recorded. Of course, a commodity might be sent to another manor belonging to the bishop, or might be received therefrom, without any reference to price or value, merely the physical loss or acquisition being recorded. In one case a horse was 'bought' from the lord's hospitium 'without price.'[3] The phrase 'without price' was seemingly put down to square the statement that the horse was 'bought.'

The reeve of Crawley had to purchase the utensils and implements, and parts thereof, needed in the regular round of work. He bought cloth for the dairy,[4] also jars,[5] tar, and salt[6]; iron[7] for the village blacksmith who repaired the carts and plows and shod the horses, the iron being purchased sometimes at great expense;[8] wheels for carts[9] and plows[10]; tiles[11] and lime,[12] nails and cleats,[13]

[1] See below, §§ 7, p. 201.
[2] MS., P. R. O., Ecclesiastical Commission, Various, 159301.
[3] See below, §§ 18, p. 298.
[4] See below, §§ 9, p. 216; §§ 10, p. 225; §§ 12, p. 243; *et passim*.
[5] See below, §§ 9, p. 216; §§ 10, p. 225; §§ 12, pp. 243, 248; §§ 13, p. 253; §§ 14, p. 262.
[6] See below, §§ 18, p. 298; §§ 19, p. 307.
[7] See below, §§ 9, p. 216; §§ 10, p. 224; §§ 14, p. 261; §§ 15, p. 272, §§ 18, p. 297.
[8] See below, §§ 10, p. 224; §§ 14, p. 261.
[9] See below, §§ 6, p. 197; §§ 7, p. 202, §§ 9, p. 216; §§ 10, p. 225; §§ 14, p. 261.
[10] See below, §§ 5, p. 189; §§ 6, p. 197; §§ 7, p. 202; §§ 8, p. 209; §§ 9, p. 216; §§ 10, p. 225; §§ 14, p. 261; §§ 15, p. 272; §§ 16, p. 280; §§ 19, p. 307.
[11] See below, §§ 18, p. 298; §§ 25, p. 479.
[12] *Ibid.*
[13] See below, §§ 7, p. 202; §§ 8, p. 209; §§ 9, p. 216; §§ 10, p. 225; *et passim*.

for building purposes; a rope and bucket[1] to serve the deep well; and oil and quicksilver[2] to cure the sheep of disease. One of the most important things purchased was the plowshare (vomer)[3] which, though of iron, was not made by the blacksmith but by more specialized workers, doubtless in Winchester.

As we have noted, the inhabitants of Crawley do not figure in the lord's accounts very directly, at least in the purchase and sale of goods. They were obliged, however, to perform certain services in carrying the lord's goods,[4] which would include his purchases and sales. They had to sell wares of their own, that is clear enough, in order to obtain money with which to pay their rents, fines, amercements, Peter's pence,[5] and such taxes as scutage (?),[6] tallage,[7] and the subsidies.[8] They probably had for sale such commodities as the following:[9] wheat, sheep, wool, pigs, and occasionally a calf and a horse; perhaps also beer of their own brewing; chickens, geese, and eggs; bacon and a little butter and cheese.[10] Doubtless the sale was at the market in Winchester to which the peasant went with his wares for centuries without change. From the late thirteenth century to the late nineteenth, Crawley women carried their few surplus goods to the butter market at the foot of the same cross in High Street. As the granddaughter of one of them recently said, "My grandmother never returned with wares unsold." A very old Winchester ordinance would not allow it. And the price received was what the market would bring. There lies the route to the Winchester market — along the Stockbridge road through the west gate which stands even now, or otherwise

[1] See below, §§ 5, p. 190; §§ 6, p. 198; §§ 7, p. 203; §§ 8, p. 209; *et passim.*

[2] See below, §§ 13, p. 253; §§ 14, p. 262.

[3] See below, §§ 9, p. 216; §§ 10, p. 224; §§ 13, p. 251; §§ 14, p. 262; §§ 16, p. 280; §§ 18, p. 298; §§ 19, p. 307.

[4] See below, §§ 11, pp. 232 ff.

[5] *Red Book of the Exchequer* (ed. by H. Hall), vol. II (1896), p. 750. De Episcopatu Wintoniensis, xvii l.

[6] Crauelega Ep*iscop*i redd*it* Comp*otum* de xx s. *The Great Roll of the Pipe for the Fourteenth Year of the Reign of Henry the Second* (1890), p. 177.

[7] See below, §§ 5, pp. 187, 189.

[8] See below, §§ 21, pp. 454 ff.

[9] See below, § 21, pp. 69 ff.

[10] Tolls on wool, cheese, butter, and wheat were specifically listed in *The Ancient Usages of the City of Winchester* (ed. by J. S. Furley, 1927), §§ 44, §§ 48.

along the Andover road through the north gate until the latter was torn down in 1781.

What these peasants purchased can be surmised, but not told exactly. Probably they bought tarts and other dainties and cutlery, pots, and other necessities at the fair of St. Giles,[1] as well as pieces of colored cloth for ornament. And in the shops of Winchester they would get their supplies of a few utensils, some iron, tar, and medicines. The purchasing power of the peasants was not large, because they had little to sell apart from their agriculture.[2] There was no manufacturing of cloth for sale in Crawley, not because of any Winchester monopoly of cloth manufacture in the district but because of that city's preëminence in the industry.[3] But there was a chance to do some spinning of the wool of their own sheep. The only specialized manufacture of Crawley seems to have been the ironworking of the blacksmith[4] and, at a later date, the making of bricks[5] and shoes.[6] Crawley has been, and is, rural and agricultural.

In buying and selling, the bishop probably had some advantage over the tenants. He certainly sold at wholesale (in grosso)[7] and may have frequently bought that way. The bishop, like the prior of St. Swithun, was specifically exempt from paying tolls on grain brought from his own barns into the City of Winchester.[8] Presumably he paid on other wares. By the royal charter of 1232, however, he was exempted from tolls throughout England, as

[1] Crawley was on one of the important roads leading to the fair: De Itin*er*e de Rodbrugge Romes*eia et* Craulye Hoc Anno ad firm*am* xl s. De Itin*er*e de Chireton' et Alresford' hoc Anno ad firm*am* iiij s. Ecclesiastical Commission, Various, 159347, memb. 24. This seems to refer to the collection of a toll on these roads during the period of the fair. Crawley is not mentioned in this connection in the charter of 1349. See G. W. Kitchin, *A Charter of Edward III Confirming and Enlarging the Privileges of St. Giles Fair, Winchester* (1886), pp. 36, 76.

[2] See below, § 21, pp. 69 ff.

[3] We have not found any grant of a monopoly of trade or manufacture made to the City of Winchester, though there were restrictions as to giving out work to people living beyond the walls.

[4] See below, §§ 5, p. 189; §§6, p. 197; §§ 7, p. 202; §§ 8, p. 209; §§ 9, p. 216; *et passim;* §§ 25, p. 485.

[5] See below, §§ 58, p. 656; §§ 59, p. 676.

[6] See below, §§ 58, p. 657; §§ 59, p. 673. Shoemaker in Crawley.

[7] See below, §§ 12, p. 241; §§ 25, pp. 474, 478.

[8] See A. W. Goodman, *Chartulary of Winchester Cathedral* (1927), p. 101.

indeed were his men or tenants.[1] It is a question, however, as to whether this applied to existing tolls or only to those yet to be established.

§ 8. *Officials in Crawley.* There were three groups of officials having to do with Crawley: (*a*) those who were wholly outside but received money or goods from the manor, such as the treasurer at Wolvesey and the treasurer of the lord's hospitium; (*b*) those who were clearly outsiders but who visited Crawley more or less regularly on official business, and (*c*) those who belonged wholly to the manor.

Of the second group the outstanding examples were the seneschal and the bailiff. The seneschal was apparently in general charge of the lord's manors. Twice a year he went to Crawley to hold the tourn. This was at hockday in the spring and at St. Martin's in the autumn. Frequent payments to this official are found entered on the Crawley records, commonly to meet the expenses connected with his visits. His salary was apparently paid by the lord independent of Crawley and its funds. In the nineteenth century the work of the seneschal was done by a deputy steward sent down to Crawley by the Ecclesiastical Commissioners.[2]

Like the seneschal, the bailiff belonged to the outside. When the accounts begin he was called the sergeant (serviens). One of these officials had charge of several manors. He was responsible for at least two duties. He came, for instance, to the Manor of Crawley to hold courts in between the sessions of the tourn.[3] And, either under the name of sergeant or bailiff, he was jointly responsible with the reeve for the manorial accounts in the thirteenth and fourteenth centuries.[4] Part of his salary was paid by Crawley.[5] The whole group of manors belonging to the bishopric of Winchester was divided into bailiwicks, Crawley being within the bailiwick of Twyford, generally along with Mardon [1] and

[1] *Calendar of Charter Rolls*, vol. I (1903), p. 145. Goodman, *op. cit.*, p. 14.
[2] See below, § 31, p. 111. [3] See below, §§ 25, p. 479; §§ 26, p. 494.
[4] See below, §§ 5, p. 188; §§ 6, p. 196; §§ 7, p. 201; §§ 12, p. 240; §§ 13, p. 250.
[5] See below, §§ 18, p. 299.
[6] See Hubert Hall, *Pipe Roll of the Bishopric of Winchester, 1208–1209* (1903), p. xvii.

Stoke.[1] Whether such an organization originally arose to meet the needs of general manorial management or pertained to the court work, is not clear. Probably it was the former function that was the more important at first, the latter later on.

The supervisor appears late upon the scene. His functions are hard to discover. He was an overseer of some kind, but whether of the lands (surveyor) or of the stock, is not clear. On one occasion, at least, he helped the seneschal hold the tourn.[2] Probably his chief special charge was to have general oversight of the livestock, particularly those leased to the various farmers of the demesnes.[3] On one occasion, he sold a cow which a tenant of Crawley had given to the lord as heriot.[4]

A fourth general official of the second class, also one of the lord's ministri, was the auditor. In the account for the year 1409–10 we find that there was an allocation or allowance of a sum of money for victuals delivered to the lord's hospitium certified by the treasurer of the hospitium to the auditor.[5] In another account of the year 1746–47 the tenant on the Crawley estate called the How or Hoo is said to be "the Lords Auditor."[6] This holding had brought in to the lord, since at least the year 1265–66, one pound of cummin[7] or the price of its commutation, 4d. It is not unlikely, though we have found no proof, that this holding in South Crawley, not far from Winchester itself, was actually possessed by the lord's auditor from at least the thirteenth century. Of course, such an auditor would not confine his activities to Crawley alone, though he might live there. He would be the auditor for the manors in general.

Of the third class of officials mentioned, the most important was the reeve who probably from time immemorial and certainly from 1208 down to the nineteenth century played his part. He was unquestionably the most important official on the manor,

1 MSS., P. R. O., Ecclesiastical Commission, Various, 155864 (8–9 Henry VIII); ibid., 155975 (Ed. VI–Mary); Ecclesiastical Commission, Court Roll, 110/1 (2–7 Elizabeth).

2 See below, §§ 25, p. 480.

3 See below, §§ 23, p. 466.

4 See below, §§ 31, p. 509.

5 See below, §§ 18, p. 299. Cf. §§ 19, p. 309.

6 See below, §§ 28, p. 501.

7 MS., P. R. O., Ecclesiastical Commission, Various, 159297, memb. 4. Cf. MS., Winchester Cathedral Chartulary, vol. III, no. 465 (9 Edward II).

taking the place of the official who was on most manors called the bailiff. In Crawley the reeve was in modern times,[1] and probably always, elected by the tenants. He was chosen from the holders of land in South Crawley, and was therefore normally a virgator or yardlander, and, of course, a bondman down to the sixteenth century. Upon the reeve devolved the management of the manor, the preparation of the accounts, and the returns of the profits from all sources. At first he was jointly responsible for the accounts with the bailiff, but sometimes he alone rendered them.[2] Later the farmer of the demesne undermined his position, and after enclosure in 1795 his office was of little importance. In the Middle Ages the reeve had held his land free from fixed rents [3] and from the ordinary services of South Crawley tenants, and received from the lord a yearly wage of 5s.[4] and special gifts of one lamb and one cheese each year.[5] On one occasion the reeve was amerced for having lessened the weight of the clove used for weighing wool.[6] There are, however, but few instances of malfeasance of office. Doubtless the reeve was one of the ablest men in Crawley. Apparently he had not only to buy and sell, and manage things generally, but to act also as granger.[7] When the demesne lands and stock were leased in the fifteenth century, it was the reeve of Crawley who took the lease.[8]

For a time there was a collector of rent who in the late fifteenth and early sixteenth centuries functioned independently of the reeve who happened to be at that time also the farmer of the demesne.[9]

The tithingman was the elected official of the tithing of Crawley and Hunton, who appears in the records from at least the year 1466[10] to the nineteenth century. He appeared at the court of the

1 See below, §§ 32, p. 512.
2 See below, §§ 18, p. 295; §§ 19, p. 304. At times there were two reeves. Cf. below, §§ 15, p. 269.
3 See, for example, §§ 6, p. 196; §§ 8, p. 206.
4 See below, §§ 11, p. 232.
5 See, for example, §§ 12, pp. 246, 247. Also §§ 11, p. 232.
6 See below, §§ 5, pp. 189, 192.
7 See below, §§ 25, p. 481.
8 See below, §§ 25, p. 473.
9 See below, §§ 25, p. 473; §§ 26, p. 489.
10 See below, §§ 30, pp. 505, 507.

hundred of Buddlesgate with five of his tithing to present all offenders. He was probably chosen at the tourn meeting in Crawley itself in the spring of the year.[1] At this tourn two affeerers were also chosen and sworn to fix the amount of amercement.[2]

The blacksmith was a tenant of North Crawley, holding his cottage, lands, shop, and tools from the lord. The tools were separately listed when the demesne was leased, and in 1449 valued at £46.[3] At this same time he had an apprentice who was enrolled for a term of twelve years.[4] In the sixteenth century his estate consisted of a shop, a messuage and ferling of land and a cottage and ferling, all in North Crawley.[5]

The following passage describes the work and status of the blacksmith about 1280.[6] 'Robert the Smith holds one cottage and ten acres of land for doing the iron-work each year on four plows. And the lord will find the iron and steel for these when it shall be necessary. And he shall have for the aforesaid work one acre of the better winter barley without the manure (?compostum) or an acre of lenten barley if no winter barley should be sown. Again, he shall have one horse free in the lord's pasture, one cheese and one lamb at his choice. He cannot marry his son or daughter nor sell his ox or his horse anymore than the aforesaid David can. He shall give pannage for his hogs and for his other beasts as the aforesaid David does. Again, he shall give a heriot as David does. And he shall do three days of boon-work in autumn along with one man. And he shall receive [food therefor] as Robert At Mere does. He shall find a man for washing [the lord's sheep] and he shall wash and shear as long as there are sheep to be washed and sheared. Again, he shall mow, spread, and gather the hay as David does. He shall give churchscot as David does. He shall fetch the lord's hay with a man and a horse, if he shall have a horse, once [a year] wherever it shall be bought. Moreover if the coulter is broken in a place called the Schonke or the plowshare in a place called the Pate, he shall repair them at the cost of the lord

1 See below, §§ 32, p. 511; §§ 33, p. 512; §§ 34, p. 514.
2 See below, for example, §§ 32, p. 511.
3 See below, §§ 25, p. 485.
4 *Ibid.*, p. 476.
5 See below, §§ 37, p. 522. Cf. also §§ 40, p. 528.
6 See below, §§ 11, pp. 237, 238.

bishop and not at his own cost. Again, he shall shoe two cart horses with the lord's horseshoes throughout the whole year and all the plowhorses once a year. . . . Roger the Smith[1] shall [*sic*]. receive from the lord a plot for making a messuage between Robert At Mere and John At Putte in the time of William Wintersull, the seneschal of the lord bishop, and he shall give 2d. to the lord at Michaelmas each year. Again, he shall find one man for shearing the [lord's] sheep for a day, and he shall do a day's boonwork in autumn. Again, the same Roger the Smith holds ten acres of land and shall give at Michaelmas a rent of 2s. 6d. for all secular service.'

There are two expressions in the accounts the meaning of which is not clear: ministri curie and famuli curie (or famuli domus), or court agents and court servants working on the home farm. Whether these were synonymous or not, and just which officials were included, is apparently never indicated in the records. We know that the famuli received grants of grain, particularly barley, and, on one occasion, included the hayward, carter, two plowmen, the shepherd's boy, and dairymaid.[2] To the ministri were given herring,[3] or other food, such as bread, beer, and cheese, for their autumn work. On at least one occasion there were said to be 149 customary tenants and eight ministri, the former working one day, the latter three days in autumn.[4] Since here could hardly be eight ministri apart from the famuli, we are inclined to conclude that one group included at least some of the other and were possibly identical. Perhaps the minstri were the famuli giving boon services and the famuli were the ministri doing the regular routine of work connected with their offices.

The hayward was an important official, apparently having charge of the crops in the fields, and receiving, at least at times, a yearly wage.[5] As we have seen, the hayward was one of the famuli, and one of the most important, standing very near to the reeve.

[1] Probably Roger was later than Robert in the village smithy.

[2] See below, §§ 18, p. 301; §§ 19, p. 310.

[3] See below, for example, §§ 12, p. 244; §§ 13, p. 254; §§ 14, p. 263. See also §§ 11, pp. 232, 236.

[4] See below, §§ 18, p. 299.

[5] See below, §§ 10, p. 225; §§ 16, p. 281; §§ 18, p. 229.

There are, however, very few details about him in the records examined.

There were generally three or four plowmen, but sometimes more. Six of them were acquitted of their fixed rent in one year and two additional ones were hired.[1] The shepherds were as important as the plowmen. We find one for the wethers, a second one for the ewes, and a third called the keeper of hogasters.[2] Three shepherds were acquitted of their fixed rent.[3] There was a cowherd,[3] but, since cows were unimportant on the Crawley demesne and probably on the tenants' lands, his office was of little importance. The swineherd was much more necessary than the cowherd, but not so important as the shepherds.

Other lesser officials were the dairymaid, the keeper of the cheese, the beer keeper, the cellarer, and the keeper of the grain in the fields.

The medieval officialdom of Crawley is, of course, not completely recorded without at least the mention of the rector or his curate, and in more modern times the churchwardens. At the present time there are also the estate manager, the gamekeeper, and the agricultural expert with his two grain bailiffs and his shepherds. These are the modern ministri curie. Of course, there are the parish clerk, the postmaster, and the schoolmistress. The constable is also there to impress his fellow villagers![4]

All in all, Crawley has been much served. There have been enough officials to get things done and to maintain the West-Saxon predisposition to believe that some were greater than others.

§ 9. *Demesne and Home Farm.* The whole manor could be divided pretty much as follows:

(1) Lord's demesne:
    Home farm
    Parts rented to tenants (special leaseholds and purprestures)

[1] See below, §§ 10, pp. 222, 225.
[2] See below, §§ 18, p. 295.
[3] See below, §§ 10, p. 222.
[4] See below, §§ 58, p. 653; §§ 59, p. 661.

(2) Tenants' land:
Customary tenements
Freehold tenements

The home farm was that part of the demesne which the lord ordinarily exploited through the reeve of the manor. It was made up of arable, pasture, meadow, woods, and waste. The size of the home farm necessarily changed somewhat from year to year as the reeve rented out more or less of the demesne to tenants. What was not rented out to them was ordinarily used by him for the lord's benefit.[1] Of course there came a time — in the early fifteenth century — when reeve cultivation was supplanted by leasing to the demesne farmer.[2]

The question of a long-time change in the size of the home farm is of greater moment than the short-time shiftings. It is difficult, however, to get precise information on this subject. The number of acres sown to grain and the number of sheep kept, as given in the following table, may be considered in this connection.

Average of Six Grains Sown by the Lord [1]			Average Number of Sheep Kept by the Lord [1]		
Period	No. of years [2]	Acres	Period	No. of years [2]	Sheep
1208–1226..........	13	$541\frac{1}{2}$	1208–1226.........	13	1866
1231–1314..........	55	$391\frac{3}{5}$	1231–1314.........	54	1581
1315–1383..........	56	$192\frac{3}{5}$	1315–1383.........	58	1530
1384–1448..........	40	$174\frac{1}{3}$	1384–1448.........	45	1486

[1] See below, §§ 20, pp, 470–504. Wheat, winter barley, spring barley, oats, peas, and vetches.
[2] The number of years during the period, for which we have figures.

So far as our figures go, the manor was at the height of its production of grain and sheep, its two chief products, in the period 1208–26.[3] For the later periods, there are three possible developments. First, the home farm may have been curtailed and the unused part rented to tenants. Secondly, the abandoned arable may have been used for pasture and fewer sheep may have been maintained. Thirdly, the abandoned arable may have been used for

[1] See the exitus manerii in §§ 9, §§ 10, §§ 12–§§ 16, §§ 18, §§ 19.
[2] See below, § 23, pp. 80 ff.
[3] See above, § 5, pp. 12 ff.

pasture and the tenants allowed more sheep per holding. The third is unlikely because, while there might have been some increase in the tenants' rights between 1226 and 1280, there was none in the subsequent periods. The first is unlikely because there was no wholesale increase in tenants' holdings nor in the size of the holding itself. Accordingly, we are left to conclude that the second development was the one which actually occurred: there was a progressive decline in arable farming and in the efficiency of animal husbandry. This view, however, is not to be accepted as proven or even demonstrated.

One of the most prominent characteristics of the demesne, as distinct from the home farm, was its shifting nature, in spite of its general and prolonged persistence.[1] Tenants' land might be drawn into the demesne.[2] Part of the demesne might be leased out,[3] or rented without a specified termination, in the form of purpresture.[4] And, as we have seen, the size of the home farm itself varied from year to year according to the advantages of renting out to tenants certain bits of land or using them directly. Moreover the tenants had certain rights of cutting wood and pasturing animals on the lord's demesne which cannot be estimated in acres, and which in practice varied from year to year as these rights were unused or exceeded.

Partly because of the somewhat shifting size of the demesne, and partly because of the inadequacy of the data, the ratio of the demesne to the tenants' lands cannot be discovered. But it can be said with some assurance that, while the tenants' arable was larger than the lord's, their pasture lands and rights were much inferior to his.

Apparently land once a part of the demesne was always so regarded. This we infer from a presentment of 1831 [5] in which a

[1] Apparently the demesne contained about 1105 acres (that is, 168 + 880 + 57 acres) in the tithe survey of about 1837. See below, §§ 57, pp. 630 and 633. If we allow that three sheep could have been pastured to an acre (Walter of Henley said two to an acre of fallow) in the period 1208–26, then the home farm alone contained 1163½ acres at that time (541½ acres sown to grain and 622 for the lord's sheep).

[2] See below, §§ 6, p. 196; §§ 8, p. 207; §§ 9, p. 214; *et passim.*

[3] See below, § 23, pp. 80 ff.

[4] See below, §§ 12, p. 241; §§ 13, p. 251; §§ 18, p. 296; §§ 19, p. 305.

[5] See below, §§ 54, p. 594.

sharp distinction was made between the inheritance custom on demesne land, which was primogeniture, and on bondland, which was cradle-hold. But it is to us an unsolved question whether, in Crawley at least, the land of customary tenants lost its status of bondland when drawn into the demesne. It is a plausible inference that it did so if it remained a part of the demesne for a long period.

When the demesne came to an end in Crawley is not heralded in the documents. The bits of demesne rented out to the customary tenants and attached to their customary holdings were lost to the demesne when the customary lands to which they were attached were enfranchised.[1] The home farm, periodically leased for a term of years[2] or for lives,[3] was apparently sold in the nineteenth century.[4]

§ 10. *Field System.* The field system of the Celts has been noted above.[5] We are here concerned with the one prevailing from at least the early thirteenth century down to enclosure in 1795, but particularly the early or medieval part. The most significant aspect of the system was the common arable fields made up of scattered strips of customary acres and roods, that is, half-acre and quarter-acre plots. Some of these tiny plots belonged to the tenants and some to the lord. About 1280 it was said that a certain tenant should receive his plowing as the plows are held,[6] that is, as the plows go from one plot to another in succession. The most significant brief expression in the Crawley records is sicut iacent, or 'as they lie.'[7] The reference is to plots as they lie in the common fields, each man's holding being scattered here and there. In the sixteenth, seventeenth, and eighteenth centuries there are explicit references to the common fields.[8]

[1] See below, § 33, pp. 117 ff.

[2] See below, §§ 18, §§ 19, §§ 23–§§ 26.

[3] See below, §§ 24, pp. 468 ff.

[4] The last lease seen was dated 19 Aug., 1805, with a regrant of 27 Nov., 1818. See MS., Millbank, Ecclesiastical Commission, $154425\frac{1}{38}$.

[5] See above, § 2, pp. 4–6.

[6] See below, §§ 11, p. 235.

[7] For example, below, §§ 7, p. 203; §§ 8, p. 208. A secondary meaning of this phrase seems to be 'unmeasured,' referring to the customary acres as they lie in the fields.

[8] For example, below, §§ 31, p. 506; §§ 37, pp. 522–524; §§ 54, pp. 588, 591; §§ 55, pp. 597 ff. and Ecclesiastical Commission, Various, 155932 (28 Elizabeth); *ibid.*, Court Roll, 92/11, fol. 59d. (2 April, 8 James I); and *ibid.*, 95/9, fol. 68 (11 March, "1626").

The possession of common or open fields, with no permanent fences or hedges separating the holdings of one man from another, is all but a universal feature of an agricultural system that is neither low nor high in its technique. In this respect Crawley was true to type. Crawley's peculiarity lay in its possession of *six* common fields, three in North Crawley and three in South Crawley.

Westfield Middlefield Homefield

North

Village

South

Westfield Homefield Eastfield

In 1612 a farthing land of North Crawley contained three (customary) acres in Homefield (one acre abutting a purrock called Overhouse, another acre lying in a furlong called Smalethornes, and the third at the farther end of the field), four acres in Middlefield (two being in a furlong called Waterslade, the other two being in Downefurlong), and two acres in Westfield (both in Gassenfurlong). In addition, there were two other acres called the Roode at the upper end of Homefield and a purrock called Overhowse.[1] In 1671 a half virgate in South Crawley, containing sixteen (customary) acres, was located in three common fields, five acres being in Eastfield (two in the furlong called Thornham), four acres and a quarter in Homefield, and four acres and a quarter in Westfield.[2] Although there is no proof that such a division of fields existed in the Middle Ages, there is no reason to doubt it. On the other hand, there is the fact that, as we read one reeve's account after another, we get the impression that what stood uppermost in the Middle Ages was the furlong rather than the field. And it is quite remarkable that perhaps two scores or more of these furlongs bore distinctive names — names indicating their use or topographical peculiarity.

Of meadow in medieval Crawley there is but little evidence. In

[1] See below, §§ 41, p. 532.
[2] See below, §§ 46, p. 541.

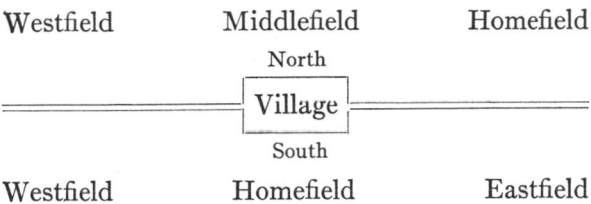

Domesday twenty-six acres were recorded.[1] About 1280 the tenants had certain rights of herbage in a plot called Mede, which may have been a meadow.[2] But as noted elsewhere, the frequent purchases of hay in Crawley are indicative of a scarcity of meadow land there, as also is the special provision that tenants were obliged to fetch hay from wherever the lord might buy it.[3] Whether the tenants had any rights in the meadow is not clear, except possibly to the herbage after the hay was cut. Of course, a meadow in upland chalk country is a rarity.

Common pasture there was in Crawley, without doubt, but there is little specific information concerning it down to its disappearance in 1795. In 1280 there was common pasture on which the tenants might keep their sheep[4] and, we may add, cattle and horses. In the modern period, for example in 1671, a tenant had 'common pasture' for a cow and other beasts of burden pertaining to his holding.[5] But this does not mean that there was one stretch of pasture land, called common pasture, set aside for the use of the tenants. It simply means that on the lord's pasture the tenants had certain rights of pasture, limited to so many animals, apparently to twenty-five sheep, one cow, and one horse.[6]

Just as there was (apparently) no common pasture set aside for the common use of tenants to the exclusion of the lord, so there was no common wood and no common waste. There were rights of cutting wood, however, just as there were rights of pasture. The woods, like the waste, belonged to the lord.

The lord, possessed of the common pasture, the meadow, the woods and the waste, and of a share of the common arable, had in addition separate plots of his own. He possessed separate pasture plots, for example, Shert or La Chert, which he might use or rent out to his tenants. He had separable arable plots, or furlongs, which he either cultivated through the reeve or let the tenants cultivate. Sometimes the tenants paid a rent, and sometimes they paid none — when it was their turn to cultivate that field in accordance with a working arrangment entered into with the lord.

[1] See below, §§ 4, p. 185.
[2] See below, §§ 11, p. 233.
[3] *Ibid.*
[4] *Ibid.*, p. 236.
[5] See below, §§ 46, p. 541.
[6] See below, § 12, pp. 44–46.

HAY HARVESTING WITH SWEEPS AND ELEVATOR

A photograph, taken about 1926 and reproduced with the permission of *Country Life*, England

For instance, it was once recorded that the reeve had sowed 131 quarters of oats on 256 acres of land, of which thirty acres were the most that belonged to the rustics.[1] But further treatment of this subject properly comes under the head of tillage, the subject of the next section.

In medieval Crawley, then, the tenants held their small tenements of arable interspersed with some of the lord's arable in the common fields.[2] They had rights in the lord's pasture (that part called the common pasture) and in the lord's meadow and woods. In addition, they had an arrangement whereby they periodically used some of the lord's furlongs. Of course, at any time, they might rent additional pasture privileges or separate plots of ground for the purpose of cultivation or pasture. In other words the tenants had only what was specifically allowed to them by custom or arrangement, all the rest belonging to the lord.

§ 11. *Medieval Tillage.* From the documents available, it is difficult to determine the nature of Crawley's agriculture. Indeed, such a task is comparable in difficulty with the interpretation of Domesday Book. About the system followed by the tenants, we get no information apart from the lord's cultivation. In all probability it was more uniform than the lord's cultivation. It is likewise probable that a double three-field system prevailed in the Middle Ages, as it did in the sixteenth century — doubtless right down to enclosure in 1795. This was a rotation of fallow, winter grain, and spring grain, separately pursued by the conservative tenants in both North and South Crawley.

We may now most profitably consider the lord's system of cultivation and then the way in which it dovetailed into that of the tenants. Although we have plenty of details about the lord's agriculture, we are left in great uncertainty at some points. The vagueness of terms is one source of difficulty. The word pastura illustrates the point. Sometimes it is winter, or stubble, pasture

[1] un*de* xxx acre s*un*t maxi*me* de t*er*ra q*ue* solebat e*ss*e rustico*rum*. MS., P. R. O., Ecclesiastical Commission, Various, 159272 (1213–14).

[2] In 7 James I (18 Sept.), the tenants seem to have had a separate field of their own: they were ordered to keep their hedges repaired between the demesne lands and the field of the tenants called Northfield. MS., P. R. O., Ecclesiastical Commission, Court Roll, 92/11, fol. 11d.

that is referred to, sometimes summer pasture (as on a permanent pasture field), and sometimes pasture on the fallow. Since pasture was commonly integrated with tillage, the subject is very pertinent here.

The lord possessed a large pasture field, called Shert, kept apart from the arable, and used or rented out to the tenants as the reeve thought best. We know something of its history from at least 1302–03 down to the present day. At first it was rented out — to persons unknown — at from 9d. to 3s. a year. Then in 1314–15 it was rented to John de Kirkeby for 3s. 4d.,[1] a rate which, with a few exceptions in the years immediately following, it bore down to 1453–54[2] and even to 1746–47.[3] During this long period it was permanent pasture. Probably at enclosure in 1795 it was turned over to tillage for the first time in centuries. Certainly in the tithe survey of 1837 it was put down as arable[4] — nearly forty acres. In 1924–25 it was growing a good stand of grain.

Puthulle, in the early fourteenth century, was used for pasturing the lord's sheep, rented sometimes when a renter could be found, sown by the lord occasionally, and sometimes held by the tenants 'in common,' that is, apparently, used for their open-field husbandry.[5] In the early fifteenth century it was again ordinarily used to pasture the lord's sheep.

The furlong, or 'field' as it is often called, of Drakenord, was frequently sold as winter pasture in the early fourteenth century. Then in the following spring it was sown to a summer crop. It was clearly recognized as one of the lord's important furlongs, though sometimes held in common.

The most interesting 'field' is Combefurlong, which has a history that has been followed year by year from 1301–02, and particularly from 1326 to almost 1426. During the hundred years indicated, there was a fourfold rotation practised by the lord, with some earlier experiments and possible straggling survivals later. First came a wheat crop followed by spring barley, this in turn by

[1] MS., P. R. O., Ecclesiastical Commission, Various, 159329.

[2] *Ibid.*, 159444.

[3] See below, §§ 28, p. 501.

[4] See below, §§ 57, p. 635.

[5] It would seem that the expressions, 'it lies in common,' 'it was sold to the homage,' and 'it was sown by the homage' are all about synonymous.

oats, and finally a fallow. Sometimes, instead of the oats, vetches were planted. In the year 1376–77, 51 acres were sown with oats, 8 with peas, and 15 with vetches — in all 74 acres.[1] This small proportion of peas and vetches was about the average. Had the full acreage (at least 82 acres of wheat had been sown in 1358–59)[2] been planted with pulse, we would have an example of legume rotation. So long as the rotation retained a fallow, it would be transitional, to be sure, but still a promise of great technical advance.

Combefurlong, like Shert, was the lord's very own, the homage having no claim upon it. Why it was set aside, we can only conjecture. Its rotation being peculiar, persistent, and an advance upon other methods of cropping, we can hardly escape concluding that this furlong was used for experimental purposes. If so, one wonders whether the experiment was empirical and original or by way of imitation of the classical models which were being studied in Italy, at least,[3] and might have been discovered for use in England by Crawley's ecclesiastical lords.

At least ten names of grain are mentioned in the reeve's accounts of the thirteenth and early fourteenth centuries, exclusive of peas, beans, and vetches. The first group is made up of winter grains: wheat, curall, mancorn, beremancorn, winter barley, and bere. The second group consists of spring grains: spring barley, oats, drage, and brotcorn. The curall is inferior wheat, which was never itself planted. The mancorn, as we judge from its position in the list, contained wheat and winter barley, probably being the same as beremancorn. The bere seems to be winter barley and the drage[4] coming in between barley and oats appears to be a mixture of the two. Brotcorn, which was used as fodder,[5] was a mixture of barley, peas, and vetches.[6] Of course, the conspicuous omission is rye, perhaps (wrongly) thought not to grow well in chalk.

[1] MS., P. R. O., Ecclesiastical Commission, Various, 159384.

[2] *Ibid.*, 159369.

[3] Petrus Crescentius (d. 1307) wrote his 'Twelve Books' largely from classical models. See N. S. B. Gras, *A History of Agriculture* (1925), pp. 36, 49.

[4] For drage (draget'), see MS., P. R. O., Ecclesiastical Commission, Various, 159316–159318 (1297–99). About 15 quarters were sown on about 40 acres, about 20 quarters of the yield being sold at an average of 4s. 7½d., 4s., and 3s. in the three respective years.

[5] See below, §§ 12, p. 245.

[6] See below, §§ 14, p. 265.

If the common three-field system prevailed in Crawley in the thirteenth and fourteenth centuries, we would expect to find that the number of acres of winter grain approximately equalled the number of acres of spring grain. The proportions in the thirteenth century, however, were roughly as follows: wheat two, barley four, and oats and peas together five. But this observation can mean nothing definite in view of the fact that we do not know that the fields were of equal size.

Fallow is often mentioned in the reeve's accounts. Its occurrence is most regular in the case of Combefurlong. On Drakenord it may have come every second year, if the meaning of pasture 'sold' or rented there is fallow pasture. Alternated with this was a grain crop. The Court Moat was frequently rented as pasture and about as frequently fallowed in the early fourteenth century, but there is no clear-cut alternation of crops and fallow. Certainly there is no trace of threefold rotation in the case of this particular piece of land. Indeed, an examination of the uses of the lord's furlongs illustrates rather a twofold and a fourfold rotation.

The situation in medieval Crawley, as revealed in the reeves' accounts, raises afresh the general question of agricultural system. We commonly speak of a two-field or a three-field system of agriculture. But this is probably very far from being as precise as we think. Two or three fields might prevail but only as very vague guides to methods followed. In Crawley, as has been said, the winter and spring crops of the lord did not equal one another, as we would expect in a three-field system. Nor did the fallow always alternate with grain, as we would expect in a two-field system.

We find as much difficulty in making an orderly system out of the elements of pasture and crops as we do out of fallow and crops. Permanent pasture existed, that is, pasture that was quite distinct from tillage in the narrow sense. But the stubble pasture and the fallow pasture were closely integrated with tillage. And we sometimes find a whole year's pasture alternated with a year's cereal crop. Lockfurlong is an example of this. Although the practices on this particular plot varied, still in the early fourteenth century it was common to find Lockfurlong alternately used for pasturing the lord's sheep and growing an oat crop. Wheat was planted on it very rarely.

When we look at the integration of the lord's tillage and the tenants' cultivation, we find as much difficulty in arriving at a simple and permanent relationship. Some furlongs were always the lord's, but otherwise there was much left to what was called the custom of the hundred which, we fancy, was another name for the arrangement arrived at in the customary court by the reeve and bailiff on the one hand and the homage of the manor on the other. Lockfurlong in 1326–27 was partly common and partly used for the lord's plow horses.[1] In the succeeding years we find it running through the gamut of fallow, wheat crop, oat crop, pulse crop, and pasture, with a strong tendency toward an alternation of oats and pasture, as has been noted. After 1378–79, however, it was very frequently set down as 'lying in common.'[2] Trendle and Holyndene were furlongs commonly linked together. About them, we have information from at least 1299–1300 to 1453–54. They belonged to the lord's demesne; and yet, the lord does not seem to have often planted grain on them. He used them for pasturing his livestock. He often rented them out for 5, 8, or 9s. a year, presumably as pasture. But the most common entry is, 'nothing because sowed by the customary tenants,' or '5s. because the land was sold to the customary tenants'; and later in the fourteenth century the expression becomes 'nothing because they lie in common.' There is a suggestion of the alternate right of the lord one year and the tenants the next year. But examination of the sequence shows that this was not regularly followed.

In the face of such irregularities and varying working arrangements — the changing customs of the hundred, it is difficult to draw sharp lines. We are inclined to set down the system as an irregular fallow system, with pasture as both separate and combined, and with the lord's demesne cultivation partly integrated with the tenants' husbandry[3] and partly separated from it. It is a plausible inference that while the tenants followed a threefold rotation, the lord maintained at one and the same time twofold,

[1] MS., P. R. O., Ecclesiastical Commission, Various, 159339.

[2] Beginning *ibid.*, 159386.

[3] See above, § 10, p. 30.

threefold, and fourfold rotations. Because of his separate furlongs such diversity was quite feasible.

About the important details of crop handling, we get little information from the documents. There was probably no special category of service for weeding or hoeing. It was apparently part of the week-work of the laborers (operarii) [1] of North Crawley. Extra work — beyond what they were able to do — was paid for at so much an acre, on one occasion one (statutory) acre and a half for 1d.[2] The annual expense for this extra work varied from year to year, amounting to 3s. 4d., 5s., 6s. 8d., and 6s.[3] Sometimes there was no additional expense for this purpose;[4] sometimes it was extra heavy, as when in 1396–97, 8s. were paid 'for weeding the lord's corn this year, and so much because of the multitude of noxious weeds called matheges.' [5]

The reeve's accounts tell us a lot about the plows used in Crawley, but, of course, not all we would like to know. The chief material was wood, particularly for the beam and wheels, as we know, and also for the handles, as we may infer. These cost very little, for they were simply cut out of timber from the lord's woods. The iron parts were the coulter, the share, and the foot-irons. Only the coulter was made by the Crawley smith. The share was apparently the most precious part of the plow: although sometimes rounded on the manor, it was always bought ready made — doubtless from the towns where it was probably made by skilled artisans. If the share broke at the pate, then it was repaired at the lord's expense; but if at any other point, it was fixed by the smith without charge to the lord. Clearly the share broke often, needed to be repaired or replaced frequently, and all in all received most anxious attention. The foot-irons were bought ready made, as were also the nails for fastening them. These foot-irons may have been attached at the forward end of the beam to keep the coulter and especially the share from digging too deeply

[1] See below, §§ 12, p. 244. [2] See below, §§ 10, p. 225.
[3] See below, §§ 10, p. 225; §§ 16, p. 281; §§ 18, p. 299; §§ 19, p. 308.
[4] See below, §§ 15, p. 273.
[5] MS., P. R. O., Ecclesiastical Commission, Various, 159403. This weed may be one of several, of which the most likely is madder (mathers), which flourishes in light or overworked soil.

into the earth. The wheels would serve the same purpose; and, if we are not mistaken, wheels and such foot-irons would not be needed on the same plow. In connection with the making and repairing of the plows, the accounts refer to expenses for trimming (scalpuland'), ironing, chipping (?chippiand'), and covering (?vestiand'). We can only conjecture what these operations really were. The most important question concerning the plow is whether the share simply dug up the earth, pushing it to either side, or whether it turned a furrow all to one side. Probably the former was the case, but there is no conclusive evidence on this subject from the Crawley records themselves.

In Domesday Book (1086) it is said there were five plows on the demesne, while the tenants are said to have possessed seven.[1] Later (1232–33) we find six new plows made for the demesne.[2] In 1389–90 there were fifteen of the twenty-five South Crawley tenants owing plowing services, who possessed no whole plows;[3] presumably the other ten actually had whole plows. Very little of the lord's plowing was done by the tenants of Crawley as special customary service, at least from the thirteenth century onward. Most of it was performed as week-work by the plowmen recruited from the North Crawley tenants who presumably had few or no plows of their own. In the customs written down about 1280 it was said that, if a certain tenant held the plow all year and inclement weather occurred after Michaelmas, so that he could not plow, then he should do only half the work required. He was himself to have the plowing of eight acres by the lord's plow at the four usual terms of the year.[4] In 1208–09 there were 13 plowmen who received 13d. for winter boon-work.[5] In 1231–32 it was stated that 11 plowmen received 11d. for boon-work and that 48 acres were plowed by 32 oxen belonging to the tenants.[6] Only 10½ plowmen could be mustered in the following year, and they received 10½d. as boon-money for spring plowing. In addition, 42 acres were plowed for the herbage of the 28 oxen by the men of the manor, that is, each ox plowing 1½ customary acres.[7] In 1256–57

[1] See below, §§ 4, p. 185.
[2] See below, §§ 8, p. 209.
[3] See below, §§ 17, p. 289.
[4] See below, §§ 11, p. 235.
[5] See below, §§ 5, p. 191.
[6] See below, §§ 7, p. 203.
[7] See below, §§ 8, p. 209.

there were only 9 plowmen, and they plowed only 9 acres, receiving therefrom 9d.[1] What was happening is fairly clear. Extra service was obtained from the plowmen on the payment of boon-money. More was obtained by making arrangements with the tenants for the pasture of their oxen. But the reliance for extra plowing was coming more and more to be put upon hired plowmen. In 1232–33, two were paid 18d. for 17 weeks' plowing,[2] and in 1256–57 they received 6s. a year.[3] On the whole it is easier to see how the lord managed to get his plowing done than it is to discover how the tenant who did not hold the lord's plow got his own done. Probably some of the North Crawley tenants who were not assumed to have plows did actually possess them. How these were rented out or loaned to fellow tenants, is not indicated.

§ 12. *Animal Husbandry.* Whether Hampshire did or did not actually get its name from the Welsh word for sheep,[4] it has at any rate for a long time been active in sheep raising. Since 1208 Crawley has been about half sheep farm and half grain farm. Cattle have never been prominent in either Hampshire or Crawley. The reason for this is that water, needed in large quantities for cattle but in much smaller for sheep, has been and is scarce on the chalk downs. This is not because rainfall is scant — the rainfall being considerable, but because what falls sinks into the ground, seldom seeking lakes, streams, ponds, or other reservoirs.

Hampshire is a land of deep wells. The precious liquid has to be sought far down, even farther today than formerly. The deepest Hampshire well seems to be in Southampton Common (1323½ feet deep),[5] the second at Otterbourne (in all 1216 feet deep?), and the third at Woolston, a suburb of Southampton (about 1100 feet?).[6] In Crawley today the deepest has been dug about 210 feet down and then a four-inch bore has been sunk 300 feet beyond. There are a few others of much less depth than this one at

[1] See below, §§ 9, p. 216. [2] See below, §§ 8, p. 210.

[3] See below, §§ 9, p. 216.

[4] Cf. J. P. Williams-Freeman, *An Introduction to Field Archaeology as illustrated by Hampshire* (1915), p. 55.

[5] Information kindly supplied by the Ordnance Survey Office, Southampton.

[6] Whitaker, W., "Some Hampshire Wells," *Papers and Proceedings*, Hampshire Field Club, and Archaeological Society, vol. VIII, pt. 1 (1917), pp. 41, 50.

EWES AND LAMBS RETURNING TO THE FOLD

A photograph, taken about 1926 and reproduced with the permission of *Country Life*, England

Crawley Court. In dry weather these wells are inadequate, probably because they have not been located where they could adequately draw upon subterranean streams. In the Middle Ages ropes (once six and another time four) [1] and buckets had to be bought for use at the well, perhaps the 210-foot well, above mentioned. Intermittently from the thirteenth century until the twentieth, it has been necessary to incur unusual charges for geting water, notably in 1921 when water had to be carted from the outside. A former resident of Crawley remembers the saying "Romsey in the mire, Crawley God help us!" [2] Romsey was on the River Test and wet enough, but Crawley had no water in sight, except in the pond at the foot of the village.

Crawley has specialized in sheep for various reasons. Sheep needed but little water. The chalky soil helped to keep down diseases that are common on low, damp lands. And there was plenty of nutritious grass growing on the downs.

Sheep were pastured in the Middle Ages and not fed on roots as today. Pulse was often given them, particularly to the mother sheep and the lambs; and when pulse was scarce, hay was provided for them.[3] Of course, pulse and grain, for example, vetches and oats were fed to the other animals, particularly the oxen and horses.[4] As is sometimes stated, the grain was fed in the sheaf and the amount only estimated, not measured.

The people of Crawley knew something of animal breeding but apparently not very much. They castrated males not needed for breeding purposes. This fact we know from two sources. There were charges for castration.[5] Also, there were classes of animals which implied castration, the oxen and the wethers. The lord's officials seem to have given at least a little attention to the choice of sires. For instance, on one occasion forty rams were brought

[1] See below, §§ 7, p. 203; §§ 8, p. 209. Cf. MS., P. R. O., Ecclesiastical Commission, Various, 159339 (1326–27).

[2] Miss Lilian J. Redstone has quoted her father, a former Crawley resident, to this effect.

[3] See below, §§ 9, p. 216; §§ 10, p. 225; §§ 18, p. 298; and §§ 19, p. 307. Six quarters of peas were given to the ewes in the time of lambing, 10–11 Henry VI. See MS., P. R. O., Ecclesiastical Commission, Various, 159449.

[4] See, for example, §§ 10, p. 226.

[5] See MS., P. R. O., Ecclesiastical Commission, Various, 159308 (1286–87). In porcell*is* castr*andis* v d.

from Fareham,[1] and on another five were received as a gift from the abbess of Harwell.[2] Of course, such instances are not conclusive, but they point in the direction of an emphasis on selection. But, so far as we know, there was complete promiscuity of animals within the flocks and herds. The common pastures themselves insured a large measure of this until the enclosure of 1795.

As might be expected, the condition of the stock was not good. There was a great deal of sterility which the reeve recorded so as to explain the small increases. One year 4 cows calved but 3 were sterile.[3] Another year (1355–56) of 475 ewes, 3 died before lambing, 6 suffered abortion, and 90 were sterile, the number of lambs being only 376.[4] Disease laid a heavy hand on these sheep. Of the 376 lambs mentioned above, 30 went as tithes, 3 as customary dues to the lord's officials, and 77 died of murrain before weaning, 6 before shearing, and 6 after shearing. The net increase from 475 ewes that the lord could enjoy was 254 lambs. A number of sheep were sold for their hides because weak.[5] Kebbs, or weak sheep, occur frequently. A good deal of care was given to the ewes and lambs at the time of lambing. The trouble came afterwards.

The disease that is recorded is nearly always murrain. This is such a general term as to mean nothing but disease. The very use of such a word to cover everything is indicative of the lack of examination of the symptoms and the causes. Occasionally it was written down in the accounts that sheep died of murrain from the sheep-pox.[6] In 1365–66 the pox prevented the sheep from giving any milk. We learn about this only because it was necessary for the reeve to explain why he had no cheese or butter to sell.[7] Tar, oil, tallow,[8] and quicksilver were purchased for smearing the sheep. Just which ones were mixed together and in what proportions is not indicated; on one occasion, it would seem, oil, copperas, verdigris, and quicksilver were bought for combining in some way.[9] On one occasion a certain friar,[10] and on another a cer-

1 See MS. P. R. O., Ecclesiastical Commission Various, 159277 (1220–21).
2 *Ibid.*, 159275 (1218–19).
3 See below, §§ 7, p. 204.
4 See below, §§ 15, p. 275.
5 See, for example, §§ 8, p. 207.
6 See below, § 25, pp. 483.
7 See MS., P. R. O., Ecclesiastical Commission, Various, 159452.
8 See below, §§ 15, p. 272; §§ 16, p. 281; §§ 18, p. 298; and §§ 19, p. 307.
9 See below, §§ 14, p. 262.
10 See below, §§ 7, p. 203.

tain Friar William,[1] were paid to visit the sheep. Once 6d. were paid for doctoring six oxen.[2]

The kind and amount of the lord's livestock are indicated in the following table.

SOURCES OF INCOME IN ANIMAL HUSBANDRY
ANNUAL AVERAGE

Source	1208–1226			1231–1314			1315–1383			1384–1448		
	£	s.	d.	£	s.	d.	£	s.	d.	£	s.	d.
Pannage	0	10	8¾	0	12	4	0	11	3	0	9	3½
Herbage	1	1	4½	0	17	4	1	8	3¾	0	16	0
Pasture	0	9	7¾	0	17	6	0	15	7¾	0	14	8
Foldage				0	4	0	0	6	2	0	0	11
Pigs in stubble							0	5	3¼	0	2	4
Lactage				0	13	1¼	1	2	1	1	4	6
Woods				2	9	5½	1	14	1	0	5	4
Underwood	1	16	8	1	11	0	1	5	2¼	1	10	8
Hides	0	2	6¼	0	4	5	0	3	8	0	2	0½
Pelts	1	8	2	1	3	11½	0	17	8½	0	16	9
Cheese	4	0	5½	4	8	2	2	3	3½			
Butter	0	2	8	0	4	9	0	3	0¼			
Wool [1]	10	9	0 [2]	24	0	0 [3]	17	0	0 [3]	16	4	0 [3]
Equines	0	4	9	0	10	2	0	10	2	0	6	1
Bovines	1	0	7¼	2	14	10¼	2	8	9¾	1	10	1
Sheep	3	4	3	5	19	11¾	12	2	0	12	11	1¾
Swine				2	0	9	1	3	10	1	0	0
Total	24	10	11¾	48	11	9¼	44	0	6	37	13	9¾

[1] Only great and lambs' wool.
[2] Estimate.
[3] Rough estimate based on amounts of wool, and prices as found in the Crawley accounts and in Rogers' materials.

The equines and bovines were for draught purposes. The few hogs were raised for the lord's larder or for sale. The sheep were chiefly for wool, with some income from the sale of hides. One year thirty wethers were sold, old and weak.[3] This is in itself indication of the purpose. The wool-producing wethers had been kept growing wool for so many years that they were no longer fit. If mutton had been a consideration, of course, they would have been sold young. The ewes were required not only to breed and grow wool but to yield a profit from milk which was sold as such

[1] See below, §§ 8, p. 209.
[2] MS., P. R. O., Ecclesiastical Commission, Various, 159301 (1272–73).
[3] See below, §§ 5, p. 189. Cf. §§ 25, p. 483.

or made into cheese. One year the lord received 20s. from the leasing of 160 ewes at 1½d. for milking purposes. It was recorded that 75 kebbs did not give milk.[1] On another occasion 10s. were derived from this lactage, or leasing for milking purposes, of 150 ewes for 7 weeks in summer.[2]

For the protection of the sheep the lord had well-sheltered sheepfolds, for repair of which there are frequent entries of expense.[3] Sheep were also folded in the fields by means of hurdles moved from place to place by the customary tenants as part of their regular service to the lord.[4]

The tenants in Crawley had their own livestock. In the thirteenth century each one was allowed to keep twenty-five sheep on the common pasture (apparently the same as the fold of the customary tenants), without paying anything for the privilege.[5] In the sixteenth century it was said that one certain tenant had pasture for twenty sheep, one cow, and one horse.[6] Whether there had been a general diminution of rights of pasture, we have not noted. If a tenant possessed over the twenty-five in the thirteenth century, he paid to the lord 1d. for three sheep in excess.[7] In the seventeenth century the excess of sheep that a holder of a yardland might possess was put at ten. Not over ten extra sheep were to be kept "from the common fould or flocke." [8] In the thirteenth century a tenant who acted as shepherd of the wethers or ewes might have thirty-one sheep on the common pasture free, and might drive them into his own fold at night.[9] Clearly then, there was a stint of the pastures, beyond which a tenant could go only if he gave extra service or paid a customary due. This stint applied to sheep, cows, and horses, but apparently not to hogs. In the Middle Ages a customary tenant in Crawley might keep

1 See below, §§ 19, p. 306.
2 See MS., P. R. O., Ecclesiastical Commission, Various, 159427 (1425–26).
3 See, for instance, §§ 12, p. 243; §§ 15, p. 272; §§ 25, pp. 479.
4 See below, §§ 11, p. 235; §§ 25, p. 486.
5 Cf. below, §§ 11, p. 236.
6 MS., P. R. O., Ecclesiastical Commission, Court Roll, 110/1, fol. 29d. (10 and 11 Sept., 4 Eliz.).
7 See below, §§ 11, p. 236.
8 MS., P. R. O., Ecclesiastical Commission, Court Roll, 95/9, fol. 68 (11 March, 1626).
9 See below, §§ 11, p. 236.

twenty-five sheep and probably one cow and one horse. If he owned only one calf (in addition to the above-mentioned animals), he probably was not required to pay any due. If he owned two calves, however, he had to take his horse from the common pastures — at least at a later date,[1] or pay 1d. a year to the lord for the extra calf.

The tenants' hogs were not limited in amount, as has been said. They might be kept freely outside the manor of Crawley, but if they were kept in the woods of Crawley with the lord's hogs, the owners should pay 2d., 1d., or ½d., according to the ages of the hogs.[2] Just what is meant by keeping hogs outside the manor,[3] just where that was, is not clear. At any rate, as we know from the entries of pannage paid, the tenants commonly found it necessary or advantageous to put their hogs in the lord's woods to eat the mast there and to dig for tubers and roots. They also frequently paid the lord for the privilege of putting their hogs on his stubble fields.[4]

How many animals the tenants had in the aggregate in the Middle Ages can only be estimated. Following is a rough reckoning.

ESTIMATE OF TENANTS' LIVESTOCK IN THE THIRTEENTH CENTURY

Equines,	25 holdings	in South Crawley,	1 each —	25[1]
Bovines,	50 "	in Crawley,	2 each —	100[2]
Sheep,	50 "	in Crawley,	25 each —	1250
Swine,	50 "	in Crawley,	10 each —	500[3]
				1875

1 Tenants of North Crawley were nearly all hand workers.
2 In the year 1256–57, the tenants had 8 oxen which were exempt from herbage because hitched to the plow; besides these there were 44 cows, 15 two-year-olds, 18 yearlings, and 23 calves. See below, §§ 9, p. 214. In addition, there were the cows which were allowed free herbage, that is about 50. In all this makes 158 bovines. This number was apparently above the average.
3 This is an allowance of one sow and her surviving farrow, along with a few yearlings. We may have given the tenants of Crawley too many pigs and not enough sheep. See below, § 21, p. 70, n. 1.

1 MS., P. R. O., Eclesiastical Commission, Court Roll, 91/6, fol. 10 (10 Sept., 41 Eliz.).
2 See below, §§ 11, p. 233.
3 For feeding swine on the road, see below, §§ 7, p. 203.
4 See MS., P. R. O., Ecclesiastical Commission, Various, 159348, *et passim*.

We may safely conclude that the allowance of pasture was not enough for the needs of the tenants in the Middle Ages. There were numerous infractions of the stint and many payments for the keeping of excess stock. An additional restriction was found in the case of bovines and equines. A customary tenant might not sell his horse or ox without the lord's consent, and the lord might buy these himself at 6d. below the anticipated market price.[1] Whether the prohibition on sale was because the lord wanted to make sure of the services due him, or whether he felt a vested interest in the stock from the fact that they had fed on the common pasture, is not clear. The latter explanation seems to be the one most valid for Crawley, because in the case of North Crawley tenants who owed no plowing or carting services, the ox and horse were not to be sold without permission if they had been raised from the calf or the colt up.[2]

The lord of Crawley had more sheep than his tenants had, but fewer equines, bovines. and swine. He had more oxen but fewer cows. The lord kept cows to breed oxen; the tenants to breed and also probably for milking purposes.

In the Middle Ages there were three sets of folds, those belonging to the lord, the one belonging to the customary tenants,[3] and private folds, for example, of the shepherds of ewes and wethers and, we may add, of the freeholders at the Hoo and at the Rookley House estate. To take care of the sheep by day and to drive them into their folds at night there were various shepherds. Apparently shepherds, swineherds, and cowherds cared for the animals of both lord and tenants. There seems to have been no keeper of horses, as has already been noted.[4]

Outstanding in the management of livestock were the combination of the interests of tenants and lord and the helplessness of both in the face of animal diseases.

[1] See below, §§ 11, pp. 233, 235.
[2] *Ibid.* p. 235.
[3] See below, §§ 9, p. 214; §§ 15, pp. 269, 270; §§ 16, p. 279; §§ 19, p. 305; §§ 25, p. 478.
[4] See above, § 17, p. 58.

§ 13. *Duality of Crawley.* The village street divides Crawley like most rural communities into two parts, North and South Crawley. There were about twenty-five peasant holdings in each.[1] Each had its three-field system, at least in modern times,[2] one managed quite apart from the other. Each section was occupied by servile tenants, succeeding to their estates by cradle-hold. And the tenants of each owed boon-works to the lord. Each had a very important official in its midst: the North had the smith, the South the reeve.

The compilers of the custumal of about 1280 were more impressed with the difference between the two sections than with their similarity. They found it more convenient to separate the two parts completely in setting forth the customs of the village.[3]

In the North the services were chiefly hand works, in the South characteristically by horse or oxen. While the North had few or no plows, the South possessed enough for their own use and the lord's help also. In the North the tenants performed the week-work, while in the South they did the special tasks, such as carting hay, wood, and manure, and riding on errands. In the North the holdings were farthing lands of $5\frac{1}{2}$ statutory acres, while in the South they were virgates of 16 statutory acres.[4] Since each was one quarter of a larger unit, the hide or what corresponded to it, in North Crawley 22 acres and in South Crawley 64 acres,[5] we can see that the two parts belonged to a different system.

The evidence covering the duality of Crawley belongs to the period from about 1280 to the seventeenth century. Since the beginning of this duality probably goes back to Anglo-Saxon times, we are left pretty much in the dark as to its origin. But in view of

[1] See below, §§ 17, p. 288. [2] See above, § 10, p. 31.

[3] See below, §§ 11, pp. 229 ff.

[4] At the tourn of St. Martin's, 3 Eliza. (1561), John Wayte paid a fine of 36s. 8d. for an estate of one messuage and a virgate of terra nativa in South Crawley, containing 32 (customary) acres; and a fine of 3s. 4d. for another estate of one toft and a ferling of terra nativa in North Crawley, containing 11 acres. MS., P. R. O., Ecclesiastical Commission, Court Roll, 110/1, fol. 10. We can find the ferling in quite modern descriptions of land units, for example, in 1806 and 1833. MS., Ecclesiastical Commission, Millbank, 153086, fol. 229; and 153113, fol. 196.

[5] Since the local or customary acre was half the later statutory acre, these numbers would be in local usage, 44 acres and 128 acres. The latter would be numerically near to the common hide of 120 acres.

the fact that the division between the two parts was so neatly done, we may conclude that it was a creation. The most likely surmise is that the lord bishop amalgamated two villages, Crawley and one other, to form a larger community. In the charter of 909 there was a separate or distinct wick called Titchfield,[1] but this is hardly pertinent in the present connection. In Domesday Book,[2] Crawley was said to have 6 villeins who may conceivably have possessed the 20 slaves (slave families) and 7 plows, and lived in South Crawley; whilst the 25 bordars may have been without plows and may have lived in North Crawley. Certainly this surmise gives to each part approximately the same number.[3] Whatever may have been the explanation of Domesday, if we are on the right track, the plain inference is that North Crawley was made up originally of Celts, without plows, doing manual labor, and possessing the Celtic land units of farthinglands or ferlings.[4] In many ways, we may infer, the two parts grew to be a single whole, without leaving a clear trace of their dual origin. If there is anything in this hypothesis, we cannot help wondering whether manorial duality occurs elsewhere.

§ 14. *Social Classes in Medieval Crawley.* There is no explicit evidence on this subject for the Anglo-Saxon period. We can, of course, argue back from thirteenth-century and Domesday records, but such a procedure is always dangerous.[5] In Domesday Book there are 6 villeins, 25 bordars, and 20 slaves. Later these were apparently shaken down into one class of customary tenants. These were the bondmen or nativi of the later Middle Ages. Their status was not emphasized until the fifteenth and sixteenth centuries. But they were unfree in so far as they could not leave the manor without the lord's consent, nor could they marry off their children without his permission. They were apparently the chief,

[1] See below, §§ 3, pp. 179, 182. [2] See below, §§ 4, pp. 185.

[3] Another surmise would be that the 6 villeins and 25 bordars lived in South Crawley, the 20 slaves in North Crawley. This would throw the balance of the two parts, which seems important, out of the issue.

[4] Vinogradoff, Sir Paul, *English Society in the Eleventh Century* (1908), p. 150. When more information is available from air photographs about the pre-Saxon field arrangements, we shall have further evidence for or against this view.

[5] See above, § 3, pp. 6 f.

or only, suitors at the manorial court in the medieval period. From them the ministri curie, or manorial officials, were chosen. They seem to have numbered about fifty tenants in the thirteenth and following centuries.

The customary tenants may have contained a sub-group of cotsetlers, about whom we have little information. In the year 1232–33 the lord planted oats on various pieces of land including twenty-four statutory acres of the land of the cotsetlers (de t*er*ra cotsetlor*um*).[1] Just what their status or economic position was we do not know. They may have been cottagers or the small holders of North Crawley. Not long after this time there were six curtilages which were leased to different people at 6d. each, one at 12d.[2] These curtilages were at least garden plots and possibly included cottages.

The two groups of customary tenants, about whom we can feel sure, are the yardlanders of South Crawley and the farthing-holders of North Crawley, already considered.[3] The former held about sixteen statutory acres of land each, the latter five and a half. The former were really cultivators of their own holdings; the latter were essentially cottagers, giving much of their time to their lord either at customary labor or task work. The latter class, farthing-holders, having about two of their acres in fallow, had only about four in crops, not sufficient to provide much grain under an inefficient system of cultivation.

Just what became of the older sons of Crawley tenants, that is, the sons who did not inherit estates, is a puzzle. Some might marry outside the manor with the lord's consent. Others could do little, at least legally, except become squatters on the lord's land or laborers for other villagers. When Robert Pottere paid 6d. to remain on the lord's land, he may have thereby acknowledged that he was an outsider with no rights, in short, a squatter or a mere inhabitant, but not a regular tenant.[4] In the period 1225–1306 there is evidence of a landless laboring class, about which,

[1] See below, §§ 8, p. 211.
[2] See MS., P. R. O., Ecclesiastical Commission, Various, 159285 (1236–37).
[3] See above, § 13, p. 47.
[4] MS., P. R. O., Ecclesiastical Commission, Various, 159304 (1277–78).

however, we can have no feeling of certainty. In the year 1235–36, as we have seen above, six curtilages rented for 6d. and one for 12d. An old house was sold for 12d. and several of them were disposed of for 11s. 6d. These were said to be in court, whether within the precint of the home farm or before the manorial court, is not clear. The 'acres' attached to some of the curtilages were eparately sold.[1]

Of freemen in medieval Crawley there is little or no evidence. We may infer that the rector was free, but he was probably always an outsider, that is, born elsewhere. The holder of the South Crawley estate called the Hoo, who may have been the lord's auditor even in the Middle Ages,[2] may have been a freeman. The tenant who possessed the holding on the extreme western part of Crawley was a freeman.[3] But how continuous he was in occupation, or how long this estate maintained its identity we have no knowledge.

The holders of the last-named tenement, at least in the year 1316 and again in 1325, were Philip Aubyn and his wife Alice. Philip Aubyn, while coroner, was elected mayor of Winchester in 1312.[4] He obtained permission in 1317 to go to the Channel Islands for grain.[5] Along with several others, he was accused of having carried off goods from a Portuguese ship which had gone ashore off the Isle of Wight but had not been wrecked.[6] And he was the patron of the church at Lainston, very near to Winchester.[7] Aubyn was apparently a capitalist who derived at least part of his income from investment. Since he could not loan openly at usury, or at what we call interest, he apparently bought rent charges.[8] To the holders of (free) tenements, he made a 'gift' — that is, in effect loaned money, receiving in return land for a period or indefinitely. He paid the tax of a twentieth in 1328 in at least four Hampshire

[1] MS., P. R. O., Ecclesiastical Commission, Various, 159284.
[2] See above, § 8, p. 23.
[3] See below, §§ 22, p. 464.
[4] *Calendar of Close Rolls, Edward II*, vol. 1307–13 (1892), p. 494.
[5] *Calendar of Patent Rolls, Edward II*, vol. 1313–17 (1898), p. 622.
[6] *Ibid.*, vol. 1317–21 (1903), p. 538.
[7] *The Registers of John de Sandale and Regaud de Asserio*, Hampshire Record Society (ed. by F. J. Baigent, 1897), pp. 157, 346.
[8] See below, §§ 22, p. 464.

manors as well as in Winchester.[1] He also had loaned £100 to a land-holder in Wiltshire.[2] But the most significant acquisition, at least for us, was of the fee made up of land in Crawley, Upper Somborne, Romsey, and Nitherden. Since there were included in this estate two acres of meadow and 500 of pasture, we may conclude it was a sheep farm. Whether he exploited this estate, which did not constitute a solid block, through a bailiff or leased it to someone else, is not known. We may conclude, at least, that since it changed hands often in a short time, it was a valuable piece of property.

Whether Philip Aubyn and the tenant at the Hoo were free suitors in the manorial court, is not known. It is not until the seventeenth century apparently that we find free suitors recorded.[3]

From the records read, we get the impression that Crawley was overwhelmingly a manor of bondmen occupying bondland throughout the Middle Ages. Freemen and freedom may have existed but they were neither vital nor important.

§ 15. *Food of the Medieval Tenants.* It is very doubtful whether there was much difference between the food of one class and that of another in Crawley. Such difference would be more in quantity and variety than in the kind of staple items. We know what food was allowed to the tenants for the services performed for the lord. Barley [4] was the chief grain given to them, but oats [5] was given at times and wheat [6] also. Oatmeal was made for porridge for the lord's servants.[7] Herring were handed out at the time of boon-work.[8] Cheese [9] went to the dairymaid, the two shepherds, the smith, and the reeve. Lambs[10] and little pigs[11] also were given, and apples [12] when picked in the orchard at Waltham.

[1] See below, §§ 21, pp. 455–456, and MS., P. R. O., Exchequer Lay Subsidies, 173/4, membs. 6d. and 17.
[2] *Calendar of Close Rolls, Edward II*, vol. 1313–18 (1893), p. 622.
[3] See below, §§ 32, pp. 511; §§ 33, pp. 512–513.
[4] See below, §§ 6, p. 198; §§ 7, p. 203, *et passim.*
[5] See below, §§ 13, p. 255.
[6] See below, §§ 14, p. 264.
[7] See below, §§ 13, p. 254; §§ 14, p. 264.
[8] See below, §§ 8, p. 209; §§ 9, p. 217.
[9] See below, §§ 7, p. 205; §§ 8, p. 212; §§ 9, p. 220.
[10] See below, §§ 9, p. 219; §§ 10, p. 228.
[11] See below, §§ 11, p. 236.
[12] See below, §§ 11, p. 236.

The tenants had their spring grain (barley and oats) and their winter grain (winter barley and probably wheat). Whether they grew any peas or beans, is unknown. Whether they ate such wheat as they might have grown or sold it to townsmen, is not clear. Unless they grew wheat it is hard to see how they fitted themselves into the scheme of a fallow rotation under the three-field system. Winter barley, at least on the lord's acres, was a minor crop as compared with wheat. Of course, the peasants may have emphasized it much more.

More certain is the existence of a supply of pork, milk, and mutton. But here the lord tended to restrict the peasants in charging a rent for the swine feeding in his woods, for the cattle feeding on his lands, and for all sheep beyond a certain number. Chickens were apparently limited only or chiefly by the measure of the industry and foresight of the peasants themselves. Geese were probably not plentiful. There were probably few or no fresh fish obtainable in Crawley itself. Rabbits were reserved for the lord and later farmed out at so much a year.[1] Nuts were occasionally collected and sold for the lord's benefit.[2] But, of course, there is no telling how many of these things were appropriated by the tenants. Berries are unrecorded, but there was no reason why the tenants could not have had apple trees as the lord had.

An interesting question is whether the tenants ate white or black bread, that is, bread made of wheaten flour or barley or rye flour. Rogers[3] thought that the English people, including the peasants, used wheaten bread. In coming to this conclusion, he was thinking chiefly of the southern and eastern parts of England, and had in mind the products of the demesne rather than of the tenants' lands. Sir William Ashley[4] has reviewed the evidence, coming to the conclusion that in medieval and early modern England, as in contemporary northern Europe, the peasants ate black bread. He is inclined to emphasize

[1] See below, §§ 26, p. 493.

[2] See below, §§ 8, p. 208.

[3] Rogers, J. E. T., *A History of Agriculture and Prices in England*, vol. IV (1882), pp. 133, 730.

[4] *The Bread of our Forefathers: An Inquiry in Economic History* (1928), pp. 132–133.

rye bread. But the use of rye bread is very doubtful in Crawley, because rye was probably not grown, at least not on the demesne. The substitute on the demesne was winter barley. It seems indeed likely that the medieval tenant in Crawley used barley for bread [1] and for beer, and oats for porridge. It would be a happy cultivator who could get enough barley bread, pork, and beer. These were nourishing and sufficiently hard to digest to meet the needs of outdoor workers: they provided the necessary resistance. It is much to be feared that beef, veal, and mutton were eaten when really unfit, that is, when the animals had died of disease. In the year 1256–57, the chines of nine hogs were sold at 2½d. cach, of four at only 1d. each because spotted (leprosi).[2] To say the least, people do not seem to have been discriminating in the eating of meat.

§ 16. *Tenure and Customs in Crawley.* The Manor of Crawley was regranted to the lord bishop in 909 apparently as free alms, owing no services to the king or state, except the trinoda necessitas — the repair of bridges, garrisoning of castles, and service in the national militia.[3] In the twelfth and thirteenth centuries, however, we know that the bishop of Winchester owed to the king sixty knights' service (once forty) for his holdings in Hampshire alone.[4] In the twelfth century he paid scutage in lieu of such service.[5] King Henry III granted to Peter des Roches, Bishop of Winchester, a number of additional privileges to be held in free alms.[6] In an account of the year 1336–37, however, the bishop paid the wages of five knights for keeping guard for ten days along the seacoast.[7] It is clear that the bishop owed and gave feudal service for his manors, but we have found no definite statement

[1] Winter barley was apparently preferred to spring barley. See below, §§ 11, p. 237.

[2] See below, §§ 9, p. 215.

[3] See below, §§ 3, pp. 179, 181.

[4] *Red Book of the Exchequer* (ed. by Hubert Hall), vol. I (1896), pp. 72, 91, 99, 148. Years 1190–91, 1194–95, 1201–02.

[5] *Ibid.*, vol. II (1896), pp. 664, 704. Years 1155–56, 1160–62.

[6] Goodman, A. W., *Chartulary of Winchester Cathedral* (1927), pp. 13–14. Date is 20 Jan., 1232 (new style).

[7] MS., P. R. O., Ecclesiastical Commission, Various, 159348. Under Wolvesey.

that he owed anything for Crawley specifically.[1] Indeed the whole flavor of Crawley life and organization was non-military. Indirectly, however, Crawley may have contributed to a feudal array in so far as the profits of the manor going to the bishop may have been used to hire knights or to buy freedom from the necessity of doing so.

When we look at the tenure, not by which Crawley itself was held from the king but by which the people within Crawley held from the lord of the manor, we find three different kinds — the customary tenure by cradle-hold, the leasehold, and the freehold. These may not be the usual designations, but we are following the Crawley evidence.

Customary tenure was all-important in Crawley from at least the thirteenth to the nineteenth century. Into the class of customary tenants seem to have gone the villeins, bordars, and slaves of Domesday Book. The customary tenants possessed bond or native land and held their land according to the customs of the manor. Chief among the customs was the payment of rents or dues of many kinds. In Crawley there was a fixed rent which in origin may have been a sum paid to be free of certain services (in Crawley most likely plowing), or it may have been the survival of an early payment by tenants who were once wholly free. There were but few rents in kind, churchscot being the outstanding if not the only example; and, of course, churchscot, as the name indicates, was originally a church due. The overwhelmingly important rent in the thirteenth century was service. In general there were two kinds, the week-work and the special task. The week-work was fixed in amount but not in nature. The nature of the special task was specified clearly enough as harvesting, carting, or carrying letters, and it was also, in most cases, fairly definite

[1] In 1316 an inquisition relative to feudal aids indicated that in the hundred of Buddlesgate there were 25 hamlets, 3 belonging to laymen, 13 to the prior of Winchester, and 9 to the bishop of Winchester. Crawley was included in these 9 hamlets. Thus our village was actually on a military list. *Inquisitions and assessments relative to Feudal Aids*, vol. II (1900), p. 309. On the general subject of the relation of the tenant holding by free alms, to military service and the commutation thereof, see Elisabeth G. Kimball, "Tenure in Frank Almoign and Secular Services," *English Historical Review*, vol. XLIII (1928), pp. 341–353.

in amount. About the decline of these customary rents more is stated elsewhere.[1]

The customary tenant owed suit of court and indeed he seems to have been all-important, so far as our records go.[2] He owed a heriot [3] — his best animal — when he succeeded his father or brother in a tenement. After the demesne had been leased to farmers, the heriots were embarassing, like the stray beasts, for they had to be sold and accounted for. They could no longer simply be added to the lord's flock or herd. Since the chief animals in Crawley were sheep, the heriot was usually a single sheep; in some cases it was a cow or bullock.

When William Stephens drowned himself in a cask of water about the year 1567 his holdings escheated to the lord, his widow receiving back some of the lands on the promise of doing heavy services in washing and shearing the lord's sheep.[4] When a tenant hanged himself, as did Henry Pitter about 1635 or 1636, his goods and chattels went to the lord, amounting in this particular case to £4 16s. in value.[5] When Peter the Blind was hanged, about 1273, his chattels, worth 33s. 6d., went to the lord.[6] And when a family died out, the tenement reverted to the lord,[7] for such use as best suited his interests. He might add the holding to the demesne; or, more likely, he would find another tenant. Apparently the lord charged varying amounts by way of fines, or accession payments. At times the fine was but two or three shillings.[8] At other times it might be one or two marks.[9] But in the sixteenth century some very high fines were collected.[10] Apparently with the rise of prices the lord was forced to get a greater income from his land. Finding rents fixed by custom, he had only the fines to fall back upon. On the whole, however, the lord seems to have derived more of his increased revenue of this type from the great number of the fines rather than from the extent of individual fines.

[1] See below § 22, pp. 74 ff. [2] See below, § 31, p. 109.
[3] See below, §§ 11, pp. 233, 237, 238; §§ 31, p. 509.
[4] MS., P. R. O., Ecclesiastical Commission, Court Roll, 110/2, fol. 9d.
[5] MS., P. R. O., Ecclesiastical Commission, Various, 159473 (11 Car. II).
[6] *Ibid.*, 159301, memb. 8. [7] See below, §§ 18, p. 297; §§ 19, p. 306.
[8] See below, §§ 19, p. 297.
[9] See below, §§ 9, p. 216; §§ 14, p. 261.
[10] See below, §§ 37, p. 521; §§ 38, p. 525.

In the sixteenth century some of the customary tenancies were called copyholds. The copyhold was simply a tenancy of bond-land, the holding of which had been recorded in the court rolls, a copy of the entry having been given to the holder of the land. Copyhold was not a category of great importance in Crawley. Indeed one can read far in the rolls without finding the name.[1] What counted was the fact that there was a definite custom known to the tenants, and, better still, entered in the court records or even in the custumal. The rents being paid yearly were fixed fast enough. The fines, however, coming only once during a generation were not so certain. But it is doubtful whether in Crawley there were any clear distinctions between copyhold and copyhold, or between one customary tenancy and another, in this respect.

One of the tag marks of customary tenure in Crawley was the fact that it involved inheritance by the youngest son, or if there were no son, by the youngest daughter. This was called borough-English, or cradle-hold inheritance.[2]

Cradle-hold probably arose in the Anglo-Saxon period. There is no evidence that the people ever wanted to get rid of it, and indeed it persisted down almost to the present time.[3] The custom had possessed some advantages. The older children would be able to provide for themselves before the father died, while the youngest and weakest would be endowed with the family holding. The widow of the deceased, and mother of the young heir, would find a logical place in the scheme of things as the holder of the tenement during her son's minority and her own chaste widowhood.[4] She was exempt from fine of entry[5] and from half the churchscot.[6] On remarriage she lost the holding but her husband might enter upon

[1] See below, §§ 31, p. 510.

[2] Not so many years ago (in the period 1900–24) there appeared in Crawley an old man, unkempt and strange, who laid claim to a tenement in the village. He told the estate agent that he was the youngest son in his family and that he had been dispossessed of his rights. When asked to produce documentary evidence of his claim, he admitted he had none. He then disappeared, never to return.

[3] See below, § 33, pp. 117 ff.

[4] See below, §§ 40, p. 529; §§ 54, p. 595.

[5] See below, §§ 11, p. 233 and §§ 54, p. 595.

[6] See below, §§ 11, pp. 236.

it, on the payment of an extra fine, and he might even become the guardian of the heir.[1]

These customs connected with bondland lasted in great strength down to the nineteenth century. Although the services were commuted in the fifteenth, seventeenth, and eighteenth centuries, still money rents continued to be collected, heriots to be compounded for, and fines to be paid down to the new land laws of 1922 and 1924 which went into effect 1 January, 1926, or even after that date until a compensation agreement had been arrived at. Indeed in November, 1924, occurred the death of a customary tenant in Crawley, which was duly noted by one of the officials in the offices of the Ecclesiastical Commission, because of the fact that a fine for the entry of a new tenant would be forthcoming.

The second general kind of tenure within the manor of Crawley was leasehold. There are clearly two parts to the story of leasehold in Crawley. One is the leasing of the demesne for a period of years, prevailing from the early fifteenth down to the nineteenth century. This, of course, was a special contract, the terms of which were open to revision whenever made. Inheritance of the lease, in the absence of a will, would apparently go to the eldest son.[2] The other kind of leasehold is less clear and of much less importance. Certain small pieces of the demesne had from time to time been granted out to tenants, apparently on indefinite leases. The purpresture, so common in Crawley, is an example of this tenure.[3] This land was said to pass from father to son by primogeniture, or inheritance of the eldest son.[4] The effect of this was lost, however, by the development of a rule that if a purpresture were attached to bondland, it should be inherited by bondland custom.[5] It was common for a customary tenant to hold bondland and purpresture and at times also gavel-land.[6]

The third tenure in Crawley was the freehold. It would seem that until at least the late thirteenth century, or perhaps the early

[1] See below, §§ 39, pp. 526, 527, 528. [2] See below, §§ 54, p. 595.

[3] Gavel-land, or gafol-land, is possibly another example. This may be assarted land of the demesne. See Nellie Neilson, "Customary Rents," *Studies in Social and Legal History* (1910), p. 47.

[4] See below, §§ 54, p. 495. [5] See below, pp. 494–495.

[6] See, for example, below, §§ 39, pp. 527–528.

fourteenth, there was no freehold in Crawley. Then two estates,[1] one called the Hoo and the other later known as the Rookley House estate,[2] were specially created, as existing somewhat outside the manor, the first away to the south and the second away to the west. From the fourteenth century on to the nineteenth we have found no cases of additional freehold in Crawley. Then came a process of enfranchisement in the nineteenth century which changed so much land into freehold that the other tenures almost disappeared and the manor became a hollow shell.[3]

§ 17. *Crawley compared with Other Communities.* Crawley was a small manor in comparison with others belonging to the bishopric of Winchester. While Crawley was set down as 28 hides in Anglo-Saxon times, Micheldever was put at 106, Farnham at 60, Downton at 55, and Alresford at 51. Of course, hidation figures were often inexact, but they serve the general purpose of showing differences in size.

The income derived by the bishop of Winchester from the various manors is indicated in the table on the following page.

Let us compare Crawley in a general way with other communities belonging to the bishop of Winchester. We have chosen to consider conditions existing at one particular time, the year 1335–36,[4] but what was true then would commonly be true before and after that time. Of course, Crawley had no shops, as had the borough of Taunton, and no castle, as had both Taunton and Farnham. There were no stalls, such as we find in Taunton, Hambledon, Witney, and Alresford. At Winchester and at Hinton there were fairs, but none at Crawley. There was no grist mill at Crawley, while we have counted over a dozen on the other manors and doubtless many more existed. Downton and Witney had both fulling mills and fishponds, Crawley none. Crawley possessed no keeper of horses, such as we find in Meon, no warren-keeper as in

[1] See above, § 14, p. 50; §§ 22, pp. 464 ff.

[2] Of course, it is just possible that the Rookley House estate was the one held by Alvin Stella in Anglo-Saxon days, as recorded in Domesday Book. See below, §§ 4, p. 185.

[3] See below, § 33, pp. 117 ff.

[4] MS., P. R. O., Ecclesiastical Commission, Various, 159347.

Burghclere, and no beadle as in Poundsford, Twyford, and Knoyle. Crawley could boast of no swans, such as both Farnham and Waltham had, and no vineyard like that at Farnham. It had no dovecot, such as was found in Brockhampton, Overton, Drakensford, and West Wycomb. It had no fish for sale as Bittern had, and little or no malt, such as we find in Farnham, Brightwell, and Wargrave. Rye was scarce in Crawley, found in Holway

INCOME FROM MANORS, 1208–09 AND 1318–19

Manor	1208–09[1] Nearest £	1316–17[2] Nearest £
West Meon	181	—
Farnham	178	185
Downton	165	437
Wargrave	138	193
Waltham	130	169
Alresford	114	97
Twyford	104	181
Crawley	47	121
Woodhay	21	60
Southwark	16	—
Ashmansworth	13	8
Beauworth	13	19
Rimpton	12	42
Fawley and Ower	10	—
Privet	6	—

[1] H. Hall, *Pipe Roll of the Bishopric of Winchester, 1208–09* (1903), pp. xlii–xliii.
[2] *The Registers of John de Sandale and Rigaud de Asserio*, Hampshire Record Society (ed. by F. J. Baigent, 1897), pp. 627–628.

(Taunton), Hambledon Church, Fareham, Adderbury, Asher, Brightwell, and Drakensford. Witney, Adderbury, and Brightwell grew the grain called dragge, while Crawley had little or none of it.

In the Crawley records we have found people called Carter, Smith, Baker, Carpenter, and Shepard, but not Fuller, Weaver, Walker, Saddler, or Miller.[1] In 1548 it was said that there was "No Towne in Englande, Village or Burrowe, but thus withe Cloathinge to bee occupied."[2] Certainly this was not true of Crawley.

[1] There was an Ivo Mersir. Whether this was a variant of Mercer, is not clear. There was also a William Toneur [Shearer?].
[2] See R. H. Tawney and E. Power, *Tudor Economic Documents*, vol. III (1924), p. 42.

Crawley produced raw wool, not woolen cloth, at least no cloth for sale so far as has been discovered. It is not unlikely that Crawley women sold some woolen yarn at Winchester and Andover, but of this there seems to be no record. There may have been some lime-burning in medieval Crawley as in Alta Clere, where tiles, shingles, and laths were also made,[1] but it is apparently only in the census of 1841 that we find someone making a business of lime-burning and brick-making.[2] There is no account of charcoal-burning and of course no smelting of any kind.

As a village, Crawley had a habit of missing things both in medieval and modern times. It escaped manufactures. It was not made into a sheep farm during the enclosure movement. Important highways avoided it. The Andover Canal was constructed to the west of Crawley and the London–Southampton–Basingstoke Canal to the east. Both the London and South Western Railroad and the Didcot Newbury and Southampton line to Oxford ignored Crawley.

Crawley was left with its sheep and its grain, its conies and its chickens, its field ways and its country roads. But, if the hypothesis already presented [3] be found to be correct, then Crawley had the distinction of being in origin a double star, albeit a small one.

§ 18. *Crawley and the Outside World.* In the Middle Ages Crawley was about as closely connected with other communities as it was at any time down to the early part of the nineteenth century. Crawley people went to Winchester about five miles away, for most of them a walk of less than two hours, to sell produce and buy supplies, as has already been said.[4] But they went to Winchester for other purposes too. Doubtless they occasionally visited the shrine of St. Swithun and viewed the Corpus Christi procession. It may be that in Anglo-Norman times they went in to catch a glimpse of the king when he wore his crown in Winchester. There is no record, and it would be hazardous to infer, that Craw-

[1] MS., P. R. O., Ecclesiastical Commission, Various, 159419, memb. xi. The year is 1416–17.

[2] See below, §§ 58, p. 656; §§ 59, p. 676.

[3] See above, § 13, pp. 47–48.

[4] See above § 7, pp. 18 ff.

ley's customary tenants ever sent their sons to a school in Winchester. In the long list of "scholars" in the public school at Winchester, in the period 1393–1887, we have found no name of a native of Crawley, except the son of a rector.[1] These scholars came commonly from towns, seldom from villages. Proximity to an educational institution is no great advantage in the face of hostile public opinion. To this day secondary education in the Winchester district, as elsewhere in England, is restricted. One little girl in 1924 said she did not plan to go to a secondary school because that was for "gentlemen's children."

The lord bishop of Winchester meant everything to Crawley people. They went to his fair at St. Giles, probably since its establishment in 1096. They carted his produce to his palaces at Wolvesey (in Winchester) and Farnham, and some of his goods for sale as far as Southwark, as has been already noted.[2] They were obliged to carry the lord's wool and cheese to Southampton and Bittern.[3] They also had to build a certain amount of paling around the park at Waltham[4] and collect apples in the orchard there.[5] And to Mardon and Overton the tenants of North Crawley had to carry the lord's letters or briefs, doubtless on foot.

Occasionally the collector of taxes had to visit Crawley. The lord's seneschal came twice a year, and the bailiff as often during certain years. Although the men of the bishop of Winchester were in 1232 exempt by royal charter from attending the shire and hundred courts,[6] we find them in the view of frankpledge of the hundred of Buddlesgate in the year 1466.[7] Cases having to do with freeholds in Crawley might be taken to the royal court at Westminster.[8]

Crawley boys, eldest sons, doubtless occasionally volunteered for military service. Possibly in early times a Crawley tenant helped guard the bishop's castle at Mardon (near Winchester).[9]

[1] See T. F. Kirby, *Winchester Scholars* (1888), p. 329.
[2] See above § 4, p. 10; § 7, pp. 18 ff.
[3] See below, §§ 17, p. 293.
[4] *Ibid.*, p. 292.
[5] See below, §§ 17, p. 293.
[6] See below, § 31, p. 107.
[7] See below, §§ 30, pp. 505 ff.
[8] See below, §§ 22, pp. 464–465.
[9] Alebroc owed 5s. in Crawley, probably in the eleventh century, which were actually rendered (possibly in military service) at Mardon. See below, §§ 5, p. 188, *et passim*.

No case of a resident knight, occupying a knight's fee has been found in Crawley proper. The king or his officials might visit Crawley,[1] and certainly during an episcopal voidance the king's officials were in command.[2]

All in all, Crawley was very much the anvil of circumstances. The West Saxons conquered the Celts and Crawley became Saxon. The religion of Rome was favored by the king of the West Saxons, and Crawley was offered up as part of the price paid for that religion. The Normans conquered England and Crawley had to accept Norman and Anglo-Norman episcopal lords — among the best it ever had. The citizens of Winchester grew rich and one of them laid his hands on a slice of Crawley land. The plague visited England and Crawley had to take its share of death. The spirit of free labor followed in the wake of death and Crawley joined in the demands for a change. In these and other ways, Crawley showed itself, not isolated but a part of a great social group, swinging into line in the Middle Ages as in the Modern Period,[3] with wide movements of great economic, social, and cultural import.

§ 19. *Prices, 1208–1448.* The first consideration in any study of prices is the units used. There was much variation from district to district in England. In Crawley, however, the standard units apparently prevailed. The hundred was made up of 5 score. The money was pounds sterling, shillings, and pence. The dry measure was the standard quarter of 8 bushels,[4] the bushel containing 4 pecks.[5] Whether this was always followed, cannot be determined. The units for reckoning wool, cheese, and butter were weys, stones, cloves, and pounds, the wey being 182 pounds avoirdupois, the stone 14, and the clove 7. An unusual weight was the mainard which was apparently 32 pounds.

We have the uneasy feeling that not all the price items are of equal value when we are trying to arrive at an average reflecting

[1] See below, §§ 10, p. 226; also MS., P. R. O., Ecclesiastical Commission, Various, 159361.

[2] For example, 22–28 Hen. III, 34–35 Hen. III, 43–46 Hen. III, etc.

[3] See below, § 45, pp. 159 ff.

[4] See, for instance, below, §§ 13, p. 253.

[5] See below, §§ 16, p. 282.

market conditions. There were sales on the market, and these are doubtless of overwhelming importance. But there were also sales per mutuum, literally 'through a loan,' and sales to the lord's officials. Yearly price variations can easily be explained.[1] Bad weather, for instance, meant high prices for grain. A horse or ox or sheep, it should be noted, was commonly bought at a higher rate than one sold. The reason for this was that when they were bought, they were in good condition for work and breeding; when sold, they were ordinarily old and weak.

By 1208, when our price materials begin, we find a genuine money economy existing as far as the exchange of goods was concerned. It was only in the latter part of the period under consideration (1208–1448), however, that we find wages and rent on a true monetary basis.

An examination of the prices of general agricultural products indicates that we may use the same periods that we found of service in a study of production.[2] These are as follows: 1208–26,[3] 1231–1314, 1315–83, 1384–1448.

The outstanding change is a rise in prices more or less progressive. This rise in price was general, not peculiar to Crawley. Fortunately we are not called upon to explain the general phenomenon. But it is of interest to correlate production on the lord's home farm with price changes. While prices were rising in the first three of our periods, the production, both of grain and animal products, declined.[4] When prices declined somewhat in the fourth period, production was further curtailed. Prices constitute no key to production. It might be thought not unlikely that during the first three periods the lure of the town would increase the cost of production by drawing off tenants and their children, thereby raising wages. But such data as we have on wages — the wages of special workers (officials) — do not indicate that wages rose before prices but lagged behind. And yet it is probable that the difficulty involved in keeping the manorial organization together in

[1] For sale on credit as a possible cause of high prices, see above, § 6, p. 16.

[2] See above, § 9, p. 28.

[3] This is, of course, too short a period to provide an adequate base. Moreover, we cannot be sure that the measures were in all cases the same as subsequently.

[4] See above, § 9, p. 28.

YEARLY AVERAGE PRICE OF GRAIN
(quarters in s. and d.)

Period	Wheat[1]		Spring barley		Oats[2]		Peas	
	Yrs.[3]	Price	Yrs.	Price	Yrs.	Price	Yrs.	Price
1208–1226...	13	3 11¼	13	2 8½	11	1 7	11	2 1½
1231–1314...	53	5 11	51	4 0¾	46	2 6½	47	4 1¾
1315–1383...	58	7 7	56	5 2	56	2 10¾	45	5 1
1384–1448...	41	5 7¾	40	3 9½	42	2 2¼	3	3 0
1208–1448[4]..	165	6 3¼	160	4 3¼	155	2 6	106	4 3½

Period	Vetches		Curall		Winter barley	
	Yrs.	Price	Yrs.	Price	Yrs.	Price
1208–1226...	8	1 11¾	9	2 8¾	10	2 2
1231–1314...	39	3 9	52	4 2¾	38	3 0½
1315–1383...	46	5 1	32	5 1½	2	3 8
1384–1448...	1	3 4				
1208–1448[4]..	94	4 3	93	4 4¾	50	2 10¾

YEARLY AVERAGE PRICE OF HORSES AND OXEN
(animals in s. and d.)

Period	Cart horses bought		Cart horses sold		Plow horses bought	
	Yrs.[3]	Price	Yrs.	Price	Yrs.	Price
1208–1226...............					5	5 5¾
1231–1314...............	5	16 11½	7	10 3	16	7 3½
1315–1383...............	19	18 11¼	11	6 11	32	12 3¼
1384–1448...............	19	20 0½	11	4 5½	8	13 6
1208–1448[4]..............	43	19 2¼	29	6 9½	61	10 7

Period	Plow horses sold		Oxen bought		Oxen sold[5]	
	Yrs.	Price	Yrs.	Price	Yrs.	Price
1208–1226.............	6	4 11¼	8	6 5¾	12	4 11½
1231–1314.............	31	4 7¾	28	10 11¾	46	9 4¾
1215–1383.............	29	5 2½	36	11 6	32	13 0
1284–1448.............	12	4 0	40	13 2	34	11 5¾
1208–1448[4].............	78	4 9¼	112	12 6	124	10 5¾

[1] In Oct., 1928, wheat in Crawley was worth about 40s. a quarter.
[2] In Oct., 1928, oats in Crawley sold at 28s. a quarter.
[3] These are the number of years in the period for which there are figures.
[4] This is the weighted average like the rest. Where figures are missing for one or more of the sub-periods, then the average is for the shorter period.
[5] In Oct., 1928, an ordinary ox or steer brought about £25.

YEARLY AVERAGE PRICE OF OTHER BOVINES AND OF PIGS

(animals in s. and d.)

Period	3-yr.-old bovines sold			Cows bought			Cows sold [1]		
	Yrs.	Price		Yrs.	Price		Yrs.	Price	
1208–1226				1	5	11½	2	4	2½
1231–1314	7	5	2	8	7	1¼	32	6	3¼
1315–1383	1	6	8	2	12	0½	9	6	10½
1384–1448	1	5	0				5	7	2
1208–1448 [2]	9	5	3¾	11	7	10¾	48	6	4¾

Period	Calves sold			Pigs bought			Pigs sold		
	Yrs.	Price		Yrs.	Price		Yrs.	Price	
1208–1226	2	0	7	1	0	8			
1231–1314	32	1	0	2	1	3½	29	2	9½
1315–1383	5	1	6½	5	2	1¾	8	2	10½
1384–1448									
1208–1448 [2]	39	1	0¾	8	1	9	37	2	9¾

YEARLY AVERAGE PRICE OF SHEEP

(animals in s. and d.)

Period	Wethers bought			Wethers sold [3]			Ewes bought			Ewes sold		
	Yrs.	Price		Yrs.	Price		Yrs.	Price		Yrs.	Price	
1208–1226				6	0	9	1	0	9¼	9	0	6½
1231–1314	2	1	1	47	1	1	2	1	4	47	0	10½
1315–1383	8	1	7¾	52	1	2¼	8	1	3	46	1	1
1384–1448				40	1	2				37	1	0
1208–1448 [2]	10	1	6½	145	1	1½	11	1	2¾	139	0	11½

Period	Rams sold			Lambs bought [4]			Lambs sold		
	Yrs.	Price		Yrs.	Price		Yrs.	Price	
1288–1226							13	0	2½
1231–1314	6	1	2¾	5	0	7½	34	0	4¼
1315–1383	44	1	1½	16	0	7¾	45	0	6
1384–1448	26	1	0	32	0	11	33	0	5½
1208–1448 [2]	76	1	1¼	53	0	9¾	125	0	5

[1] An ordinary cow (Oct., 1928) was valued at £30 in Crawley.
[2] This is the weighted average like the rest. Where figures are missing for one or more of the subperiods, then the average is for the shorter period.
[3] A wether in Oct., 1928, was worth about £3.
[4] A lamb in Oct., 1928, sold at £2.

YEARLY AVERAGE PRICE OF ANIMAL PRODUCTS AND POULTRY

Period	Cheese sold		Butter sold		Chickens sold[1]	
	Yrs.	Weys in s. & d.	Yrs.	Cloves in s. & d.	Yrs.	Each in s. & d.
1208–1226	13	7 5½				
1231–1314	53	9 4¼	36	0 4	49	0 1
1315–1383	27	10 9¾	41	0 5½	58	0 1½
1384–1448					41	0 2
1208–1448[2]	93	9 7½	77	0 4¾	148	0 1½

[1] Chickens in Oct., 1928, brought about 1s. 3d. a pound.
[2] See note 2 on the preceding page.

the face of the attraction of towns does help explain the rise in the price of foodstuffs.

Although the subject of price ratios belongs to a general study of prices, still it is interesting to note the following approximate equation for our third period (1315–83): 48 weeks' work (about the working year of an agricultural laborer) would then buy:

52 bushels of wheat, or
4 plow horses, or
7 cows, or
36 wethers, or
17 pigs, or
384 chickens.

Rough estimates seem to indicate that the ratio of the value of chickens and pork to the value of beef and mutton was not much higher then than today. In this connection we should consider the fact that bovines were valued for their labor and milk, and sheep for their wool; neither was bred with much, if any, consideration of flesh.

§ 20. *Labor and Wages.* In Crawley, as on most manors, there were three kinds of labor. First, there was customary work (opera custumaria), given by the tenant as rent for land. This was a precious commodity which the lord valued highly and the tenant gave reluctantly. It was at length commuted to a money payment.[1] The rate at which the commutation took place cannot be exactly stated, only estimated, in the form of the value of a day's work. In 1448–49 a farthing-holder in North Crawley paid 4s. to have his services commuted. For this amount, he was freed from 5 days of washing and shearing the sheep, 6 days of autumn boon-work, 50 days of autumn week-work, and 82 days of winter week-work, or in all 143 days of work.[2] This amounts to $1\frac{1}{3}$ farthings for a day's work. Of course, this was a very low valuation, arising out of the desperation of the lord's situation. Miss Levett puts the commutation value of a day's labor in the late fourteenth century at from $\frac{1}{2}$ to 1d., without food; the market value of a day's labor at 2 or 3d.[3]

When the customary work had been commuted to a money payment, more reliance for predial labor was put upon task work (ad tascham). This had been used before, but in the late fourteenth and early fifteenth centuries became of increasing importance. Hoeing, reaping, threshing, and other tasks were performed at so much per unit of work. For instance, the threshing of eight bushels of wheat was done for 2d.[4] This was done by hand and during the winter when probably there was little or nothing else to do.

Along with the task work, went time work with its rewards of wages (stipendium, vadium). Even before the commutation of customary work, this had been an important form of labor. Afterwards it became the dominant form. When tenants agreed to perform special offices, for instance of hayward and cowherd, they were given a money reward. The following table shows the amounts and changes, reckoned exactly as to amount, approximately as to dates.

The changes that took place occurred at times of great significance. One turning point in the manorial economy of Crawley was in the period 1300–15, another about 1384–1411. These two brief periods deserve minute and careful examination, such as they can-

[1] See below, § 21, pp. 69 ff.

[2] See below, §§ 25, pp. 487–489; §§ 26, p. 492. Cf. also §§ 7, p. 200.

[3] Miss A. E. Levett, "The Black Death on the Estates of the See of Winchester," *Oxford Studies in Social and Legal History*, vol. V (1916), p. 157, n. 4.

[4] See below, §§ 13, p. 253; §§ 14, p. 263.

not be given here. Economic and social forces were at work far beneath the surface of the manorial accounts which record results, not factors. The second of these periods is, of course, the time when tenants, aided by the Black Death, were rebelling against service rents. Their most dramatic protest was the Revolt of 1381. But the period 1300–15, doubtless the culmination of forces at work

YEARLY WAGE (in s. and d.)

Period	Carter	Plowman	Hayward	Cowherd	Driver	Grain Bailiff[1]	Dairy-maid	General Level
1208–1305	3 0	3 0	3 0	3 0		3 0	2 0	100[2]
1306–1410	4 0	4 0	6 8	4 0	4 0	6 8	2 0	150
1411–1453	6 0		6 8		5 0		2 6	181[3]

[1] This is an uncertain translation of messor.
[2] This taken as the base.
[3] The mean of the results when reckoned from the first and second periods.

somewhat earlier, is not so easily explained. Efforts at improvement had been going on and were now in this period renewed and accentuated. Accounting had already been elaborated; now agricultural technique was improved and labor paid a higher wage. The explanation may be that the manorial lord and his officials were trying to meet the first impact of the town on the country. It may have been that they were trying to increase their production for a town market and at the same time endeavoring to keep their tenants at home working hard, or harder than before. It may be that this was the hour of trial: when the village — the manorial village — sought to adjust itself to the rivalry of the town. Had the manor, with its servile labor system and its capacity for technical advance, been successful in its competition with the town in the period 1250–1350, we may feel sure the events of 1350–1450 would never have happened.

Apart from agricultural labor, there was the work of artisans. The chief artisan was the blacksmith who, as we have seen, was also a tenant on the manor. Besides, there were carpenters, thatchers, slaters, and tilers who repaired the buildings of the home farm, possibly also those of the tenants but to a much smaller extent. Occasionally we get specific information about the wages of such house builders and repairers. In 1355–56 a master roofer (coopertor conductor) put slates on the granary for a week at a wage of 2s. His helper received 16d. for the same period.[1] Next year a thatcher (coopertor) and his helper received 8s. 4d. for twenty days' work on the grange and cow-stable.[2] In the first case the slater and his assistant received $6\frac{2}{3}$d. a day; in the second the thatcher and his helper 5d. a day. Not a little miscellaneous information of this kind could be culled from the Crawley records, a great deal from the pipe rolls of the whole bishopric. We wonder just where these house builders came from — the town or the country — and we would like to learn about their ways of contracting, travelling, and providing materials for work.

The big gap in the wage records comes in the period after 1450. During this time lessees of the home farm and yeoman farmers were dominant. They kept few records and these have apparently all disappeared.

At present, wages in Crawley appear, on the surface at least, to be relatively good.[3] The poorest agricultural laborers receive the minimum wage of the district, which is about 30s. a week. The week is 51 hours, Saturday afternoon being a half holiday. The laborers get pay for overtime. At certain seasons a bonus is paid. The workers get their cottages at a reasonable rate, as also the milk they use — both from the owner of Crawley Court. And a bonus of 50 per cent is reported to be given to them for the purchase of clothing — the aim being to induce them to wear better clothes. Formerly laborers on the Crawley estate were paid two thirds of their wages when ill. But since the incoming of a minimum wage (1924), this has been discontinued. In 1924 there was an old-time worker, a carpenter, one who had helped build Crawley Court in 1877, and who in old age was living in a cottage free of rent and, apparently, of all other cares, except those of bodily infirmity.

§ 21. *The Peasant's Money Income.* We have no direct and specific information about the peasant's income that is anything like complete. We may infer a good deal, however, from what we

[1] See below, §§ 15, p. 273.
[2] See below, §§ 16, p. 281.
[3] See also, below, § 38, p. 136.

learn from the reeve's accounts,[1] the custumal, and the court rolls, about his income and outgo. It is most useful in our reckoning to consider only money receipts and disbursements.

Let us consider the incomes of a yardlander of South Crawley and a farthinglander of North Crawley. In order to get some idea of variations, we take them and their fortunes at two different times, first, the year 1257–58, which was a good year, and secondly, the year 1306–07, which was unfavorable. The yardlander, or virgator, normally held a tenement of 16 statutory acres, 5 of which, we shall assume, were devoted to wheat, 6 to barley and oats, and the remaining 5 left fallow. The farthinglander on the other hand, had only 5½ acres, 2 of which we shall allot to spring barley, 2 to oats, and 1½ to fallow.[2] We shall assume the normal circumstance that the yardlander held no office and that the farthinglander was a week-worker also doing no special work as shepherd, cowherd, or the like. While the former had a fair amount of land and a good deal of free time, the latter had little land and only 4 days a week for himself and he had those during only 40 weeks a year. The first was a team worker, the latter a hand worker.

The virgator would receive as the net produce from his 5 acres of wheat, at one quarter an acre (the average for that year), just 5 quarters. Out of this he would probably have to give to the rector 4 bushels as tithe. Thus he would have 4½ quarters for sale, at the prevailing rate of 8s. a quarter. For his family, we assume five in all, he would need for bread and pottage at least 5 quarters of

[1] About the year 1252 a tenant called Ingeram encroached upon the lord's wood. The whole tithing was amerced 6s. 8d. for not producing him for trial: Ingeram had fled.

He left behind his chattels which are listed in detail:

Animals: 2 cart horses, 2 cows, 2 steers, 1 yearling, 1 calf, 39 ewes, 27 wethers, 11 hogasters, 26 lambs, 5 pigs, 4 little pigs, and 12 hens.
Grain: 6 bushels of wheat, 5⅜ quarters of barley, and 3 bushels of oats.
Honey: ¼ of 7 hives; 7d. for honey.
Clothing: 1 tunic, 1 counterpane, 2 shirts.

At about the same time John Carter also fled, leaving behind 1 weak plow horse, 2 ewes, 1 wether, and 1 lamb. And his widow paid a fine of 10s. for his land. See MS., P. R. O., Ecclesiastical Commission, Various, 159291 (1252–53).

[2] If the two-field system prevailed, instead of the three-field, the reckoning would be a little different.

barley and oats. His net yield, at the average rate for the year, would be 5 quarters of barley and 3½ quarters of oats from 3 acres devoted to each. It is very doubtful whether he would have any of either of these grains for sale, after he had taken out the 5 quarters for bread and pottage and another 3½ quarters for beer or ale. We shall assume that he has one extra plow horse — for sale this year. His 25 sheep might be divided as follows: 9 ewes, 6 wethers, 4 hogasters, and 6 lambs. Four of the wethers he might sell as old and feeble. About 19 good great fleeces would come in, of which he might use 9 for homespun purposes, and sell 10. Perhaps 4 lambs' fleeces were worth selling. We shall allow him two cows and two calves. He might sell one of the calves. Of his 10 pigs, he might sell 4 at least. We assume that he used all the pelts he had, all the chickens (after paying 4 for churchscot), all the geese, all the eggs and the milk and cheese. Here we may be out a few shillings but not very much.

The financial position of the virgator for the year 1257–58, the gains and losses of other years disregarded, would then be somewhat as follows:

		s.	d.
Money income:			
Wheat, 4½ quarters	sold at 8s. each	36	0
Plow horse	sold at 6s.	6	0
Wethers	4 sold at 8d.	2	8
Great fleeces	10 sold at $3\frac{8}{10}$d. (average)	3	2
Lambs' fleeces	4 sold at 1d.	0	4
Calf	1 sold at 1s. 2d.	1	2
Pigs	4 sold at 3s.	12	0
		61	4
Money outgo:			
Fixed rent to the lord		5	0
Rent for extra herbage for cow and calf		0	7
Rent for extra pasture		0	2
		5	9
Money surplus for expenditure		55	7

For the year 1306–07, the situation would not be so favorable. The partial failure of crops in Crawley, however, was somewhat compensated for by high prices for animals and animal products. This year the virgator's position would be as follows:

			s.	d.
Money income:				
Wheat, $1\frac{1}{4}$ quarters		sold at 7s.	8	9
Plow horse		sold at 10s.	10	0
Wethers	4	sold at 1s. 1d.	4	4
Great fleeces	10	sold at 5d.	4	2
Lambs' fleeces	4	sold at $1\frac{1}{2}$d.	0	6
Calf		sold at 1s.	1	0
Pigs	4	sold at 3s. 5d.	13	8
			42	5
Money outgo (as in 1257–58)			5	9
Money surplus for expenditure			36	8

The lot of the farthinglander was far harder, as has been said. For the year 1257–58 he would have only $3\frac{2}{5}$ quarters of barley (net yield) and $2\frac{2}{5}$ quarters of oats. These would provide his family with bread, pottage, and a little beer. The items may be listed thus:

			s.	d.
Money income:				
Barley and oats, no surplus				
Horse		none kept		
Wethers	4	sold at 8d.	2	8
Great fleeces	10	sold at $3\frac{4}{5}$d.	3	2
Lambs' fleeces	4	sold at 1d.	0	4
Calf	1	sold at 1s. 2d.	1	2
Pigs	4	sold at 3s.	12	0
			19	4
Money outgo:				
Fixed rent to the lord			2	8
Rent for extra herbage for cow and calf			0	7
Rent for extra pasture			0	2
			3	5
Money surplus for expenditure			15	11

In 1306–07 the situation would be much worse for the farthingholder. His grain would not be sufficient for bread, pottage, and beer or ale. If we assume that he made little or no beer or ale, he would have to buy $4\frac{3}{10}$ quarters of barley and oats at an average of 4s. a quarter. In order to make up the deficiency in grain, he would have to economize elsewhere, perhaps sell all 19 great fleeces, leaving none this year for homespun.

			s.	d.
Money income:				
Barley and oats, only a deficit				
Horse	none kept			
Wethers	4 sold at 1s. 1d.		4	4
Great fleeces	19 sold at 5d.		7	11
Lambs' fleeces	4 sold at $1\frac{1}{2}$d.		0	6
Calf	sold at 1s.		1	0
Pigs	4 sold at 3s. 5d.		13	8
			27	5
Money outgo:				
Fixed rent to the lord			2	8
Rent for extra herbage for cow and calf			0	7
Rent for extra pasture			0	2
Purchase of $4\frac{3}{10}$ quarters barley and oats at 4s.			17	$2\frac{1}{2}$
			20	$7\frac{1}{2}$
Money surplus for expenditure			6	$9\frac{1}{2}$

Of course, what we should like to know is what expenditures were considered necessary by the two classes of tenants. For both there were the upkeep of the house buildings and the purchase of utensils. For both there were the attractions of the village inns and especially of the fair of St. Giles where a few pennies could easily be squandered. Spices and medicines would be regarded as necessary. The virgator would also have the upkeep of his cart and plow. He might buy a cap for himself and some colored cloth for his wife. The farthinglander probably would have no such aspirations. Most clothing, shoes, shirts, and belts would be homemade for both families.

For the purchase of all these things (for five people) in 1257–58, the virgator had 55s. 5d., or the value of over 18 pigs; while the farthinglander had 15s. 9d., or the value of over 5 pigs. In 1306–07, the virgator had only 36s. 8d., or the value of nearly 11 pigs; while the farthinglander had only 6s. $9\frac{1}{2}$d., or the value of just 2 pigs. It is to be noted, that according to our reckoning the farthinglander had skimped himself in the matter of homemade clothing this year.

Such reckoning as this does not deserve to be taken very seriously. And yet, it is probably not far wrong. The virgator of South Crawley was pretty well off; the yardlander of the North was on a subsistence basis. The former could stand a bad crop without physical suffering; the latter certainly could not. It was animal husbandry based on pasture rights that made life fairly easy for the one and possible for the other. Pestilences and revolts would possibly aid the small tenants of North Crawley; they could hardly be any injury. It is small wonder then that it was in North Crawley, among the hand or week workers living at a low point of physical endurance, there was a scarcity of tenants when the crises of 1349–50 and 1381 came along. The lord bishop had forgotten part of his flock; and that part just bolted when the chance came. Of course, one cannot help wondering just what part of Crawley is in a similar condition today. A ship is usually not much stronger than its rottenest timber.

It almost goes without saying that the tenants had income other than material goods. They had a measure of assurance in the very possession of a lord that in time of at least the worst famines they would receive aid. As against the outside world of men they had an interested protector in their lord bishop. Moreover, that part of the populace called the homage, had the satisfaction of knowing that they shared in the management of the manor, though at times this may have been regarded as a burden. This is similar to the position which in our day is demanded on behalf of industrial workers. The homage chose the tithingman and also the reeve (or bailiff, as he would have been commonly called elsewhere). The members of the homage were the suitors of the courts of the manor. Sometimes they chose new tenants for vacant holdings.[1] And, possibly above all else in their estimation, they had the right to determine the course of agricultural routine and operation; at least such was the case in the early Modern Period, and doubtless also in the Middle Ages.

§ 22. *Commutation of Service Rents.* The system of predial services lay near to the heart of the manor, in fact may be regarded as the heart itself. Of course it is conceivable that a lord might work a home farm wholly by means of hired labor, but such a

[1] In 1315–16 Robert Meriweder was elected by the whole tithing (decenna) to a cottage and ten acres which had escheated to the lord. MS., P. R. O., Ecclesiastical Commission, Various, 159330.

method would not be practicable if the labor was free and was paid a competitive wage.[1] Under such circumstances the large-scale agriculture of the lord, working through a reeve or bailiff, could not compete with the small holdings of the tenants themselves. The direct utilization of the home farm depended, in the long run, upon unfree labor. The lord's advantage came through the low wage which he paid to the workers in the form of land and food allowances.

Into the reeve's accounts creeps the practice of commutation in the form of works relaxed (opera relaxata) or works sold (opera vendita). There were at least three kinds of relaxations: (*a*) work given up for the season because of bad weather, (*b*) surplus work willingly commuted or relaxed for the time being because not wanted, and (*c*) much needed labor relaxed or commuted unwillingly. This third kind of commutation might prove to be for but a period if the lord could find another tenant, or it might be permanently if no such tenant was forthcoming.

When the extant accounts of the Manor of Crawley begin (1208–09), all the services due to the lord in the form of rent were apparently rendered. There seem to have been about thirteen laborers who presumably did daily service in the autumn and two days a week during the rest of the year. In addition there were eight or nine who acted as special officials.[2] Others probably did special services in harvest and at other times, just as we find them doing later in the century.

A change in the management of the manor seems to have occurred about 1231–32. In that year, we find only six laborers doing the daily service during the autumn and two-days-a-week work during the rest of the year. In other words, there were seven week-workers fewer than the usual number; and indeed, we find seven tenements entered under 'defects of rents.' In one case it is stated that the land is vacant. What is cause and what effect is difficult to determine. Certainly there was a diminution in the number of acres in the home farm cultivated and in the number of

[1] The assumption here is that the agricultural laborer and the reeve at the time would have given little or no better service if free.

[2] See below, §§ 5, p. 188. Cf. also, §§ 6, p. 196.

the lord's sheep kept. Whether the diminution in week-workers caused, or resulted from, the diminution in the lord's cultivation and animal husbandry, is not clear. At any rate, there was no commutation, so far as can be learned. By 1256–57 there were ten laborers doing week-work.[1] The old number had not been quite restored. In the custumal of about 1280 there were four clear cases of commutation of services — apparently of the holders of small tenements in North Crawley.[2] They were apparently all farthing-holders who had done week-work. The arrangement appears new, being tagged onto the end of the services that were performed. Here we seem to have a clear case of labor services sold because not required by the lord, presumably because of a diminution in both land cultivation and animal husbandry.

The next period, 1315–83, saw further reduction in cultivation on the home farm, a rise in the wages paid to the various special workers, ministri curie, and a further decline in the number of week-workers. This third phase occurred chiefly after the Black Death. In 1355–56 and 1356–57 only five week-workers performed their services.[3]

In the period 1384–1448 there was further curtailment of activity on the home farm. The wages of the ministri curie were increased, at least from 1411 onward. And both week-work and other services diminished. In 1389–90 there were rendered or acquitted 700 autumn week-works out of a total of 950, and 984 winter week-works out of a total of 1394.[4] In all, 69 per cent of all works were either rendered or acquitted for special service.

The Black Death and Revolt of 1381 had come and gone.[5] At least the first hit Crawley hard. The impact was met, as apparently similar pressure had been met before, by curtailment of the work on the home farm and by an increase in the wages of the special workers. It was a new device when in 1407 the home farm

[1] See below, §§ 9, p. 214. Cf. also, §§ 10, p. 222.

[2] See below, §§ 11, p. 238.

[3] See below, §§ 15, p. 271; §§ 16, p. 279.

[4] See below, §§ 17, p. 286.

[5] On the subject of the commutation of service rents and its relation to the Black Death and Revolt of 1381, see the works of J. E. Thorold Rogers, T. W. Page, H. L. Gray, and especially Miss A. E. Levett (for the Winchester group of manors).

was leased to the reeve.[1] In the accounts of 1409–10 and 1410–11 all the week-works had apparently disappeared with the possible exception of the winter week-works of three farthing-holders in North Crawley.[2] In the account for 1448–49 we find that the three farthing-holders had apparently commuted all their services.[3] This was the first year of a new lease of the home farm — for a period of eight years.

Now, the interesting question is whether the leasing of the home farm or the commutation of labor came first. We have put the question to two scholars who have long worked in the medieval field, and received opposite replies as to the general development in England. In Crawley it is clear that all week-works had been lost before the regular policy of leasing the home farm had been adopted. They had been lost through acquittance, default, and especially commutation. On the other hand, practically none of the non-week-works had been commuted. So, it appears that both our experts would have been right for Crawley: week-works had been commuted before leasing and non-week-works afterwards. The lord and the farmer, realizing the importance of the subject, inserted in the first account under the lease of 1448 just what services were due and what were not. The table on the following page gives a summary of the situation.

What has usually not been appreciated is that the demesne farmer received with his lease not only the land, buildings, implements, and livestock, but also uncommuted services.[4] In the year 1448–49 the general farmer, or farmer of the home farm, received 859 works, or days of service, along with the plowing of 10 acres and the harrowing of 69 acres. In the account for 1513–14, it is stated that the customary works, not commuted, belonged to the farmer with his farm, except the carriage of wood.[5] And in 1562 occurred an interesting case of a revival or adaptation of predial services. One of the lord's bondmen, possessing a virgate of bondland in South Crawley and also a farthing of bondland, a farthing

[1] See below, §§ 18, pp. 293 ff.

[2] See below, §§ 18, p. 296; §§ 19, p. 305.

[3] See below, §§ 25, pp. 474, 477.

[4] See below, §§ 23, p. 466; §§ 25, p. 475; §§ 26, p. 490.

[5] See MS., P. R. O., Ecclesiastical Commission, Various, 155861 (5–6 Henry VIII).

of gavel-land, and a pightle of purpresture land in North Crawley, drowned himself in a cask of water. His holdings accordingly escheated to the lord. The recipient of these escheated lands was permitted to farm out to the widow of the deceased a messuage and six acres of land on condition that she wash the lord's sheep

TABLE SHOWING SERVICES IN 1448–49[1]

Service	Due	Acquitted[2]	Defaulted[3]	Commuted	Rendered
	Acres	Acres	Acres	Acres	Acres
Plowing	25	1	14	....	10
Harrowing	90	12	...	9	69
	Works	Works	Works	Works	Works
Carrying the fold	75	3	...	....	72
Carrying the manure	186	12	...	....	174
Mowing the meadow	50	8	...	....	42
Carrying the wood	49	1	...	....	48
Washing and shearing sheep	297	43	27	....	227
Carrying corn	150	6	...	....	144
Shocking corn	6	...	...	....	6
Autumn boon-work	262	45	17	54	146
Autumn week-work	950	200	...	750	...
Winter week-work	1558	410	82	1066	...
Total[4] Works	3,583	728	126	1,870	859

[1] See below, §§ 25, pp 635–640
[2] Acquitted through service — by such officials and special workers as reeve, plowmen, and shepherds
[3] Defaulted means that for some special reason, not expected to be permanent, the service was not rendered. In the case of plowing it was the lack of whole plows on the part of South Crawley tenants — an old condition. In the other cases it was due to estates being at the time in the hands of the lord.
[4] The acres are not included in the total works (days of labor).

(leased to the general farmer) for two days (each year) and shear them for three days (a year), no other service being required.[1]

In the account for 1503–04 we find that the custom of carrying the lord's wood, mentioned above, which had not been at all commuted in 1389–90 or 1448–49, was sold apparently to the tenants themselves.[2] The sale continued to recur in this form down to enclosure,[3] that is, as a kind of special quit rent. The custom of

[1] See MS., P. R. O., Ecclesiastical Commission, Court Roll 110/2, fol. 9d. (10 Sept., 4 Elizabeth).
[2] See below, §§ 26, p. 492.
[3] See MS., Millbank, Ecclesiastical Commission, 158298 (year 1790).

carrying the lord's manure lasted down to 1690 when it was commuted.[1] But the washing and shearing of sheep, and possibly a few other customs, remained until 1795 when they were commuted under the enclosure act.[2] In 1601 a customary tenant was amerced half a mark for not washing and shearing the lord's sheep as he ought according to the custom of the manor as expressed in the old custumal. When a tenement was leased, the condition was made that the services that were due should be rendered. This held right down to the time of enclosure, and, as a traditional procedure, even after that date.[3] It was thought in 1794 that the surviving dues owed to the lord were worth £12 10s.[4] Probably this sum included both uncommuted services and such a payment as churchscot. For these straggling rights the lord received a final payment in the form of land.

My lord bishop of Winchester, savior of souls, was a zealous shepherd when it came to human services owed to him. He clung tenaciously to the servitudes his tenants bore in his favor. In order to hold to the service system he restricted his home farm and then leased it; he sold services where he could not exact them. He kept what services he could, to lease along with the sheep to the general farmer. Some of the sheep gave wool, some services.

Look upon England and then upon France, Germany, and other Continental European countries! That England gave up her manorial system in the fifteenth century, that is, gave up cultivation of the home farm by a reeve and the exaction of services, is the accepted theory; while parts of France held much of theirs until the Revolution, and Prussia until the early part of the nineteenth century. But, if Crawley be at all typical of England, we need to reconsider this judgment. Manorial origins have been much studied in England and the early commutation of labor also. But manorial survivals, and particularly the survival of predial services, have been lightly passed over. Perhaps Crawley was peculiar, and Church estates backward. But also, perhaps not. It is at least significant that there probably were more semi-manorial

[1] See below, §§ 35, pp. 516, 517. [2] See below, §§ 55, pp. 596 ff.
[3] See MS., Millbank, Ecclesiastical Commission, 153076, fol. 159 (4 April, 1795).
[4] See below, § 30, p. 105.

survivals in Crawley in 1795 than there were in French manors, if indeed any at all remained in France. What a lot of land laws in the nineteenth and twentieth centuries have been necessary to modernize the surviving medieval system! And it was only yesterday (1926) that the quit rents, paid in lieu of services, general and special, were (practically) abolished. What a contrast between the leadership of England in industry and transportation on the one hand and her backwardness in land tenure on the other! And what a contrast, indeed, between the agricultural progress of England and her agrarian conservatism!

§ 23. *Leasing of the Demesne.* A lease is a contract to give something to somebody for an understood period, to be used, within limits, as the lessee sees fit. In the Crawley documents the term used is commonly farming (ad firmam dimittere) in contradistinction to renting (locare) or selling the right to (vendere) for a year or other short period. There can be no doubt that the periodic renting was a step to leasing or farming. The sow was put out to farm, 1370–1448,[1] and the uncertainties of pig raising given up by the lord. Later the conies were leased for a long period at a time.[2] Land was first rented for a year, then leased for increasing periods. Various bits of demesne were rented, some as additions to the holdings of customary tenements and some as separate and distinct holdings. For instance, about 1287–88 the lord's seneschal handed over to three tenants of Wodecote (in South Crawley) twenty acres of demesne land carefully measured, free from all secular services (but not from churchscot?) for their lives and for their heirs' lives.[3] The estates at Wodecote were off on the borders of the manor, far from the village. They seem to have had a somewhat separate existence, though not so much removed from the village as the Hoo or the Rookley House estate.

No effort has been made to discover the first instance of leasing in Crawley. At least as early as 1402–03, however, a virgate of bondland and twenty-two acres of purpresture in Wodecote, just

[1] See MS., P. R. O., Ecclesiastical Commission, Various, 159380 to 159440. See especially below, §§ 18, p. 302.

[2] See below, §§ 26, p. 493.

[3] See below, §§ 11, p. 238.

mentioned, were leased for twelve years.[1] This may have been a suggestion or model for leasing the home farm in 1407. Just what the legal arrangement was for the lease of the home farm we do not know. It was a contract (convencio) made with the counsel of the lord bishop,[2] but certainly not regarded as a great departure in the management of the manor.

The essence of the leasing of the demesne, or home farm, was the development of an attitude toward the reeve who managed it. During the thirteenth century the lords of Crawley gave not a little attention to the working of the manor. The reeve did his work and accounts were based on what he was able to accomplish under supervision. In the fourteenth century, however, responsibility was shifted gradually to the shoulders of the reeve. Probably shortly after the famine of 1316 and 1317 there was a tendency to hold the reeve responsible for a certain standard of production. At this very time there was doubtless a corresponding tendency on the part of the lord to give up the initiation of agricultural practices. Then after the Black Death this tendency was accentuated owing to the difficulties involved in dealing with unwilling tenant laborers. From about 1370 onwards, we see the same more clearly. In other words, there was a movement on foot — even before the Black Death — to put the responsibility of cultivation upon the reeve and a preference for a certain minimum of income over the ups and downs of crop variation. Whether this preference grew partly out of the famine difficulties of 1316 and 1317, the sharp practices of reeves, the wars with Scotland and France, or a growing interest, on the part of the bishops, in church building and the founding of colleges, is not easily determined. At any rate the leasing of the demesne was the logical result of forces which were rather slow in working themselves out. The new situation may perhaps be otherwise expressed by saying that, as the entrepreneurial ability of the reeves increased with the incoming of commercial practices, the bishops took advantage of the fact to concentrate on the things in which they were specially interested.

[1] See below, §§ 18, p. 296.
[2] *Ibid.*, p. 300.

Since we do not possess the lease of 1407, we do not know just how it read. A complication arises out of the fact that the lessee was also the reeve of the manor. It is difficult to tell just when he is accounting for things as lessee and when as reeve. Apparently the chief profit that the reeve could hope for arose out of the returns from grain cultivation. If the price of grain was high, only so much had to be accounted for. If it was low, then more was due to the lord. As before, the wool was sent to the lord's palace of Wolvesey for sale there. Other products were sold for the lord's profit. Perhaps we can put the matter this way: the reeve leased the grain lands, the uncommuted services, and the implements (utensilia). The implements included three plows and one cart, all with their full equipment.[1] On the whole, we get the impression that the home farm was in a rather poor condition at this time.

The permanent leasing of the home farm occurred in the period from 1448 to the nineteenth century. According to the arrangement of 1448, the lessee paid £6 13s. 4d. in money each year and the wool produced during the year. By 1487 the yield of wool had been given up, the farmer paying £6 13s. 4d. for the grain and £15 3s. 4d. for the livestock, and, of course, also for the lands and buildings connected therewith, along with the implements and uncommuted services.[2] The money payments continued thus until the nineteenth century. The livestock came to include only sheep. The number of sheep included in the lease was increased. And there was apparently a gradually diminishing amount of arable and also of equipment, apart from buildings. As is indicated elsewhere,[3] we lack information about the premiums paid for the lease. Just before enclosure it was stated that the bishop of Winchester ordinarily gave a lease for twenty-one years with fines for renewal increased "in proportion to what improvements had been made."[4]

The first farmers of the demesne were of the soil of Crawley. There were William Cuppere, the reeve, in 1407; William Sely,

[1] See below, §§ 18, p. 303.
[2] See below, §§ 23, pp. 466 ff. and §§ 26, pp. 489 ff.
[3] See below, § 24, p. 86.
[4] Driver, A. and W., *General View of the Agriculture of the County of Hants* (1794), p. 21.

reeve, in 1448; John Coupere in 1487 with a 21-year lease; and Henry Coupere in 1491 with a 30-year lease. Later farmers were William Seynthyll, Gilbert Coke, and, by 1570, Thomas Percy. There came John Holwey, alias Edmondes, followed by Percy Edmondes. While the first four farmers were Crawley tenants, the others were apparently from elsewhere. And this was to be typical of the subsequent period. As more and more capital was required to carry on the business of agriculture, outsiders came to have an advantage. And as more and more capital came in, the element of a residence, a fine place to live and hunt, came to the foreground.[1]

The steps in the history of farming seem to be somewhat as follows. The sow was farmed in 1370, part of Wodecote in 1402, and the home farm tentatively in 1407 and as a permanent policy in 1448. In the sixteenth century farming (or leasing) somebody's land, in addition to cultivating one's own, became a common practice.[2] In the development of this practice, the reeve played the chief part. What became of the able Coupere family,[3] is not indicated in the records. Both the Selys and Couperes disappeared — the fate also of the Waytes, Pitters, and Perns, yeoman farmers all, in the late nineteenth century.

§ 24. *The Lord's Receipts.* For the period from 1208 to 1790 we have the details of money income from Crawley in great fullness, except for the fines on the renewal of leases. Some of the chief items are shown in the table on the following page.

Up to the time the home farm was leased to the demesne farmer, there were ups and downs in the returns to the lord, that are startling. The three chief variants were court dues, profits from animal husbandry, and profits from grain cultivation. The introduction of demesne farming in place of reeve cultivation brought in both evenness and certainty.

The approximate total money receipts of the lord from his Manor of Crawley is indicated in the table on page 85.

There were probably four periods in the history of Crawley, as

[1] For a continuation of this subject for a later period, see below, § 29, p. 99.

[2] See below, §§ 36, p. 519; §§ 37, p. 522.

[3] See below, §§ 49, p. 545; John Coper made a will (1513) leaving his farm of Little Somborne, an adjoining parish, to his son and (apparently) son-in-law.

reckoned from the standpoint of the lord's income. First, there was the pre-manorial period, during which the lord received probably only rents in kind. About this we know nothing specifically.

CHIEF ITEMS OF THE LORD'S RECEIPTS

	1208–09			1309–10			1408–09			1503–04		
Fixed Rent (net)[1]......	9	9	0	10	5	7	11	15	11	13	10	8
Sale of Services........	None			None			2	11	4	2	6	8
Court Dues[2]..........	2	17	6	6	0	10	2	13	1	1	16	10
Animal Husbandry.....	13	4	$3\frac{1}{2}$[3]	59	11	7	19	10	0[3]	None		
Grain Cultivation......	9	14	6	44	12	$9\frac{1}{2}$[4]	28	18	5	None		
Farm of Home Farm....	None			None			None			21	16	8
Total Income..........	46	16	2	157	8	8	74	14	4	43	13	11

	1625–26			1735			1790			1912		
Fixed Rent (net)[5].....	13	15	11	13	16	9	13	16	9	0	6	5[5]
Sale of Services.......	2	8	0	2	8	0	2	8	0	None		
Court Dues[6]..........	0	16	10	10	0	8	Omitted[6]			0	6	9
Animal Husbandry....	None			None			None			None		
Grain Cultivation.....	None			None			None			None		
Farm of Home Farm...	26	16	8	21	16	8	21	16	8	None		
Total Income..........	51	3	4	55	7	7	41	8	9	0	13	2

1 Exclusive of the pound of cummin, at first paid in kind, later in money, for the estate called the Hoo.
2 Includes tithingpenny, fines, heriots, marriage payments, amercements, strays sold.
3 The value of the wool sent to Wolvesey this year was estimated. This item is therefore only an approximation.
4 Unusually high.
5 Really quit rent. The year 1912 is conspicuous because it showed a return, most years before and after showing none.
6 Omitted from the account consulted.

Secondly, there was the manorial period (from Anglo-Saxon times to 1448), during which the lord received not only rents in money and in kind but services on the home farm, from which profits were derived. The third period extended from the early fifteenth century to the nineteenth, during which the lord was once again (largely) a rent taker and the collector of payments connected with such jurisdictional rights as could be enforced. Then, fourthly, the value of the demesne and of the rights over tenants'

LORD'S ANNUAL RECEIPTS FROM CRAWLEY

Years	Reeve's Yield	Demesne Farmer's Rent	Net Income in Money	Remarks
	£ s. d.	£ s. d.	£ s. d.	
1065–66	.. .. ..	None	35 0 0	From Domesday Book
1085–86	.. .. ..	None	35 0 0	" " "
1208–26	.. .. ..	None	54 5 9	Yearly av. — reeves' accts.
1231–1314	.. .. ..	None	85 14 5¼	" " " "
1315–83	.. .. ..	None	82 3 4¾	" " " "
1384–1448	.. .. ..	.. .. ..	72 7 1¾	" " " "
1449–54	[30 10 3]	6 13 4(?)	37 3 7	Livestock not farmed
1503–04	[21 17 3]	21 16 8[1]	43 13 11	MS., Millbank, E. C., 155648
1546–47	[27 10 7]	21 16 8	49 7 4	MS., P. R. O., E. C., V., 155886
1570–71	31 5 9	21 16 8	53 2 5	" " " " 159473
1625–26	24 6 8	26 16 8	51 3 4	" " Exch. Aug., Misc. 312
1647–48	.. .. ..	.. .. .	[41 6 6¾]	$\frac{1}{20}$th of sale price
1733[2]	24 0 4	21 16 8	[44 16 11]	Includes Pigeons Hold
1735[3]	33 10 11	21 16 8	[55 7 7]	Complete. Taxes not deducted
1750–51[4]	23 8 3	21 16 8	[45 4 11]	Fines, heriots, and taxes not included
1773[5]	19 19 7	21 16 8	[41 16 3]	Fines, heriots, and taxes not included
1790[6]	19 12 1	21 16 8	[41 8 9]	Fines, heriots, and taxes not included
1796[7]	[22 14 7]	21 16 8	44 11 5	Complete — Pigeons Hold and fees
1807[8]	[21 18 9]	21 16 8	42 15 5	Pigeons Hold, but no fees
1912[9]	None	None	0 13 2	Possibly incomplete

[1] The amount since at least 1487. See below, §§ 23, p. 466.
[2] MS., Millbank, Ecclesiastical Commission, 158264.
[3] *Ibid.*, 158265. [4] *Ibid.*, 158274. [5] *Ibid.*, 158284. [6] *Ibid.*, 158298.
[7] *Ibid.*, 158299, 158250½, and 158250$\frac{2}{2}$. [8] *Ibid.*, 158300.
[9] *Ibid.*, "Crawley Manor, List of Tenants."

lands were transferred into money in the nineteenth century, whereupon the lord became practically a taker of interest and dividends.[1]

[1] Reference is here made to the action of the Ecclesiastical Commissioners, who, upon enfranchising the land, apparently invested the proceeds largely in securities. Partly from these investments, which yield interest and dividends, the bishops of Winchester derive their salary.

In all probability the change from the first to the second stage involved not only an increase in total yield but also much greater certainty. The next change brought even greater certainty but less income. In the face of the growing difficulties and general social uneasiness of the fifteenth century, the smaller certain profit was not at the time to be regarded as a net loss. Nevertheless, as the value of money began to decline in the sixteenth century, there developed a serious problem of finding new sources of revenue. For the lord bishop of Winchester this meant (*a*) charging an ever-increasing premium on the lease of the home farm, and (*b*) exacting such fines for entry as could be justified. These helped to compensate, if indeed they did not fully make up for any loss through fixity of money income in the face of the falling value of money.[1] Unfortunately we do not possess statistics of the premiums charged for the various leases, though we know that at times they were very high.[2] Of course, it is the progressive increase of such premiums that explains how it was possible to charge no more for the rent of the home farm in 1807 than in 1487, and no more for the rent of the pasture field called Shert in 1746–47 than in 1314–15.[3] The transmutation into money of the rights of landlord and manorial lord, that is, rights over the demesne and over the tenants' land,[4] made the lord subject to changing values of the monetary medium, from which it was difficult for him to escape.

§ 25. *Rents.* A rent is here taken to be a payment for the use of the lord's property. The reason for the payment is often difficult

[1] Total Income of the bishopric of Winchester. (It is doubtful whether these totals are quite comparable.)

1208–09	£2,720	(Hubert Hall, *Pipe Roll of the Bishopric of Winchester*, 1903, p. xliii.)
1316–17	£ 5,249	(*The Registers of John de Sandale*, etc., ed. by Baigent, 1897, p. 628.)
1503–04	£ 3,953	(MS., Millbank, Ecclesiastical Commission, 159648.)
1596	£ 2,300(?)	(Estimate of the yearly rents. MS., Br. M., Lansdowne, vol. 82, no. 32. Incomplete statement (?).
1829–31 (av.)	£11,151	(Sir L. T. Dibdin and S. E. Downing, *The Ecclesiastical Commission: A Sketch of its History and Work*, 1919, p. 12.)

[2] See below, §§ 24, pp. 468 ff.

[3] See above, § 11, p. 34.

[4] Part of this is dealt with under the head of the enfranchisement of land. See below, § 33, pp. 117 ff.

to find. In the case of churchscot, the rent or customary payment attached to various holdings and varying from one to four chickens, arose out of the custom of making a contribution for church purposes. Whether this was for festive or other use, is not stated. At any rate, in some fashion it came to be paid to the lord. Each year 125 chickens were due, from at least 1256–57 [1] to enclosure in 1795.[2] It is not unlikely that this payment is the oldest one about which we have specific information.

Apart from churchscot, the only regular rent in kind was one pound of cummin paid by the holder of the estate called the Hoo or the How. This appears about 1267;[3] and, in one form or another, the item occurs in the accounts until at least 1746–47. While churchscot was a church due originally, this payment in kind was of the nature of a seignorial due, somewhat like a petty sergeanty. Just what service the holder gave to the lord for his tenement (later called Hoo Close), that would justify so small a nominal payment, is not stated in any records read, though one supposition is that the holder may have been the episcopal auditor.[4]

The chief rents paid in medieval Crawley were service rents. In return for the privilege of occupying certain tenements, the holders gave to the lord services of various kinds. These are dealt with elsewhere.[5]

Quit rents were ordinarily money payments to free the tenant from some other kind of payment. In Crawley 4d. were later paid in lieu of the pound of cummin, mentioned above. But more important than this, was the rent paid to be quit of services. This is the 'works sold,' as recorded in the reeves' accounts, or the commuted labor as ordinarily spoken of.[6]

There was also a fixed money payment (gabulum assisum or redditus assisus) which occurs in the records from at least 1208

[1] See below, §§ 9, p. 220.

[2] See MS., Millbank, Ecclesiastical Commission, 158298 (year 1790). Cocks and hens, 125. Deducted for lands, 12 and for widows, 10. Net total is 103.

[3] See MS., P. R. O., Ecclesiastical Commission, Various, 159298.

[4] See below, §§ 28, p. 501.

[5] See above, § 13, pp. 22 ff.; § 14, pp. 48 ff.; § 16, pp. 53 ff.

[6] See above, § 22, p. 75.

down to enclosure as a fairly steady item. What it amounted to in early times may be seen in the following table.[1]

AVERAGE YEARLY FIXED RENT

Period	Years [1]	Net Rent £	s.	d.
1208–1226	13	9	11	2
1231–1314	55	9	18	0
1315–1383	63	11	19	0
1384–1448	42	11	14	10

[1] That is, the number of years for which there are figures.

The unsettled question is the meaning of fixed rent. We know it was paid in hard cash, but can only surmise its origin. More of it was paid by South Crawley tenants, who, we have surmised, were originally freemen, than by North Crawley tenants, who may have been an enslaved (Celtic?) group. It might seem therefore to reflect an early condition of freedom. The other explanation is, however, that fixed rent arose from some early, and forgotten, commutation of services. Thus the first view indicates a free origin, the latter servile. It is not improbable that both hold true, the first for South Crawley, the second for North Crawley. Certainly there were tenants in North Crawley who paid varying amounts of fixed rent, some even higher amounts than any paid in the south part.[2] Still it remains true that as between the two parts the South paid money and the North services — even the objectionable week-work.

All of the rents so far considered have been customary, that is, fixed by custom and not changeable. Rack rents are hard to find in medieval Crawley, and we cannot be sure when we come across them. Perhaps we may distinguish between nominal rack rents and real rack rents. The nominal rack rent is a payment for land rented freely to anyone by the lord, legally at the highest market price but actually at a much lower and more stable rate. Some of the pasture fields came under this heading. Perhaps we ought to put into this category the two inns which paid 1s. each from 1218–19 to 1278–79. Some of the special estates, like the later Pigeons

[1] For the amounts paid in later years, see above, § 24, p. 83.
[2] See below, §§ 11, pp. 232 and 237.

Hold, may have also belonged to this class. The pightles, or small bits of purpresture, constitute another example. The most interesting case, however, is the plot of a small number of acres of arable rented from year to year. The following table gives the details of such rentals for the first century of the accounts.

RENT OF ARABLE LAND

Period	Years [1]	Av. "acres" rented	Av. rental per "acre"	Av. rental [2] per statutory acre
1208–1222..................	11	15.87	4 d.	8 d.
1231–1307..................	45	16.76	8½d.	17 d.
1208–1307..................	56	16.58	7¾d.	15½d.

[1] Years for which there are figures.
[2] The rental value of land in Crawley (Oct., 1928) is given by Professor Wibberley as from 10s. to 15s. an acre; the selling value £15 to £20 an acre. Mr. J. O. Robertson, estate agent, at the same date put it thus: the approximate value of land with suitable buildings in this district is £10 an acre. The average rent per acre of such land would be 10s., but anyone wishing to rent grass land alone would have to pay from 30s. to 40s. per acre for good meadows.

These seem to be unusually high rates and may in fact be competitive rents. In 1381 the rebels just outside of London asked for land at 4d. an acre. In certain parts of northern England, until the early sixteenth century, 4d. an acre was the common rate.[1]

Any effort to study rents statistically in the Middle Ages is confronted with insuperable difficulties. In most cases various things were paid, especially money and services. The lord's home farm presents another type of difficulty, at least in the Modern Period. The rental fixed in the fifteenth century prevailed until the nineteenth, as we have already seen. But the rack renting, which does not appear on the surface, is hidden in the premiums which the lord received on giving the lease. A similar situation in connection with the tenants' lands occurred in the sixteenth century: the old rents were left, but heavy fines were charged on entry. Indeed, rather consistently the lords of Crawley seem to have charged at first customary rents and then only nominal rack rents. The idea of benevolence and custom probably underlay the situation, as indeed is the case with the rental of cottages in Crawley today.

About the renting of tenants' land by tenants, from the sixteenth to the nineteenth century, we have but little information.

[1] See, for example, G. H. Tupling, *Rossendale* (1927), p. 162.

Whether they too leased at a nominal rack rent and charged a premium for the lease, we do not know.

§ 26. *Economic Attitudes in Medieval Crawley.* There was, of course, no formulated theory in medieval Crawley, in the sense in which we speak of Wyclif's theory of dominium. There was no complete consciousness of social and economic conditions and therefore no agreement on the subject. The people of Crawley lacked a language to express generalizations and they lacked a leader. The Bible would have helped, but they read it not. The rector could have applied its examples to their position and become their leader, but he had no such ambition, so far as can be learned.

What is here referred to is the unformulated, partly conscious ideas which the tenants of Crawley probably accepted or held. Of course, such ideas, being unexpressed and not wholly conscious, are not to be uncovered now with any degree of certainty. We have no other method open to us except inference from medieval action, subsequent position, and what men of modern selfishness and ignorance would probably have thought.

Probably the most pronounced attitude that the medieval peasants of Crawley struck was toward their lord, the bishop of Winchester. Him they had never or rarely seen — just as the head and assistants of a department store have never seen the owner of it, or the superintendent and workers of a mine have never seen the president of the company that owns or operates the property. Probably the tenants of Crawley disliked the services which they had to perform, particularly the week-work due from North Crawley tenants. The neglectful or despiteful way that some did it, as indicated by the court rolls, suggests that some of them did the least possible work that would be accepted. Probably the only compensation that they saw was the corrodies and the special gifts made by the lord at boon-work. Having all too little pasture and woodland, they doubtless held that the lord had not played fair with them. Whether the people of Crawley ever held to the common peasant tradition of an original freedom and ownership of the land, is not known. One would judge from the cost of locks and the appointment of keepers of corn in the field that there was a more or less tacit understanding that it was more of a crime to be caught stealing the lord's goods than actually doing so.

There can be little doubt that the peasants of Crawley came to object to manorial economy, preferring to cultivate their own holdings and such additions as they could procure, rather than to spend part of their time on the lord's land. Certainly commutation of labor on the demesne was first demanded and then partially attained, before the lord gave up his cultivation of the demesne. What the tenants preferred was to pay more money rent and less labor service. There would be little question that at the same time they thought too high the rent of both demesne lands and their own customary tenements. On the whole, the chief and unmistakable inference is that the tenants preferred collective peasant economy to manorial economy. Doubtless this preference was based partly on feeling but partly also on rational economic grounds. Circumstances were later to make the change more favorable than they could have dreamed — favorable to the strong and the careful, while disastrous to the careless and the unfortunate.

The open-field system with its tiny plots cultivated under a communal system of regulations, the Crawley peasants probably thought the only method. Certainly they clung to it down to modern times. Their chief anxiety in this connection was to keep the hedges and fences, balks and hurdles in proper condition, to prevent injury to their various holdings, and to keep open the roads and lanes.

They probably accepted the fallow system of cultivation, thinking that the land needed a rest or at least the tonic that a fallow brings. It is not unlikely that there was a tradition that rye did not grow well on their chalk soil. Manuring they thought worth while, but probably resented having to cart the lord's out to his fields. A good piece of pasture they thought had best be kept separate from tillage. And they probably thought that seed from their own ground was as good as any other.

In animal husbandry, the peasants of Crawley believed in, and practised, castration. Though they wisely refused to follow a natural system in this respect, they accepted animal diseases as they came along, probably as the work of an evil spirit, at the very time that the lord made an effort to obviate or mitigate the worst attacks. Certainly breeding was considered to be an animal function, in which man had a share only in helping parturition. One man's sheep were as good as another's. There was complete democracy in animal intercourse and a fine socialism in sharing diseases and parasites.

The size of their holdings, the peasants were dissatisfied with. They added little bits of the lord's demesne, purprestures, to round out their all-too-small tenements. They held their allowances of pasture inadequate, as we have seen, particularly in dry years. Oxen to them were probably preferable to horses, because better at the plow in a hard soil like Crawley's, and because worth more when killed or when sold in old age.

Barley and oats the peasants of Crawley thought the best food for themselves, while wheat was more suitable for sale in the town market. Prices they doubtless thought were manipulated by the town dealers. And, at the top of their little world, the reeve, their chosen boss, was probably secretly despised, because he was one of themselves. Of course, one cannot help wondering whether the peasants had an absolutely free choice of reeve. In any case, there would be pressure to elect the most capable tenant. To them intrinsic merit would not be equivalent to the strength and power ascribed to strangers or to those of a higher social class.

People of medieval Crawley, we may do you wrong! But there is argument for, and in some cases present survival of, the attitudes, ideas, and weaknesses here indicated. Doubtless not all reacted alike to all situations. The chief characteristic in common was the lack of a theory of how things could be done differently and better.

§ 27. *Rise of Personal Freedom.* Probably personal freedom had existed in Crawley before the lord bishop came into its affairs. Apparently also some measure of servitude was there, particularly in North Crawley. Serfs and slaves there were in Domesday Book (1086). In the period 1086–1248 the voice of freedom seems to have got no farther than the freeing of the slaves, and the levelling of all the people to the rank of serfs. One of the disabilities of serfs was that they were not permitted to live outside the manor. From 1248 to the Black Death of 1349, however, there were tenants in Crawley who were willing to pay an annual fee for the privilege of remaining away from the manor, while others fled, leaving their land and goods behind them.[1] This was the annual recognition so often found in the reeves' accounts. When fully expressed, the item read something like this: 6d. from Robert Sewyne, the lord's bondman (nativus), for the privilege of remaining wherever he wishes, with the understanding that he come back at the two lawdays — under the pledge of Robert le Bonde and John Trigg.[2] Sometimes there was the additional statement that the person in question might remain at Sparsholt, or elsewhere, and should still regard himself as the lord's bondman.[3] Just why such persons wanted to live elsewhere, we do not know. We rather plausibly surmise that the older sons saw advantages elsewhere and that in many cases the aged simply wished to live out their days with daughters or sisters married elsewhere.

From 1248 to 1312 the yearly payments for annual recognition were small, ranging from 6d. (for one person) to 2s. 6d. From 1317 to 1346 the amount received each year from this source was from 4s. to 9s. During each of the two years 1347–48 and 1348–49, only 6d. and 12d. were paid for the privilege. Then during the long stretch from 1349 to 1433 the lord apparently collected no fees for annual recognition. Flight from the manors in England was probably so common in the confusion following the Black Death and Revolt of 1381, that anyone getting away could stay away without much risk. But from 1433 to at least 1598 various sums were collected on the occasion of annual recognition under the name of chevage, the amounts ranging from 8d. to 4s. a year up to 1454. In 1448–49 it was stated that two persons were to remain in Canford and one at Sparsholt. Under the same heading of chevage is an entry of 8d. for the privilege of being apprenticed

[1] See above, § 21, p. 70, n. 1.
[2] See below, §§ 14, p. 259.
[3] See below, §§ 25, p. 476; cf. also, §§ 26, p. 491.

to the blacksmith.[1] In 1598, John Wilkins paid for the privilege of living away from the manor for seven years, while John Browning paid for being away for ten years. Both were to perform the customs and services due to the lord, both being put under pledge. Both were called customary tenants.[2]

Another clear mark of servile status, other than chevage or annual recognition, was the payment of a fee for the privilege of getting married, especially away from the manor. This is the well-known maritagium or merchet. It runs through the Crawley accounts (1208–1448) as a regular item. Even in 1570–71 one of the customary tenants, Thomas Wayte, paid 3s. 4d. for the privilege of marrying his three daughters outside the manor.[3]

Clear marks of the survival of a servile status are found in the occurrence of chevage, merchet, and the use of the terms bondman (nativus) and bondwoman (nativa). In 1515–16 the collector of rents, Thomas Davy, was labelled the lord's bondman.[4] In 1570–71, six out of ten persons, whose services had been commuted, were specifically put down as bondmen (nativi).[5] They were all farthing-holders of North Crawley, where the servile status probably remained longest. Even in 1625–26, and possibly later, divers tenants paying the lord for the commutation of their services were called bondmen.[6] After Queen Elizabeth had commuted 200 bondmen on the Duchy of Lancaster in 1575, however, it must have been difficult for other lords to hold their tenants to the old servile status.

We may infer that the chief factor in the rise of personal freedom in Crawley was the decline in predial services. The latter followed the former about 200 years. This was a big lag, to be sure, but the system of binding men to the soil and otherwise curtailing their liberty had become rooted in the legal system and would not at once disintegrate. There was also probably the ques-

[1] See below, §§ 25, p. 476.

[2] MS., P. R. O., Ecclesiastical Commission, Court Roll, 158008 (113/7), fol. 42 (26 March, 40 Eliz.).

[3] *Ibid.*, Various, 159473 (one of 103 rolls).

[4] *Ibid.*, 155863 (7–8 Henry VIII).

[5] *Ibid.*, 159473 (one of 103 rolls).

[6] MS., P. R. O., Exchequer Augmentation, Miscellaneous 312, fols. 68 and 69 (1–2 Charles I).

tion, long after the 1380's and even after 1448, of a possible return to customary services. A second factor was doubtless the cumulative effect of the influence of the spirit and example of personal freedom in the towns. The encroachment of the royal courts on manorial courts was a notable and more tangible influence.

No Magna Carta of personal freedom was inscribed in Crawley. A free status came without leaving a precise mark. In 1553 Randolph Davy, being a bondman, had committed the offence of leasing his messuage and farthingland without the lord's consent. In the entry it is written in that he has been manumitted (manumissus).[1] We have noted no other reference so specific. But the general story is clear enough. The term bondman was gradually superseded by the very different phrase, customary tenant, which had itself long been in use. Merchet and chevage ceased to be recorded. But, of equal significance, the newly freed persons, beginning to make use of their personal freedom by moving about, developed a market for land that had not before existed in Crawley.

§ 28. *Rise of a Market for Land: Old Units split up.* In the Middle Ages, in Crawley, a family held its tenement until it died out or until it deserted without claim. In the sixteenth century, however, a very different situation arose: the tenant could leave his holding and at the same time retain his title. Or, put in other words, the copyholder could derive an income from his copyhold without actually working it. This was closely akin to the new position of the capitalist: he could loan his money freely at interest, deriving an income therefrom quite apart from the actual use of the capital. Of the parallel development in the use of land we need a good deal of investigation.

There sprang up in the sixteenth century a market for land, made possible by the developing freedom of the individual and the lord's need for a greater money income. As time went on, the rise in prices became a factor also. Land came to be readily transferred from person to person, but the transfer was not free. If a tenant wanted to lease his holding to someone else, he could get

[1] See below, §§ 36, p. 519.

the lord's permission to do so for a specified period, on condition that he pay the lord a fine for the privilege and that the under-tenant meet all the obligations connected with the land he occupied. So many transactions of this kind were put through that a separate set of records, apart from the ordinary court rolls, was required. These are the books of fines which are very numerous for the whole bishopric of Winchester. They run from 1507–08 to 1766–67,[1] becoming voluminous in the reign of Elizabeth. A few significant extracts relating to Crawley are to be found printed below.[2]

Although the books of fines contain fines for the entry of a son upon his family inheritance and for the entry of a new tenant to a tenement that had escheated to the lord, as in the Middle Ages, they also record, and most characteristically, the fine for permission to lease or sublet a holding. Of course this was pure gain to the lord. All the old customs were due as before: there was now this additional revenue from the incoming of the new class of tenants. The raising of the fines for entry seems to have been the order of the day. The following case illustrates both the increase in fines and the new system of the farming or leasing of a tenant's land. In the year 1553 Randolph Davy, the lord's bondman, was said to have leased his holding without the lord's consent. Accordingly, his estate escheated to the lord; but it was given back on condition that it bear henceforth the old fine and an increase (in all 5s. 4d.), the privilege of leasing the holding being now granted.[3]

Besides the new use for the fine on entry, there was a new use for the surrender. The surrender was the return of the title to the lord, enrollment taking place as a matter of record. This was, of course, no new practice, though there are few instances in the medieval period. But in the sixteenth century and particularly in the seventeenth and eighteenth, the surrender was used for a new purpose — to facilitate the mortgage of land. For a study of both the transfer of estates and the loaning of money on the security of

[1] MSS., P. R. O., Ecclesiastical Commission, Court Rolls 108/1 to 135/5.

[2] See below, §§ 36 to §§ 40, pp. 518–530.

[3] See below, §§ 36, p. 519.

bondland, the books of surrenders of the bishopric of Winchester are invaluable. They run from about 1552 to 1763–64.[1] Thereafter the entries occur in the ordinary court rolls. It should be noted that the books of fines and books of surrenders are nothing but special kinds of court records. A few samples of the surrenders are printed below in this book.[2]

Our interest in surrenders centers in the transfer of land and its economic and social significance. There was a great deal of consolidation of tenements, three, four, or more being piled up to form a new unit, without the individuality of the several tenements being disturbed. This was not new in kind, only in extent.[3] Cottagers were, however, separated from their arable and pasture lands. This was more novel. In 1560 a single cottage in North Crawley was given over to a woman and her husband, each paying a fine, without reference to any land or garden attached.[4] In the year 1610–11 a tenant received the lord's permission to lease a cottage with yard and garden (or orchard).[5] In 1612 Ambrose Davy surrendered a farthingland in North Crawley along with the right of pasturing one cow, to the use of Richard Davy. But Ambrose reserved for his own use the messuage in which he lived, together with the barns and other buildings. He also reserved for himself a cottage with a yard and garden (or orchard) at the time occupied by a kinsman.[6]

The leasing of unattached land is illustrated by the case of Thomas Syms, who in 1553 obtained a licence to put to farm to anyone a parcel of twenty acres of bondland in the furlong of Wheatgarstens for the period of five years.[7] In 1634 Richard Syms loaned money to Richard Pucknoll (the blacksmith?) in the form of a mortgage on the latter's holding of a farthingland and an extra rood.[8]

Many bits of land and rights connected therewith were attached to a single messuage (or farmstead), thereby creating a

[1] MSS., P. R. O., Ecclesiastical Commission, Court Rolls, 136/1 to 143/8.

[2] See below, §§ 41 to §§ 48, pp. 531–543.

[3] See below, §§ 37, pp. 521, 522; also below, § 32, pp. 111 ff.

[4] See below, §§ 37, p. 522.

[5] See below, §§ 40, p. 529.

[6] See below, §§ 41, pp. 531–532.

[7] See below, §§ 36, p. 519.

[8] See below, §§ 43, p. 535.

larger unit for cultivation. A late instance of this is found in a surrender made for the purpose of a mortgage in 1671. The whole estate involved was made up of (*a*) a messuage (or homestead) with a virgate of bondland and a pittle (or pightle, probably purpresture land), (*b*) part of a granary (or barn), orchard, and yard with a half virgate of land, and (*c*) a virgate with 1½ acres of purpresture land, all in South Crawley.[1]

The new market for land, then, involved the splitting up of old units to form new ones. These new units were ordinarily larger than the medieval average, but some were smaller, consisting of a cottage, yard, and at most an acre or two of arable or pasture.[2] A second result was the incoming of a new class of undertenants,[3] some of whom were regarded as threatening to the parish. Of course, there could be no fear that the new yeoman farming class would ever become a charge to the parish, but with the landless agricultural laborer renting one of the extra, or tied, cottages of a farmer, the situation was very different. Perhaps these were the subtenants[4] of whom complaint was made, or the inhabitants[5] referred to in the court rolls in contradistinction to the freeholders and customary tenants. A third result was the transfer of title, without reference to the nature of the unit, particularly by means of the surrender for the purpose of a mortgage. Apparently (we have no statistics), the earlier mortgage loans were made by one Crawley tenant to another and at a high rate of interest. Later the loans were frequently made by persons living in towns, even at a distance, and at a lower rate of interest.[6] Of this last development we have evidence from the seventeenth to the nineteenth century. In 1831 James Holdaway, of Crawley, borrowed £300 from Henry Twynam, of Bishopstoke, on the security of his tenement. The mortgage loan not having been repaid, the tenement was forfeited.[7]

[1] See below, §§ 46, pp. 539–540.
[2] See below, §§ 37, pp. 520, 521 ff.
[3] William Wayte, having received a subtenant, or *inmat*, against the statute, is ordered to remove him. See MS., P. R. O., Ecclesiastical Commission, Court Roll, 92/11, fol. 11 (18 Sept., 7 James I).
[4] See below, §§ 31, p. 510.
[5] See below, §§ 34, p. 514.
[6] See below, §§ 46, p. 540; §§ 48, p. 543.
[7] See MS., Millbank, Ecclesiastical Commission, 153118, fols. 173–178 (13 July).

It ought to be noted that it was a tremendous convenience for a tenant to be able to realize on his holding either by a loan or through an income in the form of rent. It was now possible, for instance, for an heiress to marry outside the manor without losing her inheritance.[1] And it was possible for a cultivator to borrow fairly large sums, we trust for the purpose of improving his holdings. But the practice of borrowing, with land as security, was likely to be dangerous. In 1613 Ambrose Davy had to mortgage his land to John Wilkins,[2] who had to mortgage his in 1635 to William Browning;[3] the last named in 1679 mortgaged his land to John Godwin,[4] who in 1686 mortgaged his to an outsider.[5]

There is no evidence that the rise of a market for land with its concomitant consolidation of holdings led to any improvement in agricultural methods. This came later — after enclosure. But a further stage in the development of a competitive money economy was reached. In the long process of attaining this goal, there were at least three stages. First, there was the marketing of goods by both lord and tenant. Secondly, there was the payment of money for services and rents. And thirdly, there was developed a practice of subletting and even mortgaging land. Personal property was sold first, then labor, then land. Freedom lay in the trail of money. But freedom meant opportunity for the capable, loss for the incapable. Some families rose, others fell. Out of it all came a yeoman class of farmers and a landless, or semi-landless, class of laborers. The old simplicity of virgates in South Crawley and farthinglands in North Crawley was passing. And in its stead had come the ceaseless change in the size and ownership of holdings, which went on with rapid acceleration well into the nineteenth century.

§ 29. *Gentleman Lessees of the Home Farm.* The first farmers or lessees of the home farm had been reeves and bondmen. This continued to be true for over a century. Then in the second half of the sixteenth century, and early part of the seventeenth, the situation changed. Whether John Holwey, alias Edmondes, who was

[1] See below, §§ 40, p. 529.

[2] See below, §§ 42, p. 533.

[3] See below, §§ 44, p. 537.

[4] See below, §§ 47, p. 541.

[5] See below, §§ 48, pp. 543–544.

the farmer in the latter part of the reign of Elizabeth was of the old type, is not known to us. But Sir Gerard Fleetwood, about whom there is not a little information, belonged to a new class.[1] He was a gentleman of capital and outside connections for whom Crawley was both a residence and a source of income. Just why outsiders should have come in, why they should have brought large amounts of capital, can only be inferred. Crawley was a pleasant place in which to live, or could be made such. But this was probably not the only attraction. There was opportunity for gain in Crawley in both grain cultivation and sheep raising, especially at a time of rising prices (1560–1640).

With the personalities, social indulgences, and family scandals of the occupants of the home farm we are not much concerned. But their social rank and especially the sources of the family fortunes are of considerable importance. Into Crawley were poured considerable sums of money; out of it at times not a little was extracted. Those who occupied the manor house dazzled the villagers with their aristocratic connections and lavish entertainment. While several of the later gentlemen were generous in their treatment of the poor, at least one was thought to have done the smaller people much harm by enclosure.

Sir Gerard Fleetwood, already noted above, became the lessee of the home farm in 1606, as we know from the accounts which he along with the reeve turned in to the lord.[2] He held a leasehold for two lives. In the period 1646–50 he was in hot water, having made false declarations of his taxable property. He was a man of wealth, his estate being put down as worth £3,420 in 1648.[3] His farm (or lease) of Crawley was said in 1646 to be worth £100 a year above the rent paid to the lord.[4] His yearly income from estates sequestered was put at £500.[5] He held other estates in

[1] For some of the facts used in this section, see F. W. Pledge, *Crawley* (1907), ch. XII.

[2] MS., P. R. O., Ecclesiastical Commission, Various, 155938 (Mich., 4 Jac. I — Mich., fol.).

[3] *Calendar of Proceedings of the Committee for Advance of Money*, pt. II (1888), p. 757.

[4] MS., P. R. O., State Papers, Domestic, Interregnum, Committee for Compounding, vol. CLXXVIII, p. 95.

[5] MS., P. R. O., Exchequer Depositions, County Southampton, 13 Charles II, Mich. 1 [1661].

Hampshire and in Buckinghamshire, with a mortgage on a manor in Gloucestershire. He had made large loans to several persons. The son of a courtier, he probably derived his capital from court patronage, as well as the land, and a profitable marriage. He is said to have built the manor house which lasted for two centuries, though much remodelled on later occasions.

The Henleys came to Crawley from Henley, Somersetshire, in 1666, remaining in the direct line or on the female side until 1791. They were country gentlemen, public officials, and politicians. Of a good deal of ability, two of their number gained considerable success in law, one becoming Lord Chancellor and attaining the title of Earl of Northington. Some of their capital may have come in early days from agriculture, but in later times it grew through office holding and profitable marriages. Through this connection Crawley was brought near to the very Crown of England.

In 1791 the lease of the home farm of Crawley was sold to Richard Meyler, the son of a slave trader and slave owner with a plantation in Jamaica. The new occupant had added to his wealth by marriage. His greatest accomplishment was the enclosure of 1795. Returning from Jamaica in 1805, he died at sea. His young son, possessing a princely income, purchased a seat in parliament (for Winchester) and treated the poor of Crawley on the occasion. He was a great benefactor of the poor and an admirer of fine horses. Rather fittingly he died hunting. In the Middle Ages kings had sent their officers and dogs to Crawley, but in the time of the Meylers a king-to-be actually went there in person. But this was to be almost the climax of a brilliant court period. The heirs to the real estate of the second Meyler who had held for three lives, as had the Henleys before them, were neither rich nor ambitious. The manor house went to ruin and the farm was neglected. In 1869 it was sold to Baron Ashburton, who not only failed to build up the estate but further impoverished it. The new owner bought the lease, not to provide himself with a residence, but for gain. The Ashburton family had looked in upon Crawley in the person of the first baron about 1828, as the holder of an estate but not the manor farm.[1] Indeed, the first Lord Ashburton,

[1] See below, §§ 57, p. 630.

ever to be remembered in Canadian history, was a great landowner in Hampshire, as his will indicates.[1] It is not unlikely that this son of a great banker, and himself an able man of business, derived not a little of his capital from his rich American wife. Perhaps it was, in part at least, the early circumstance of his family's owning an estate in Crawley that brought the later Lord Ashburton to Manor Farm. At any rate, it was during this time, 1869–74, that the home farm was at its lowest point since the early seventeenth century. The strength of the village at that moment lay in its yeoman farmers, not in its demesne farmer and certainly not in its cottagers. It is at least an interesting coincidence that the year 1874 saw the last manorial court in Crawley that was attended by the homage.

We would like to know what Fleetwood, the Henleys and their kinsmen, the Meylers and theirs, and Lord Ashburton did for the agriculture of the village. Great changes were taking place in agrarian conditions and in agricultural technique at the time in question all over England. But the part played by these people is not easy to discover. Richard Meyler, who enclosed the land, did not himself cultivate the home farm but sublet it to another person.[2] In all probability this was the normal condition. It is difficult to see how persons with such wide interests outside of Crawley and commonly in non-agricultural pursuits — in public office, in parliament, in investment, and in banking — could, in the face of social activities, drinking, and hunting, do very much to improve agriculture — at least directly. There is one respect in which the lessees of the home farm were not only of no help to agriculture but a positive hindrance. The hunting necessary for a gentleman's entertainment was decidedly harmful to his own agriculture (or his tenants') and to that of his neighbors. It is to be remembered that the hunting rights of the lord of the manor were reserved on the occasion of enclosure (1795). Presumably these were transferred to the demesne farmer, or as he is here called, the lessee of the home farm. The greatest claim to agricultural advance on the part of the lessee of the home farm in Crawley could

[1] See MS., Millbank, Ecclesiastical Commission, 153129, pp. 234–236.
[2] See below, §§ 55, p. 614.

be made out for the period 1795–1818. But this whole subject would need, and does need, very special study. Indeed the very reputation of the gentlemen is at stake!

§ 30. *Enclosure.* The planting of hedges around the sheepfolds was a common practice in Crawley during the thirteenth and fourteenth centuries.[1] Hedges were also made around copses [2] and plantations(?) [3] and between the court and the fields. A new ditch was dug to enclose a field in 1411–12.[4] The farmer of the demesne was required by the lease of 1491 to keep up the hedges at his own expense.[5]

We might infer from the fact that the lord possessed separate furlongs of his own, notably Shert and Combefurlong, that he would hasten to shut them off permanently from the common fields. There is, however, no conclusive evidence for this. Movable hurdles were erected here and there at need; and when it was specially necessary to protect these or other plots, such a device might have been adopted.

For the existence of enclosure (probably piecemeal) in the sixteenth and seventeenth centuries there is somewhat more evidence, though we do not know when the enclosure actually took place. The lord's wood at Northwood had long been enclosed.[6] The tenants in Crawley were ordered in 1625 to keep their hedges up on the side of the land of the demesne farmer.[7] In 1652 there is a reference to "hedge tearing" [8] which may, or may not, have a bearing upon enclosure. The repair of gates and hedges was strongly enjoined.[9] In 1664 it was ordered at the hocktide session of the tourn "That all those that milke cowes that they keepe them in their ingrounds upon paine of v s. every one."[10] Just what

[1] See below, §§ 5, p. 190; §§ 12, p. 243; §§ 14, p. 262.
[2] See below, §§ 12, p. 243; §§ 15, p. 273; §§ 16, p. 281; §§ 18, p. 299; §§ 25, p. 480.
[3] See below, §§ 19, p. 308.
[4] *Ibid.*, *pro* camp*o* includend*o*.
[5] See below, §§ 26, p. 493.
[6] MS., P. R. O., Ecclesiastical Commission, Various, 155854 (21–22 Hen. VII); 155861 (5–6 Hen. VIII); and *ibid.*, Court Roll, 95/7, fol. 94 (20 March, 1625).
[7] *Ibid.*, Court Roll, 95/7, fol. 94.
[8] *Ibid.*, 99/7, fol. 12.
[9] See below, §§ 34, p. 515.
[10] MS., P. R. O., Ecclesiastical Commission, Court Roll, 100/5, fol. 67.

the "ingrounds" were, is not clear; but the suggestion is something enclosed.

When the wholesale and complete enclosure of Crawley took place in 1795, reference was made to seven, or possibly eight, plots called "ancient enclosures" — Hookfield, Hundred Acres, and others.[1] Apparently much of the Manor Farm (the demesne) and some of the land of the yeoman farmers (such as Thomas Pern, George Godwin, Charles Paige, and John Birch) had been enclosed before 1795. But the big event occurred in that year.

The adjoining parishes of Barton Stacey,[2] Leckford, and King's Somborne had been previously enclosed, respectively in 1758, 1780, and 1784. On the other hand, Chilbolton was finally enclosed in 1838 and King's Worthy in 1852. Thus we see that Crawley occupied no unusual position in the district.

In the enclosure act of 1794 the episcopal lord of Crawley and his demesne farmer were given special consideration, as also the rector. It was specifically stated that the enclosure "shall not extend to, or take Effect in, or upon, any Part of the said Manor Farm,"[3] that is, the demesne farm. Five plots, however, were excepted — they might be thrown into the pot for enclosure and re-allotment. Apparently they amounted to 273½ acres and were exchanged for 268 acres.[4] Some of them had already been enclosed, but it might and did become necessary to include them for purposes of adjustment. Of course, all this is just additional evidence that the demesne had already been enclosed. Clearly the advantages gained in the past were not to be lost.

The bishop was not only to have his demesne disturbed very little, but he was to be compensated for the loss of his share of the commons. He was to receive one fiftieth of the commons, downs, and waste and one thirtieth of the common woods in lieu of his rights thereto. His share was to be put as near to the mansion

[1] See below, §§ 56, pp. 625–628.

[2] See MS., P. R. O., Close Roll, no. 6006, pt. 10, nos. 13–16 (31 George II), with plan showing holdings of two Crawley yeoman farmers, Robert Pitter and Thomas Godwin.

[3] See below, §§ 55, p. 606.

[4] See MS., Millbank, Ecclesiastical Commission, 154427½ (lease endorsed 19 Aug., 1805).

house as possible.[1] The "Dues and Services" (probably chiefly washing and shearing the lord's sheep) still owed by copyhold tenants were to be estimated and their value (thought to be worth £12 10s.) was to be handed over to the lord bishop in the form of land adjoining the demesne. Apparently these rights netted the bishop 109¾ acres.[2] There were reserved to the lord bishop (1) rents, heriots, and other dues, (2) fines and suit of court, (3) the lord's rights of hunting, hawking, fishing, and fowling in all common fields, woods, downs, meadows, and waste now enclosed, and (4) general supervision over the timber. The first two groups were stern realities, as the records at Millbank show, while the second two probably had little import.

Well, it is pretty clear that the lord of the manor was not to be made to suffer by enclosure. Nor was the rector to lose. Of course, the expense of getting the act put through parliament, doing the surveying, and making the allotments was to be borne by the beneficiaries.[3] Anyone could force his nearest neighbor to contribute to the cost of hedging.[4] The enclosure was between friends. The position of the small people of the community is considered elsewhere.[5]

Henceforth in Crawley there were no commons of any kind. There was no common or group legislation on agricultural matters of any importance. There were no services to be done, except attendance at the court sessions. But the courts remained, also the demesne, customary tenure with all its incidents (except predial service), and the lord's hunting rights. The outstanding accomplishment of the enclosure was the extinction of old agricultural methods. The remains of the fallow system and permanent pasture were abolished. The scattered strips, with the régime involved, of course, disappeared. Joint use of common pasture and waste was at an end. Probably complete individualism in the use of the woods soon followed. Crawley's old agricultural house was cleaned up in 1795.

[1] See below, §§ 55, p. 611.
[2] See note 4 on preceding page.
[3] See below, §§ 55, p. 614.
[4] See below, §§, 55, p. 607.
[5] See below, § 32, pp. 115 ff.

§ 31. *The Courts of Crawley: their Decline after Enclosure.* The courts of Crawley were held from at least 1208 up to and including 1874, though they had but little vigor after 1795, when enclosure took place in Crawley. Having touched upon their work at various points, we may now outline their early history, indicating the forces at work making for their destruction.

There were two great lawdays in Crawley, in the spring and autumn, when the tourn and the 'court' met — together, as we should judge from the records. The tourn was always the institution that was emphasized. Over it, the seneschal[1] presided. Later it was the steward.[2] This official went from manor to manor according to a regular schedule.[3] At a later day, at least, there was a clerk who was paid a fee or wage for his work.[4] The chief business was done by the presentment of the tithingman and his fellows, the tithingman being himself elected in the court.[5] Presumably, then, what the seneschal or steward accepted from this jury of tithingman and his twelve associates, was regarded substantially as a judgment.

The jurisdiction of the tourn can be made out from the court rolls with difficulty. It is at times impossible to discover whether it is the tourn or the 'court' that is functioning. Clearly the defaults in attendance constituted an important part of their work. Those not appearing paid an amercement in accordnace with their status as free suitors, customary tenants, or mere inhabitants, at the respective rates of 6d., 4d., and 3d. for each offence.[6] The deaths of old tenants and the incoming of new ones were duly presented.[7] The tithingman might present that all was well and have that opinion accepted; or he might be judged to have done his pre-

[1] See above, § 8, p. 22.

[2] See below, §§ 24, p. 471; §§ 28, p. 502.

[3] In the year 1784, twenty-two tourns were to be held in their respective manors between 14 Sept. and 29 Oct. (inclusive), Crawley's tourn coming 27 Oct. See MS., Millbank, Ecclesiastical Commission, 158240⅔.

[4] See below, §§ 23, p. 468.

[5] See below, §§ 30, p. 507; §§ 32, p. 512; §§ 33, p. 513; §§ 34, pp. 514, 515; §§ 35, p. 517. At St. Martin's tourn, 15 Elizabeth, the tithingman of Crawley was amerced 8d. for not having served distraint on a tenant in a plea for debt. MS., P. R. O., Ecclesiastical Commission, Court Roll, 90/5, fol. 76. Cf. fol. 49d.

[6] See below, §§ 31, p. 509; §§ 33, p. 513; §§ 34, p. 514; §§ 35, p. 517; §§ 54, p. 588.

[7] See, for example, §§ 31, p. 509; §§ 33, p. 513.

senting badly. In that case the whole tithing was amerced.[1] Whether an offence against the rules of cultivation was presented in the tourn is not clear, but such seems to have been the case. Presumably many offences to be regarded as criminal would come under the jurisdiction of the tourn, such as sursisa (contempt of court),[2] stultiloquium (mistaken pleading),[3] mellea (breach of peace),[4] and transgressio (trespass).[5] Also the enforcement of the assize of bread and ale, a very rare occasion in Crawley.[6]

The tourn was also called a hundred, the records referring to it as the hundred of hockday and St. Martin's.[7] We should call it a private hundred, doing about the same business as the sheriff's tourn in the hundred of Buddlesgate. When it came into existence is not clear. Possibly it was just developed by the bishop without royal authorization. But by the charter of 1232, it would seem, some such court was authorized in all the manors of the bishop of Winchester. The charter gave to the bishop, his men, and his fees, freedom from the "suits of shires and hundreds." [8] By implication the bishop might hold his own private hundred court. Another name for the court is leet.[9] We have not found it called the view of frankpledge.

If this was a private hundred court, the lord's tourn or leet, what tithing made the presentments? The public tithing was Crawley and Hunton. We have found no indication of the participation of Hunton or that the public tithing was the one in question. In other words, there seem to have been two tithings, or frankpledge groups, the public and the private.[10]

[1] De vj s. viij d. de T*ithinga* de Craule *quia* min*us* bene *pre*sent ad hund*redum* s*an*cti M*artini*. MS., P. R. O., Ecclesiastical Commission, Various, 159310 (1287–88).

[2] See below, §§ 5, p. 189; §§ 29, p. 505.

[3] See below, §§ 6, p. 197.

[4] See below, §§ 6, p. 197; §§ 7, p. 202.

[5] See below, §§ 9, p. 216; §§ 10, p. 224.

[6] See below, §§ 29, p. 504, for a possible instance.

[7] See below, §§ 9, p. 215; §§ 10, p. 224. We find agricultural practices called the customs of the hundred rather than of the manor: for instance, the furlong of Drakenore was not 'sold' as pasture, because it was sowed this year by the custom of the hundred. MS., P. R. O., Ecclesiastical Commission, Various, 159341 (1327–28).

[8] See above, § 7, p. 22, n. 1.

[9] See below, §§ 33, p. 512; §§ 54, p. 588.

[10] See, for example, the tithing of Crawley in MS., P. R. O., Ecclesiastical Commission, Various, 159310. Year 1287–88.

The most interesting, as well as the most persistent, item entered in the rolls is the tithingpenny [1] or certum. This was a custom, tax, or tribute paid by the suitors, probably for the expenses of the court — particularly to reimburse the clerk, we may infer. It was commuted in Crawley from so much paid by each suitor to a fixed sum from the manor, the amount being a mark of silver (13s. 4d.) a year,[2] which was paid continuously down to quite modern times.[3]

The second court was sometimes called the court baron [4] or customary court.[5] It was held along with the tourn and, as we have seen, is hardly to be distinguished from the tourn. Who presided over it, is not indicated. When it was held apart from the tourn, that is, oftener than twice a year, the presiding official was the bailiff.[6] The important element in the court was the homage, as distinct from the tithingman and his twelve associates. If we were to use the well-known sources of information, it would be easy to generalize about the court baron, but, as far as the Crawley records are concerned, it is more to the point to consider the two courts together.

Following are the chief categories of business coming before the combined tourn and court baron. There were fines, or payments, for the settlement of claims to property or other rights.[7] When a fine was put down, the entry constituted a record of value to all concerned. A special use of the fine is found in case of the surrender, or turning back to the lord the title to a piece of land, so that it might be transferred to a third party, commonly for the purpose of a mortgage.[8] Wills were often enrolled, especially in modern times. Escheats were occasionally recorded.[9] Marriages

[1] See below, §§ 12, p. 242; *et passim.*

[2] Cf. below, §§ 9, p. 215; §§ 10, p. 224.

[3] See below, §§ 28, p. 501.

[4] See below, §§ 33, p. 512; §§ 54, p. 588.

[5] "General Court Baron or Customary Court," held 30 March, 1809. See MS., Millbank, Ecclesiastical Commission, 153089.

[6] See below, §§ 25, p. 479; §§ 26, p. 494. Cf. §§ 15, p. 272; §§ 16, p. 280; §§ 18, p. 297; §§ 19, p. 307. See above, § 8, p. 22.

[7] See below, §§ 14, p. 261; §§ 15, p. 272; §§ 16, p. 280; §§ 18, p. 280; §§ 19, p. 306. Also below, §§ 36–40, pp. 518–530.

[8] See below, §§ 41–48, pp. 531–543.

[9] See below, §§ 15, p. 272; §§ 18, p. 297; §§ 19, p. 306.

constituted a common source of income.[1] Fines and marriages were indeed often put together.[2] Chevage,[3] or a payment for the privilege of remaining outside the manor, is a customary due arising from a source quite similar to that of the marriage payment, namely, the servile status of the tenant. Chevage was accompanied by an annual recognition of the tenant's subordinate status. Amercements, or payments for the infraction of a law or custom, were an uncertain and varying source of income. The amounts were fixed in some, if not in all, cases by the affeerers[4] who were elected for the purpose. The occurrence of extrahure,[5] or strays, generally sheep, cows, and horses, is a reminder of the fact that the fields, or many of them, were unenclosed. An iron wheelbarrow was once presented as treasure trove.[6] There were also, as has been said, the tithingpenny payments, defaults of attendance, and the election of tithingman and reeve to be set down.

In the management of agriculture the court played an important part. During the Middle Ages it enforced the customs of the manor, primarily designed to keep the people in their proper position as tenants. Bad sowing,[7] plowing,[8] and guarding of the woods[9] were all duly amerced. Offences against the woods[10] and the pasture[11] were common, probably chiefly in the form of unauthorized use. In the Modern Period there is a good deal of evidence of the legislative capacity of the court in regulating the plowing, use of the pastures, the making of hedges and gates, and the like.[12]

The suitors of the tourn and court baron (or customary court) were from first to last almost wholly customary tenants. This gives special point to our calling the court, held along with the tourn, the customary court rather than the court baron, particularly during the period from the thirteenth to the early seven-

[1] See below, §§ 6, p. 197; *et passim*.
[2] See below, §§ 12, p. 242; *et passim*.
[3] See below, §§ 25, p. 476. Cf. §§ 26, p. 491.
[4] See above, § 8, p. 25.
[5] See, for example, §§ 30, p. 506.
[6] See MS., P. R. O., Ecclesiastical Commission, Court Roll, 90/3, fol. 96.
[7] See below, §§ 5, p. 189.
[8] See below, §§ 10, p. 224.
[9] See below, §§ 10, p. 224.
[10] See below, §§ 5, p. 189; §§ 29, p. 504.
[11] See below, §§ 6, p. 197; §§ 9, p. 216; §§ 10, p. 224; §§ 29, p. 504.
[12] See, for example, §§ 31, p. 508; §§ 34, p. 515; §§ 54, pp. 587–589.

teenth century. When the two free suitors of the estate called the Hoo and the other called Rookley House came to be mentioned in the sixteenth century, it was to record their non-attendance.[1] On at least one occasion Rookley House was called 'the manor of Rokley.'[2]

Besides the tourn and 'court,' there was a private court for Crawley tenants, at least in the nineteenth century.[3] It seems to have consisted of the lord's representative and the party or parties concerned. Apparently it did about the same work as the general tourn and court held in combination. In addition, the bishop of Winchester had what was called the "Cheyney Court," a court of record, especially for the collection of debts. Crawley was, at the end of the eighteenth century, one of about 200 places within the jurisdiction of this court.[4]

The language that prevails in the Crawley court records down to the eighteenth and nineteenth centuries is Latin, except for the period 1651–57[5] and now and then elsewhere. The bulk of these records is very large, the early ones being kept at the Public Record Office, the later (1754 f.) at the Millbank office of the Ecclesiastical Commissioners. The last entry that we have noted for Crawley was dated 3 February, 1919, when John Marsh paid 1s. 3d., apparently on entry upon a customary tenement.

A marked decline in the courts of Crawley occurred in the period 1795–1859.[6] Nevertheless throughout this time they were

[1] See below, §§ 31, p. 509; §§ 32, p. 511; §§ 33, p. 513; §§ 34, p. 514.

[2] See MS., P. R. O., Ecclesiastical Commission, Court Roll, 92/12, fol. 29. Date is 24 Sept., 9 James I.

[3] See MS., Millbank, Ecclesiastical Commission, 153107, fols. 43–50 (1828) and 153116, fols. 202 and 283 (1836).

[4] See *The Hampshire Repository*, vol. II (n. d., for 1799), pp. 305–306.

[5] See MS., P. R. O., Ecclesiastical Commission, Court Roll, 99/7, fols. 11–20.

[6] Probably the last full court was held 24 Aug., 1859:

The Queen's Jury and Homage

William Pern	William Tibble
George Pern	George Grigg
Rob*ert* Waight	George Lansley
George Godwin	William Barter
Charles Ewens	J. M. Davis
Lewis Godwin	J. H. Courtney
John Gruncell	

[There was a fine of 3d. for a cottage and curtilage of yearly rent of 12d.] MS., Millbank, Ecclesiastical Commission, 153140, fol. 328.

held to perform the routine of business. But vigor had gone. With enclosure went the management of agriculture. Communal cultivation disappeared. Henceforth the chief business was to present the reeve and tithingman, and to record the deaths of customary tenants [1] and an occasional will.

From 1859 to 1872 the courts met but with a diminishing homage. From 1872 to and including 1874 [2] they met but with no business. From 1875 to 1899 there were no courts at all. In the year 1899 one of the deputy stewards was sent down by the Ecclesiastical Commissioners to hold a court. The court was there, but no homage was present and there was no business to perform.[3] As the deputy steward put it orally, henceforth Crawley was a "dead manor." And yet the court rolls remain, and at any time transactions may be entered therein as a matter of record. Presumably compensation agreements under the acts of 1922 and 1924 extinguishing customary tenure will be entered on the rolls (really folio volumes). When the last bit of land is enfranchised, Crawley will indeed be a dead manor, but still a manor.

The enclosure of land had dealt a heavy blow, but the diminution of the smaller customary tenants, through the consolidation of holdings [4] and the enfranchisement of lands [5] robbed the courts of both homage and business.

§ 32. *Yeoman Farmers and Cottagers, 1550–1850.* At the time of the rise of personal freedom, the development of a market for land, the incoming of gentleman lessees, the enclosure of the land, and the decline of courts, the old customary tenants were gradually being sifted out into two classes — yeoman farmers and cot-

1 See below, §§ 54, p. 594.

2 Apparently the last court held in the long chain of sessions from the Middle Ages occurred 25 March, 1874:

Tourn of Hock with the Court Baron
The Homage
George Rawlins } Sworn
George Godwin }
Nil

MS., Millbank, Ecclesiastical Commission, 210159, fol. 212.

3 See *ibid.*, vol. 1898–1900, fol. 149. The date is 8 May, 1899.

4 See below, § 32, pp. 111 ff.

5 See below, § 33, pp. 117 ff.

tagers. By cottagers is meant customary tenants with an hereditary claim upon their houses. By yeoman farmers is meant customary tenants possessing a messuage and one or more holdings of bond or customary land, and, in addition, land farmed or leased from the other tenants. Ultimately this land, squeezed by economic processes from their neighbors, came to be theirs by virtue of purchase from the former holders (often by means of a mortgage) or by fining for it when it escheated to the lord. The yeoman farmers were free men in person, but they were not free holders in Crawley — not until they enfranchised their land, chiefly after 1841.

For a study of the yeomen in Crawley we have some of their wills, the court rolls, books of fines, books of surrenders, churchwardens' accounts, the national subsidies, the tithe survey of 1837, the census enumerations of 1841 and 1851, and the county directories. Not a single account book of this class has been found.[1] A few of the wills are printed in this volume. John Coper, who probably died in 1514, bequeathed to different members of his family and to his servants almost 300 sheep. He held a tenement in Crawley and a leasehold in Little Somborne.[2] William Coper who died about 1517, left to his servant, Robert Chyddyn (an agricultural laborer?), four sheep. The rest of his goods went to his wife and son. But he also gave to his son 90s.,[3] which would be equal to about 100 bushels of wheat in value. In 1616 Richard Beche died, leaving personal property to the value of £82 11s. 8d. and a half virgate of land rented from John Monke, a fellow customary tenant. In the inventory of personal property there is no money but a fair amount of grain and livestock, the latter consisting of 4 horses, 3 kine, a bullock, and 69 sheep.[4] William Godwin, probably of Rookley House,[5] made his will in 1656. It is eloquent testimony of success in agriculture. He bequeathed £1,050

[1] The last of the Perns of Crawley, living in London, says he has no records. This is Ernest G. Pern, Esq., an assessor and valuer for insurance in London.

[2] See below, §§ 49, p. 545.

[3] See below, §§ 49, p. 546.

[4] *Ibid.*, pp. 546–547.

[5] See the surrenders made 7 Aug., 10 Charles I (1634), to William Godwin, senior, of Rookley. MS., P. R. O., Ecclesiastical Commission, Court Roll, 138/2, fol. 131.

TABLE SHOWING GENESIS OF CRAWLEY LANDHOLDERS

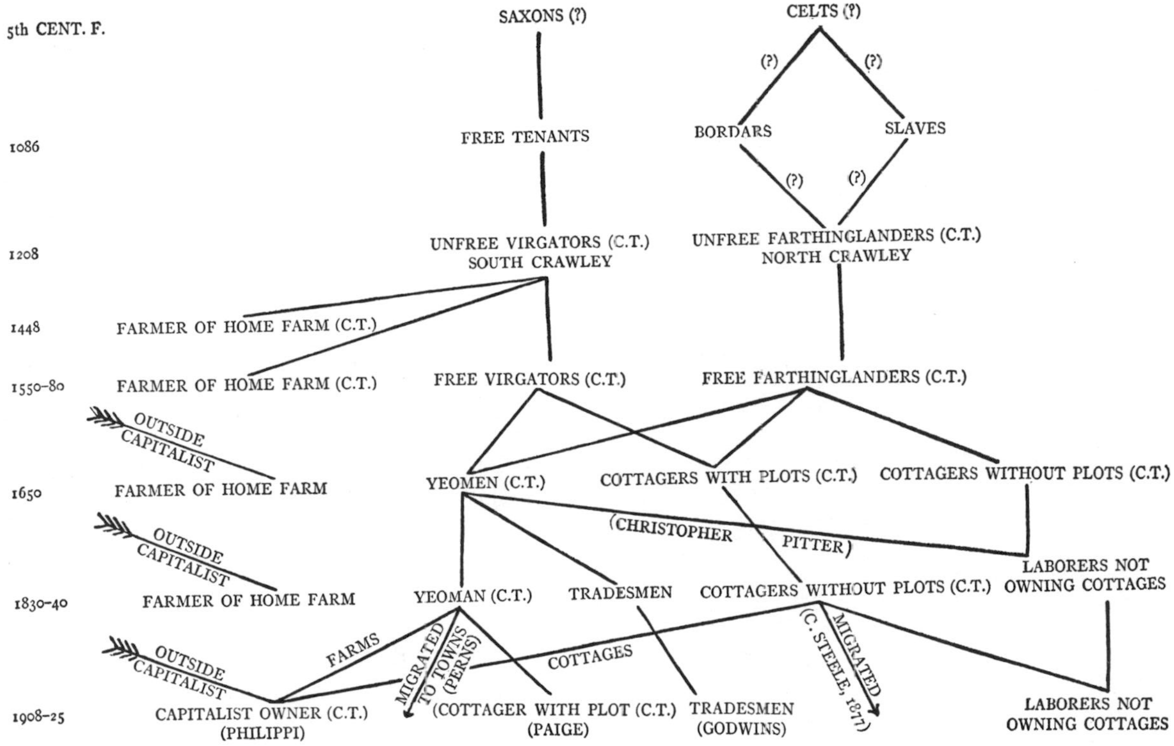

C. T. = customary tenants

in money to his family, £2 to the poor, and £4 to his executors. He had other chattels and estates in Crawley and elsewhere.[1] John Pitter's will of 1761 gave to a son and two daughters £250. Much other property was not specified, except in a general way as "money Goods Bills Bonds Nots of hand." [2] Besides these there were probably landed estates in Crawley. The climax was reached in the will of Thomas Pern, dated 1815. The money devised alone amounted to £5,300. The whole estate seems to have been worth close to £12,500.[3]

Perhaps it was Thomas Pern, son of the Thomas Pern above mentioned, who in 1837 owned and occupied 570½ acres and rented 709 acres more from others.[4] This same estate was put down as 1,280 acres and employing 40 laborers, in the census of 1851.[5] One might question whether such a large estate was worked as a single unit. One credible informant has handed on the information that Pern, whether our Thomas Pern who died in 1852, or his successor, is not known, worked one estate himself and left the others in the hands of farm bailiffs. On the death of Thomas Pern, it is interesting to note, 14 heriots were compounded for £38 19s.[6]

By 1837 six yeoman farmers occupied practically the whole of the (civil) Parish of Crawley; and by 1850 they had it all, except the cottages. Only two of the six belonged to families that had been in Crawley since the sixteenth century. These were Robert Waight and Charles Paige, the two smallest holders of the six. At the top of the list [7] was Thomas Pern, just considered, whose family was relatively new, being probably an eighteenth-century importation.[8] The Selys and Coupers of the fifteenth century had long disappeared. The Brownings and Godwins, so prominent in the seventeenth century, were not in the list, though the Godwin family were in the village as tradesmen. The Pitters had sunk to the agricultural laboring class, Christopher dying at the age of

[1] See below, §§ 49, p. 548.
[2] See below, §§ 49, p. 548.
[3] See below, §§ 49, p. 549.
[4] See below, §§ 57, p. 630.
[5] See below, §§ 59, p. 668.
[6] See MS., Millbank, Ecclesiastical Commission, 153134, p. 34. Cf. pp. 38 and 46.
[7] See below, §§ 59, p. 668.
[8] See F. W. Pledge, *Crawley* (1907), p. 198.

74 in the year 1855.[1] Probably for biological reasons which fortunately we do not need to consider, some families died out. For economic reasons which we cannot easily uncover, others went to the wall or stepped over into neighboring parishes, there to carry on their occupations.

These yeoman farmers drew a strong bow in sheep and grain farming. They made agriculture pay dividends. Probably this was possible partly because of the heavy war demands of the period 1793–1815 and the heavy peace demands of an industrial population, 1815–50, and partly because they introduced improved methods. About the latter we know almost nothing. When these yeomen acted as churchwardens, they not only kept the church in repair but they gave considerable sums as bounties for the killing of sparrows and hedgehogs.[2] They helped the lessee of the home farm put through the enclosure of common lands. They also encroached on their fellow tenants, reducing some to the status of cottagers with small plots and then taking either their small plots, or, in some cases, both cottages and plots.

What was happening may be illustrated by the accompanying table which is meant to be a rough guide rather than a complete or final representation.

The story that this table tells, at least in the latter part, the one in which we are at the moment interested, is that there was a re-alignment of tenants. The virgators and farthinglanders, once they were free, soon found a new level. The higher level was the yeoman class, the lower the cottager class. The way in which the cottager class came into existence has already been indicated: the market for land created them.[3] At this point we are interested in their later history. When some of the customary tenants parted with their fields to their fellow villagers, the yeomen, they retained nothing but their cottages, yards, and outbuildings. Others, however, kept about an acre of arable and a close or paddock for pasture.

[1] As recorded in the Parish Register, Crawley Church.
[2] See below, §§ 52, pp. 564, 570–572.
[3] See above, § 28, pp. 95 ff.

It was a significant further step, in the social differentiation of the population, when the cottagers lost their remaining agricultural lands. Among the petitioners for the enclosure in 1794 was John Glide, who stood apparently between the yeoman group of Perns, Waights, Godwins, Pitters, and Paiges on the one hand and the humble cottagers on the other. He had at least three pieces of land allotted to him on enclosure.[1] When he died, the Widow Waight took over at least part of his holdings, paying a fine of 39s. 8d., as recorded in 1799.[2] A more humble recipient of small favors at the feast of 1795 (enclosure) was John Birch and Martha his wife — John Birch had paid a fine of 6d. for a tenement in 1785 [3] and on enclosure received at least one allotment.[4] By 1837 John Birch had disappeared and with him his name. In 1810 John Tigwell paid a fine to have possession of a cottage, garden, barn, stable, and two pieces of land containing 1½ acres.[5] This was all that was left of a messuage and farthingland, known in the records as Newlands,[6] and containing originally 5½ acres and an extra rood. The name of Tigwell does not occur in either the tithe survey of 1837 or the census of 1841.

Especially after enclosure, the little tenements of a cottage and a small plot of land did not last long in Crawley. Richard Trift, apparently entering into his heritage in 1779, died about 1822, his daughter Kitty, the wife of Richard Turton, succeeding to his holding. Once this tenement had consisted of a cottage, yard, and 2½ acres of land in North Crawley, but by 1822 there remained only the cottage and yard.[7] The Turtons still occupied the cottage in 1837 when the tithe survey was made. In 1859 William Barter paid a fine of 3d. for another cottage and yard which had once been part of a holding containing 2½ acres.[8]

Yeoman farmers were getting the bits of land attached to the

[1] See MS., Millbank, Ecclesiastical Commission, 153107, pp. 24–25 (entry of 10 April, 1827).

[2] *Ibid.*, 158253½ (Hock, 1799). Cf. also, below, §§ 21, p. 462.

[3] As in the second note above.

[4] *Ibid.*, 158241¼. Cf. also, below, §§ 21, p. 462.

[5] *Ibid.*, 153090, fol. 65.

[6] See below, §§ 37, p. 524.

[7] In order to get the tenement, Kitty paid 3d. fine, her husband 1½d. extra. MS., Millbank, Ecclesiastical Commission, 153102, pp. 186–190.

[8] *Ibid.*, 153140, p. 328.

cottages. Under the year 1806, there is an entry to the effect that George Godwin, yeoman, paid a fine of 9d. to the lord for five acres of bondland and common pasture for ten sheep in South Crawley, the cottage and blacksmith's shop belonging thereto being reserved to John Butterley.[1] In 1857 a gardener, named William Allen, surrendered a messuage and garden which was handed over to George Lansley, a bricklayer,[2] who in turn surrendered it in 1869, the holding this time going to William Best, gentleman, of Winchester. But what interests us most in this connection is that this holding of a messuage and garden was but part of a larger tenement, "the barn close and land lying on the North part of the messuage aforesaid late surrendered to Thomas Pitter."[3] In the late eighteenth and early nineteenth centuries the court records are full of fines and surrenders indicating the admission of yeoman farmers to cottages, the plots attached to cottages, or to both together. Thomas Pern paid £3 6d. on the receipt of 13 holdings in 1785, and 6d. for another later in the same year. In 1786 he paid £2 17s. 8d. for six holdings, and then 1s. for two more. In 1791 he paid 5s. for one holding.[4] Apparently he held $15\frac{3}{4}$ yardlands (or virgates) on enclosure, the ruins of old South Crawley tenements.[5]

By the time of the tithe survey in 1837 the Perns, Pitters, Godwins, Waights, and Paiges had just about done their work. There were only three cottages and gardens having extra land in 1837, if we have read the survey aright. Two of these had paddocks attached, together probably amounting to less than 2 roods, and belonging to members of the Godwin family, surviving yeomen, not cottagers. The other had a paddock of nearly 4 roods and belonged to R. J. T. Williamson, who occupied it.[6] This is not a Crawley name. Whence Williamson came and whither he went, we do not know. But he had gone when the census of 1841 was taken.

It is clear enough that by 1837 the cottagers had lost their little plots and the yeomen had taken them. Moreover, the yeomen

[1] MS., Millbank, Ecclesiastical Commission, 153086, p. 229.
[2] *Ibid.*, 153137, p. 325 (11 Sept., 1857).
[3] *Ibid.*, 153150, p. 224 (29 Sept., 1869).
[4] *Ibid.*, $158241\frac{1}{4}$, $158241\frac{3}{4}$, $158242\frac{1}{3}$, $158247\frac{1}{2}$.
[5] See below, §§ 56, p. 622. [6] See below, §§ 57, p. 649.

had taken many of the cottages also, tying them to their own growing estates for the use of their agricultural laborers. The census of 1851 is a scroll which one might think had been written to record the details of the triumph of the yeomen of Crawley: they possessed the (civil) parish, except for a few cottages which one might fancifully think had been left as a memorial of the fact that "once there had been cottagers in Crawley."

§ 33. *Enfranchisement of Land.* The partial emancipation of the land from predial services had taken place on a large scale in the fourteenth and fifteenth centuries in Crawley.[1] The freeing of the individual in a legal way had occurred in the sixteenth century. The final legal emancipation came to the community only in the nineteenth century, when the land was enfranchised, that is, when the surviving semi-manorial or seigniorial incidents were abolished. Up to this enfranchisement the land of Crawley had been bondland, held by customary or copyhold tenure. It had been subject to fine for entry, quit and fixed rents,[2] heriots, escheats, and suit of court. The act of enfranchising the land did away with all of these customs, except escheats and suit of court which probably came to an end everywhere in England under the Birkenhead Act and its amendments on 1 January, 1926.

Enfranchisement may occur in at least two ways. The lord of the manor may, under the common law, convey a piece of bondland, or copyhold, as it is commonly called, to the holder in fee simple. Or the change may be made under the numerous acts of parliament passed 1841–94. In the period 1841–1924 there occurred 24,882 cases of enfranchisement in England on 2,678 manors, the payments being made in cash amounting to £2,863,030.[3]

The Ecclesiastical Commissioners, who were the lords of Crawley from 1869 onwards, apparently began their enfranchisement,

[1] See above, § 22, pp. 74 ff.

[2] The customary rents had been commuted on enclosure in 1795, the lord receiving land in lieu of his rights to customary services or rents. See below, §§ 55, pp. 596, 611.

[3] *Annual Report of Proceedings under A.— The Tithe Acts B.— The Copyhold, Inclosure, Commons and certain other Acts For the Year 1924.* Ministry of Agriculture and Fisheries (1925), p. 7.

at least on a large scale, under authorization by an order in council dated 31 March, 1870. After that date they were quite active in enfranchisement, as their reports to the government indicate.

We have no record of emancipation in Crawley except for the period 1871–1910, when about 40 per cent of the acreage of the civil parish was put upon the basis of freehold. Presumably before 1869 the bishops of Winchester had emancipated the rest of the land, probably much of it since 1841.

In the period 1871–1910, nine cases [1] of enfranchisement occurred in Crawley. At least seven cottages were included, and 1,458½ acres in all were involved. Payments totalling £2,534 12s. were made to the Ecclesiastical Commissioners. The rate per acre for land alone varied a good deal, for instance from 101s. 10d. in 1872 for what was probably Northwood Park to 10s. 8d. in 1896 for a large block of arable. In 1875 Adam S. Kennard, son of a London banker, enfranchised a number of well-known fields, some such as Shert and Peach Hill of long historic record, at 46s. an acre, the total acreage involved being 736. At twenty years' purchase this would amount to a rental of 2s. 4d. an acre. Such a sum doubtless represented, at least roughly, the disability of servitude that was extinguished.

It is notable that the enfranchisers during this period were all, or almost all, outsiders. They were either very definitely outsiders or in one case a man who bore a name new to the village. The chief enfranchisers were Mrs. George Pern in 1882 and 1896 and Adam S. Kennard, the greatest of them all. Clearly it was London banking capital which here played the larger part in enfranchisement.

The instance of enfranchisement of the year 1871 bears a statement as to the significance of the act. The land in question (containing two cottages) was to be "as Freehold henceforth and for ever discharged by these presents from all fines quit rents heriots and all incidents of Copyhold or Customary tenure." [2] But dur-

[1] MS., Millbank, Ecclesiastical Commission, vol. 210191, pp. 284–286, 355–359, 646–663; *ibid.*, vol. 210192, pp. 307–309, 540–542; *ibid.*, vol. 1893–98, pp. 321–325, 374–378; *ibid.*, vol. 1899–1903, pp. 200–202, 300–302; and *ibid.*, vol. 1910– pp. 40–42.

[2] *Ibid.*, vol. 210191, pp. 284–286.

ing the period 1910–26, there were a number of bits of land which were still copyhold, customary tenements, or bondland. In fact, there were at least eleven pieces which awaited the coming into effect of the new land law. In 1912 the present owner of Crawley Court paid 6s. 7d. fine and 6s. 2d. quit rent for seven pieces of land on which were apparently located six cottages or tenements. During the same year his sister paid a fine of 2d. and a quit rent of 3d. for one rood and 24 perches of land. A small bit of land was apparently not claimed by the heir. The Jolly Sportsman Inn, which lost its licence in 1914, was possibly entered upon in 1919, but apparently without the payment of a fine or quit rent. Besides these there is in Crawley the Paige cottage (still occupied by one member of the Paige family), which until at least 1926 was bondland and held by customary tenure. Beginning 1 January, 1926, under the acts of 1922 and 1924, customary land becomes freehold, but only in a limited sense until the customary tenant enters upon a compensation agreement (of enfranchisement) with the lord, the fines, heriots, quit rents, and other incidents being due until that time.

Enfranchisement brought land, or other tenement, out of the legal mesh of the manorial and seigniorial system. Again we note that England did not destroy the obvious anomaly of an antiquated system during the great era of reform. France had made the change during its Revolution and the United States shortly after the American Revolution.

§ 34. *Lords of Crawley: their Passing and their Contributions.* For over a thousand years the lords of Crawley were bishops. How many, if any, of the first five (635–705) bishops of the West Saxons were really lords of Crawley, we do not know. The most that they could have done for the village was to introduce Christianity.

The twenty-eight (705–1070) Anglo-Saxon bishops of Winchester played a greater part. They introduced the manorial system and possibly manorial accounting. They gave to Crawley protection against all except the Danes and the king. They gave to Crawley a church and probably a rector. They probably welded together two communities, possibly one Celtic, the other West Saxon, to form a united Crawley, North and South.

There were twenty-five (1070–1551) pre-Reformation bishops, some of whom knew Crawley directly and several of whom exerted considerable influence upon its development. What Bishop Henry of Blois (1109–71) did for his estates, besides build castles, we do not know. But Peter des Roches (1205–38) was a great administrator, as well as a statesman and international figure. He may not have cared much for the next world, but he cared for his manors. Probably the whole manorial system was at its height under his rule. From the king he secured privileges that tended to promote the welfare of his lands. Judging from the improvements in accounting and from agricultural advance, we are inclined to think that several of Bishop Peter's early successors were also able administrators. Other bishops of the period were distinguished in their own several ways, but without helping their estates in any outstanding fashion. William of Edyngton (1346–66) introduced the perpendicular style into England. William of Wykeham (1367–1404) founded colleges at Oxford and Winchester, but he seems to have done more to spend the income from his estates than to build them up.[1] And yet we must recall the fact that he bequeathed to Crawley a cape and a chalice! William Waynflete (1447–86) was fond of learning, a founder of schools, and lord chancellor of England. He it was who treated with Jack Cade, the peasant leader, with promises of pardon. He gave to Crawley the permanent policy of leasing the demesne. That is, during practically the first year of his episcopate, he gave up the struggle to maintain the old-time reeve cultivation. In view of the difficulties, we can only sympathize with this commonsense procedure: the old way could be conserved no longer, even by an ecclesiastical corporation.

The twelve post-Reformation (1551–1647) bishops of Winchester were about as conspicuous for their mediocrity as great officials

[1] Miss A. E. Levett has suggested that William of Wykeham was a more important factor than the Black Death in the commutation of labor services (that is, service rents), his motive being a larger money income for his colleges. See "The Black Death on the Estates of the See of Winchester," *Oxford Studies in Social and Legal History*, vol. V (1916), p. 160.

can well be. They accepted the general drift to personal freedom; and they allowed a market for land to develop. Of course they did their ecclesiastical duty in swinging most of their villages and villagers over to the Protestant faith. Apparently they merely followed an earlier practice when they licensed prostitutes in Southwark. These were the well-known "Winchester geese" of Shakespeare's day.

From 1647 to 1662 there was no bishop of Winchester. Even in 1646 the episcopal lands had been sequestered, being vested in trustees, by the parliamentary party. In 1648 (12 March) Crawley was sold to John Pigeon for £826 11s. 6d., the whole of the Winchester estates amounting to the enormous figure of £103,664 4s. 11¾d.[1] Who the new lord, John Pigeon, was, we have not discovered. Like other Commonwealth lords, he substituted the English for the Latin language in the court records, an example not completely followed.

Eleven ever-to-be-forgotten bishops (1662–1869) complete the episcopal period of the Crawley lordship. Some of these lord bishops were great partisans; most of them were lax in church affairs. The negligent, noisy Hoadly may be passed over. But Brownlow North (1781–1820) deserves consideration. This was the lord who enclosed Crawley, in coöperation with his lessee Richard Meyler, son of a slave owner of Jamaica. North spent much money on building, but he was a nefarious nepotist and luxurious lounger, passing many years in Italy with his fashion-loving wife. Crawley's last lord bishop was Charles Richard Sumner (1827–69), called "the last of the old prince bishops."

In 1869, three weeks after Bishop Sumner's retirement, Crawley was taken over by the Ecclesiastical Commissioners who have been the lords of the manor ever since.[2] They hold all, or almost all, of the Crawley records. The Ecclesiastical Commission was appointed and incorporated in 1836. It was the fruit of the age of reform which sought to correct old abuses. The government of the day was particularly anxious to bring about a greater measure of

[1] See MS., Br. M., Add. 9049, fols. 13d. and 27.

[2] MS., Millbank, Ecclesiastical Commission, vol. 153150 (11 Nov.). Confirmed by Mr. Hugh De Bock Porter, Official Solicitor and Assistant Steward of the Manors.

equality in the incomes of ecclesiastical incumbents. Some had enormous revenues; others almost starved. The annual average income of the bishopric of Winchester for the three years 1828–31 was £11,151, while for the bishopric of Chichester it was £4,229 and for the bishopric of Rochester £1,459.[1] The plan has worked well in the accomplishment of the main purpose aimed at. As we have noted, the Ecclesiastical Commissioners were liberal, not conservative, in the granting of enfranchisements. They can hardly be blamed for not at once putting an end to the antiquated customs which they found so strongly entrenched.

Crawley and the Church have gone a long way together. The Church has always been exacting and conservative. It has been more interested in taking out than in putting back. It has regarded the salvation of souls as its proper function. What material contributions were made to Crawley's social life came before 1350. The Church left much undone: it soon gave up its effort to improve agricultural technique; it did not save the small holders; and it did not introduce popular education until the early nineteenth century. The bishops could hardly be expected to be great shepherds of souls, national administrators, and patrons of architecture and learning, and at the same time promote manorial economy or village welfare. And yet, there was the example of thirteenth-century bishops. One wish we may finally express is that students investigate the subject of the administration of Winchester's bishops.[2]

It is a plausible surmise that the failure of the manorial lords, lay and ecclesiastical, helped to make a middle class socially necessary. The lords as a class, and the bishops of Winchester in particular, from the fourteenth century onward, had a psychology of enjoyment and expending, not of saving and re-investing. In a material way this meant stagnation. The people who were capable of planning, saving, and improving, developed as an urban middle class. The capital which this class amassed in dealing in personal property it invested heavily, in the sixteenth and

[1] See Sir L. T. Dibdin and S. E. Downing, *The Ecclesiastical Commission: a Sketch of its History and Work* (1919), pp. 12–13.

[2] Miss A. E. Levett of King's College, London, has the possibilities well in mind, with students already at work on the subject.

following centuries, in landed property. Therein did it come to supplant the manorial lords who could not, or did not, measure up to the social needs of men and communities. Incidentally it is a matter of interest that it was these persons — tradesmen, artisans, merchants, and their auxiliaries, the scribes and lawyers, who evolved a protesting religion, established Protestantism, and reformed surviving Catholicism. There is also at least a suggestion that the failures of Crawley's bishops in material matters prepared the way for a Protestant bourgeoisie of bankers and manufacturers.

§ 35. *The Capitalist Owner acquires all the Yeomen's Farms by 1902–08.* Gradually as the lord of the manor lost his rights or sold them, and accordingly receded into the background, there came in a rich capitalist owner who bought his way into the manor and substantially into the position occupied by the lord bishop of Winchester in the palmy days of manorialism and feudalism.

As we have seen, Lord Ashburton possessed the home farm from 1869 to 1874. At the latter date, he sold his possession to Adam Steinmetz Kennard [1] (1833–1915), whose father was a banker as his father had been before him.[2] Kennard bought one holding after another, including six cottages and gardens between 1875 and 1883. These and other holdings of arable and pasture he enfranchised.[3] That is, he bought the lord off his own estates. He tore down the old and delapidated manor house, erecting in its stead the present Crawley Court, a representation of which is shown on the preceding page. Doubtless Kennard, anticipating a legacy which never actually came to him, sank a lot of capital in Crawley, in purchasing possession and enfranchisement, and in building the great house with its spacious grounds and fine old trees. Kennard was a London banker who sought the distinction that country associations bring. He became a justice of the peace for Hampshire and High Sheriff in 1885.[4] In spite of his

[1] See MS., Millbank, Ecclesiastical Commission, 210160, pp. 377–410.

[2] Burke, J. B. *A Genealogical and Heraldic Dictionary of the Landed Gentry* (1879), p. 896.

[3] See above, § 33, p. 118.

[4] Walford, Edward, *The County Families of the United Kingdom* (*1890 and 1900*), *s. v.*

ambitions and expenditures, however, he saw but little of Crawley and apparently lived in Crawley Court only a short time. His will, dated 1909, seems to indicate that he was far from being a rich man at his death.

In 1900 Kennard sold out to Otto Ernst Philippi, who was born in Hamburg, Germany, and had been successful in the business of J. P. Coates and Company of Glasgow, Scotland. Philippi brought his family with him and also Mr. J. O. Robertson, who has been the estate agent ever since. Clearly Philippi was a remarkable man, but he had the common weakness of the industrialist — a desire to attain the prestige of a country family. His choice of Crawley, as a substitute for Glasgow, seemed a wise one for his family. And yet one of his sons, preferring industry to agriculture and town life to rural existence, has long resided in or near Glasgow and is active in his father's former business.

The new capitalist owner, Philippi, acquired not only the home farm but the yeomen's farms. The yeomen had been triumphant by 1850, as we have seen. By September, 1902, they had left the village or lost their status of yeomen, their holdings going to the man who could command outside capital, that is, to the one whose income did not depend upon agriculture.

The Waights or Waites had been in Crawley since at least 1523.[1] In 1837 Robert Waight held $164\frac{1}{2}$ acres which he is put down as both occupying and owning, and a few more acres leased.[2] In 1851 he possessed 176 acres with 8 laborers, and 8 women and girls in his service.[3] In a directory for 1867 he was recorded as landowner and farmer. In 1879 he died at the age of 78.[4] This seems to have been the last of the family in Crawley, certainly as yeoman farmers. In the early part of the nineteenth century the family was migrating to the towns, one being a carpenter and cabinet maker in New Alresford, while another was a watchmaker in Birmingham, Worcestershire.[5] Perhaps if we could follow the family we should find that it had gone to successes elsewhere, but it really seems to have lost its vigor.

[1] See below, §§ 50, p. 552. [2] See below, §§ 57, p. 631.
[3] See below, §§ 59, pp. 659, 672.
[4] As recorded in the Parish Register, Crawley Church.
[5] MS., Millbank, Ecclesiastical Commission, 153099. Year 1821.

The Godwins were at their height in the seventeenth century.[1] Prominent at enclosure in 1795, they were out of the running by 1837. They had become small tradespeople in the village by 1841, and as such they have remained to this day in the capacity of bakers and shopkeepers.

The Perns seem to have been a fairly short-lived but very vigorous family. They are said to have acquired much of their property through intermarriage. In 1875, George Pern, landowner and farmer as he is called in the directories, died at the age of 43. His widow continued to live in the village, cultivating the estate, at least part of which had been enfranchised, by means of a farm bailiff. Shortly after her death in 1902 the trustees of the estate sold the heavily mortgaged Pern farms to Philippi.[2] The loss of the Perns was a real blow to Crawley, for they had made agriculture a success. In a sense the Philippi family is the occupational descendant of the Perns. The mantle of the old has fallen upon the new.

The Paige family has been in Crawley probably since the fifteenth century. It was prominent in 1523, active in enclosure in 1795, but the least of the six farmers in 1837. In 1863 the Crofts Farm of 47 acres with 27 in arable belonged to the Paige family.[3] In 1920 Thomas Paige, the last male representative in Crawley, died at the age of 70 years. The Paige estate today (1925) is really a cottage with a plot, a degeneration from a yeoman farm. But it is not part of the Crawley Court estate, at least not yet. The cottage, near the pond, is a somewhat picturesque and unregenerated dwelling. A picture of it is here reproduced as frontispiece.[4] It is thatched and has the old type of heavy timbered ceiling and a deep fire-place. The floors are brick covered with some kind of oiled cloth. Attached to the cottage is a plot of about 1½ acres. The Paige descendant and occupant married a poor but spirited thatcher from Wiltshire, who had thatched some of Philippi's houses. He is now old and a pensioner. This customary-tenant family has survived through, and degenerated from, the yeoman

[1] See below, §§ 21, p. 457; §§ 49, p. 547.

[2] We have been informed indirectly by one of Mrs. Pern's sons that the sale occurred only in 1908.

[3] See MS., Millbank, Ecclesiastical Commission, 153144, p. 202. [4] House at left.

class. This old family and the pond at their door have come down from the Middle Ages together. It seemed rather pathetic that the old couple should have been boarding for a few weeks during the summer some poor children sent down from London for the country air.

This is the end of the yeomen of the Village of Crawley! How are we to explain their going? Locally it is said that the yeoman families died out. That is in a sense true, but in another sense it is not. The families did not die out — only that part remaining in the village died out. Had the family occupations and estates been prosperous and promising, the families would probably have supplied representatives to continue the business of farming. Another explanation given for their passing by persons still on the ground is "the bad year in 1879 when the wheat was brought in 'in cartloads, sopping wet like manure.'" Farmers were obliged, it was said, to mortgage their holdings and never were able to pay off the mortgage. This is at least suggestive of the truth, but the well-to-do yeoman farmers were able to withstand a single crop failure. What they could not do was compete with American wheat and Australian wool and mutton. From about 1873 to perhaps 1914 was a trying time for Crawley's agriculture. It was chiefly a question of how much money one was willing and able to lose. Those Crawley cottagers who had gone to America and to Australia were wreaking vengeance on the yeoman farmers who had taken the holdings of their families.

As has been said, in the Village of Crawley there are no yeoman farmers. There have been no farms separate from the Crawley Court estate since 1902. But this does not apply to the Parish of Crawley as a whole.

There are other gentlemen in the parish besides the Philippis. Rookley House, situated on the extreme west of the parish, apart from the village, is a fine residence which has attached to it Rookley Farm, now used for dairy purposes. The estate has recently changed hands, the name of the farmer in 1927 being W. H. Ruffle. Both the occupant of the House and of the Farm are at present outsiders.

In 1872 a London merchant, Philip Vanderbyl, bought off the

yeoman family of Fifield, contemporaries of the Perns. Vanderbyl built in 1883 a fine house on this estate, which is now called Northwood Park but in the Middle Ages Wodecote. Later the house was used for a private school. Attached to this estate is Home Farm containing about 125 acres. The chief function of the Farm, when visited in 1925, was to supply eggs from 500 fowl and milk from 10 cows to the school. The farmer, a friendly and none too happy man living out of town for his health's sake, held by a lease from the owner of the estate, Thomas Eastman, of Guildford, Sussex. It was a three-year lease containing a stipulation that a four-crop rotation should be followed. The farmer had a laborer's cottage, and two laborers to do the work of the farm. Of the 125 acres, 24 were in copse (the old medieval source of firewood), 86 in grass, 12 in grain and potatoes, and 3 in yard and garden. The lease was worth £200 a year. Since our visit in 1925 another farmer has taken over the holding.

Another place of residence in Crawley with a farm attached is Littleton House owned by Arthur E. Deane, a town banker. His farmer, James Grey, has 500 acres in all, part being in Crawley and paid in the adjoining Parish of Littleton.

The rest of the Parish of Crawley is not following the course of events in the Village of Crawley. While the owner of Crawley Court has bought up cottages and farms to manage all as a single indivisible unit, the other three estates have their subordinate farmers. The gentleman landowner in these cases provides the land and improvements and also advice in management (in the lease). The farmer supplies the capital and management. The manual work is done by laborers living in tied cottages. This is more typical of England as a whole than is the Crawley Court estate.

§ 36. *The Capitalist Owner acquires the Laborers' Cottages by 1908.* The first Philippi was more of a builder than an agriculturist. He would have the carts off on some construction enterprise when they were needed in the fields. He erected several new cottages in the village, and reconstructed others. In the work of reconstruction he used timbers from old buildings in order to give the newly built or freshly altered cottages the appearance of age. There is no doubt that in removing thatched roofs, installing wooden floors instead of the old brick or dirt floors, and putting in more windows, he greatly improved the dwellings. But he gave to Crawley the appearance of a model village, almost devoid of a single striking corner or nook. Much of it is neat, all of it seems clean, but none of it is the object of an artist's pilgrimage. Such, we suppose, is the inevitable effect of the impact of industrial capital upon rural life. Crawley had become, however, a finer village in which to live.

Soon after his arrival, Philippi let it be known that he would pay a good price for cottages. Presently the owners were offering them for sale, in some cases stipulating that they should never in their lifetime be turned out. The purchase was completed by June, 1908. The former owner of the last cottage bought still (1927) occupies the cottage. We do not feel sure that every last cottager's house was bought, but there was probably not more than one outstanding. Later (1911) the old rectory was acquired. This left in the village not more than three residences not tied to Crawley Court. They were the new rectory, the cottage belonging to a decayed yeoman — not cottager — family (Paige), and one (possible) cottager's house to which title may or may not be very clear. Of course, we are here speaking of the village, not the parish. In so far as Philippi possessed a few unenfranchised pieces of land, he was a customary tenant. But he it was who dealt the final blow to the surviving customary tenants who parted with their cottages and gardens.

The cottagers of Crawley had gone off gradually. The earlier ones in the late eighteenth and early nineteenth centuries went without leaving a trace behind them. Some doubtless went to the colonies or to America, but most probably to the neighboring towns and to London, and possibly through London drifting to the industrial North. William Bagshaw, who had gone to Australia, transferred his tenement in 1875 through intermediaries to Kennard.[1] Charles Steele, son of Charles Steele, a carpenter, after migrating to Iowa, U.S.A., surrendered his cottage and garden to

[1] See MS., Millbank, Ecclesiastical Commission, 210160, pp. 6–8.

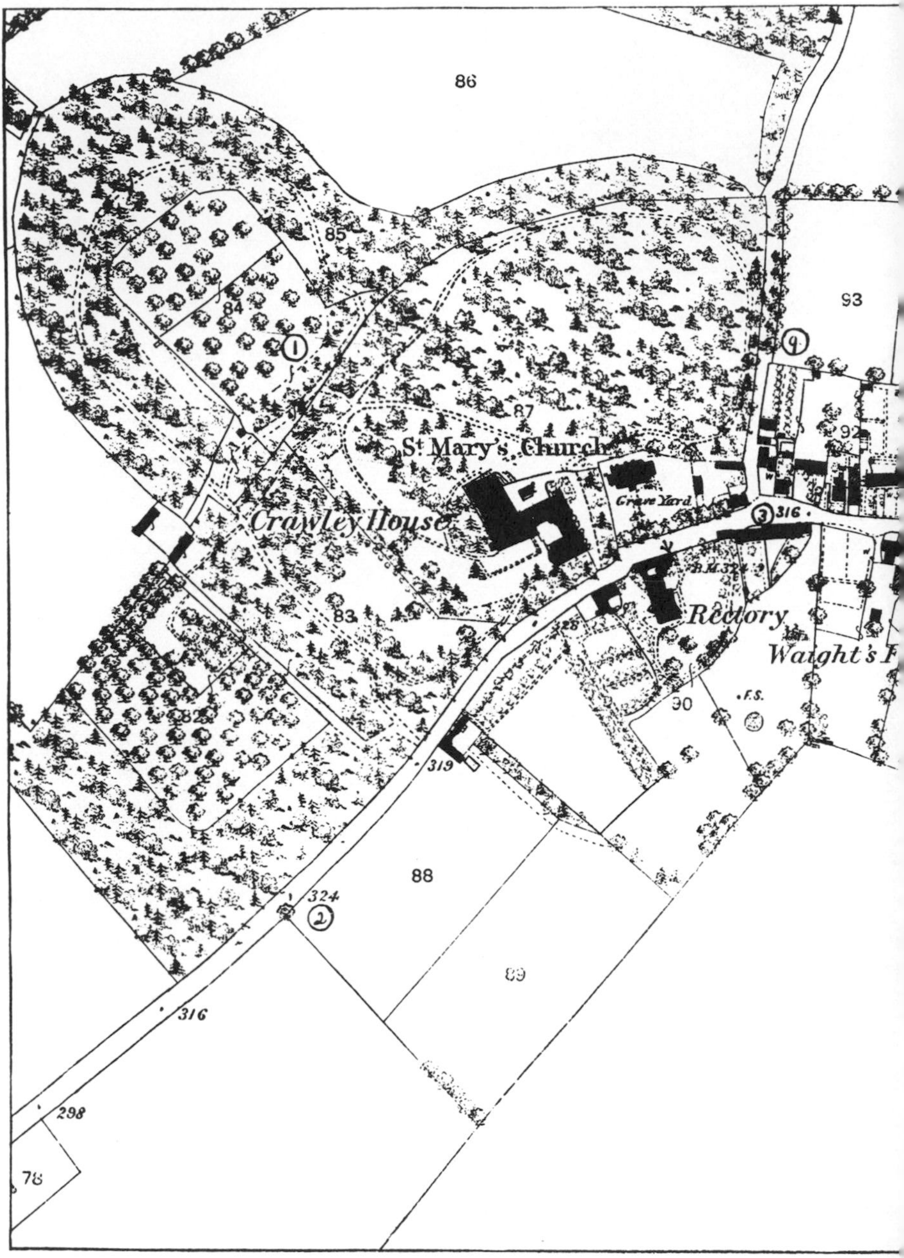

The Survey of 1908 shows changes as indicated by the following number

① Location of the present Crawley Court taking the pla
of the old Crawley House.

② Cemetery.

③ Houses almost all removed here.

④ Allotment gardens. Waight's Farm disappears.

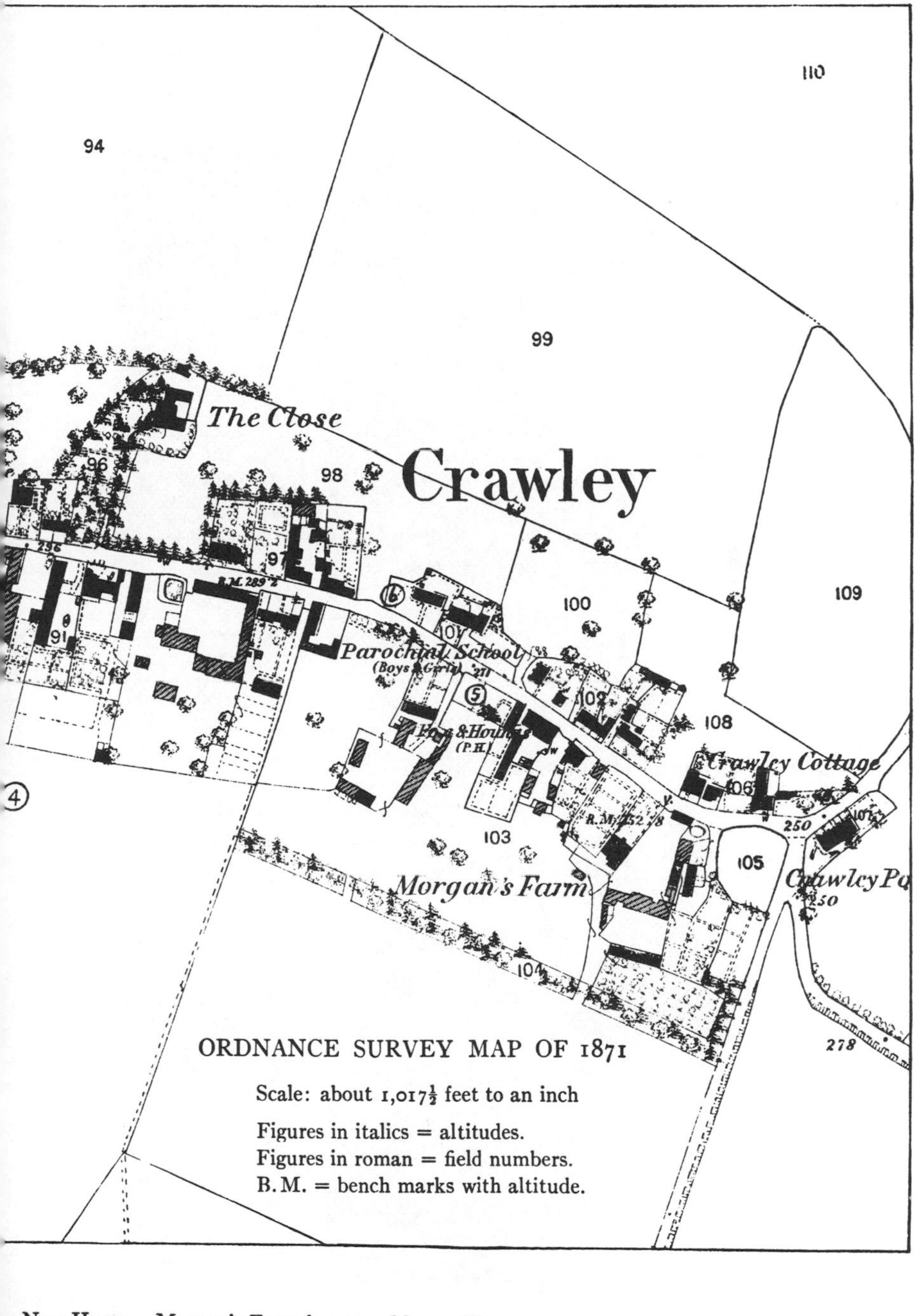

ORDNANCE SURVEY MAP OF 1871

Scale: about 1,017½ feet to an inch

Figures in italics = altitudes.
Figures in roman = field numbers.
B. M. = bench marks with altitude.

New House. Morgan's Farm becomes Manor House.
Baptist Chapel (new). The Close becomes White House.
New House (P. O.).
Cricket Ground.
Smithy.

CRAWLEY COURT

A photograph

a builder in Winchester in the year 1878.[1] William Wheeler had died intestate, leaving his tenement and stable (The Jolly Sportsman) to his only child (a daughter) and customary heir who was living in New South Wales (1889).[2] Thirty years later the right to this tenement was inherited apparently by this woman's son, but we have not learned that he ever entered upon his inheritance.

The cottagers of Crawley sometimes lost their cottages through mortgage;[3] sometimes they merely moved off without regard to impending possession; sometimes they sold out to others. At any rate, the parting with the cottage was often connected with migration, planned or accomplished. Since 1908 it has not been possible for cottage-dwellers to sell their cottages for migration, because they possess none to sell. And yet, they are so relatively well off today that they do not need to go away — except the young people, more of whom enter agriculture than can be accommodated on the Crawley Court estate.

The existence of an agricultural proletariat is found not only in very recent times but (apparently) also in the period about 1235–1306. At this earlier time, several curtilages were let by the lord each year at 6d. or 12d. each, the arable acres being rented out separately. Just what was behind this situation in the Middle Ages is not clear. It was at any rate relatively short-lived. Fortunately for the lord bishop, it did not exist as an explosive element during the troublesome period 1349–83. Obviously today, the agricultural proletariat, in a time of crisis, might be expected to identify itself with the more numerous proletarian class in the towns. And yet, the landless peasantry of southern England, generally speaking, appears to be psychologically as conservative as the Russian peasantry. This Russian peasantry, however, maintained its claim upon most of the soil and now has it all.

[1] *Ibid.*, 210161, p. 286 (4 Dec., 1877) and *ibid.*, 210162, p. 53.

[2] *Ibid.*, 237131, p. 409 (10 Oct.).

[3] E. g., James Davis of Barton Stacey acquired through a mortgage a holding in Crawley, including a blacksmith's shop. MS., Millbank, Ecclesiastical Commission, 153136, p. 326 (26 Sept., 1856).

§ 37. *The New Manorialism.* On the ruins of the old manorial system has been erected a new one. In the (civil) parish there is one man dominant over about 3,164 acres called the Crawley Court estate.[1] In the Middle Ages there had been one lord over the whole (civil) parish of about 3,600 acres. Now, as then, there is a desire for an income from the land. There is today an officialdom much like that existing in the Middle Ages. There is at present an estate agent who corresponds roughly to the bailiff who accounted (jointly with the reeve) for the year's receipts and disbursements. And today there is an agricultural expert, or farm manager, who is much like the reeve of the Middle Ages, for upon his shoulders fall the general policy and details of agricultural management. There are the shepherds today as then. And the modern grain bailiff is apparently somewhat like the old messor and perhaps hayward in one. Today the laborers know their fields as they must have in the Middle Ages. There is the same subservience of attitude (or is it merely deference?) and probably the same undercurrent of discontent. And now, as then, there is the same slovenliness of work and dislike of the official immediately in charge of operations.[2] Today there is a patronage by the capitalist owner comparable to that of the medieval lord. Today milk is given at a low rate and houses at a less than market rate. The clothing of the laborers is partly paid for and the poor are helped where this is necessary. In the medieval period, the lord gave wood, pasture, corrodies, and boon feasts. And in the Middle Ages, as now, Rookley House estate was a thing apart from the village, which looked then, as it does now, to Winchester for supplies, the sale of products, and amusement.

As is to be expected, the new manorialism differs much from the old. The new is based upon capitalism, the old upon a grant of lordship by the king. In the present manor there are practically no customary tenants with rights enforceable in the courts; there are today only inhabitants — laborers, residents, tradesmen, and officials. On the medieval manor the tenant who was also a laborer, had the security of tenure that was based on custom

[1] See below, § 38, p. 134.

[2] See also, below, § 38, pp. 136–137.

which indeed had the effect of law. Today the laborer merely occupies the estate owner's cottage at a rental of about 3s. (this being the rate allowed by the national law, the market rate for a five-roomed cottage being about 10s.). Although this laborer has no legal security, the force of custom and public opinion may keep him, often does keep him, in the cottage long after his services prove to be ineffective. Of course, there is now no personal servitude: anyone may go away without being called a fugitive or without paying an annual due for the privilege of being away. Today there are national or semi-national officials who play a fairly important rôle. There are the postmistress, the schoolmistress, and the tax collector. There has been a shop since the early nineteenth century. Today the village is a place where outsiders come to live and where there is some social intercourse and intellectual life, not paralleled in medieval Crawley. There is no legal court today, but there is Crawley Court, the name surviving through the house in which the court had been held. However, the present Crawley Court (the great house of the village) never actually witnessed a legal session. And it is probable that its immediate predecessor, the mansion of Fleetwood, let the court meet in one of the inns.

The capitalist owner of Crawley, Colonel George Philippi, is a young man, educated at Exeter College, Oxford, who has seen some civil and military service. His wife is a brilliant as well as beautiful lady whose portrait was on view at the exhibition of the Royal Academy in London, 1925. All in all, the Philippi family stands for a high order of social life, in which entertainment, hunting, and fishing, as well as foreign travel, play a prominent part. In their midst are beauty, order, command, service, liberality, and good cheer. Here the tradition of simplicity and enjoyment is maintained. Nothing like this prevailed in medieval Crawley. For these things or their counterpart, it was necessary to go to the lord's palace at Wolvesey, at Farnham, or elsewhere. The new "lord" of Crawley, probably like the old, gives only general attention to the business of management, but it is a sympathetic and intelligent oversight.

The capitalist owner has an attitude of progressivism. He wants to improve rather than maintain conditions. This may have existed in the thirteenth century and in the early fourteenth, but it cannot be put down as a medieval characteristic. Today there is but one agricultural unit in the Village of Crawley, while in the Middle Ages there were over fifty. Today the fields are consolidated, while in the medieval period they were in the form of scattered strips. Today the agricultural methods of Crawley stand out as a model for other villages and other lands, while in the Middle Ages Crawley had apparently no such leadership. Today the secular arm is in control and it seeks and uses special knowledge.

But it is somewhat misleading to compare modern conditions, the "manorialism" of the last twenty years (1908–28), with the manorialism of the Middle Ages. Conditions really changed much from year to year in the medieval period. The lord was the hammer in Crawley until about the middle of the thirteenth century; thenceforth, to an increasing extent, he was pretty much the anvil. In the sixteenth and early seventeenth centuries, however, he again made an effort to control the situation. Economic circumstances and legal system have played their part. In modern times there is and is likely to be a similar see-saw of events. During the war, 1914–18, there was outward prosperity in Crawley, followed by enormous agricultural losses about 1918–22. Since 1925, by herculean efforts, losses have almost been changed into gains, but with more recent difficulties cropping up. All this belongs to the following section.

§ 38. *The New Agricultural Technique and Farm Management.* It would be quite possible to piece together and eke out the probable story of Crawley's agricultural technique from general histories of Hampshire from the eighteenth century onward. Real Crawley material on this subject, however, is very scant. About 1799 it was stated that land was sown on an average of twice in four years, that the average rental was 8s. per acre, and the price of labor 9s. per week.[1] We can compare the uses to which the lands of the parish were put at four different times as follows.

[1] *The Hampshire Repository*, vol. II (for 1799), p. 278.

USE OF THE LAND IN THE (CIVIL) PARISH OF CRAWLEY

Use	1795[1] Acres	1795[1] %	1837[2] Acres	1837[2] %	1871[3] Acres	1871[3] %	1928[4] Acres	1928[4] %
Arable........	2,938	85.2	2,803	80.5	3,006	86.5	2,000	57.1
Pasture.......	280	8.1	420	12.1	182	5.2	500[5]	14.3
Wood........	228	6.7	257	7.4	288	8.3	1,000[6]	28.6
Total.......	3,446	100.0	3,480	100.0	3,476[7]	100.0	3,500	100.0

1 The figures found in *The Hampshire Repository* referred to in the note above were almost certainly from the lost survey made on the occasion of enclosure in 1795.
2 See below, §§ 57, p. 633.
3 *Ordnance Survey of England, Book of Reference to the Plan of the Parish of Crawley* (1872).
4 Really the Crawley Court estate, part of which lies outside the parish. Rough estimates.
5 Pasture and down.
6 Wood and waste land.
7 In addition, there were 131 acres as follows: 80 acres in houses, orchards, etc., and 51 acres in roads and water.

Figures for the number of sheep kept are hard to find. Following are all that have been discovered.

SHEEP IN CRAWLEY

Date	No.	Remarks
About 1794............	1,200	Apparently in the (civil) Parish of Crawley[1]
1890..................	1,845	On Kennard's own estate (Home Farm)[2]
1925..................	2,200	On the Crawley Court estate[3]

1 Driver, A. and W. *General View of the Agriculture of the County of Hants* (1794), p. 25.
2 *The Hampshire Down Flock Book*, vol. I (1890), p. 18. This flock had been established in 1884.
3 Information supplied by Professor T. Wibberley, of Crawley.

Such information as is contained in this table is indeed scant. A few generalizations, however, may be made. The sheep must have been fed, to quite a large extent, upon the lands used for arable purposes, after the crops had been harvested in the case of grains, and on root crops as a substitute for harvesting or gathering. Doubtless many were fed on turnips right in the fields. The best balanced agriculture of the period 1795–1871 would seem to have been in 1837, when the six yeoman farmers were in full command. By 1871 pasture had been cut down to a little over 5 per cent of the total. This seems to point to a preponderance of grain cultivation. If so, it shows why the American competition of the late 1870's and the following decades was such a serious matter.

The outstanding characteristics of the Crawley Court estate are its size and (until Sept., 1928) its operation as practically a single unit. Inquiries during 1924–25 brought somewhat divergent statements as to the size of the estate. An exact reckoning, however, has now been made.[1]

Estate up to 1920	2,744	acres
Acquired in 1920	500	"
Acquired in 1928	858	"
Total	4,102	"

Of these 4,102 acres, 938 lie outside the civil parish. These totals include park and woodlands, and also land covered by buildings.

During the War of 1914–18 heavy demands were put upon Crawley as upon other villages in England. Land was sown to grains without adequate preparation of the soil and without being kept clean and in good tilth. After the War, came a period of five years during which there was an average annual loss on the Crawley Court estate alone of about £8,000, as we have been informed. The seed used was not good. Not enough sheep were kept. Part of the soil was wasted by fallowing. Of the 2,400 acres, 1,200 were said to have been bare fallow or barren land in 1922.[2] And methods of purchasing supplies and selling products were antiquated. For instance, 100 bags of corn would be sold at a Winchester public house to some local dealer. This was clearly unworthy of a great establishment such as the Crawley Court estate. It is no wonder that, in the face of general hard times for agriculture, such methods should have brought a large deficit. In order to reduce this loss, Professor Thomas Wibberley was brought in as agricultural expert and farm manager.

Professor Wibberley, the son of a Lancashire yeoman, was born on a farm in Ireland, and was given four years of special academic training in agriculture. For six years he was County Instructor in County Limerick, in which capacity he advocated a

[1] By Mr. J. O. Robertson, estate agent, and set forth in a letter of 29 Jan., 1929.

[2] See H. G. Robinson, "A Modern Super-Farm: The Crawley Court Estate," *Country Life* (7 Aug., 1926), p. 195.

continuous-cropping system to the great benefit of the farmers.[1] For a time he was associated with Sir Horace Plunkett and indeed he often displays some of the enthusiasms of that leader. By experience and by training he seemed to be admirably equipped to pull the Crawley Court estate out of the hole agriculturally. Judging from results and from the number of people who visit the scene of his activities, we think it probable that he has realized some of his expectations. And yet Professor Wibberley is enough of a theorist and idealist not to be satisfied himself with a single job, once the routine has been worked out.

The whole Crawley Court estate was mapped out by Professor Wibberley, different colors indicating the crops used in the various rotations. Better seed was introduced and the sheep were bred upwards. Fallow was eliminated as so much loss. Some of the barren wastes were brought under cultivation, and during the process these were called by the incredulous the Professor's folly. But sure enough promising crops are coming where rabbits would have formerly almost starved.

The basic assumption was that Crawley's climate was wet and that therefore sheep raising, rather than grain cultivation, would deserve the greater emphasis. Accordingly, it was planned to devote from one-half to two-thirds of the land to sheep,[2] the rest to grain. Of course, the sheep were not to be fed on permanent pastures, but on vetches, kale, rape-kale, white mustard, swedes, and turnips, not cut or pulled but growing in the field. If heavy rains injured the grain, they would improve these fodder crops. And feeding the sheep right in the fields would save the labor of harvesting and serving out fodder to the sheep. Here were good factory principles: to diversify products so as to insure safety and to economize on labor. It is the ideal of the system practised to follow each crop, either when harvested or eaten by sheep, by the tractor plow a few days after the harvester or the sheep have left. Here is another factory principle — the elimination of waste.

In cropping, Professor Wibberley follows several courses, the

[1] See Thomas Wibberley, N. D. A., N. D. D., *Farming on Factory Lines: Continuous Cropping for the Large Farmer* (2d ed., 1919), p. 21.

[2] Some dairy cattle were included.

chief of which are set forth below.[1] The main aims seem to be variety of crops for marketing and for feeding, and keeping the land clean and fertile.

Artificial fertilizers of considerable variety are used on Crawley's weak soil. They are bought in large quantities from Germany, South America, or elsewhere, as the prices fluctuate up or down. Guano has been used, but an artificial guano is now being made by Messrs. James Carter and Company of London under the direction of Professor Wibberley. Similarly this firm advertises special fertilizers for wheat, barley, and oats, following the experiences and experiments of Professor Wibberley. A mixture called Phos-Nitrine, the outcome of research on the part of Professor Wibberley, is said to be not only a fertilizer but a charlock-killer.

Crawley's influence radiates not only in these respects but also, and perhaps chiefly, through its seeds. Professor Wibberley has developed special strains of wheat — Yeoman, Little Joss, and Square Head Masters, each having some notable points of strength. His special pride is a hybrid called rape-kale. If this luxurious plant is sown on good land in spring, a crop can be cut in the early part of the winter and the stubble left to grow again for feeding the sheep in the spring.[2]

The labor problem is a difficult one in Crawley as elsewhere. In the past Professor Wibberley has been inclined to blame the farmer for labor difficulties, but he is not now uncritical of the hands he has to employ.[3] Some fifty-odd laborers are apparently used in Crawley. They distrust book learning and shy at any methods that are new. The worst of them receive a minimum wage of about 30s. a week; the best receive a bonus for extra work accomplished in the prevailing week of 51 hours. All get paid for overtime.[4] The laborers will not work in the rain and are said to keep a

[1] See §§ 62, p. 693.

[2] See *Forage Cropping* by Professor T. Wibberley, F. L. S., N. D. A., etc. Published for James Carter and Company of London.

[3] And yet on leaving Crawley 29 Sept., 1928, he said: "Nowadays I do not think a better gang of labourers could be obtained anywhere in England."

[4] Under the Agricultural Wages Act of 1924, minimum wages were fixed for the administrative Counties of Southampton and the Isle of Wight in 1927 as follows: 30s. for a week of 51 hours in the summer and 48 hours in the winter, with lower rates for younger people down to 9s. a week for a boy of 14 years. These rates apply to

cow from calving in order to get overtime for watching her. They have heard socialists speak in Crawley and in Winchester. One of their number was dubbed a Bolshevik. He did look shaggy like the Russian of tradition. But he had had a hard time in finding employment in the village or elsewhere. Probably he had his side of the case. Labor is spread over the year in Crawley more evenly than before and accordingly costs less per acre. In August, 1925, gypsies were employed — they come year after year to shock the wheat. Their representative asked for a higher wage but was peremptorily refused. It seemed that a refusal was expected. It is interesting to note that some Irish had been in Crawley in 1851,[1] doubtless helping solve the problem of seasonal demands prevalent even on the best managed farms. They were there in families in 1851 as the gypsies were in 1925.

In order to get results, it has been necessary, of course, to work through foremen. Under Professor Wibberley are two grain bailiffs, a chief dairyman and his two assistants, and a head shepherd. It is interesting to note in Crawley, what one hears about occasionally elsewhere in England, that the young people, even the sons of shepherds, will not themselves become shepherds, the work being so exacting, particularly at the time of lambing, that there is no free time for recreation. Animal husbandry as a whole is no longer popular. England, classic land of animal breeders, is thought by some to be about to undergo an agricultural revolution that is hardly yet recognized. When the new agricultural régime was introduced into Crawley, it is interesting to note, one of the grain bailiffs was chosen from among the villagers and was told to make no suggestion but to obey orders for a whole year. He

---

males. The minimum wages were 5d. an hour for a female of 18 years or over. Overtime was to be at the minimum of 8d. an hour for males of 21 years or over, down to 3½d. an hour for boys of 14. A special overtime rate for workers caring for animals was fixed at a minimum of 7½d. for males of 21 or over, and 3d. for boys of 14 years. *London Gazette*, Friday, 4 Feb., 1927.

The standard weekly rate of wages, Mr. J. O. Robertson says, is for a bailiff 60s., a shepherd 35s. 6d., a laborer 30s. 6d., and a plowman 36s. 6d. In the last three cases, where a cottage is provided, 3s. per week should be deducted as rent. It is not usual in Crawley to hire labor by the year. At harvest time every available man goes into the fields, being paid his normal wage, plus 8d. per hour for overtime.

[1] See below, §§ 59, p. 670.

did so with wry face, but at the end of the period had some helpful recommendations to make.

The results of the new agricultural régime have been favorable in some respects. The yield of grain has been increased, for example, from 20 bushels of wheat per acre to 44 bushels. Wheat and other grains from Crawley have been fast gaining a reputation for seed. And the enormous deficit of the years from about 1918 to 1922 had been reduced for a few years — apparently up to 1926. The June frost and mildew of 1926, however, played havoc in Crawley as elsewhere in England. In 1927 there was wet weather for harvesting, and also low prices for grain, and, we may add, for meat — due to the meat war. In addition, there was a serious drought in Crawley in spring and summer. But the diversification of crops and interests on the Crawley Court estate offset these disadvantages to the very maximum. Even in the breeding of the sheep there is diversity, about equal emphasis being put on wool and mutton.

Conditions on the Crawley Court estate can be further understood by a statistical presentation of the chief details, which is found below.[1] Although the figures referred to appear favorable, the situation is not all one-sided. If a diversified system of agriculture is to be continued, there is some question whether it would not be better to divide the estate into two farms of about 1,200 acres each. The system of "feeding off," plowing, and planting, all in rapid succession falls down when the weather is unfavorable. The land, indeed, in 1926 and 1927 could be cleaned with difficulty. By 1928, however, it had been put into good shape again. The prevalence of shooting in Crawley is, of course, bad for agriculture and discouraging to efforts at improvement. For days before shooting is to take place, laborers must not go into certain fields to disturb the game. Indeed the game-keeper and the agricultural expert are inevitably rival potentates in the domains of Crawley. But the owner of Crawley Court seems to hold to the view that it would cost him as much to hire his shooting elsewhere as it would to do it at home. But, bad as this is, the chief criticism that occurs to us is the labor situation. Although it is probably

[1] See §§ 62, p. 696.

true that the laborers are better off than the village people have ever been in Crawley's history, that is, better off in a material way, their income being greater, still they do not have the feeling of possession. Colonel Philippi and especially Professor Wibberley seem to have had this situation in mind. A scheme of profit-sharing is at least a possibility, but there would be great difficulty in the management, so long as about one-fifth of the laborers are inefficient and non-coöperative. Opinion is, of course, dead against removing a villager from his cottage. If Crawley could only supply to England an example of the solution of a labor difficulty — a human and economic problem — as it has an example of fine agricultural technique, it would be even more worthy of wide-spread attention and study. The difference between material success and human failure is great in Crawley. To build up some of the old yeoman qualities would be an even finer feat than building up fertility on a barren upland. The small-holdings movement in England has been almost a failure up to date. Men do not want to establish small units only to starve. And starve they do, apart from some few kinds of specialization. But agriculture, carried on in big units, with plenty of capital, and under skilled management has something to promise by way of returns to all concerned. Perhaps the new "manorialism" is just beginning, with profit-sharing as a future step, some kind of joint working arrangement comparable with that of the Middle Ages. But there is the serious question whether social selection has not already played havoc with the people of Crawley. They lack ambition, vigor, initiative, zest, and promise. In England's agricultural situation, however, this condition is in no sense peculiar. The great question, it seems, is whether these shortcomings are social or biological; that is, whether they reflect the prevailing outer circumstances of life or have become ingrained in the very fabric of the human mechanism. The development of the American negro seems to suggest that environment is the great conditioning circumstance and that physical and nervous energy arise within the individual in response to favorable circumstances and opportunities.

But even as these lines were being written (September, 1928) comes word of important changes. The Crawley Court estate is being divided, not in ownership but in use. In fact, the estate is now cut up into five parts, not including the tiny allotments which have been in existence for some time. The most important of the parts consists of 1,700 acres which have been rented to a Scotsman, who has had twenty years' experience as a cattleman in Hampshire. He pays 10s. an acre for the land, but has stipulated that water be provided by the owner. Accordingly, fresh wells are to be dug or driven. The 1,700 acres are to be used as a cattle farm. The new wells are to solve the age-long objection to cattle — the scarcity of water. Herein the estate seems to be passing from an intensive agriculture to a more extensive system, from experimental work to production for profits, from grain to milk, from the traditional breeding of sheep to their casual purchase and sale, and from a position of almost national interest to local commonplaceness. In spite of efforts now being made to retain practically all of the laborers, there may actually prove to be a surplus of hands. If all that is involved means letting go the laborers coming in from outside the parish, Crawley itself will not suffer, but the district as a whole may be the loser.

The second part of the estate is made up of over 300 acres which have been rented to a neighbor who will carry on the usual Hampshire mixed farming with sheep and cattle. The Forestry Commission has rented the third part — 315 acres which have been planted with spruce, larch, and other soft woods, as part of the national reforestation policy. The owner receives 2s. 6d. an acre and retains the sporting rights to the land. The Commission pays the rates and other charges. The fourth part consists of about twenty acres which have been taken by the County Council and sub-let to a former sailor under the back-to-the-land movement. In addition, there is a fifth part, comprising plantations, sporting lands, and meadows, retained by the owner of the estate.

The passing of the big farming venture is chiefly the result of a failure to pay dividends. The deficit for the year ending 31 March, 1928, was about £6,500. This was too high a price to pay for cleaning and bringing the land into a relatively high state of fertility. The cost of raising grain and sheep was apparently higher than the price that was determined by international conditions would justify. This high cost was due to the expense of management, the free use of fertilizers, and the intensive application of labor. Professor Wibberley had been turning more and more from practical farm management to the production of special strains of seeds. Apparently the seed grain did not bring in a sufficiently high price, or there was not enough of the total yield sold as such. Professor Wibberley sometimes thought of his work as comparable to the experimentations of the agricultural revolution of the eighteenth century, in which the gentlemen of England sank a great deal of money. In addition, one cannot help feeling that the laborers of the village were a prejudiced jury ready to hear evidence in favor of the old order. Working the estate so intensively involved a good deal of anxiety and not a little fussing. Quiet and seclusion have been impossible. And in the background has been the imponderable fact that sport had been interfered with.

The possibility of cultivating the estate as one unit under an expert and with profit-sharing laborers has now been postponed. A new stage seems to have arrived: the leasing of the parts, the shifting of the burden of making profits to people using smaller units. Herein do we find somewhat of a parallel with the fifteenth-century practice of leasing. After an effort to cultivate the home farm by a manager (the reeve), the medieval lord turned to leasing. Whereas this early lessee was engaged largely in sheep raising, the lessee of the chief part of the present estate is engaged in an apparently unprecedented effort to make cattle profitable in Crawley. Truly Crawley is not as it used to be: rye now grows there and water can be found for cattle.

§ 39. *Annals of Crawley.* What Crawley has done year after year, no one can now discover. Most of the events were repetitions, trivial, and worthy only of oblivion. On the other hand, much we should like to know is unrecorded. We could read into Crawley's history the happenings of the district, but that would be going backwards in historical method. We note here only the things happening to or in Crawley that are for one reason or another significant. The dates in italics are only approximate.

643 Two Crawley boundary marks mentioned in a grant of adjoining villages.
909 Crawley regranted to the bishop of Winchester. At least a lordship, if not a manor.
1086 The Domesday inquest shows Crawley to be a manor.
1167 Paid to the royal exchequer 20s.
1207 Crawley men visited Mardon and got into a fight.
1231 Curtailment of cultivation of the home farm.
1235 Existence of agricultural laborers to 1305, their curtilages and acres being rented separately from year to year.
1280 Customs of Crawley recorded by inquest.
1306 Wages of special workers increased.
1315 Further curtailment of the activities of the home farm.
1349 The Black Death, subsequent years being reckoned from it.
1384 Further curtailment of home farm.
1389 69 % of all labor services were still rendered or acquitted for special services.
1407 Lease of the demesne or home farm.
1411 Wages of special workers increased.
1448 Lease of home farm a permanent policy. End of the manor in an economic sense.
1523 Crawley men in arms.
1648 John Pigeon became the lord of Crawley.
1656 William Godwin, land grabber, died.
1660 Restoration to the bishop of Winchester.
1690 Carting manure commuted.
1738 Disastrous fire while the people were in the harvest fields.[1]
1758 Dispute and suit concerning the Stockbridge road.
1795 Survey and enclosure of lands.
1797 Parish spent 10s. 6d. for ringing bells — victory over the Dutch.
1805 Parish paid 15s. to celebrate Nelson's victory.
1813 Parish paid 16s. for ringing bells — Wellington's victory.
1835 A school established, reconstituted 1846.
1837 Tithe survey.
1871 Ordnance survey.
1874 Last manorial court held.
1877 The new Great House, or Crawley Court, built.
1879 Crop failure, yeomen being hard hit.
1880 Cottages and woodyard in the upper village burned.

---

[1] Eighteen sufferers were given sums from two to twenty-five pounds sterling from a relief fund. Cf. MS., Br. M., Add. 33278, fol. 112 (14 July, 1739, the date of the decision to distribute funds).

1884 Archdeacon Jacob, rector of Crawley, died.
1896 Advowson of the church passed into the hands of a layman.
1902 Last of the yeoman farmers.
1907 Pledge's *Crawley* was privately printed.
1908 Last of the laborers' cottages bought up.
Last of the yeoman farms bought up. One big farm in Crawley.
1910 Crawley and Hunton separated after over 1000 years together.
1914 One of the two inns lost its licence.
1921 Excessive drought, history thereby repeating itself.
1922 Employment of an agricultural expert — intensive agriculture.
1926 Abolition of bondland and customary payments provided for.
1928 Leasing to various farmers — less intensive agriculture.
1929 Excessive drought. Water and gas piped from Winchester.

It is of the nature of annals that they do not record some of the most important developments. Far-reaching changes occur without a single date to mark their progress. Most of these are described elsewhere in this book. The most intimate pictures of Crawley are provided by the medieval manorial accounts and by the modern parish records. Since the year 1208, it is not at all true that "annals of the poor" are either "short" or "simple." They have just not been studied or set down. The events that linger in memory are soon to be lost as the actors leave the scene. A few recollections of the living have been gathered and used in this volume to supplement the deeds set down in writing. It is notable how small a part Crawley played in the news items of the journals of neighboring towns.

§ 40. *The Church, Past and Present.* The church building at Crawley, which is made from the stone of the district, was much repaired in the early nineteenth century, and in 1887 it was restored on a considerable scale.[1] In the present edifice are parts of the fourteenth-century church and even fragments of a Norman building. The church as it stands is without distinction on the inside except for its gloominess, or on the outside, except for its deep porch and neighboring lime trees.

The first mention of the church at Crawley seems to be in Domesday Book.[2] It was no doubt in existence in 909 and earlier,

[1] See F. W. Pledge, *Crawley* (1907), pp. 158–159.
[2] See below, §§ 4, p. 185.

when Crawley had attached to it the subordinate community of Hunton, doubtless even then also ecclesiastically dependent. It is a plausible inference that in earliest days the rector of Crawley journeyed to Hunton to perform such services as were necessary, but that later he appointed a curate to officiate at Hunton — and, we may add, sometimes another at Crawley to free himself for other duties. Walter Perys, whose will was probated in 1539, was rector of Crawley and Hunton and also of Meonstoke and Soberton, with curates in all four parishes.[1] The patronage of Hunton, that is, the right to appoint the curate there, was in the hands of the rector of Crawley until 1910, when Hunton was exchanged with the Dean and Chapter of Winchester for Littleton, the adjoining parish to the southward.

The first reference to the parson of Crawley, which we have noted, is in a reeve's account of 1231–32, where there was said to be a defect in the churchscot of cocks and hens due from the t*er*ra q*ua*m vicari*us* tenet.[2] Of course, one cannot be certain whether a vicar is actually meant rather than a rector (parsona) or more likely a curate. It is not clear that Fremund Lebrun, who was made papal chaplain in 1259, was really rector of the Crawley with which we are concerned, though such seems to have been the case.[3] Probably because of the fact that the rector of Crawley had a considerable income and because the parish was near to Winchester, the living was much sought after. It was given to men of distinction as well as to those whose chief strength was their influence at court or with the bishop of Winchester. For several of them Crawley seemed to be quite salubrious and their work not overtaxing: Michael Renniger in the sixteenth century, Robert Wiseman in the eighteenth, and Philip Jacob in the nineteenth, all held the living for over fifty years each. Others occupied the incumbency almost as long. Some of the rectors, being active and useful men, sought and held other preferments also. Matthew Woodford, who participated in the enclosure of 1795, is a case

[1] MS., Prerogative Court of Canterbury, 2 Alenger. Will dated 31 Oct., 1538; probated 4 Feb., 1539.

[2] See below, §§ 7, p. 205.

[3] *Calendar of Entries in the Papal Registers relating to Great Britain and Ireland, Papal Letters*, vol. I, 1198–1304 (1893), pp. 367, 457, 460.

in point.[1] Few of the rectors, as we might perhaps expect, were of the peasant or proletarian class. Charitable as many were, their origins could hardly help influencing their sympathies on such an occasion as enclosure.

The chief source of income for this fat living was the tithe. But we get surprisingly little information on this subject. During the Middle Ages the lord bishop gave to the rector one tenth of the yearly increase of his cattle, sheep, and hogs, as well as of his wool, but no tithe was paid on his grain, so far as the accounts indicate. What the tenants paid is never stated. At the time of enclosure, no provision was made with regard to the tithes, though of course the glebe was duly arranged for. In 1837 the lands of Crawley were surveyed and each piece of ground given a number on a map and put down as owing so much tithe in the form of money. Then the obligation was expressed in the form of a total rent charge. For Crawley the amount was £662 10s.[2] This has varied from year to year with the price of grain in accordance with the original plan. The whole arrangement has given dissatisfaction at one time or another to all persons concerned. After years of agitation the British parliament has at last (1925) established a fixed valuation for the rent charge and provided for the extinction of the tithe throughout the nation.[3] This would seem to be an heroic measure, but in fact it is to be done gradually over a period of eighty-five years. During this long term, Crawley land owners, whether they are adherents of the Church or not, are to pay the annual tithe and enough in addition to amortize the whole obligation. Truly the British are a patient, long-suffering people.[4] Outsiders may well hesitate between admiration for their respect for private property and vested interest on the one hand and astonishment at their lack of courage in meeting an anomalous situation in a logical and obvious fashion. The whole plan is perhaps more patently absurd in Crawley than in most parishes in England, for there the chief land-owner seems to care as little for the Church as do his laborers.

[1] See below, §§ 55, pp. 605, 615; §§ 56, p. 626. [2] See below, §§ 57, p. 649.

[3] See the act of 15 and 16 George V, ch. 87. *The Public General Statutes, 1925*, vol. II (1925), pp. 1720–39.

[4] Professor Wibberley puts the tithe in Crawley (Oct., 1928) at 4s. to 5s. an acre.

The living of Crawley was assessed at £20 in the taxation of Pope Nicholas, put down in the King's Book of 1535 as of the net value of £35 13s. 4d.,[1] and in 1928 as bringing in a net income of £604.[2] Besides this there is the rectory which the incumbent is supposed to enjoy.

The patronage of the church in Crawley, that is, the right to appoint the rector, was in the hands of the bishop of Winchester until 1860, when it was handed over to Queen's College, Oxford, by an exchange arrangement. In 1896 it was sold to Mr. George Bliss, an outsider, who presented the living to his nephew. Sold several times since, and once it was offered at a bargain, the patronage has been owned twice by women [3] who were interested, one in getting her husband into the living and the other in getting her husband into a more congenial one by exchange. Of course it is not considered as simony when a parson has a relative or kinsman buy a living for him, any more than it is considered un-Christian to force a non-believer to contribute to the support of the Church. Anomalous as the system of patronage or advowson is, it leads to many excellent appointments and a few very bad ones. It has this one very unfortunate and inescapable effect, however, that it gives to an outsider power over the affairs of a congregation, not because of his wisdom or holiness, but because of his wealth. In reply to such an accusation, there is much sophistry expressed, but the fact remains — an unreformed Church of England.

Until the early nineteenth century the rector of Crawley had not only a handsome income but a very beautiful residence opposite the church itself. This dwelling had a large garden, with a chestnut avenue, and remains of a sixteenth-century building with an old polished oak ceiling.[4] Being rather expensive to maintain, it was transferred in 1911 to the owner of Crawley Court, later to be used as the dwelling of a member of his family.[5] Doubtless it

[1] See F. W. Pledge, *Crawley* (1907), pp. 165–167.

[2] See the *Diocesan Year Book* for 1928.

[3]

Patron	Mrs. Edith A. Churchill	10 July, 1914
Rector	The Rev. J. W. Churchill	8 Aug., 1918
Patron	Mrs. Dorothy Simeon	9 Aug., 1920
Rector	The Rev. J. P. Simeon	2 May, 1921.

[4] See F. W. Pledge, *Crawley* (1907), p. 168.

[5] Cf. MS., Millbank, Ecclesiastical Commission, vol. 1909–14, pp. 49–53 and 245.

THE OLD RECTORY

A photograph

AËRIAL PHOTOGRAPH OF THE VILLAGE SHOWING PRESENT-DAY ALLOTMENTS

Taken in 1922 at 10,000 feet in the air and reproduced with the permission of the Ordnance Survey Office

will continue to be difficult for rectors to accept the loss of such an attractive residence so conveniently located. The actual rectory of today is a prosaic dwelling almost poked out of the village far from the church in the direction of Winchester whence Christianity had originally come.

Now, it seems that this is really symbolic of the present condition of things. The Church means very little to the people of Crawley. They send their children to Sunday School, but apart from the harvest festival and a few fine Sunday evenings the attendance is now (1928) about seven. As one of the natives said in 1925, the rector preaches well but he cannot compete with the chapel, or Gospel Hall as it is now called. In this Hall there is unlettered zeal, such as can be appreciated by the audience of over a score of dissenters. Apart from the retired admiral there is but little encouragement for the Church from above. The owner of Crawley Court has no interest in formal religion, and the agricultural expert and his family arc Catholics.[1] So between the aversion of non-conformists and Catholics on the one hand and the indifference of both the high and low on the other, there is only the shell of a congregation. Of course, this is not peculiar to Crawley nor yet to Britain. The old bassoon no longer plays, and the bellringers have recently ceased to function, because the rector would not consent to their leaving before the end of the service.

In the past, some rectors of Crawley have held many preferments and neglected all. For over a generation the right to appoint the rector has been bought and sold by those having personal or family interests. And now the tithes are paid directly and indirectly by persons caring nothing for the uses to which they are put or by those who are positively hostile to the whole system. But these anomalous conditions on the inside are but minor factors in the situation, as compared with what is happening in the outside world upon which Crawley looks — with eyes through the moving pictures and with ears through the radio — it is too much to add with the eyes of the understanding in a search for objective

[1] In 4 Charles I we find Joan Wayte, widow, set down as a Catholic recusant, and, of course, others as adhering to Catholicism at a later date. See MS., P. R. O., Exchequer Lay Subsidies, 175/522.

truth. It is, of course, a misfortune that the rectors of Crawley have not remained long enough in the village during recent years to gain a sympathetic understanding of the problems of the young people.

§41. *Parish and School.* The old ecclesiastical parish of Crawley included Hunton, but since 1910, as we have seen, Littleton has taken the place of Hunton. The Civil or Rural Parish of Crawley is apparently identical in boundaries with the Manor of Crawley. It is this parish that has been the unit for census enumeration and for administration generally. The Rural Parish is supposed to meet each year in the form of a primary assembly or Parish Meeting as it is called. This Parish Meeting, made up of adult males and females who own or occupy property, elects the Parish Council, and the chairman; the former for a period of three years, the latter for one year. The Parish Council, meeting once a year, in the spring, elects the overseers of the poor, the treasurer, and the clerk. The office of clerk for many years has been in the hands of members of the Cox family, the incumbent until recently being a gardener on the Crawley Court estate. Probably the most active member of the Council[1] is the chairman, Mr. J. O. Robertson, the estate agent of Crawley Court. It should be added that his knowledge and administrative ability are also at the service of other local government organizations in the county, for he is a justice of the peace and a member of the Winchester Rural District Council (since 1908). On the whole one can say that the Parish Council of Crawley, as is often charged, is not independent of the local "lord" or squire. In other words it is ability and property that guide the destinies of the parish and not mere noses and hands.

The Parish Council has the power to provide buildings, acquire property for recreation, look after wells, footpaths, and the cemetery, provide fire engines, remedy offensive ditches and ponds, and provide allotments. The Parish Council rents from the owner of Crawley Court such land as is necessary to be divided into garden allotments. Apparently only about three quarters of the

[1] Other members (Oct., 1928) are G. Philippi, F. W. Pledge, F. Turton, and R. Davis (the paid clerk).

allotments available have been taken, many of the people already having small gardens attached to their houses. The Parish Council has been pretty well stripped of its functions by national statutes which have erected new units or have given away some of the powers of the parish to old units. The Rural District Council has charge of sanitation, housing, maternity and child welfare, and many other matters. There is a Poor Law Union which, through its guardians, looks after the poor, though there are none (1924–25) in Crawley to be cared for — thanks to the existence of the old-age pension system. The County Council has charge of education, public libraries, agriculture, small holdings, the main roads, people mentally afflicted, those suffering from tuberculosis and venereal diseases, and the granting of licences. No one in Crawley seems to have applied for a small holding until very recently.[1]

In the Middle Ages men were hanged for felony, their goods going to the lord. It would appear, indeed, that there were more crimes then than now. "In the last twenty-seven years" [1901–28, as has been reported to us], "there has not been a single 'crime' in the parish. By that I mean what is termed a penal offence. We occasionally get what is known as a petty offence, such as breaking the motoring regulations, poaching, or licensing offences. I do not remember a single case of drunkenness. Only the other day, however, [a resident in the village] was summoned for employing a male servant without first obtaining a licence (cost 15s.). He pleaded ignorance and got off."[2]

People living in Crawley have been theoretically able to obtain an education in various ways at various times. In the Middle Ages there was apparently no school in the parish. The rector or the curate would have been available for instruction, and there were monastic organizations in the general district which gave some instruction. Winchester College was not officially founded until 1382. During approximately 500 years following, no son of Crawley's soil became a "scholar" in that College.[3] Some may have actually attended, but they were most likely to be the sons

[1] See below, § 38, p. 141.

[2] A written statement made in October, 1928.

[3] See above, § 18, p. 61.

of the parson — following the establishment of Protestantism. Now, this school is only five miles away from Crawley. Clearly physical proximity is ineffective in the face of social custom and economic condition.

Book learning was pretty scarce in Crawley until the nineteenth century. Most Crawley tenants had to make a sign of the cross or some other simple mark in lieu of a signature. How the reeve got along unless by tallies (notched sticks) and pictorial language, we cannot imagine. Of course, he may have been able to obtain the help of the rector or even of the episcopal auditor. But in the nineteenth century the yeoman farmers at least were given an elementary training at some neighboring school. One informant has stated that it was at a private school in Twyford. It is true that Sunday Schools, which might have been used by some of the better tenants, were established early — at Basingstoke in 1524, Southampton in 1550, Newport in 1614, Alton in 1638, Odiham in 1694, Alresford in 1696, and so on.[1]

In the very midst of Crawley there was finally set up an elementary school. In 1832 or 1835 the rector, Philip Jacob, established a small school, which was maintained, at least partly, at his expense. In 1846 the same rector received a grant of this school from the lord bishop, "for the education of Children and Adults or Children only of the labouring Classes of and in the said Parish of Crawley which said School shall always be united to the incorporated National Society for promoting the education of the Poor in the Principles of the Church of England."[2] Like parochial schools generally in England, this one is not at once to be distinguished by the eye of the visitor from the residences of the people of the village. The founder of the present Crawley Court family, a beneficent gentleman and a great builder, replaced the old thatched roof and added a section.

This parochial school, having accommodation for nearly 100 students, actually had 84 in attendance, 1927–28, divided as follows:

[1] See *The Victoria History of the Counties of England, Hampshire and the Isle of Wight*, vol. II (1903), p. 387.

[2] MS., Millbank, Ecclesiastical Commission, 153126, pp. 340, 352.

From the Village of Crawley	29
From the rest of the parish	12
Outside the (civil) parish[1]	43

This attendance is at least an improvement over that of 1862, which was 46 and of 1867, which was 71.

There are only three teachers for all the grades. For instance, one teacher has to teach four standards of work in the upper group consisting of children whose ages range from ten to fifteen years. Bearing in mind this fact and that the parents of the children are agricultural laborers, we are not surprised that only about two or three, on graduation, go each year to a secondary school. In the majority of cases the boys go into agriculture, the girls into domestic service. The next choice for the boys is motor work or gardening, for the girls clerkships.[2] Apart from the estate office, there seems to be no clerical opening at all in Crawley. Accordingly the school, preparing for clerical training, helps to drain off the best brains from the village. This is a part of the social selection now going on. The towns draw off Crawley girls for office work and for domestic service.[3] The Crawley men seem to make up the loss by marrying girls from other rural parishes.

There is in the Village of Crawley a tutor, F. W. Pledge, Esq., M.A., who has lived in Crawley for over twenty years and who prepares young men for Cambridge and Oxford. The young men are in residence with their tutor during the few months necessary. Mr. Pledge lives in the old Pern house, now called Manor House. Thus do residents take the place of yeoman farmers.

Out on the borders of Crawley, in the direction of Winchester, in the parish but not in the village, is a large public school called Clayesmore School. It occupies about 250 acres of Northwood Park, with which we have long been familiar. It takes boys from the age of eight upwards and provides facilities for manual work as well as for book studies. Its students are introduced to wireless

[1] Chiefly from Littleton, now part of the ecclesiastical parish, and adjacent to Crawley.

[2] Much of this information has come from Mrs. Margaret Fish, the headmistress.

[3] Miss Lilian J. Redstone has been particularly helpful in supplying information from her father for the period about 1845–75, and for the present.

operating as well as to golf. It is young, erected on the ruins (apparently) of Eastman's Royal Naval Academy, established in the 1890's and housing a population of 151, including teachers, students, and servants, in the census of 1921.[1] It is perhaps unnecessary to say that the new school is in no way a rival of Winchester College, which is less than three miles distant.

Few of the people of Crawley Village have received any considerable education in the world of books. Primary education is theirs today, but in the few cases where it leads anywhere, it is away from the village. Other people come to the Parish of Crawley for secondary education, but this is quite apart from the villagers. For a long time, the villagers had no faith in education, removing their children from the primary school as soon as the law would allow it. Now, seeing the greater earning power that sometimes results, they allow their children to stay on in continuation classes. And they themselves, in later life, do some reading, whereas twenty years ago adult reading was non-existent. To help out in this adult education is a branch of the county library used by about seventy persons and housed in the school. At last a new force has entered the village: whether it will make for the permanent well-being of the village itself is, however, a matter that cannot yet be determined.

§ 42. *Population and Well-being.* It is not possible to state the population of Crawley before the first census (1801). From first to last there is the question of two units, the village on the one hand and the (civil) parish on the other. And for the early centuries, for which only estimates are possible, there is the problem of the squatters, or the mere inhabitants, as distinct from the recognized tenants. Even the recent census figures are misleading, because since the 1890's there has been a large school for boys on the border of the parish but in no very real sense a part of the (civil) parish. The following table gives the population as estimated (in brackets) or as enumerated at various times.

It would seem that the two high points in the history of the parish were about 1307 and about 1875. The low spots seem to have

[1] See below, §§ 60, pp. 683–684.

POPULATION OF THE (CIVIL) PARISH OF CRAWLEY

Year	Population	Year	Population
1086	[260][1]	1851	403
1256	[370][2]	1861	397
1307	[400][3]	1871	411
1673	[180][4]	1881	455
1801	324[5]	1891	410
1811	298	1901	366[6] [502]
1821	354	1911	481[7]
1831	372	1921	412[6] [563]
1841	372		

1 The number of tenants (we assume families) as given in Domesday Book (see below, §§ 4, p. 185) is 51. At 5 to a family this gives 255. A household of 5 is allowed to the rector.

2 During the year 1256–57 there were 278 men along with the keepers of the grain doing harvesting for the lord (see below, §§ 9, p. 217). If we allow one-quarter of the population to have been children or feeble, this gives an approximate total of 370.

3 In 1307–08 there were 312 men along with the ministri curie doing harvesting (see below, §§ 14, p. 263).

4 On the occasion of the levy of the hearth tax in 1673 there were 23 taxable households and 13 non-taxable or 36 in all (see below, §§ 21, pp. 459–462). At 5 to a household, we have 180, a surprisingly low figure. How much reliance is to be placed upon the hearth tax returns is uncertain.

5 From this point on, we follow the census enumeration.

6 The net population after the new boys' school has been deducted.

7 The school was on a holiday at the time of the enumeration and its population therefore not included.

been about 1673 and 1811. If we were more certain of all this, we should have more zeal in trying to explain the situations. The year 1307 was well before the Black Death, and the year 1881 was just after the beginning of the decline of agriculture and the decay of the yeoman farmers. In 1673 the exchange of tenements had doubtless pushed out many families; and in 1811 the combined effects of enclosure, poor law, and war brought the parish into decay. Conditions were in some respects even worse after the death of the younger Meyler, lessee of the home farm, in 1818.

About the number of houses in Crawley we have even more fragmentary evidence, as is indicated in the next table.

It is clear from the second table following that there has been a diminution in the child population. During the period in question there has probably been a tendency for laborers with large families to move away. Old people, at least in recent years, have, however, preferred the quiet of village life and have deliberately sought residence in Crawley as in other villages.

NUMBER OF HOUSES

Year	In the Village	In the Parish	Vacant
1086		[52] [1]	
1673		36	0
1837		[37] [2]	
1841		81	1
1851		79	3
1891		86	0
1901		85	10
1927	[67] [3]		

[1] See below, §§ 4, p. 185. Reckoning uncertain.
[2] See below, §§ 57, pp. 635–646. The count here is necessarily uncertain.
[3] See below, §§ 61, p. 685.

NUMBER OF CHILDREN IN THE (CIVIL) PARISH OF CRAWLEY [1]

Year	Number of Children	Percentage of Total Population
1841	123	33.1
1851	164	40.7
1871	150	36.5
1881	168	36.9
1891	147	35.9
1901	109	30.0
1911	127	26.4
1921	103	25.0

[1] See below, §§ 60, p. 679.

The census of 1927 shows a large measure of well-being in Crawley. This consists in ownership, not of land and houses but of furniture, clothing, bicycles, radios, and automobiles. The income in good homes, schooling, recreation, free time, clothing, and food is probably greater than at any time in Crawley's history. Thus this village population is comparable with townspeople, the rank and file of whom own little but enjoy much. What the villagers lack today is independence, self-esteem, and a feeling of equality. Some are disgruntled, but most of the older people seem content.

Once there were slaves in Crawley; now there are none. Later there were only serfs in the village, while now all are legally free. Once there were many poor receiving relief, now there are none except the aged. But throughout its history Crawley has faced both social subordination and monotony of work. The deadliness of the village's life increases as the young people become fewer and the old predominate. But this is somewhat offset by the greater amount of traffic along the village street. Whereas in the thirteenth century, and apparently up to the late war, there were two inns in Crawley, there is but one now. In 1924–25 the sole remaining public place of jollification — The Jolly Sportsman has gone — was a prosaic and uninviting spot. In marked contrast to this was the warm glow of the Irishman's house — the residence of the agricultural expert, and the quiet geniality of the Scotsman's fireside — the dwelling of the estate agent. Both of these had young people much astir. In the homes of the aged there was nothing but dull, blank quiet — such as was probably most desired.

§ 43. *Occupations, Medieval and Modern.* For a study of occupations in Crawley we have the manorial accounts, the court rolls, the censuses of 1841, 1851, and 1927, and the parish registers. We can hardly compile any statistics of medieval occupations but we can draw some general conclusions. Crawley was even more overwhelmingly agricultural at that time than it is today. And, except for a period in the Middle Ages, there was no agricultural laboring class as there is today.[1]

Of housework in medieval Crawley we have no information. It is doubtful whether there was a class of domestic servants before the rise of the yeoman farmers in the sixteenth century.[2] Such domestic service as existed was doubtless casual and supplied by very young unmarried daughters.

Of specialized manufacture in medieval Crawley there is no information, except for the work of the blacksmith and house builders, and the dairy. Most of the manufacture of ordinary cloth and clothing, boots, shoes, belts and harness, and wooden utensils and implements doubtless took place in the home. There is no indication that Crawley ever attained sufficient skill in these

[1] Cf. MS., P. R. O., Ecclesiastical Commission, Various, 159285 (1236–37). De 12d. de vet*er*i domo Rob*erti* Cawe.

[2] In 1561 there is an instance of outside domestic service: John Wayte, of the yeoman family, had a gardener with a tenement. MS., P. R. O., Ecclesiastical Commission, Court Roll, 110/1, fol. 10.

pursuits to lead to the making of a surplus for sale. In this respect Crawley was a bit unusual.[1]

There was no tradesman in medieval Crawley, no baker, grocer, or the like. The nearest to public servants were the innkeepers, the rector, and at times a curate. There was no policeman or his counterpart, unless the reeve be considered as such. There was an agricultural officialdom in the Middle Ages, however, as there is today.[2]

The nearest to independents, or residents, in Crawley in the Middle Ages were the widows, who by custom were permitted to occupy the family cottage until the youngest child and heir became of age or until re-marriage. There were no attractive houses such as the White House, the old Rectory, and the present Manor House.

For the Modern Period we have some statistics that are significant.

OCCUPATIONS OF ADULTS IN CRAWLEY

(Classified)

Classes	1841[1] No.	1841[1] %	1851[1] No.	1851[1] %	1927[2] No.	1927[2] %
Agriculture	69	61.61	63	54.78	44	42.31
Housework	12	10.71	17	14.78	32	30.77
Industry, transportation	18	16.07	19	16.52	17	16.34
Trade	3	2.68	3	2.61	2	1.92
Public service	2	1.79	7	6.09	4	3.85
Independent	3	2.68	1	0.87	5	4.81
Yeomen	5	4.46	5	4.35	0	0.00
Total with occupations	112	100.00	115[3]	100.00	104	100.00
Total population	372		403		222	
% with occupations		30.11		28.53		46.85

[1] For the (civil) Parish of Crawley (that is, the village, Rookley, Northwood Park, and Littleton House, to use present-day names).
[2] For the Village of Crawley alone.
[3] In addition there was one banker, the son of a lady who was an annuitant.

Unfortunately the first two years being for the civil parish and the third for the village only, the data are not quite comparable. There is no reason to expect, however, that the results would be very different if we had figures for the civil parish in 1927. It is

[1] See above, § 17, pp. 58 ff. [2] See above, § 8, pp. 22 ff.

noteworthy that there has been a decline, absolute and relative, in the number of persons engaged in agriculture. The decline shown by the figures for 1927 may be due to the more efficient use of labor under the present management. It is also due to the fact that some of the agricultural laborers employed in Crawley in 1927 actually resided in adjoining parishes.

The increase in the number of adult household servants is remarkable. It is doubtless due to the development of Crawley as a place of residence and still more to the fact that Crawley Court employs many more servants than did the Manor House in 1841 and 1851.

The number of persons engaged in trade and industry has not changed very much. Today the baker and the storekeeper appear to be the only tradesmen. There is in Crawley today no physician, dentist, lawyer, or artist. There is no kinema. There is a garage, however, as well as a blacksmith's shop.

We have noted no one in Crawley who now earns his living through sport, except the gamekeeper. In 1871 there were fifteen persons, in 1881, twenty-one, and in 1891 eighteen, listed as trainers and grooms in the racing stables of Crawley. None were set down in 1901.[1] England has taught the world how to save time through the use of machinery, how to waste it through sport. In the latter, Crawley has played its part particularly in the eighteenth and early nineteenth centuries.

Child labor is a notable feature of the census enumeration of 1851. It is much less today. It would appear to have been at a minimum in 1881, when only one person under fifteen years was reported as employed — as an agricultural laborer. In Crawley, as in other purely rural communities, the two chief prospective occupations, as has already been said, are agriculture for boys and domestic service for girls. And in these two occupations there are not enough openings in Crawley to meet the needs of the young people.[2] The result is a constant drainage of the youth of the village and the parish to other places.

[1] See below, §§ 60, p. 679–682.

[2] Mrs. Adam S. Kennard has stated (privately) that it was her policy at the end of last century to take servants from elsewhere rather than from Crawley itself.

§ 44. *Notable Personalities.* We shall not try to uncover true greatness in men, as it has come to the village and departed again. It is enough that the various persons mentioned are notable for one act or another, one characteristic or another. The first man in Crawley, whether in the ecclesiastical or civil parish we do not know, about whom we have any information is Alvin Stilla. Alvin was a prosperous bondman who bore the distinction of having two names. Richard, the reeve, was the first (1208) Crawley official of whom record remains. Ingeram was a fugitive about 1252 — gone to parts unknown. The rector of Crawley, Fremund Lebrun, was appointed papal chaplain in 1259. Without stating that he was illegitimate, he secured the archdeacony of Waterford. Elected to the archbishopric of Dublin, he was not allowed to take possession.[1] In the early fourteenth century, Philip Aubyn of Winchester was an investor in lands and rich hypothecator of tenements, who included Crawley in his net. William Sely was the first reeve-farmer (1407). John Page was a rich and able archer ready to do his bit in 1523. John Edmondes was the patriotic subscriber of £25 to aid in the defence of England against the Armada.[2]

Sir Gerard Fleetwood (about 1580–1663) was a master dissimulator and apparently the father of Crawley's line of gentlemen. The second Anthony Henley (d. 1745) was an impudent libertine who died young for his country's good. During the American Revolution His Royal Highness, the Duke of Cumberland, occupied Rookley House[3] in ignorance and in profligacy. As an example to his community, George Godwin, yeoman farmer, did his duty year after year in the capacity of churchwarden through one of Crawley's most trying periods — the late eighteenth and early nineteenth centuries. This was at the time when the second Richard Meyler was young, dashing, and playing the lord bountiful. Poor old Richard Bright, who was almost arrested as an intruder on his own estate — the home farm — was a misogynist, a gentleman, and a geologist. At the same time, Thomas Pern was

[1] *Calendar of Entries in the Papal Registers relating to Great Britain and Ireland, Papal Letters*, vol. I, 1198–1304 (1893), pp. 367 (1259), 389 (1263), 457 and 460 (1279).

[2] See F. W. Pledge, *Crawley*, p. 131.

[3] See below, §§ 52, p. 575; §§ 53, p. 579.

the most envied farmer in Crawley. At Rookley House Thackeray probably came to know the yeomen — perhaps finding in their midst the model for Sir Pitt Crawley, who was at least in outline a real character. In the Village of Crawley, Archdeacon Jacob, the rector, ministered to men's bodies and to their souls, much as a missionary does to Hottentots at the present time. His medicine chest was their magic box. The first Philippi arrived in 1900, a feverish builder, determined to make the old village into a new one and still look old.

Today there is in Crawley the astute and generous James Ogilvie Robertson, the estate agent, who has brought to the Crawley estate the carefulness, integrity, and intelligence of the Scots' land that gave him birth. Professor Wibberley has the lively imagination of his native land, for some years placed at the service of Crawley's mediocre soil. F. W. Pledge is the modest scholar who looks out upon the world with calm judgment, getting his abiding satisfactions from the simpler things of life. Below his house is old-man Kelly, a thatcher warming himself by the flickering fire of his wife's yeoman ancestry. Carpenter Broadway is retired, lame, voluble, and reminiscent. Harry Thick, the under-carpenter, is an ardent leader in Gospel Hall, getting trade away from the rector of the parish. The slouching Bolshevik of the village bears no name known to us, but he appeared unhappy and unkempt. The innkeeper's wife is very properly stolid and inscrutable. Admiral Sir Montagu and Lady Browning maintain the best traditions of the navy in their faithful attendance at church.

§ 45. *Recent Outside Influences.* The traditional attitude of scholars has been to regard the medieval manor as isolated, self-sufficing, and living without much influence from the rest of the world. This is not based on a very large measure of reality, but arises from a feeling for contrasts. The present is a commercial, inter-related world: the past must have been quite divided and pent up, each part living in and for itself. This view is not accepted here. Crawley was never a thing apart — at least never in historic times.[1]

[1] See above, § 7, pp. 18 ff.; § 18, pp. 60 ff.

In the Middle Ages Winchester was the towering city just beyond whose walls Crawley found security and peace. Crawley was within the influence of that center, from which both religion and material goods were obtained. But in the modern world, the dominating influences have been the nation and the metropolis. The nation had begun to have influence even in the Middle Ages when it taxed the village, made military levies, and began to encroach upon the manorial courts. In the sixteenth century it gave Crawley a new religion — Protestantism. It was even more liberal in offering to Crawley's youth the opportunity of military service than it had been in the Middle Ages. It enclosed Crawley's land by act of parliament. It gave to Crawley a post office and has had much influence upon primary education. Recently (1924) the state has fixed a minimum wage for agricultural laborers, male and female.

London gave to Crawley capital in the families of the Barings and Kennard. The latter invested heavily in Crawley at a time when the village needed building up. Crawley became a pleasant place to live in once again. Of course, through trade, London has scoured the world for things which Crawley might buy, and has always been ready to receive the products of the village — at a price.

Scotland has given to Crawley David Waite, who was steward or land agent at least from 1841 to 1851. It has also given Mr. Robertson and the Philippi family. Since 1900 Glasgow influence has taken the place of London's on the side of capital and management.

Ireland has also had its influence. In 1851 three families of Irish laborers and servants apparently occupied cottages and two families of Irish trampers slept in a stable.[1] The present rector comes from the north of Ireland and the agricultural expert from the south.

America began to influence Crawley — in common with the rest of Western Europe — through its outpourings of gold and silver, which caused prices to rise. Apparently this was one of the forces leading to the formation of the class of yeoman farmers who

[1] See below, §§ 59, pp. 670, 674.

encroached upon their neighbors, reducing them to cottagers. It probably also forced the lord bishop of Winchester to increase his fines for entry and in general to develop a more elaborate system of fines, whereby he encouraged the exchange of land among his tenants for the sake of the fees coming to him. The American slave trade and slave plantations had their influence through the rich Meyler family, as has already been noted. The low price of grain beginning in the 1870's was partly due to the great increase in the surplus wheat that America offered to Europe. This lowering of the price hit the yeomen a staggering blow and caused the rectors of Crawley to lose part of their tithe. American machinery is even now in use in Crawley. And the American kinema pictures, nightly on view in Winchester, help to create unrest among the young people of Crawley, inculcating what seems to be a negative condition of mild discontent with what exists, without putting much that is positive and attainable in its place.

§ 46. *Summary*. We shall not try to recount even the most important happenings in the history of our village of the Hampshire Downs. The chief phases in its development may, however, be noted. If our surmise be correct, there were originally two villages existing side by side on the territory now occupied by the Manor of Crawley. One was Celtic, the older of the two. The other was Saxon, lying to the south. How or when the two grew together is unknown. Then came the lordship of the bishops, during which some kind of tribute was probably more or less systematically collected. The manorialization of Crawley had taken place, at least in structure, by the time of Domesday Book. By that date the lord was deriving from the village not only lordship rents but an income from unfree predial services on his home farm.

So far as we know, this was a régime of small holders and small tenements. The ups and downs of these small people cannot now be discovered for the earliest times. While they seem to have been held pretty much in check and in control in the period 1208–30, under the firm hand of Bishop Peter des Roches, they appear to have been restless in the period 1231–1314. From 1315 to 1383 the restlessness continued, aided by general circumstances, and apparently led to a diminution in the size of the home farm and a rise in the wages of special workers. In the period 1384–1448 the small people succeeded in getting free from the most objectionable services, the lord meeting his difficulties by leasing the home farm. Just what happened during the hundred years following 1448 is not clear, but the small tenantry appear to have maintained their position as a class.

The rise of a middle class of yeoman farmers occurred in the sixteenth century. This class was the dynamic factor on the manor until about 1880. It made an increasingly good income until the nineteenth century, but tended to become less and less numerous. Finally it proved unable to withstand oversea competition.

Outside capital had entered Crawley at least by the seventeenth century in the person of the lessee of the home farm. In the late eighteenth and nineteenth centuries capital was poured into the village. When the yeomen could no longer hold their own, the person possessing capital was there to supplant them. The holder of the home farm, commanding a stream of outside capital, could and did buy off the yeomen. He also bought off the surviving cottagers. Whilst the yeomen had taken the fields of the smaller villagers, the capitalist took their cottages. Whilst there had been perhaps a half dozen agricultural laborers, owning neither land nor cottages, in the period 1235–1306, there is now (1928) a village full of such proletarians.

On the whole, we can say that the village has never been isolated, at least not in historic times, and has constantly been buffeted by external circumstances of a material and non-material nature. As the ownership of property has become more restricted, so has the flow of material income become larger and more dependable. As the rank and file of Crawley people have lost control of the management of the soil, their share of the soil's surplus has increased. The subconscious feeling of inequality, however, burns deep down in the human make-up. Whether the laborer would be willing to pay the price of a poorer income for more control remains to be seen.

After some labor, we have been able to decipher on a village tombstone the following couplets, doggerel in form but significant in meaning.

Crawley is a village with a crooked street,
Where in its midst all the forces meet;
Once its sons had risen to moderate heights,
Few of them have recently demanded any rights.

Even as we were reading this, there "echoed" back from the walls of the village church, seemingly through the old lime trees of the Court:

Rights are for those who fight even as they lose,
Under such circumstances Crawley men refuse;
England made her choice long years ago —
Wealth, great cities, industries — all villages know.

PART II

DOCUMENTS AND STATISTICS

DOCUMENTS AND STATISTICS

§§ 1. Original Grant of Chilcomb, about A.D. 643, and of the Winchester Circuit of Villages up to the Boundary of Crawley.

Two kings are said to have participated in this donation, Kinegils (608–639) and his son, Kinewalc (639–666).

In 633 Birinus, a Continental missionary, went to England and baptized Kinegils. The plans and efforts of Kinegils to found a great endowed church at Winchester are said to have failed.

Kinewalc actually built the Church of Winchester, endowing it with the village of Chilcomb, just southeast of Winchester, and, as the story goes, with all the land in the immediate vicinity of Winchester. The date of the grant is not clear. It may not have been quite as early as 643, if, as Bede says, Kinewalc was a pagan until 646. He returned from exile in that year (according to Bede) and perhaps then or (as the Anglo-Saxon Chronicle says) in 648, he built the cathedral church.

The narrative as it stands here, while not above suspicion, is probably correct in a general way. The part relating to Kinewalc is perhaps more worthy of credence than the story of Kinegils.

The chief question has to do with the amount of land actually granted at the time. The village of Chilcomb was clearly granted, but the so-called seven-league circuit (the larger Chilcomb) may have been either a later addition or an ecclesiastical encroachment. The latter is certainly doubtful, because it would have been too obvious, the land in question being rather too extensive and too central to be wrongfully claimed. Both the village of Chilcomb and the Chilcomb circuit were later attached to the Church of Winchester as distinct from the episcopal establishment.

Crawley, the village of our special interest, is nowhere mentioned. In 661 the Bishop obtained Alresford, just outside the grand circuit on the northeastern side. Possibly Crawley, to the northwest, came into the Bishop's net at about the same time. At any rate, this document has for us great significance when read with the two that follow.

The chronicle from which this excerpt has been taken was written by one probably a resident of Winchester. It was compiled from charters and perhaps other sources, the earliest now lost to us. It may have owed something to Bede. Its late composition is indicated in part by the use of the term manerium. The manuscript is in the Corpus Christi College Library at Cambridge, and appears to be the original of part of the version printed by the Master of the Rolls as the *Annales Monasterii de Wintonia.* The numerous marginal notes are particularly valuable for the chronology.

Kinegilsus[1] filius celrici rex Westsaxonum (.DC.VIII.). Iste pendam regem merciorum fines suos egressum taliter semel excepit. quod ulterius nihil minus cogitabat. quam cum illo contendere. Istum batizauit sanctus birinus episcopus (.DC.XXXIII.).[2] Baptizatur ab eodem birino filius Kinegilsi Kinewalcus. et omnes saxones eiusdem regni credentes baptizati sunt. Iste dedit sancto birino ciuitatem dorcacestram ut sederet interim in ea. donec conderet ecclesiam tanto sacerdote dignam in regia ciuitate. In uotis enim eius erat in Wintonia edificare templum precipuum. et collectis iam plurimis ad opus edificii: terram totam ambientem Wintoniam. á centro Wintonie usque ad circumferentiam ab omni parte linea exeunte .vii. leucas habentem edificande ecclesie in dotem dare disposuit. Que quia letifera preuentus egritudine per se complere non potuit: uicario usus est. uocatumque ad se filium suum Kinewalcum fecit iurare coram sancto birino in animam suam. quod ipse ecclesiam sede pontificali dignam constureret in Wintonia. et terram quam circinauerat eidem ecclesie: ad opus ministriorum eius ex parte sua deo offerret. et in ius perpetuum confirmaret.

Kinewalcus filius Kinegilsi rex britonum (.DC.XXXIX.). Iste post uexationes quas pertulit (.DC.XLI.) á Penda rege merciorum propter repudium filie sue. ecclesiam pulcherrimam construxit in Wintonia (.DC.XLIII.). et totam terram quam pater uouerat. ecclesie contulit et confirmauit (.DC.XLIII.).[3] Agilberto uero episcopo dorcacestrie successore birini. diffugiente ad uotum regis sedem transferre Wintoniam: rex qui linguam Agilberti quia gallus erat parum nouerat. fecit sibi

[1] MS. 339, Corpus Christi Library, Cambridge, fol. 10 r. and v. Many marginal notes in the original are omitted here. The dates are taken from the margin.

[2] Sanctus Birinus uenit in angliam, in the margin.

[3] Ciltecumba data est ecclesie Wintoniensi (.DC.XLIII.), in the margin.

nacta occasio*ne* sac*r*ari i*n* ep*iscop*um noue sedis q*ue*nda*m* saxo*n*am no*min*e Wine (.DC.LII.). *et* diuisa *est* diocesis una i*n* duas (?.DC.LX.). Apposuit Kinewalc*us* rex post oblat*io*nem pat*r*is facta*m* d*e* ciltecu*m*ba: de suo p*ropri*o dono ditare Wint*oniensem* eccl*esiam*. cui t*ri*a maneria. s*cilicet*. Duntun. Alresford. *et* Wordiam c*on*tulit (.DC.LXI.). et i*n* illa humat*us est* (.DCLXVI.).

TRANSLATION

Kinegils son of Celric [became] king of the West-Saxons (in 608). He once suffered so much from an attack on his boundaries by Penda king of the Mercians that he no longer thought of anything less than fighting with him. The holy bishop Birinus baptized him (in 633). Kinewalc son of Kinegils was baptized by the same Birinus and all the Saxons of the same realm were baptized as believers. He gave to the holy Birinus the City of Dorchester in which to dwell against the time when he would found a church in the royal city worthy of such a priest. For it was his intention to build in Winchester a temple of the first order, and when he had collected a great amount of building material, he determined to hand over as a gift the whole land around Winchester, seven leagues round about with Winchester as the center, for the purpose of building the church. But because, when prevented by a threatening illness, he could not himself fulfill his plan, he deputed the task to another; and having called into his presence his son Kinewalc, he caused him to swear upon his soul in the presence of the holy Birinus that he would construct in Winchester a church worthy of the pontifical see, and the land which surrounded the same church he would offer to God on his part for the use of his [Birinus'] ministry, and would confirm in perpetual right.

Kinewalc son of Kinegils [became] king of the Britons (in 639). After the annoyances which he had suffered (in 641) from Penda king of the Mercians because of the repudiation of his daughter, he [Kinewalc] built in Winchester a surpassingly beautiful church (in 643), and the whole land which his father had pledged, he granted and confirmed to the church (in 643). But Agilbert, who succeeded Birinus as bishop of Dorchester, opposed the king's desire to transfer the see to Winches-chester. The king who was unacquainted with the language of Agilbert who was a Gaul [1] seized a favorable opportunity to consecrate as bishop of the new see a certain Saxon called Wine (in 652); and the diocese was divided into two parts (? in 660). Kinewalc, the king, after he had given effect to his father's gift of Chilcomb, took the further step of enriching the church of Winchester with his own gift of three manors,

[1] Probably a Frenchman.

that is, Downton, Alresford, and Worthy (in 661); and in that [church] he was buried (in 666).

§§ 2. The Chilcomb Charter of Winchester Territory up to the Boundary of Crawley: Re-grant of Part of the original Donation (of about A.D. 643) made in 909.

After the long and somewhat unfortunate incumbency of Denewulf, 879–909, the See of Winchester was occupied by Frithestan, a monk, later a saint, to whom were re-granted many estates recently alienated.

There are at least four holdings, or groups of holdings, mentioned in this badly drawn charter. First, there is the wide circuit on all sides of the city of Winchester, rather liberally said to have been seven miles or seven leagues round about,[1] but actually possessing a very uneven boundary. The limits of this area are set forth in the Anglo-Saxon part of the document, which apparently constitutes the oldest section of the charter.

Secondly, there was the southeastern part of this original grant, probably with Chilcomb as the first or the central estate. It is possible that the land book, or charter of possessions, was actually kept at Chilcomb.[2] Later this area was said to consist of nine contiguous manors.

Thirdly, there were the two non-contiguous estates, Nursling to the south and Chilbolton to the north, which were included in the beneficial hidation of Chilcomb. Actually this latter unit contained more than 100 hides, but it was officially assessed at only 100. Even more, as a special favor to the Church, it was with magnificent beneficence put down as only one hide. This was the rating for the payment of taxes to the West-Saxon kings. What these taxes were in 909 is, we suppose, not now to be determined. Of course, such a splendid gift leads one somewhat to suspect the genuineness of the whole grant and particularly this part of it.[3] But we are compelled to leave the matter thus without settlement and without prejudice.

[1] See above, §§ 1, pp. 167, 168, 169.
[2] See J. M. Kemble, *Codex Diplomaticus*, vol. III (1845), p. 203.
[3] See F. W. Maitland, *Domesday Book and Beyond* (1897), p. 497.

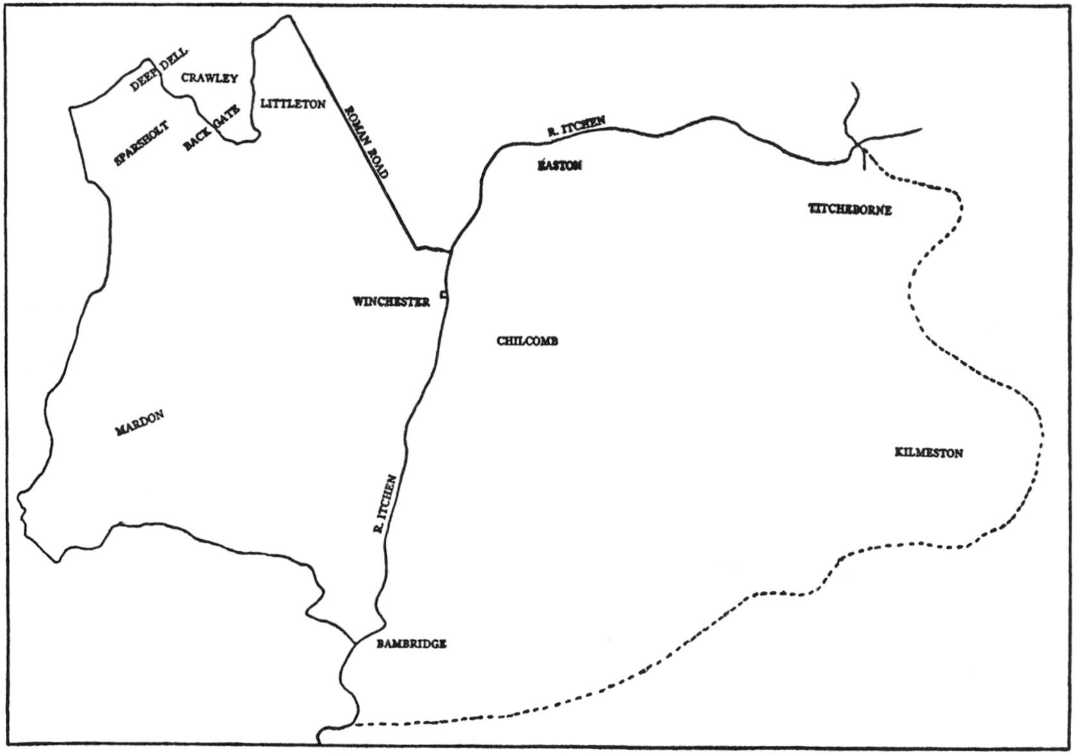

TENTATIVE MAP SHOWING APPROXIMATE EXTENT OF THE CHILCOMB GRANT OF ABOUT A.D. 643

Fourthly, there were Downton (including Ebblesburn) in Wiltshire and Beddington in Surrey. These estates, rightly belonging to the Church of Winchester, were actually in the possession of the king but on his death were to be restored to the bishopric.

For our purposes, the most interesting part of the whole charter is the description of the territory north and west of the Itchen. It is very difficult, if not impossible, to identify the boundary places. This may be because the hamlets or villages had been destroyed in these parts, presumably by the Danes in the ninth century. Or it may be that the names commonly referred to marks, spots, fields, and the like, rather than to settlements. However, Crawley, a village, and Titchfield, a village or hamlet, are actually mentioned.

The most pertinent question for our village study is whether Crawley was just inside, or just outside, the grant. Certainly the boundaries of Crawley were also part of the boundaries of the original seventh-century grant of a wide circuit about Winchester. If the Crawley boundary marks have been rightly identified, notably deep-dell and back-gate, the northern limits of the original grant were actually the southern boundary of Crawley. Thus Crawley was apparently just outside the great original grant. Some time later, perhaps soon after 643, it too was granted to the See of Winchester.

The date of the charter is clearly 909, the calendar year and its position in the indiction agreeing perfectly.

In witness to the charter were Plegmund, Archbishop of Canterbury (889–914), Wulfsige, Bishop of London (about 901–910), Wighelm, probably Bishop of Selsey, Ceolmund, Bishop of Rochester (897–926), and many others. The list of witnesses should be compared with the one in §§ 3.

✝ Cum presentis uitæ series mutabilium uarietur discursu. Et preterita obliuione tradantur nisi litterarum apicib*us* elucubrata posteris clarescunt.[1] Ego eaduueardus diuina largiente clementia angulsaxo-

[1] MS., Br.M., Harl. 43 C. I. This is a carefully written version of about the twelfth century. It affects classical forms and literary expressions. As it stands, it is a very questionable document, though many of its parts cannot be doubted with

num rex tempore quo diucesim uuentanæ eccl*esi*æ In duas diuisi parrochias obnixæ rogatus fui a frithestano quem tunc predictæ eccl*esi*æ ep*iscopu*m constitueram. ut nouarum astipulatione litteraru*m* s*anct*æ eccl*esi*æ testamenta uti olim ab antecessorib*us* meis cynegislo atq*ue* cynewalho.[1] multisq*ue* eorum successorib*us* deuote tradita atq*ue* restaurata fuerant confirmans renouarem ob æternæ beatitudinis p*ræ*mium et p*ro*speru*m* huius uitæ excursu*m*. terra*m* quæ undique adiacet ciuitati quæ in exordio chr*isti*anæ religionis birino [2] uenerabili ep*iscop*o p*ræ*dicante. beato petro eiusq*ue* coap*osto*lo paulo concessa fuerat Consilio optimatum meoru*m* usus cu*m* territoriis antiquis cartulis insertis. C. uidelicet mansas. licet spatiosior ab incolis estimari ualeat. Ita ut in ipsius terræ quantitate quod ep*iscop*o aratur et q*uo*d coloni inhabitant p*ro* una tantu*m*modo cassato reputetur qui ciltancumb ab hui*us* patriæ peritis uocatur. auos atauos p*ro*auos atauosque sp*iritu*s s*anct*i igne succensos deuotissime imitans itidem corroborando æterna largior hereditate. Quam ob rem tam ego sceptra anglorum patrio more regens qua*m* plegmund dorubernensis eccl*esi*æ archiep*iscopus* ceteriq*ue* utriusq*ue* ordinis sufraganei quoru*m* inferiu*s* uocabula litteraru*m* notulis designantur. In no*min*e alm*a*e trinitatis atq*ue* indiuiduæ unitatis p*ræ*cipimus tam frithestano eiusdem uuentanæ sedis ep*iscop*o quam cunctis eius successorib*us*. ut nulli seculariu*m* militu*m* nec ipsud rus nec aliud quotlibet ad eccl*esi*am d*e*i p*er*tinens p*ro* munere quotlibet dare p*ræ*sumant. Seculares igitur ep*iscop*orum dicione subiecti Intra ambitu*m* hui*us* spatiosæ telluris diuersis in uillis degentes censu*m* episcopali sede p*er*soluant. Et expeditione*m* pontis. arcisue restauratione*m* dum necessitas incubuerit incunctant*er* p*er*agant. Et has .C. mansas om*ni* obsequio defendant. Ita ut ciltancumb cu*m* suis appendiciis p*ro* una tantu*m*modo mansa ut olim constitutum fuerat reputetur; Moderno temp*o*re uti antiquit*us* constitutum fuerat hnut scillinge et ceolbolding tun in quantitate horum C. cassatorum p*er*sistant. hoc quoq*ue* In nomine alm*a*e trinitatis Et indiuiduæ unitatis obnixæ flagitam*us* et beati petri ap*osto*lorum principis auctoritate p*ræ*cipimus. ut rura quæ ab antecessorib*us* suis maximæ a denewulfo ad animæ suæ periculum diuersis seculariu*m* p*er*sonis acommodata fuerant dum oportunu*m* fuerit statuto a p*ræ*decessorib*us* epi*scopi*s temp*o*re sine ullo contrauersionis obstaculo In qualicumq*ue* sint p*ro*uincia *ve*l episcopatu uuentane cathedr*a*e. restituantur. si aut*em* reditu*m* accelerare uoluerit eorum. in ipsius consistat arbitrio. p*ræ*cipue dum beatæ memoriæ theodorus hoc olim interdixerat nefas. ne scilicet ep*iscop*o-

any reason. This present version is also to be compared with that in the *Codex Wintoniensis*, printed by W. de G. Birch, *Cartularium Saxonicum*, vol. II (1887), pp. 286–289.

[1] See above §§ 1.

[2] See above §§ 1.

rum quispiam chr*isto* collatam a catholicis possessione*m* p*ro* quolibet munere temerariu*s* dare *vel* acco*m*modare p*ræ*sumeret p*ræ*sumentem equidem anathematis uinculo inretitum sinodali damnauit concilio. et tam inlicitu*m* ac inconueniens datum successores nullatenus stare permitterent iussit. ne prauo antecessoru*m* consilio successores ad hanc deducerentur inopia*m*. ut chr*isti* pauperib*us* quid erogarent non haberent; C. mansæ in duntun.[1] et in ebles burnan.[2] quas mihi p*ræ*fatus acommodauit ep*iscopus*. et lxx in beaddingtune.[3] quas mihi denewulf ac*c*omodauerat presul si hoc illi placuerit. ut his uita comite fruar. post obitum meum uuentane eccl*esiæ* libere restituantur. n*os*-*t*ris salubrib*us* obtemperantes preceptis p*ræ*senti prosperitate et futura beatitudine iocundi p*er*fruantur. si autem temerariu*s* quispia*m* nefas superiu*s* interdictu*m* ullo modo p*ræ*sumerit. anathema sit et auctoritate beati petri ap*osto*loru*m* principis. pauliq*ue*. quorum subalmæ trinitatis possessio est quod a nobis modo renouatur. damnat*us* intereat. nisi cum eiulato magno quod contra n*os*tr*u*m decretum minuendo p*ræ*sumens abstulit. penitendo ante obitum suu*m* satisfaciens restituerit. Hæc cartula scripta ert [4] anno domin*icæ* incarnat*ionis* .DCCCC VIIII. Indictione. XII. his limitib*us* hoc rus undiq*ue* circumdatur. et intra ambitum suu*m* multas uillas complectitur quaru*m* nomina incolis. liquido clarescunt. hnut scillinc tamen et ceolbolding tún. quia [ha]e du*a*e uillæ contiguæ non sunt .C. manentiu*m* quantitatem p*er*ficientes indumentis cleri deseruientes. non his limitib*us*; set p*ro*-priis et ratis terminis ambiuntur.[5]

✝ Ærest on icenan æt brombrigce up ⁊ lang weges to hlidgeate. thanon ⁊ lang slades to beánstede. th*onne* [6] be hagen to searnægles forda. th*onne* up be swætheling to sugebroce thæt forth be mearce to cules felda. forth be gehrihtum gemære to stodleage. swa to ticnes felda. th*onne* to mearcdene. swa to tæppeleage. swa forth to scipleage. th*onne* to bradan ersce. swá to thære ealdan cwealmstówe. th*onne* forth be deopan delle. th*onne* be craweleainga mearce to bacegeate. forth be mearce to thæm ealdan falde. swá north ⁊ east to hearpathe. a be hearpathe to heafod stoccu*m*. swá be hide burninga gemære on icenan. th*onne* úp be streame. th*onne* swá with easton

[1] Downton, Wilts, was said to have been given by Cynewalch to the church in Winchester.

[2] Ebblesburn, or Bishopston, in Downton.

[3] Beddington in Surrey.

[4] The manuscript has ert. This may be an error for est or erat. If the latter, it is evidence of the charter having been pieced together: it *had* been written, etc. The *Codex Wintoniensis*, however, has est, which is the more likely.

[5] For an attempt to reconstruct this grant, see the map following p. o.

[6] There is some question as to whether þ should be transliterated as th*onne* or th*aet*. We have followed the reading of the second manuscript version, as printed by Birch.

wordige thonan be rihtre mearce to thæm gemær thornan. th*onne* to thære readan rode. swâ forth be ealdormonnes mearce. a be mearce. th*onne* hit cimth on icenan. úp be streame to alres forda. thonon on ticceburnan. up ⁊ lang burnan. to hearpathe swa to tyrngeate withinnan tha æfisc to sceap wican. th*onne* be riht gemære to ellenforda. swa to bradan dene. th*onne* to meoluc cumbe. swa to meolæn beorge. ⁊ lang weges to wealthæminga mearce. be rihton gemære to hige leage. th*onne* to clænefelda. swâ on are dene forth be hagan on sceatte leage. th*onne* forth on icenan be northan stanforde. swâ mid streame thæt hit cymth eft on brom bricge.

✝ Ego eadweard rex hanc restaurationem a me renouatam signum s*anct*e crucis propria manu scribendo firmaui.

✝ ego plegmund archiep*iscopus* mellifluam donationem præfati regis subscripsi cum signaculo s*anct*e crucis.

✝ ego frithestan ep*iscopus* cum consilio eiusdem regis conroboraui atq*ue* conexi cum triumpho regis æterni.

✝ ego wulfsige ep*iscopus* consens*i* et subs*cripsi*
✝ ego wighelm ep*iscopus* consens*i* et subs*cripsi*
✝ ego ceolmund ep*iscopus* cons*ensi* et subs*cripsi*
✝ ego æthelweard frater regis
✝ ego æthelstan filius regis
✝ ego ælfweard filius regis
✝ ego ordlaf dux
✝ ego osferth dux
✝ ego beorhtulf dux
✝ ego ordgar dux
✝ ego heahferth dux
✝ Wærulf presbit*er*
✝ æthelstan presbit*er*
✝ beornstan presbit*er*
✝ eahlstan presbit*er*
✝ deormund minist*er*
✝ wihtbrord minist*er*
✝ odda minist*er*
✝ ælfwold minist*er*
✝ ælfred minist*er*
✝ athulf minist*er*
✝ æthelferth minist*er*
✝ ælfric minist*er*
✝ wulfhelm minist*er*
✝ uffa minist*er*
✝ ælfstan minist*er*
✝ ælfred minist*er*
✝ ælfstan minist*er*
✝ ælfstan minist*er*
✝ wulfhere minist*er*
✝ athulf minist*er*
✝ wulfhun minist*er*
✝ wullaf minist*er*
ælred
æthelnoth
ælfric.

TRANSLATION

Since the course of this life is varied by the fluctuation of changing circumstances and past events are lost in oblivion, unless they are illuminated and made clear by literary records, I, Edward, by divine bountiful mercy king of the Anglo-Saxons, at the time when I divided the diocese of the church of Winchester into two parishes, was urgently requested by Frithestan whom I had at that time made bishop of the aforesaid church, to confirm and renew the grants to the holy church, by assenting to new writings as once they had been devoutedly granted and restored by my ancestors Cynegisl and Cynewalh and many of their successors, for the sake of the reward of eternal happiness and the successful consumation of this life. The land which lies on all sides of the city, which at the time of the introduction of the Christian religion as the result of the preaching of the venerable Birinus had been granted to the blessed Peter and his co-apostle Paul, I in co-operation with the counsel of my optimates, imitating most faithfully my grand-parents, great-grand-parents, great-great-grand-parents, and ancestors who were consumed with the fire of the holy ghost, likewise corroborate and grant in eternal possession, along with the territories included in the old charters, that is, 100 hides (mansæ), perhaps reckoned rather larger by the inhabitants, with the restriction that in respect of the amount of the land itself which is plowed for the bishop and which the tenants occupy, there shall be computed but one hide (cassatus) which is called Chilcomb by the well informed people of this country.

On which account, both I, ruling by ancient custom the kingdom of the Angles, and Plegmund, archbishop of the Church of Canterbury, and other suffragans of both orders whose names are indicated below by literary marks, in the name of the kindly trinity and the undivided unity, enjoin upon both Frithestan the bishop of the same See of Winchester and all his successors, that they shall not presume to give to any secular knight for any consideration whatsoever either the land itself or anything else belonging to the Church of God. Accordingly, the secular people subject to the jurisdiction of the bishops living in the divers manors within the circuit of this wide estate shall pay rent to the episcopal see and collectively serve in the army and aid in the upkeep of the bridge and castle as long as it may be necessary, and defend these hundred hides with complete submission, on the understanding that Chilcomb with its appendices be reckoned as only one hide, as once it had been constituted. In modern times, as had been of old determined, let Nursling and Chilbolten be included in the amount of these hundred hides. This also in the name of the kindly trinity and undivided unity we earnestly entreat and by the authority of the blessed Peter, chief of the apostles, we order that the estates which by his ancestors, and most of all by Denewulf at the peril of his soul, had been granted to divers secular persons, shall be, in conformity with the period fixed by the preceding bishops, restored to the Cathedral of Winchester without any obstacle or contravention, in whatever province or bishopric they may be.

Moreover, if he [the bishop] should wish to hasten their return, let him stand in judgment of the same. Especially in view of the fact that

Theodorus of blessed memory had once forbidden this as a crime, that is, that no bishop should be so rash as to presume to give, or grant for any office, a possession conferred upon Christ by Catholics, if he did so presume, he entangled him in the meshes of anathema and condemned him by synodal council. He ordered his successors by no means to permit the illicit and unseemly gift to stand, lest, because of the wicked policy of their predecessors, his successors be reduced to such poverty that they would not have anything left to contribute to Christ's poor.

The hundred hides in Dunton and in Ebblesburn which the aforesaid bishop granted to me and 70 in Beddington which Bishop Denewulf had granted to me, if it should be His pleasure that I might enjoy life possessed of these, are to be freely restored after my death to the Church of Winchester.

May they [my successors], obedient to these my salutary commands, enjoy to the full present prosperity and future bliss.

Moreover, if anyone be so rash as to presume in any way to commit the crime above forbidden, let him be anathema and let him stand condemned by the authority of the blessed Peter, chief of the apostles, and of Paul, for it is their possession held in the title of the kindly trinity that we are now renewing, unless with great lamentation and in penitence he should make satisfactory restitution before his death for what presumptiously he has taken in violation of our decree.

This charter has been written in the year of the incarnation of our Lord 909, in the twelfth of the indiction.

By these bounds this estate is on all sides surrounded, and within its circuit it embraces many manors, the names of which are well known to the inhabitants.

Nursling and Chilbolton, nevertheless, which make up the quantity of 100 hides and which provide for the upkeep of the clergy, because these two manors are not contiguous, are not surrounded by these bounds but by their own and proper limits.

First on the Itchen at Brombridge, up along the road to Lidyate, then along the slade to Bunstead, then by the hedge to sear-nail's (?) ford, then up by Swathling to sow-brook (?), then forth by the boundary to Cowlsfield, forth by the right boundary to Studley, so to Titchfield, then to mark dean, so to Tapley, so forth to Shipley, then to the broad stubble-field, so to the old killing-place, then forth by the deepdell, then by Crawley boundary to the back-gate, forth by the boundary to the old fold, so north and east to the highway, right along by the highway to Head Stoke (?), so by Headbourne boundary onto the Itchen, then up by the stream, then right near Easton-Worthy, then by the right boundary to the boundary thorns, then to the red cross, so forth near the alderman's boundary, always near the boundary, until it comes onto the Itchen, up near the stream to Alresford, then to

Titchburn, up along the burn to the highway, so to the turn-gate within the border to the sheep-fold, then near the right boundary to Ellenford (?), then to the broad valley, then to the milk-valley (?), then to the milk-hill (?), along the road to Waltham boundary, by the right boundary to Higely (?), then to the open-field, so to the ore-valley (?), forth by the hedge to the corner meadow, then forth to the Itchen by North Stoneford, so along the stream until it comes again to Brombridge.

I, Edward the King, have confirmed this restoration renewed by me by writing with my own hand the sign of the holy cross.

I, Plegmund the Archbishop, have subscribed to this mellifluous gift of the aforesaid king by the device of the holy cross.

I, Frithstan the Bishop, with the counsel of the same king have confirmed this and connected it with the triumph of the eternal king.

I, Wulfsige the Bishop, have consented and subscribed.

[Here follow the names of additional witnesses to the charter.]

§§ 3. Confirmation of Crawley to the Bishop of Winchester, about 909.

The form of the name, Crawan-lea, indicates that the meaning is meadow, or clearing, of the crows. The name is obviously Anglo-Saxon, not Celtic. There are about ten different Crawleys in various parts of England.

Long in the possession of Winchester, but temporarily alienated or lost, Crawley was again granted, this time by King Edward (901–924), to the new Bishop Frithstan (909–931). The estate was confirmed to Winchester after a period of disturbance probably caused by the Danish wars. The re-grant was in free alms, except for the threefold duty of serving in the militia, repairing bridges, and keeping up the castle (in Winchester).

Crawley itself was said to contain twenty mansæ or hides, in all about 2400 acres, while the survey of 1871 gave to the Parish of Crawley 3607 acres. The boundaries of the Parish are today very irregular. They may have been the same in 909. If identification of the places named is correct, the boundary marks, as here set forth, are made to run around in the direction of the hands of a clock, starting from a prominent field (or lea) just north of the village itself.

The noteworthy economic features are four in number. (1) Meadows (leas) predominated. Of course, the word "lea" may really be applied to any cleared ground. (2) The prominence of ditches is notable. These were probably field marks and roads rather than for drainage. In a chalk-down country, they would hardly be drainage ditches. (3) Crawley does not stand alone. To it was attached the sub-manor (?) of Hunton, or Hinton (physically located within the adjoining Parish of Wonston), northeast of Crawley. More difficult to identify is the first of the two dependent communities mentioned, Titchfield, the bounds of which are also set forth. Titchfield was a village or hamlet, near Crawley, as is indicated in the preceding document (§§ 2). (4) There seem to have been three kinds of roads, the highway or army-road, the village street, and the field ways.

The original document of 909 has itself apparently disappeared. The copy we have, the one here reproduced, is found in the Codex Wintoniensis, the great manuscript source of early land grants made to Winchester. This Codex, probably written in an eleventh- or twelfth-century hand, is now preserved in the British Museum. Although there are many inaccuracies and uncertainties in this copy of the charter, and in the Codex generally, there is no reason to doubt the authenticity of the document in question.

DONUM EDWARDI REGIS TO CRAWELEA[1]

Clamante divine auctoritatis agiographo commonemur ut terrena presentis s*ecu*li lucra dantes. celestia eterne beatitudinis emolumenta iugi indeffessoq*ue* adquiramus labore. Ideoq*ue* incertum futuri temporis statum mutabilitatemq*ue* certis dinoscens indiciis. totis uiribus prout posse dederit qui cuncta creauit subnixe delibero ut redemptoris n*ost*ri possessionem ecclesiis iure deligatam in priorem s*anct*e religionis statum sertis roborata[m] litterulis medullitus consolidarem. Qua propter ego Eadwardus diuina indulgente clementia angul saxonum

[1] Ms., Br. Mus., Add. 15350, fols. 54–55. The best printed text of this charter is found in J. M. Kemble's *Codex Diplomaticus Aevi Saxonici*, vol. V (1847), no. MXCVI, pp. 183–185. The charter is partly reproduced in W. de G. Birch's *Cartularium Saxonicum*, vol. II (1887), pp. 304–305; and also in H. Pierquin's *Recueil Général des Chartes Anglo-Saxonnes* (1912), pp. 448–449. Birch's version has been reproduced in F. W. Pledge's *Crawley* (1907), pp. 13–16, together with a translation (pp. 16–18).

rex rogatus fui á meo dilecto episcopo. Frithestano. territoria eccl*esi*e dei cui deseruiebat p*er*tinentia nouis litterarum ápicib*us* renouare. Et ueterum librorum monimenta recenti recuperata auctoritate restaurare. Id circo uotis eius libenter obtemperans renouare studui territorium illius telluris que noto Crawanléa. appellatur uocabulo. quantitate. xx et. viij. constans manentium. xx. scilicet æt Crawanléa. et. viij. In hundatvne reverende Trinitati. beatoq*ue* ap*osto*lorum principi. eiusq*ue* có-ap*ostu*lo Paulo. uti antecessores n*ost*ri priscis dederant temporibus renouando iterum deuotus eterna largior hereditate. Sit igitur prefatum rus cui*us* ego cum optimatum meorum consilio libertatem fideliter renouaui eterna iocunditate gloriosum cum omnibus sibi rite p*er*tinentibus pratis uidelicet. Pascuis. Siluis. expeditionis laborem pontis arcísue restauratione[m?] tantummodo p*er*soluat. Alias iocundetur et*er*na lib*er*tate. Si quis autem diaboli pellectus instinctu hanc p*er*petuam n*ost*re renouationis libertatem uiolare u*e*l minuere audax. p*re*sumpserit á s*anct*a [1] corporis et sanguinis d*omi*ni n*ost*ri ihe*s*u Chr*ist*i communione et s*anct*a dei ecclesia ac s*anct*orum omnium contubernio segregatus eterna inferni miseria dampnatus intereat. Si non satisfactione congrua humiliter correctus emendauerit. quod concontra n*ostru*m tumidus deliquit decretum. His limitib*us* hoc rus circumdatur.

Ærest to beast man léa. thonne north to lunden hærpathe. swa to winstanes stapole. of tham stapóle to thære díc. forth and lang díc. útt to stræt. ⁊ swa suth ⁊ lang díc. oth fora geán thane níwan stán. thonne west ⁊ lang díc. óf thære díc innan sceaftes hangran. swa forth be æfisc tó fearn leage suth be herpathe. thonne tó baccan geáte. ⁊ swa ford be efisc to lippan hamme. th*onne* to tham scamelan. swa forth tó beatan stapóle. thæt west ⁊ lang dæne tó deopan delle. thæt west ⁊ lang slades to swinburnan. swa north of thone æthena byrigels. thonne ⁊ lang dæne. of feárn dúne. thet forth to screótes dúne. swa on sænget thorn. thet to trind lea. swa on bæstman lea. This sind tha wíc. the hyrath therto. Ærest æt ticcenesfelda wícum. swa north ⁊ lang hagan thæt man cymth to fearbúrnan. thæt forth to mearc déne heafdu*m*. swa north tó seaxes seathe. swa suth thónan of hit cymth to thære holding stówe. thonne ther suth ⁊ lang hagan óf hit cymth æft to ticcefeldes wicum. To hundatúne. ærest fram thære ea foran gean thæs abbodes byrig. thonne swa north and lang thæs grenan weges. tó cram mære. thonne thær úp to tham hricge. thæt ⁊ land [sic] dúne to cealc grafan. thonne innan cealc gráf on thóne wyl. swa on thæt ruge dæl. thonan east on thone wég. ⁊ lang weges upp to tham ricge. swá north to thám thórne. thær se stapul stent. swa ⁊ lang weges to tham slade. thonne be slade to thære byrig.

[1] The word archam is deleted and á s*anct*a written above.

swa nyther 7 lang weges on thóne forth. forth be éa oth hit cymth æft to thæs abbodes byrig.
Ego Eadwardus Rex hanc restaurationem á me renouatam signum s*anct*e crucis propria manu scribendo firmaui.
Ego Plegmund archiepiscopus mellifluam donationem prefati regis subscribsi cum signaculo s*anct*e crucis.
Ego Frithestan. episcopus cum consilio eiusdem regis hoc roboraui atq*ue* conexi cum triumpho Regis eterni.
Ego Wulfsige ep*iscopus* cons*ensi* 7 s*ubscribsi*.
Ego Wighelm ep*iscopus* cons*ensi* 7 s*ubscribsi*.
Ego Ceolmund ep*iscopus* cons*ensi* 7 s*ubscribsi*.
Ego Æthelweard ep*iscopus* cons*ensi* 7 s*ubscribsi*.

Ego Æthelstan	filius regis.	Ego Æthelferth	min*ister*.
Ego Ælfweard	filius regis.	Ego Wulfhearth	min*ister*.
Ego Offerth	Dux.	Ego Ælfric	min*ister*.
Ego Ordlaf	Dux.	Ego Wulfhelm	min*ister*.
Ego Beorhtulf	Dux.	Ego Vffa	min*ister*.
Ego Ordgar	Dux.	Ego Ælfstan	min*ister*.
Ego heafferd	Dux.	Ego Ælfred	min*ister*.
Ego Werulf	pr*es*b*y*t*e*r.	Ego Ælfstan	min*ister*.
Ego Æthestan	pr*es*b*y*t*e*r.	Ego Wulfhere	min*ister*.
Ego Beornstán	pr*es*b*y*t*e*r.	Ego Athulf	min*ister*.
Ego Ealhstan	pr*es*b*y*t*e*r.	Ego Wulfhun	min*ister*.
Ego Deormod	min*ister*.	Ego Wullaf	min*ister*.
Ego Withbrord	min*ister*.	Ego Buga	min*ister*.
Ego Odda	min*ister*.	Ego Ælfreth	min*ister*.
Ego Ælwold	min*ister*.	Ego Æthelnoth	min*ister*.
Ego Elred	min*ister*.	Ego Wulfric	min*ister*.
Ego Athulf	min*ister*.		

GIFT OF EDWARD THE KING TO CRAWELEA

By the call of the holy writ of divine authority we are admonished to give up the earthly gains of this world, and to acquire with the untiring labor of the yoke the heavenly rewards of eternal bliss. Therefore, perceiving by definite signs the uncertain condition and mutability of the future, I confidently resolve by all the strength given to me by Him who has created all things, to restore completely the possession of our Redeemer lawfully granted to the churches, to the former state of holy religion, and to confirm it in legal form. Wherefore I, Edward, by the kindness of divine mercy king of the Anglo-Saxons, was asked by my dear bishop Frithstan to restore by new written documents the territories belonging to the church of the God whom it served, and to give back again the muniments of charters (*libri*) recovered by recent authority. For this reason willingly complying with his wishes I have sought to restore the territory of that estate which is called in common speech Crawanlea amounting to xx and viii hides (*manentes*), that is xx at Crawanlea and viii in Hundatune, to the holy trinity and blessed prince of the apostles and his co-apostle Paul. As our ancestors had given it in former times, I, again piously renewing, grant the same in perpetual inheritance. Accordingly let the aforesaid estate, the liberty of which I, with the counsel of my optimates, have faithfully restored, be illustrious in eternal bliss with all the things properly pertaining to it, that is, meadows, pastures, woods. Only it shall be responsible for service in the army and for the upkeep of bridge or castle. Otherwise it shall be enjoyed in eternal freedom. Moreovcr, if any audacious one, seduced by diabolical instigation, should presume to violate or diminish this perpetual liberty of our restoration, cut off from the holy communion of the body and blood of our lord Jesus Christ and the holy church of God and from the association of all the saints, let him be condemned to the eternal torment of hell, unless, by a suitable satisfaction, having been put right, he humbly make amends for what in his swollen pride he has done against our decree.

By these bounds the estate is surrounded.

First to beastman-lea,[1] then north to the London highway,[2] then to Winstan's post,[3] from that post to the ditch,[4] further along the ditch, out to the street,[5] and then south along the ditch, until (one comes) opposite the new stone, then west along the ditch, from the ditch inside shaftshanger,[6] then onward by the edge to fern-lea south by the highway,[7] then to back-gate,[8] and so forth by the edge to lippanham,[9] then

[1] Beastman-lea survives in the reeves' accounts as Bassumly, one of the important furlongs, in North Crawley.

[2] London highway or army road cannot with certainty be identified. It may be the Winchester-to-Andover road on the eastern boundary of Crawley Parish, or possibly an old road in northwestern Crawley running directly toward the Salisbury-to-London road.

[3] Winstan's post, probably a special boundary mark. Reference may be to the Crawley-Wonston parish boundary.

[4] The Anglo-Saxon dic, possibly earthen bank or turf-dike, but more probably a sunken ditch dividing cultivated plots, sometimes used as a road.

[5] It is tempting to regard this as the main street of Crawley village, or an extension of the same, possibly later obliterated, running off to the north.

[6] Sceaftes hangra, or shaftshanger, probably shaft-green (village green, with a maypole, being the later equivalent).

[7] Possibly the Winchester-to-Stockbridge road.

[8] Back-gate has been associated with Backet Close in South Crawley. See F. W. Pledge, *Crawley* (1907), p. 17. Meaning may be ridge-gate. Although both tradition and the tithe map put back-gate in South Crawley, there may have been another spot so called in earlier times, for of course the name is generic. If it were in North Crawley, there would be an argument for including Crawley in the grant of 643.

[9] Lippanham, a hamlet or homestead, not now to be identified. Or, possibly a meadow or other piece of land.

to the bench,[1] then onward to beatan-post, then west along the low ground to the deep dell,[2] then west along the slade to swineburn,[3] then north as far as the heathen burial-place,[4] then along the low ground as far as fearn down, then onward to screotes down,[5] then to saenget thorn,[6] then to trind-lea,[7] then to beastman-lea.

These are the wicks [8] which belong thereto.

First at ticcenesfield [9] wick then north along the hedge until one comes to fearburn, then forth to the mearc dene headland, then north to Saxon pit,[10] then south thence until it comes to the holding place,[11] then there south along the hedge until it comes again to ticcefield wick.

To Hundatune. First from the river[12] opposite the abbot's grave, then north along the green way to cram meare,[13] then there up to the ridge, then along the down to the chalk pit, then within the chalk pit to the well, then to the rough dell, then east to the road, along the road up to the ridge, then north to the thorn, where the post stands, then along the road to the slade, then along the slade to the grave, then down along the road to the ford, onward by the river, until it comes again to the abbot's grave.

I, Edward the King, have confirmed this restoration renewed by me by writing with my own hand the sign of the holy cross.

I, Plegmund the Archbishop, have subscribed to this mellifluous gift of the aforesaid king by the device of the holy cross.

I, Frithestan the Bishop, with the counsel of the same king have confirmed this and connected it with the triumph of the eternal king.

I, Wulfsige the Bishop, have consented and subscribed.

[Here follow the names of additional witnesses to the charter.]

[1] Raised ground, or possibly shambles.

[2] Thought to be the modern Dibdell's Field on the boundary of Crawley and King's Somborne. F. W. Pledge *Crawley* (1917), p. 17.

[3] Probably the same as Somborne, the adjoining parish on the west.

[4] Doubtless a Celtic or pre-Celtic mound.

[5] The meaning of screot is not clear; possibly crevice.

[6] Saenget thorn, doubtless a thorn tree, such as we find in other Anglo-Saxon charters. It may be burned thorn.

[7] Trind-lea, circular field, the later Trindley Field.

[8] Wicks may mean homesteads or hamlets. It is a plausible inference that this group of homesteads (if such it was) explains the duality of North and South Crawley, each with its set of customs. It may have been an early berewick of Crawley's, later quite merged. Conceivably also a berewick later separated.

[9] Apparently the name Titchfield has been lost, if it was a part of Crawley proper. Meaning originally, kid's field.

[10] Possibly rock-pit. Not unlikely a pit dug as a water reservoir in a district where water was periodically scarce.

[11] Meaning of holding place unknown

[12] A tributary of the River Test.

[13] Crammer or crane's pond.

§§ 4. Crawley in Domesday Book, 1086.

Crawley was very clearly a manor with all the equipment of manorial agriculture. The bishop's arable demesne had five plows or plowlands, which amounted to about 600 acres, if we are to equate plowland to hides, the latter being commonly of 120 acres. When we consider the smaller amount of land cultivated by the bishop at a somewhat later date,[1] the demesne appears large. Of course, the explanation may be that part of it was later granted out to the tenants in the form of small holdings.

The tenants' land carried seven plows, therefore amounting probably to about 840 acres. Since there were at least thirty-one land-holding tenants or families (six villeins and twenty-five bordars), the average holding would be about 27 acres. Under the three-field system, which at any rate prevailed at a later date, this would allow to each family about eighteen acres of cereals under cultivation each year. Of course if the slaves were land-holders, the average size would be smaller, about 16½ acres which is much nearer to thirteenth-century conditions.

The amount of woodland — for fifteen pigs — seems to be an understatement. But the meadowland — twenty-six acres — is quite in keeping with the general impression one gets of a shortage of hay in Crawley, notably in the thirteenth century.

There was a second estate which we may surmise to have been Hunton.[2] It was held by Alvin who is given a surname, quite an exceptional possession at this time. It is said that he was unable to go anywhere. This places serfdom, or a measure of it, in the Anglo-Saxon period, quite specifically. And this serf was a holder of three hides. Doubtless Alvin had been a sub-tenant, a mesne lord, holding of the bishop, as is said, in paragio, or in partible socage. His successor, Hugo, was probably a Norman follower of the king.

The demesne of the subordinate community possessed one plow and the tenants had one. This makes the sub-manor about 240

[1] See above, § 9, p. 28.

[2] Or possibly the Rookley House estate, in the seventeenth century called the "manor of Rookley." See above, § 14, p. 50; § 16, p. 58; § 31, p. 110.

acres, while in the nineteenth century Hunton was put down as 1075 acres. This discrepancy somewhat impairs the identification of the sub-manor as Hunton.

In Crawley proper there were twenty slaves and in the subordinate community nine. Whether these were individual adult slaves or households (families), is not clear. The ratio is ten slaves to a plowland in Crawley and nine in the subordinate part. Apparently slave labor constituted an important part of the economy of the manors. The large proportion of slaves probably helps to account for the relatively large demesnes. The bordarii, or cottage-men (cottagers), are clearly the normal citizens of each manor. In later documents there is a class of cotsettlers who may be descendants of either the slaves or the cottagers. Two hundred years later there were but two names for classes, customary tenants and cotsettlers. Just how villagers, cottagers, and slaves were shaken down into these two classes must remain an unrecorded story.

Crawley is a clear case of beneficial hidation, not so striking, however, as the larger Chilcomb. The manor could support fourteen plows, was actually using twelve, and was assessed at six and one-half (hides). Thus the benefit was almost fifty per cent, if our equation of plows, plowlands, and hides be correct. Or we may put it another way. In 909 there were said to be twenty hides in Crawley. In 1086 the manor was assessed at six and a half hides. Assuming that the demesne of the bishop was exempt for tax purposes, we have to put down a slight special benefit, that is, one-half hide, the difference between seven plows (plowlands or hides) on the one hand and six and one-half hides on the other. In this connection it is hard to escape the conclusion that, if Crawley had been actually made up of twenty hides in 909 and was using only 12 plows (or twelve hides) in 1086, there must have been either a big decline in agriculture or perhaps a splitting off of one of the appendages (Titchfield?).

The total size of Crawley cannot be determined from the Domesday description. Apparently 1440 acres (12 plowlands) were being cultivated, while 1680 (14 plowlands) might have been brought under the plow. Since the manor (apparently) had the same bounds in 909 as it has today, it actually possessed a little over 3600 acres. Thus less than one half was in arable. The value of the manor of Crawley is put down as £28, while Hunton was worth £7. In all probability this is a rough average of the net yearly income which the bishop received from manor and sub-manor. Out of this income he would be expected to pay a tax (Danegeld), whenever it happened to be levied, of about 2 s. a hide. This would amount to 19 s., that is, $(6\frac{1}{2} + 3) \times 2$ s., on the two manors, or a little over $2\frac{1}{2}\%$ of the estimated net income of a year.

IN[1] BITELESIETE HUNDRET[2]

Ipse episcopus[3] tenet Crawelie in dominio.[4] Semper[5] fuit in episcopatu. Tempore Regis Edwardi et modo se defendit pro vi hidis et dimidia. Terra[6] est xiiii carucis. In dominio[7] sunt v caruce et vi villani et xxv bordarii cum vii carucis et xx serui et xxvi acre prati. Silua de xv porcis, et Ecclesia. De hac terra[8] huius Manerii tenet Hugo iii hidas. Aluuinus Stilla[9] tenuit in paragio de episcopo non potuit ire quolibet. Ibi in dominio[7] est una caruca et ii villani et v bordarii cum i caruca. Ibi ix serui. Silua de vi denariis. Tempore Regis Eduardi totum Manerium ualebat[10] xxxv libras[11] et postea xxviii libras. Modo dominium[9] episcopi xxxv libras. Quod Hugo tenet vii libras.

IN BUDDLESGATE HUNDRED [12]

The bishop himself holds Crawley in demesne. It always belonged to the bishopric. In the time of King Edward it was, as now, assessed at $6\frac{1}{2}$ hides. There is land for 14 plows. In the demesne are 5 plows, and 6 villeins and 25 bordars with 7 plows, and 20 slaves, and 26 acres of meadow. There is woodland worth 15 swine, and there is a church.

[1] *Domesday Book, Hampshire* (photo-zincographed ed., 1864), p. VI.
[2] Modern Buddlesgate Hundred.
[3] Bishop of Winchester.
[4] Possession.
[5] As far back as memory or records go; certainly after A.D. 643.
[6] Terra arabilis.
[7] The bishop's own land — cultivated for his direct benefit.
[8] Land in a general sense.
[9] Written above Aluuinus.
[10] "Was worth," in the sense of bringing in a net income to the bishop.
[11] The old Saxon or Tower, pound (of silver) of 5400 grains, changed in 1527 to the troy pound of 5760 grains.
[12] This translation is partly based on the one found in *The Victoria History of the Counties of England, Hampshire and the Isle of Wight*, vol. I (1900), p. 460.

Of this land of this manor, Hugh holds 3 hides. Alwin Stilla held them in parage from the bishop; he could not go anywhere. There is in the demesne 1 plow, and 2 villeins and 5 bordars with 1 plow. There are 9 slaves. There is woodland worth 6 pence. In the time of King Edward the whole manor was worth 35 pounds, and afterwards 28 pounds. Now the bishop's demesne is worth 35 pounds. What Hugh holds is worth 7 pounds.

§§ 5. Reeve's Account, 29 Sept., 1208—28 Sept., 1209.

The officials who rendered this account were the bishop's sergeant and the manorial reeve. In this particular account there were two reeves, probably one succeeding the other. It is likely that the sergeant was the same as bailiff, or, at least in his position, similar to the bailiff of a later date, having oversight of several manors. But when we look through the collection of accounts, we find that the one official who was consistently and persistently responsible for the yearly accounts was the reeve (prepositus). Accordingly we may call these the reeves' accounts, although the generally accepted designation is bailiffs' accounts.

The date of this account is probably the same as that of the whole pipe roll of which it is but a part. This is the fourth year of Bishop Peter des Roches. The bishop was consecrated 25 September, 1205, but did not receive the temporalities until 24 March, 1206. Accordingly it is a question whether we should start with 1205 or 1206, or indeed with the year 1204 when the preceding bishop had died. Since the custom was to date from the consecration, however, we may conclude that the date was 1208–1209,[1] probably September to September. Since the agricultural year was Michaelmas to Michaelmas, the date is probably 29 September to 28 September.

This is the very first of the long series of accounts running on until the middle of the fifteenth century.[2] It is, of course, not the first roll that was prepared for the bishop. The earliest extant pipe roll of the royal exchequer is from the year 1130. It is prob-

[1] See Hubert Hall, *The Pipe Roll of the Bishopric of Winchester, 1208–1209* (1903), p. ix. For this Crawley document, see *ibid.*, pp. 50–52.

[2] See below, §§ 25, pp. 473 ff.; also Hubert Hall, "A List of Rent Rolls of the Bishopric of Winchester," *Economica*, no. 10 (Feb., 1924), pp. 52–61.

ably a matter of chance that none for the bishopric of Winchester goes back that far. How much the episcopal accounts owed to the royal exchequer of England and how much to the Frankish imperial system would be a matter of speculation and surmise.

The sources of income are:

	£.	s.	d.
Fixed rent (net)	9	9	0
Animal husbandry	14	17	2
Grain cultivation	9	14	6
Court profits	2	17	6
Tallage [1]	9	18	0
	46	16	2

An interesting speculation has to do with the origin of the fixed rent. Did it come from labor dues early commuted or was it merely the rent newly imposed upon, and collected from, free tenants? In other words, did it spring from a very dependent (or servile) community rising in the social scale or from a fairly independent community sinking down? If the explanation of the duality of Crawley be correct,[2] both explanations may indeed hold for the same manor, about one third of the fixed rent being paid by the once-submerged North Crawley and the other two thirds by the freer South Crawley.

In the statement of income it is clear that while the lord was engaged in a varied animal (and grain) culture, the emphasis was upon sheep, the swine and cattle being relatively insignificant. And this account illustrates very well why at least cattle were not more emphasized. They had in this year of great dryness to be sent to Mardon, doubtless for both hay and water.

Among the items of court returns is the payment of a large fine of 8 s. for having land. Probably this was for original possession rather than for inheritance. The commonest offence was trespass on the lord's wood, a fact which indicates either that the forest was already small, which is unlikely, or that the lord was reserving the forest strictly for exploitation and for sport. The two amercements for sowing the lord's land badly are significant. From the

[1] There was a national tallage in 1206 and a thirteenth in 1207. See S. K. Mitchell, *Studies in Taxation under John and Henry III* (1914), pp. 82, 84–92.

[2] See above, § 13, pp. 47 ff.

recurrence of this kind of entry we may judge that the remedy was not effective. The reeve was heavily amerced for having reduced the weight of the lord's clove used in selling wool, whereby he cheated the merchants with whom he dealt, to the damage of the credit of the lord bishop.

The expenses were for the upkeep of the plows and carts, the sheepfold, and the grange. A rope and bucket had to be purchased, rather significantly in a dry year. The wells were deep and the amounts of water required were great.

The manor's outside connections were commonly with Wolvesey to which the usual tithes of sheep and swine, the churchscot of hens and cocks, the surplus crops, and money rents were sent. But relations with Mardon (parish of Hursley) were also close. A tenant, Alebroc, had gone there, and there he was allowed to pay his dues. This entry goes marching on gloriously through the generations of reeves and of accounts. To Mardon, Crawley also sent wheat and barley and the cows and the bull. From it Crawley received sheep. Here were two manors, both near Winchester and near one another, which were at this time worked together. The advantage of such a procedure is obviously similar to the advantage of a big firm's management of several factories. But the working of the plan was not always smooth. The court entries indicate that when the Crawley men had been in Mardon the year before, they had got into a fight and had to be put into the stocks. They were this year amerced at home for the offence.

The yearly chronicle of the village's existence begins in 1208. It is, indeed, to be a long succession of many small events with a few major developments here and there.

CRAWEL*EIA* [1]

Ric*ardus* Ser*uiens* *et* Her*bertus* *et* Arnold*us* p*re*po*siti* redd*unt* xxxviij s. ij d. ob. de Rerag*io* ann*i* p*re*t*eriti*. *Et* Quieti sunt. Id*em* r*eddunt* co*m*-*potum* de x li. xij d. de toto Gab*u*lo ass*iso* pret*er* t*er*ras iiij carucar*iorum* j Fabri j Porcar*ii* ij Bercar*iorum* xiij Op*er*ar*iorum* q*ui* se defend*unt* p*er* Op*er*a sua. In Quiet*ancia* j p*re*po*siti* v s. In Def*ec*tu Gab*u*li t*er*re str*ong*' t*r*acte in D*omi*ni*um* ij s. In Def*ec*tu Gab*u*li t*er*re de Alebroc v s. qui

[1] MS., P. R. O., Ecclesiastical Commission, Various, 159270.

modo redduntur apud meredonam. *Summa* Quietanciarum *et* Defectuum xij s. *Summa* remanens ix li. ix s.

Idem *reddunt compotum* de xxxij s. v d. de Pannagio. Et de iij s. viij d. de Herbagio. Et de xx s. de iiij Bobus uiuis venditis. Et de ij s. vj d. de Coriis ij Bouum venditis. Et de ij d. de ij pellibus vitulorum anno preterito mortuorum venditis. Et de viij s. iiij d. de xxx multonibus veteribus *et* debilibus viuis venditis. Et de xiiij s. x d. ob. de C xv pellibus Ouium mortuarum venditis. Et de viij s. viij d. ob. de xlv agnis viuis venditis. Et de viij s. x d. de C iiij pellibus agnorum mortuorum venditis. Et de ix s. x d. de terra locata hoc anno. Et de x d. de Butiro vendito. Et de lxiij s. de C lxiij Caseis remanentibus anno preterito qui fecerunt ix pondera venditis. Et de xxiiij s. de iiij^{xx} iiij Caseis hujus anni qui fecerunt iij pondera dimidium venditis. Et de C s. de CCCC iiij^{xx} ix velleribus grossis que fecerunt iij pondera iiij partem ponderis *et* CC i velleribus agnorum que fecerunt dimidium pondus venditis. *Summa* xiiij li. xvii s. ii d. Idem *reddunt compotum* de vij li. xv s. iiij d. de lxj quarteriis dimidio frumenti venditis. Et de xj s. iij d. de v quarteriis Curailli venditis. Et de xxv s. viij d. de xij quarteriis dimidio Ordei venditis. Et de ij s. iij d. de j quarterio dimidio pisarum venditis. Summa ix li. xiiij s. vj d. DE PURCHasiis Idem reddunt compotum de xx s. de tota villata pro pleuina hominum qui fuerunt in Cippo apud meredonam pro mellea anno preterito. Et de xx s. de Herberto preposito pro Claue dimittendo. Et de ij s. de Willelmo palmer pro Sursisa. Et de xij d. de Ivone Coch pro forisfacto Bosci. Et de vj d. de Willelmo Tole pro simili. Et de xviij d. de Roberto Longo pro simili. Et de xij d. de Hugone Niwem' pro terra Episcopi male seminata. Et de xij d. de Odone pro simili. Et de vj d. de Sewale pro forisfacto Bosci. Et de vj d. de Tanculfo pro simili. Et de vj d. de Roberto de Insula pro simili. Et de xij d. de Ricardo de Vinea pro simili. Et de viiij s. de Roberto milite pro terra habenda. *Summa* lvij s. vj d. Idem *reddunt compotum* de ix li. xviij s. de Tallagio. *Summa* tocius Recepte xlvj li. xvj s. ij d.

Liberatio[1] In liberatis Johanni Decano C s. iij ob. tam de Reragio anni preteriti venditionum. Eidem de Purchasiis xx s. per j talliam. Eidem de Blado vendito xl s. per j talliam. Eidem de Tallagio ix li. xviij s. per j talliam. Eidem de termino Natalis xlv s. j d. per j talliam. Eidem de iij terminis sequentibus vj li. xv s. per j talliam. Eidem ix li. xij d. per j talliam. *Summa* tocius liberationis xxxiiij li. xij d.

Expensa In ferramentis iiij carrucarum x aurorum per annum xiiij s. ij d. In vj paribus Rotarum Emptis ad Carrucas iiij Carucis factis de Nouo *et* in Carucis reparandis ij s. iiij d. In j Careta ferrata Empta ix s. viij d. In j Careta reparanda ix d. In j Sella perono peronello Emptis

[1] In the margin.

ad Caret*am* xiiij d. In Capistr*is* Empt*is* iij ob. In vi Bob*us* Empt*is* xxxv s. ij d. In p*re*car*iis* Hyem*alibus* de xiij Caruc*ariis* xiij d. In fossand*is* lx p*er*tic*is* C*ir*ca B*er*car*iam* xv s. In Sepe facienda c*ir*ca B*er*car*iam* xij d. In j Noua porta facienda an*te* B*er*car*iam* xij d. In porta Cur*ie* rep*ar*and*a* vij d. In pariet*ibus* Daer*ie* *et* Granar*ii* faciend*is* ij s. j d. In p*re*dic*t*is Domib*us* *et* j B*er*car*ia* et ij Grang*iis* cooperiend*is* v s. j d. In Serr*ur*is rep*ar*and*is* iiij d. In Corda *et* Vtre ad put*eum* Empt*is* multocie*ns* p*ro*p*ter* nimia*m* Siccitat*em* xx d. In xxxviij Clat*is* ad fald*am* x d. In Custo Daer*ie* iiij s. j d. In Pull*is* Empt*is* c*ontra* Pentecost*en* p*er* p*re*ceptu*m* Senesc*alli* s*cilicet* lxiiij pull*is* iij s. v d. ob. In lxxij acr*is* Blad*i* Sarcland*is* xvj d. In c*orredio* magi*st*ri R*oberti* Basse*t*[1] ibid*em* ix s. ob. In c*orredio* Thom*e* de Wichton*a* ibid*em* in Aupt*umno* p*er* v sept*imanas* vj s. ij d. p*er* die*m* ij d. In caneuaz Empt' ad inponend*am* lana*m* xvj d. ob. In Solid*o* iiij Bouar*iorum* p*er* ann*um* xvj s. In Solid*o* j Haiward*i* iij s. In Solid*o* j Daie iij s. In lib*er*at*ione* R*icardi* de Foxcot*e* S*er*uient*is* p*er* annu*m* lx s. x d. S*umma* x li. iiij d. S*umma* toci*us* lib*er*at*ionis* *et* Exp*ense* xliiij li. xvj d. debent liiij s. x d.

Exit*us* Grang*ie* Id*em* r*eddunt* c*ompotum* de lxvj q*uarteriis* dim*idio* de Toto Exitu fr*umenti*. Et de xxvj q*uarteriis* recept*is* de M*er*edon*a*. S*umma* iiij^{xx} xij q*uarteria* dim*idium*. In Se*m*in*e* iiij^{xx} x acr*arum* xxvj q*uarteria*. In Pan*e* p*re*car*iarum* aupt*umnalium* v q*uarteria*. In S*upra*uend*itis* lxj q*uarteria* dim*idium*. De p*re*cio sup*er*i*us* R*espondent*. Id*em* r*eddunt* c*ompotum* de v q*uarteriis* de toto Exit*u* Curaill*i*. In vend*itis* tot*um*. De p*re*cio sup*er*i*us* R*espondent*. Id*em* r*eddunt* c*ompotum* de c xlvij q*uarteriis* dim*idio* de Toto Exitu Ordei. In Se*m*in*e* c lxxiij acr*arum* lvij q*uarteria*. In miss*is* ap*ud* Cumb*am* ad Seme*n* *et* ibi lib*er*at*is* R. de deneford*e* vj q*uarteria*. In miss*is* ap*ud* meredon*am* xxij q*uarteria*. In c*orrediis* iiij bouar*iorum* j Haiward*i* j Daie p*er* ann*um* xxxix q*uarteria*. In m*er*cede *et* c*orredio* j H*er*ciat*or*is a festo s*ancti* mich*aelis* usq*ue* Pasch*am* iij q*uarteria*. In Porc*is* pascend*is* viij q*uarteria*. In S*upra*uend*itis* xij q*uarteria* dim*idium*. Id*em* r*eddunt* c*ompotum* de cc j q*uarteriis* de toto Exitu auen*e*. In Se*m*in*e* cc iiij^{xx} vj acr*arum* c iiij q*uarteria*. In miss*is* ap*ud* m*er*edon*am* viij q*uarteria*. In miss*is* ap*ud* Wlues*eiam* *et* ibi lib*er*at*is* J*ohanni* Decan*o* xxx q*uarteria* p*er* ij tall*ias*. In miss*is* ap*ud* Wlues*eiam* *et* lib*er*at*is* P*etro* Ace ad p*re*b*endam* Ep*iscop*i xviij q*uarteria*. In p*re*b*enda* R*oberti* Basse*t* iij q*uarteria*. In p*re*b*endam* x aur*orum* p*er* ann*um* xxxviij q*uarteria*. Id*em* r*eddunt* c*ompotum* de ij q*uarteriis* dim*idio* de toto Exitu pisar*um*. In Se*m*in*e* iiij acr*aram* j q*uarterium*. In S*upra*uend*itis* j q*uarterium* dim*idium*. Quiet*i*.

Instaur*um*. Id*em* r*eddunt* c*ompotum* de x aur*is* rem*anentibus* ann*o*

[1] Probably the seneschal of the bishop of Winchester.

p*re*t*er*ito. Om*n*es rem*anent*. Id*em* r*eddunt* co*mpotum* de xxxvij bob*us* rem*anentibus* ann*o* p*re*t*er*ito. Et de vj p*ost*ea Empt*is*. Et de ij adiu*n*ctis de Instaur*o*. S*umma* xlv. In viuis vend*itis* iiij. De p*re*cio sup*er*i*us* R*espondent*. In mort*uis* ij. S*umma* vj. Et rem*anent* xxxix Bou*es*. Id*em* r*eddunt* co*mpotum* de xij vacc*is* j Taur*o* rem*anentibus* ann*o* p*re*t*er*ito. Et de iij vacc*is* adiu*n*ctis de Instaur*o*. S*umma* xv vacc*e* j Taur*us*. Om*n*es rem*anent et* sunt missi apud m*er*edon*am*. Id*em* r*eddunt* co*mpotum* de ij Bouett*is* iij Genic*ulis* rem*anentibus* ann*o* p*re*t*er*ito. In adiu*n*ctis Bob*us* ij. In adiu*n*ctis vacc*is* iij. Nich*il* rem*anet*. Id*em* r*eddunt* co*mpotum* de iiij vitul*is* rem*anentibus* ann*o* p*re*t*er*ito. In mort*uis* ij. Et rem*anent* ij. Id*em* r*eddunt* co*mpotum* de CCCC iiij^xx Ou*ibus* rem*anentibus* ann*o* p*re*t*er*ito. Et de C x adiu*n*ctis de Instaur*o*. S*umma* D iiij^xx x. In mort*uis* an*te* p*ar*tu*m* x p*ost* p*ar*tu*m et* an*te* tons*ionem* viij p*ost* tons*ionem* viij. S*umma* xxvj. Et rem*anent* D lxiiij Ou*es*. Id*em* r*eddunt* co*mpotum* de CCC xlv mult*onibus* rem*anentibus* ann*o* p*re*t*er*ito. Et de C xxvij adiu*n*ctis de Instaur*o*. S*umma* CCCC lxij. In viuis vend*itis* xx. In mort*uis* an*te* Tons*ionem* xxxiiij. In mort*uis* p*ost* tons*ionem* vj. S*umma* lx. Et rem*anent* CCCC xij mult*ones*. Id*em* r*eddunt* co*mpotum* de CC xviij hogg*astris* ann*o* p*re*t*er*ito agn*is*. Et de xlviij recept*is* de m*er*edon*a*. S*umma* CC iiij^xx vj. In mort*uis* an*te* tons*ionem* xlix. Et rem*anent* CC xxxvij un*de* C x sunt Gerc*ie* Iuncte Ou*ibus* C xxvij s*unt* mar*es* iuncti multon*ibus*. Id*em* r*eddunt* co*mpotum* de CCCC liij agn*is* p*ro*uent*is* hoc ann*o*. Et de iij p*ro*vent*is* de Gerc*iis* q*uia* xvij Ou*es* fuer*unt* steriles. In Dec*ima* xlv. In c*on*suet*udinibus* j fabri ij B*er*cari*orum et* Custod*is* agnor*um* iiij. In viuis vend*itis* xlv. In mort*uis* an*te* Tons*ionem* iiij^xx xiij. In mort*uis* p*ost* tons*ionem* xj. S*umma* C iiij^xx xviij. Et rem*anent* CC lviij. Id*em* r*eddunt* co*mpotum* de DCCCC iiij^xx x Vell*eribus* Lan*e* Crisp*e et* Gross*e*. In Dec*imis* iiij^xx xix. In c*on*suet*udinibus* ij B*er*cari*orum* Daie iij. In vend*itis* DCCC iiij^xx viij q*ue* fec*erunt* ij pond*era* Lan*e* minut*e* iij pond*era* Lan*e* Gross*e et* iiij p*ar*te*m* j pond*eris*. Id*em* r*eddunt* co*mpotum* de CC j Vell*eribus* Lan*e* agn*ine* q*uia* lxviij subtil*es* agni n*on* fuer*unt* tons*i*. In S*upra*uend*itis* CC j q*ue* fec*erunt* dim*idium* pond*us*. Id*em* r*eddunt* co*mpotum* de C lxxvj Case*is* q*ui* incep*er*unt fi*er*i viij° Id*us* Ap*ri*l*is et* desier*unt* iiij k*alendas* Octob*ri*s ut*roque* die co*mputato*. In Dec*ima* xvij. In c*on*suet*udinibus* B*er*car*ii* fabri Daie iij. In miss*is* ap*ud* Wluese*iam* xxiiij. In p*re*car*iis* aupt*umnalibus* xiiij. In S*upra*uend*itis* iiij^xx iiij. Et rem*anent* xxxiiij Cas*ei*. Id*em* r*eddunt* co*mpotum* de xxxiiij Porc*is* rem*anentibus* ann*o* p*re*t*er*ito. Et de xxiij de Exit*u* eor*undem*. S*umma* lvij. In Dec*ima* ij. In c*on*suet*udine* porc*arii* j. In Lard*ario* Winton*ie* xv. In mort*uis* vij. S*umma* xxv. Et rem*anent* xxxij Porc*i*. Id*em* lib*er*auer*unt* Rad*ulfo* Salserio ap*ud* Wluese*iam* xxx pull*os*. Id*em* r*eddunt* co*mpotum* de lxj Gall*inis* de Ch*er*iset. Et de lxiiij E*m*pt*is*. In lib*er*at*is* J*ohanni* Decan*o* iiij^xx xj. Et rem*anent* xxxiiij *et* p*reter*ea xxviij Capon*es* de adq*uisi*ti*one* R*icardi* S*er*uientis. Id*em* *reddunt compotum* de iiij Baco*nibus* recept*is* de Wlues*eia*. In p*recariis* aupt*umnalibus* totu*m* Exp*endiderunt*. *Summa* Tot*ius* Deb*iti* liiij s. x d. Soluit p*ost* *com*pot*um* *et* Quiet*us* est p*er* totu*m*.[1]

CRAWLEY

Richard the sergeant, Herbert and Arnold the reeves, pay 38s. 2½d. arrears of the past year. And they are quit.

The same render account of £10 12d. from the whole fixed gafol, except for the lands of 4 plowmen, 1 smith, 1 swineherd, 2 shepherds, 13 laborers who answered by their own works. For acquittance of 1 reeve, 5s. For default of gafol for Strong's land drawn into the demesne, 2s. For default of gafol of the land of Alebroc, 5s. which are now paid at Mardon. Sum of acquittances and defaults, 12s. Sum remaining, £9 9s.

The same render account of 32s. 5d. from pannage. And 3s. 8d. from herbage. And 20s. from the sale of 4 live oxen. And 2s. 6d. from the sale of the hides of 2 oxen. And 2d. from the sale of 2 pelts of calves that died in the past year. And 8s. 4d. from the sale of 30 live wethers, old and feeble. And 14s. 10½d. from the sale of 115 pelts of dead ewes. And 8s. 8½d. from the sale of 45 live lambs. And 8s. 10d. from the sale of 104 pelts of dead lambs. And 9s. 10d. from land let this year. And 10s. from the butter sold. And 63s. from the sale of 163 cheeses, remaining from the past year which made 9 weys. And 24s. from the sale of 84 cheeses of this year which made 3½ weys. And 100s. from the sale of 489 great fleeces which made 3¼ weys, and 201 lambs' fleeces which made ½ wey. Sum, £14 17s. 2d.

The same render account of £7 15s. 4d. from the sale of 61½ quarters of wheat. And 11s. 3d. from the sale of 5 quarters of curall. And 25s. 8d. from the sale of 12½ quarters of barley. And 2s. 3d. from the sale of 1½ quarters of peas. Sum, £9 14s. 6d.

From court dues. The same render account of 20s. from the whole township for the plevin of the men who were in stocks at Mardon for 'ficht-wite' the past year. And 20s. from Herbert the reeve for diminishing the clove. And 2s. from William Palmer for contempt of court. And 12d. from Ivan Coch for trespass in the woods. And 6d. from William Tole for the same. And 18d. from Robert Long for the same. And 12d. from Hugh Niweman for having sown the bishop's land badly. And 12d. from Odo for the same. And 6d. from Sewale for trespass in the woods. And 6d. from Tanculf for the same. And 6d. from Robert de Insula for the same. And 12d. from Richard de Vinea for the same. And 8s. from Robert Knight for having land. Sum, 57s. 6d.

[1] These two concluding sentences are in a different hand.

The same render account of £9 18s. for tallage. Sum of the total receipt, £46 16s. 2d.

The delivery. For delivery to John the Deacon of 100s. ¾d. as well from arrears of the sales of the past year. The same [officials make delivery] from court dues, 20s. by 1 tally. The same from the sale of grain, 40s. by 1 tally. The same from tallage, £9 18s. by 1 tally. The same from Christmas term, 45s. 1d. by 1 tally. The same from the three following terms, £6 15s. by 1 tally. The same, £9 12d. by 1 tally. Sum of the total delivery, £34 12d.

Expense. For the ironwork on 4 plows, 10 plow-horses throughout the year, 14s. 2d. For 6 pairs of wheels bought for the plows, 4 plows made new, and for repairing plows, 2s. 4d. For the purchase of 1 iron cart, 9s. 8d. For repairing 1 cart, 9 d. For 1 saddle, and leather trappings, small leather trappings bought for the cart, 14d. For halters purchased, 1½d. For the purchase of 6 oxen, 35s. 2d. For winter boon days of 13 plowmen, 13d. For ditching 60 perches around the sheep-fold, 15s. For making a hedge around the sheep-fold, 12d. For making 1 new gate in front of the sheep-fold, 12d. For repairing the gate of the courtyard, 7d. For building walls of the dairy and granary, 2s. 1d. For roofing the aforesaid houses, 1 sheep-fold, and 2 granges, 5s. 1d. For repairing locks, 4d. For rope and bucket at the well bought many times on account of excessive drought, 20d. For 38 hurdles for the fold, 10d. For outlay on the dairy, 4s. 1d. For hens bought against the time of Pentecost by the order of the seneschal, namely, 64 hens, 3s. 5½d. For the hoeing of 72 acres of corn, 16d. For the food allowance of Master Robert Basset in the same place, 9s. ½d. For food allowance of Thomas de Wichtona at the same place in autumn for 5 weeks, 6s. 2d., per day 2d. For canvas bought for wrapping wool, 16½d. For the payment of 4 oxherds, by the year, 16s. For the payment of 1 hayward, 3s. For the payment of 1 dairy-woman, 3s. For the payment of Richard de Foxcote, the sergeant, for the year, 60s. 10d. Sum, £10 4d. Sum of the total payment and expense, £44 16d. And they owe 54s. 10d.

Yield of the Grange. The same render account of 66½ quarters of the total yield of wheat. And of 26 quarters received from Mardon. Sum, 92½ quarters. For the seed of 90 acres, 26 quarters. For the bread of autumn boon-days, 5 quarters. Above sold, 61½ quarters. For the price they account above. The same render an account of 5 quarters of the total yield of curall. Sold, all; for the price they account above. The same render account of 147½ quarters of the total yield of barley. For the seed of 173 acres, 57 quarters. Sent to Cumbe for seed and there delivered to R. de Deneforde, 6 quarters. Sent to Mardon, 22 quarters. For the allowances of 4 oxherds, 1 hayward, 1 dairy-woman, by the year, 39 quarters. For the wages and allowance of 1 harrower from the feast of St. Michael until Easter, 3 quarters. For feeding pigs, 8 quarters. Sold above, 12½ quarters. The same render account of 201 quarters of the total yield of oats. For the seed of 286 acres, 104 quarters. Sent to Mardon, 8 quarters. Sent to Wolvesey and there delivered to John the Deacon, 30 quarters, by 2 tallies. Sent to Wolvesey and delivered to Peter Ace for the bishop's provender, 18 quarters. For provender of Robert Basset, 3 quarters. For the provender of 10 plow-horses for the year, 38 quarters. The same render account of 2½ quarters of the total yield of peas. For the seed of 4 acres, 1 quarter. Sold above, 1½ quarters. They are quit.

Stock. The same render account of 10 plow-horses remaining from the past year. All remain. The same render account of 37 oxen remaining from the past year. And of 6 afterwards bought. And of 2 added from the stock. Sum, 45. Sold alive, 4. For the price they account above. Dead, 2. Sum, 6. And there remain 39 oxen. The same render account of 12 cows, 1 bull, remaining from the past year. And 3 cows added from the stock. Total 15 cows, 1 bull. All remain and are sent to Mardon. The same render account of 2 bullocks, 3 heifers, remaining from the past year. Added to oxen, 2. Added to cows, 3. None remain. The same render account of 4 calves remaining from the past year. Died, 2. And 2 remain. The same render account of 480 ewes remaining from the past year. And of 100 added from the stock. Sum, 590.[1] Died before lambing, 10; after lambing and before shearing, 8; after shearing, 8. Sum, 26. And 564 ewes remain. The same render account of 345 wethers remaining from the past year. And of 127 added from the stock. Sum, 462.[2] Sold alive, 20. Died before shearing, 34. Died after shearing, 6. Sum, 60. And 412 wethers remain. The same render account of 218 two-year old sheep, lambs of the past year. And of 48 received from Mardon. Sum, 286.[2] Died before shearing, 49. And 237 remain, of which 110 are young ewes added to the sheep; 127 are young wethers added to the wethers. The same render account of 453 lambs born this year, and 3 born of young ewes, because 17 ewes were barren. For the tithe, 45. For the customary allowance of 1 smith, 2 shepherds, and the keeper of the lambs, 4. Sold alive, 45. Died before shearing, 93. Died after shearing, 11. Sum, 198. And 258 remain. The same render account of 990 fleeces of curly and great wool. For the tithes, 99. For the customary allowance of 2 shepherds, a dairy-woman, 3. Sold, 888 which made 2 weys of fine wool, 3 weys of great wool and ¼ of 1 wey. The same render account of 201 fleeces of lambs' wool because 68 delicate lambs were not shorn. Sold above, 201 which made half a wey. The

[1] Corrected total. [2] Incorrect total.

same render account of 176 cheeses which were begun eight days before the Ides of April and were finished four days before the Calends of October, both days being reckoned. For the tithe, 17. For the customary allowance of the shepherd, smith, dairy-woman, 3. That sent to Wolvesey, 24. For autumn boon days, 14. Above sold, 84. And 34 cheeses remain. The same render account of 34 pigs remaining from the past year. And 23 from the yield of the same. Sum, 57. For the tithe, 2. For the customary allowance of the swineherd, 1. For the larder at Winchester, 15. Dead, 7. Sum, 35. And 32 pigs remain. The same delivered to Radulf Salserio at Wolvesey, 30 chickens. The same render account of 61 hens of churchscot. And of 64 purchased. Delivered to John the deacon, 91. And 34 remain, and in addition 28 capons of the aquisition of Richard the sergeant. The same render account of 4 flitches of bacon received from Wolvesey. For autumn boon-days they used up the whole.

Sum of the total debt, 54s. 10d. He paid after the account and is quit for the whole.[1]

§§ 6. Reeve's Account, 29 Sept., 1210—28 Sept., 1211.

At this time — less than 150 years after the Conquest — there were apparently very few Anglo-Saxon names of persons in Crawley. Whether this meant new blood in the village or simply imitation of the conquerors' names is not clear. The higher officials of the bishop were commonly not Saxons.

The list of fines and amercements is more than usually interesting. The payment for marrying off a daughter is a commonplace; but 10s. paid by a male tenant for getting married is out of the ordinary. One wonders whether he was marrying outside the manor; [2] it could hardly be a case of marrying a free woman on the manor. Four were amerced for wrongly maintaining some cause. Perhaps it was connected with the concealing of a man (or his offence), for which the whole tithing was amerced 20s. Fines were paid for having land (an entry fee?), for having chattels (after forfeiture for a crime?), and for the commutation of labor services. Amercements were paid for trespass on the forest and the pasture and for mistakes in pleading. The payment of 14s.

[1] A later entry in an official hand.

[2] An Alan paid 10s. this same year in Mardon for having the widow of Peter. It may be that he was a resident of Crawley and there paid 10s. for marrying outside the manor, and 10s. in addition for having a widow on another manor (Mardon) belonging to the bishop.

for hay for feeding sheep and the use of oats for feeding oxen during the winter and of barley for feeding swine throughout the year are unusual occurrences, not singly but in conjunction. It was a difficult year in animal husbandry, ten tenants being amerced for trespass on the lord's pasture.

Seldom do we get more information about Crawley's relations with the outside world than in this account. There was the usual yield of stock for the bishop's use at Wolvesey Palace. Chickens were sent to Clere (in northern Hampshire) and 723 fleeces (amounting to four weys and seven cloves) to Southwark,[1] the bishop's manor, just across the Thames from London. From Twyford came 149 wethers and from Downton (in Wilts) 51 lambs. In such instances we observe the effective utilization of a group of estates for the supplying of stock and in the case of Southwark for the sale of products. It would seem that Roger Wacelin, whatever his title, was a kind of business agent for the whole group of episcopal manors.

Some values are of interest. Land was leased, apparently for a year, at a little less than 5d. per acre. Oxen, doubtless in good condition, were bought for a little under 6s. 5d. each. Wethers were sold at 5½d. each. Thus the man who paid 10s. for getting married, gave the equivalent of an ox, three wethers, and the annual rent of five acres of land.

CRAWELEIA[2]

R[icardus] seruiens *et* E[rnaldus?] p*re*po*situs* r*eddunt* comp*otum* de x li. xij d. p*reter* iiij carucar*ios* j fab*rum* j Porcar*ium* ij b*er*car*ios* [x]iij op*er*atore*s* q*ui* se defend*unt* p*er* op*er*ationes suas. In Q*uiet*a*ncia* j p*re*-p*ositi* v s. In def*ectu* Gab*u*li [terre] str*on*ge t*ra*ct*e* i*n* d*omi*nic*um* ij s. In def*ectu* t*er*re de Alebroke v s. q*ui* m*odo* reddunt*ur* apud m*er*edun*am*. S*umma* Q*ui*et*anciarum et* def*ectuum* xij s. S*umma* Reman*ens* ix li. ix s.

[Exitus manerii.] Id*em* r*eddunt* co*mpotum* de xxviij s. vj d. de pannag*io*. De viij s. de ij bob*us* viu*is* vend*itis*. De xij s. vj d. de xxx m*atri*-*cibus* ou*ibus* viu*is* vend*itis*. De vij s. iiij d. de xvj Mult*onibus* viu*is* vend*itis*. De iiij d. ob. de pell*ibus* iij Mult*onum*. De iij d. de pell*ibus* ij ouiu*m*. De iij s. de herbag*io*. De iiij s. j d. de xviij agn*is* viu*is* ven-

[1] That the wool was really sent to London is indicated by the item of expense, 18d. for wool sent to London.

[2] MS., P. R. O., Ecclesiastical Commission, Various, 159270A.

FACSIMILE OF PART OF A REEVE'S ACCOUNT, 1210–11

VILLAGE STREET SHOWING THE INN AT THE RIGHT

A photograph

d*itis*. De ij s. iiij d. de Coriis ij bou*um* Mort*uorum* vend*itis*. De x d. de Coriis ij aur*orum*. De ix s. ix d. de pell*ibus* xxvij ouiu*m* xlix Mult*onum* iij hogg*astrorum* mort*uorum* vend*itis*. De iiij s. viij d. ob de pell*ibus* iiij^{xx} vij agn*orum* et rott*orum*. De xlv s. de vj pond*eribus* dim*idio* Cas*ei*. De viij d. de butir*o* vend*ito*. De vij s. de vij pet*ris* lane agnin*e*. De ix s. vj d. de t*er*ra locata scilic*et* xxiiij acr*is*. *Summa* vij li. iij s. x d.

[Bladum.] Id*em* *reddunt* co*mpotum* de xvj s. vj d. de xj q*uarteriis* Ord*ei* vend*itis*. De vj li. vij d. de xxij q*uarteriis* frum*enti* vend*itis*. De vj s. de iij q*uarteriis* de Curall*o* vend*itis*. De xxxix s. xj d. de xxj q*uarteriis* ordei vend*itis*. De xviij d. de j q*uarterio* pisar*um*. De v s. de v q*uarteriis* auen*e* vend*itis*. *Summa* ix li. ix s. vj d.

De Purch*asia*. Id*em* *reddunt* co*mpotum* De iiij s. de Will*elmo* sewin' p*ro* fil*ia* Marit*anda*. De ij s. de Rob*erto* fil*io* alan*i* p*ro* manutenem*ento*. De xij d. de pet*ro* p*ro* sim*i*li. De xviij d. de Ivone fil*io* edwin*i* p*ro* sim*i*li. De vj d. de yuone f*ra*tre steph*ani* p*ro* sim*i*li. De xij d. de Joh*anne* Mer*catore* p*ro* t*er*ra h*abend*a. De xij d. de Ernal*do* p*ro* sim*i*li. De vj d. de Rob*er*ti [sic] Joh*annis* f*ra*tre p*ro* sim*i*li. De xij d. de yuone fil*io* Wiand' p*ro* sim*i*li. De vj d. de Will*elmo* toneur p*ro* sim*i*li *et* de iij s. de eod*em* p*ro* relaxat*ione* op*er*is. De iij s. de yvon*e* palm*er* p*ro* forisf*ac*to pasture. De vj d. de Ric*ardo* de vinea p*ro* stultiloq*uio*. De xij d. de Ric*ardo* Carewin' p*ro* sim*i*li. De vj d. de Nigell*o* fab*ro* p*ro* forisfact*o* pasture. De vj d. de Gilb*erto* Jobi p*ro* sim*i*li. De vj d. de Rob*erto* p*ro* sim*i*li. De xij d. de Ivone palm*er* p*ro* sim*i*li. De xij d. de Joh*anne* fil*io* alueue p*ro* sim*i*li. De vj d. de Will*elmo* b*er*car*io* p*ro* sim*i*li. De vj d. de Rand*ulfo* b*er*car*io* p*ro* sim*i*li. De vj d. de yuone lude p*ro* sim*i*li. De xij d. de panchulf' *et* saual' p*ro* sim*i*li. De vj d. de hug*one* niweman*n* p*ro* sim*i*li. De xx s. de thething*a* p*ro* quod*am* hom*ine* co*n*celat*o*. De xij d. de Wiand' p*ro* fil*ia* sua marit*anda*. De xviij d. de dauid*o* p*ro* sim*i*li. De ij s. de alexand*ro* p*ro* t*er*ra sua relaxata. De xij d. de Will*elmo* fil*io* fab*ri* p*ro* mell*ea*. De ij s. de hawis*ia* vid*ua* p*ro* stultiloq*uio*. De xij d. de Ric*ardo* biscop p*ro* relaxatio*ne* op*er*is. De x s. de Alan*o* fil*io* Will*elmo* p*ro* se maritand*o*. De iiij s. de Will*elmo* dod' p*ro* catall*is* suis h*abe*ndis. *Summa* lxxj s. *Summa* toti*us* Recept*e* xxix li. xiij s. iiij d.

Liberat*io*. In lib*er*at*ione* J[ohanni] decano p*er* j Talli*am* xviij li.

Expens*e*. In ferram*enti*s iij Caruc*arum* p*er* annu*m* *et* j caruc*e* p*er* iij t*er*minos anni xiij s. ix d. In iiij p*aribus* rotar*um* ad caruc*as* empt*is* *et* caruc*is* *et* h*er*ciis de nouo f*ac*tis ij s. x d. In Rot*is* empt*is* ad bigas ij s. iiij d. In big*is* ligand*is* *et* ferr*o* empt*o* ad id*em* iij s. vj d. ob. In big*is* exuland*is* iij d. In paronis *et*(?) paronell*is* Capistr*is* *et* vnct*o* xj d. ob. In v bob*us* empt*is* xxxj s. xj d. In ij aur*is* empt*is* x s. j d. In poll*is* p*arand*is ad noua*m* g*ra*ngia*m* vj d. In g*ra*ngi*a* releuand*a* *et* alia repar*and*a vij s. ij d. In boueri*a* G*ra*ngi*a* *et* ceteris domib*us* cooperiend*is* *et* rep*ar*and*is* vij s. v d. ob. In b*er*cari*a* cooperiend*a* *et* rep*ar*and*a* ij s. In xj *q*uart*eriis* dim*idio* auen*e* empt*is* ad sem*entem* xij s. j d. In dim*idio* *q*uart*erio* fab*arum* empt*o* ad sem*entem* xiiij d. In cord*a* *et* utre ad puteu*m* viij d. In xj clat*ibus* miss*is* ad W*o*lues*eiam* vj d. In Cust*o* daerie v s. iij ob. In c xviij acr*is* sarcland*is* iij s. v d. In sarplariis ad lana*m* *im*ponend*am* ij s. iiij d. In lana pond*e*rand*a* *et* saccand*a* vij d. In clat*ibus* p*a*rand*is* ad fald*am* xx d. In lana cariand*a* ap*u*d lond*oniam* xviij d. In bucatt*is* *et* tinis *et* cet*e*ris p*a*ram*en*tis iiij d. In j porcaria de nouo faciend*a* xviij d. In iij ventila[b]r*is*[?] j Corbell*a* xvj d. In feno empt*o* ad op*us* ouiu*m* xiiij s. In p*r*ecar*iis* hyemal*ibus* de xiij Caruc*ariis* xiij d. In c ij pell*ibus* agnin*is* p*a*rand*is* xviij d. In iij serruris empt*is* v d. In solid*o* iij bouar*iorum* p*er* annu*m* *et* j bouar*ii* p*er* iij t*e*rminos xv s. In sol*ido* j haiward*i* j daie vj s. In exp*ensis* R[ogeri] Wacel*ini* viij d. In expens*is* Mauric*ii* de Turvill*e* p*er* iij dies v s. iiij d. ob. S*umma* vij li. xix s. ob. S*umma* lib*erationum* *et* exp*ensarum* xxv li. xix s. ob. Et debet lxxv s. iij d. ob. vnd*e* p*re*po*situs* soluit xxxv s. iij d. ob. Et R[icardus] Morel[lus] h*a*buit xl s. p*ro* lib*eratione* sua Q*u*iet*us*.

Exit*us* G*r*angiar*um*. Id*em* r*eddunt* co*mpotum* de lxvj *q*uart*eriis* dim*idio* frum*enti* de toto exit*u*. In se*mine* iiij^{xx} vj acr*arum* xxvj *q*uar*teria*. In Miss*is* ap*u*d W*o*lues*eiam* ix *q*uart*eria* dim*idium*. In sup*ra*vend*itis* xxxj *et* Q*u*iet*us* *est*. Id*em* r*eddunt* co*mpotum* de v *q*uart*eriis* Curall*i*. In p*r*ecar*iis* autu*m*pn*alibus* ij *q*uart*eria*. In sup*ra*vend*itis* iij *et* q*u*iet*us* *est*. Id*em* r*eddunt* co*mpotum* de lxj *q*uart*eriis* ij buss*ellis* Ordei heim*alis*. In se*mine* c vij acr*arum* xxxvj *q*uart*eria*. In porc*is* pascend*is* p*er* totu*m* ann*um* xviij *q*uart*eria* ij buss*elli*. In sup*ra*vend*itis* vij *et* Q*u*iet*us* *est*. Id*em* r*eddunt* co*mpotum* de c x *q*uart*eriis* dim*idio* j Buss*ello* de exitu ordei. In se*mine* iiij^{xx} xj acr*arum* dim*idie* xl *q*uart*eria* dim*idium* j buss*ellus*. In co*rredio* iij bouar*iorum* j haiward*i* xxviij *q*uart*eria*. In lib*e*rat*ione* j bouar*ii* iij *q*uart*eria* ij buss*elli*. In lib*era*-*tione* daie v *q*uart*eria* ij buss*elli*. In co*rredio* *et* mercede cui*us*da*m* heri-ciat*oris* [sic] iij *q*uart*eria*. In miss*is* ap*u*d W*o*lues*eiam* ij *q*uart*eria*. In p*r*ecar*iis* autumpn*alibus* iij *q*uart*eria*. In sup*ra*vend*itis* xxv *q*uar*teria*. Id*em* r*eddunt* co*mpotum* de cc j *q*uart*eriis* ii buss*ellis* auene. De xj *q*uart*eriis* dim*idio* empt*is* ad sem*entem*. S*umma* cc xij *q*uart*eria* dimi*dium* ij buss*elli*. In se*mine* cc xxvj acr*arum* c j *q*uart*eria* dim*idium*. Lib*e*rat*a* G. Marescall*i* ap*u*d m*e*reduna*m* x *q*uart*eria*. In p*r*ebend*a* R[ogeri] Wacelin*i* dim*idium* *q*uart*erium* j Buss*ellus*. In p*r*ebend*a* M[auricii] de Turuill*e* dim*idium* j Buss*elli*. In p*r*ebend*a* x aur*orum* p*er* ann*um* xl *q*uart*eria*. In miss*is* ap*u*d W*o*lues*eiam* xl *q*uart*eria*. In bob*us* sustinend*is* in hieme xv *q*uart*eria*. In sup*ra*vend*itis* v *q*uart*eria* *et* q*u*iet*us*. Id*em* r*eddunt* co*mpotum* de ij *q*uart*eriis* dim*idio* de Exitu pisar*um*. In se*mine* j *q*uart*erium* dim*idium* j buss*ellus*. In sup*ra*ven*ditis* j *q*uart*erium* *et* Quiet*us*.

De Instauro. Idem *reddunt compotum* de xxxiij bobus rem*anentibus* ann*i* p*reteriti*. De ij adiunct*is* de Instaur*o*. De j iuuent*o*. De v empt*is*. S*umma* xlj. In mort*uis* ij. In viv*is* vend*itis* ij. S*umma* iiij. Et rem*anent* xxxvij. Id*em* r*eddunt* c*ompotum* de x aur*is* reman*entibus* ann*i* p*reteriti*. De ij postea empt*is*. S*umma* vij. In mort*uis* ij. Et rem*anent* x. Id*em* r*eddunt* c*ompotum* de ij bouett*is* rem*anentibus* ann*i* p*reteriti*. In adiunct*is* bob*us* ij *et* n*ih*il rem*anet*. Id*em* r*eddunt* co*mpotum* de D xiij ouib*us* rem*anentibus* ann*i* p*reteriti*. De xx adiunct*is* de instaur*o*. S*umma* D xxxiij. In viu*is* vend*itis* xxx. In mort*uis* an*te* p*ar*tu*m et* tons*ionem* xij. In mort*uis* p*ost* p*ar*tu*m et* an*te* tons*ionem* xij Post partu*m et* tons*ionem* v. S*umma* lix. Et rem*anent* CCCC lxxiiij. Id*em* r*eddunt* c*ompotum* de CCC lxj mult*onibus* rem*anentibus* ann*i* p*reteriti*. De xvj de adiunct*is* de i*n*staur*o*. De C xlix recept*is* de Twiford*ia* p*ost* tons*ionem*. S*umma* D xxvj. In viu*is* vend*itis* xvj. In mort*uis* an*te* Tons*ionem* xxxv. In mort*uis* p*ost* tons*ionem* xvij. S*umma* lxviij. Et reman*ent* CCCC lviij. Id*em* r*eddunt* c*ompotum* de xxxix hog*astris* rem*anentibus* ann*i* p*reteriti* agn*is*. In [1] adiunct*is* ouib*us* xx. In adiunct*is* mult*onibus* xvj. In mort*uis* an*te* tons*ionem* ij p*ost* tons*ionem* j et n*ih*il remanet. Id*em* r*eddunt* c*ompotum* de CCCC xxiiij agnis p*r*ouent*is* h*oc* ann*o* q*ui*a xlvij erant st*er*iles. De lj recept*is* de D[u]nton*ia*. S*umma* CCCC lxxv. In dec*ima* xlij. In c*onsuetudine* b*er*car*ii* haiward*i* fab*ri* ij b*er*car*iorum* Custod*is* agnor*um* vj. In viu*is* vend*itis* xxviij. In mort*uis* an*te* sep*ar*ati*onem* C xxxix. In mort*uis* post sep*ar*ationem *et* an*te* tons*ionem* xl Post tons*ionem* x vn*de* C ij pell*es* miss*e* erant ad W*o*lues*eiam* de p*r*ecio aliar*um* sup*er*i*us* respond*ent*. S*umma* CC lv. Et rem*anent* CC xx. Id*em* r*eddunt* c*ompotum* de xlviij porc*is* rem*anentibus* ann*i* p*reteriti*. De vij porcell*is* p*r*ouent*is* de suib*us*. S*umma* lv. In Miss*is* ap*u*d W*o*lues*eiam* xvj. In mort*uis* viij. S*umma* xxiiij. Et rem*anent* xxxj. Id*em* r*eddunt* c*ompotum* de DCCC vj vell*eribus* Gross*e* lane *et* crisp*e*. In decim*a* iiij^{xx}. In c*onsuetudine* ij b*er*car*iorum* j daie iij. In Miss*is* ap*u*d suwerk' *et* ibi lib*eratis* R[ogero] Wacelin*o et* Joh*anni* caretar*io* DCC xxiij q*ue* fecer*unt* iiij pond*era* vij claues vn*de* iij pond*era* erant c*r*isp*a* j pond*us* vij Claues Gross*a*. Id*em* r*eddunt* de C iiij^{xx} iij vell*eribus* lan*e* agn*ine* q*ui*a xlvij erant adeo c*r*ispi q*uod* n*on* fuer*unt* tons*i*. In sup*ra*vend*itis* tot*um* q*uod* fecit vij claues. Id*em* r*eddunt* c*ompotum* de C lxiij case*is* q*ui* inceper*unt* f*ieri* xij K*alendas* Maii *et* desier*unt* die s*ancti* mich*aelis* ut*roque* die c*o*mput*ato*. De xix case*is* f*ac*tis an*te* ablact*ationem*. S*umma* C iiij^{xx} ij. In dec*ima* xviij. In c*onsuetudine* p*r*e*positi* haiward*i* fab*ri* b*er*car*ii* Daie v. In p*r*ecar*iis* autu*m*pn*alibus* xij. In miss*is* ap*u*d W*o*lues*eiam* xij q*ui* fecer*unt* j pond*us*. In sup*ra*vend*itis* C xxxv q*ui* fecer*unt* vj pond*era* dim*idium*. Id*em* r*eddunt* c*ompotum* de lxxvj Gall*inis* reman*entibus* ann*i* p*reteriti*. De lx de Cheriset*o* h*uius*

[1] MS. has Id*em*.

anni. *Summa* c xxxvj. In miss*is* ap*ud* clere lib*eratis* R. salsar*io* iiij^{xx} p*er* j tall*iam*. In miss*is* ap*ud* W*o*lues*eiam et* lib*eratis* J[ohanni] dec*ano* xlv. In exp*ensis* R[ogeri] Wacelin*i* iiij. In mort*uis* vij. Id*em* r*eddunt* c*ompotum* de xiiij Chapon*ibus* rem*anentibus* ann*i* p*reteriti*. In miss*is* ap*ud* W*o*lues*eiam* vj. In mort*uis* ij. Et rem*anent* vj.

§§ 7. Reeve's Account, 29 Sept., 1231—28 Sept., 1232.[1]

The arrears of the past year were very large. They were paid off, but new ones, only one quarter less, were again incurred.

This was clearly a trying year for animal husbandry. There was a scarcity of rainfall, for ropes and buckets had to be bought for the well, the swine had to be pastured elsewhere, and a large sum had to be spent on hay.

At least 48 acres of the lord's demesne lay in common fields. Three acres and one half in the common fields were leased. There were six laborers (operarii) and a cowherd who were acquitted of their money rent, 2s. 8d. each, in return for regular work. They are said to give two days a week, and every day during autumn. Probably the only extra service given was from Lammas-day to Michaelmas. For these fifty-odd days they received a money allowance of 32d. and doubtless some food. It probably amounted to less than 1d. a day. Some of the tenants had died. Seven cottages and holdings of land were vacant, and constituted a considerable loss to the lord. Doubtless this explains the acquittance of the cowherd and the six laborers in return for the special autumn work: they were probably doing the work of the deceased tenants.

Oxen which were hitched to the plow, to plow the lord's land, paid no herbage. Each one plowed one acre and a half. These were probably customary acres, just one half the size of the measured acres (acre per perticam). The sheep had been sick, doubtless with the usual murrain. To bring relief, oil had been bought and a friar had been paid for visiting them.

Here, as elsewhere, it was the furlongs which were prominent, not the larger divisions of the arable into sections (campi or "fields"). They bore names of landmarks and topographical peculiarities. They persisted through the centuries, while the

[1] The date is 27 Peter des Roches.

big sections ("fields") of the manor seemed more elastic and nebulous.

The payment made twice a year, later called tithingpenny, was this year changed from 5s. to 6s. 8d., a rate kept through the centuries.

We have here three names for the Crawley organization, villa, villata, and tithinga. The first is equivalent to manor, the second to township, and the third to the frankpledge group of the men of Crawley.

CRAWEL*EIA* [1]

R[icardus] [2] s*er*uiens [et] W[illelmus] p*re*p*ositus* r*eddunt* co*m*p*otum* de xix li. xvj s. j d. de Rerag*io* anni p*re*t*eriti*. In lib*erato* R. de Clinch' p*er* j tall*iam* tot*um et* q*uieti*. Id*em* r*eddunt* co*m*p*otum* de xiij li. viij s. vj d. de Gab*u*lo assis*o*. In q*uie*t*ancia* p*re*p*ositi* v s. v carucar*iorum* j fab*ri* j porcar*ii* iij b*er*car*iorum* p*er* ann*um* xxvj s. viij d. cuil*ibet* ij s. viij d. In quiet*ancia* j vaccar*ii* p*er* annu*m* ij s. viij d. vj op*er*ar*iorum* p*er* ann*um* op*er*ant*ium* ij dies i*n* ebd*omada et* cotidie i*n* aut*umpno* xvj s cuil*ibet* ij s. viij d. S*umma* l s. iiij d. In def*ectu* t*er*r*e* strong' t*r*act*e* i*n* d*ominicum* ij s. In def*ectu* t*er*re Will*elmi* de curia t*r*act*e* i*n* d*ominicum* ij s. viij d. In def*ectu* t*er*re de Alebroc v s. q*ui* m*odo* reddunt*ur* ap*ud* m*er*edon*am*. In def*ectu* t*er*re Rob*erti* cawe h*oc* anno ij s. viij d. In defectu terre Rob*erti* osm*undi* h*oc* anno ij s. viij d. In def*ectu* t*er*re Rog*eri* koie h*oc* anno ij s. viij d. In def*ectu* t*er*re osm*undi* vacantis h*oc* anno ij s. viij d. In def*ectu* t*er*re Rog*eri* coc ij s. viij d. In def*ectu* t*er*r*e* Will*elmi* longi h*oc* anno ij s. viij d. In def*ectu* t*er*re Ace h*oc* anno ij s. viij d. S*umma* xxviij s. iiij d. S*umma* Quiet*anciarum et* def*ectuum* lxxviij s. viij d. S*umma* Rem*anens* ix li. ix s. x d.

Id*em* r*eddunt* co*m*p*otum* de iij s. vij d. ob. de pannag*io*. De xxiijs. v d. ob. de h*er*bag*io* de bob*us* n*on* iunct*is* ad car*ucam* s*cilicet* de q*uolibet* boue *et* q*ua*libe*t* uacca plene etatis ocioso vj d. *et* bouett*o* iij annor*um* iij d. *et* de annali ij annor*um* ij d. *et* de bouetto annic*u*lo j d. *et* memorand*um* q*uod* q*ui*libet bos *et* vacc*a* iuncti ad car*ucam* arab*unt* j acr*am* dimi*diam* ep*iscop*o *et* ideo par*iter* respondent h*oc* anno de h*er*bag*io* q*uia* multi boues erunt arabiles. De xxvj s. de iiij bob*us*. De xiiij d. de aur*o* eg*ro*to. De ix s. de ij aur*is*. De vj d. de cor*io* j aur*i*. De ij s. vj d. de j vacc*a*. De xij d. de cor*io* j vacc*e*. De iij ob. de cor*io* j vitul*i*. De xxxiij s. iiij d. de l ouib*us*. De iiij s. vij d. de pell*ibus* xxij ou*ium* an*te* tons*ionem*. De xxxix s. de xxxix mult*onibus* De ij s. ix d. de pell*ibus* xj mult*onum* an*te* tons*ionem*. De v s. de pell*ibus* xxx hog*astris* an*te* ton-

[1] MS., P. R. O., Ecclesiastical Commission, Various, 159282, memb. VI.
[2] In the margin In oct*abis* S*ancti* Mart*ini*.

sionem. De xv d. de pell*ibus* vj ou*ium* xij mult*onum* xj hog*astrorum* post tons*ionem*. De iij s. iij ob. de vj agnis. De vj s. iij d. de pell*ibus* lxvij agn*orum*. De ix d. ob. de xix rott*is*. De xiiij li. ix s. de vij pond*eribus* vj clau*is* lan*e* gr*o*sse *et* agn*ine*. De iiij s. iij d. de lockis. De iiij li. viij s. de xj pond*eribus* cas*ei*. De xiiij s. de ij pond*eribus* cas*ei*. De xxj d. de Butiro. De xx d. de xx cas*eis* yem*alibus*. De xij d. de tab*er*na. De ij s. de pastur*a* locata h*oc* anno. De ij s. vj d. de mesuag*io* vid*ue* Will*elmi* Longi Locat*o* h*oc* anno. De ij s. vj d. de mesuag*io* Rob*erti* cawe locat*o* h*oc* anno. De ij s. vj d. de mesuag*io* Rog*eri* keue locat*o* h*oc* anno. De ij s. vj d. de mesuag*io* osm*undi* locat*o* h*oc* anno. De ij s. vj d. de mesuag*io* ace locat*o* h*oc* anno. De xxj d. de iij acr*is* dim*idia* sic*ut* iacent locat*is* h*oc* anno. *Summa* xxviij li. xix s. iiij d. ob.

Blad*um* vend*itum*. Id*em* r*eddunt* c*om*p*otum* de xviij li. viij s. ix d. de iiij^{xx} x q*uarteriis* vj b*ussellis* fr*umenti*. De xv s. iiij d. de v q*uarteriis* curall*i*. De ix li. ij s. ix d. de lxxj q*uarteriis* dim*idio* manc*orni*. De ix li. xviij s. vj d. de lxvj q*uarteriis* ordei. De xj li. v s. ij d. de c xxxv *quarteriis* dim*idio* auen*e*. De xx d. de dim*idio* q*uarterio* fab*arum*. De ix s. ix d. de iij q*uarteriis* ij b*ussellis* pis*arum*. De vj s. viij d. de ij q*uarteriis* dim*idio* vesc*iarum*. *Summa* l li. viij s. vij d.

Purch*asia*. Id*em* r*eddunt* c*om*p*otum* de v s. de edm*undo* p*ro* bosco. De vj d. de Alano p*ro* pastur*a*. De vj d. de Joh*anne*. De vj d. de Will*elmo*. De vj d. de Rob*erto*. De vj d. de Rog*ero* *et* Joh*anne*. De xij d. de od*er*ino. De ij s. de Yuone *et* filio suo. De vj d. de fil*io* Rog*eri*. De xij d. de Will*elmo*. De vj d. de Alano. De xij d. de odiern'. De v s. de t*it*h*inga* p*ro* occas*ione*. De vj d. de vid*ua* Hug*onis*. De vj d. de Joh*anne*. De vj d. de Rog*ero*. De vj d. de edelot p*ro* def*ectu* op*er*is. De vj d. de Reg*inaldo*. De vj d. de Will*elmo*. De vj d. de Reg*inaldo*. De vj d. de Rog*ero*. De vj d. de Rob*erto*. De vj d. de Yuon*e*. De ij s. de Eudun*e*. De iij s. de Rob*erto* Huggel' p*ro* fine t*erre*. De vj d. de Will*elmo*. De xxvj s. viij d. de Oderino p*ro* melle*a*. De vj s. viij d. de Nich*olao* de puteo p*ro* t*ra*nsg*ressione*. De xxxiij s. iiij d. de tota villat*a* p*ro* si*mi*li. De vj s. viij d. de t*it*h*in*ga p*ro* occas*ione*. De xiij s. iiij d. de edelot*a* p*ro* se mar*ianda*. De vj d. de Joh*anne* Wippe p*ro* pastur*a*. *Summa* c xvj s. ij d. *Summa* toti*us* Recept*e* iiij^{xx} xiiij li. xiij s. xj d. ob.

Lib*eratio*. In lib*eratis* R. de clinch' p*er* j tall*iam* lxix li. ij s. vj d.

Exp*ense*. In ferr*amentis* iiij car*ucarum* p*er* ann*um* *et* j car*uce* p*er* xvij sept*imanas* *et* *in* ferr*amentis* xj aur*orum* xiiij s. ij d. ob. In iiij pari*bus* rot*arum* ad car*ucas* xiiij d. In iij car*ucis* de nouo f*act*is *et* Jugis *et* h*er*ciis xvj d. In j pari rot*arum* ad big*am* ij s. v d. In eisd*em* uet*er*i f*er*ro ligand*is* *et* m*er*cede fab*ri* xix d. In big*a* axand*a* *et* clut*is* *et* vnct*o* ix d. ob. In p*er*onell*o* *et* bac*is* ix d. In viij capistr*is* fac*tis* de pil*o* au*er*o*rum* ij d. In feno empt*o* xxj s. In iiij bob*us* xxv s. x d. ob. In iij hostiis fac*tis* ad b*er*car*iam* viij d. In aula *et* g*ra*ngia cooperiend*is* iij s. vj d.

In j serur*a* ad gr*a*nar*iam* ij d. In iiij^{xx} crat*is* ad fald*am* xx d. In vj cord*is* ad puteu*m* vj d. In ij ut*ribus* ad id*em* v d. ob. In p*re*car*iis* *con*-*cedebantu*r xj car*ucariis* xj d. *et* xlviij acre sic*ut* iacent arate s*unt* h*oc* anno de xxxij bob*us* ho*minum* uille s*cilicet* p*ro* q*uo*libe*t* boue j acra dim*idia*. In xxij q*uarteriis* fr*umenti* ad sem*en* e*mp*t*is* iiij li. x s. viij d. In xxij q*uarteriis* dim*idio* manc*orni* lxv s. iij d. In dim*idio* q*uarterio* ord*ei* xvj d. In porcis pasc*andis* p*er* uia*m* ap*ud* Iuingeh' vj d. In ij q*uarteriis* auen*e* ij s. xj d. ob. In blado sarcland*o* vj s. ij d. In t*ri*tu-r*andis et* vent*ilandis* lxij q*uarteriis* fr*umenti* x s. iiij d. In t*ri*tur*andis et* vent*ilandis* xlviij q*uarteriis* manc*orni* iiij s. In t*ri*tur*andis et* vent*ilan*-*dis* xij q*uarteriis* auen*e* vj d. In vj sacc*is* xij d. ob. In custo daer*ie* v s. j d. In ouib*us* medic*andis* v d. In exp*ensa* fr*at*ris uisitantis oue*s* viij d. In xxvj vlnis canabi ad lana*m* iij s. ix d. ob. In ead*em* saccand*a* vij d. In M allec*iis* ad iij p*re*car*ia* aut*umnalia* iij s. vj d. q*uia* n*on* h*ab*uer*un*t carne*m* neq*ue* case*um*. In stip*endiis* ij caruc*ariorum* p*er* ann*um* vj s. In stip*endiis* ij car*ucariorum* p*er* xvij sept*imanas* xviij d. In stip*endiis* j caret*tarii et* j haiward*i* vj s. In stip*endio* daie ij s. In lib*eratis* s*er*uient*i* lx s. x d. S*umma* xvij li. xs. iijd. ob. S*umma* liberat*ionis et* exp*ensarum* iiij^{xx} vj li. xij s. ix d. ob. Deb*ent* viij li. xiiij d. vn*de* posuit i*n* xx q*uar*-*teriis* fr*umenti* dim*idio* ad sem*en* lxvj s. ij d. In xxj q*uarteriis* dim*idio* manc*orni* ad id*em* xliiij s. vij d.

Exit*us* gr*angie*. Id*em* r*eddunt* co*mpotum* de iiij^{xx} x q*uarteriis* vj b*us*-*sellis* de exitu fr*umenti*. De xxij q*uarteriis* empt*is*. S*umma* C xij q*uar*-*teria* vj b*usselli*. In se*mine* lxiiij acr*arum* p*er* pertic*am* i*n* dunstanefur-lang' xxij q*uarteria*. In sup*r*auend*itis* iiij^{xx} x q*uarteria* vj b*usselli*. Id*em* r*eddunt* co*mpotum* de v q*uarteriis* curall*i*. In sup*r*auend*itis* tot*um*. Id*em* r*eddunt* co*mpotum* de lxxj q*uarteriis* dim*idio* de exitu manc*orni*. De xxij q*uarteriis* dim*idio* empt*is*. S*umma* iiij^{xx} xiiij. In se*mine* lvj acr*arum* p*er* pertic*am* ap*ud* huitthorne xxij q*uarteria* dim*idium*. In sup*r*auend*itis* lxxj q*uarteria* dim*idium*. Id*em* r*eddunt* co*mpotum* de C lxv q*uarteriis* iij b*ussellis* de exitu ordei. De dim*idio* q*uarterio* empt*o*. In se*mine* iiij^{xx} v acr*arum* dim*idie* p*er* pertic*am* i*n* midfurlang' *et* buri-furlang' xlij q*uarteria* iij b*usselli*. In co*rr*ed*io* j caret*tarii* ij caruc*ari*-*orum* p*er* ann*um* xix q*uarteria* dim*idium*. In co*rr*ed*io* ij car*ucariorum* p*er* xvij sept*imanas* iiij q*uarteria* ij b*usselli*. In co*rr*ed*io* j haiward*i* vj q*uarteria* dim*idium* Daie a*b* purif*icatione* Be*ate* mar*ie* usq*ue* fest*um* s*ancti* mich*aelis* iij q*uarteria* ij b*usselli*. In co*rr*ed*io* j h*er*ciat*oris* p*er* xij sept*imanas* j q*uarterium*. In porc*is* sust*inendis* ij q*uarteria* dim*idium*. In co*rr*ed*io* porcar*ii* euntis ap*ud* Yuingeh'o c*um* porcis ad pastur*am* dim*id*-*ium* q*uarterium*. In iij p*re*car*iis* aut*umnalibus* iiij q*uarteria*. In ele-m*osina* ep*isco*p*i* xij q*uarteria*. In sup*r*auend*itis* lxvj q*uarteria*. In miss*is* ap*ud* Wlues*eiam* iiij q*uarteria*. Id*em* r*eddunt* co*mpotum* de CCC vj q*uarteriis* vj b*ussellis* de exitu auen*e*. De ij quart*eriis* empt*is*. In se*mine* c lxvj acr*arum* p*er* p*er*tica*m* c xxx q*uarteria* ij b*usselli* qui jacent i*n* lo*n*gfurland' et hillefurlang' *et* iux*ta* b*er*cari*am*. In p*rebenda* xj auro*rum* i*n* yeme xxiij q*uarteria*. In bob*us* sust*inendis* xx q*uarteria*. In sup*ra*uend*itis* c xxxv q*uarteria* dim*idium*. Id*em* r*eddunt* co*mpotum* de vj b*ussellis* fab*arum*. In plant*acione* ij b*usselli*. In sup*ra*uend*itis* dim*idium* q*uarterium*. Id*em* r*eddunt* co*mpotum* de v q*uarteriis* j b*ussello* de exitu pis*arum*. In se*mine* v acr*arum* dim*idie* p*er* p*er*tica*m* j q*uarterium* vij b*usselli*. In vend*itis* iij q*uarteria* ij b*usselli*. Id*em* r*eddunt* co*mpotum* de v q*uarteriis* vesc*iarum*. In se*mine* j acr*e* dim*idie* p*er* p*er*tic*am* ij q*uarteria* dim*idium*. In sup*ra*uend*itis* ij q*uarteria* dim*idium*.

Instauru*m*. Id*em* r*eddunt* co*mpotum* de xij auri*s* rem*anentibus*. De ij de test*amento*. S*umma* xiiij. In vend*itis* iij. In mort*uo* j. Et Rem*anent* x. Id*em* r*eddunt* co*mpotum* de xxxix bob*us* rem*anentibus*. De iiij e*mpti*s. S*umma* xliij. In vend*itis* iiij. Et Rem*anent* xxxix. Id*em* r*eddunt* co*mpotum* de ix vacc*is* rem*anentibus*. In vend*ita* j. In mort*ua* j. Et Rem*anent* vij. Id*em* r*eddunt* co*mpotum* de iij annal*ibus* rem*anentibus*. O*mne*s rem*anent*. Id*em* r*eddunt* co*mpotum* de iij annal*ibus* anno p*reterito* vitul*is*. In mort*uo* j. Et Rem*anent* ij. Id*em* r*eddunt* co*mpotum* de iiij vitul*is* p*r*o*uen*t*is* h*oc* anno de vacc*is* q*uia* iij erant st*e*ril*es*. Et Rem*anent*. Id*em* r*eddunt* co*mpotum* de DC xx ouib*us* rem*anentibus*. De c l adiunct*is*. S*umma* DCC lxx. In vend*itis* ad f*estum* s*ancti* mart*ini* l. In mort*uis* an*te* p*ar*tu*m* xiiij p*ost* p*ar*tu*m et* an*te* tons*ionem* viij p*ost* tons*ionem* vj. S*umma* lxxviij. Et Rem*anent* DC iiij^{xx} xij.

Id*em* r*eddunt* co*mpotum* de CCC iiij^{xx} xij mult*onibus* rem*anentibus*. De c lj adiunct*is*. S*umma* D xliij. In vend*itis* xxxix. In mort*uis* an*te* tons*ionem* xj p*ost* tons*ionem* xij. S*umma* lxij. Et Rem*anent* CCCC iiij^{xx} j. Id*em* r*eddunt* co*mpotum* de CCC xlij hog*astris* ann*o* p*reterito* agn*is*. In mort*uis* an*te* tons*ionem* xxx p*ost* tons*ionem* xj. In adiunct*is* ouib*us* c l *et* mult*onibus* c lj *et* ni*hi*l rem*anet*. Id*em* r*eddunt* co*mpotum* de D xx agnis p*r*o*uen*t*is* h*oc* anno de ouib*us* q*uia* xx fuer*unt* st*e*ril*es et* xvj fecer*un*t aborsu*m*. In dec*ima* lij. In co*n*suet*udine* p*re*po*siti* fab*ri* iij b*er*cari*orum* v. In mort*uis* an*te* sep*ara*t*ionem* lxvij p*ost* sep*ara*t*ionem* xix. S*umma* c xliij. Et Rem*anent* CCC lxxvij. Id*em* r*eddunt* co*mpotum* de xliij porc*is* rem*anentibus*. De xxij de exitu. S*umma* lxv. In dec*ima* ij. In co*n*suet*udine* porcar*ii* j. In miss*is* ap*ud* dunt*oniam* ad lard*arium* xix. S*umma* xxij. Et Rem*anent* xliij vn*de* j uerr*es* iiij sues xix sup*e*rannat*i* xix Juniores. Id*em* r*eddunt* co*mpotum* de MCC ij vell*eribus* gr*ossis*. In dec*ima* vj^{xx}. In co*n*suet*udine* iij b*er*cari*orum et* daie iiij. In sup*ra*uend*itis* M lxxviij q*ue* fec*erunt* vij pond*era* vj clau*os*. Id*em* r*eddunt* co*mpotum* de v cas*eis* f*ac*tis an*te* ablact*ationem*. De CC xxx q*ue* i*nc*ep*erunt* fi*eri* xv K*alendas* maii *et* desier*unt* iiij K*alendas* octobr*is* q*uia* fecer*un*t binos p*er* lxv dies. In dec*ima* xxiij. In consuet*udine* p*re*po*siti* fab*ri* ij b*er*-

car*iorum* Daie v. In miss*is* ap*ud* Wlues*eiam* xij q*ue* fecer*unt* j pond*us*. In sup*rauendi*t*is* c iiij[xx] xv.

Id*em reddunt compotum* de xx cas*eis* f*ac*tis i*n* yem*e*. In sup*r*auend*itis* tot*um*.

Id*em reddunt compotum* de c xxiij gall*inis* de ch*e*ris*eto*. In def*ectu* p*ro* mort*uis* x. In def*ectu* vij cotar*iorum* vaccant*ium* h*oc* anno xxx *et* t*er*re q*ua*m vicari*us* tenet. In miss*is* ap*ud* Wlues*eiam* iiij[xx] iij.

§§ 8. Reeve's Account, 29 Sept., 1232—28 Sept., 1233.

This year the Crawley account occurs right at the beginning of the pipe roll of the bishop, a rather unusual happening. It is well written and, except for the very end, is almost perfectly legible. The account was made up on Thursday, the day after All Souls, or 3 November, to run from Michaelmas in the twenty-eighth year of Bishop Peter des Roches to the Michaelmas following.

There is every evidence of an effort toward efficiency. Defaulted estates were leased out or drawn into the demesne. The fines and amercements were heavy. A relatively large sum was realized from collecting nuts. A windfall was sold. The land was carefully measured. A friar came to inspect the sheep and two other persons to view the corn in the granges. Many repairs were carried through. Whether all this was owing to the influence of the able bishop or to one of his officials is, of course, not indicated.

A great deal of information concerning fields is set forth in this account. The fields (campi) are really furlongs or shots. They are aggregations of small strips of land used by lord and tenants. The other meaning of fields, two or three big sections of the whole village arable, is not found in this account. One of the furlongs, called basumli, doubtless got its name from the boundary meadow called beast-man lea in the charter of 909.[1] Another is called sturte, elsewhere cherte and shert, and today recognized as shirt. If we have identified this field rightly, what was for long after this date a permanent pasture, was at the time of this account sown to mixtil.

The lord's demesne was in this particular year larger than it would have otherwise been, being made up of the regular demesne, estates drawn into the demesne, and the land of cottagers (cot-

[1] See above, §§ 3, pp. 179, 181.

setli) temporarily cultivated. All in all, it amounted to over 400 statutory acres.[1] It lay, of course, scattered among the various furlongs, as is indicated by the use of the word iacent, they (the acres) lie.

The income from animals and animal products (including a small amount from other sources) was £36. 3s. 6½d.; while from grain it was £49. 4s. 8d. While some of the barley and oats were given out as food allowances or fed as fodder, the wheat was sold for hard cash. This was a typical condition. The lord paid no tithes on grain but he did on cattle, sheep, swine, wool, and cheese.

Amercements for the following offences are notable: keeping the sheep badly, keeping (withholding?) two of the (lord's) colts, ineffective guarding of the (lord's) sheaves, bad shearing of the (lord's) sheep, concealing or (withholding) labor service, taking rabbits in the (lord's) warren, the wrongful collection of manure, witholding the (lord's) horseshoes, despising the lord's service, and offences against the thorn hedges, the plowing, and especially the forest. There were fines for having land, for commuting labor, and for the privilege of marrying. The reeve paid 13s. 4d. for the privilege of marrying his son to an heiress and for having her land. This fine, or accord, amounted to almost twenty-eight bushels of wheat. A widow was allowed to marry outside the manor. By custom she would have to give up her holding. Being of little use to the lord, she was allowed to depart on the payment of the value of three wether sheep.

It is said that 192 cheeses make 15½ weys and two quarters of a hundredweight. From other sources,[2] we learn that the wey contained 182 pounds. Accordingly the average weight of these cheeses was 15 pounds.

ROTULUS ANN*I* VICESIM*I* OCT*I* PONT*IFICATUS* DOM*I*NI P*ETRI* WINTO*NIENSIS* EPIS*COPI*

CRAWELEIA DIE JOUIS IN CRASTINO ANIMARU*M*[3]

Will*elmus* Seruiens et Will*elmus* p*re*posit*us* Reddunt compotum De viij li. xiiij d. De areragio anni p*reteriti*. In lib*eratis* D*om*ino Rob*erti*

[1] For the average size of the desmesne, see above, § 9, pp. 27 ff.

[2] See above, § 19, p. 62.

[3] MS. P. R. O., Ecclesiastical Commission, Various, 159283.

de clunapp' tot*um* p*er* j talliam et Quiet*i* sunt. Idem Reddu*n*t compot*um* De xiij li. viij s. vj d. De toto Gabulo assiso. In Quiet*ancia* vnius p*repositi* p*er* annu*m* v s. In Quiet*anciis* vj caruc*ariorum* et j fabri et j porcarii et iiij bercar*iorum* p*er* annum xxxij s. sing*ulus* ij s. viij d. In quiet*ancia* j vacc*arii* p*er* annu*m* ij s. viij d. In quiet*anciis* vj op*era*r*iorum* op*er*anciu*m* p*er* duos dies in sept*imana* et In autu*m*pno quolib*et* Die xvj s. Sing*ulus* ij s. viij d. S*umma* lv s. viij d. In defectu terre st*r*onge t*r*actum in dominicu*m* ij s. In defectu terre Will*elm*i de curia t*r*act*um* in d*omi*nicu*m* ijs. viij d. In defectu de Alebroc v s. Qui m*odo* redduntu*r* apud meredune. In defectu t*er*re Rob*erti* cauwe h*oc* anno ij s. viij d. In defectu t*er*re Rog*er*i Coye h*oc* anno ij s. viij d. In defectu t*er*re Osm*undi* uacant*is* h*oc* anno ij s. viij d. In defcctu t*er*re Rog*er*i cohc [sic] h*oc* anno ij s. viij d. In defectu t*er*re Will*elm*i long' ij s. viij d. Su*mma* Defect*uum* xxiij s. Su*mma* quiet*anciarum* et defect*uum* lxxviij s. viij d. Su*mma* Remanens ix li. ix s. x d.

Exitus. Idem Reddu*n*t Compotum de iij s. iiij d. De pannagio. Et de xxiij s. iiij d. De herbagio de bob*us* et vacc*is* non iunct*is* ad carucam s*cilicet* de quolib*et* boue et qualib*et* uacc*a* plene etatis ocioso vj d. et bouetto t*r*ium annor*um* iij d. et de bouiculo duor*um* annor*um* ij d. et bouett*o* anniculo siue de dim*idio* anno j d. Et memorand*um* quod quilib*et* bos et uacc*a* iuncta ad carucam arabit ep*iscop*o vnam acram et dim*idiam* et de xxxvj s. iiij d. de vj bob*us* uiuis uend*itis* et de ij s. iij d. de corio j bou*is* mort*ui* uend*ito* et de iij d. de iij cori*is* annal*ium* mort*uorum* uend*itis* et de xl s. viij d. de lxj mat*ricibus* ou*ibus* uiu*is* uend*itis* ad festum s*anct*i martini sing*ula* viij d. et de xxvj s. ix d. de C vij pell*ibus* de mat*ribus* ante tons*ionem* uend*itis* quelib*et* iij d. et de ix d. de xviij pell*ibus* de mat*ribus* mort*uis* vend*itis* p*ost* tons*ionem* et de l s. de l mult*onibus* uiu*is* uend*itis* ad festum s*anct*i martini et de xiij s. iij d. de liij pellibus mult*onum* mort*uorum* uend*itis* ante tons*ionem* quelib*et* iij d. et de viij d. ob de xvij pell*ibus* mult*onum* debil*ium* uend*itis* p*ost* tons*ionem* et de xiij s. vj d. de liiij pell*ibus* hog*astrorum* mort*uorum* uend*itis* an*te* tons*ionem* quelib*et* iij d. q*uia* uenditi fuerunt cum pell*ibus* mult*onum* et de vij d. de xiiij pell*ibus* hog*astrorum* p*ost* tons*ionem* et de xvij d. de vj agn*is* debilib*us* uend*itis* et de xx s. iiij d. de CC pell*ibus* agn*orum* mort*uorum* uend*itis* ante sep*ara*tio*n*em et de xliiij mort*uis* uend*itis* p*ost* sep*ara*cio*n*em et de j d. de iiij pell*ibus* agn*orum* uend*itis* p*ost* tons*ionem* et de xvj li. viij s. de viij pond*eribus* lane g*r*osse uend*ite* cum CC xlix vell*eribus* agnor*um* uend*itis* s*cilicet* quo*d*libe*t* pond*us* xlj s. et de v s. vj d. De lock*is* uend*itis* et de vj li. xiiij s. vij d. de xv pond*eribus* dim*idio et* ij quart*eronis* casei uend*itis*. Et de ij s. viij d. de butir*o* uend*ito* et de xij d. de Gunnilda p*ro* tab*er*na p*er* annu*m* et de vj d. de Agnet*e* p*ro* tab*er*na p*er* dim*idium* annu*m* et de xvij d. de pastura locata et de ij s. vj d. de mesuagio Rob*erti* Cauwe locato h*oc* anno et de ij s.

vj d. de mesuagio Rog*eri* Coye locato h*oc* anno et de ij s. vj d. de mesuagio Osm*undi* locato h*oc* anno. Et de ij s. vj d. de mesuagio Rel*ict*e Will*elm*i long' locato h*oc* anno *et* de vj d. de j p*ar*ua acra locata h*oc* anno sic*ut* iacet et de iiij s. vj d. de nucib*us* colligend*is* et de xij d. de quodam fusto st*rat*o p*er* uentu*m*. Su*mm*a xxxvj li. iij s. vij d. ob.

Blad*um* uend*itum*. Idem Reddunt Compotum de xviij li. xvj s. vj d. de iiij^{xx} xviij quart*eriis* dim*idio* ij bussell*is* frum*en*ti uenditi et de xiiij s. v d. de v q*uarteriis* ij buss*ellis* de curall fr*umento* uend*ito* et de viij li. xv s. vj d. ob. de lxxj q*uarteriis* de mancor*no* vend*ito* et de x li. x s. ij d. de lxxiiij quart*eriis* dim*idio* ord*ei* uend*iti* et de ix li. xviij s. v d. ob. de c vj q*uarteriis* ij buss*ellis* auen*arum* uend*itarum* et de xiij d. ob. de iij buss*ellis* fabar*um* uend*itarum* et de iiij s. xj d. ob. de ij quart*eriis* j buss*ello* pisaru*m* uend*itarum* et de iij s. vj d. de j quart*erio* vj buss*ellis* de uesc*ia* uend*itis*. Su*mm*a xlix li. iiij s. viij d.

Purch*asia*. Idem Reddu*n*t Compotu*m* de vj s. viij d. hundr*edi* p*ro* occ*asion*e Relax*ata et* de xiij s. iiij d. de Will*elmo* p*re*po*sito* p*ro* filio suo t*er*ram et vxore*m* Recept*o* et de v s. de alicia uidua p*ro* filia sua maritand*a* et de vj s. viij d. de Will*elmo* filio Rob*erti* p*ro* fine t*er*re et de vj s. viij d. de Rob*erto* st*ro*nge p*ro* simili et de xij d. de Ric*ardo* dun p*ro* pleuina et de vj d. de Rand*olpho* dun p*ro* simili et de vj d. de steph*ano* filio Rand*olphi* p*ro* agn*is* male retent*is* et de vj d. de Rob*erto* milit*e* p*ro* pastura et de vj d. de H*en*ric*o* bouar*io* p*ro* melle*a* et de vj d. de Sym*one* de Wudecote p*ro* pleuina et de xij d. de ywon*e* messo*re* p*ro* op*er*e Rob*erti* vggel et de xij d. de Ric*ardo* p*ro* simili et de ij s. de Rob*erto* vggel p*ro* op*er*e relax*ato* int*er* festu*m* s*anc*ti mich*aelis et* hockeday et de vj d. de Ada et Will*elmo* de Wordie p*ro* custodia ij pullor*um* et de vj d. de Will*elmo* fil*io* Ren*er* p*ro* del*ict*o spinar*um* et de vj d. de Nich*olao* fil*io* Joh*annis* p*ro* del*ict*o bosci et de vj d. de ywon*e* blundo p*ro* simili et de xij d. de Rog*ero* cupping p*ro* simili et de vj d. ywon*e* palm*er* p*ro* pastura et de vj d. de Nich*olao* de puteo p*ro* del*ict*o bosci et de xij d. de Rog*ero* filio Hug*onis* p*ro* h*er*ciatura. Et de vj s. viij d. de Hundr*edo* p*ro* occ*asion*e relax*ata* et de iij s. de lucia uidua p*ro* se mar*itanda* ext*ra* t*er*ram epi*scopi* et de vj d. de Will*elmo* bele p*ro* del*ict*o pleuin*e* et de vj d. de ywon*e* paum*er* p*ro* simili et de vj d. de ywon*e* m*er*sir p*ro* simili *et* de vj d. de Will*elmo* fil*io* odon*is* p*ro* garb*is* stulte capt*is* et de vj d. de Rob*erto* milite p*ro* del*ict*o arure et de vj d. de Waut*er* caruc*ario* p*ro* ferr*amentis* equi retent*is* et de vj d. de Joh*anne* caruc*ario* p*ro* past*ur*a et de xij d. de Rel*ict*a Rand*olphi* p*ro* sim*i*li et de xij d. de Odine p*ro* mala tons*ione* et de vj d. de Joh*anne* caruc*ario* p*ro* op*er*e co*n*celato et de vj d. de alano car*ucario* p*ro* simili et de vj d. de Alexand*ro* p*ro* simili et de vj d. de Waut*er* p*ro* simili et de vj d. de Rog*ero* cupping p*ro* delicto pasture et de vj d. de albrea de Wudecote p*ro* simili et de vj d. de Will*elmo* cupping p*ro* lepore capt*o* in Warenn*a* et de vj d. de rel*ict*a Rand*olphi* p*ro* simili et de vj s. viij d. de yuon*e* blundo p*ro* sorore sua mar*itanda* ext*ra* t*er*ram epis*copi* et de vj s. viij d. de Will*elmo* b*er*car*io* p*ro* se ip*so* mar*itando* et de xij d. de quodam ext*ra*neo p*ro* del*ict*o garbe et de vj d. de thoma papa p*ro* pastura et de vj d. de ywon*e* palm*er* p*ro* fimo iniuste collecta et de vj d. de Ren*er* maiore p*ro* mell*ea* et de vj d. de alb*rea* de Wudecote p*ro* del*icto* op*er*is et de vj d. de Rob*erto* st*ro*nge p*ro* past*ura* et de xij d. de osm*undo* p*ro* blado dat*o* equo et de vj d. de steph*ano* beste p*ro* op*er*e d*omi*ni desp*i*cat*o*. Su*mma* iiij li. viij s. iiij d. Su*mma* Tocius Recepte iiij^{xx} xix li. vj s. v d. ob. In lib*eratis* D*omi*no R*oberto* de clunapp' lxix li. xvij s. iij d. p*er* j t*alliam*.

Exp*ensa*. In feram*en*to iiij caruc*arum* p*er* annu*m* et j caruc*e* p*er* xvij sept*imanas* et in ferr*amento* xj auer*orum* p*er* annu*m* xiij s. ij d. ob. In ij parib*us* rotaru*m* ad carucas vj d. ob. In vj caruc*is* de nouo faciend*is* xj d. In j biga f*ra*cta rep*a*rand*a* et axand*a* sepi*us* p*er* annu*m* et in clut*is* ferr*i* et in clau*is et* in uncto ad eand*em* p*er* annu*m* xj d. In vno panell*o* et j coll*ar*i et in ij bac*is* et in una sella ad bigam et in uno paron*o* xiij d. et in decem capist*ris* de pilo auer*is* faciend*is* ij d. In feno falcando scil*icet* ix falcatorib*us* h*oc* anno p*er* ij dies p*ro* cibo et m*er*cede vj s. singulus iiij d. p*er* diem p*ro*pt*er* difficultate*m* falcand*i*. In vij op*er*ar*iis* locat*is* ad fenu*m* spargendu*m* quia op*er*arii colleg*er*unt stipulam p*er* j diem v d. q. s*cilicet* singul*us* p*er* diem iij q. In vj bob*us* e*m*pt*is* l s. viij d. in xx porc*is* e*m*pt*is* p*er* sen*escallum* xxxvij s. vj d. ob. sing*ulus* xxij d. ob. In uno hostio de nouo faciend*o* ad g*ra*ngiam et in hostio aule rep*a*rand*o* et in ij port*is* rep*a*rand*is* de parco xij d. ob. in g*ra*ngiis et aula et bouar*ia* et b*er*car*ia* p*er* tempestate*m* f*ra*ct*is* cooperand*is* iiij s. vij d. In ser*is* ad daeriam et g*ra*ngiam iij d. ob. In clat*is* ad fald*am* faciend*am* xx d. In iiij cord*is* et in uno vt*re* ad puteu*m* e*m*pt*is* vj d. ob. In p*re*car*iis* arure in *quadragesima* s*cilicet* de x caruc*ariis* dim*idio* x d. ob. et xlij acr*is* sicut iacent arantur p*ro* h*er*bag*io* de xxviij bob*us* p*er* h*omi*nes uille s*cilicet* p*ro* quolib*et* bou*e* j acr*a* dim*idia*. In xx *quarteriis* dim*idio* frum*en*ti e*m*pt*is* ad seme*n* lxvj s. ij d. In xxj q*uarteriis* dim*idio* de mancor*no* e*m*pt*is* ad seme*n* xliiij s. vij d. In j q*uarterio* ord*ei* e*m*pt*o* ij s. in iij q*uarteriis* iij buss*ellis* auen*arum* e*m*pt*is* iiij s. vij d. In blado sarcland*o* v s. vj d. In lxvj q*uarteriis* dim*idio* frum*enti* et v q*uarteriis* de currall fr*umento* t*ri*turand*is* et uent*ilandis* xj s. xj d. sing*ulus* ij d. In xxix q*uarteriis* de mancor*no* t*ri*turand*is* et uent*ilandis* ij s. v d. singulus j d. In xlvij q*uarteriis* dim*idio* ord*ei* t*ri*turand*is* et uent*ilandis* iij s. xj d. ob. In v sacc*is* e*m*pt*is* ad bladu*m* xvj d. In custo Daerie s*cilicet* sale p*ri*sur*a* oll*is* uasis et aliis necc*essariis* vj s. iiij d. In exp*ensa* fr*atr*is Will*elm*i uisitat*i* ou*es* et Will*elmi* cl*er*ici et Ric*ardi* Wautehus' qui affuerunt ad uidendu*m* bladu*m* in g*ra*ngiis xviij d. ob. In xxvj ulnis de canabo e*m*pt*is* ad lanam saccand*am* iiij s. iiij d. et p*ro* lana saccand*a* et filo vij d. In M allec*ium* e*m*pt*is* ad ij p*re*car*ia* autu*m*pni iiij s. ij d. ob.

quia non habuerunt aliud companagium. In blado ligando et deligando et siccando in tempore pluios' scilicet lxviij acre ij s. v d. hoc anno. In stipendio duorum carucariorum per annum vj s. In stipendio ij carucariorum per xvij septimanas xviij d. In stipendio j caretarii per annum iij s. In stipendio j messoris per annum iij s. In stipendio Daie a purificatione usque ad festum sancti michaelis ij s. In expensa senescalli iiij s. ix d. In liberatione Willelmi seruientis per annum lx s. x d. Summa xviij li. iij s. v d. q. Summa liberationis et Expensarum iiij^{xx} viij li. viij d. q. Et Debet xj li. v s. ix d. q. vnde posuit In semine in xix quarteriis dimidio frumenti c s. xj d. Et In xvij quarteriis dimidio mancorni emptis ad semen lj s. vij d. ob. Et ad huc habent emere semen.

Exitus grangie.   Idem Reddunt Compotum de iiij^{xx} xviij quarteriis dimidio ij bussellis de toto exitu frumenti. Et de xx quarteriis dimidio postea emptis. Summa c xix quarteria ij busselli. In semine lxviij acrarum dimidia mensuratis per perticam xx quarteria dimidium vnde vj acre dimidia iacent in campo qui uocatur northbery et xvj acre iacent in campo qui dicitur bassumliforlang et xlvj acre iacent in campo de Westgarstun. In suprauenditis iiij^{xx} xviij quarteria dimidium ij busselli. Idem Reddunt compotum de v quarteriis ij bussellis de toto exitu curall' frumenti. In suprauenditis totum. Idem Reddunt Compotum de lxxj quarteriis de toto exitu mestiliorum et de xxj quarteriis dimidio postea emptis. Summa iiij^{xx} xij quarteria dimidium. In semine liiij acrarum dimidia ij uirgis mensuratis per perticam xxj quarteria dimidium vnde xxxiij acre iacent in beriforlang et in middelforland et iiij in bassumliforland et in campo de sturte viij acre dimidia. Et in huldelande ix acre ij uirge. In suprauenditis lxxj quarteria. Idem Reddunt compotum de c iiij^{xx} j quarteriis dimidio de toto exitu ordei et de j quarterio postea empto. Summa c iiij^{xx} ij quarteria dimidium. In semine iiij^{xx} ix acrarum iij perticis xliij quarteria dimidium vnde xlv acre iacent in haseleforland et ewedelforland et xliiij acre iij pertice in danstanfurland et in yurchenefurland. In Conredio vnius caretarii per annum vj quarteria dimidium. In conredio duorum carucariorum per annum xiij quarteria. Et In conredio ij carucariorum per xvij septimanas iiij quarteria ij busselli. Et In conredio j messoris per annum vj quarteria dimidium et j Daie a festo purificationis usque ad festum sancti Michaelis iij quarteria ij busselli. Et In conredio vnius herciatoris per xij septimanas j quarterium. In porcis et purcellis sustinendis ij quarteria. Et in tribus precariis autumpni iiij quarteria de cetero non computabuntur tot quarteria. In missis apud Wlueseiam liberatis Johanni clerico viij quarteria. Et in Elemosina episcopi precepto suo xvj quarteria. In suprauenditis lxxiiij quarteria dimidium. Idem Reddu*n*t Compotu*m* De cc lxxiiij q*uarteriis* ij buss*ellis* De toto exitu auene et de iij q*uarteriis* iij buss*ellis* p*os*t*ea* e*m*pt*is*. Su*mma* cc lxxvij q*uar*-t*eria* dim*idium* j buss*ellus*. In se*mine* c iiij^xx xiiij acr*arum* p*er* p*er*tic*am* cxxviij q*uarteria* dim*idium* vn*de* lxxvij acr*e* iacent in campo de ha*m*me *et* iux*ta* b*er*c*ariam* *et* in puteshulle l et in bassu*m*ly xxxvij et in b*ro*cfurland vj et de t*er*ra cotsetlor*um* xxiiij. In p*re*benda Will*elmi* cl*er*ici et fr*atr*is Will*elmi* iij buss*elli*. In p*re*benda xj auer*orum* in yeme xxij q*uar*-t*eria* dim*idium*. Et In bob*us* sustinendis p*er* estima*tionem* garbar*um* xx q*uarteria*. In sup*ra*uend*itis* c vj q*uarteria* ij buss*elli*. Idem Redd*unt* co*m*potu*m* de iiij buss*ellis* de toto exitu fabaru*m*. In plantat*ione* j buss*ellus*. In sup*ra*uend*itis* iij buss*elli*. Idem Reddu*n*t Comp*otum* de iij q*uarteriis* dim*idio* iij buss*ellis* de toto exitu pisaru*m*. In se*mine* v acr*arum* j q*uarterium* dim*idium* ij buss*elli* qui iacent in b*ro*cfurlang'. In sup*ra*uend*itis* ij q*uarteria* j buss*ellus*. Idem Redd*unt* co*mpotum* de iij q*uarteriis* dim*idio* de toto exitu ucsc*ie*. In se*mine* v acr*arum* dim*idia* j q*uarterium* dim*idium* ij buss*elli* qui iacent in b*ro*cfurland. In sup*ra*-uend*itis* j q*uarterium* dim*idium* ij buss*elli*.

Instauru*m*. Idem r*eddunt* co*mpotum* de x auer*iis* Rem*anentibus* ann*o* p*reterito* et de j eq*uo* de testame*n*to ywon*is* coc. Su*mma* xj. Et om*nes* Rem*anent*. Idem Redd*unt* co*mpotum* de j pullo p*ro*uento de instauro et Rem*anet*. Id*em* r*eddunt* co*mpotum* de xxxix bob*us* remanent*ibus* anno p*reterito* et de iij adiunct*is* et de vj p*os*t*ea* e*m*pt*is*. Su*mma* xlviij. In viu*is* uend*itis* vj. in mortuo j. Su*mma* vij. Et Rem*anent* xlj. Id*em* r*eddunt* co*mpotum* de vij vacc*is* Rem*anentibus* ann*o* p*reterito*. Et o*mnes* Rem*anent*. Idem r*eddunt* co*mpotum* de iij bouiculis Rem*anentibus* ann*o* p*reterito*. In adiu*n*ct*is* cu*m* bob*us* iij et nich*il* Rem*anet*. Id*em* r*eddunt* co*mpotum* de ij annalib*us* Rem*anentibus* ann*o* p*reterito* vnde alt*er* est bouicul*us* et alt*era* est juuent*a*. Et Rem*anent*. Id*em* r*eddunt* co*m*-p*otum* de iiij annalib*us* Rem*anentibus* ann*o* p*reterito* uit*ulis*. In mor-t*uis* iij. Et Rem*anet* j. Id*em* r*eddunt* co*mpotum* de v uitulis p*ro*uent*is* ex vacc*is* hoc anno q*uia* duo uacc*e* erant steriles. In decim*a* j q*uia* vij superer*ant* in ann*o* p*reterito*. In mort*uo* j et Rem*anent* iij. Id*em* r*ed*-d*unt* co*mpotum* De dc iiij^xx xij mat*ricibus* o*uibus* Rem*anentibus* ann*o* p*reterito*. Et de c lvj adiunct*is* de Instaur*o*. Su*mma* dccc xlviij. In uiu*is* uend*itis* ad festu*m* s*an*ct*i* m*ar*tini lxj. In mort*uis* an*te* p*ar*tu*m* xvij. In mort*uis* p*ost* p*ar*tu*m* *et* an*te* tons*ionem* iiij^xx x. In mort*uis* p*ost* tons*ionem* xviij. Su*mma* c iiij^xx vj. Et Rem*anent* dc lxij. Id*em* r*ed*-d*unt* co*mpotum* De cccc iiij^xx j mult*onibus* Rem*anentibus* ann*o* p*reterito* et de c liij adiu*n*ct*is*. Su*mma* dc xxxiiij. In uiuis uend*itis* ad festu*m* s*an*ct*i* m*ar*tini l. In mort*uis* an*te* tons*ionem* liij. In mort*uis* p*ost* ton-s*ionem* xvij. Su*mma* c xx. Et Rem*anent* d xiiij. Id*em* r*eddunt* co*mpo*-t*um* de ccc lxxvij hog*astris* Reman*entibus* ann*o* p*reterito* agn*is*. In mor-t*uis* an*te* tons*ionem* liiij. In mort*uis* p*ost* tons*ionem* xiiij. In adiunct*is* cum mat*ribus* c lvj. In adiunct*is* cu*m* mult*onibus* c liij. Et nich*il* Re-m*anet.* Id*em* r*eddunt* c*ompotum* de D lix agn*is* p*r*ouent*is* de mat*ribus* h*oc* anno q*uia* xvij matre*s* fuer*unt* mort*ue* an*te* p*artum* et lxj vend*itis* et xxxj stereles et xxiiij abort*e*. In decim*a* lv. In c*on*suet*udine* p*r*epo*siti* fab*ri* et iij b*er*car*iorum* v. In mort*uis* an*te* sep*ar*at*io*nem cc. In mort*uis* p*ost* sep*ar*ati*o*nem et an*te* tons*ionem* xliiij. In mort*uis* p*ost* tons*ionem* iiij. In sup*r*auend*itis* vj. Su*mma* ccc xiiij. Et Rem*anent* cc xlv. Id*em* r*eddunt* c*ompotum* de xliij porc*is* Rem*anentibus* ann*o* p*r*et*erito* et de xiiij p*r*ouent*is* de suib*us* hoc anno et de xx p*os*tea e*mpt*is*. Su*mma* lxxvij. In decima j. In c*on*suet*udine* porc*arii* j. In mort*uo* j. In missis ap*ud* Wlues*eiam* ad lardar*ium* xvj. Su*mma* xix. Et Rem*anent* lviij un*de* j est uerre*s* iiij sues xlj s*up*erannati *et* xij p*o*rcell*i*. Id*em* r*eddunt* c*ompotum* de MCC xxv uell*eribus* lane g*r*osse. In decim*a* c xxij. In c*on*suet*udine* t*r*i*um* b*er*car*iorum* *et* Daie iiij. In sup*r*auend*itis* M iiij^{xx} xix que fec*er*u*nt* cu*m* lana agn*orum* viij pond*era*. Id*em* r*eddunt* c*ompotum* de cc xlix [velleribus] [1] agn*orum*. In sup*r*auend*itis* cu*m* lan*a* ou*ium* totu*m*. [Idem reddunt compotum] [1] de ix caseis fact*is* an*te* plen*am* ablactat*io*nem et de cc xlij caseis qui incep*er*unt fi*eri* v° id*us* ap*r*ilis et desier*unt* fi*eri* Die s*an*c*t*i mich*aelis* vt*r*oq*ue* die co*m*[putato quia fece-] [1] runt binos caseos per lxviij dies . . . . [1] In decim*a* xxv. In c*on*suet*udine* p*r*epo*sit*i fab*ri* *et* duor*um* b*er*car*iorum* et Daie v. In sup*r*auend*itis* c iiij^{xx} xij qui fec*er*unt xv pond*era* dim*idium* *et* ij q*uarteronos*. . . . [1] casei qui fec*er*unt j po*ndus*. . . . [1] [Idem reddunt compotum de]. . . . [1] gall*is* de chiriset*o*. In def*ec*tu uiror*um* *et* mulier*um* h*oc* ann*o* x. Et in def*ec*tu vj cotsetlor*um* *et* t*er*re uicar*ii* xxvj. In [missis]. . . . [1] pachu' lxxj.

§§ 9. Reeve's Account, 29 Sept., 1256—28 Sept., 1257.[2]

This is a long, full, and well-paragraphed account. The arrears of last year were £22. 6s. 4d., and of this year £47. ¼d., a very large sum. Nine weys and three cloves of wool, probably 1659 pounds avoirdupois, were sold on credit to Lady Alice Hachard and Jordan le Draper. The price was £18. 4s. 7½d. or about 2⅔d. a pound.

Here we find 4d. paid for 12 sheep kept in the tenants' fold, the common fold of the village, beyond the number of 25 allowed to each of the tenants, particularly in North Crawley.

We are told that a wey (pondus) of cheese consisted of 26 cloves.

[1] MS. torn.

[2] The date given here (following Hall) may be at least a year too early. This account precedes the one following. See below, §§ 10, p. 221, n. 1.

Probably the clove was of seven pounds. If so, the wey of cheese was in Crawley the same as the wey of wool. An unusually large amount of butter was sold. Whether it was from cows' or sheeps' milk, is not stated. A small amount of honey was found and sold for 4d.

A tenant paid 6d. as annual recognition of the fact that he was the lord's man. He was probably required to make the payment for the privilege of remaining outside of the manor. The tithing paid the tithing penny, as is stated, for the occasion (or obligation of attendance), which was due at the two hundred courts and which had been commuted to a fixed sum.

The chief officials were the seneschal who made at least two visits to Cawley during the year, probably to hold the court, the bailiff, the sergeant who received 13s. 4d. for a winter toga, and the reeve. The dairymaid received 2s. a year and the hayward 3s., each with extra allowances. On three boon-days 900 herring were given to about 300 workers, including 278 men and keepers of the grain, on the occasion of the lord's reaping. That these were all tenants is impossible. Many were the children, and perhaps the wives, of the tenants. Some may have been gypsies or other wandering strangers.

We are told of eight oxen hitched to the plow. In all, there were two cart horses, eight plow horses, and thirty-nine oxen, belonging to the lord. Thirteen young pigs died of the pox.

In the expense accounts we learn of the main hall (aula, where the court was probably held), the chamber, the kitchen, and the bake-house. Probably these and other buildings and out-buildings making up the Crawley Court of the time, were located near the village church not far from the present Court.

CRAUUELEG*A* [1]

Arrer*agium*. Joh*anne*s s*er*uiens *et* yuo p*re*p*ositu*s R*eddunt* c*om*p*otum* de xxij li. vj s. iiij d. de arrer*agio* anni p*re*ter*i*t*i* vn*de* In lib*e*rat*ione* d*omi*no martino de s*anct*a cruce p*er* j tall*iam* tot*um* *et* q*u*iet*i* s*un*t.

Redd*itus*. Id*em* R*eddunt* c*om*p*otum* de xiij li. xj s. de Redd*itu* ass*iso* p*er* ann*um* in man*er*io de Craweleg*a*. Summ*a* ead*em*.

[1] MS., P. R. O., Ecclesiastical Commission, Various, 159292, memb. VI.

Quiet*ancie*. In quiet*ancia* j p*re*pos*iti* p*er* ann*um* v s. In aq*ui*et*anciis* [vj] caruc*ariorum* j fab*ri* j porcar*ii* j vaccar*ii* iij b*er*car*iorum* p*er* ann*um* xxxij s. quil*ibet* illor*um* ij s. viij d. In aq*ui*et*anciis* x op*er*ar*iorum* op*er*anc*ium* p*er* ann*um* p*er* ij dies In ebdom*ada* a fest*o* s*anct*i mich*aelis* us*que* ad autu*m*p*num* et In autu*m*pn*o* cotidie xxvj s. viij d. quil*ibet* ij s. viij d. Summ*a* aquiet*anciarum* lxiij s. viij d.

Def*ec*tus. In def*ec*tu t*er*re stronge capt*e* In d*omi*nic*um* ij s. In def*ec*tu t*er*re Will*elmi* de cur*ia* capt*e* In d*omi*nic*um* ij s. viij d. In def*ec*tu t*er*re de alebrok*e* v s. qui modo reddunt*ur* apud m*er*edun*am*. In def*ec*tu t*er*re Rob*erti* coya capt*e* In d*omi*nic*um* ij s. viij d. In def*ec*tu Rob*er*t*i* coche capt*e* In d*omi*nic*um* ij s. viij d. In def*ec*tu t*er*re Rog*er*i porcar*ii* tract*e* in d*omi*nic*um* ij s. viij d. In def*ec*tu t*er*re Ric*ardi* vaccar*ii* capt*e* In d*omi*nic*um* ij s. viij d. Summ*a* def*ectuum* xx s. iiij d. Summ*a* quiet*anciarum et* def*ec*tu*u*m iiij li. iiij s. Summ*a* Remanens ix li. vij s.

Exit*us* man*er*ii. Id*em* R*eddunt* co*m*p*otum* de viij s. viij d. de pannag*io* porcor*um* ad fest*um* s*anct*i martini. Et de xxx s. viij d. de h*er*bag*io* xliiij vacc*arum* xv bouett*orum* xviij annal*ium* xxiij vitul*orum* n*on* junct*orum* ad caruc*am* videl*icet* de q*ualibet* vacc*a* vj d. de q*uolibet* bouett*o* iij ann*orum* iij d. de q*uolibet* annal*i* ij d. de q*uolibet* vitul*o* j d. *unius* anni siu*e* dimid*ii* anni *et* no*n* plus q*uia* viij bou*es* fu*eru*nt junct*i* ad caruc*am et* d*omi*n*u*s h*ab*uit de tremeys*io* de quol*ibet* boue junct*o* ad caruc*am* arur*am* j acr*e et* dimid*ie*. Et de iiij d. de xij bident*ibus* Inuent*is* In fald*a* homin*u*m ult*ra* xxv s*cilicet* p*ro* iij bident*ibus* j d. Et de ij s. j d. de h*er*bag*io* c agn*orum* ad festum s*anct*i Joh*annis* bapt*iste* videl*icet* p*ro* iiij agn*is* j d. Et de ij s. vj d. de pastur*a* h*oc* ann*o* locat*a*. Et de xiij s. de ij affr*is* vend*itis*. Et de ij s. viij d. de j pullan*o* vend*ito*. Et de xlviij s. de vj bob*us* vet*er*ib*us* vend*itis* vn*de* iij bou*es* vendeb*antur* quil*ibet* p*ro* viij s. *et* ij ut*er*q*ue* p*ro* vij s. vj d. Et j bos p*ro* ix s. Et de xxiij s. x d. de iiij vacc*is* vet*er*ib*us* vend*itis* vnde iij vacce q*ualibet* vendeb*atur* p*ro* vj s. et j pro v s. x d. Et de viij s. de j taur*o* vend*ito*. Et de iiij s. de j bouic*u*lo vend*ito*. Et de vj li. xiij s. iiij d. de c l mult*onibus* In fest*o* s*anct*i martini vend*itis* p*recium* cui*us*l*ibet* viij d. Et de v s. de xv agnis ser*o* nat*is* vend*itis*. Et de ij s. j d. de cor*io* j bouis mort*ui* de mor*ina* vend*ito*. Et de vij d. de lxxiij pell*ibus* pellut*is* mult*onum* ouiu*m* mat*ricium et* hogg*astrorum* mort*uorum* de mor*ina* an*te* tons*ionem* vend*itis*. Et de xij d. de xvj pell*ibus* multon*um et* mat*ricium* ou*ium* mort*uorum* de mor*ina* stati*m* post tons*ionem* vend*itis*. Et de xiij s. x d. de cc xxj pell*ibus* agn*orum* mor*tuorum* de mor*ina* an*te* sep*ar*ac*io*nem vend*itis*. Et de ij d. ob. de ix pell*ibus* rottor*um* mor*tuorum* de mor*ina* vend*itis*. Et de xviij li. iiij s. vij d. ob. de ix pond*eribus* iij clau*is* lane gross*e* vend*itis* p*recium* pond*eris* xl s. Et de xxv s. viij d. de xiij pett*ris* lan*e* agn*ine* vend*itis* p*recium* petr*e* xxij d. Et de x s. de x pet*ri*s lok*o*-

rum lane vend*itis*. Et de ij s. vj d. de xxvj cas*eis* de Rewaynn' vend*itis*
qui fec*er*unt vj clau*os*. Et de ix li. iiij s. x d. de xx pond*eribus* dim*idio*
cas*eorum* vend*itis* pr*ecium* pond*eris* ix s. *et* ponder*antur* p*er* xxvj clau*os*.
Et de x s. de j pond*ere* viij clau*is* dim*idio* butyri vend*itis*. Et de vij s.
v d. de iiij*ˣˣ* ix gall*inis* de c*onsuetudine* vend*itis*. Et de xij d. de quod*am*
curtillag*io* q*uod* q*uon*dam fuit Roger*i* porcar*ii* cu*m* dimid*ia* acr*a* locat*o*
hoc ann*o*. Et de xviij d. de q*uodam* curtill*agio* q*uod* q*uon*dam fuit
Robert*i* casye. Et de ij s. de arr*er*ag*io* eiusd*em* curtill*agii* de ij ann*is*
pr*oximo* pret*er*it*is*. Et de x s. vj d. de xxj acr*is* locat*is* hoc ann*o* que
sup*er*ius c*om*putant*ur* In def*ec*tu. Et de ij s. de ij tab*er*nis. Et de ij s.
ij d. ob. de xiij eschinis porc*orum* vend*itis* vnd*e* le ix pr*ecium* c*uius*l*ibet*
ij d. ob. *et* le iiij quil*ibet* j d. q*uia* lepr*os*i. Et de ij s. viij d. ob. de xiij
exit*ibus* porc*orum* vend*itis* pr*o* quol*ibet* ij d. ob. Et de ij s. de ij pet*ris*
vnct*i* porc*orum* vend*itis*. Et de xxxij s. viij d. de xiiij bacon*ibus* vend*i-*
tis pr*ecium* bacon*is* ij s. iiij d. Et de iiij d. de melle Inuen*to* vend*ito*.
Et hoc ann*o* n*on* R*esp*ond*ent* de op*er*ac*io*ne relax*ata* prop*ter* temp*us* in
autu*m*pn*o*. Summ*a* lj li. xj s.

R*ecognitio*. Id*em* R*eddunt* c*om*potum de vj d. de Rob*er*t*o* cupping'
pr*o* annua r*ecog*nit*io*ne. Summ*a* vj d.

Fr*umentum* vend*itum*. Id*em* R*eddunt* c*om*potum de xiiij li. vij s. x d.
de xxxviij q*uarteriis* j b*us*s*ello* frum*en*ti vnd*e* xj q*uarteria* pr*ecium*
q*uart*erii vj s. viij d. *et* v q*uarteria* pr*ecium* q*uart*erii vij s. vj d. Et
xxij q*uarteria* j b*us*s*ellus* pr*ecium* q*uart*erii viij s.

Curall*um*. Id*em* R*eddunt* c*om*potum de xxij s. vj d. de iij q*uart*eriis
iij b*us*s*ellis* curall*i* vend*itis* pr*ecium* q*uart*erii vj s. viij d.

Ord*eum* yem*ale*. Id*em* R*eddunt* c*om*potum de c xij s. iij d. de xxvj
q*uart*eriis ord*ei* yem*al*is vend*itis* vnd*e* ix q*uarteria* pr*ecium* q*uart*erii
ij s. x d. *et* xiij q*uarteria* pr*ecium* q*uart*erii iij s. j d. Et xiiij q*uarteria*
pr*ecium* q*uart*erii iij s. iiij d.

Vet*us* ord*eum*. Id*em* R*eddunt* c*om*potum de lxxix s. ix d. de xiiij
q*uart*eriis dimid*io* vet*er*is ord*ei* pr*ecium* q*uart*erii v s. vj d.

Ord*eum* Id*em* R*eddunt* c*om*potum de xxj li. xj s. de iiij*ˣˣ* ij q*uart*eriis
ord*ei* vend*itis* vnd*e* xl q*uarteria* pr*ecium* q*uart*erii v s. Et xlij q*uar-*
teria pr*ecium* q*uart*erii v s. vj d.

Auen*a*. Id*em* R*eddunt* c*om*potum de xviij li. vj s. ix d. de c xvj q*uar-*
teriis dimid*io* ij b*us*s*ellis* Auen*e* vend*itis* vnd*e* xij q*uarteria* pr*ecium*
q*uart*erii ij s. viij d. *et* xiij q*uarteria* dim*idium* pr*ecium* q*uart*erii ij s.
x d. Et xxiij q*uarteria* pr*ecium* q*uart*erii iij s. Et lxviij q*uarteria* ij
b*us*s*elli* pr*ecium* q*uart*erii iij s. iiij d.

Vesc*ia*. Id*em* R*eddunt* c*om*potum de v s. v d. de j q*uart*erio v b*us*s*ellis*
vesc*ie* vend*itis* pr*ecium* q*uart*erii iij s. iiij d. Summ*a* lxv li. v s. v d.

P*er*quisit*a*. Id*em* R*eddunt* c*om*potum de xiij s. iiij d. de ti*th*ing*a* de
crawel*ega* pr*o* occas*io*ne relax*ata* ad hundr*eda* sanc*ti* mart*ini* *et* hokeday.

Et de xij d. de symone cupping p*ro* del*icto* pastur*e*. Et de xij d. de Will*elmo* lombhurd' p*ro* simil*i*. Et de vj d. de Will*elmo* Koc p*ro* simil*i*. Et de vj d. de Gilb*erto* b*er*car*io* *et* sociis suis p*ro* t*ransgressione*. Et de ij s. de hugone de Wodecote p*ro* del*icto* past*ure*. Et de xij d. de nich*olao* p*ape*(?) p*ro* simil*i*. Et de ij s. de Will*elmo* cupping p*ro* t*ransgressione*. Et de iij s. de Will*elmo* cupping' p*ro* Inq*uisicione* h*abend*a. Et de ij s. de felicia nept*a* nich*olai* p*ape*(?) p*ro* se marit*anda*. Et de x s. de Rog*ero* fil*io* Yuonis p*ro* fine t*er*re. Et de xiij s. iiij d. de Rob*erto* fil*io* Yuonis p*ro* si*m*ili. Et de iij s. iiij d. de Joh*ann*e lambhurd' p*ro* Julian*a* fil*ia* sua mar*itanda*. Et de xiij s. iiij d. de felic*ia* fil*ia* Roger*i* pape p*ro* t*er*ra q*ue* fuit matild*e* fil*ie* steph*ani* ad op*us* Will*elmi* filii *et* h*ere*d*is* ip*s*ius matild*e* us*que* ad etate*m* sua*m* legittima*m*. Et de xij d. de symone cupping p*ro* del*icto* pastur*e*. Et de xij d. de Joh*anne* Gode p*ro* simil*i*. Et de xx s. de Rob*erto* fab*ro* p*ro* fine t*er*re. Et de vj d. de Alano pac p*ro* del*icto* pastur*e*. Et de xij d. de Will*elmo* Koc p*ro* simil*i*. Et de vj d. de Will*elmo* lomhurd' p*ro* simil*i*. Et de ij s. de Rob*erto* cupping p*ro* simil*i*. Et de vj d. de Rob*erto* strong*e* p*ro* simil*i*. Et de xij d. de Nich*olao* fil*io* odonis p*ro* simil*i*. Et de vj d. [de] pap(?) p*ro* simil*i*. Et de xij d. de eadmu*ndo* de Wodecote p*ro* simil*i*. Summ*a* iiij li. xv s. x d. Summ*a* toci*us* recept*e* c xxx li. xix s. x d.

Exp*ensa* neccess*aria*. In ferro *et* ascer*o* emp*tis* ad iiij caruc*as* p*er* ann*um* *et* ad j caruc*am* t*em*p*ore* seme*nt*is ordei *et* auene v s. *et* Rem*anet* j gadd'. In ij vom*er*ib*us* emp*tis* xiiij d. In eisd*em* attorniand*is* ij d. In xij long*is* ferr*is* empt*is* ad caruc*as* ij s. x d. ob. Et Rem*anent* vj long*a* ferr*a*. In ij p*aribus* rot*arum* emp*tis* ad caruc*as* vj d. In j noua caruc*a* ferr*o* lig*ata* j d. In ferr*amentis* viij affr*orum* p*er* ann*um* ij s. v d. In p*recio* ix caruc*ariorum* q*ui* araue*r*unt ix acr*as* ix d. In ij bob*us* emp*tis* xvj s. vj d. In stip*end*i*is* ij caruc*ariorum* p*er* ann*um* vj s. In vj capist*ris* de p*ro*p*rio* pilo fac*tis* j d. ob. Summ*a* xxxv s. vij d.

Expens*a* carett*arum*. Id*em* R*eddunt* co*mpotum* de j par*i* Rot*arum* emp*to* ad carett*am* xxij d. ob. In d*ic*t*is* Rot*is* cu*m* vet*er*i ligatur*a* lig*atis* cu*m* clau*is* ad id*em* *et* cu*m* stipend*io* fab*ri* xxiij d. ob. In ferr*amentis* ij eq*uorum* carett*ariorum* p*er* ann*um* ij s. iiij d. In carett*is* emend*is* p*er* annu*m* v d. In carett*is* axand*is* iij d. In clut*is* clauis emp*tis* ad carett*as* vij d. In ij colar*ibus* emp*tis* xij d. In j sell*a* emp*ta* iij d. In h*a*rnas*io* emend*o* cu*m* albo cor*io* iiij d. In stip*end*i*o* j carett*arii* p*er* ann*um* iij s. In ij capist*r*is de p*ro*p*ri*o pil*o* fac*tis* ob. In j trubla ferr*o* ligand*a* j d. Summ*a* xij s. j d. ob.

Expens*a* daer*ie*. In ij q*uarteriis* sal*is* *et* vj b*ussellis* emp*tis* ad saland*a* xxij pond*era* dimid*ium* cas*ei* ij s. ix d. In linea tela emp*ta* ad daer*iam* vij d. ob. In p*ressur*a emp*ta* vj d. In oll*is* empt*is* iiij d. In vtens*iliis* daer*ie* emend*is* ij d. ob. In j tina emp*ta* iij d. ob. In stip*end*i*o* daye p*er* annu*m* ij s. Summ*a* vj s. viij d. ob.

Expens*a* Necc*essar*ia. In Grang*ia* coop*er*iend*a et* emend*a* p*er* loca iij s. iiij d. In aula cam*er*a coq*ui*na coop*er*iend*is et* emend*is* ij s. In j ser*rura* emp*ta* ad hostiu*m* Granar*ii* ij d. ob. In j b*er*car*ia* coop*er*iend*a et* eme*n*d*a* iij d. In xviij clatis ad fald*am* fac*tis et* virg*is* ad id*em* colli-g*endis* iiij d. ob. In fen*o* emp*to* ad oue*s* sustinend*as* in yem*e* xv s. In c lvj acr*is* bladi sarcland*is* ad tasch*am* iiij s. iiij d. videl*icet* iij acr*e* sic*ut* jacent j d. In j bukett*o* emp*to* ad puteu*m* iij d. In xij ulnis de canab*o* emp*tis* ad sacc*os* blad*i* ij s. In xxxij uln*is* de canabo emp*tis* ad ix pon-d*era* iij cl*avos* lan*e* gross*e* iiij s. vij d. In fil*o* ad id*em* j d. In ead*em* lan*a* saccand*a et* pond*er*and*a* ix d. In stipend*io* j hayward*i* p*er* ann*um* iij s. In exp*ensa* duor*um* G*arcionum et* oliu*er*i(?) sen*escalli* p*er* om*n*es suos aduent*us et* p*er* iij tall*ias* xv s. iij d. In exp*ens*is seruicnt*is* p*er* ann*um* lx s. x d. amodo paria*ntur* exp*ense* sen*escalli et* lib*er*ac*io* ball*ivi*. In fine om*n*ium expens*arum*. Summ*a* c xij s. iij d.

Bect*aria*.[1] In viij q*uarteriis* frum*en*ti t*r*itur*andis et* vent*ilandis* ad tasch*am* xviij d. *et* op*er*ar*ii* t*r*itur*averunt* xl q*uarteria* di*midium*. In xxxj q*uarteriis* ord*ei* yem*alis* t*r*itur*andis et* vent*ilandis* ad tasch*am* iij s. ij d. ob. q. p*ro* q*uolibet* sext*ario* v d. In lxv q*uarteriis* di*midio* ordei t*r*itu-r*andis et* vent*ilandis* ad tasch*am* vj s. x d. p*ro* q*uolibet* sext*ar*io v d. *et* op*er*ar*ii* t*r*itur*averunt* c q*uarteria*. In l q*uarteriis* aucn*e* t*r*itur*andis et* vent*ilandis* ad tasch*am* iij s. j d. ob. p*ro* q*uolibet* sext*ar*io iij d. Et op*er*ar*ii* t*r*itur*averunt* c lx q*uarteria*. Summ*a* xiiij s. viij d. q.

Expens*a* autu*m*pn*alia*. In dcccc all*eciis* emp*tis* ad iij p*r*ecar*ias* au-tu*m*pn*ales* de cc lxxviij homi*n*i*bus* cu*m* custod*ibus* blad*i* metend*is* c xij acr*as* p*er* pertic*am* iiij s. Summ*a* iiij s.

Exp*ensa* forinseca. Id*em* R*eddunt* co*mpotum* In nouo furno leuand*o et* domu ult*ra* furnu*m* facie*n*d*a* de nou*o* xxiij d. Summ*a* xxiij d.

Expens*a* forinseca. In vj vacc*is* emp*tis* xliij s. vn*de* iiij vacc*e* eme-ba*ntur* p*ro* xxviij s. Et j vacc*a* p*ro* viij s. iiij d. Et j p*ro* vj s. viij d. In lxxiij pell*ibus* piland*is* vij d. In dimid*io* q*uarterio* sal*is* emp*to* ad salan-d*os* xiiij bac*ones* vij d. ob. In lard*ario* fac*iendo* iiij d. ob. In lib*eratis* s*er*uienti p*ro* Roba yemali xiij s. iiij d. Summ*a* lxvij s. xj d. Summ*a* toti*us* expens*e* xij li. v s. ij d. q.

Lib*er*at*io*. In lib*er*ati*one* Do*mi*no Walt*ero* de brich' thes*aurario* Wulues*eie* p*er* j tall*iam* liij li. x s. Summ*a* lib*er*ac*io*nis et expens*e* lxv li. xv s. ij d. ob. q. Et deb*en*t lxv li. iiij s. vij d. ob. q. vn*de* xviij li. iiij s. vij d. ob. sunt sup*er* d*omi*nam Alic*iam* hachard' *et* Jord*anum* le Draper de ix pond*eribus* iij clau*is* lane eis vend*itis*. Et debet de clar*o* xlvij li. q.

Exit*us* g*rangie*. fr*umentum*. Id*em* R*eddunt* co*mpotum* de lij q*uar*-t*eriis* j b*ussello* de tot*o* exit*u* fr*umenti* vn*de* In semi*ne* lvj acr*arum* p*er*

[1] Bateria, beating or threshing.

per*ticam* In hoa *et* In haselforlong' *et* In norbury xiiij q*uarteria*. In suprauend*itis* xxxviij q*uarteria* j b*ussellus*.

Curall*um*. Ide*m* R*eddunt* co*mpotum* de iij q*uarteriis* iij b*ussellis* de tot*o* exit*u* curall*i* vn*de* In sup*r*auend*itis* iij q*uarteria* iij b*usselli*.

Ord*eum* yemal*e*. Id*em* R*eddunt* co*mpotum* de xxxvj q*uarteriis* de tot*o* exit*u* ord*e*i yemal*is* vn*de* In sup*r*auend*itis* xxvj q*uarteria et* eq*ui*.

Ord*eum* vet*us*. Id*em* R*eddunt* co*mpotum* de xiiij q*uarteriis* dimid*io* de tot*o* exit*u* vet*er*is ord*e*i rem*anentibus* ann*o* p*reterito* p*er* estima-c*ionem* in tass*is* vn*de*. In sup*r*auend*itis* xiiij q*uarteria* dimid*ium et* eq*ui*.

Ord*eum* nouu*m*. Id*em* R*eddunt* co*mpotum* de c lxxv q*uarteriis* ij b*ussellis* de tot*o* exit*u* ord*e*i vn*de* In sem*i*n*e* c xvj acr*arum* p*er* p*er*tic*am* In langlond' *et* Ewedelforlong lviij q*uarteria*. In lib*eratione* j carett*arii* j mess*oris* ij caruc*ariorum* p*er* annu*m* xxvj q*uarteria* p*er* viij sept*i*-*manas* q*uilibet* p*er*cip*it* q*uarterium*. In lib*eratione* j daye a fest*o* s*anct*i mich*aelis* us*que* ad purificac*io*nem b*eat*e mar*ie* di*midium* q*uarterium*. In lib*eratione* ei*us*de*m* daye a p*u*rificac*ione* us*que* ad fest*um* s*anct*i mich*aelis* iij q*uarteria* ij b*usselli*. In porc*is* sustinend*is et* porcell*is* In yeme ij q*uarteria*. In m*er*cede j h*er*ciator*is* ad seme*n* auen*e et* ord*e*i dimid*ium* q*uarterium*. In iij p*recariis* autu*mpnalibus* de cc lxxviij ho*minibus* cu*m* custod*ibus* blad*i* metend*is* c xij acr*as* fr*umenti* ord*e*i *et* auen*e* p*er* p*er*tic*am* iij q*uarteria*. In sup*r*auend*itis* iiij^{xx} ij q*uarteria*.

Auen*a*. Id*em* R*eddunt* co*mpotum* de cc lxj q*uarteriis* dimid*io* de tot*o* exit*u* auen*e* vn*de* In se*mi*n*e* c lx acr*arum* p*er* p*er*tic*am*. In putteshull' *et* tr*i*ndly *et* basmeli c q*uarteria* ij b*usselli*. In p*rebenda* ij eq*uorum* carett*ariorum* p*er* ann*um* xiij q*uarteria* ij b*usselli*. In p*rebenda* viij affr*orum* a nat*ali* d*omi*ni us*que* ad Inue*ntionem* s*anct*e cruc*is* ix q*uar*-*teria* ij b*usselli*. In xl bob*us* sustinend*is* p*er* estim*ationem* garb*arum* a nath*ali* d*omi*ni us*que* ad Inuenc*ionem* s*anct*e cruc*is* xxj q*uarteria*. In p*rebenda* eq*uorum* d*omi*ni sen*escalli* p*er* ij aduent*us* suos p*er* ij tall*ias* j q*uarterium*. In sup*r*auend*itis* c xvj q*uarteria* dimid*ium* ij b*usselli*.

vesc*ie*. Id*em* R*eddunt* co*mpotum* de ij q*uarteriis* de tot*o* exit*u* vesci-*arum* q*uia* eq*ui* carett*arii* pasceb*ant* fruct*um* j acr*e et* dimid*ie* vn*de* In se*mi*n*e* j acr*e et* di*midie* iij b*usselli*. In sup*r*auend*itis* j q*uarterium* dimid*ium* j b*ussellus et* eq*ui*.

Instaur*um*. Id*em* R*eddunt* co*mpotum* de ij equis rem*anentibus* ann*o* p*reterito*. Et Rem*anent* ij equi carett*arii*.

Affr*i*. Id*em* R*eddunt* co*mpotum* de viij affr*is* rem*anentibus* ann*o* p*re*-*terito*. Et de j p*r*ouent*o* de h*er*iett*o* Rob*er*t*i* filii p*re*pos*iti*. Et de j emp*to*. S*umma* x affr*i* vn*de* in sup*r*auend*itis* ij affr*i*. S*umma* ij. Et Rem*anent* viij aff*ri*.

Pullan*us*. Id*em* R*eddunt* co*mpotum* de j pullan*o* rem*anente* ann*o* p*reterito* ex etate j anni. In sup*r*auend*ito* j pullan*us*. Et n*ichil* Rem*anet*.

Boues. Id*em* R*eddunt* *compotum* de xli bo*bus* rem*anentibus* ann*o* p*re*t*erito*. Et de iij adiunct*is* *et* de ij emp*tis*. *Summa* xlvj vn*de* In mor*ina* j. In sup*ra*uend*itis* vj. *Summa* vij. Et Rem*anent* xxxix boues.

Taur*i*. Id*em* R*eddunt* *compotum* de ij taur*is* rem*anentibus* ann*o* p*re*t*erito*. In sup*ra*uend*ito* j. Et Rem*anet* j taur*us*.

vacce. Id*em* R*eddunt* *compotum* de xvij vacc*is* rem*anentibus* ann*o* p*re*t*erito*. Et de ij adiunct*is*. Et de vj emp*tis*. *Summa* xxv vn*de* In sup*ra*uend*itis* iiij. *Summa* iiij. Et Rem*anent* xxj vacc*e*.

Bouett*i*. Id*em* R*eddunt* *compotum* de vj bouett*is* rem*anentibus* ann*o* p*re*t*erito* bouic*u*l*is* vn*de* In adiunct*is* bob*us* iij In adiunct*is* vacc*is* ij. In sup*ra*uend*ito* j. *Summa* vj. Et nich*il* Rem*anet*.

Bouicul*i*. Id*em* R*eddunt* *compotum* de vj bouicul*is* rem*anentibus* ann*o* p*re*t*erito* annal*ibus*. Et Rem*anent* vj bouic*u*l*i* vn*de* v sunt mascul*i*.

Annal*es*. Id*em* R*eddunt* *compotum* de vij annal*ibus* rem*anentibus* ann*o* p*re*t*erito* vitul*is*. Et Rem*anent* vij annal*es*.

vitul*i*. Id*em* R*eddunt* *compotum* de xij vitul*is* p*ro*uent*is* ex predi*ct*is vacc*is* h*oc* ann*o* q*uia* vij fu*erunt* [steriles] *et* iiij vendebant*ur* an*te* vitu*la*t*ionem* vn*de* In dec*ima* j. Et Rem*anent* xj vitul*i*.

Multon*es*. Id*em* R*eddunt* *compotum* de DC mult*onibus* rem*anentibus* ann*o* p*re*t*erito*. Et de lvj adiunct*is*. Summ*a* DC lvj vn*de* In sup*ra*uend*itis*. In fest*o* s*anc*ti martin*i* C l mult*ones*. In mor*ina* an*te* tons*i*o*nem* xix. In mor*ina* p*ost* tons*ionem* ix. *Summa* C lxxviij. Et R*emanent* CCCC lxxviij mult*ones*.

Ou*es* mat*rices*. Id*em* R*eddunt* *compotum* de DCCC xxvj ou*ibus* mat*ri*c*ibus* rem*anentibus* ann*o* p*re*t*erito*. Et de iiij^{xx} xv adiunct*is*. *Summa* DCCCC xxj [unde][1] In sup*ra*uend*itis* C in fest*o* s*anc*ti martin*i*. In mor*ina* an*te* p*a*rtu*m* x. In mor*ina* post p*a*rtu*m* *et* an*te* tons*ionem* xxij. In mor*ina* post t*onsionem* vij. *Summa* C xxxix. Et Rem*anent* DCC iiij^{xx} ij.

Hogg*astri*. Id*em* R*eddunt* *compotum* de C lxxiij hogg*astris* Rem*anentibus* [anno] p*re*t*erito* agni*s*. De q*uibus* In mor*ina* an*te* tons*ionem* xxij. In adiunct*is* mult*onibus* lvj. In adiunct*is* ou*ibus* mat*ricibus* iiij^{xx} xv. *Summa* C lxxiij. Et nich*il* R*emanet*.

Agni. Id*em* R*eddunt* *compotum* de DC iiij^{xx} iij agn*is* p*ro*uent*is* ex mat*ribus* h*oc* ann*o* q*uia* xviij fu*erunt* st*e*ril*es* *et* xv fec*er*unt aborsu*m* vn*de* In dec*ima* lxviij. In *consuetudine* j *prepositi* ij b*e*rcar*iorum* j fabri iiij. In mor*ina* an*te* sep*aracionem* CC xx. In mor*ina* p*ost* sep*aracionem* *et* an*te* tons*ionem* ix. In viu*is* vend*itis* xv. *Summa* CCC xvj. Et Re*manent* CCC lxvij agni.

lan*a* gross*a*. Id*em* R*eddunt* *compotum* de MCCC xlix vell*eribus* lan*e* gross*e* vn*de* In dec*ima* C xxxiiij. In *consuetudine* ij b*e*rcar*iorum* j daye

[1] Manuscript has exp', a mistake for unde.

iij. S*umma* c xxxvj vell*era*. Et In sup*ra*uend*itis* MCC xij vell*era* q*ue* fec*er*unt ix pond*era* iij clau*os*.

lan*a* agn*ina*. Id*em* R*eddunt* co*mpotum* de ccc lxvij vell*eribus* lane agn*ine*. In sup*ra*uend*itis* om*n*ia q*ue* fec*er*unt xiiij pett*ras*.

Porc*i*. Id*em* R*eddunt* co*mpotum* de j verre rem*anente* ann*o* p*reterito*. Et de j adiunct*o*. S*umma* ij. Et R*emanent* ij verre*s*.

Sues. Id*em* R*eddunt* co*mpotum* de iiij suib*us* rem*anentibus* ann*o* p*reterito*. Et de vij adiunct*is*. S*umma* xj vn*de* in occis*is* ad lard*arium* vij. S*umma* vij. Et Rem*anent* iiij sues.

Porc*i*. Id*em* R*eddunt* co*mpotum* de xix porc*is* mascul*is* rem*anentibus* ann*o* p*reterito*. Et de xviij adiunct*is*. Sum*ma* xxxvij. De quib*us* in occis*is* ad lard*arium* vij. S*umma* vij. Et R*emanent* xxx porc*i*.

Hogg*etti*. Id*em* R*eddunt* co*mpotum* de xxviij hogg*ettis* rem*anentibus* ann*o* p*reterito* porcell*is*. In mor*ina* ij. In adiunct*o* u*erribus* j. In adiunct*is* suib*us* vij. In adiu*n*ct*is* porc*is* mascul*is* xviij. S*umma* xxviij. Et n*ihil* R*emanent*.

Porcell*i*. Id*em* R*eddunt* co*mpotum* de xxxvij porcell*is* porcell' [sic] ex p*redict*is suib*us* h*oc* ann*o* q*uia* ij sues no*n* porcellau*eru*nt n*isi* semel vn*de* In dec*ima* iij. In mor*ina* xiij de veroll'. S*umma* xvj. Et R*emanent* xxj porcell*i* vn*de* vij fue*ru*nt porcell*i* mens*is* april*is* *et* viij fuerunt porcelli mens*is* Julii. Et vj su*n*t modo lactante*s*. Et sci*endum* q*uod* xvj su*n*t mascul*i*.

Cas*ei*. Id*em* R*eddunt* co*mpotum* de xxvj cas*eis* f*ac*tis de Rewaynn*o* h*oc* anno vn*de* In sup*ra*uend*itis* om*ne*s q*ui* fec*er*unt v clauos.

Cas*ei*. Id*em* R*eddunt* co*mpotum* de xx cas*eis* f*ac*tis an*te* ablactac*ionem*. Et de ccc iij cas*eis* qui Incep*er*u*n*t fi*eri* iiij die Idus ap*rilis* *et* desieru*n*t die s*anct*i mich*aelis* vtroq*ue* die co*mput*at*o* q*uia* fec*er*unt bin*os* cas*eos* p*er* c xxx dies. S*umma* ccc xxiij vn*de* In decim*a* xxxij. In co*nsuetudine* j p*repositi* j b*er*c*arii* j fab*ri* j daye iiij cas*ei*. In sup*ra*uend*itis* cc iiij^xx vij qui fec*er*unt xx pond*era* dimid*ium*.

Gall*ine*. Id*em* R*eddunt* co*mpotum* de c xxv Gallinis de co*nsuetudine* de Cher*iseto* vn*de* In def*ec*tu t*er*re Rob*er*t*i* stronge capt*e* In d*ominicum* iiij Gall*ine*. In def*ectu* t*er*re Will*elmi* de cur*ia* capt*e* In d*ominicum* iiij Gall*ine*. In def*ectu* t*er*re Rob*er*t*i* coya capt*e* In d*ominicum* iiij Gall*ine*. In def*ectu* t*er*re Rob*er*t*i* coche capt*e* in d*ominicum* iiij Gall*ine* p*ro* simil*i*. In def*ec*tu t*er*re Rog*eri* porcar*ii* p*ro* simil*i* iiij gall*ine*. In def*ec*tu t*er*re Ric*ardi* vaccar*ii* p*ro* simil*i* iiij Gall*ine*. In def*ec*tu t*er*re Rob*er*t*i* cawe p*ro* simil*i* iiij Gall*ine*. In def*ec*tu t*er*re Gunilde vidue ij q*uia* vidua est. In def*ec*tu t*er*re agnet*e* vidue ij q*uia* vidua est. In def*ec*tu t*er*re alani caruc*arii* ij q*uia* viduar*ius* est. S*umma* xxxvj. Et In sup*ra*uend*itis* iiij^xx ix.

Pelle*s* gross*e*. Id*em* R*eddunt* co*mpotum* de xix pell*ibus* mult*onum* mort*uorum* de mor*ina* an*te* tons*ionem*. Et de xxxij pell*ibus* ouiu*m* mat*ricium* mort*uarum* de mor*ina* an*te* tons*ionem*. Et de xxij pell*ibus* hogg*astrorum* mort*uorum* de mor*ina* an*te* tons*ionem*. *Summa* lxxiij vn*de* In sup*r*apelluc*tis* om*nes*. Id*em* R*eddunt* co*mpotum* de lxxiij pell*ibus* pelluc*tis* vnde In sup*r*auend*itis* om*nes*.

Pell*es*. Id*em* R*eddunt* co*mpotum* de ix pell*ibus* mult*onum* mort*uorum* de mor*ina* post tons*ionem*. Et de vij pell*ibus* ouiu*m* mat*ricium* mort*uarum* de mor*ina* post tons*ionem*. *Summa* xvj vnde In sup*r*auend*itis* om*nes*.

Pell*es* agn*ine*. Id*em* R*eddunt* co*mpotum* de cc xlv pell*ibus* agn*orum* mort*uorum* de mor*ina* an*te* sep*aracion*em. Et de ix pell*ibus* mort*uorum* de mor*ina* post sep*aracion*em *et* an*te* tons*ionem*. *Summa* cc liiij vn*de* In dec*ima* xxiiij. In sup*r*auend*itis* cc xxx.

Bacon*es*. Id*em* R*eddunt* co*mpotum* de xiij bacon*ibus* posit*is* In lard*ario* h*oc* ann*o* vnde In sup*r*auend*itis* om*nes*.

Eschin*es*. Id*em* R*eddunt* co*mpotum* de xiiij eschines porcor*um* vn*de* In c*onsuetudine* porcar*ii* j. In sup*r*auend*itis* xiij. Et eq*ui*.

Exit*us*. Id*em* R*eddunt* co*mpotum* de xiiij exit*ibus* porcor*um* vn*de* In c*onsuetudine* porcar*ii* j. In sup*r*auend*itis* xiij. Et eq*ui*.

Vnct*um*. Id*em* R*eddunt* co*mpotum* de vnct*o* xiiij porcor*um* vnde In sup*r*auend*ito* totu*m* qui fecit iij pet*r*as.

§§ 10. Reeve's Account, 29 Sept., 1257—28 Sept., 1258.

This account is very much like the preceding one. It is included here so as to provide a basis of comparison of details in successive years.

The same officials were responsible for this account as for the last, paid their arrears for the previous year, and incurred none for this. Probably this was due to the presence of a royal agent who collected £113. 19s. 4d., while only £21. 16s. were paid to the episcopal treasurer. The date is somewhat uncertain.[1]

The receipts this year were considerably larger than for last year. Barley alone brought £44. 19s. 8d. The cheeses, weighing about 15½ pounds apiece, were not so numerous as they would have been if the weather had not been so wet and the sheep so affected by murrain. At least a large amount of the cheese, if not all of it, must have been from sheep's milk. It is alleged that the cost of repairing the plows was high because the ground was

[1] The roll is for the eighth year of the Lord A[ylmer], elect of Winchester. It follows the document which we have printed above (in §§ 9).

so stony — hardly a sudden occurrence in any village, but possibly to be explained by the baking of the soil through drought during one of the plowing seasons.

CRAUULEGA[1]

Arreragium. Johannes seruiens et yuo prepositus Reddunt compotum de xlvij li. q. de arreragio anni preteriti vnde In liberatis domino W. de brich' thesaurario de Wulueseia per j talliam totum. Et quieti sunt.

Redditus. Idem Reddunt compotum de xiij li. xj s. de toto Redditu assiso per annum. In manerio de Crauuely. Summa eadem.

Quietancie. In acquietancia j prepositi per annum v s. In quietanciis vj carucariorum j fabri j porcarii j vaccarii iij bercariorum per annum xxxij quilibet illorum ij s. viij d. In quietanciis x operariorum operancium per annum per ij dies. In ebdomada a festo sancti michaelis usque ad autumpnum et in autumpno cotidie xxvj s. viij d. quilibet ij s. viij d. Summa lxiij s. viij d.

Defectus. In defectu terre stronge capte in dominico ij s. In defectu terre Willelmi de curia capte In dominicum ij s. viij d. In defectu terre de alebrok' v s. qui modo redduntur apud meredunam. In defectu terre Roberti coya capte In dominicum ij s. viij d. In defectu terre Roberti coche capte in dominicum ij s. viij d. In defectu terre porcarii capte in dominicum ij s. viij d. In defectu terre Ricardi vaccarii capte In dominicum ij s. viij d. Summa defectuum xx s. iiij d. Summa quietanciarum et defectuum iiij li. iiij s. Summa Remanens ix li. vij s.

Exitus manerii. Idem Reddunt compotum de ix s. viij d. de pannagio porcorum ad festum sancti martini. Et de xxxiij s. x d. de herbagio xlviij vaccarum xviij bouettorum xx annalium xxiiij vitulorum non junctorum ad carucam videlicet de qualibet vacca vj d. de quolibet bouetto iij annorum iij d. de quolibet annali ij d. de quolibet vitulo j d. j anni siue dimidii anni et non plus quia iiij boues fuerunt juncti ad carucam et dominus habuit ad tremes de quolibet boue juncto ad carucam aruram j acre et dimidie. Et de vj d. de xviij bidentibus juuentis In falda hominum ultra xxv videlicet pro iij bidentibus j d. Et de ij s. ij d. de herbagio C iiij agnorum ad festum beati Johannis baptiste videlicet pro iiij agnis j d. Et de iiij s. de pastura hoc anno locata. Et de lv s. viij d. de vij bobus veteribus In festo sancti martini venditis vnde j bos vendebatur pro xiij s. et ij boues vendebantur pro xx s. Et ij boues vendebantur pro x s. Et j bos vendebatur pro vj s. Et j bos vendebatur pro vj s. viij d. Et de xviij s. de iij vaccis venditis vnde ij vacce vendebantur utroque pro vj s. vj d. et j vacca vendebatur pro v s. Et de iij s. vj d. de iij vitulis venditis quilibet pro xiiij d. Et de xxij s. viij d. de xxiiij multonibus veteribus in festo sancti martini venditis precium

[1] MS., P. R. O., Ecclesiastical Commission, Various, 159293.

cui*us*l*ibet* viij d. Et de l s. de lxxv ou*ibus* mat*ricibus* vet*eribus* in festo s*anct*i mart*ini* vend*itis* p*recium* cui*us*l*ibet* viij d. Et de iij s. ix d. ob. de xiij agn*is* sero natis vend*itis*. Et de xvj d. de cor*io* j vitul*i* mor-t*ui* de mor*ina* vend*ito*. Et de xij d. de cor*io* j annal*is* mort*ui* de mor*ina* vend*ito*. Et de vj d. de xlvj pell*ibus* pelluc*tis* mult*onum* mat*ricium* ou*ium et* hogg*astrorum* mort*uorum* de mor*ina* an*te* tons*ionem* vend*itis*. Et de x d. de xiij pell*ibus* mult*onum et* ou*ium* mat*ricium* mort*uorum* de mor*ina* statim post tons*ionem* vend*itis*. Et de xij s. xj d. ob. de CC vij pell*ibus* agnor*um* mort*uorum* de mor*ina* an*te* sep*aracion*em vend*itis*. Et de vij d. ob. de xxix pell*ibus* rottor*um* mort*uorum* de mor*ina* ven-d*itis*. Et de xxj li. xiiij s. iiij d. de x pond*eribus* xj clau*is* lan*e* grosse vend*itis* p*recium* pond*eris* xlj s. viij d. Et de xxxij s. de xvj pet*ris* lane agnine vend*itis*. Et de xij s. de xij pet*ris* lok*orum* lane vend*itis*. Et de ij s. viij d. de xxiiij cas*eis* de Rewann*o* vend*itis* qui fec*erunt* vj clau*os*. Et de vij li. iij d. de xvj pond*eribus* dimid*io* cas*ei* vend*itis* p*recium* pond*eris* viij s. vj d. *et* ponder*antur* p*er* xxvj cl*avos*. Et de vij s. vij d. de j ponder*e* butyr*i* vend*ito*. Et de vij s. vij d. de iiij^{xx} xj gall*inis* de cons*uetudine* vend*itis*. Et de xij d. de quod*am* curtillag*io* quod q*uan*-d*am* fuit Rog*er*i porcar*ii* cu*m* dimid*ia* acr*a* locat*o* h*oc* ann*o*. Et de xviij d. de quod*am* curtill*agio* quod q*uond*a*m* fuit Rob*ert*i cawe. Et de xij s. de xxiiij acr*is* locat*is* h*oc* ann*o* q*ue* sup*er*i*us* comp*utabuntur* In def*ec*tu. Et de ij s. de ij tab*er*nis. Et de v s. vij d. ob. de xxvij eschinis porcor*um* vend*itis* p*recium* cui*us*l*ibet* ij d. ob. Et de v s. vij d. de xxvij exit*ibus* porcor*um* vend*itis* p*recium* cui*us*l*ibet* ij d. ob. Et de x s. vj d. de xj pet*ris* dimid*ia* vnct*i* porcor*um* vend*itis*. Et de lxxij s. iiij d. de xxviij baconib*us* vend*itis* p*recium* bacon*is* ij s. vij d. Et de v s. de j verr*e* vend*ito*. Et de iij d. de mell*e* vend*ito*. Et de ij s. de j carett*a* vend*ita*. Sum*ma* xlviij li. xv s. ij d. ob.

Annua recognic*io*. Id*em* R*eddunt* co*mpotum* de vj d. de Rob*erto* cupping' p*ro* annua recognic*ione*. Summ*a* vj d.

Frum*entum* vend*itum*. Id*em* R*eddunt* co*mpotum* de xxiij li. xix d. de liiij q*uarteriis* ij b*ussellis* frum*en*ti vend*itis* vnde v q*uarteria* p*recium* q*uarterii* vj s. viij d. *et* ij q*uarteria* p*recium* q*uarterii* vij s. vj d. *et* xiiij q*uarteria* p*recium* q*uarterii* viij s. Et xxix q*uarteria* ij b*usselli* p*recium* q*uarterii* ix s. *et* iiij q*uarteria* p*recium* q*uarterii* ix s. vj d.

Curall*um*. Id*em* R*eddunt* co*mpotum* de xxx s. de v q*uarteriis* curall*i* vend*itis* p*recium* q*uarterii* vj s.

Ord*eum*. Id*em* R*eddunt* co*mpotum* de xliiij li. xix s. viij d. de C lvij q*uarteriis* dimid*io* iij b*ussellis* ord*ei* vend*itis* vn*de* xiiij q*uarteria* dimi-d*ium* p*recium* q*uarterii* v s. Et xij q*uarteria* p*recium* q*uarterii* v s. ij d. Et xxxvj q*uarteria* p*recium* q*uarterii* vj s. ij d. *et* xij q*uarteria* p*recium* q*uarterii* vj s. iiij d. *et* lxxvj q*uarteria* p*recium* q*uarterii* v s. vj d. *et* vij q*uarteria* iij b*usselli* p*recium* q*uarterii* vj s. viij d.

Auena. Id*em* R*eddunt* com*potum* de xvij li. viij s. xj d. de c xvij q*uarteriis* dimid*io* auen*e* vend*itis* vnde xij q*uarteria* p*recium* q*uarterii* ij s. iiij d. Et vj q*uarteria* p*recium* q*uarterii* ij s. vj d. Et lxxvj q*uar*-*teria* dimid*ium* p*recium* q*uarterii* iij s. *et* xvij q*uarteria* p*recium* q*uar*-*terii* iij s. j d. Et vj q*uarteria* p*recium* q*uarterii* iiij s.

Visch*ie*. Id*em* R*eddunt* com*potum* de ix d. de ij b*ussellis* vesch*iarum* vend*itis*. Summ*a* iiij^{xx} vij li. xj d.

P*er*quis*ita*. Id*em* R*eddunt* com*potum* de xiij s. iiij d. de t*it*h*inga* de craweleia p*ro* occ*as*ione relax*ata* ad hundr*edum* s*ancti* martini *et* hok-*edaye*. Et de vj d. de Nich*olao* de puteo p*ro* t*ra*nsgr*essione*. Et de xij d. de Dauid' de Wodecote p*ro* simil*i*. Et de vj d. de Rob*erto* coche p*ro* simil*i*. Et de iiij s. de symo*ne* cupping' p*ro* simil*i*. Et de xij d. de Rob*erto* stronge p*ro* simil*i*. Et de vj d. de Rog*ero* strutare p*ro* del*icto* bosci. Et de ij s. de Joh*anne* gode p*ro* del*icto* pastur*e*. Et de xij d. de symone de Wodecote p*ro* simil*i*. Et de vj d. de hug*one* de Wodecote p*ro* simil*i* t*ra*nsgr*essione*. Et de xij d. de Rob*erto* coche p*ro* del*ic*to pas-tur*e*. Et de ij s. de ad*a* brian p*ro* simil*i*. Et de xij d. de Rob*erto* caret-t*ario* pro pleuin*a*. Et de vj d. de Will*elmo* lamhurd p*ro* t*ra*nsgr*essione*. Et de vj d. de Walt*ero* coop*er*ator*e* p*ro* simil*i*. Et de vj d. de Ranulfo dou p*ro* pleuin*a*. Et de vj d. de Rog*ero* burnard' p*ro* del*icto* pastur*e*. Et de ij s. de Will*elmo* bele p*ro* matild*a* *et* Julian*a* fil*iabus* suis mari-t*andis*. Et de ij s. de Joh*anne* porcar*io* p*ro* fine t*er*re. Et de xij d. de alano pac p*ro* del*icto* pastur*e*. Et de xij d. de Gun*n*ild*a* vidua p*ro* simil*i*. Et de vj d. de Joh*anne* martin p*ro* simil*i*. Et de xij d. de Jo-h*anne* lomhurd' p*ro* mala arr*ura*. Et de vj d. de Will*elmo* fil*io* hugon*is* p*ro* del*icto* pastur*e*. Et de xij d. de steph*ano* vacc*ario* p*ro* t*ra*nsgr*es*-*sione*. Et de vj d. de Rob*erto* fab*ro* p*ro* del*icto* pastur*e*. Et de xij d. de elya ak*er*man p*ro* simil*i*. Et de xij d. de Joh*anne* martin p*ro* simil*i*. Et de xij d. de Alano pac p*ro* simil*i*. Et de xij d. de Rob*erto* stronge p*ro* simil*i*. Et de vj d. de Will*elmo* p*re*po*sito* p*ro* del*icto* bosci. Et de xij d. de Nich*olao* de puteo p*ro* del*icto* pastur*e*. Et de vj d. de matild*a* de lamara p*ro* simil*i*. Et de vj d. de Joh*anne* cok p*ro* simil*i*. Et de v s. de Will*elmo* Cupping' p*ro* plur*ibus* t*ra*nsgr*essionibus*. Et de ij s. de sy-mo*ne* cupping' p*ro* mal*a* custod*ia* bosci. Et de xij d. de dyonis*io* de somburne p*ro* del*icto* pastur*e*. Et de ij s. de Ric*ardo* cran p*ro* del*icto* bosci. Et de xij d. de Joh*anne* lamhurde p*ro* del*icto* pastur*e*. Et de ij s. de nich*olao* fil*io* odonis p*ro* Juliana fil*ia* sua mar*itanda*. Et de iiij s. de Rog*ero* marde p*ro* t*ra*nsgr*essione*. Summ*a* lxiij s. iiij d. Summ*a* tocius recept*e* c xlviij li. vj s. xj d. ob.

Expens*a* neccess*ar*ia. In ferr*o* *et* ac*er*o emp*tis* ad iiij caruc*as* p*er* ann*um* *et* ad j caruc*am* temp*ore* sem*ent*is ord*ei* *et* auen*e* vij s. h*oc* anno t*am* q*uia* t*er*ra pet*ro*sa. Et Rem*anent* ij gadd'. In ij vom*er*ib*us* emp*tis* xiiij d. In eisd*em* atornand*is* ij d. In ix long*is* ferr*is* empt*is* ad caruc*as* ij s. ij d. Et Rem*anent* vj long*a* ferr*a*. In iiij p*a*rib*us* Rotar*um* emp*tis* ad caruc*as* xiij *d*. In iij nou*is* caruc*is* ferr*o* lig*atis* iij d. In ferr*amentis* viij affr*orum* p*er* ann*um* ij s. iiij d. In p*recio* xj caruc*ariorum* q*ue* arau*erunt* xj acr*as* xj d. In stip*endiis* ij carucar*iorum* p*er* ann*um* vj s. In viij capistris de p*ro*p*rio* pil*o* fac*tis* ij d. S*umma* xxj s. iij d.

Exp*ensa* carett*e*. In j par*i* Rot*arum* ad carett*am* xxij d. In j ligatur*a* ad eand*em* emp*ta* viij s. In stip*endio* fab*ri* qui d*ic*t*a*s Rot*as* ligauit iiij d. In ferr*amentis* ij equor*um* carett*ariorum* p*er* ann*um* ij s. v d. ob. In carett*a* em*end*a p*er* ann*um* ij d. In carett*a* axand*a* ij d. In clutis cl*avis* emp*tis* ad carett*am* vj d. In j colar*e* emp*to* iiij d. ob. In j par*i* tract*uum* emp*to* iij d. In j cord*a* emp*ta* iiij d. In stip*en*d*io* j carett*arii* p*er* ann*um* iij s. Summ*a* xvij s. vj d.

Expens*a* daeri*e*. In ij q*uarteriis* sal*is* emp*tis* ad salandu*m* xviij pond*era* case*i* iiij s. In linea tela emp*ta* ad daer*iam* vj d. In p*ressura* emp*ta* vj d. In oll*a* *et* picher*a* emp*tis* iiij d. ob. In stip*endio* daye p*er* ann*um* ij s. Summ*a* vij s. iiij d. ob.

Exp*ensa* necc*essar*ia. In g*rangia* coop*er*iend*a* *et* emend*a* p*er* loca xiij d. *et* In j b*er*car*ia* largiend*a* In longitud*ine* cu*m* iiij furcis xx d. In dictam b*er*car*iam* Walland*o* ij s. ix d. In d*ic*t*am* b*er*car*iam* coop*er*iend*o* o*mn*i*n*o de nouo v s. In virg*is* ad id*em* colligend*is* *et* ad Wallur*am* ij s. In stipul*is* collig*endis* ad idem xxij d. In stipul*is* mixt*is* cu*m* feno colligend*is* ad sustent*ationem* ou*ium* xxij d. In xlij clatis ad fald*am* cu*m* virgis ad id*em* collig*endis* x d. ob. In feno emp*to* ad oues sustinend*as* in yeme xviij s. In c xx acr*is* bladi sarcland*is* ad tasch*am* iij s. iiij d. videl*icet* iij acre sicut jacent j d. In j bukett*o* emp*to* ad puteu*m* iij d. In xij ulnis de canabo emp*tis* ad sacc*os* bladi ij s. Et in xxxvj ulnis de canabo emp*tis* ad x pond*era* xj clau*os* lane gross*e* v s. iij d. In filo ad id*em* emp*to* j d. In ead*em* lana saccand*a* *et* po*nderanda* x d. In stip*en*d*io* j hayward*i* p*er* annu*m* iij s. Summ*a* xlix s. ix d. ob.

Tritur*atio*. In xx q*uarteriis* frum*en*ti t*ri*tur*andis* *et* vent*ilandis* ad tasch*am* iij s. ix d. p*ro* q*uo*l*ibet* sext*ario* ix d. *et* op*erarii* t*ri*tur*averunt* xliiij q*uarteria*. In c xvj q*uarteriis* ordei t*ri*tur*andis* *et* vent*ilandis* ad tasch*am* xij s. j d. p*ro* q*uolibet* sext*ario* v d. *et* op*erarii* t*ri*tur*averunt* c viij q*uarteria*. In xlvj q*uarteriis* auen*e* t*ri*tur*andis* *et* vent*ilandis* ad tasch*am* ij s. x d. ob. p*ro* quol*ibet* sext*ario* iij d. et op*erarii* t*ri*turau*erunt* c lxij q*uarteria*. Summ*a* xviij s. viij d. ob.

[Expensa] Autu*mp*n*alia*. In dcccc allec*iis* emp*tis* ad iij p*recarias* autu*m*pni de cc lxxviij homi*nibus* cu*m* custod*ibus* bladi metent*ibus* c viij acr*as* p*er* p*er*tic*am* iij s. iiij d. Summ*a* iij s. iiij d.

Expens*a* forins*eca*. In iij vacc*is* emp*tis* xviij s. viij d. ob. vn*de* j vacc*a* emebat*ur* p*ro* vij s. v d. Et j vacc*a* emebat*ur* p*ro* iiij s. j d. ob. In j q*uarterio* j b*ussello* sal*is* emp*tis* ad salsand*um* xxviij bacon*es* ij s. iij d. In lard*ario* fac*iendo* ix d. In xlvj pell*ibus* piland*is* iiij d. ob. In elemos*inis* d*omi*ni el*ec*t*i* p*er* p*re*cept*um* suu*m* fac*tis* a x[a] die ap*ri*l*is* us*que* ad septimu*m* diem Julii videl*icet* p*er* iiij[xx] viij dies xj s. quol*ibet* die j d. ob. In lib*eratione* seruient*is* p*er* ann*um* lx s. x d. In expens*is* sen*escalli* p*er* j tall*iam* xvj d. Summ*a* iiij li. xv s. iij d. Summ*a* tocius expens*e* x li. xiij s. ij d. ob.

Lib*eratio*. In lib*eratis* d*omi*no W. de brich' thesaur*ario* Wulues*eie* p*er* j tall*iam* xxj li. xvj s. In lib*eratis* eid*em* *et* d*omi*no W. de Insula sibi ex p*a*rte d*omi*ni Reg*is* associat*o* p*er* aliam tall*iam* c xiij li. xix s. iiij d. Summ*a* vt*r*ius*que* lib*er*ate c xxxv li. xv s. iiij d. Summ*a* tocius lib*er*at*e* *et* expens*e* c xlvj li. viij s. vj d. ob. Et sunt sup*er* d*omi*nu*m* Elec*tu*m p*ro* xij q*uarteriis* auen*e* Lib*eratis* Joh*anni* le g*ra*nt xxxvj s. Et sunt sup*er* eund*em* d*omi*nu*m* elec*tu*m p*ro* xxix Gall*inis* lib*er*at*is* philippo emptor*i* suo ij s. v d. Et sic quiet*us* est.

Exit*us* *grangie*. frum*entum*. Id*em* R*eddunt* c*om*p*otum* de lxix q*uarteriis* ij b*ussellis* de tot*o* exit*u* frum*en*ti vn*de* In semi*ne* de lxiiij acr*is* p*er* p*er*tic*am* In Danstonfurlo*n*g xv q*uarteria* In sup*ra*uend*itis* liiij q*uarteria* ij b*usselli*.

Curall*um*. Id*em* R*eddunt* c*om*p*otum* de v q*uarteriis* de tot*o* exit*u* curall*i* vnde In sup*ra*uend*itis* totu*m*.

Ord*eum*. Id*em* R*eddunt* c*om*p*otum* de cc lvij q*uarteriis* j b*ussello* de tot*o* exit*u* ordei vn*de* In semi*ne* c xxviij acr*arum* p*er* p*er*tic*am* In haselforlong'. Et In langelong' *et* In serelond' lxiiij q*uarteria*. In lib*eratis* j carett*ario* j messar*io* ij caruc*ariis* p*er* ann*um* xxvj q*uarteria* p*er* viij sept*imanas* quil*ibet* p*er*cipit q*uarterium* In lib*erata* j daye a fest*o* s*anc*t*i* mich*aelis* us*que* ad p*ur*ificat*ionem* be*ate* mar*ie* dimid*ium* q*uarterium*. In lib*erata* eiusd*em* daye a purific*ati*one us*que* ad fest*um* s*anc*t*i* mich*aelis* iij q*uarteria* ij b*usselli*. In porc*is* *et* porcell*is* sustinend*is* In hyeme ij q*uarteria*. In m*er*cede j h*er*ciator*is* ad sem*entem* auen*e* *et* ord*ei* dimid*ium* q*uarterium*. In iij p*re*car*iis* autumpnal*ibus* de cc lxxviij homin*ibus* cu*m* custod*ibus* bladi metent*ibus* c viij acr*as* p*er* p*er*tic*am* frum*enti* ord*ei* *et* auen*e* iij q*uarteria*. In sup*ra*uend*itis* clvij q*uarteria* dimid*ium* ij b*usselli*.

Auen*a*. Id*em* R*eddunt* c*om*p*otum* de cc lxiiij q*uarteriis* de tot*o* exit*u* auen*e* vnde in semi*ne* de c lxij acr*is* p*er* p*er*tic*am* in brockely *et* lonforlong' *et* In hamme c ij q*uarteria*. In p*re*b*enda* ij equoru*m* carett*ariorum* p*er* ann*um* xiij q*uarteria*. In p*re*b*enda* viij affr*orum* a natiuitat*e* d*omi*ni us*que* ad fest*um* s*anc*t*i* Joh*annis* ante porta*m* latina*m* ix q*uarteria* dimid*ium* quia tractau*er*unt multu*m* ad h*er*ciam temp*o*re sem*ent*is ord*ei*. In xxxvj bob*us* sustinend*is* p*er* estimac*ionem* Garbaru*m* a natiuit*ate* d*omi*ni us*que* ad festu*m* s*anc*t*i* Joh*annis* an*te* port*am* lat*inam* xxj q*uarteria* dimid*ium* q*uia* diu arau*er*unt ad sem*entem* ord*ei* *et* h*ab*uerunt duram t*er*ram. In p*re*b*enda* equoru*m* d*omi*ni sen*escalli* p*er* suos aduen-

tos per j tall*iam* dimid*ium quarterium*. In sup*ra*uend*itis* c xvij *quarteria* dimid*ium et* eque.

veschie. Id*em* R*eddunt* c*ompotum* de j q*uarterio* de toto exit*u* veschi*arum* quia equi carettar*ii* pascebant fruct*us* vnius acr*e* vnde In semi*ne* iij acr*arum* per pertic*am* vj b*usselli*. In sup*ra*uend*itis* ij b*usselli*.

Instaur*um*. Equi. Id*em* R*eddunt* c*ompotum* de ij equis carett*ariis* remanent*ibus* ann*o* p*re*t*erito*. Et Rem*anent* ij equi carett*arii*.

Affr*i*. Id*em* R*eddunt* c*ompotum* de viij affr*is* rem*anentibus* anno p*re*t*erito*. Et Rem*anent* viij affri.

Boues. Id*em* R*eddunt* c*ompotum* de xxxix bob*us* rem*anentibus* ann*o* p*re*t*erito*. Et de iiij adiunct*is*. Summ*a* xliij vnde In viu*is* vend*itis* vij. Summ*a* vij. Et Rem*anent* xxxvj.

Taur*us*. Id*em* R*eddunt* c*ompotum* de j taur*o* rem*anente* ann*o* p*re*t*erito*. Et Rem*anet* j taur*us*.

Vacc*e*. Id*em* R*eddunt* c*ompotum* de xxj vacc*is* rem*anentibus* ann*o* p*re*t*erito*. Et de ij adiunct*is*. Et de iij s*upra* empt*is*. Summ*a* xxvj vnde In sup*ra*uend*itis* iij vacc*e*. S*umma* iij. Et Rem*anent* xxiij vacc*e*.

Bouett*i*. Id*em* R*eddunt* c*ompotum* de vj bouett*is* rem*anentibus* ann*o* p*re*t*erito* bouicul*is* vn*de* In adiunct*is* bob*us* iiij. In adiunct*is* vacc*is* ij. Summ*a* vj. Et nich*il* Rem*anet*.

Bouicul*i*. Id*em* R*eddunt* c*ompotum* de vij bouicul*is* rem*anentibus* ann*o* p*re*t*erito* annal*ibus* vn*de* In mor*ina* j. Et Rem*anent* vj bouicul*i* vnde iiij mascul*i*.

Annal*es*. Id*em* R*eddunt* c*ompotum* de xj annal*ibus* rem*anentibus* ann*o* p*re*t*erito* vitul*is* vnde In mor*ina* j. Et Rem*anent* x annal*es* vnde viij fu*eru*nt mascul*i*.

Vitul*i*. Id*em* R*eddunt* c*ompotum* de xiiij vitul*is* p*ro*uent*is* ex p*re*dic*t*is vacc*is* h*oc* ann*o* quia vj vacce fu*eru*nt steril*es et* iij vendebant*ur* an*te* vitul*ationem et* iij emebant*ur* sine vitul*is* vn*de* In *decima* j. In sup*ra*uend*itis* iij q*uia* fu*eru*nt debil*es et* tarde vitul*antes*. S*umma* iiij. Et Rem*anent* x vitul*i*.

Multon*es*. Id*em* R*eddunt* c*ompotum* de cccc lxxviij multon*ibus* rem*anentibus* ann*i* p*re*t*eriti*. Et de c lxxvj adiunct*is*. Summ*a* dc liiij vnde In sup*ra*uend*itis* in fest*o* s*anc*t*i* mart*ini* xxxiiij. In mor*ina* an*te* tons*ionem* xvij. In mor*ina* post tons*ionem* vj. S*umma* lvij. Et R*emanent* d iiij^{xx} xvij mult*ones*.

Ou*es* mat*rices*. Id*em* R*eddunt* c*ompotum* de dcc iiij^{xx} ij ou*ibus* mat*ricibus* rem*anentibus* ann*o* p*re*t*erito*. Et de c iiij^{xx} adiunct*is*. Et de j cumeling*o*. Summ*a* dcccc lxiij vnde In sup*ra*uend*itis* In fest*o* lxxv. In mor*ina* an*te* part*um* v. In mor*ina* post part*um et* an*te* tons*ionem* xiij. In mor*ina* post tonsio*nem* vij. Summ*a* c. Et Rem*anent* dccc lxiij sues [sic] mat*ri*ces.

Hogg*astri*. Id*em* R*eddunt* c*ompotum* de ccc lxvij hogg*astris* Rem*an*-

entibus anno *preterito* agnis vn*de* In mor*ina* an*te* tons*ionem* xj. In adiunct*is* multon*ibus* c lxxvj. In adiunct*is* ou*ibus* mat*ricibus* c iiij^xx^. Summ*a* ccc lxvij hogg*etti*. Et nich*il* Rem*anet*.

Agni. Id*em* R*eddunt* co*mpotum* de dc lxxiij agnis p*r*ouent*is* ex p*re*d*ic*tis mat*ribus* h*oc* ann*o* q*uia* xxj fu*erunt* sterile*s* *et* ix fece*runt* aborsu*m* vn*de* In dec*ima* lxvij. In consuet*udine* j p*re*p*osit*i ij b*e*rcar*iorum* j fab*ri* iiij. In mor*ina* an*te* sep*a*rac*io*nem cc vij p*ost* sep*a*rac*io*nem *et* an*te* tons*ionem* x. In mor*ina* p*ost* tons*ionem* xix. In viu*is* vend*itis* xiij sero nat*is*. S*umma* ccc xx. Et Rem*anent* ccc liij agn*i*.

Lana gross*a*. Id*em* R*eddunt* co*mpotum* de md xviij vell*eribus* lan*e* gross*e* vnde In dec*ima* [c lj]. Sum*ma* c lj. In cons*uetudine* ij b*e*rcar*io*-*rum* j daye iij. Sum*ma* c liiij uell*era*. In sup*r*auend*itis* mccc lxiiij vell*era* q*ue* fece*runt* x vell*era* [sic] xj cl*avos*.

Lana agn*ina*. Id*em* R*eddunt* co*mpotum* de ccc iiij^xx^ v vell*eribus* lan*e* agn*ine* vn*de* In sup*r*auend*itis* om*n*ia q*ue* fec*er*unt xvj pett*r*as.

Porc*i*. Id*em* R*eddunt* co*mpotum* de ij verr*ibus* rem*anentibus* ann*o* p*re*ter*ito* vnde In sup*r*auend*itis* j verr*es*. Et Rem*anet* j verr*es*.

Sues. Id*em* R*eddunt* co*mpotum* de iiij suib*us* rem*anentibus* ann*o* p*re*-*terito*. Et de v adiunct*is*. Sum*ma* ix vn*de* In occis*is* ad lardar*ium* v. Sum*ma* v. Et Rem*anent* iiij sues.

Porci. Id*em* R*eddunt* co*mpotum* de xxx porc*is* mascul*is* rem*anentibus* ann*o* p*re*ter*ito*. Et de xvj adiunct*is*. Sum*ma* xlvj vn*de* In occis*is* ad lardar*ium* xxiij. Sum*ma* xxiij. Et Rem*anent* xxiij porc*i* mascul*i*.

Hogg*etti*. Id*em* R*eddunt* co*mpotum* de xxj hogg*ettis* rem*anentibus* ann*o* p*re*ter*ito* porcell*is* vn*de* In adiunct*is* suib*us* v. In adiunct*is* mascu-l*is* [xvj]. Sum*ma* xxj. Et nich*il* Rem*anet*.

Porcell*i*. Id*em* R*eddunt* co*mpotum* de xxxviij porcell*is* porcellat*is* ex p*re*d*ic*tis suib*us* h*oc* ann*o* quia j sus n*ichil* porcellauit vn*de* In *decima* iij In mor*ina* x. Sum*ma* xiij. Et Rem*anent* xxv vn*de* x fu*er*unt porcel-lat*i* mens*e* marcii. Et ix fu*er*unt porcell*ati* mens*e* Julii *et* vj fu*er*unt m*odo* lactantes. Et sciend*um* quod xix sunt mascul*i*.

Cas*eus* yem*alis*. Id*em* R*eddunt* co*mpotum* de xxiiij cas*eis* f*ac*tis In yeme vn*de* In sup*r*auend*itis* om*ne*s qui fec*er*unt vj clau*os*.

Cas*eus* estiual*is*. Id*em* R*eddunt* co*mpotum* de xxij cas*eis* f*ac*tis an*te* ablactac*io*nem. Et de c iiij^xx^ xviij cas*eis* f*ac*tis h*oc* ann*o* qui Incep*er*unt fieri xviij° die Kal*endas* maii *et* desierunt die s*anct*i mich*aelis* vt*r*oq*ue* die comp*utato* quia fec*erunt* binos case*os* p*er* xxix dies. S*umma* cc xx cas*ei* vn*de* In dec*ima* xxij In con*suetudine* j p*re*p*o*siti j b*e*rcar*ii* j fabri j daye iiij. In sup*r*auend*itis* c iiij^xx^ xiiij cas*ei* qui fec*erunt* xvj pond*era* dimid*ium*. Et h*oc* ann*o* tam par*um* p*ro*p*ter* temp*us* pluuios*um* in estate *et* p*ro*p*ter* morinam agnor*um*.

Gall*ine*. Id*em* R*eddunt* co*mpotum* de c xxv Gall*inis* de consuet*udine* de cheris*eto* vn*de* In def*e*ctu t*er*re Rob*er*ti stronge capte In d*ominicum* iiij. In def*ec*tu t*er*re Will*elmi* de curi*a* capt*e* In d*omi*nic*um* iiij. In defectu t*er*re Rob*erti* coya capt*e* In d*omi*nic*um* iiij. In def*ec*tu t*er*re coche tract*e* In d*omi*nic*um* iiij. In def*ec*tu t*er*re Rog*eri* porcar*ii* tra*c*te In d*omi*nic*um* iiij. In def*ec*tu t*er*re Ric*ardi* vaccar*ii* p*ro* simil*i* iiij. In def*ectu* t*er*re Rob*erti* cawe p*ro* si*mi*li iiij. In def*ec*tu t*er*re Gunild*e* ij q*uia* vid*ua* est. In def*ec*tu t*er*re agnet*e* vid*ue* ij q*uia* vid*ua est*. In de*fectu* t*er*re alani akerman ij q*uia* vid*uarius*. S*umma* xxxiiij. In s*upra*ue*n*d*itis* iiij[xx] xj Gall*ine*.

Corei. Id*em* R*eddunt* c*om*p*otum* de core*o* j bouicul*i* mort*ui* de mori*na*. Et de coreo j annal*is* mort*ui* de mori*na*. Sum*ma* ij vn*de* In sup*ra*uend*itis* om*ne*s.

Pell*es* gross*e*. Id*em* R*eddunt* c*om*p*otum* de xvij pell*ibus* mult*onum* mort*uorum* de mori*na* an*te* tons*ionem*. Et de xviij pell*ibus* oui*um* ma*tricium* mort*uarum* de mori*na* an*te* tons*ionem*. Et de xj pell*ibus* hog*gastrorum* mort*uorum* de mori*na* an*te* tons*ionem*. S*umma* xlvj vn*de* In sup*ra*pellut*is* om*ne*s.

Pell*es* [pellute]. Id*em* R*eddunt* c*om*p*otum* de xlvj pell*ibus* pellut*is* vnde In sup*ra*uend*itis* om*ne*s.

Pell*es* nude. Id*em* R*eddunt* c*om*p*otum* de vj pell*ibus* multon*um* mor*tuorum* de mori*na* post tons*ionem*. Et de vij pell*ibus* oui*um* mat*ricium* mort*uarum* post tons*ionem*. Sum*ma* xiij vnde In sup*ra*uend*itis* om*ne*s.

Pell*es* agn*ine*. Id*em* R*eddunt* c*om*p*otum* de cc vij pell*ibus* agn*orum* mort*uorum* de mori*na* an*te* sep*ara*cio*n*em. Et de x pell*ibus* mort*uorum* de mori*na* post sep*aracio*nem *et* an*te* tons*ionem*. Et de xix pell*ibus* mort*uorum* de mori*na* post tons*ionem*. S*umma* cc xxxvj vnde In sup*ra*uend*itis* om*ne*s.

Bacones. Id*em* R*eddunt* c*om*p*otum* de xxviij baconi*bus* positis In lardar*ium* hoc ann*o* vn*de* In sup*ra*uend*itis* om*ne*s.

Eschines. Id*em* R*eddunt* c*om*p*otum* de xxviij eschinis porcor*um* vnde In consuet*udine* j porcar*ii* j. Et In sup*ra*uend*itis* xxvij.

Exit*us*. Id*em* R*eddunt* c*om*p*otum* de xxviij exit*ibus* porcor*um* vnde In consuet*udine* j porcar*ii* j. Et In sup*ra*uend*itis* xxvij.

Vnct*um*. Id*em* R*eddunt* c*om*p*otum* de vnct*o* xxviij porcor*um* vnde In sup*ra*uend*ito* tot*um* qui fecit xj petras.

§§ 11. Custumal of Crawley, about 1280.

This enumeration of the customs due to the lord of Crawley from his tenants is taken from a fine large custumal, still unprinted, listing the customs, military and non-military, of the various manors and boroughs belonging to the bishopric of Winchester. The non-military customs were paid in kind, in money, or in agricultural services. They were written down from the oral statements of jurors, sworn for the purpose. The names of the Crawley jurors, however, are not given.

The custumal, in the form we have it, was written in the early fifteenth century, as is evident from internal evidence. But it is based upon much earlier originals, at least in the case of the Crawley entry. The probable date is about 1280 when there was a voidance in the bishopric. The names in this custumal are found rather plentifully in the reeve's accounts[1] of the decade of 1280.

The most striking feature of the Crawley part of the custumal was the division of the manor into North and South Crawley. Each of these parts, separated presumably by the village street, was as different from one another as one manor was from another. In South Crawley the tenants were holders of virgates or half-virgates (except one who held two virgates), while in North Crawley the tenants held only about eleven acres (farthingland). In South Crawley the tenants did boon-work or other special tasks, while in the North they owed week-work. In the South they did the more interesting and less menial tasks, while in the North they did the heavier and more continuous labor, especially caring for the animals. In the South the tenants owed service with plows and beasts of burden, while in the North they owed hand labor. In fact, one would think that South Crawley was originally a community of free men, while North Crawley was originally a private estate of slaves.

Of course there were many conditions common to both North and South Crawley. All the customs mentioned came from unfree tenants: all were restricted in the matter of marrying off their children and in the sale of their beasts of burden. All apparently alike owed a heriot to their lord. Suit of court may have been obligatory on tenants regardless of their residence in the North or South.

There was a third division, really a part of South Crawley, called Wodecote. This was apparently the modern Northwood

[1] See particularly MS., P. R. O., Ecclesiastical Commission, Various, 159312 and 159313.

Park. At least three of the four tenants mentioned as resident there had been given lands carved out of the demesne, for which they paid money rents.

It is to be noted that the tenants are not called Liberi, Consuetudinarii, and Cotarii, as they are for instance in West Wycombe. They were all just holders of estates of such-and-such a size owing the customs indicated. Of course, there is no indication that the list of tenants is complete. A free tenant owing only a rent in money or in kind, but no services, might be omitted. Indeed Stephen Fromond was apparently such a tenant paying a pound of cummin each year for his holding, which was apparently an estate in South Crawley quite apart from the village group of houses. It is likely that he and the rector were the only freemen in the village organization, and both almost certainly from other parishes.

Not a little is said about commutation. Those in South Crawley, doing no week-work, paid money. This was conceivably in lieu of services already commuted. The men of Wodecote are stated to pay in lieu of all secular services. But this was simply on account of their holding demesne lands. Four others, however, each holding 10 acres, paid 2s. 6d., 2s. 9d., 3s., and 5s. to be free of such services. These are the clearest cases of commutation, all coming at the end of the document. They appear to have been added to the main body of the document at a later date. The Philip Hoyville mentioned was apparently seneschal to John of Pointoise about 1287–88. The exact dates of these commutations are quite uncertain, but they probably belong to the late thirteenth century.

Outside services were due, chiefly for carrying, for example, writs to Mardon and Overton, firewood and oats to Wolvesey (the bishop's seat in Winchester), wool and cheese to Winchester, Southampton, and Bittern, and building timbers from Mardon to Crawley. There was haying to be done at Wolvesey and apples to be gathered at Waltham.

CRAULEY [1]

Redd*it*us Et S*er*uicia illius villat*e* de Suth [Crawley].

Rob*er*tus At Mere tenet di*midi*am virg*atam* t*er*r*e* dab*it* de redd*itu* Annuali iij s. ix d. ad iiij^or^ t*erminos* videli*c*et ad festum S*anct*i Mich*ael*is xij d. Nat*a*lis d*omi*ni xj d. ad Pasch*am* xj d. ad festum S*anct*i Joh*ann*is Bap*tis*te xj d. It*em* Adiuuab*it* ad falcand*um* sp*ar*gend*um et* leuand*um* cum co*mmunitate* tocius ville vj acr*as* p*r*ati in p*r*ato de Wulues*eia* et adiuuab*it* cariar*e* fenu*m* de p*r*edi*c*tis vj acr*is* In Cur*iam* de Wulues*eia et* mullo*n*em inde componer*e*. It*em* inueniet iij dies p*r*ecar*ios* in Autumpn*o* ad q*ua*mlib*e*t p*r*ecar*iam* j hom*in*em *et* h*ab*ebit de d*omi*no j pane*m* Melior*em* ob*olatam* legum*inis et* iij alec*ia* ad principal*em* p*r*ecar*iam* panem legume*n* iij alec*ia et* q*ua*rta*m* s*er*uisie. Et om*n*es Ministri tocius Curie h*ab*ebunt p*r*ansu*m* sicut p*r*edi*c*ti p*r*ecar*iarii*. It*em* deb*et* adiuuar*e* cariar*e* bladum d*omi*ni p*er* totum Autumpn*um* q*uan*d*o* nec*cess*e fu*er*it si aute*m* cariat p*er* j die*m* integ*rum* h*ab*ebit ij garbas ad suum pastum de tali bl*ad*o sicut cariant si p*er* dimid*ium* diem j garba*m*. deb*et* esse p*re*pos*itus* Berebrut*us* Wodwardus Cust*os* casei *et* votenn*a*ri*us*. *et* q*uan*d*o* si custos casei p*ro*uideat se vt tass*a* d*omi*ni sint ben*e* ordinat*a*. si Aute*m* p*re*pos*itus* recipiet de d*omi*no ad stipend*ium* p*er* Annu*m* v s. j agnu*m* elect*um* parit*er et* caseum. Item Rob*er*t*u*s At Mere portab*it* breuia d*omi*ni sicut Alii vicini sui videli*c*et Apud Merdon*am* vel Ap*ud* Ouerton*am*. deb*et* ducere semel ad Wulues*eiam* j q*uarterium* Auene si d*omi*n*u*s fu*er*it ibid*em*. deb*et* adiuuar*e* facer*e* xvj p*er*tic*as* de hagio circa p*ar*cu*m* de Walth*a*m cu*m* co*mmunitate* tocius ville. It*em* inueniet cu*m* co*mmunitate* tocius ville v hom*in*es ad colligend*um* mala in gardino de Walth*a*m q*ua*mdiu fu*er*int ad colligend*um et* molend*um et* sing*u*lis eor*um* recipiet p*er* diem x mala p*ro*pt*er* p*r*ansu*m*. It*em* cariabit semel j carect*atam* Buste c*ontr*a Nat*alem* d*omi*ni apud Wulues*eiam*. Et om*n*es tenent*es* sicut Rob*er*tus At Mere nisi si*n*t in s*er*uici*o* d*omi*ni deb*ent* Adiuuare cu*m* equo *et* carect*a* ad duce*n*du*m* fenu*m* d*omi*ni ad oue*s* v*bi* fu*er*int emp*te*. Ita q*uo*d possint ir*e et* redir*e* p*er* j diem ad cust*um* p*r*op*rium*. deb*ent* Ararare [sic] j acr*am* sicut iacet in campo d*omi*ni ad p*r*ecar*ium* vna cum sociis suis Iumctis [sic]. ad illu*m et* singul*is* Caruc*arius*. h*ab*ebit de d*omi*no j d. It*em* Rob*er*t*us* At Mere h*er*ciabit ij acr*as* Auen*e* sicut iacent *et* sem*in*ab*it et* queret in granar*io* d*omi*ni cum p*ro*p*r*iis sactis *et* h*ab*ebit x virg*as* choruli ad h*ar*nasiu*m et* om*n*is [sic] hom*in*es qui h*er*ciant h*ab*ebunt spinas ad coop*er*iend*um* terra*m* p*r*edi*ctam*. It*em* ducet faldam d*omi*ni q*uan*d*o* deb*et* Amoueri v*idelicet* v clates. It*em* inueniet j ho*min*em ad oue*s*

[1] MS., Br. M., Egerton 2418, Episcopatus Wintoniensis consuetudines, fols. 6–8. The manuscript bears the heading Consuetudinarius Maneriorum Episcopatus Wintoniensis.

d*omi*ni lauand*as et* tondeb*it* q*ua*mdiu fu*er*int ad lauand*as et* tond*en*-*das*. Item deb*et* adiuuar*e* ad ducend*a* Fima d*omi*ni semel in Anno videli-*c*et infra festu*m* Penthecost*e et* festum s*anct*i Petri Aduinc*u*la. Et deb*et* ducer*e* in om*n*ib*us* locis *ita* q*uo*d non vltra puthulle ad custum p*ro*-p*rium*. Item ducet fima de Barcario In camp*um* Austral*em* v*bi* d*omi*no placu*er*it vel Drakenorye ita q*uo*d no*n* vltra limict*es* virid*as*. deb*et* ducere lana*m* d*omi*ni *et* caseu*m* videlic*et* Winton*iam* vel apud Hampto-*niam* vel apud Bittern*e*. It*em* si domin*us* volu*er*it edificare queret mere-*mium* in p*ar*co de Mardon*a* ad custu*m* p*ro*priu*m* s*ed* non p*ro*strabunt Arbores si Rob*ertus* At Mere sit Decennar*ius* respondeb*it* cu*m* tota decen*na* sua p*er* Annu*m* j marc*am*. Non p*otest* maritar*e* filiu*m* nec filiam nec vender*e* boue*m* nec equu*m* suu*m* absq*ue* licencia d*omi*ni si ip*su*m equu*m* Aut boue*m* aut pull*um* aut Ani*m*al nutteret.[1] Et dab*it* idem An*im*a*l* d*omi*no si ip*sum* volu*er*it de p*re*cio vj d. min*us* q*ua*m Alibi vender*e* pot*er*it. It*em* Rob*ertus* At Mere cu*m* tota villa h*ab*ebit bestias suas in h*er*bagio d*omi*ni *et* dab*it* Annuati*m* ad pannag*ium* p*ro* bestia de etate vj d. *et* de dimid*ia* etate iij d. pro bouet*to* ij d. *et* p*ro* vitulo j d. si ip*sum* vitul*um* intrat h*er*bagiu*m* d*omi*ni. Et soluet vnusquisq*ue* pan-nag*ium* suu*m* die s*anct*i Martini eode*m* die recipiet h*er*bag*ium* voc*atum* Mede *et* erunt in eodem usq*ue* Penthecost*en* Die Penthecost*es* recipiet pastura*m* vocat*am* Hulde *et* h*ab*ebit usq*ue* Nat*a*l*em* s*anct*i Joh*ann*is Bapt*ist*e Die s*anct*i Joh*ann*is B*aptiste* recipiet h*er*bagiu*m* vocatum gore s*ed* bost*ie*[2] d*omi*ni debent p*re*ceder*e et* erun*t* in Eode*m* h*er*bag*io* usq*ue* ad exaltac*io*nem s*anct*e Cruc*is* die s*anct*e Cruc*is* intrabu*n*t in stipul*am* post best*ias* d*omi*ni *et* ibit in eadem pastur*a* om*n*ib*us* loc*is* post an*i*-*ma*l*i*a d*omi*ni Except*a* pastu[r]a ult*ra* Puthulle *et* erunt in h*er*bag*io* usq*ue* festu*m* s*anct*i Marti*ni* p*ro* pannag*io* p*re*dict*o*. It*em* Rog*er*us At Mere dab*it* pannag*ium* p*ro* porcis suis videlic*et* p*ro* porco j anni ij d. *et* dimid*ii* anni j d. *et* p*ro* porcello ob. si porc*i* d*omi*ni sint in pessona bosc*i* de Crauley porci Rob*er*ti Att Mere erunt in eodem bosc*o* cu*m* tota villa p*ro* pannag*io* p*re*dict*o*. si porci Rob*er*t*i* At Mere si*n*t in pessona an*te* Festu*m* s*anct*i Mich*ae*lis ex*tra* villa*m* de Crauly no*n* dab*it* pannag*ium* p*ro* porcis suis n*isi* mora*m* faciant in t*err*a d*omi*ni post fest*um* s*anct*i Mart*ini*. Item omnis [sic] tenente*s* sicut Rob*ertus* At Mere faciu*nt* in estate mull*o*nem de stramine remanen*ti* in Cur*ia*. Item Rob*er*tus At Mere dabit h*er*iett*um et* vxor sua no*n* emet terr*am* sua*m* post obitu*m* viri sui. Et q*uando* aliquis Wudredi[3] de Crauly capit introitu*m* t*err*e sue non op*er*ab*it* p*ro* t*err*a sua an*te* falcat*ionem* p*ra*ti de Wulues*eia* s*ed* dab*it* redd*itum* sic*ut* Alii vicini sui. Joh*anne*s Att Putte tenet j virg*a*-*tam* t*err*e *et* dimid*iam*. dab*it* de Redd*itu* p*er* annu*m* xj s. iij d. Et idem s*er*uic*ium* sic*ut* Rob*ertus* At Mere p*re*t*er* q*uo*d inueniet ad q*ua*mli*bet*

[1] For nutrieret. [2] For bestie.

[3] Probably for Hundredi.

p*recariam* Autumpn*i* iij ho*min*es ad tassum j ho*min*em. Et ad fenu*m* cariand*um* j ho*min*em plus q*ua*m p*redict*us Rob*ertus* At Mere *et* ad lauand*um* j ho*min*em. Et [ad] tond*endum* ij ho*mines*. Will*el*m*us* Coche tenet j virg*atam* t*erre* *et* dabit viij s. Et id*em* s*e*ruic*i*um sicut Rob*ertus* At Mere p*reter* q*uo*d inueniet ad q*ua*mlibet p*recariam* Autumpn*i* ij ho*mines*. Et ad suu*m* tond*endum* ij ho*min*es plusq*ua*m p*redic*tus Rob*er*tus At Mere. Steph*an*us Baker ten*et* j virg*atam* t*erre* *et* dab*it* viij s. Et id*em* s*e*ruic*ium* sicut Will*el*m*us* Choche. Joh*ann*es Dauid tenet di*midi*am virg*atam* t*erre* *et* dab*it* iiij s. Et idem s*e*ruic*ium* sicut Rob*er*tus At Mere. Steph*an*us Cl*er*icus tenet di*midi*am virg*atam* t*erre* *et* dab*it* iiij s. Et id*em* s*e*ruic*iu*m sicut Rob*ertus* At Mere. Rad*ul*-*f*us de Somburne ten*et* di*midiam* virg*atam* t*erre* *et* dab*it* iiij s. *et* idem s*e*ruic*ium* sicut Rob*er*tus At Mere. Will*el*m*us* Gille tenet di*midi*am virg*atam* t*erre* p*ro* iiij s. *et* idem s*e*ruic*ium* sicut Rob*er*tus Att*e* Mere. Rob*ertus* Forist*er* tenet ij virg*atas* t*erre* *et* dab*it* xvj s. *et* idem s*e*ruiciu*m* sicut Rob*er*tus At Mere preter q*uo*d inueniet iiij ho*min*es ad q*ua*mli-bet p*recariam* Autumpn*i*. Et semi*na*b*it* *et* h*er*ciab*it* viij acr*as* auen*e*. Et ad lauand*um* j ho*min*em. Et ad tondend*um* iiij ho*min*es. Walt*er*us Thouckeff*e* tenet di*midiam* virg*atam* t*erre* *et* dab*it* iiij s. *et* idem s*e*rui-*cium* sicut Rob*ertus* At Mere. Rog*er*us Gille ten*et* di*midi*am virg*atam* t*erre* *et* dab*it* iiij s. *et* idem seruic*ium* sicut Rob*ertus* At Mere. Will*el*-m*us* Beale tenet j virg*atam* t*erre* *et* dab*it* viij s. *et* idem s*e*ruic*ium* sicut Will*el*m*us* Choche. Joh*ann*es Gode tenet j virg*atam* t*erre* *et* dab*it* viij s. Et id*em* s*e*ruic*ium* sicut Will*e*lm*us* Choche. Steph*an*us At Soler tenet j virgat*am* terr*e* *et* dab*it* viij s. *et* idem s*e*ruic*ium* sicut Will*e*lm*us* Choche. Rob*ertus* Muryweder tenet di*midi*am virg*atam* t*erre* *et* dab*it* iiij s. *et* idem s*e*ruic*iu*m sicut Rob*ertus* At Mere. Dauid Martyn' tenet di*midi*am virg*atam* t*erre* *et* dabit iiij s. *et* idem s*e*ruic*ium* sicut Rob*er*tus At Mere. Thom*as* Carpynter tenet j virg*atam* t*erre* *et* dab*it* viij s. *et* idem s*e*ruic*iu*m sicut Will*el*m*us* Choche. Ric*ard*us de Aula tenet j vir-g*atam* *et* dab*it* viij s. *et* idem s*e*ruic*iu*m sicut Will*e*lm*us* Choche. Ro-g*er*us Marday tenet di*midi*am virg*atam* t*erre* *et* dab*it* iij s. ix d. Et id*em* seruic*iu*m sicut Rob*er*tus At Mere. Rob*er*tus Bunde tenet j vir-g*atam* t*erre* *et* dab*it* vij s. ix d. *et* idem s*e*ruic*ium* sicut Will*el*m*us* Choche. Joh*ann*es Bele tenet di*midiam* virg*atam* t*erre* *et* dabit iiij s. *et* id*em* s*e*ruic*ium* sicut Rob*ertus* At Mere. Will*el*m*us* Randulf' tenet di*midi*am virg*atam* terr*e* *et* dab*it* iiij s. *et* idem s*e*ruic*iu*m sicut Rob*ertus* At Mere. Rob*ertus* lange tenet j virg*atam* t*erre* *et* dabit vij s. vj d. *et* id*em* s*e*ruic*ium* sicut Will*el*m*us* Choche. Hugo Bele tenet j virg*atam* t*erre* *et* dabit viij s. *et* idem s*e*ruic*ium* sicut Will*el*m*us* Choche. Rog*er*us Sewyne tenet di*midiam* virg*atam* t*erre* *et* dab*it* iiij s. *et* idem seruic*ium* sicut Rob*ertus* At Mere.

S*um*m*a* den*ariorum* de Suth [Crawley] vij li. xviij s. ij d.

Memorand*um* qu*o*d Rector de Crawley h*abe*b*i*t vj vaccas *et* j Taur*um* in pastura cu*m* a*nim*alib*us* d*omi*ni. Et lx oue*s* matrice*s* *et* j hurtard*um* cu*m* ouib*us* d*omi*ni ex cons*uetudine* vel iiij^{xx} iiij oue*s* *et* j hurtard*um* pro sex vaccis et Tauro cu*m* ouib*us* d*omi*ni ex co*n*venc*ione* vt p*atet* A*nno* xxxvij° Will*elm*i Wykh*a*m.[1]

Redd*it*us *et* S*er*uicia de North' [Crawley]

Dauid*us* Knyght' tenet j mes*uagium* *et* x acr*as* t*er*re faciend*o* p*ro* eis quali*be*t septim*ana* int*er* festum S*anct*i Mich*ae*lis Arch*angel*i *et* gulam August*i* duo op*er*a scil*icet* p*ro* op*er*e tritur*andi* iij b*ussellos* frumenti v b*ussellos* ordei vel v b*ussellos* ordei yemal*is* vel iij b*ussellos* pis*arum* vel iij b*ussellos* vesc*iarum* vel xij b*ussellos* Auen*e* *et* valet opus ob. q. Et si h*ab*eat equ*u*m h*er*ciab*it* j acr*am* in quadrag*esima* sicut iacet. Et recipiet p*ro* h*er*ciatura sicut Rob*ertus* At Mere. It*em* metet quali*be*t die in Autumpn*o* q*ua*mdiu durau*er*it di*midi*am acr*am* frumenti vel di*midiam* acr*am* ordei vel di*midiam* acr*am* ordei yemal*is* vel di*midi*am acr*am* pis*arum* vel di*midi*am acr*am* vesc*iarum* vel acr*am* Auene. deb*et* collig*er*e ligar*e* tassar*e* p*re*dict*um* blad*um* in campo glaniar*e* si necc*esse* fuerit *et* mu*n*dar*e*. Et h*a*bebit p*ro* cuiusli*be*t di*midia* acr*a* j garbam de eod*em* blado cresc*enti* sup*er* ip*s*am de q*uo*cu*n*q*ue* elig*er*e voluerit. debet elig*er*e ligame*n* suu*m* de blado longior*e* in d*ict*a terr*a* Ex*cepto* blado de Tuff' ad d*ict*am garbam ligand*am* aut recipiet garba*m* per corrigea*m* videlic*e*t a planta ped*is* usq*ue* ad genua *et* post Autumpn*um* fac*iet* q*u*ali*be*t die di*midium* op*us* usq*ue* ad fest*um* s*anct*i Mich*ae*lis. si Aut*em* Cust*odierit* oue*s* aut Al*ias* best*ias* Aut si tenuerit caruc*am* non op*er*ab*it* p*ost* Messione*m*. It*em* inueniet vj ho*min*es ad iij dies p*re*car*ios* messionis in Autumpn*o* *et* h*a*bebit quili*be*t eor*um* p*ro* diet*a* j pan*em* melior*em* ob. legume*n* iij Alec*ia* *et* eod*em* on*ere* recipiet comestu*m* sicut Alii p*re*car*iarii*. cust*odiet* best*ias* vel oue*s* vel porc*os* vel tenebit car*ucam*. si aut*em* custodi[e]r*it* oue*s* Aut Al*ias* best*ias* aut si custodierit porc*os* *et* tempestas in Autumpn*o* euener*it* opus illius dieti non computet*ur*. si Autem tenuer*it* caruca*m* p*er* totum Annu*m* *et* tempest*as* euener*it* post fest*um* s*anct*i Mich*ae*lis ita q*uo*d non errar*e* pot*er*it op*er*abit dimid*ium* opus. Et h*ab*ebit Arrura*m* ad viij acr*as* de caruc*a* d*omi*ni ad iiij^{or} t*er*min*os* videlic*e*t ad fest*um* s*anct*i Mich*aelis* ij acr*as* Pascha ij acr*as* Nat*alem* s*anct*i Joh*ann*is Bapt*ist*e ij acr*as* *et* ad Nat*alem* d*omi*ni ij acr*as*. si Aut*em* custodier*it* Multone*s* Aut oue*s* matrice*s* h*ab*ebit Arrur*am* v acr*arum* de caruc*a* d*omi*ni ad iiij t*er*min*os*. Et recipiet Arrur*am* sua*m* sicut caruc*e* tene*ntur*. deb*et* collig*er*e stipul*am* virgas ad clat*es* wyxand*as* ad cust*um* p*ro*p*ri*um *et* predict*as* stipul*am* *et* virg*as* cariab*it* ad fald*am* *et* clat*es* wixab*it*. Et h*ab*ebit ramicul*os* quos eisd*em*

[1] This memorandum has been inserted after the rest had been written down. It records an agreement of 1393 or 1394.

virg*is* absciderit. Et si custod*ierit* Multon*es* h*ab*ebit j vellus *et* j Agnu*m* elect*um*. Et si custodier*it* oue*s* matr*ices* h*ab*ebit j vellus *et* j Agnu*m* elect*um et* j caseu*m*. non potest maritar*e* filiu*m* n*ec* filia*m* n*ec* vender*e* bouem n*ec* eq*u*um suu*m* si ip*sum* boue*m* aut equu*m* a vitulo aut a pullo nutrierit absq*ue* licencia d*omi*ni. Et dab*it* idem Aueriu*m* d*omi*no si ip*sum* volu*er*it de p*recio* vj d. Minus q*ua*m Alibi vender*e* potuerit. dab*it* Schirichet*um* videli*c*et iij gallin*as et* j gall*um*. Wydyari*us* n*ec* vidua non dabu*n*t n*isi* dimid*ium* churichet*um et* faciet sect*am*. si Aut*em* Dauid Knyght' egrotau*er*it non calumpniabit*ur* p*er* xl dies de Aliquo labore. It*em* falcab*it* sp*ar*get p*ra*tu*m* vocat*um* litelmede ap*ud* Wulues*eiam* cu*m* p*ar*ticip*ibus* suis. si Aut*em* custod*ierit* porc*os* d*omi*ni h*ab*ebit v porc*os* cu*m* porc*is* d*omi*ni quiet*os et* j porcellu*m* de d*omi*no p*er* Annu*m* de p*ri*mo exit*u* mense marc*is et* h*ab*ebit blad*um* q*uo*d calcat*um et* remissu*m* loco q*uo* blado d*omi*ni fuerit tassat*um* in campo p*er* Autumpn*um*. It*em* h*ab*ebit tot*um* exit*um* vnius porc*i* cum eskine. Et fugabit porc*os* ad pessona*m* quocu*n*q*ue* d*omi*nus volu*er*it *et* eos in pessona custodiet *et* recipiet bladu*m* sic*ut* Alii Ministr*i* isti*us* Cur*ie*. si Aut*em* custodier*it* vaccas *et* Alias bestias h*ab*ebit cum eis in pastur*a* d*omi*ni v best*ias*. Et dab*it* p*ro* best*ia* ad f*es*tum s*anct*i Mart*in*i s*ecun*d*u*m quantitat*em* etat*um* suar*um*. si Aut*em* custodier*it* multon*es* au*t* oues matric*es* h*ab*ebit xxxj biden*tes* cu*m* ou*ibus* d*omi*ni quiet*os* de pastura. Et qualib*e*t nocte fugabunt*ur* ad fald*am* sua*m* p*ro*p*ri*am. si fu*er*it in nullo officio non h*ab*ebit nisi xxv biden*tes* eunt*es* in co*mmun*i pastur*a* quietos *et* quali*be*t nocte fugabunt*ur* ad faldam suam p*ro*p*ri*am. dabit heriett*um* sicut Rob*er*t*us* At mere. Et pannag*iabit* porc*os* suos *et* p*ro* Aliis bestiis *et* d*omi*n*us* si inueniet h*er*bag*ium* sicut Rob*ertus* p*re*dict*us*. It*em* inueniet ho*min*em ad oue*s* d*omi*ni lauand*as et* tondeb*it* q*ua*mdiu fu*er*unt ad lauandas *et* tondend*as*. Et q*uando* Dauid*us* obierit vx*or* sua no*n* metet terram suam. Will*el*m*us* Wyte tenet *et* facit in om*n*ib*us* sicut Dauid*us* Kyngt [sic]. Simon Kok*e* tenet *et* facit in om*n*ib*us* sicut p*re*dict*us* Dauid*us*. Ywon' Hewolf*e* tenet *et* facit in om*n*ib*us* sicut p*re*d*ict*us Dauid. Will*el*m*us* Cupper ten*et et* facit in om*n*ib*us* sicut p*re*d*ict*us Dauid. Joh*ann*es Carpent*er* tenet *et* facit in om*n*ib*us* sicut p*re*d*ict*us Dauid*us*. Joh*ann*es Pack*e* tenet *et* facit in om*n*ib*us* sicut p*re*d*ict*us Dauid. Simon Kyngt' tenet *et* facit in om*n*ib*us* sicut p*re*d*ic*t*us* Dauid. Joh*ann*es Neweman' tenet *et* facit in om*n*ib*us* sicut p*re*d*ict*us Dauid. Joh*ann*es Prust tenet *et* facit in om*n*ib*us* sicut p*re*d*ict*us Dauid. Rob*ertus* Carter ten*et et* facit in om*n*ib*us* sicut p*re*d*ict*us Dauid. Will*el*m*us* Wyndute tenet *et* facit in om*n*ib*us* sicut p*re*d*ict*us Dauid. Rob*ertus* Blackewyne tenet *et* facit in om*n*ib*us* sicut p*re*d*ict*us Dauid*us*. Alan*us* Kyngt' ten*et et* facit in om*n*ib*us* sicut p*re*dict*us* Dauid. Joh*ann*es Elys tenet *et* facit in om*n*ib*us* sicut p*re*d*ict*us Dauid. Rob*er*tus Elis tenet *et* facit in om*n*ib*us* sicut p*re*d*ict*us Dauid. Joh*anne*s Martyn' tenet *et* facit in om*n*ib*us* sicut p*re*d*ic*tus Dauid. Rob*er*tus Faber tenet j Cotagiu*m* *et* x acr*as* t*er*r*e* ad faciend*um* p*er* Annu*m* Ferram*enta* ad iiij^or^ caruc*as*. Et D*omin*us inueniet ad eas Ferr*um* *et* ac*er*um cu*m* nece*ss*e fu*er*it. Et h*ab*ebit p*ro* p*re*d*ic*t*o* op*er*e j acr*am* ordei yemal*is* melior*is* sin*e* compost*o* vel acr*am* ordei quadrages*imalis* si nullus ordei yemal*is* fu*er*it seminatu*m*. It*em* h*ab*ebit j equu*m* quietu*m* in pastur*a* d*omi*ni *et* j caseu*m*. Et j Agnu*m* elect*um*. Non potest maritar*e* filiu*m* nec filia*m* sua*m* nec vender*e* boue*m* nec equ*u*m suu*m* Ma*g*is q*ua*m p*re*dictus Dauid. dab*it* pannag*ium* p*ro* porcis *et* p*ro* Aliis bestiis suis sicut p*re*d*ic*tus Dauid. It*em* dab*it* h*er*iett*um* sicut Dauid. Et faciet iij dies p*re*cari*os* in Autumpn*o* cu*m* j ho*min*e. Et recipiet sicut Rob*er*tus At Mere. Inueniet ho*min*em ad lauand*um* *et* tondeb*it* q*ua*mdiu fu*er*it ad lauand*um* *et* tondeb*it*. Item falcab*it* sp*ar*get *et* collig*et* fenu*m* sicut Dauid*us*. dab*it* chirichet*um* sicut Dauid. queret Fenu*m* d*omi*ni cu*m* j homi*ne* *et* equo si equu*m* h*ab*u*er*it p*er* vna*m* vice*m* vbi fu*er*it emp*tum*. si Aut*em* Cult*er* Frangat*ur* loco quo d*icitu*r Schonke Aut vomer loco quo d*icitu*r Pate emendet ad custu*m* d*omi*ni Ep*iscop*i. Et no*n* ad cust*um* p*ro*p*rium*. It*em* Ferret ij equos carect*arios* cu*m* Ferrur*is* d*omi*ni p*er* totum Annu*m* *et* sem*el* in Anno om*n*is Affr*os*. Thom*as* Melewarde tenet j Cotag*ium* *et* x acr*as* terr*e* redd*endo* p*er* Annu*m* iiij s. ad iiij t*er*m*inos*. h*er*ciab*it* ij acr*as* in *quadragesima* s*ine* h*ab*uer*it* equ*um* s*ine* non. Et si h*ab*u*er*it equ*um* h*er*ciabit iij acr*as* in eade*m* seyson*a*. dabit chirichet*um* sicut Dauid lauab*it* *et* tondeb*it* sicut Dauid*us* falcab*it* sp*ar*get colliget fenu*m* *et* cariab*it*. dabit pannag*ium* *et* faciet p*re*car*ia* sicut Dauid*us*. Item custodiet best*ias* vel multon*es* vel oue*s* matr*ices* vel Agnu*m* vel porc*os* sicut Dauid*us* *et* om*n*ia Alia s*er*uicia sicut Dauid*us* faciet Ex*cepto* q*uo*d non erit Carucar*ius* nec op*er*abit quali*be*t septim*ana* inter festum s*anct*i Mich*ael*is *et* guglam Augusti sic*ut* p*re*dictus Dauid. Et si fu*er*it in Aliquo officio Allocabu*n*tur ei p*er* Annu*m* ij s. viij d. de redd*it*u suo. si Aut*em* in nullo officio s*it* cariet Fima d*omi*ni sic*ut* Rob*er*tus At Mere. Will*el*m*us* Gilb*ertus* tenet j Cotag*ium* xvj acr*as* t*er*re redd*endo* p*er* Annu*m* iiij s. vj d. Et faciet in om*n*ib*us* sicut Thom*as* Melward*e*. Rob*er*tus Wetherhurde tenet *et* facit in om*n*ib*us* sicut Will*el*m*us* Gilb*er*t. Will*el*m*us* de Wodecote ten*et* j mes*uagium* *et* j virg*atam* t*er*re redd*endo* p*er* Annu*m* ad iiij t*er*m*inos* x s. h*er*ciabit vj acr*as* in *quadragesima* p*re*c*ium* acre j d. ob. falcabit sp*ar*get *et* Collig*et* pratum. Et lauab*it* *et* tondeb*it* oue*s*. Cariabit Fenu*m*. op*er*ab*it* int*er* gulam Augusti *et* f*estu*m s*anct*i Mich*ael*is sicut p*re*d*ic*tus Dauid. dabit chirichet*um* h*er*iett*um* sicut Dauid. non p*otest* maritar*e* filiu*m* n*ec* filiam n*ec* vender*e* equu*m* nec boue*m* suu*m* si ip*su*m tenuerit sicut Dauid*us*. cariab*it* fenum *et* ex*trahiet* fima sicut Robertus At Mere. cariabit j carect*am* busce apud Wulues*eiam* cont*ra* Nat*a*le*m*. It*em* ducet ib*id*em q*ua*rt*erium* Auen*e* si d*omi*nu*s* Fu*er*it. Erit Wodewardus si d*omi*nu*s* volu*er*it *et* tunc erit quiet*us* de om*n*ib*us* s*er*uic*iis* ex*cepto* toto redd*itu* suo *et* faciet sect*am*. Rob*ertus* de Wodecote tenet j mes*uagium et* di*midi*am virg*atam* terre redd*endo* p*er* Annu*m* v s. ad iiij t*erminos et* faciet om*n*ia Alia s*er*uicia sicut p*redict*us Will*elmu*s ex*cepto* q*uo*d no*n* h*er*ciabit nisi ij acr*as* in *quadragesima*. Will*elmu*s Wodecote ten*et* j mes*uagium et* j acr*am* terre [reddendo] p*er* Annu*m* xij d. ad iiij t*erminos*. falcab*it* sp*ar*get fenu*m* in p*ra*to de Wulues*eia* cu*m* p*ar*ticip*ibus* suis. dab*it* ij gallinas de chiriche*to* p*recium* j gall*ine* j d. Et faciet ij p*recari*a in Autumpn*o*. Inueniet j ho*min*em ad oues tondend*as* p*er* ij dies. dab*it* pannag*ium* p*ro* porc*is* suis. dab*it* h*er*iett*um et* faciet sect*am*.

P*hilippus* Hoyuille sen*eschalus* Ep*iscop*i Wintoni*ensis* Anno d*omini* J*ohann*is [1] Ep*iscop*i vj^to^ tradid*it* o*m*nib*us* homi*nibus* de Wodecote videli*cet* Will*el*mo fil*io* Hug*onis et* Rober*to* de Wodecote *et* Will*el*mo de ead*em et* hered*ibus* illor*um* xx acr*as* terr*e* de d*omini*co Arpenti de Wedgarstu*m* mensurat*as* p*er* p*er*tic*am* d*om*ini Reg*is* redd*endo* inde An*n*uati*m* p*ro* om*ni* secular*i* s*er*uic*io* x s. ad iiij t*ermin*o*s*. Matilda vidua ten*et* j mesuag*ium et* iij acr*as terre* redd*endo* p*er* annu*m* ij s. ad iiij t*ermino*s Et faciet om*n*ia Alia s*er*uicia sicut Will*elmu*s de Wodecote. Dauid Knigt' ten*et* j mes*uagium et* j acr*am* terr*e* redd*endo* p*er* Annu*m* xij d. ad iiij t*ermin*o*s* Et dab*it* j gallu*m* de Chiriche*tto et* j die*m* p*recar*i*um* in Autumpn*o et* faciet sect*am*. Rob*ertus* Choche ten*et* j mes*uagium et* iij acr*as* terre redd*endo* p*er* Annu*m* iij s. ad iiij t*ermin*o*s et* dab*it* pannag*ium* p*ro* porcis suis *et* p*ro* Aliis best*iis et* dab*it* h*er*iett*um* Et faciet sect*am*. Will*elmu*s Rayson' tenet j Cotag*ium et* x acr*as terre* p*er* Annu*m* v s. ad iiij t*ermin*o*s*. Inueniet j homine*m* ad ou*es* tondend*as* p*er* j diem *et* faciet p*recar*i*um*. Simon Cocks tenet x acr*as terre reddendo* p*er* Annu*m* ij s. vj d. ad iiij t*ermin*o*s* Et faciet sect*am*. Rog*er*us Faber recipiet A d*omi*no Aream ad co*m*ponend*um* messuag*ium* temp*ore* Will*el*mi Wintersull' sen*eschall*i D*omi*ni Ep*iscop*i int*er* Rob*ertum* At Mere *et* Joh*ann*em At Putte Et dat d*omi*no die s*anct*i Mich*aelis* singul*i* Anno ij d. It*em* Inueniet j homine*m* ad ou*es* tondend*as* p*er* j diem *et* faciet j die*m* p*recar*i*um* in Autumpn*o*. It*em* idem Rog*er*us Faber tenet x acr*as terre* Et dab*it* de redd*itu* die s*anct*i Mich*ael*is ij s. vj d. p*ro* om*n*i s*er*uicio se*cu*lari. Steph*anu*s Palm*ere* tenet j messuag*ium et* x acr*as* terre redd*endo* p*ro* om*ni* se*cu*lari s*er*uicio die s*anct*i Mich*aelis* v s. Et faciet sect*am*. Joh*ann*es Carpentir ten*et* x acr*as* terr*e* redd*endo* die s*anct*i Mich*ael*is iij s. p*ro* om*n*i seruicio. Et faciet sect*am*. Will*elmu*s Cupp*er* tenet x acr*as* terr*e* redd*endo* die s*anct*i Mich*ael*is ij s. ix d. p*ro* om*n*i seruic*io*. It*em* Will*el*m*u*s Cupper tenet voreacr*am* redd*endo* Annuatim iij d.

[1] John of Gerveys, 1262–68, or John of Pointoise, 1282–1305.

§§ 12. Reeve's Account, 29 Sept., 1305—28 Sept., 1306.

The lord sold many things: pannage for hogs, agistment of cattle, pastures, right to fold sheep, cattle, sheep, wool, grain, cheese, butter, hides, cider, underwood, services, permission to remain outside of the manor, right to marry, and justice. The sale of oxen, recorded in this account, is notable. Apparently the older ones were being eliminated and some of the younger ones also. The gradation of prices is indicative of close market valuation — 4s. 3d., 5s., 5s. 6d., 6s., 6s. 8d., 7s., 7s. 6d., 9s. 9d., and 10 s.

The lord had 90 acres [1] of wheat in the field (furlong) called Drakenord, 129 acres of barley in the east part of Puthulle and in Langelond, and 142 acres of oats in the east part of Puthulle. The location of four other kinds of grain is not stated. Clearly the lord's demesne was in several places. It is stated that the lord did not sell pasture rights opposite Norhbury because the field was fallowed.

The Crawley court was made up of at least the hall, the chamber, the grange, the cow stable, and the poundfold, all apparently surrounded by a moat and perhaps also by a hedge. At least one of the walls of the chamber, and probably all of them, were made of stone.

One thousand herring were bought for 6s. 8d. for giving to 305 men and the officials of the court engaged in reaping all of the bishop's wheat and fifty (customary) acres of his barley and oats. This work was to be performed at the three boon-works of reaping the lord's wheat, reaping his barley, and reaping his oats. But the meaning is not that there were actually 305 tenants and so many officials, but that, on the occasion of these boon-works, the tenants, working themselves, also provided others to help. David Knight of North Crawley had been required, about 1280, to furnish six men for three boon-works.[2] Perhaps these workers included his wife and children.

That theft was a common risk in medieval Crawley is indicated by the frequent expenses incurred for the purchase of locks and

[1] These were apparently customary acres, half the size of the statutory acres.

[2] See above, §§ 11, p. 235.

the hiring of a special watchman to guard the grain lying in the fields at night.

CRAULE[1]

Arr*eragium*. Henr*icus* Baret Ball*ivus et* Nich*ol*aus de Aula p*r*eposi*tus* Redd*unt* comp*otum* de iiij li. xix s. vj d. de Arr*eragio* anni p*r*et*eriti*. Et in lib*eratis* D*omi*no S. de Farh*a*m thes*aurario* Wolues*eie* p*er* j t*alliam* totu*m*. Et quieti sunt.

Redd*itus*. Iid*e*m Redd*unt* comp*otum* de lxj s. iiij d. de toto Redd*itu* ass*iso* ad Nat*alem* d*omi*ni. Et de lxj s. iiij d. ad Pasch*am*. Et de lxj s. iiij d. ad f*estu*m Nat*alis* s*anct*i Joh*an*nis Bapt*ist*e. Et de iiij li. xvij s. vij d. ad f*estu*m s*ancti* Mich*ae*lis. S*umma* xiiij li. xix d.

Acq*uie*t*ancie*. In acq*uie*t*ancia* j p*r*epo*siti* p*er* annu*m* v s. In acq*uie*t*anciis* vj caruc*ariorum et* j fabri p*er* annu*m* xviij s. viij d. cui*us*l*ibet* ij s. viij d. In acq*uie*t*anciis* ij Bercar*iorum* p*er* annu*m* v s. iiij d. In acq*uie*t*anciis* viij op*erar*i*orum* operanc*ium* p*er* duos dies in Ebdom*ada* a f*est*o S*anct*i Mich*ae*lis usq*ue* ad gula*m* Augusti *et* in aut*umpno* q*uo*l*ibet* die op*er*abili xxj s. iiij d. cui*us*l*ibet* ij s. iiij d. *et* j vaccar*ii* p*er* annu*m* ij s. viij d. In acq*uie*t*ancia* j porcar*ii* q*ua*si p*er* j t*ermi*n*um* viij d. S*umma* liij s. viij d.

Def*ect*us. In defect*u* t*erre* Le stronge tr*acte* in d*omi*nicu*m* ij s. In defect*u* t*erre* Will*elm*i de Cur*ia* tr*acte* in d*omi*nic*um* p*er* annu*m* ij s. viij d. In def*ectu* t*erre* de Alebrok*e* q*ui* modo respondit ap*u*d m*er*don*am* v s. In def*ectu* t*erre* Rob*er*ti Couch' tract*e* in d*ominicum* p*er* annu*m* ij s. viij d. In def*ectu* t*erre* Rob*er*ti Coye tr*acte* in d*ominicum* p*er* annu*m* ij s. viij d. In def*ectu* t*erre* Rog*er*i Le Porchir tr*acte* in do*mi*-*nicum* p*er* ann*um* ij s. viij d. In def*ectu* t*erre* Ric*ard*i vaccar*ii* tr*acte* in d*ominicum* p*er* annu*m* ij s. viij d. S*umma* xx s. iiij d. S*umma* acq*uie*t*anciarum* et defect*uum* lxxiiij s. S*umma* Redd*ituum* Rem*anens* x li. vij s. vij d.

Cyminu*m*. Idem R*eddunt* c*ompotum* de j l*ibra* Cymini de Redd*itu* Ric*ard*i Fromond Et in liber*ata* apud Wolues*eiam*.

Exitus maner*ii*. Id*em* r*eddunt* c*ompotum* de iiij s. j d. de pannag*io* porcor*um* hoc a*nno* vide*licet* p*ro* ix porc*is* s*uper*annat*is* j porc*o* t*ri*um t*ermi*n*orum et* lix porcell*is* sep*ar*at*is* vide*licet* p*ro* porc*o* s*uper*annat*o* ij d. p*ro* porc*o* iij t*ermi*n*orum* j d. ob. *et* p*ro* porcell*o* sep*a*rat*o* ob. Et de xx d. de pannag*io* xx vitul*orum* ad f*estu*m s*anct*i martin*i*. Et de xxxj s. de xlix vacc*is* xvj Bouett*is et* xv Bouicul*is* de pannag*io* ad La hokkeday vide*licet* p*ro* vacc*a* vj d. p*ro* bouet*to* iij d. *et* p*ro* bouic*u*lo ij d. D*e* ou*ibus* inuent*is* in fald*a* ho*m*inu*m* vel vill*at*e vlt*ra* c*er*tu*m* num*er*u*m* xxv n*ichil*

[1] MS., P. R. O., Ecclesiastical Commission, Various, 159321. Most marginal notes are here omitted.

hoc a*nno*. Et de xx d. de iiij^{xx} agn*is* sep*ar*at*is* in pastur*a* vsq*ue* f*estu*m Nat*alis* s*anc*ti Joh*an*nis Bapt*ist*e. Et de iij s. ij d. de pastur*a* vend*ita* in bosco in yeme. Et de ij s. vj d. de pastur*a* vend*ita* ad equos in estat*e* in bosco. D*e* pastur*a* de Puthull*e* n*ichil* hoc a*nno* p*ro* multon*ibus* d*omi*ni. Et de viij s. de pastur*a* de Trendly *et* Holyndane vend*ita* hoc a*nno*. D*e* pastur*a* de Drakenord n*ichil* hoc a*nno* q*uia* sem*inata* hoc a*nno*. D*e* pastur*a* de Combforlang*e* n*ihil* q*uia* sem*inata* pis*is*. D*e* past*ura* circa fossat*um* iux*ta* Norhbury n*ichil* h*oc* a*nno* quia camp*us* Warect*us*. D*e* pastur*a* de Locforlang*e* n*ichil* hoc a*nno* p*ro* auer*is* d*omi*ni. Et de ij s. de pastur*a* de shret' vend*ita* hoc a*nno*. Et de lxx s. xj d. de xj bob*us* vend*itis* v*nde* ij p*recium* vt*ri*usq*ue* iiij s. iij d. ij p*recium* vt*ri*usq*ue* v s. j p*recium* v s. vj d. j p*recium* vj s. *et* j p*recium* vj s. viij d. j p*recium* vij s. j p*recium* vij s. vj d. j p*recium* ix s. ix d. *et* j p*recium* x s. Et de ix s. vj d. de j taur*o* vend*ito*. Et de xxxiiij s. ij d. de vij vacc*is* ad f*estu*m s*anc*ti martin*i* vend*itis* v*nde* ij p*recium* ut*ri*usq*ue* iiij s. j p*recium* iiij s. vj d. j p*recium* iiij s. ij d. j p*recium* v s. j p*recium* vj s. j p*recium* vj s. *et* j p*recium* vj s. vj d. Et de x s. vj d. de iij bouet*tis* vend*itis* p*recium* c*uius*l*ibet* iij s. vj d. Et de iij s. ij d. de iij vitul*is* vend*itis*. Et de xij d. de iiij agnis debil*ibus* po*st* tons*ionem* vend*itis*. D*e* Lan*a* g*ro*ssa n*ichil* v*e*l agn*ina* nichil hic q*uia* mictebat*ur* ap*u*d Wolues*eiam*. Et de vij s. ij d. de Lan*a* fract*a* vend*ita*. D*e* Case*o* yem*ali* n*ichil*. Et de lxj s. viij d. q. de v pond*eribus* viij clau*is* *et* di*midio* case*i* estiual*is* vend*itis* v*nde* iiij pond*era* p*recium* c*uius*l*ibet* xij s. *et* j pond*us* viij cl*avi* *et* di*midius* p*recium* pond*eris* x s. vj d. Et de v s. viij d. ob. de xvj cl*avis* Butir*i* vend*itis*. Et de viij s. j d. de iiij^{xx} xvij gall*inis* de cher*iseto* vend*itis*. Et de xij d. de cor*io* j affr*i* de mor*ina* vend*ito*. Et de xxj d. de cor*io* j bou*is* de mor*ina* vend*ito*. Et de iiij s. ij d. de cor*iis* *et* Carn*e* ij Bou*um* de mor*ina* vend*itis*. Et de xxvij s. de xxvj pell*ibus* mult*onum* xxxvj pell*ibus* ou*ium* matr*icium* *et* xlvj pell*ibus* hogastr*orum* de mor*ina* an*te* tons*ionem* vend*itis* p*recium* c*uius*l*ibet* iij d. Et de xij d. de vij pell*ibus* mult*onum* *et* xj pell*ibus* ou*ium* matr*icium* de mor*ina* post tons*ionem* vend*itis* in g*ro*sso. Et de xv s. iij d. ob. q. de CC xlv pell*ibus* agn*orum* de mor*ina* an*te* sep*ar*ac*ionem* vend*itis* p*recium* pell*is* ob. q. Et de xvj d. ob. de xxxiij pell*ibus* agn*orum* de mor*ina* p*o*st sep*ar*ac*ionem* *et* an*te* tons*ionem* vend*itis*. Et de ij d. de vij pell*ibus* agnor*um* de mor*ina* p*o*st tons*ionem* vend*itis*. Et de x s. de j dol*eo* cic*e*re vend*ito*. Et de ij s. de Ric*ard*o Capell' p*ro* op*er*ib*us* vj acr*arum* t*er*r*e* t*r*adit*arum* s*ibi* *et* suis relax*atis*. Et de xij d. de quod*am* c*ur*tillagio q*uo*d q*uo*nd*am* fuit Rog*er*i Le Porchyr locat*o* hoc a*nno*. Et de xij s. de xxiiij acr*is* t*er*re d*omi*nice locat*is* hoc a*nno* q*ue* s*u*p*er*ius co*m*putant*ur* in defect*ibus*. Et de ij s. de q*uo*d*am* curtillag*io* q*uo*d q*uo*nd*am* fuit Rob*er*ti Coche. Et de lxiiij s. vj d. de xxij acr*is* subbosci vend*itis* p*recium* acr*e* ij s. xj d. *et* iiij d. plus in toto. Et de xj d. de j Cultr*o* vend*ito*. S*umm*a xx li. x s. ij d.

Vend*itio* s*uper* comp*otum*. D*e* Reb*us* vend*itis* s*uper* comp*otum* vij li. ij s. viij d. q. S*umma* vij li. ij s. viij d. q.

Recogn*itiones*. Iidem R*eddunt* c*ompotum* de vj d. de Rob*er*to Le Pak' p*ro* ann*ua* recogn*itione*. Et de vj d. de Rob*er*to Le Pott*ere* p*ro* si*mi*li. Et de iij d. de Joh*anne* Le Walsch' p*ro* si*mi*li. Et de iij d. de Rog*ero* Elys pro ann*ua* Recogn*itione* vt possit s*er*uire ex*tra* lib*er*tate*m* *et* seq*ui* decen*nam* sua*m* *et* venire ad duos Laghedays. Et de iij d. de Rob*er*to Elys p*ro* si*mi*li. S*umma* xxj d.

Item Recogn*itiones*. Id*em* r*eddunt* c*ompotum* de j cultro de Recog*nitione* Rob*er*ti Coleman vt possit morar*i* *et* s*er*uir*e* ex*tra* lib*er*tate*m* *et* n*ihil*omin*us* seq*ui* decen*nam* sua*m* *et* venir*e* ad ij Laghedays *et* vend*ito* s*uper*i*us*.

Recogn*itio* Cere. Id*em* r*eddunt* c*ompotum* de di*midia* li*bra* cere de Joh*anne* Le Cart*ere* p*ro* ann*ua* Recogn*itione* vt h*ab*eat lic*entiam* mand*i* alibi q*uam* s*uper* terra*m* d*omi*ni. Et debet sequi decen*nam* sua*m* ad ij Laghedays p*er* pl*egium* Rob*er*ti Le Bunde *et* Rob*er*ti Meryweder. Et liber*atum* apud Wolues*eiam*.

Vend*itio* Blad*i*. Idem R*eddunt* c*ompotum* de xv li. ix s. j d. ob. de xlvj q*uarteriis* j b*ussello* fr*umenti* vend*itis* v*nde* xlj q*uarteria* ij b*usselli* p*recium* q*uarterii* vj s. viij d. *et* iiij q*uarteria* vij b*usselli* p*recium* q*uarterii* vij s. Et de xxvj s. vj d. de v q*uarteriis* j b*ussello* Curall*i* vend*itis* p*recium* q*uarterii* v s. ij d. Et de xvj d. de ij b*ussellis* Brotcorn vend*itis*. S*umma* xvj li. xvj s. xj d. ob.

Fines *et* mar*itagia*. Idem Redd*unt* c*ompotum* de vj s. viij d. de Decena de Craule p*ro* thechingp*enny* ad hundr*edum* s*an*c*t*i mart*ini*. Et de vj s. viij d. p*ro* eod*em* ad hundr*edum* de Hock*e*. Et de ij s. de Joh*anne* fil*io* Joh*annis* Nichole Natiuo d*omi*ni p*ro* Alic*ia* q*ue* fuit vx*or* Will*elmi* Le Cup*ere* q*uonia*m tenuit ad viduet*atem* h*abenda*. Et de ij s. de Nich*olao* atte Halle p*ro* Lucya filia Ric*ard*i atte Halle mar*itanda* ex*tra*. S*umma* xvij s. iiij d.

P*er*quis*ita*. Idem R*eddunt* c*ompotum* de xxiiij s. vij d. de minut*is* p*er*q*uisitis* Cur*ie* hoc a*nno*. S*umma* xxiiij s. vij d. S*umma* vt*ri*usq*ue* xlj s. xj d. S*umma* toci*us* Recept*e* lvij li. xij d. ob. q.

Cust*us* Caruc*arum*. In ferr*o* *et* acero e*mptis* ad ferram*entum* iiij Caruc*arum* p*er* annu*m* ix s. In ij vom*eribus* e*mptis* xviij d. In iiij ferr*is* pedal*ibus* e*mptis* xvj d. In iij par*ibus* rotaru*m* e*mptis* ad Caruc*as* ix d. In j noua Caruc*a* fac*ienda* iij d. In m*er*em*io* scapuland*o* ad Caruc*as* ij d. ob. In Caruc*is* ferr*o* lig*andis* ij d. In ferr*amentis* vj affr*orum* p*er* annu*m* iij s. In capistr*is* de p*ro*p*ri*o pilo fac*iendis* j d. o*b*. In xvj bobus e*mptis* ad Caruc*as* vij li. iiij s. iij d. v*nde* xij p*recium* c*uius*l*ibet* ix s. viij d. *et* iiij p*recium* c*uius*l*ibet* vij s. iij d. plus in toto. In j affr*o* e*mpto* ad Caruc*am* v s. ij d. In stip*endiis* ij Caruc*ariorum* fugat*orum* p*er* annu*m* vj s. S*umma* viij li. xj s. viij d. ob. q.

Empc*io* Blad*i*. In xxix q*uarteriis* *et* di*midio* b*ussello* ord*ei* e*mptis* ad liber*atas* famul*is* *et* ad seme*n* vj li. xiiij s. iij d. ob. v*nde* x q*uarteria* p*recium* q*uarterii* iiij s. ix q*uarteria* di*midius* b*ussellus* p*recium* q*uarterii* iiij s. vj d. *et* x q*uarteria* p*recium* q*uarterii* v s. iiij d. s*cilicet* j d. ob. q. plus in toto. In xvij q*uarteriis* fr*umenti* e*mptis* p*recium* q*uarterii* vj s. c ij s. In xxxviij q*uarteriis* Auen*e* e*mptis* p*recium* q*uarterii* ij s. vj d. iiij li. xv s. In ij q*uarteriis* di*midio* vesc*iarum* p*recium* q*uarterii* vj s. xv s. S*umma* xvij li. vj s. iij d.

Cust*us* carect*arum*. In clut*is* clau*is* *et* vncto e*mptis* ad Carect*as* per annu*m* vj d. In veter*e* caret*ta* g*ro*pand*a* *et* emen*da* iiij d. In ferr*amento* j equi Caret*tarii* p*er* annu*m* xij d. In stipe*ndio* j Caret*tarii* p*er* annu*m* iij s. In j sacco e*mpto* vj d. ob. In albo cor*io* e*mpto* ad h*ar*nes*ium* Caret*tarum* vj d. S*umma* v s. x d. ob.

Custus Daer*ie*. In Linea tela *et* Laneo panno e*mptis* ad dayer*iam* hoc a*nno* vj d. In iiij b*ussellis* *et* di*midio* sal*is* empt*is* xij d. In p*re*sura e*mpta* iiij d. In j coler*a* e*mpta* j d. In oll*is* *et* patell*is* terr*enis* e*mpt*is ij d. ob. In vncto e*mpto* ad oue*s* vng*endas* xlviij s. viij d. In bercar*ia* ou*ium* matr*icium* coop*er*iend*a* *et* emend*a* ad tasch*am* cu*m* par*ietibus* d*ict*e B*er*car*ie* emend*is* xxiij d. In j porta fac*ienda* ad domu*m* hogastr*orum* xj d. *ob.* q. In Crechis fac*iendis* circa Bercar*iam* ou*ium* matri*cium* ad tasch*am* v s. In v crechiis eme*ndis* in d*ict*a Bercaria astantib*us* p*er* med*ium* d*ict*e Bercari*e* cu*m* iij truncis fac*tis* ad ferur*am* *et* p*ro* serur*is* cu*m* clau*ibus* ad d*ict*os truncos p*ro* t*ribus* Bercar*iis* ij s. vj d. In lvij cleiis fac*iendis* ad fald*am* xxij d. In lxxij p*er*tic*is* fossat*i* circa Berca*riam* hogastr*orum* fodiend*is* cu*m* plantis ad idem collig*endis* ix s. p*ro* p*er*tica j d. ob. In j haya c*irca* d*ictu*m fossat*um* fac*ienda* xviij d. In iiij vacc*is* e*mptis* xxviij s. vj d. v*nde* j p*recium* vij s. vj d. *et* iij p*recium* c*uius*lib*et* vij s. In j hurt*ardo* e*mpto* iij s. ij d. In iiij^{xx} xiiij agnis e*mptis* an*te* tons*ionem* lxxiij s. j d. ob. v*nde* x p*recium* c*uius*lib*et* iij d. ob. q. *et* iiij^{xx} iiij p*recium* c*uiuslibet* x d. In lv agnis e*mptis* p*o*st tons*ionem* lviij s. x d. v*nde* xxviij p*recium* c*uius*lib*et* xij d. *et* xxxvij p*recium* c*uius*lib*et* x d. In stipend*io* j daye p*er* annu*m* ij s. In feno e*mpto* ad inst*aurum* c iiij s. ob. Et totu*m* Rem*anet* ad inst*aurum* p*ro* a*nno* fut*uro*. S*umma* xvij li. iij s. ij d. q.

Custus domor*um*. In aula g*rangia* *et* bouer*ia* coop*er*iend*is* *et* eme*ndis* iiij s. vj d. In j muro Lapideo in Cam*era* ex p*ar*te Aust*ra*li Aule eme*ndo* *et* fac*iendo* vij d. In j muro Lapideo int*er* aula*m* *et* g*rangiam* cooperiend*o* *et* eme*ndo* xviij d. In xix p*er*tic*is* fossat*i* fodiend*is* circa Cur*iam* ij s. iiij d. ob. p*ro* p*er*tica j d. ob. In ij v*er*tinell*is* e*mptis* ad porta*m* Pundfald*e* ij d. ob. In serur*a* eme*nda* ij d. In iij acr*is* clastur*e* p*ro*st*er*nend*is* p*ro* haiis claud*endis* iiij s. In cicera e*mpta* p*ro* doleo p*er*impl*en*do xxij d. ob. In iiij q*ua*rentenis *et* xv p*er*tic*is* haye claud*endis* circa nouu*m* Copiciu*m* in bosco v s. x d. p*ro* q*uarentena* xvj d. S*umma* xxj s. ob.

T*rituratio*. In xlv q*uarteriis* v b*ussellis* fr*umenti* t*ri*turand*is* ad tasch*am* vij d. q. p*ro* q*uarterio* Ras*o* ij d. In eisd*em* vent*ilandis* ix d. p*ro* x b*ussellis* q. In xxiiij q*uarteriis* di*midio* ord*ei* t*ri*tur*andis et* vent*ilandis* ad tasch*am* iij s. ob. q. p*ro* q*uarterio* Ras*o* j d. ob. In v q*uarteriis* vj b*ussellis* Auen*e* t*ri*tur*andis et* vent*ilandis* ad tasch*am* v d. ob. q. In iij q*uarteriis* vj b*ussellis* pis*arum et* vesci*arum* t*ri*tur*andis et* vent*ilandis* vij d. ob. pro q*uarterio* ij d. Et residuu*m* blad*i* t*ri*turabat*ur* p*er* op*er*a. In vadiis ij g*ar*c*io*num exist*entium* vlt*ra* t*ri*tur*ationem* iiij s. p*er* ij t*erminos*. S*umma* xvj s. vj d. q.

Cust*us* Aut*umpnalis*. In blad*o* sarcland*o* vlt*ra* illud q*uo*d op*er*ar*ii* sarclauer*unt* vj s. In M allec*iis* e*mptis* ad iij p*re*car*ias* in autu*m*pn*o* de CCC v ho*minibus* cu*m* ministr*is* Cur*ie* met*entibus* iiij^xx x acr*as* fr*umenti et* l acr*as* ord*ei et* Auen*e* sicut iace*n*t vj s. iij d. In stipe*ndio* j ho*min*is custod*ientis* blad*um* in camp*o* p*er* noct*em et* auxil*iantis* carcare Car*ectas* iij s. In stipe*ndio* j messor*is* p*er* annu*m* vj s. viij d. S*umma* xxj s. vj d.

Expens*e* sen*escalli*. In expe*nsis* sen*escalli* ad ij hundr*eda* p*er* annu*m* vj s. vij d. S*umma* vj s. vij d.

Expens*a* For*ensica*. In donis dat*is* familie d*omi*ni Reg*is et* Regin*e* ij s. viij d. S*umma* ij s. viij d. S*umma* o*mnium* Expens*arum* xlvj li. xv s. ix d. q. Et debet x li. v s. iij d. ob.

Alloc*atio* Liber*ata*. In alloc*atione* preposi*ti* p*ro* xx q*uarteriis* fr*umenti* liber*atis* ad f*estu*m Int*ro*nizac*io*nis d*omi*ni vj li. xiij s. iiij d.

Liber*atio*. In Liber*atis* d*omi*no S. de Farham thes*aurario* Wolues*eie* p*er* j t*alliam* xlij s. S*umma* o*mnium* Alloc*ationum et* Lib*erationum* xix li. vij s. iiij d. Et sic debent de Claro xxix s. xj d. ob.

Exitus g*rangie*. Fr*umentum*.[1] Ide*m* R*eddunt* c*ompotum* de lxviij q*uarteriis* iij b*ussellis* de exit*u* fr*umenti* de g*rangia* in g*ranario* mens*ura* Ras*a* Et de xvij q*uarteriis* rec*eptis* de p*re*pos*ito* de merdone. S*umma* iiij^xx v q*uarteria* iij b*usselli*. De q*uibus* in se*mine* de iiij^xx x acr*is* sicut iacent in Camp*o* de Drakenord' xv q*uarteria* di*midium* vid*elicet* in acr*a* j b*ussellus* di*midius et* j q*uarterium* iij b*usselli* plus in toto. In lib*eratis* j messor*i* p*er* annu*m* q*ui* capit q*uarterium* p*er* viij sept*imanas* iij q*uarteria* ij b*usselli et* cap*it* residuu*m* de ordeo inferi*us*. Et in vend*itis* xlvj q*uarteria* j b*ussellus*. Et in vend*itis* s*up*er comp*otum* xx q*uarteria* di*midium* p*ro* vj li. xvj s. viij d.

Curall*um*. Ide*m* r*eddunt* c*ompotum* de v q*uarteriis* ij b*ussellis* de toto exit*u* Curall*i* mens*ura* Ras*a*. Et in vend*itis* v q*uarteria* j b*ussellus*. Et in vend*itis* sup*er* comp*otum* j b*ussellus* p*ro* vij d. ob.

Ord*eum*.[2] Id*em* r*eddunt* c*ompotum* de xxxviij q*uarteriis* di*midio* de toto exit*u* ord*ei* de g*rangia* in g*ranario* mens*ura* Ras*a*. Et de xxix q*uar*-

[1] Marginal note: R*eddunt* [or R*espondent* de] i q*uarterium* iii b*ussellos* min*us* se*mine* q*uarto*.

[2] Marginal note: R*eddunt* viii q*uarteria* di*midium* min*us* se*mine* [illegible; etc.].

teriis di*midio* b*ussello* de e*mpcis*. S*umma* lxvij q*uarteria* iiij b*usselli* di*midius*. De q*uibus* in se*mine* in c xxix acr*is* sicut iacent in ca*m*po ex p*ar*te orient*ali* de Puthull*e* *et* in La Langelond' xxxvj q*uarteria* vj b*usselli* sic cap*it* acr*a* ij b*ussellos* j p*eccum* plus in toto iij b*usselli* di*midius* j p*eccum* in Liber*atione* j Carect*arii* ij fugator*um* p*er* annu*m* q*ui* capi*unt* q*uarterium* p*er* viij sept*imanas* xix q*uarteria* di*midium*. In libera*tione* j Daye a f*esto* s*ancti* mich*ae*lis usq*ue* f*estum* Pur*ificationis* bea*te* mar*ie* di*midium* q*uarterium*. In lib*eratione* eius*dem* a f*esto* Pur*ificationis* usq*ue* f*estum* s*ancti* mich*ae*lis q*ue* cap*it* q*uarterium* p*er* xij septi*manas* ij q*uarteria* vj b*usselli* *et* di*midius*. In lib*eratione* j h*er*ciator*is* t*em*pore vt*r*iusq*ue* se*ment*is vj b*usselli*. In lib*eratione* j custod*is* agno*rum* p*er* ix sept*imanas* in aut*umpno* *et* ante j q*uarterium*. In Lib*eratione* j s*er*uient*is* q*ui* capit q*uarterium* p*er* viij sept*imanas* p*er* annu*m* iij q*uarteria* ij b*usselli* *et* capit residuu*m* de fr*umento* s*uperius*. In expe*nsis* iij p*r*ecar*iarum* in aut*umpno* iij q*uarteria* *et* debe*nt* fieri de q*uarterio* c panes.

Auen*a*. Idem R*eddunt* co*mpotum* de xxviij q*uarteriis* iij b*ussellis* de toto exit*u* Auen*e* de g*rangia* in g*ranario* mens*ura* Ras*a*. Et de xv q*uarteriis* dat*is* bob*us* p*er* est*imationem* in garb*is*. Et de xxxviij q*uarteriis* rec*eptis* de p*reposito* de M*er*don*a*. Et de iij b*ussellis* rec*eptis* de Brotcorn. S*umma* iiij^{xx} j q*uarteria* *et* vj b*usselli*. D*e* q*uibus* in se*min*e de c xlij acr*is* sicut iacent in ca*m*po ex p*ar*te orient*ali* de Puthulle lx q*uarteria* j b*ussellus* in acr*a* sicut iacet iij b*usselli* di*midium* *et* ij q*uarteria* plus in toto. In p*r*eben*da* vj affr*orum* a f*esto* Nat*alis* D*omi*ni vsq*ue* La Hokkeday v q*uarteria* j b*ussellus*. In p*r*eben*da* bou*um* p*er* est*imationem* in garb*is* xv q*uarteria*. In p*r*eben*da* j equi caret*tarii* p*er* annu*m* j q*uarterium* di*midium*.

Pis*e*. Iid*em* r*eddunt* co*mpotum* de iij q*uarteriis* ij b*ussellis* de toto exit*u* pis*arum* de g*rangia* in g*ranar*i*o* mens*ura* Ras*a*. Et in se*min*e totu*m*.

Vesc*ie*. Id*em* r*eddunt* co*mpotum* de iiij b*ussellis* de toto exit*u* vesc*iarum* de g*rangia* in g*ranar*i*o* mens*ura* Ras*a*. Et de ij q*uarteriis* di*midio* rec*eptis* de empc*is* de p*reposito* de M*er*done. S*umma* iij q*uarteria* Et in se*mine* totu*m*.

Brotcorn. Id*em* r*eddunt* co*mpotum* de vij b*ussellis* Brotcorn. De q*uibus* in dat*is* porc*is* ij b*usselli*. In mixt*is* cu*m* Auena ad p*r*eben*dum* equor*um* iij b*usselli*. Et in vend*itis* ij b*usselli*.

Instauru*m*. Equi Care*ttarii*. Id*em* r*eddunt* co*mpotum* de j equo caret*tario* Rem*anente* a*nno* p*r*et*erito*. Et Rem*anet* j equs [sic] Caret*tarius*.

Affr*i*. Id*em* r*eddunt* co*mpotum* de vj affr*is* Rem*anentibus* anno p*re*t*erito*. Et de j de em*pto*. S*umma* vij. De q*uibus* in morin*a* j. Et Rem*anent* vj affr*i*.

Boues. Id*em* r*eddunt* co*mpotum* de xxx bob*us* rem*anentibus* anno preterito. Et de xvj de emptis. Summa xlvj. De quibus in morina iij. In venditis xj. Summa xiiij. Et Remanent xxxij.

Taurus. Iidem reddunt compotum de j tauro remanente anno preterito. In vendito j. Et nihil Remanet.

Vacce. Idem reddunt compotum de xiij vaccis remanentibus anno preterito. Et de j adiuncta. Et de j prouenta de Herietto Alani Le Knyght post vitulationem. Et de j prouenta de estrahura. Et de iiij de empcis post vitulationem. Summa xx. De quibus in venditis ante vitulationem vij. Et Remanent xiij.

Bouetti. Idem reddunt compotum de iiij bouettis remanentibus anno preterito bouiculis. De quibus in adiunctis vaccis j. In venditis iij. Summa iiij. Et nihil Remanet.

[Ann]ales. Idem Reddunt compotum de iij annalibus remanentibus anno preterito vitulis. Et Remanent iij Annales vnde ij masculi.

Vituli. Idem reddunt compotum de iiij vitulis de exitu dictarum vaccarum quia iiij steriles. De quibus in decima pro anno preterito et anno presente j. In venditis iij. Et nihil Remanet.

Multones. Idem reddunt compotum de CC iiij^{xx} vj multonibus remanentibus anno preterito. Et de iiij^{xx} xix adiunctis. Summa CCC iiij^{xx} v. De quibus in morina ante tonsionem xxvj. Et post tonsionem vij. Et Remanent CCC lij multones.

Hurtardi. Idem Reddunt compotum de x hurtardis Remanentibus anno preterito. Et de j de empco post tonsionem. Et Remanent xj hurtardi.

Oues matrices. Idem reddunt compotum de D xxvj ouibus matricibus remanentibus anno preterito. Et de C j adiunctis de instauro. Summa DC xxvij. De quibus in morina ante Agnilationem xxj post Agnilationem et ante tonsionem xv. Et post tonsionem xj. Summa xlvij. Et Remanent D iiij^{xx} oues matrices.

Hogastri. Iidem Reddunt compotum de CC vj hogastris remanentibus anno preterito Agnis. Et de xl receptis de preposito de Merdona ante tonsionem. Summa CC xlvj. De quibus in morina ante tonsionem xlvj. In adiunctis multonibus iiij^{xx} xix et cum ouibus matricibus C j. Et nihil Remanet.

Agni. Iidem reddunt compotum de CCC iiij^{xx} xviij agnis de exitu dictarum ouium matricium quia C vij fuerunt steriles et abortiue. Et de iiij^{xx} iiij emptis de preposito de Weregraue ante tonsionem. Et de x de emptis ante tonsionem. Et de lxv de emptis post tonsionem. Summa D lvij. De quibus in morina ante separacionem CC lxxij. In decima xij. In morina post separacionem et ante tonsionem xxiij. In morina post tonsionem vij. In venditis iiij post tonsionem. In consuetudine j prepositi ij Bercariorum j fabri iiij. Et in venditis super compotum x agni pro v s. Summa CCC xxxij. Et Remanent CC xxv.

Porc*i*. Id*em* r*eddunt* com*potum* de x porc*is* rec*eptis* de p*re*pos*ito* de Twyford v*nde* j sus. Et de xx porc*is* rec*eptis* de Henr*ico* Baret p*ro*-uent*is* de e*mptis* apud Pridye. S*umma* xxx. D*e* q*uibus* in miss*is* ap*ud* M*er*don*am* x v*nde* j sus. Et Rem*anent* xx porc*i*.

Porcell*i*. Id*em* r*eddunt* com*potum* de v porcell*is* de exit*u* j suis. Et in miss*is* ap*ud* merdon*am* o*m*nis cu*m* sue. Et n*ihil* Rem*anet*.

Lan*a* g*rossa*. Id*em* r*eddunt* com*potum* de cc lx veller*ibus* multon*um* x veller*ibus* hurt*ardorum* cccc iiij^{xx} x veller*ibus* ou*ium* matr*icium* cc hogastr*orum* p*r*ouen*torum* ad tons*ionem* hoc a*nno*. S*umma* dcccc lx. De q*uibus* in dec*ima* iiij^{xx} xvj. In cons*uetudine* ij Bercar*iorum* j daye iij. S*umma* iiij^{xx} xix. In miss*is* ap*ud* Wolues*eiam* dccc lx vell*era* q*ue* fece-*runt* v pond*era* di*midium* ij cl*avos*. Et in vend*ito* s*upe*r comp*otum* j pro iiij d. ob. q.

Lan*a* Fract*a*. Id*em* R*eddunt* com*potum* de vj cl*avis* j li*bra* de Lana fract*a*. Et in vend*itis* totu*m*.

Lan*a* Agn*ina*. Id*em* r*eddunt* com*potum* de c iiij^{xx} j vell*eribus* agno-*rum* p*r*ouen*torum* ad tons*ionem* hoc a*nno*. In miss*is* ap*ud* Wolues*eiam* o*m*nia q*ue* fec*erunt* ix cl*avos*.

De Cas*eo* yem*ali* n*ihil*.

Cas*eus* estiual*is*. Id*em* r*eddunt* com*potum*[1] de c lxx cas*eis* f*act*is hoc a*nno* q*ui* inceper*unt* fieri ydus ap*rilis* *et* desier*unt* fieri die S*anct*i mich*ae*-*lis* utr*oque* die co*m*putat*o*. De q*uibus* in dec*ima* xvij. In cons*uetudine* j p*re*pos*iti* j Bercar*ii* j Fabr*i* *et* j daye iiij. S*umma* xxj. Et in vend*itis* c xlix q*ui* fec*erunt* v pond*era* viij cl*avos* di*midium*.

Butir*um*. Id*em* r*eddunt* com*potum* de xvij cl*avis* butir*i* de exit*u* dayer*ie* hoc a*nno*. Et in vend*itis* totu*m*.

Gallin*e*. Id*em* r*eddunt* com*potum* de c xxv gallin*is* p*r*ouen*tis* de Cheri-*setto*.[2] De q*uibus* in def*ectu* t*erre* Le Stronge tr*acte* in d*ominicum* iiij. In def*ectu* t*erre* Will*elm*i de Curi*a* iiij. In def*ectu* Cur*tilagii* Rob*er*ti Coche iiij. In def*ectu* t*erre* Le Swon p*ro* eode*m* iiij. In def*ectu* t*erre* Ric*ard*i vaccar*ii* iiij. In def*ectu* t*erre* Ric*ard*i Knaue p*ro* eod*em* iiij. In def*ectu* t*erre* Eme Martyn q*uia* vidua ij. In def*ectu* t*erre* Buwolf' p*ro* eod*em* ij. S*umma* xxviij. Et in vend*itis* iiij^{xx} xvij.

Cori*a*. Iid*em* r*eddunt* com*potum* de j cor*io* affr*i* iij cor*iis* bou*um* de mor*ina*. In vend*itis* o*m*nia.

Pell*es* g*rosse*. Id*em* r*eddunt* com*potum* de xxvj pell*ibus* multon*um* xxxvj pell*ibus* ou*ium* matr*icium* xlvj pell*ibus* hogastr*orum* de mor*ina* an*te* tons*ionem*. S*umma* c ix. Et in vend*itis* o*m*nis.

Pell*es* nude. Id*em* r*eddunt* com*potum* de vij pell*ibus* multon*um* xj

[1] Marginal note: Vacca R*eddit* de ij s. vj d. oue*s* de j d. o*b*. *et* hoc p*ro*pt*er* m*axi*-*mam* siccitate*m* in est*ate* hoc a*nno* iiij d. min*us* in toto.

[2] Marginal note: M*emorandum* q*uod* p*re*ceptu*m* est p*re*pos*ito* q*uo*d emat iiij Auc*as* *et* j Ancere*m* v gallinas *et* j gallu*m* q*uia* on*e*rabit*ur* de exit*u* in anno fut*uro*.

pell*ibus* ou*ium* matr*icium* de mor*ina* po*s*t tons*ionem*. S*umma* xviij. Et in vend*itis* o*m*nis.

Pell*es* Agn*ine*. Id*em* r*eddunt* co*mpotum* de cc lxxij pell*ibus* agn*orum* de mor*ina* an*te* sep*araci*o*nem*. De q*uibus* in deci*ma* xxvij. Et in vend*itis* cc xlv. Et de xxiij pell*ibus* agn*orum* de mor*ina* po*s*t sep*aracionem* *et* an*te* tons*ionem* *et* vij po*s*t tons*ionem*. S*umma* xxx. Et in vend*itis* o*m*nis.

Cic*er*a. Id*em* r*eddunt* co*mpotum* de j doleo Cic*er*e rem*anente* a*nno* p*re*ter*ito*. Et de j de exit*u* gardini hoc a*nno*. S*umma* ij. In vend*ito* j. Et Rem*anet* j dol*eum*.

Vtens*ilia*. Id*em* r*eddunt* co*mpotum* de j cacab*o* j olla enea j pocinet' j patell*a* j lauacr*o* cu*m* pelu*e* j serur*a* rem*anentibus* a*nno* p*re*ter*ito*. Et Rem*anent* hec o*m*nia.

Caret*ta*. Et de j caret*ta* rem*anente* a*nno* p*re*ter*ito*. Et Rem*anet* j caret*ta*.

§§ 13. Reeve's Account, 29 Sept., 1306—28 Sept., 1307.

This account is of great value because of its detail. We are told, to give but one illustration of the detail, that certain men paid annually for the privilege of serving beyond the liberty of Crawley, with the understandng that they follow their tithing at the two law-days; that is, that they be present at the tourns of Hock and St. Martin. Five paid in money, one in wax, and one a plow. The sums or values paid were 3d., 6d., and 12d. We are not told whether these people were older sons who were destined by the custom of Crawley not to inherit their father's holding, or whether they were themselves tenants who, for the time being, were arranging to have someone else perform their service and look after their holdings. Probably the former is the explanation, particularly in the case of the larger sums paid.

There seems to be a clear case here of an outsider, William Bonde of Niwenton, paying a composition or fine for marrying an heiress and for having her messuage and virgate. A large sum was exacted, 20s., or the price of two good oxen.

There were sheepfolds for ewes, wethers, and hogasters. These had buildings with walls and roofs and were provided with cribs. Oil, quicksilver, and copperas were purchased for smearing the sheep, doubtless as a preventative of murrain. The price paid was 54s. 5d., almost the price (61s. 5d.) of 59 ewes sold this year.

The lord sowed 431 (customary) acres of grain in five different 'fields,' or furlongs as we should perhaps say. All but 20 acres of peas are stated to be 'as they lie,' that is, to be in half (statutary) acre strips. But this arable demesne, being in only five furlongs, could not have been scattered all over the village. In Puttes-hulle, 176 acres of oats were sown; in Drakenore, 117 acres of barley and 20 acres of vetches; and in Combforlange and opposite Northbery, 98 acres of wheat. Apparently, at this time, the lord used certain large furlongs exclusively or largely for himself, passing them on in rotation to the tenants in subsequent years. Trendlye and Holindane were not the lord's this year, to be used either as pasture or as arable, because they belonged to the men of the manor and were sowed with grain. The word pasture seems to have had at least two meanings here, permanent pasture as in the case of Schoret or Shert, and fallow pasture as in the case of Lok-forlang and all, or almost all, other furlongs.

One wey (pondus) of wool was sold 'to a certain merchant' this year. The lactage of cows and sheep, apparently the right to milk them, was sold for 12s. 10d. Cider of both last year and this year was sold. Here as elsewhere it is stated that certain articles, such as fowl and cider, were sold on account (super compotum), which we take to mean entered on a separate account because the items were small and individually unimportant. One entry has 36s. 9¾d. 'from things sold on account.' There is no indication of a charge or future payment.

In connection with the lord's gifts to his boon-workers it is stated that one quarter, apparently, of barley ought to make 100 loaves of bread. Clearly either the loaves were very large or very heavy.

It is recorded that 6s. 8d. were paid to the taxers and collectors of the thirtieth. This was a subsidy imposed by parliament in 1306 to be collected 2 February—3 November, 1307. It was due only in the country, the towns being liable to a twentieth. It was an actual thirtieth of the movable property possessed by both peasants and lords, by both poor and rich. Such exemptions as were allowed, for armor, jewelry, clothing, and plate, would affect Crawley but little. The assessors of the shire were to appoint twelve residents of each hundred who, together with four men and the reeve of each manor, were to assess the tax.[1] Apparently the reeve of Crawley collected the tax and then handed it over to the officials above named, whether of the hundred or the shire is not stated.

CRAULEE [2]

Compotus eiusd*e*m Manerii.

Arreragi*um*. Ric*ar*dus Wodelok' Ball*ivus* *et* Nich*ola*us de Aula p*re*positus reddunt comp*otum* de xxix s. xj d. ob. de arr*eragio* anni p*re*ter*iti*. In lib*eratis* d*om*ino Symon*i* de Farh*a*m Thes*aurario* Wolues*eie* p*er* j t*alliam* tot*um* *et* q*uieti* sunt.

Redditus assis*us*. Iidem r*eddunt* c*ompotum* de lxj s. iiij d. de toto Reddit*u* assis*o* ad Nat*alem* d*omi*ni. Et de lxj s. iiij d. ad Pasch*am*. Et de lxj s. iiij d. ad f*estu*m Nat*alis* s*anc*ti Joh*annis* Bapt*ist*e. Et de iiij li. xvij s. vij d. ad f*estu*m s*anc*ti mich*aelis*. S*umma* xiiij li. xix d.

Acquietanc*ie*. In acq*uie*t*ancia* j p*re*p*osit*i v s. In acq*uie*t*anciis* vj Caruc*ariorum* *et* j Fabr*i* p*er* annu*m* xviij s. viij d. cuil*ibet* ij s. viij d. In acq*uie*t*anciis* ij b*er*cari*orum* p*er* ann*um* v s. iiij d. In acquiet*anciis* viij oper*ariorum* op*er*anci*um* p*er* ij dies in ebdom*ada* a f*est*o s*anc*ti mich*aelis* usq*ue* Gula*m* Augusti *et* in Aut*umpno* q*uo*libe*t* die op*er*abil*i* xxj s. iiij d. cuil*ibet* ij s. iiij d. In acq*uie*t*ancia* j porc*arii* fere p*er* d*imidium* ann*um* xv d. In acquiet*ancia* j vaccar*ii* p*er* ann*um* ij s. viij d. S*umma* liiij s. iij d.

Defectus. In def*ec*t*u* t*erre* le Stronge t*racte* in do*minicum* ij s. In def*ec*t*u* t*erre* Will*elm*i de Curi*a* p*ro* eodem p*er* ann*um* ij s. viij d. In def*ec*t*u* t*erre* de Alebrok' q*ui* m*odo* respond*it* apud M*er*don*am* v s. In def*ec*t*u* t*erre* Rob*er*ti Couche t*racte* in do*minicum* p*er* ann*um* ij s. viij d. In def*ec*t*u* t*erre* Rob*er*ti Caye p*ro* eodem ij s. viij d. In def*ec*t*u* t*erre* Rog*er*i le Porchir p*ro* eodem p*er* annu*m* ij s. viij d. In def*ec*t*u* t*erre* Ric*ard*i vaccar*ii* p*ro* eodem p*er* annu*m* ij s. viij d. S*umma* xx s. iiij d. S*umma* acquiet*anciarum* *et* defec*t*us lxxiiij s. vij d. S*umma* Redd*itus* Rem*anens* x li. vij s.

Ciminum. Idem r*eddunt* c*ompotum* de j l*ibra* Cimini de Redd*itu* Ric*ard*i Fromond'. Et in lib*erata* apud Wolues*eiam*.

Exitus manerii. Idem r*eddunt* c*ompotum* de xxiij d. o*b*. de pannag*io* porc*orum* ad f*estu*m s*anc*ti martini vid*elicet* p*ro* v Porc*is* sup*er*ann*atis* j t*rium* t*ermi*n*orum* *et* xxiiij porcell*is* sep*ara*t*is* s*cilicet* pro Porco sup*er*ann*ato* ij d. Et pro Porco iij t*ermi*n*orum* j d. ob. *et* p*ro* Porcell*o* sep*ara*t*o* o*b*. Et de iiij d. de Pannag*io* iiij vit*ulorum*. Et de xxv s. ij d. de xlvj

[1] *Rotuli Parliamentarum*, vol. I (1767), pp. 269–270.

[2] MS. P. R. O., Ecclesiastical Commission, Various, 159322.

vaccis vj Bouett*is* Et iiij bouicul*is* de pannag*io* de la Hok' vid*elicet* p*ro* vacc*a* vj d. p*ro* Bouett*o* iij d. *et* p*ro* Bouic*ulo* ij d. [De o][1]uib*us* inuent*is* in F[alda] . . . [nihil] [1] *quia non* excedebant num*erum* xxv. Et de xxj d. de iiij^{xx} iiij Agn*is* sep*aratis* in Pastur*a* [usque] [1] f*estu*m Nat*alis* . . . .[1] De Pastur*a* in bosc*o* vend*ita* in yeme n*ihi*l hoc anno. Et de ix s. viij d. de Pastur*a* vend*ita* ad equos in estate in Bosco vid*elicet* ad xiiij eq*uo*s p*ro* eq*uo* viij d. D*e* Pastur*a* de Puthulle n*ihil* hoc anno p*ro* mult*onibus* d*omi*ni. D*e* Pastur*a* de Trendlye *et* holindane n*ihil* hoc anno q*uia* se*min*abat*ur et* est t*erra* hom*inum* ville. D*e* Pastur*a* de Drakenore n*ihil* q*uia* se*mina*t*ur* cu*m* ordeo. De Pastur*a* de Combforlang' n*ihil* hoc a*nno* q*uia* se*min*abat*ur* fr*ument*o d*omi*ni. Et de viij d. de Pastur*a* circa Fossat*um* iux*ta* Northbur*y* vend*ita*. D*e* Pastur*a* de Lokforlang' n*ihil* hoc a*nno* p*ro* auer*is* d*omi*ni. Et de ij s. de Pastur*a* de Schoret vend*ita* hoc anno. Et de lix s. de viij bob*us* vend*itis* vn*de* j p*recium* v s. vj d. *et* j p*recium* vj s. *et* j p*recium* vj s. vj d. *et* ij p*recium* vt*ri*usq*ue* viij s. iij d. *et* j p*recium* viij s. vj d. *et* j p*recium* ix s. *et* j p*recium* vij s. Et de xlj s. ij d. de viij vacc*is* vend*itis* vn*de* ij p*recium* utr*i*usq*ue* iiij s. *et* j p*recium* v s. *et* j p*recium* iiij s. vj d. *et* ij p*recium* vt*ri*usq*ue* v s. vj d. *et* j p*recium* v s. viij d. *et* j p*recium* vij s. Et de ij s. de ij vitul*is* vend*itis*. Et de lxix s. ix d. de liiij multon*ibus* in t*er*m*in*o S*anc*ti m*a*rtini vend*itis* p*recium* cui*us*l*ibet* xv d. o*b*. Et de lxj s. v d. o*b*. de lix ou*ibus* matr*icibus* in T*er*m*in*o S*anc*ti Mart*ini* vend*itis* p*recium* cui*us*l*ibet* xij d. ob. Et de xxv s. de l agn*is* vend*itis*. Et de vj s. x d. de ij Porc*is* vend*itis*. Et de vj s. iiij d. o*b*. de iiij cl*avis* vj l*ibris* lan*e* fract*e* vend*itis*. D*e* cas*eo* yem*ali* hoc a*nno* n*ihil*. Et de lxv s. de vj pond*eribus* di*midio* cas*ei* estiual*is* vend*itis* p*recium* pond*eris* x s. Et de vj s. viij d. de xix clau*is* Butir*i* vend*itis*. Et de xxj s. de lxiij pell*ibus* g*ro*ss*is* de mor*ina* an*te* tons*ionem* vendit*is* p*recium* pell*is* iiij d. Et de xvj d. de iiij pell*ibus* multon*um* x pell*ibus* ou*ium* m*a*t*ricium* de mor*ina* p*o*st tons*ionem* vend*itis* in gross*o*. Et de vj s. iiij d. de lxxvj pell*ibus* agn*orum* de mor*ina* an*te* sep*ar*at*ionem* vend*itis*. Et de j d. de vij pell*ibus* Agn*orum* de mor*ina* p*ost* tons*ionem* vend*itis*. Et de xj s. iij d. de iiij^{xx} x gallin*is* vend*itis* p*recium* Galline j d. ob. Et de iiij d. de c ou*is* vend*itis*. Et de xj s. de j dol*eo* cisere vend*ito* q*uia* debil*is* sine vase. Et de ij s. de Ric*ard*o cappellano p*ro* oper*ibus* vj acr*arum* t*er*r*e* t*ra*duct*e* s*ibi et* suis relax*ate*. Et de xij d. de quod*am* Curtillag*io* quod q*uond*a*m* fuit Rog*er*i le Porchir locato hoc anno. Et de xij s. de xxiiij acr*is* t*er*r*e* d*ominici* loc*ate* hoc a*nno* q*uia* s*u*p*er*i*us* comp*utatur* in def*ec*t*u*. Et de ij s. de quod*am* Curtillag*io* quod q*uond*a*m* fuit Rob*er*ti Couch'. Et de xl s. de iiij^{xx} vij roffr*is* vendit*is* in Bosco hoc a*nno*. Et de xvij s. iij d. de vj acr*is* di*midia et* q*uar*ta p*ar*te vni*us* acr*e* subbosci vend*itis* p*recium* acr*e* ij s. vj d. o*b*. *et* o*b*. q. plus in toto. Et de xij d. de j Cultr*o* de ann*ua* recogni-

[1] Manuscript torn.

tione vend*ito*. Et de xj s. de iij affr*is* vend*itis* vn*de* ij p*recium* cui*us*l*ibet* iiij s. *et* j p*recium* iij s. *Summa* xxvj li. ij s. iiij d. ob.

Vend*itio* Sup*er* Comp*otum*. Et de xxxvj s. ix d. *ob*. q. de reb*us* ven-d*itis* s*up*er Comp*otum*. *Summa* xxxvj s. ix d. ob. q.

Annua Recogn*itio*. Iidem r*eddunt* c*ompotum* de vj d. de Rob*er*to Pak' p*ro* annua recogn*itione*. Et de vj d. de Rob*er*to le Porck p*ro* s*im*ili. Et de iij d. de Joh*anne* le Wolsche p*ro* s*im*ili. Et de iij d. de Rog*er*o Elys p*ro* s*im*ili vt possit seruir*e* ex*tra* lib*ertatem et* seq*ui* decen-*nam* sua*m et* venir*e* ad duas laghedays. Et de iij d. de Rob*er*to Elys p*ro* eodem. S*umma* xxj d.

Item Recogn*itio*. Idem r*eddunt* c*ompotum* de j Cultr*o* de recogn*i*-*tione* Rob*er*ti Coleman vt possit morari *et* seruir*e* ex*tra* lib*ertatem et* n*ihilominus* seq*ui* decen*nam* sua*m et* venir*e* ad duas laghedays *et* [in] vend*ito* sup*erius*.

Recogn*itio* Cere. Id*em* r*eddunt* c*ompotum* de di*midia* li*bra* Cer*e* de Joh*anne* le Cart*er*e p*ro* annua recogn*itione* vt h*ab*eat licenc*iam* man-end*i* alibi q*uam* sup*er* t*erram* d*omini et* d*ebet* seq*ui* decen*nam* sua*m et* duos lagedays p*er* pl*egium* Rob*ert*i le Bonde *et* Rob*ert*i Meriweder. Et lib*erata* apud Wolues*eiam*.

Vend*itio* Blad*i*. Fr*umentum*. Idem r*eddunt* c*ompotum* de iiij li. ix s. iiij d. de xvj q*uarteriis* fr*ument*i vend*itis* vn*de* ij q*uarteria* p*recium* q*uarterii* v s. *et* xiiij q*uarteria* p*recium* q*uarterii* v s. viij d. Curall*um*. Idem r*eddunt* c*ompotum* de viij s. de ij q*uarteriis* Curall*i* vend*itis*. Pis*e*. Idem r*eddunt* c*ompotum* de xvij s. ij d. o*b*. de iij q*uarteriis* v b*us*-*sellis* di*midio* Pis*arum* vend*itis* p*recium* q*uarterii* iiij s. viij d. Vesc*ie*. Idem r*eddunt* c*ompotum* de xvij s. vj d. de iij q*uarteriis* vj b*ussellis* ves-*ciarum* vend*itis* p*recium* q*uarterii* iiij s. viij d. S*umma* vj li. xij s. ob.

Fines *et* maritag*ia* cu*m* Tethingp*enny*. Iidem r*eddunt* c*ompotum* de vj s. viij d. de Dec*enna* de Craule p*ro* teghing*a* ad hundr*edum* s*anct*i m*art*i*ni*. Et de vj s. viij d. p*ro* eodem ad hundr*edum* de Hock*e*. Et de xx s. de Will*elmo* Bonde de Niwenton' p*ro* Alic*ia* la Lang' *et* p*ro* j mes*uagio et* j v*irgat*a t*erre* sue h*abendis*. Et de ij s. de Steph*ano* le Baker' p*ro* Dionis*ia* fil*ia* sua marit*anda* ex*tra*. S*umma* xxv s. iiij d.

Perquisit*a*. Iidem r*eddunt* c*ompotu*m de xxj s. iiij d. de minut*is* p*er*-quis*itis* Cur*ie* hoc anno. S*umma* xxj s. iiij d. S*umma* vt*ri*usq*ue* lvj s. viij d. S*umma* Toci*us* Rec*epte* xlvij li. xvj s. vij d. ob. q.

Custus caruc*arum*. In Ferr*o et* acer*o* emp*tis* ad ferr*amentum* iiij Caru-c*arum* p*er* ann*um* x s. iiij d. In ij vomer*ibus* e*mptis* ij s. In iiij ferr*is* pedal*ibus* e*mptis* cu*m* clau*is* ad idem xv d. In iiij par*ibus* rotar*um* ad Caruc*as* e*mptis* xvj d. In ij nouis Caruc*is* fac*iendis* vj d. In ferr*o* j caruce lig*ando* j d. In ferr*amentis* vj affr*orum* p*er* ann*um* iij s. vj d. In p*recariis* vij Caruc*ariorum* aranc*ium* vij acr*as* ad sem*entem* yem*alem et* q*ua*d*r*a*gesimalem* vij d. In Capistr*is* p*ro*p*ri*o pilo fac*iendis* j d. In iij bob*us* e*mptis* ad Caruc*as* xxix s. j d. q. vn*de* ij p*recium* vt*ri*usq*ue* ix s. *ob*. *et* j p*recium* xj s. q. In ij affr*is* e*mptis* xix s. ix d. In stip*endiis* ij Caruc*ariorum* p*er* ann*um* viij s. In xij jug*is* e*mptis* x d. In iiij car*ec*-t*atis* foragi*i* e*mptis* ad suste*n*taci*on*em bou*um* viij s. ij d. S*um*m*a* iiij li. v s. vj d. q.

Empcio Blad*i*. In iiij q*uarteriis* v b*ussellis* di*midio* ordei e*mptis* xviij s. ix d. p*recium* q*uarterii* iiij s. S*umma* xviij s. ix d.

Custus car*ectarum*. In Clut*is* clau*is* *et* vncto e*mptis* ad Car*ect*as viij s. In car*ect*is gropp*an*d*is* *et* emend*is* clau*is* e*mptis* ad idem *et* car-*ectis* emend*is* de Carpent*ario* xix d. In ferr*amentis* ij eq*uorum* Car*ec*-*tariorum* p*er* ann*um* ij s. vj d. In stip*endio* j car*ectarii* p*er* ann*um* iiij s. In albo Cor*io* ad h*ar*nes*ium* emp*to* iiij d. In ij car*ec*till*is* de p*ro*p*ri*o m*er*emi*o* fac*iendis* vij d. In j Potto fac*iendo* ad fim*a* ex*tra*hend*a* iiij d. In j Car*ect*a emp*ta* xviij s. vj d. q. In j par*i* t*ractarum* e*mpto* iiij d. ob. S*um*m*a* xxix s. j d. ob. q.

Custus Daer*ie*. In Line*a* tela *et* lane*o* Pann*o* empt*is* ad Daer*iam* vj d. In vij buss*ellis* sal*is* emp*tis* xxj d. In p*r*essur*a* e*mpta* iiij d. In oll*is* *et* patell*is* terr*enis* emp*tis* ad daer*iam* iiij d. In vnct*o* viuo arg*ento* *et* cope-*r*ose emp*tis* ad bident*es* vngend*as* liiij s. v d. In par*ietibus* bercar*ie* hogastr*orum* em*endis* xij d. In Crech*is* fac*iendis* in eadem b*er*car*ia* ad Tasch*am* iiij s. In b*er*car*iis* multon*um* *et* ou*ium* m*a*t*ricium* cooper*iend*is* *et* emend*is* p*er* loca ad Tasch*am* xxj d. In j int*er*clause de nouo fac*iend'* in b*er*car*ia* multon*um* xij d. In vtens*iliis* Daer*ie* emend*is* *et* j patell*a* en*ea* emend*a* ix d. In iij vacc*is* emp*tis* xxiiij s. iiij d. vn*de* j p*recium* vij s. iij d. j p*recium* viij s. iij d. *et* j p*recium* viij s. x d. In ij suib*us* cu*m* v porcell*is* emp*tis* vij s. vj d. In j anc*ere* *et* iiij auc*is* emp*tis* xx d. In v gal-lin*is* *et* j gall*o* emp*tis* viij s. *ob*. In xj capon*ibus* e*mptis* p*recepto* d*omi*ni iij s. xj d. In stip*endio* j Daye p*er* ann*um* ij s. In feno emp*to* ad sus-tent*ionem* Bident*ium* vid*elicet* xj mullon*ibus* feni lj s. Et rem*anet* in-teg*ra* lit*era* in Bert*ona* ad Instaur*um* p*ro* anno futur*o*. In xxv cleiis de p*ro*p*r*iis virg*is* fac*iendis* viij d. S*umma* vij li. xvij s. vij d. *ob*.

Custus domor*um*. In g*ra*ng*ia* ordei discoop*er*t*a* Watuland*a* viij d. In g*ra*ng*ia* fr*umen*ti *et* dict*a* g*ra*ng*ia* ordei coop*er*iend*is* p*er* loca ij s. x d. In j bukett*o* aq*ua*tico ad puteu*m* emp*to* iiij d. q. In j Picos*o* emp*to* iij d. In j besc*a* ferrand*a* j d. In iij q*uarent*en*is* *et* v p*er*tic*is* haye claud*end*is c*ir*ca copiciu*m* in Bosco iij s. vij d. ob. p*ro* q*uarent*en*a* xiiij d. In j serur*a* cu*m* claue emp*ta* ad host*ium* g*r*an*arii* v d. S*umma* viij s. ij d. ob. q.

Tritur*atio*. In xix q*uarteriis* fr*umen*ti t*r*itur*andis* ad Tasch*am* iij s. iij d. ob. p*ro* q*uarterio* de viij b*ussellis* Ras*is* ij d. In eisdem vent*andis* iiij d. ob. q. In vij q*uarteriis* di*midio* ordei t*r*itur*andis* *et* vent*andis* ad Tasch*am* xj d. q. In ij cribr*is* emp*tis* iij d. In vad*io* Rob*er*ti de Bern-cestr' Berebrett*i* exist*entis* vlt*ra* t*r*itur*ationem* *et* p*ro* Blado ventand*o* v s. j d. *ob*. p*er* t*alliam*. S*um*m*a* x s.

Custus Autumpn*i*. In Blad*o* sarcland*o* vlt*ra* illud q*uod* op*erarii* sarclau*er*unt vj s. In M allec*iis* emp*tis* ad iij p*recarias* Aut*umpnales* de ccc ij ho*minibus* cu*m* ministr*is* Cur*ie* metent*ibus* iiij^xx xviij acr*as* fr*umenti* xxxij acr*as* auen*e* *et* xxiiij acras Pis*arum* *et* vesc*iarum* sicut iacent v s. x d. In stipe*ndio* j ho*minis* custod*ientis* Blad*um* in camp*is* p*er* noct*em* *et* auxiliant*is* Carcare Car*ectas* iij s. In stip*endio* j messor*is* p*er* annu*m* vj s. viij d. In vad*io* Joh*annis* le Kyng' existent*is* apud Craule p*er* xxviij dies Aut*umpnales* iij s. vj d. p*er* t*alliam*. S*umma* xxv s.[1]

Expen*se* Sen*escalli* *et* Ball*ivi*. In expen*sis* R. de Bereford' tenent*is* Turn*um* s*ancti* martini iij s. v d. p*er* t*alliam*. In expen*sis* Ric*ard*i Wadeloke . . . [per][2] suos aduent*us* x s. j d. S*umma* xiij s. vj d.

Expen*se* For*insice*. In solut*is* Tax*atoribus* [?] *et* collector*ibus* xxx^e vj s. viij d. S*umma* vj s. viij d. S*umma* Om*n*ium Expen*sarum* xvij li. xiiij s. v d. q. Et d*ebent* xxxli. ij s. ij d. ob.

lib*eratio*. In lib*eratis* d*omi*no Sym*oni* de Farham Thes*aurario* Woluese*ie* p*er* j t*alliam* xviij li. Et sic d*ebent* de Claro xij li. ij s. ij d. ob.

Exitus g*rangie*. Fr*umentum*.[2] Idem r*eddunt* co*mpotum* de xxxviij q*uarteriis* de toto exit*u* fr*umenti* mens*ura* ras*a*. De quib*us* in se*mine* s*upe*r iiij^xx xviij acr*as* sicut iacent in Campo de Combforlang*e* *et* iux*ta* Northber*y* xviij q*uarteria* vij b*usselli* s*cilicet* in a[cra][3] j b*ussellus* di*midium* *sed* iij b*usselli* plus in toto. In lib*eratis* j messor*i* p*er* annu*m* iij q*uarteria* ij b*usselli* *et* cap*it* residuu*m* de ordeo inferi*us* *et* cap*it* q*uarterium* per v[iij][3] sept*imanas*. Et in vend*itis* xvj q*uarteria*.

Curall*um*. Id*em* redd*unt* Comp*otum* de ij q*uarteriis* Curall*i* de toto exitu . . . .[3] [Et] in vend*itis* Tot*um*.

Ord*eum*. Iid*em* r*eddunt* comp*otum* de lviij q*uarteriis* di*midio* de toto exit*u* ord[ei de gr][3]ang*ia* in Granar*io*. E[t de][3] iiij q*uarteriis* v b*ussellis* di*midio* de empc*ione*. S*umma* lxiij q*uarteria* j b*ussellus* di*midius*. De quib*us* in se*mine* sup*er* c xvij acr*as* sicut iacent in Campo de Drakenore ex p*ar*te Orient*ali* de Puthull*e* xxxiij q*uarteria* j b*ussellus* s*cilicet* in ac*ra* ij b*usselli* j p*eccum* set vj b*usselli* j pek*um* min*us* in toto. In lib*eratione* j Carectar*ii* ij Fugator*um* p*er* annu*m* q*ui* cap*iunt* q*uarterium* p*er* x sept*imanas* xv q*uarteria* iiij b*usselli* di*midius*. In lib*eratione* j Daye a Festo s*ancti* mich*ae*lis vsq*ue* F*estu*m Pur*ificationis* b*eat*e mar*ie* di*midium* q*uarterium*. In lib*eratione* eiusdem a F*est*o Pur*ificationis* vsq*ue* Festum s*ancti* mich*ae*lis q*ue* capit q*uarterium* p*er* xij sept*imanas* ij q*uarteria* vj b*usselli* di*midius*. In lib*eratione* j h*er*ciator*is* ad vt*ram*q*ue* semen[tem] vj b*usselli*. In lib*eratione* j Custod*is* Hogastr*orum* Agno-

[1] The manuscript is torn and wrinkled from here on for several lines.

[2] Marginal note on frumentum, other notes being omitted here: R*espondent* de i q*ua*r*terio* ii b*ussellis* plus se*mine* alt*ero* *et* di*midio*.

[3] Torn off.

rum per annu*m* qui cap*it quarterium per* x sept*imanas* v q*uarteria* j b*us*-*sellus* di*midius*. In lib*eratione* j haiwardi *per* annu*m* qui cap*it quarterium per* viij sept*imanas* iij q*uarteria* ij b*usselli et* capit residuu*m* de fr*umento* sup*erius*. In Expens*is* iij p*recariarum* iij q*uarteria*. Et debent fieri de q*uarterio* c panes. S*umma* lxiij q*uarteria* j b*ussellus* di*midius*.

Auene. Iidem r*eddunt* Comp*otum* de lxxix q*uarteriis* de toto exit*u* auen*arum* mens*ura* ras*a*. Et de xij q*uarteriis per* estim*ationem* dat*is* bob*us* in Garb*is*. S*umma* iiij^{xx} xj q*uarteria*. D*e* quib*us* in se*mine* sup*er* c lxxvj acr*as* sicut iacent in Campo de Putteshull*e* ex p*ar*te Orient*ali* de Puthull*e* lxvj q*uarteria* j b*ussellus scilicet* in acr*a* iij b*usselli sed* j b*ussellus* plus in toto. In p*rebenda* vj affr*orum* a Festo Nat*alis* d*omi*ni vsq*ue* Hockeday v q*uarteria* di*midium*. In p*rebend*a boui*um per* est*imationem* in garb*is* xij q*uarteria*. In p*rebenda* ij eq*uorum* Car*ectariorum per* annu*m* iiij q*uarteria* vj b*usselli*. In p*rebenda* eq*uorum* d*omi*ni Rad*ulphi* de Bereford j b*ussellus*. In p*rebenda* eq*uorum* Ball*ivi* p*er* suos aduent*us* di*midium* q*uarterium*. In Farin*a* f*ac*ta ad Potag*ium* famulor*um* ij q*uarteria*. S*umma* iiij^{xx} xj q*uarteria*.

Pis*e*. Iidem r*eddunt* comp*otum* de viij q*uarteriis* ij b*ussellis* di*midio* de toto exit*u* Pis*arum* mens*ura* ras*a*. De quib*us* in se*min*e sup*er* xx acr*as* in Campo de Gerdelond' iiij q*uarteria* v b*usselli scilicet* in acr*a* ij b*usselli sed* iij b*usselli* min*us* in Toto. Et in vend*itis* iij q*uarteria* v b*usselli* di*midius*.

Vesc*ie*. Iidem r*eddunt* Comp*otum* de viij q*uarteriis* ij b*ussellis* de toto exit*u* vesc*iarum* mens*ura* ras*a*. Et de j q*uarterio* dat*o* ou*ibus* in siliquis. S*umma* ix q*uarteria* ij b*usselli*. De quib*us* in se*mine* sup*er* xx acr*as* sicut iacent in Campo de Drakenore iiij q*uarteria* di*midium scilicet* in acr*a* ij b*usselli sed* di*midium* q*uarterium* min*us* in Toto. In Dat*is* ou*ibus* mat*ricibus* in yeme in siliquis j q*uarterium*. S*umma* vj q*uarteria* di*midium*. Et in vend*itis* iij q*uarteria* vj b*usselli*.

Instaur*um*. E*qui* Car*e*ctar*ii*. Iid*em* redd*unt* comp*otum* de j eq*uo* Car*ectario* rem*anente* anno p*re*terito. Et de j de emp*to*. S*umma* ij. Et rem*anent* ij eq*ui* Car*ectarii*.

Affri. Iidem r*eddunt* c*ompotum* de vj affr*is* Rem*anentibus* anno p*re*terito. Et de ij de emp*tis*. S*umma* viij. D*e* quib*us* in vend*itis* iij. S*umma* iij. Et rem*anent* v affri.

Boues. Iidem r*eddunt* comp*otum* de xxxij bob*us* Rem*anentibus* anno p*re*terito. Et de iij de emp*tis*. S*umma* xxxv. D*e* quib*us* in vend*itis* viij. S*umma* viij. Et rem*anent* xxvij Boues.

Vacc*e*. Iidem r*eddunt* c*ompotum* de xiij vacc*is* rem*anentibus* a*nno* p*re*terito. Et de iij de Emp*tis* vn*de* j an*te* vitul*ationem et* ij p*ost* vitul*ationem*. S*umma* xvj. D*e* quib*us* in vend*itis* viij an*te* vit*ulationem*. S*umma* viij. Et rem*anent* viij vacc*e*.

Bouic*u*li. Iidem r*eddunt* comp*otum* de iij bouic*u*lis Rem*anentibus* *anno* pr*eterito* annal*ibus*. Et rem*anent* iij bouic*u*li vnd*e* ij masc*u*li.[1] D*e* annalib*us* n*ihil* q*uia* a*nno* pr*eter*ito no*n* rem*anent* vituli.

Vituli. Iid*em* r*eddunt* comp*otum* de vj vitul*is* de exit*u* d*icta*r*um* vacc*arum*. D*e* quib*us* in Decim*a* n*ihil* hoc anno. Et in vend*itis* ij. Et rem*anent* iiij vit*u*li.

Multon*es*. Iid*em* r*eddunt* Comp*otum* de ccc lij multon*ibus* Rem*anentibus* a*nno* pr*eter*it*o*. Et de c viij adiu*n*ct*is*. S*um*m*a* cccc lx. D*e* quib*us* in mor*ina* xviij an*te* tons*ionem*. Et p*ost* tons*ionem* iiij. Et in vend*itis* an*te* Tons*ionem* liiij. S*um*m*a* lxxvj. Et rem*anent* ccc iiij^{xx} iiij multon*es*.

Hurtard*i*. Iid*em* r*eddunt* Comp*otum* de xj hurtard*is* rem*anentibus* a*nno* pr*eter*it*o*. Et rem*anent* xj hurtard*i*.

Oues matr*ices*. Iid*em* r*eddunt* comp*otum* de d iiij^{xx} ou*ibus* matr*icibus* Rem*anentibus* a*nno* pr*eterito*. Et de iiij^{xx} xvj adiu*n*ct*is*. S*um*m*a* dc lxxvj. D*e* quib*us* in mor*ina* an*te* Agn*ilationem* xxj. Et p*ost* Agn*ilationem* *et* an*te* Tons*ionem* iij. Et p*ost* tons*ionem* x. In vend*itis* in t*er*mi*n*o s*anc*t*i* martini lix. S*um*m*a* iiij^{xx} xiij. Et rem*anentibus* d iiij^{xx} iij oues matr*ices*.

Hogastr*i*. Iid*em* r*eddunt* comp*otum* de cc xxv hogastr*is* rem*anentibus* a*nno* pr*eter*it*o* Agn*is*. De quib*us* in mor*ina* an*te* Tons*ionem* xxj. In adiu*n*ct*is* cu*m* multon*ibus* c viij. Et cu*m* ou*ibus* matr*icibus* iiij^{xx} xvj. S*um*m*a* cc xxv. Et n*ihil* rem*anet*.

Agni. Iid*em* redd*unt* Comp*otum* de cccc xxix Agn*is* de exit*u* d*icta*r*um* ou*ium* matr*icium* q*uia* lxj fuer*unt* st*er*il*es* *et* x fecerunt aborsum. Et de lxj rec*eptis* de Rector*e* eccl*es*ie de Chilbolton' an*te* tons*ionem*. Et de x de dono an*te* tons*ionem*. S*um*m*a* d. De q*uibus* in mor*ina* an*te* sep*aracionem* iiij^{xx} iiij. In Decim*a* xxxiiij. In mor*ina* p*ost* separ*ationem* *et* an*te* tons*ionem* xj. Et p*ost* tons*ionem* vij. In Cons*uetudine* j pr*e*p*osit*i ij berc*ariorum* *et* j fabr*i* an*te* tons*ionem* iiij. In vend*itis* p*re*posit*o* de Merewell' l an*te* tons*ionem*. S*um*m*a* c iiij^{xx} x. Et rem*anent* ccc x Agni.

Porc*i*. Iid*em* r*eddunt* comp*otum* de xx Porc*is* rem*anentibus* anno p*re*t*er*it*o*. D*e* quib*us* in lib*er*at*is* ad Expens*as* d*om*i*n*i apud Wytteneye xviij. In vend*itis* ij. S*um*m*a* xx. Et n*ihil* rem*anet*.

Sues. Iid*em* r*eddunt* c*ompotum* de ij suib*us* de emp*tis*. Et rem*anent* ij sues.

Porcell*i*. Iid*em* r*eddunt* Comp*otum* de xvj porcell*is* de exit*u* d*icta*r*um* suu*m*. Et de v de emp*tis* cu*m* j sue. S*um*m*a* xxj. De quib*us* in Decim*a* j. In Cons*uetudine* j Porc*arii* n*ihil* q*uia* no*n* fuit ibi Porcar*ius* n*isi* p*er* p*a*ruu*m* temp*us*. Et rem*anent* xx Porcell*i*.

Lan*a* grossa. Iid*em* r*eddunt* comp*otum* de cc iiij^{xx} vell*eribus* multon*um*. Et de xj vell*eribus* Hurt*ardorum* cccc iiij^{xx} xvij vell*eribus* ou*ium* matr*icium*. Et de cc iiij vell*eribus* Hogastr*orum* p*r*ouen*torum* ad Tons*ionem*. S*um*m*a* dcccc iiij^{xx} xij vell*era*. D*e* quib*us* in decim*a* iiij^{xx} xix.

[1] Corrected from masc*u*hi.

In Cons*uetudine* ij b*er*car*iorum et* j Daye iij. In lib*eratis* cuide*m* m*er*catori p*recepto* d*omi*ni C xxvij q*ui* fecerunt j pond*us*. In vend*itis* p*re*p*osit*o xxxviij que fecer*unt* vij clau*os*. S*um*m*a* CC lxvij. In miss*is* apud Wolue*seiam* DCC xxv vell*era* q*ue* fec*erunt* iiij pond*era* xxiij clau*os* di*midium*. Et in vend*itis* s*up*er comp*otum* xxxviij vell*era* pro xvij s. v d.

Lan*a* fract*a*. Iidem r*eddunt* Comp*otum* de iiij clau*is* vj li*bris* lan*e* fract*e* ad tons*ionem* p*ro*uent*is*. Et in vend*itis* totu*m*.

Lan*a* Agn*ina*. Iide*m* reddu*n*t c*om*p*otum* de CCC xvij vell*eribus* Agn*inis* ad tons*ionem* p*ro*uent*is*. Et in miss*is* apud Wolues*eiam* o*mn*ia q*ue* fecer*unt* xxiij clau*os* ij li*bras*.

Cas*eus* est*iu*al*is*. Iidem redd*unt* c*om*p*otum* de C lxxiij cas*eis* f*ac*t*is* hoc anno ex d*ic*t*is* ou*ibus* m*a*tric*ibus et* vacc*is* qui Incep*er*unt fieri Die Lune p*roximo* an*te* F*estu*m S*anc*torum Tiburt*i et* Valer*ii et* desier*unt* fieri die S*anc*ti mich*aelis* vt*ro*q*ue* die Comp*utato*. D*e* quib*us* in Decim*a* xvij. In Cons*uetudine* b*er*car*ii* j p*re*p*osit*i j Fabr*i et* j Daye iiij. S*um*m*a* xxj. Et in vend*itis* C lij qui fecer*unt* vj pond*era* xiiij clau*os*.

D*e* Cas*eo* yem*ali* n*ihil* hoc anno.

De lacta*gio* vend*ito* c*om*p*utato* xij s. x d. vt vacc*e et* oue*s* respond*entur* sup*ra*.

Butir*um*. Iidem r*eddunt* c*om*p*otum* de xix clau*is* Butir*i* de toto exit*u* Daer*ie*. Et in vend*ito* Totu*m*.

De cor*io* n*ihil*.

Pell*es* grosse. Idem r*eddunt* c*om*p*otum* de xviij pell*ibus* multon*um* xxiiij pell*ibus* ou*ium* matr*icium et* xxj pell*ibus* Hogastr*orum* de mor*ina* an*te* Tons*ionem*. S*um*m*a* lxiij. Et in vend*itis* omn*es*.

Pell*es* Nude. Iidem r*eddunt* c*om*p*otum* de iiij pell*ibus* multon*um* x pell*ibus* ou*ium* matr*icium* de mor*ina* p*ost* Tons*ionem*. S*um*m*a* xiiij. Et in vend*itis* omn*es*.

Pell*es* Agn*ine*. Iidem r*eddunt* c*om*p*otum* de iiij^{xx} iiij pell*ibus* Agn*orum* de mor*ina* an*te* separ*ationem*. D*e* quib*us* in dec*ima* viij. Et in vend*itis* lxxvj. Et de xj pell*ibus* post separ*ationem et* an*te* Tons*ionem*. Et de vij post Tons*ionem*. S*um*m*a* xviij. Et in vend*itis* omn*es*. Et in vend*itis* supe*r* Comp*otum* xj pell*es* pro xj d.

Auc*e*. Iidem r*eddunt* comp*otum* de iiij auc*is et* j ancer*e* de emp*tis*. Et de x de exit*u*. S*um*m*a* xv. D*e* q*ui*b*us* in dec*ima* j. Et in vend*itis* s*up*er Comp*otum* ix auc*e* p*ro* iij s. Et rem*anent* v Auc*e* vn*de* j ance*r*.

Gallin*e*. Idem r*eddunt* c*om*p*otum* de v gallin*is et* j gallo de emp*tis*. Et de C xxv gallin*is* p*ro*uent*is* de ch*er*iset*o*. S*um*m*a* C xxxj. D*e* quib*us* in def*ectu* t*er*r*e* le strong*e* t*r*act*e* in d*ominicum* iiij. In def*ectu* t*er*r*e* Wil*lelm*i de Cur*ia* p*ro* s*im*il*i* iiij. In def*ectu* t*er*r*e* Rob*er*t*i* Coche p*ro* s*im*il*i* iiij. In def*ectu* t*er*r*e* le Swon p*ro* s*im*il*i* iiij. In def*ectu* t*er*r*e* Ric*ard*i Vaccar*ii* p*ro* s*im*il*i* iiij. In def*ectu* t*er*r*e* Ric*ard*i Knaue p*ro* s*im*il*i* iiij. In def*ectu* t*er*r*e* Emme Martyn q*uia* vidua ij. In def*ectu* t*er*r*e* Bewolf*e* p*ro* eod*em* ij. In def*ec*tu t*err*e Pet*r*onill*e* Elys q*uia* vidua ij. In def*ec*tu t*err*e Wyndout q*uia* vidua ij. In def*ec*tu t*err*e Alici*e* le Knight q*uia* vidua ij. S*umma* xxxiiij. In vend*itis* iiij^{xx} x. Et in vend*itis* s*up*er Comp*otum* j p*ro* j d. o*b*. Et rem*anent* v gall*ine* *et* j gall*us*.

Capon*es*. Iidem r*eddunt* c*ompotum* de xx caponi*bus* f*ac*tis hoc a*nno* de Pulc*inis*. Et de xv de emp*tis*. S*umma* xxxv. Et rem*anent*.

Pulc*ini*. Iidem r*eddunt* c*ompotum* de xx pulc*inis* de exit*u* gallin*arum* hoc a*nno*. In Caponi*bus* f*ac*tis sup*erius* om*nes*. Et n*ihil* rem*anet*.

Oua. Iidem r*eddun*t c*ompotum* de cc ou*is* de exit*u* gallin*arum*. Et in vend*itis* infra c. Et in vend*itis* s*up*er Comp*otum* c oua p*ro* iiij d.

Ciser*a*. Id*em* r*eddunt* c*ompotum* de j dole*o* Cisere Rem*anente* a*nno* p*re*te*rito*. Et de xxxv lagen*is* f*ac*tis hoc a*nno*. In vendito j dol*eum*. Et in vend*itis* s*up*er Comp*otum* xxxv lagen*e* p*ro* ij s. ij d. q.

Vtens*ilia*. Iidem r*eddunt* c*ompotum* de j Cacabo j oll*a* en*ea* j pocinet' j patell*a* j lauacr*o* cu*m* pelu*e* j secur*i* de rem*anentibus* *et* j picos*o* emp*to* hoc a*nno* *et* de j dole*o* de Rem*anente*. Et rem*anent* h*ec* o*mn*ia.

Caret*ta*. Iidem r*eddunt* c*ompotum* de j Caret*ta* ferr*ata* Rem*anente* a*nno* p*re*te*r*ito. Et rem*anet* j Caret*ta* ferrat*a*.

§§ 14. Reeve's Account, 29 Sept., 1307—28 Sept., 1308.

This is a badly written and irregular account with unusual abbreviations, but of value as a continuation of the two previous ones, particularly in the matter of the use of fields and furlongs.

The cost of iron was very high this year, leading to unusual expenditures for the repair of plows. The reeve of Crawley was worked rather hard in being required to send (perhaps personally to deliver) pigs to the bishop's palace at Farnham and chickens to his residence at Marwell, and to convey a tun of wine from Winchester to Northampton. For these services, however, he received allowances.

In the business of the manor it was necessary to castrate twenty-four young cocks for the bishop's table, and, for his purse, to sell an ox that was old and almost dead.

To the lord's servants (famuli) were given a mixture of a little wheat and a lot of barley. These servants were the hayward, two drovers, a dairymaid, a harrower, a plowman, and the keeper of the hogs and lambs. Cheeses were given to the reeve, the shepherd, the smith, and the dairymaid. The distinction between the famuli and the ministri (who helped reap and bind the grain) is not made clear.

CRAULEE[1]

Arreragi*um*. Ric*ardus* Wodelok Ball*iuus* *et* Dauid Martyn p*re*pos*itus* Reddu*n*t comp*otum* de xij li. ij s. ij d. ob. de Arrerag*io* Anni p*ret*eriti. Et In lib*eratis* D*omi*no Symo*ni* de Farh*am* thesaur*ario* Wolues*eie* per vnam talliam totum. Et quieti sunt.

Redd*itus*. Iidem R*eddunt* c*ompotum* de lxj s. iiij d. de toto Redd*itu* assis*o* ad Nat*alem*. Et de lxj s. iiij d. ad Pasch*am*. Et de lxj s. iiij d. ad f*estu*m Nat*alis* *s*a*nc*t*i* Joh*ann*is Bapt*iste*. Et de iiij li. xvij s. vij d. ad f*estu*m *s*a*nc*t*i* mich*ae*l*is*. Sum*ma* xiiij li. xix d.

Aquiet*ancie*. In aquiet*ancia* j p*re*pos*iti* p*er* ann*um* v s. In acquiet*anciis* iiij caruc*ariorum* *et* j fabri p*er* ann*um* xiij s. iiij d. cuil*ibet* ij s. viij d. In aq*uie*t*anciis* ij b*er*car*iorum* p*er* ann*um* v s. iiij d. In aq*uie*t*anciis* x op*er*ar*iorum* op*er*anc*ium* p*er* ij dies in ebdo*mada* a f*esto* s*anc*t*i* mich*aelis* usq*ue* Gul*am* Aug*us*ti *et* in Aut*umpn*o quol*ibet* die op*erabili* xxvj s. viij d. cuil*ibet* ij s. viij d. In aquiet*ancia* j porcar*ii* p*er* ann*um* ij s. viij d. In acquiet*ancia* j vaccar*ii* p*er* ann*um* ij s. viij d. S*um*m*a* lv s. viij d.

Def*ectus*. In def*ectu* t*er*re Le Strong*e* t*r*act*e* in do*minicum* ij s. In def*ectu* t*er*r*e* Will*elm*i de Curi*a* p*ro* eod*em* p*er* ann*um* ij s. viij d. In def*ectu* t*er*re de Alebroc q*ui* modo r*es*p*o*nd*it* apud M*er*don*am* v s. In def*ectu* t*er*r*e* Rob*ert*i Coche t*r*act*e* in do*minicum* p*er* ann*um* ij s. viij d. In def*ectu* t*er*re Rob*er*t*i* Coye p*ro* eodem ij s. viij d. In def*ectu* t*erre* Rog*e*ri Le Porcher p*ro* eod*em* p*er* ann*um* ij s. viij d. In def*ectu* t*er*re Ric*ard*i vaccar*ii* p*ro* eodem p*er* ann*um* ij s. viij d. S*um*m*a* xx s. iiij d. S*um*m*a* Aquiet*anciarum* *et* def*ectuum* lxxvj s. S*um*m*a* Redd*itus* rem*anentis* x li. v s. vij d.

Ciminu*m*. Iid*em* r*eddunt* c*ompotum* de j lib*ra* Cymin*i* de Redd*itu* R' F*r*omo*n*d. Et lib*erata* ap*ud* Wolu*e*seiam.

Recogn*itiones*. Iide*m* r*eddunt* c*ompotum* de vj d. de Rob*erto* Pak*e* p*ro* ann*ua* recogn*itione*. Et de vj d. de Rob*erto* Pott*e*re p*ro* si*m*ili. Et de iij d. de Joh*anne* Walsch*e* pro si*m*ili. Et de iij d. de Rog*ero* Elys p*ro* si*m*ili ut possit s*er*uir*e* ex*tra* lib*er*tate*m* *et* seq*ui* dece*nn*a*m* suam *et* venir*e* ad duos Laghedayes. Et de iij d. de Rob*erto* Elys pro si*m*ili. Et de vj d. de Rob*erto* Sewyne Natiuo d*omi*ni ut possit morari vbi volu*er*it *et* venir*e* ad ij laghedaes p*er* pl*egium* Rob*er*t*i* le Bonde *et* Joh*ann*is Tryg'. S*um*m*a* ij s. iij d.

It*em* recogn*itio*. Et de j cultro de Recogn*itione* Rob*er*t*i* Coleman ut possit morari *et* s*e*ruir*e* ex*tra* lib*er*tate*m* *et* n*ihilominus* seq*ui* dece*nna*m suam *et* venir*e* ad ij Lagh*e*daes. In vend*ito* inferi*us*.

Cer*a*. Et de di*midia* lib*ra* cere de Joh*anne* le Cart*e*re p*ro* ann*ua* recogn*itione* ut h*ab*eat lic*entiam* manendi alibi q*ua*m sup*er* t*er*ram d*omi*ni

[1] MS., P. R. O., Ecclesiastical Commission, Various, 159323.

et d*ebet* seq*ui* dece*nnam* sua*m* ad duos Laghedaes p*er* p*legium* Rob*er*ti le Bond et Rob*er*ti murieweder. Et lib*era*t*a* apud Wolues*eiam*.

Ex*itus* maner*ii*. Iidem r*eddunt* c*ompotum* de iij s. ij d. ob. de pannag*io* porcor*um* ad f*est*um s*anc*ti m*ar*t*in*i v*idelicet* p*ro* porco s*uper*ann*ato* ij d. p*ro* porco t*ri*um t*erminorum* j d. ob. p*ro* porco di*midii* ann*i* j d. *et* p*ro* porcell*o* sep*ar*ato ob. Et de xviij d. de pannag*io* c viij vit*ulorum*. Et de xxiiij s. ix d. de xlv vacc*is* ij bouett*is et* x bouic*ulis* de pann*agio* ad La Hocked*ay* v*idelicet* p*ro* vacc*a* vj d. p*ro* bouett*o* iij d. *et* p*ro* bouic*ulo* ij d. De ou*ibus* inuent*is* in fald*a* hom*inum* ville n*ihil* hoc anno q*uia* no*n* excedebant num*erum* xxv. Et de ij s. iiij d. ob. q. de c xiij Agn*is* sep*ar*atis in past*ura* d*omi*ni usq*ue* f*est*um s*anc*ti Joh*annis* Bapt*ist*e p*ro* agno q. D*e* past*ur*a yem*ali* vend*ita* in bosco n*ihil* hoc ann*o*. Et de iiij s. viij d. de past*ur*a vend*ita* ad vij eq*uo*s in bosco i*n* estat*e* p*ro* eq*uo* viij d. D*e* past*ura* de Puthull*e* n*ihil* hoc a*nno* p*ro* multon*ibus* d*omi*ni. Et de viij s. de past*ur*a de Trendlye *et* Holyndan*e* vend*ita* hoc ann*o*. D*e* past*ur*a de Comforlang*e* n*ihil* q*uia* sem*inabatur* fr*umento*. Et de xij d. de past*ura* foss*ati* c*irc*a Cur*iam* vend*ita*. D*e* past*ur*a de Drakenord*e* n*ihil* hoc a*nno* q*uia* hom*in*es ville se*minauer*u*n*t d*ict*um camp*um* ordeo *et* Auen*is*. D*e* past*ura* de Locforlong*e* n*ihil* q*uia* sem*inabatur* c*um* auen*is* d*omi*ni. Et de ij s. de past*ur*a de Schret vend*ita* hoc anno. Et de xlviij s. de xv acr*is* di*midia et* t*erti*a p*ar*te j acre subbosci vend*itis* p*recium* acre iij s. Et de xxxj s. viij d. de xxiiij roffr*is* veter*ibus* vend*itis*. Et de xij d. de j cultro de Recogn*itione* vend*ito*. S*umma* vj li. xiij s. j d. ob. q.

vend*itio* s*up*er comp*otum*. C*omputatum* Est de lij s. xj d. ob. de diu*er*sis rebus vend*itis* sup*er* comp*otum*. S*umma* lij s. xj d. ob.

vend*itum* Instaur*i*. Iidem R*eddunt* c*ompotum* de lij s. vj d. de vj bob*us* vend*itis* v*nde* j p*recium* iiij s. vj d. q*uia* debil*is et* fere mort*uus* ij p*reciu*m vt*ri*usq*ue* ix s. *et* iij p*recium* cui*us*l*ibet* x s. Et de iij s. de iij vitul*is* vend*itis*. Et de xlv s. de xxxvj multon*ibus* in f*est*o s*anc*ti Mart*ini* vend*itis* p*reciu*m cui*us*l*ibet* xv d. Et de iiij li. iiij s. vj d. de iiij^{xx} ou*ibus* matr*icibus* in f*est*o s*anc*ti Mart*ini* vend*itis* vn*de* j p*reci*u*m* vj d. ij p*recium* ut*ri*usq*ue* vij d. vij p*recium* cui*us*l*ibet* xij d. *et* lxx p*recium* cui*us*l*ibet* xiij d. Et de iij s. de iij Agn*is* an*te* tons*ionem* vend*itis*. Et de xxvij s. de ix porcis vend*itis* ad exp*ensas* d*omi*ni p*recium* cui*us*l*ibet* iij s. Et de iij s. de xviij li*bris* lan*e* fract*e* vend*itis*. Et de xvj d. de xxxij li*bris* case*i* yem*alis* vend*itis*. Et de iiij li. de viij pond*eribus* case*i* estiu*alis* vend*itis* p*recium* pond*eris* x s. Et de iij s. iiij d. de x clau*is* butyr*i* vend*itis* p*recium* clau*i* iiij d. Et de x s. v d. de ix pell*ibus* multon*um* j pell*e* hurt*ardi* xj pell*ibus* ou*ium* matr*icium et* xiij pell*ibus* hogastr*orum* de mor*ina* an*te* tons*ionem* vend*itis* v*nde* xxij p*recium* cui*us*l*ibet* iij d. ob. *et* xij p*recium* cui*us*l*ibet* iiij d. Et de xv d. de vj pell*ibus* multon*um* ix pell*ibus* ou*ium* matr*icium* de mor*ina* post tons*ionem* vend*itis*. Et de iiij s. vij d. de l pell*ibus* agn*orum* de mor*ina* an*te* sep*aratio*nem *et* v post sep*arationem et* an*te* tons*ionem* vend*itis* p*recium* pell*is* j d. Et de j d. de iiij pell*ibus* Agn*orum* de mor*ina* post tons*ionem* vend*itis*. Et de iiij s. de xij Auc*is* vend*itis* p*recium* cui*us*l*ibet* iiij d. Et de xj s. iiij d. ob. de iiij^{xx} xj gall*inis* vend*itis* p*recium* gall*ine* j d. ob. Et de v s. x d. de xxxv capon*ibus* vend*itis* p*recium* capon*is* ij d. Et de xij d. de CCC ou*is* vend*itis*. S*umma* xvij li. xiiij d. ob.

vend*itio* Blad*i*. Iidem r*eddunt* co*mpotum* de ix li. xiiij s. vj d. de xxvij q*uarteriis* di*midio* fr*umenti* vend*itis* v*nde* x q*uarteria* vj b*usselli* p*recium* q*uarterii* vj s. viij d. *et* xvj q*uarteria* vj b*usselli* p*recium* q*uarterii* vij s. iiij d. Et de xiiij s. de ij q*uarteriis* v b*ussellis* curall*i* vend*itis* p*recium* q*uarterii* v s. iiij d. Et de lxxvij s. viij d. de xxvij q*uarteriis* j b*ussello* di*midio* Auen*arum* vend*itis* v*nde* viij q*uarteria* j b*ussellus* di*midius* p*recium* q*uarterii* ij s. viij d. xv q*uarteria* p*recium* q*uarterii* ij s. x d. *et* iiij q*uarteria* p*recium* q*uarterii* iij s. iiij d. Et de lxvij s. iiij d. de xij q*uarteriis* v b*ussellis* pis*arum* vend*itis* p*recium* q*uarterii* v s. iiij d. Et de lviij s. vij d. ob. de xij q*uarteriis* iiij b*ussellis* di*midio* vesc*iarum* vend*itis* p*recium* q*uarterii* iiij s. viij d. S*umma* xx li. xij s. j d. ob.

Fin*es*. Iid*em* r*eddunt* co*mpotum* de vj s. viij d. de dece*nna* de Craul*e* p*ro* t*het*h*ing*penn*y* ad hundr*edum* sa*nct*i mart*ini*. Et de vj s. viij d. de ead*em* p*ro* eod*em* ad hundr*edum* de Hock*e*. Et de xxvj s. viij d. de Wil*lelmo* fil*io* Joh*annis* Goude p*ro* j mess*uagio et* j virg*ata* t*er*r*e* q*ue* fu*er*u*nt* matill' Goude m*at*ris sue h*abendis* in Craul*e*. S*umma* xl s.

Perq*uisita*. Iid*em* r*eddunt* co*mpotum* de xxij s. viij d. de minut*is* p*er*quis*itis* cur*ie* hoc ann*o*. S*umma* xxij s. viij d. S*umma* vt*ri*usq*ue* lxij s. viij d. S*umma* toci*us* Recept*e* lx li. v s. vij d. q.

Custus caruc*arum*. In ferro *et* ac*er*o emp*tis* ad ferrame*n*ta iij caruc*arum* p*er* ann*um* ix s. ij d. *et* tantu*m* hoc ann*o* p*ro*p*ter* magna*m* caristiam ferr*i*. In j vom*ere* emp*to* x s. In eod*em* rest*r*ing*endo* j d. In j vom*ere* fract*o* refic*iendo et* emend*o* ij d. ob. In iiij ferr*is* pedal*ibus* emp*tis* xvj d. ob. In clau*is* ad idem iij d. In v rotul*is* emp*tis* ad caruc*as* x d. In j nou*a* caruc*a* fac*ienda et* al*ia* veter*a* emend*a* v d. In caruc*a* ferr*o* lig*anda* j d. ob. In ferr*amentis* vj Affr*orum* p*er* ann*um* in ped*ibus* ant*erioribus et* post*erioribus* iiij s. vj d. In p*re*car*iis* viij caruc*ariorum* in *quadragesima* q*ui* arau*er*u*n*t viij acr*as* viij d. In viij capistr*is* de p*ro*p*rio* pilo fac*iendis* ij d. In stip*endiis* ij carucar*iorum* p*er* ann*um* viij s. S*umma* xxvj s. vij d. ob.

Emp*tio* blad*i et* instaur*i*. In vij b*ussellis* di*midio* ord*e*i emp*tis* ad lib*eration*em famulor*um* iiij s. v d. In j affr*o* emp*to* ix s. viij d. In j affr*o* emp*to* xiij s. q. In j sue *et* vj porcell*is* emp*tis* iij s. vj d. S*umma* xxx s. vij d. q.

Car*ecte*. In j p*ari* rot*arum* emp*to* ad car*ectam* iij s. j d. In iiij c*ircul*is ligni emp*tis* iij d. In eisd*em* rot*is* ax*andis* iij d. In gross*is* clau*is* clut*is et* grop*is* emp*tis* ad id*em* iij s. vj d. In stip*endio* fabri lig*antis* d*ic*tas Rot*as* cu*m* j vet*er*i ligatur*a* *et* d*ic*ta ligat*ur*a elong*anda* cum ferr*o* emp*to* ad id*e*m xiij d. In clut*is* *et* clau*is* ad car*ectam* ix s. ob. In vet*er*i car*ecta* gr*o*pand*a* p*er* ann*um* ij d. ob. In j colar*a* emp*ta* vij d. In ferr*amentis* ij eq*uorum* car*ectariorum* p*er* ann*um* iij s. ij d. In j strigili ij d. In j p*a*ri t*r*actar*um* iiij d. ob. In vj uln*is* caneuas*ii* emp*tis* ad iij saccos bladifer*os* inde fac*iendos* xxj d. In stip*endio* j car*ectarii* p*er* ann*um* iiij s. S*umma* xix s. iij d. ob.

Cust*us* daer*ie*. In line*a* tela *et* lan*eo* pann*o* viij d. ob. In oll*is* *et* patell*is* terr*enis* emp*tis* v d. In p*re*sur*a* vj d. ob. In vij b*ussellis* sal*is* emp*tis* ad id*em* xx d. ob. In stip*endio* Daie p*er* ann*um* ij s. In deci*ma* vj vitul*orum* iij d. S*umma* v s. vij d. ob.

Cust*us* bercar*ie*. In vnct*o* cop*er*ose v*er*idigr*is* *et* viuo arg*ento* emp*tis* ad oue*s* vng*endas* p*er* ann*um* lj s. viij d. In rubio color*e* emp*to* iij d. In feno emp*to* ad bident*es* sustin*endas* *in* yem*e* xxv s. vij d. In feno emp*to* *in* estate p*ro* a*nno* fut*ur*o lij s. vij d. In xxv cleiis fac*iendis* ad fald*am* de p*ro*p*ri*is virg*is* x d. In b*er*car*ia* multon*um* ou*ium* matr*icium* *et* hogg*astrorum* coop*er*ienda p*er* loca iij s. In cc lxj p*er*tic*is* fossat*i* fod*iendis* *circa* bercar*iam* multon*um* ou*ium* matr*icium* *et* hogg*astrorum* xxxviij s. o*b*. q. p*ro* p*er*tica ob. q. cu*m* planc*is* ad id*em*. In iiij [acris] di*midia* s*u*bbosci p*ro*st*er*nend*is* v s. vij d. ob. p*ro* d*ic*ta Bercar*ia* v*idelicet* in ac*ra* xv d. In cc lxj p*er*tic*is* haie claud*endis* sup*er* d*ic*t*um* foss*atum* *circa* d*ic*tas b*er*car*ias* v s. v d. q. p*ro* p*er*tic*a* q. In veter*ibus* haiis claud*endis* *et* emend*is* *circa* bercar*iam* ou*ium* matr*icium* iij d. In vj nou*is* post*ibus* p*ro* ij nou*is* portis ad b*er*car*ias* fac*iendis* ad tasch*am* xij d. In vj cleiis emp*tis* ad p*re*d*ic*tas portas ij d. In j vet*er*i porta ad b*er*car*iam* hog*astrorum* emend*a* j d. In stip*endio* j custod*is* hogastr*orum* p*er* iij t*er*min*o*s iij s. In m*e*rem*io* p*ro*st*er*nend*o* *et* scapul*is* ad B*er*car*iam* ou*ium* matr*icium* elongand*is* viij [d.?].[1] In b*er*car*ia* ou*ium* matric*ium* elong*anda* de viij copul*is* furtar*um* ad tasch*am* xxv s. v d. In yvo[ne] cem*entario* die lu*ne* q*uando* leuau*i*t d*ic*tam g*r*ang*iam* xvj d. In m*e*rem*io* s*ar*rando ad d*ic*tam bouer*iam* iiij s. iiij d. In d*ic*ta bercar*ia* Watelanda una cu*m* p*a*riet*ibus* Wandend*is* ad tascham v s. In vj acr*is* di*midia* stipul*e* ad d*ic*tam b*er*car*iam* xij d. ob. p*ro* ac*ra* ij d. o*b*. q. In forag*io* emp*to* ad coop*er*t*ur*am d*ic*t*e* b*er*car*ie* xj s. In d*ic*ta b*er*car*ia* coop*er*ie*nda* ad tasch*a*m v s. vj d. In fundam*en*to lapid*ibus* fac*iendo* *et* pariet*ibus* d*ic*t*e* bercar*ie* plastr*andis* ad tasch*am* v s. In xij bord*is* emp*tis* ad iij nou*a* host*ia* ibidem fac*ienda* ij s. In c l flornayl emp*tis* ad d*ic*ta host*ia* vj d. In iij p*a*rib*us* v*e*rcinell*arum* *cum* gunnis ij s. vj d. S*umma* xij li. xij s. vij d.

Custus dom*orum*. In Aul*a* coq*u*ina g*r*ang*ia* f*r*u*menti* ordei *et* Auen*e* recop*er*iend*is* *et* emend*is* p*er* loca ad Tasch*a*m ix s. j d. ob. In j serr*ura* cu*m* clau*ibus* emp*ta* ad hostiu*m* g*r*ang*ie* f*r*u*menti* iij d. In palicio emend*o* *circa* Cur*iam* *cum* clau*ibus* emp*tis* ad id*em* vj d. In c xxj p*er*tic*is*

[1] Probably viij d. though xvij would add up better.

haie claud*endis* copiciu*m* *cum* claust*ura* p*ro*sternend*a* ad idem iiij s. q. p*ro* xl p*er*tic*is* xvj d. In pesso*na* emp*ta* p*ro* xj porc*is* agistat*is* in p*ar*te de M*er*edon*a* p*er* vj sep*timanas* v s. p*ro* porco p*er* sept*imana*m [—].[1] In pesson*a* emp*ta* ad ij porcell*os* agistat*os* ibidem p*er* idem temp*us* ij s. vj d. p*ro* porcell*o* per sept*imana*m ob. Summa xxj s. x d. ob.

Tritur*atio*. In xxix q*uarteriis* fr*umen*ti t*ritur*a*ndis* ad tasch*a*m mens*ura* ras*a* iiij s. x d. p*ro* q*uarterio* ij d. In eisdem ventand*is* v s. q. p*ro* x b*ussellis* q. In xxv q*uarteriis* di*midio* orde*i* t*ritur*a*ndis* ad tasch*a*m mens*ura* ras*a* ij s. vj d. ob. p*ro* x b*ussellis* j d. ob. In eisd*em* ventand*is* vj d. In xliij q*uarteriis* Auen*e* t*ritur*a*ndis* *et* vent*andis* ad tasch*am* mens*ura* ras*a* iij s. vij d. p*ro* x b*ussellis* j d. In ix q*uarteriis* vesc*iarum* mens*ura* ras*a* tritur*andis* xviij d. In eisd*em* vent*andis* j d. ob. q. p*ro* x b*ussellis* q. In vad*io* Gilb*er*t*i* Pymor exist*entis* ult*ra* tritur*ationem* *et* fac*ientis* exit*um* g*r*ang*ie* p*er* xlv dies p*er* t*alliam* v s. vij d. ob. In vad*io* Henr*ici* Le Douly fac*ientis* exit*um* g*r*ang*ie* p*er* ix dies xiij d. ob. In vad*io* eiusd*em* Henr*ici* p*er* c xlj dies fac*ientis* exit*um* g*r*ang*ie* xvij s. vij d. ob. S*umm*a xxxvij s. x d. ob.

Autump*n*us. In Blado sarclando ult*ra* illud q*uo*d op*erarii* sarcl*averunt* iiij s. In pane empt*o* ad iij p*re*car*ias* aut*um*pni *nihil* *quia* h*a*bueru*n*t Blad*um* de g*r*ang*ia*. In xxj clau*is* case*i* emp*tis* pro def*ec*tu Allec*ium* ad iij p*re*car*ias* aut*um*pn*i* de ccc xij hom*inibus* cu*m* ministr*is* cur*ie* met*entibus* *et* lig*antibus* c xij acr*as* fr*umen*ti xxx acr*as* Auen*e* xx acr*as* pis*arum* *et* vesc*iarum* sicut iacent vj s. vj d. *et* quil*ibet* ho*mo* h*ab*uit q*ua*dr*am* case*i*. In vad*io* Pet*ri* le Caungeby exist*entis* in camp*is* t*em*p*o*re nocturno p*ro* blado custod*iendo* *et* auxil*iando* carcare car*ectas* p*er* xlij dies v s. iij d. p*er* die*m* j d. ob. In vad*io* Joh*annis* Wynerd exist*entis* in grang*ia* *et* in camp*is* p*er* vices p*er* xxxv dies p*ro* blad*o* decim*ando* in g*r*ang*ia* *et* tassand*o* iiij s. iiij d. ob. p*er* diem j d. *ob*. In stip*end*i*o* j messor*is* p*er* ann*um* vj s. viij d. S*umma* xxvj s. ix d. ob.

Expens*e* sen*escalli* *et* ball*ivi*. In exp*ensis* sen*escalli* Rad*ulph*i de Bereford ad t*ermin*u*m* s*anc*ti m*ar*ti*ni* iij s. vj d. p*er* tall*iam*. In expen*sis* Ric*ardi* Wodeloc ball*ivi* p*er* suos aduent*us* iiij s. S*umma* vij s. vj d. S*umma* om*nium* expen*sarum* xxj li. viij s. viij d. Et d*ebent* xxxviij li. xvj s. x d. ob. q.

Allocac*iones*. In alloc*atione* p*re*po*sito* p*ro* ix porc*is* liber*atis* ad expe*nsas* dom*us* d*omi*ni apud Farnham p*er* p*rimum* brev*e* xxxvij s. In alloc*atione* eide*m* xiiij s. ij d. p*ro* v q*uarteriis* lib*eratis* ad expe*nsas* dom*us* d*omi*ni apud M*er*ewell' p*o*st f*estu*m Nat*alis* d*omi*ni p*er* idem brev*e*. In alloc*atione* eide*m* vij s. vj d. p*ro* lx gall*inis* lib*eratis* ad expens*as* Dom*us* d*omi*ni apud Merewell' post f*estu*m Nat*alis* d*omi*ni p*er* idem brev*e*. In alloc*atione* eide*m* xviij s. p*ro* j car*ecta* locat*a* p*ro* j dole*o* vini car*iando* de Wynton*ia* usq*ue* Nor*th*ampton*iam* p*er* sec*und*um brev*e*. In alloc*atione*

[1] Omitted in manuscript.

eid*em* xxxix s. iiij d. p*ro* iiij dol*eis* cisere emp*tis* *et* liber*atis* ad exspens*as* dom*us* d*omi*ni p*er* terciu*m* bre*ve*. In alloc*atione* lix sterlingor*um* p*ro* vad*io* liber*ato* Henr*ico* Baret Anno Consecr*ationis* D*omi*ni H*enrici* ep*iscop*i secundo p*er* q*uar*tu*m* bre*ve*. S*umma* vij li. xv s. viij [d.].

Lib*eratio*. In liber*atis* D*omi*no Sym*oni* thes*aurario* Wolues*eie* xviij li. xiij s. S*umma* om*nium* allocacion*um* *et* liberat*ionis* xxvj li. viij s. viij d. Et d*ebent* de claro xij li. viij s. ij d. ob. q.

Exit*us* gr*angie*. Fr*umentum*. Idem R*eddunt* co*mpotum* de xlviij q*uar-teriis* de toto ex*itu* fr*umenti* mens*ura* ras*a* Et de ij q*uarteriis* de emp*tis* de p*reposit*o de m*erdona*. S*umma* l q*uarteria*. D*e* quib*us* in se*mine* sup*er* iiij^{xx} xvj acr*as* sicut iacent in camp*is* de la Langelond Schortelond *et* iux*ta* la Greneweye *et* la Geredelond xix q*uarteria* ij b*usselli* v*nde* In ac*ra* j b*ussellus* di*midius* set j q*uarterium* ij b*usselli* plus in toto. In mixc*is* cu*m* ordeo ad lib*eratio*nem hayward*i* iij q*uarteria* ij b*usselli*. Et in vend*itis* xxvij q*uarteria* di*midium* *et* eque.

Curall*um*. Iid*em* r*eddunt* co*mpotum* de ij q*uarteriis* de toto ex*itu* Curall*i* mens*ura* ras*a*. Et in vend*itis* totu*m*.

Ord*eum*. Iidem R*eddunt* co*mpotum* de lxvij q*uarteriis* de toto ex*itu* orde*i* mens*ura* ras*a*. Et de vij b*ussellis* di*midio* de emp*tis*. S*umma* lxvij q*uarteria* vij b*usselli* di*midius*. De quib*us* in se*mine* iiij^{xx} vij acr*a-rum* sicut iace*nt* in camp*is* de buryforlong Combforlang' *et* Drakenord xxvj q*uarteria* ij b*usselli* i*n* ac*ra* iij b*usselli* s*ed* ij b*usselli* plus in toto. In exp*ensis* iij p*recariarum* iij q*uarteria* *et* debent fi*eri* de q*uarterio* c panes. In inferi*us* ad lib*eratio*nem fam*ulorum* xxviij q*uarteria* iij b*us-selli* di*midius*. Et In vend*itis* sup*er* comp*otum* ij b*usselli* p*ro* xv d.

Auen*a*. Iidem R*eddunt* co*mpotum* de c xxiiij q*uarteriis* iij b*ussellis* de toto ex*itu* Auen*e* mens*ura* rasa. Et de xv q*uarteriis* dat*is* bob*us* p*er* estim*ationem* in garb*is*. S*umma* c xxxix q*uarteria* iij b*usselli*. D*e* quib*us* In se*mine* c lxvij acr*arum* sicut iacent in camp*is* iux*ta* Drakenord Brokkele Middelforlang Locforlang*e* *et* ap*u*d le Smalethornes lxxiij q*uarteria* vij b*usselli* in ac*ra* iij b*usselli* di*midius* *et* vj b*usselli* di*midius* plus in toto. In p*rebend*a vj affr*orum* a f*est*o Nat*alis* d*omi*ni usq*ue* Hocked[aye] ix q*uarteria* q*uia* araue*run*t ante p*ra*nd*ium* *et* poste*a*. In p*rebend*a ij eq*uorum* care*ctariorum* p*er* annu*m* vij q*uarteria* j b*ussellus* *et* tant*um* hoc anno q*uia* q*uar*ta Caruc*a* p*ro*strat*a* *et* equ*i* car*ectarii* ali-qu*ando* ibant ad Caruc*am* al*iquando* ad h*e*rciam *et* car*ectam*. In p*re-*b*enda* bou*um* p*er* estim*ationem* in garbis xv q*uarteria*. In p*rebend*a eq*uorum* Rad*ulph*i de Bereford ad t*ermi*n*um* s*anc*t*i* martin*i* j b*ussellus* di*midius* p*er* t*alliam*. In farin*a* f*act*a ad potag*ium* famul*orum* ij q*uar-teria*. Et in vend*itis* xxvij q*uarteria* j b*ussellus* di*midius*. Et in vend*itis* sup*er* comp*otum* v q*uarteria* p*ro* xiij s. iiij d. *et* eque.

Pis*e*. Iid*em* r*eddunt* co*mpotum* de xvij q*uarteriis* iij b*ussellis* de toto ex*itu* pis*arum* mens*ura* ras*a*. Et de iiij b*ussellis* dat*is* ou*ibus* matr*icibus* in siliq*uis* t*em*p*ore* Agn*ilationis*. *Summa* xvij q*uarteria* vij b*usselli*. D*e* quib*us* In se*mine* sup*er* xxij acr*as* sic*ut* iace*n*t in Camp*is* de Drakenord *et* subt*er* Puthulle iiij q*uarteria* vj b*usselli* in acr*a* ij b*usselli* vj b*usselli* min*us* in toto. In ou*ibus* sustin*endis* in yem*e* t*em*p*ore* Agnicl*ationis* [sic] di*midium* q*uarterium*. Et In vend*itis* xij q*uarteria* v b*usselli*.

Vesce. Iidem R*eddunt* co*mpotum* de xviij q*uarteriis* vj b*ussellis* de toto ex*itu* vesc*arum* mens*ura* ras*a*. Et de j q*uarterio* di*midio* dat*is* bid*entibus* in yem*e*. *Summa* xx q*uarteria* ij b*usselli*. D*e* quib*us* In se*mine* sup*er* xxviij acr*as* sicut iace*n*t i*n* camp*is* de Danestan*e* *et* sub*ter* puthull*e* vj q*uarteria* j b*ussellus* di*midius* in acr*a* ij b*usselli* *sed* vj b*usselli* di*midius* min*us* in toto. In bident*ibus* sustin*endis* in yem*e* j q*uarterium* di*midium*. Et In vend*itis* xij q*uarteria* di*midium* di*midius* b*ussellus* *et* eque.

Broctcorn*um*. Iidem r*eddunt* co*mpotum* de ij q*uarteriis* broctcorn*i* ord*ei* iiij q*uarteriis* di*midio* b*ussello* broctcorn*i* pis*arum* *et* iij q*uarteriis* vesc*arum*. *Summa* ix q*uarteria* di*midius* b*ussellus*. Et in vend*itis* sup*er* comp*otum* tot*um* p*ro* xxx s. ij d. ob.

Lib*eratio* fam*ulorum*. Iidem R*eddunt* co*mpotum* de iij q*uarteriis* ij b*ussellis* fr*umenti* xxviij q*uarteriis* iij b*ussellis* ord*ei* sup*erius* rece*ptis* ad lib*erationem* fam*ulorum*. *Summa* xxxj q*uarteria* v b*usselli* di*midius*. D*e* quib*us* In lib*eratione* j haywardi p*er* ann*um* vj q*uarteria* di*midium* v*nde* medi*um* fr*umenti* *et* capit q*uarterium* ad viij sept*imanas*. In lib*eratione* j car*ucarii* ij fug*atorum* p*er* ann*um* q*uorum* quil*ibet* cap*it* q*uarterium* p*er* x sept*imanas* xv q*uarteria* iiij b*usselli* di*midius*. In lib*eratione* j Daye a f*esto* s*anc*ti mich*aelis* usq*ue* fest*um* Puri*ficationis* be*ate* mar*ie* di*midium* q*uarterium*. In lib*eratio*ne eiusd*em* a f*esto* Puri*ficationis* usq*ue* f*est*um s*anc*ti mich*aelis* *qui* cap*it* q*uarterium* p*er* xij sept*imanas* ij q*uarteria* vj b*usselli* di*midius*. In lib*eratione* j h*er*ciator*is* ad vtr*amque* seme*ntem* v b*usselli*. In dat*o* j caruc*ario* ad seme*ntem* *quadragesime* a festo Puri*ficationis* be*ate* mar*ie* usq*ue* hock*e* qui ibat ad caruc*am* eq*uinam* p*ost* prandi*um* di*midium* q*uarterium*. In lib*eratione* j custod*is* hogg*ettorum* *et* Agn*orum* p*er* ann*um* *qui* cap*it* q*uarterium* p*er* x sept*imanas* v q*uarteria* j b*ussellus* di*midius*. Sum*ma* xxxj q*uarteria* v b*usselli* di*midius*. Et eque

Instaur*um*. Equi car*ettarii*. Iidem R*eddunt* co*mpotum* de ij equ*is* car*ettariis* rem*anentibus* anno p*re*terito. Et Rem*anent* ij equi car*ettarii*.

Affr*i*. Iid*em* r*eddunt* co*mpotum* de v affr*is* rem*anentibus* anno p*re*terito. Et de ij emp*tis*. *Summa* vij. D*e* quib*us* In mor*ina* j. Et Rem*anent* vj Affr*i*.

Boues. Iid*em* r*eddunt* co*mpotum* de xxvij bob*us* rem*anentibus* a*nno* p*reterito* Et de j adiu*n*cto. *Summa* xxviij. D*e* quib*us* in vend*itis* vj. Et Rem*anent* xxij boue*s*.

Taur*us*. Iidem R*eddunt compotum* de j taur*o* adiu*n*ct*o* hoc ann*o*. Et Rem*anet* j taur*us*.

vacc*e*. Iid*em* r*eddunt* c*ompotum* de viij vacc*is* rem*anentibus* a*nno* p*reterito*. Et de j adiu*n*ct*a*. S*umma* ix. Et Rem*anent* ix vacce.

Bouett*i*. Iid*em* r*eddunt compotum* de iij bouet*us* rem*anentibus* a*nno* p*reterito* bouic*ulis*. De quib*us* In adiu*n*ct*o* cu*m* bob*us* j Cum Taur*o* j *et* Cum vacc*is* j. Et n*ihil* rem*anet*. De bouic*ulis* hoc a*nno* n*ihil* q*uia* rem*anent* Annal*es* a*nno* p*reterito*.

Annal*es*. Iid*em* r*eddunt* co*mpotum* de iiij Annal*ibus* rem*anentibus* a*nno* p*reterito* vitul*is*. Et Rem*anent* iiij Annal*es* v*nde* ij masc*uli*.

Vit*uli*. Iidem r*eddunt compotum* de vj vitul*is* de ex*itu* vacc*arum* q*uia* iij st*e*ril*es*. De quib*us* In vend*itis* iij. Et Rem*anent* iij vit*u*li quor*um* j masc*ulus*.

Multon*es*. Iid*em* r*eddunt* c*ompotum* de ccc iiij^{xx} iiij multon*ibus* re-m*anentibus* a*nno* p*reterito*. Et de c liij adiu*n*ct*is*. S*umma* d xxxvij. D*e* quib*us* In mor*ina* an*te* tons*ionem* ix. Et post tons*ionem* vj. In vend*itis* in t*ermino* s*anc*ti martin*i* xxxvj. S*umma* lj. Et Rem*anent* cccc iiij^{xx} vj m*u*lton*es*.

Hurt*ardi*. Iid*em* r*eddunt* c*ompotum* de xj hurt*ardis* rem*anentibus* a*nno* p*reterito*. Et de j adiunct*o*. S*umma* xij. De quib*us* in mor*ina* post tons*ionem* j. Et Rem*anent* xj Hurt*ardi*.

Matr*es*. Iid*em* r*eddunt* c*ompotum* de d iiij^{xx} iij ou*ibus* matr*icibus* re-m*anentibus* a*nno* p*reterito*. Et de c xliij adiu*n*ct*is*. S*umma* dcc xxvj. D*e* quib*us* in mor*ina* an*te* agn*ilationem et* tons*ionem* viij. Et p*os*t agn*ila-tionem et* an*te* tons*ionem* iij. Et p*os*t tons*ionem* ix. In vend*itis* In f*es*t*o* martin*i* iiij^{xx}. S*umma* c. Et Rem*anent* d c xxvj ou*es* matr*ices*.

Hogastr*i*. Iid*em* r*eddunt* c*ompotum* de ccc x Hogastr*is* rem*anentibus* anno p*re*t*e*rito Agn*is*. D*e* quib*us* In mor*ina* an*te* tons*ionem* xiij. In adiu*n*ct*is* multon*ibus* c liij. Et cu*m* hurt*ardis* j. Et cu*m* ou*ibus* matr*ici-bus* c xliij. Et n*ihil* rem*anet*.

Agni. Iidem R*eddunt* c*ompotum* de cccc xliiij Agn*is* de ex*itu* matr*i-cium* quia xlvj steril*es* v f*ecerunt* abors*um*. Et de ij Rec*eptis* de Henr*ico* le Duk*e* p*os*t tons*ionem*. S*umma* cccc xlvj. De quib*us* in mor*ina* an*te* sep*aratio*nem lv. In decim*a* xxxviij. In mor*ina* p*os*t sep*aratio*nem *et* an*te* tons*ionem* v. Et post tons*ionem* iiij. In cons*uetudine* j p*re*posit*i* ij b*ercariorum et* j fabr*i* iiij. In vend*itis* an*te* tons*ionem* iij. S*umma* c ix. Et Rem*anent* ccc xxxvij Agn*i*.

Porc*i*. Iid*em* r*eddunt* c*ompotum* de xx porc*is* adiu*n*ct*is* de Hogett*is*. D*e* quib*us* In vend*itis* ix. Et Rem*anent* xj porc*i*.

Sues. Iid*em* r*eddunt* comp*otum* de ij Suib*us* Rem*anentibus* a*nno* p*re-terito*. Et de j de emp*ta* in aut*umpno*. S*umma* iij. Et Rem*anent* iij sues.

[Hoggetti]. Iid*em* r*eddunt* c*ompotum* de xx Hoggett*is* rem*anentibus* a*nno* p*reterito* porcell*is*. In adiunct*is* porc*is* om*nes et* n*ihil* rem*anet*.

Porcell*i*. Iid*em* r*eddunt* co*mpotum* de xvj porcell*is* de exit*u* suu*m*. Et de vj de emp*tis* sup*erius* cu*m* sue. Et de ij recep*tis* de Henr*ico* le Douke. S*umma* xxiiij. D*e* quib*us* j [sic.]. In mor*ina* iij. In cons*uetudine* j porcar*ii* j. Et In vend*itis* sup*er* comp*otum* vj pro ij s. Et Rem*anent* xiij porcell*i*.

Lan*a*. Iidem r*eddunt* co*mpotum* de ccc xxxix veller*ibus* multon*um* xj veller*ibus* hurt*ardorum* cccc iiij^xx xij vell*eribus* ou*ium* matric*ium* *et* cc iiij^xx xvij vell*eribus* hogastr*orum* p*rouentis* ad tons*ionem*. S*umma* MC xxxix. D*e* quib*us* In decim*a* xiij. In cons*uetudine* ij b*ercariorum* j Daye iij. S*umma* C xvj. In miss*is* apud Wolues*eiam* M xxiij veller*a* q*ue* fec*erunt* vij pond*era* di*midium* vij clau*os*.

Lan*a* fract*a*. Iidem r*eddunt* co*mpotum* de xviij clau*is* lan*e* fract*e*. Et In vend*itis* tot*um*.

Lan*a* Agn*ina*. Iid*em* r*eddunt* co*mpotum* de ccc xx vell*eribus* lan*e* p*ro*u*entis* ad tons*ionem* q*uia* xix agn*i* adhuc no*n* tond*ebantur*. In miss*is* apud Wolues*eiam* tot*um* q*uod* pond*eravit* xxv clauos.

Cas*eum* yem*ale et* esti*vale*. Iidem r*eddunt* co*mpotum* de xxxij cas*eis* yem*alibus* fact*is* p*er* colle*c*tam lact*e*. Et In vend*itis* totu*m*.

Iid*em* r*eddunt* co*mpotum* de C lxxij cas*eis* fact*is* q*ui* incep*erun*t f*ieri* die Jou*is* p*roximo* an*te* f*estu*m s*anc*to*rum* Tyburt*i et* valer*ii et* desieru*n*t die s*anc*ti mich*aelis* ut*ro*q*ue* die comp*utato*. De quib*us* In d*ecim*a xvij. In cons*uetudine* j p*re*pos*it*i j b*er*car*ii* j fabri *et* j Daye iiij. S*umma* xxj. Et In vend*itis* C lj qui f*ecerunt* viij pond*era*. Et In vend*itis* sup*er* comp*otum* de lactag*io* pro iiij s. ij d.

Butir*um*. Iidem R*eddunt* co*mpotum* de x clau*is* butir*i*. Et In vend*itis* totu*m*.

Cor*ium*. Id*em* r*eddunt* co*mpotum* de j cor*io* affr*i* de mor*ina*. In dealbat*o* ad H*a*rnes*ium* j. Et Rem*anet* j cor*ium* dealbat*um*.

Pell*es* grosse. Iid*em* r*eddunt* co*mpotum* de ix pell*ibus* multon*um* j pell*e* hurt*ardi* xj pell*ibus* ou*ium* matr*icium et* xiij pell*ibus* hogastr*orum* de mor*ina* p*o*st tons*ionem*. S*umma* xxxiiij. Et vend*ebantur*.

Pell*es* Nude *et* Agn*ine*. Iid*em* r*eddunt* co*mpotum* de vj pell*ibus* multon*um et* ix pell*ibus* matr*icium* ou*ium* de mor*ina* p*o*st tons*ionem*. Et In vend*itis* om*nis*. Et de lv pell*ibus* agn*orum* de mor*ina* an*te* separ*acio*nem *et* v post sep*aracio*nem *et* an*te* tons*ionem*. D*e* quib*us* In decim*a* v. Et In vend*itis* lv. Et de iiij pell*ibus* agn*orum* de mor*ina* p*o*st tons*ionem*. In vend*itis* om*ne*s.

Auc*e*. Iid*em* r*eddunt* co*mpotum* de j anc*er*e *et* iiij auc*is* rem*anentibus* a*nno* pret*erito*. Et de xx de ex*itu*. S*umma* xxv. D*e* quib*us* In decim*a* ij. In vend*itis* xij. Et In vend*itis* s*up*er comp*otum* vj p*ro* ij s. Et Rem*anent* iiij Auce *et* j ancer.

Gallin*e*. Iid*em* r*eddunt* [compotum] de j gall*o et* v gallin*is* rem*anentibus* a*nno* pret*erito*. Et C xxv de ch*eriseto*. S*umma* C xxxj. D*e* quib*us* In def*ectu* t*er*re le Strong*e* t*ra*c*te* in do*minicum* iiij. In def*ectu* t*erre* Wil-l*elm*i de Cur*ia* p*r*o eode*m* iiij. In def*ectu* t*er*re Robe*rt*i Couch*e* p*ro* si*mi*li iiij. In def*ectu* t*erre* swon p*ro* si*mi*li iiij. In def*ectu* t*erre* Ric*ard*i vac-car*ii* p*r*o si*mi*li iiij. In def*ectu* t*erre* Ric*ard*i Cnaue p*r*o si*mi*li iiij. In de-f*ectu* t*erre* Emme martyn q*uia* vid*ua* ij. In def*ectu* t*erre* Buewolf p*ro* eod*em* ij. In def*ectu* t*erre* Pet*r*onill*e* Elys p*r*o eod*em* ij. In def*ectu* t*er*re Wyndhut ij. In def*ectu* t*er*re Alic*ie* Knyght ij. S*umma* xxxiiij. In ven-d*itis* iiij^{xx} xj.

Capon*es*. Iid*em* r*eddunt* co*mpotum* de xxxv capon*ibus* rem*anentibus* a*nno* p*reterito*. Et de xxiiij f*act*is Hoc ann*o*. D*e* quib*us* In vend*itis* xxxv. Et Rem*anent* xxiiij capon*es*.

Pulcin*i*. Id*em* r*eddunt* co*mpotum* de xxvj pulc*inis* de ex*itu*. D*e* quib*us* in mor*ina* ij. In capon*ibus* f*act*is xxiiij *et* n*ihil* r*emanet*.

Oua. Iid*em* r*eddunt* co*mpotum* de CCC ou*is* de ex*itu* gall*inarum*. In vend*itis* o*mn*ia.

cisera. De cicera n*ihil* hoc a*nno*.

Vtensil*ia*. Iid*em* r*eddunt* co*mpotum* de j cacabo j oll*a* en*ea* j pocin*n*et' j patell*a* j lauacr*o* cu*m* pelui j secur*i* j picos*o* j dol*eo* vacuo de Rem*anen-tibus*. Et Rem*anent*.

Car*ecte*. Iid*em* r*eddunt* co*mpotum* de j car*ecta* ferr*ata* rem*anente* a*nno* p*reterito*. Et de j Renouata. S*umma* ij. De quib*us* j p*ur*ificat*a*. Et Rem*anet* j carec*ta* ferro ligat*a*.

§§ 15. Reeves' Account, 29 Sept., 1355—28 Sept., 1356.

This account, which is carelessly written and contains many irregularities in abbreviation, is dated the eleventh year of Bishop William (of Edington) and the eighth year of the pestilence. It was rendered by two reeves jointly. This year the seneschal held the two tourns as usual, while the bailiff held five courts in addition. The bailiff received 40s. from Crawley and the rest of his wages from other manors.

The great calamity that sweeps across the account is the pestilence of 1348–49. Holdings were vacant, services commuted, and few customary tenants remained to reap the grain. The son and heir of Richard Fromond paid the rent for one of his father's estates, a toft called "the howe," but refused to pay a fine or composition for another, a toft of a half virgate of bondland in Wodecote, which thereupon escheated to the lord. Clearly, agricultural holdings were not in demand. Probably the young Fromond saw no chance of hiring labor to help him cultivate this second tenement.

The second misfortune was the dryness of the year, which forced the lord to buy hay for the sheep. Dryness on the chalk downs was obviously a serious matter, for water was hard to obtain for the cattle and fodder for the numerous sheep.

A master tiler (coopertor conductor) and his helper (garcio suus) were employed for a week to cover the granary with slates, the former receiving 2s., the latter 18d. The slates were apparently fixed in mortar.

Again we find reference to the fold of the customary tenants, that is, apparently the common fold in contradistinction to the lord's folds. If the tenants kept over twenty-five sheep in their own fold, they paid a custom to the lord. It is not here stated whether this was twenty-five sheep for each tenant or for the whole group of tenants. As we know from other sources, however, the former was the case.[1]

There is an interesting entry that has to do with the accounting practices of the time. The reeves were allowed 30s., "without writ," for divers charges and discharges in the current account. Whether this was to cover errors or unusual emergencies is not stated.

Crawley was linked up with a fair, probably the great fair of St. Giles, when it sent oats to Wolvesey for use at the fair.[2] And it evidently was of considerable service to an episcopal manor, Stoke, when it sent a ram and forty-nine ewes. But whether these were simply to replenish the stock of a sister manor or were of unusual quality to aid in keeping up the breed is not indicated.

CRAULEE[3]

Comp*otus* Joh*ann*is att*e* Hull*e* *et* Joh*ann*is att*e* Putte p*re*p*osit*or*um* ib*id*em de anno Cons*ecrationis* d*omi*ni Will*elm*i Wynton*iensis* Epis*copi* xj^{mo}

Arrer*agium*. Idem r*espondent* de vj li. ix s. xj d. de arr*eragio* comp*oti* p*re*cedent*is* Quos lib*eraverunt* d*omi*no Joh*ann*i Payn Thes*aurario* de Wolues*eia* p*er* j tall*iam*. Et quiet*us* est.

[1] See above, § 12, pp. 44-45.
[2] See above, § 7, p. 21; § 18, p. 61.
[3] MS., P. R. O., Ecclesiastical Commission, Various, 159366.

Redd*itus*. Et de lxiiij s. vj d. de tot*o* redd*itu* ass*iso* ad f*estu*m Nat*alis* d*omi*ni. Et de lxvij s. x d. de tot*o* redd*itu* ass*iso* ad f*estu*m Pasch*e*. Et de lxiiij s. vj d. de tot*o* redd*itu* ass*iso* ad f*estu*m Nat*alis* s*anct*i Joh*annis* Bapt*iste*. Et de c iiij s. j d. de tot*o* redd*itu* ass*iso* ad f*estu*m s*anct*i Mich*ael*is. S*umma* xv li. xj d.

Acquiet*ancie*. In acq*uietancia* j p*re*po*sit*i p*er* annu*m* v s. In acq*uie*-*tanciis* ij caruc*ariorum et* j fabr*i* p*er* a*nnu*m viij s. cuil*ibe*t ij s. viij d. In acq*uietancia* j b*er*car*ii* m*u*lton*um* p*er* annu*m* ij s. viij d. S*umma* xv s. viij d.

Defe*ct*us cust*umariorum*. In def*ectu* redd*itus* t*erre* Will*elm*i le Stronge t*ra*ct*e* in d*omi*nico p*er* a*nnu*m ij s. In def*ectu* t*erre* Will*elm*i de Curi*a* p*ro* si*mi*li ij s. viij d. In def*ectu* t*erre* de Alebrok*e* q*ui* modo rem*anet* apud M*er*don*am* v s. In def*ectu* t*erre* Rob*er*ti Crouch*e* t*ra*c*t*e in d*omi*nico p*er* annu*m* ij s. viij d. In def*ectu* t*erre* Rob*er*ti Coye p*ro* si*mi*li ij s. viij d. In def*ectu* t*erre* porcar*ii* ij s. viij d. In def*ectu* t*erre* Ric*ardi* vaccar*ii* p*ro* si*mi*li ij s. viij d. S*umma* xx s. iiij d.

Def*ect*us p*er* pestil*entiam* hoc anno viij°. In def*ectu* redd*itus* j mes-*suagii* j ferling*i* t*erre* nat*ive* q*ue* fuer*unt* Joh*annis* Moraunt*e* in man*u* d*omi*ni p*er* mort*em* eiusd*em* in pestil*entia* n*ihil* q*uia* p*re*d*ict*us redd*itus* vid*elicet* iiij s. le*vatus* de ex*itu*. D*e* xxj s. de redd*itu* j mes*suagii* j virg*ate* t*erre et* xxij acr*arum* t*erre* p*ur*p*restu*r*e* que fuer*unt* Rob*ert*i Wodecote n*ihil* q*uia* leu*atus* de ex*itu* in past*ura* vend*ita* p*ro* bid*entibus* d*omi*ni hoc anno. D*e* ij s. viij d. de redd*itu* j mes*suagii* j ferling*i* t*erre* nat*ive* que fuer*unt* Thome Symond n*ihil* q*uia* leu*atus* de ex*itu*. D*e* ij s. viij d. de redd*itu* j mes*suagii* j ferling*i* t*erre* nat*ive* que fuer*unt* Joh*ann*is Body n*ihil* q*uia* leu*atus* de ex*itu*. S*umma* acquiet*anciarum et* defe*ct*us xxxvj s. S*umma* redd*ituum* rem*anentium* de Clar*o* xiij li. iiij s. xj d.

Ciminu*m*. Et de j l*ibra* Cimin*i* de redd*itu* Joh*ann*is fil*ii et* her*edis* Ric*ard*i Fromond p*ro* j croft*o* voc*ato* howe. Et lib*erata* Thes*aurario* de Wolues*eia*.

Exit*us* maner*ii*. Et de xvij s. viij d. de pannag*io* porc*orum* intr*ato*-*rum* ad f*estu*m s*anct*i Mart*in*i. D*e* pesson*a* in bosc*o* n*ihil* hoc a*nno*. Et de ij s. j d. de pannag*io* vitul*orum*. Et de xxix s. vj d. de xlviij vacc*is et* xxiij bouic*ulis* ad hock*e* hoc anno p*ro* vacc*a* vj d. *et* p*ro* bouic*ulo* ij d. Et de xxiij s. iiij d. de vij acr*is* subbosc*i* vend*itis* p*recium* acr*e* iij s. iiij d. D*e* past*ura* yem*ali* in bosc*o* n*ihil* hoc a*nno* p*ro* def*ectu* emp*toris*. Et de x s. viij d. de pastur*a* est*ivali* vend*ita* ib*ide*m hoc a*nno*. D*e* past*ura* bid*entium* in bosc*o* n*ihil* hoc a*nno* q*uia* depasc*abatur* cu*m* hog*ast*ris d*omi*ni. Et de v s. de pastur*a* in Drakenorth*e* vend*ita*. D*e* past*ura* in Trendele *et* Halydon*e* n*ihil* p*ro* def*ectu* emp*toris*. D*e* pastur*a* in Com-forlonge n*ihil* q*uia* se*minabatur* cu*m* orde*o*. D*e* past*ura* in Bassamlee n*ihil* q*uia* depasc*abatur* cu*m* bid*entibus* d*omi*ni. D*e* ou*ibus* in fald*a* cus-tum*ariorum* n*ihil* q*uia* no*n* excedunt c*er*tu*m* num*erum* xxv hoc a*nno*.

Et de vij s. j d. de porc*is* agist*atis* in stipul*a* d*omi*ni hoc anno. D*e* pas*tura* fossat*i* circ*a* Cur*iam* n*ihil* hoc anno. Et de xviij d. de pastur*a* in lokforlang*e* *et* markforlang*e* vend*ita*. Et de iij s. iiij d. de pastur*a* de la Sherte vend*ita* homag*io*. D*e* pastur*a* in Puthull*e* n*ihil* p*ro* def*ec*tu emp*toris*. Et de vj s. viij d. de Alic*ia* Pours p*ro* op*eribus* t*er*r*e* Rob*ert*i Bonde relax*atis*. Et de vj s. viij d. de Roger*o* Crop p*ro* op*eribus* t*er*r*e* Ric*ard*i Alayn relax*atis*. Et de vj s. viij d. de Joh*anne* Wodecote p*ro* op*eribus* t*er*r*e* Walt*er*i Shawe r*e*lax*atis* p*er* a*nnu*m q*ua*m diu d*omi*no placu*er*it. D*e* v s. de Steph*ano* Knyght' p*ro* op*eribus* Nich*ola*i Pope p*ro* tene*mento* qu*o*d Joh*anne*s att*e* Hall*e* te*net* n*ihil* q*uia* fec*it* op*era*. Et de v s. de Joh*anne* Cart*er*e p*ro* op*eribus* t*er*r*e* Steph*an*i Cart*er*e p*at*ris sui relax*atis* p*er* a*nnum*. D*e* vj s. viij d. de Gilb*ert*o Sely p*ro* op*eribus* Walt*er*i Coleman n*ihil* q*uia* fec*it* op*era*. Et de vj s. viij d. de Joh*anne* Trygg*e* p*ro* op*eribus* t*er*r*e* Rob*er*ti Trigg*e* p*at*ris sui relax*atis*. D*e* vj s. viij d. de Rob*er*to Wodecote p*ro* op*eribus* t*er*r*e* Henr*ici* Martyn n*ihil* q*uia* fec*it* op*era*. Et de vj s. viij d. de Walt*er*o Hodeman p*ro* op*eribus* t*er*r*e* Joh*annis* veynes relax*atis*. D*e* Rog*er*o Gibbes p*ro* op*eribus* t*er*r*e* Edith*e* Gibbes n*ihil* q*uia* fec*it* op*era*. D*e* vj s. viij d. de Gilb*er*t*o* Niweman p*ro* op*eribus* t*er*r*e* Will*elm*i Elys n*ihil* q*uia* fec*it* op*era*. Et de vj s. viij d. de Will*elm*o Bolkhurst p*ro* op*eribus* t*er*r*e* Joh*anni*s att*e* Neweweye relax*atis*. Et de vij s. iiij d. de xxij auc*is* vend*itis* p*recium* cuiusl*ibe*t iiij d. Et de v s. de xxiiij capon*ibus* vend*itis* p*recium* cuiusl*ibe*t ij d. ob. Et de viij s. iij d. de lxvj gall*is* *et* gallin*is* vend*itis* p*recium* cuiusl*ibe*t j d. ob. Et de viij d. de cc ou*is* vend*itis*. Et de ij s. xj d. de v cl*avis* lan*e* f*ra*cte vend*itis*. Et de xviij s. viij d. de iiij pell*ibus* hurt*ardorum* xvij m*ulto*n*um* xxviij ou*ium* matr*icium* *et* iiij^{xx} iiij hog*astrorum* dc mor*ina* an*te* tons*ionem* vend*itis* p*recium* pell*is* hurt*ardi* m*ulto*n*is* *et* ou*is* ij d. *et* hog*ast*ri j d. ob. Et de x d. de v pell*ibus* m*ulto*n*um* *et* v pell*ibus* ou*ium* matr*icium* de mor*ina* post tons*ionem* vend*itis*. Et de vj s. v d. de lxxvij pell*ibus* agn*orum* de mor*ina* an*te* sep*ara*c*ionem* vend*itis* p*recium* pell*is* j d. Et de vj d. de xij pell*ibus* agn*orum* de mor*ina* post sep*ara*c*ionem* vend*itis* p*recium* pell*is* ob. Et de xxiiij s. iij d. de iiij^{xx} xvij cas*eis* vend*itis* ad diu*ersa* p*recia*. Et de vij d. de j cl*avo* butir*i* vend*ito*. Et de iiij s. de j veter*e* oll*a* en*ea* dirrupt*a* vend*ita*. S*umma* xj li. iiij s. vij d.

Vend*itio* bl*ad*i. Et de xxiiij li. v s. de lxix q*uarteriis* fr*umen*ti vend*itis* vn*de* vj p*recium* q*uarterii* vij s. iiij d. *et* lxiij p*recium* q*uarterii* vij s. Et de viij li. vij s. j d. de xlj q*uarteriis* iij b*ussellis* di*midio* ordei vend*itis* vn*de* ij q*uarteria* p*recium* q*uarterii* iiij s. viij d. *et* xxxix q*uarteria* iij b*usselli* di*midius* p*recium* q*uarterii* iiij s. Et de xlij s. viij d. ob. q. de xvj q*uarteriis* iij b*ussellis* auen*e* vend*itis* vn*de* ij q*uarteria* di*midius* b*ussellus* p*recium* q*uarterii* iij s. *et* xiij q*uarteria* ij b*usselli* di*midius* vend*ita* hosp*itio* d*omi*ni *et* apud Wolues*eiam* p*ro* feria x q*uarteria* iij b*usselli* p*recium* q*uarterii* ij s. viij d. *et* ij q*uarteria* vij b*usselli* di*midius* p*recium* q*uarterii* ij s. Et de xxxvij s. vj d. de ix q*uarteriis* iij b*ussellis* pis*arum* vend*itis* p*recium* q*uarterii* iiij s. S*umma* xxxvj li. xij s. iij d. ob. q.

Vend*itio* staur*i*. Et de vj s. de j affr*o* vend*ito*. Et de lxvj s. iiij d. de lvij m*u*lton*ibus* vend*itis* post ton*sionem* vn*de* xxix hosp*itio* d*omi*ni p*re*c*ium* cap*itis* xij d. *et* xxviij p*recium* cap*itis* xvj d. Et de l s. de j hurt*ardo* xlix ou*ibus* matr*icibus* post ton*sionem* vend*itis* p*re*pos*it*o de Stoke p*recium* cap*itis* xij d. S*umma* vj li. ij s. iiij d.

Fin*es et* marit*agia*. Et de xiij s. iiij d. de Tethe*penny* ad t*erminum* s*anct*i Marti*ni et* Hock*e*. Et de vij s. de Gilb*erto* Valk*er* p*ro* j toft*a* di*midia* virg*at*a t*er*r*e* nat*iv*e apud Wodecote que fuer*unt* Ric*ard*i Fromond *et* que deuen*erunt* in man*us* d*omi*ni ta*mquam* esc*aete* eo q*uo*d Joh*ann*es fil*ius* eiusd*em* Ric*ard*i p*ro* eisd*em* finir*e* recus*averit* h*abendis*. S*umma* xx s. iiij d.

P*er*quis*ita*. Et de viij s. de p*er*quis*itis* t*ur*ni s*anct*i Mart*ini*. Et de xv d. de p*er*quis*itis* j Cur*ie* tent*e* an*te* d*ictu*m t*ur*nu*m*. Et de iiij s. vj d. de p*er*quis*itis* t*ur*ni de Hock*e*. Et de ij s. iij d. de p*er*quis*itis* ij Cur*iarum* tent*arum* an*te* d*ictu*m t*ur*nu*m*. Et de iij s. v d. de p*er*quis*itis* ij Curi*arum* tent*arum* post d*ictu*m t*ur*nu*m*. S*umma* xxix s. v d.

Vend*itio* S*up*er Comp*otum*. Et de xxv s. vj d. de reb*us* vend*itis* s*up*er comp*otum*. S*umma* xxv s. vj d. S*umma* to*talis* Rece*pte* lxx li. ix s. iiij d. ob. q.

Cust*us* caruc*arum*. In ferr*o et* acer*o* emp*tis* p*ro* ferr*amentis* iij caru*carum* p*er* a*nnu*m xvj s. In j vom*er*e fac*iendo* viij d. In iij ferr*is* ped*alibus* emp*tis* xviij d. In ij par*ibus* rot*arum* p*ro* caruc*is* xij d. In iij caruc*is* de nou*o* fac*iendis* xij d. In j cultr*o* dirrupt*o* emen*do* ij d. In ferr*amentis* vj affr*orum* iij s. In stip*endiis* ij bouar*iorum et* j fug*atoris* p*er* a*nnu*m xij s. In j se*milione* e*mpto* de lign' ix d. ob. S*umma* xxxvij s. j d. ob.

Cust*us* carect*arum*. In vj clut*is* emp*tis* xij d. In carect*a* axand*a* iiij d. In vnct*o* iiij d. In alb*o* core*o* viij d. In ferr*amentis* iij eq*uorum* v s. In stip*endio* j carect*arii* p*er* a*nnu*m iiij s. In j sell*a* carect*arii* emp*ta* iiij d. ob. S*umma* xj s. viij d. ob.

Emp*tio* staur*i*. In j affr*o* emp*to* ix s. S*umma* ix s.

Cust*us* b*er*car*ie*. In ij barell*is* tarr*e* emp*tis* p*ro* vnctur*a* bid*entium* x s. In vnct*o et* cep*o* ad id*em* xx s. In bercar*ia* m*u*lton*um* Watilland*a et* coop*erienda* p*er* vic*es* ij s. vj d. In b*er*car*ii* p*re*car*ia* p*ro* bid*entibus* vnguend*is* de p*recio* ix d. In stip*endiis* ij b*er*car*iorum* ou*ium* matr*icium et* hog*astrorum* p*er* a*nnu*m viij s. In pann*o* lan*eo et* line*o* emp*to* vj d. In sal*e* emp*to* xij d. In p*re*ssur*a* ij d. ob. In oll*a et* patell*a* lut*i* emp*tis* iij d. In stoppl*es* [?] emp*tis* vj d. In oll*a* ene*a* cont*inente* v lag*enas* di*midiam* ponder*ante* xlij l*ibras* x s. In stip*endio* j daye p*er* annu*m* ij s. In fen*o* emp*to* p*ro* sust*inendis* bid*entibus* lxiij s. vt testi*catur* p*er* balli*vum*. In pastur*a* de t*er*r*a* de Wodecote emp*ta* p*ro* bid*entibus* d*omi*ni xxj s. hoc anno p*ro* def*ec*tu pastur*e* *et* p*ro*pt*er* magn*am* sicc*itatem* in estat*e*. S*umma* vj li. xix s. viij d. ob.

Cust*us* dom*orum*. In j coop*er*tor*e* conduct*ore* p*ro* g*ra*nar*io* cu*m* sclat*is* coop*eriendo* p*er* j sept*imanam* ij s. In stip*endio* garc*ionis* sui p*er* idem temp*us* xvj d. In sclat*is* ad idem emp*tis* iij d. In ij q*uarteriis* calc*is* ad id*em* xvj d. In lath*es* *et* lathnail xij d. In crest*ura* iij d. In D kernill*is* j d. ob. In j mur*o* petr*e* int*er* bouar*iam* *et* port*am* de nou*o* fac*iendo* ad tas*cham* iij s. In d*icto* mur*o* coop*eriendo* iij d. In g*rangia*[1] pis*arum* *et* vesc*iarum* coop*er*iend*a* p*er* iij dies xij d. In iij quarent*enis* claustur*e* c*irca* coopic*ium* claud*endis* iiij s. vj d. p*ro* quarent*ena* xviij d. S*umma* xv s. ob.

De sarc*ulatione* *et* falc*atione* n*ihil* hoc anno.

Cust*us* aut*umpni*. In pan*e* ad iij p*recarias* de CC xix ho*minibus* cust*umariis* qui mess*uerunt* lxxviij acr*as* f*rumenti* xxxj acr*as* auen*e* q*uas*i p*er* j diem cu*m* ministr*is* Cur*ie* ix s. j d. ob. cuil*ibe*t eor*um* pan*is* de ob. In cas*eis* p*ro* eisd*em* iiij s. vj d. ob. q. cuil*ibe*t eor*um* cas*eum* de q. In c*eruis*ia p*ro* eisd*em* emp*ta* xxij d. In xlviij acr*is* di*midia* cuiuscu*m*q*ue* gen*er*is bl*ad*i met*endis* lig*andis* *et* adhim*endis* xxij s. ij d. ob. videl*icet* p*ro* acr*a* v d. ob. plus in tot*o* ob. p*rete*rea cust*umarii* mess*uerunt* *et* lig*averunt* C xix acr*as* de cons*uetudine* p*ro* Nydripe. In stip*endio* j haiward*i* p*er* *annu*m vj s. viij d. S*umma* xliiij s. iiij d. ob. q.

Tritur*atio* *et* vent*ilatio*. In iiij^{xx} viij q*uarteriis* vij b*ussellis* f*rumen*ti iij q*uarteriis* j b*ussello* Cur*alli* xiij q*uarteriis* iij b*ussellis* pis*arum* *et* vj q*uarteriis* ij b*ussellis* vesc*iarum* t*ritur*a*ndis* ad t*ascham* xviij s. vij d. q. p*ro* q*uarterio* ij d. In C xvj q*uarteriis* ordei t*ritur*a*ndis* ad tas*cham* xiiij s. vj d. p*ro* q*uarterio* j d. ob. In lxxiiij q*uarteriis* iij b*ussellis* auen*e* t*ritu*r*andis* ad t*ascham* vj s. ij d. q. p*ro* q*uarterio* j d. In med*ietate* toc*ius* bl*ad*i vent*ilanda* ad t*ascham* iij s. j d. ob. q. p*ro* q*uarterio* q. S*umma* xlij s. v d. q.

Exp*ense* sen*escalli*. In exp*ensis* Sen*escalli* ven*ientis* ib*idem* p*ro* t*urnis* tenend*is* xiij s. iij d. p*er* ij bill*as*. S*umma* xiij s. iij d.

Vad*ia* ball*ivi*. In vad*iis* Rog*er*i Haiwode ball*ivi* in p*arte* vad*iorum* suor*um* xl s. *et* res*iduum* cap*tum* in al*iis* maner*iis*. S*umma* xl s. S*umma* xl s. S*umma* om*nium* exp*ensarum* xvij li. xij s. viij d. Et deb*ent* lij li. xvj s. viij d. ob. q.

Alloc*atio* s*ine* bre*vi*. Ind*entura* alloc*ationis* p*repositi*s xix d. in j dol*eo* vini car*iando* de Suth*amptonia* usq*ue* merewell*e* cu*m* p*rebenda* equ*orum* car*iantium* d*ictu*m vinu*m*. Et eid*em* xxx s. de diu*ersis* s*upe*ron*eratis* *et* dis*oneratis* in p*resenti* comp*oto*. S*umma* xxxj s. vij d.

Alloc*atio* p*er* bre*ve*. Et eid*em* xxxiiij s. ix d. quos lib*eravit* d*omi*no Joh*anni* Bleobury Garderob*ario* hosp*itii* d*omi*ni in diu*ersis* victual*iis* p*er* Indentur*am*. S*umma* xxxiiij s. ix d.

[1] Before *grangia* is the word def*ec*tib*us* stricken through.

Liberatio denariorum. Et liberavit domino Johanni Payn Thesaurario de Wolueseia xxxj li. xij s. ij d. ob. Summa xxxj li. xij s. ij d. ob. Summa omnium allocationum et liberationum xxxiij li. xviij s. vj d. ob. Et debet xvij li. xviij s. ij d.

Frumentum. Idem reddunt [compotum] de iiij^{xx} viij quarteriis vij bussellis frumenti receptis de exitu per talliam contra Johannem Palmere. Summa iiij^{xx} viij quarteria vij busselli frumenti. De quibus in semine super lxxviij acras terre per perticam in Ger'delonde xix quarteria iiij busselli super acram ij busselli. In pane furniato pro expensis Senescalli venientis ibidem pro turnis tenendis iij busselli per billam. In venditis lxix quarteriis. Summa que supra. Et eque.

Curallum. Et de iij quarteriis j bussello Curalli receptis de exitu per talliam contra eundem. Et totum computatur in mixtura ad liberationem famulorum. Et eque.

Ordeum. Et de C xvj quarteriis ordei receptis de exitu per talliam contra eundem. Summa C xvj quarteria. De quibus in semine super lxxv acras dimidiam per perticam in la Combe xxxvij quarteria vj busselli super acram iiij busselli. In dono Senescalli ij bercariis ij busselli. In mixtura ad liberationem famulorum xxxvj quarteria iiij busselli dimidius. In venditis xlj quarteria iij busselli dimidius. Summa que supra. Et eque.

Auena. Et de lxxiiij quarteriis iij bussellis auene receptis de exitu per talliam contra eundem. Et de x quarteriis per estimationem in garbis. Summa iiij^{xx} iiij quarteria iij busselli. De quibus in semine super iiij^{xx} ij acras in Markforlange per perticam xlj quarteria super acram iiij busselli. In datis bobus per estimationem in garbis viij quarteria. In sustentacione ouium et agnorum tempore agnellationis ij quarteria per estimationem. In prebenda iiij equorum carectariorum per annum v quarteria. In prebenda vj affrorum per annum vij quarteria. In farina fracta pro potagio famulorum iij quarteria iiij busselli. In prebenda equorum Senescalli venientis ibidem pro turnis tenendis j quarterium per billam. In venditis xvj quarteria iij busselli unde hospitio domini xiij quarteria ij busselli dimidius. Et super compotum iiij busselli pro[-]. Et eque.

Pise. Et de xiij quarteriis iij bussellis pisarum receptis de exitu per talliam contra eundem. Et de iij quarteriis per estimationem in siliquis. Summa xvj quarteria iij busselli. De quibus in semine super xvj acras per perticam in Drakenorthe iiij quarteria super acram ij busselli. In sustentacione ouium in yeme per estimationem iij quarteria. In venditis ix quarteria iij busselli. Summa que supra. Et eque.

Vescie. Et de vj quarteriis ij bussellis vesciarum receptis de exitu per talliam contra eundem. Et de vj quarteriis per estimationem in siliquis.

Summa xij *quarteria* ij *busselli*. D*e* quib*us* in se*mine* su*per* xxv acr*as* p*er* p*er*tic*am* in Drakenorth*e* vj *quarteria* ij *busselli* su*per* acr*am* ij *busselli*. In sust*entacione* o*uium* matr*icium* in yem*e* vj *quarteria*. *Summa* que s*upra*. Et eq*ue*.

Lib*eratio* famul*orum*. Et de iij *quarteriis* j *bussello* Cur*alli* xxxvj *quarteriis* iiij *bussellis* di*midio* ord*ei* rec*eptis* sup*ra* ad lib*erationem* famu*lorum*. *Summa* xxxix *quarteria* v *busselli* di*midius*. D*e* quib*us* in libe*ratione* haiward*i* j carect*arii* ij caruc*ariorum et* ij b*ercariorum* o*uium* matr*icium et* hog*astrorum* p*er* a*nnum* xxxj *quarteria* j *bussellus* qui*libet* capi*ens quarterium* ad x sept*imanas*. In lib*eratione* j garc*ionis* auxil*iantis* b*ercariis* temp*ore* agn*ellationis et* custod*ientis* agn*os* p*er* se a t*empore* sep*aracionis* usq*ue* tons*ionem* j *quarterium*. In lib*eratione* j dai*e* p*er* a*nnum* iij *quarteria* ij *busselli* capi*entis quarterium* ad xvj sept*imanas*. In lib*eratione* j fug*atoris* eunt*is* ad iij caruc*as* ad ij seison*as et* aux*iliantis* carect*ariis* p*ro* di*uersis* car*ectatis* p*er* a*nnum* iiij *quarteria* ij *busselli* di*midius* capi*entis quarterium* ad xij sept*imanas*. *Summa* que s*upra*. Et eque.

Equi. Et de iij eq*uis* de rem*anentibus*. Et rem*anent* iij eq*ui*.

Affr*i*. Et de vj affr*is* de rem*anentibus*. Et de j de e*mpto*. *Summa* vij. D*e* quib*us* in vend*ito* j. Et rem*anent* vj affr*i*.

Boues. Et de xx bob*us* de rem*anentibus*. Et rem*anent* xx bou*es*.

Hurt*ardi*. Et de xv hurt*ardis* de rem*anentibus*. Et de v de adiu*nctis*. *Summa* xx. D*e* q*uibus* in mor*ina* an*te* tons*ionem* iiij. In vend*ito* p*ost* tons*ionem* p*re*pos*ito* de Stok*e* j. *Summa* v. Et rem*anent* xv hurt*ardi*.

M*u*ltone*s*. Et de D xxvj m*u*lton*ibus* de rem*anentibus*. Et de lxxix de adiu*nctis*. D*e* quib*us* in mor*ina* an*te* tons*ionem* xvij *et* post tons*ionem* v. In vend*itis* post tons*ionem* lvij vn*de* hosp*itio* d*om*ini xxix. *Summa* lxxix. Et rem*anent* D xxvj m*u*ltone*s*.

Oues matr*ices*. Et de CCCC lxxv o*uibus* matr*icibus* de rem*anentibus*. Et de iiij^{xx} ij de adiu*nctis*. *Summa* D lvij. D*e* quib*us* in mor*ina* an*te* agn*ellationem* iij *et* post agnel*lationem et* an*te* tons*ionem* xxv *et* post tons*ionem* v. In vend*itis* p*re*pos*ito* de Stoke post tons*ionem* xlix. *Summa* iiij^{xx} ij. Et rem*anent* CCCC lxxv matre*s*.

Hog*astri*. Et de CC l hog*astris* de rem*anentibus*. *Summa* CC l. D*e* quib*us* in mor*ina* an*te* tons*ionem* iiij^{xx} iiij. In adiu*nctis* cu*m* hurt*ardis* v *et* cu*m* m*u*lton*ibus* lxxix *et* cu*m* o*uibus* matr*icibus* iiij^{xx} ij. Et n*ihil* rem*anet*.

Agn*i*. Et de CCC lxxvj agn*is* de ex*itu et* no*n* de plur*ibus* q*uia* iij matre*s* mor*tue* an*te* agn*ellationem* iiij^{xx} x fuer*unt* sterile*s et* vj fecer*unt* abort*um*. *Summa* CCC lxxvj. D*e* quib*us* in mor*ina* an*te* sep*aracionem* lxxvij. In de*cima* xxx. In cons*uetudine* p*re*pos*iti* fabr*i et* b*er*car*ii* m*u*lton*um* iij. In mor*ina* post sep*aracionem et* an*te* tons*ionem* vj *et* post tons*ionem* vj. *Summa* C xxij. Et rem*anent* CC liiij agn*i*.

Auc*e*. Et de j ancer*o* *et* iiij mariol*es* de rem*anentibus*. Et de xxiiij de ex*itu*. S*umma* xxix. D*e* quib*us* in dec*ima* ij. In vend*itis* xxij. S*umma* xxiiij. Et rem*anent* j ance*r* *et* iiij mariol*es*.

Capon*es*. Et de xxiiij capon*ibus* de rem*anentibus*. Et de xxiiij de pulc*inis* fac*t*is. S*umma* xlviij. D*e* quib*us* in vend*itis* xxiiij. Et rem*anent* xxiiij Capon*es*.

Gall*us* *et* gallin*e*. Et de j gall*o* *et* v gallin*is* de rem*anentibus*. Et de c xxv de Ch*e*r*iseto* ad f*estum* s*anc*ti Martin*i*. S*umma* c xxxj. D*e* quib*us* in def*ectu* t*er*r*e* le Stronge t*r*act*e* in d*omi*nico p*er* a*nnum* iiij. In def*ectu* t*er*r*e* Will*elm*i de Cur*ia* p*ro* sim*i*li iiij. In def*ectu* t*er*r*e* Rob*er*ti Crouch*e* p*ro* sim*i*li iiij. In def*ec*tu t*er*r*e* Will*elm*i le Swon p*ro* sim*i*li iiij. In def*ectu* t*er*r*e* Ric*ard*i vaccar*ii* p*ro* sim*i*li iiij. In def*ectu* t*er*r*e* Ric*ard*i Cnaue p*ro* sim*i*li iiij. In def*ectu* Rog*er*i Crop Alic*ie* Hodeman Rog*er*i Gibbes Joh*annis* Cart*er*e Joh*an*nis Trigg*e* Junior*is* Joh*an*nis Trigg*e* senior*is* Rad*ulph*i Smyth*e* q*uia* viduar*ii* *et* vidua xiij p*ro* q*uo*l*ibe*t ij. In def*ectu* t*er*r*e* Joh*an*nis Body Joh*an*nis Coup*er*e Thom*e* Symond *et* Joh*an*nis Moraunt*e* xvj p*ro* quol*ibe*t iiij. In def*ectu* t*er*r*e* Rob*er*ti Wodecote p*ro* iij ten*ementis* in man*ibus* d*omi*ni p*er* pestil*entiam* v. In vend*itis* lxvj. S*umma* c xxv. Et rem*anent* j gall*us* *et* v gallin*e*.

Pulcin*i*. Et de xxiiij pulc*inis* de ex*itu*. Et comp*utantur* in cap*onibus* fa*ct*is. Et n*ihil* rem*anet*.

Oua. Et de cc ou*is* de ex*itu*. Et vend*ita* inf*ra*. Et n*ih*il rem*anet*.

Vell*era*. Et de xj vell*eribus* hurt*ardorum* D ix m*u*lton*um* cccc xlviij ou*ium* *et* c lxvj hogr*orum* p*r*ouen*tis* ad ton*sionem*. S*umma* MC xxxiij. D*e* quib*us* in dec*ima* c lxiij. Et lib*erata* apud Wolues*eiam* M xx q*ue* fecer*unt* iiij sacc*os* xvj cl*avos*. Et n*ihil* rem*anet*.

Lan*a* agn*ina*. Et de cc lx vell*eribus* agn*inis* p*r*ouen*tis* ad ton*sionem*. Et lib*erata* apud Wolues*eiam* que fecer*unt* xij cl*avos*. Et n*ihil* rem*anet*.

Lan*a* f*racta*. Et de v cl*avis* lan*e* f*r*act*e* p*r*ouen*tis* ad ton*sionem*. Et vend*ita* inf*ra*. Et n*ihil* rem*anet*.

Pell*es* lanut*e*. Et de iiij pell*ibus* hurt*ardorum* xvij m*u*lton*um* xxviij ou*ium* m*a*tric*ium* *et* iiij^{xx} iiij hog*astrorum* de mor*ina* an*te* tons*ionem*. S*umma* c xxxiij. Et vend*ite* inf*ra*. Et n*ihil* rem*anet*.

Pell*es* nud*e*. Et de v pell*ibus* m*u*lton*um* v ou*ium* m*a*tric*ium* de mor*ina* post ton*sionem*. Et vend*ite* inf*ra*. Et n*ihil* rem*anet*.

Pell*es* agn*ine*. Et de lxxvij pell*ibus* agn*orum* de mor*ina* an*te* sep*ara*c*ionem*. D*e* quib*us* in dec*ima* viij. In vend*itis* lxix. S*umma* que s*upra*. Et n*ihil* rem*anet*.

Pell*es* Rott*orum*. Et de xij pell*ibus* agn*orum* rott*orum* de mor*ina* post sep*aracionem*. Et vend*ite* inf*ra*. Et n*ihil* rem*anet*.

Cas*eus*. Et de c x cas*eis* fac*t*is in est*ate*. S*umma* c x. D*e* q*ui*b*us* in dec*ima* xj. In cons*uetudine* p*re*posit*i* *et* fabr*i* ij. In vend*itis* iiij^{xx} xvij. Et n*ihil* rem*anet*.

Butir*um*. Et de j cl*avo* butir*i* de ex*itu*. Et vend*itum* inf*ra*. Et n*ihil* rem*anet*. S*ed* onera[n]t*ur* de xxiiij s. de lact*agio* s*up*er co*mpotum* vt ou*es* r*eddunt* de[1] ij d. cu*m* ij cas*eis* dat*is* de cons*uetudine* p*recium* xij d.

§§ 16. Reeves' Account, 29 Sept., 1356—28 Sept., 1357.

This document like the preceding one is dated not only in the year of the bishop but in the year of the pestilence. The tenement of Robert Wodecote was not given out to a new tenant, doubtless because there was none who wanted it, but sold for 21s., as pasture for sheep. Another tenement escheated to the lord, because there was none of the family of the late owner to claim it. Eleven persons are said to hold the tenements of others, six having the services commuted (five for 6s. 8d. and one for 5s.), and five performing the services due. In one instance, it is said, the commutation was at the lord's pleasure, in another case for the year. Clearly the commutation was meant to be temporary.

One tenant paid 18d. for marrying his daughter within the manor; a woman paid 2s. for getting married outside the manor.

To the lord's hospitium, perhaps guest house, were sent various goods. Sheep and oats were entered as sold to the hospitium and the price put down. This does not mean credited to Crawley as against the hospitium, but actually sold. The price is clearly entered. Doubtless cash was received. It was the lord's palace at Farnham and his hospitium there that were drawing foodstuffs and, as in this case, money also, away from the accustomed residence at Wolvesey. This meant a longer haul for Crawley people.

This year there was such lack of straw that bruer (heath?) had to be cut for covering the wattles of the sheepfold. And there was also the greatest lack of oats, so great that only a small amount could be given to the oxen.

We find a rather precise statement here about the measures used. The acres sown with wheat were statutory acres (per p*er*tic*am*). And the amount of wheat sown was exactly stated as 20 quarters 7 bushels, less 2½ bushels by standard measure (per

[1] For ad. Each sheep brought in 2d., either in the form of milk or the rental for milking.

stand*ardum*). Here is specific indication that the official units were being used.

CRAULEE [1]

Comp*otus* Joh*ann*is att*e* Putte *et* Joh*ann*is att*e* Halle p*re*pos*iti* ib*id*em de Anno Cons*ecrationis* d*omi*ni Will*elm*i Wynt*oniensis* Ep*iscop*i xij^{mo}.

Arr*eragium*. iidem r*eddunt* comp*otum* de xvij li. xviij s. ij d. q. de arr*eragio* comp*oti* p*recedentis*. O*mn*es lib*erate* d*omi*no Joh*ann*i Payn Thes*aurario* de Wolues*eia* p*er* j t*alliam*. Et quietus est.

Redd*itus*. Et de lxiiij s. vj d. de tot*o* redd*itu* ass*iso* ad f*estu*m Nat*alis* d*omi*ni. Et de lxvij s. x d. de tot*o* redd*itu* ass*iso* ad f*estu*m Pasch*e*. Et de lxiiij s. vj d. de tot*o* redd*itu* ass*iso* ad f*estu*m Nat*alis* s*anct*i Joh*ann*is Bapt*iste*. Et de c iiij s. j d. de tot*o* redd*itu* ass*iso* ad f*estu*m s*anct*i Mich*ael*is. S*umm*a xv li. xj d.

Acq*uietancie*. In acq*uietancia* j p*re*pos*iti* p*er* a*nnum* v s. In acq*uietanciis* ij caruc*ariorum et* j fabr*i* p*er* a*nnum* viij s. cuil*ibe*t ij s. viij d. In acq*uie*t*ancia* j b*er*car*ii* m*ulto*n*um* p*er* a*nnum* ij s. viij d. S*umm*a xv s. viij d.

Def*ectu*s. In def*ectu* redd*itus* t*er*r*e* Will*elm*i le Stronge t*ra*ct*e* in d*ominicum* p*er* a*nnum* ij s. In def*ectu* t*er*r*e* Will*elm*i de Cur*i*a p*ro* si*mi*li ij s. viij d. In def*ectu* t*er*r*e* de Alebrouk*e* q*ui* m*odo* rem*anet* apud M*er*don*am* v s. In def*ectu* t*er*r*e* Rob*er*ti Crouch*e* t*ra*ct*e* in d*ominicum* p*er* a*nnum* ij s. viij d. In def*ectu* t*er*r*e* Rob*er*ti Coye p*ro* si*mi*li ij s. viij d. In def*ectu* t*er*r*e* porcar*ii* ij s. viij d. In def*ectu* t*er*r*e* Ric*ard*i vactar*ii* ij s. viij d. S*umm*a xx s. iiij d.

Def*ectus* ca*usa* pestil*entie* h*oc* anno ix^{o}. D*e* xxj s. de redd*itu* j mes*suagii* j v*irgate* t*er*r*e* nat*ive et* xxij acr*arum* t*er*r*e* p*ur*p*re*st*ure* q*ue* fu*erunt* Rob*er*ti Wodecote n*ihil* q*uia* le*vatus* de ex*itu* in pas*tura* vend*ita* p*ro* bid*entibus* d*omi*ni h*oc* a*nno*. D*e* ij s. viij d. de redd*itu* j mess*uagii* j ferling*i* t*er*r*e* nat*ive* q*ue* fu*erunt* Thom*e* Symond n*ihil* q*uia* le*vatus* de ex*itu*. D*e* ij s. viij d. de redd*itu* j mess*uagii* j ferling*i* t*er*r*e* nat*ive* q*ue* fu*erunt* Joh*ann*is Body n*ihil* q*uia* le*vatus* de ex*itu*. S*umm*a n*ihil*. S*umm*a acq*uietanciarum et* def*ec*tus xxxvj s. S*umm*a redd*itus* rem*anen*t*is* de Clar*o* xiij li. iiij s. xj d.

Cymynu*m*. Et de j l*ib*r*a* cimini de redd*itu* Joh*ann*is fil*ii et* her*ed*is Ric*ard*i Fromond p*ro* j cr*o*fto voc*ato* howe. Et lib*erata* Thes*aurario* de Wolues*eia*.

Ex*itus* maner*ii*. Et de xij s. vij d. de pan*nagio* porc*orum* intr*atorum* ad f*estu*m s*anct*i martin*i*. D*e* pesson*a* in bosc*o* n*ihil* h*oc* a*nno*. Et de xij d. de pannag*io* vitul*orum*. Et de xxvij s. viij d. de xlvij vacc*is et* xxv bouic*ulis* ad hock*e* h*oc* a*nno* p*ro* vacc*a* vj d. *et* p*ro* bouic*u*lo ij d. Et de xvj s. viij d. de v acr*is* s*u*bbosc*i* vend*itis* p*recium* acr*e* iij s. iiij d. D*e*

[1] MS., P. R. O., Ecclesiastical Commission, Various, 159367.

pas*tura* yem*ali* in bosc*o* n*ihil* h*oc* a*nno* p*ro* def*ectu* em*ptoris*. Et de vj s. viij d. de pas*tura* estiu*al*i vend*ita* ib*id*em h*oc* a*nno*. D*e* pas*tura* bid*en*-*tium* in bosc*o* n*ihil* q*uia* dep*ascata* cu*m* hog*astris* d*omi*ni. Et de v s. de pas*tura* in Drakenorth*e* vend*ita*. D*e* pas*tura* in Trendele *et* holydon*e* n*ihil* h*oc* a*nno* q*uia* se*mi*na*ta*. D*e* pas*tura* in Combforlang n*ihil* q*uia* se*mi*nat*a* cu*m* auen*a*. D*e* pas*tura* in Bassamlee n*ihil* q*uia* dep*ascata* cu*m* bid*entibus* d*omi*ni. D*e* ou*ibus* in fald*a* cust*umariorum* n*ihil* h*oc* a*nno* q*uia* no*n* exced*unt* c*er*tu*m* num*er*u*m* xxv h*oc* a*nno*. Et de v s. iij d. de porc*is* agist*atis* in stipul*a* d*omi*ni h*oc* a*nno*. Et de vj d. de pas*tura* fos-sat*i* c*irca* Cur*iam* vend*ita*. D*e* pas*tura* in lokforlang*e* *et* markforlang*e* n*ihil* q*uia* dep*ascata* cu*m* bid*entibus* d*omi*ni. Et de iij s. iiij d. de pas-*tura* in la Sherte vend*ita* homag*io*. D*e* pas*tura* in Puthull*e* n*ihil* p*ro* def*ectu* em*ptoris*. Et de xij d. de reng*ia* c*irca* fr*umentu*m iux*ta* b*ar*-ton*am* b*er*car*ie*. Et de vj s. viij d. de Ad*a* Pours p*ro* op*eribus* t*err*e Rob*er*ti Bonde relax*atis*. Et de vj s. viij d. de Rog*er*o Crop p*ro* op*eri*-*bus* t*err*e Ric*ar*d*i* Alayn relax*atis*. Et de vj s. viij d. de Joh*ann*e Wode-cote p*ro* op*eribus* t*err*e Walt*er*i Shawe relax*atis* p*er* a*nnum* q*uam*diu d*omi*no plac*uerit*. D*e* v s. de Steph*an*o Knyght p*ro* op*eribus* t*err*e Nich*ol*a*i* Pope q*uo*nd*am* Joh*ann*is att*e* Hall*e* n*ihil* q*uia* fec*it* op*er*a. Et de v s. de Joh*ann*e Cart*er*e p*ro* op*eribus* t*err*e Steph*an*i Cart*er*e p*at*ris sui relax*atis* p*er* a*nnum*. D*e* vj s. viij d. de Gilb*er*to Sely p*ro* op*eribus* t*err*e Walt*er*i Cole n*ihil* q*uia* fec*it* op*er*a. Et de vj s. viij d. de Joh*ann*e T*r*igge p*ro* op*eribus* t*err*e Rob*er*ti T*r*igge p*at*ris sui relax*atis*. D*e* vj s. viij d. de Rob*er*to Wodecote p*ro* op*eribus* t*err*e Henr*ic*i Martyn n*ihil* q*uia* fec*it* op*er*a. Et de vj s. viij d. de Will*elm*o Hodeman p*ro* op*eribus* t*err*e Joh*ann*e [for Johannis] Veynes relax*atis*. D*e* Rog*er*o Gibbes p*ro* op*eribus* t*err*e Edith*e* Gibbes n*ihil* q*uia* fec*it* op*er*a. D*e* vj s. viij d. de Gilb*er*t*o* Nyweman p*ro* op*eribus* t*err*e Will*elm*i Elys n*ihil* q*uia* fec*it* op*er*a. Et de vj s. viij d. de Will*elm*o Bokhurst p*ro* op*eribus* t*err*e Jo-h*ann*is att*e* Nyweye relax*atis*. Et de vij s. iiij d. de xxij auc*is* vend*itis* p*re*c*ium* cui*usli*b*et* iiij d. Et de v s. de xxiiij cap*onibus* vend*itis* p*recium* capon*is* ij d. ob. Et de viij s. iij d. de lxvj gallin*is* vend*itis* p*recium* cui*usli*b*et* j d. ob. Et de viij d. de CC ouis vend*itis*. Et de ij s. iiij d. de iiij cl*avis* lane f*r*acte vend*itis*. Et de vj s. ij d. de x pell*ibus* mult*onum* xij ou*ium* *et* xvij hog*astrorum* de mor*in*a an*te* tons*ionem* vend*itis* p*re*-*cium* pell*is* mult*onis* ij d. ob. *et* ou*is* ij d. *et* hog*astri* j d. ob. Et de x d. de iiij pell*ibus* mult*onum* *et* vj ou*ium* de mor*ina* p*ost* tons*ionem* vend*itis* p*recium* pell*is* j d. Et de v s. de lx pell*ibus* agn*orum* de mor*ina* an*te* sep*aracionem* vend*itis* p*recium* pell*is* j d. Et de iiij d. ob. de ix pell*ibus* agn*orum* de mor*ina* p*ost* sep*aracionem* vend*itis* p*recium* pell*is* ob. Et de xlviij s. de iiij^{xx} xvij cas*eis* vend*itis* ad diu*er*s*a* p*recia*. Et de xxj d. de ij cl*avis* butir*i* vend*itis* p*recium* cl*avi* vij d. Et de vij s. de j veter*e* carect*a* vend*ita*. S*umm*a x li. xvij s. iiij d. ob.

Vend*itio* bl*adi*. Et de xxix li. viij s. viij d. de lxxiij q*uarteriis* vj b*us-sellis* fr*umenti* vend*itis* vn*de* ij q*uarteria* p*recium* q*uarterii* vij s. iiij d. *et* lxxj q*uarteria* vj b*usselli* p*recium* q*uarterii* viij s. Et de x s. de iiij q*uarteriis* auene nou*i* gr*a*ni vend*itis* hosp*itio* d*omi*ni. S*umma* xxix li. xviij s. viij d.

Vend*itio* stauri. Et de v s. de j eq*uo* debil*i* vend*ito*. Et de iij s. iiij d. de j affr*o* debili vend*ito*. Et de lxij s. iij d. de lxj m*ultonibus* vend*itis* vn*de* xlvj hosp*itio* d*omini* p*recium* cap*itis* xij d. *et* xv p*recium* cap*itis* xiij d. Et de lxx s. de iiij hurt*ardis* lxvj ou*ibus* matric*ibus* vend*itis* p*re-cium* cap*itis* xij d. Et de v s. vj d. de xj agn*is* de ex*tractis* an*te* ton-*sionem* vend*itis* p*recium* cap*itis* vj d. S*umma* vij li. vj s. j d.

Fin*es et* mar*itagia*. Et de xiij s. iiij d. de Teth*ingapenny* ad t*urnum* s*anct*i Martin*i et* hock*e*. Et de xviij d. de Rob*er*to Trigge p*ro* Alic*ia* fil*ia* sua mar*itanda* inf*ra*. Et de xij d. de Ric*ardo* Veynes p*ro* j mes*suagio* j Cotl*and* t*erre* nat*ive* in Craule q*ue* fu*erunt* Rob*er*ti Lamh*er*de *et* q*ue* de-u*enerunt* in man*us* d*omini* ta*mquam* esc*aeta* eo q*uo*d n*u*ll*us* de sang*uine* lic*et* p*ro*clam*atio* f*act*a fuerit sec*un*d*um* cons*uetudinem* maner*ii* p*ro* eisd*em* finir*e* cur*avit* ad h*oc* co*m*puls*us* h*abendis*. Et de ij s. de C*hri*stin*a* Pak*e* p*ro* se mar*itanda* ex*tra*. S*umma* xvij s. x d.

P*er*quis*ita*. Et de xxj d. de p*er*quis*itis* t*ur*ni s*anct*i martin*i*. Et de xvij d. de p*er*quis*itis* j Cur*ie* tent*e* an*te* d*ictum* t*urnum*. Et de xviij d. de p*erquisitis* t*ur*ni de hock*e*. Et de ix d. de p*er*quis*itis* j Cur*ie* tent*e* an*te* d*ict*u*m* t*ur*nu*m*. Et de ij s. ix d. de p*er*quis*itis* ij Cur*iarum* tent*a-rum* p*ost* d*ict*u*m* t*ur*nu*m*. S*umma* viij s. ij d.

Vend*itio* s*up*er Comp*otum*. Et de xiiij s. iij d. de reb*us* vend*itis* s*up*er comp*otum*. S*umma* xiiij s. iij d. S*umma* to*talis* Rec*epte* lxiij li. vij s. iij d. ob.

Cust*us* caruc*arum*. In ferr*o et* acer*o* e*mptis* p*ro* ferr*amentis* iij caruc*a-rum* p*er* a*nnum* xvj s. In iij ferr*is* ped*alibus* emp*tis* xviij d. In ij par*ibus* rot*arum* p*ro* caruc*is* xij d. In j cultr*o* dirrupt*o* emen*do* ij d. In j vom*ere* xx d. In j caruc*a* de nou*o* fac*ienda* iiij d. In caruc*is* chipp*andis et* vest*i-andis* vj [d.]. In ferr*amentis* vj eq*uorum* iiij s. In stip*endiis* ij bouar*io-rum et* j fug*atoris* p*er* a*nnum* xij s. S*umma* xxxvij s. ij d.

Cust*us* carect*arum*. In j par*i* bridd*es* vj s. viij d. In j lig*atura* cu*m* gr*opis* gr*ossis et* munut*is* cl*avis* xxv s. In d*ict*a carect*a* lig*anda* xij d. In mod*iis* d*ict*e carect*e* ferr*o* frett*andis* xviij d. In d*ict*a carect*a* ax*anda* vj d. In vj clut*is* xij d. In vnct*o* iiij d. In par*i* tract*uum* vj d. In j colar*i* x d. In alb*o* cor*io* vj d. In ferr*amentis* iij eq*uorum* v s. In sti-p*endio* j carect*arii* p*er* a*nnum* iiij s. S*umma* xlvj s. x d.

Emp*tio* bl*adi*. In xx q*uarteriis* vij b*ussellis* fr*umenti* emp*tis* p*ro* se*mine* vij li. xiij s. j d. p*recium* q*uarterii* vij s. iiij d. In xxviij q*uarteriis* vj b*ussellis* ord*ei* e*mptis* vj li. xvij s. iij d. vn*de* vj q*uarteria* iiij b*usselli* p*recium* q*uarterii* iiij s. *et* xxij q*uarteria* ij b*usselli* p*recium* q*uarterii* v s.

In xxiiij *quarteriis* vij b*ussellis* di*midio* auen*e* e*mptis* iiij li. iij s. v d. q. vn*de* viij q*uarteria* p*recium* q*uarterii* ij s. viij d. *et* xvj q*uarteria* vij b*us-selli* di*midius* p*recium* q*uarterii* iij s. viij d. In iij q*uarteriis* j b*ussello* di*midio* vesc*iarum* emp*tis* xxv s. vj d. p*recium* q*uarterii* viij s. S*umma* xix li. xix s. iij d. q.

Emp*tio* st*auri*. In j eq*uo* e*mpto* xviij s. vj d. S*umma* p*atet*.

Cust*us* b*ercarie*. In j barell*o* tarr*e* de magn' bond' *et* vij lag*enis* *et* di*midia* [pinguis] p*ro* vnct*ura* bid*entium* x s. In vnct*o* *et* cep*o* ad id*em* xx s. In rub*eo* color*e* vj d. In xxx clat*ibus* fac*iendis* xv d. In bruer*a* falc*anda* p*ro* clat*ibus* Wesc*iandis* hoc a*nno* p*ro* def*ectu* st*ramin*is xiij d. In pas*tura* e*mpta* de ten*emento* q*uo*d fuit Robert*i* Wodecote in man*ibus* d*omi*ni p*ro* bid*entibus* xxj s. In fen*o* p*ro* sust*entacione* bid*entium* ann*i* futur*i* e*mpto* lx s. In stip*endiis* ij b*er*car*iorum* ou*ium* *et* hog*astrorum* p*er* a*nnum* viij s. In pan*no* line*o* *et* lane*o* e*mpto* v d. In p*re*ssur*a* ij d. In oll*is* *et* patell*is* lut*i* iiij d. In j form*a* p*ro* case*o* vj d. In stip*endio* j daie ij s. S*umma* vj li. v s. iij d.

Cust*us* dom*orum*. In stip*endio* j coop*er*t*oris* coop*erientis* s*upe*r g*ran-giam* *et* bouar*iam* p*er* xx dies viij s. iiij d. p*er* die*m* cu*m* suo aux*iliatore* v d. In ij q*uarentenis* circ*a* copic*ium* de nou*o* claud*endis* iij s. p*ro* q*ua-rentena* xviij d. S*umma* xj s. iiij d.

Sarc*ulatio* *et* falc*atio*. In om*ni*bu*s* bl*ad*is d*om*ini sarc*ulandis* ad t*as-cham* v s. S*umma* p*atet*.

Cust*us* aut*umpni*. In pan*e* emp*to* ad iij p*recarias* de CC xxviij ho*mini-bus* custum*ariis* cu*m* ministr*is* Cur*ie* q*ui* mess*uerunt* lxxvj acr*as* f*ru-menti* p*er* pertic*am* ix s. vj d. cuil*ibe*t eoru*m* pan*is* de ob. In case*o* p*ro* eisd*em* iiij s. ix d. c*uilibet* eoru*m* case*um* de q. In c*er*uisi*a* xx d. p*re*ter*ea* mess*e* *et* lig*ate* fu*erunt* xvij acr*e* ord*ei* lxv acr*e* auen*e* *et* iiij acr*e* vesc*iarum* p*er* p*er*tic*am* de cons*uetudine* p*ro* Niedacr*a*. In lxj acr*is* di*midia* ord*ei* xij acr*is* pis*arum* xvj acr*is* vesc*iarum* met*endis* *et* lig*andis* ad t*ascham* xxxv s. ij d. ob. p*ro* acr*a* p*er* pertic*am* v d. In stip*endio* j haiward*i* p*er* a*nnum* vj s. viij d. S*umma* lvij s. ix d. ob.

Trit*uratio*. In xxj q*uarteriis* vj b*ussellis* f*rumen*ti iij q*uarteriis* ij b*us-sellis* pis*arum* ij q*uarteriis* v b*ussellis* vesc*iarum* t*riturandis* ad t*ascham* p*re*t*erea* lij q*uarteria* iiij b*usselli* t*riturata* p*er* op*er*a iiij s. vij d. p*ro* q*uarterio* ij d. In xlix q*uarteriis* iij b*ussellis* ord*ei* t*riturandis* ad t*as-cham* vj s. ij d. p*ro* q*uarterio* j d. ob. In xxxj q*uarteriis* iij b*ussellis* auen*e* t*riturandis* ad t*ascham* ij s. vij d. q. p*ro* q*uarterio* j d. In medi-*etate* toci*us* bl*ad*i q*ui* [for quod] trit*uratum* ad t*ascham* vent*ilanda* xiij d. ob. p*ro* q*uarterio* q. S*umma* xiiij s. vj d.

Expense Sen*escalli*. In exp*ensis* Thom*e* de Pentelowe sen*escalli* ven-*ientis* ib*id*em p*ro* t*u*rnis te*nendis* xiiij s. ix d. ob. q. p*er* ij bill*as*. S*umma* p*atet*.

Vad*ia* ball*iui*. In vad*iis* Roger*i* Haiwod*e* ball*iui* in p*a*rte vad*iorum* suor*um* xl s. *et* resid*uum* cap*it* in al*iis* maner*iis*. S*umma* xl s. S*umma* om*nium* exp*ensarum* xxxviij li. x s. v d. ob. Et deb*ent* xxiiij li. xvj s. x d.

All*ocatio* s*ine* br*evi*. Ind*e* all*ocantur* p*re*pos*it*o vj d. p*ro* exp*ensa* j ho*min*is ad eq*uum* car*iantem* poletr*iam* ap*ud* Farnh*a*m p*ro* hosp*itio* d*omi*ni con*tra* Nat*alem*. Et eid*em* ij s. ix d. de p*re*ben*da* eq*ui* car*iantis* poletr*iam* *et* al*ia* vict*ualia* ad hosp*itium* d*omi*ni. Et eid*em* xxiij s. de diu*ersis* onerat*is* *et* dis*allocatis* in p*re*s*enti* comp*oto*. S*umma* xxvj s. iij d.

All*ocatio* p*er* br*eve*. Et eidem viij li. xij s. vij d. q*uo*s lib*eraverunt* d*omi*no J*ohanni* Bleobur*y* Gard*erobario* d*omi*ni in pecun*ia* *et* diu*ersis* vict*ualibus* p*ro* eod*em* hosp*itio* vn*de* in pecun*ia* c xiij s. iiij d. S*umma* viij li. xij s. vij d.

Lib*eratio* den*ariorum*. Et lib*eraverunt* d*omi*no Joh*ann*i Payn Thes*aurario* de Wolues*eia* p*er* j t*alliam* x li. x s. ix d. S*umma* p*atet*. S*umma* om*nium* allo*cationum* *et* lib*erationum* xx li. ix s. vij d. Et deb*ent* de Clar*o* iiij li. vij s. iij d.

Fr*umentum*. Idem r*espondent* de lxxiiij q*uarteriis* ij b*ussellis* de tot*o* ex*itu* p*er* t*alliam* con*tra* Gilb*er*t*u*m Dauy vn*de* lij q*uarteria* iiij b*usselli* *triturata* p*er* op*era*. Et de xx q*uarteriis* vij b*ussellis* de emp*tis*. S*umma* iiij^{xx} xv q*uarteria* j b*ussellus*. De q*uibus* in se*mine* s*up*er lxxvj acr*as* p*er* p*er*tic*am* Byesteputhull*e* xx q*uarteria* vij b*usselli* s*up*er acr*am* ij b*usselli* j p*eccum* mi*nus* in to*to* ij b*usselli* di*midius* *et* t*antu*m q*uia* p*er* stand*ardum*. In pan*e* furn*iato* p*ro* exp*ensis* Sen*escalli* veni*entis* ib*ide*m p*ro* t*ur*nis te*nendis* iiij b*usselli* p*er* ij bill*as*. In vend*itis* lxxiij q*uarteria* vj b*usselli*. S*umma* que s*upra*. Et eq*ue*.

Ord*eum*. Et de xlix q*uarteriis* iij b*ussellis* rec*eptis* de ex*itu* p*er* t*alliam* con*tra* eu*ndem*. Et de xxviij q*uarteriis* vj b*ussellis* de emp*tis*. S*umma* lxxviij q*uarteria* j b*ussellus*. De q*uibus* in se*mine* s*up*er lxxiij acr*as* p*er* p*er*tic*am* in Geredelond*e* *et* Langelond*e* xxxviij q*uarteria* iiij b*usselli* s*up*er acr*am* iiij b*usselli* p*eccum* mi*nus* in to*to* ij b*usselli* p*eccum* *et* t*antum* c*au*sa q*ue* s*upra*. In mix*tur*a ad lib*erationem* famul*orum* xxxix q*uarteria* v b*usselli*. S*umma* que s*upra*. Et eq*ue*.

Auena. Et de xxxj q*uarteriis* iij b*ussellis* auen*e* rec*eptis* de ex*itu* p*er* t*alliam* con*tra* eund*em*. Et de v q*uarteriis* p*er* estim*ationem* in garb*is*. Et de xxiiij q*uarteriis* vij b*ussellis* di*midio* de emp*tis*. Et de iiij q*uarteriis* de ex*itu* nou*i* gr*a*ni. S*umma* lxv q*uarteria* ij b*usselli* di*midius*. De q*uibus* in se*mine* s*up*er lxv acr*as* p*er* p*er*tic*am* in la Combe *et* Haselforlang*e* xxxvj q*uarteria* iiij b*usselli* di*midius* s*up*er acr*am* iiij b*usselli* di*midius* *et* t*antu*m c*au*sa q*ue* s*upra*. In dat*is* bobus p*er* estim*ationem* in garb*is* v q*uarteria* *et* no*n* plus h*oc* a*nno* p*ro* maxi*mo* def*ectu* auen*e*. In p*re*ben*da* iiij eq*uorum* carect*ariorum* p*er* a*nnum* v q*uarteria*. In p*re*-

ben*da* vj affr*orum* p*er* a*nnum* vij q*uarteria*. In far*ina* fac*ta* p*ro* pot*agio* fam*ulorum* iij q*uarteria* iiij b*usselli*. In p*re*ben*da* equ*orum* Sene*scalli* ven*ientis* ib*idem* p*ro* t*urnis* te*nendis* j q*uarterium* ij b*usselli* per ij bill*as*. In vend*itis* hosp*itio* d*omi*ni iiij q*uarteria*. Et s*uper* com*potum* iij q*uar*-*teria* p*ro*[—]. S*umma* que s*upra*. Et eq*ue*.

Pis*e*. Et de iij q*uarteriis* ij b*ussellis* pis*arum* rec*eptis* de ex*itu* p*er* t*alliam* con*tra* eund*em*. Et de j q*uarterio* iiij b*ussellis* p*er* estim*ationem* in garb*is*. S*umma* iiij q*uarteria* vj b*usselli*. D*e* q*uibus* in se*mine* s*up*er xij acr*as* p*er* pertic*am* in la Combe iij q*uarteria* ij b*usselli* s*up*er acr*am* ij b*usselli* pec*cum* mi*nus* in to*to* j b*ussellus et* t*antu*m c*au*sa q*ue* s*upra*. In sustent*atione* ou*ium* in yem*e* j q*uarterium* iiij b*usselli*. Et eq*ue*.

Vesc*ie*. Et de ij q*uarteriis* v b*ussellis* vesc*iarum* rec*eptis* de ex*itu* p*er* t*alliam* con*tra* eund*em*. Et de ij q*uarteriis* p*er* estim*ationem* in siliq*uis*. Et de iij q*uarteriis* j b*ussello* di*midio* de emp*tis*. S*umma* vij q*uarteria* vj b*usselli* di*midius*. D*e* q*uibus* in se*mine* s*up*er xx acr*as* p*er* pertic*am* in la Combe v q*uarteria* v b*usselli* s*up*er acr*am* ij b*usselli* pec*cum et* t*an*-*tu*m c*au*sa q*ue* s*upra*. In sust*entatione* ou*ium* in yem*e* ij q*uarteria*. In vend*itis* s*up*er comp*otum* j b*ussellus* di*midius* p*ro* [—]. Et eq*ue*.

Lib*erati*o Fam*ulorum*. Et de xxxix q*uarteriis* v b*ussellis* ord*ei* rec*eptis* vt s*upra* p*ro* lib*erationibus* fam*ulorum*. S*umma* xxxix q*uarteria* v b*us*-*selli*. D*e* q*uibus* in lib*eratione* j haiward*i* j Carect*arii* ij caruc*ariorum et* ij b*ercariorum* ouiu*m et* hog*astrorum* p*er* a*nnum* xxxj q*uarteria* j b*ussel*-*lus* q*uilibe*t cap*it* q*uarterium* ad x sept*imanas*. In lib*eratione* j garc*onis* aux*iliantis* b*ercariis* t*em*p*o*re agnel*lationis et* custod*ientis* agn*os* p*er* se a t*em*p*o*re sep*aracionis* usq*ue* tons*ionem* j q*uarterium*. In lib*eratione* j daie p*er* a*nnum* iij q*uarteria* ij b*usselli* cap*ientis* q*uarterium* ad xvj sept*imanas*. In lib*eratione* j fug*atoris* eunt*is* ad iij caruc*antes* ad ij seison*as et* aux*iliantis* carect*ariis* p*ro* diu*ersis* cariag*iis* p*er* a*nnum* iiij q*uarteria* ij b*usselli* cap*ientis* q*uarterium* ad xij sept*imanas*. Et eq*ue*.

Equi. Et de iij eq*uis* de rem*anentibus*. Et de j de emp*to*. S*umma* iiij. D*e* q*uibus* in vend*ito* j. Et rem*anent* [iij] equi.

Affr*i*. Et de vj affr*is* de rem*anentibus*. Et de j de h*erie*t*to* Gilb*er*t*i* valk*er*. S*umma* vij. Ind*e* in vend*ito* j. Et rem*anent* vj affr*i*.

Boues. Et de xx bob*us* de rem*anentibus*. Et rem*anent* xx bou*es*.

Hurt*ardi*. Et de xv hurt*ardis* de rem*anentibus*. Et de iiij de adiu*nc*-t*is*. S*umma* xix. D*e* q*uibus* in vend*itis* p*re*posit*o* de Stoke p*ost* ton-*sionem* iiij. Et rem*anent* xv hurtard*i*.

M*u*lton*es*. Et de D xxvj m*ulto*n*ibus* de rem*anentibus*. Et de C xix de adiu*nc*t*is*. S*umma* DC xlv. D*e* q*uibus* in mor*ina* an*te* tons*ionem* x *et* p*ost* tons*ionem* iiij. In vend*itis* lx p*ost* tons*ionem* vnd*e* hosp*itio* d*omi*ni xlvj. S*umma* lxxv. Et rem*anent* D lxx m*u*lt*ones* vnd*e* xliiij keb*bati*.

Oues. Et de CCCC lxx ou*ibus* de rem*anentibus*. Et de C xiiij de adiu*nc*-t*is*. S*umma* D iiij^{xx} ix. D*e* q*uibus* in mor*ina* an*te* agn*ellationem* viij *et* post agnellationem et ante tonsionem iiij et post tonsionem vj. In venditis post tonsionem lxvj vnde preposito de Stoke lj. Summa iiij^{xx} iiij. Et remanent D v oues vnde xxx kebbate.

Hogastri. Et de CC liiij hogris de remanentibus agnis. De quibus in morina ante tonsionem xvij. In adiunctis cum multonibus C xix cum hurtardis iiij et cum matricibus C xiiij. Et eque.

Agni. Et de CCC lxxv agnis de exitu et non de pluribus quia viij oues mortue ante agnellationem iiij^{xx} j fuerunt steriles et xij fecerunt abortum. Summa CCC lxxv. De quibus in morina ante separacionem lxvj. In decima xxxj. In consuetudinibus prepositi fabri et bercarii multonum iij. In morina post separacionem et ante tonsionem iiij et post tonsionem v. In venditis ante tonsionem xj de extractis. Summa C xx. Et remanent CC lv agni.

Auce. Et de j ancere et iiij marioles de remanentibus. Et de xxiiij de exitu. Summa xxix. De quibus in decima ij. In venditis xxij. Et remanent j ancer et iiij mariole.

Capones. Et de xxiiij caponibus de remanentibus. Et de xxiiij factis de pulcinis. Summa xlviij. De quibus in venditis xxiiij. Et remanent xxiiij capones.

Gallus et galline. Et de j gallo et v gallinis de remanentibus. Et de C xxv de Cheriseto ad festum sancti Martini. Summa C xxxj. De quibus in defectu terre le Stronge tracte in dominicum per annum iiij. In defectu terre Willelmi de Curia pro simili iiij. In defectu terre Roberti Crouche pro simili iiij. In defectu terre Willelmi Le Swon pro simili iiij. In defectu terre Ricardi vaccarii pro simili iiij. In defectu terre Ricardi Cnaue pro simili iiij. In defectu terre Rogeri Crop Alicie Hodeman Rogeri Gibbes Johannis Cartere Johannis Trigge Junioris Johannis Trigge senioris et Radulphi Smyth quia viduarii et vidua xiiij pro quolibet ij. In defectu terre Johannis Body Johannis Coupere Thome Symond et Johannis moraunt xvj pro quolibet iiij quorum tenementa sunt in manibus domini per obitum eorum in pestilentia. In defectu terre Roberti Wodecote pro iij tenementis que tenentur in manibus domini per pestilentiam v. In venditis lxvj. Summa C xxv. Et remanent j gallus et v galline.

Pulcini. Et de xxiiij pulcinis de exitu. Et omnes fiunt in capones. Et nihil remanet.

Oua. Et de CC ouis de exitu gallinarum. Et omnia vendita infra. Et nihil remanet.

Vellera. Et de xv velleribus hurtardorum D xvj multonum CCCC lxiij ouium et CC xxxvij hogastrorum prouentis ad tonsionem. Summa MCC xxxj. De quibus in decima C xxiij. Liberata apud Wolueseiam MC viij vellera que fecerunt v saccos xix clavos j libram.

Lana agnina. Et de CC lx velleribus agninis prouentis ad tonsionem h*oc* a*nno*. Et o*mn*ia lib*erata* apud Wolues*eiam* pond*erantia* xij cl*avos* vj l*ibras*.

Lan*a* f*racta*. Et de iiij cl*avis* lan*e* f*racte* de ex*itu* h*oc* a*nno*. Et vend*ita* inf*ra*. Et n*ihil* rem*anet*.

Pell*es* lanut*e*. Et de x pell*ibus* mult*onum* xij ouiu*m* *et* xvij hog*astrorum* de mor*ina* an*te* tons*ionem*. Et vend*ite* inf*ra*. Et n*ihil* rem*anet*.

Pell*es* nud*e*. Et de iiij pell*ibus* m*ultonum* *et* vj ou*ium* de mor*ina* p*ost* tons*ionem*. Et vend*ite* inf*ra*. Et n*ihil* rem*anet*.

Pell*es* agn*ine*. Et de lxvj pell*ibus* agn*orum* de mor*ina* an*te* sep*ara*c*ionem*. D*e* q*uibus* in dec*ima* vj. In vend*itis* lx. Et n*ihil* rem*anet*.

Pell*es* rott*orum*. Et de iiij pell*ibus* agn*orum* de mor*ina* post sep*ara*c*ionem* *et* an*te* tons*ionem*. Et vend*ite* inf*ra*. Et n*ihil* rem*anet*.

Pell*es* nud*e* agn*ine*. Et de v pell*ibus* agn*orum* nud*is* de mor*ina* p*ost* tons*ionem*. Et vend*ite* inf*ra*. Et n*ihil* rem*anet*.

Cas*eus*. Et de c x cas*eis* f*act*is de lact*e* ouiu*m*. D*e* q*uibus* in dec*ima* xj. In cons*uetudine* p*re*pos*it*i *et* fab*ri* ij. In vend*itis* iiij[xx] xvij. Et n*ihil* rem*anet*.

Butir*um*. Et de iij cl*avis* butir*i* de ex*itu*. Et vend*iti* inf*ra*. Et n*ihil* rem*anet*.

S*ed* oner*a*[n]t*ur* de ix d. s*u*p*er* comp*otum* vt oue*s* r*eddunt* ij d. de lact*agio* cu*m* ij cas*eis* dat*is* de custum*a* [?] app*reciatis* ad xij d.

§§ 17. Account of Customary Works, 29 Sept., 1389—28 Sept., 1390.

This document is a part of the reeve's account for the twenty-third year of Bishop William of Wykeham. Although it does not purport to include all the services — only customary services being dealt with — as a matter of fact it comprehends virtually all received by the lord from the Manor of Crawley. There may have been a free tenant, for example, on the estate called the Hoo, but neither he nor his services were very important.

Unfortunately the text of this document is very uncertain because the manuscript is torn in places and at many spots otherwise illegible. It has been found necessary to interpolate words and figures from other sources.[1] This is, of course, a dangerous procedure, but the reader is given due warning of the situation. The paragraphing, which is not found in the manuscript, has been introduced to facilitate reading.

[1] Especially from Ecclesiastical Commission, Various, 159827; also 155828, 159428, and 159445.

Those services which were more or less uncertain in amount come at the end of the document. They include carrying letters and briefs, carting oats to the lord's palace, enclosing Waltham park, carting hay wherever bought, gathering apples at Waltham, carting wool and cheese, and aiding in building. The fixed services, that is, fixed in amount, are set forth in the following table.

TABLE SHOWING SERVICES DUE, RENDERED, AND NOT RENDERED

Service	Due	Acquitted	Defaulted	Rendered
Plowing	25 acres	1 acre	15 acres	9 acres
Harrowing	90 "	11 "	11 "	68 "
Total acres	115	12	26	77
Carrying the sheepfold	75 works	3 works	0 works	72 works
Carting etc. manure	186 "	12 "	0 "	174 "
Cutting etc. hay	50 "	8 "	5 "	37 "
Carrying wood to Wolvesey	25 "	1 "	0 "	24 "
Washing and shearing sheep	297 "	43 "	37 "	217 "
Autumn boon-works	265 "	63 "	44 "	158(?) "
Autumn[1] week-works (every work-day)	950 "	450 "	250 "	250 "
Carrying grain	150 "	6 "	0 "	144 "
Shocking grain	6 "	0 "	0 "	6 "
Winter[2] week-works (2 days a week)	1394 "	656 "	410 "	328 "
Total works	3398	1242	746	1410

[1] From 1 Aug. to 28 Sept., 8 weeks and 2 days (less holidays).
[2] From 29 Sept. to 31 July, 43 weeks and 6 days (less 3 holy weeks).

Of the 1242 works acquitted, 836 were for service (of the reeve, smith, three shepherds, and three plowmen) and 406 were temporarily commuted. If we add the services acquitted for special duties, to those actually rendered, we find that 2246 works out of 3398 due were received by the lord. In other words, while only 41.5 % of the works were directly performed, 69 % were rendered directly or indirectly.

There were three holders of farthinglands in North Crawley, who had had their week-works commuted, at least temporarily, that is, 150 autumn works and 256 winter works.

Just as there were eight officials or servants of the manor who had some of their services commuted because of their special duties, so there happened to be eight other tenants who did not perform their obligations. Probably in all cases this was due to the fact that their tenements were in the lord's hands.

In contemplating the great number and range of the services due and rendered, we should not forget the fact that the tenants received benefits. The officials were given various allowances such as lambs and cheese, as we know from the reeve's accounts. The tenants, here as generally, were given food at boon-work; but also at certain other tasks they received at least partial payment for what they did. For plowing, the customary tenant received 1 d. per acre; for sowing and carrying the lord's seed into the granary, he received ten twigs of hazelwood for his 'harness'; and for cutting, binding and gathering the lord's grain at summer work, he received one sheaf per acre. It is said that a winter, or manual, work was worth ¾d., which means probably, not that any such sum was given by way of allowance but that this was the rate of commutation.

In connection with the haying there are said to have been fifty tenants, as also for the shearing of the sheep. But for autumn work there were forty-eight tenants in all. The following table indicates the size of their holdings.

Customary Tenants and their Holdings

1	tenant, holding 2 virgates of 32 acres	64 acres
12	tenants, each holding 1 virgate of 32 acres	384 "
14	" " " ½ " " 16 "	224 "
17	" " " 1 farthingland of 11 acres	187 "
4	" " " 1 cottage	0 "
48	tenants, holding	859 "

Since these were customary acres, the extent of the customary tenants' arable land was at this time 429½ statutory acres. In a manor of about 3600 acres, this left a large amount of land for common pasture, woods, and waste and for the use of the lord. There can be little doubt that much of the lord's large demesne was used for sheep pasture at this time.

Crawley Manor is here divided into three parts, North, South, and Wodecote, made up of holdings as follows:

South Crawley

1 holding of 2 virgates
11 holdings of 1 virgate
13 holdings of ½ virgate

Wodecote (physically in South Crawley [1])

1 virgate
½ virgate
1 cottage

North Crawley

3 cottages
17 farthinglands

Both North and South Crawley were prominent in harrowing, haying, autumn boon-works, and in washing and shearing the lord's sheep. But it is in North Crawley, on the farthinglands, that we find the hardest-worked tenants on the manor. They owed the week-work, every work-day from 1 August to 28 September, and two days a week from 29 September to 31 July.

The poorest of the tenants, cottagers and farthing holders, lived in North Crawley. They gave week-work which was manual labor. The tenants of South Crawley were the élite of the village. They had beasts of burden and carts. Their distinctive service, at least that part of it limited in amount, was carting manure, hay, wood, and grain for the lord. But at this particular time, they could hardly be regarded as a prosperous class because fifteen of them had no whole plows of their own.

Why the lord went to the trouble of having all these customary services set down in account form, when he already had them duly recorded in his custumal,[2] is not stated. We may infer, however, that the enforcement or collection of the same was in question or perhaps even difficult. The lord seems here to be on the defensive. A comparable statement of customary services is found in various

[1] In 1872 R. H. Fifield of Littleton surrendered to Philip Vanderbyl, merchant, of London, "One Messuage one toft and one yard and a half of bondland in Crawley on the South part called Woodcott." MS., Millbank, Ecclesiastical Commission, 210157, p. 357 (6 April).

[2] See above, §§ 11, pp. 229 ff.

reeve's accounts in subsequent years; and it is seen to be a gradually diminishing list. Some of the items, however, linger on to 1690 and even to the enclosure in 1795.

OP*ER*A CUSTUMAR*IA* [1]

Et de arur*a* xxv acr*arum* p*r*oueni*ente* de j Custum*ario* ten*ente* ij virg*atas* t*er*re xj virg*atariis* *et* xiij semivirgat*ariis* in Craule in p*ar*te Aust*ra*l*i* quor*um* quili*be*t Caruc*am* h*ab*ens integr*am* arab*it* j acr*am* sic*ut* iac*et* ad sem*en* yem*ale* vel q*uadragesimal*e p*er*ci*pien*do de d*omi*no p*ro* arura cuiusli*be*t acre j d. Arura S*umm*a xxv acre. De quib*us* in acq*uie*-*tancia* j p*re*pos*it*i ten*entis* j virg*atam* t*er*re in p*ar*te aust*ral*i arur*a* j acre. In def*ectu* xv Cust*umariorum* q*ui* no*n* h*abent* Caruc*as* integr*as* arur*a* xv acr*arum*. In t*er*ris d*ominicis* arand*is* h*oc* a*nno* arur*a* ix acr*arum* sic*ut* iac*ent* que fac*iunt* iiij acr*as* di*midiam* p*er* pertic*am*. S*umm*a que sup*ra*. Et eq*ue*.

Et de herc*iatura* iiij^{xx} ix [2] acr*arum* p*r*oueni*ente* de p*re*dict*o* Custum*a*-*rio* tenent*e* ij virg*atas* t*er*re qui h*erciabit* viij acr*as* xj virg*atariis* et xiij se*mi*virg*atariis* in Craule in parte boriali [3] *et* j [semi]virg*atario* in Wodecote quor*um* quil*ibe*t herc*iabit* ij acr*as* iij Cot*agiariis* de Craule in p*ar*te borial*i* quor*um* quili*be*t h*erciabit* iij acr*as* *et* xvij ferl*ingatariis* de Craule in p*ar*te borial*i* quor*um* quili*be*t h*erciabit* j acr*am* *et* j virg*atario* in Wodecote qui herc*iabit* vj acr*as* sic*ut* iac*ent* siue hundr' [4] equ*um* siue no*n* *et* eas semi*na*b*it* *et* sem*en* ad g*ranar*ium d*omi*ni in p*ropriis* sacc*is* quer*et* p*er*ci*piente* quol*ibe*t de d*omi*no x virg*as* coruli p*ro* h*ar*nes*io* suo. H*ercia*-*tura* S*umm*a iiij^{xx} x acre. De quib*us* in acq*uietancia* j p*re*pos*it*i ten*entis* j virg*atam* t*er*re h*erciatura* ij acr*arum*. In acq*uietancia* j fabri iij caru-*cariorum* *et* ij b*er*car*iorum* quol*ibe*t ten*en*te j ferl*ingatam* t*er*re herc*ia*-*tura* vj acr*arum*. In acq*uietancia* j b*er*car*ii* ten*en*tis j cot*agium* herc*ia*-*tura* iij acr*arum*. In def*ectu* j virg*ate* t*er*re q*uo*ndam Rob*er*ti Wodecote q*uia* in man*u* d*omi*ni h*erciatura* vj acr*arum*. In def*ectu* j ferl*ingate* t*er*re q*uo*nd*am* Joh*annis* Body j ferl*ingate* t*er*re [quondam Johannis] Symond' j ferl*ingate* t*er*re q*uo*nd*am* Joh*annis* Morant j ferl*ingate* t*er*re q*uo*nd*am* Thome Wayte et j ferl*ingate* t*er*re q*uo*nd*am* Walt*er*i Aleyn q*uia* in man*u* d*omi*ni h*erciatur*a v acr*arum*. In t*er*ris d*ominicis* h*ercian*-*dis* ad semen auen*e* h*oc* a*nno* h*erciatura* lxviij acr*arum* sic*ut* iac*ent* que fac*iunt* xxxiiij acr*as* [per perticam. Summa] que sup*ra*. Et eq*ue*.

Et de lxxv op*eribus* p*r*oueni*entibus* de xxv Cust*umariis* in Craule in p*ar*te Austral*i* quor*um* quili*be*t port*abit* v clat*es* ad fald*am* d*omi*ni de

[1] MS., P. R. O., Ecclesiastical Commission, Various, 159396, memb. 24.
[2] An error for iiij^{xx}x.
[3] An error for austral*i*.
[4] Probably for habebit.

campo in [1] campum quosciens fuerit admouenda. Et estimatur quod fieri poterit communibus annis per iij vices. [Et si] dominus [vlter]ius indigeat vlterius operentur. Portacio falde Summa lxxv opera. De quibus in acquietancia j prepositi iij opera. In falda domini portanda de campo in campum lxxij opera. Et eque.

Et de C iiij^{xx} operibus cariacionis et implecacionis fimorum prouenientibus de xxv custumariis in Craule in parte [australi] et iij[?] cotagariis in parte boriali et ij Custumariis de Wodecote quorum quilibet inueniet j operarium cum equis et Carectis pro fimis in Carectas implendis et vsque in campum cariandis donec totaliter percarientur. Et estimatur quod fieri poterit communibus annis per vj dies. Et si [dominus] plura opera indigeat plura facient. Et si tanta non indigeat per minora sint quieti. Et de vj operibus implecacionis prouenientibus de j Custumario qui inveniet j operarium pro carectis cum fimis implendis per tempus predictum. Cariacio et implecacio fimorum summa C iiij^{xx} vj opera. De quibus in [acquietancia] j prepositi et j bercarii xij opera. In fimis domini in Carectas implendis (per tempus predictum) [2] et in campum cariandis hoc anno C lxxiiij opera. Summa que supra. Et eque.

Et de l operibus falcacionis spargacionis leuacionis mulliones cariacionis et tassacionis prouenientibus de xxv Custumariis in [Craule in parte] australi et xxv custumariis in parte boriali qui in communi falcabunt spargent leuabunt mulliones cariabunt et tassabunt vj acras prati domini apud Wolueseiam nichil pro eodem percipiendo Falcacio prati de Wolueseia Summa l opera. De quibus in acquietancia j prepositi j fabri iij carucariorum et iij bercariorum [vi]ij opera in defectu [v ferlingatariorum?] quorum tenementa remanent in manu domini vt supra v opera. In feno predictarum vj acrarum prati apud Wolueseiam falcando spargendo leuando mulliones cariando et tassando xxxvij opera. Summa que supra. Et eque.

Et de xxv operibus cariacionis busce prouenientibus de xxv custumariis [in parte australi de Craule] quorum quilibet cariabit j Carectam busce vsque Wolueseiam contra Natalem domini nichil pro eodem percipiendo. Cariacio busce vsque Wolueseiam Summa xxv opera. De quibus in acquientancia j prepositi j opus. in busca vsque Wolueseiam carianda contra Natalem domini [x]xiiij opera. Et eque.

Et de C operibus locionis prouenientibus de l Custumariis in Craule et Wodecote quorum quilibet inueniet j operarium pro bidentibus domini lauandis. Et estimatur quod fieri poterit communibus annis per ij dies. Et si dominus plura opera indigeat plura facient quousque totaliter [perfic]iebatur[?]. Et de [C iiij^{xx}] xv operibus tonsionis prouenientibus de predictis l Custumariis quorum j inueniet (per diem iiij) [3] operarios j per diem iij operarios x quilibet illorum ij operarios et xxxviij quilibet

[1] Altered from ad. [2] Struck through. [3] Interlineated.

illor*um* p*er* diem j op*er*ar*ium* p*ro* biden*tibus* d*omi*ni tond*endis*. Et esti*matur* q*uo*d fieri pot*er*it co*mmuni*b*us* annis per iij dies. Et si [dominus plura opera indigeat] plura fac*ient*. Et si tant*a* no*n* indig*eat* p*ro* pauc*ioribus* sint quieti. Et de ij op*er*ibus (indig')[1] tons*ionis* p*r*oueni*entibus* de ij Cust*umariis* in north Craule [quorum vter]q*ue* inue*n*iet j op*er*ar*ium* p*er* j diem p*ro* biden*tibu*s d*omi*ni tond*endis* ut sup*ra*. Loc*io* [et tonsio bidentium Summa CC iiij^{xx} xvij opera. De quibus in] acq*uietancia* j p*re*pos*iti* viij op*er*a. In acq*uietancia* j fabri iij carucar*iorum et* iij b*er*car*iorum* xxxv op*er*a. In defectu j virg*ate* t*er*re j s*em*ivirgat*e et* j cotag*ii* in Wodecote et [v ferlingatarum] in Northcraule q*uia* in man*u* d*omi*ni vt sup*ra* xxxvij op*er*a. In bident*ibus* d*omi*ni lavand*is et* tond*endis* CC xxvij op*er*a. Et eq*ue*.

Et de CC lj[2] op*er*ibus p*re*car*ii* p*r*oueni*entibus* de xlviij Cust*umariis* in Craule et Wodecote quor*um* j inue*n*iet iiij op*er*ar*ios* ad iij p*re*car*ia* p*er* iij dies j inue*n*iet iij op*er*arios *et* [xxxij] quili*be*t illor*um* inue*n*iet ij op*er*a*rios et* xiiij quili*be*t inue*n*iet j op*er*ar*ium* ad [iij] p*recaria* in a*utumpno* [pro bladis domini metendis ligandis et adimendis ad] cibu*m* d*omi*ni. [Et de iiij operibus] p*re*ca*rii* p*recarii* [sic] p*r*oueni*entibus* de ij Cust*umariis* quor*um* vt*er*q*ue* inue*n*iet j op*er*ar*ium* ad ij precaria ad cibu*m* d*omi*ni vt sup*ra*. Et de iij op*er*ibus p*re*car*ii* p*r*oueni*entibus* de iij Cus*tumariis* quor*um* quili*be*t inue*n*iet j op*er*ar*ium* ad j p*re*car*ium* ad cibum [domini] vt sup*ra*. [Precaria autumpnalia Summa CC lxv opera.] De quib*us* in acq*uientancia* j p*re*pos*iti* iij caruc*ariorum* et iij b*er*car*iorum* xlij op*er*a cuili*be*t vj op*er*a. In acq*uietancia* j Wodeward*i* n*ihi*l q*uia* nullus de Cust*umariis* h*oc* anno. In acq*uietancia* j fabri iij op*er*a. In acq*uientancia* iij[?] ferling*atariorum* quor*um* op*er*a relax*ata* ut inf*ra* xviij op*er*a cuili*be*t vj op*er*a. In def*ectu* j virg*ate et* j s*em*ivirgat*e* in Wodecote *et* v ferling*atarum* in Craule q*uia* in man*u* d*omi*ni vt s*upra* xlij op*er*a cuili*be*t vj op*er*a. In def*ectu* j cot*agii* in Wodecote q*uia* in man*u* d*omi*ni vt s*upra* ij op*er*a. In lv acr*is* frum*enti* met*endis* lig*andis* et adim*endis* C lv op*er*a. s*umma* q*ue* sup*ra*. Et eq*ue*.

Et de DCCCC l op*eribus* p*r*oueni*entibus* de xi[x] Cust*umariis* in Northcraule quor*um* quil*ib*et op*er*abi*t* j opus quoli*be*t die op*er*abili inter gul*am* aug*usti et* fest*um* s*anct*i mich*ae*lis exc*ep*t*is* dieb*us* festi*ui*s in quib*us* operari no*n* deb*ent*. Et q*uando* mec*unt* mec*ent* p*ro* j op*er*e di*midiam* acr*am* fr*umen*ti orde*i* pis*arum* vel vesc*arum* vel j acr*am* auen*arum* sic*ut* iac*et* perci*piend*o de d*omi*no p*ro* messe*ndo*[3] lig*ando et* adim*endo* cuiusli*be*t acr*e* j garb*am*. S*umma* DCCCC l op*er*a. De quib*us* in acq*uietancia* iij caruc*ariorum et* iij b*er*car*iorum* CCC op*er*a. In acq*uietancia* iij ferling*atarum* in Northcraule quor*um* op*er*a relax*ata* vt sup*ra* C l op*er*a. In def*ectu* v ferl*ingatarum* q*uia* in man*u* d*omi*ni vt sup*ra* CC l op*er*a. In ac-

[1] Struck through.

[2] Apparently an error for CC lxv.

[3] Error for metendo.

quietancia iiij ferlingatariorum operancium hoc anno pro diebus festivis contingentibus in diebus suis operabilibus hoc anno xxiiij opera. In xxxvij acris dimidia ordei et xxxviij acris auenarum pro [1] perticam metendis ligandis et adimendis cc xxvj opera pro acra ordei iiij opera et pro acra auenarum ij opera. Summa que supra et eque.

Et de c l operibus cariacionis prouenientibus de xxv Custumariis in Suthcraule quorum quilibet cariabit blada domini donec totaliter intrantur. Et estimatur quod fieri poterit communibus annis per vj dies. Et si dominus plura opera indigeat plura facient. Et si tanta non indigeat per pauciora sint quieti. Cariacio bladi summa c l opera. De quibus in acquietancia j prepositi vj opera. In bladis domini cariandis hoc anno c xliiij opera. Et eque.

Et de vj operibus tassacionis prouenientibus de j Custumario in Suthcraule qui inueniet j operarium pro bladis domini tassandis quousque totaliter tassentur. Et estimatur quod fieri poterit communibus annis per vj dies. Et si dominus plura opera indigeat plura facient. Et si tanta non indigeat per minora sint quieti. Tassacio bladi Summa vj opera. Et computatur in bladis domini tassandis. Et eque.

Et de MCCC iiij^{xx} xiiij operibus prouenientibus de xvij Custumariis de Northcraule quorum quilibet operabit ij opera qualibet septimana inter festum Sancti Michaelis et gulam Augusti exceptis inde iij septimanis [festivis] videlicet Natalis domini Pasche et Pentecostes in quibus non operabunt nec superius oneratur in capiti de quolibet iiij^{xx} ij opera. Et quando triturant quilibet illorum triturabit iij bussellos frumenti vel v bussellos ordei iij bussellos pisarum vel vescarum vel vj bussellos auenarum pro j opere et valet opus ob. q. Opera manualia summa MCCC [iiij^{xx} xiiij]. De quibus in acquietancia iij carucariorum et ij bercariorum CCCC x opera cuilibet iiij^{xx} ij opera. In acquietancia iij ferlingatarum quorum opera relaxata vt supra cc xlvj opera. In defectu v ferlingatarum quia in manu domini vt supra cccc x opera cuilibet iiij^{xx} ij opera. In liiij quarteriis iiij bussellis frumenti iij quarteriis Curalli iij quarteriis iiij bussellis pisarum et iiij quarteriis vj bussellis [vescarum triturandis et] ventilandis c lxxv opera pro vj bussellis j opus. In iiij^{xx} xv quarteriis v bussellis ordei triturandis et ventilandis c liij opera pro v bussellis j opus. Summa que supra. Et eque.

Et sciendum est quod omnes Custumarii de Northcraule portabunt litteras vel brevia vsque Merdon vel Ouerton quosciens vel quando neccesse fuerit. Et eciam cariabunt j quarterium [auenarum] vsque Wolueseiam pro mora domini ibidem vnde ij Custumarii de Wodecote Debent eciam claudere et sustinere in communi cum auxilio omnium Custumariorum de Suthcraule xvj perticas palicii circa parcum de Waltham. Debent eciam querere et cariare cum equis et carectis suis fenum pro

[2] Error for per.

aueris d*omi*ni vbicu*n*que empt*um* fu*er*it. [Ita] q*uo*d possint ire *et* redire p*er* j die*m*. Et deb*ent* p*re*d*ic*ti Cust*umarii* de Suthcraule in co*mmun*i inue*n*ire v homi*n*es ad college*nda* poma in gardi*n*o de Walth*am*. It*em* deb*ent* car*iare* lana*m* vel cas*eum* d*omi*ni vsq*ue* Hampton*iam* vel Byt*er*ne. Et si d*omin*us volu*er*it aliq*uam* domu*m* edificar*e* deb*ent* querer*e* mere*mium* [apud] M*er*don et car*iare* vsq*ue* Craule. Et fac*ient* mullione*s* de st*ra*mi*n*e rem*anente* in Cur*ia* q*uando* neccess*e* fu*erit*. Op*er*a fac*ienda* in co*mmuni*.

§§ 18. Reeve's Account 29 Sept., 1409—28 Sept., 1410.

This account states that it runs from Michaelmas for one whole year. We know from other accounts too that this was the general practice — to begin the agricultural year at Michaelmas.

The new circumstance is that the Manor of Crawley has, apparently for the first time, been leased to the reeve. Since this was the third year, the lease probably began 29 September, 1407. This may be regarded as a landmark for Crawley. The present lease was to run for twelve years. It seems to have involved very largely the grain farming, that part of the management of the manor which had become so difficult — in view of the scarcity of tenants and their unwillingness to give services in kind. At any rate, when the price of grain was high, the reeve accounted for only a small fixed amount; when it was low, he accounted for a greater yield. Here was a chance for some profits on the part of the reeve, with but slight variation in the income of the lord.

An instance also occurs of the leasing of a tenant's holding. It is said that this was the eighth of the twelve years which the lease was to run. The period accordingly was from 1402 to 1414. The holding was Robert Wodecote's virgate of bondland together with his 22 acres of purpresture land leased to Robert Crompe.

The second chief interest of the account lies in the sale or commutation of labor services. Eleven persons paid for commutation, three for autumn week-works and eight for all week-works. At least we infer that week-works were the only ones involved. All the commuters were holders of farthinglands to which the week-works in Crawley were attached.

Difficulties between King Henry IV and his kinsman, Henry,

Bishop of Winchester, are indicated by the reference to the escheator. Apparently the situation was not ironed out until 1412.

There are several indications of the breakdown of reeve cultivation (sometimes called bailiff farming). There was the commutation above mentioned. There was a diminishing supply of laborers for the harvest. And there was a lease in operation. None of these things necessarily involved any great change, but they were the entering wedge to new conditions.

The lord possessed certain furlongs or fields; at least he had a special interest in them. La Sherte and Trendale and Holyndane he sold for pasture. One he sowed to grain. Three he used for pasturing his own stock. And two, Drakenorth and Bashamle, lay in common. Whether this meant for the use of both lord and tenants, or only tenants, is not indicated.

On the market, probably at Winchester, the reeve sold 25 6/8 quarters of wheat, 10 being at 8s. 8d. and 15 6/8 at 8s. He also sold 56 wether kebbs at 14d. each. Probably on the same market, he bought a horse — for 34s. 1d. Eight quarters of wheat were sold for a loan (per mutuum) at 10s. a quarter, while the rest of the wheat brought 8s. 8d. and 8s. It would seem that the 8 quarters were sold on credit, and at a sufficiently high rate to justify our seeing usury or interest in the transaction. Sales on credit are extremely rare in Crawley accounts.

The parson (or rector) of the church of Crawley paid 12d. for a piece of demesne land. Whether it was for pasture or tillage is not stated.

There was no ewe's milk this year because of the dryness of the summer. A stray wether is accounted for. Indeed this is a rather new item, to be found frequently in the accounts and court rolls, however, from the early fifteenth to the late eighteenth century. As before, we note the allowances or credits given to the reeve, probably to cover special circumstances. Sometimes these were authorized by writs and sometimes not.

New hedges were being made around the coppice, between the court and a field, and around the woods. Of course, the arable fields were still generally unenclosed in Crawley.

Families that recur in Crawley for generations are found in this account, notably the Selys, Davys, and Waytes. The last-named family was represented in the village until the late nineteenth century, that is, for about 500 years. At the time of the present account the family resided in North Crawley, in later centuries in South Crawley. There are many indications that the Wayte family became one of the most propserous in Crawley.

CRAULE[1]

Comp*ot*us Will*elm*i Cupp*er*e p*re*pos*it*i ib*id*em a festo S*anct*i Mic*hael*is anno t*ra*nsl*ationis* d*omi*ni Henr*ici* Beaufort Ep*iscop*i Wynton*iensis* v[to] vsq*ue* idem f*estu*m extu*n*c p*ro*xim*um* seque*n*s a*nno* d*ict*i Ep*iscop*i vj[to] p*er* A*nnum* integ*rum*.

Arr*eragium*. Idem r*eddit* de xviij s. vj d. de arr*eragio* vlti*mi* Comp*ot*i a*nni* p*re*cedent*is* vt p*atet* in ped*e* ib*ide*m. S*umma* xviij s. vj d.

Redd*itu*s assis*i*. Et de lxiiij s. vj d. de to*to* r*eddit*u assis*o* ad f*estu*m Nat*alis* d*omi*ni. Et de lxvij s. x d. de to*to* r*eddit*u assis*o* ad f*estu*m Pasch*e*. Et lxiiij s. vj d. de to*to* r*eddit*u assis*o* ad f*estu*m Nat*alis* S*anct*i Joh*an*nis Bapti*st*e. Et de c iiij s. j d. de to*to* r*eddit*u assis*o* ad fest*um* S*anct*i Mich*ael*is. Et de xij d. de Symone Membury p*ar*sona eccl*es*ie de Craule de incr*emento* redd*itus* p*ro* j p*ar*cella t*er*re de d*omi*nico d*omi*ni apud Puthulle ad iiij t*er*mi*n*os. S*umma* xv li. xxiij d.

Acquiet*ancie* redd*itus*. In Acq*uietancia* r*edditus* j p*re*pos*it*i p*er* Ann*um* v s. In acq*uietanciis* r*edditus* iij Caruc*ariorum et* j Fabri p*er* annu*m* x s. viij d. cuil*ibe*t ij s. viij d. In acq*uietanciis* r*edditus* j b*er*car*ii* multon*um* j b*e*rcar*ii* ou*ium* m*a*tricium *et* j Cust*odis* Hog*astrorum* p*er* Annu*m* viij s. cuil*ibet* ij s. viij d. S*umma* xxiij s. viij d.

Defect*us* redd*itus*. In def*ectu* r*edditus* t*er*re Will*elm*i Stronge tract*e* in do*minicum* p*er* annu*m* ij s. In def*ectu* r*edditus* t*er*re Will*elm*i de Curi*a* p*ro* sim*i*li ij s. viij d. In def*ectu* r*edditus* terr*e* de Alebrok*e* q*ui* mod*o* rem*anet* apud m*er*don*am* p*er* annu*m* v s. In def*ectu* r*edditus* t*er*re Rob*er*ti de Crouche tract*e* in d*ominicum* p*er* annu*m* ij s. viij d. In de*f*ectu r*edditus* t*er*re Rob*er*ti Coye p*ro* sim*i*li ij s. viij d. In def*ectu* r*eddi*-*tus* t*er*re Porcar*ii* p*ro* sim*i*li ij s. viij d. In def*ectu* r*edditus* t*er*re vaccar*ii* p*er* annu*m* ij s. viij d. S*umma* xx s. iiij d.

Def*ectus* redd*itus* p*er* pestill*entiam*. In def*ectu* r*edditus* j virg*ate* t*er*re nat*ive et* xxij acr*arum* t*er*re p*ur*p*re*st*u*re que fu*it* Rob*er*ti Wodecote mod*o* rem*anentis* in man*ibus* d*omi*ni p*er* annu*m* xxj s. S*umma* xxj s. S*umma* acquiet*anciarum et* defettus Reddit*us* lxv s. S*umma* Redditus rema-nent*is* de claro xj li. xvj s. xj d.

[1] MS., P. R. O., Ecclesiastical Commission, Various, 159412, memb. 24.

Ciminu*m*. Et de j l*ib*r*a* Cimin*i* de redd*itu* Joh*an*nis Fromond*e* p*ro* j croft*a* voc*ata* le howe. Et lib*erata* sup*er* sc*accarium*. Et eq*ue*.

Ex*itus* ten*ementi* in man*ibus* d*omi*ni. Et de xxij s. de ex*itu* j virg*ate* t*er*re nat*iue et* xxij acr*arum* t*er*re p*ur*prest*ur*e que fu*it* Rob*er*ti Wodecote sic dimiss*arum* Rob*er*to Crompe ad t*erminum* xij annor*um* hoc a*nno* viij°. S*um*m*a* xxij s.

Vend*itio* op*erum*. Et de iiij s. de henr*ico* Wodecote p*ro* op*eribus* j ferl*ingi* t*er*re s*ibi* relax*atis* du*m* d*omi*no placu*er*it. Et de iiij s. de Joh*an*ne Sely p*ro* op*eribus* j ferl*ingi* t*er*re s*ibi* relax*atis*. Et de iiij s. de Rob*er*to Sely p*ro* op*eribus* j ferl*ingi* t*er*re s*ibi* relax*atis*. Et de vj s. viij d. de Will*el*mo Vayne p*ro* op*eribus* j ferl*ingi* t*er*re sibi relax*atis*. Et de iiij s. de Joh*an*ne lange p*ro* op*eribus* j ferl*ingi* t*er*re s*ibi* relax*atis*. Et de viij s. de Joh*an*ne Belle p*ro* op*eribus* ij ferl*ingorum* t*er*re s*ibi* relax*atis*. Et de iiij s. de Will*el*mo hodman p*ro* op*eribus* j ferl*ingi* t*er*re s*ibi* relax*atis*. Et de vj s. viij d. de Joh*an*ne Mulward p*ro* op*eribus* j ferl*ingi* t*er*re s*ibi* relax*atis*. Et de x s. de op*eribus* autu*m*pn*alibus* iij ferl*ingorum* t*er*re *videlicet* Joh*an*nis Baret Rog*eri* Gybbes *et* Joh*an*nis Dauy eisde*m* relax*atis* c*aus*a inopie eoru*n*dem ad volunt*atem* d*omi*ni p*ro* quol*ibe*t iij s. iiij d. S*um*m*a* lj s. iiij d.

Ex*itus* man*er*ii. Et de xiij s. de pannag*io* porc*orum* ad f*estu*m s*anc*ti martin*i*. Et de xij d. de pannag*io* vit*u*lor*um* hoc anno. Et de xv s. de pann*agio* xxvj vacc*arum et* xij bouic*u*lor*um* ad t*erminum* de hock*e* p*ro* vacc*a* vj d. *et* p*ro* bouic*u*lo ij d. Et de xxxv s. de vij acr*is* sub*b*osc*i* vend*itis* p*ro* acr*a* v s. D*e* past*ura* yem*ali* in bosc*o* vend*ita* n*ihil* quia depascit*ur* cu*m* hog*astr*is d*omi*ni. Et de v s. de pas*tura* in Trendale *et* holyndan*e* vend*ita*. D*e* pas*tura* in Drakenorth*e* vend*ita* n*ihil* q*uia* iac*et* in co*mmun*i. Et de iiij s. ij d. de porc*is* agist*atis* in stipul*a* d*omi*ni hoc a*nno*. D*e* past*ura* fossat*i* c*irc*a Curi*am* n*ihil* quia p*ro* equis d*omi*ni. D*e* pas*tura* in Locforlang*e et* markforlang*e* n*ihil* quia se*mi*nab*atur*. D*e* pas*tura* in Bashamle n*ihil* q*uia* iac*et* in co*mmun*i. Et de iij s. iiij d. de pas*tura* in la Sherte vend*ita* homag*io* p*er* a*nnum*. D*e* past*ura* c*ir*ca b*ar*tonas b*er*cari*arum* n*ihil* quia p*ro* equis d*omi*ni. D*e* pastur*a* in Puthulle n*ihil* p*ro* biden*tibus* d*omi*ni. D*e* ou*ibus* in fald*a* Cust*umariorum* n*ihil* quia no*n* exced*unt* c*er*tu*m* num*er*u*m* xxv hoc anno. Et de vij s. iiij d. de xxij auc*is* vend*itis* p*recium* cap*itis* iiij d. Et de viij s. de xxiiij Capon*ibus* vend*itis* p*recium* cap*itis* iiij d. vnde hospic*io* d*omi*ni xiiij. Et de xiiij s. x d. de iiij^{xx} iij gall*is et* gall*in*is vend*itis* p*recium* cap*itis* ij d. Et de xij d. de cor*iis* ij equor*um* de mori*na* vend*itis*. Et de xiiij d. de cor*io* j bouis de mor*ina* vend*ito*. Et de vij s. viij d. de pell*ibus* xxiiij multon*um* ix ou*ium* m*atricium et* xij hog*astrorum* de mori*na* an*te* tons*ionem* vend*itis* p*recium* pell*is* multon*is* iiij d. m*atricis* ij d. *et* hog*astri* j d. ob. Et de x d. de pell*ibus* vij multon*um et* iij m*atricium* de mor*ina* post tons*ionem* p*recium* pell*is* j d. Et de ij s. v d. de pell*ibus* xlj agn*orum* de mori*na* an*te* sep*aracionem* vend*itis* p*recium* duodeci*m* viij d. Et de iij d. de pell*ibus* iij agnor*um* rott*orum* de mori*na* post sep*aracionem et* an*te* tons*ionem*. Et de x d. de pellectr*ia* xx agnor*um* de mori*na* post ton*sionem* vend*ita* p*recium* pell*is* ob. Et de xx d. de ij cl*avis* lane fracte vend*itis*. Et de xvj s. vj d. de xj cl*avis* lan*e* agn*ine* vend*itis* p*recium* cl*avi* xviij d. D*e* lact*e* ou*ium* m*a*tric*ium* n*ihil* q*uia* no*n* lact*abant* c*aus*a scic*itatis* in estat*e*. Et de x d. de cc ouis gall*inarum* vend*itis*. D*e* equis agist*atis* in bosco d*omi*ni n*ihil* p*ro* biden*tibus* d*omi*ni. Et de iij s. iiij d. de Joh*ann*e Wayte p*ro* pas*tura* l biden*tium* cu*m* multon*ibus* d*omi*ni annex*ata* ad ij ferl*ingos* t*er*re nat*ive* S*um*m*a* vij li. ij s. ij d.

Vend*itio* bl*adi*. Et de xv li. viij d. de xxxiiij q*uarteriis* vj b*ussellis* fru*menti* vend*itis* vnd*e* p*er* mut*uum* viij q*uarteria* p*recium* q*uarterii* x s. *et* in foro xxvj q*uarteria* vj b*usselli* vnd*e* x q*uarteria* p*recium* q*uarterii* viij s. viij d. *et* xv q*uarteria* vj b*usselli* p*recium* q*uarterii* viij s. Et de xv li. de l q*uarteriis* ordei vend*itis* p*recium* q*uarterii* vj s. Et de lxiij s. iiij d. ob. de xxj q*uarteriis* j b*ussello* auen*e* vend*itis* p*recium* q*uarterii* iij s. S*um*m*a* xxxiij li. iiij s. ob.

Vend*itio* Staur*i*. Et de lxxvij s. iiij d. de lxviij multon*ibus* k*ebbatis* post tons*ionem* vend*itis* vnd*e* hospic*io* d*omi*ni xij p*recium* cap*itis* xij d. *et* in foro lvj p*recium* cap*itis* xiiij d. Et de lxxvij s. de ij hurt*ardis et* lxv m*a*tric*ibus* k*ebbatis* vend*itis* p*recium* capit*is* xiiij d. Et de viij li. vj s. viij d. de c hog*astris* an*te* tons*ionem* vend*itis* s*er*uient*i* de Walth*am* laurens p*recium* cap*itis* xx d. Et de ix s. iiij d. de xiiij agn*is* ext*ract*is vend*itis* p*recium* cap*itis* viij d. Et de xx s. de porcell*is* de ex*itu* j suis sic dimiss*e* ad firm*am* hoc anno. S*um*m*a* xvij li. x s. iiij d.

Fines. Et de xiij s. iiij d. de tuth*yngpenny* ad t*ur*nos s*anc*ti Mart*ini et* hock*e*. Et de iij s. iiij d. de Alic*ia* Hankyn p*ro* C*ri*stina filia sua mari*tanda* ex*tra*. Et de vj d. de Thoma Aleyn p*ro* j tofto *et* j ferl*ingo* t*er*re nat*ive* in Craule in p*ar*te boriali que q*uond*a*m* fu*erunt* Joh*ann*is Moraun*t et* que deuen*erunt* in man*us* d*omi*ni tanq*ua*m esc*aeta* sua eo q*uo*d null*us* de sang*uine* d*ic*ti Joh*ann*is lic*et* p*ro*clam*atio* fac*t*a fuerit *secundum* cons*uetudinem* maneri*i* p*ro* eisdem finir*e* cur*avit* ad hoc compuls*us* h*abe*nd*is*. Et de v s. de Joh*ann*e Gibbes p*ro* Joh*ann*a filia sua mar*itanda* ex*tra*. S*um*m*a* xxij s. ij d.

Perquis*ita*. Et de xxij d. de p*er*quis*itis* t*ur*ni s*anc*ti Mart*ini*. Et de iiij s. iiij d. de p*er*quis*itis* t*ur*ni de hock*e*. Et de vij s. viij d. de p*er*quis*itis* Cur*ie* tent*e* int*er* d*ic*tos ij t*ur*nos. Et de vj s. de p*er*quis*itis* Cur*ie* tent*e* post d*ic*t*u*m t*ur*nu*m* de hock*e*. S*um*m*a* xix s. x d.

Vend*itio* sup*er* compo*tum*. Et de ix s. de diu*ersis* vend*itis* sup*er* com*potum* vt ex*tra*. S*um*m*a* ix s. S*um*m*a* to*talis* Rec*epte* cum arr*er*a*gio* lxxvj li. xvj s. iij d. ob.

Cust*us* caruc*arum*. In fer*o et* acer*e* emp*tis* p*ro* ferram*entis* iij Caruc*arum* p*er* annu*m* xvj s. viij d. In j nou*a* Caruc*a* emp*ta* xij d. In eade*m* lig*anda* iij d. In caruc*is* chippi*andis et* vest*iandis per* annu*m* vj d. In iij ferr*is* pedal*ibus* emp*tis* xviij d. In iij p*aribus* rot*arum* p*ro* Caruc*is* emp*tis* ij s. In iiij jug*is* fac*iendis* iiij d. In j vom*ere* emp*to* xx d. In iiij capistr*is* emp*tis* iiij d. In stapul*is et* annul*is* ferr*i* fract*is* refic*iendis* viij d. In P*recariis* viij caruc*arum* de cust*umariis qui* arrau*erunt* viij acr*as* sic*ut* iac*ent* viij d. In xviij bob*us* ferr*andis et* it*erum* affirm*andis* ij s. iiij d. In ferr*amentis* iiij affr*orum per* annu*m* vj s. In stipen*diis* ij fug*atorum per* annu*m* viij s. In iij h*erciis* fac*iendis* viij d. S*umma* xliij s. v d.

Cust*us* Carect*arum*. In viij clut*is* cu*m* clau*is* emp*tis* p*ro* Carect*is per* annu*m* xx d. In carect*a* ax*anda* vj d. In vncto ad idem emp*to* vj d. In iij coler*is* emp*tis* ij s. iij d. In ij p*aribus* tract*uum* emp*tis* xij d. In albo coreo emp*to* xij d. In iij capistr*is* emp*tis* iij d. In j scala p*ro* carect*a* emp*ta* viij d. In ferr*amentis* iij equor*um per* annu*m* vj s. In stip*endio* j carect*arii per annum* iiij s. S*umma* xvij s. x d.

Emp*tio* St*auri*. In j equo emp*to* in foro xxiiij s. j d. In j equo emp*to* de hospici*o* d*omi*ni sine p*recio*. In iij bob*us* emp*tis* xlij s. p*recium* capi*tis* xiiij s. In lj agnis emp*tis* lv s. iij d. p*recium* cap*itis* xiij d. in co*m*-*mun*i. S*umma* vj li. xvj d.

Cust*us* b*ercarie*. In ij barell*is* tarre emp*tis* xj s. In vncto ad id*em* emp*to* xiiij s. In lx clat*ibus* fac*iendis* iij s. iiij d. p*ro* duoden*a* viij d. In rub*ea* pet*ra* emp*ta* xij d. In fil*o et* ynde emp*tis* j d. In feno emp*to* p*ro* sust*entacione* biden*tium* in yem*e* xxx s. *et* tantu*m* c*au*sa paucitat*is* de puls' hoc anno. In ij bu*ssellis* sal*is* emp*tis* p*ro* potagi*o* fam*ulorum* xvj d. In portand*a* fald*a* de campo in campu*m* xij d. In stip*endio* j coop*er*-tor*is* coop*erientis* sup*er* b*er*car*iam* m*a*tric*ium per* iiij dies xvj d. In ij suis s*er*uitor*ibus per* id*em* tempus xij d. In j quarent*ena et* xxx p*er*t*icis* nou*e* haie circa b*er*car*iam* claud*endis* ij s. xj d. p*ro* quar*entena* xx d. In stip*endio* j daye p*er* annu*m* ij s. vj d. In j nou*o* t*ri*pod*e* emp*to* xij d. S*umma* lxx s. vj d.

Cust*us* domor*um* cu*m* necc*essar*iis. In iij m*ille* teg*u*lis plan*is* emp*tis* xvj s. vj d. In c huptil*es et* gut*er*til*es* emp*tis* iiij s. vj d. In stip*endiis* ij Coop*er*tor*ium* coop*erientium* sup*er grangiam* aula*m et* cameras p*er* iiij sept*imanas* xvj s. cap*ientium* int*er* se p*er* sept*imanam* ij s. In iij q*uar*-t*eriis* calc*is* emp*tis* ij s. In cccc lath*is* emp*tis* ij s. iiij d. In iiij m*ille* lath*e*nall*es* emp*tis* iiij s. viij d. p*recium* m*ille* xiiij d. In bordnall*es* emp*tis* ij d. In xij m*ille* tylpynn*es* emp*tis* ij s. In ij serur*is* cu*m* clau*ibus* emp*tis* p*ro* ij stab*u*lis viij d. In ferram*entis* emp*tis* p*ro* ij hostiis xvj d. In stip*endiis* ij Carpent*ariorum per* ij sept*imanas* fac*ientium* noua*m* portam iux*ta* punfald*am* gransull' aula*m et* cam*er*am ix s. cap*ientium* int*er* se p*er* sept*imanam* iiij s. vj d. In j vet*er*lok' cu*m* cathen*a* nou*a* emp*t*' p*ro* equis affirm*andis* xij d. In aliis cathenis emp*tis* vj d. In j sacco emp*to* xij d. In j cribr*o et* ridell*is* emp*tis* iiij d. ob. In fimis in camp*is* sp*ar*gend*is* xij d. In iiij quarent*enis et* x p*er*tic*is* nou*e* haie circa copic*ium* claud*endis* vij s. j d. p*ro* quarent*ena* xx d. In haiis int*er* Cur*iam et* campu*m* claud*endis* ij s. In ij quarent*enis et* x p*er*tic*is* nou*e* haie circa boscu*m* claud*endis* iij s. ix d. pro quarent*ena* xx d. In g*rossis* clau*is* emp*tis* p*ro* ostio g*rangie* iiij d. S*umma* lxxvj s. ij d. ob.

Sarcl*atio*. In bl*adis* d*omi*ni sarcland*is* hoc anno ad t*asc*h*a*m vj s. viij d. S*umma* vj s. viij d.

Trit*uratio et* vent*ilatio*. In iij q*uarteriis* vj b*ussellis* pis*arum et* v q*uarteriis* vesc*iarum* trit*urandis* ad t*asc*ham ij s. ij d. p*ro* q*uarterio* iij d. In iiij[xx] q*uarteriis* v b*ussellis* ordei trit*urandis* ad t*asc*ham xiij s. v d. p*ro* q*uarterio* ij d. In lij q*uarteriis* auen*e* trit*urandis* ad t*asc*ham vj s. vj d. p*ro* q*uarterio* j d. ob. In mediet*ate* d*icti* bl*adi* vent*ilanda* ad t*asc*ham que fac*it* lxxj q*uarteria* j b*ussellum* di*midium* ij s. p*ro* iij q*uarteriis* j d. S*umma* xxiiij s. j d.

Cust*us* autu*mpni*. In pan*e et* comp*a*nag*io* emp*tis* p*ro* c xlix cust*umariis* q*uadra* p*er* j diem *et* viij ministr*is* Cur*ie* p*er* iij dies que [sic] messuer*unt* lj acr*as et* comport*averunt* l acr*as* fr*umenti* p*er* pertic*am* vij s. ij d. ob. cuil*ibe*t pan*is* p*recium* ob. In s*er*uis*ia* emp*ta* p*ro* eisdem ij s. In cas*eo* emp*to* p*ro* eisdem iij s. vij d. q. cuil*ibe*t cas*eum* p*recium* q. In x acr*is* fr*umenti* l acr*is* ordei xv acr*is* pis*arum* xx acr*is* vesc*iarum et* xl acr*is* auen*e* met*endis* lig*andis et* comport*andis* ad t*asc*ham c j s. iij d. p*ro* acr*a* ix d. In stip*endio* j haiward*i* p*er* annu*m* vj s. viij d. S*umma* vj li. viij d. ob. q.

Expen*se* sen*escalli*. In expen*sis* Ric*ar*d*i* Wyot sen*escalli* tenent*is* t*ur*nos s*an*c*t*i Mart*ini et* hock*e* p*er* ij bill*as* sigill*atas* vj s. iiij d. In j b*ussello* fr*umenti* emp*to et* dat*o* fam*ulis* p*er* bill*am* sen*escalli* xij d. S*umma* vij s. iiij d.

Vad*ia* ball*ivi*. In vad*iis* Thom*e* Boson' Ball*ivi* in p*ar*tem solu*tionis* vad*iorum* suor*um* p*er* annu*m* xl s. *et* res*iduum* cap*it* in aliis man*eriis*. S*umma* xl s.

Expen*sa* For*ensica*. In xij multon*ibus* fug*atis* usq*ue* Walth*a*m iiij d. S*umma* iiij d. S*umma* Om*nium* Expen*sarum* xxvj li. viij s. v d. q. Et debet l li. vij s. x d. q.

Alloc*atio* sine bre*vi*. Inde allo*cantur* eidem iij s. de stip*endiis* fam*ulorum* superius dis*allocatis*. Et eidem lxiij s. q. de diu*ersis* sup*eronerationibus et* dissall*ocationibus* tam ext*er*ius q*uam* infer*ius* sibi fact*is* in hoc p*re*sent*i* comp*oto*. Et eidem xx s. de feno emp*to* p*ro* mult*onibus et* al*iis* bi[dentibu]s sup*er*ius dis*allocatis*. S*umma* iiij li. vj s. q.

Alloc*atio* p*er* bre*ve*. Et eidem xvj s. viij d. quos lib*eravit* Joh*an*ni Reede Thes*aurario* hosp*itii* d*omi*ni in p*re*c*io* diu*ersorum* victual*ium* sup*er* expen*sas* d*icti* hospic*ii* p*r*out pat*et* p*er* euiden*ciam* eiusdem Joh*annis* auditor*i* sup*er* hu*n*c comp*otum* direct*am*. S*umma* xvj s. viij d.

Lib*e*racio d*e*nar*iorum*. Et in d*e*nar*iis* lib*e*rat*is* Joh*an*ni Arnold Rec*eptori* de Wolues*eia* p*er* j t*alliam* xliiij li. vj s. viij d. S*umma* xliiij li. vj s. viij d. S*umma* om*nium* Alloc*ationum et* lib*erationum* xlix li. ix s. iiij d. q. Et debet xviij s. vj d. Et to*tum* in man*ibus* Esc*aetoris*.

Frumentu*m*. Will*elmus* Cupp*ere* p*re*pos*itus* ib*idem* on*eravit* se de l q*uarteriis* fr*umen*t*i* de ex*itu grangie* mens*ura* ras*a* trit*uratis* p*er* op*er*a ex conuenc*ione* fac*t*a cu*m* consilio d*omi*ni ad r*eddend*u*m* annuati*m* lx q*uarteria* fr*umen*t*i* n*isi* p*recium* q*uarterii* fr*umen*t*i* excedit vj s. viij d. Et si excedat d*ictu*m p*reciu*m vj s. viij d. tu*n*c r*espondebit* de l q*uar- teriis*. Et sic illam conuenc*ionem* s*er*uando de anno in annu*m* ad t*ermi- nu*m xij anno*rum* hoc anno t*er*cio. Et reddet comp*otum* de vend*itioni- bus* d*ic*t*i* fr*umenti et* alio*rum* bladoru*m* ac de aliis exit*ibus* hui*us* man*er*ii. Et satisfaciet d*omi*no sup*er* comp*otum* p*er* pleg*ium* Thome Cupp*ere* Joh*ann*is Wylde Joh*ann*is Sely *et* Joh*ann*is Mulward. S*umma* l q*uar- teria*. D*e* quib*us* in se*min*e sup*er* lx acr*as* t*er*re p*er* p*er*tic*am* xv q*uar- teria* sup*er* acr*am* ij b*usselli*. In pane furn*iato* p*ro* expen*sis* sen*escalli* tenent*is* t*ur*nos s*anc*t*i* Mart*ini et* hocke p*er* ij bill*as* sigill*atas* ij b*usselli*. In vend*itis* inf*ra* xxxiiij q*uarteria* vj b*usselli*. S*umma* que s*upra*. Et eq*ue*.

Ord*eum*. Et de c q*uarteriis* ordei de ex*itu grangie* mens*ura* ras*a* tri- t*uratis* vnde p*er* op*er*a xix q*uarteria* iij b*usselli et* ad t*asc*ham iiij^{xx} q*uar- teria* v b*usselli* ex conuenc*ione* fac*t*a cu*m* consilio d*omi*ni ad r*eddendum* annuati*m* c xx q*uarteria* ordei n*isi* p*recium* q*uarterii* ordei excedat v s. Et si excedat d*ictu*m p*recium* v s. tunc r*espondebit* de c q*uarteriis* ordei. S*umma* c q*uarteria*. D*e* quib*us* sup*er* l acr*as* t*er*re p*er* p*er*tic*am* xxv q*uarteria* sup*er* acr*am* iiij b*usselli*. In mix*tis* inferi*us* ad lib*erationem* fam*ulorum* xxv q*uarteria*. In vend*itis* inf*ra* l q*uarteria*. S*umma* que sup*ra*. Et eque.

Pis*e*. Et de iij q*uarteriis* vj b*ussellis* pis*arum* de ex*itu* trit*uratis* ad t*asc*ham. Et de v q*uarteriis* de eodem ex*itu* p*er* est*imationem* in sili- q*uis*. S*umma* viij q*uarteria* vj b*usselli*. D*e* quib*us* sup*er* xv acr*as* t*er*re p*er* p*er*tic*am* iij q*uarteria* vj b*usselli* sup*er* acr*am* ij b*usselli*. In sust*en- tatione* ou*ium* m*atricium* temp*or*e agnell*ationis* p*er* est*imationem* in sili- quis v q*uarteria*. S*umma* que sup*ra*. Et eq*ue*.

Vesce. Et de v q*uarteriis* vesc*arum* de ex*itu* trit*uratis* ad t*asc*ham. Et de x q*uarteriis* de eodem ex*itu* p*er* est*imationem* in siliq*uis*. S*umma* xv q*uarteria*. D*e* quib*us* in se*min*e sup*er* xx acr*as* t*er*re p*er* p*er*tic*am* v q*uarteria* sup*er* acr*am* ij b*usselli*. In sust*entatione* biden*tium* in yeme equo*rum et* alio*rum* aueriorum p*er* est*imationem* in siliq*uis* x q*uarteria*. S*umma* que sup*ra*. Et eque.

Auene. Et de lij q*uarteriis* auen*arum* de ex*itu grangie* trit*uratis* ad t*asc*ham. Et de viij q*uarteriis* de eodem ex*itu* p*er* est*imationem* in garb*is* ex conuenc*ione* fac*t*a cu*m* consilio d*omi*ni ad r*eddendum* annua-t*im* iiij^xx q*uarteria* auen*arum* n*isi* p*re*ci*um* q*uarterii* auen*arum* excedat ij s. iiij d. Et si excedit d*ictum* p*recium* ij s. iiij d. tunc r*espondebit* de lx q*uarteriis* auen*arum*. S*umma* lx q*uarteria*. D*e* quib*us* in se*mi*ne sup*er* xl acr*as* t*er*re p*er* p*er*tic*am* xx q*uarteria* sup*er* acra*m* iiij b*usselli*. In p*re*ben*da* bou*um* p*er* est*imationem* in garb*is* vj q*uarteria*. In p*re*ben*da* equor*um* carect*ariorum* p*er* annu*m* iiij q*uarteria*. In p*re*ben*da* affr*orum* p*er* ann*um* ij q*uarteria*. In far*ina* f*ac*ta p*ro* pot*agio* fam*ulorum* p*er* annu*m* ij q*uarteria* iiij b*usselli*. In p*re*ben*da* equor*um* sen*escalli* ten*entis* t*ur*nos s*anc*ti Mart*ini* *et* hock*e* p*er* ij bill*as* sigill*atas* j q*uarterium* iij b*usselli*. In vend*itis* inf*ra* xxj q*uarteria* j b*ussellus*. Et sup*er* comp*otum* iij q*uarteria* p*ro* ix s. S*umma* que sup*ra*. Et eque.

Lib*eratio* fam*ulorum*. Et de xxv q*uarteriis* ord*ei* rec*eptis* sup*ra* p*ro* lib*eratione* fam*ulorum*. S*umma* xxv q*uarteria*. D*e* quib*us* in lib*eratione* j haiward*i* j carect*arii* *et* ij caruc*ariorum* p*er* annu*m* xx q*uarteria* vj b*usselli* quil*ibe*t cap*iens* q*uarterium* ad x sept*imanas*. In lib*eratione* j garcionis [1] auxil*iantis* bercar*io* m*a*tric*ium* temp*ore* agnell*ationis* j q*uarterium*. In lib*eratione* j daie p*er* a*nnum* iij q*uarteria* ij b*usselli* que cap*it* q*uarterium* ad xvj sept*imanas*. S*umma* que sup*ra*. Et eq*ue*.

Equi. Et de iij equis de rem*anentibus*. Et de ij de emp*tis* vn*de* de hospic*io* d*omi*ni j. S*umma* v. D*e* quib*us* in mori*na* ij. Et rem*anent* iij equi.

Affr*i*. Et de iiij affr*is* de rem*anentibus*. S*umma* iiij. Et rem*anent* iiij affr*i*.

Boues. Et de xviij bob*us* de rem*anentibus*. Et de iij de emp*tis*. S*umma* xxj. D*e* quib*us* in mori*na* j. Et rem*anent* xx bou*es* vn*de* ij K*ebbati*.

Multon*es*. Et de D ij multon*ibus* de rem*anentibus*. Et de C vj de hog*astris* adiu*n*ct*is*. Et de j de ex*trah*ura sup*er*ann*ato*. S*umma* DC ix. D*e* quib*us* in mori*na* an*te* tons*ionem* xiiij. In mori*na* post tons*ionem* vij. In vend*itis* post tons*ionem* lxviij vn*de* hospic*io* d*omi*ni xij. S*umma* iiij^xx ix. Et rem*anent* D xx multon*es*.

Hurt*ardi*. Et de xj hurt*ardis* de rem*anentibus*. Et de vj de hog*astris* adiu*n*ct*is*. S*umma* xvij. D*e* quib*us* in vend*ito* post tons*ionem* j. Et rem*anent* xvj hurt*ardi*.

Matric*es*. Et de CCC iiij^xx v m*a*tric*ibus* de rem*anentibus*. Et de iiij^xx vij de hog*astris* adiu*n*ct*is*. Et de j de ex*trah*ura sup*er*ann*ata*. S*umma* CCCC lxxiij. D*e* quib*us* in mori*na* ix vn*de* an*te* agnell*ationem* iiij. In mori*na* post tons*ionem* iij. In vend*itis* post tons*ionem* lxv. S*umma* lxxvij. Et rem*anent* CCC iiij^xx xvj m*a*tric*es*.

Hog*ast*ri. Et de CCC xj hog*astris* de rem*anentibus* agnor*um*. S*umma* CCC xj. D*e* quib*us* in mori*na* an*te* tons*ionem* xij. In adiu*n*ctis sup*ra* cu*m* multon*ibus* C vj cu*m* hurt*ardis* vj *et* cu*m* m*a*tric*ibus* iiij^xx vij. In

[1] The manuscript has garcoinis.

vend*itis* ante tons*ionem* seruient*i* de Walth*am* laurens c. S*umma* que s*upra*. Et n*ihil* rem*anet*.

Agni. Et de ccc lj agnis de ex*itu* d*ictarum* m*atricium et* no*n* plur*es* quia iiij m*atrices* moreb*antur* an*te* agnell*ationem et* xxx fu*erunt* ster*iles* hoc anno. Et de lj de emp*tis* an*te* tons*ionem*. S*umma* cccc ij. D*e* quib*us* in morin*a* an*te* sep*aracionem* xlj. In *decima* xxxj. In cons*uetudinibus* p*re*pos*iti* Fabri b*er*car*ii* mult*onum et* b*er*car*ii* ou*ium* m*atricium* an*te* tons*ionem* iiij. In vend*itis* de ex*tractis* an*te* tons*ionem* xiiij. In morin*a* post sep*aracionem et* an*te* tons*ionem* v. In morin*a* post tons*ionem* xx. S*umma* c xv. Et rem*anent* cc iiij^{xx} vij agni.

Sus. Et de j sue de rem*anente*. Et rem*anet* j sus. D*e* porcell*is* de ex*itu* eiusdem suis n*ihil* hic quia inf*ra* in den*ariis* ad firm*am*.

Auce. Et de j anc*ere et* iiij auc*is* mar*ioles* de rem*anentibus*. Et de xxiiij de ex*itu*. S*umma* xxix. D*e* quib*us* in *decima* ij. In vend*itis* inf*ra* xxij. Et rem*anent* j anc*er et* iiij auc*e* mar*iole*.

Capon*es*. Et de xxiiij capon*ibus* de rem*anentibus*. Et de xxiiij de puls*inis* inferi*us* f*act*is. S*umma* xlviij. D*e* quib*us* in vend*itis* inf*ra* xxiiij. Et rem*anent* xxiiij capon*es*.

Galli *et* gallin*e*. Et de j gallo *et* v gall*i*nis de rem*anentibus*. Et de c xxv de churs*eto* ad f*estum* s*anct*i Mart*ini*. S*umma* c xxxj. D*e* quib*us* in defect*u* t*er*re le Strong*e* tract*e* in d*omi*nic*um* p*er* annu*m* iiij. In def*ectu* t*er*re Will*elm*i de Curi*a* p*ro* si*mi*li iiij. In def*ectu* t*er*re Rob*er*ti de Cruce p*ro* si*mi*li iiij. In def*ectu* t*er*re le swon p*ro* si*mi*li iiij. In def*ectu* t*er*re Ric*ard*i vaccar*ii* p*ro* si*mi*li iiij. In def*ectu* t*er*re Ric*ard*i Knaue p*ro* si*mi*li iiij. In def*ectu* terre q*uo*nd*a*m Rob*er*ti Wodecotte p*ro* iij di*midiis* virg*atis* t*er*re q*uia* in man*ibus* d*om*ini xij. In def*ectu* t*er*re Joh*ann*is Dauy q*uia* no*n* h*abuit* vxore*m* ij. In def*ectu* t*er*re Rog*er*i Lyght*e* p*ro* si*mi*li ij. In def*ectu* t*er*re Amicie Wodecote quia no*n* h*abuit* viru*m* ij. In vend*itis* inf*ra* iiij^{xx} iij. S*umma* c xxv. Et rem*anent* j gallus *et* v gallin*e*.

Puls*ini*. Et de xxiiij puls*inis* de ex*itu*. Et omn*es* comp*utantur* in capon*ibus* sup*er*ius f*act*is. Et n*ihil* rem*anet*.

Oua. Et de cc ouis de ex*itu* gallin*arum*. Et vend*ita* inf*ra*. Et n*ihil* rem*anet*.

Lana grossa. Et de vell*eribus* cccc iiij^{xx} ix multon*um* xj hurt*ardorum* ccc lxxvij ou*ium* m*atricium et* c iiij^{xx} xix hog*astrorum* p*ro*uen*tis* ad tons*ionem* hoc a*nno*. S*umma* m lxxvj. D*e* quib*us* in *decima* c vij vell*era*. In lib*eratione* Rec*eptori* de Wolues*eia* dcccc lxix vell*era* lan*e* pond*erantia* iij sacc*os* xv cl*avos*. S*umma* que sup*ra*. Et eque.

Lana fracta. Et de ij cl*avis* lan*e* fract*e* de coll*ecta* b*er*car*ie* ad tons*ionem* hoc anno. Et vend*iti* inf*ra*. Et n*ihil* rem*anet*.

Lana agn*ina*. Et de vell*eribus* ccc vij agn*orum* p*ro*uen*tis* ad tons*ionem* hoc anno. Et vend*ita* inf*ra* pond*erantia* xj cl*avos*. Et n*ihil* rem*anet*.

Cor*ia*. Et de cor*iis* ij equor*um et* j bouis de mor*ina* vt sup*ra*. Et vend*ita* inf*ra*. Et n*ihil* rem*anet*.

Pell*es* lanut*e*. Et de pell*ibus* xiiij multon*um* ix m*a*tric*ium et* xij hog*a*-*st*r*orum* de mor*ina* an*te* tons*ionem*. Et vend*ite* inf*ra*. Et n*ihil* rem*anet*.

Pell*es* nud*e*. Et de pell*ibus* nud*is* vij multon*um et* iij ou*ium* m*a*tri-c*ium* de mor*ina* post tons*ionem*. Et vend*ite* inf*ra*. Et n*ihil* rem*anet*.

Pell*es* agn*ine*. Et de pell*ibus* xlj agn*orum* de mor*ina* an*te* sep*ara*-c*ionem*. Et vend*ite* inf*ra*. Et n*ihil* rem*anet*.

Pell*es* rott*orum*. Et de pell*ibus* v agn*orum* rott*orum* de mor*ina* post sep*aracionem et* an*te* tons*ionem*. Et vend*ite* inf*ra*. Et n*ihil* rem*anet*.

Pellect*ria*. Et de pell*ectria* xx agn*orum* de mor*ina* post tons*ionem*. Et vend*ita* inf*ra*. Et n*ihil* rem*anet*.

Vtens*ilia*. Et de iij Caruc*is* cu*m* iij p*a*rib*us* ferram*entorum et* tot*o* app*a*rat*u* ferr*i* p*ro* xvj bob*us* v herc*iis* lign*i* j s*emilione* j b*ussello* ferr*o* lig*ato* j p*icoso* ij sacc*is* j ventilabr*o et* j sporta bl*a*d*i*fer*a* de rem*anen-tibus*. Et rem*anent*. Et de j Carecta ferr*o* lig*ata* cu*m* corda *et* scala j sella Carecta v coler*is* iiij p*a*rib*us* tract*uum et* v capistr*is* de rem*anen-tibus*. Et rem*anent*. Et de j olla en*ea* cont*inente* v lagen*as* j posnet*o* j patella cont*inente* v lagen*as* j patell*a* cont*inente* xij lagen*as* j lathe j vat p*ro* daier*a* j tina j t*ri*pod*e* ij formis p*ro* cas*eo* j siuera rotat*a* [?] de rem*anentibus*. Et rem*anent*. Et de xj Cracch*is* p*ro* biden*tibus* de rem*anentibus*. Et rem*anent*.

§§ 19. Reeve's Account, 29 Sept., 1410—28 Sept., 1411.

In most respects this account runs quite parrallel to the one preceding, as is to be expected. But still it is important to have it for purposes of comparison, particularly in the matter of fields and yields.

Three heriots are recorded, a bullock, a wether, and a ewe. It is stated that half a virgate contains sixteen (customary) acres. Two tourns and two extra courts (customary courts or courts baron) were held this year.

The most striking entry is the amercement of 20s. paid by the tenants for refusing to shear the lord's lambs, as they had been accustomed to do. Why the lambs were specially singled out, is not stated. The general obligation of shearing the lord's sheep seems to have survived until enclosure in 1795.

New hedges were made around a coppice and a plantation(?). A trench or moat was dug and planted, apparently between the yards of the sheepfolds, in order to enclose a field. Probably this was not an arable field, certainly not one of importance.

Officials mentioned are the seneschal who held the two tourns, the bailiff who probably held the other two separate courts, the treasurer of the lord's hospitium, the receiver (of money and wool) at Wolvesey Palace, the reeve who also was the general farmer, the escheator, and the court 'household' and 'ministers.'

CRAULE [1]

Comp*ot*us Will*elm*i Cupp*er*e p*re*po*s*iti ib*ide*m A festo S*anc*ti Mich*ael*is Anno t*ranslationis* D*omi*ni Henr*ici* Beaufort Ep*iscop*i vj vsq*ue* idem festu*m* extunc p*ro*ximu*m* sequens Anno vij^{mo}. Et Anno regni regis Hen*ricus* xij^{mo} *et cetera.*

Arreragia. Idem redd*it* de xviij s. vj d. de arr*eragiis* vlt*im*i Comp*ot*i Anni p*re*ced*entis*. S*umma* xviij s. vj d.

Redd*it*us assis*i*. Et de lxiiij s. vj d. de toto r*eddit*u ass*is*o ad f*est*um Nat*alis* D*omi*ni. Et de lxvij s. x d. de to*to* r*eddit*u ass*is*o ad f*est*um Pasche. Et de lxiiij s. vj d. de to*to* r*eddit*u ass*is*o ad f*est*um S*anc*ti Joh*ann*is Bapt*ist*e. Et de c iiij s. j d. de to*to* r*eddit*u ass*is*o ad f*est*um S*anc*ti Mich*ael*is. Et de xij d. de Symone Membury P*ar*sona eccl*es*ie de Craule de incr*emen*to r*eddit*us p*ro* j p*ar*cell*a* t*er*r*e* de d*omi*nic*o* d*om*i*ni* apud Puthull*e* ad iiij^{or} t*er*m*in*os. S*umma* xv li. xxiij d.

Acquiet*ancie* reddit*us*. In acquiet*ancia* j p*re*po*s*iti p*er* annu*m* v s. In acq*uietanciis* r*edditus* iij Caruc*ariorum et* j fabri p*er* annu*m* x s. viij d. cuil*ibe*t ij s. viij d. In acq*uietanciis* r*edditus* b*er*car*ii* multon*um* j b*er*car*ii* ou*ium* m*a*tric*ium et* j custod*is* hog*astrorum* p*er* a*nnum* viij s. cuil*ibe*t ij s. viij d. S*umma* xxiij s. viij d.

Defect*us* redd*itus*. In defect*u* r*edditus* t*er*r*e* Will*elmi* Stronge t*r*act*e* in d*ominicum* p*er* annu*m* ij s. In def*ectu* r*edditus* t*er*r*e* Will*elm*i de Curi*a* p*ro* si*m*ili ij s. viij d. In defect*u* r*edditus* t*er*r*e* de alebrok*e* q*ui* mo*do* rem*anet* apud M*er*don*am* p*er* annu*m* v s. In defectu r*edditus* terre Rob*er*ti de Crouche tract*e* in d*ominicum* p*er* a*nnum* ij s. viij d. In de*fectu* r*edditus* terre Rob*er*ti Coye p*ro* si*m*ili ij s. viij d. In def*ectu* r*edditus* t*er*re porcar*ii* p*ro* si*m*ili ij s. viij d. In def*ectu* r*edditus* t*er*re vaccar*ii* p*ro* si*m*ili ij s. viij d. S*umma* xx s. iiij d.

Defect*us* redd*itus* p*er* pestill*entiam*. In defect*u* j virg*ate* t*er*r*e* nat*ive et* xxij acr*arum* t*er*r*e* p*ur*p*res*t*ur*e q*ue* fu*erunt* Rob*er*ti Wodecote mo*do* reman*entium* in man*ibus* d*om*i*ni* p*er* annu*m* xxj s. S*umma* xxj s. S*umma* acq*uietanciarum et* defect*uum* redd*itus* lxv s. S*umma* redd*itus* rem*anens* de claro xj li. xvj s. xj d.

[1] MS., P. R. O., Ecclesiastical Commission, Various, 159413, memb. 25.

Cimin*um*. Et de j l*ibra* Cimini de r*eddit*u Joh*ann*is Fromond' p*ro* j croft*a* voc*ata* le Howe. Et lib*erata* sup*er* scacc*arium*. Et eq*ue*.

Ex*itus* ten*ementi* in man*ibus* d*omi*ni. Et de xxij s. de ex*itu* j virg*ate* t*er*re nat*ive et* xxij acr*arum* t*er*re p*ur*prest*ure* q*ue* fu*erunt* Rob*erti* Wodecote sic dimiss*arum* Rob*er*to Crompe ad t*ermi*n*um* xij annor*um* h*oc* a*nno* ix°. S*umma* xxij s.

Vendic*io* op*er*u*m*. Et de iiij s. de Henr*ico* Wodecote p*ro* op*er*ib*us* j ferl*ingi* t*er*re s*ibi* relax*atis* du*m* d*omi*no plac*uerit*. Et de iiij s. de Joh*ann*e Sely p*ro* op*er*ib*us* j ferl*ingi* t*er*re s*ibi* relax*atis*. Et de iiij s. de Rob*er*to Sely p*ro* op*er*ib*us* j ferl*ingi* t*er*re sibi relax*atis*. Et de vj s. viij d. de Joh*ann*e Sely p*ro* op*er*ib*us* j ferl*ingi* t*er*re nup*er* Will*elm*i Vayne. Et de iiij s. de Joh*ann*e Lange p*ro* op*er*ib*us* j ferl*ingi* t*er*re sibi relax*atis*. Et de iiij s. de Will*elm*o Sewel p*ro* op*er*ib*us* j ferl*ingi* t*er*re nup*er* Joh*ann*is Belle. Et de iiij s. de Will*elm*o Fernhull*e* p*ro* op*er*ib*us* j ferl*ingi* t*er*re nup*er* Joh*ann*is Belle. Et de iiij s. de Thom*a* Aleyn p*ro* op*er*ib*us* j ferl*ingi* t*er*re nup*er* Will*elm*i Hodeman. Et de vj s. viij d. de Joh*ann*e Mulward p*ro* op*er*ib*us* j ferl*ingi* t*er*re s*ibi* relax*atis*. Et de x s. de op*eri*b*us* autu*m*pn*alibus* iij ferl*ingorum* t*er*re videl*ice*t Will*elm*i Hodeman Rog*er*i Gibbes Will*elm*i Fernhull*e* eisdem relax*atis* c*aus*a inopie eoru*n*dem ad voluntate*m* d*omi*ni p*ro* quol*ibe*t iij s. iiij d. S*umma* lj s. iiij d.

Exit*us* maner*ii*. Et de xj s. viij d. de pann*agio* porc*orum* ad f*est*u*m* s*anc*ti Mart*in*i. Et de xij d. de pann*agio* vitulor*um* hoc anno. Et de xv s. ij d. de pann*agio* xxvj vacc*arum et* xiij bouic*u*lor*um* ad t*ermi*n*um* de hock*e* videl*ice*t p*ro* vacc*a* vj d. *et* p*ro* bouic*u*lo ij d. Et de xxv s. de v acr*is* subbosc*i* vend*itis* p*re*c*ium* acr*e* v s. *et* eo min*us* p*ro* clausur*a* haiar*um* c*ir*ca nouu*m* fossat*um* plantatu*m*. D*e* past*ura* yem*ali* in bosc*o* vend*ita* n*ihil* q*uia* depasc*itur* cu*m* hog*astris* d*omi*ni. D*e* past*ura* in Trendale *et* Holyndon*e* n*ihil* q*uia* iac*et* in co*mmun*i. Et de v s. de past*ura* in Drakenorth*e* vend*ita* hoc anno. Et de iiij s. iiij d. de porc*is* agist*atis* in Stipull*a* d*omi*ni hoc anno. D*e* past*ura* fossat*i* c*ir*ca Cur*iam* n*ihil* q*uia* p*ro* equis d*omi*ni. D*e* past*ura* in Markforlang*e et* locforlang*e* n*ihil* q*uia* iac*et* in co*mmun*i *et* p*ro* biden*tibus* d*omi*ni. D*e* past*ura* in Bashamle n*ihil* p*ro* biden*tibus* d*omi*ni. Et de iij s. iiij d. de past*ura* in la Schorte vend*ita* homag*io* p*er* annu*m*. D*e* past*ura* c*ir*ca b*ar*ton*am* berc*ar*i*e* n*ihil* q*uia* p*ro* equis d*omi*ni. D*e* past*ura* in Puthull*e* n*ihil* p*ro* biden*tibus* d*omi*ni. D*e* ou*ibus* in fald*a* Cust*umariorum* n*ihil* q*uia* no*n* exced*unt* c*er*tu*m* num*er*u*m* xxv hoc anno. Et de vij s. iiij d. de xxij auc*is* vend*itis* p*re*c*ium* cap*itis* iiij d. Et de viij s. de xxiiij capon*ibus* vend*itis* p*re*c*ium* ca*pitis* iiij d. Et de xiij s. x d. de iiij^{xx} iij gall*is et* gall*in*is vend*itis* p*re*c*ium* cap*itis* ij d. Et de xij d. de Cor*eo* j bouis de mor*ina* vend*ito*. Et de xxxij s. viij d. ob. de pell*ibus* lv multon*um* xxx ou*ium* m*at*ric*ium et* lxxv hog*astrorum* de mor*ina* an*te* tons*ionem* vend*itis* p*re*c*ium* pell*is* multon*is* iij d. m*at*ric*is* ij d. *et* hog*astri* j d. ob. Et de xviij d. de Pell*ibus* x mult*onum et* viij m*a*tric*ium* de mori*na* post ton-s*ionem* vend*itis* p*recium* pell*is* j d. Et de iij s. viij d. ob. de pell*ibus* iiij^{xx} xviij agn*orum* de mori*na* ante sep*aracionem* vend*itis* p*recium* pell*is* ob. Et de xx d. ob. de pell*ibus* xxvj agn*in*is rott*is et* xv pellect*is* vend*itis* p*recium* pell*is* ob. Et de ij s. vj d. de iij cl*avis* lane fract*e* ven-d*itis*. Et de xvj s. vj d. de xj cl*avis* lan*e* agn*ine* vend*itis* p*recium* cl*avi* xviij d. Et de xx s. de lactag*io* c lx m*a*tric*ium* vend*ito* vt r*edditur* p*ro* oue j d. ob. *et* no*n* plur*es* quia lxv k*ebbate* no*n* lactab*ant*. Et de x d. de cc ouis gallin*arum* vend*itis*. Et de iij s. de equis agist*atis* in bosc*o* d*omi*ni hoc anno. Et de iij s. iiij d. de Joh*an*ne Wayte p*ro* pas*tura* l biden*tium* cu*m* mult*onibus* d*omi*ni annex*ata* ad ij ferl*ingos* t*er*re. S*umma* ix li. xvij d. ob.

Vend*itio* bl*adi*. Et de xiiij li. iiij d. de xliiij q*uarteriis* iiij b*ussellis* fr*umenti* vend*itis* vn*de* p*er* mut*uum* xx q*uarteria* p*recium* q*uarterii* vj s. viij d. *et* in foro xxiiij q*uarteria* iiij b*usselli* p*recium* q*uarterii* vj s. Et de xij li. x s. de l q*uarteriis* ord*e*i vend*itis* p*recium* q*uarterii* v s. Et de lxiiij s. x d. ob. de xxj q*uarteriis* v b*ussellis* auen*e* vend*itis* p*recium* q*uarterii* iij s. S*umma* xxix li. xv s. ij d. ob.

Vend*itio* st*auri*. Et de iiij s. de j equo debil*i* vend*ito*. Et de lxx s. de vj bob*us* vend*itis* vnde hosp*itio* d*omi*ni ij p*recium* ca*pitis* xij s. *et* in foro iiij vn*de* iij p*recium* ca*pitis* xij s. *et* j infirm*us* p*recium* x s. Et de v s. de j bouec*ta* fec*unda* de h*eriet*to vend*itis*. Et de iiij li. x s. viij d. de iiij^{xx} iiij multon*ibus* k*ebbatis* post tons*ionem* vend*itis* vn*de* xl p*recium* ca[pitis] xiiij d. *et* xliiij p*recium* ca[pitis] xij d. Et de lxiij s. de v hurt*ardis et* lviij m*a*tric*ibus* k*ebbatis* post tons*ionem* vend*itis* p*recium* cap*itis* xij d. Et de v s. de xij agnis ext*ractis* ante tons*ionem* vend*itis* p*recium* cap*itis* v d. Et de xx s. de Porcell*is* de exit*u* j suis sic dimiss*is* ad firm*am* hoc anno. S*umma* xij li. xvij s. viij d.

Fines. Et de xiij s. iiij d. de tuth*ingpenny* ad t*ur*nos S*anc*ti Mart*ini et* hock*e*. Et de iij s. iiij d. de Roberto fil*io* Rad*ulph*i Smyth*e* p*ro* j me-s*uagio et* di*midia* virg*ata* t*er*re nat*ive* cont*inente* xvj acr*as* in Craule que fu*it* Will*elm*i Smyth*e* p*at*ris sui h*abe*nd*is*. Et de ij s. de Joh*an*ne Sely p*ro* j mes*uagio et* j ferl*ingo* t*er*re nat*ive* in Craule que fu*it* Will*elm*i Vayne *et* que deuen*it* in man*us* d*omi*ni tanq*uam* esc*aeta* sua eo q*uo*d null*us* de sa*nguine* lic*et* p*ro*clam*atio* f*act*a fuerit s*ecundum* cons*uetudinem* man*er*ii p*ro* eisd*em* finire Cur*avit* h*abe*nd*is*. Et de iij s. iiij d. de Rob*er*to fil*io* Joh*an*nis Wodecote p*ro* j mes*uagio et* j ferl*ingo* t*er*re nat*ive* in Craule in p*ar*te boriali que fu*erunt* p*re*dic*t*i Joh*annis* p*at*ris su*i* h*abe*nd*is*. Et de iij s. iiij d. de Joh*an*ne Dauy p*ro* Joh*an*na Cupp*er*e cu*m* t*er*ra sua vide-*lic*et j mes*uagio et* j virg*ata* t*er*re nat*ive* in Craule in p*ar*te aust*r*ali h*abe*nd*a*. S*umma* xxxv s. iiij d.

P*er*quis*ita*. Et de ij s. vij d. de p*er*quis*itis* t*ur*ni S*anc*ti Mart*ini*. Et de v s. x d. de p*er*quis*itis* t*ur*ni de hock. Et de vij s. de p*er*quis*itis* Cur*ie* tente inter dictos ij turnos. Et de vij s. x d. de perquisitis Curie tente post dictum turnum de hocke. Et de xx s. de tenentibus quia recusaverunt tondere agnos domini sicut consueuerunt. Summa xliij s. iij d.

Venditio super compotum. Et de vij li. xiij s. viij d. de diuersis venditis super compotum vt extra. Summa vij li. xiij s. viij d. Summa totalis Recepte cum Arreragiis lxxix li. xv s. iij d.

Custus carucarum. In ferro et acere emptis pro ferramentis iij Carucarum per annum xvj s. viij d. In j noua Caruca empta xij d. In eadem liganda iij d. In Carucis chippiandis et vestiandis per annum vj d. In iij ferris pedalibus emptis xviij d. In iij paribus rotarum pro Carucis emptis ij s. In iij jugis faciendis iij d. In ij vomeribus emptis iij s. iiij d. In iiij capistris emptis iiij d. In stapulis et annulis ferreis fractis reficiendis viij d. In ij herciis emptis xij d. In precariis viij Carucarum de Custumariis qui arauerunt viij acras sicut jacent viij d. In xviij bobus ferrandis et iterum affirmandis iiij s. vj d. In ferramentis iiij affrorum per annum vj s. In stipendiis ij fugatorum per Annum viij s. Summa xlvj s. viij d.

Custus Carecte. In viij clutis cum clauis emptis pro carecta per annum xx d. In carecta axanda vj d. In vncto ad idem empto vj d. In iij Coleris emptis ij s. iij d. In ij paribus tractuum emptis xiiij d. In Albo Coreo empto xij d. In iij Capistris emptis iij d. In j corpore Carecte de nouo empto cum toto apparatu iij s. iiij d. In j corda pro carecta empta xx d. In ferramentis iij equorum per annum vj s. In stipendio Carectarii per annum iiij s. Summa xxij s. iiij d.

Emptio bladi et stauri. In ij quarteriis vesciarum emptis pro semine x s. In j equo empto xxiiij s. In v bobus emptis lxx s. precium capitis xiiij s. In c xliij agnis emptis vij li. ix s. v d. ob. precium capitis xij d. ob. plus in toto vj d. Summa xij li. xiij s. v d. ob.

Custus bercarie. In j barello dimidio tarre empto vj s. viij d. In vncto ad idem empto xiiij s. In xlviij clatibus faciendis ij s. pro duodena viij d. In rubea petra empta xij d. In filo et ynde emptis j d. In feno empto pro sustentatione bidentium in yeme xxvj s. viij d. In iiij barellis salis emptis pro daieria et potagio famulorum ij s. iiij d. In falda portanda de campo in campum xij d. In puls' et feno emptis in yeme pro sustentatione matricium et agnorum xiij s. iiij d. In stipendio j coopertoris cooperientis super bercariam per ij dies viij d. In ij suis seruitoribus per idem tempus viij d. In stramine ad idem ij s. vj d. In iij quarentenis noue haie circa bartonam falcandis v s. pro quarentena xx d. In vj clatibus faciendis pro portis vj d. In solutione pro excambio j olle enee pro potagio famulorum vij s. In coagulis emptis vj d. In panno lineo et laneo ad daieriam vij d. In ij formis pro caseo emptis ix d. In ollis et patellis luti emptis iiij d. In stipendio j daie per annum ij s. In ostio bercarie emenda cum vertinellis emptis vij d. Summa iiij li. viij s. viij d.

Cust*us* dom*us* cum necc*essar*iis. In iij quarent*enis et* xxxvj p*er*tic*is* nou*i* fossat*i* fodiend*is et* plantand*is* int*er* b*ar*ton*as* b*er*car*iarum* usq*ue* Puthull*e* p*ro* camp*o* includend*o* xxvj s. dando p*ro* p*er*tic*a* ij d. In ij b*us*-*sellis* fr*umen*t*i* dat*is* in conuenc*ione* p*re*dict*a* xviij d. In vij q*ua*rent*enis et* xxxij p*er*tic*is* nou*e* haie fac*iendis* p*ro* plantic' ex vt*raque* p*ar*te includend' xix s. vj d. p*ro* quarent*ena* ij s. vj d. In busc*a* ad id*em* p*ro*-st*ernenda* iiij s. In j sacc*o* emp*to* xij d. In j cribr*o et* j ridell*o* emp*tis* iiij d. ob. In fimis in camp*is* sp*argend*is xij d. In j vet*er*lok' cum cathen*a* ferr*ea* emp*t'* xiiij d. In j sport*a* bl*ad*ifer*a* emp*ta* xviij d. In j seuera rot*ata* emp*ta* xij d. In ij quarent*enis et* xx p*er*tic*is* nou*e* haie circa copic*ium* claud*endis* iiij s. ij d. p*ro* q*ua*rent*ena* xx d. In j t*ri*bul*o* ferr*eo* emp*to* v d. In ostio g*rangie* em*endendo* cu*m* ferram*entis et* clau*is* emp*tis* xv d. S*umma* lxij s. x d. ob.

Sarcl*atio*. In bl*ad*is d*omi*ni sarcland*is* hoc anno ad t*asc*h*a*m vj s. S*umma* vj s.

Trit*uratio et* vent*ilatio*. In iij q*uarteriis* vj b*ussellis* pis*arum et* iij q*uarteriis* vesc*iarum* trit*urandis* ad t*asc*ham xx d. q. p*ro* q*uarterio* iij d. In iiij^{xx} xvij q*uarteriis* iiij b*ussellis* ordei trit*urandis* ad t*asc*ham xvj s. iij d. p*ro* q*uarterio* ij d. In lij q*uarteriis* auen*e* trit*urandis* ad t*asc*h*a*m vj s. vj d. p*ro* q*uarterio* j d. ob. In mediet*ate* d*ict*i bl*ad*i vent*ilanda* ad t*asc*h*a*m que fac*it* lxxviij q*uarteria* j b*ussellum* ij s. ij d. p*ro* iij q*uar*-*teriis* j d. S*umma* xxvj s. vij d.

Custus autumpn*i*. In pane *et* comp*anagio* emp*tis* p*ro* c xlix Cust*u*-*mariis* q*uarterium* per vnu*m* diem *et* viij m*inistr*is Cur*ie* p*er* iij dies qui mess*uerunt* lig*averunt et* comport*averunt* l acr*as* fr*umen*t*i* p*er* pertic*am* vij s. ij d. ob. cuil*ibe*t pan*is* p*recium* ob. In s*er*uisia empt*a* p*ro* eisdem ij s. In cas*eo* emp*to* p*ro* eisd*em* iij s. vij d. q. cuil*ibe*t cas*eum* p*recium* q. In x acr*is* fr*umen*t*i* l acr*is* ordei xv acr*is* pis*arum* xx acr*is* vesc*iarum et* xl acr*is* auen*e* met*endis* lig*andis et* comport*andis* ad t*asc*h*a*m c j s. iij d. p*ro* acr*a* ix d. In stip*endio* j haiward*i* p*er* annu*m* vj s. viij d. S*umma* vj li. viij d. ob. q.

Expen*se* sen*escalli*. In expen*sis* Ric*ard*i Wyot senescall*i* ten*entis* t*ur*nos S*anc*t*i* Mart*ini et* Hock*e* p*er* ij bill*as* sigill*atas* vj s. iiij d. ob. S*umma* vj s. iiij d. ob.

Vad*ia* balliui. In vad*iis* Thome Boson' ball*ivi* in p*ar*te*m* sol*utionis* vad*iorum* suor*um* p*er* a*nnum* xl s. *et* res*iduum* cap*it* in al*iis* maneriis. S*umma* xl s. S*umma* om*nium* expen*sarum* xxxiij li. xiij s. viij d. q. Et debet xlvj li. xviij d. ob. q.

Alloc*atio* sine br*evi*. Inde alloc*antur* ei xxij s. de feno emp*to* p*ro* multon*ibus* hog*astris et* m*a*tric*ibus* sibi sup*er*i*us* dis*allocati*. Et eidem v s. de expen*sis* fam*ulorum* sibi sup*er*ius dis*allocati*. Et eidem vij li. xiij s. iiij d. de sup*eroneratio*n*ibus* g*ranurii* [1] in dorso eo q*uo*d p*recium* q*uarterii*

[1] Probably for granarii.

ord*ei et* auen*e* excedit p*recium* in dorso specificat*um*. Et eid*em* xxviij s. viij d. ob. q. de diu*ersis* sup*eronerationibus et* disalloc*ationibus* in hoc present*i* comp*oto sibi* fact*is*. S*umma* x li. ix s. ob. q.

Alloc*atio* p*er* bre*ve*. Et eidem xxiiij s. quos lib*eravit* Joh*ann*i Arnold' Rec*eptori* de Wolues*eia* p*er* manus Joh*ann*is Reede Thes*aurar*ii hosp*itii* d*omi*ni in p*recio* ij bou*um* sup*er* expens*as* hospic*ii* p*r*out p*atet* p*er* euidenc*iam* eiusd*em* Joh*ann*is auditor*i* sup*er* hu*n*c comp*otum* direct*am*. S*umma* xxiiij s.

Lib*erati*o denar*iorum*. Et lib*eravit* Joh*ann*i Arnold' Rec*eptori* de Wolues*eia* per j t*alliam* xxx li. S*umma* xxx li. S*umma* Omn*ium* Alloca*tionum et* lib*erationum* xlj li. xiij s. ob. q. Et debet de claro iiij li. viij s. vj d. vn*de* in man*ibus* Esc*aetoris* xviij s. vj d. Qui on*erantur* in p*roxim*o comp*oto* Anni subseq*uentis* in tit*u*lo de Arr*eragiis*.

F*rumentum*. Will*el*mu*s* Cupp*er*e p*re*pos*it*us ib*idem* r*espondebit* de lx q*uarteriis* fr*umen*t*i* de ex*itu* g*rangie* mens*ura* ras*a* trit*uratis* p*er* op*er*a ex c*er*ta conuenc*ione* f*act*a cu*m* consil*io* d*omi*ni ad r*edd*end*um* annuati*m* lx q*uarteria* fr*umen*t*i* n*isi* p*recium* q*uarterii* fr*umen*t*i* exced*at* vj s. viij d. Et si exced*at* d*ict*um p*recium* vj s. viij d. tunc r*espondebit* de l q*uarteriis*. Et sic illa*m* conuenc*ionem* s*er*uando de Anno in A*nnum* Ad t*er*min*um* xij Anno*rum* hoc anno iiij^{to}. Et redd*et* comp*otum* de vend*itione* d*ict*i fr*umenti et* alio*rum* bl*ad*o*rum* ac de al*iis* exit*ibus* hui*us* man*er*ii. Et satisfaciet d*omi*no sup*er* comp*otum* p*er* pl*egi*um Thom*e* Cupp*er*e Joh*ann*is Wilde Joh*ann*is Sely *et* Joh*ann*is Mulward. S*umma* lx q*uarteria*. D*e* quib*us* in se*min*e sup*er* lx acr*as* t*erre* p*er* p*er*tic*am* xv q*uarteria* sup*er* acr*am* ij b*usselli*. In pane furn*iato* p*ro* expen*sis* sen*escalli* ten*entis* t*ur*nos S*anc*t*i* Mart*ini et* Hocke p*er* ij bill*as* sigill*atas* ij b*usselli*. In vend*itis* inf*ra* xliiij q*uarteria* iiij b*usselli*. In dat*is* fam*ulis* Cur*ie* p*er* bill*as* sen*escalli* ij b*usselli*. S*umma* que sup*ra*. Et eq*ue*.

Ord*eum*. Et de c xx q*uarteriis* ordei de ex*itu* g*rangie* mens*ura* ras*a* tr*ituratis* vn*de* p*er* op*er*a ij q*uarteria* iiij b*usselli et* ad tasc*h*am iiij^{xx} xvij q*uarteria* iiij b*usselli* ex c*er*ta conuenc*ione* f*act*a cu*m* consil*io* d*omi*ni ad r*eddendum* annuati*m* c xx q*uarteria* ordei n*isi* p*recium* q*uarterii* exced*at* v s. Et si exced*at* d*ict*um p*recium* v s. tunc r*espondebit* de c q*uarter*iis ordei. S*umma* c xx q*uarteria*. D*e* quib*us* In se*min*e sup*er* l acr*as* t*err*e p*er* p*er*tic*am* xxv q*uarteria* sup*er* acr*am* iiij b*usselli*. In mix*tis* inferi*us* ad lib*erationem* fam*ulorum* xxv q*uarteria*. In vend*itis* inf*erius* l q*uarteria*. Et sup*er* comp*otum* xx q*uarteria* p*ro* c s. S*umma* que s*upra*. Et eq*ue*.

Pis*e*. Et de iij q*uarteriis* vj b*ussellis* pis*arum* de ex*itu* trit*uratis* ad tasc*h*am. Et de v q*uarteriis* de eodem ex*itu* p*er* est*imationem* in siliq*uis*. S*umma* viij q*uarteria* vj b*usselli*. D*e* quib*us* In se*min*e sup*er* xv acr*as* t*er*re p*er* p*er*tic*am* iij q*uarteria* vj b*usselli* sup*er* acr*am* ij b*usselli*. In sust*entatione* ou*ium* m*atricium* temp*ore* agnell*ationis* p*er* est*imationem* in siliq*uis* v q*uarteria*. S*umma* que s*upra*. Et eq*ue*.

Vesce. Et de iij q*uarteriis* vesc*arum* de ex*itu* trit*uratis* ad t*asc*h*am*. Et de xij q*uarteriis* de eodem ex*itu* p*er* estim*ationem* in siliq*uis*. Et de ij q*uarteriis* de emp*tis* p*ro* se*mine*. S*umma* xvij q*uarteria*. D*e* quib*us* In se*mine* sup*er* xx acr*as* p*er* p*er*tic*am* v q*uarteria* sup*er* acr*am* ij b*usselli*. In susten*tatione* biden*tium* in yem*e* equor*um* *et* alior*um* au*er*ior*um* p*er* est*imationem* in siliq*uis* xij q*uarteria*. S*umma* que sup*ra*. Et eq*ue*.

Auen*a*. Et de lxxij q*uarteriis* auen*e* de ex*itu* gr*angie* trit*uratis* ad t*asc*h*am*. Et de viij q*uarteriis* de eod*em* ex*itu* p*er* est*imationem* in garb*is* ex conuenc*ione* f*act*a cu*m* consilio d*omi*ni ad r*eddendum* annuati*m* iiij[xx] q*uarteria* auene n*isi* p*recium* q*uarterii* auen*e* exced*at* ij s. iiij d. Et si exced*at* d*ictu*m p*recium* ij s. iiij d. tunc r*espondebit* de lx q*uarteriis* auen*e*. S*umma* iiij[xx] q*uarteria*. D*e* quib*us* In se*mine* sup*er* xl acr*as* t*er*re p*er* p*er*tic*am* xx q*uarteria* sup*er* acr*am* iiij b*usselli*. In p*re*ben*da* bou*um* p*er* est*imationem* in garb*is* vj q*uarteria*. In p*re*ben*da* equor*um* Carect*ariorum* p*er* a*nnum* iiij q*uarteria*. In p*re*ben*da* affr*orum* p*er* a*nnum* ij q*uarteria*. In far*ina* f*act*a p*ro* potag*io* fam*ulorum* p*er* annu*m* ij q*uarteria* iiij b*usselli*. In p*re*bend*a* equor*um* sen*escalli* ten*entis* t*ur*nos s*anct*i Mart*ini* *et* Hock*e* p*er* ij bill*as* sigill*atas* vij b*usselli*. In vend*itis* inf*ra* xxj q*uarteria* v b*usselli*. Et sup*er* comp*otum* xxiij q*uarteria* p*ro* liij s. viij d. S*umma* que sup*ra*. Et eque.

Lib*eratio* famul*orum*. Et de xxv q*uarteriis* ordei rec*eptis* sup*ra* p*ro* lib*eratione* fam*ulorum*. S*umma* xxv q*uarteria*. D*e* quib*us* In lib*eratione* j haywardi j Carect*arii* *et* ij Caruc*ariorum* p*er* annu*m* xx q*uarteria* vj b*usselli* quil*ibe*t cap*iens* q*uarterium* ad x sept*imanas*. In lib*eratione* j garc*ionis* auxil*iantis* b*er*car*io* m*atricium* temp*ore* agnell*ationis* j q*uar-terium*. In lib*eratione* j daie p*er* a*nnum* iij q*uarteria* ij b*usselli* que cap*it* q*uarterium* ad xvj sept*imanas*. S*umma* que supra. Et eq*ue*.

Equi. Et de iij equis de rem*anentibus*. Et de j de emp*to*. S*umma* iiij. D*e* quib*us* In vend*ito* j debil*is*. Et rem*anent* iij equi.

Affr*i*. Et de iiij affr*is* de rem*anentibus*. S*umma* iiij. Et rem*anent* iiij affr*i*.

Boues. Et de xx bob*us* de rem*anentibus*. Et v de emp*tis*. S*umma* xxv. D*e* quib*us* In mor*ina* j. In vend*itis* inf*ra* vj vn*de* hospic*io* d*omi*ni ij. S*umma* vij. Et rem*anent* xviij boues.

Bouett*i*. Et de j bouett*a* fe*cunda* de h*er*iecto Thom*e* Cupp*er*e. Et vend*itus* inf*ra*. Et n*ihil* rem*anet*.

Multon*es*. Et de D xx multon*ibus* de rem*anentibus*. Et de C xxxiij de hog*astris* adiu*nctis*. Et de j de h*er*iect*o* Will*elm*i Smyth*e* ante ton-s*ionem*. S*umma* DC liiij. D*e* quib*us* in mori*na* ante tons*ionem* lv. In mori*na* post tons*ionem* x d. [sic]. In vend*itis* post tons*ionem* iiij[xx] iiij. S*umma* C xlix. Et rem*anent* D v multones.

Hurt*ardi*. Et de xvj hurt*ardis* de rem*anentibus*. Et de ij de hog*astris* adiu*n*ct*is*. S*umma* xviij. D*e* quib*us* in vend*itis* post tons*ionem* v. Et rem*anent* xiij hurt*ardi*.

M*a*trice*s*. Et de ccc iiij^{xx} xvj m*a*tric*ibus* de rem*anentibus*. Et de lxxvij de hog*astris* adiu*n*ct*is*. Et de j de h*erietto* Joh*an*nis Wodecote. S*umma* cccc lxxiiij. D*e* quib*us* in mori*na* ante tons*ionem* xxx vn*de* ante agnellac*ionem* xxij. In mori*na* post tons*ionem* viij. In vend*itis* post tons*ionem* lviij. S*umma* iiij^{xx} xvj. Et rem*anent* ccc lxxviij m*a*trice*s*.

Hog*astri*. Et de cc iiij^{xx} vij hog*astris* de rem*anentibus* agn*is*. D*e* quib*us* in mori*na* ante tons*ionem* lxxv. In adiu*n*ct*is* s*upra* cum multon*ibus* c xxxiij cu*m* hurt*ardis* ij *et* cu*m* m*a*tric*ibus* lxxvij. S*umma* que sup*ra*. Et eq*ue*.

Agni. Et de ccc xxiij agnis de ex*itu* dict*arum* m*a*tric*ium* *et* no*n* pluri*bus* q*uia* xxij m*a*trices morieb*antur* ante agnell*ationem* *et* lij fu*erunt* st*e*ril*es* hoc anno. Et de c xliij de emp*tis* ante tons*ionem*. S*umma* cccc lxvj. D*e* quib*us* in mori*na* ante sep*aracionem* iiij^{xx} xviij. In *decima* xxij. In cons*uetudine* p*re*pos*iti* fabri b*e*rcar*ii* multon*um* *et* b*e*rcar*ii* ou*ium* m*a*tric*ium* ant*e* tons*ionem* iiij. In vend*itis* de ext*r*act*is* ante tons*ionem* xij. In mori*na* post sep*aracionem* *et* ant*e* tons*ionem* xxvj. In mori*na* post tons*ionem* xv. S*umma* c lxxvij. Et rem*anent* cc iiij^{xx} ix Agni.

Sus. Et de j sue de rem*anente*. Et rem*anet* j sus. D*e* porcell*is* de ex*itu* eiusdem suis n*ihil* hic q*uia* inf*ra* in den*ariis* ad fi*rmam*.

Auce. Et de j anc*er*e *et* iiij auc*is* mar*ioles* de rem*anentibus*. Et de xxiiij de ex*itu*. S*umma* xxix. D*e* quib*us* in *decima* ij. In vend*itis* inf*ra* xxij. Et rem*anent* j anc*er* *et* iiij auc*e* mar*iole*.

Capones. Et de xxiiij capon*ibus* de rem*anentibus*. Et de xxiiij de pulc*inis* inferi*us* fac*t*is. S*umma* xlviij. D*e* quib*us* in vend*itis* inf*ra* xxiiij. Et rem*anent* xxiiij capones.

Galli *et* galline. Et de j gallo et v gall*in*is de rem*anentibus*. Et de c xxv de churs*etto* ad f*est*um S*anc*ti Mart*ini*. S*umma* c xxxj. D*e* quib*us* In def*ectu* t*er*r*e* le stronge t*r*ac*t*e in d*ominicum* p*er* a*nnum* iiij. In def*ectu* t*er*re Will*elmi* de Cur*ia* p*ro* sim*i*li iiij. In def*ectu* t*er*re Rob*er*ti de Cruce p*ro* sim*i*li iiij. In def*ectu* t*er*re le Swon p*ro* sim*i*li iiij. In def*ectu* t*er*re Ric*ar*di Vaccar*ii* p*ro* sim*i*li iiij. In def*ectu* t*er*re Ric*ar*di Knaue p*ro* sim*i*li iiij. In def*ectu* terr*e* q*uo*nd*a*m Rob*er*ti Wodecote p*ro* iij di*midiis* virg*atis* t*er*re quia in man*ibus* d*omi*ni xij. In defect*u* t*er*re Joh*annis* Dauy q*uia* no*n* h*ab*et vx*or*em ij. In def*ectu* t*er*re Rog*er*i light' p*ro* sim*i*li ij. In def*ectu* t*er*re Amicie Wodecote q*uia* no*n* h*ab*et viru*m* ij. In ven-d*itis* inf*ra* iiij^{xx} iij. S*umma* c xxv. Et rem*anent* j gallus *et* v galline.

Pulcin*i*. Et de xxiiij pulc*inis* de ex*itu*. Et om*n*es comp*utantur* in capon*ibus* superius fac*t*is. Et n*ihil* rem*anet*.

Oua. Et de cc ouis de ex*itu* gallin*arum*. Et vendunt*ur* inf*ra*. Et n*ihil* rem*anet*.

Lana grossa. Et de vell*eribus* cccc lxvj mult*onum* xvj hurt*ardorum* ccc lxvij ou*ium* m*atricium et* cc xij hog*astrorum* p*r*ouen*torum* ad tonsi*onem* hoc anno. S*umma* M lxj. D*e* quib*us* in *decima* C vj veller*a*. In lib*eratis* Rece*ptori* de Wolues*eia* DCCCC lv vell*era* lan*e* pond*erantia* ij sacc*os* xlviij cl*avos*. S*umma* que sup*ra*. Et n*ihil* rem*anet*.

Lana fract*a*. Et de iij cl*avis* lan*e* fract*e* de collect*is* b*er*car*iarum* ad tons*ionem* hoc anno. Et vend*untur* infra. Et n*ihil* rem*anet*.

Lana Agn*ina*. Et de vell*eribus* ccc iiij agn*orum* p*r*ouen*torum* ad tons*ionem* hoc anno. Et vend*untur* inf*ra* pond*erantia* xj cl*avos*. Et n*ihil* rem*anet*.

Cor*ia*. Et de cor*io* j bouis de mor*ina* vt sup*ra*. Et vend*itur* inf*ra*. Et n*ihil* rem*anet*.

Pell*es* lanut*e*. Et de pell*ibus* lv mult*onum* xxx ou*ium* m*a*tric*ium et* lxxv hog*astrorum* de mor*ina* an*te* tons*ionem*. Et vend*untur* inf*ra*. Et n*ihil* rem*anet*.

Pell*es* nude. Et de pell*ibus* nud*is* x multon*um et* viij ou*ium* m*a*tric*ium* de mor*ina* post tons*ionem*. Et vend*untur* inf*ra*. Et n*ihil* rem*anet*.

Pell*es* agn*orum*. Et de pell*ibus* iiij^{xx} xviij agn*orum* de mor*ina* ante sep*a*rac*ionem*. Et vend*untur* inf*ra*. Et n*ihil* rem*anet*.

Pell*es* rott*orum*. Et de pell*ibus* xxvj agn*orum* rott*orum* de mor*ina* post sep*aracionem et* ante tons*ionem*. Et vend*untur* inf*ra*. Et n*ihil* rem*anet*.

Pellect*ria*. Et de pellect*ria* xv agn*orum* de mor*ina* post tons*ionem*. Et vend*itur* inf*ra*. Et n*ihil* rem*anet*.

Vtensilia. Et de iij caruc*is* cu*m* iij p*a*rib*us* ferram*entorum et* to*to* app*a*ratu ferr*i* p*ro* xvj bob*us* v h*er*c*iis* lign*i* j se*mi*l*i*on*e* j b*i*g*a* ferr*o* lig*ata* j p*icoso* ij sacc*is* j ventilabr*o et* j sport*a* bl*a*difer*a* de rem*anentibus*. Et rem*anent*. Et de j Carect*a* ferr*o* lig*ata* cu*m* Corda *et* scala j sell*a* Carect*aria* v coler*is* iij p*a*ribus t*r*act*uum et* v capist*r*is de rem*anentibus*. Et rem*anent*. Et de j oll*a* en*ea* cont*inente* v lagen*as* j posnet*o* j patell*a* cont*inente* v lagen*as* j patell*a* cont*inente* xij lagen*as* j lathe j vat p*ro* daier*ia* j tina j t*ri*pod*e* ij formis p*ro* case*o* j t*ri*bul*o* j siuera rot*ata* de rem*anentibus*. Et rem*anent*. Et de xj cracch*is* de rem*anentibus*. Et rem*anent*.

§§ 20. Statistics of Income, Outgo, Production, and Prices, 1208—1448.

The reeves' accounts, which provide the statistical details set forth in this section, begin only in 1208. About 1448 these accounts become what we may regard as substantially rentals, with few price entries. There are many missing rolls, sometimes the loss being due to voidances in the see of Winchester, sometimes to the accidental loss of the pipe rolls in which the accounts had been enrolled.

At least as early as the 1340's there was a tendency for the reeves' returns to become standardized, and even more so from about 1370 onwards. The value of the statistics after the lease of 1407 is, of course, greatly diminished. The yearly averages (in roman type) which are found in the manuscripts themselves are not so accurate as those (in italics) which are worked out, because in the case of the former the total price is said to be greater or smaller by a few pence. Of course the discrepancy is slight.

Where the manuscript could not be read because torn, the fact has been indicated by M.T. (manuscript torn); and where dulled or blurred, by Ill. (illegible). Figures which were not in the original manuscripts have generally been italicized.

The dating of documents has been a difficult and uncertain matter. We have accepted the revised dating of Dr. Hubert Hall and Sir William Beveridge, checking up the sequence of documents by an examination of various items. The amount of money owing to the lord in one document should be the arrears in the next year's account. The number of lambs and wethers of one account is found entered in the account for the following year. By such comparisons, the sequence can be determined with certainty. And for our purpose, in most cases the sequence has been of greater significance than the precise year. Indeed, for the determination of the yield of grain per acre this has been absolutely vital.

Much of the price material here presented in detail has already been summarized for the chief sub-periods of the period 1208–1448.[1]

[1] See above, § 19, pp. 62–66.

CHIEF SOURCES OF THE LORD'S INCOME

Year	Fixed rent											Grain sold			Stock sold			Yield of the manor			Sum total received		
	Gross			Acquit-tance		Default		Net			Rent thru pestilence												
	£	s.	d.	s.	d.	s.	d.	£	s.	d.		£	s.	d.	£	s.	d.	£	s.	d.	£	s.	d.
1208–09	10	12	0	5	0	7	0	9	9	0		9	14	6				14	17	2	46	16	2
1210–11	10	12	0	5	0	7	0	9	9	0								7	3	10	29	13	4
1211–12	13	2	6	61	0	7	0	9	14	6		15	14	11				19	8	7½	48	15	0½
1213–14	13	2	9	55	8	12	4	9	14	9			8	10				29	4	2½	49	19	9½
1215–16	13	3	9	55	8	105	8	5	2	5		9	13	8				23	2	2½	39	9	11½
1217–18	13	3	9	51	8	17	8	11	13	3½		9	2	0½				10	2	0½	38	14	2½
1218–19	13	5	2	51	8	17	8	9	15	10		9	9	8				16	7	0	40	10	8
1219–20	13	5	2	51	8	17	8	9	15	10		15	8	2½				19	9	2	48	10	6½
1220–21	13	5	2	55	8	12	4	9	17	2		25	1	8							67	9	7
1223–24	13	5	8	50	4	17	8	9	17	8		19	18	9				28	7	8½	62	6	9½
1224–25	13	7	0	50	4	17	8	9	19	0		29	13	7½				23	7	6½	65	19	6
1225–26	13	7	0	55	8	15	0	9	16	4		29	6	2				38	2	7	79	16	3
1226–27	13	7	6	44	4	23	0	10	0	10		42	2	4				32	4	11½	87	13	0½
1231–32	13	8	6	50	4	28	4	9	9	10		50	8	6				28	19	4½	94	13	11½
1232–33	13	8	6	55	8	23	0	9	9	10		49	4	8				36	3	7½	99	6	5½
1235–36	13	8	6	47	8	33	8	9	7	2		40	11	3				45	17	3½	97	14	8½
1236–37	13	8	6	47	8	33	8	9	7	2		62	11	3				49	12	3	124	3	9
1244–45	13	9	6	52	4	31	0	9	6	2		33	0	0				39	3	11½	107	7	10½
1245–46	13	9	6	57	0	25	8	9	6	10		37	11	4				36	14	6½	88	8	4½
1246–47	13	9	6	58	4	25	8	9	5	6		67	1	1½				45	13	11	124	9	10½
1247–48	13	9	6	58	4	25	8	9	5	6		60	10	0½				42	14	3½	116	7	10
1248–49	13	10	0	63	8	20	4	9	0	6		30	0	7½				42	7	1¼	84	7	6¾
1251–52	13	9	6	63	8	20	4	9	7	0		30	19	10½				36	10	7½	82	7	4
1252–53	13	11	0	63	8	20	4	9	7	0		28	7	4½				46	5	2	90	10	0½
1253–54	13	11	0	63	8	20	4	9	7	0		24	5	6				48	7	3½		[M.T.]	
1254–55	13	11	0	63	8	20	4	9	7	0		25	3	5½				45	5	8	83	15	7½
1256–57	13	11	0	63	8	20	4	9	7	0		65	5	5				51	11	0	130	19	10

1257–58	13	11	0	63	8	20	4	9	7	0		87	0	11		48	15	2½	148	6	11½
1264–65	13	11	1	58	4	20	4	9	12	5		36	9	9		15	2	6	64	1	10
1265–66	13	11	2	55	0	20	4	9	15	10		34	6	6		25	1	2¾	87	6	0¾
1267–68	13	11	2	51	8	20	4	9	19	2		32	19	9		15	2	4¾	64	0	15¾
1268–69	13	11	2	51	8	20	4	9	19	2		36	16	5		62	4	10	111	5	11
1270–71	13	11	2	51	8	20	4	9	19	2		41	14	1		21	8	6	75	11	3
1271–72	13	11	2	51	8	20	4	9	19	2		32	4	4		15	0	14	62	15	10
1272–73	13	11	2	51	8	20	4	9	19	2		18	7	5½		48	17	5	99	2	2½
1273–74	13	11	2	51	8	20	4	9	19	2		19	13	0							
1274–75	13	11	2	51	8	20	4	9	19	2		43	4	10		54	14	6½	111	0	0½
1276–77	13	11	2	51	8	20	4	9	19	2		52	5	6½		65	5	1½	130	11	6
1277–78	13	11	2	51	8	20	4	9	19	2		52	17	8		56	11	11½	122	2	3½
1282–83	13	11	2	51	8	20	4	9	19	2		56	10	10½		12	4	10½	94	3	3
1283–84	13	11	2	51	8	20	4	9	19	2		12	11	2½		6	9	0½	30	18	6
1284–85	13	11	2	51	8	20	4	9	19	2		15	9	8		15	6	9½	48	17	3½
1285–86	13	11	2	51	8	20	4	9	19	2		24	4	9½		29	15	6½	77	6	1
1286–87	13	11	2	51	8	20	4	9	19	2		19	0	1¼		28	4	7¾	61	1	6
1287–88	14	0	14	57	0	20	4	10	3	10		17	18	7		23	18	9¼	56	3	4¼
1288–89	14	0	14	55	8	20	4	10	5	2		20	5	3		27	18	11	60	13	11
1289–90	14	0	14	55	8	20	4	10	5	2		35	12	4½		35	16	2	83	10	9½
1290–91	14	0	14	55	8	20	4	10	5	2		34	13	6		32	2	3¼	79	14	11¼
1291–92	14	0	14	55	8	20	4	10	5	2		18	9	3		36	19	8	48	14	2
1292–93	14	0	14	55	8	20	4	10	5	2		15	9	9½		35	19	11	74	16	8½
1296–97	14	0	14	55	8	20	4	10	5	2		35	0	5½		18	13	1	68	0	15½
1297–98	14	0	14	54	8	20	4	10	6	2		39	3	7½		23	2	7½	74	15	11
1298–99	14	0	14	55	8	20	4	10	5	2		44	3	9		14	18	3½	70	18	2½
1299–00	14	0	18	55	8	20	4	10	5	6		36	17	11		22	4	9½	71	7	4½
1300–01	14	0	19	55	8	20	4	10	5	7		8	3	5		18	0	11	38	15	6
1301–02	14	0	19	55	8	20	4	10	5	7		23	19	8		19	19	0	56	3	3
1302–03	14	0	19	55	8	20	4	10	5	7		25	11	8½		24	13	0½	63	7	7
1304–05 [1]	11	0	4	34	4	15	3	8	10	8			4	3¼		8	13	10	20	4	0
1305–06	14	1	7	53	8	20	4	10	7	7		16	16	11½		20	10	2	57	1	0¾
1306–07	14	1	7	53	3	20	4	10	7	0		6	12	0½		26	2	4½	47	16	7¾
1307–08	14	1	7	55	8	20	4	10	5	7		20	12	1½		6	13	1¾	60	5	7¼

1. This account is for only part of the year; some figures, however, seem to be complete in certain cases.

CHIEF SOURCES OF THE LORD'S INCOME (Continued)

Year	Fixed rent: Gross £	s.	d.	Acquittance s.	d.	Default s.	d.	Net £	s.	d.	Rent thru pestilence	Grain sold £	s.	d.	Stock sold	Yield of the manor £	s.	d.	Sum total received £	s.	d.
1308–09	14	1	7	55	8	20	4	10	5	7		23	4	3¼		67	4	5¼	108	13	7
1309–10	14	1	7	55	8	20	4	10	5	7		44	12	9½		96	7	0½	157	8	8
1310–11	14	1	7	55	8	20	4	10	5	7		26	6	8		75	14	2¼	115	16	1
1311–12	14	1	7	55	8	20	4	10	5	7		19	7	2¾		65	4	6¼	76	12	4¼
1312–13	14	1	7	53	0	20	4	10	8	3		36	5	3½		70	12	11¼	120	2	2¾
1313–14	14	1	9	50	4	20	4	10	11	1		39	4	4¼		80	13	5½	133	4	4½
1314–15	14	1	9	50	4	20	4	10	11	1											
1315–16[1]	9	4	1½	42	3	19	1	6	2	9½		57	6	1		32	11	10½	138	13	7¼
1316–17[1]	14	1	9	53	0	20	4	10	8	5		68	0	1¼		65	8	3¼	151	11	5¼
1317–18	14	1	9	53	0	20	4	10	8	5		45	7	4		69	10	4½	129	4	5¼
1318–19	14	1	9	53	0	20	4	10	18	0[2]		32	17	5		141	14	3½	194	14	6½
1320[1]	8	3	8	21	2	10	2	6	12	4							97	2¾	14	3	8¾
1320–21	14	11	1	47	8	20	4	11	3	1						95	4	11¼	111	13	1½
1324–25	14	11	3	39	8	20	4	11	11	3		49	12	4¼			116	1	73	4	3¾
1325–26	14	11	3	39	8	20	4	11	11	3		42	5	7¾		8	2	5	68	2	11
1326–27	14	11	3	45	0	20	4	11	5	11		20	1	11		37	7	4¼	71	9	10
1327–28	14	12	9	45	0	20	4	11	7	5						45	9	2	69	4	4¼
1328–29	15	0	11	45	0	20	4	11	15	7		31	17	7		122	6	8	143	5	11
1329–30	15	0	11	45	0	20	4	11	15	7		45	2	2¼		54	18	6¼	70	1	7¼
1330–31	15	0	11	45	0	20	4	11	15	7		28	[——][3]				[M.T.]		68	1	5
1331–32	15	0	11	45	0	20	4	11	15	7		31	18	0		109	13	8½	125	12	4½
1332–33	15	0	11	45	0	20	4	11	15	7		21	9	8¼		71	8	11¾	86	9	8¾
1334–35	15	0	11	42	4	20	4	11	18	3		27	18	11[4]		17	8	0	70	13	0
1335–36	15	0	11	42	4	20	4	11	18	3		31	11	3¾[4]		19	12	11¼	70	5	1
1336–37	15	0	11	42	4	20	4	11	18	3		25	2	2¾[4]		9	6	8½	49	11	0¾
1337–38	15	0	11	42	4	20	4	11	18	3						31	4	0¾	46	3	9¼
1338–39	15	0	11	42	4	20	4	11	18	3						29	11	6	43	18	0

1339–40	15 0 11	42 4	20 4	11 18 3		19 5 0½	57 0[5]	9 3 6	45 5 2
1340–41	15 0 11	42 4	20 4	11 18 3		18 12 10	61 8	7 13 4¾	45 4 0¾
1341–42	15 0 11	45 0	20 4	11 15 7		22 11 8½	7 15 2	7 18 7	51 17 7½
1342–43	15 0 11	45 0	20 4	11 15 7		22 16 4	8 8 8	7 13 8	54 10 3½
1343–44	15 0 11	45 0	20 4	11 15 7		34 19 2¼[6]		7 5 11½	67 12 5¾
1344–45[1]	11 16 10	44 8	15 3	6 16 11[2]		26 5 8¼	58 7 8½	7 16 4½	101 12 9¼
1345–46[1]	15 0 11	43 8	20 4	11 16 11		17 3 6	46 6	5 8 9	58 1 10½
1346–47	15 0 11	45 0	20 4	11 15 7		32 18 10¾	40 4	9 3 10¾	59 19 5
1347–48	15 0 11	45 0	20 4	11 15 7		37 11 5	9 2 6	9 15 8	69 19 10
1348–49	15 0 11	22 8	20 4	12 17 11		14 0 8½	8 16 8	118 0½	55 0 2¼
1349–50	15 0 11	21 0	26 4	12 13 7		27 6 11¾	12 2 4	10 2 1¾	48 7 3¾
1350–51	15 0 11	15 8	29 10	12 15 5		31 14 8	16 9 4	10 3 1¼	76 13 5
1351–52	15 0 11	15 8	45 0	12 0 3		49 0 4¼	21 6 8	10 6 1	97 3 7¼
1352–53	15 0 11	15 8	24 7	13 0 8		29 15 10	10 17 6	11 6 2½	70 1 2½
1353–54	15 0 11	15 8	25 2	13 0 1		19 15 6	8 19 5	11 17 0	57 18 1
1354–55	15 0 11	15 8	26 4	12 18 11		26 19 0½	12 4 2	12 13 5	69 8 9½
1355–56	15 0 11	15 8	20 4	13 4 11		36 12 3¾	6 2 4	11 4 7	70 9 4¾
1356–57	15 0 11	15 8	20 4	13 4 11		29 18 7	7 6 1	10 17 4½	63 7 3½
1357–58	15 0 11	21 0	20 4	12 19 7		41 0 1½	8 17 5	10 8 10½	78 9 1½
1358–59	15 0 11	21 0	20 4	12 19 7		46 9 2¼	11 9 7	11 7 8½	80 3 4¾
1359–60	15 0 11	21 0	20 4	12 19 7		29 10 3	13 19 3	10 12 3½	69 0 8
1360–61	15 0 11	21 0	20 4	12 19 7		38 6 4½	[M.T.]	[M.T.]	66 11 8¾
1361–62	15 0 11	21 0	20 4	12 19 7		22 5 7¾	12 3 8	8 10 10¾	62 11 1
1362–63	15 0 11	21 0	20 4	12 19 7		15 18 8¼	11 17 5	9 2 9¼	52 11 3½
1363–64	15 0 11	21 0	20 4	12 19 7		47 14 8	16 9 10	8 18 0	89 8 0
1364–65	15 0 11	21 0	20 4	12 19 7		26 18 0	12 9 9	9 3 4¼	65 11 7¼
1365–66	15 0 11	23 8	20 4	12 16 11		19 3 5½	7 4 8	9 2 10½	175 4 1½
1366–67	15 0 11	26 4	20 4	12 14 3			13 12 11	8 17 8	103 4 8¼
1367–68	15 0 11	23 8	22 4[7]	*12 14 11*		40 18 6½	18 5 2	10 2 8¼	120 9 7½
1368–69	15 0 11	21 0	22 4	12 17 7		42 2 9½	19 4 6	11 9 1½	93 19 2¼
1369–70	15 0 11	23 8	20 4	12 16 11		69 10 4	23 16 5	14 17 1	138 6 3¼
1370–71	15 0 11	23 8	20 4	12 16 11		42 13 8	19 2 4	13 14 10¼	109 18 7¼

1. This account is for only part of the year; some figures, however, seem to be complete in certain cases.
2. Sic.
3. Manuscript is torn.
4. Includes amount from sale of stock.
5. Hitherto these amounts are included in figures under yield of the manor or as is specially noted in the grain sold figures.
6. Includes stock sales.
7. Increase in default is due to pestilence.

CHIEF SOURCES OF THE LORD'S INCOME (CONTINUED)

Year	Fixed rent												Grain sold			Stock sold			Yield of the manor			Sum total received		
	Gross			Acquit-tance		Default		Net			Rent[1] thru pestilence													
	£	s.	e.	s.	d.	s.	d.	£	s.	d.	s.	d.	£	s.	d.	£	s.	d.	£	s.	d.	£.	s.	d.
1371–72	15	0	11	23	8	20	4	12	16	11			39	15	9	18	9	2	11	16	8	108	14	5
1372–73	15	0	11	23	8	20	4	12	16	11			33	1	9½	13	19	8	13	6	6¼	108	11	6¾
1373–74	15	0	11	22	4	20	4	12	18	3			31	7	6	6	1	10	14	9	6	90	8	10½
1375–76	15	0	11	23	8	41	4[2]	11	15	11			34	1	1	19	16	11				106	0	8½
1376–77	15	0	11	23	8	20	4	12	16	11			21	12	5	14	1	4				63	0	6¾
1377–78	15	0	11	23	8	41	4[2]	11	15	11			22	11	10¼	11	14	10	10	[——][3]		67	2	5¾
1378–79	15	0	11	23	8	41	4	11	15	11			27	3	10	12	8	2	10	11	0	70	19	0½
1379–80	15	0	11	23	8	41	4	11	15	11			22	10	6	15	18	3	11	7	0	78	0	10
1381–82	15	0	11	23	8	41	4	11	15	11			14	5	10½				27	10	3	[Ill.]		
1382–83	15	0	11	23	8	41	4	11	15	11			17	17	6½	23	[——][3]		8	4	9½	74	14	0
1383–84	15	0	11	23	8	41	4	11	15	11			17	10	11½	16	1	4	7	19	8	62	11	5¼
1384–85	15	0	11	23	8	41	4	11	15	11			16	8	9	21	0	0	9	13	9	68	9	0½
1385–86	15	0	11	23	8	41	4	11	15	11			31	8	6	18	2	4	11	10	1	81	1	2
1387–88	15	0	11	23	8	41	4	11	15	11			22	10	9	10	5	2				58	7	11½
1388–89	15	0	11	23	8	41	4	11	15	11			20	8	1	14	3	4	11	17	9	65	3	8
1390–91	15	0	11	23	8	41	4	11	15	11			*37*	*18*	*11*		[M.T.]		9	4	*6*	91	5	4
1392–93	15	0	11	23	8	41	4	11	15	11			20	13	9	*15*	*10*	*2*	9	4	11½	64	18	4½
1393–94	15	0	11	23	8	41	4	11	15	11			19	4	10	14	2	10	8	19	1	65	19	2
1394–95	15	0	11	23	8	41	4	11	15	11			18	1	3½	10	3	0	10	12	2½	60	17	7½
1395–96	15	0	11	23	8	41	4	*11*	*15*	*11*			18	12	4¾	15	12	6	8	6	8½	62	19	3¾
1398–99	15	0	11	23	8	41	4	11	15	11	9	0	15	4	7½		[M.T.]		9	15	9	57	4	3½
1399–00	15	0	11	*23*	*8*	41	4	11	15	11	9	0	21	8	3½	13	18	10	8	13	2	65	15	10½
1400–01	15	0	11	23	8	41	4	11	15	11	9	0	18	13	6	*20*	*16*	*1*	10	0	6½	73	12	10½
1402–03	15	*0*	*11*	23	8	41	4	11	15	11	*8*	*8*		[M.T.]			[M.T.]			[M.T.]		83	19	10½

1406–07	15	0	11	23	8	41	4	11	16	11	22	0	19	12	8	15	2	6				64	19	5½
1408–09	*15*	*0*	*11*	23	8	41	4	11	15	11	22	0	28	18	5	17	9	8	8	18	5	74	14	4
1409–10	15	1	11	23	8	41	4	11	16	11	22	0	33	4	0½	17	10	4	7	2	2	76	16	3½
1410–11	15	1	11	23	8	41	4	11	16	11	22	0	29	15	2½	12	17	8	9	1	5½	79	15	3
1411–12	15	1	11	23	8	41	4	11	16	11	22	0	28	18	9	15	12	8	8	16	10	75	14	0
1412–13	15	1	11	23	8	41	4	11	16	11	22	0	19	6	0	14	6	8	7	0	1½	77	4	8½
1413–14	15	1	11	23	8	41	4	11	16	11	22	0	15	5	3	18	5	2	6	17	6	75	1	7
1414–15	15	1	11	23	8	41	4	11	16	11	22	0	6	9	0	18	18	0	7	7	9½	71	5	10½
1418–19	15	1	11	23	8	41	4	11	16	11	22	0	6	11	10	21	17	0	8	1	2½	73	17	11½
1419–20	15	1	11	23	8	41	4	11	16	11	22	0	12	14	11	18	12	0	7	5	9½	76	13	11½
1420–21	15	1	11	23	8	42	4	11	15	11	22	0	7	19	6	22	11	0	5	7	7	79	3	9
1421–22	15	1	11	23	8	42	4	11	15	11	22	0	11	13	4½	17	16	10	6	1	1	98	14	6½
1422–23	15	*0*	*11*	23	8	45	0	11	12	3	28	8	7	5	5½	14	1	8	6	11	10½	79	9	1
1423–24	15	0	11	23	8	45	0	11	12	3	28	8	8	3	6½	8	6	1	5	19	6	62	10	6½
1424–25	15	0	11	24	8[4]	45	0	11	12	3	28	8	9	7	11	5	10	11	8	4	10	63	8	11
1425–26	15	0	11	23	8	45	0	11	12	3	28	8	8	15	2	6	16	2	6	9	8½	73	5	9½
1427–28	15	0	11	23	8	45	0	11	12	3	28	8	8	6	4½	14	8	9	5	5	11½	85	1	10¾
1429–30	15	0	11	23	8	45	0	11	12	3	28	8	10	7	0	20	0	6	5	2	3	78	5	3½
1430–31	15	0	11	23	8	45	0	11	12	3	28	8	10	5	9½	16	1	11	5	0	1½	78	4	9
1431–32	15	0	11	23	8	45	0	11	12	3	28	8	9	13	0½	10	19	2	5	18	1½	77	11	7
1432–33	15	0	11	23	8	45	0	11	12	3	28	8	10	8	2¼	14	5	2	5	15	3	91	11	3¼
1433–34	15	0	11	23	8	45	0	11	12	3	28	8	6	3	2½	15	0	8	5	12	0½	68	12	7
1434–35[5]	15	0	11	23	8	45	0	11	12	3	28	8	8	9	5	10	9	0	6	0	1	65	14	7½
1435–36	15	0	11	23	8	45	0	11	12	3	28	8	6	7	0	9	14	10	5	10	0	66	12	7¼
1438–39	15	0	11	23	8	45	0	11	12	3	28	8	16	19	4	11	1	4	5	4	8	71	19	4
1440–41	15	0	11	23	8	45	0	11	12	3	28	8	7	2	10½	13	5	10	5	13	2	66	0	0½
1441–42	15	0	11	23	8	45	0	11	12	3	28	8	4	15	5½	12	19	8	5	4	11	63	4	6½
1447–48	15	2	7	23	8	42	4	11	16	7	22	0	10	13	8	10	16	10	5	10	5½	56	3	5½
1448–49	15	2	7	23	8	42	4	11	16	7	22	0	15	14	8¾	4	18	1	11	0	1½	67	7	4½

1. Rents from tenements vacant because of pestilence.
2. Increase in default is due to pestilence.
3. MS. torn.
4. Sic.
5. Beginning at this point is an item, called chevage, of 8d., which continues through the following 4 years here represented. In 1447–48 it became 2s. 8d.; and in 1448–49, 3s. 4d.

SOME IMPORTANT ITEMS IN THE LORD'S INCOME

Year	Pannage		Herbage		Pasture		Lactage	Foldage		Curtilage		Agistment	Underwood			Woods		Acres rented			Court dues		Recognition		Commutation of services		Inns rented		Sold on account [1]
	s.	d.	s.	d.	s.	d.		s.	d.	s.	d.		acres	s.	d.	s.	d.	acres	s.	d.	s.	d.	s.	d.	s.	d.	s.	d.	
1208–09	32	5	3	8															9	10	57	6							
1210–11	28	6	3	0														24	9	6	71	0							
1211–12	4	8½	24	11½	5	4													10	3	77	0							
1213–14	5	8	17	5	3	0									8			2	0	9	50	10							
1215–16	11	4	24	8	4	0													10	9	31	8							
1217–18	6	5	22	9	22	0													13	7	50	2							
1218–19	4	0	27	1	16	0										1	0		14	2	98	2					2	0[2]	
1219–20	5	8	21	3½	30	2													25	5	77	4					1	6	
1220–21	8	8	27	1	19	6												4	1	3	96	4					2	0	
1223–24	11	5	24	4	1	6												14	4	0	82	8			1	2			
1224–25	9	2	28	1	2	0								1	1			9	2	10	49	4			1	4	1	0	
1225–26	7	0	27	5	1	6				1	6[3]			131	6½			10	3	3	51	2			2	4	1	0	
1226–27	4	7	26	0½	1	0				6	6[3]			13	5			7	3	4	65	7			6	0	2	0	
1231–32	3	7½	23	5½	2	0				12	6[3]							3½	1	9	116	2					1	0	
1232–33	3	4	23	4	1	10				10	0[3]			4	6			1	0	6	88	4					1	6	
1235–36	15	6	32	0						3	0[4]					10	0	9½	4	9	39	0					none		
1236–37	6	10	32	3½						4	0[5]					14	0	12½	6	3	53	0					0	6	
1244–45	8	5½	37	1	49	3				6	3			28	9½	171	10	14	7	0	63	0			40	0	2	0	
1245–46	12	9	35	7	41	0				3	6[3]							36	17	7	95	8					1	0	
1246–47	8	5½	36	1½						3	9							22	10	9	49	4					2	0	
1247–48	6	1	36	8	9	0				1	3			75	0			21	10	6	78	0					1	0	
1248–49	6	1½	37	8	11	6				1	0			58	4			17	8	6	53	10					2	0	
1251–52	7	7½	31	8	10	6		2	8	2	6			32	8			31	15	6	109	10		6	5	6	2	0	
1252–53	8	1½	32	7½	12	3		3	2	2	6					28	8	28	14	0	130	6		6	4	0	2	0	
1253–54	[Ill.]		31	5½	10	7				2	6			30	0	112	0	23	11	6	[M.T.]			6	5	6	2	0	
1254–55	8	8	32	7	6	2		1	10	2	0							20	10	0	78	6	1	0	8	0	2	0	

1256–57	8	8	32	9	2	6				4	4	6						21	10	6	95	10		6			2	0
1257–58	9	8	36	0	4	0					2	6						24	12	0	63	4		6			2	0
1264–65	5	9½	38	6½	27	6					3	0				22	0	24	12	0	50	8	2	0			2	0
1265–66	10	7	52	0	31	6					3	0				18	0	24	12	0	58	0	2	0	2	0	2	0
1267–68[6]	12	4½	36	4½	35	4½			1	2	3	0		8	0			24	12	0			52	0	2	0	2	0
1268–69	5	10	37	0	36	1			1	3	3	0						24	12	0	59	8	51	6	2	0	2	0
1270–71	8	6½	38	4	45	6			1	3	3	0						24	12	0	48	0	1	6	2	0	2	0
1271–72	9	10	40	9	3	0			1	3	3	0						24	12	0	74	6	1	6	2	0	2	0
1272–73	7	7½	54	0	12	6			1	4	3	0						24	12	0	44	10	1	6	2	0	2	0
1273–74	14	1	39	15	14	3			1	5	3	0						24	12	0	44	0	1	6	2	0		
1274–75	10	10	41	7	16	0			3	10	3	0						24	12	0	60	0	1	6	2	0	1	0
1276–77	12	1½	43	7	11	8			2	8	3	0						24	12	0	60	8	1	0	2	0	1	0
1277–78	3	7	41	1	10	2			2	10	3	0		56	0			24	12	0	52	0	1	6	2	0	1	0
1282–83	9	8	31	5	11	2			2	2	3	0		18	0			24	12	0	306	10	1	6	2	0		
1283–84	10	8			54	11½			3	0											36	7	1	6	2	0		
1284–85	4	6	34	2	30	11			3	9				8	4	91	11				160	8	2	0	4	6		
1285–86	9	10	54	8½	37	2½			4	6	13	0		25	3½			24	12	0	284	7	2	0	2	0		
1286–87	11	1½	101	2	17	6			3	9	49	0									70	11	2	0	2	0		
1287–88	11	6	52	13	15	6			4	1	3	0						24	12	0	79	11	2	3	2	0		
1288–89	12	0	50	0	17	0			3	6	3	0		18	0			24	12	0	42	1	2	6	2	0		
1289–90	13	8	36	6	21	0			2	1	3	0						24	12	0	34	7	2	6	2	0		
1290–91	8	8	35	8½	23	8			2	3	3	0						24	12	0	43	6	2	6	2	0		
1291–92	8	9	29	5	28	10			2	4	3	0		22	0			24	12	0	57	8			2	0		
1292–93	[Ill.]		[Ill.]		39	11			[Ill.]		3	0						24	12	0	56	9	2	6	2	0		
1296–97	4	7	22	3	13	0			2	8	3	0						24	12	0	90	1	2	6	2	0		
1297–98	3	5	25	0	12	0			2	1	3	0						24	12	0	41	5	2	3	2	0		
1298–99	4	7	30	2		9					3	0						24	12	0	29	1	1	9	2	0		
1299–00	5	1	27	4		6					3	0						24	12	0	37	5	1	9	2	0		
1300–01	10	2½	32	7	5	3	24	8½	12	0	3	0						24	12	0	43	10	1	9	2	0		
1301–02	6	2½	45	4	11	9	20	4	2	8	3	0						24	12	0	37	3	1	9	2	0		
1302–03	[Ill.]						14	4			3	0						24	12	0	55	7	1	9	2	0		
1304–05	43	4[7]			14	8	6	6			3	0				29	1	23	12	0	54	2	1	3	2	0		

1. Not on credit but entered on the back of the account either because sold late or in small amounts; or possibly just charged against the reeve.
2. Rent from 2 inns.
3. Messuage rent.
4. Messuage rent, 4s. 6d.
5. Messuage rent, 5s.
6. Beginning with this year is the yearly rental of 1 lb. of cummin from the estate called the Hoo. For income from churchscot see the chickens account.
7. Herbage included.

SOME IMPORTANT ITEMS IN THE LORD'S INCOME (CONTINUED)

Year	Pannage [1]		Herbage		Pasture		Lactage		Foldage		Curtilage		Agistment	Underwood			Woods		Acres rented			Court dues		Recognition		Commutation of services		Inns rented	Sold on account	
	s.	d.	s.	d.	s.	d.	s.	d.	s.	d.	s.	d.		acres	s.	d.	s.	d.	acres	s.	d.	s.	d.	s.	d.	s.	d.		s.	d.
1305–06	36	9			17	4					3	0		22	64	6			24	12	0	41	11	1	9	2	0		142	. 8¼
1306–07	48	6			14	1	12	10			3	0		6½	17	3	40	0	24	12	0	56	8	1	9				36	9¾
1307–08	29	0½			9	0¾											31	8	15½	48	0	62	8						52	11½
1308–09	[M.T.]						3	11						9	27	0						25	10							
1309–10	12	9½	29	11	10	0	22	8						5	15	0						120	10	3	3					
1310–11	11	6½	25	0	13	2	5	1¼						5	16	6	6	4				67	6	3	3					
1311–12	38	6½			15	1								10	35	10½	19	4				79	8	2	3					5
1312–13	32	5			13	6	7	8						10	40	0						53	6						8	0½
1313–14	11	6	30	4	11	4								10	40	0	120	0				53	3	2	3					
1314–15	13	11	32	0	12	4								10	41	0								2	3					
1315–16	10	10½	26	3	12	4								5	10	0						23	4						260	10
1316–17	3	3	25	11	9	4																43	2						109	2¾
1317–18	5	1½	28	11	10	4	7	11						5	10	0						74	3	4	0					
1318–19	[M.T.]				6	9	7	10½						10	30	0						181	1							
1320			9	8	1	8																		54	0					
1320–21	10	6½	13	11	11	4								6	26	0						100	10	5	0					
1324–25 [2]	31	0			17	11			5	0				3	12	0	21	0				106	8	5	6	6	8		12	5½
1325–26	31	9			24	3			1	4				5	15	0	18	0				84	6	9	6	6	8		29	6¼
1326–27	33	4			26	0								5	16	8						45	6¼	9	0	6	8			1½
1327–28	6	11½	23	1	25	8								1½	5	0						239	2	8	6	6	8			
1328–29	4	5½	34	5	31	8								3	10	0						176	3	7	6	6	8			
1329–30	1	0	40	0	17	4	75	10														60	0	7	6	6	8			
1330–31	11	0	33	5	24	4																89	8	7	6	6	8			
1331–32	3	8	57	7½	22	4	31	0						5	17	6						75	5	7	0	6	8			
1332–33	4	11	39	2	32	8								8½	25	6						58	2	7	0	6	8			

1334–35	35 11		16 8	6 9	10 0			6 18 9	16 8			78 1	7 0	6 8		26 9
1335–36	37 2½		11 4		8 4			5 15 0	19 6			96 10	8 0	6 8		38 9
1336–37	38 4½		15 6	16 0½				6½ 19 9	14 2			39 2	6 9	6 8		18 0½
1337–38	6 0	40 9½	21 4					5 15 0				56 0	5 6	6 8		23 6
1338–39	5 8½	38 7½	3 10					3 11 0				42 5	5 6	6 8		4
1339–40	6 11½	24 18	21 10	3 2½			2 4					31 11	5 3	6 8		3 2½
1340–41	4 10	22 8	18 10					11 4½				71 3	5 3	6 8		1 6
1341–42	3 2½	23 2	21 8				2 3½	15 0			9	45 1	5 3	6 8		6 3
1342–43	4 11	23 9	25 1				5 6					69 0½	5 0	6 8		2 0
1343–44	4 11½	23 0	11 4						17 3			58 4	4 6	6 8		5 6
1344–45	3 5	25 9	6 8								50 0	42 2	0	0		2 5
1345–46	5 0	44 0	10 10	6 2			5 0					40 11	4 6	13 4		14 9½
1346–47	5 3½	28 4	10 10				4 0	10 33 4	16 6			32 0	4 6	13 4		4 2½
1347–48	5 4½	31 11	11 10					6 20 0				29 11	4 0	13 4		3
1348–49	1 10	26 3	22 5	22 0								243 4	6	13 4		22 11
1349–50	3 4		11 8				6 0	6 20 0	1 4			16 1	1 0	70 0		19 1¾
1350–51	9 11	28 9	13 9					4½ 15 0						75 0		31 6¾
1351–52	5 10	29 2	16 2				6 2	10 0			10	65 0		70 0		25 3
1352–53	5 9½	32 8	19 6				4 5	13 4			6 4	81 1		70 0		20 11
1353–54	10 7	35 2	18 2					6 20 0			1 7	46 10		70 0		39 3
1354–55	13 5	36 3	17 6					6½ 21 8				84 8		70 0		7 8
1355–56	19 9	29 6	9 10				7 1	7 23 4			24 0	49 5		70 0		25 6
1356–57	13 7	27 8	15 6				5 3	5 16 8				26 0		70 0		14 4
1357–58	17 3	24 0	18 4					6 20 0				60 9		[Ill.]		42 4½
1358–59	19 0	27 1	16 6					8 26 8				[Ill.]		70 0		10 1
1359–60	17 8	26 7	12 10					8 27 6				[Ill.]		63 4		9 8
1360–61	16 5	24 1	12 10					8 28 4						[Ill.]		16 1
1361–62	12 5	23 6	19 10					5 16 8				12 3½		70 0		
1362–63	9 2	23 4	15 10	1 4½				5½ 8 4				34 10		70 0		18 0
1363–64	14 7	24 0	11 0					6 20 0				60 11		70 0		5 0
1364–65	10 7	25 5	18 0					6½ 21 8				75 5		70 0		5 6
1365–66[3]	18 0½	27 9	10 10					7 23 4				97 5		70 0		

1. Herbage included where the figure is large.
2. For this and the two following years the lord received as agistment of pigs on stubble, 4s. 3½d., 2s. 11d., 2s. 2½d. respectively.
3. This year occurs the sum of £121 18s. 9½d. as outside receipts (forensica recepta), probably from other manors. The next year the amount from the same was £29 9s. 0½d.

SOME IMPORTANT ITEMS IN THE LORD'S INCOME (CONTINUED)

Year	Pannage s. d.	Herbage s. d.	Pasture s. d.	Lactage s. d.	Foldage	Curtilage	Agistment s. d.	Underwood acres	Underwood s. d.	Woods s. d.	Acres rented acres	Acres rented s. d.	Court dues s. d.	Recognition s. d.	Commutation of services s. d.	Inns rented	Sold on account s. d.
1366–67	13 5½	24 0	14 0	28 0			8 5	3	10 0				69 11		70 0		11 0
1367–68	14 11½	23 8	12 4	30 6			9 0½	5	16 8			2 3	84 6	50 0	65 0		21 3½
1368–69	16 5½	25 2	12 10	31 2			6 0½	12	41 8			3 10	43 7		65 0		12 1
1369–70	15 7½	28 8	17 10	56 2			7 2½	23	76 8			12 0	89 8		65 0		185 10½
1370–71	23 1½	31 10	18 4					16	64 0				108 0		70 0		219 3
1371–72	17 11	29 4	13 0				9 6	9	46 3			8 3	54 6		70 0		43 0
1372–73	25 9½	29 11	10 4										148 10		60 4½		227 7
1373–74	17 5	27 6	11 4				7 6	12	62 6				43 11		38 4		114 7½
1375–76	17 6½	38 0	11 10				7 1	12	60 0				53 9		26 0		16 2
1376–77	15 6½	[M.T.]	[M.T.]					7½	37 6				32 6		26 10½		13 0
1377–78	7 3	25 4	[M.T.]	17 6			7 3	10	50 0						25 1½		
1378–79	17 9	25 2	13 4	18 9			6 9	8	40 0	2 6			74 2		25 0		26 0½
1379–80													131 6		18 4		84 5
1381–82	9 10	16 6	8 4	17 6				5	29 4½				35 0		25 0		41 2
1382–83	14 11	14 6	[Ill.]				6 0	[Ill.]					60 0		25 0		166 8
1383–84	5 6½	19 4	10 4	20 0			6 0	8½	42 6				46 9		32 6¾		46 0
1384–85	16 4	17 6	21 0	31 3				9½	47 6				74 10		25 0		80 6½
1385–86	15 4½	17 10	8 4				5 8	14½	72 6				41 0		25 0		2 4
1387–88	12 8½	17 0	29 4				3 2	5	25 0				50 10		18 4		14 5
1388–89	15 1	17 2	29 10	31 3			4 4	16	83 9				91 0		18 4		20 3
1390–91	[Ill.]	42 8	12 7	40 0				6	33 9						18 4		[M.T.]
1392–93	13 10	17 6	35 4	25 8			4 6	7	36 3				34 6		18 4		31 1
1393–94	10 3½	18 6	36 4	6 8			4 8		41 3				75 2		18 4		45 0
1394–95	5 9	19 4	37 2	25 0			4 10	8	40 7½				69 9		18 4		42 1½
1395–96	3 4	18 8	[M.T.]	25 0			5 4	4	22 6				36 6		47 0		33 3½
1398–99	14 9½	13 8	33 0	27 6			4 4	8	40 0				31 9		47 0		75 11

1399–00	16 11	13 2	34 0	20 0			[Ill.]	7 35 *0*			34 11		47 0		72 1
1400–01	17 5	[Ill.]	37 9	*30 0*				6 30 0			81 6		47 0		62 0
1402–03	14 6	24 0	[M.T.]	37 6											
1406–07		14 0		23 7			4 0	8 40 0			39 3		51 4		54 2
1408–09	14 5	14 6	6 8	30 0				6 32 6			53 1		51 4		6 0
1409–10	25 0	15 0	11 8	0			4 2	7 35 0			42 0		51 4		9 0
1410–11	12 8	15 2	8 4	20 0			4 4	5 25 0	3 0		78 7		51 4		153 8
1411–12	13 1	15 6	11 8	25 0			4 0	5 26 3	3 0		43 8		51 4		3 4
1412–13	14 6	14 6	11 8	0			3 10	6 30 0	3 0		61 11		54 4		205 4
1413–14	7 14	15 0	15 0	0				5 25 0	2 4		61 8		51 4		152 6
1414–15	4 2	15 0	11 8	20 0			4 0	6½ 30 7½	2 0		46 11		51 4		85 5
1418–19	13 11	14 6	11 8	10 5			3 2	7 35 0	15 0		36 6		51 4		92 8
1419–20	7 2	9 2	11 8	26 0			2 5	6 31 3	12 10		73 2		51 4		89 4
1420–21	3 5	8 0	9 0				2 0	5½ 27 6	2 0		44 11		48 8		150 0
1421–22[1]	14 1	10 6	9 0				2 0	5½ 28 8	1 0		33 10		48 8		124 0
1422–23	3 0	8 0	3 4	25 0			2 0	5½ 28 1½	1 0		39 6		48 8		82 7
1423–24	2 10½	10 0	4 4				2 0	3½ 18 3	10 0		37 10		48 8		65 6
1424–25	9 11½	16 0	8 10				2 0	4 21 3			27 6		48 8		129 8
1425–26	1 6	16 0	9 8	10 0				4 20 0			70 8		48 8		144 6
1427–28		16 0	8 4				10	2 10 0					48 8		110 6
1429–30	3 9	16 0	8 10	0			1 0	4 20 0			38 5		48 8		161 9½
1430–31	2 5½	16 0	9 0				1 0	3 18 9			28 5		48 8		151 6
1431–32	1 7	16 0	9 0				1 0	4½ 22 6			36 0		48 8		194 9
1432–33	9 10½	16 0	9 0				1 0	4½ 22 6			63 7		48 8		143 10
1433–34	1 8	16 0	9 0				1 0	3½ 17 6			26 5		48 8		211 2
1434–35	2 9	16 0	9 0				1 0	3½ 17 6			29 4		48 8		185 4½
1435–36	8 11	16 0	9 0				1 0	3 15 0			27 2		48 8		274 8¼
1438–39	8 10	16 0	9 0				1 0	4 20 0			28 2		48 8		147 1
1440–41	1 3	16 0	8 4				1 4	4 20 0			43 8		48 8		155 9
1441–42	1 11½	16 0	8 4				11	3½ 18 1½			37 4		48 8		[M.T.]
1447–48	1 2	16 0	8 4				6	2½ 12 6			38 1		46 0		224 6¼
1448–49[2]	10 4	16 0	8 4				0	3½ 17 6			39 7		46 0		173 7½

1. Beginning this year the income from farm of the conies was 3s. 4d. each year.
2. This year the manor was farmed at £6 13s. 4d.

OUTGO OF THE MANOR

Year	Arrears paid to bishop			Delivery to bishop			Regular expense			Allocation			Hay bought		Amount owing			Net amount owing		
	£	s.	d.	£	s.	d.	£	s.	d.	£	s.	d.	s.	d.	£	s.	d.	£	s.	d.
1208–09				33	1	0	10	0	4							54	10			
1210–11				18	0	0	7	19	0½							75	3½			
1211–12				37	4	0	8	10	9							60	3½			
1213–14				29	1	0	8	14	1						12	4	8½			
1215–16				33	2	9½	5	18	10							8	4			
1217–18				1	17	5½	14	12	11½						2	19	9½			
1218–19		59	9	17	16	2½	13	0	4						9	14	0¾	4	11	0¾
1219–20	9	14	3½	26	17	2	14	12	7½						7	0	10			
1220–21	7	0	9	44	8	0	14	16	6				14	0	8	5	1			
1223–24	3	3	0½	47	0	0	12	6	1				15	8	3	0	8½			
1224–25	3	0	8½	40	0	5½	13	12	3½				25	6	11	16	6			
1225–26	11	16	11	34	1	1½	31	12	11½				26	6	14	2	2			
1226–27	14	2	2	25	1	0	20	9	4						42	2	8½			
1231–32	19	16	1	66	2	6	17	10	3½				21	0	8	1	2			
1232–33	8	1	2	69	17	3	18	3	5¼						11	5	9¼			
1235–36	15	15	4½	74	0	0	13	6	4½				16	6	11	8	4			
1236–37	11	8	4	70	13	8	17	19	2½				13	11½	35	10	10½			
1244–45	22	14	5	38	13	0	37	5	3¾				12	9	31	9	6¾			
1245–46	31	10	0	73	0	0	11	14	8½				11	10	3	13	8			
1246–47	3	13	8	109	0	0	10	16	10				7	0	4	13	0½			
1247–48	4	13	0½	76	13	9	16	6	5½				12	0	23	7	7½			
1248–49	23	7	7½	48	4	11½	16	2	7						24	6	2½			
1251–52	3	9	3	32	3	4	21	19	0½				24	0				6	18	11½
1252–53	6	18	11½	34	10	4	11	15	3½				20	0				44	4	5
1253–54	44	4	5	36	6	0	10	4	3	17	13	9			39	11	0½	21	17	3½
1254–55	21	17	3½	38	15	0	14	15	8½						30	4	11	11	11	2
1256–57	22	6	4	53	10	0	12	5	2¼				15	0	65	4	7¾	47	0	0¼

1257–58	47	0	0	135	15	4	10	13	2½				18	0		38	5 [1]			
1264–65	1	13	3	48	0	6¼	10	11	0¼				10	0	5	10	3½ [1]			
1265–66	0	0	0	78	4	3¾	6	18	0				6	0	2	4	9 [1]			
1267–68	11	12	2	30	13	8	16	4	8¾									12	10	11
1268–69	12	16	10	41	10	0	4	15	7½									9	8	10
1270–71	12	13	8¼	21	0	0	30	3	2½	10	3	0						14	5	0½
1271–72	14	5	0½	32	2	0	19	17	4	19	18	4	24	0				17	4	6½
1272–73	17	4	6½	34	0	0	18	13	11	31	1	4	27	8				10	6	0
1273–74	10	6	0	47	10	0	18	14	9	32	8	8						12	12	6
1274–75	12	12	6	50	0	0	14	18	3	26	10	7½						20	11	2
1276–77	11	12	8½	75	10	0	17	8	5	28	19	8	35	7	37	13	1	8	13	5
1277–78	8	13	5	50	0	0	14	13	10	24	14	6	35	1				32	13	11½
1282–83	2	8	11¾	39	2	0	48	3	9		35	8			45	19	6	5	1	10
1283–84	5	1	10	16	0	0	8	14	7½						22	3	10¾	6	3	10
1284–85	6	3	10¾				17	15	11									31	1	4¼
1285–86				59	2	4¾	18	3	8¼											
1286–87				33	13	9	17	16	10¼		3	9						8	10	10¾
1287–88	8	10	10¾	29	0	0	11	11	9¼		12	6	16	2				14	19	1
1288–89	14	3	1	25	0	0	13	6	7¾				17	1	47	7	3¼	22	7	3¼
1289–90	13	7	3¼	17	2	2¾	16	5	5¼	21	8	0	16	1	67	5	4¼	28	15	1½
1290–91	19	0	1½	17	1	0		[Ill.]			40	0	17	2		[Ill.]			[Ill.]	
1291–92	33	0	1¼	44	1	6¾	9	3	5½						59	10	8½	15	9	1¾
1292–93	15	9	1¾	27	0	0	12	12	1½	18	0	0	17	0	52	4	7	7	4	7
1296–97				27	0	0	16	3	7				18	0	52	7	5½	25	7	5½
1297–98	25	7	5½	35	2	1	12	2	9½				24	0	62	13	3½	27	12	5½
1298–99	27	12	5½		23	4	20	5	1½	20	5	8	30	0				29	4	1
1299–00	29	4	1				28	16	5	4	0	0			42	10	11½	37	15	11½
1300–01	37	15	11½	11	6	4	38	15	6									7	8	8
1301–02	7	8	8	27	14	4	13	8	8¾						42	14	6¼	15	0	2¼
1302–03	15	0	2¼	28	6	11	16	12	10½				58	0	46	14	9½	18	10	9½
1304–05				5	0	0	10	4	8¼				36	0	9	19	6	4	19	6
1305–06	4	19	6										104	0½						

1. Paid in kind.

OUTGO OF THE MANOR (CONTINUED)

Year	Arrears paid to bishop			Delivery to bishop			Regular expense			Allocation			Hay bought		Amount owing			Net amount owing		
	£	s.	d.	£	s.	d.	£	s.	d.	£	s.	d.	s.	d.	£	s.	d.	£	s.	d.
1306–07		29	11½	18	0	0	17	14	5¼				51	0	20	2	2½	12	2	2½
1307–08	12	2	2½	18	13	0	21	8	8	7	15	8	78	2	38	16	10¾	12	8	2¾
1308–09	12	8	2¾	26	11	0	16	13	11	49	3	5¾	48	9	91	19	8	17	5	2¼
1309–10	17	5	2¼	32	4	0	45	12	1	53	14	8	83	0	111	16	7	25	17	11
1310–11	25	17	11	20	0	0	34	3	2	49	1	11	141	11	81	12	11	12	11	0
1311–12	12	11	0	42	0	0	26	7	5½				87	0	50	4	10¾	8	4	10¾
1312–13	8	4	10¾	48	5	0	31	14	0¾	36	3	3	121	0	88	8	2	3	19	11
1313–14	3	19	11	46	0	0	33	1	3	34	9	9	163	0	100	3	1¾	19	13	4¾
1314–15	19	13	4¾	43	0	0	32	8	7½	30	7	8¼	120	0	87	11	0¾	14	3	4½
1315–16	14	3	4½	13	4	0	60	9	5	50	17	3¾			78	4	2¼	14	2	10½
1316–17				81	18	2¼	30	6	0¾	39	7	2¼	76	8	121	5	4½			
1317–18				46	16	5	28	2	2	54	5	10¼	70	0	101	2	3¼			
1318–19				83	15	11½	20	18	4	90	0	3	68	0	173	16	2½			
1320[1]							14	2	8½				60	0			12¼			
1320–21				60	4	2¼	20	8	6½	31	1	1¾	56	0	91	5	4			
1324–25	3	0	0¼	62	0	4½	11	3	11						62	0	4½			
1325–26				54	0	0	10	10	6	5	6	5			57	12	5			
1326–27				18	6	7½	31	9	9¼	21	13	5¼	25	8	40	0	0¾			
1327–28				31	0	0	25	4	10		33	4			43	19	5¼	11	6	1¼
1328–29	11	6	1¼	106	17	4	16	1	10¾	6	0	0			127	4	0¼	14	6	8¼
1329–30	14	6	8	33	10	0	19	10	9½	9	10	0			50	10	9½	7	10	9¾
1330–31	7	10	9¾	45	0	0	12	10	0	3	11	11	81	1	55	11	5	8	19	6
1331–32	8	19	6	45	0	0	20	3	7	39	5	9	58	0	105	8	9½	21	3	0½
1332–33	21	3	0½	28	0	0	22	7	5½	29	1	5	68	0	64	2	3¼	7	10	0¼
1334–35	7	16	0	34	0	9½	21	15	10		52	3	48	0	48	17	2	12	4	1½
1335–36	12	4	1½	50	0	0¼	12	3	4		7	1½	38	0	58	1	9	7	14	7¼
1336–37	7	14	7¼	26	0	0	13	1	10		15	8	42	1¼	36	9	2¾	9	13	6¾

1337–38	9	13	6¾	21	11	0	11	13	5		21	8			34	10	4¼	11	17	8¼
1338–39	11	17	8¼		[M.T.]		14	5	1						29	12	11	5	8	7
1339–40	5	8	7	16	0	0	16	0	9	6	6	4	78	8	28	16	5	6	10	1
1340–41	6	10	1	17	0	0	21	8	4¾	1	13	0	48	6	23	15	8	5	2	8
1341–42	5	2	8	23	12	2	18	17	2		53	4	70	8	33	0	5½	6	14	11½
1342–43	6	14	11½	28	0	0	20	3	11		40	6	50	9	34	6	4½	4	5	10½
1343–44	4	5	10½	42	0	0	20	11	6		11	6	53	0	47	0	11¾	4	0	5¾
1344–45	11	5	0¾	76	18	7¾	19	2	1½	4	7	3	42	0	82	10	7¾		24	9
1345–46		50	0	10	3	0¾	46	15	5		23	4¾	72	11	11	6	5½			
1346–47				37	3	3	22	13	2		3	0	40	0	37	6	3			
1347–48				52	11	9	40	14	1½		3	0	43	4	54	5	8½		31	0½
1348–49		31	0½	29	3	0	19	2	9½		52	4	45	0	35	17	4¾	4	2	0¾
1349–50	4	2	0¾	40	6	4	21	3	5½	4	19	10½	25	8	47	3	10½		37	8
1350–51		37	8	24	0	0	28	12	9½	7	9	7¼	20	0	48	0	7½	16	0	11¼
1351–52	16	0	11¼	50	7	4	17	18	5¾		24	4	41	0	79	5	1½	27	13	5½
1352–53	27	13	5½	31	0	0	26	18	10¼		30	8	60	0	43	2	4¼	10	11	8¼
1353–54	10	11	8	23	8	0	16	12	3¾	5	13	7			41	5	9¼	12	3	7¼
1354–55	12	3	7	36	11	10¾	22	3	5¾	4	3	6½	40	0	47	5	4¾	6	9	11
1355–56	6	9	11	31	12	2½	17	12	8	3	6	4	63	0	52	16	8¾	17	18	2¼
1356–57	17	18	2¼	10	10	9	38	10	5½	9	18	10	60	0	24	16	10	4	7	3
1357–58	4	7	3	45	12	8	19	11	10½	5	5	0			58	17	3	7	19	7¼
1358–59	7	19	7	48	2	3	25	16	0¾	6	19	9	60	0	55	2	0			
1359–60[2]													60	0	41	3	9¼			
1360–61				40	11	6¼	25	7	11½		12	3	52	6						
1361–62							26	[——][3]					60	0						
1362–63							21	19	3½	30	12	0	60	0	30	12	0			
1363–64				58	4	6	24	18	8	6	4	10	60	0	64	9	4			
1364–65				43	12	3¼	20	13	10		25	6	60	0	44	17	9¼			
1365–66							140	9	6¾		14	8	20	0	34	14	6¾	33	19	10¾
1366–67	33	19	10¾	4	11	10½	67	6	7		13	8	60	0	35	18	1	30	12	6
1367–68	30	12	6	31	0	0	71	14	10½	12	5	2½	60	0	48	14	8¾	5	9	6¼
1368–69	5	9	6¼	59	6	2	29	12	6	2	10	6¼	60	0	64	6	8¼		50	0

1. For only part of the year.
2. Mostly illegible.
3. Illegible.

OUTGO OF THE MANOR (Continued)

Year	Arrears paid to bishop			Delivery to bishop			Regular expense			Allocation			Hay bought		Amount owing			Net amount owing		
	£	s.	d.	£	s.	d.	£	s.	d.	£	s.	d.	s.	d.	£	s.	d.	£	s.	d.
1369–70		50	0	100	14	9	27	16	6¼	3	11	3	60	0	109	0	9	5	3	8
1370–71	5	3	8	56	0	0	23	8	3½	9	11	10¾	60	0	86	10	3¾	20	18	5
1371–72	20	18	5	65	0	0				4	19	0			10	11	7½	13	1	7½
1372–73	13	1	7½	61	0	0	24	3	6¾	8	8	0	60	0	84	8	0	15	0	0
1373–74	15	0	0	17	0	0	71	9	1¾	1	19	8¾	60	0	18	19	8¾			
1375–76	24	3	8	80	16	3½	21	17	9¼	2	16	7¾	60	0	84	2	11¼		10	0
1376–77		10	0	37	4	0	18	9	0¾	4	12	6	60	0	44	11	6		55	0
1377–78		55	0	16	0	0	43	12	7¼	5	9	10½	63	0	23	9	10½		40	0
1378–79		40	0	40	4	4	27	2	6¼		12	2¼	61	0	43	16	6¼		60	0
1379–80		60	0	54	11	8	21	8	2½		24	3½	62	0	56	12	7½		16	8
1381–82	4	10	0	38	12	0	21	15	4	3	0	8¼	53	4	49	7	0¼		13	4
1383–84		50	0	32	10	0	24	10	4¾		21	0½	60	0	38	1	0½	4	10	0
1384–85	0	0	0	32	10	4	24	15	0	6	17	0½	51	8	43	14	0½	4	6	8
1385–86	4	6	8	53	11	4	20	8	7¾	6	12	6¼			60	12	6¼		8	8
1387–88		21	8	32	15	0	23	7	5¼		45	6¼	43	0	35	0	6¼			
1388–89				38	16	0	18	11	3½	3	16	4½	39	0	46	12	4½	4	0	0
1390–91		70	0		[M.T.]		18	1	6¼						73	3	9¾	2	16	8
1392–93		73	4	36	16	4	17	10	8¾	6	6	3¾	40	0	47	7	7¾	4	5	0
1393–94	4	5	0	39	1	4	19	9	0½	4	6	9½	40	0	46	10	1½	3	2	0
1394–95	3	2	0	37	15	0	18	12	8¾	2	14	10¾	45	0	42	12	8¾	2	5	0
1395–96	2	5	0	32	17	8	23	4	2	2	15	9¾	36	0	39	15	1¾	4	1	8
1398–99				29	0	4	24	9	4	1	18	0½	36	8	32	[—— [1]]			36	8
1399–00		36	8	36	0	0	19	10	0¾	5	3	9¾	26	8	46	5	9¾	5	2	0
1400–01	5	2	0	30	13	4	30	0	10¼	12	18	8¼	30	0	43	12	0¼			

1402–03				37	10	0	28	13	11¾	17	15	10¾	46	8	55	5	10¾			
1406–07		18	6	33	16	8	28	16	10¾		27	4¾	26	8	36	2	6¾			
1408–09		18	6	42	13	0	28	3	4¼	2	19	5¾	26	8	46	10	11¾		18	6
1409–10		18	6	44	6	8	26	8	5¼	5	2	8¼	30	0	50	7	10¼		18	6
1410–11		18	6	30	0	0	33	13	8¼	11	13	0¾	26	0	46	1	6¾	4	8	6
1411–12	4	8	6	28	11	8	33	3	8½	8	15	5½	26	8	42	10	3½	5	3	2
1412–13	5	3	2	28	11	8	26	2	9¼	9	18	7¾	26	8	48	18	9¾	10	8	6
1413–14	10	8	6	21	5	0	32	10	1	7	1	1½	26	8	44	14	7½	16	8	6
1414–15	16	8	6	28	0	0	25	4	4¼	4	13	0¼			46	1	6¼	13	8	6
1418–19				32	0	0	22	2	6¼	5	6	11¼			51	15	6¼	14	8	6
1419–20	14	8	6	34	3	0	19	16	3¼		50	6¼	16	0	56	17	8¼	20	4	2
1420–21	20	4	2	10	10	4	21	7	7¾	7	7	3¼	24	0	57	16	1¼	39	18	6
1421–22	39	18	6	44	10	0	19	12	8¾	4	13	4¾			79	1	9¾	29	18	5
1422–23	29	18	5	33	9	11	21	14	8	4	16	0	20	0	57	14	5	19	8	6
1423–24	19	8	6	22	0	0	21	5	1½	2	6	11	20	0	41	5	5	16	18	6
1424–25	16	18	6	6	10	0	28	7	11½	3	10	1½	20	0	35	0	11½	25	0	0
1425–26	25	0	0	18	0	0	18	2	11¼	7	0	4¼	15	0	55	2	10¼	30	2	6
1427–28	33	12	5	34	0	0	21	0	0½		19	5¼	15	0	63	11	10¼	24	12	5
1429–30	17	5	9	33	0	4	18	12	2	4	5	4½	15	0	59	13	1½	22	7	5
1430–31	22	7	5	*31*	*10*	*2*	18	9	5½	4	4	2½	22	6	59	15	3½	24	0	11
1431–32	24	0	11	19	1	6	22	6	3		18	3	24	0	55	5	4	35	5	7
1432–33	35	5	7	56	7	1	17	15	4		59	4¼	18	0	74	15	11¼	14	8	6
1433–34	14	8	6	*27*	*13*	*11½*	23	3	5¼		65	0¼	34	0	45	10	1½	14	11	2
1434–35	14	11	2	17	3	4	32	12	3¾		30	5¾	24	0	33	2	3¾	14	8	6
1435–36	14	8	6	17	13	4	19	14	5½	14	16	3¾	12	0	46	18	1¾	14	8	6
1438–39	14	8	6	12	5	8	33	16	0¼	11	9	1¾	21	4	38	3	3¾	14	8	6
1440–41	14	8	6	25	7	1	20	7	1½	5	17	4	21	4	45	12	11	14	8	6
1441–42	14	8	6	21	19	9¼	21	16	3¼						41	8	3¼	19	8	6
1447–48		12	7¾	24	6	8	20	6	3¼	2	4	6½	24	0	35	17	2¼	9	5	11¾
1448–49	8	13	4	32	0	0	19	0	2¾	5	11	1¾			48	7	1¾	10	16	0

1. Manuscript torn.

CLASSIFIED ITEMS OF EXPENSE

Year	Plow			Cart		Dairy [1]			Sheepfold [2]			Threshing		Autumn boon-work etc. [3]		House		Seneschal [4]		Miscel-laneous		Hoeing and weeding	
	£	s.	d.	s.	d.	£	s.	d.	£	s.	d.	s.	d.	s.	d.	s.	d.	s.	d.	s.	d.	s.	d.
1251–52		72	1½	12	1		6	8½															
1253–54		41	11	24	8		5	8½															
1254–55	5	9	3½	19	3		6	3										60	10				
1256–57		35	7	12	1½		6	8½															
1257–58		21	3	17	6		7	4½				18	8½	3	4			95	3				
1264–65		49	0	10	6½		91	7½				11	4¾	7	7	8	2½	32	7				
1265–66		38	5	17	7½		17	11				10	5½	6	9			35	0				
1267–68		35	11½	19	9		14	0				6	0¾	11	7½	25	0	105	0				
1268–69		30	8	8	7½		20	8½				5	2	16	10	16	5½	85	0				
1270–71	9	16	2½	10	7½		16	9½				1	11½	16	1	6	7½	62	0				
1271–72	9	7	10½	11	11½		47	1½				2	8	25	9	11	4½	65	6				
1272–73	10	8	10	11	1½		46	8½				1	4½	25	4	14	6½	62	4				
1273–74	5	11	5	21	9½		60	0				5	3	27	8½	13	2	86	9				
1274–75		32	10	33	3½		58	5				6	7	25	1	14	0½	62	10½				
1276–77	6	3	10½	12	10		54	5				5	9	22	4½	4	10½	78	4½				
1277–78		57	0	21	7½		65	2½				14	11	23	0	21	0	73	1				
1282–83		52	0	35	4¼		46	0¼				3	1	7	8	16	3¾	39	4				
1283–84		23	5	18	9½		36	10						7	7½	17	10	11	1				
1284–85		[M.T.]		12	2	4	7	7½				6	6	22	7	24	9	21	7½				
1285–86	7	0	6½	19	1	4	13	7½				20	5	16	0	16	5	40	2				
1287–88	4	0	9¾	13	5½		49	6¾				9	11¾	14	10	6	7½	56	6				
1288–89	4	7	10¾	36	9		56	10½				2	5½	14	4½	10	9	57	0				
1289–90	3	8	5¼	15	3		57	4½				1	1½	37	10½	5	10	46	8				

1290–91	3	9	2¼	30	3¾		47	9¾				6	3¼	50	11	21	7	[Ill.]	
1291–92		53	2	8	9½		56	2½				6	6	22	0	10	9½	7	3
1292–93		36	8	16	11½	6	7	4½				5	0	37	0	7	5	5	0½
1296–97		37	8	15	6	5	19	5½				28	8	24	2	5	11	34	8
1297–98		[M.T.]		[M.T.]			75	1				15	0	28	0	31	11½	45	7½
1298–99		69	8	16	7	10	10	5				16	6	28	4	11	0	45	7½
1299–00		30	0				22	8				14	8	28	0	13	4	8	1
1300–01		31	11	10	8½	11	17	5½				6	3	13	6	18	8½	25	3½
1301–02		61	0¼	16	4½		79	5½				20	5	33	10	6	5¼	24	4½
1302–03		62	3½	23	5		66	5½				27	5½	23	0	8	7	12	11
1304–05		68	2	25	0¼		76	1½						20	3	8	9		
1306–07	4	5	6¼	29	1¾	7	17	7				10	0	[M.T.]		8	2¾	13	6
1307–08		26	7½	19	3½							37	10½	26	9½	21	10½	3	6
1308–09		76	8	11	7¾		12	6	6	13	5	45	9	22	6	31	4¾		
1309–10		69	7¾	38	4¼		7	0½	34	7	10	38	6½	24	4	35	9½	11	6½
1310–11		61	4½	31	2		7	4	15	15	0	31	10¼	17	11	37	5¼	9	13
1311–12	4	14	9¾	12	1½		8	8¼	17	3	7¼	13	7	19	11	30	11½	3	8½
1312–13	4	13	2½	21	1		8	1	17	8	6	24	2¼	37	0	18	5	13	7
1313–14	5	10	10	52	7		17	0		15	4	26	1½	16	6			35	10½
1314–15		[M.T.]							24	12	0½	25	4½	33	5	22	2	10	3
1315–16	9	2	1½	57	4		22	7½	13	17	4	18	5	72	10	9	10[5]		
1316–17	4	9	8	18	9½		47	4	17	9	7	21	6¼	37	2	16	3	25	9
1317–18		44	10½	28	6		7	0½	13	2	10	22	9			42	3	106	6
1318–19		40	4	13	11		5	6	12	4	2	20	6	23	8	18	9	51	6
1320	8	7	10½	6	1		78	11						20	4	3	6	6	0
1320–21		39	10½	20	11		5	11½	7	4	8	20	6	28	11½	29	7	65	5
1324–25		29	0	28	0					19	2	20	3½	22	0	79	4¾	10	1
1325–26		26	2½	11	5					8	5			11	6	17	11	16	11½

1. Dairy sometimes includes the sheepfold expenses.
2. Sheepfold sometimes includes the dairy expenses.
3. Includes the cost of gifts to boonworkers and the expense of weeding, mowing, and other services in autumn.
4. Seneschal sometimes includes the expense of bailiff.
5. New building this year amounted to £28 8s. 11d.

CLASSIFIED ITEMS OF EXPENSE (Continued)

Year	Plow			Cart		Dairy			Sheepfold			Threshing		Autumn boon-work, etc.			House[1]			Seneschal[2]		Miscel-laneous[3]		Hoeing and weeding	
	£	s.	d.	s.	d.	£	s.	d.	£	s.	d.	s.	d.	£	s.	d.	£	s.	d.	s.	d.	s.	d.	s.	d.
1326–27		52	1½	25	2½		8	4½		79	6	13	6¼		16	9½		36	7						
1327–28		25	4	10	4	7	19	0				3	6½		17	6				6	5½				
1328–29		26	5	12	1	6	12	10½				8	9¼		13	2		12	0	10	8				
1329–30		26	6	30	9		68	1½				6	4		13	2		10	2	11	0½				
1330–31		24	8	10	3		4	11	5	6	4½	3	0½		13	2		9	11	2	10				
1331–32		30	1	12	5½		6	8	5	4	5				31	4		7	7	5	9¾				
1332–33		31	2	28	6½		6	3	6	7	8	3	6		37	0		13	6	7	3½				
1334–35		30	8	26	11		3	6	4	5	9½				36	6		31	5	4	10	14	6½		
1335–36		28	4	11	9½		5	2½		75	10				37	11½		15	2	4	0½	15	0		
1336–37		29	1¼	24	11½		5	7		77	5¾				35	8½		13	7½	2	1½	12	10		
1337–38		55	0½	12	1		5	7		79	3				36	8½		20	5½	2	8	21	7½		
1338–39		30	6½	27	4		5	5	5	0	2½				35	8½		14	9	43	11½	15	1		
1339–40		32	7	22	1		3	7½	5	16	4½				35	1		4	8	3	9	14	4		
1340–41		30	6	14	0		4	2	4	9	2				36	8½		4	0	52	3¼	60	5		
1341–42		33	8½	32	1		4	0	5	3	3				46	2½		19	6½	8	3	16	9½		
1342–43		33	4	12	6		5	0	4	5	9½				51	5½		12	4	7	1	14	3		
1343–44		36	2	12	3		7	5½	5	3	0				30	5½		36	0	6	11				
1344–45		23	2	28	7		4	10	4	0	6				31	11½		35	9	12	6				
1345–46		29	1½	13	7		6	4	6	2	10				24	11½		17	1	6	0				
1346–47		31	4	9	6					76	5½				37	2½		19	8	3	0				
1347–48		26	10	12	3		76	9							34	0½		20	5	3	6				
1348–49		19	4	22	9					75	9	30	11½		17	6		5	10	8	4				
1349–50		36	7	10	9	6	5	2				49	6¾	4	12	9		19	10	5	9½				
1350–51		35	9	44	11				4	7	1	33	1¼	5	3	8¼		20	2½	11	10			5	0

1351–52	36	3	13	8	4	4	10				34	1¼	4	9	9		21	0	14	0½			3	4
1352–53	38	1	21	5	5	19	6				33	1	5	6	7¼		10	10	8	11½			5	0
1353–54	37	7	12	7					77	8			4	18	9½		10	5	13	5				
1354–55	36	11	47	7				6	3	2	43	4½	4	1	10¾		56	0	14	6½				
1355–56	37	1½	11	8½				6	19	8½	42	5¼		44	4¾		15	0½	13	3				
1356–57	37	2	46	10				6	5	3	14	6		57	9½		11	4	14	9¾				
1357–58	33	3	15	2				8	5	8	26	8¾		61	11		11	8	52	11¾			5	0
1358–59	33	9	15	0				7	14	3	31	5¼		65	1		4	8	15	3½			5	0
1359–60	33	10	15	2				6	9	10½	[Ill.]			74	7		12	8	[Ill.]				3	0
1360–61	33	2	47	6				7	0	1				30	2		18	2	18	3			1	6
1361–62	36	2	20	0				7	8	5	21	10½		58	11½				[M.T.]				5	7
1362–63	34	10	13	11				7	6	7	24	0		[Ill.]			28	0					5	0
1363–64	34	7	49	4				7	8	6	41	7½		68	0		21	8	18	1			4	4
1364–65	33	10	14	5				6	19	6	31	8½		78	1		10	7½	13	8	11	10	5	6
1365–66	35	4	16	1				5	2	10	26	6¾	4	4	4	11	17	5[4]	7	6	8	2	4	2
1366–67	40	9	16	7				7	10	4			4	1	6		27	4	224	7	10	0		
1367–68	38	8	46	2				7	10	8	50	10	4	3	10		10	11[5]	16	6	19	4	4	0
1368–69	42	7	14	5½				6	19	3	49	7		66	4		3	0[5]	8	11½	9	9	5	0
1369–70	39	5	34	9				7	0	0½	38	8		64	4¾			11	7	11	6	5	10	0
1370–71	37	0	17	10				6	7	9	46	11		51	7		7	4	8	10½	11	1	9	10
1371–72	34	0	19	7				6	9	10	49	0		57	10		2	6	11	2½	5	6	8	0
1372–73	34	5	15	5				7	19	0	37	5		61	7¾		5	10	10	2	1	8	8	0
1373–74	34	8	49	10				6	9	0	20	11		62	8¾				7	7				
1375–76	35	2	15	2				6	8	5				52	2¾		22	3	12	10½			7	0
1376–77	[M.T.]		34	1				6	10	5				57	2¾				12	3			6	8
1377–78	35	4	16	1				[M.T.]			[M.T.]			[M.T.]										
1378–79	37	4	44	7				5	19	10	15	8		56	8¾		11	2	13	0½			8	0

1. House sometimes includes miscellaneous expenses.
2. Expenses of seneschal sometimes include those of the bailiff.
3. Includes necessary and small items (necessaria, minuta).
4. New building included.
5. In 1367–68 and 1368–69 new building expenses amounted to £52 17s. 11d.

CLASSIFIED ITEMS OF EXPENSE (Continued)

Year	Plow			Cart		Dairy			Sheepfold			Threshing		Autumn boon-work, etc.			House			Seneschal		Miscel-laneous		Hoeing and weeding	
	£	s.	d.	s.	d.	£	s.	d.	£	s.	d.	s.	d.	£	s.	d.	£	s.	d.	s.	d.	s.	d.	s.	d.
1379–80		37	9	18	3				6	13	7	3	9							10	4				
1381–82		38	9	46	7				5	19	3	8	8¼		47	5¾				6	8				
1383–84		39	5	14	0				6	5	0½				37	11¼		11	1	13	5			8	0
1384–85		38	11	47	7				5	2	9½	13	5¾		71	3¾				14	3			8	0
1385–86		36	4	18	1				5	11	7	23	1		73	7¾		20	5	9	4			8	0
1387–88		38	4	46	8				4	13	9	13	6		58	7¼		14	2	2	9			6	8
1388–89		36	1	14	9				4	9	0	12	4		59	10¼		32	9½	2	5			6	6
1390–91		35	5	[M.T.]					4	6	3				61	5¾		32	2						
1392–93		36	8	16	7				3	18	10	10	4½		47	6¼		23	8	3	8			6	0
1393–94		35	7	21	1				4	8	10	16	1½		61	0		14	0	2	9			5	0
1394–95		36	2	16	6				4	7	9	13	6¾		65	8		37	7	2	0			5	0
1395–96		35	9	18	10				3	17	8	3	0	5	6	4		15	9	2	8			6	0
1398–99		33	10	[M.T.]					3	17	2	18	2¼	6	4	11¼		45	6½	[M.T.]				5	4
1399–00		33	11	19	5				3	6	11	21	1½	5	15	1¼		42	0½	3	8½			8	8
1400–01		46	10	53	6				5	17	8	19	8	6	1	1¼		61	10½	20	0			8	4
1402–03		39	5	53	0				11	11	8	23	2	5	18	1½		14	3½	11	3			9	0
1406–07		38	8	48	1				3	2	5	24	7½	5	16	2¾		58	11½	8	10			6	0
1408–09		42	8	19	5				3	14	8	24	1	6	0	8¾		58	10½	5	5			6	0
1409–10		43	5	17	10				3	10	6	24	1	6	0	8¾		76	2½	7	4			6	8
1410–11		46	8	32	4				4	8	8	26	7	6	0	8¾		62	10½	6	4½			6	0
1411–12		46	9	49	7				4	2	3	30	0¼	6	11	11¾		38	5	11	11½			6	0
1412–13		46	10	18	5				3	7	1	20	6½	6	9	5¾		61	7	7	10			6	0

1413–14	47	1	49	3		2	19	10	23	6½	6	3	7½		48	9	7	8		6	0
1414–15	46	6	21	9		3	16	9	7	6	6	4	5¾		29	8	5	4		6	0
1418–19	48	2	49	7		3	13	3	7	9	5	18	7¾		14	1	4	4½		6	0
1419–20	45	11	20	3		2	18	4	15	8½	6	5	3¾		11	4	5	5		6	0
1420–21	44	0	21	5		3	7	0	8	1½	6	6	11¾		45	3½	5	8		8	0
1421–22	43	2	17	11			18	10	14	4	6	2	9¾				4	4		3	4
1422–23	41	10	19	11			54	4½	19	2½	5	18	3½		36	0	5	0½		3	4
1423–24	36	5	20	3			54	4	22	7½	5	9	9½		16	9	7	4		2	0
1424–25	40	3	46	7			51	6	17	4½	5	9	9½		59	7½	6	3		2	0
1425–26	40	3	16	1			44	6	21	11¾	5	6	0½		27	5	3	0		1	8
1427–28	40	5	18	9			45	2	30	5	5	6	10½		51	10½	7	3½			
1429–30	40	0	16	10			43	0	28	5½	5	6	10½		26	7	6	6			
1430–31	39	10	14	9			47	5	28	1	5	6	9½		34	10	7	1			
1431–32	37	11	17	11			53	1	32	2	5	6	9½		28	7½	8	5			
1432–33	38	7	18	0			52	6	28	9	5	6	9½		13	9½	6	3			
1433–34	34	1	47	8½			48	3	26	[—][1]	5	6	9½		38	8½	8	5½			
1434–35	33	8	20	2		9	10	8	29	9¾	5	6	9½		52	7½	9	3			
1435–36	33	8	17	11			67	2½	28	3½	5	6	9½		11	9½	12	9½			
1438–39	36	8	48	0		4	1	3½	28	7¼	5	5	3½	14	1	7	14	11			
1440–41	41	11½	16	0			55	3	30	5¼	5	8	3½		7	0¾	8	9½			
1441–42	36	1	19	4			[M.T.]		25	7¼	5	14	3½		51	2	10	11			
1447–48	40	11	22	6			63	11	32	4¾	6	4	7		20	10	13	9½			
1448–49		[2]					43	0	34	2¼			[2]		35	10½	13	10			

1. Manuscript torn.

2. Nothing because of the lease of the home farm.

WHEAT[1]

Year	Total Yield[2]	No. of acres sown	Total amt. of seed	Av. seed per acre	Net yield[3]	Av. net yield per acre	Amount sold	Total sale price			Av. sale price per qr.		No. given to officials	No. bought	Total purchase price			Av. purchase price		No. sent away	Remarks
	Qrs.		Qrs.	Qrs.	Qrs.	Qrs.	Qrs.	£	s.	d.	s.	d.	Qrs.	Qrs.	£	s.	d.	s.	d.	Qrs.	
1208–09	66½	90	26	.289			61½	7	15	4	2	6¼	5								26 from Mardon
1210–11	66½	96	26	.271	70½	.734	31	6	0	7	3	10¾								9½	
1211–12	96½	104	26½	.255			51	6	7	3½	2	6								19	
1213–14	90	104	27	.260			3		9	0	3	0								60	
1215–16	91	99	24	.242			40½	6	5	10	3	1¼								26½	
1217–18	46½	35	9	.257	18	.514	24½	6	5	3	5	1¼	5							8	
1218–19	27	83	24	.289	25⅞	.312	1½		6	0	4	0	2								
1219–20	49⅞	60	14½	.242	32¾	.546	47¾	6	15	8½	2	10	2⅛	14½		50	3½	3	5½		curall included
1220–21	47¼	101	26½	.262			20¾	4	15	4	4	9									
1223–24	85½	116	22⅝	.195	42⅞	.370	58½	8	7	7½	2	10½		5⅜		14	5½	2	8¼	10	[4]
1224–25	65½	98	19½	.199	55⅛	.563	46	15	3	9	6	7¼		2½						17	[5]
1225–26	74⅝	80½	18	.222	22	.273	72⅝	18	3	5	5	0	1¼	18¼	4	0	3½	4	4¾		[6]
1226–27	40	90	18⅞	.210			37	9	5	10	5	0¼		17⅛[7]	4	3	3½	4	10¼	3	[8]
1231–32	90¾	64	22	.344	76¾	1.199	90¾	18	8	9	4	0¾		22	4	10	8	4	1½		
1232–33	98¾	68½	20½	.299			98¾	18	16	6	3	9¾		20½		66	2	3	2¾		
1235–36	67⅜	83½	18	.216	84	1.006	51⅞	10	0	9	3	10½									2½ from a fugitive
1236–37	102	79½	17	.214			102	21	15	5	4	3¼		17		64	1	3	9¼		
1244–45	111¾	109	18⅞	.173	58⅜	.536	88¼	11	3	2½	2	6¼	3½	18⅞		60	6½	3	2½	20	
1245–46	77¼	51	15¼	.299	42½	.833	51½	9	18	4	3	10¼	5	1½		2	0	1	4	5	
1246–47	57¾	57	17¾	.311	83½	1.465	35	12	16	5	7	4	5								
1247–48	101¼	56	15¾	.281	40⅜	.721	85½	25	17	9½	6	0¾									
1248–49	56⅛	45	11½	.256			40⅝	7	2	1¼	3	6	4								
1251–52	88	63	15⅜	.244	52⅝	.835	72⅝	13	14	0½	3	[illegible]¼									
1252–53	67¼[9]	66	16½	.250	12⅜	.188	43½	12	8	6	5	8½									
1253–54	28⅞	61	15¼	.250	57¼	.939	15¼	2	14	6	3	7									[10]
1254–55	72½	48	12	.250			61½	8	6	10	2	8½									[11]
1256–57	52⅛	56	14	.250	55¼	.987	38⅛	14	7	10	7	6½									

1257–58	69¼	64	15	.234			54¼	23	0	19	8	6							
1264–65	45⅜	50	12½	.250	38⅞	.778	32⅞	9	6	10½	5	8¼							
1265–66	51⅜	52	12⅛	.233			39¼	9	16	6	5	0							
1267–68	44½	52	13	.250	36	.692	27½	6	3	11	4	6	4						
1268–69	49	54	14	.259			27	7	12	7	5	7¾	8						
1270–71	41¾	76	19	.250	27	.355	33¾	12	17	1	7	7½	6	17					
1271–72	46	60	15	.250	61	1.017	24	11	6	0	9	5	7						
1272–73	76	64	16	.250	48¼	.754	52	14	10	7	5	7	8						
1273–74	64¼	70	17	.243	43½	.621	39¼	13	4	10½	6	9	8						
1274–75	60½	61	15¼	.250			37¼	12	14	2	6	10	8						
1276–77	77	70	18	.257	78¼	1.118	51	19	5	6	7	6¾	8						
1277–78	96¼	66	16¼	.246			72	18	9	9	5	1¾	8						
1282–83	34⅛	60	14⅛	.235	15¾	.263	34⅛	13	13	0	8	0		14⅛				6	3
1283–84	29 15/16	84	16⅛	.192	23	.274	13 9/16	5	8	6	8	0							
1284–85	39⅛	64	16⅛	.252	26⅛	.408	22¼	4	18	1½	4	5	1¾	1					
1285–86	42¼	88	15½	.176	36 1/16	.410	22⅝				4	6	4⅜						
1286–87	51 9/16	91	16⅜	.180	80¼	.882	31 7/16				4	8	3¾						
1287–88	96⅝	73	13 11/16	.188	33	.452	80	11	13	8	2	11	3						
1288–89	46⅝	86	15¾	.183	55½	.645	28⅛	5	2	2½	3	7½	2¾						
1289–90	71¼	84	15⅜	.183	29⅛	.347	67¾	20	6	6	6	0	4½	16⅜					
1290–91	44½	84	15½	.185	50¼	.508	44½	17	0	12	7	8		15½				5	7
1291–92	65¾	82	15⅜	.188	33⅜	.407	50⅜	16	15	10	6	8							
1292–93	48¾	98	18⅛	.185			30⅜	10	10	5½	6	11¼	¼						
1296–97	73⅞	96	18	.188	61⅜	.639	55⅜	19	7	7	7	0	½						
1297–98	79⅜	96	18	.188	69¾	.727	60⅞	24	7	0	8	0	½						
1298–99	87¾	96	18	.188	51¾	.539	69¼	24	0	20	6	11½	½						
1299–00	69¾	96	18	.188	3⅝	.038	69¼	29	4	7	8	5¼	½	18	6	15	5	7	6¼
1300–01	21⅝	95	17¾	.187	41	.432	8¾		14	9	5	0	3¾	8½		56	8	6	8
1301–02	58¾	89	16¾	.188	29⅝	.333	40	11	18	2	5	11½	2⅞	¾		4	6	6	0
1302–03	46⅜	90	20	.222			31⅜	8	4	10	5	3	3¼	8¼		39	3	4	9
1304[12]	1 1/16												1 9/16	½		1	6	3	0
1305–06	85⅜	90	15½	.172	22⅝	.251	66⅝	22	5	9½	6	8¼	3¼	17[13]		102	0	6	0

1. Frumentum. 2. From 1264–65 to 1286–87 includes an increment. 3. Obtained by subtracting the amount of seed from the yield found in the account of the following year. 4. Seventeen and a quarter left over, 17 remain. 5. Seventeen left over, 1 remains. 6. One left over, 2 remain. 7. One qr. of rye bought and mixed with wheat and mancorn for seed. 8. Two left over, 2 remain. 9. Six bushels received from the goods of Ingeram, a fugitive. Eight qrs. curall sold. 10. Forty-five from previous year, 4 from a fugitive, and 5/8 from John Carter. 11. Forty-five left over, 44 remain. 12. Michaelmas — 5 Dec. 13. Bought at Mardon.

WHEAT (Continued)

Year	Total yield	No. of acres sown	Total amt. of seed	Av. seed per acre	Net yield	Av. net yield per acre	Amount sold	Total sale price			Av. sale price per qr.		No. given to officials	No. bought	Total purchase price			Av. purchase price		No. sent away	Remarks
	Qrs.		Qrs.	Qrs.	Qrs.	Qrs.	Qrs.	£	s.	d.	s.	d.	Qrs.	Qrs.	£	s.	d.	s.	d.	Qrs.	
1306–07	$38\frac{1}{8}$	98	$18\frac{7}{8}$	.193	$20\frac{1}{8}$	.297	16	4	9	4	5	7	$3\frac{1}{4}$								
1307–08	48	96	$19\frac{1}{4}$	.201	$26\frac{3}{4}$	.279	$27\frac{1}{2}$	9	14	6	7	1	$3\frac{1}{4}$	2							
1308–09	46	95	$20\frac{5}{8}$	.217	$56\frac{5}{8}$	.596	$22\frac{1}{8}$	8	17	0	8	0	$3\frac{1}{4}$								
1309–10	$77\frac{1}{4}$	90	16	.178	10	.111	58	23	0	6	7	$11\frac{1}{4}$	$3\frac{1}{4}$								
1310–11	26	95	17	.179	$24\frac{1}{8}$	.254	$5\frac{3}{4}$		51	10	9	$0\frac{1}{4}$	$3\frac{1}{4}$								
1311–12	$41\frac{1}{8}$	84	$15\frac{1}{4}$	.182	$60\frac{1}{2}$	.720	$22\frac{5}{8}$	6	18	9	6	$1\frac{1}{2}$	$3\frac{1}{4}$								
1312–13	$75\frac{3}{4}$	101	$18\frac{7}{8}$	.187	$60\frac{3}{8}$	.598	$53\frac{5}{8}$	16	0	21	6	0	$3\frac{1}{4}$								
1313–14	$79\frac{1}{4}$	99	$18\frac{9}{16}$	.188	$41\frac{7}{8}$	.423	$57\frac{7}{16}$	19	2	11	6	8	$3\frac{1}{4}$								
1314–15	$60\frac{3}{8}$	103	$19\frac{1}{4}$	.187	$18\frac{1}{2}$	.180	$37\frac{7}{8}$		[M.T.]				$3\frac{1}{4}$								
1315–16	$37\frac{3}{4}$	100	$18\frac{3}{4}$ [1]	.188	$46\frac{3}{8}$	.464	$25\frac{11}{16}$	24	8	1	19	0	$2\frac{7}{16}$	$9\frac{1}{8}$							
1316–17	$65\frac{1}{8}$	95	$17\frac{5}{8}$	.186	$40\frac{1}{2}$	.426	$47\frac{3}{8}$	40	10	9	17	$1\frac{1}{4}$	$\frac{1}{8}$								
1317–18	$58\frac{1}{8}$	89	$16\frac{1}{2}$	.185	$55\frac{1}{4}$	.621	$41\frac{1}{2}$	19	9	0	9	$4\frac{1}{2}$	$\frac{1}{8}$								
1318–19	$71\frac{3}{4}$	123	$19\frac{3}{4}$	.161			$45\frac{1}{4}$	11	6	3	5	0									
1320–21	$75\frac{3}{8}$	63 [2]	$19\frac{1}{2}$	.310			$55\frac{7}{8}$	18	5	3	6	$6\frac{1}{2}$									
1324–25	$58\frac{3}{8}$	57	$17\frac{3}{4}$	.311	$74\frac{3}{8}$	1.305	$40\frac{5}{8}$	17	8	5	8	7									
1325–26	$92\frac{1}{8}$	$49\frac{1}{2}$	$15\frac{1}{2}$	.313	$50\frac{1}{8}$	1.013	$76\frac{5}{8}$	21	16	$5\frac{1}{2}$	5	$8\frac{1}{4}$									
1326–27	$65\frac{5}{8}$	60	$18\frac{1}{4}$	.304	$36\frac{7}{8}$	.615	$47\frac{3}{8}$	12	12	8	5	4									
1327–28	$55\frac{1}{8}$	51	$15\frac{5}{8}$	.306	$43\frac{1}{8}$	.846	$39\frac{1}{2}$	11	12	4	5	$10\frac{1}{2}$									
1328–29	$58\frac{3}{4}$	57	$17\frac{7}{8}$	.314	$41\frac{1}{8}$	.721	$40\frac{7}{8}$	13	12	6	6	8									
1329–30	59	48	$15\frac{1}{8}$	.315	$35\frac{1}{4}$	.734	59	21	13	4	7	$4\frac{1}{4}$		$15\frac{1}{8}$							
1330–31	$50\frac{13}{32}$	60	$18\frac{3}{4}$	.313	$57\frac{7}{8}$	.965	28	13	4	[—] [3]			$\frac{1}{16}$								$3\frac{17}{32}$ extra sold
1331–32	$76\frac{5}{8}$	46	$13\frac{9}{16}$	.295	$37\frac{1}{8}$	.807	$61\frac{7}{8}$	27	11	6	8	11	$\frac{1}{8}$								
1332–33	$50\frac{5}{8}$	58	$18\frac{1}{4}$	.315			32	10	5	4	6	5	$\frac{3}{8}$								
1334–35	$49\frac{7}{8}$	56	$17\frac{1}{2}$	.313	36	.643	$44\frac{3}{8}$	13	7	$5\frac{1}{2}$	6	$0\frac{1}{4}$		12		62	0	5	2		
1335–36	$53\frac{1}{2}$	52	$16\frac{1}{8}$	.310	$47\frac{1}{8}$	.906	$37\frac{3}{8}$	11	8	0	6	$1\frac{1}{4}$									
1336–37	$63\frac{1}{4}$	54	$16\frac{5}{8}$	.308	$41\frac{5}{8}$	.771	$46\frac{5}{8}$	11	13	$0\frac{1}{2}$	5	0									
1337–38	$58\frac{1}{4}$	48	$14\frac{15}{16}$	.311	$37\frac{1}{8}$	.773	$43\frac{5}{16}$	9	18	$0\frac{1}{4}$	4	$6\frac{3}{4}$									

1338-39	52	54	16⅞	.313	9½	.176	35½	5	18	4	3	4						
1339-40	26⅜	48	15⅛	.315	36⅞	.768	11¼	4	6	0	7	7¾						
1340-41	52	51	16 1/16	.315	44 11/16	.876	35 15/16	8	13	0	4	9¾						
1341-42	60¾	50½	15¾	.312	31¼	.619	54⅞	15	8	2	5	7½	⅛					
1342-43	47	52	16¼	.313	32⅜	.623	35⅞	9	5	7	5	2		5⅛	43 8	4 8		
1343-44	48⅝	43	13½	.314	49⅞	1.160	35⅛	13	3	11	7	6¼						
1344-45	63⅜	56	17¼	.308	49½	.884	46⅛	11	3	3½	4	10						
1345-46	66¾	54	16⅞	.313	32¾	.606	49⅞	13	11	5½	5	5¼						
1346-47	49⅝	66	16½	.250	36½	.553	33⅛	13	9	10	8	1¾						
1347-48	53	62	15½	.250	43⅝	.704	37½	15	0	12	8	0¼						
1348-49	59⅛	69½	17⅜	.250	31	.446	29½	7	15	9	5	3¼						[4]
1349-50	48⅜	60	15¼	.254	36¼	.604	33¼	13	11	10	8	2						
1350-51	51½	65½[5]	16⅜	.250	46¼	.706	34¾	16	15	8	9	8	¼					
1351-52	62⅝	63½	15⅞	.250	96⅝	1.522	46½	32	11	0	14	0	¼					[6]
1352-53	112½	76	19	.250	45⅜	.597	68¾	22	18	4	6	8	24¼					½ sold extra
1353-54	64⅜	70	17½	.250	37⅝	.538	44½	13	7	0	6	0	¾					1⅝ sold extra
1354-55	55⅛	66	16½	.250	72⅜	1.097	38⅛	15	2	7	7	11¼	½					[6]
1355-56	88⅞	78	19½	.250	54¾	.702	69	23	5	0	6	8¾	⅜					
1356-57	74¼	76	20⅞	.275	55⅛	.725	73¾	29	8	8	7	11¾	½	20⅞	7 13 1	7 4		
1357-58	76	75	19⅛	.255	54⅞	.732	55	23	7	3	8	6	½					1⅜ sold extra
1358-59	74	82	20½	.250			73 1/16	29	8	7¼	7	0	⅜	20	6 10 0	6 6		
1359-60	[M.T.]	78	[M.T.]				39½	15	16	0	8	0						
1360-61	67	78	19½	.250	54¼	.696	47	17	4	8	7	4	½					
1361-62	73¾	76	19	.250	13⅜	.176	54¼	15	16	2	5	10	½					
1362-63	32⅜	76	19	.250	46¼	.609	10⅞	5	8	9	10	0	½					2 sold extra
1363-64	65¼	66	16½	.250	37¾	.572	48¼	25	8	0	10	6¼	½					
1364-65	54¼	68	17	.250	19¼	.283	36¾	15	18	6	8	8	½					
1365-66	36¼	[M.T.]	16½				19 9/16	6	10	5	6	8	3/16					
1366-67	16½	66	16½	.250	45	.682												
1367-68	61½	68	17	.250	48⅛	.708	44⅛	19	16	4	8	11¾	⅜					
1368-69	65⅛	65	16¼	.250	35	.538	50¼	20	2	0	8	0	⅛	1½	11 0	6 4		
1369-70	51¼	68	17	.250	59½	.875	46⅝	39	19	2	17	1¾	⅛	12½	5 16 8	9 4		

1. The manuscript has 44¾.
2. The acres are per perticam. The antithetical expression seems to be sicut iacent.
3. Manuscript torn.
4. Sold 2¼ extra, 10 remaining.
5. The acres from this year onward are commonly designated per perticam.
6. Sixteen and one half — *per* magn*am* mens*uram*.

WHEAT (Continued)

Year	Total yield	No. of acres sown	Total amt. of seed	Av. seed per acre	Net yield	Av. net yield per acre	Amount sold	Total sale price			Av. sale price per qr.		No. given to officials	No. bought	Total purchase price		Av. purchase price		No. sent away	Remarks
	Qrs.		Qrs.	Qrs.	Qrs.	Qrs.	Qrs.	£	s.	d.	s.	d.	Qrs.	Qrs.	s.	d.	s.	d.	Qrs.	
1370–71	76½	69	17¼	*.250*	*60⅜*	*.879*	59	23	4	0	7	*10¼*	¼							
1371–72	77⅝	64	16	*.250*	*32⅞*	*.514*	61⅛	20	7	6	6	8	½	7	46	8	*6*	*8*		
1372–73	48⅞	63	15¾	*.250*	*54¼*	*.861*	46	21	13	9	*9*	*5¼*	¼							
1373–74	70	58	14½	*.250*			47¾	15	18	4	*6*	*8*								7¾ sold extra
1375–76	43¼	56	14	*.250*	*34¼*	*.612*	28½	13	6	0	9	4	¾							
1376–77	48¼	69	17⅜	*.252*	*42¼*	*.612*	30¾	8	4	0[1]	5	4	⅛							
1377–78	59⅝	64	16	*.250*	*49½*	*.773*	43 7/16						3/16							
1378–79	65½	65	16¼	*.250*	*22⅜*	*.344*	49	11	13	0	*4*	*9*	¼							
1379–80	38⅝	60	15	*.250*			23⅜						¼							
1381–82	30	62	15½	*.250*			11 13/16		66	11¼	5	8[3]	9/16							2⅛ sold extra
1382–83[2]							37⅞	10	2	0	*5*	*4*								
1383–84	46	66	16½	*.250*	*42¼*	*.640*	25¾	6	17	4½	5	4	¼							3½ sold extra
1384–85	58¾	66	16½	*.250*	*38¾*	*.587*	41⅜	10	0	17	*4*	*10½*	⅜							
1385–86	55¼	58	14½	*.250*			40 7/16	12	11	7	*6*	*2¾*	5/16							
1387–88	60¼	54	*13½*	*.250*	*39⅛*	*.725*	43 3/16	9	0	13	*4*	*2¼*	⅝							2⅝ sold extra
1388–89	52⅝	60	15	*.250*			37⅛	7	15	6	*4*	*2¼*								
1390–91	39¼	[M.T.]	14½				24⅝	12	6	3	10	0	⅛							
1392–93	63½	58	14½	*.250*	*43½*	*.750*	45 7/16	8	11	9	*3*	*9¼*	9/16							3 sold extra
1393–94	58	60	15	*.250*	*46*	*.767*	39⅝	8	14	6	*4*	*4¾*	½							2⅞ sold extra
1394–95	61	56	14	*.250*	*32*	*.571*	46⅞	10	16	5½	*4*	*7½*	⅛							
1395–96	46	58	14½	*.250*			25 3/16	7	5	0	*5*	*9*	7/16							5⅞ sold extra
1398–99	42⅛	60	15	*.250*	*34½*	*.575*	26 13/16	6	18	0	*5*	*1¾*	3/16							

1399–00	$49\frac{1}{2}$	48	12	.250	$26\frac{7}{8}$	.560	$37\frac{3}{8}$	11	7	5	6	1	$\frac{1}{8}$					
1400–01[4]	$38\frac{7}{8}$	60	15	.250			$23\frac{3}{4}$	9	8	6	7	$11\frac{1}{4}$	$\frac{1}{8}$					
1402–03	$48\frac{1}{2}$	60	15	.250			$33\frac{1}{4}$	[M.T.]					$\frac{1}{4}$					
1406–07	$53\frac{1}{2}$	60	15	.250			$38\frac{3}{8}$	9	2	5	4	9	$\frac{1}{8}$					
1408–09	50	60	15	.250	35	.583	$34\frac{3}{4}$	12	10	3	7	$2\frac{1}{2}$	$\frac{1}{4}$					
1409–10	50	60	15	.250	45	.750	$34\frac{3}{4}$	15	0	8	8	$7\frac{3}{4}$	$\frac{1}{4}$					
1410–11	60	60	15	.250	45	.750	$44\frac{1}{2}$	14	0	4	6	$3\frac{1}{2}$	$\frac{1}{2}$					
1411–12	60	60	15	.250	45	.750	$44\frac{7}{16}$	12	10	4	5	$7\frac{1}{2}$	$\frac{1}{2}$					
1412–13	60	60	15	.250	44	.733	$41\frac{3}{4}$	10	15	$7\frac{1}{2}$	5	2	$\frac{1}{2}$					
1413–14	59	60	15	.250	$20\frac{1}{2}$	.342	$43\frac{1}{2}$	10	11	4	5	0	$\frac{1}{2}$					
1414–15	$35\frac{1}{2}$	60	15	.250			20		95	6	4	$9\frac{1}{4}$	$\frac{1}{2}$					
1418–19	26	60	15	.250	$41\frac{1}{4}$	.688	$17\frac{7}{8}$		93	5	5	$2\frac{3}{4}$	$\frac{1}{8}$					7 qrs. old
1419–20	$56\frac{1}{4}$	60	15	.250	27	.450	$41\frac{1}{8}$	10	19	4	5	4	$\frac{3}{16}$					
1420–21	42	60	15	.250	26	.433	$26\frac{7}{8}$	8	7	0	6	$2\frac{1}{2}$	$\frac{1}{8}$					
1421–22	41	60	15	.250	39	.650	$25\frac{7}{8}$	7	6	11	5	8	$\frac{1}{8}$					
1422–23	54	60	15	.250	$25\frac{1}{2}$	.425	$38\frac{7}{8}$	7	19	5	4	$1\frac{1}{4}$	$\frac{1}{8}$					
1423–24	$40\frac{1}{2}$	60	15	.250	$34\frac{1}{2}$	.575	$18\frac{1}{2}$	4	6	8	4	$8\frac{1}{4}$	$\frac{1}{2}$					$6\frac{1}{2}$ sold extra[5]
1424–25	$49\frac{1}{2}$	60	15	.250	41	.683	$30\frac{5}{16}$	9	0	17	5	$11\frac{3}{4}$	$\frac{1}{8}$					$12\frac{1}{16}$ sold extra[6]
1425–26	56	60	15	.250			$41\frac{7}{8}$	9	4	3	4	$4\frac{3}{4}$	$\frac{1}{8}$					
1427–28	$48\frac{1}{2}$	60	15	.250			18		72	0	4	4	$\frac{1}{4}$					$15\frac{1}{4}$ sold extra
1429–30	41	60	15	.250	$33\frac{1}{2}$	.558	$25\frac{7}{8}$	9	8	9	7	$3\frac{1}{2}$	$\frac{1}{8}$					
1430–31	$48\frac{1}{2}$	60	$15\frac{1}{4}$	.254	$33\frac{1}{4}$	.554	$33\frac{11}{32}$	10	13	$3\frac{1}{2}$	6	$4\frac{3}{4}$	$\frac{1}{8}$					
1431–32	$48\frac{1}{2}$	60	15	.250	$25\frac{7}{8}$	.431	$21\frac{3}{8}$	4	19	9	4	8	$\frac{1}{8}$					12 sold extra
1432–33	$40\frac{27}{32}$	60	15	.250	$35\frac{1}{2}$	.592	$25\frac{27}{32}$	9	4	$7\frac{3}{4}$	7	$1\frac{3}{4}$	$\frac{1}{8}$					
1433–34	$50\frac{1}{2}$	60	15	.250	41	.683	20	4	16	8	4	10	$\frac{1}{4}$					$15\frac{1}{4}$ sold extra
1434–35	56	60	15	.250	41	.683	$40\frac{5}{8}$	8	19	1	4	5	$\frac{3}{8}$					
1435–36	56	60	15	.250			$40\frac{5}{8}$	9	14	4	4	$9\frac{1}{2}$	$\frac{3}{8}$					
1438–39	$22\frac{31}{32}$	56	14	.250			$8\frac{23}{32}$	5	16	3	13	4	$\frac{1}{4}$					
1440–41	57	60	15	.250	$37\frac{1}{2}$	.625	$41\frac{23}{32}$	7	9	$2\frac{1}{2}$	3	7	$\frac{1}{4}$					
1441–42	$52\frac{1}{2}$	56	14	.250			$38\frac{1}{4}$	7	13	$1\frac{1}{2}$	4	0	$\frac{7}{32}$					
1447–48	$54\frac{15}{16}$	60	15	.250	$43\frac{3}{32}$	.552	$11\frac{11}{16}$		70	$1\frac{1}{2}$	6	0	$\frac{7}{32}$					$28\frac{1}{16}$ sold extra
1448–49	$58\frac{3}{32}$	60	15	.250			$42\frac{29}{32}$	10	2	5	4	$8\frac{1}{2}$	$\frac{6}{32}$					

1. Ms. has £18 4s., obviously an error.
2. Ms. in bad condition.
3. Sold per mutuum.
4. The stereotyped data would indicate a lease arrangement even at this date.
5. Eight qrs. remain in sheaf.
6. Eight qrs. from the previous year.

CURALL

Year	Total yield	Amount sold	Total sale price		Average sale price per qr.		Food Allowance	Year	Total yield	Amount sold	Total sale price per qr.		Average sale price		Food Allowance
	Qrs.	Qrs.	s.	d.	s.	d.	Qrs.		Qrs.	Qrs.	s.	d.	s.	d.	Qrs.
1208–09	5	5	11	3	2	3		1257–58	5	5	30	0	6	0	
1210–11	5	3	6	0	2	0		1264–65	8	8	32	0	4	0	
1211–12	12	10	14	1	1	5	2	1265–66	9	9	32	9	3	$7\frac{3}{4}$	
1213–14	11	8	7	2	0	$10\frac{3}{4}$	3	1267–68	$3\frac{1}{2}$	$3\frac{1}{2}$	13	2	3	$9\frac{1}{4}$	
1217–18	$2\frac{5}{8}$	$2\frac{5}{8}$	8	$0\frac{3}{4}$	3	$0\frac{3}{4}$		1268–69	$4\frac{1}{8}$	$4\frac{1}{8}$	17	$10\frac{1}{2}$	4	4	
1218–19	10						10	1270–71	$2\frac{3}{4}$	$2\frac{3}{4}$	14	$4\frac{1}{2}$	5	$2\frac{3}{4}$	
1220–21		2	5	6	2	9		1271–72	$2\frac{1}{2}$	$2\frac{1}{2}$	16	0	6	8	
1223–24	$5\frac{1}{2}$	$5\frac{1}{2}$						1272–73	3	3	13	0	4	4	
1224–25	$3\frac{1}{2}$	$3\frac{1}{2}$	15	11	4	$6\frac{1}{2}$		1273–74	4	4	18	$11\frac{1}{2}$	4	9	
1225–26	4	4	14	9	3	$8\frac{1}{4}$		1274–75	5	5	25	0	5	0	
1226–27	$3\frac{1}{2}$	$3\frac{1}{2}$	13	$9\frac{1}{2}$	3	$11\frac{1}{4}$		1276–77	3	3	16	0	5	4	
1231–32	5	5	15	4	3	$0\frac{3}{4}$		1277–78	$3\frac{1}{2}$	$3\frac{1}{2}$	13	5	3	10	
1232–33	$5\frac{1}{4}$	$5\frac{1}{4}$	14	5	2	9		1282–83	$2\frac{3}{4}$	$5\frac{7}{16}$	27	2	5	0	
1235–36	4	4	10	1	2	$6\frac{1}{4}$		1283–84	$3\frac{3}{16}$	$3\frac{1}{8}$	16	9	5	$4\frac{1}{4}$	
1236–37	5	5	16	3	3	3		1284–85	$5\frac{1}{2}$	$5\frac{1}{2}$	14	8	2	8	$\frac{3}{8}$
1244–45	19	19	40	0	2	$1\frac{1}{4}$		1285–86	$17\frac{7}{8}$	$17\frac{1}{2}$	40	10	2	4	
1245–46	$9\frac{1}{2}$	$9\frac{1}{2}$	30	8	3	$2\frac{3}{4}$		1286–87	$11\frac{9}{16}$	$10\frac{13}{16}$	34	$10\frac{1}{2}$	3	$2\frac{3}{4}$	$\frac{9}{16}$
1246–47	$5\frac{1}{2}$	$5\frac{1}{2}$	24	6	4	$5\frac{1}{2}$		1287–88	$13\frac{1}{2}$	10	17	4	1	$8\frac{3}{4}$	$3\frac{1}{2}$
1247–48	$8\frac{3}{8}$	$8\frac{3}{8}$	31	$1\frac{1}{2}$	3	$8\frac{1}{2}$		1288–89	$10\frac{1}{2}$	$6\frac{3}{4}$	16	8	2	$5\frac{1}{2}$	$3\frac{3}{4}$
1248–49	$5\frac{1}{2}$	$5\frac{1}{2}$	15	8	2	10		1289–90	$4\frac{1}{2}$	$4\frac{1}{2}$	22	6	5	0	
1251–52	9	9	24	0	2	8		1290–91	$1\frac{1}{2}$	$1\frac{1}{2}$	9	0	6	0	
1252–53	8	8	40	6	5	$0\frac{3}{4}$		1291–92	$\frac{1}{4}$	$\frac{1}{4}$	0	15	5	0	
1253–54	3	3	8	0	2	8		1292–93	$4\frac{3}{8}$	$4\frac{3}{8}$	23	4	5	4	
1254–55	$6\frac{1}{2}$	$6\frac{1}{2}$	13	$10\frac{1}{2}$	2	$1\frac{1}{2}$		1296–97	5	5	20	0	4	0	
1256–57	$3\frac{3}{8}$	$3\frac{3}{8}$	22	6	6	8		1297–98	3	3	12	0	4	0	

1298–99	2	2	8	0	4	0	
1300–01	12 1/4	5 5/8	19	3	3	5	6 5/8
1301–02	12 1/16	12 1/16	45	6	3	9 1/4	
1302–03	18 7/8	18 7/8	56	7 1/2	3	0	
1305–06	5 1/4	5 1/4	26	6	5	2	
1306–07	2	2	8	0	4	0	
1307–08	2	2 5/8	14	0	5	4	
1308–09	9 9/16	9 9/16	63	4	6	8	
1309–10	9 3/16	9 3/16	54	8 1/2	5	11 1/2	
1310–11	4 1/4	4 1/4	39	6	9	3 1/2	
1311–12	16 9/16	16 5/16	62	9	3	10 1/4	1/4
1312–13	8 7/8	8 3/4	35	0	4	0	1/8
1313–14	5	5	25	0	5	0	
1314–15	5 3/8	5 3/8	[M.T.]				
1315–16	9 3/8	9 3/8	105	0	11	2 1/2	
1316–17	9 1/8	9 1/8	91	3	10	0	
1317–18	13 3/8	13 3/8	92	3	6	10 3/4	
1318–19	19 3/8	12 3/8	49	6	4	0	7
1320–21	9 1/4	9 1/4	39	0	4	2 1/2	
1324–25	15 1/4	15 1/4	76	3	5	0	
1325–26	8 1/2	8 1/2	34	0	4	0	
1328–29	6 3/4	6 13/16	40	10 1/2	6	0	
1329–30	13 7/8	13 7/8	55	6	4	0	
1330–31	2 1/2	2 1/2	15	0	6	0	
1331–32	3 3/4	3 3/4	22	6	7	0	
1332–33	6 3/8	6 3/8	23	3	3	7 3/4	
1334–35	9 1/4	9 1/4	37	0	4	0	
1335–36	2 7/8	2 7/8	11	6	4	0	
1336–37	4 5/8	4 5/8	18	6	4	0	
1337–38	10 15/16	6 15/16	22	9 1/2	3	3 1/2	

1338–39	8 3/4	8 3/4	20	5	2	4	
1339–40	4	4	16	0	4	0	
1340–41	7 5/8	7 5/8	30	6	4	0	
1341–42	6 5/8	6 1/8	26	0	4	3	1/2
1342–43	7	7	28	0	4	0	
1343–44	9 3/4	9 3/4	58	6	6	0	
1344–45	7 1/4	7 1/4	29	0	4	0	
1345–46	6 1/2	6 1/2	21	8	3	4	
1346–47	2 1/2	2 1/2	15	0	6	0	
1347–48	2 5/8	2 5/8	17	6	6	8	
1348–49	4 5/8						4 5/8
1349–50	3 11/16						3 11/16
1350–51	3	1 1/2	9	0	6	0	1 1/2
1351–52	1 1/2						1 1/2
1352–53	1 1/2						1 1/2
1353–54	2 1/8						2 1/8
1354–55	1 5/8						1 5/8
1355–56	3 1/8						3 1/8
1357–58	1 1/8						1 1/8
1358–59	1/2	1/2	2	6	5	0	
1360–61	2						2
1361–62	1						1
1362–63	1 7/8	1 7/8	11	3	6	0	
1363–64	4 1/8	4 1/8	22	0	5	4	
1364–65	4	4	20	0	5	0	
1365–66	[M.T.]						
1367–68	3						3
1368–69	4 5/8						4 5/8
1369–70	1/2						1/2
1370–71	1 1/4						1 1/4

CURALL (Continued)

Year	Total yield	Amount sold	Total sale price	Average sale price per qr.	Food allowance	Year	Total yield	Amount sold	Total sale price	Average sale price per qr.	Food allowance
	Qrs.	Qrs.	s. d.	s. d.	Qrs.		Qrs.	Qrs.	s. d.	s. d.	Qrs.
1371–72	$\frac{1}{2}$	$\frac{1}{2}$	2 4	*4 8*		1414–15	2				2
1372–73	$\frac{1}{2}$				$\frac{1}{2}$	1418–19	2				2
1376–77	1				1	1419–20	$3\frac{3}{8}$				$3\frac{3}{8}$
1377–78	$1\frac{1}{2}$				$1\frac{1}{2}$	1420–21	3				3
1378–79	2				2	1421–22	4				4
1379–80	2				2	1422–23	6				6
1381–82	3				3	1423–24	4				4
1383–84	2				2	1424–25	1				1
1384–85	3				3	1425–26	4				4
1388–89	$3\frac{1}{2}$				$3\frac{1}{2}$	1427–28	4				4
1390–91	$2\frac{1}{2}$				[M.T.]	1429–30	4				4
1392–93	4				4	1430–31	4				4
1393–94	3				3	1431–32	4				4
1394–95	2				2	1432–33	4				4
1395–96	3				3	1433–34	2				2
1398–99	3				3	1434–35	4				4
1399–00	3				3	1435–36	4				4
1400–01	3				3	1438–39	1				1
1402–03	4				4	1440–41	3				3
1406–07	$2\frac{1}{2}$				$2\frac{1}{2}$	1441–42	$3\frac{1}{8}$				$3\frac{1}{8}$
1412–13	2				2	1447–48	$5\frac{1}{32}$				$5\frac{1}{32}$
1413–14	1				1	1448–49	2				2

SPRING BARLEY[1]

Year	Total Yield	Number of acres sown	Total amount of seed	Average seed per acre	Net yield	Average net yield per acre	Amount sold	Total sale price			Average sale price per qr.		Food allowance	For feed	Number bought	Total purchase price		Average purchase price	Number sent away	Remarks
	Qrs.		Qrs.	Qrs.	Qrs.	Qrs.	Qrs.	£	s.	d.	s.	d.	Qrs.	Qrs.	Qrs.	s.	d.	s. d.	Qrs.	
1208–09	147½	173	57	.329			12½		25	8	2	0¾	42	8					28	
1210–11	110⅝	91½	40⅝	.444	82½	.902	32		56	5	1	9¼	42½						2	see w. barley
1211–12	123½	89	29½	.331			39½		77	4	1	11½	44						10½	
1213–14	113	94	32½	.346			37		72	8	1	11½	43½							
1215–16	79	77	30⅜	.394			10½		24	6	2	4	36⅞						2	
1217–18	66⅝	74	25⅛	.340	68½	.926	5½		20	2	3	8	30⅝						5	
1218–19	93⅝	62	23	.371	74⅞	1.208	30	4	6	0	2	10½	40⅝							
1219–20	97⅞	83	29⅛	.351	57⅞	.697	17⅛		38	7	2	3	45⅛		3½	8	2½		10	
1220–21	87	75	26½	.353			11¾		34	6	2	11¼	48¾							
1223–24	100⅜	104½	38½	.368	111¼	1.065	28½		54	1	1	10¾	39⅞		6½	10	3			
1224–25	149¾	102	37	.363	70½	.691	33½	5	12	2	3	4¼	26¼						53	
1225–26	107½	108	39½	.366	129¾	1.201	32¾	6	11	0	4	0	41	2½	9¼	28	3½			1 remains
1226–27	169¼	116	42½	.366			74½	15	4	1	4	1	54¾	2	4½	10	1			
1231–32	165⅜	85½	42⅜	.406	139⅛	1.627	66	9	18	6	3	0	51	2½	½	1	4		4	
1232–33	181½	89	43½	.489			74½	10	10	2	2	9¾	54½	2	1	2	3		8	
1235–36	202⅝	99½	46	.462	190⅛	1.911	120¼	12	15	3½	2	1¼	40⅜	1						2
1236–37	236⅛	102	43¾	.429			154⅝	21	10	6¼	2	9½	37¾	1½	1½	3	3			
1244–45	236¾	166	52½	.316	225⅜	1.358	140⅝	10	4	0½	1	5½	40⅛	1						2½ in malt
1245–46	277⅞	80½	42½	.528	156¾	1.947	199½	21	4	9½	2	1½	32¾	2⅝						
1246–47	199¼	102	52½	.515	143⅞	1.411	107½	23	10	10	4	4½	35¼	4						
1247–48	196⅜	110½	58¼	.527	164½	1.489	104⅜	23	19	9½	4	7¼	30¾	3						
1248–49	222¾	115	56⅛	.488			130⅞	14	5	2¾	2	2¼	30¼	2½						
1251–52	154¾	79	43¼	.547	83¼	1.054	76½	9	10	9	2	6	33¼	1¾						
1252–53	126½	84	48	.571	111⅜	1.326	48¼	11	3	9	4	7¾	33¾	1⅞						
1253–54	159⅜	82	46½	.567	134	1.634	87	8	13	2	2	0	33¾	2⅛						20 left over[3]
1254–55	180½	80	44½	.556			119¾	9	12	6	1	7¼	33¾	2½						20 left over[4]

1. Ordeum. 2. From a fugitive. 3. From the goods of Ingeram, 5⅜ qrs. 4. From the previous year; 10 qrs. from a fugitive.

SPRING BARLEY (Continued)

Year	Total yield	Number of acres sown	Total amount of seed	Average seed per acre	Net yield	Average net yield per acre	Amount sold	Total sale price			Average sale price per qr.		Food allowance	For feed	Number bought	Total purchase price		Average purchase price		Number sent away	Remarks
	Qrs.		Qrs.	Qrs.	Qrs.	Qrs.	Qrs.	£	s.	d.	s.	d.	Qrs.	Qrs.	Qrs.	s.	d.	s.	d.	Qrs.	
1256–57	175¼	116	58	.500	*199⅛*	*1.717*	96½	25	10	9	*5*	*3½*	33¼	2							14½ old grain
1257–58	257⅛	128	64	.500			157⅞	44	19	8	*5*	*8½*	33¼	2							
1264–65	165⅞[1]	105	52⅜	.499	*98⅞*	*.942*	86⅛	15	12	10½	*3*	*7½*	26¾	⅝							
1265–66	151¼	105	52½	.500			71½	11	14	9	*3*	*3½*	26¾	½							
1267–68	82½	110	55	.500	*90⅛*	*.819*	32½	4	6	8	2	8	43½[2]		17						
1268–69	145⅛	112	56	.500	*97*	*.866*	60⅜	11	4	6½	*3*	*8¾*	28¾								
1270–71	153	131	65½	.500	*86⅛*	*.657*	56¾	15	13	4	*5*	*6¼*	30¾								
1271–72	151⅝	124	62	.500	*41⅞*	*.338*	59⅞	18	7	5½	*6*	*1¾*	29¾								
1272–73	103⅞	126	63¾	.506	*96¾*	*.768*	8⅜		37	1½	4	6	30¼	1½							
1273–74	160½	134	67½	.504	*100¼*	*.748*	61¼	14	4	11	*4*	*7¾*	30¼	1½							
1274–75	167¾	127	63½	.500			72½	17	11	6	*4*	*10¼*	30¼	1½							
1276–77	171½	106	53	.500	*126¾*	*1.196*	86¼	24	12	9	*5*	*8½*	29¾	2½							
1277–78	179¾	102	52	.510			95	19	0	0	4	0	30¼	2½							
1282–83	98⅜	147	49¼	.335	*42 13/16*	*.291*	98⅜	21	13	6	4	*5*	32[3]		49¼			4	0		
1283–84	92 1/16	127	46⅞	.369	*74*	*.583*	15⅝	3	14	1½	4	*9*	33 1/16		3½			4	8		
1284–85	120⅞	73½	36¾	.500	*63*	*.857*	51¼	7	8	5	*2*	*10¾*	32	⅞							
1285–86	99¾	90	42⅞	.476	*85½*	*.950*	19⅛	*3*	*1*	4	3	2½	37	¾							
1286–87	128 7/16	105	43⅝	.415	*76⅜*	*.727*	47 5/16	*8*	7	4½	*3*	6½	3								
1287–88	120	128	48	.375	*94½*	*.738*	31		54	8	*1*	*9¼*	37⅜	¾							2½ remain
1288–89	142½	134	48⅞	.365	*81⅝*	*.609*	51¼	7	10	10	*2*	*11¼*	42⅛	2½							2½ old grain
1289–90	130½	142	52⅝	.371	*69¼*	*.488*	41	10	5	0	5	0	40⅞	1							
1290–91	121⅞	122	45½	.373	*35*	*.287*	29⅞	8	19	3	6	0	46½								
1291–92	80½	105	39⅜	.375	*58¾*	*.560*							46⅝	¾	6¼	18	9	3	0		
1292–93	98⅛	118	44⅜	.376			13¼		70	8	5	4	45½		5	16	8	3	4		
1296–97	116½	106	40	.377	*41½*	*.392*	34½	8	12	6	5	0	33	⅝							8⅜[4]
1297–98	81½	101	38	.376	*70¾*	*.700*	15¾		77	6	5	0	27¾								

1298–99	108¾	88	36⅜	.413	66	.750	45⅝	11 8 1½	5 0	26¾					
1299–00	102⅜	95	35⅝	.375	33⅛	.349	40	8 0 0	4 0	26¾					
1300–01	68¾	102	38¼	.375	53⅜	.523	18⅜	4 5 0	4 7½	44⅛					
1301–02	91⅝	115½	43¼	.374	67½	.584	22¼	4 9 11	4 0½	29⅞		3¾	12 4	3 4	
1302–03	110¾	166	40½	.244			58⅝	9 9 4	3 2¾	30⅛		18½	69 6	3 9	
1304–05	57 9/16	146	46	.315			7/16	1 6	3 5¾	18 5/16		7 3/16	32 4½	3 6	
1305–06	38½	129	36¾	.285	21¾	.169				30 13/16		29 1/16	134 3½	4 7½	
1306–07	58½	117	33⅛	.283	33⅞	.290				30 1/16		4 11/16	18 9	4 0	
1307–08	67	87	36¼	.417	50¾	.583	¼	0 15	5 0	31 7/16		15/16	4 5	4 8½	
1308–09	87	101	36½	.361	75¾	.750	16	4 16 0	6 0	34⅜					
1309–10	112¼	98	35⅝	.363	60½	.617	37 13/16	11 14 5	6 2½	38 13/16					
1310–11	96⅛	90	33⅛	.368	59 23/32	.664	27 3/16	8 13 11	6 4¾	35 13/16					
1311–12	93 1/16	112	40⅝	.363	88⅜	.789	17 11/32	4 0 11½	4 8	35 1/16					
1312–13	129	100	39⅝	.396	91	.910	55 13/16	11 3 3	4 0	33 9/16					
1313–14	130⅝	113	36⅞	.326	74¼	.657	53 7/16	13 0 6¼	4 10½	40 5/16					
1314–15	111⅛	103	32⅝	.317	66 13/16	.649	37⅜	[M.T.]		41⅛					
1315–16	99 1/32	105	33⅞	.323	68	.648	28	22 8 0	16 0	37 7/16					
1316–17	101⅞	99	33	.333	83¾	.846	32 1/16	17 8 9	10 10½	36 13/16					
1317–18	116¾	95	31⅜	.330	98⅛	1.033	53⅝	10 14 6	4 0	31¾					
1318–19	129½	96	31⅞	.332			68¾	12 1 8	3 6¼	28⅞					
1320–21	99½	62	31⅛	.502			33½	7 0 6	4 2¼	34⅞					
1324–25	115⅛	55	27½	.500	73⅜	1.334	66 3/16	17 16 8¾	5 4¾	21 7/16					
1325–26	100⅞	63	31⅜	.498	40⅞	.649	48 1/16	10 8 5	4 4	21 7/16					
1326–27	72¼	60	30⅛	.502	45 3/16	.753	18⅜	4 5 9	4 8	23¾					
1327–28	75 5/16	58	28⅞	.498	42⅞	.739	17 5/16	4 8 3¼	5 1¼	29⅛					
1328–29	71¾	49½	24¾	.500	68⅛	1.376	32	8 0 0	5 0	29 1/16		14 1/16	79 4½	5 7¾	
1329–30	92⅞	53½	26¾	.500	52⅞	.988	36 1/16	9 4 4¼	5 1¼	30 1/16					
1330–31	79⅝	47	23⅜	.497	34⅛	.726	27⅛	10 12 2	7 9¾	29 1/16					
1331–32	57⅛	56	27⅞	.498	51⅝	.922				31⅝		2 7/16	13 4½	6 8	
1332–33	79½	52½	26⅜	.502			17 7/15	4 3 1½	4 9¼	35¾					
1334–35	73⅛	56	27⅞	.498	60½	1.080	16 13/16	66 5½	3 11½	28 7/16					
1335–36	88⅜	52½	26¼	.500	43¾	.833	36 5/16	8 9 5½	4 8	25 13/16					
1336–37	70	46	23⅛	.503	39⅛	.851	21 1/16	4 0 6¾	3 10	25 13/16					
1337–38	62¼	48	23⅞	.497	66¾	1.391	16 1/16	53 6½	3 4	22 5/16					

1. From 1264–65 to 1286–87, the figures here given for total yield include increment.
2. Of this, 15¾ were bought for food allowance.
3. For food allowance.
4. Eight and three-quarters qrs. barley with 4 qrs. oats used for sowing drage.

SPRING BARLEY (CONTINUED)

Year	Total yield	Number of acres sown	Total amount of seed	Average seed per acre	Net yield	Average net yield per acre	Amount sold	Total sale price			Average sale price per qr.		Food allowance	For feed	Number bought	Total purchase price			Average purchase price		Number sent away	Remarks
	Qrs.		Qrs.	Qrs.	Qrs.	Qrs.	Qrs.	£	s.	d.	s.	d.	Qrs.	Qrs.	Qrs.	£	s.	d.	s.	d.	Qrs.	
1338–39	$90\frac{5}{8}$	$50\frac{1}{2}$	25	.495	$67\frac{7}{8}$	1.344	$39\frac{9}{16}$	4	12	$3\frac{3}{4}$	2	4	$26\frac{1}{16}$									
1339–40	$92\frac{7}{8}$	46	$22\frac{7}{8}$	.497	$59\frac{5}{8}$	1.296	$44\frac{3}{16}$	10	1	8	4	$6\frac{3}{4}$	$25\frac{15}{16}$									
1340 41	$82\frac{1}{2}$	43	$21\frac{3}{8}$	.497	39	.907	$34\frac{13}{16}$	6	19	0	4	0	$26\frac{3}{16}$									
1341–42	$60\frac{3}{8}$	$54\frac{1}{4}$	$27\frac{1}{4}$	.500	$63\frac{3}{8}$	1.168	$7\frac{11}{16}$		35	$10\frac{1}{2}$	4	8	$25\frac{9}{16}$									
1342–43	$90\frac{1}{2}$	50	28	.560	65	1.300	$36\frac{3}{16}$	7	1	6	3	11	$26\frac{5}{16}$									
1343–44	93	60	30	.500	$55\frac{1}{8}$	.919	$36\frac{3}{16}$	9	17	$1\frac{1}{2}$	5	$5\frac{1}{4}$	$26\frac{13}{16}$									
1344–45	$85\frac{1}{8}$	48	24	.500	42	.875	$34\frac{5}{16}$	6	6	7	3	$8\frac{1}{4}$	$26\frac{13}{16}$									
1345–46	66	57	$28\frac{1}{2}$	.500	$60\frac{7}{8}$	1.068	$11\frac{9}{16}$		46	3	4	0	$25\frac{15}{16}$									
1346–47	$89\frac{3}{8}$	58	$27\frac{3}{8}$	.472	$63\frac{3}{4}$	1.099	$35\frac{7}{8}$	9	11	$7\frac{1}{2}$	5	4	$26\frac{1}{16}$									
1347–48	$91\frac{1}{8}$	64	32	.500	72	1.125	$32\frac{13}{16}$	9	17	5	6	$0\frac{1}{4}$	$26\frac{5}{16}$									
1348–49	104	$50\frac{1}{2}$	$25\frac{1}{4}$	.500	$50\frac{3}{8}$	.998	$25\frac{1}{16}$		75	$2\frac{1}{4}$	3	0	$26\frac{13}{16}$									30 remain
1349–50	$105\frac{5}{8}$	60	$29\frac{7}{8}$	.498	$77\frac{5}{8}$	1.294	$38\frac{5}{16}$	4	17	3	2	$6\frac{1}{2}$	$37\frac{7}{16}$									30 grs. [1]
1350–51	$107\frac{1}{2}$	$73\frac{1}{2}$	$36\frac{3}{4}$	.500	$64\frac{3}{8}$	.876	$27\frac{7}{8}$	9	5	10	6	8	$42\frac{7}{8}$									
1351–52	$101\frac{1}{8}$	72	36	.500	$25\frac{3}{8}$	.352	$25\frac{1}{8}$	9	1	7	7	$2\frac{3}{4}$	40									
1352–53	$61\frac{3}{4}$	$73\frac{1}{2}$	$36\frac{3}{4}$	.500	$50\frac{1}{2}$	.687	23	6	11	8	5	$8\frac{3}{4}$	2									
1353–54	$87\frac{1}{4}$	62	$31\frac{1}{4}$	.504	$66\frac{3}{4}$	1.077	$14\frac{3}{8}$		57	9	4	0	$37\frac{9}{16}$									4 sold extra
1354–55	98	76	38	.500	78	1.026	$21\frac{15}{16}$	4	7	9	4	0	$38\frac{1}{16}$									
1355–56	116	$75\frac{1}{2}$	$37\frac{3}{4}$	.500	$11\frac{5}{8}$	.154	$41\frac{7}{16}$	8	7	1	4	$0\frac{1}{2}$	$36\frac{13}{16}$									
1356–57	$49\frac{3}{8}$	73	$38\frac{1}{2}$	.527	$61\frac{3}{4}$	.846							$39\frac{5}{8}$		$28\frac{3}{4}$	6	17	3	4	$9\frac{1}{4}$		
1357–58	$100\frac{1}{4}$	64	$32\frac{1}{2}$	.508	$72\frac{7}{8}$	1.139	$31\frac{3}{4}$	9	10	6	6	0	$34\frac{1}{4}$									$6\frac{1}{8}$ sold extra
1358–59	$105\frac{3}{8}$	67	$33\frac{1}{2}$	.500			$36\frac{1}{2}$	9	2	6	5	0	$35\frac{3}{8}$									
1359–60							[M.T.]	7	13	1	5	0										
1360–61	$121\frac{3}{8}$	72	36	.500	51	.708	52	13	[M.T.]				$33\frac{3}{8}$									
1361–62	87	65	$32\frac{1}{2}$	.500	$42\frac{1}{8}$	.648	$20\frac{1}{8}$	5	0	$7\frac{1}{2}$	5	0	$34\frac{3}{8}$									
1362–63	$74\frac{5}{8}$	64	32	.500	$78\frac{1}{2}$	1.227	$7\frac{1}{4}$		43	6	6	0	$35\frac{3}{8}$									
1363–64	$110\frac{1}{2}$	60	30	.500	$60\frac{3}{8}$	1.006	$45\frac{1}{8}$	12	0	8	5	4	$35\frac{3}{8}$									

1364–65	90⅜	61	30½	.500	69¾	1.143	24½	6	2	6	5	0	35⅜						
1365–66	100¼	60	30	.500	31⅛	.519	44 1/16	8	16	3	4	0	26 3/16						
1366–67	61⅛	63	31½	.500	70½	1.119							29⅝						
1367–68	102	62	31	.500	81¼	1.310	43 13/16	11	13	8	5	4	27 3/16						
1368–69	112¼	60	30	.500	75	1.250	51½	12	17	6	5	0	30¾						
1369–70	105	60	30	.500	105	1.750	45 5/16	27	15	5	12	3	29 11/16						
1370–71	135	56	28	.500	84⅛	1.502	46¾	14	0	10½	6	0	28 15/16						31¼ sold extra
1371–72	112⅛	57	28½	.500	68⅛	1.195	49⅝	11	11	7	4	8	25						9 sold extra
1372–73	96⅝	48	24	.500	96	2.000	65⅜	28	15	7½	8	9¾	24½						
1373–74	120	48	24¼	.505			58⅛	11	12	6	4	0	24						13⅝ sold extra
1375–76	102⅜	49	24½	.500	83½	1.704	52⅞	15	17	3	6	0	25						
1376–77	108	57	28½	.500	86	1.509	55[2]	11	0	0	4	0	24						½ sold extra
1377–78	114½	50	25	.500	100¼	2.005	66						23½						
1378–79	125¼	48	24	.500	73½	1.531	78¼	13	0	10	3	4	23						
1379–80	97½	48	24	.500			50½						23						
1381–82	102	50	25	.500			50½	9	5	2	3	8	22						4½ sold extra
1382–83							37⅞	6	18	10½	3	8							
1383–84	100	51	25½	.500	52½	1.029	50	8	6	8	3	4	23						1½ sold extra
1384–85	78	50	25	.500	88⅞	1.778	25⅞	5	16	3	4	4	22						14⅛ sold extra
1385–86	113⅞	52	26	.500			66⅞	13	7	8	4	0	21						
1387–88	124½	47	24	.511	101½	2.160	78½	11	15	6	3	0	22						
1388–89	125½	51	25½	.500			78½	10	9	4	2	8	21½						
1390–91	113½	52	26	.500			65	21	13	4	6	8	22½						
1392–93	117	51	25½	.500	81½	1.598	66½	11	1	8	3	4	21						4 sold extra
1393–94	107	52	26	.500	65½	1.260	56	9	6	8	3	4	22						3 sold extra
1394–95	91½	53	26½	.500	76	1.434	33⅝	6	14	6	4	0	23						8⅜ sold extra
1395–96	102½	52	26	.500			54½	9	19	10	3	8	22						
1398–99	96¼	53	26½	.500	79½	1.500	47¾	7	14	6	3	2¾	22						
1399–00	106	52	26	.500	67½	1.298	58	11	3	2	4	0	22						
1400–01	93½	53	27	.509			44½	9	12	10	4	4	22						
1402–03	108	50	25	.500			61¾	[M.T.]					21¼						
1406–07	112	50	25	.500			64½	10	14	12	3	4	22½						
1408–09	100	50	25	.500	75	1.500	50	13	6	7	5	4	25						
1409–10	100	50	25	.500	95	1.900	50	15	0	0	6	0	25						

1. From the previous year.

2. Six qrs. sold for the lord's dogs and 49 per mutuum.

SPRING BARLEY (Continued)

Year	Total yield	Number of acres sown	Total amount of seed	Average seed per acre	Net yield	Average net yield per acre	Amount sold	Total sale price	Average sale price per qr.	Food allowance	For feed	Number bought	Total purchase price	Average purchase price	Number sent away	Remarks
	Qrs.		Qrs.	Qrs.	Qrs.	Qrs.	Qrs.	£ s. d.	s. d.	Qrs.	Qrs.	Qrs.	s. d.	s. d.	Qrs.	
1410–11	120	50	25	*.500*	*95*	*1.900*	70	17 10 0	5 0	25						
1411–12	120	50	25	*.500*	*95*	*1.900*	70	11 13 4	3 4	25						
1412–13	120	49	24½	*.500*	*95½*	*1.949*	72½	10 17 6	3 0	23						
1413–14	120	48	24	*.500*	*48*	*1.000*	71¾	11 18 14	3 4	24¼						
1414–15	72	48	24	*.500*			25	4 7 3	*3 6*	23						
1418–19	72	48	24	*.500*	*48*	*1.000*	25	4 17 4	*3 10¾*	23						
1419–20	72	56	28	*.500*	*56*	*1.000*	22⅜	4 14 7	*4 2¾*	21⅝						
1420–21	84	52	26	*.500*	*65*	*1.250*	16	64 0	*4 0*	22						20 sold extra
1421–22	91	48	24	*.500*	*24*	*.500*	46	8 13 4	*3 9¼*	21						
1422–23	48	48	24	*.500*	*48*	*1.000*	13	34 8	*2 8*	*19*		8	28 8	3 4		
1423–24	72	52	26	*.500*	*26*	*.500*	16¼	54 2	*3 4*	21¼						8½ sold extra
1424–25	52	52	[M.T.]				19⅝			22		15⅝	52 1	3 4		
1425–26	78	48	24	*.500*			33	5 4 6	*3 2*	21						
1427–28	72	48	24	*.500*			21½	75 0	*3 5¾*	21						5½ sold extra
1429–30	72	48	24	*.500*	*47*	*.979*	27	5 13 11	*4 2¾*	21						
1430–31	72[1]	48	24	*.500*	*60*	*1.250*	16½	57 0	3 *5½*	21						10½ sold extra
1431–32	84	48	24	*.500*	*48*	*1.000*	39	6 0 7	*3 1*	21						
1432–33	72	48	24	*.500*	*54*	*1.125*	27	5 6 8	*3 11½*	21						
1433–34	78	48	24	*.500*	*62*	*1.292*	31	5 13 8	*3 8*	23						
1434–35	86	48	24	*.500*	*71*	*1.479*	41	5 19 0	2 10¼	21						
1435–36	95	48	24	*.500*			51	7 13 0	3 0	21						
1438–39	84	48	24	*.500*			35¾	14 8 8	*8 1*	24¼						
1440–41	84	48	24	*.500*	*48*	*1.000*	36	4 16 0	2 8	24						
1441–42	72	48	24	*.500*			30⅝	4 1 8	*2 8*	21⅞		4½				
1447–48	95 31/32	48	24	*.500*	*72*	*1.500*	36 11/16	6 2 3½	3 4	19 31/32						15 11/32 sold extra
1448–49	96	48	24	*.500*			72	10 5 11	3 0							

1. Includes 1 qr. of Cornebote.

Year	Total yield	Number of acres sown	Total amount of seed	Average seed per acre	Net yield	Average net yield per acre	Amount sold	Total sale price			Average sale price per qr.		Feed	Number bought	Total purchase price		Average purchase price		Number sent away	Remarks
	Qrs.		Qrs.	Qrs.	Qrs.	Qrs.	Qrs.	£	s.	d.	s.	d.	Qrs.	Qrs.	s.	d.	s.	d.	Qrs.	
1210–11	61¼	107	36	.336	87½	.818	7 [2]						18¼							
1211–12	123½	120	34½	.288			51	4	0	4½	1	7	12						26	
1213–14	85⅝	124	35½	.286			38⅝		66	9	1	8¾	11½							
1215–16	64	117	28½	.244			17½		33	4	1	10¾	8						10	
1217–18	39	123	34	.276	42⅛	.342	3½		10	6	3	0	1½							
1218–19	76⅛	100	30	.300	59	.590	46⅛	4	12	3	2	0								
1219–20	89	97	27½	.284	58	.598	87	5	16	10½	1	4	2	27½						
1220–21	85½	118	35½	.301			47½	6	13	9	2	9¾	2½							
1223–24	104 [3]	118	39½	.335	43⅜	.368	69½	5	11	0¾	1	7¼	2½	4¼	5	11½	1	4¾		32 remain
1224–25	80⅞ [4]	109	32	.294			35¼	5	6	0	3	0	27½						6	
1225–26	6¼ [5]	56	17¾	.317	26½	.473								1		2½				12½ remain
1226–27	44¼	53	15	.283			44¼	6	3	11	2	9½		15	27	6½	1	10		
1231–32	71½	56	22½	.402	48½	.866	71½	9	2	9	2	6¾		22½	65	3	2	10¾		
1232–33 [6]	71	54½	21½	.394			71	8	15	6½	2	5¾		21½	44	7	2	0¾		
1235–36	49½	68½	18¾	.274	36⅜	.531	31¼		73	10	2	4¼								½ from fugitive
1236–37	55⅛	68	19½	.287			55⅛	7	5	6½	2	7¾		19½	41	7	2	1½		
1244–45 [6]	53	66	12½	.189	30	.455	50½		77	1½	1	6¼		12½	20	10¾	1	8		2½ in malt
1245–46 [6]	42½	40	15	.375	28⅜	.709	27½		68	8½	2	6								
1246–47 [6]	43⅜	31	11⅞	.383	12⅛	.391	31½	8	1	10	5	1¾								
1247–48	24	21	7½	.357	7	.333	22		45	4	2	0¾		5½	20	9	3	9¼		
1248–49	14½						14½		30	0	2	0¾								
1251–52	21½	13	6½	.500	15	1.154	15		35	0	2	4								
1252–53	21½	21	10½	.500	44	2.095	11		44	0	4	0								
1253–54	54½	24	11½	.479	33	1.375	45		55	0	1	2¾								3 from Ingeram
1254–55	44½	17	8½	.500			36		58	4	1	7½								
1256–57	36						36	5	12	3	3	1½								
1264–65	38¼	24½	12⅛	.495	34⅝	1.413	26⅛	4	3	1	3	2¼								
1265–66	46¾	22½	11¾	.522			35		77	8	2	2¾								
1267–68	11⅜	40	11⅜	.284	23¾	.594														
1268–69	35⅛	45	11¼	.250			23⅞	4	11	6	3	10								

1. Ordeum hiemale. This seems to be the same as berecorn. And it seems impossible to distinguish either from mancorn or mixtil, terms which are themselves frequently used interchangeably.
2. Accounted for in sale of spring barley.
3. Left over from the previous year 35¼.
4. Left over 32.
5. Left over 12½. Mixed with wheat, 2 qrs.
6. Mixtil, not winter barley alone.

WINTER BARLEY OR BERECORN (Continued)

Year	Total yield	Number of acres sown	Total amount of seed	Average seed per acre	Net yield	Average net yield per acre	Amount sold	Total sale price			Average sale price per qr.		Feed	Number bought	Total purchase price		Average purchase price		Number sent away	Remarks
	Qrs.		Qrs.	Qrs.	Qrs.	Qrs.	Qrs.	£	s.	d.	s.	d.	Qrs.	Qrs.	s.	d.	s.	d.	Qrs.	
1270–71	24½	5	3½	*.700*	*3*	*.600*	24½	4	10	0	*3*	*8*								
1271–72	6½	8	2⅞	*.359*	*5⅝*	*.703*	5		12	6	2	6	1½	2⅞						
1272–73	8½	12	3½	*.292*	*7¼*	*.604*	5		18	4	*3*	8								
1273–74	10¾	15	4½	*.300*	*12*	*.800*	6¼		17	10	*2*	*10¼*								
1274–75	16½	14	4¼	*.304*			12¼		44	0	3	8								
1276–77	14¼	24	8½	*.354*	*19*	*.792*	5¾		25	10½	4	6								
1277–78	27½	20	7	*.350*			20½	4	2	0	4	0								
1282–83	17	46	11⅝	*.253*	*2¾*	*.598*	17	5	2	0	6	0		11½			*4*	*3*[1]		
1283–84	14⅜	12	4	*.333*	*3⅛*	*.260*	10⅜		34	7	3	4								
1284–85	7⅛		3⅝		*5¾*		3½		6	5	1	10								
1285–86	9⅜		5		*1¾*		7⅛		*15*	*5¼*	2	2		2¾						
1286–87	6¾	16	4½	*.281*	*7½*	*.469*	1¾		*4*	*8*	2	8	½							¾ yld curall
1287–88	12	17	3⅝	*.213*	*4⅜*	*.257*	6⅞		11	5½	1	8	1½							
1288–89	8	16½	3½	*.212*	*4½*	*.273*	3¾		8	9	*2*	*4*	¾							
1289–90	8						3		9	0	3	0	5							
1290–91		4	1	*.250*	*1⅞*	*.469*								1	3	0	3	0		
1291–92	2⅞	11	2⅞	*.261*	*4⅜*	*.398*														
1292–93	7¼	27	6¾	*.250*									½							
1296–97	13	20	5	*.250*	*9⅝*	*.481*	13		43	4	3	4		5						
1297–98	14⅝	24	6	*.250*	*10⅝*	*.443*	7⅝		30	6	*4*	*0*		1						
1298–99	16⅝	24	6	*.250*	*10⅜*	*.432*	10⅝		42	6	4	0								
1299–00	16⅜	12	3	*.250*	*1⅛*	*.094*	15⅜		46	1½	3	0	1	3	15	0	5	0		
1300–01	4⅛	9	2⅛	*.236*	*2⅛*	*.236*							2							
1301–02	4¼												4¼							
1305–06	⅞						¼		1	4	*5*	*4*	⅝							
1307–08	9 1/16[2]						9 1/16		30	2½	*3*	*4*								
1334–35			1⅝											1⅝	5	5	3	4		
1335–36	4⅜		2				2⅛		7	1	3	4	¼							
1336–37	3 3/16						3 3/16		12	9	4	0								

Year	Yield	Yield in sheaf	Number of acres sown	Total amount of seed	Average seed per acre	Net yield	Average net yield per acre	Amount sold	Total sale price	Average sale price per qr.	Food allowance	For feed	Number bought	Total purchase price	Average purchase price	Number sent away	Remarks
	Qrs.	Qrs.		Qrs.	Qrs.	Qrs.	Qrs.	Qrs.	£ s. d.	s. d.	Qrs.	Qrs.	Qrs.	s. d.	s. d.	Qrs.	
1208–09	201		286	104	.364						3	38				56	
1210–11	201¼		226	101½	.449	199⅜	.882	5	5 0	1 0	11¼	55	11½	12 1		40	
1211–12	300⅞		264½	121⅝	.460			6	8 0	1 4	3	67¼				103	
1213–14	216½		256	131	.512			1	1 8	1 8		49½				35	
1215–16	210⅜		228½	112	.490			5	8 4	1 8		38⅞				54	
1217–18	149⅜		220	110	.500	123	.559	1	2 0	2 0		26⅞	3½	7 1		15	
1218–19	233		241	117	.485	143	.595					9	100			7	
1219–20	260½		383	192	.501	135⅜	.353	16	17 0	1 0¾		32½				20	
1220–21	327⅜		218	126¼	.579			153	11 9 9	1 6	2⅛	25				21	
1223–24	217⅛		221½	116½	.526	112	.506	42	52 6	1 3	⅝	28¾	4½	4 3½		33¾	
1224–25	228½		234	107	.457	66	.282	24	48 0	2 0	4½	31½				62	
1225–26	173		224	112	.500	144⅜	.645	38½	77 0	2 0		26¼	3¾	6 0½			
1226–27	256⅜		284	124½	.438			102⅜	9 12 5½	1 10½	4	27½	2	3 0		4	
1231–32	306¾		166	130¼	.785	144	.867	135½	11 5 2	1 8		43	2	2 11½			
1232–33	274¼		194	128½	.662			106¼	9 18 5½	1 10½	⅜	42½	3⅜	4 7			
1235–36	291⅝		167	120¼	.720	154¾	.927	128½	13 5 0½	2 0¾	1⅜	43					1½ from f ˙tive
1236–37	275		166	123½	.744			110	11 3 0½	2 0¼	1½	42	2	3 2½			
1244–45	283¾		213	99¼	.466	70⅝	.332	92½	5 15 7½	1 3	7	42				43	
1245–46	169⅞ [1]		131½	97⅜	.740	144⅝	1.100				9½	43				20	
1246–47	242 [2]		97½	72½	.744	80½	.826	116	14 19 7½	2 7		53½					
1247–48	153 [3]		117	79½	.679	137⅛	1.172	32	101 0	3 2		41½					
1248–49	216⅝		180	89¼	.496			77⅜	6 6 7½	1 7¾		50					
1251–52	197		158	97½	.617	53⅞	.341	58	116 0	2 0		41½					
1252–53	151⅜ [4]		168	106¼	.632	130¾	.778	4¼	10 7	2 6		41¼					
1253–54	237		160	100⅜	.627	103⅜	.646	96½	8 10 8	1 9¼	¼	41⅝					1¾ from fugitive

1. In addition there were 17 qrs. of oats mixed with barley, 12½ qrs. sown on 16½ acres, 4½ sold for 7s. 1½d.
2. In addition there were 48 qrs. of draget, 6 qrs. sown on 8 acres, 42 sold for 111s. 5d.
3. Eighteen qrs. of mixtil in the yield and amount sold.
4. In addition there were 3 bus. received from the goods of Ingeram, a fugitive.

OATS (Continued)

Year	Yield	Yield in sheaf	Number of acres sown	Total amount of seed	Average seed per acre	Net yield	Average net yield per acre	Amount sold	Total sale price	Average sale price per qr.	Food allowance	For Feed	Number bought	Total purchase price	Average purchase price	Number sent away	Remarks
	Qrs.	Qrs.		Qrs.	Qrs.	Qrs.	Qrs.	Qrs.	£ s. d.	s. d.	Qrs.	Qrs.	Qrs.	s. d.	s. d.	Qrs.	
1254–55	203¾		183	114½	.626			40½	60 11	1 6	⅜	48½					
1256–57	261½		160	100¼	.627	163¾	1.023	116¾	18 6 9	3 1¾		44½					
1257–58	264		162	102	.630			117½	17 8 9	2 11½		44½					
1264–65	161¾[1]	21	148	98½	.666	114	.770	41¼	4 16 7	2 4		43					
1265–66	191½	21	149	99	.664			70½	6 6 10	1 9½		43					
1267–68	173⅜	28	198	99½	.503	116⅜	.588	54	108 0	2 0		58⅞	12				
1268–69	194⅞	21	224	112	.500			48½	6 6 10	3 0		55⅜					
1270–71	168⅝	21	212	105	.495	62½	.295	34	4 17 0	2 10¼		54½					
1271–72	146½	21	217	106	.488	13¼	.061	10½	31 6	3 0		51					
1272–73	98¼	21	170	90	.529	94⅜	.555	10	30 0	3 0		51	31¾				
1273–74	163⅜	21	168	90	.536	92⅞	.553	38¾	5 13 3	3 4¾	12	42⅛				1	
1274–75	161⅞	21	164	88	.537			43¼	6 11 5	3 4		51⅝					
1276–77	139¼	21	157	83	.529	118¼	.753	26	4 6 8	3 4		51¼					
1277–78	180¼	21	159	84	.528			66	8 16 0	2 8		51¼					
1282–83	119¾	16	172	72¾	.423	24⅜	.142	135⅞	14 4 10½	2 1¼		36	108¾		2 0		
1283–84	81⅛	16	175	67⅝	.386	38⅛	.218					34¼	3⅞		2 6		1 from 1282–83
1284–85	87¾	18	174	93	.534	127⅞	.735	15⅜	30 10½	2 0		30¾	30¾				15 new grain
1285–86	200⅞	20	160	81⅜	.509	50⅜	.315	76	9 13 8	2 6		63½					
1286–87	111¾	20	203	85½	.421	65	.320					47¼	1				
1287–88	130½	20	200	84¼	.421	94⅜	.472	19	31 8	1 8		47¼					
1288–89	158⅝	20	199	82	.412	59⅛	.297	46¾	102 4½	2 2¼		49⅞					
1289–90	121⅛	20	184	77⅞	.423	90⅝	.493	21¼	63 9	3 0		43	1				
1290–91	148½	20	261	98	.375	16⅛	.618	29	4 7 0	3 0		41½					
1291–92	94⅛	20	193	72⅜	.375	38¾	.201					41¾					
1292–93	91⅛	20	187	70	.374							30⅝					incomplete
1296–97	132¼	20	167	62⅝	.375	74⅜	.445	19	57 0	3 0		70⅝					
1297–98	117	20	173	65	.376	42¼	.244	30½	4 11 6	3 0		41½					

1298–99	87¼	20	176	65¾	.374	36¼	.206					41½					
1299–00	82	20	162	60¾	.375	72⅝	.448	3½	11 8	3 4		41¾	4	13 4	3 4		
1300–01	112⅜ [2]	21	238	89¼	.375	76½	.321	6⅛	13 8	2 2¾		43					
1301–02	145¾ [3]	20	222½	83⅜	.375	71⅜	.321	43	4 7 8	2 0½		43⅝					
1302–03	134¾	20	212	80⅛	.378			30 9/16	71 3¾	2 4		44 1/16					
1304–05	62¼		156	54⅛	.347			1⅜	2 9	2 0		8	1¼	3 9			
1305–06	28⅜	15	142	60⅛	.423	30⅞	.217					21⅝	38⅜	95 0			
1306–07	79	12	176	66⅛	.376	73¼	.416				2	22⅞					
1307–08	124⅜	15	167	73⅞	.442	57¾	.346	32 3/16	91 0	2 10	2	31 5/16					
1308–09	116⅝	15	176	74⅜	.423	68⅞	.391	20 7/16	54 6	2 8	2½	34⅛					
1309–10	128¼	15	154	65¾	.427	74⅝	.485	40 5/16	6 0 2	2 11¾		36 15/16					
1310–11	125⅜	15	166	71¾	.432	45⅛	.272	34⅜	5 14 7	3 4	2½	31¾					
1311–12	101⅞	15	170	73⅛	.430	66½	.391	4 13/16	14 5¼	3 0		39					
1312–13	124⅝	15	170	73	.429	48⅞	.288	29 3/16	4 17 3½	3 4		37 7/16					
1313–14	106⅞	15	168	72¼	.430	68½	.408	9⅛	30 5	3 4	3	37½					
1314–15	125¾	15	168	72⅜	.431	56½	.336	27⅞	[M.T.]			40½					
1315–16	113⅞	15	111	74½	.671	46	.414	13¼	5 6 0	8 0	3	38⅛					
1316–17	105½	15	146	62⅜	.427	54	.370	18⅜	4 12 8¼	5 1	2½	37¼					
1317–18	101⅜	15	130	55⅜	.426	65½	.504	21¾	4 18 3	4 6¼		39 3/16					
1318–19	105⅞	15	125	52⅛	.417			30	60 0	2 0	2½	37⅛	⅞	0 21			
1320–21	136⅛		80½	50¼	.624			49 15/16	7 7 9¾	2 11½	3¼	32 11/16					
1324–25	114¼	8½	91½	57¼	.626	58⅞	.643	39¼	5 19 7	3 0½	1½	24¼					
1325–26	107⅝	8½	82½	51½	.624	45⅝	.553	38½	5 4 3¼	2 8	1½	24⅝					
1326–27	88¼	8⅞	80	51¼	.641	54¾	.684	18¼	54 9	3 0	1½	26⅛					
1327–28	95¾	10¼	78	48½	.622	35¼	.452	32⅝	72 1	2 2½	1½	26⅜	4½	10 4			1½ sold extra
1328–29	76¼	7½	74	46⅛	.623	54½	.736	17	45 4	2 8	2	19	⅜	0 12			
1329–30	90⅝	10	59½	37⅛	.624	51	.857	40	110 0	2 9	2	21½					
1330–31	78⅝	9½	64	40¼	.629	40¼	.629	30½	4 17 0	3 2¼	2⅜	15					
1331–32	73	7½	68	42⅜	.623	58¼	.857	11 9/16	34 9¼	3 0	7¾	18¾					
1332–33	92⅛	8½	71	44⅜	.625			30 29/32	65 9¾	2 1½	3 17/32	21¾					
1334–35	62½	8½	61	38⅛	.625	58½	.959	15½	51 4	3 3¾	2¼	19 11/16	4 19/32	12 2	2 7¾		
1335–36	88⅛	8½	74	46⅛	.623	31⅞	.431	28 15/32	66 5¼	2 4	2¼	19 25/32					
1336–37	70	8	67½	42⅛	.624	34¼	.507	13⅞	32 0½	2 3¾	2¼	19¾					
1337–38	68⅜	8	60	37⅝	.627	37⅛	.619	14¾	29 6	2 0	2	22					

1. Beginning here, the total yield means only the 'total yield of the grange in the granary.' The grand total is found by adding to this amount the number of qrs. fed in sheaf.
2. In addition 3½ curall and 1½ berecorn.
3. In addition 4¼ berecorn.

OATS (Continued)

Year	Yield	Yield in sheaf	Number of acres sown	Total amount of seed	Average seed per acre	Net yield	Average net yield per acre	Amount sold	Total sale price			Average sale price per qr.		Food allowance	For feed	Number bought	Total purchase price		Average purchase price		Number sent away	Remarks
	Qrs.	Qrs.		Qrs.	Qrs.	Qrs	Qrs.	Qrs.	£	s.	d.	s.	d.	Qrs.	Qrs.	Qrs.	s.	d.	s.	d.	Qrs.	
1338–39	66¾	8	[M.T.]	32⅛		34¼		19 19/32		30	11¾	1	7									
1339–40	58⅜	8	57	35⅝	.625	25¾	.452	7⅞		23	7½	3	0	2	20⅞							
1340–41	53⅜	8	71½	44⅝	.624	43¼	.605							2	22 3/16	7 7/16	19	10	2	7		
1341–42	77⅞	10	57½	36	.626	45⅜	.789	26⅞		60	4	2	3	2	22 31/32							
1342–43	71⅜	10	61½	38	.618	51 1/16	.830	19½		49	4	2	6¼	2⅜	21½							
1343–44	80 1/16	9	67	41¾	.623	58⅜	.871	23 3/32		62	3¼	2	8¼	2¼	21 31/32							
1344–45	90⅛	10	49	30½	.622	24⅝	.503	44 13/16	4	16	4¾	2	2	2⅛	22 11/16							
1345–46	47⅛	8	50½	31½	.624	55	1.089	1⅜		4	1½	3	0	1⅞	19 3/16							1⅛ sold extra
1346–47	78½	8	64	40	.625	51¾	.809	25 1/16		74	6¼	2	11¾	2	19 7/16							
1347–48	81⅝	10	71	35½	.500	57⅛	.805	31 15/32	4	15	4½	3	0¼	2	22⅝							
1348–49	83⅝	9	74	37	.500	41	.554	31 29/32		49	9½	1	6¾	2	21 23/32							
1349–50	70	8	67	33⅝	.502	17¼	.257	20 15/32		68	1	3	4	3½	20 13/32							
1350–51	45⅞	5	73	36½	.500	37 11/16	.516	½						3½	18	7⅝	35	7	4	8		
1351–52	66 3/16	8	64	32	.500	8¼	.129	18 3/16	4	10	11¼	5	0	3½	20½							
1352–53	32¼	8	65	32½	.500	45¼	.696							3½	20 5/16	16 1/16	17	11½	4	8		
1353–54	67¾	10	69	34½	.500	55⅜	.803	20		40	0	2	0	3½	22 11/16	4 11/16	9	4½	2	0		1¾ sold extra
1354–55	79⅞	10	69	34½	.500	49⅞	.723	27 11/16		73	10	2	8	3½	23 7/16							¾ sold extra
1355–56	74⅜	10	82	41	.500	0		16⅜		42	8¾	2	7¼	3½	23							½ sold extra
1356–57	35⅜	5	65	36 9/16	.563	55 7/16	.853	4		10	0	2	6	3½	18¼	24 15/16	83	5¼	3	4¼		3 sold extra
1357–58	83	9	74½	37⅝	.505	51½	.691	26¼		76	0	2	10¾	3½	21¾							2¾ sold extra
1358–59	80⅛	9	68	34	.500			29 13/16		79	3	2	8¼	3½	21 15/16							
1359–60	[M.T.]							19⅜		45	2½	2	4									
1360–61	97½	10	84	42	.500	20	.238	39⅞	[M.T.]					3½	22⅜							
1361–62	53	9	68	34	.500	58	.853	2⅝		8	10¼	3	4	3½	21 15/16							
1362–63	82½	9½	61	31	.508	64⅞	1.064	34⅛	5	8	8¼	3	2¼	3½	23⅜							
1363–64	86⅜	9½	60	30	.500	50	.833	39¼	5	16	8	2	11¾	3½	23⅛							
1364–65	70½	9½	60	30	.500	40½	.675	23⅞		62	0	2	7¼	3½	22⅝							

1365–66	61	9½	56	[M.T.]				18⅝		43	5½	2	4	3½	[M.T.]	
1366–67	45½	9½	57	28½	.500	70⅞	1.243	1½		3	0	2	0	3½	21½	
1367–68	91⅜	8	58	29	.500	70½	1.216	45 9/16	7	11	10½	3	4	3½	21 5/16	
1368–69	89½	10	56	28	.500	42¼	.754	47 9/16	6	6	10	2	8	3½	20 7/16	
1369–70	60¼	10	58	29	.500	58	1.000	20 9/16	5	7	10	5	3	3	19 11/16	
1370–71	79	8	60	30	.500	64⅝	1.077	25 7/16	4	3	10½	3	4	3	17½	11 1/16 sold extra
1371–72	86⅝	8	64	32	.500	32	.500	34¼	4	11	4	2	8	2	17	
1372–73	56	8	55	27½	.500	41¼	.750	16 7/16		52	6½	3	2¼	2½	17 7/16	
1373–74	60¾	8	50	25	.500			18⅝		49	8	2	8	2	17	5⅝ sold extra
1375–76	55⅝	8	50	25	.500	40½	.810	18¾		62	6	3	4	2½	17⅜	
1376–77	57½	8	51	25½	.500	38¼	.750	20¾[1]		48	5	2	4	2½	16¾	
1377–78	55¾	8	52	26	.500	44¼	.851	18⅜						2½	16⅞	
1378–79	62¼	8	50	25¼	.505	50½	1.010	25		50	0	2	0	2½	16½	
1379–80	67¾	8	52	26	.500			29¾							17½	
1381–82	53¼		48	24	.500			17 5/16		33	9½	1	11½	2½	16 11/16	¾ sold extra
1382–83		8						6¼		16	8	2	8			
1383–84	64	8	49	24	.490	41	.837	20⅛		46	11½	2	4	2½	17⅞	7½ sold extra
1384–85	57	8	[Ill.]	24		57½		4¾		11	1	2	4	2½	[Ill.]	17 sold extra
1385–86	73½	8	42	21	.500			41 31/32		109	5	2	7¼	2½	16 1/32	
1387–88	56½	8	42	21	.500	52½	1.250	21½		34	2	1	7	2½	15¼	3¼ sold extra
1388–89	65½	8	41	20½	.500			21⅝		43	3	2	0	2½	15⅜	13½ sold extra
1390–91	51⅛	8	41	20½	.500			19 13/16		79	3	4	0	2½	15 13/16	
1392–93	39½	8	34	17	.500	34	1.000	7⅝		20	4	2	8	2½	15⅝	4¾ " "
1393–94	43	8	36	18	.500	27	.750	8⅞		23	8	2	8	2½	15½	6¾ " "
1394–95	37	8	40	20	.500	32½	.813	3⅜		10	4	3	0¾	2½	14⅛	6½ " "
1395–96	44½	8	44	22	.500			11 13/16		27	6¾	2	4	2½	11 13/16	4⅜ " "
1398–99	54½	8	34	17	.500	36	1.059	30⅞		60	10½	1	11¾	2½	12½	
1399–00	45	8	38	19	.500	38	1.000	18⅝		42	4½	2	3¼	2½	12⅞	
1400–01	49	8	36	18	.500			22⅞		57	2	2	6	2½	13⅝	
1402–03	40¼	8	36	18	.500			11¾		31	4	2	8	2½	14	2 sold extra
1406–07	51½	8	34	17	.500			26¾		49	0	1	10	2½	13¼	
1408–09	52	8	40	20	.500	40	1.000	24⅞		67	6	2	8½	2½	13	
1409–10	52	8	40	20	.500	60	1.500	24⅛		72	4½	3	0	2½	13⅜	
1410–11	72	8	40	20	.500	60	1.500	44⅝	5	18	6½	2	8	2½	12⅞	

1. Sold per mutuum.

OATS (Continued)

Year	Yield	Yield in sheaf	Number of acres sown	Total amount of seed	Average seed per acre	Net yield	Average net yield per acre	Amount sold	Total sale price			Average sale price per qr.		Food allowance	For feed	Number bought	Total purchase price	Average purchase price	Number sent away	Remarks
	Qrs.	Qrs.		Qrs.	Qrs.	Qrs.	Qrs.	Qrs.	£	s.	d.	s.	d.	Qrs.	Qrs.	Qrs.	s. d.	s. d.	Qrs.	
1411–12	72	8	40	20	.500	60	1.500	$43\frac{3}{4}$	4	18	5	2	3	$2\frac{1}{2}$	$9\frac{3}{4}$					
1412–13	72	8	38	19	.500	61	1.605	$43\frac{5}{8}$		77	5	1	$9\frac{1}{4}$	$2\frac{1}{2}$	$14\frac{7}{8}$					
1413–14	$69\frac{3}{4}$	$10\frac{1}{4}$	32	16	.500	32	1.000	$43\frac{1}{2}$		87	0	2	0	$2\frac{1}{2}$	18					
1414–15	40	8	34	17	.500			$12\frac{3}{4}$		30	0	2	$4\frac{1}{4}$	$2\frac{1}{2}$	$15\frac{3}{4}$					
1418–19	$41\frac{1}{2}$	8	32	16	.500	32	1.000	$14\frac{1}{2}$		33	10	2	4	$2\frac{1}{2}$	$16\frac{1}{2}$					
1419–20	41	7	34	17	.500	$25\frac{1}{2}$	.735	$15\frac{1}{8}$		30	4	2	0	$2\frac{1}{4}$	$13\frac{1}{4}$					
1420–21	$34\frac{1}{2}$	8	34	17	.500	$32\frac{1}{2}$	.941	$10\frac{1}{4}$		18	6	1	$9\frac{3}{4}$	$2\frac{1}{2}$	$12\frac{3}{4}$					
1421–22	$41\frac{1}{2}$	8	32	16	.500	$31\frac{1}{2}$	.984	$18\frac{9}{16}$		37	$4\frac{1}{2}$	2	$0\frac{1}{4}$	$2\frac{1}{2}$	$12\frac{7}{8}$					
1422–23	$39\frac{1}{2}$	8	32	16	.500	$33\frac{1}{2}$	1.047	$16\frac{15}{16}$		33	11	2	0	$2\frac{1}{2}$	$12\frac{1}{16}$					
1423–24	$41\frac{1}{2}$	8	32	16	.500	32	1.000	$20\frac{13}{16}$		36	$0\frac{1}{2}$	1	$8\frac{3}{4}$	$2\frac{1}{2}$	$10\frac{3}{16}$					
1424–25	40	8	32	16	.500	32	1.000	$3\frac{1}{4}$		6	6	2	0	$2\frac{1}{2}$	$12\frac{3}{4}$					$13\frac{1}{2}$ sold extra
1425–26	40	8	32	16	.500			$17\frac{1}{8}$		30	11	1	$9\frac{3}{4}$	$2\frac{1}{2}$	$12\frac{3}{8}$					
1427–28	48	8	32	16	.500			$25\frac{3}{4}$		45	$2\frac{1}{4}$	1	9	$2\frac{1}{2}$	$11\frac{23}{32}$					
1429–30	48	8	32	16	.500	40	1.250	$26\frac{3}{8}$		66	$1\frac{1}{2}$	2	6	$2\frac{1}{2}$	$11\frac{1}{8}$					
1430–31	48	8	32	16	.500	40	1.250	26		58	0	2	$2\frac{3}{4}$	$2\frac{1}{2}$	$11\frac{1}{2}$					
1431–32	48	8	32	16	.500	40	1.250	$26\frac{1}{4}$		39	$4\frac{1}{2}$	1	6	$2\frac{1}{2}$	$11\frac{1}{4}$					
1432–33	48	8	32	16	.500	$38\frac{7}{8}$	1.215	$26\frac{19}{32}$		58	$8\frac{1}{4}$	2	$2\frac{1}{2}$	$2\frac{1}{2}$	$11\frac{1}{8}$					
1433–34	$46\frac{7}{8}$	8	32	16	.500	48	1.500	$25\frac{1}{2}$		54	11	2	$1\frac{3}{4}$	$2\frac{1}{2}$	$11\frac{7}{8}$					
1434–35	52	12	32	16	500	48	1.500	$30\frac{1}{8}$		44	$4\frac{1}{2}$	1	$5\frac{3}{4}$	$2\frac{1}{2}$	$15\frac{1}{2}$					
1435–36	56	8	32	16	.500			$32\frac{7}{16}$		54	$4\frac{1}{4}$	1	8	$2\frac{1}{2}$	$13\frac{1}{16}$					
1438–39	48	8	32	16	.500			$24\frac{1}{4}$		81	6	3	$4\frac{1}{4}$	$2\frac{1}{2}$	$13\frac{1}{4}$					
1440–41	64		32	16	.500	40	1.250	$29\frac{9}{16}$		39	5	1	4	$2\frac{1}{2}$	$15\frac{15}{16}$					
1441–42	48	8	32	16	.500			$21\frac{13}{16}$		29	1	1	4	$2\frac{1}{2}$	$15\frac{11}{16}$					
1447–48	56	8	32	16	.500	48	1.500	$12\frac{3}{4}$		21	3	1	8	$2\frac{1}{2}$	$15\frac{23}{32}$					$17\frac{1}{32}$ sold extra
1448–49	59	5	32	16	.500			42		70	11	1	8	1	5					

PEAS

Year	Yield	In pod	Number of acres sown	Total amount of seed	Average seed per acre	Net yield	Average net yield per acre	Amount sold	Total sale price		Average sale price per qr.		Feed	Number bought	Total purchase price		Average purchase price		Remarks
	Qrs.	Qrs.		Qrs.	Qrs.	Qrs.	Qrs.	Qrs.	s.	d.	s.	d.	Qrs.	Qrs.	s.	d.	Qrs.		
1208–09	2½		4	1	.250			1½	2	3	1	6							
1210–11	2½			1⅝		3⅝		1	0	18	1	6							
1211–12	5¼		4	1¼	.313			4	5	10	1	5½							
1213–14	2⅜		4	1	.250			1⅜	2	9	2	0							
1215–16	2			1				1	0	20	1	8							
1217–18	1½		3	1	.333	2⅛	.708	½	0	18	3	0							
1218–19	3⅛		4	1⅛	.281	1⅝	.406	2	3	4	1	8							
1219–20	2¾		3½	¾	.214			2	4	0	2	0							
1220–21	½		2½																
1223–24	3		5	1	.200	1¼	.250	2	4	5½	2	2¾							
1224–25	2¼		5	⅞	.175			1⅜	5	5	3	11¼							
1225–26	⅞		5	⅞	.175	7⅜	1.475												
1226–27	8¼		9½	2¼	.237			6	20	0	2	4							
1231–32	5⅛		5	1⅞	.375	2	.400	3¼	9	9	3	0							
1232–33	3⅞		5	1¾	.350			2⅛	4	11½	2	4							
1235–36	2½		3	½	.167			2	4	4	2	2							
1236–37	⅜		[M.T.]					¼	0	7	2	4							
1244–45			4	⅝	.156	1⅞	.469							⅝	0	11½	1	6½	
1245–46	2½		3½	1	.286	2 7/16	.696	1⅜	3	8	2	8	⅛						
1246–47	3 1/16		3	7/16	.146	1 11/16	.563	2½	12	8	5	0¾	⅛						
1247–48	2⅛		2	½	.250	¼	.125	1½	7	0	4	8	⅛						
1248–49	¾		2	½	.250			½	0	12	2	0	⅛	½	0	12	2	0	⅛ extra used
1251–52	2¼		3	¾	.250			1¼	2	11	2	4	¼						
1256–57								1⅝	5	5	3	4							
1257–58	1		3	¾	.250			¼	0	9	3	0							

PEAS (Continued)

Year	Yield	In pod	Number of acres sown	Total amount of seed	Average seed per acre	Net yield	Average net yield per acre	Amount sold	Total sale price		Average sale price per qr.		Feed	Number bought	Total purchase price		Average purchase price		Remarks
	Qrs.	Qrs.		Qrs.	Qrs.	Qrs.	Qrs.	Qrs.	s.	d.	s.	d.	Qrs.	Qrs.	s.	d.	s.	d.	
1264–65	3⅝		3	⅞	*.292*	*4⅛*	*1.375*	2¾	9	2	3	4							
1265–66	5		4	1	*.250*			4	12	0	3	0							
1267–68	2½		4	1	*.250*	*3*	*.750*	1½											
1268–69	4			1				3	12	0	4	0							
1270–71	8		8	2	*.250*	*7⅞*	*.984*	10½	*70*	*0*	6	8	½						
1271–72	9⅞		4	1	*.250*			7⅞	52	6	6	8							
1272–73	¾		6	1½	*.250*	*5*	*.833*	¾	3	4½	*4*	*6*	⅛	1⅝					
1273–74	6½		6	1½	*.250*	*5½*	*.917*	5	26	8	5	4							
1274–75	7		5	1¼	*.250*			5¾	28	9	5	0							
1276–77	2¼			1		*4⅝*		1¼	7	6	6	0							
1277–78	5⅝		5	1½	*.300*			4⅛	16	6	4	0							
1282–83	2		11	1 11/16	*.153*	*2 11/16*	*.244*	1 15/16	7	1½	3	4		1⅝			3	4	
1283–84	4⅜		9	1	*.111*			3⅜	16	10½	6	0							
1284–85	6			3½		*7½*		2½	7	6	3	0							
1285–86	11		8	1½	*.188*	*6⅛*	*.766*	10	30	0	3	0		½					
1286–87	7⅝		14	3	*.214*	*8*	*.571*	4½	*13*	*6*	3	0							
1287–88	11		11	2½	*.227*	*3⅛*	*.284*	4¼	5	8	0	16	1¼						3 remain
1288–89	5⅝		12	2½	*.208*	*1⅛*	*.094*	2¾	9	2	3	4	⅜						
1289–90	3⅝		12	2½	*.208*	*11*	*.917*	1⅛	5	7½	5	0							
1290–91	13½			3⅞		*4⅝*		9⅝	57	9	6	0							
1291–92	8½			3⅞				4⅝	24	8	5	4							
1292–93	3⅞			2⅜		*1*		1	5	4	5	4	½						
1296–97	3⅜			1		*2⅛*		2	8	0	*4*	*0*							
1297–98	3⅛			1½		*3¼*		1⅝	8	1½	*5*	*0*							
1298–99	4¾			1⅝		*2¾*		3⅛	15	7½	*5*	*0*							
1299–00	4⅜			1¼		*4¼*		3⅛	10	5	3	4							

1300–01	5½			3⅛		3⅜		2⅜	6 4	2 8				
1301–02	6½			3		4¾		3⅛	9 4½	3 0	⅜			
1302–03	7¾		15	2½	.167			5	16 8	3 4	¼			
1304–05	2⅝			2⅝										
1305–06	3¼			3¼		5 1/16								
1306–07	8 5/16		20	4⅝	.231	13¼	.663	3 11/16	17 2½	4 8				
1307–08	17⅜	½	22	4¾	.216	15/16	.043	12⅝	67 4	5 4	½			
1308–09	5 11/16		21	4⅜	.208	⅞	.042	1 5/16	8 9	6 8				
1309–10	5¼		18	3 11/16	.205	11 7/16	.635	1 9/16	9 4½	6 0				
1310–11	15⅛		24	4⅞	.203	11¾	.490	9½		6 1¼	¾			
1311–12	16 21/32		19½	4⅝	.237	13⅜	.686	11¼	51 0	4 6½	25/32			
1312–13	17½	½	28	7 1/16	.252	13 13/16	.493	9⅞	39 9	4 0¼				
1313–14	20⅞		24	6⅛	.255	13⅞	.578	13	65 0	5 0	1¾			
1314–15	20		26	6½	.250			11⅜	[M.T.]		2⅛			
1315–16	5¾			5¾		4 11/16								
1316–17	10 7/16		18	4½	.250	11⅛	.618	5 15/16	79 2	13 4				
1317–18	15⅝		21	4⅞	.232	19⅛	.911	10¾	71 8	6 8				
1318–19	24			4½				19½	63 6	3 3				
1320–21	15½		17½	4⅜	.250			11⅛	46 10½	4 2½				
1324–25	14⅝		18	4½	.250	10⅛	.563	10⅛	48 6½	4 9½				
1325–26	14⅝		17	4¼	.250	3⅞	.228	10⅜	44 6	4 3½				
1326–27	3⅛	5	18½	4½	.243	6 9/16	.355	1⅞	8 9	4 8	5	3¼		
1327–28	11 1/16		15	3⅝	.242	8⅝	.575	4⅛			3½	¼	0 12	4 0
1328–29	12¼		15	3⅞	.258	11⅞	.792	8⅜	17 6	2 1				
1329–30	15¾		13	3¼	.250	1	.077	12½	72 4	5 9½				
1330–31	4¼		17	4¼	.250	5¾	.338							
1331–32	10		13	3¼	.250	6⅜	.490	5¾	40 3	7 0	1			
1332–33	9⅝		13	3¼	.250			5¼	26 3	5 0	1⅛			
1334–35	4¼	1	13	3¼	.250	8⅞	.683				2			
1335–36	10⅛	2	13	3¼	.250	6	.462	6⅞	27 6	4 0	2			
1336–37	7¼	2	12½	3⅛	.250	7⅜	.590	4⅛	16 6	4 0	2			
1337–38	8½	2	12	3⅛	.260	6⅝	.552	5⅜	16 1½	3 0	2			

PEAS (CONTINUED)

Year	Yield	In pod	Number of acres sown	Total amount of seed	Average seed per acre	Net yield	Average net yield per acre	Amount sold	Total sale price		Average sale price per qr.		Feed	Number bought	Total purchase price		Average purchase price		Remarks
	Qrs.	Qrs.		Qrs.	Qrs.	Qrs.	Qrs.	Qrs.	s.	d.	s.	d.	Qrs.	Qrs.	s.	d.	s.	d.	
1338–39	7¾	2	11½	2⅞	.250	3¼	.283	4⅞	14	7½	3	0	2						
1339–40	4⅛	2	13	3¼	.250	5⅝	.433	⅞	4	8	5	4	2						
1340–41	7⅜	1½	13½	3⅜	.250	3½	.259	4	16	0	4	0	1½						
1341–42	6⅞		13	3¼	.250	5¾	.442	3⅝	14	6	4	0							
1342–43	9		11	3	.273	8¾	.795	6	24	0	4	0							
1343–44	11 23/32		14	3½	.250	6	.429	8 7/32	41	1	5	0							
1344–45	9½		14	3½	.250	1¼	.089	6	20	0	3	4							
1345–46	4¾		19	4¾	.250	13⅞	.730												
1346–47	18⅝		14	3½	.250	14¾	1.054	15⅛	85	9	5	8							
1347–48	18¼		16	4	.250			14¼	76	0	5	4							
1348–49	2½			2½		3¾													[Ill.]
1349–50	3¼	3	3½	⅞	.250	5⅝	1.607	2⅜	12	8[illegible]	5	4							3 remain
1350–51	6½			3		⅝		3½	23	4	6	8							
1351–52	3⅝		12	3	.250	⅜	.031						⅝						
1352–53	3⅜		12	3	.250	5	.417	⅜	2	6	6	8¼							
1353–54	5	3	12	3	.250	7⅞	.656	2	6	0	3	0	3						
1354–55	7⅞	3	10½	2⅝	.250	13¾	1.310	5¼	17	6	3	4	3						
1355–56	13⅜	3	16	4	.250	¾	.047	9⅜	37	6	4	0	3						
1356–57	3¼	1½	12	3¼	.271	7¼	.604							1½					
1357–58	10½		13	3¼	.250	7¾	.596	7¼	42	0	6	0							
1358–59	11		12	3	.250			8	32	0	4	0							
1359–60	[Ill.]							6¼	29	3	4	8¼							
1360–61	5	1	12	3	.250	1¾	.146	2	10	0	5	0	1						
1361–62	3¾	1	11	2¾	.250	5½	.500	1	5	0	5	0	1						
1362–63	7¼	1	10	2½	.250	8	.800	4¾	28	6	6	0	1						
1363–64	8½	2	10	2½	.250	3	.300	6	32	0	5	4	2						

1364–65	3½	2	12	3	.250			½	2	6	5	0	2						
1365–66	[M.T.]	2	11	3	.273	*1½*	*.136*	3½	11	8	3	4	2						
1366–67	2½	2	10	2½	.250	*5*	*.500*						2						
1367–68	5½	2	12	3	.250	*9*	*.750*	2½	13	4	*5*	*4*	2						
1368–69	10	2	12	3	.250	*6¼*	*.521*	6½	31	9½	*4*	*10¾*	2½						
1369–70	7¼	2	13	3¼	.250	*4⅜*	*.337*	3½	46	8	13	4	2½						
1370–71	5⅛	2½	10½	2⅝	.250	*8⅛*	*.774*	2½	15	0	6	0	2½						
1371–72	8¼	2½	12	3	.250	*7*	*.583*	5¼	24	6	4	8	2½						
1372–73	4½	5½	14	3½	.250	*7¼*	*.518*	1			6	0	5½						
1373–74	4¼	6½	10	2½	.250			1¾ [2]					6½						
1375–76	2¼	3½	8	2	.250	*4*	*.500*	¼ [3]					3½						
1376–77	2	4	8	2	.250	*6½*	*.813*						4						
1377–78	4½	4	10	2½	.250	*5¾*	*.575*	2					4						
1378–79	2¼	6	9	2½	.278	*10*	*1.111*	2					4						
1379–80	2½	10	10	5	.500			2	6	8	*3*	*4*	8						1 extra sold
1381–82	2½	4	10	2½	.250								4						
1383–84	2¾	5	11	2¾	.250	*4*	*.364*	1					4						
1384–85	2¾	4	8	2	.250	*5*	*.625*	1¼					4	½	2	0	*4*	*0*	
1385–86	3	4	12	3	.250								4						
1387–88	3	4	12	3	.250	*4½*	*.375*						4						
1388–89	3½	4	14	3½	.250								4						
1390–91	4¾	4	14	3½	.250			1¼					4						
1392–93	3½	4	14	3½	.250	*7*	*.500*						4						
1393–94	6½	4	14	3½	.250	*5¼*	*.375*	3					4						
1394–95	4¾	4	15	3¾	.250	*4¾*	*.317*						4	½	*2*	*0*			1½ sold extra
1395–96	3½	5	14	3½	.250			1					4						
1398–99	4	5	16	4	.250	*5*	*.313*	1	3	4	*3*	*4*	4						
1399–00	4	5	16	4	.250	*6*	*.375*						5						
1400–01	5	5	16	4	.250			1½	4	0	*2*	*8*	5						
1402–03	4	5	16	4	.250								5						
1406–07	3¾	5	15	3¾	.250								5						
1408–09	3¾	5	15	3¾	.250	*5*	*.333*						5						

1. Sold for 31s. 4d. — 2⅜ qrs. peas and 3½ qrs. vetches.
2. One and three-quarters peas and 5 qrs. vetches sold for 27s.
3. Two bus. peas and 5⅜ qrs. vetches sold for 35s. 3d.

PEAS (Continued)

Year	Yield	In pod	Number of acres sown	Total amount of seed	Average seed per acre	Net yield	Average net yield per acre	Amount sold	Total sale price		Average sale price per qr.		Feed	Number bought	Total purchase price		Average purchase price		Remarks
	Qrs.	Qrs.		Qrs.	Qrs.	Qrs.	Qrs.	Qrs.	s.	d.	s.	d.	Qrs.	Qrs.	s.	d.	s.	d.	
1409–10	3¾	5	15	3¾	.250	5	.333						5						
1410–11	3¾	5	15	3¾	.250	5	.333						5						
1411–12	3¾	5	15	3¾	.250	5	.333						5						
1412–13	3¾	5	15	3¾	.250	5	.333						5						
1413–14	1¾	5	15	3¾	.250	3	.200						5	2	6	8	3	4	
1414–15	2¼	5	14	3½	.250								5	1¼			5	0	
1418–19	3¼	5	13	3¼	.250	6	.462						5						
1419–20	2¾	6½	11	2¾	.250	6¼	.568						6½						
1420–21	3	6	12	3	.250	6½	.542						6						
1421–22	3½	6	16	4	.250	4	.250						7						(?)
1422–23	2	6	12	3	.250	6	.500						6	1	3	4	3	4	
1423–24	3	6	12	3	.250	5	.417						6						
1424–25	2	6	12	3	.250	6	.500						6	1	4	0	4	0	
1425–26	3	6	12	3	.250								6						
1427–28	3	6	12	3	.250								6						
1429–30	3	6	12	3	.250	6	.500						6						
1430–31	3	6	12	3	.250	6	.500						6						
1431–32	3	6	12	3	.250	6	.500						6						
1432–33	3	6	12	3	.250	6	.500						6						
1433–34	3	6	12	3	.250	6	.500						6						
1434–35	3	6	12	3	.250	6	.500						6						
1435–36	3	6	12	3	.250								6						
1438–39	3	6	12	3	.250								6						
1440–41	6		12	3	.250	6	.500	2	6	0	3	0	4	3	8	0	2	8	
1441–42	3	6	12	3	.250								6						
1447–48	3	6	12	3	.250	6	.500						6						
1448–49	3	6	12	3	.250								6						

Year	Yield	In pod	Number of acres sown	Total amount of seed	Average seed per acre	Net yield	Average net yield per acre	Amount sold	Total sale price		Average sale price per qr.		For feed	Number bought	Total purchase price		Average purchase price		Remarks
	Qrs.	Qrs.		Qrs.	Qrs.	Qrs.	Qrs.	Qrs.	s.	d.	s.	d.	Qrs.	Qrs.	s.	d.	s.	d.	
1208–09																			
1210–11														½[1]	0	14	*2*	*4*	
1211–12	1¾[1]			½				1¼[2]	2	2	*1*	*8¾*							
1213–14																			
1215–16																			
1217–18	9⅝		11	2⅝	*.239*	*7⅜*	*.670*	5½	14	6	*2*	*7¾*							1½ sent away
1218–19	10		10	2¼	*.225*	*7⅜*	*.738*	1¼	2	1	*1*	*8*	6½						
1219–20	9⅝		6	1½	*.250*	*1¾*	*.292*	3⅛	5	2½	*1*	*8*	5						
1220–21	3¼		7	1½	*.214*			1¼	2	10	*2*	*3¼*	½						
1223–24	2⅛		5	1	*.200*	*1¼*	*.250*	⅝	0	15½	*2*	*5*	½						
1224–25	2¼		6	1¼	*.208*			1	2	2½	2	2½							
1225–26	¾		4	¾	*.188*	*2¾*	*.688*												
1226–27	3½		7	1¾	*.250*			1¾	2	3	*1*	*3½*							
1231–32	5		1½[3]	2½		*1*	*.667*	2½	6	8	*2*	*8*							
1232–33	3½		5½	1¾	*.318*			1¾	3	6	*2*	*0*							
1235–36	1		3	½	*.167*			½	0	12	*2*	*0*							
1236–37																			
1244–45	1⅜		10	1⅜	*.138*	*4⅝*	*.463*												
1245–46	6		8	2⅜	*.297*	*4¾*	*.594*	3⅝	7	3	*2*	*0*							
1246–47	7⅛		6½	2	*.308*	*6⅞*	*1.058*	5⅛	22	8	*4*	*5*							
1247–48	8⅞		3½	1⅞	*.536*			7	28	0	4	0		¼[1]	0	18	*6*	*0*	
1248–49			4	1	*.250*									1	0	20	1	8	
1251–52	1⅜		3½	⅞	*.250*			½	0	14	*2*	*4*							
1252–53			2	½	*.250*	⅝	*.313*							½	2	4	*4*	*8*	
1253–54	1⅛		3	¾	*.250*	½	*.167*	½	[M.T.]										
1254–55	1¼		3	¾	*.250*			½	0	12	*2*	*0*							
1256–57	2		1½	⅜	*.250*	⅝	*.417*	1⅝											

1. Beans. 2. The amount is 1 qr. and 1 stri*cum*. The latter is taken to be 2 bushs. 3. This is 1½ acres p*er* perti*cam*. The amount is probably incorrect.

VETCHES (Continued)

Year	Yield	In pod	Number of acres sown	Total amount of seed	Average seed per acre	Net yield	Average net yield per acre	Amount sold	Total sale price		Average sale price per qr.		For feed	Number bought	Total purchase price		Average purchase price		Remarks
	Qrs.	Qrs.		Qrs.	Qrs.	Qrs.	Qrs.	Qrs.	s.	d.	s.	d.	Qrs.	Qrs.	s.	d.	s.	d.	
1257–58	1		3	¾	.250			¼											
1264–65	3⅝		4½	1⅛	.250	2⅛	.472	2¾	9	2	3	4							
1265–66	3¼		4	1	.250			2¼	6	0	2	8							
1267–68	4		8	2	.250	6	.750	2											
1268–69	8			2				6	20	0	3	4							
1270–71	7⅛		8	2	.250	4¼	.531	5⅛	25	7½	5	0							
1271–72	6¼		6	1½	.250			4¾	28	6	6	0							
1272–73	⅜		7	1⅞	.268	2¼	.321							1½					
1273–74	4⅛		8	2	.250	7	.875	2⅛	9	11	4	8							
1274–75	9		6	1½	.250			7½	30	0	4	0							
1276–77	5¼		10	1½	.150	6	.600	3¾	21	3	5	8							
1277–78	7½		6	1½	.250			6	20	0	3	4							
1282–83	3⅛		12	1¾	.146			3⅛	13	6	4	4¾		1¾	5	3	3	0	
1283–84	1⅜							1⅜											
1284–85	4⅜			3		15½		1⅜	3	8	2	8							
1285–86	18½		10	2½	.250	4	.400	15⅝	41	8	2	8	⅜						
1286–87	6½		15	3⅛	.208	2¾	.183	3⅛			3	0	¼						
1287–88	5⅞		15½	3	.194	1½	.097	1⅞	3	1½	1	8	1						
1288–89	4½		13	2⅝	.202			1⅞	6	3	3	4							
1289–90	2½		12	2½	.208	5⅛	.427												
1290–91	7⅝			2⅞		2⅛		3¼	19	6	6	0	1½						
1291–92	5			2⅝		⅛		1½	7	6	5	0	⅞						
1292–93	2¾			1½									¼						
1296–97	4⅝			1⅝		3⅜		3	12	0	4	0							
1297–98	5			2		4⅝		3	12	0	4	0							
1298–99	6⅝			2¼		4⅜		4⅜	16	6	4	0							
1299–00	6⅝			2⅛		2		4½	15	0	3	0							

1300–01	$4\frac{1}{8}$			$4\frac{1}{8}$		$3\frac{5}{8}$													
1301–02	$7\frac{3}{4}$			$3\frac{1}{4}$		$4\frac{11}{16}$		$4\frac{1}{2}$	9	0	2	0							
1302–03	$7\frac{15}{16}$			$3\frac{1}{4}$				$4\frac{5}{16}$	12	$11\frac{1}{4}$	3	0	$\frac{3}{8}$						
1304–05																			
1305–06	$\frac{1}{2}$			3		$6\frac{1}{4}$								$2\frac{1}{2}$[1]	15	0	6	0	
1306–07	$8\frac{1}{4}$	1	20	$4\frac{1}{2}$	.225	$15\frac{3}{4}$	.788	$3\frac{3}{4}$	17	6	4	8	1						
1307–08	$18\frac{3}{4}$	$1\frac{1}{2}$	28	$6\frac{3}{16}$	.221	$12\frac{3}{4}$	.455	$12\frac{9}{16}$	58	$7\frac{1}{2}$	4	8	$1\frac{1}{2}$						
1308–09	$18\frac{15}{16}$		27	$6\frac{5}{32}$	.228	$4\frac{3}{4}$	.176	$10\frac{25}{32}$	64	$8\frac{1}{4}$	6	0	2						
1309–10	$8\frac{3}{8}$	$2\frac{1}{2}$	26	$5\frac{7}{8}$	.226	$8\frac{5}{8}$	.332	$2\frac{1}{2}$	15	8	6	$3\frac{1}{4}$	$2\frac{1}{2}$						
1310–11	12	$2\frac{1}{2}$	28	6	.214	$10\frac{1}{2}$	.375	6	36	0	6	0	$2\frac{1}{2}$						
1311–12	$16\frac{1}{2}$		$24\frac{1}{2}$	$5\frac{11}{16}$	.232	$2\frac{15}{16}$	.120	$10\frac{1}{2}$	40	4	3	10	$\frac{5}{16}$						
1312–13	$8\frac{5}{8}$		$23\frac{1}{2}$	$5\frac{7}{8}$	.250	$11\frac{3}{4}$	.500	$2\frac{3}{4}$	8	3	3	0							
1313–14	$13\frac{7}{8}$	$3\frac{3}{4}$	35	$8\frac{3}{4}$	.250	$5\frac{3}{8}$	.154	$5\frac{1}{8}$	20	6	4	0	$3\frac{3}{4}$						$1\frac{3}{4}$ from peas
1314–15	$14\frac{1}{8}$		42	$10\frac{1}{2}$	.250			$6\frac{3}{4}$	[M.T.]										$2\frac{1}{8}$ from peas
1315–16	[$\frac{3}{8}$]			$3\frac{7}{8}$		$1\frac{5}{8}$								$3\frac{1}{2}$	42	0	12	0	Incomplete
1316–17	$5\frac{1}{2}$			$4\frac{3}{8}$		$7\frac{1}{8}$		$1\frac{1}{8}$	15	0	13	4							
1317–18	$11\frac{1}{2}$			$5\frac{1}{4}$		9		$6\frac{1}{4}$	41	8	6	8							
1318–19	$14\frac{1}{4}$			6				$8\frac{1}{4}$	16	6	2	0							
1320–21	$10\frac{1}{8}$		17	$4\frac{1}{4}$	.250			$5\frac{7}{8}$	24	$1\frac{1}{2}$	4	$1\frac{1}{4}$							
1324–25	$16\frac{3}{8}$		$17\frac{1}{2}$	$4\frac{3}{8}$	.250	$10\frac{1}{4}$	.586	11	49	4	4	$5\frac{3}{4}$							[*sic*]
1325–26	$14\frac{5}{8}$		$16\frac{1}{2}$	$4\frac{1}{8}$	.250	$3\frac{1}{8}$	.189	$10\frac{1}{2}$	45	0	4	$3\frac{1}{2}$							
1326–27	$1\frac{1}{4}$	6	17	$4\frac{1}{8}$	.243	$7\frac{7}{8}$	.463						6	$2\frac{7}{8}$					
1327–28	12			$3\frac{5}{8}$		$8\frac{1}{8}$		$\frac{5}{8}$	2	6	4	0	$3\frac{1}{8}$						$4\frac{5}{8}$ sold extra
1328–29	$11\frac{3}{4}$		10	$2\frac{1}{2}$	.250	7	.700	$9\frac{1}{4}$	53	$1\frac{1}{2}$	5	9							
1329–30	$9\frac{1}{2}$		10	$2\frac{1}{2}$	.250			7	42	0	6	0							
1330–31			8	2	.250	$2\frac{1}{4}$	.281	2	18	0	9	0							
1331–32	$4\frac{1}{4}$		$10\frac{1}{2}$	$2\frac{5}{8}$	.250	$6\frac{1}{2}$	.619	$\frac{9}{16}$	3	$11\frac{1}{4}$	7	0	$1\frac{1}{16}$						
1332–33	$9\frac{1}{8}$		11	$2\frac{3}{4}$	.250			$5\frac{3}{8}$	25	11	4	$9\frac{3}{4}$	1						
1334–35	$4\frac{7}{8}$	$\frac{1}{2}$	22	$5\frac{3}{8}$	.244	$13\frac{7}{8}$	.631	$\frac{1}{2}$	1	8	3	4	$\frac{1}{2}$						1 from peas
1335–36	$19\frac{1}{4}$		32	8	.250	$10\frac{1}{8}$	.316	$11\frac{1}{4}$	32	2	2	$10\frac{1}{4}$							
1336–37	$18\frac{1}{8}$		27	$6\frac{3}{4}$	.250	$14\frac{3}{8}$	.532	$11\frac{3}{8}$	45	6	4	0							
1337–38	$21\frac{1}{8}$		24	$6\frac{1}{8}$	.255	$10\frac{1}{4}$	.427	15	42	4	2	$9\frac{3}{4}$							

1. Purchased from the reeve of Mardon.

VETCHES (CONTINUED)

Year	Yield	In pod	Number of acres sown	Total amount of seed	Average seed per acre	Net yield	Average net yield per acre	Amount sold	Total sale price		Average sale price per qr.		For feed	Number bought	Total purchase price		Average purchase price		Remarks
	Qrs.	Qrs.		Qrs.	Qrs.	Qrs.	Qrs.	Qrs.	s.	d.	s.	d.	Qrs.	Qrs.	s.	d.	s.	d.	
1338–39	14⅜	2	23	5¾	.250	13⅜	.582	8⅝	22	6½	2	7¼	2						
1339–40	16⅛	3	24	6	.250	6⅛	.255	10⅛	54	0	5	4	3						
1340–41	10⅛	2	27	6¾	.250	5¾	.213	3⅜	13	6	4	0	2						
1341–42	8	4½	26	6½	.250	15	.577	1½	6	0	4	0	4½						
1342–43	14½	7	28	7	.250	23⅛	.826	7½	30	0	4	0	7						
1343–44	23⅛	7	31½	7⅞	.250	19	.603	15¼	76	3	5	0	7						
1344–45	16⅞	10	31	7¾	.250			9⅛	30	5	3	4	10						
1345–46	5		24	6	.250	14¾	.615							1					Incomplete
1346–47	12¾	8	34	8½	.250	20⅜	.599	4¼	24	6	5	9¼	8						
1347–48	20⅞	8	32	8	.250	2¼	.070	12⅞	64	4½	5	0	8						
1348–49	6¼	4	25	6¼	.250	9⅜	.375						4						
1349–50	10⅝	5	28½	7⅛	.250	18	.632	3½	18	8	5	4	5						
1350–51	19⅛	6	28	7	.250	8⅝	.308	12⅛	90	0	6	8	6						
1351–52	12⅝	3	19	4⅞	.257	3⅝	.191	7¾	56	10	7	4	3						
1352–53	5½	3	20	5	.250	12¼	.613	½	3	4	6	8	3						
1353–54	14¼	3	24	6	.250	22⅞	.953	8¼	24	9	3	0	3						
1354–55	25⅞	3	27	6¾	.250	5½	.204	19⅛	57	4½	3	0	3						
1355–56	6¼	6	25	6¼	.250								6						
1356–57	2⅝	2	20	5⅝	.281	8⅞	.444	3/16					2	3 3/16					
1357–58	13½	1	23	5¾	.250	13¼	.576	7⅜	44	3	6	0	1						⅜ sold extra
1358–59	16	3	24	6	.250			10	33	4	3	4	3						
1359–60	[Ill.]							11	46	8	4	3							
1360–61	12	5	20	5	.250	6	.300	8					4						
1361–62	7	4	16	4	.250	6½	.406	3	15	0	5	0	4						
1362–63	6½	4	14	3½	.250	11⅝	.830	3	18	0	6	0	4						
1363–64	10⅛	5	14	3½	.250	7	.500	6⅝	35	4	5	4	5						
1364–65	6	4½	14	3½	.250	10½	.750	2½	12	6	5	0	4½						

1365–66	9½	4½	[M.T.]	3		*4½*		6½	21	8	3	4	4½						
1366–67	3½	4	12	3	*.250*	*9⅜*	*.781*	½	0	20	*3*	*4*	4						
1367–68	8⅜	4	16	4	*.250*	*12*	*.750*	4⅜	23	4	*5*	*4*	4						
1368–69	11	5	20	5	*.250*	*10*	*.500*	7	35	0	5	0	4						
1369–70	10	5	18	4½	*.250*	*6⅝*	*.368*	5½	55	0	10	0	5						
1370–71	5⅝	5½	16½	4⅛	*.250*	*16⅞*	*1.023*	1½	9	0	6	0	5½						
1371–72	12½	8½	7	4¼	*.607*	*9¾*	*1.393*	8¼	38	6	4	8	8½						
1372–73	7¼	6¾	25	6¼	*.250*	*12¼*	*.490*	1	6	0	6	0	6¾						
1373–74	10	8½	20	5	*.250*			5					8½						
1375–76	12⅝	6½	28	7	*.250*	*7*	*.250*	5⅝					4						2½ sold extra
1376–77	7½	6½	15	3¾	*.250*	*8¾*	*.583*	3¾					6½						
1377–78	*6*	6½	24	6	*.250*	*7⅛*	*.297*						6½						
1378–79	3⅛	10	18½	4⅝	*.250*			3⅞					8	1½					[M.T.]
1381–82	4½	10	18	4½	*.250*								10						
1383–84	4¾	10	19	4¾	*.250*	*10*	*.526*	2					8						
1384–85	4¾	10	19	4¾	*.250*	*9¾*	*.513*						10						
1385–86	4½	10	18	4½	*.250*								10						
1387–88	5½	10	22	5½	*.250*	*9½*	*.432*						10						
1388–89	5	10	20	5	*.250*								10						
1390–91	5	10	20	5	*.250*								10						
1392–93	5	10	20	5	*.250*	*9¾*	*.488*						10						
1393–94	4¾	10	19	4¾	*.250*	*10¼*	*.539*						10						
1394–95	5	10	22	5½	*.250*	*9½*	*.432*						10	½					
1395–96	5	10	20	5	*.250*								10						
1398–99	6	10	24	6	*.250*	*11*	*.458*						10						
1399–00	7	10		5½		*9½*		2½	8	4	*3*	*4*	10						
1400–01	5	10	20	5	*.250*								10						
1402–03	5	10	20	5	*.250*								10						
1406–07	5	10	20	5	*.250*								10						
1408–09	5	10	20	5	*.250*	*10*	*.500*						10						
1409–10	5	10	20	5	*.250*	*10*	*.500*						10						
1410–11	3	12	20	5	*.250*	*10*	*.500*						12	2	10	0	*5*	*0*	

VETCHES (Continued)

Year	Yield	In pod	Number of acres sown	Total amount of seed	Average seed per acre	Net yield	Average net yield per acre	Amount sold	Total sale price		Average sale price per qr.		For feed	Number bought	Total purchase price		Average purchase price		Remarks
	Qrs.	Qrs.		Qrs.	Qrs.	Qrs.	Qrs.	Qrs.	s.	d.	s.	d.	Qrs.	Qrs.	s.	d.	s.	d.	
1411–12	5	10	20	5	.250	10	.500						10						
1412–13	5	10	20	5	.250	10	.500						10						
1413–14	5	10	20	5	.250	10	.500						10						
1414–15	4	10	20	5	.250								10	2¼	11	2½	5	0	
1418–19	5	10	20	5	.250	9	.450						10						
1419–20	4	10	16	4	.250	8½	.531						10						
1420–21	4	8½	16	4	.250	8	.500						8½						
1421–22	4	8	16	4	.250	8	.500						8						
1422–23	4	8	16	4	.250	8	.500						8						
1423–24	4	8	16	4	.250	8	.500						8						
1424–25	4	8	16	4	.250	8	.500						8						
1425–26	4	8	16	4	.250								8						
1427–28	4	8	16	4	.250								8						
1429–30	4	8	16	4	.250	8	.500						8						
1430–31	4	8	16	4	.250	8	.500						8						
1431–32	4	8	16	4	.250	8	.500						8						
1432–33	4	8	16	4	.250	8	.500						8						
1433–34	4	8	16	4	.250	8	.500						8						
1434–35	4	8	16	4	.250	8	.500						8						
1435–36	4	8	16	4	.250								8						
1438–39	4	8	16	4	.250								8						
1440–41	10		8	2	.250	10	1.250	3	8	0	2	8	6	1	2	8			
1441–42	4	8	16	4	.250								8						
1447–48	4	8	16	4	.250	8	.500						8						
1448–49	4	8	16	4	.250								8						

CART HORSES[1]

Year	Number left over	Number bought	Total purchase price s.	d.	Total number in account	Number sold	Total sale price s.	d.	Number died	Number remaining
1246–47	1				1	1	8	0		
1251–52	2	1	12	1	3				1	2
1252–53	2				4[2]	2	19	0		2
1253–54	2	1			3				1	2
1254–55	2				2	1[3]	6	8		2
1256–57	2				2					2
1257–58	2				2					2
1264–65	2				2					2
1265–66	2				2					2
1267–68	2				2					2
1268–69	2				2					2
1270–71	2				2					2
1271–72	2				2					2
1272–73	2				2					2
1273–74	2				2					2
1274–75	2	1			3	1	11	0		2
1276–77	2				2					2
1277–78	2				2					2
1282–83	2				2					2
1283–84	2				2					2
1284–85	2				2					2
1285–86	2	1			3				1	2
1286–87	2				2					2

Year	Number left over	Number bought	Total purchase price s.	d.	Total number in account	Number sold	Total sale price s.	d.	Number died	Number remaining
1287–88	2				2					2
1288–89	2	1			3				1	2
1289–90	2	1			3				1	2
1290–91	2	1			3	1	3	0		2
1291–92	2				2					2
1292–93	2				2					2
1296–97	2				2					2
1297–98	2				2					2
1298–99	2				2					2
1299–00	2				2					2
1300–01	2				2					2
1301–02	2				2					2
1302–03	2	1	15	0	3					3
1304–05		2	21	4	2					1
1305–06	1				1					1
1306–07	1	1			2					2
1307–08	2				2					2
1308–09	2				2					2
1309–10	2	1	24	$0\frac{1}{4}$	3	1	7	0		2
1310–11	2				2					2
1311–12	2				2					2
1312–13	2				2					2
1313–14	2	1	23	0	3					3

1. Equus. 2. Two additional cart horses came from the chattels of Ingeram, the fugitive. 3. Heriot.

CART HORSES (CONTINUED)

Year	Number left over	Number bought	Total purchase price s.	d.	Total Number in account	Number sold	Total sale price s.	d.	Number died	Number remaining
1314–15	4	1			5	1	26	8	1	3
1315–16	3	1			4				1	3
1316–17	3				3	1	10	0		2
1317–18	3				3					3
1318–19	3				3					3
1320 [1]	3				3					3
1320–21	3				3	1	6	6		2
1324–25	2				2					2
1325–26	2				2					2
1326–27	2				2					2
1327–28	2				2					2
1328–29	3	1	10	0¼	4	1	3	0	1	2
1329–30	2	1			3					2
1330–31	2	1	14	6	3	1	5	0		2
1331–32	2	1	16	0¼	3				1	2
1332–33	2	1	13	6	3					3
1334–35	2	2	25	0	4					2
1335–36	2	1	17	0	3	1	6	8		2
1336–37	2	1			3					3
1337–38	3				3					3
1338–39	3				3					3
1339–40	3				3					3
1340–41	3	1	18	0	4	1	5	0		3

Year	Number left over	Number bought	Total purchase price s.	d.	Total number in account	Number sold	Total sale price s.	d.	Number died	Number remaining
1341–42	3				3					3
1342–43	3				3					3
1343–44	3				3					3
1344–45	3				3				1	2
1345–46	2	1	16	0	3					3
1346–47	3				3	1	5	6		2
1347–48	3				3					3
1348–49	3				3					3
1349–50	3				3					3
1350–51	3				3					3
1351–52	3	1	12	0	4				1	3
1352–53	3	1	15	0	4	1	6	8		3
1353–54	3				3					3
1354–55	3				5	1	16	0	1	3
1355–56	3				3					3
1356–57	3	1	18	6	4	1	5	0		3
1357–58	3				3					3
1358–59	3				3					3
1361–62	3				3					3
1362–63	3				3					3
1363–64	3	1	23	2	4					3
1364–65	3	1	21	8	4	1	6	8	2	1
1365–66	[M.T.]	2	44	8½	3					3

1366–67	3				3					3
1367–68	3				3					3
1368–69	3				3					3
1369–70	3				3					3
1370–71	3				3					3
1371–72	3	2	56	8	5				2	3
1372–73	4				4					4
1373–74		1	26	8	1					
1375–76	4				4					4
1376–77	4	1	22	0	5				1	4
1377–78	4	1			5				1	4
1378–79	4	1	20	0	5				1	4
1379–80	4				4					4
1381–82	4	1	20	0	6				2	4
1384–85	4	2	42	0	6				2	4
1385–86	4	1	27	8	5					5
1387–88	5				5					5
1388–89	5				5					5
1390–91	5				5					5
1392–93	6	1	17	6	7	1	10	0	2	4
1393–94	4				4					4
1394–95	4				4					4
1395–96	5	1	16	8	6	1		20	1	4
1398–99	4	1	20	0	5	1	1	8		4
1399–00	4				4					4
1400–01	5	1	21	0	6	1	5	0	1	4
1402–03	4				4					4
1406–07	3				3					3

1408–09	4	1			6	2	8	8	1	3
1409–10	3	1	24	1	5				2	3
1410–11	3	1	24	0	4	1	4	0		3
1411–12	3	1	20	0	4	1	4	0		3
1412–13	3				3					3
1413–14	3	2	40	0	5	1	3	4	1	3
1414–15	3	1	20	0	4				1	3
1418–19	3				3					3
1419–20	3				3					3
1420–21	3				3					3
1421–22	4				4	1	6	8		3
1422–23	3				3					3
1423–24	3	1	16	8	4	1	3	4		3
1424–25	3	1	18	0	4				1	3
1425–26	3				3					3
1427–28	3	1			4				1	3
1429–30	3				3					3
1430–31	4				4				1	3
1431–32	3	1	20	0	4				1	3
1432–33	3	1	20	0	4				1	3
1433–34	4	1	23	0	5	1	5	0	1	3
1434–35	3	1			4				1	3
1435–36	3				3					3
1438–39	3	1			4					4
1440–41	3	1	16	0	4				1	3
1441–42	3	1	18	0	4				1	3
1447–48	2	1	20	0	3					3
1448–49	4				4				1	3[2]

1. 17 Ap.–28 Sept.

2. Valued at 13s. 4d. each.

PLOW HORSES[1]

Year	Number left over	Number of increase[2]	Number bought	Total purchase price		Average purchase price		Total number in account	Number sold	Total sale price		Average sale price[3]		Number died	Number remaining	Remarks
				s.	d.	s.	d.			s.	d.	s.	d.			
1208–09	10							10							10	
1210–11	10		2	10	1	*5*	*0½*	12						2	10	
1211–12	10	2						12	1	6	8	6	8	1	10	
1213–14	9	2						11	1	6	8	6	8		10	
1215–16	10							10							1	9 sent away
1217–18	5		5	30	9	*6*	*1¾*	12	1	2	0	2	0	1	10	
1218–19	10							10							10	
1219–20	10		3	13	8	*4*	*6¾*	13	1	4	8	4	8	1	11	
1220–21	11		4					15						5	10	
1223–24	9	1	1	6	6	6	6	10							10	
1224–25	11	1						12	1	5	6	5	6	1	10	
1225–26	10	1	1	5	1	5	1	12						2	10	
1226–27	10	2						12	1	3	0	3	0	1	10	
1231–32	12	2						14	3	10	2	*3*	*4¾*	1	10	
1232–33	10	1						11							11	
1235–36	12	2						16	1	6	6	6	6	3	12	
1236–37	12							12						1	*11*	
1244–45	14							14	3	9	3	*3*	*1*	1	10	
1245–46	10							10							10	
1246–47	10	4						14	3	4	6	*1*	*6*	2	9	
1247–48	9		4	29	2	*7*	*3½*	13						1	12	
1248–49	12	1	1	10	0	10	0	14	2	5	6	*2*	*9*		12	
1251–52	7		3	19	6	*6*	*6*	10	1	6	5½	6	5½	1	8	
1252–53	9		1	6	6	6	6	10	1	4	6	4	6	1	8	
1253–54	8		1	5	11	5	11	9						1	8	

1254–55	8	1	4	30	2	7	6½	13	4	19	4	*4*	*10*	1	8	
1256–57	9	1	1					11	2	13	0	*6*	*6*		8	1 sold as colt
1257–58	8							8							8	
1264–65	11	1						12	2	10	0	5	0	1	9	
1265–66	9		1	7	0	7	0	10	1	4	0	4	0	1	8	
1267–68	8	10[4]	1					19	2	9	0	*4*	6		10	7 sent to Mardon
1268–69	10								2	16	6	*8*	3		10	
1270–71	8	3	1					12	2	10	0	*5*	*0*	1	9	
1271–72	9		1					10	3	15	0	*5*	*0*	1	6	
1272–73	6	1	3					10						3	7	
1273–74	7		4					11						4	7	
1274–75	7	1						8							8	
1276–77	7							7	1	3	2	3	2		6	
1277–78	6							6							6	
1282–83	7		2					9	2	12	2	*6*	*1*	2	5	2 added to cart horses
1283–84	5	1	1					7							7	
1284–85	7		1					8	1	2	8	2	8		7	
1285–86	7							7						4	3	
1286–87	3	1	6					10	1	2	6	2	6	2	7	
1287–88	7		1	7	1	7	1	8	1	5	6	5	6	1	6	
1288–89	6							6							6	
1289–90	6							6							6	
1290–91	6	1	1					8	2	4	0	*2*	*0*		6	
1291–92	6	2						8	2	6	0	3	0		6	
1292–93	6	1	1	6	2	6	2	8	1	7	0	7	0	1	6	
1296–97	6		1					7						1	6	
1297–98	6							6							6	
1298–99	6							6							6	
1299–00	6							6						1	5	
1300–01	5	1						6	1	3	0	3	0		5	
1301–02	5	1	1					7						1	6	
1302–03	6		1	4	0	4	0	7						1	6	

1. Affri.
2. Increase includes heriots, animals received by testament, and animals strayed in.
3. Generally low because of old and weak animals sold. Occasionally a valuable heriot sold.
4. Received from Overton.

PLOW HORSES (CONTINUED)

Year	Number left over	Number of increase	Number bought	Total purchase price s.	Total purchase price d.	Average purchase price s.	Average purchase price d.	Total number in account	Number sold	Total sale price s.	Total sale price d.	Average sale price s.	Average sale price d.	Number died	Number remaining	Remarks
1304–05	6		1	4	0	4	0	7	1	2	5	2	5		6	
1305–06	6		1	5	2	5	2	7						1	6	
1306–07	6		2	19	9	*9*	*10½*	8	3	11	0	*3*	*8*		5	
1307–08	5		2[1]	13	0¼	*6*	*6*	7						1	6	
1308–09	6		3	33	6¾	*11*	*2¼*	9	2	15	10	*7*	*11*	1	6	
1309–10	6	1						7	1	6	8	6	8		6	
1310–11	6							6							6	
1311–12	6							6							6	
1312–13	6	1	1	12	0	12	0	8	1	2	0	2	0		7	
1313–14	7		1					8	1	6	8	6	8	1	6	
1314–15	6	2						8	2	16	8	*8*	*4*		6	
1315–16	6	2						8	1	5	0	5	0	1	6	
1316–17	6	1	1	16	4	16	4	8	2	12	0	6	0		6	
1317–18	6	1	1	15	0	15	0	8	2	13	8	*6*	*10*		6	
1318–19	6	1	2	20	0	*10*	0	9						3	6	
1320	6		5	93	6	*18*	*8½*	11							11	
1320–21	11		1	18	0	18	0	12							12	
1324–25	6							6							6	
1325–26	6	2	1	10	0	10	0	9	2	6	0	*3*	*0*		6	1 sent to Mardon
1326–27	6	1	1	14	6	14	6	8	2	13	0	*6*	*6*		6	
1327–28	6	2						8	2	26	0	*13*	*0*		6	
1328–29	6		1	9	6¼	9	6¼	7	1	6	8	6	8		6	
1329–30	6	1	1	[M.T.]				8	2	6	10	*3*	*5*		6	
1330–31	6		1	7	6	7	6	7	1	4	0	4	0		6	
1331–32	6		2	21	0½	*10*	*6¼*	8	2	11	0	5	6		6	

1332–33	6							6							6	
1334–35	6							6							6	
1335–36	6							6	1	4	6	4	6		5	
1336–37	5							5							5	
1337–38	5	1						6							6	
1338–39	6							6							6	
1339–40	6	1						7	1	3	6	3	6		6	
1340–41	6		1	10	0	10	0	7						1	6	
1341–42	6		1	7	6	7	6	7	1	2	6	2	6		6	
1342–43	6		2	17	0	*8*	*6*	8	2	13	8	*6*	*10*		6	
1343–44	6		3	22	3	*7*	*5*	9	3	16	0	*5*	*4*		6	
1344–45	6	1						7	1	2	0	2	0		6	
1345–46	6		4	30	0	*7*	*6*	10						1	6	3 to army
1346–47	6		1	8	0	8	0	7	1	7	0	7	0	1	6	
1347–48	6	2						8	2	11	0	*5*	*6*		6	
1348–49	6	13	1	9	0	9	0	20	12	34	3	*2*	*10¼*	1	7	
1349–50	7	1						8	1	1	6	1	6	1	6	
1350–51	6							6							6	
1351–52	6		1	8	6	8	6	7	1	6	0	6	0		6	
1352–53	6		2	22	0	*11*	*0*	8	2	7	6	*3*	*9*		6	
1353–54	6							6							6	
1354–55	6							6							6	
1355–56	6		1	9	0	9	0	7	1	6	0	6	0		6	
1356–57	6	1						7	1	3	4	3	4		6	
1357–58	6							6							6	
1358–59	6	1						7							6	1 stolen
1359–60	6		1	12	0	12	0	7	1	3	6	3	6		*6*	
1360–61	6	5	1	10	6	10	6	12	3	15	0	*5*	*0*		6	3 sold — no price given
1361–62	6							6							6	
1362–63	6		2	21	0	*10*	6	8	2	17	0	*8*	*6*		6	
1363–64	6	1						7	1	10	0	10	0		6	
1364–65	6							6						5	1	

1. The price is given for only one.

PLOW HORSES (CONTINUED)

Year	Number left over	Number increase	Number bought	Total purchase price s.	d.	Average purchase price s.	d.	Total number in account	Number sold	Total sale price s.	d.	Average sale price s.	d.	Number died	Number remaining	Remarks
1365–66	1	5	5	62	8	*12*	*6½*	6							6	
1366–67	6		2	27	0	*13*	*6*	8						2	6	
1367–68	6							6							6	
1368–69	6							6							6	
1369–70	6							6							6	
1370–71	6	1	2	33	0	*16*	*6*	9	1	3	4	3	4	4	3	1 sold extra
1371–72	3		1	18	0	*18*	*0*	4						2	2	
1372–73	2		1	20	0	20	0	3							3	
1373–74			1	13	4	13	4									Ms. incomplete
1375–76	3							3							3	
1376–77	3							3							3	
1377–78	3							3							3	
1378–79	3		1	18	6	18	6	4						1	3	
1379–80	3		1	15	0	15	0	4						*1*	3	
1381–82	3	1	2	32	0	16	0	6						3	2	[M.T.]
1384–85	[Ill.]		3	[Ill.]												
1385–86	3							3							3	
1387–88	3		1	12	0	12	0	4						[Ill.]	3	
1388–89	3							3							3	
1390–91	3	1						4	1	7	6	7	6		3	
1392–93	3							3							3	
1393–94	3	*1*	1	13	4	13	4	5	1	2	0	2	0	1	3	
1394–95	3							3							3	
1395–96	3							3							3	
1398–99	3							3							3	

1399–00	3							3							3	
1400–01	3	2						5	2	8	6	*4*	*3*		3	
1402–03	3							3							3	
1406–07	4							4							4	
1408–09	4							4							4	
1409–10	4							4							4	
1410–11	4							4							4	
1411–12	4							4							4	
1412–13	4	2						6	2	5	0	2	*6*		4	
1413–14	4							4							4	
1414–15	4							4							4	
1418–19	4	2						6	2	23	4	*11*	*8*		4	
1419–20	4	2						6	2	12	0	*6*	*0*		4	
1420–21	4		1	16	0	16	0	5	1	2	0	2	0		4	
1421–22	4							4							4	
1422–23	4							4							4	
1423–24	4							4							4	
1424–25	4							4							4	
1425–26	4	1						5	1	1	8	1	8		4	
1427–28	4		1					5						1	4	
1429–30	4		1	13	4	13	4	5						1	4	
1430–31	4							4							4	
1431–32	4							4							4	
1432–33	4		1	16	0	16	0	5						1	4	
1433–34	4							4							4	
1434–35	4	2	1					7	3	4	4	*1*	*5¼*		4	
1435–36	4	2						6	2	9	6	*4*	*9*		4	
1438–39	4		1					5	1	1	0	1	0		4	1 plow horse and 1 cart horse bought for 40s.
1440–41	4		1	12	0	12	0	5						1	4	
1441–42	4		1	13	4	13	4	5						1	4	
1447–48	4		1	12	0	12	0	5	1	3	4	3	4		4	
1448–49	4							4							4[1]	

1. Valued at 6s. 8d. each.

OXEN

Year	Number left over	Number of increase[1]	Number bought	Total purchase price s.	Total purchase price d.	Average purchase price s.	Average purchase price d.	Total number in account	Number sold	Total sale price s.	Total sale price d.	Average sale price s.	Average sale price d.	Number died	Number sent away	Number remaining
1208–09	37	2	6					45	4	20	0	5	0	2		39
1210–11	33	3	5	31	11	6	4¾	41	2	8	0	4	0	2		37
1211–12	37		6					43	4	14	9	3	8¼	2		37
1213–14	32		5					37	4	18	0	4	6	1	1[2]	31
1215–16	33		1					34							34	
1217–18	15	8	9	61	9	6	10¼	32	8	30	0	3	9	4		20
1218–19	21		7					28	3	12	0	4	0	1		24
1219–20	24	10[3]	4	21	10	5	5½	38	1	3	6	3	6		9	28
1220–21	28	2	4	26	0	6	6	34	2	11	6	5	9			32
1223–24	36		3	17	0	5	8	39	3	21	0	7	0	1		35
1224–25	35		6	35	6	5	11	41	2	11	0	5	6	1		38
1225–26	38		7	51	5	7	4	45	6	33	5	5	7	1		38
1226–27	38		7	54	3	7	9	45	6	44	0	7	4	1		38
1231–32	39		4	25	10½	6	5¾	43	4	26	0	6	6			39
1232–33	39	3	6	50	8	8	5¼	48	6	36	4	6	0¾	1		41
1235–36	36	2	7	66	9½	9	6½	45	5	44	0	8	9½	6		34
1236–37	34	3	6	56	0	9	4	43	2	19	0	9	6	3		38
1244–45	32	2	10	83	3½	8	4	44	5	32	6	6	6			39
1245–46	39	5	8	72	4½	9	0½	52	5	53	0	10	7		3	44
1246–47	44	2	7	83	8½	11	11½	53	12	116	4	9	8¼		4	37
1247–48	37	2						39	4	46	7	11	7¾	1	2	32
1248–49	32		5	40	9	8	1¾	37	6	42	6	7	1			31
1251–52	33		13	114	0	8	9¼	46	6	36	6	6	3	2		38
1252–53	38		5	46	2	9	2¾	43	6	60	0	10	0	1		36
1253–54	36	6	2	17	0	8	6	44	4					1		39
1254–55	39	5	7	59	6	8	6	51	6	40	0	6	8	3		42

1256–57	41	3	2	16	6	8	3	46	6	48	0	8	0	1		39
1257–58	39	4						43	7	55	8	7	11½			36
1264–65	36	2	3	29	c	9	8	41	5	33	0	6	7			36
1265–66	36		1	10	0	10	0	37								37
1267–68	34	75 [4]	1					110	4	32	0	8	0	1	61 [5]	44
1268–69	44							44	10	96	0	9	7¼	1		33
1270–71	32		6					38	4	52	10	12	8½	2		32
1271–72	32		15					47	8	73	6	9	2¼	8		31
1272–73	31	3	6					40	1	9	0	9	0	3		36
1273–74	36	4	4					44	6	63	0	10	6	1		37
1274–75	37	3	1					41	6	66	0	11	0			35
1276–77	34	2	8					44	9	71	0	7	10¾			35
1277–78	35	3	3					41	5	42	6	8	6			36
1282–83	33		4	26	8	6	8	37	4	31	0	7	9	2		30
1283–84	30		2					32						1		31
1284–85	31	1	8					40	4	30	0	7	6	2		34
1285–86	34		9					43	3	29	0	9	8	1		39
1286–87	39	1	11					51	6	55	0	9	2	9		36
1287–88	36		4	40	8½	10	2	40	5	33	0	6	7¼	1		34
1288–89	34	2	6					42	6	34	6	5	9	1		35
1289–90	35		4					39	4	36	6	9	1½			35
1290–91	35	1	3					39	6	54	0	9	0	1		32
1291–92	32	4	2					38	4	36	0	9	0			34
1292–93	34	1						35	2	16	0	8	0			33
1296–97	30							30								30
1297–98	30	3						33	2	14	0	7	0	2		29
1298–99	29	1	3	40	0	13	4	33						3		30
1299–1300	30	3	4	38	0	9	6	37	6	63	0	10	6	1		30
1300–01	30							30								30
1301–02	30	2	5					37						2		35
1302–03	35	2	4	34	11½	8	9	41	6	45	0	7	6	1		34

1. Includes those brought from elsewhere.
2. For the use of the legate(?).
3. From Cornwall.
4. From Overton.
5. Sixty of these to Mardon.

OXEN (Continued)

Year	Number left over	Number of increase	Number bought	Total purchase price s.	d.	Average purchase price s.	d.	Total number in account	Number sold	Total sale price s.	d.	Average sale price s.	d.	Number died	Number sent away	Number remaining
1304–05	30	2						32						2		30
1305–06	30		16	144	3	9	0¼	46	11	70	11	6	5¼	3		32
1306–07	32		3	29	1¼	9	8½	35	8	59	0	7	4½			27
1307–08	27	1						28	6	52	6	8	9			22
1308–09	22		1	15	0	15	0	23	5	[M.T.]						18
1309–10	18	3	2	42	0¼	21	0	23	1	11	0	11	0			22
1310–11	22		2	32	11	16	5½	24	4	61	6	15	4½			20
1311–12	20	2	4	69	6	17	4½	26	3	54	0	18	0	1		22
1312–13	22	4	3	55	0	18	4	29	5	84	0	16	9¾			24
1313–14	24		4	72	0	18	0	28	4	75	0	18	9	1		23
1314–15	23	2						25	5	76	0	15	2½			20
1315–16	20	2	1					23						1		22
1316–17	22	2	3	48	0	16	0	27						1		26
1317–18	26	2						28	4	63	0	16	0			24
1318–19	24	3						27	2	32	0	16	0	3		22
1320	16							16								16
1320–21	16	3						19	15	225	0	15	0			4
1324–25	16		1	16	0	16	0	17								17
1325–26	17		4	59	0	14	9	21	3	20	0	6	8			18
1326–27	18		1	15	0	15	0	19								19
1327–28	19							19	2	38	0	19	0			17
1328–29	17							17								17
1329–30	17		6	[M.T.]				23	1	4	0	4	0			22
1330–31	22		2	22	6	11	3	24	6	76	8	12	9¼			18
1331–32	18		3	42	4	14	1¼	21	2	30	0	15	0	1		18
1332–33	18							18								18

1334–35	18		6	80	0	13	4	24	6	63	0	*10*	*6*			18
1335–36	18		2	29	0	14	6	20	2	24	0	*12*	*0*			18
1336–37	8[1]		3	36	11	*12*	*3¾*	11	2	26	10	*13*	*5*			9
1337–38	19		2	25	6	*12*	*9*	21								21
1338–39	21							21	2	16	0	*8*	*0*			19
1339–40	19		3	31	3	*10*	*5*	22						3		19
1340–41	19		9					28	3	17	8	*5*	*10¾*	3		22
1341–42	22		5	58	4	*11*	*8*	27	4	35	0	*8*	*9*			23
1342–43	23		2	23	2	*11*	*7*	25	5	44	0	*8*	*9½*			20
1343–44	20							20	2	19	6	*9*	*9*			18
1344–45	18		5	66	10	*13*	*4½*	23	6	67	0	*11*	*2*			17
1345–46	17		2	24	6	*12*	*3*	19						1		18
1346–47	18		3	38	10	*12*	*11¼*	21	3	32	0	*10*	*8*			18
1347–48	18							18								18
1348–49	18		2	16	0	*8*	*0*	20						*1*		19
1349–50	19		1	10	0	10	0	20								20
1350–51	20							20								20
1351–52	20							20								20
1352–53	20							20								20
1353–54	20							20								20
1354–55	20							20								20
1355–56	20							20								20
1356–57	20							20								20
1357–58	20		1	14	0	14	0	21						1		20
1358–59	20							20								20
1359–60	20		2	26	2	*13*	*1*	22	2	[Ill.]						20
1360–61	20		3	33	0	*11*	*0*	23								23
1361–62	23							23	3	33	0	*11*	*0*			20
1362–63	20		1	14	6	14	6	21						1		20
1363–64	20							20								20
1364–65	20							20								20
1365–66	20		4	66	0	*16*	*6*	24	4	80	0	20	0			[M.T.]

1. Ms. probably in error. Should be 18 left over and 19 remaining.

OXEN (Continued)

Year	Number left over	Number of increase	Number bought	Total purchase price		Average purchase price		Total number in account	Number sold	Total sale price		Average sale price		Number died	Number sent away	Number remaining
				s.	d.	s.	d.			s.	d.	s.	d.			
1366–67	20		2	38	0	19	0	22	2	36	0	18	0			20
1367–68	20		4	73	9	18	5¼	24	4	78	0	19	6			20
1368–69	20		5	91	10	18	2½	25	2	36	0	18	0	3		20
1369–70	20		5	94	0	18	9½	25	5	88	4	17	8			20
1370–71	20		4	62	0	18	0	24								24
1371–72	24		2	36	0	18	0	26	5	86	0	17	2½	1		20
1372–73	20		5	90	0	18	0	25	2	33	0	16	6	3		20
1373–74			4	79	0	19	9									
1375–76	24		5	83	4	16	8	29	6	75	8	12	7¼	1		22
1376–77	22		5	70	8	14	2	27	4	48	0	12	0	1		22
1377–78	22		5					27	3					2		22
1378–79	22		3	36	0	12	0	25	6	73	8	12	3¼	1		18
1379–80	18		4	40	0	10	0	22	2							20
1381–82	23		4	53	4	13	4	27	5	62	6	12	6			22
1382–83									2	30	0	15	0			
1383–84									3	30	4	10	1¼			
1384–85	20		3	37	4	12	5¼	23	5	60	0	12	0			[M.T.]
1385–86	18		3	40	6	13	6	21	3	33	0	11	0			18
1387–88	21		3	30	0	10	0	24	3	[Ill.]				2		19
1388–89	19		3	30	0	10	0	22	3	30	4	10	1¼			19
1390–91	18		3					21	3	36	0	12	0			18
1392–93	18		1	14	0	14	0	19	1	12	0	12	0			18
1393–94	18		3	41	4	13	9¼	21								21
1394–95	21		2	29	0	14	6	23	3	33	0	11	0			20
1395–96	20		2	29	0	14	6	22	2	24	0	12	0			20
1398–99	18		3	46	0	15	4	21	3	40	0	13	4			18

1399–00	18		1	15	6	15	6	19	1	13	4	13	4			18
1400–01	18		6	90	0	15	0	24	5	65	0	*13*	*0*	1		18
1402–03	18		2	34	0	17	0	20	2	[M.T.]						18
1406–07	18		4	52	0	13	0	22	4	44	0	11	0			18
1408–09	18		5	62	0	14	6	23	2	24	0	*12*	*0*	3		18
1409–10	18		3	42	0	14	0	21						1		20
1410–11	20		5	70	0	14	0	25	6	70	0	*11*	*8*	1		18
1411–12	18		6	84	0	14	0	24	5	48	0	*9*	*7¼*	1		18
1412–13	18		2	28	0	14	0	20	2	22	0	*11*	*0*			18
1413–14	18		3	36	0	12	0	21	3	33	0	*11*	*0*			18
1414–15	18		2	26	8	*13*	*4*	20	2	22	0	*11*	*0*			18
1418–19	18		2	24	0	*12*	*0*	20	2	24	0	*12*	*0*	1		17
1419–20	17		4	52	0	*13*	*0*	21	4	44	0	*11*	*0*			17
1420–21	17		3	36	0	*12*	*0*	20	3	30	0	*10*	*0*			17
1421–22	17		2	25	0	*12*	*6*	19	2[1]	18	0	*9*	*0*			17
1422–23	17		2	24	0	*12*	*0*	19	2	20	0	*10*	*0*			17
1423–24	17		3	37	8	*12*	*6¾*	20	2	20	0	*10*	*0*	1		17
1424–25	17		2	24	0	*12*	*0*	19						2		17
1425–26	17		1	12	0	12	0	18						1		17
1427–28	*17*		2	*28*	*0*	14	0	19	2	26	0	13	0			17
1429–30	17		4	64	0	*16*	*0*	21	3	45	0	15	0	1		17
1430–31	17		2	26	8	13	4	19	1	12	0	12	0	1		17
1431–32	17		3	36	0	12	0	20	2	24	0	12	0	1		17
1432–33	17		1	12	0	12	0	18	1	12	0	12	0			17
1433–34	17		4	52	0	*13*	*0*	21	3	36	0	*12*	*0*	1		17
1434–35	17		4	48	0	12	0	21	3	33	0	11	0	1		17
1435–36	17		4	50	4	*12*	*7*	21	3	36	0	12	0	1		17
1438–39	17		1	13	0	13	0	18						1		17
1440–40	17		1	14	0	14	0	18	1	12	0	12	0			17
1441–42	17		3	35	0	*11*	*8*	20	1	10	0	10	0	2		17
1447–48	17		2	22	0	11	0	19	1	10	0	10	0	1		17
1448–49	17							17								17[2]

1. Of these 1 sold dead at 8s.

2. Valued at 11s. each.

THREE-YEAR-OLD BOVINES[1]

Year	Number left over	Number added to oxen	Number added to cows	Number added to bulls	Number sold	Average sale price		Year	Number left over	Number added to oxen	Number added to cows	Number added to bulls	Number sold	Average sale price	
						s.	d.							s.	d.
1208–09	2	2	3					1291–92	4	2	2				
1210–11	2	2						1292–93	5	1	2	1	1	6	8
1219–20	2							1296–97	2		1				
1220–21	2							1297–98	7	3	3	1			
1235–36	2	2						1298–99	4	1	3				
1236–37	3[2]	3						1299–00	4	3	1				
1244–45	8	2	5		1			1300–01	3		3				
1245–46	9	3	5		1	5	6	1301–02	4	1	2	1			
1246–47	6							1302–03	4	2	2				
1247–48	6	2	4					1304–05	6	2	4				
1248–49	6		2					1305–06	4		1		3	3	6
1253–54	10	6	3	1				1307–08	3	1	1	1			
1254–55	11	5	5	1				1309–10	4	2	2				
1256–57	6	3	2		1	4	0	1310–11	3		2	1			
1257–58	6	4	2					1311–12	4	2	2				
1264–65	4	2	1	1				1312–13	4	4					
1272–73	5	4	1					1313–14	3		3				
1273–74	9	4	4	1				1314–15	3	2	1				
1274–75	8	3	4		1	7	0	1315–16	3	2	1				
1276–77	6	2	2		2	5	0	1317–18	5	2	3				
1277–78	10	3	6	1				1318–19	6	3	3				
1286–87	5							1320–21	4	3					
1287–88	2		1	1				1331–32	1				1	6	8
1288–89	4	1	3					1410–11	1				1	5	0
1290–91	4	1			3	4	6								

1. Bovetti.   2. Three heifers left over and sold at 5s. 4d. each.

COWS

Year	Number left over	Number of increase	Number bought	Total purchase price s.	Total purchase price d.	Average purchase price s.	Average purchase price d.	Total number in account	Number sold	Total sale price s.	Total sale price d.	Average sale price s.	Average sale price d.	Number died	Number remaining	Remarks
1208–09	12	3						15							15	
1217–18			9												9	9 with 5 calves for 55s. 6d.
1218–19	9	1						10	3	15	9	5	3		7	
1219–20	7	1						8							8	
1220–21	8	2						10	1	3	2	3	2		9	
1223–24	1							1							1	
1224–25	1							1							1	
1225–26	1		8					9							9	8 with 7 calves for 53s.
1226–27	9		1	5	11½	5	11½	10							10	
1231–32	9							9	1	2	6	2	6	1	7	
1232–33	7							7							7	
1235–36	12							12	1	9	0	9	0	1	10	
1236–37	10							10	2	12	2	*6*	*1*		8	
1244–45	5		2	14	6	*7*	*3*	7							7	
1245–46	7	5						12	1	4	0	4	0		11	
1246–47	11							11	1	3	0	3	0		10	
1247–48	10	4						14							14	
1248–49	14	2	2					18						1	17	2 with 1 calf for 15s. 6d.
1251–52	10		4					14							14	4 with calves for 28s. 5d.
1252–53	14	2	3					19	4	28	0	*7*	*0*		15	
1253–54	15	3						18	4	27	0	*6*	*9*		14	
1254–55	14	5						19	5	28	0	*5*	*7¼*		14	
1256–57	17	2	6	43	0	*7*	*2*	25	4	22	10	*5*	*8½*		21	
1257–58	21	2	3	18	8½	*6*	*2¾*	26	3	18	0	*6*	*0*		23	

COWS (CONTINUED)

Year	Number left over	Number of increase	Number bought	Total purchase price s.	Total purchase price d.	Average purchase price s.	Average purchase price d.	Total number in account	Number sold	Total sale price s.	Total sale price d.	Average sale price s.	Average sale price d.	Number died	Number remaining	Remarks
1264–65	6	1	2	14	0	7	0	9							9	
1265–66	9								9	44	6	4	11¼			
1268–69			3					3							3	
1270–71	3		16					19	3	26	6	8	10		16	
1271–72	16	8						24						8	16	
1272–73	16	1						17	4	28	0	7	0	1	12	
1273–74	12	4						16	2	14	0	7	0		14	
1274–75	14	4						18							18	
1276–77	18	3						21	3	23	0	7	8	1	17	
1277–78	17	6						23	3	21	0	7	0		20	
1282–83			4	26	8	6	8	4							4	
1283–84	4	10						14								
1284–85	14							14							10	4 sent to Mardon
1285–86	10		2					12							12	
1286–87	12	4						16						5	11	
1287–88	11	1						12	1	3	0	3	0		11	
1288–89	11	3						14	2	7	0	3	6	1	11	
1289–90	11							11						1	10	
1290–91	10							10	1	6	0	6	0		9	
1291–92	9	2						11	3	20	0	6	8		8	
1292–93	8	2						10							10	
1296–97	15	1[1]						16	2	10	0	5	0	1	13	
1297–98	13	4						17	2	10	0	5	0	1	14	
1298–99	14	3						17						3	14	
1299–1300	14	1	6	44	0	7	4	21	6	49	0	8	2		15	

1300–01	15	3	2					20	3	18	0	6	0		17	
1301–02	17	2						19							19	
1302–03	19	2						21	4	24	0	6	0		17	
1304–05	10	4						14						1	13	
1305–06	13	3	4	28	6	7	1½	20	7	34	2	4	10½		13	
1306–07	13		3	24	4	8	1¼	16	8	41	2	5	1¾		8	
1307–08	8	1						9							9	
1308–09	9							9	2	16	0	8	0		7	
1309–10	7	3						10							10	
1310–11	10	3						13	3	30	0	10	0		10	
1311–12	10	2						12	2	16	0	8	0		10	
1312–13	10							10	2	18	0	9	0		8	
1313–14	8	3						11							11	
1314–15	11	1						12	2	17	0	8	6		10	
1315–16	10	1						11	6	40	0	6	8		5	
1316–17	5	2	3	37	4	12	5¼	10							10	
1317–18	10	3						13	2	20	0	10	0		11	
1318–19	11	4						15	1	8	1	8	1		14	
1320	13							13							13	
1320–21	13							13	2	17	0	8	6	1	10	
1327–28		1	2	23	4	11	8	3	3	29	4	8	0[2]			
1348–49		9½						9½	7½	18	9	2	6½	1		9½ were heriots
1349–50	1							1	1	4	0	4	0			
1360–61		2						2						2		
1361–62	2							2	2	12	0	6	0			
1366–67		1						1	1	8	0	8	0			
1390–91		2						2	2	15	8	7	10			
1418–19		2						2	2	16	0	8	0			
1425–26		1						1	1	6	0	6	0			
1430–31		2						2	2	14	0	7	0			
1438–39		1						1	1	7	0	7	0			

1. One-half heriot added and sold for 2s.

2. This is the price of 1 cow before calving; the other two were sold with their calves at 10s. 4d. and 11s.

CALVES

Year	Number of increase	Number bought	Total purchase price s.	Total purchase price d.	Average purchase price s.	Average purchase price d.	Total number in account	Number for tithe	Number sold	Total sale price s.	Total sale price d.	Average sale price s.	Average sale price d.	Number died	Number remaining
1208–09	4						4							2	2
1218–19	4						4		1		8		8		3
1219–20	7						7	1							6
1220–21	5						5								5
1223–24	1						1		1		6		6		
1225–26		7					7								7
1226–27	9						9								9
1231–32	4						4								4
1232–33	5						5	1						1	3
1235–36	10						10	1	2					1	6
1236–37	6						6		1 [1]						5
1244–45	3						3								3
1245–46	7						7								7
1246–47	7						7		2	2	3	1	1½	3	2
1247–48	10						10	1	3	3	2	1	0¾		6
1248–49	9	2					11	1	4	3	6		10½	1	5
1251–52	8	4					12	1						1	10
1252–53	10	1					11	1						1	9
1253–54	10						10	1						1	8
1254–55	6						6								6
1256–57	12						12	1							11
1257–58	14						14	1	3	3	6	1	2		10
1264–65	8						8		4	4	0	1	0		4
1265–66	4						4		3					1	
1270–71		11					11		2	1	8		10		9
1271–72	13						13	1						1	11
1272–73	10						10	1	1		14		14		8
1273–74	13						13	1	4	4	6	1	1½		8
1274–75	16						16	1	5	6	6	1	3½		10

1276–77	13				13	1	2	2	0	1	0	1	9
1277–78	14				14	1	3	2	4		9¼	3	7
1283–84	7				7							1	6
1284–85	8				8	1	2		23		11½	4	
1285–86	9				9	1							8
1286–87	8				8							6	2
1287–88	5				5								5
1288–89	7				7							4	3
1289–90	8				8	1						2	5
1290–91	7				7	1	2		12		6		4
1291–92	6				6		1		12		12	2	3
1292–93	6				6	1						2	3
1296–97	14				14	1	6	3	6		7	1	6
1297–98	12				12	1	6	3	8		7¼		5
1298–99	11				11	1	5	3	7		8¾	2	3
1299–00	13				13	1	7	4	0		7		5
1300–01	16				16	2	5	4	2		10	3	6
1301–02	13				13	1	5	5	0	1	0	1	6
1302–03	13				13	1	7	5	10		10	1	4
1304–05	8				8		4	2	8		8	1	3
1305–06	4				4	1	3	3	2	1	0¾		
1306–07	6				6		2	2	0	1	0		4
1307–08	6				6		3	3	0	1	0		3
1308–09	7				7	1	2	3	0	1	6		4
1309–10	8				8	1	3	4	6	1	6		4
1310–11	8				8	1	3	4	6	1	6		4
1311–12	7				7		3	4	3	1	5	1	3
1312–13	5				5		1		14		14	1	3
1313–14	6				6		1		16		16	1	4
1314–15	8				8		2	2	5	1	2½	1	5
1315–16	7				7		1	1	4	1	4		6
1316–17	8				8		1		16	1	4		7
1317–18	8				8		1	1	6	1	6	1	6
1318–19	10				10	1	2	3	0	1	6		7
1320–21	11				11	1	1	2	0	2	0		8[1]

1. Sold dead — for 3d.

HIDES[1] SOLD

Year	Horse	Total sale price s.	d.	Ox	Total sale price s.	d.	Cow	Total sale price s.	d.	Calf	Total sale price s.	d.	Yearling[2]	Total sale price s.	d.	Two-year old[3]	Total sale price s.	d.
1208–09				2	2	6				2		2						
1210–11	2		10	2	2	4												
1211–12	1		6	2	2	2												
1213–14				1	1	8												
1215–16				1	2	0												
1217–18				4	5	2												
1218–19				1	1	7							1		4½			
1219–20	1		7															
1220–21	5	3	9½															
1223–24				1	2	0												
1224–25	1		7	1	1	6												
1225–26	2		11	1	1	8												
1226–27	1		7	1	1	10												
1231–32	1		6				1	1	0	1		4½						
1232–33				1	2	3							3		3			
1235–36	3	2	0	6	12	10	1	1	6	1		1	2		4			
1236–37	1		10	3	6	6												
1244–45	1		10							1		3						
1245–46																		
1246–47	2	1	6							3		4	3		11			
1247–48	1		10	1	2	0												
1248–49							1		6	1		2½				1[4]		3
1251–52	1		17	2	4	0												
1252–53	1		8	1	1	7½												
1253–54	1		9	1	1	6				1		2				2	1	4

1254–55	1		7	3	4	7							2		8			
1256–57				1	2	1												
1257–58										9	1	4	1	1	0	1		
1264–65	1		10															
1265–66	1		10													1	1	0
1267–68				1	2	8												
1268–69				1	3	0												
1270–71	1		8	2	5	2												
1271–72	1		10	8	18	10	8	9	6	1						1	1	6
1272–73	3	2	0	3	7	2	1	1	4				3		9			
1273–74	1		10															
1274–75													2		8			
1276–77							1		10	1		2	1		4			
1277–78										3		6						
1282–83	2		13	2	3	6												
1283–84				1	1	10												
1284–85				2	4	2				3			+1		6			
1285–86	5	3	4½	1	2	1												
1286–87	9	1	3	9	9	3	5	4	2	6		3½	4		4			
1287–88	1		8	1		12							2		3			
1288–89	1		9	1	1	4	1	1	0	4			+1		6			
1289–90	1		8				1		10	2		2				1		2
1290–91				1	1	6												
1291–92										2		2						
1292–93	1	1	0							2		3						
1296–97	1	1	0				1	1	6	1		1				1		7
1297–98							1	1	0				1			+1	1	1
1298–99				3	9	0	3	4	4	2		3	2		8			
1299–00	1	1	0	1	3	0												
1300–01										3		3						
1301–02	1		11	2	4	6½				1		1	1		1½	1		6
1302–03	1	1	0	1	1	6				1		1½						

1. Coria, of bovines usually dying of disease. 2. Annales. 3. Boviculi. 4. A three-year old or bovettus.

HIDES SOLD (CONTINUED)

Year	Horse	Total sale price		Ox	Total sale price		Cow	Total sale price		Calf	Total sale price		Yearling	Total sale price		Two-year old	Total sale price	
		s.	d.		s.	d.		s.	d.		s.	d.		s.	d.		s.	d.
1304–05				2	6	4	1	3	0	1		1						
1305–06	1	1	0	1	1	9												
1308–09	1		11															
1311–12				1						1		2½	1		6			
1312–13										1		2						
1313–14	1	1	0	1						1		3						
1315–16	2	2	3	1	3	0												
1317–18										1		2	1		8			
1318–19	3	3	0	3	9	0												
1320–21							1	1	8							1[1]	1	0
1331–32	1	1	0	1	2	8												
1339–40				3	4	6												
1340–41	1		9	3	4	0												
1344–45	1		8															
1345–46	1		8	1	2	6												
1358–59	1		8															
1362–63				1	3	0												
1364–65	7	2	8															
1365–66	3	1	6															
1366–67	2	1	0															
1368–69				3	7	0												
1370–71	4	3	0															
1371–72	4	2	4	1	2	0												
1372–73	1	1	0	3	6	0												
1373–74	1		6															

1376–77	1		8	1	1	6								
1377–78	1		8	2	3	0								
1378–79	2	1	4	1	1	6								
1381–82	5	2	6											
1382–83				5	7	6								
1383–84	1		8	1	1	6								
1384–85	5	3	4											
1387–88	1			+2	3	8								
1392–93	2													
1393–94	1		8											
1396–97	1		8											
1400–01	1		8	1	1	6								
1408–09	1			+3	6	2								
1409–10	2	1	0	1	1	2								
1410–11				1	1	0								
1411–12				1	1	8								
1418–19				1	1	4								
1423–24				1	1	4								
1424–25	1			+2	3	8								
1425–26				1	1	8								
1427–28	1			+1	1	4								
1429–30	1			+1	2	4								
1430–31	1			+1	2	4								
1431–32	1			+1	2	6								
1432–33	2	1	8											
1433–34	1			+1	1	10								
1434–35	1			+1	2	6								
1435–36				1	1	6								
1438–39				1	1	6								
1440–41	2	1	6											
1441–42	2			+2	3	10								
1447–48				1	1	4								
1448–49	1		2											

1. Bovettus.

WETHERS[1]

Year	Number left over	Number from stock[2]	Number bought	Total purchase price £ s. d.	Average purchase price s. d.	Total number in account	Number sold	Total sale price £ s. d.	Average sale price s. d.	Number died	Number remaining	Remarks
1208–09	345	127				472	20	8 4	0 5	40	412	
1210–11	361	15				526	16	7 4	0 5½	52	458	149 came from Twyford
1211–12	458	88				546				96	380	70 sent to Waltham
1213–14	462	112				574	30	24 2	0 9¾	42	499	3 for boon days
1215–16	520	219				739	20[3]			10	684	25 sent away
1217–18		144	3			148	28[4]			5	113	2 killed, 87 added
1218–19	200	105				305	16			7	282	
1219–20	282	114				396	32[5]			6	358	
1220–21	358	160				538	30			17	491	
1223–24	420	150				574	48	36 8	0 9¼	28	498	4 from Twyford
1224–25	498	133				631	70	73 4	1 0½	63	498	
1225–26	498	104				609	95[6]	4 7 1	0 11	109	397	
1226–27	397	90				487	33	32 0	0 11¾	25	429	
1231–32	392	151				543	39	39 0	1 0	23	481	
1232–33	481	153				634	50	50 0	1 0	70	514	
1235–36	393	169				563	10	12 6	1 3	15	538	1 from Dunton
1236–37	538	42				580	48	57 0	1 2¼	15	517	1 sold dead
1244–45	276	89				365	13	13 5	1 0½	34	319	
1245–46	319	47				366	24	30 0	1 3	22	318	2 more sold
1246–47	318	107	314			769	23	29 3	1 3¼	52	694	
1247–48	694	22				716	92	4 13 2	1 0¼	78	284	262 sent away
1248–49	284	80				364	58	60 8	1 0½	45	261	
1251–52	380	64	50	50 0	1 0	494	41	41 0	1 0	31	422	
1252–53	422	108				530	34	34 0	1 0	19	477	
1253–54	477	213				690	67	67 0	1 0	100	523	
1254–55	523	96				619	80	53 4	0 8	64	475	

1256–57	600	56				656	150	6	13	4	*0*	*10¾*	28	478	
1257–58	478	176				654	34		22	8	0	8	23	597	
1264–65	179	38				217	39		32	6	0	10	22	156	
1265–66	156	43				199	70		66	8	*0*	*11½*	16	113	
1267–68	54	18				72	4		4	0	*1*	*0*	7	61	
1268–69	61	24				85	4		3	8	0	11	6	75	
1270–71	69	20	40			129	7		7	0	*1*	*0*	9	113	
1271–72	113	134				746[7]	22		25	7	*1*	*2*	69	505	150 sent to Mardon
1272–73	505	178				744	60						117	567	61 from outside
1273–74	567	127	15			709	130	6	3	0	*0*	*11¼*	58	521	
1274–75	521	81				602	53		49	10	*0*	*11¼*	41	508	
1276–77	502	91				593	98	5	14	6	*1*	*2*	89	406	
1277–78	406	92				498	43		45	2½	*1*	*0½*	25	430	
1282–83	177	53				235							21	214	5 from Mardon
1283–84	214	38				252	18						23	211	
1284–85	211	90				307	19		19	0	*1*	*0*	8	280	
1285–86	180	49				329	20		*25*	*10*	1	3½	41	268	
1286–87	268	10				278							41		
1287–88	237	30				267	5		4	7	0	11	33	229	
1288–89	229	67				296	28		25	8	*0*	*11*	39	229	
1289–90	229	54	206			489	13		10	5	*0*	*9½*	13	349	114 sent to Mardon
1290–91	349	81				430							2	423	5 added to rams
1291–92	423	88				511	87	*5*	*1*	*6*	0	14	9	415	
1292–93	415	93				508	69	4	6	3	*1*	*3*	13	426	
1296–97	312	26	37			375	42		42	0	1	0	13	320	
1297–98	320	17				337	27		27	0	*1*	*0*	10	300	
1298–99	300	90	111			501	50		55	0	*1*	*1¼*	42	409	
1299–00	409	148				557	38		39	8	*1*	*0½*	59	460	
1300–01	460	75	18			553	72		75	0	*1*	*0½*	15	383	83 sent to Waltham
1301–02	383	132				515	47		54	10	0	14	35	433	
1302–03	433	120				553	89	4	9	0	0	12	25	439	
1304–05	204	126				330							6	286	38 to the lord (?)

1. Multones. Total number in account includes a few items not here listed.
2. Occasionally includes strays, etc.
3. Twenty wethers and 28 ewes sold for 34s. 2d.
4. Twenty-eight wethers and 67 ewes sold for 53s. 0¾d.
5. Thirty-two wethers and 22 ewes sold for 33s. 9d.
6. From Overton 16, and 8 more sold.
7. Of these, 499 from outside.

WETHERS (Continued)

Year	Number left over	Number from stock	Number bought	Total purchase price £	s.	d.	Average purchase price s.	d.	Total number in account	Number sold	Total sale price £	s.	d.	Average sale price s.	d.	Number died	Number remaining	Remarks
1305–06	286	99							385							33	352	
1306–07	352	108							460	54		69	9	0	15½	22	384	
1307–08	384	153							537	36		45	0	*1*	*3*	15	486	
1308–09	486	165							651	37		48	8	*1*	*3¾*	12	601	1 sold extra
1309–10	601	190							791	241	20	12	8	*1*	*8½*	20	530	
1310–11	530	100							630							14	616	
1311–12	616	151							767	187	13	2	6½	*1*	*4¾*	18	562	
1312–13	562	124	60		70	0	0	14	746	157	13	1	8	1	8	27	562	
1313–14	562	65							627	103	9	0	3	0	21	85	439	
1314–15	439	37							476	45		52	6	0	14	25	406	
1315–16	406	141							547	163	12	15	0	*1*	*6¾*	24	360	
1316–17	360	142							502	54	5	8	0	2	0	19	429	
1317–18	429	109							538	60	6	0	0	*2*	*0*	12	466	
1318–19	466	139							605	420	42	13	2	*2*	*0¼*	12	173	
1320	65	137							202							1	201	
1320–21	201	46							247	10		20	0	2	0	3	234	
1323[1]									157									
1324–25	152								152									152 sent to Twyford
1325–26	280								280								280	From other manors
1326–27	280		85	6	0	5	*1*	*5*	365	18		25	6	*1*	*5*	16	331	
1327–28	331	136	25		41	8	*1*	*8*	492	40		59	0	*1*	*5¾*	9	443	
1328–29	443								443	439	40	16	8	*1*	*10¼*	4		
1329–30		239							239							12	227	
1330–31	227	162							389							10	379	
1331–32	379	94	50	4	13	9	1	10½	523	100	10	0	0	2	0	4	419	
1332–33	419	151							570	65	4	10	10	*1*	*4¾*	3	502	20 of 65 to Wolvesey @ 14d.

1334–35	148	20						168	12		8	0	0	8	1	155	
1335–36	155							155							4	151	
1336–37	151	64						214	7		9	4	*I*	*4*	1	206	
1337–38									29		31	5	0	13			
1338–39	287	86						373	58		58	0	0	12	24	291	
1339–40	291	10						301							78	223	
1340–41	223	24						247	22		16	6	*0*	*9*	17	208	
1341–42	208	71						279	70		58	4	*0*	*10*	2	207	
1342–43	207	66						273	59		47	3	0	9	5	209	
1343–44	209	127						336	53		49	7	*0*	*11¼*	7	276	
1344–45	276	130						406	389[2]	22	8	10	*I*	*1¾*	9		
1345–46		230	40			1	6¼	310							6	304	
1346–47	304	116	30	30	0	*I*	*0*	450	24				0	10	22	404	
1347–48	404	104						508	34		42	6	0	15	47	427	
1348–49	427	83						509	91		49	9	*0*	*6½*	*9*	409	Ms. in bad cond.
1349–50	409	207						616	153	5	16	6	0	*9*	18	445	
1350–51	*445*	144						589	77		75	0	*0*	*11¾*	6	506	
1351–52	506	101						607	90	4	10	0	*I*	*0*	13	504	
1352–53	504	102						606	80	5	9	4	*I*	*4½*	11	515	
1353–54	515	109						624	79	4	10	9	*I*	*1¾*	17	526	2 sold extra
1354–55	526	94						620	79		79	0	0	12	15	526	
1355–56	526	79						605	57		66	4	*I*	*2*	22	526	
1356–57	526	119						645	61		62	3	0	12	14	570	
1357–58	570	117						687	44		47	8	0	13	27	616	
1358–59	616	115						731	161		[Ill.]				44	526	
1359–60	526	117						643	100	6	0	0	*I*	*2½*	17	526	
1360–61	526	131	61	61	0	*I*	*0*	718	12		10	0	*0*	*10*	118	588	
1361–62	588	46	38	50	8	0	16	672	134	6	15	8	*I*	*0*	12	526	
1362–63	526	109						635	31		46	6	0	18	18	586	
1363–64	586	*106*						692	145	10	3	10	*I*	*5*	21	526	
1364–65	526	86						612	70	4	19	2	0	17	16	526	
1365–66	*526*	[M.T.]						628	12		30	0	2	6½	*59*	557	

1. Only one quarter of the year.

2. Eight wethers and 7 ewes sold for 8s. 9d. not included.

WETHERS (CONTINUED)

Year	Number left over	Number from stock	Number bought	Total purchase price			Average purchase price		Total number in account	Number sold	Total sale price			Average sale price		Number died	Number remaining	Remarks
				£	s.	d.	s.	d.			£	s.	d.	s.	d.			
1366–67	557	114							671	106	8	3	2	1	$6\frac{1}{2}$	15	550	
1367–68	550	100							650	84	7	7	8	1	9	16	550	
1368–69	550	110							660	100	9	1	4	1	$9\frac{3}{4}$	10	550	
1369–70	600	110							710	97	8	9	0	1	9	13	600	Ms. frayed
1370–71	550	99							649	87	7	11	8	1	9	11	551	
1371–72	551	47							598	72	6	18	0	1	11	18	508	
1372–73	508	149							657	55		92	6	1	8	217	385	
1373–74	385	33	351	59	11	2	3	$4\frac{3}{4}$	769	15		22	6	1	6	35	719	
1375–76	560	116							676	80	5	15	0	1	$5\frac{1}{4}$	34	562	
1376–77	562	114							676	68	4	9	4	1	$3\frac{3}{4}$	61	547	
1377–78	547	57	80						684	88						64	532	
1378–79	532	112							644	76	4	15	0	0	15	39	529	
1379–80	529	113							642	91						21	530	
1381–82	589	67							656	106	6	15	11	1	$3\frac{1}{2}$	28	522	
1382–83										65	5	9	0	1	8			
1383–84										5		8	4	1	8			
1384–85	622	[M.T.]								86		90	0	1	$0\frac{1}{2}$		[M.T.]	
1385–86	523	134							657	106	5	12	0	1	$0\frac{3}{4}$	23	528	
1387–88	521	99							620							63	557	
1338–89	557	96							653	102	5	2	0	1	0	30	521	
1390–91	527	74							601	64		66	0	1	$0\frac{1}{4}$	9	528	
1392–93	529	110							639	104	6	1	4	1	2	15	520	
1393–94	520	101							621	62		60	2	0	$11\frac{3}{4}$	26	533	
1394–95	533	140							673	79		80	0	1	0	67	527	
1395–96	527	114							641	103	5	5	10	1	$0\frac{1}{4}$	44	494	
1398–99	492	66							558	74	4	4	6	1	$1\frac{3}{4}$	20	464	

1399–00	464	116				580	40		37	0	*0*	*11*	71	469	
1400–01	469	103				572[1]	55	*3*	*5*	*7*	*1*	*2¼*	12	415	10 to the lord
1402–03	508	104				612	209		[M.T.]				12	391	
1406–07	466	101				567	36		42	0	0	14	17	514	
1408–09	509	65				574	58		69	8	*1*	*2½*	14	502	
1409–10	502	107				609	68		77	4	*1*	*1¾*	21	520	
1410–11	520	134				654	84	4	10	8	*1*	*1*	65	505	
1411–12	505	98				603	63	4	4	0	0	16	36	*504*	
1412–13	504	78				582	63	4	4	0	*1*	*4*	15	504	
1413–14	504	93				597	40		46	8	0	14	44	513	
1414–15	513	91				604	80	4	13	4	0	14	20	504	
1418–19	505	73				578	54	4	10	0	*1*	*8*	21	503	
1419–20	503	100				603	37		37	0	*1*	*0*	13	553	
1420–21	553	91				644	91		93	4	*1*	*0¼*	*35*	518	
1421–22	518	102				620	82	4	12	8	*1*	*1½*	38	500	
1422–23	*500*	105				*605*	68		79	4	0	14	32	505	
1423–24	505	78				583	40		46	8	*1*	*2*	53	490	
1424–25	479	53	11			543	43		50	2	0	12	*82*	418	
1425–26	418	135	2			555	36		41	0	0	14	17	502	
1427–28	507	76				583	64		74	8	0	14	18	501	
1429–30	515	60				575	48		64	0	0	16	11	516	
1430–31	516	81				597	64	4	3	7	*1*	*3¾*	13	520	
1431–32	520	82				602	46		52	6	0	14	43	513	
1432–33	513	74				587	56		59	4	*1*	*1¾*	39	492	
1433–34	492	88				580	45		*55*	*0*	*1*	*2¾*	43	492	
1434–35	492	122				614	54		60	8	*1*	*1½*	73	487	
1435–36	487	94				581	26		39	0	0	18	52	503	
1438–39	399	153				552	97	7	18	2	*1*	*7½*	9	446	
1440–41	490	82				572	26		34	4	*1*	*4*	47	482	17 went to ewes
1441–42	482	54				536	18		19	0	*1*	*0¾*	24	494	
1447–48	527	110				637	61		71	2	0	14	70	506	
1448–49	506	90				596	40		43	4	0	13	77	470	9 went to ewes

1. This number is not fully accounted for.

EWES[1]

Year	Number left over	Number from stock, etc.	Number bought	Total purchase price (£ s. d.)	Average purchase price (s. d.)	Total number in account	Number sold	Total sale price (£ s. d.)	Average sale price (s. d.)	Number died	Number remaining	Remarks
1208–09	480	110				590				26	564	
1210–11	513	20				533	30	12 6	0 5	29	474	
1211–12	474	83				557	45	22 6	0 6	109	403	
1213–14	684	108				792	50	27 1	0 6½	23	716	3 for boon days
1215–16	770	218				988	28			25	910	25 sent away
1217–18	10	503	20[2]			533	67			25	439	2 killed
1218–19	439	78				517	1	0 8	0 8	15	466	36 sent away
1219–20	466	123				589	22			10	557	
1220–21	557	125	60	46 5½	0 9¼	742	40	20 0	0 6	15	687	
1223–24	861	143				1004	55	22 1	0 4¾	54	895	
1224–25	895	192				1087	70	46 8	0 8	100	917	
1225–26	917	121				1038	93	52 6	0 6¾	99	832	14 more sold
1226–27	832	94				926	75	47 8	0 7½	42	809	
1231–32	620	150				770	50	33 4	0 8	28	692	
1232–33	692	156				848	61	40 8	0 8	125	662	
1235–36	829	223				1052	57	47 6	0 10	45	950	
1236–37	950	73				1023	52	43 4	0 10	31	940	
1244–45	490	107				597	20	13 4	0 8	16	561	
1245–46	561	40				601	32	25 10	0 9¾	36	533	
1246–47	533	127	107			767	40	33 4	0 10	36	691	
1247–48	691	35				968	49	40 0	0 9¾	56	863	242 came from Mardon
1248–49	863	127				990	110	62 6	0 6¾	83	797	
1251–52	723	99	50	50 0	1 0	872	76	50 8	0 8	55	741	
1252–53	741	114[3]				855	54	36 0	0 8	26	775	
1253–54	775	226				1001	56	37 4	0 8	49	896	
1254–55	896	97				993	90	60 0	0 8	34	869	

1256–57	826	95				921	100						39	782	
1257–58	782	181				963	75		50	0	0	8	25	863	
1264–65	228	38				266	20		16	8	0	10	16	230	
1265–66	230	32				262	70		66	8	*0*	*11½*	13	179	
1267–68	139	28				167	30		25	0	0	10	7	130	
1268–69	130	25				155	10		8	4	0	10	4	141	
1270–71	137	20	92			249	15		12	6	0	10	10	224	
1271–72	224	732[4]				956	16		12	0	0	9	35	855	50 sent to Mardon
1272–73	855	162				1017	123	4	19	3	*0*	*9¾*	60	834	
1273–74	834	139	11			984	150	6	3	14	0	10	80	754	
1274–75	754	75				829	80		70	0	0	5½	16	733	
1276–77	739	109				848	110	5	19	2	1	1	50	688	
1277–78	688	112				800	107	5	15	0	*1*	*1*	35	658	
1282–83	253	62				315							55	260	
1283–84	260	30				290	21[5]						7	262	
1284–85	262	80				342	22		22	0	1	0	11	309	
1285–86	309	29				338	24		*25*	*0*	1	0½	76	238	
1286–87	238	10				248	14		14	0	*1*	*0*	15	*219*	
1287–88	219	33				252	6		5	6	0	11	5	241	
1288–89	241	68				309	12		10	0	0	10	28	269	
1289–90	269	45	4			318	16		12	8	*0*	*9½*	10	231	61 sent to Mardon
1290–91	231	72				303							2	301	
1291–92	301	87				388	40		40	0	*1*	*0*	5	343	
1292–93	343	89				432	25						12	395	
1296–97	336	46				382	26		23	10	0	11	33	323	
1297–98	323	57				380	23		19	2	0	10	10	347	
1298–99	347	101	111			559	10		10	0	*1*	*0*	35	514	
1299–1300	514	151				665	69		54	3	*0*	*9½*	82	514	
1300–01	514	86	50			650	31		31	0	1	0	33	536	50 sent away
1301–02	536	131				667	55		45	10	0	10	37	575	
1302–03	575	127				702	74		61	8	0	10	26	522	80 sent to Mardon
1304–05	488	111				599							16	526	57 sent away

1. Oves matrices.
2. Twenty ewes and 3 wethers bought for 24s. 5d.
3. From the goods of Ingeram, 41.
4. Of these, 560 from dominus Ricardus Capellanus.
5. Twenty-one ewes and 18 wethers sold for 38s. 9d.

EWES (CONTINUED)

Year	Number left over	Number from stock, etc.	Number bought	Total purchase price			Average purchase price		Total number in account	Number sold	Total sale price			Average sale price		Number died	Number remaining	Remarks
				£	s.	d.	s.	d.			£	s.	d.	s.	d.			
1305–06	526	101							627							47	580	
1306–07	580	96							676	59		61	5½	1	0½	34	583	
1307–08	583	143							726	80	4	4	6	*1*	*0¾*	20	626	
1308–09	626	156							782	70	4	1	8	1	2	15	697	
1309–10	697	195	50	4	7	6	1	8	942	237	15	2	0	*1*	*3¼*	31	674	
1310–11	674	159							833	250	14	7	6	*1*	*1¾*	20	563	
1311–12	563	174							737	128	7	17	9			23	588	sale includes 2 rams
1312–13	588	164							752	67	4	3	9	1	3	30	655	
1313–14	655	106							761	150	9	7	6	1	4	56	555	
1314–15	555	69							624	40		46	8	1	2	76	508	
1315–16	508	175							683	150	9	7	6	*1*	*3*	16	516	
1316–17	516	172							688	60	3	11	8	*1*	*2½*	16	*512*	100 sold — no price given
1317–18	512	137							649	137	10	5	6	1	6	18	494	
1318–19	494	139							633	413	30	19	6	1	6	17	203	
1320	195	142							337								337	
1320–21	336	69							405							10	395	
1323–24									429									
1324–25	417								417									417 to Twyford
1325–26									385								385 [1]	
1326–27	385		80	8	0	0	*2*	*0*	465	50	5	0	0	2	0	27	388	
1327–28	388	145	32		45	8	*1*	*5*	565	59		96	8	*1*	*7¾*	11	489	6 sold extra
1328–29	489								489	165	*11*	10	10	*1*	*4¾*	4	320	
1329–30	320	237							557							13	494	50 sent to Mardon
1330–31	494	169							663	76		80	10	*1*	*0¾*	23	564	
1331–32	564	97							661	185	10	12	6	*1*	*1¾*	9	466	
1332–33	466	141							607	97	4	15	7	*0*	*11¾*	8	502	

1334–35	259	169							423							14	409	[*sic*]
1335–36	409								409	52		55	4	*1*	*0¾*	9	348	
1336–37	348	76							424	28		26	6	*0*	*11¼*	6	390	
1337–38	390	122							512	33		22	0	0	8	14	465	
1338–39	465	128							593	60		41	8	*0*	*8¼*	26	507	
1339–40	507	13							520	92		53	6	*0*	*7*	81	347	
1340–41	347	31							378	22		16	6	*0*	*9*	19	337	
1341–42	337	89							426	71		55	10	*0*	*9½*	8	347	
1342–43	347	97	60		45	0	*0*	*9*	504	66		49	6	0	9	17	421	
1343–44	421	163							584	99		66	0	0	8	*15*	470	
1344–45	470	287							757	588	30	11	6	*1*	*0½*	15	147	7 sold with wethers
1345–46	147	316	10		16	8	*1*	*8*	473	52[2]		46	6			14	358	50 added to wethers
1346–47	358	112	26		26	0	*1*	*0*	496	17						40	439	
1347–48	439	140							579	121		6	12	0	12	24	434	
1348–49	434	137							572	109		58	7	*0*	*6½*	12	451	
1349–50	451	193							644	159	6	2	8	*0*	*9¼*	23	442[3]	
1350–51	442	108	77				0	10	627	103	4	18	2	*0*	*11½*	12	462	50 added to wethers
1351–52	462	98							560	89[4]	4	10	0	0	12	16	457[5]	
1352–53	457	68	30		37	6	1	3	555	73		73	0	0	12	23	459	
1353–54	459	87							546	74		*74*	*0*	0	12	13	459	
1354–55	459	122							581	95		*95*	*0*	0	12	11	475	
1355–56	475	82							557	50		50	0	0	12	33	475	sale includes 1 ram
1356–57	*475*	114							589	70		70	0	0	12	18	505	sale includes 4 rams
1357–58	505	109							614	124	5	19	0			19	475	sale includes 4 rams
1358–59	475	94							569	70		[Ill.]				22	477	
1359–60	477	88							565	73		69	2	*0*	*11¼*	15	477	
1360–61	477	137							614	32						201	381	
1361–62	381	58	84	4	18	0	1	2	523	40		40	0	0	12	13	470	
1362–63	470	114							584	101	5	12	11	*1*	*1½*	13	470	
1363–64	470	119							589	102	5	13	10	*1*	*1½*	17	470	
1364–65	470	82							552	69		73	9	0	13	17	470	sale includes 4 rams
1365–66	470	[M.T.]								32		34	8	0	13			sale includes 5 rams

1. Received from Twyford and Mardon.
2. Includes 1 ram.
3. Castrated and added to the wethers, 20.
4. Includes 3 rams.
5. Castrated and added to the wethers, 1.

EWES (CONTINUED)

Year	Number left over	Number from stock, etc.	Number bought	Total purchase price £ s. d.	Average purchase price s. d.	Total number in account	Number sold	Total sale price £	s.	d.	Average sale price s.	d.	Number died	Number remaining	Remarks
1366–67	470	41				511	27		29	3	0	13	15	470	sale includes 1 ram
1367–68	470	92				562	66		75	8			24	474	sale includes 2 rams
1368–69	474	111				585	100	6	7	1	1	3¼	12	473	
1369–70	473	129				602	113	7	7	1			12	479	sale includes 2 rams
1370–71	479	86				565	67	4	4	2	1	3	17	472	8 sold extra
1371–72	472	155				627	82	4	14	6	0	14	30	469	incomplete
1372–73	469	209				678	66	5	2	8	1	6¾	138	475	
1373–74	475	52				527	20		26	8	1	4	35	472	
1375–76	420	161	31			612	116	8	8	9	1	5½	31	465	
1376–77	465	108				573	54		54	0	0	12	60	461	sale includes 2 rams
1377–78	461	116				577	64						50	463	
1378–79	463	94				557	50		50	0	1	0	38	469	
1379–80	469	139				608	118						29	461	
1381–82	424	58				482	49		52	6	1	1	14	423	sale includes 4 rams
1382–83							29		29	0					sale includes 2 rams
1383–84							50		50	4					sale includes 1 ram
1384–85	[M.T.]						58		58	0				421	sale includes 2 rams
1385–86	421	79				500	61						15	424	
1387–88	430	109				539	40		40	0	0	12	81	419	sale includes 1 ram
1388–89	419	86				505	53		53	0	0	12	33	419	
1390–91	419	66				485	46		46	6	1	0	12	429	sale includes 2 rams
1392–93	420[1]	112				537	73		73	0	1	0	36	429	sale includes 1 ram
1393–94	429	93				522	62		62	0	1	0	34	428	sale includes 2 rams
1394–95	417	112				529	63		63	0	1	0	46	423	sale includes 3 rams
1395–96	423	102				525	78		79	4	1	0¼	29	420	sale includes 2 rams
1398–99	415	76				491	42		42	0	0	12	21	418	10 others sold

1399–00	418	63				481	45	*46*	*0*	*0*	*12¼*	44	392	
1400–01	392	128				520	76					26	418	
1402–03	424	70				494	73	[M.T.]				12	*409*	
1406–07	338	87				425	60	76	4	*1*	3¼	9	357	1 ram included in sale
1408–09	346	100				446	50	49	0	0	12	15	385	4 rams included in sale
1409–10	385	88				473	67	77	0	0	14	12	396	2 rams included in sale
1410–11	396	78				474	63	63	0	0	12	38	378	5 rams included in sale
1411–12	378	60				438	38	37	0	0	12	27	375	2 rams included in sale
1412–13	375	72				447	59	59	0	0	12	13	379	4 rams included in sale
1413–14	379	80				459	57	57	0	0	12	28	376	2 rams included in sale
1414–15	376	72				448	58	58	0	0	12	12	381	3 rams included in sale
1418–19	390	49				439	46	46	0	0	12	8	385	
1419–20	385	62				447	48	48	0	*1*	*0*	11	390	2 rams included in sale
1420–21	390	79				469	56	51	8	*0*	*11*	23	392	2 rams included in sale
1421–22	392	77				469	70	58	4	0	10	10	390	1 ram included in sale
1422–23	390	83				473	66	55	0	0	10	15	392	
1423–24	392	50				442	40	34	4	*0*	*10¼*	28	375	1 ram included in sale
1424–25	375	70				445	34					60	351	
1425–26	351	111				462	43	43	0	0	12	11	410	2 rams included in sale
1427–28	411	60				471	45	45	0	0	12	21	406	1 ram included in sale
1429–30	401	60				461	47	54	10	0	14	14	402	2 rams included in sale
1430–31	402	75				477	44	51	6	0	14	21	413	1 ram included in sale
1431–32	413	86				499	50	50	0	0	12	50	401	2 rams included in sale
1432–33	401	60				461	50	55	10	0	14	30	383	2 rams included in sale
1433–34	383	80				463	45			1	0	34	384	
1434–35	384	79				463	34	31	2	0	11	49	380	
1435–36	380	70				450	28	32	8	0	14	18	404	
1438–39	366	88				454	46	42	2	0	11	10	399	1 ram included in sale
1440–41	405	94				499	30	22	6	0	13	52	417	
1441–42	417	49				466	37	24	8	0	8	20	410	1 ram included in sale
1446–47	408	101				509	38	28	6	0	9	10	461	
1447–48	461	37				498	52[2]	42	4			55	393	3 rams included in sale
1448–49	393	56				449	32	24	0	0	9	66	351	

1. This should probably be 425.

2. One more sold extra.

LAMBS

Year	Number of increase	Number bought	Total purchase price		Average purchase price		Total number in account	Number for tithe	Number sold	Total sale price		Average sale price		Number for customary payment	Number given to St. Anthony	Number died	Number remaining	Remarks
			s.	d.	s.	d.				s.	d.	s.	d.					
1208–09	456						456	45	45	8	$8\frac{1}{2}$	*0*	$2\frac{1}{4}$	4		104	258	
1210–11	424						475	42	18	4	1	*0*	$2\frac{3}{4}$	6		189	220	51 were received from Overton
1211–12	376						776	37	145	20	$11\frac{3}{4}$	*0*	*$1\frac{3}{4}$*	5		198	391	400(?) were from Overton
1213–14	598						610	59	72	11	$4\frac{1}{2}$	*0*	*2*	6		79	394	12 came from Clere
1215–16	674						674	67	60	11	8	*0*	$2\frac{1}{4}$	7		83	457	
1217–18	305						305	30	18	3	7	*0*	$2\frac{1}{2}$	6		66	185	
1218–19	381						381	38	36	8	0	*0*	$2\frac{3}{4}$	6		*47*	254	
1219–20	425						425	42	10	2	5	*0*	*3*	6		72	295	
1220–21	494						898	49	18	3	$10\frac{1}{2}$	*0*	$2\frac{1}{2}$	6		218	607	404 were received from Menes
1223–24	728						728	72	105	26	$2\frac{1}{2}$	*0*	*3*	6		142	403	
1224–25	735						735	73	55	13	$3\frac{1}{2}$	*0*	*3*	6		347	254	
1225–26	660						660	66	16	3	$7\frac{1}{2}$	*0*	$2\frac{3}{4}$	6		360	212	
1226–27	702						702	70	6	0	19	*0*	$3\frac{1}{4}$	6		250	370	
1231–32	520						520	52	6	3	$3\frac{1}{2}$	*0*	*$6\frac{1}{2}$*	5		86	377	[*sic*]
1232–33	559						559	55	6	0	17	*0*	$2\frac{3}{4}$	5		248	245	
1235–36	722						722	73	5	2	1	*0*	*5*	5		503	147	[*sic*]
1236–37	835						835	83	56	12	9	*0*	$2\frac{3}{4}$	5		80	*611*	
1244–45	*342*						*342*	44	9	2	9	*0*	$3\frac{3}{4}$	4		194	91	
1245–46	482						482	48	19	6	$9\frac{1}{2}$	*0*	*$4\frac{1}{4}$*	4		83	328	
1246–47	457	10					467	45	10	2	$11\frac{1}{2}$	*0*	$3\frac{1}{2}$	4		313	95	
1247–48	591						707	59	6	2	$2\frac{1}{2}$	*0*	*$4\frac{1}{2}$*	4		307	331	116 came from Mardon
1248–49	685						685	68	8	2	$3\frac{1}{2}$	*0*	$3\frac{1}{2}$	4		417	188	
1251–52	602						602	22[1]	17	4	3	*0*	*3*	4		406	153	
1252–53	652						679	56	18	4	6	0	3	4		95	506	27 from a fugitive
1253–54	675						675	25	8	2	0	*0*	*3*	4		422	216	
1254–55	731						731	46	10	2	6	*0*	*3*	4		289	382	

1256–57	683						683	68	15	5	0	*0*	*4*	4		229	367	
1257–58	673						673	67	13	3	9½	*0*	*3½*	4		236	353	
1264–65	184	150	56	3	0	4½	334	12	60	9	0	*0*	*1¾*	4		81	177	
1265–66	197						197	9	80	23	4	*0*	*3½*	4		104		
1267–68	95						95	7						4		32	52	
1268–69	108[2]						124	5						4		64	51	16 from elsewhere
1270–71	110	51					161	6						4		45	106	
1271–72	649	67	45	2	*0*	*8*	716	30						4		389	293	
1272–73	666						666	40	12	3	0	*0*	*3*	4		303	307	
1273–74	610	40					650	21	13	3	9½	0	3½	4		417	195	
1274–75	617	46					663	28	16	5	4	0	4	4		335	276	[*sic*]
1276–77	556	58	45	11	0	9½	614	24	5	2	1	0	5	4		332	249	
1277–78	520	36	18	0	*0*	*6*	556	23						4		299	230	
1282–83	235						235	11						4		128	92	
1283–84	228						228	19						4		31	174	
1284–85	233						233	20						4		33	176	
1285–86	252						252							4		209	39	
1286–87	207						207	11						4		105	87	
1287–88	199						199	19						4		37	139	
1288–89	212						212	14						4		93	101	
1289–90	235						235	18						4		53	160	
1290–91	235						235	20						4		28	183	
1291–92	256						256	22						4		38	192	
1292–93	295						295							4		69	191	Ms. incomplete
1296–97	256						256	25						4		130	97	
1297–98	269						269	27	10	3	4	0	4	4		23	205	
1298–99	379	16					395	22	12	5	0	0	5	4		101	256	
1299–00	330						330	19						4		154	153	
1300–01	398						398	34						4		74	286	
1301–02	392						392	32						4		88	268	
1302–03	328						328	28						4		66	231	[*sic*]
1304–05	384						577	11	20	4	0	*0*	*2½*	4		336	206	193 from elsewhere

1. In payment of the tithe, henceforth, allowance was made for the death of lambs before weaning.
2. Sixteen from the shepherd for badly caring for the lambs after shearing.

LAMBS (Continued)

Year	Number of increase	Number bought	Total purchase price s.	Total purchase price d.	Average purchase price s.	Average purchase price d.	Total number in account	Number for tithe	Number sold	Total sale price s.	Total sale price d.	Average sale price s.	Average sale price d.	Number for customary payment	Number given to St. Anthony	Number died	Number remaining	Remarks
1305–06	398	159	131	11½	0	10	557	12	14	6	0	0	5	4		302	225	
1306–07	429						500	34	50	25	0	0	6	4		102	310	71 from elsewhere
1307–08	444						446	38	3	3	0	1	0	4		64	337	2 from elsewhere
1308–09	472						545	43	50	29	2	0	7	4		47	401	73 from elsewhere
1309–10	536						536	42	40	16	8	0	5	4		164	286	
1310–11	550						550	49	43	18	0	0	5	4		104	350	
1311–12	463						463	40	40	16	5½	0	5	4		72	307	
1312–13	457						457	32	21	9	7½	0	5½	4		145	254	[*sic*]
1313–14	483						483	17	16	5	0	0	4	3		327	120	
1314–15	399	300					699	15	60	27	11	0	5½	3		292	329	
1315–16	433						433	40	13	6	8	0	6¼	2		44	334	
1316–17	361						370	34	25	10	5	0	5	3		38	270	9 from elsewhere
1317–18	429						429	38	30	15	0	0	6	4		57	300	
1318–19	423						423	38	20	10	0	0	6	4		61	300	
1320	124						124									1	123	
1320–21	302	67	44	8	0	8	369	28	40	30	0	0	9	4		38	259	
1323–24							385											
1326–27	349	62	41	4	0	8	411	32	25	16	8	0	8	4		60	290	
1327–28	303	170	110	6	0	7¾	473	27	2					4		64	376	
1328–29	304						682	28	25	10	5	0	5	4		43	582	378 from elsewhere
1329–30	303						467	26	23	9	7	0	5	4		56	358	164 from elsewhere
1330–31	334						334	30	32	24	0	0	9	4		29	239	
1331–32	442						442	41	57	40	7½	0	8½	4		35	305	
1332–33	442						442	42	40	18	4	0	5½	4		27	329	
1334–35	205						205	17	141	70	6	0	6	3		44		
1335–36	304						304	24	34	17	0	0	6	3		91	152	

1336–37	317						317	29						3		27	258	
1337–38	340	46					386	31	37	10	9½	0	3½	3		43	272	
1338–39	355	29	12	1	0	5	384	12	18	4	6	0	3	3		257	94	
1339–40	326	75	25	0	0	4	401	3						3		328	67	
1340–41	268						268	22	24	6	0	0	3	3		42	177	
1341–42	261						261	21						4		57	179	
1342–43	342	106	53	0	0	6	448	30	27	13	6	0	6	4		51	336	
1343–44	374	155	76	6	0	6	529	29[1]	68	31	0	0	5½	4		107	321	
1344–45	400						400	36	52	15	10½	0	3¾	4		59	250	[*sic*]
1345–46	115	164	86	0	0	6¼	279	9						3		30	237	
1346–47	273	217	113	2	0	6	490	10						4		249	227	
1347–48	368	82	52	11	0	7½	450	27						4		125	294	
1348–49	404	185	45	0	0	3	589	33	60	12	0	0	2½	4		92	400	
1349–50	421						421	36	1	0	5	0	5	3		23	359	
1350–51	404	160	80	0	0	6	564	37	109	51	2	0	5½	3		50	365	
1351–52	418						418	39	110	55	0	0	6	3		90	176	
1352–53	375						375	32	32	16	0	0	6	3		98	210	
1353–54	411						411	32	30	30	0	0	4	3		121	225	
1354–55	408						408	37	74	49	2	0	8	3		44	250	
1355–56	376						376	30						3		89	254	
1356–57	375						375	31	11	5	6	0	6	3		75	255	
1357–58	397						397	33	33	8	3	0	3	3		90	238	
1358–59	401						401	33						3		82	283	
1359–60	397						397	33	15	6	3	0	5	3		65	281	
1360–61	408						408	33[2]						3		269	103	
1361–62	331						331	31	40	20	0	0	6	3		24	233	
1362–63	413						413	39	100	56	8	0	6¾	3		31	240	
1363–64	393	36	33	0	0	11	429	26						3		160	240	
1364–65	390	14	12	10	0	11	404	31	21	7	0	0	4	3		109	240	
1365–66	[M.T.]																	
1366–67	380						593[3]	30	48	28	0	0	7	4	1	103	408	213 from Mardon
1367–68	424						632	38	79	59	0	0	9	4	1	72	438	208 from Mardon

1. The manuscript has C or 100, an error for 29.
2. Corrected from 34.
3. Perhaps 594.

LAMBS (CONTINUED)

Year	Number of increase	Number bought	Total purchase price		Average purchase price		Total number in account	Number for tithe	Number sold	Total sale price		Average sale price		Number for customary payment	Number given to St. Anthony	Number died	Number remaining	Remarks
			s.	d.	s.	d.				s.	d.	s.	d.					
1368–69	404						621	37	56	36	8	0	8	4	1	63	460	217 from Mardon
1369–70	408						656	33	64	45	4	*0*	*8½*	5	1	100	453	248 from Mardon (?)
1370–71	405						653	35	66[1]	47	8	*0*	*8¾*	5		83	456	248 from Mardon
1371–72	408						643	33	50	25	0	0	6	4	1	126	429	235 from Mardon
1372–73	406						628	31	55	27	6	0	6	4		417	121	220 from Mardon
1373–74	281	120	140	0	*1*	*2*	567	22	20	10	0	*0*	*6*	4		223	*298*	166 from Mardon
1375–76	382						382	36	7	2	11	*0*	*5*	4	1	33	300	[*sic*]
1376–77	289						289	23						4		106	156	
1377–78	355	110					465	27	22					4		122	290	
1378–79	379	100	111	8	*1*	*1½*	479	24	12	5	0	*0*	*5*	4		173	266	
1379–80	381	61					441	34	15					4	1	62	326	[*sic*]
1381–82	378						378	36	14	9	4	0	8	4		19	305	
1382–83									13	6	6	*0*	*6*					
1383–84									67	55	6	*0*	*10*					
1384–85		9	9	0	*1*	*0*			11	5	6	*0*	*6*					
1385–86	*396*						*396*	38	20					4	1	22	311	
1387–88	334						334	20	6	2	6	0	5	4		*140*	[Ill.]	
1388–89	368	65	47	6¾	*0*	*8¾*	433	29	16	8	0	0	6	4	1	85	298	
1390–91	*399*						399	38	16	9	4	*0*	*7*	4			[M.T.]	
1392–93	361	80					441	30	30	12	6	*0*	*5*	4	1	72	304	
1393–94	383	60	50	0	0	10	443	31	26	8	8	*0*	*4*	4		81	301	
1394–95	348	87	65	6	*0*	*9*	435	29	21	7	0	*0*	*4*	4	1	74	306	
1395–96	361	140	122	6	0	10½	501	24	50	16	8	*0*	*4*	4		133	270	20 sold extra
1398–99	365	80	60	0	0	9	445	28	*12*	7	6	*0*	*7½*	4		*111*	290	
1399–00	380	26	21	8	0	10	406	37	14	7	0	0	6	4		23	328	
1400–01	343	45	37	6	*0*	*10*	388	33	32					4		14	306	

1402–03	390						390	*36*	20	[M.T.]				4		45	285	
1406–07	304	123	173	1	*1*	*5*	427	24	24	16	6	*0*	*8¼*	4		76	299	
1408–09	307	60	60	0	*1*	*0*	367	29	4	0	20	*0*	*5*	4	*19*		311	
1409–10	351	51	55	3	*1*	*1*	402	31	14	9	4	0	8	4		66	287	
1410–11	323	143	149	5½	0	12½	466	22	12	5	0	0	5	4		139	289	
1411–12	316	120	121	9	*1*	*0¼*	436	26	18	8	8	*0*	*5¾*	4		91	297	
1412–13	326	97	97	0	0	12	423	28	18	8	6	*0*	*5¾*	4		69	304	
1413–14	316	192	160	0	0	10	508	17	20	8	4	0	6	4		160	307	
1414–15	325	88					413	27	24	10	0	0	5	4	1	54	303	
1418–19	341	68	56	8	0	10	409	29	19	10	4	*0*	*6½*	4	1	50	306	
1419–20	336	62	51	8	*0*	*10*	398	32	14	7	0	*0*	*6*	4	1	23	324	
1420–21	338	59	49	0	*0*	*10*	397	32	12	4	0	*0*	*4*	4	1	31	317	
1421–22	352	47					399	31	15	5	0	0	4	4	1	48	300	
1422–23	341	64	42	8	0	8	405	29	18	6	6½	0	4	4	1	59	294	
1423–24	323	64					387	29	11	5	6	*0*	*6*	4	1	62	280	
1424–25	261	120	120	0	1	0	381	22	9	3	9	0	5	4	1	48	297	
1425–26	311	60	50	0	0	10	371	29	8	3	4	0	5	4	1	27	302	
1427–28	364	50	41	8	*0*	*10*	414	32	20	8	4	0	5	4	1	64	293	
1429–30	365						365	36	14	7	0	0	6	4		16	295	
1430–31	326	36	36	0	0	12	362	31	10	5	0	0	6	4		32	285	
1431–32	337	144	123	4	*0*	*10¼*	481	18	18	9	0	0	6	4	1	162	278	
1432–33	360	16	16	0	0	12	381	33	10	4	0	*0*	*4¾*	4	1	41	292	[*sic*]
1433–34	344	31	28	5	0	11	375	31	5	2	6	0	6	4		41	294	
1434–35	312	100	100	0	0	12	412	23	3	0	18	0	6	4		119	263	
1435–36	330	52	39	0	0	9	382	29						4	1	46	302	
1438–39	344						344	31						4		33	276	
1440–41	332	60	60	0	0	12	392	27						4		71	290	
1441–42	380	18	18	0	0	12	398	33						4		77	284	
1446–47	164	147	110	3	0	9	311									9	302	[*sic*]
1447–48	365	40	33	4	0	10	405	32						4		65	304	
1448–49	332	240	200	0	0	10	572	6						4		289	273	

1. Seven sold extra. Totals do not quite balance, as frequently elsewhere.

RAMS

Year	Number left over	Number of increase	Number bought	Total purchase price s.	Total purchase price d.	Average purchase price s.	Average purchase price d.	Total number in account	Number sold	Total sale price s.	Total sale price d.	Average sale price s.	Average sale price d.	Number died	Number remaining	Remarks
1244–45									1	1	2	1	2			
1245–46									2	1	8		*10*			
1290–91		8						8								
1291–92	8	6						14	1	1	2	1	2			
1305–06	10		1	3	2	3	2	11							11	
1306–07	11							11							11	
1307–08	11	1						12						1	11	
1308–09	11	3						14							14	
1309–10	14	7						21	1	1	0	1	0		20	
1310–11	20	8						28	9	18	6	*2*	*0¾*		19	
1311–12	19	7	7	18	0	*2*	*7*	33	2					2	29	
1312–13	29	2						31							31	
1313–14	31							31						1	30	
1314–15	30	2						32	2	2	4	*1*	*2*	7	23	
1315–16	23	3						26	3	4	6	*1*	*6*	2	21	
1316–17	21	5						26	3					1	22	
1317–18	22	*3*						25	4	8	0	*2*	*0*	1	20	
1318–19	20	5						25	2	4	0	*2*	*0*	2	21	
1320	16							16							16	
1320–21	16	4						20	1	2	0	2	0		19	
1324–25	15							15								15 sent to Twyford
1325–26		9[1]						9							9	
1326–27	9							9							9	
1327–28	9	7	10	16	8	*1*	*8*	26	10	15	0	*1*	*6*	2	14	
1328–29	14							14	2	2	8	*1*	*4*		12	
1329–30	12	6						18							12	6 sent to Mardon

1330–31	12	6						18	3	3	2	*1*	*1*	2	13	
1331–32	13	6						19	7	9	2	*1*	$3\frac{3}{4}$		12	1 added to wethers
1334–35	14							14	3	3	6	*1*	*2*	2	9	
1335–36	9							9	2	2	4	*1*	*2*		7	
1336–37	7	5						12	2	2	0	*1*	*0*		10	
1337–38	10	4						14	1	0	12	1	0	2	11	
1338–39	11	3						14							14	
1339–40	14							14						7	7	
1341–42	8	5	3					16	4	3	6	*0*	$10\frac{1}{2}$		12	
1342–43	12	4						16	1						15	
1343–44									2	1	4	*0*	*8*			
1344–45	18	8						26	13	13	9	*1*	$0\frac{3}{4}$	4	9	
1345–46	9	8						17	1	0	9	0	9	1	15	
1346–47	15	5						20	2					3	15	
1347–48	15	3						18	2	2	0	*1*	*0*	1	15	
1348–49	15	6						21						3	18	
1349–50	18	6						24	3	3	2	*1*	*1*	1	19	1 sold extra
1350–51	19	4	2	2	4	*1*	*2*	25	5	5	0	*1*	*0*	1	19	
1351–52	19	3						22	3	*3*	*0*	1	0		19	
1352–53	19	3						22	5	5	0	*1*	*0*		17	
1353–54	17	3						20	5	*5*	*0*	1	0		15	
1354–55	15	5						20	5	*5*	*0*	1	0		15	
1355–56	15	5						20	1	1	0	1	0	4	15	
1356–57	15	4						19	4	4	0	1	0		15	
1357–58	15	4						19	4						15	
1358–59	15	4						19	3	3	0	*1*	*0*	1	15	
1359–60	*15*	*4*						19	3	3	0	*1*	*0*	1	15	
1360–61	15	4						19	2	1	8		*10*	2	15	
1361–62	15	3						18	3	3	0	*1*	*0*		15	
1362–63	15	4						19	4	4	4	*1*	*1*		15	
1363–64	15	5						20	2	2	2	*1*	*1*	3	15	
1364–65	15	6						21	4	*4*	*4*	1	1	2	15	

1. All from Twyford and Mardon.

RAMS (CONTINUED)

Year	Number left over	Number of increase	Number bought	Total purchase price s.	Total purchase price d.	Average purchase price s.	Average purchase price d.	Total number in account	Number sold	Total sale price s.	Total sale price d.	Average sale price s.	Average sale price d.	Number died	Number remaining	Remarks
1365–66	15	5						20	5	*5*	*5*	1	1		[M.T.]	
1366–67	15	1						16	1	1	1	1	1		15	
1367–68	15	3						18	2					1	15	
1368–69	15	2						17	1	1	2	1	2	1	15	
1369–70	15	2						17	2	*2*	*4*	1	2		15	
1370–71	15	3						18						3	15	
1371–72	15	6						21	5	5	8	*1*	*1¾*	1	15	
1372–73	15	8						23	3	4	0	*1*	*4*	6	14	
1375–76	12	5						17	1	1	3	1	3		16	
1376–77	16	3						19	2	*2*	*0*	1	0	2	15	
1377–78	15	6						21	2					4	15	
1378–79	15	3						18	1	1	0	1	0	3	14	
1381–82	15	*4*						19	4	4	6	*1*	*1½*		15	
1382–83									2	2	0	*1*	*0*			
1383–84									1	1	0	1	0			
1384–85	15	3						18	2	*2*	*0*	1	0		[M.T.]	
1385–86	15	4						19	*3*					1	15	
1387–88	15	5						20	1	1	0	1	0	4	15	
1388–89	15	2						17						2	15	
1390–91	15	2						17	2	*2*	*0*	1	0		*15*	
1392–93	15	7						22	1	1	0	1	0	6	15	
1393–94	15	6						21	2	2	*0*	1	0	3	16	
1394–95	16	4						20	3					2	15	
1395–96	15	2						17	2	*2*	*0*	1	0	1	14	
1398–99	15	4						19						*4*	15	
1399–00	15	3						18	2	*2*	*0*	1	0	2	14	

1400–01	14	4				18	3					1	14	
1402–03	14	3				17	2					1	14	
1406–07	8	9				17	1	1	4	1	4		16	
1408–09	13	2				15	3	3	0	1	0	1	11	
1409–10	11	6				17	1	1	0	1	2		16	
1410–11	16	2				18	5	1	0	1	0		13	
1411–12	13	4				17	2	2	0	1	0		15	
1412–13	15	2				17	4	4	0	1	0		13	
1413–14	13	3				16	2	2	0	1	0	2	12	
1414–15	12	3				15	3	3	0	1	0	1	11	
1418–19	11	2				13						1	12	
1419–20	12	3				15	2	1	0	1	0	1	12	
1420–21	12	2				14	2					1	11	
1421–22	11	2				13	1		10		10	1	11	
1422–23	11	2				13						2	11	
1423–24	11	1				12	1					2	9	
1424–25	9	3				12						4	8	
1425–26	8	5				13	2	2	0	1	0		11	
1427–28	10	3				13	1	1	0	1	0		12	
1429–30	11	3				14	2	2	4	1	2	1	11	
1430–31	11	3				14	1	1	2	1	2	1	12	
1431–32	12	4				16	2	1	0	1	0	2	12	
1432–33	12	2				14	2	0	11		11	1	11	
1433–34	11	3				14	1	1	0	1	0	1	11	
1434–35	11	3				14						3	11	
1435–36	11	3				14						2	12	
1438–39	12	2				14	1	0	11		11	1	12	
1440–41	12	2				14						4	10	
1441–42	10	3				13	1	0	8		8	1	11	
1446–47	10	3				13	1	0	9	0	9		12	
1447–48	12	4				16	3					1	12	
1448–49	12	3				15						5	10	

SHEEP'S WOOL [1]

Year	Total number	Number for tithe	Number for customary payment	Number sold	Total weight sold [2]				Total sale price			Average sale price per wey [3]		Number sent to Wolvesey	Total weight sent				Number of plucked [4]	Number remaining
	Fleeces	Fleeces	Fleeces	Fleeces	W.	St.	C.	Lb.	£	s.	d.	s.	d.	Fleeces	W.	St.	C.	Lb.	Fleeces	Fleeces
1208–09	990	99	3	888	4	4			5	0	0	*23*	2½							
1210–11	806	80	3											723 [5]	4		6			
1211–12	808	80	3	725	4				7	0	0	*35*	*0*							
1213–14	1250	125	3	1122	*7⅚				15	3	4	*38*	*8¾*							
1215–16	1594	159	4	1431	10				17	6	8	*34*	*8*							
1217–18	656	65	3											588	4					
1218–19	776	76	3	687	5				5	13	0	*22*	*7¼*							
1219–20	928	92	3	833	6				7	0	12	*23*	*6*							
1220–21	1197	119	3	1075	8	2			10	0	18	*24*	*8½*							
1223–24	1426	142	4	1280	7	1			9	16	4	*27*	*9*							
1224–25	1503	150	4	659	4				5	0	0	*25*	*0*							690
1225–26	1933	124	4	1208	7				10	10	0	*30*	*0*							597
1226–27	1253	125	4	1124	10½				13	18	2	*26*	*6*							
1231–32	1202	120	4	1078	7		6		14	9	0	*39*	*11½*							
1232–33	1225	122	4	1099	* 8				16	8	0	*41*	*0*							
1235–36	1520	152	4	1364	*10		7		21	0	12½	*41*	*0*							
1236–37	1473	[M.T.]		1321	*11		6½		24	3	9	*43*	*0*							
1244–45	*891*	89	3	799	* 5		1		10	0	18	*40*	*0*							
1245–46	866	86	3	777	5		8		13	5	8½	*50*	*0¾*							
1246–47	1417	96	3	1318	9		16		20	19	10	*43*	*8*							
1247–48	1147	114	3	1030	6				13	10	0	46	8							
1248–49	1079	108	3	968	7		8		15	16	3½	43	4							
1251–52	1081	108	3	970	7½		2		16	8	4	*43*	*4*							
1252–53	1272	127	3	1142	11				22	0	0	*40*	*0*							

1253–54	1445	144	3	1298	* 9½			17	9	9	36	8					
1254–55	1466	137	3	1326	*10	5		18	13	9	36	8					
1256–57	1349	134	3	1212	9	3		18	4	7½	*40*	*0*					
1257–58	1518	151	3	1364	10	11		21	14	4	41	8					
1264–65	436	40	3														
1265–66					4½	22		10	13	11	40	0					393
1267–68	225	21	3	201	1	10			60	0	*43*	*4*				21	
1268–69	220	22	3										195[6]				
1270–71	209	19	3	187	1	4			53	4	*46*	*2¾*				14	
1271–72	1535	89	3	1443	11	3		24	0	9	43	4				153	
1272–73	1437	123	3	1311	10	12		24	8	2½	46	8				204	
1273–74	1451	129	3	1319	11½	6		27	7	5	*46*	*8*				159	
1274–75	1337	125	3	1212	*10½	3		26	10	7½	50	0				87	
1276–77	1318	109	3	1206	*10	6		28	19	8	56	8				219	
1277–78	1193	110	3	1080	* 9	7		24	14	6	53	4				90	
1282–83	478	48	3										427				
1283–84	482	48	3										431				
1284–85	592	59	3										530				
1285–86	511	51	3	457	* 3			8	0	0	53	4					
1286–87	459	46	3	410	* 3	3		9	14	5	*62*	*4¾*					
1287–88	479	48	3	428	* 4	2		12	4	0	60	0					
1288–89	501	50	3	448	* 4	4		12	8	0	60	0					
1289–90	764	55	3	706	* 6½	6¾		21	4	2	*62*	*9*					
1290–91	733	73	3	657	* 5	12		16	7	8	60	0					
1291–92	772	77	3	692	* 5	6		14	0	0	53	4					
1292–93	842	84	3	755	6			18	0	0	60	0					
1296–97	628	62	3	563	4			6	0	0	*30*	*0*					
1297–98	651	65	3	583	* 4	5	4	11	0	21½	*52*	*7½*					
1298–99	966	96	3										867	5	5		
1299–00	851	83	3										765	3	18		
1300–01	935	93	3	10					2	11			829				

1. Lana grossa (great fleeces). 2. In sacks, weys, stones, cloves, and pounds.
3. The wey was 182 lbs. The price of one lb. of wool in Crawley in Oct., 1928, was about 18d. The average price here given sometimes is for lamb's as well as sheep's wool, where the asterisk occurs. 4. Fleeces that were plucked were not subject to the tithe. 5. Sent to Southwerk. 6. Sent to Clere.
* These totals (found in the original accounts) include lamb's wool, the amounts of which are indicated in the tables for lamb's wool, following.

SHEEP'S WOOL (Continued)

Year	Total number	Number for tithe	Number for customary payment	Number sold	Total weight sold				Total sale price			Average sale price per wey			Number sent to Wolvesey	Total weight sent				Number of plucked	Number remaining
	Fleeces	Fleeces	Fleeces	Fleeces	W.	St.	C.	Lb.	£	s.	d.		s.	d.	Fleeces	W.	St.	C.	Lb.	Fleeces	Fleeces
1301–02	1035	103	3												929	6½		3			
1302–03	978	*97*	*3*												878	4		18			
					Sack	W.		C.								Sack	W.		C.		
1304–05	926	92	3												831		3		24		
1305–06	960	96	3	1						0	4¾				860		5½		2		
1306–07	992	99	3	38[1]				7		17	5		*64*	*10¼*	725		4		23½		
1307–08	1139	113	3												1023		7		8		
1308–09	1319	132	3	1185	*	11			45	0	0¾		74	4	(1185)						
1309–10	1535	153	3	1479	*	14½		5	48	19	6		66	8							
1310–11	1476	147	3	1324[2]		12			36	0	0		60	0							
1311–12	1418	142	2												1274		12		4		
1312–13	1432	143	2	1287	*	11		17	32	0	11		55	0							
1313–14	1294	129	2	1163	*	9		25	34	9	9		66	8							
1314–15	1055	105	2	949	*	8		3	30	7	8¼		66	8							
1315–16	1111				* 6	1		1	39	2	3¾		60	0							
1316–17	1098	109		989	*	11		21	39	7	2¼		66	8							
1317–18	1194	119	2	1073	*	10		23	37	12	8¼		67	4							
1318–19	1242	124	2	1116	*	13		3	51	17	11		*79*	*1¾*							
1320	124			124				9		25	3¾		2	9¾[3]							
1320–21	665	66	2	597	*	6		13	31	0	13¾	4	5	0							
1326–27	670	67	2	601[4]	* 2			25	18	0	18¼	6	13	4[5]	(601)						
1327–28	922	92	2												828						
1328–29	366	36	2												328						
1329–30	811	81													730						
1330–31	994	99													895						

														Sack	C.	Lb.		
1331–32	1108	111		997	* 6	10	38	3	9	*6*	*3*	*6*[5]						
1332–33	1193	119	2	1072	* 6	34$\frac{3}{7}$	28	17	5	4	6	8[5]						
1334–35	586	58		528	2	7	8	10	9½	*4*	*0*	*0*[5]						
1335–36	531	53	2	476	* 2	9	10	10	0¼	*4*	*16*	7¾[5]						
1336–37	645	64½											580½	3	6			
1337–38	834	83											751					
1338–39	909	91											818					
1339–40	594	59											535					
1340–41	560	56											504					
1341–42	652	65	2										585					
1342–43	779	78	2										699	3	9			
1343–44	924	92	2										830	3	23			
1344–45	1034	103	2										929	4	48			
1345–46	741	38	2										701[6]	2	16			
1346–47	861	86	2										773	3	8			
1347–48	1048	105	2										941	3	33			
1348–49	1080	109											971					
1349–50	1052	105	1										946	4	19			
1350–51	1176	117											1059	6				
1351–52	1161	116											1045	5	20			
1352–53	1127	112											1015	5	46			
1353–54	1171	117											1055	5	14			
1354–55	1202	120											1082	5	13	4		
1355–56	1133	113											1020	4	16			
1356–57	1231	123											1108	5	19	1		
1357–58	1222	122											1100		51			
1358–59	1167	117											1050	4	10			
1359–60	1245	124											1121	4	20			
1360–61	1208	121											1087	4	40			
1361–62	1013	101											912	4	41			
1362–63	1213	121											1092	4	42			

1. Handed over to a certain merchant, 127 fleeces (1 wey) extra. 2. Two fleeces in addition were sold for 12d. 3. Average price given in cloves.
4. Sent to Wolvesey and there sold. 5. Average price given in sacks. 6. Sold at Wolvesey for £12 6s. 1½d.

SHEEP'S WOOL (Continued)

Year	Total number	Number for tithe	Number for customary payment	Number sold	Total weight sold			Total sale price			Average sale price per wey		Number sent to Wolvesey	Total weight sent			Number of plucked	Number remaining
	Fleeces	Fleeces	Fleeces	Fleeces	Sack	C.	Lb.	£	s.	d.	s.	d.	Fleeces	Sack	C.	Lb.	Fleeces	Fleeces
1363–64	1213	121											1092	4	34			
1364–65	1206	120											1086	4	29			
1365–66	1095	109											986	4	23			
1366–67	1194	119											1000					
1367–68	1197	120											1077	5	16			
1368–69	1246	124											1122	5	8			
1369–70	1060	126											1035	4	47			92[1]
1370–71	1183	118		92[1]		23			23	0	0	12	1065	4	9			
1371–72	1162	*116*[2]											843	4	7			
1372–73[3]	1215	121	1	33	1	6		4	16	8	0	20	1059	3	20			
1373–74						45[1]												
1375–76	1254	125	1	63[1]		12	3½		14	6	0	14	1020[4]	2	46			96
1376–77	1185	118	2										831	2	37			234[1]
1377–78	1137	110	2										1025[5]	2	39			
1378–79	1153	115	2										1036	2	39			
1379–80	*1216*	121	2										1093	3	23			
1381–82	1226	122	2										1102	3	14			
1385–86	1203	120	2										1081	2	16			
1388–89	1140	114	2										1024	2	50			
1390–91	1149	115	*2*										[M.T.]					
1392–93	1160	116	2										1042	3	1			
1393–94	1211	121	2										1088	3	2			
1394–95	1119	112	2										[Ill.]	2	28			
1395–96	1148	115	*2*										1031	3	4			
1398–99	1018	102	2										914	2	40			

1399–00	1047	105						942	3	8			
1406–07	947	106						841	2	41			
1408–09	1013	101						912	3				
1409–10	1076	107						969	3	15			
1410–11	1061	106						955	2	48			
1411–12	1014	107						907	2	36			
1412–13	1029	113						916	3				
1413–14	1016	108						908	2	16			
1414–15	1045	104						941	3	2			
1418–19	953	114						839	2	42			
1419–20	1064	118						946	3	6			
1420–21	1055	119						936	3	34			
1421–22	1115	112						1003	3				
1422–23	*1049*	105						944	3	8			
1423–24	999	100						899	2	48			
1424–25	881	87						*794*	2	15			
1425–26	1010	101						909	3	11			
1427–28	1151	115						1035	2	49			[*sic*]
1429–30	987	120						867	3	6			
1430–31	1030	117						913	2	22			
1431–32	1101	110						991	2	38			
1432–33	976	114						862	2	33			
1433–34	979	98						878	2	39			[*sic*]
1434–35	1034	105						929	2	4			
1435–36	976	106						870	2	23			
1438–39	905	100						805	2	46			
1440–41	994	111						883	2	30			
1441–42	995	113						882	2	38			
1446–47	1015	101						914	2¾	6	1		
1447–48	968	103						865	2	49			
1448–49	957	96						861	2	36			

1. Refuse fleeces, sometimes not counted in the number of yield. 2. Corrected from 516. 3. Data uncertain. Manuscript partly illegible.
4. Sold extra, 11, 5. In addition were 39 refuse, sent to Wolvesey.

LAMB'S WOOL [1]

Year	Number of yield	Number sold [2]	Total weight sold				Total sale price		Average sale price		Number sent to Wolvesey	Total weight sent			
	Fleeces	Fleeces	W.	St.	C.	Lb.	s.	d.	s.	d.	Fleeces	W.	St.	C.	Lb.
1208–09	201	201	½												
1210–11	183	183		7			7	0	* 1	0					
1211–12	396	396	1 1/12				26	0	† 24	0					
1213–14	394	394													
1217–18	194										194	½			
1218–19	61	61	11/12				17	6	† 19	1					
1219–20	301	301	1				27	8	† 27	8					
1220–21		664	1 7/12				38	0	† 24	0					
1223–24	449	449	1				25	0	† 25	0					
1224–25	150	150		7			9	0	* 1	3½					
1225–26				6			7	6	* 1	3					
1226–27		270	½	3			17	0	* 1	9½					
1232–33	249	249													
1235–36	172	172													
1236–37	516	516													
1244–45	[M.T.]			4			8	4	* 2	1					
1245–46	332	332		11		2	22	7½	* 2	0¼					
1246–47	95	95		4			9	4	* 2	4					
1247–48	155	155	2				53	4	† 26	8					
1248–49	180	180		8			12	0	* 1	6					
1251–52	149	149			10		16	8	† 43	4					
1252–53	508	508	1				26	8	† 26	8					
1253–54	223	223	½												
1254–55	387	387	½		2										

1256–57	367	367		14			15	8	*	*1*	*1½*		
1257–58	385	385		16			32	0	*	*2*	*0*		
1264–65	185 [3]												
1267–68	205	205		7			14	0	*	*2*	*0*		
1268–69	38	38		1		2	2	10	*	*2*	*4*		
1270–71	54	54		1½			3	6	*	*2*	*4*		
1271–72	319	319			13		21	11	‡	*1*	*8¼*		
1272–73	321	321	½		1		25	1½	‡	*1*	*9½*		
1273–74	201	[Ill.]			10		17	11	‡	*1*	*9½*		
1274–75	280	280	½										
1276–77	263	263											
1277–78	236	236											
1282–83	105											105	3
1283–84	173											173	
1284–85	173											173	
1285–86	60	60											
1286–87	87	87											
1287–88	149	149											
1288–89	101	101											
1289–90	244	244											
1290–91	185	185											
1291–92	192	192			12		14	7	‡	0	15		
1292–93	191	191			12½								
1296–97	134	134			7	4	4	1	‡	0	7		
1298–99	256											256	21
1299–00	159											159	8
1300–01	289											289	
1301–02	283											283	15
1302–03	234											234	8

* Average price per stone. † Average price per wey. ‡ Average price per clove.

1. Lana agnina. 2. Number sold is not always for the same years as the number produced. Where price is not indicated, see the sheep's wool account.
3. These remain weighing 9 cloves.

LAMB'S WOOL (Continued)

Year	Number of yield	Number sold	Total weight sold				Total sale price		Average sale price		Number sent to Wolvesey	Total weight sent			
	Fleeces	Fleeces	W.	St.	C.	Lb.	s.	d.	s.	d.	Fleeces	W.	St.	C.	Lb.
1304–05	179	179			9		16	6	‡ 0	22					
1305–06	181										181				
1306–07	317										317			23	2
1307–08	320										320			25	
1308–09	401	401	1		4						401				
1309–10	306	306													
1310–11	360	360			20		46	1¾	‡ 2	3½					
1311–12	323										323			21	
1312–13	266	266			13										
1313–14	124	124			10										
1314–15	402	402	1												
1315–16	340	340	1		3										
1316–17	265	265	1		1										
1317–18	300	300	1												
1318–19	304	304			27										
1320	268	268			21										
1320–21															
1326–27	301										301				
1327–28	401				26						401				
1328–29	585										585				
1329–30	367										367				
1330–31	239										239				
1331–32	307	307			21										
1332–33	333	333			30	3									

1334–35								
1335–36	164	164	9					
1336–37								
1337–38	317					317		
1338–39	105					105		
1339–40	87					87		
1340–41	182					182		
1341–42	183					183		
1342–43	341					341	30	
1343–44	327					327	22	
1344–45	272					272		
1345–46	241					241	19[1]	
1346–47	301					301	23	
1347–48	310					310	21	
1348–49	473					473		
1349–50	313					313	15	
1350–51	475					475	22	
1351–52	342					342	18	
1352–53	251					251	30	
1353–54	285					285	20	
1354–55	302					302	13	3
1355–56	260					260	12	
1356–57	260					260	12	6
1357–58	251					251	12	
1358–59	294					294	14	
1359–60	283					283	13	
1360–61	291					291	14	
1361–62	234					234		

1. Sold for 38s. 9½d. at 2s. 0½d. per clove.

‡ Average price per clove.

LAMB'S WOOL (CONTINUED)

Year	Number of yield	Number sold	Total weight sold				Total sale price		Average sale price		Number sent to Wolvesey	Total weight sent			
	Fleeces	Fleeces	W.	St.	C.	Lb.	s.	d.	s.	d.	Fleeces	W.	St.	C.	Lb.
1362–63	241										241			22	
1363–64	218										218			14	
1364–65	240										240			17	
1365–66	230										230			16	
1366–67	[M.T.]													32	
1367–68	483										483			33	
1368–69	470										470			34	
1369–70	[M.T.]													37	
1370–71	483										483			30	
1371–72	444										444			38	
1375–76	304										304			14	
1376–77	172										172			7	
1377–78	303										303			7	
1378–79	276										276			5	
1379–80	329										329			12	
1381–82	307										307			12	
1385–86	315										315			12	
1388–89	304										304			10	
1390–91	320										[M.T.]				
1393–94	307	*307*					9	8							
1394–95	313	*313*			11		13	3½	*1*	*2½* [1]					
1395–96	300										300			11	
1398–99	309	309			12	6	14	4	*1*	*1¼*					
1399–00	339	339			11		12	10	1	2					
1400–01	321	321			14		16	4	0	14					

1406–07	322	322	12		19	0	0	19		
1408–09	314	314	12		20	0	0	20		
1409–10	307	307	11		16	6	0	18		
1410–11	98	98	11		16	6	0	18		
1411–12	306	306	10		15	0	0	18		
1412–13	337	337	10		13	4	0	16		
1413–14	321	321	11		13	9	0	15		
1414–15	306	306	10		11	8	0	14		
1418–19	321	321	10		8	4	0	10		
1419–20	331	331	13		13	0	*1*	*0*		
1420–21	330	330	12		12	0	*1*	*0*		
1421–22	301	301	11		9	2	*0*	*10*		
1422–23	308	308	12		10	0	*0*	*10*		
1423–24	310	310	11		11	0	*1*	*0*		
1424–25	310	310	12		14	0	*1*	*2*		
1425–26	312	312	12		14	0	0	14		
1427–28	304	304	9		10	6	*1*	*2*		
1429–30	302	302	10		11	8	0	14		
1430–31	264	264	8		8	0	0	12		
1431–32	222	222	6		6	0	0	12		
1432–33	280	280	9		9	0	0	12		
1433–34	302	302	9		10	6	0	14		
1434–35	296	296	7		8	9	0	15		
1435–36	309	309	8		7	1	0	11		
1438–39	279	279	9		11	3	0	15		
1440–41	303	303	7	4	9	5	0	15		
1441–42	315	315	6	1						
1446–47	164	164	3	1½	3	1½	0	12		
1447–48			7	5	6	5½	0	10		
1448–49				4	0	6	*0*	*10½*		

1. Henceforth prices are per clove.

BROKEN WOOL

Year	Total weight sold				Total sale price		Average sale price per clove		Year	Total weight sold [1]				Total sale price		Average sale price per clove	
	W.	St.	C.	Lb.	s.	d.	s.	d.		W.	St.	C.	Lb.	s.	d.	s.	d.
1219–20					3	0			1272–73		3		4	4	0	0	7¼
1220–21					3	3			1273–74		3			4	3	0	8½
1223–24					5	0			1274–75		3		4	4	10	0	8¾
1224–25					4	3			1276–77		6			14	3	1	2¼
1225–26					3	9			1277–78		6			15	0	1	3
1226–27					3	5			1284–85		5		2	6	6	0	7½
1231–32					4	3			1285–86			16		11	8	0	8¾
1232–33					5	6			1286–87		3			2	6	0	5
1235–36					10	0			1287–88		6			6	0	0	6
1236–37					10	3			1288–89			2		0	22	0	11
1244–45		10			14	8	0	8¾	1289–90			6	6	4	0	0	7
1246–47					6	4			1290–91				11	0	13¾	0	8¾
1247–48					4	0			1291–92			8		6	0	0	10 [2]
1248–49					4	2			1292–93			20		8	4	0	7
1251–52					4	6			1296–97					3	0		
1253–54		6			5	2	0	5¼	1299–00			7		6	1½	0	10
1254–55		5½			4	7	0	5	1300–01			2		2	4	0	14
1256–57		10			10	0	0	6	1301–02			5		4	4	0	10½
1257–58		12			12	0	0	6	1302–03			4		3	6	0	10½
1264–65			5		3	4	0	8	1304–05			7	2	6	5½	0	10½
1265–66		1			0	12	0	6	1305–06			6	1	7	2	1	2
1267–68		2		4	2	3	0	6	1306–07			4	6	6	4	1	3¾
1268–69				8	0	8	0	7	1307–08				18	3	0	1	2
1270–71		1			0	12	0	6	1308–09			2		2	4	0	14

1309–10	4		6	1½	0	10½	1345–46	3	0	21	0	7
1310–11	5		3	7¾	0	8½	1346–47	4	2	4	0	7
1311–12	5	1	4	6	0	10½	1347–48	6	3	4	0	6¾
1312–13	10		11	8	0	14	1349–50	2	0	8	0	4
1313–14	9		10	6	0	18	1350–51	2	0	8	0	4
131—15	6		6	0	1	0	1351–52	3	0	12	0	4
1315–16	3		3	6	1	2	1352–53	4	0	42	0	10½
1316–17	2		2	0	1	0	1353–54	3	0	21	0	7
1317–18	2		2	0	1	0	1354–55	4	2	4	0	7
1318–19	3		3	6	1	2	1355–56	5	2	11	0	7
1320–21	3		3	6	0	14	1356–57	4	2	4	0	7
1326–27	2		2	4	0	14	1357–58	5	2	11	0	7
1328–29	7		8	2	0	14	1358–59	4	2	4	0	7
1329–30	8		9	4	0	14	1359–60	3	0	21	0	7
1330–31	6		7	0	0	14	1360–61	3				
1331–432	5		5	10	1	2	1361–62	2	0	14	0	7
1332–33	5		3	4	0	8	1362–63	2	0	14	0	7
1334–35	2		0	21	0	10½	1363–64	2	0	14	0	7
1335–36	3		2	7½	0	10½	1364–65	2	0	14	0	7
1336–37	2	3	2	1½	0	10½	1365–66	2	0	14	0	7
1337–38	4		2	11	0	8¾	1366–67	3	3	6	0	14
1338–39	5	3	3	2	0	7	1367–68	4	4	8	1	2
1339–40	11		6	5	0	7	1368–69	3	2	7½	0	10½
1340–41	5		4	4½	0	10½	1369–70	8	8	0	1	0
1341–42	4		2	4	0	7	1370–71	9	7	10	0	10½
1342–43	5		2	11	0	7	1371–72	6	5	3	0	10½
1343–44	4		2	4	0	7	1375–76	2	2	0	1	0
1344–45	3		0	21	0	7	1376–77		3	0		

1. In weys, stones, cloves, and pounds.

2. Discrepancies in the original manuscripts are numerous from this point onwards.

BROKEN WOOL (Continued)

Year	Total weight sold				Total sale price		Average sale price per clove	
	W.	St.	C.	Lb.	s.	d.	s.	d.
1377–78			3		3	0	*1*	*0*
1378–79			8		8	0	*1*	*0*
1381–82			7		7	0	*1*	*0*
1382–83			3½		3	6	*1*	*0*
1383–84			7		7	0	*1*	*0*
1384–85			4		4	0	*1*	*0*
1385–86			5					
1387–88			5		4	2	*0*	*10*
1388–89			6		5	0	*0*	*10*
1390–91			2		0	20	*0*	*10*
1392–93			7		5	10	*0*	*10*
1393–94			[M.T.]		5	6½		
1394–95			11		8	11	*0*	*9¾*
1395–96			7		5	10	*0*	*10*
1398–99			6		[M.T.]			
1399–00			2					
1400–01			2		0	20	*0*	*10*
1402–03			3		2	6	*0*	*10*
1406–07			4		3	4	*0*	*10*
1408–09			2		0	20	*0*	*10*
1409–10			2		0	20	*0*	*10*
1410–11			3		2	6	*0*	*10*
1411–12			3		2	6	*0*	*10*
1412–13			2		0	20	*0*	*10*
1413–14			3		2	6	*0*	*10*
1414–15			2		0	20	*0*	*10*
1418–19			2		0	21	*0*	*10½*
1419–20			1½		0	21	*0*	*14*
1420–21			1½		0	18	*0*	*12*
1421–22			2		0	20	*0*	*10*
1422–23			1½		0	15	*0*	*10*
1423–24			2		0	20	*0*	*10*
1424–25			3		2	6	*0*	*10*
1425–26			1½		0	15	*0*	*10*
1427–28			2		2	0	*1*	*0*
1429–30			2		2	0	*1*	*0*
1430–31			3		3	0	*1*	*0*
1431–32			3		3	6	*1*	*2*
1432–33			2½		2	6	*1*	*0*
1433–34			2		2	0	*1*	*0*
1434–35			3		3	0	*1*	*0*
1435–36			4		4	0	*1*	*0*
1438–39			1		0	10	0	10
1440–41			5		4	2	*0*	*10*
1441–42			2½		2	1	*0*	*10*
1447–48			1		0	10	0	10
1448–49			2½		2	1	*0*	*10*

PELTS[1] SOLD

Year	Wether	Total sale price s.	d.	Ram	Ewe	Total sale price s.	d.	Hogaster	Total sale price s.	d.	Lamb	Total sale price s.	d.	Number for tithe	Rotter[2]	Total sale price s.	d.	Plucked[3]	Total sale price s.	d.	Remarks
1208–09					115	14	10½				104	8	10								
1210–11	52				+ 29			+ 3	10	4½	87				+[–]	4	8½				
1211–12					254	29	10				189				+ 9	12	0				
1213–14					62	9	0				73	5	7		6		3				
1215–16	35[4]	5	2½								60	11	8								
1217–18	42[4]	3	0¾								66	3	0								
1218–19	31[4]	3	3								47	3	4								
1219–20	33[4]	2	10								42	4	2		30	1	8				
1220–21	42[4]	5	4								61	5	1		157	7	4				
1223–24	82[4]	18	5					70	11	8	16	12	0		46	2	2				
1224–25	38				+ 55			+ 60	28	0	312	33	3		35	1	7				
1225–26	236[4]	45	4								276	24	8		84	3	9				
1226–27	67[4]							+ 28	11	5	228	21	9		22		11				
1231–32	21				+ 28			+ 41	13	7	67	6	3		19		9½				
1232–33	70	13	11½		125	27	6	68	14	1	248	20	5								
1235–36	70	6	7½		45	10	9	69	12	1	503	44	10								
1236–37	14	3	11		31	7	5	32	5	8	80	8	6½								
1244–45	9		13½		5		7½				294	26	9								
1245–46	14	2	3½		26	4	4				83	7	4								
1246–47	20	1	2		11		9				227	26	0		86	3	7				
1247–48	20	6	8					18		10	251	28	9		52	2	4				
1248–49	383	37	8					97	6	1½					59	2	5½				383 includes 11 ewes and 12 lambs
1251–52					18	2	0				363	19	10	37	6		1½	76		8	
1252–53					20	1	6				81	6	8	8	14		6	36		4	20 includes ewes and hogasters
1253–54	26	1	7½								365	17	8½	40	17		5	190	1	6½	

1. Pelles (sheep skins). In many cases the animals died of murrain. Sales were often in grosso. Pelts of sheared and unsheared sheep have not been (and in many cases could not be) kept separate.
2. Rotters seem to have been lambs suffering from rot; the tithe was taken from the pelts of lambs which had died before weaning.
3. Pelles pellute, of sheep that died before shearing.
4. Pelles grosse, including pelts of wethers, ewes, and sometimes hogasters.

PELTS SOLD (Continued)

Year	Wether	Total sale price s.	Total sale price d.	Ram	Ewe	Total sale price s.	Total sale price d.	Hogaster	Total sale price s.	Total sale price d.	Lamb	Total sale price s.	Total sale price d.	Number for tithe	Rotter	Total sale price s.	Total sale price d.	Plucked	Total sale price s.	Total sale price d.	Remarks
1254–55	29	1	11								264	11	0	26	25		6½	80		6½	29 includes ewes
1256–57	16	1	0								221	13	10	24	9		2½	73		7	1
1257–58	6				+ 7		10				207	12	11½		29		7½	46		6	
1264–65	22				+ 16			+ 12	5	6	52	4	4	5	24		9				
1265–66	16				+ 13	4	2	37	3	10¼	95	7	11	10							
1267–68	2				+ 2		2				18	1	6	1	13		6				
1268–69	3				+ 1		2				49	4	1	5	10		4½				
1270–71	4				+ 5		9				39	3	3		2		1	21		2	
1271–72	5				+ 5		10				309	25	9		46	1	6	153	1	3	64 wethers sold extra
1272–73	82				+ 12	17	10				229	19	1		49	1	9	204	1	6	
1273–74	9				+ 8	1	5				352	21	3	39	26		11½	159	1	4	
1274–75	7				+ 2	1	0				298	23	10	33	8		3	87		8	
1276–77	3				+ 2		3				269	23	5		34	2	3	219	2	3	
1277–78	5				+ 11	1	2				256	26	8	28	15	1	0	90	1	4	
1282–83	19				+ 52			+ 17	9	7½	93	3	10½		25		1				
1283–84	45	6	8								27	1	8	3				10		5	45 includes ewes and hogasters
1284–85	8				+ 11			+ 24	2	9	24	1	5		7		2				
1285–86	41				76			98			183			19							
1286–87	3		4		53	11	0	19	1	7	75	4	8½		33						
1287–88	25				+ 4	7	3	24	4	0	25	1	6¾		21		10½				21 incl. 8 wethers and 1 ewe
1288–89	38	9	6		26			+ 4	5	0	87	5	3	6							
1289–90	13				+ 16			+ 2	4	6	48	3	0	3							
1290–91	1				+ 2			+ 4	2	4	26	1	8	2							
1291–92	9				+ 5			+ 3	2	10	32	2	6	3	3		1½				
1292–93	13				+ 12			+ 7	3	0	32	1	4	3	44		11				
1296–97	33				+ 13			+ 65	3	6	130	4	0								Sold in grosso
1297–98	10				+ 10			+ 22	5	7	23	1	4								

1298–99	25				+ 42			+ 29	21	9	95	5	1½							
1299–00	59				+ 82			+165	39	5	122	7	2	13	19		6			
1300–01	15				+ 33	7	6	21	2	7	53	3	3½		10		4			
1301–02	35				+ 37			+ 23	23	4	62	5	2		20		5			
1302–03	25				+ 26			+ 21	12	6	66	3	1							
1304–05	6				+ 16	2	4				309	17	8	27						
1305–06	33				+ 47			+ 46	29	0	285	16	10¼	27						
1306–07	67	22	4		10						83	6	5	8						22 lambs sold extra
1307–08	15			+1	+ 20			+ 13	11	8	54	4	8							
1308–09	12				+ 15			+ 14	10	4	44	3	8							
1309–10	51	12	3					19	1	7	114	9	6	11	39	1	5			51 includes ewes
1310–11	21				+ 13			+ 21	7	2	89	11	1½	5	10		2			
1311–12	43				+[—]			+ 18	12	2½	56	7	2		6		1½			
1312–13	26				+ 30			+ 17	27	0	121	14	1		12	1	0			
1313–14	85			+1	+ 56			+ 83	77	11	297	36	0½	30						[2]
1314–15	20				11						238			25	29					M.T. for price
1315–16	24			+2	+ 17	12	9	11	2	9	37	4	1½		4		4			
1316–17	19			+1	+ 16			+ 15	14	5	24	3	0	2	9		9			
1317–18	12			+1	+ 18	9	6	15	3	9	42	5	3	4	11		11			
1318–19	12			+2	+ 17	11	2	17	5	8	42	4	11		15	1	3			
1320	1		3								1		0½							
1320–21	3				+ 10	3	7	4	1	4	36	3	6	2						36 includes 6 rotters
1326–27	16				+ 27	13	4				58	4	10							
1327–28	9				+ 11			+ 9			+62	13	1							
1328–29	4	1	4		4	1	4	4	1	0	35	2	11	2	6		6			
1329–30	12				+ 13	2	10	100	25	0	43	3	3½	4	8		8			
1330–31	10			+2	+ 23	8	6	22	5	6	25	2	1		1		1			
1331–32	4		9		10	2	7	2		6	27	3	1½		5		5			
1332–33	3		3		8	1	8	6	1	6	20	1	6	1	6		6			
1334–35	1			+2	+ 14			+ 26	6	9	32	2	8		9		3			
1335–36	4	1	4		9	2	3				68	4	11	6	17		8½			
1336–37	1				+ 6	1	6	7	1	4½	21	1	9		4		1			

1. Eighty-nine includes ewes and hogasters.

2. One wether pelt sold at 6d., 1 hogaster at 3d., 1 ewe at 4d., 1 ram at 4d.

PELTS SOLD (Continued)

Year	Wether	Total sale price		Ram	Ewe	Total sale price		Hogaster	Total sale price		Lamb	Total sale price		Number for tithe	Rotter	Total sale price		Lamb skin after shearing[1]	Total sale price		Remarks
		s.	d.			s.	d.		s.	d.		s.	d.			s.	d.		s.	d.	
1337–38	4			+1	+14	2	11	17	2	1½	35	2	5		5		2½				
1338–39	24				+26	9	0	55	4	7	224	15	0	23	10		5				
1339–40	78			+7	+81	36	1	71	8	10½	289	22	8	29	12		6				
1340–41	17				+9	7	2	11	1	4½	29	2	1¼	2	11		5½				
1341–42	2				+8	2	1	10	1	8	50	3	9½	5	5		5				
1342–43	5				+16	4	4	12	2	0	40	3	1½	4	7		7				
1343–44	7			+1	+15	5	2	10	1	8	85	6	9½	8	14	1	2				
1344–45	10			+4	+15	4	11	8	1	4	34	3	8	4	12	1	0				
1345–46	6			+1	+14	3	3	20	3	3	21	1	7	2	7		7				
1346–47	22			+3	+40	11	10½				225	15	8¼	16	8		4				
1347–48	47			+1	+24	12	5	40	5	0	115	7	10	9	12		6				
1348–49	10			+3	+12	1	9	6	6	8	76	1	6		9		2				
1349–50	18			+1	+23			+14	3	10	66	2	6¾								66 includes 5 rotters
1350–51	6				+12			+6	2	8	31	1	3	3	16		3¾				
1351–52	33					4	8				22		11	2	66	1	4½				33 includes the others
1352–53	11				+23			+3	5	4	145	5	2	5							
1353–54	17				+13			+11	6	7	78	6	6	8	36		9				
1354–55	15				+11			+4	4	7	31	2	7	3	10		2½				
1355–56	22			+4	+33			+84	19	6	89	6	11	8							
1356–57	14				+18			+17	7	0	69	5	4½	6							
1357–58	19				+19			+26	8	6½	63	5	3	7	20		10				
1358–59	44			+1	+22			+25	20	2½	59	4	11	6	6		3	11		2½	
1359–60	17			+1	+15			+26	[Ill.][2]		56	4	8	6	1		0½	2		0½	
1360–61	28			+2	+52			+9	15	11½	76	4	9		188	1	4				
1361–62	12				+13			+2	3	10½	22	1	3¼	2	3		1½				
1362–63	18				+13			+6	5	11½	22	1	4½	2	6	3	0				
1363–64	21			+3	+17			+12	7	2	116	7	3	13	17		8½	14		3½	
1364–65	16			+2	+18			+16	7	11	75	4	8	8	12		6	14		3½	

1365–66	59			+ 91		+ 15	24	4	148	8	10½	16	3		1½	3		0½	
1366–67	15			+ 15		+ 17	7	11½	72	4	6		15		7½	8		2	
1367–68	16		+1	+ 25		+ 19	10	6½	39	2	4¾		15	10	7½	14		2½	
1368–69	10		+1	+ 12		+ 7	7	8	37	3	1		16		8	10		2	
1369–70	13			+ 12		+ 8	7	3	54	3	4		16		8	7		1	
1370–71	11		+3	+ 18		+ 18	11	3	51	3	2¼		21		10½	5			
1371–72	18		+1	+ 30		+ 95	27	0	68	4	3		37	1	4	14		3	
1372–73	217		+6	+138		+ 66	59	0	69	4	3¾		20		6	320	2	8	
1373–74	—[3]		—[3]	—[3]		—[3]	29	4	57	3	7						1	6	
1375–76	34			+ 31		+ 18	18	9	22	1	4	2	6		3	4		1	
1376–77	61		+2	+ 60		+ 33	29	9	51	3	2¼	6	33	1	4½	16		4	
1377–78	64		+4	+ 50		+ 77	44	11	79	4	4		21		10½				
1378–79	39		+3	+ 38		+ 81	32	10	134	7	9		26	1	0				
1379–80	14			+ 16		+ 8			45						3				[M.T.]
1381–82	28			+ 14		+ 12	11	10	17		11								
1382–83	8			+ 9		+ 8	6	3	4		1								
1383–84	31		+3	+ 19		+ 26	16	8	18	1	2½		2		1	4		2	
1384–85	9			+ 16		+ 11	6	9											
1387–88	63		+4	+ 81		+ 15	25	4	139	7	10								
1388–89	30		+2	+ 33		+ 54	18	10	73	4	0		6		6				
1390–91	9			+ 12		+ 9	4	6	20	1	3		6		3				
1392–93	—[3]		—[3]	—[3]		—[3]	13	4		2	4								
1393–94	26		+3	+ 35		+ 24	12	5		3	9								
1394–95	67		+2	+ 7		+ 45	19	11½	60	3	4		7						
1395–96	44		+1	+ 39		+ 50	16	10	119	4	11		4			+10		7	
1398–99	20		+4	+ 21		+ 34	12	8	85	4	8		3			+ 7		5½	
1399–00	72		+1	+ 44		+ 6	9	11	11		6		1			+11		6	
1400–01	12		+1	+ 26		+ 31	10	0½	10		6					3		1½	
1402–03	6		+1	+ 8		+ 9	4	1½[4]											
1406–07	17			+ 9		+ 28	9	8	67	[M.T.]			3			6			
1408–09	14		+1	+ 15		+ 21	8	2½	14		8		2			+ 3		2½	
1409–10	31			+ 12		+ 12	8	6	41	2	5		3		3	20		10	

1. Pellectule. These have occurred before, but henceforth are specially named.
2. One wether pelt sold for 2d., 1 ewe sold for 2d., 1 hogaster sold for 1½d., 1 ram sold for 2d.
3. Number not given.
4. One wether pelt sold for 3d., 1 ewe for 2d., 1 ram for 2d., 1 hogaster for 1½d.

PELTS SOLD (CONTINUED)

Year	Wether	Total sale price		Ram	Ewe	Total sale price		Hogaster	Total sale price		Lamb	Total sale price		Number for tithe	Rotter	Total sale price		Lamb skin after shearing	Total sale price		Remarks
		s.	d.			s.	d.		s.	d.		s.	d.			s.	d.		s.	d.	
1410–11	65				+ 38			+ 75	34	2½	98	3	8½		26			+15	1	8½	
1411–12	36				+ 27			+ 67	19	4½	58	2	5		8			+21		14½	
1412–13	15				+ 13			+ 45	10	1½	40	1	8								
1413–14	44			+2	+ 28			+ 57	20	8½	146	6	1					14		7	
1414–15	19			+1	+ 12			+ 32	9	9	51	2	1½					3		1½	
1418–19	21			+1	+ 8			+ 21	8	4½	45	1	10½					5		2	
1419–20	13			+1	+ 11			+ 5	4	8½	14		7					9		3	
1420–21	35			+1	+ 23			+ 11	11	5	18		9					13		4	
1421–22	38			+1	+ 10			+ 20	10	7	27	1	6½					11		3	
1422–23	32			+2	+ 15			+ 27	13	6½	45	1	10½					14		4	
1423–24	53			+2	+ 28			+127	27	10½	32	1	3					30	1	3	
1424–25	68			+3	+ 50			+163	46	2½	35	1	5½					13		6	
1425–26	17				+[—][1]			+ 26	7	10	17		8½					10		5	
1427–28	18				+ 21			+ 39	11	10½	44	1	10					20		10	
1429–30	11			+1	+ 14			+ 15	5	9½	9		3					7		3	
1430–31	13			+1	+ 21			+ 19	8	5½	17		5½					15		4	
1431–32	43			+2	+ 50			+ 62	21	9	154	4	3½					8		2	
1432–33	39			+1	+ 30			+ 27	12	3½	33		11					8		2	
1433–34	43			+1	+ 34			+ 13	14	5½	33		11					8		2	
1434–35	73			+3	+ 49			+ 38	26	7	85	2	4					34		8	
1435–36	52			+2	+ 18			+ 50	16	11	39	1	1					7		2	
1438–39	9			+1	+ 10			+ 17	6	0½	39		7½					3		1	
1440–41	47			+4	+ 52			+ 13	18	8½	58	1	2½					13		3	
1441–42	24			+1	+ 20			+ 42	13	4½											
1446–47	15				+ 8	1	11½											9			
1447–48	70			+1	+ 55			+ 81	25	10	44		11					21		2	
1448–49	77			+5	+ 66			+122	28	5	271	3	9					18		1½	

1. Manuscript torn.

Year	Number left over	Number made	Number sold	Total weight sold[2]			Total sale price			Average sale price per wey		Number for customary payment	Number for tithe	Number sent to Wolvesey	Total weight sent			Number for boon days	Number remaining
	Cheeses	Cheeses	Cheeses	W.	C.	Lb.	£.	s.	d.	s.	d.	Cheeses	Cheeses	Cheeses	W.	C.	Lb.	Cheeses	Cheeses
1208–09	163	176	247	12				87	0	7	3	17	17	24					34
1210–11		182	135	6½				45	0	6	11	5	18	12					
1211–12	[?]	215	166	7				56	0	8	0	6	21	27				12	
1213–14		247	202	14				119	0	8	6	5	24	10				5	
				2				14	0	7	0							6	
1215–16		94	14	1½				10	9	7	2	6	9	65					
1217–18		210	68	4				28	0	7	0	7	17	77				6	
			32					2	6				3						
1218–19		225	88	8				64	0	8	0	10	26	22	2				60
			23					0	16				2						
		72[3]	72					6	0										
1219–20	60	194	178	11				77	0	7	0	10	19	20	2				27
		36	24					1	6½				3						9
1220–21	9[3]	322	253	17 1/12				119	7	7	0	9	32	6					1
		29[3]	29					1	8										
			30	2				14	0	7	0								
1223–24		[M.T.]	183	16			6	2	8	7	8		25	9	1				27
1224–25	27	166	142	9			4	2	0	9	1¼	5	16	18					12
1225–26	11	217	137[4]	12¼			4	1	6	6	8¼	5	20	27					17
1226–27	17	200	131	15				112	6	7	6	5	20	49[5]					12
1231–32		235[6]	195	11			4	8	0	8	0	5	23	12					
		20	20					1	8										
				2				14	0	7	0								
1232–33		251	192	15 7/9(?)			6	14	7	8	6¼	5	25	[M.T.]					
1235–36	21	235	228	19			8	11	0	9	0	5	33						
		39	39					3	0										
1236–37		312		25			11	5	0	9	0	5	31						
		[M.T.]	31					2	0										

1. Probably made from sheep's milk. 2. In weys, cloves, and pounds. 3. Made of cows' milk.
4. Sold extra, 11 cheeses for 11d. 5. Including outside gifts. 6. Summer cheeses, those following in the next line being winter cheese.

CHEESE (Continued)

Year	Number left over	Number made	Number sold	Total weight sold			Total sale price			Average sale price per wey		Number for customary payment	Number for tithe	Number sent to Wolvesey	Total weight sent	Number for boon days	Number remaining
	Cheeses	Cheeses	Cheeses	W.	C.	Lb.	£.	s.	d.	s.	d.	Cheeses	Cheeses	Cheeses	W. C. Lb.	Cheeses	Cheeses
1244–45				10	10		4	3	2½	8	0						
			35					3	2								
1245–46		210	185	25½			6	19	6	5	5¾	4	21				
		39	36					3	4				3				
1246–47		212	184	12			6	0	0	10	0	4	21	3			
		44	40					3	8				4				
1247–48		198	175	12½				112	6	9	0	4	19				
		33	30					2	0				3				
1248–49		185	155	12			4	16	0	8	0	4	18	8			
		9	9						5¾								
1251–52		214	187	10½			4	14	6	9	0	4	23				
		16	16					0	12								
1252–53		242	214	19½	1		7	6	6	7	6	4	24				
		19	19					1	4								
		15[1]	15					0	6								
1253–54		198	167	10			4	12	6	9	3	4	19				
		21	21					1	7								
					7			0	6								
1254–55		184	162	16			6	18	8	8	8	4	18				
		22	22		4			1	8								
1256–57		323	287	20½			9	4	10	9	0	4	32				
		26	26		6			2	6								
1257–58		244[2]	218	16½	6		7	2	11	8	6½	4	22				
1264–65		201	51	1½	6			14	0	8	0	4	17				129
1265–66		178	158	6	4			63	0	7	6	4	16				
				6½				44	0	8	0						
1267–68		165	145	5				45	0	9	0	4	16				
1268–69		160	140	5				50	0	10	0	4	16				
1270–71		180	158	8½				81	0	9	6¼	4	18				

1271–72		191	168	9½			4	10	3	9	6	4	19				
1272–73		190	167	13				117	0	9	0	4	19				
1273–74		191	167	13			6	10	0	10	0	4	19				
1274–75		188	166	10½				105	0	10	0	4	18				
		15	15					1	8								
1276–77			166	10				100	0[3]	10	0						
1277–78		198	166	10				100	0[4]	10	0	4	28				
1282–83		159	43	1				10	0	10	0	4	16	96	3½		
						25		2	4								
1283–84		169										4	17	118	6		30¾
1284–85		182	43	1				6	8	6	8	4	18	117	6½		
1285–86		171	150	3½				*31*	*6*	9	0	4	17				
		16	16					1	2								
1286–87		167	121	4				36	0	*9*	*0*	4	16				26
		18	18					1	0								
1287–88		185	163	6½				52	0	*8*	*0*	4	18				
		20	20					1	1								
1288–89		179	158	4				38	0	9	6	4	17				
		19	19						9								
1289–90		190	167	8			4	0	0	*10*	*0*	4	19				
		12	12						6								
1290–91		176	155	7				70	0	10	0	4	17				
		5	5						5								
1291–92		171	150	7½				75	0	10	0	4	17				
		17	17						11								
1292–93		184	162	7½				67	6	9	0	4	18				
		21	21					1	6								
1296–97		168	148	6								4	16				
		22	22														
1297–98		170	150	6½				52	0	8	0	4	17				
		27	27					1	7								
1298–99		167	147	7			4	13	4	13	4	4	16				
		24	24					1	8								
1299–00		176	146	7	6			72	6	10	0	4	16				
		26	26					1	10								

1. Little cheeses.
2. Only 220 summer cheeses, the summer being rainy and the sheep much infected with murrain.
3. In addition, there were 20d. from cheese de rewanno (winter cheese).
4. Similarly an extra 2s. from winter cheese.

CHEESE (Continued)

Year	Number left over	Number made	Number sold	Total weight sold			Total sale price			Average sale price per wey		Number for customary payment	Number for tithe	Number sent to Wolvesey	Total weight sent	Number for boon days	Number remaining
	Cheeses	Cheeses	Cheeses	W.	C.	Lb.	£.	s.	d.	s.	d.	Cheeses	Cheeses	Cheeses	W. C. Lb	Cheeses	Cheeses
1300–01		170	150	6	3½			61	3	9	11¾	4	16				
		28	28		9	2		3	7	9	9						
1301–02		168	148	7½	12			66	1	8	4	4	16				
					5	1		1	6								
1302–03		165	145	7½				67	6	9	0	4	16				
					9			2	8								
1304–05		167	147	3	7			29	3	9	0	4	16				
1305–06		170	149	5	8½			61	8	11	7	4	17				
1306–07		173	152	6½				65	0	10	0	4	17				
1307–08		204	183	8		32	4	16	0	11	9	4	17				
1308–09		164	144	9			4	10	0	10	0	4	16				
		6	6		16			1	9	7	7						
1309–10		163	143	7			4	4	0	11	0	4	16				
					5			1	8								
1310–11		158	139	8½	6			104	6¾	12	0	4	15				
					6			2	0								
1311–12		160	140	8½				102	0	12	0	4	16				
1312–13		136	119	5	25			64	9¾	11	0	4	13				
1313–14		135	118	7			4	4	0	12	0	4	13				
1314–15		130	113	6	17							4	13				
1315–16		131	114[1]	4	14			60	0	13	4	3	13				
1316–17		130	113	6			4	0	0	13	4	4	13				
1317–18		132	115	6	7			68	9	11	0	4	13				
1318–19		134	118	8½			4	13	6	11	0	3	13				
1320		165	145	4				53	4	13	4	3	16				
			1						6								
1320–21		178	158	7	7		4	16	8	13	4	3	17				
1326–27[2]		152	134	5				55	0	11	0	3	15				
1327–28		121	106	4½	5			51	5¾	11	0	3	12				

1329–30		131	115	3		36	0	12	0	4	13				
1330–31		154	135	3½		42	0	12	0	4	15				
1331–32		171	150	5½		55	0	10	0	4	17				
1332–33		144	126	5½		55	0	10	0	4	14				
1334–35		127	112	3		40	0	13	4	3	12				
1335–36		159	140	3	20	46	8	*12*	*4½*	3	16				
1336–37		157 [3]	139	5½		55	0	10	0	3	16				
1337–38		154	136	8		64	0	8	0	3	15				
1338–39		154	136	4	7	42	6	*9*	*11½*	3	15				
1339–40		95	83	2		20	0	*10*	*0*	3	9				
1340–41		145 [3]	123	4½		40	6	9	0	3	13				
1341–42		150	132	3½		31	6	9	0	3	15				
1342–43		126	111	5½		48	0	9	0	3	12				
1343–44		130	114	4		40	0	*10*	*0*	3	13				
1344–45		100	87	3		30	0	*10*	*0*	3	10				
1345–46		112	98	1½		15	0	*10*	*0*	3	11				
1346–47		110	96	2		20	0	*10*	*0*	3	11				
1347–48		134	118	5		50	0	10	0	3	13				
1349–49		92	81	3		30	0	*10*	*0*	2	9				
1350–51		100	88			38	2			2	10				
1351–52		110	97			41	7			2	11				
1352–53		100	90			42	2				10				
1353–54		110	97			43	7			2	11				
1354–55		109	96			53	11			2	11				
1355–56		110	97			24	3			2	11				
1356–57		110	97			48	0			2	11				
1357–58		110	87			43	9			2	11				
1358–59		110	97			46	2			2	*11*				
1359–60		100	88			44	0			2	10				
1360–61		30	25			8	4			2	3				
1361–62		100	88			32	1½			2	10				
1362–63		110	97			32	0			2	11				
1363–64		100	88			22	3			2	10				
1364–65		100	88			23	0			2	10				

1. Sold extra, 1 for 6d.
2. The number of ewes milked was 340 in 1326–27; 193 in 1329–30; 273 in 1330–31; 332 in 1331–32; 344 in 1332–33; 324 in 1344–45; 104 in 1345–46, and 323 in 1347–48.
3. Error in manuscript.

BUTTER [1]

Year	Total weight sold [2]				Total sale price		Average sale price per clove	
	W.	St.	C.	Lb.	s.	d.	s.	d.
1208–09					0	10		
1210–11					0	8		
1211–12					2	0		
1213–14					0	9		
1215–16					0	12		
1217–18					3	0		
1218–19					3	3		
1219–20					2	6		
1220–21					6	0		
1223–24					5	0		
1224–25					2	7		
1225–26					4	0		
1226–27					3	0		
1231–32					0	21		
1232–33					2	8		
1235–36					4	9½		
1236–37					6	0		
1244–45					2	8		
1245–46					5	8		
1246–47					5	2		
1247–48					4	8		
1248–49					5	3		
1251–52	½				3	10	0	3½
1252–53	⅚				5	10	0	3¼
1253–54		10			4	2	0	2½
1254–55		13			5	5	0	2½
1256–57	1		8½		10	0	0	3½
1257–58	1				7	7	0	3½
1264–65			10	2	3	0	0	3½
1265–66			5		0	17½		3½
1267–68			3½		0	12	0	3½
1268–69			3		0	10½	0	3½
1270–71			4		0	20	0	5
1271–72			8		2	4	0	3½
1272–73			10		3	0	0	3½
1273–74	½				4	0	0	3¾
1274–75	½				5	0	0	4¾
1276–77	½		5		7	6	0	5
1277–78	½		4		7	0	0	5
1285–86			6	1				
1290–91			8		3	4	0	3½
1291–92			8	3	3	5½	0	3½
1292–93			16		4	8	0	3½
1296–97			14					
1297–98			12		3	9½	0	3½
1298–99			18		6	0	0	4

1299–00		21		7	6	0	4¼
1300–01		12	3	3	7½	0	3½
1301–02		15		4	8	0	3¾
1302–03		18		5	6	0	3¾
1304–05		6		0	23	0	3¾
1305–06		16		5	8	0	4¼
1306–07		19		6	8	0	4¼
1307–08		10		3	4	0	4
1308–09	½	6		5	3½	0	3½
1309–10		12		5	2	0	5¼
1310–11	½			6	0	0	5½
1311–12		18		7	8½	0	5¼
1312–13		16		8	0	0	6
1313–14		18		9	0	0	6
1314–15		21		[M.T.]			
1315–16		14		7	0	0	6
1316–17	½			6	8	0	6¼
1317–18	½			5	6	0	5
1318–19	½			6	0	0	5½
1320–21		10		5	0	0	6
1321–22		13		6	8	0	6¼
1326–27		20		8	4	0	5
1227–28		19		7	8	0	4¾
1329–30		7		2	11	0	5
1330–31		8		3	4	0	5
1331–32		14		5	0	0	4¼
1332–33		26		5	0	0	2½
1334–35		6		3	0	0	6

1335–36	5		2	6	0	6
1336–37	10		4	4½	0	5¼
1337–38	14		4	0	0	3½
1338–39	7		2	6	0	4¼
1339–40	5		0	21½	0	4¼
1340–41	14		4	6	0	4
1341–42	6		2	3	0	4½
1342–43	8		3	0	0	4½
1343–44	8		3	0	0	4½
1344–45	4		0	14	0	3½
1345–46	2		0	9	0	4½
1347–48	6	4	2	4	0	4¼
1349–50	3½		0	12	0	3½
1350–51	5		0	17½	0	3½
1351–52	2		0	7	0	3½
1352–53	3		0	21	0	7
1353–54	3		0	21	0	7
1354–55	3		0	21	0	7
1355–56	1		0	7	0	7
1356–57	3		0	21	0	7
1357–58	3		0	21	0	7
1358–59	3		0	21	0	7
1359–60	3		0	21	0	7
1360–61	1		0	7	0	7
1361–62	3		0	21	0	7
1362–63	3		0	21	0	7
1363–64	3		0	21	0	7
1364–65	3		0	21	0	7

1. The accounts do not indicate whether it was made from the milk of sheep or of cows.

2. In weys, stones, cloves, and pounds.

PIGS[1]

Year	Number left over	Number of increase	Number bought	Total purchase price s.	Total purchase price d.	Average purchase price s.	Average purchase price d.	Total number in account	Number sold	Total sale price s.	Total sale price d.	Average sale price s.	Average sale price d.	Number died	Number of tithe	Number for customary payment	Number sent away	Number killed for larder	Number remaining
1208–09	34	23						57						7	2	1	15		32
1211–12	31	19	7					57							1		22		34
1213–14	32	26						58						2	1	1	19		34
1215–16	37	10						47						4	1	1	23		18
1217–18	26	31	2					59						4	3	1	15		36
1218–19	36	11						47						4	1	1	9		32
1219–20	32	43						75						4	4	1	12		54
1220–21	54	24	7	4	8	*0*	*8*	85						4	2	1	25		53
1223–24	88	33	[M.T.]					123						5	3	1	53		61
1224–25	61	16	61					138						4	1	1	6		126
1225–26	126	26						152						5	2	1	100		44
1226–27	44	40						84						6	4	1	17		56
1231–32	43	22						65							2	1	19		43
1232–33	43	14	20	37	6½	1	7	77						1	1	1	16		58
1235–36	60	31						91	1[2]	2	1	2	1	3	3	1	41		43
1236–37	43	17						60						6	1	1	[M.T.]		
1244–45	[M.T.]													1	4	1	137		2
1245–46	70	49						119	8	17	9	*2*	*2¾*	5	4	1	16	9	76
1246–47	76	20[3]						97	1					6	2	1	20	6	61
1247–48	61	22[3]						84	9[4]	20	6½	*2*	*3½*	1	2	1	10		60
1248–49	36	19						55						2			36	4	12[5]
1251–52	30							30						2					28
1252–53	25	35[6]						66						5			25		34

1253–54	27	18				45						1				26	18
1254–55	18	35				53										16	37
1256–57	19	18				37						7					30
1257–58	30	16				46						23					23
1264–65	10	5				15	10	30	0	*3*	*0*						5
1265–66	27					27	*23*[7]	51	0			4					
1267–68	2					2											2
1268–69		1	13			*14*						1					13
1270–71	31	21				52										10	42
1271–72	42	27				69	40[8]	100	0	2	6						29
1272–73	29	40				69	30[9]	55	0	*1*	*8*						30
1273–74	30	15				45	24	77	10	*3*	*3*						21
1274–75	21	25	5			51	23	80	6	3	6	1					27
1276–77	53	27				80	37	120	6	*3*	*3*						43
1277–78	43	25				68	35	105	0	3	0	2					31
1283–84	17					17											*17*
1284–85	19	11				30	13	26	0	2	0						17
1285–86	14	15	7			41	19	*57*	*0*	3	0	2					20
1286–87	20	21				41	12	29	8	*2*	$5\frac{3}{4}$	5					*24*
1287	24	14				38											38
1288	38	16				54	16	44	0	*2*	*9*						38
1289–90	38	8				46	16	40	0	2	6						30
1290–91	30	11				41	25	50	0	2	0						16
1291–92	16	16				32	17	46	4	*2*	$8\frac{3}{4}$						15
1292–93	15	14				29	17	36	0	*2*	$1\frac{1}{2}$						12
1296–97	16	13				29	10	22	6	2	3						19
1297–98	19	11				30	12	24	0	*2*	*0*						18

1. Porci, chiefly male porkers, not including suckling pigs.
2. One of the three that died.
3. One of these arrived by chance.
4. In addition a boar was sold for 10s.
5. One added to the sows.
6. Includes 4 from the chattels of a fugitive.
7. Fourteen sows included in amount from sale.
8. Really sold to the bishop's larder.
9. Sold extra, 9.

PIGS (Continued)

Year	Number left over	Number of increase	Number bought	Total purchase price		Average purchase price		Total number in account	Number sold	Total sale price		Average sale price		Number died	Number of tithe	Number for customary payment	Number sent away	Number killed for larder	Number remaining
				s.	d.	s.	d.			s.	d.	s.	d.						
1298–99	18	13						31	11	22	0	2	0						20
1299–00	20	15						35	12	27	0	2	3						23
1300–01	23	13						37	10	32	0	3	2½						27
1301–02	27	29						56	26	67	4	2	7						30
1302–03	30	18						48	25	64	7	2	7						23
1305–06		30[1]						30									10		20
1306–07	20							20	2	6	10	3	5				18		
1307–08		20						20	9	27	0	3	0						11
1308–09	11	14						24	9	37	0	4	1¼						16
1309–10	16	22						38						3			4		31
1310–11	31	20						51	13	67	0	5	2						38
1311–12	38	19						57	15	49	0	3	6	16					26
1312–13	26		1	1	0	1	0	27	17	66	0	3	10½				10		
1324–25			5	10	0	2	0												5
1325–26	5		12	30	0	2	6	17	5	13	4	2	8						12
1326–27	12		7	17	10	2	7	19	14	43	6	3	0½						5
1327–28	5		14	32	6	2	4	19	7	20	0	2	10¼						12
1328–29	12							12	12	33	0	2	6						
1334–35		4[1]						4	4	8	0	2	0						
1335–36			3	4	0	1	4		3	8	0	2	8						
1369–70	9							9	9	30	0	3	4						
1370–71	12							12	12	48	0	4	0						

1. Received from elsewhere.

Year	Number left over	Number due from Churchscot	Number default	Number sold	Total sale price s.	Total sale price d.	Average sale price s.	Average sale price d.	Sent to Wolvesey	Number remaining
1208–09		61[1]							91	34
1210–11	76	60							45[2]	
1211–12		110	20						60	30
1213–14		110	33						71[3]	
1215–16		110	35						75	
1217–18		110	20						78	12
1218–19	12	110	24						96	2
1219–20	2	110	28						67	17
1220–21	17	110	22						92	13
1223–24	11	110	21	[M.T.]					30[4]	
1224–25	2	121	25						95	3
1225–26	3	123	25						101	
1226–27		123	30						93	
1231–32		123	40						83	
1232–33	[M.T.]	*123*	42							
1235–36	37	123	52						37[5]	65
1236–37	65	123	[M.T.]							
1244–45				78	6	6		*1*		
1245–46	2	125	38	22	0	22		*1*	65	2
1246–47	2	125	38	67	5	7		*1*		22
1247–48	22	125	40	60	5	0		*1*		47
1248–49	47	125	32	116	9	8		*1*		24
1251–52		125	36	89	7	5		*1*		
1252–53		125[6]	36	89	7	5		*1*		
1253–54		125	36	89	7	5		*1*		
1254–55		125	36	89	7	5		*1*		

Year	Number left over	Number due from Churchscot	Number default	Number sold	Total sale price s.	Total sale price d.	Average sale price s.	Average sale price d.	Sent to Wolvesey	Number remaining
1256–57		125	36	89	7	5		*1*		
1257–58		125	34	91	7	7		*1*		
1264–65		125	32	93	7	9		*1*		
1265–66		125	32	93	7	9		*1*		
1267–68		125	36	89	7	5		*1*		
1268–69		125	36	89	7	5		*1*		
1270–71		125	37	88	7	0		*1*		
1271–72		125	36	89	7	6		*1*		
1272–73		125	38	87	7	3		*1*		
1273–74		125	42	83	6	11		*1*		
1274–75		125	38	87	7	3		*1*		
1276–77		125	40	85	7	1		*1*		
1277–78		125	40	85	7	1		*1*		
1282–83		125	28	97	8	1		*1*		
1283–84		125	28	97	8	1		*1*		
1284–85		125	34	91	6	8		*1*		
1285–86		125	34	91	7	7		*1*		
1286–87		125	28	97	8	1		*1*		
1287–88		125	26	99	8	4		*1*		
1288–89		125	26	99	8	4		*1*		
1289–90		125	26	99	8	4		*1*		
1290–91		125	26	99	8	4		*1*		
1291–92		125	26	99	8	4		*1*		
1292–93		125	30	95	7	11		*1*		
1296–97		125	30	95	6	11		*1*		
1297–98		125	32	93	8	1		*1*		

1. This year 64 were bought. 2. This year 80 were sent to Clere, 4 paid to the seneschal, and 7 died. 3. Six were paid to the seneschal. 4. Sent to Mardon. 5. Six were paid to the seneschal. 6. In addition 12 from the chattels of Ingeram were sold for 12d.

CHICKENS (CONTINUED)

Year	Number left over	Number due from Churchscot	Number default	Number sold	Total sale price s.	Total sale price d.	Average sale price s.	Average sale price d.	Number remained	Number remaining
1298–99		125	28	97	8	1		1		
1299–00		125	30	95	7	9		1		
1300–01		125	30	95	7	11		1		
1301–02		125	30	95	7	11		1		
1302–03		125	32	93	7	9		1		
1305–06		125	28	97	8	1		1		
1306–07	6 bot.	125	34	91	11	4		1½		
1307–08	6	125	34	91	11	4½		1½	6	
1308–09	6[1]	125	58	91	11	4½		1½	6	
1309–10	6[1]	125	57	92	11	6		1½	6	
1310–11	6[1]	125	55	94	11	9		1½	6	
1311–12	6[1]	125	33	92	11	6		1½	6	
1312–13	6[1]	125	31	94	11	8		1½	6	
1313–14	6[1]	125	55	94	6	9		1	6	
1314–15	6[1]	125	57	92	[M.T.]				6	
1315–16	6[1]	125	57	92	7	8		1	6	
1316–17	6	125	38	87	10	10½		1½	6	
1317–18	6	125	38	87	10	10½		1½	6	
1318–19	6	125	38	87	10	10½		1½	6	
1320–21	6	125	38	87	10	10½		1½	6	
1324–25	6	125	36	89	11	1½		1½	6	
1325–26	6	125	31	94	11	9		1½	6	
1326–27	6	125	31	94	11	9		1½	6	
1327–28	6	125	30	95					6	
1328–29	6	125	30	95	11	10½		1½	6	
1329–30	6	125	32	93	11	7		1½	6	

Year	Number left over	Number due from Churchscot	Number default	Number sold	Total sale price s.	Total sale price d.	Average sale price s.	Average sale price d.	Number remained	Number remaining
1330–31	6	125	32	93	11	7		1½	6	
1331–32	6	125	36	89	11	1½		1½	6	
1332–33	6	125	38	87	10	10½		1½	6	
1334–35	6[2]	125	28	97	12	1½		1½	6	
1335–36	6	125	30	95	11	10½		1½	6	
1336–37	6	125	26	99	12	4½		1½	6	
1337–38	6	125	34	97	12	1½		1½		
1338–39		125	22	97	12	1½		1½	6	
1339–40	6	125	30	95	11	10½		1½	6	
1340–41	6	125	32	93	11	7½		1½	6	
1341–42	6	125	32	93	11	7½		1½	6	
1342–43	6	125	32	93	11	5½		1½	6	
1343–44	6	125	30	95	11	10½		1½	6	
1344–45	6	125	34	97	12	7½		1½		
1346–47	6	125	30	95	11	10½		1½	6	
1347–48	6	125	32	93	11	7½		1½	6	
1348–49	6	125	32	93	11	7½		1½	6	
1349–50	6	125	62	63	7	10½		1½	6	
1350–51	6	125	64	61	7	7½		1½	6	
1351–52	6	125	64	61	7	7		1½	6	
1352–53	6	125	59	66	8	3		1½	6	
1353–54	6	125	59	66	8	3		1½	6	
1354–55	6	125	59	66	8	3		1½	6	
1355–56	6	125	59	66	8	3		1½	6	
1356–57	6	125	59	66	8	3		1½	6	
1357–58	6	125	59	66	8	3		1½	6	

1358–59	6	125	57	68	8	6		1½	6	
1359–60	6	125	62	63	7	10½		1½	6	
1360–61	6	125	62	63	7	10½		1½	6	
1361–62	6	125	61	59 [3]	6	8½		1½	6	
1362–63	6	125	63	57 [3]	7	1		1½	6	
1363–64	6	125	70	55	6	10		1½	6	
1364–65	6	125	70	55	6	10		1½	6	
1365–66	6	125	66	59	7	4½		1½	6	
1366–67	6	125	70	55 [4]	6	10½		1½	6	
1367–68	6	125	55	70	9	5½		1½	6	
1368–69	6	125	68	57	9	6		2	6	
1369–70	6	125	68	57	9	6		2	6	
1370–71	6	125	60	65	10	10		2	6	
1371–72	6	125	56	69	11	6		2	6	
1372–73	6	125	60	65	10	10		2	6	
1373–74	6	125	62	63	11	2		2	6	
1375–76	6	125	56	69	11	6		2	6	
1376–77	6	125	54	71	11	10	0	2	6	
1377–78	6	125	54	71	11	10	0	2	6	
1378–79	6	125	54	71	11	10	0	2	6	
1379–80	6	125	54	71					6	
1381–82	6	125	45	75	12	6		2	6	
1383–84				75	12	1		2		
1384–85				75	12	6		2		
1385–86	6	125		75	12	7		2		
1387–88				71	11	10		2		
1388–89	6	125	54	71	11	10		2	6	
1390–91	6	125	48	77	12	10		2	6	
1392–93	6	125	48	77	12	10		2	6	
1393–94	6	125	42	83	13	10		2	6	
1394–95	6	125	42	83	13	10		2	6	
1395–96	6	125	42	83	13	10		2	6	
1398–99	6	125	52	73	12	2		2	6	

1399–00	6	125	51	74	12	2	2	6
1400–01	6	125	52	73	12	2	2	6
1402–03	6	125	60	65	12	6	2¼	6
1406–07	6	125	40	85	[M.T.]			6
1408–09	6	125	40	85	14	2	2	6
1409–10	6	125	42	83	14	10	2	6
1410–11	6	125	42	83	13	10	2	6
1411–12	6	125	42	83	13	10	2	6
1412–13	6	125	30	95	14	2	2	6
1413–14	6	125	40	85	14	2	2	6
1414–15	6	125	40	85	14	2	2	6
1418–19	6	125	38	87	14	6	2	6
1419–20	6	125	46	79	13	2	2	6
1420–21	6	125	44	81	13	6	2	6
1421–22	6	125	46	79	13	2	2	6
1422–23	6	125	56	69	11	6	2	6
1423–24	6	125	56	69	11	6	2	6
1424–25	6	125	56	69	11	6	2	6
1425–26	6	125	58	67	11	2	2	6
1427–28	6	125	56	69	11	6	2	6
1429–30	6	125	60	65	10	10	2	6
1430–31	6	125	60	65	10	10	2	6
1431–32	6	125	60	65	10	10	2	6
1432–33	6	125	60	65	10	10	2	6
1433–34	6	125	60	65	10	10	2	6
1434–35	6	125	62	63	10	6	2	6
1435–36	6	125	64	61	10	2	2	6
1438–39	6	125	64	61	10	2	2	6
1440–41	6	125	56	69	11	6	2	6
1441–42	6	125	52	73	12	2	2	6
1447–48	6	125	30	95	15	10	2	6
1448–49	6	125	32	93	15	6	2	6

1. An increase of 24 was accounted for — used as capons. These are separately accounted for in the documents.
2. Six were bought.
3. Sold extra, 5.
4. Sold to the executors at the hospitium 23 and on the market 32, both for 1½d. each.

§§ 21. National Subsidies levied in Crawley, 1328, 1628, 1673, 1799, and 1812.

(*a*) Subsidy of a Twentieth on Movable Goods, 1328.

The parliament held at Lincoln, 15–23 September, 1327, granted a subsidy of a twentieth on all movable goods, the proceeds to be used for the defence of the realm against the Scots.[1] Its collection was ordered in November, 1327, one half being due by 2 February, the other half by 25 June, 1328. The present account includes both halves, or in the words of the account, "the whole twentieth." Thus, it was made up after 25 June, 1328.

The tax was to be paid by countrymen and townsmen alike. The smallest sum paid in Crawley was 8d., the tax on goods worth a mark of silver, or 13s. 4d. But in villages other than Crawley as little as 7d. was collected. How much was exempt, or what the rate of valuation was, is not stated.

In Crawley twenty-eight, out of a total of about fifty tenants, paid the tax, ranging from 8d. to 30s. each. Eleven paid from 8 to 10d., sixteen from 1 to 3s., and one 30s. Philip Aubyn, who paid the highest amount, was responsible for almost half the total tax. He stood at the top of the list also in Sparkford and Sparsholt.[2]

Some of the names besides Aubyn's are new or recent acquisitions, such as Snow, Fawes, Marde, and Strupe. In the list for Hursley (or Mardon) we find the name of Alebrok, a family once resident in Crawley. And in Sparsholt Richard Fromond paid his tax. To this man, or to one of like name, twenty-five acres of land had been granted in Crawley in the year 1316.[3] In Crawley the family regularly paid to the lord of the manor one pound of cummin as a yearly rent. Just why he paid no twentieth on the occasion of the present levy in Crawley is hard to explain, unless he paid in Sparsholt or elsewhere for his Crawley holding. If such a thing were possible and actually done, then all estimates of the tax due in Crawley, and all generalizations therefrom are false.

[1] *Rotuli Parliamentorum*, vol. II (about 1783), p. 425.
[2] For Philip Aubyn, see § 14, pp. 50–51.
[3] Goodman, A. W., *Chartulary of Winchester Cathedral* (1927), p. 200.

Taxacio tocius vicesime d*omi*no Regi concesse in Com*itatu* Suth*amp*-t*onie* facta per Joh*anne*m de Tycheburne et Joh*anne*m de Roches Anno Regni Regis Edwardi tercii a conquestu primo.[1]

Hundr*edu*m de Buttlesgate.

Villata de Mulebrok*e*. S*umma* xx s. p*r*ob*ata*.

Villata de Nhut Schullyng*e*. S*umma* xxx s. vj d. p*r*ob*ata*.

Villata de Muchelmersch*e*. S*umma* xliiij s. xj d. p*r*ob*ata*.

Villata de Hoghton'. S*umma* x s. v d. p*r*ob*ata*.

Villata de Hurselygh*e*. S*umma* vj li. xviij d. ob. p*r*ob*ata*.

Villata de Compton'. S*umma* xlv s. j d. p*r*ob*ata*.

Villata de Sparkeforde.

D*e* Ph*ilipp*o Aubin xiij s. ij d.
D*e* Joh*anne* le Schut xv d.
D*e* Joh*anne* le Cart*ere* ij s.
D*e* Rel*icta* le Sefte xij d.
D*e* Joh*anne* Archir viij d.
D*e* Joh*anna* Thurmound v s.
D*e* Ad*a* Shire vij d.
D*e* Priore S*ancti* Swith*un*i Wynton*ie* vij s. vj d.
S*umma* xxxj s. ij d. p*r*ob*ata*.

Villata de Oterbourne. S*umma* xiij s. vij d. ob. p*r*ob*ata*.

Villata de Craulye.

D*e* Joh*anne* Light xij d.
D*e* Rob*er*to Hughet xviij d.
D*e* Rog*er*o Dauy x d.
D*e* Rob*er*to le Bunde viij d.
D*e* Steph*ano* le Cart*ere* ix d.
D*e* Will*elmo* le Longe ij s.
D*e* Rob*er*to Bele viij d.
D*e* Joh*anne* le Coupere ix d.
D*e* Rob*er*to le Bunde x d.
D*e* Rob*er*to Rankin xij d.
D*e* Alicia Gibbes xij d.
D*e* Joh*anne* Snow x d.
D*e* Steph*ano* le Carpentir xviij d.
D*e* Rob*er*to Dauy xij d.
D*e* Rob*er*to Munweder xij d.
D*e* Thom*a* le Wilde ij s.
D*e* Albreda Falkes xviij d.
D*e* Joh*anne* le vayne x d.
D*e* Chr*ist*ina Marde viij d.

[1] MS., P. R. O., Exchequer Lay Subsidy, 173/4. For all but three of the townships the names of the tax payers and the amount of their taxes have been omitted.

D*e* Nich*ola*o de Aula iij s.
D*e* Gilb*er*to Dauy viij d.
D*e* Steph*ano* Pistore ij s.
D*e* Albreda atte Putte iij s.
D*e* Joh*anne* Kirkebi iij s.
D*e* Rob*er*to de Wodecote xij d.
D*e* Gilb*er*to Prat xij d.
D*e* Ric*ardo* Strupe viij d.
D*e* Ph*ilipp*o Aubin xxx s.
S*umma* lxiiij s. viij d. p*ro*b*ata*.
Villata de Chilebolton'. S*umma* xxiiij s. iij d. ob. p*ro*b*ata*.
Villata de Wonsynton'. S*umma* xix s. j d. ob. p*ro*b*ata*.
Villata de Spersolte.
D*e* Ph*ilipp*o Aubin xx s.
D*e* Walt*er*o de Layneston' viij d.
D*e* Ric*ardo* Waryn xij d.
D*e* Walt*er*o de Maundeuille xij d.
D*e* Rob*er*to le Pere ij s.
D*e* Rob*er*to Archemer viij d.
D*e* Rog*er*o atte Dane ij s.
D*e* Rob*er*to Dauy ij s.
D*e* Henr*ico* Gileput viij d.
D*e* Will*elm*o Bigge viij d.
D*e* Rob*er*to Body ij s.
D*e* Walt*er*o Alayn x d.
D*e* Matill' Herfen iij s.
D*e* Thom*a* Inge iiij s.
D*e* Galfr*id*o de Westely ij s. iij d.
D*e* Joh*anne* Chiron iij s. iij d.
D*e* Rob*er*to Bekke viij d.
D*e* Valentino Bekke iij s. iiij d.
D*e* Ric*ardo* Fromond iij s. iiij d.
D*e* Andr*ea* Payn ij s.
S*umma* lv s. iiij d. p*ro*b*ata*.
Villata de Wyke. S*umma* x s. j d. p*ro*b*ata*.
Villata de Fulflode. S*umma* x s. vij d. p*ro*b*ata*.
Villata de Eledestoke. S*umma* liiij s. vj d. p*ro*b*ata*.
Villata de Hunton'. S*umma* xix s. j d. p*ro*b*ata*.
Villata de Littleton'. S*umma* vij s. iij d. p*ro*b*ata*.
S*umma* toci*us* Hundr*e*d*i* xxix li. ij s. ij d. p*ro*b*ata*.

(*b*) List of Payers of Taxes on Personal and Landed Property, [about Sept.], 1628.

A subsidy of 2s. 8d. per pound sterling was granted by parliament in June, 1628.[1] It was to be levied on every person (except orphans) having at least three pounds' worth of property in goods. Debts owed were to be deducted; and personal apparel, other than jewelry, was to be exempt. Papal recusants and aliens were to pay at double the rate. There was also a subsidy on real estate, including annuities, at the rate of 4s. a pound sterling, with a double rate for papal recusants and aliens.

Barring orphans, there were apparently only eight persons in Crawley who possessed personal property to the value of three

CRAWLYE[2]

Sir Gerrard Fleetwood kt.	*goods*	—	xij li.	xxxij s.
Wm Godwine	*goods*	—	v li.	xiij s. iiij d.
Richard Allen	*goods*	—	iij li.	viij s.
Joseph Hewett	*goods*	—	iij li.	viij s.
Richard Page	*goods*	—	iij li.	viij s.
Richard Beech	*goods*	—	iij li.	viij s.
Joan*e* Wayte vid*ua*[2]	la*nds*	—	xx s.	viij s.
Sess*ores:*[3]				
John Wilkins	*goods*	—	vj li.	xvj s.
Richard Pucknall	*goods*	—	v li.	xiij s. iiij d.
			Sum*ma* v li.	xiiij s. viij d.

HUNTON

Mary Goddard vid*ua*	*goods*	—	iij li.	viij s.
Richard Smith	*goods*	—	iij li.	viij s.
John Twyne	*goods*	—	iiij li.	x s. viij d.
Thomas Bulpitt	ann'	—	xx s.	iiij s.
John Purchell	ann'	—	xx s.	iiij s.
Sess*ores:*[4]				
Wm Jeffery sen*ior*	*goods*	—	vj li.	xvj s.
Wm Jeffery ju*nior*	*goods*	—	iij li.	viij s.
			Sum*ma* lviij s. viij d.	

[1] *The Statutes of the Realm*, vol. V (1819), pp. 39–52.

[2] MS., P. R. O., Exchequer Lay Subsidies, 175/522. The third of five entire subsidies granted by parliament, 4 Car. I.

[3] Before this name occurs "Rec. Con.", a convicted recusant.

[4] Assessors.

BUDDLESGATE HUNDRED[1]

Village	No. of persons taxed	Tax £	s.	d.
Nursling	12	7	8	0
Milbrooke	25	10	1	4
Compton	10	14	18	0
Michelmersh	26	11	6	0
Crawlye	9	5	14	8
Hunton	7	2	18	8
Wonston	8	3	14	8
Stoke Charitie	4	2	2	8
Littleton	4	2	1	4
Houghton	7	2	17	4
Sparsholte	10	9	1	4
Chilbolton and Bramsbury'	14	8	0	0
Otterborne	12	2	14	8
Week and Fulflood'	6	3	17	4
Hurslye	37	23	7	4

Summ*a* tot*a*lis istius Hundred*i* c x li. iij s. iiij d.

pounds sterling. This is a striking commentary on the material well-being of the village, that so few had grain, stock, implements, and household goods worth three pounds. Of course part of the explanation probably is that the valuation or assessment was low.

Only one had taxable lands, and she paid at a double rate because a Roman Catholic recusant. No one in Crawley had annuities worth as much as one pound sterling, while there were two such in Hunton.

The most interesting question has to do with land and landholding. Here is a list of the most important tenants, only one, however, being subject to the land tax. If we are to interpret the meaning of the statute imposing the tax, the plain inference is that there was at this time only one fee simple or copyhold in Crawley that was regarded as worth 20s. a year. That was held by Widow Wayte. The demesne, farmed by Sir Gerrard Fleetwood, was a leasehold and as such not subject to the tax. The meaning of "worth 20s.," or "of the yearlie value of twentie

[1] Summary, not an exact reproduction, of the manuscript.

shillinges," as the statute has it, is apparently the annual rental paid by the tenant to the lord.

(*c*) The Hearth-Tax Assessment, 1673.

In 1662 a tax was imposed, of 2s. "for every Fire Hearth and Stove," [1] or on all "Chimneyes Fire Hearthes or Stoves." [2] It had to be paid by the occupier. Exemption was allowed for the very poor, but none was granted to anyone having over two chimneys, fire-places, or stoves.[2] Those who were "certificated" were exempt on account of poverty. The others were taxed. There appear to have been in Crawley at the time thirty-six occupiers, thirteen of whom were too poor to be taxed.

It is interesting to note that while a Widow Wayte was one of the best-off tenants in Crawley in 1628, on the present occasion (doubtless) another Widow Wayte was among the poor thirteen. We wonder whether economic misfortune or religious dissent had borne down the more heavily on this stalwart Crawley family.

Since there were no vacant houses recorded, we may conclude that there were approximately 36 cottages in Crawley Parish at this time, and somewhat fewer in the village itself. We find it difficult to accept these returns as they stand.

CRAULEY [3]

Sr Kingeman Lucy	xvj
Dr Darrell	vj
Mr. Turner	ij
Richard Long	ij
James Wade	j
John Petter	j
Rob*ert* Baker	ij
George Perton	j
Rich*ard* Beath	iiij
Rob*ert* Petter	iij
Widdow Page	j
Edward Butler	ij
Wm Wilkins	iij
Widd*ow* Allen	ij
Wm Browning	j

[1] 14 Car. II, ch. 10. *The Statutes of the Realm*, vol. V (1819), pp. 390–393.

[2] Cf. 16 Car. II, ch. 3, § 6. *Ibid.*, p. 516. The tax imposed in 1662 was continued until 1689.

[3] MS., P. R. O., Exchequer Lay Subsidies, 176/569 (memb. 22 for Crawley alone). Endorsed "25 Car. II." Heading partly gone; "1673" is clear.

John Trifell	iiij
Wm Pett	j
Wm Harris	j
Ambrose Beate	j
Rookely Farme	iiij
Widd*ow* Page	j
Wm Harris a forge	j
Edward Butler	ij
Rich*ard* Partridge Coll*ector* Ambrose Beate Titheman	l xij

PERSONS CERTIFICATED

Richard Sheppard	j
Oliver Poole	j
Wm Poole	ij
Ambrose Houchin	j
Tho*mas* Allin	j
Richard Franklin	ij
Robert Wilkins	j
John Gregory	j
Widd*ow* Waite	ij
John Page	j
Rowland Hall	j
Wm Buman	ij
Edward Rostlide	j
	xvij

SUMMARY FOR BUDDLESGATE[1]

Village	No. of persons not certified	No. of their hearths	No. of persons certified	No. of their hearths
Hunton	13	37	0	
Compton	19 + a forge	74[2]	0	
Houghton	31	52	13	16
Chilboulton	26 [1][3]	53	8	10
Michelmersh	72 [1]	164	30	38
Sparkford	10 [1]	70[4]	0	
Sparshalt	20 [1]	37	19	26
Stoke Charity	12	37		
Bransbury	7	20		
Wonston	21	46	12	16
Otterborne	18 [3]	43	14	18
Littleton	7 [1]	18		
Weeke	9 [1]	19		
Hursley	97 [2]	281	64	80
Crauley	23	62	13	17
Nurseling	34 [2]	103	14	19
Millbrooke	46 [3]	110	18	25

[1] This is a summary of the manuscript, not an exact reproduction.
[2] Including forge. [3] [ ] = "voyd" = vacant. These are reckoned in the totals.
[4] The Hospitall of St. Crosse — l [hearths].

VACANT HOUSES ("VOYD")[1]

Chilboulton	1	house	with	2	hearths
Michelmersh	1	"	"	1	"
Sparkford	1	"	"	2	"
Sparshalt	1	"	"	6	"
Otterborne	3	"	"	(2, 2, 1)	"
Littleton	1	"	"	2	"
Weeke	1	"	"	3	"
Hursley	2	"	"	(2, 2)	"
Nurseling	2	"	"	(2, 2)	"
Millbrooke	3	"	"	(3, 4, 5)	"

[1] Not a verbatim reproduction of the manuscript.

(*d*) Crawley Land Tax, 1799–1800 and 1812–13.

The land tax is, of course, very old in England. The rate at the time of the document here published was 4s. on the pound sterling of annual value. It was levied on tenements and lands, including the glebe lands of the rector, and on thithes.[1] By a statute of 1798 the land tax was made perpetual, but redemption was provided for. Anyone wishing to free himself from future payment might redeem his land by paying into the government 3% consolidated or reduced annuities producing the annual returns equal to the tax redeemed, plus 10%.[2] These accounts show that three Crawley proprietors had taken advantage of this provision before the specified limit — 25 March, 1799. It is to be noted that while there were 12 proprietors in 1799, there were only 11 in 1812; and that while there were 9 occupiers in 1799, there were 12 in 1812.

We may analyze the situation in another way. Among the landholders in Crawley in 1799 were the occupants of the home farm, Rookley House, and the rectory and glebe land, and also the yeoman farmers, all of whom were taxed; and in addition, there were a few small holders who were exempt from the tax because their tenements were "not of the full yearly value of twenty Shillings

[1] 38 George III, ch. 5, § 80 (1797). *The Statutes at Large*, vol. 36–38 George III (1811), p. 511.

[2] 38 George III, ch. 60. *The Statutes at Large*, vol. 35–38 George III (1798), pp. 788–790, 807–808. Cf. also 39 George III, ch. 6. *Ibid.*, vol. 39–40 George III (1800), pp. 12–13.

in the whole."[1] The great majority of families in Crawley were, of course, exempt, because they were of the laboring class who lived commonly in cottages tied to the holdings of the yeoman farmers. The five or six yeomen were as often lessees of the lands of others as proprietors of holdings of their own. Thomas Pern was the foremost representative of his class.[2]

LAND TAX RATE FROM APRIL 5, 1799, to APRIL 5, 1800[3]

Proprietors	Occupiers	£	s.	d.
Rich:^{d} Meyler Esqr	Himself	1	16	4
D^{o} Late Hankins &c.	D^{o}		10	
D^{o} Late Loomers	Ja^{s} Allen		2	
D^{o}	Rich:^{d} Bailey	29	1	8
D^{o} Late Ferrell's Included	Thos Pern	12	19	11
Archdeacon Woodford	Thos Pern &c.	25	9	1
General Bathurst	Rich:^{d} Bailey	1	6	
Mr Morrifs (Rookley)	Geo: Read	24	13	6
Thos Pern Senr	Himself		4	
Mrs Morgan	Thos Pern		17	8
Jno Pern	Geo Godwin	4	·	
Geo Godwin	D^{o}	5	14	
Mr Birch	Jno Pickering	2	5	
Ana Waight	D^{o}	1	5	10
Robt Fifield	Himself	1	18	
Charles Paige	Himself	1	4	8
		£ 113	7	8

Jno Pickering } afsessor & collector.

June 26th 1799 allowed & confirmed by us. Wm Goffe

C. Wade B^{m} Tawney

[1] See 38 George III, ch. 5, § 80 (1797). *Ibid.*, vol. 36–38 George III (1811), p. 511.

[2] See above, § 32, p. 147, and § 35, p. 165.

[3] MS., the Castle, Winchester. Copied by Miss E. Barber.

LAND TAX RATE [from 1812 to 1813]

Proprietors	Occupiers	Crawley Land Tax Redeemed			From what time	Land Tax not Redeemed		
		£	s.	d.		£	s.	d.
Wm Morgan	Thos Pern	0	17	8				
G. Godwin & Perns	Himself	4	0	0	March 25			
Chas Morris Esqre	L. J. Allee	19	15	3	1799.			
		24	12	11				
Rd Meyler Esqre	T.B.LethbridgeEsq					1	16	1
do Late Hankings	do					0	9	11
do farm	Wm Wade					28	17	4
do Late Loomers	James Allen					0	2	0
do Late Perns	Thos Pern					12	18	0
Hble Hutton A. G. Legge	Rector Parsonage					25	5	4
G. Lovel Esqre	Himself					5	10	5
G. Godwin	Himself					5	13	2
John Birch	Himself					2	4	9
Rot Waight	John Birch					1	5	8
Rot Fifield	Himself					1	17	9
Chas. Paige	Himself					1	4	6
do Late Bathurst	Himself					1	5	10
Thos Pern	Himself					0	4	0
		24	12	11		£88	14	9

G. Godwin Thos Pern Assers 1812

Confirmed & allowed by us.
May 6 1812 H. Lee.
N. Westcomb

§§ 22. Tenements in Crawley and other Communities nearby held by Philip Aubyn and Alice his Wife by Pleas of Contract in the King's Court, 1316 and 1325.

In the first of these cases, held before the king's court, in the octaves of Saint Michael, 10 Edward II, Richard, son of Richard de Sutton, brought suit against Robert Gereberd for one messuage, three carucates of land, and two acres of meadow with their appurtenances, in Crawley, Upper Somborne, and Romsey. These tenements were at the time held of Robert Gereberd by Philip Aubyn and Alice his wife for the life of Alice, to revert to Robert. Now, however, on the payment of 100 marks of silver to Robert, Richard gets the reversion, to hold of the chief lords of the fee by the services pertaining thereto. In this way, Robert was eliminated from the scene. He had alienated his rights for the life of Alice. Now he permanently alienates them to Richard.

Probably this was a case of a rent-charge which Philip Aubyn of Winchester had bought from Robert, doubtless in the form of a loan to Robert. Then Robert sold his remaining rights.

It would seem that we have here a case of enfranchised land, a freehold, at this time or earlier carved out of three manors, and now alienated by fine in the king's court. The Crawley part of this holding may be the Rookley House estate, adjoining Upper Somborne, on the extreme western boundary of Crawley.

Later, in 1325, the same estate, with 500 acres of meadow added, at least part of which was probably in Nitherden (Netherton?), again came before the royal court. This time Philip Aubyn and Alice his wife were the petitioners and John de Marlebergh, chaplain, the defendant. A contract was made in the court which recognized the right of John to the estate. But John now hands it over to Philip Aubyn and Alice his wife, in return for a gift from Philip. The various tenements of this estate are henceforth to belong to Philip and Alice and the heirs of Philip, who are to hold forever from the chief lords of that fee (or estate) by the services pertaining thereto.

In some way, after 1316, Philip and Alice had given up or sold their claim, as had Richard de Sutton. How many transactions had ensued, we do not know. But Philip and Alice got complete and permanent possession as under-tenants.

It would seem that this was one step in the breaking up of the Manor of Crawley, which, however, did not go far. The tenement of Crawley, forming part of this inter-manorial freehold, was probably cut out of the manor by enfranchisement. That it was the holding of Alvin recorded in Domesday Book is unlikely, Alvin's holding being rather too large. But this possibility should not be ruled out. The enfranchisement of land was ultimately to help kill the manor, but single acts were more threatening than dangerous. Whether the holder of this estate in the Middle Ages was also a free suitor in the Crawley court is not indicated in any records examined.

(*a*) Hec[1] est finalis concordia facta in Curia d*omi*ni Regis apud Westm*onasterium* in Octab*is* Sancti Mich*ae*lis Anno regni Regis Edwardi

[1] MS., P. R. O., Feet of Fines, Southampton, 10–12 Ed. II, no. 5.

filii Regis Edwardi decimo coram Will*el*mo de Bereford Gileberto de Roubiry Johanne de Benstede, Henrico le Scrop' Joh*anne* Bacun, *et* Joh*anne* de Mutford Justiciariis *et* aliis d*omi*ni Regis fidelibus, tunc ibi presentib*us* Inter Ric*ardu*m filiu*m* Ric*ard*i de Sutton' querent*em*, *et* Rob*ertu*m Gereberd deforc*iantem*, de vno Mesuagio trib*us* Carucatis terre *et* duab*us* acris p*ra*ti cum pertin*enciis* in Craule Vpsunbourne et Romesie que Ph*illip*us Aubyn et Alicia vx*or* eius tenent ad terminu*m* vite ip*s*ius Alicie. Vnde pl*acitu*m conuencionis sum*monitum* fuit int*er* eos in eadem Curia. Scil*ice*t q*uo*d p*redic*tus Rob*er*tus recogn*oui*t p*re*d*ic*ta ten*ementa* cum pertin*enciis* esse Jus ip*s*ius Ric*ard*i Et concessit p*ro* se *et* her*edibus* suis q*uo*d p*redic*ta ten*ementa* cum pertin*enciis* que p*redic*ti Ph*illip*us *et* Alicia tenuerunt ad t*er*minu*m* vite ip*s*ius Alice ex dimissione p*redic*ti Rob*er*ti in p*redic*t*is* villis, die quo hec concordia facta fuit, *et* que post decessum ip*s*ius Alicie ad p*redic*tu*m* Rob*er*t*um* *et* her*edes* suos debuerunt reu*er*ti; post decessum ip*s*ius Alicie integre remaneant p*redic*to Ric*ard*o *et* her*edibus* suis Tenenda de Capit*alibus* d*omi*nis feodi illius p*er* s*er*uicia que ad p*redic*ta ten*ementa* p*er*tinent imp*er*pet*uu*m. Et p*redic*tus Rob*er*tus *et* her*ede*s sui warantizabu*n*t p*re*d*ic*to Ric*ard*o *et* her*edibus* suis p*redic*ta ten*ementa* cum p*er*tin*enciis* sicut p*redic*t*u*m est, cont*ra* omnes ho*min*es imp*er*pet*uu*m. Et p*ro* hac recognicione, concessione, warantia, fine *et* concordia, idem Ricardus dedit p*redic*to Rob*er*to Centum Marcas argenti. Et hec concordia facta fuit p*re*sentib*us* p*redic*tis Ph*illip*o *et* Alicia *et* eam concedentib*us* *et* fecerunt p*redic*to Ric*ard*o fidelitatem in eadem Curia.

(*b*) Hec[1] est finalis concordia facta in Curia d*omi*ni Regis apud Westm*onasterium* a die S*anc*t*e* Trinitatis in quindecim dies Anno regni Regis Edwardi filii Regis Edwardi decimo octauo; coram Willelmo de Bereford Joh*anne* de Mutford Will*el*mo de Herle Joh*anne* de S*to*nore *et* Joh*anne* de Bousser Justic*iariis* *et* aliis d*omi*ni Regis fidelib*us* tunc ibi presentibus Int*er* Phill*ipu*m Aubyn *et* Aliciam vx*or*em eius querent*es* p*er* Thomam de Crukern' positum loco ip*s*ius Alicie ad lucrand*um* vel p*er*dend*um* et Joh*anne*m de Marlebergh' capellanum deforc*iantem* de vno mesuagio trib*us* carucatis t*er*re duab*us* acris p*ra*ti *et* quingentis acris pasture cum pertin*enciis* in vpsumburn' Nitherden' Craule ct Romesye Vnde pl*acitu*m conuen*cio*nis sum*monitum* fuit int*er* eos in eadem Curia. Scil*ice*t q*uo*d p*redic*tus Ph*illip*us recogn[*ovit*] p*redic*ta ten*ementa* cum p*er*tin*enciis* esse jus ip*s*ius Joh*anni*s Vt illa que idem Joh*anne*s h*ab*et de dono p*redic*ti Ph*illip*i. Et p*ro* hac recognic*io*ne fine *et* concordia idem Johannes concessit predic*tis* Ph*illip*o *et* Alicie p*redic*t*a* ten*ementa* cum p*er*tin*enciis* Et illa eis reddidit in eadem Curia Habend*a*

[1] MS., P. R. O., Feet of Fines, Southampton, 18–20 Ed. II, no. 5. See also Inquisition Misc., Chancery File 113, no. 4 (18 March, 4 Ed. III).

et Tenend*a* eisdem Ph*illip*o *et* Alicie *et* her*edibus* ip*s*ius Ph*illip*i de Capi-t*alibus* d*omi*nis feodi illius p*er* s*er*uicia que ad p*redict*a ten*ementa* p*er*ti-nent imp*erpetuu*m.

§§ 23. Part of a Lease of the Demesne, 24 March, 1487.

Only a part of a lease of the demesne is here reproduced. The lessee was John Couper, apparently a member of an old Crawley family. The lease was to run for twenty-one years. It has been taken from a rental of the third year (1489–90) of the lease.

The lessee contracted to pay £6. 13s. 4d. as the farm of the lands and £15. 3s. 4d. as the farm of the stock. The lessee was to repair all the thatched roofs and the earthen walls, while the lord would repair the tiled roofs and the stone walls. The lessee, or farmer (of the demesne) as he is called in the records, was to repair all the hedges and trenches (fossata), and keep the buildings and stock in good condition. The farmer was to provide meat, drink, and lodging (?lecticuna), hay, litter, and one quarter of oats for the seneschal, supervisor, and other officials of the lord, while they were holding the court and supervising the demesne and stock. He was to pay each year to the lord's clerk 13s. 4d. for holding the courts and writing the rolls and estreats (extracts).

The farmer was to have the demesne lands and, we may add, buildings, pertaining to husbandry, the stock, and, we may add, implements, three acres of underwood for his haybote[1] and firebote,[2] and a gown of the livery of the bishop's valetti (?Toga de Sect*a* valect*orum*). He was to return things as he found them, or the price of the same, at the choice of the lord. He was to occupy the lands, subject to the customs as found in the lord's custumal. And the lord might enter and distrain, if the rent were not paid. To the lord were reserved many incidents connected with lordship and also fixed rents, services commuted, the pannage of pigs, and woods and underwood. The items that were reserved occur in the accounts[3] which exist in plenty down to about the middle of the eighteenth century.

[1] The privilege of taking bushes for planting as hedge fences.

[2] The privilege of taking underbrush material for firewood.

[3] For an actual account of Crawley under a similar lease, see below, §§ 26, pp. 489 ff.

The prominence of the livestock is notable. The farmer was to receive from the lord 440 wethers, 10 rams, 300 ewes, and 200 hoggets, or 950 sheep in all. He was not to overstock the pastures of the lord and of the lord's other tenants beyond 1,300 sheep, 10 cart- and plow-horses, and 20 oxen.

In this document we see clearly that the demesne of Crawley was a sheep and grain farm, as indeed Crawley is to this day.

Et[1] de vj li. xiij s. iiij d. de firma man*erii* ib*idem et* om*nium* t*erra*r*um* d*omi*nical*ium* prator*um et* pasturar*um* ad husb*andriam* pertin*entium* sic*ut* dimiss*orum* Joh*anni* Coup*er* p*er* reu*er*end*um* in Chr*ist*o p*a*trem *et* d*ominum* d*omi*n*um* Petrum Courteney Winton*iensem* Ep*iscopu*m p*er* Indentur*am* p*ro* t*er*mino xxj Anno*rum* hoc Anno t*er*cio. Et de xv li. iij s. iiij d. de firma cccc xl Multon*um* x hurterd*orum* ccc M*a*tric*ium et* cc hogg*astrorum* soluend*o* ad duos Anni t*er*minos p*r*incipales v*idelicet* ad festa Pasche *et* Sancti Mich*ae*lis Arch*angel*i per equales porc*io*nes sic*ut* dimiss*orum* p*r*efat*o* Joh*anni* Coup*er* p*er* p*r*edict*um* d*ominu*m Ep*is*-*copu*m p*er* indentur*am* p*r*edict*am* p*ro* t*er*mi*no* p*r*edi*ct*o hoc An*no* ut sup*ra* Redd*itu* assis*o* pannag*io* porc*orum* Custum*ariis* op*eribus* in dena-*riis* extent*is* ward*is* marit*agiis* Releuiis finib*us* heriett*is* bosc*is et* sub-bosc*is* Escaet*is* For*isfacturis* Am*er*ciame*n*t*is* Turn*is et* Cur*iis* Maner*ii* p*r*edict*i* Exc*eptis et* penit*us* d*omi*no Reseruat*is*. Et p*r*edict*us* Joh*anne*s Firmar*ius* om*n*es dom*os* maner*ii* p*r*edict*i* stra*min*e coop*er*t*as* ut in coop*er*tur*is* necnon muros terreos ear*und*em ben*e et* suffic*ien*t*er* repara-b*it* virgulabit *et* sustentab*it* sumpt*ibus* suis p*r*opriis *et* expens*is* dura*n*te t*er*mi*no* p*r*edicto. Et p*r*edict*us* d*omi*n*us* Ep*iscop*us om*n*es dom*os* Maner*ii* p*r*edic*ti* tegulis coop*er*t*as et* omnes muros petrinos ut in coo-p*er*tur*is et* gross*o* meremio b*en*e *et* suffic*ien*t*er* rep*a*rabit *et* sustentab*it* sumpt*ibus* suis p*r*opriis *et* expens*is* durant*e* t*er*mi*no* sup*ra*dict*o*. Et p*r*edict*us* Joh*anni*s Firmar*ius* om*n*es cepes haias *et* fossat*a* Maner*io* p*r*edict*o* p*er*tin*entia* bene *et* sufficient*er* faciet *et* escurabit *et* plantabit sumpt*ibus* suis p*r*opriis *et* expen*sis* durant*e* t*er*mi*no* p*r*edict*o*. Et ea o*mn*ia ac domos vt p*r*edic*i*tur o*m*ni suo incumben*te* bene *et* sufficient*er* rep*ara*t*a* vnacu*m* toto staur*o* ta*m* uiuo quam mort*uo* p*r*ovt in dorso hui*us* lib*ri* specificat*ur* in adheo bono statu quo recepit vel melior*i* in fine t*ermi*n*i* sui p*r*edict*i* dimittet *et* relib*erabit* vel p*r*ec*ium* inde ad elec-cionem d*omi*ni. Et p*r*edict*us* Joh*anne*s h*a*bebit tres acr*as* subbosci in bosc*o* d*omi*ni ib*ide*m temp*o*re seisionab*i*li p*ro* suo haibote *et* Firebote Annuatim p*er* visum *et* dilib*er*ac*io*nem ministror*um* d*omi*ni ib*ide*m *et* vnam Togam de Sect*a* valect*orum* d*omi*ni vel vj s. viij d. ad eleccionem d*omi*ni t*er*mino p*r*edict*o*. Et p*r*edict*us* firmar*ius* inueniet Sen*esca*lo

[1] MS., P. R. O., Ecclesiastical Commission, Various, 155847.

Sup*er*uis*ori et* Aliis ministr*is* d*omi*ni t*a*m p*ro* Turn*is et* Cur*iis* tenend*is* q*ua*m p*ro* dominio [1] *et* staur*o* sup*er*uidend*is* lectic*una* [?] fenu*m et* littura*m et* ad quemli*be*t Turnu*m* j q*uart*e*rium* Auen*arum* in quoli*be*t eor*um* aduent*u* durante t*er*mino sup*ra*dict*o*. Et si contigat p*re*dict*um* Annualem redd*itu*m A retro fore in p*ar*te vel in toto post Aliqu*em* t*er*minum p*re*no*mina*t*um* p*er* quindicem dies non solut*um* ex tunc bene licebit p*re*fat*o* d*omi*no Ep*iscop*o *et* successor*ibus* suis in Maner*io* p*re*dict*o* cu*m* om*n*i*bus* suis p*er*tinen*tiis* int*r*a*re et* distringer*e et* districti*onem* ib*id*em capt*am* abduc*er*e imp*ar*car*e et* penes se retiner*e* quousq*ue* de p*re*dict*o* Annual*i* redd*itu* cu*m* arr*eragiis* si que fu*er*int [?] plenar*ie* fu*er*it satisfect*us et* p*er*solut*us*. Et si nulla sufficiens districti*o* in p*re*dict*o* Maner*io* cum suis reint*ra*re in manus suas reassum*er*e dictu*m* que Joh*ann*em Totalit*er* expeller*e* hac indentur*a* in Aliquo non obstante. Et p*re*dict*us* firmar*ius* soluet Annuati*m* Cl*er*ico d*omi*ni p*ro* Officio suo Attend*endo* p*ro* Curiis tenend*is* ac Rotul*is et* Ex*tr*act*is* [2] earu*nd*em Necno*n* Rotul*is* comp*o*t*urum* scribend*is et* Aliis necessar*iis* eid*em* Officio p*er*tinenc*ibus* attend*endis* tresdecem solidos *et* quatuor denari*os* Prouiso ecia*m* q*uo*d tam p*re*dict*us* firmar*ius* q*ua*m tenente*s* d*omi*ni ib*id*em h*a*bebunt *et* occupabu*n*t t*erras et* pastur*as et* prat*a* maner*ii* antedict*i* s*ecundu*m vsum *et* Cons*uetudinem* ab antiquo vsitat*a et* p*ro*ut in Custum*ario* d*omi*ni magis Ap*er*te *et* clarius patet. Et q*uo*d p*re*dict*us* firm*arius* non onorabit nec oner*e* faciet pastur*as* d*omi*ni *et* tenent*ium* suor*um* vlt*ra* num*erum* Aquor*um* [3] *et* affror*um* xx boum *et* MCCC biden*cium* p*er* Annu*m* durante t*er*mino p*re*dicto. In cui*us* rei testimoniu*m* vni p*ar*ti har*um* Indentur*arum* penes p*re*fat*um* Joh*ann*em Coup*er*e Rem*anenti* sup*ra*dict*us* d*omin*us Ep*iscop*us sigillu*m* suu*m* apposuit Alt*er*i vero p*ar*t*i* har*um* Indentur*arum* penes p*re*fat*um* d*ominu*m Ep*iscop*um rem*anenti* p*re*fat*us* Joh*ann*es Coup*er*e sigillum suu*m* apposuit. dat*um* ap*ud* Suthwalth*a*m vicesimo quarto die mens*is* Marcii Anno regni R*egis* Henric*i* siptimi [sic] secundo. S*umma* xxj li. xvj s. viij d.

§§ 24. Part of a Lease of the Demesne, 20 July, 1787.

This lease was granted to the three persons named, to hold until the death of the last survivor. But it was actually surrendered, 2 April, 1796, to Richard Meyler. Apparently when this surrender took place, the present lease was underscored in those parts which were to be omitted in the new lease. The part relating to Norwood or Northwood Park was so dealt with; as also those lines referring to services commuted to money payments, the overstock-

[1] Altered from domino.

[2] Manuscript has Exctr'.

[3] Error for Equor*um*.

ing of the pastures, and the three acres of wood for hedgebot, firebot, and plowbot. The enclosure of 1795 had seemingly robbed these items of their significance.[1]

On the whole, the most surprising feature of this lease is the fact that there had been so few changes, at least on the surface, in a period of exactly 300 years.[2] Even the sums paid remained the same, that is £6. 13s. 4d. for the lands and £15. 3s. 4d. for the stock. It would appear incredible that during this long period of rising prices there should have been no increase in the rental received for the demesne lands and equipment. Perhaps we can explain this, in small part at least, by a diminution in what was leased. The tendency was for the equipment to decline or deteriorate. Some of the services also disappeared, notably the carriage of manure in 1690. But this was a small item, and, as is observed elsewhere,[3] may not actually have been a loss. But the chief explanation, and it is sufficient, lies in the lump sum paid down on entry upon the demesne lands and goods. It is said that on the present occasion Sir Willoughby Aston paid £21,000 for possession.[4] If we assume that the lease might have run for forty years, a generous period, then the annual rental implied was £500; if the period proved to be thirty years, then it was £700. At any rate some such sum should be added to the nominal one expressed in the lease itself.

The bishop "Doth [5] for himself and his Successors demise grant and to farm let unto the said Sir Willoughby Aston All that the Scite of the Manor of Crawley with the Appurtenances in the County of Southampton And also all Houses and other Edifices built upon the said Scite And all Lands Arable Meadows Feedings Pastures Hereditaments Ways Paths and other Appurtenances to the said Scite of the Manor of Crawley aforesaid belonging or appertaining *And also all that Pasture called the Park under Norwood Together with the works of the Tenants of the said Manor*

[1] See below, §§ 55, pp. 596 ff.
[2] See the preceding document, §§ 23, pp. 466 ff.
[3] See below, §§ 35, p. 516.
[4] Pledge, F. W. *Crawley* (1907), p. 142.
[5] MS., P. R. O., Ecclesiastical Commission, Millbank, 154425⁴⁄₃₃.

not being in Money[1] And that Stock and Store of the said Lord Bishop as well living as dead now being upon the Scite and other the Premises which said Stock and Store the said Sir Willoughby Aston for himself his Heirs Executors Administrators and Assigns doth hereby covenant and agree to return and deliver up unto the said Lord Bishop or his Successors in as good State and Condition as he the said Sir Willoughby Aston received the same or the Value thereof in Money at the Election of the said Lord Bishop or his Successors at the End or other sooner Determination of this present Demise which shall first happen (Except and always reserved out of this present Demise unto the said Lord Bishop and his Successors all Rents of Assize Pawnage of Hogs Custom Work of Tenants there being in Money Wards Marriages Reliefs Fines Herriots Woods Underwoods Escheats Forfeitures Amerciaments Perquisites Turns of Courts and all Views of Frankpledge whatsoever to the said Scite of the said Manor and all other the Premises belonging or appertaining *And also Except and always reserved to the Tenants of the Manor aforesaid the Feeding and depasturing for their Cattle in the said Place called the Park under Norwood heretofore granted or antiently granted* To have and to hold the said Scite of the said Manor and all the said Houses Lands Meadows Feedings Pastures and other the Premises with their and every of their Appurtenances together with the said Stock and Store as well living as Dead (except before excepted) unto the said Sir Willoughby Aston his Heirs and Assigns from the making hereof for and during the Term of the natural Lives of the said Sir Willoughby Aston party hereto The Right Honourable Bridget Tollemache widow commonly called Lady Bridget Tollemache Sister of the said Robert Earl of Northington deceased and of Valentine Henry Wilmot Son of Henry Wilmot of Farnborough Place in the said County of Southampton Esquire and for and during the natural Life of the longest liver of them Yielding and Paying therefore yearly unto the said Lord Bishop and his Successors at his and their Exchequer at Wolvesey in the

[1] Underlined here and elsewhere by pencil, doubtless for omission in the subsequent lease (1796). For the lease of 1805 and the regrant of 1818 to Richard Bright, see MS., Millbank, Ecclesiastical Commission, 154425⅓3.

said County of Southampton for the said Lands Six Pounds thirteen Shillings and four Pence of lawful Money of Great Britain at the two most usual Feasts or Terms of the year (that is to say) the Feasts of Saint Michael the Archangel and the Annunciation of the blessed Virgin Mary by even and equal Portions for the said Lands And for the said Stock and Store yearly at the Feast of Saint Peter at Bonds and Saint Michael the Archangel the yearly Rent of Fifteen Pounds three Shillings and four Pence of like lawful Money by even and equal Portions free of all Taxes whatsoever And also Yielding and Paying and Performing yearly unto and for the said Lord Bishop and his Successors all other Rents and Services for the aforesaid Scite of the said Manor and other the Premises or for any Part or Parcel thereof heretofore due and Payable." [Right of re-entry to the bishop and his successors if the two said rents be in arrears by the space of 28 days after any of the said feasts.]

The lessee was to make repairs on the house and other buildings at his own cost, and to allow "the Steward Overseer and Bailiff and Clerk of the Bishoprick of Winchester And also to and for the Clerk of the Bailiwick of Twyford for the time being and every of them and to and for such others as they shall bring with them for the keeping of the Courts of the said Manor Sufficient Meat Drink and Lodging and also Hay Litter and Oats for their and every of their Horses twice in every year when they shall come to the said Manor to keep Courts there at the Discretion of the Steward and Overseer of the said Lord Bishop and his Successors And also that he the said Sir Willoughby Aston his Heirs and Assigns shall and will also yearly and every year during the Continuance of this present Demise and Grant at his and their own proper Costs and Charges pay or cause to be paid unto the said Clerk of the said Bishop and his Successors of the Bailwick of Twyford aforesaid for the time being for his Office in the said Manor of Crawley to be done and performed for the Courts there to be holden and the Rolls and Extracts to be made And also for writing and transcribing the Rolls of Accounts of the said Manor and other necessary Duties to the said Office of Clerk belonging or appertaining thirteen Shillings and four Pence of lawful Money of

Great Britain *And the said Lord Bishop for himself and his Successors doth agree to and with the said Sir Willoughby Aston his Heirs and Assigns by these Presents that he the said Sir Willoughby Aston his Heirs and Assigns together with the other Tenants there of the said Lord Bishop and his Successors shall and may during the Continuance of the Estate hereby granted have hold and enjoy the said Lands Meadows and Pastures of the said Manor of Crawley according to the Customs and Usage there antiently observed and as in the Records of the said Lord Bishop and of his Predecessors may more plainly and at large appear Yet that he the said Sir Willoughby Aston his Heirs or Assigns do not nor shall overcharge or burthen the Pastures of the said Lord Bishop and his Successors or of his or their Tenants there with above ten Horses and Mares twenty Oxen and One thousand three hundred Sheep and Feeding Cattle yearly during the term aforesaid without the License of the said Lord Bishop or his Successors in Writing And that he the said Sir Willoughby Aston his Heirs and Assigns shall and may have yearly during the Continuance of the Estate hereby granted three Acres of wood in the woods of the said Lord Bishop and his Successors there to be cut at seasonable times for his and their Hedge boot Fire boot and Plough boot by the Assignment and Delivery of the General Woodward for the time being of the said Lord Bishop and his successors* and shall and may also have and take upon the Premises hereby granted reasonable Howse boot for the repairing of the Premises by the Assignment and Delivery of the General Woodward for the time being of the said Lord Bishop and his Successors as often and as need shall require during the said Term hereby granted And Lastly the said Lord Bishop hath constituted made and ordained And by these Presents doth constitute make and ordain John Fleetwood of the City of Winchester Gentleman and Henry Seally of Alresford in the said County of South*amp*ton Esquire jointly and severally his true and lawful Attornies and Deputies for him the said Lord Bishop and in his Name into the aforesaid Scite of the Manor and other the Premises or any Part thereof in the name of the whole to enter and full and peaceable Possession and Seizin thereof to take and the like full and peaceable possession and Seisin thereof or of any Part thereof in the name of the whole to the said Sir Willoughby Aston or to his certain Attorney to give and deliver To have and to hold the said Scite of the said Manor with the Appur*tenance*s and all and singular other the Premises with their Appurt*enance*s unto the said Sir Willoughby Aston his Heirs and Assigns for and during the Term of the Lives of him the said Sir Willoughby Aston Lady Bridget Tollemache and Valentine Henry Wilmot and the longest liver of them according to the Form Effect and true Meaning of this present Indenture hereby ratifying and confirming whatsoever his said Attornies or either of them shall lawfully do or cause to be done in or concerning the Premises by virtue of these Presents In Witness whereof the said Parties to these Presents have hereunto interchangeably set their Hands and Seals the Day and year first above written.

§§ 25. Reeve's Account, being the Accounts of the Collector of Rents and of the Farmer[1] of the Home Farm, 29 Sept., 1448 — 28 Sept., 1449.

There are four parts to this account: (1) the income or receipts, (2) the outgo or disbursements, (3) the stock account, and (4) the customary services. The first and last are of most importance.

Among the receipts, a notable item is the sum of £6. 13s. 4d. for the farm of the demesne lands (and equipment, excluding most of the stock). The farmer, who was also the reeve, obtained the arable and pasture lands, the swine, geese, capons, and eggs. He had taken a lease for eight years, the present year being the first. Later farms or leases included all the livestock. Henceforth there was no break in the practice of leasing the home farm.

The farmer of the demesne was William Sely, a Crawley serf or customary tenant. He was also granger and reeve. He was the first of an unbroken line of cultivators who were ultimately to push the lord out of the manor.

Significant items entered under income are defects in rent because of the pestilence (including that of 1348–49), chevage or head tax paid by the serfs, the yield of lands and tenements in the

[1] In the account for the following year, the heading is as follows: Comp*ot*us Will*el*mi Sely firmar*ii et* Joh*ann*is Sely sen*ioris* Collect*oris* Re*dditus* ib*idem*. MS., P. R. O., Ecclesiastical Commission, Various, 159441, memb. 15.

hands of the lord, and the sale or commutation of services. The custom of foldage is paid by the tenants because their sheep exceeded the fixed number of twenty-five which each tenant was apparently allowed to keep in the common fold.

It is difficult to separate the duties at this time of the farmer and reeve on the one hand and the collector of rents on the other. Later their offices and accounts were somewhat more distinct.

John Couch, the lord's serf, paid 8d. as his annual due for having permission to exercise the art of blacksmith along with John Starlynge, the existing blacksmith. He was to remain within the lord's domain of Crawley by the custom of apprenticeship for the period of twelve years. In other words he was bound out to the village blacksmith to learn the trade. We are surprised to read, however, of the custom of apprenticeship in Crawley. Whether it was a peculiarly local custom or had been imported from the towns is uncertain.

Various commodities were sold on the market, doubtless in Winchester. They were cocks and hens, wheat, barley, oats, and sheep. Lamb skins were sold 'in gross.' It is stated also that 240 lambs were purchased on the market for £10.

Money economy was dominant in Crawley. Not only were goods bought and sold, but the demesne was leased for money, and many of the customary services were commuted to money payments.

All the week-works, both those of the autumn and winter, had been commuted. About 16½ per cent of the aggregate of the autumn boon-works, harrowing, and washing and shearing of sheep had been also commuted. It was chiefly the farthingland holders of North Crawley who had got free from customary services. Three had commuted their labor obligations in olden times (ab antiquo), nine had done so temporarily and at the will of the lord, and three had left their holdings. The tenants of North Crawley, who had been the most heavily burdened, were the first to break the bonds of predial service. They had been primarily laborers, because of the smallness of their holdings — five acres and one-half.

Without week-work, the lord could hardly hope to carry on grain cultivation. His solution was, of course, to lease the demesne lands. Thus the sequence of cause and effect seems to be (1) the difficulty of enforcing week-work, (2) the leasing of the demesne lands, and (3) the leasing of livestock along with the lands.

Some of the old services, however, were still exacted for the benefit of the lord and the farmer. There had been no diminution in many services since 1390 [1] — in plowing, carrying the sheepfold, carting manure and wood, mowing the meadow at Wolvesey, and the carriage and shocking of the grain. But these were insignificant in comparison with the services which had been commuted. With the exception of mowing the hay at Wolvesey, all these services went to the farmer, some at the time of this account, others later.

The blacksmith's equipment is enumerated in detail and valued at £46. The supervisor helped the seneschal hold the tourn at this time. A storm had blown down the sheepfold and unroofed the hall. From Michelmarsh, seven miles away, 1,200 tiles were brought for the repairs. Two of the harrows belonging to the demesne were equipped with iron pegs, four with wooden ones. Wethers, to the number of 46, died of sheep-pox (in veroll*e et* rub*eo* morbo).

CRAULE [2]

Comp*ot*us Will*el*mi Sely p*re*pos*iti* ib*ide*m Anno regni Regis Henr*ici* sexti xxviij° Et anno Cons*ecrationis* D*om*ini Will*el*mi Waynflete Wynton*iensis* Ep*iscop*i t*er*cio.

Arr*eragia*. Id*e*m Will*elmu*s Sely respond*it* de viij li. xiij s. iiij d. de arr*eragiis* vltimi comp*oti* sui anni p*roximo* p*re*ced*entis*. S*umma* viij li. xiij s. iiij d.

Redd*itus* Assis*i*. Et de lxiiij s. vj d. de toto re*dditu* assis*o* ib*ide*m ad festum Natal*is* d*omi*ni. Et de lxvij s. x d. de to*to* re*dditu* assis*o* ib*ide*m ad fes*tu*m Pasche. Et de lxiiij s. vj d. de toto re*dditu* assis*o* ib*ide*m ad festum Natiuitat*is* s*anct*i Joh*an*nis Baptiste. Et de c iiij s. j d. de toto re*dditu* assis*o* ib*ide*m ad festum s*anct*i Mich*ae*lis arch*angel*i. Et de xx d. de Will*el*mo Sely de increm*ento* redd*itus* p*ro* iiij acr*is* t*er*r*e* de d*ominic*o d*omi*ni in la Estfeld*e* iux*ta* le Puttehilles p*er* ann*um*. S*umma* xv li. ij s. vij d.

[1] See above, §§ 17, pp. 285 ff.

[2] MS., P. R. O., Ecclesiastical Commission, Various, 159440, membs. 18 and 19.

Acquiet*ancie* Re*dditus*. Inde in acquiet*ancia* redd*itus* vnius p*r*eposi*ti* p*er* ann*um* v s. In acquiet*anciis* redd*itus* j fabri *et* iij Carucar*iorum* p*er* ann*um* x s. viij d. cuil*ib*et eor*um* ij s. viij d. In acquiet*anciis* redd*itus* bercar*ii* multon*um* j b*er*car*ii* ouiu*m* m*a*tric*ium* *et* j Custod*is* hog*astro*-*rum* p*er* ann*um* viij s. cuil*ib*et eor*um* ij s. viij d. S*umma* xxiij s. viij d.

Def*ec*tus Redd*itus*. In def*ectu* redd*itus* [terre] Will*elm*i le Straunge tract*e* in d*ominicum* p*er* ann*um* ij s. In def*ectu* redd*itus* t*err*e Will*elm*i de Curia p*ro* consi*m*ili ij s. viij d. In def*ectu* redd*itus* t*err*e Rob*er*ti de Crouch t*r*act*e* in d*ominicum* p*er* ann*um* ij s. viij d. In def*ectu* re*dditus* t*err*e Will*elm*i de Alebroke qui modo rem*anet* apud M*er*don*am* p*er* an-*num* v s. In def*ectu* redd*itus* t*err*e Rob*er*ti Coye p*ro* consi*m*ili ij s. viij d. In def*ectu* redd*itus* t*err*e porcar*ii* p*ro* consi*m*ili ij s. viij d. In def*ectu* redd*itus* t*err*e Ric*ard*i vaccar*ii* p*ro* consi*m*ili ij s. viij d. S*umma* xx s. iiij d.

Def*ec*tus Redd*itus* p*er* pestillenc*iam*. In def*ectu* redd*itus* j virgat*e* t*err*e nat*ive* *et* xxij acr*arum* t*err*e p*ur*p*restur*e que fuer*unt* Rob*er*ti Wode-cote m*odo* rem*anentium* in man*ibus* d*omi*ni p*er* ann*um* xxj s. In def*ectu* redd*itus* j place*e* t*err*e nup*er* Rog*er*i lyght postea Rad*ulph*i lange xij d. q*uia* trad*itur* Johanni lange nisi p*ro* xij d. p*er* ann*um*. S*umma* xxij s. S*umma* acquiet*anciarum* *et* def*ectuum* re*dditus* lxvj s. S*umma* Re*dditus* rem*anens* de claro xj li. xvj s. vij d.

Chiuagiu*m*. Et de viij d. de ann*uali* recogn*itione* Joh*an*nis Cupp*er*e sen*ioris* nat*ivi* d*omi*ni vt possit morar*i* ex*tra* do*minicum* d*omi*ni q*uam*-diu d*omi*no placu*er*it *et* venire ad turnu*m* de hock*e* *et* maner*e* nat*ivus* d*omi*ni vt p*r*ius. Et de viij d. de Joh*an*ne filio henr*ici* Dauy nat*ivo* d*omi*ni ann*uali* recogn*itione* vt possit morar*i* ex*tra* lib*ertates* d*omi*ni Ep*iscop*i Wynton*iensis* vi*delicet* apud Caneford*e* q*ua*mdiu d*omi*no pla-cu*er*it *et* venir*e* ad turnu*m* de hock*e* p*er* ann*um* *et* maner*e* nat*ivus* d*omi*ni vt p*r*ius de Craule p*er* pl*egium* Joh*an*nis Dauy sen*ioris* *et* Joh*an*nis Dauy jun*ioris*. Et de viij d. de Rog*er*o filio Rob*er*ti Wodecote nat*ivo* d*omi*ni de annuali recognic*ione* vt possit morar*i* ex*tra* lib*er*tat*es* d*omi*ni vi*delicet* apud Caneford*e* q*uam*diu d*omi*no placu*er*it *et* venir*e* ad turnu*m* de hock*e* p*er* ann*um* *et* maner*e* nat*ivus* d*omi*ni de Craule vt prius p*er* pl*egi*u*m* Thome Wayte. Et de viij d. de Joh*an*ne filio Steph*an*i Couche nat*ivo* d*omi*ni de annuali pensione p*ro* licencia h*ab*end*a* ad arte*m* fabri-cal*em* excercend*am* cu*m* Joh*an*ne Starlynge *et* cu*m* eodem Joh*an*ne Star-lynge inf*ra* do*minicum* d*omi*ni de Craule moratur more app*re*ntic*ii* a festo s*anc*ti Mich*ae*lis arch*angel*i anno xxvij° Reg*is* Henr*ici* sexti vsq*ue* ad fine*m* t*ermi*ni xij annor*um* extunc p*roximo* seq*uen*t*ium* plenar*ie* complend*i* p*er* pleg*ium* eiusdem Joh*an*nis Starlynge. Et de viij d. de Rob*er*to Dauy nat*ivo* d*omi*ni de ann*uali* recogn*itione* vt possit morar*i* ex*tra* do*minicum* d*omi*ni vi*delicet* apud Sp*ar*sholte q*uam*diu d*omi*no placu*er*it *et* venire ad turnu*m* de Hock*e* p*er* a*nnum* *et* maner*e* nat*ivus* d*omi*ni de Craule vt prius p*er* pleg*ium* Joh*an*nis Starlynge Smyth*e*. S*umma* iij s. iiij d.

Ciminu*m*. Et de j l*ibra* Cimini de redd*itu* Mich*aeli*s Skyllynge p*ro* j crofto voc*ato* le howe nup*er* Joh*an*nis Esteneye. Et lib*er*at*a* Thes*au*-*rario* de Woluesey sup*er* s*caccarium*. Et eq*ue*.

Exit*us* t*errarum et* ten*ementorum* in man*ibus* d*omi*ni exist*entium*. Et de xxij s. de exit*u* j virg*ate* t*erre* nat*ive et* xxij ac*rarum* t*erre* p*urpresture* que fuer*unt* Rob*er*ti Wodecote sic dimiss*arum* Mich*aelo* [sic] Skyllynge p*er* fine*m* p*er* ann*um*. S*umma* xxij s.

Vend*itio* Op*er*um. Et de iiij s. de Ric*ard*o Chidden' pro op*er*ib*us* j ferling*i* t*erre* nat*ive* nup*er* henr*ici* Wodecote sic sibi relax*atis* dum d*omi*no placu*er*it. Et de iiij s. de Rog*er*o Couche nat*ivo* d*omi*ni p*ro* op*er*ib*us* j ferling*i* t*erre* nat*ive* nup*er* Joh*an*nis Sely jun*ioris* prius Ade purs sic sibi relax*atis* dum d*omi*no placu*er*it. Et de iiij s. de Ric*ard*o Sely nat*ivo* d*omi*ni p*ro* op*er*ib*us* j ferling*i* t*erre* nat*ive* q*uo*nd*a*m Rob*er*ti Sely voc*ati* Bodyeslond sic sibi relax*atis* dum d*omi*no placu*er*it. Et de iiij s. de Joh*an*ne Gybbes al*ias* Joh*an*ne Rog*er*e nat*ivo* d*omi*ni p*ro* op*er*i-b*us* j ferling*i* t*erre* nat*ive* nup*er* Joh*an*nis Sely sen*ioris* voc*ati* Vaynes sic sibi relax*atis* du*m* d*omi*no placu*er*it. Et de iiij s. de Joh*an*ne Whete-lond p*ro* op*er*ib*us* j ferling*i* t*erre* nat*ive* nup*er* Joh*an*nis lange sic sibi relax*atis*. Et de iiij s. de Ric*ard*o Palm*er*e p*ro* op*er*ib*us* j ferling*i* t*erre* nat*ive* nup*er* Will*elm*i Sewale prius Joh*an*nis Belle sic sibi relax*atis* du*m* d*omi*no placu*er*it. Et de iiij s. de Joh*an*ne Sely filio Will*elm*i Sely nat*ivi* d*omi*ni p*ro* op*er*ib*us* j ferling*i* t*erre* nat*ive* nup*er* Thome Corbet' prius Joh*an*nis Belle voc*ati* Symond' sic sibi relax*atis* dum d*omi*no placu*er*it. Et de iiij s. de Rob*er*to Wayte nat*ivo* d*omi*ni p*ro* op*er*ib*us* j ferl*ingi* t*erre* nat*ive* nup*er* Thome Aleyne prius Will*elm*i Hodeman' sic sibi re-lax*atis* dum d*omi*no placu*er*it. Et de iiij s. de Thoma Dauy nat*ivo* d*omi*ni p*ro* op*er*ib*us* j ferling*i* t*erre* t*erre* [sic] nat*ive* q*uo*nd*a*m Rog*er*i lyght sic sibi relax*atis* dum d*omi*no placu*er*it. Et de x s. de op*er*ib*us* iij ferling*orum* t*erre* nat*ive* vi*delicet* Will*elm*i hodeman' Rog*er*i Gybbes *et* Will*elm*i Fernehull*e* sic eisde*m* relax*atis* causa inopie eor*und*em pro qual*ibe*t iij s. iiij d. S*umma* xlvj s.

Exit*us* man*er*ii. Et de x s. iiij d. de pannag*io* porcor*um* custum*ario*-*rum* ad festum *sanct*i Martini. Et de xvj s. de pannag*io* vaccar*um et* bouic*ulorum* ad t*ur*num de hock*e* sic dimiss*o* hoc anno. Et de xvij s. vj d. de iij acr*is* di*midia* subbosc*i* in Northewode hoc anno vend*itis* p*recium* acr*e* v s. D*e* scrugg*is* ib*idem* nich*il* hoc anno vend*itis*. D*e* pas-tur*a* in Drakenorth*e* nich*il* hic q*uia* p*er*tin*et* firmar*io*. Et de v s. de pas-tur*a* in Trendle *et* holyngdane sic tenent*ibus* hoc anno vend*ita*. D*e* porc*is* agist*atis* in stepu*l*is d*omi*ni nich*il* q*uia* p*er*tin*ent* firmar*io*. D*e* pastur*a* fossat*i* circa Curia*m* nich*il* p*ro* sim*i*li *et* p*ro* multon*ibus* d*omi*ni in estate. D*e* pastur*a* in lokfurlange *et* makfurlange nich*il* p*ro* sim*i*li. D*e* pastur*a* in Bash*a*mle nich*il* p*ro* si*mi*li. Et de iij s. iiij d. de pastur*a* in Sherte sic vend*ita* homagi*o* hoc anno. D*e* pastur*a* voc*ata* Bewes circa b*a*rton*am* bercar*ie* n*ichil* p*ro* si*mi*li *et* p*ro* bid*entibus* d*omi*ni. D*e* pastur*a* in Pytteshille nich*il* q*uia* p*ro* bident*ibus* om*nin*o. Et de ix d. de diu*er*sis tenent*ibus* p*ro* bid*entibus* in fald*a* custum*ariorum* exced*entibus* cert*um* num*erum* xxv hoc anno. D*e* auc*is* neq*ue* de capon*ibus* nich*il* hic q*uia* p*er*tin*ent* firmar*io*. Et de xv s. vj d. de iiij[xx] xiij gallis *et* gall*in*is de churs*etto* in foro vt ex*tra* vend*itis*. D*e* x d. de cc ouis galli*narum* nich*il* hic q*uia* p*er*tin*ent* firmar*io*. Et de ij d. de Corr*io* j equi de ex*tra*hur*a* de mori*na* vt ex*tra* vend*ito*. Et de xxiiij s. j d. de pellib*us* lanut*is* xlvj multon*um* iiij hurt*ardorum* xlvj m*a*tric*ium* *et* c xxij hog*astrorum* de mori*na* vt ex*tra* ante tons*ionem* vend*itis* p*recium* pell*is* multon*is* ij d. hurt*ardi* *et* m*a*tric*is* j d. ob. et hog*ast*ri j d. Et de iiij s. iiij d. de pellib*us* nud*is* xxxj multon*um* j hurt*ardi* *et* xx m*a*tric*ium* de mori*na* post tons*ionem* vt ex*tra* p*recium* pell*is* j d. Et de iij s. ix d. de pellib*us* cc lxxj agnor*um* de mori*na* ante tons*ionem* vt ex*tra* vend*itis* in gross*o*. Et de j d. ob. de pellectul*is* xviij agnor*um* de mori*na* post tons*ionem* vt ex*tra* vend*itis* in gross*o*. Et de ij s. j d. de ij cl*avis* di*midio* lane fract*e* de Collect*ione* b*er*car*ie* ad tons*ionem* vend*itis* vt ex*tra*. Et de vj d. de iiij l*ibris* lane agnor*um* vt ex*tra* hoc anno vend*itis* p*recium* l*ibre* j d. ob. D*e* lactag*io* ouiu*m* m*a*tric*ium* nich*il* q*uia* non lactabant*ur* hoc anno. Et de iij s. iiij d. de firma Cunic*u*lor*um* in Northewode p*er* ann*um*. Et de vj li. xiij s. iiij d. de firma Man*er*ii *et* om*nium* t*errarum* d*omi*nical*ium* p*ra*-t*orum* *et* pastur*arum* ad husbondriam p*er*tin*entium* sic dimiss*orum* Wil*lel*mo Sely ad t*er*m*in*um octo annor*um* hoc anno p*ri*mo. S*umma* xj li. j d. ob.

Vend*itio* blad*i*. Et de lx s. de xij q*uart*er*iis* fr*umen*ti hospic*io* d*omi*ni hoc anno vend*itis* p*recium* q*uar*t*er*ii v s. Et de lxj s. vj d. ob. q. de xij q*uart*er*iis* ij b*ussellis* j p*ecco* *et* di*midio* fr*umen*ti in foro vt ex*tra* vend*itis* p*recium* q*uart*er*ii* v s. Et de vij li. xvij s. j d. ob. de lij q*uart*er*iis* iij b*ussellis* ordei in foro vt ex*tra* vend*itis* p*recium* q*uart*er*ii* iij s. Et de xxxvj s. xj d. ob. de xxj q*uart*er*iis* v b*ussellis* auenar*um* in foro vt ex*tra* vend*itis* p*recium* q*uart*er*ii* xx d. S*umma* xv li. xiiij s. viij d. ob. q.

Vend*itio* stauri. Et de xij d. de j vit*u*lo de ex*tra*hur*a* vt ex*tra* vend*ito*. Et de xliij s. iiij d. de xl multon*ibus* kebb*atis* ante tons*ionem* in foro vt ex*tra* vend*itis* p*recium* ca*pitis* xiij d. Et de xxiiij s. de xxxij m*a*tric*ibus* kebb*atis* post tons*ionem* vt ex*tra* vend*itis* p*recium* ca*pitis* ix d. Et de xxix s. ix d. de xlij hog*astris* de peiorib*us* ex*tractis* fe*cundis*[1] post tons*ionem* in foro vt ex*tra* vend*itis* p*recium* ca*pitis* viij d. ob. D*e* xx s. de exit*u* j suis nich*il* hic q*uia* p*er*tin*et* firmar*io*. S*umma* iiij li. xviij s. j d.

[1] Compare; Hurt*ardi*. . . . In vend*itis* vt infra q*uia* lana gross*a* ext*ractis* post tons*ionem* q*uia* invtil*ibus* p*ro* stauro iiij. MS., P. R. O., Ecclesiastical Commission, Various, 159443, memb. 22.

Fines *et* marit*agia*. Et de xiij s. iiij d. de Tuht*ingpenny* ad Turnu*m* s*ancti* martini *et* hock*e*. Et de vj s. de Rob*er*to filio Rob*er*ti Wayte nat*ivo* d*omi*ni p*ro* j mes*suagio* di*midie* virgat*e* t*erre* nat*ive* in Craule in p*ar*te australi ex reddic*ione* Rob*er*ti Dauy nat*ivi* d*omi*ni h*ab*end*o*. Et de ij s. de Rob*er*to Dauy nat*ivo* d*omi*ni p*ro* licenc*ia* h*ab*end*a* trahend*i* moram ex*tra* d*ominicum* d*omi*ni ap*ud* Sp*ar*sholte *et* venire ad turnum de hock*e* vt prius. S*umma* xxj s. iiij d.

P*er*quis*ita* Cur*ie*. Et de iij s. v d. de p*er*quis*itis* turni s*anc*ti Martini. Et de v s. ij d. de p*er*quis*itis* turni de hock*e*. Et de vj s. de p*er*quis*itis* Cur*ie* tent*e* p*er* balliu*um* int*er* d*ic*tos ij turnos. Et de iij s. viij d. de p*er*-quis*itis* Cur*ie* tent*e* p*er* balliu*um* post d*ictu*m turnu*m* de hock*e*. S*umma* xviij s. iij d.

Vend*itio* sup*er* Comp*otu*m. Et de viij li. xiij s. vij d. q. de diu*ersis* reb*us* sup*er* comp*otu*m vt ex*tra* vend*itis*. S*umma* viij li. xiij s. vij d. ob. [sic] S*umma* t*otalis* Rece*ptarum* cum arr*eragiis* lxvij li. vij s. iiij d. ob.

D*e* Custub*us* Caruc*arum* nich*il* hic q*uia* p*er*tin*ent* firmar*io*.

Empc*io* blad*i et* stauri. In cc xl agnis post tons*ionem* in foro vt ex*tra* empt*is* p*recium* ca*pitis* x d. x li. S*umma* x li.

Cust*us* Bercar*ie*. In stipend*iis* iij Carpent*ariorum* de nou*o* grundsil-land*orum* b*er*cariam orienta*lem* p*ro* maiori p*ar*te p*er* x dies quol*ibe*t ca*piente* p*er* diem v d. xij s. vj d. In stipend*io* j Carpent*arii* de nou*o* cum m*erem*i*o* d*omi*ni grundsill*antis* residuu*m* eiusdem b*er*car*ie* orien-*talis* ad t*asc*ham cum balli*vo* faci*entis* necnon afforc*iantis et* emend*entis* lez Rakk*es* in eadem b*er*car*ia* v s. j d. In d*ic*t*o* m*erem*i*o* ad idem *et* virg*is* p*ro* p*ar*iett*ibus* p*ro*str*andis et* in carect*is* car*iandis* ij s. x d. In d*ic*t*o* m*erem*i*o* in Carect*is* de North*e*wode vsq*ue* b*er*car*iam* p*er* v dies cari-*ando* dand*o* p*ro* carect*a* p*er* diem xvj d. vj s. viij d. In solut*is* p*ro* sti-pend*io* vnius Cementar*ii* de nou*o* pynnant*is* d*ic*tam b*er*caria*m* vndiq*ue* in circuitu ad t*asc*ham cum balli*vo* fact*am* iij s. v d. In luto ad idem fodiend*o et* lucrand*o* viij d. In clau*is* p*ro* lez Rakk*es* affirm*andis* empt*is* ij d. In solut*is* p*ro* j Carect*ario* conduct*ore* p*ro* cilicib*us et* aqua p*ro* le pynnynge domus car*iandis* p*er* ij dies ca*piente* p*er* diem xiiij d. ij s. iiij d. In solut*is* p*ro* stipend*io* j hom*in*is brudant*is* d*ic*t*am* dom*um* in circuitu p*er* vj dies ca*pientis* p*er* diem iiij d. ij s. In solut*is* p*ro* stipend*io* j carect*arii* p*er* ij dies *et* di*midium* p*ro* d*ic*t*is* virg*is* ad idem de North*e*wode car*iandis* ca*pientis* p*er* diem xij d. ij s. vj d. In ij Carect*atis* pisar*um* p*ro* m*at*ric*ibus* hoc anno empt*is* dand*o* p*ro* carec-*tata* ij s. iiij s. In xx p*er*tic*is* haye apud b*er*caria*m* int*er* Croft*am* mul-ton*um et* le brodecrofte hoc anno claud*endis* p*ro* p*er*tic*am* ob. x d. S*umma* xliij s.

Custus Domor*um*. In solut*is* p*ro* stipend*io* vnius tegulatoris tegent*is* cu*m* tegul*is* sup*er* austral*em* p*ar*tem aule total*iter* discoop*er*t*e* p*er* xvj dies ca*pientis* p*er* diem v d. vj s. viij d. In mcc teg*u*lis plan*is* ad idem empt*is* p*recium* M*ille* vj s. viij d. viij s. In solut*is* p*ro* eisd*em* tegul*is* de Muchelmersshe vsq*ue* Maneriu*m* car*iandis* qui distant int*er* se p*ro* vij milliar*ia* ij s. In DC latth*is* ad id*em* empt*is* p*recium* c*entene* vj d. iij s. In iij M latthnayllis ad id*em* empt*is* p*recium* M*ille* xiiij d. iij s. vj d. In MD tylepynnes ad id*em* empt*is* p*recium* M*ille* ij d. iij d. In ij Ouesbordes [1] ad id*em* empt*is* iiij d. In Euesbordn*ayllis* ad idem empt*is* j d. ob. In iiij q*uarteriis* calc*is* vst*ulate* ad idem empt*is* p*recium* q*uarterii* vj d. ij s. In x b*ussellis* zabuli ad idem empt*is* x d. In stipend*io* vnius cementar*ii* conduct*oris* p*ro* bouaria *et* stab*u*lis subt*er* lez grundsill*es* scrutant*is* *et* pynnant*is* p*er* vij dies ca*pientis* p*er* diem v d. ij s. xj d. In viij carect*atis* Cilic*um* ad idem collig*endis* *et* car*iandis* dand*o* p*ro* Carect*ata* ij d. xvj d. In v carect*atis* luti ad id*em* fodiend*is* *et* Car*iandis* x d. In iiij b*ussellis* zabuli ad idem empt*is* iiij d. In ij quarent*enis* *et* x p*er*tic*is* haie circa copic*ium* in North*e*wode hoc anno claud*endis* dand*o* p*ro* quarent*ena* xx d. iij s. ix d. S*umma* xxxv s. x d. ob. *et cetera*.

Trit*uratio* *et* Ventul*atio*. In xxxix q*uarteriis* iij b*ussellis* iij p*eccis* fru*menti* j q*uarterio* vij b*ussellis* Curalli iij q*uarteriis* pisar*um* *et* iiij q*uarteriis* vescar*um* triturand*is* ad t*as*cham dand*o* p*ro* q*uarterio* iij d. xij s. j d. In lxxvj q*uarteriis* iij b*ussellis* ordei trit*urandis* ad t*asc*ham dand*o* p*ro* q*uarterio* ij d. xij s. viij d. ob. q. In xxxviij q*uarteriis* v b*ussellis* auenar*um* trit*urandis* ad t*asc*ham dand*o* p*ro* q*uarterio* j d. ob. iiij s. x d. In toto bl*ado* p*re*dic*to* ventul*ando* ad t*asc*ham cuius Summ*a* cont*inet* C lxiij q*uarteria* ij b*ussellos* iij p*ecca* dand*o* p*ro* sing*u*lis iij q*uarteriis* j d. iiij s. vj d. ob. S*umma* xxxiiij s. ij d. q. De Cust*ubus* (?) autumpn*alibus* nich*il* hic q*uia* p*er*tin*ent* firmar*io*.

Expens*e* sen*escalli* t*errarum* *et* sup*er*uisoris. In expens*is* Ric*ard*i Waller armig*eri* sen*escalli* t*errarum* d*omi*ni *et* Magi*st*ri Ric*ard*i Eweyn sup*er*uis*oris* tenenc*ium* Turnos s*anc*ti Martini *et* hock*e* p*er* ij bill*as* sigillat*as* xiij s. x d. S*umma* xiij s. x d.

Feod*um* balliui. In feod*o* Ric*ard*i Newport armig*er*i ball*iv*i ib*ide*m p*er* j ann*um* integru*m* ca*pientis* sec*und*um Rata*m* x m*arcarum* p*er* an*num* xxvj s. viij d. Residuu*m* capit in aliis man*er*iis. Et in feod*o* eiusd*em* ball*iv*i anno p*re*ced*enti* no*n* alloc*antur* xxvj s. viij d. S*umma* liij s. iiij d.

Expens*e* for*insece* null*um*. S*umma* Om*nium* expens*arum* xix li. ij d. ob. q. Et debet xlviij li. vij s. j d. ob. q.

Alloc*atio* sine bre*vi*. Inde alloc*antur* eid*em* de diu*er*sis sup*er*on*eribus* *et* dis*allocationibus* tam interius q*uam* exterius in hoc p*re*senti comput*o* sibi fact*is* lj s. j d. ob. q. S*umma* lj s. j d. ob. q.

Alloc*atio* p*er* breve. Et in denar*iis* lib*er*atis Will*elm*o Porte Thes*aurario* de Woluesey ad manus M*agis*tri Thome Walkyngton' Thes*aurarii*

[1] For eavesboards.

hospic*ii* d*omi*ni vt in p*re*c*io* xij q*uarteriorum* fr*umen*t*i* p*re*c*ium* q*uar*-t*erii* [v s.] [1] eid*em* hospic*ii* lib*er*at*orum* p*ro*ut pat*et* p*er* euidenc*iam* eiusd*em* hospic*ii* sup*er* hunc comp*otu*m ostens*am* *et* exa*mi*nat*am* lx s. S*umma* lx s.

Lib*er*ac*io* Denar*iorum*. Et in denariis lib*er*at*is* Will*el*mo Porte Thes*aurario* de Wolues*eia* p*er* manus Will*elm*i Sely nup*er* p*re*pos*iti* de arre*ragiis* vij li. vj s. viij d. Et eid*em* Thes*aurario* p*er* manus eiusd*em* Will*elm*i g*ra*ngiat*oris* ib*id*em hoc anno de exit*ibus* liij s. iiij d. Et eid*em* Thes*aurario* p*er* manus eiusd*em* Will*elm*i Sely firmar*ii* ib*id*em hoc anno de exit*ibus* vj li. xiij s. iiij d. Et eid*em* Thes*aurario* p*er* manus Joh*an*nis Dauy Collect*oris* redd*itus* ib*id*em h*oc* a*nno*. D*e* nouis exit*ibus* huius anni xv li. vj s. viij d. S*umma* xxxij li. S*umma* alloc*ationum* Solut*ionum* *et* lib*er*at*ionum* xxxvij li. xj s. j d. ob. q. Et debet adhuc x li. xvj s. Vnde sup*er* Will*elmu*m Sely nup*er* p*re*pos*itu*m ib*id*em de arr*eragiis* anni p*re*ced*entis* nich*il*. Sup*er* eund*em* Will*elmu*m Sely g*ra*ngiat*orem* ib*id*em hoc anno de exit*ibus* huius anni ix li. Sup*er* eund*em* Will*elmu*m Sely firma*rium* ib*id*em hoc anno de exit*ibus* huius anni nich*il*. Et sup*er* Joh*an*nem Dauy Coll*ectorem* redd*itus* ib*id*em hoc anno de exit*ibus* hui*us* anni xxxvj s.

Frumentu*m*. Will*el*m*u*s Sely firmar*ius* *et* g*ra*ngiat*or* ib*id*em respond*et* de xxxix q*uarteriis* iij b*ussellis* iij p*eccis* fr*umen*t*i* de toto exit*u* g*ra*n-giat*oris* mens*ura* ras*a* trit*uratis* ad t*as*cham. Et on*era*t*ur* de xviij q*uar*-t*eriis* v b*ussellis* vt r*espondet* se*paratim* iiij[to].[2] S*umma* lviij q*uarteria* j b*ussellus*. D*e* quib*us* in semi*n*e sup*er* lx acr*as* t*erre* p*er* p*er*tic*am* in Shepehousfeld*e* alias Estfeld*e* xv q*uarteria* sup*er* acr*am* ij b*usselli*. In pane furni*a*t*o* p*ro* expens*is* Ric*ard*i Waller armig*er*i sen*escalli* *et* Magistri Ric*ard*i Eweyn' sup*er*uis*oris* t*errarum* d*omi*ni tenent*ium* turnos s*an*c*t*i Martini *et* hock*e* p*er* ij bill*as* sigill*atas* j b*ussellus* j p*eccum* *et* d*imidium*. In vendic*is* hospic*io* d*omi*ni xij q*uarteria*. In vend*itis* in foro vt infra xij q*uarteria* ij b*usselli* p*eccum* *et* d*imidium*. Et sup*er* comp*otu*m xviij q*uarteria* v b*usselli* p*ro* iiij li. x d. q. S*umma* que sup*ra*. Et eq*ue*.

Curallum. Et de j q*uarterio* viij [sic] b*ussellis* Curalli de exit*u* dic*t*i fr*umen*t*i* trit*uratis* ad t*as*cham. Et vend*untur* vt infra. Et nich*il* rem*anet*

Ordeum. Et de lxxvj q*uarteriis* iij b*ussellis* ordei de toto exit*u* g*ra*n-*gie* mens*ura* ras*a* trit*uratis* ad t*as*ch*am*. Et on*era*t*ur* de xix q*uarteriis* v b*ussellis* vt r*espondet* se*paratim* iiij[to]. S*umma* iiij^{xx} xvj q*uarteria*. D*e* q*u*ib*us* in se*mi*n*e* sup*er* xlviij acr*as* t*erre* p*er* p*er*tic*am* in Greneweyesfeld*e*

[1] Left blank, obviously v s.

[2] Apparently the full expression is Et oneratur de xviij quarteriis v bussellis super compotum ut respondet separatim iiij[to]. See above, § 6, p. 15.

xxiiij q*uarteria* sup*er* acr*am* iiij b*usselli*. D*e* lib*eracione* famulor*um* nich*il* q*uia* p*er* firmar*ium*. In vendic*is* in foro vt infra lij q*uarteria* iij b*usselli*. Et sup*er* comp*otu*m xix q*uarteria* v b*usselli* p*ro* lviij s. ix d. ob. S*umma* que sup*ra*. Et eq*ue*.

Pise. Et de iij q*uarteriis* pisar*um* de exit*u* g*rangie* mens*ura* ras*a* trit*uratis* ad t*asc*h*am*. Et de vj q*uarteriis* de eodem exit*u* p*er* estimac*ionem* in siliq*uis*. S*umma* ix q*uarteria*. D*e* quib*us* in se*min*e sup*er* xij acr*as* t*erre* p*er* p*er*tic*am* in Bastnorthbury iij q*uarteria* sup*er* acr*am* ij b*usselli*. In sustent*atione* ouiu*m* m*at*ric*ium* temp*or*e agnell*ationis* p*er* estim*ationem* in siliquis vj q*uarteria*. S*umma* que sup*ra*. Et eq*ue*.

Vesce. Et de iiij q*uarteriis* vescar*um* de exit*u* g*rangie* mens*ura* ras*a* trit*uratis* ad t*asc*h*am*. Et de viij q*uarteriis* de eodem exit*u* p*er* estim*ationem* in siliq*uis*. S*umma* xij q*uarteria*. D*e* quib*us* in se*min*e sup*er* xvj acr*as* t*erre* p*er* p*er*tic*am* in Bastnorthbury iiij q*uarteria* sup*er* acr*am* ij b*usselli*. In sustent*atione* bident*ium* equor*um* *et* auer*orum* d*om*ini in yem*e* p*er* estim*ationem* in siliq*uis* viij q*uarteria*. S*umma* que sup*ra*. Et eq*ue*.

Auene. Et de xxxviij q*uarteriis* v b*ussellis* auen*arum* de exit*u* g*ran*g*ie* mens*ura* ras*a* trit*uratis* ad t*asc*h*am*. Et de v q*uarteriis* de eodem exit*u* p*er* estimac*ionem* in garb*is*. Et on*era*t*ur* de xx q*uarteriis* iij b*ussellis* vt r*espondet* s*eparatim* iiij*to*. S*umma* lxiiij q*uarteria*. D*e* quib*us* in se*min*e sup*er* xxxij acr*as* t*erre* p*er* p*er*tic*am* in haselfurlange xvj q*uar*t*eria* sup*er* acr*am* iiij b*usselli*. In p*re*bend*a* m*at*ric*ium* temp*or*e yemal*i* p*er* estim*ationem* in garb*is* v q*uarteria*. D*e* p*re*bend*a* bou*um* equor*um* *et* affror*um* in yem*e* nich*il* hic q*uia* p*er* firmar*ium*. In p*re*bend*a* Ric*ard*i Waller senesc*alli* *et* mag*ist*ri Ric*ard*i Eweyn' sup*er*uisor*is* t*errarum* d*om*ini tenenc*ium* turn*os* s*anc*ti Martini *et* hock*e* p*er* ij bill*as* sigillat*as* j q*uarterium*. In vend*itis* in foro xxj q*uarteria* v b*usselli*. Et sup*er* comp*otu*m xx q*uarteria* iii b*usselli* p*ro* xxxiij s. xj d. ob. S*umma* que sup*ra*. Et eq*ue*.

Lib*eratio* famulor*um* null*um* q*uia* p*er* firmar*ium*.

S*umma* acrar*um* hoc anno semi*n*atar*um* c lxviij acr*e*.

Equi. Et de iij equis de rem*anentibus*. Et de j de ex*tra*hur*a* sup*er*ann*ato*. S*umma* iiij. D*e* quib*us* in morin*a* de ex*tra*hur*a* j. Et rem*anent* iij equi p*recium* ca*pitis* xiij s. iiij d. in man*ibus* d*ic*ti firmar*ii* ad relib*erandum* in fine t*er*m*in*i sui vel p*recium* eoru*n*dem ad voluntat*em* d*om*ini.

Affri. Et de iiij affr*is* de rem*anentibus*. S*umma* iiij. Et rem*anent* iiij affr*i* p*recium* ca*pitis* vj s. viij d. in man*ibus* d*ic*ti firmar*ii* ad relib*eran*d*um* vt sup*ra*.

Boues. Et de xvij bob*us* de rem*anentibus*. S*umma* xvij. Et rem*anent* xvij boues p*recium* ca*pitis* xj s. in man*ibus* d*ic*ti firmar*ii* ad r*eliberan*d*um* vt sup*ra*.

D*e* Tauris vaccis bouett*is* Bouic*ulis et* Annal*ibus* null*um*.

Vit*u*li. Et de j vit*u*lo p*r*ouen*to* de ex*tra*hur*a* sup*er*ann*ato*. Et vend*itur* vt infra. Et nich*il* rem*anet*.

Multones. Et de D vj multon*ibus* de rem*anentibus*. Et de iiij^{xx} x de hogastr*is* inferius adiunct*is* post tons*ionem*. S*umma* D iiij^{xx} xvj. D*e* quib*us* in morin*a* ante tons*ionem* in verolle *et* rub*io* morbo xlvj vnde iiij kebb*ati*. In adiunct*is* cu*m* m*a*tric*ibus* inferius q*uia* fe*cundis* eunt*ibus* in num*ero* multon*um* post tons*ionem* ix. In morin*a* post tons*ionem* in veroll*e* xxxj vn*de* ij kebb*ati*. In vend*itis* in foro vt inf*ra* ante tons*ionem* xl kebb*ati*. S*umma* C xxvj. Et rem*anent* CCCC lxx multon*es* p*ro* stauro.

Hurt*ardi*. Et de xij hurt*ardis* de rem*anentibus*. Et de iij de hog*astris* inferius adiunct*is* post tons*ionem*. S*umma* xv. D*e* quib*us* in morin*a* ante tons*ionem* iiij. In morin*a* post tons*ionem* j kebb*atus*. S*umma* v. Et rem*anent* x hurt*ardi* p*ro* stauro.

M*a*trices. Et de CCC iiij^{xx} xiij m*a*tric*ibus* de rem*anentibus*. Et de ix recept*is* de fald*a* multon*um* sup*ra* post tons*ionem* eunt*ibus* ib*ide*m in num*ero* multon*um*. Et de xlvij de hog*ast*ris inferius adiunct*is* post tons*ionem*. S*umma* CCCC xlix. D*e* quib*us* in morin*a* in veroll*e et* in rubio morbo ante tons*ionem* xlvj vnde v keb*bati et* vn*de* ante agnella*cionem* xvj. In morin*a* post tons*ionem* xx vn*de* x kebb*ati*. In vend*itis* in foro vt inf*ra* post tons*ionem* xxxij. S*umma* iiij^{xx} xviij. Et rem*anent* CCC lj m*a*trice*s* p*ro* stauro.

Hog*ast*ri. Et de CCC iiij hog*astris* de rem*anentibus* agnor*um*. S*umma* CCC iiij. D*e* quib*us* in morin*a* in veroll*e et* rubio morbo ante tons*ionem* C xxij. In adiunct*is* sup*ra* cum multon*ibus* iiij^{xx} x cum hurt*ardis* iij cu*m* m*a*tric*ibus* xlvij. In vend*itis* in foro vt infra de peiorib*us* ex*tra*ct*is* fe*cundis* post tons*ionem* xlij. S*umma* que sup*ra*. Et eq*ue*.

Agni. Et de CCC xxxij agnis de exit*u* d*ictarum* ouiu*m* m*a*tric*ium et* non de plur*ibus* q*uia* xvj m*a*trice*s* morieb*antur* ante agnella*cionem* ix m*a*trice*s* rec*epte* de fald*a* multon*um* adiung*ebantur* post temp*us* agnella*cionis* xlvij hog*ast*ri adiung*ebantur* post temp*us* agnell*ationis* xxj p*r*oiecer*unt* agn*os* suos abortiuos *et* xxiiij fuer*unt* sterile*s* hoc anno. Et de CC xl agn*is* in foro vt ex*tra* hoc anno post tons*ionem* empt*is*. S*umma* D lxxij. D*e* quib*us* In morin*a* ante sep*ara*cio*nem et* tons*ionem* CC lxxj. In decima vj *et* non de plur*ibus* q*uia* CC xl de empc*is* non decimant*ur* hic. In Cons*uetudine* p*re*pos*iti* fabri b*er*car*ii* multon*um et* b*er*car*ii* ouiu*m* m*a*tric*ium* iiij. In morin*a* post tons*ionem et* post sep*ara*cio*nem* xviij. S*umma* CC iiij^{xx} xix. Et rem*anent* CC lxxiij agni triati p*ro* stauro.

Veller*a*. Et de veller*ibus* CCCC xx multon*um* viij hurt*ardorum* CCC xlvij m*a*tric*ium et* C iiij^{xx} ij hog*astrorum* p*r*ouen*torum* ad tons*ionem* hoc anno. S*umma* DCCCC lvij. D*e* quib*us* In decim*a* iiij^{xx} xvj vellera In lib*er*at*is* Thes*aurario* de Woluesey DCCC lxj vell*era* pond*erantia* ij saccos xxxvj cl*avos*. S*umma* que sup*ra*. Et eq*ue*.

Lana fract*a*. Et de ij cl*avis* di*midio* lane fract*e* de collect*io*ne b*er*car*ie* ad tons*ionem* hoc anno. Et vend*untur* vt infra. Et nich*il* rem*anet*.

Corr*eum*. Et de Corr*eo* vnius equi de ex*tra*hur*a* de mori*n*a vt sup*ra*. Et vend*itur* vt inf*ra*. Et nich*il* rem*anet*.

Pelles lanut*e*. Et de pell*ibus* lanut*is* xlvj multon*um* iiij hurt*ardorum* xlvj m*a*tric*ium et* c xxij hog*astrorum* de mori*n*a vt sup*ra* ante tons*ionem*. Et vend*untur* vt infra. Et nich*il* rem*anet*.

Pelles nud*e*. Et de pellib*us* nud*is* xxxj multon*um* j hurt*ardi et* xx m*a*tric*ium* de mori*n*a vt sup*ra* post tons*ionem*. Et vend*untur* inf*ra*. Et nich*il* rem*anet*.

Pell*es* agnor*um*. Et de pellib*us* cc lxxj agnor*um* de mori*n*a vt sup*ra* post tons*ionem*. Et vend*untur* vt inf*ra*. Et nich*il* rem*anet*.

Pellectul*e*. Et de pellectul*is* xviij agnor*um* de mori*n*a vt sup*ra* post tons*ionem*. Et vend*untur* vt infra. Et nich*il* rem*anet*.

D*e* Apris null*um* de rem*anentibus*.

Sues. Et de j sue de rem*anente*. S*umma* j. Et rem*anet* j sus p*recium* iiij s. in man*ibus* d*icti* firmar*ii* ad relib*er*and*um* in fine t*er*m*in*i sui.

De porc*is et* hoggett*is* null*um*.

De porcell*is* de exit*u* d*ict*e suis nich*il* hic q*uia* p*er*tin*ent* firmar*io*.

Auce. Et de j anc*er*e *et* iiij auc*is* mariol*es* de rem*anentibus*. S*umma* v. Et rem*anent* j anc*er et* iiij^{or} auce mariol*e* p*recium* ca*pitis* iiij d. ad relib*er*and*um* vt sup*ra*.

Capones. Et de xxiiij capon*ibus* de rem*anentibus*. S*umma* xxiiij. Et rem*anent* xxiiij capon*es* p*recium* ca*pitis* iiij d. in man*ibus* d*icti* firmar*ii* ad relib*erandum* vt sup*ra*.

Galli *et* galline. Et de j gallo *et* v gall*in*is de rem*anentibus*. Et de c xxv de churs*etto* custum*ariorum* ad festu*m* s*anct*i Martini. S*umma* c xxxj D*e* quib*us* In def*ectu* t*er*r*e* le Straunge t*r*act*e* in d*ominicum* p*er* ann*um* iiij. In def*ectu* t*er*r*e* Will*elm*i de Curia p*ro* consi*m*ili iiij. In def*ectu* t*er*r*e* Rob*er*ti de Crouche p*ro* consi*m*ili iiij. In def*ectu* t*er*r*e* porcarii p*ro* consi*m*ili iiij. In def*ectu* t*er*r*e* Ric*ard*i vaccar*ii* iiij p*ro* consi*m*ili. In def*ectu* t*er*r*e* Ric*ard*i Knave p*ro* consi*m*ili iiij. In def*ectu* churs*etti* t*er*r*e* Thome Roger al*ias* Gibbes Rob*er*ti filii Rob*er*ti Wayte Thome Dauy Joh*ann*is filii Will*elm*i Sely quia viduar*ii et* vidue *et* non coniug*ati* viij cui*uslibe*t eor*um* ij. In vend*itis* in foro vt infra iiij^{xx} xiij. S*umma* c xxv. Et rem*anent* j gall*us et* v galli*n*e.

D*e* pulcinis de exit*u* galli*narum* p*redictarum* nich*il* quia p*er*tin*ent* firmar*io*.

D*e* ouis de exit*u* d*ictarum* galli*narum* n*ichil* p*ro* si*m*ili.

Vtens*ilia*. Et de iij Caruc*is* cu*m* iij p*aribus* ferram*entorum et* toto app*a*rat*u* ferr*i* p*ro* xvj bob*us* p*recium* in toto xx s. ij h*e*rciis cu*m* cauill*is* ferr*eis* p*recium* int*er* se ij s. vj d. iiij h*e*rciis ligni p*recium* int*er* se xviij d.

j se*m*ilion*e* p*recium* viij d. j b*ussello* j p*ecco* ferr*o* lig*atis* p*recium* inte*r* se xviij d. j ventil*abro* p*recium* xij d. ij sacc*is* p*recium* inte*r* se xiiij d. j sport*a* bl*a*difer*a* p*recium* xij d. j Carect*a* ferr*o* lig*ata* cum corp*ore* *et* scala p*recium* xvj s. viij d. j Cella Carect*a*ria p*recium* viij d. vj Coler*is* p*recium* inte*r* se iij s. iiij p*a*ribu*s* tractuu*m* p*recium* inte*r* se iij s. iiij d. j corda carett*a*ria p*recium* xx d. iij Capistr*is* Corr*ei* p*recium* inte*r* se xviij d. ij Capistr*is* canab*i* nulli*us* valoris. Et de j olla enea cont*inente* v lagen*as* p*recium* vj s. viij d. j posnet*o* nulli*us* valor*is* j patell*a* enea cont*inente* v lagen*as* nulli*us* valor*is* j patell*a* ene*a* cont*inente* xij lagen*as* p*recium* ij s. j lache nulli*us* valor*is* j vate p*ro* daire nulli*us* valor*is* j Cuba null*ius* valor*is* j tripod*e* ij formis p*ro* casiis j tribul*o* ferr*ato* j cenevector*io* *et* xij cracches non app*reciatis* q*uia* null*ius* valor*is* j cribr*o* *et* j ridell*o* p*recium* inte*r* se v d. de rem*anentibus*. Et hec om*n*ia rem*anent* in Man*ibus* d*ic*t*i* firm*arii* ad relib*e*rand*um* in fine te*rmin*i sui vel p*re*-*cium* eor*un*dem *et cetera*.

Vtensilia fabri. Et de j magno anfeld*o* j Pykehorne ferr*at*' non ponder*atis* j p*a*ri de belowes *et* ij forehamers j handehamer ij p*a*ribu*s* tonges j p*a*ri pynsc*e*ris j Wasshe[r] j herthstaf' j botre *et* j Cawcer ferr*i* ponde-*rantibus* in toto in tot*o* [sic] inte*r* se xlvj l*ibras*. Et hec om*n*ia rem*anent*.

Op*e*ra Custum*aria*. Arur*a*. Et de arur*a* xxv acr*arum* te*rre* p*ro*ueni-*ente* de j Custum*ario* tenent*e* ij virg*atas* te*rre* xj virg*atariis* *et* xiij semiuir*gatariis* in Craule in p*ar*te Australi quor*um* quil*ib*et Caruca*m* h*ab*ens integra*m* arab*it* j acra*m* ad seme*ntem* yemale*m* vel *quadragesimalem* p*er*cipi*ente* de d*omi*no p*ro* arur*a* cuiusl*ib*et acr*e* j d. S*umma* xxv op*er*a. D*e* quibu*s* In acquiet*ancia* j p*re*posi*ti* tenent*is* j virg*atam* te*rre* in p*ar*te australi arur*a* de j acr*a*. In def*ectu* xv Custum*ariorum* qui non h*ab*ent Caruc*am* integr*am* hoc anno xiiij acr*e*. In te*rris* d*omi*ni arand*is* x acr*e* sic*ut* iac*ent* que fac*iunt* v acr*as* p*er* pertic*am*. S*umma* que sup*ra*. Et eq*ue*.

Herciatur*a*. Et de h*er*ciatur*a* iiij^{xx} x acr*arum* te*rre* p*er* pertic*am* p*ro*ueni*ente* de dict*o* Custum*ario* tenent*e* ij virg*atas* te*rre* qui h*er*ciab*it* viij acr*as* xj virg*atariis* *et* xiiij semiu*irgatariis* in Craule in p*ar*te austral*i* j semiu*irgatario* in Wodecote quorum quil*ib*et h*er*ciab*it* ij acr*as* iij Cotag*iis* in Craule in p*ar*te boriali quor*um* quil*ib*et h*er*ciab*it* iij acr*as* xvij ferling*is* te*rre* in Craule in p*ar*te borial*i* quor*um* quil*ib*et h*er*ciab*it* j acr*am* j virg*ata et* d*imidia* in Wodecote que h*er*ciab*unt* vj acr*as* sicut iac*ent* siue h*ab*uerint equ*um* siue non *et* eas se*min*abu*n*t *et* seme*n* in g*ra*ng*ia* d*omi*ni in p*ro*p*ri*is sacc*is* querent p*er*cipient*ibus* de d*omi*no x virgas Cornli p*ro* hernes*io* suo. S*umma* iiij^{xx} x acr*e*. D*e* acquiet*ancia* vnius p*re*pos*iti* tenent*is* j virg*atam* te*rre* herciatur*a* iiij acr*arum*. In acquiet*anciis* j fabri iij Carucar*iorum et* iiij b*er*car*iorum* quol*ib*et tenent*e* j ferling*um* terre herciatur*a* viij acr*arum*. In acquiet*ancia* j ferling*i* terre henr*ici* Wodecote j ferling*i* terre Joh*ann*is Sely j ferling*i* terre Roberti Sely j ferl*ingi* terre Will*elm*i Vayne j ferling*i* terre Joh*ann*is lange ij ferling*orum* terre Joh*ann*is Belle j ferling*i* terre Joh*ann*is hodeman' *et* j ferling*i* terre Joh*ann*is Mullewarde quor*um* opera vend*ebantur* infra in denar*iis* herciatur*a* ix acr*arum*. In terr*is* dominical*ibus* ad semen auenar*um* hoc anno herciand*um* lxix acre sicut iac*ent* que faci*unt* xxxiiij acr*as* *et* di*midiam* per perticam. Summa que supr*a*. Et eq*ue*.

Portac*io* falde. Et de lxxv oper*ibus* prouen*ientibus* de xxv Custumar*iis* in Craule in p*ar*te austral*i* quor*um* quil*ibet* portab*it* v clat*es* ad faldam dom*ini* de campo in Campu*m* quociens necc*esse* fuerit ad mouend*um*. Et esti*matur* qu*od* fieri poter*it* comm*unibus* annis per iij dies. Et si dom*inus* plura opera indige*at* plura operent*ur*. Summa lxxv opera. De quib*us* In acquiet*ancia* vnius prepos*iti* iij opera. In falda dom*ini* hoc anno de campo in Campu*m* portand*a* lxxij opera. Summa que supr*a*. Et eq*ue*.

Cariac*io* *et* implicac*io* fimor*um*. Et de c iiij^xx oper*ibus* cariac*ionis* *et* implic*acionis* fimor*um* prouen*ientibus* de xxv Custum*ariis* in p*ar*te australi de Craule iij Cotag*iis* in p*ar*te boriali *et* ij custum*ariis* in Wodecote quor*um* quil*ibet* inveniet j oper*arium* cum equis *et* carect*is* pro fimis in Carect*is* implend*is* *et* vsq*ue* in Campu*m* cariand*is* quousq*ue* total*iter* percariet*ur* pro quol*ibet* vj opera. Et esti*matur* qu*od* fieri poter*it* com*munibus* annis per vj dies. Et si dom*inus* plura opera indig*eat* plura faci*antur* etcetera. Et si tant*um* non indig*eat* pro paucior*ibus* sint quieti. Et de vj oper*ibus* implicac*ionis* prouen*ientibus* de j Custum*ario* qui inveniet j hom*inem* pro carect*a* cum fimis implend*a* per temp*us* predict*um*. Summa c iiij^xx vj opera. De quib*us* In acquiet*anciis* vnius prepos*iti* *et* j bercarie xij opera. In fimis in Carect*is* implend*is* *et* in campu*m* cariand*is* c lxxiiij opera. Summa que supr*a*. Et eq*ue*.

Falcac*io* Prat*i* de Woluesey. Et de l oper*ibus* falcac*ionis* sp*ar*gac*ionis* leu*acionis* mullion*es* cariac*ionis* *et* tass*acionis* feni prouen*ientibus* de xxv Custum*ariis* in Craule in p*ar*te australi *et* xxv Custum*ariis* in p*ar*te boriali qui in comm*uni* falcab*unt* sp*ar*gent leu*abunt* mullion*es* cari*abunt* *et* tass*abunt* fenum vj acr*arum* prati dom*ini* in Woluesey nich*il* pro eodem percipiend*o*. Summa l opera. De quib*us* In acquiet*anciis* vnius prepos*iti* j fabri iij Carucar*iorum* *et* iij bercar*iorum* viij opera. In feno predict*o* vj acr*arum* prati dom*ini* de Woluesey falc*ando* sp*ar*gendo leuando mullion*es* cari*ando* *et* tass*ando* xlij opera. Summa que supr*a*. Et eq*ue*.

Cariac*io* bosci. Et de xxiiij oper*ibus* cari*acionis* bosc*i* de reman*entibus*. Et de xxv oper*ibus* cariac*ionis* bosci prouen*ientibus* de xxv Custum*ariis* de Craule in p*ar*te australi quor*um* quil*ibet* cari*abit* j Carecta-

tam bosci vsq*ue* Woluesey cont*ra* festum Natal*is* d*omi*ni nich*il* p*ro* eodem p*er*cipiend*o*. S*umma* xlix op*era*. D*e* quib*us* In acquiet*ancia* j p*re*posi*ti* j opus In bosco vsq*ue* Woluesey car*iando* cont*ra* festum Natal*is* d*omi*ni. S*umma* j. Et rem*anent* xlviij op*era*.

Loc*io et* tons*io* bident*ium*. Et de c op*er*ib*us* loc*i*onis p*r*oueni*entibus* de l Custum*ariis* in Craule *et* Wodecote quor*um* quil*ibe*t inveniet j ope*rarium* p*ro* bident*ibus* d*omi*ni leuand*is*. Et estimat*ur* q*uo*d fieri pot*er*it co*mmun*ib*us* annis p*er* ij dies. Et si d*ominu*s plur*a* op*era* indig*eat* plur*a* fac*iantur* quousq*ue* total*ite*r p*er*ficit*ur*. Et de c iiij^{xx} xv op*eribus* ton*sionis* p*r*oueni*entibus* de p*r*edict*is* l Custum*ariis* quor*um* j inveniet p*er* diem iiij op*er*ar*ios* j p*er* diem iij op*er*ar*ios* x quil*ibe*t eor*um* p*er* diem ij op*er*ar*ios et* xxxviij quil*ibe*t eor*um* p*er* diem j op*er*ar*ium* p*ro* bident*ibus* d*omi*ni tond*endis*. Et esti*matur* q*uo*d fieri pot*er*it co*mmun*ibus annis p*er* iij dies. Et si d*ominus etcetera*. Et si tant*um etcetera*. Et de ij op*er*ib*us* Cons*ionis*[sic] p*r*oueni*entibus* de ij Custum*ariis* in Northe Craule quor*um* vt*er*q*ue* inveniet j op*er*ar*ium* p*er* j diem p*ro* bident*ibus* d*omi*ni tond*endis* vt sup*ra*. S*umma* cc iiij^{xx} xvij op*er*a. D*e* quib*us* In acquie*tancia* vnius p*re*posi*ti* viij op*era*. In acquiet*anciis* j fabri iij b*ercario*-*rum et* iij Carucar*iorum* xxxv op*er*a cuil*ibe*t v op*era*. In def*ectu* j vir*gate* j semiu*irgate* ac j Cotag*ii* in Wodecote quia in man*ibus* d*omi*ni xxxvij [sic] op*era* cuil*ibe*t ix op*era*. In bident*ibus* d*omi*ni lauand*is et* tond*endis* cc xxvij op*era*. S*umma* que sup*ra*. Et eq*ue*.

Precari*a* Autumpn*alia*. Et de cc lv op*er*ib*us* p*r*ecar*iis* p*r*oueni*en*-*tibus* de xlviij Custum*ariis* in Craule *et* Wodecote quor*um* j inveniet iiij op*er*ar*ios* ad iij p*r*ecari*a* p*er* iij dies j inueniet iij op*er*ar*ios* xxxij quil*ibe*t illor*um* ij op*er*ar*ios et* xiiij quil*ibe*t illor*um* j op*er*ar*ium* ad p*r*edict*a* iij p*r*ecari*a* in autumpno p*ro* bl*a*dis d*omi*ni metend*is* ligand*is et* adimand*is* ad cibum d*omi*ni. Et de iiij op*eribus* p*r*ecar*iis* p*r*oueni*entibus* de ij Cus*tumariis* quor*um* vt*er*q*ue* inveniet j op*er*ar*ium* ad ij p*r*ecari*a* ad cibu*m* d*omi*ni vt sup*ra*. Et de iij op*er*ib*us* p*r*ecar*iis* p*r*oueni*entibus* de iij Cus*tumariis* quor*um* quil*ibe*t inveniet j op*er*ar*ium* ad j p*r*ecar*ium* ad cibu*m* d*omi*ni vt sup*ra*. S*umma* cc lxij op*era*. D*e* quib*us* In acquiet*anciis* j p*r*eposi*ti* iij Caruc*ariorum et* iij b*er*car*iorum* xlij op*er*a cuil*ibe*t vj op*era*. D*e* acquiet*ancia* j Wodward*i* nich*il* q*uia* null*us* hoc anno. In acquie*tancia* j fabri iij op*era*. In acquiet*anciis* ix ferling*orum* t*er*r*e* quor*um* op*er*a vend*ita* vt sup*ra* liiij op*er*a cuil*ibe*t vj op*era*. In acquiet*anciis* j virgat*e* t*er*r*e et* j semiu*irgate* t*er*r*e* in Wodecote q*uia* in man*ibus* d*omi*ni xij op*era*. In def*ectu* j cotag*ii* in Wodecote quia in man*ibus* d*omi*ni ij op*era*. In acquiet*ancia* j ferling*i* t*er*r*e* nup*er* Joh*ann*is Sely quia in man*i*-*bus* d*omi*ni iij op*era*. In xl acr*is* fr*umen*t*i* metend*is* lig*a*nd*is et* adimand*is* c xlvj op*era*. S*umma* que sup*ra*. Et eq*ue*.

Opera Autumpn*alia*. Et de dcccc l op*er*ib*us* autumpn*alibus* p*r*oueni-*entibus* de xix Custum*ariis* in Northe Craule quor*um* quil*ibe*t operab*it* j opus quol*ibe*t die op*er*ab*i*li int*er* gulam augusti *et* festum s*anc*t*i* Mich*ael*is exc*eptis* diebu*s* fest*iv*is in quibu*s* op*er*ari non deb*ent et quando* metent debent meter*e* p*ro* j op*er*e di*midiam* acr*am* fr*ument*i ordei pisa*rum* vel vesc*iarum* vel j acr*am* auen*arum* sic*ut* iac*ent* p*er*cipient*ibus* de d*om*ino p*ro* mess*ione* ligac*ione et* adimac*ione* cuiusl*ibe*t acr*e* j garba*m*. S*umma* DCCCC l op*er*a. D*e* quibu*s* In acquiet*anciis* iij Carucar*iorum et* iij b*er*car*iorum* CC op*er*a. In acquiet*anciis* iij ferling*orum* t*er*r*e* in North*e* Craule quor*um* op*er*a relax*ata* de antiquo C l op*er*a. In acquiet*anciis* ix ferling*orum* t*er*r*e* sup*er*ius vend*ita* du*m* d*om*ino placu*er*it CCCC l op*er*a cuil*ibe*t l op*er*a. In acquiet*anciis* iij ferling*orum* op*er*abil*ium* qui solu*n*t pro op*eribus* autumpnal*ibus* vt pat*et* infra eisdem relax*ata* c*aus*a inopie eoru*n*dem C l op*er*a. S*umma* que sup*ra*. Et eque.

Cariac*io* bl*ad*or*um*. Et de C l op*eribus* cariac*ionis* bl*ad*or*um* p*rou*en*ientibus* de xxv Custum*ariis* in Craule quor*um* quil*ibe*t car*iabit* blad*um* d*omi*ni donec total*ite*r intrent*ur*. Et esti*matur* q*uo*d fieri pot*er*it co*m*mu*n*ibu*s* annis p*er* vj dies. Et si d*ominu*s plur*a etcetera*. Et si tant*um etcetera*. S*umma* C l op*er*a. D*e* quibu*s* In acquiet*ancia* vnius p*re*posi*ti* vj op*er*a. In bl*ad*is d*omi*ni car*iandis* hoc anno C xliiij. Et eque.

Tass*acio* bl*ad*or*um*. Et de vj op*er*ibu*s* tass*acionis* bl*ad*or*um* p*r*oueni*entibus* de j Custum*ario* in Suth*e* Craule qui inveniet j ho*min*em p*ro* bl*ad*is d*omi*ni tassand*is* donec total*ite*r tassentur. Et esti*matur* quod fieri pot*er*it co*mmun*ibu*s* annis p*er* vj dies. Et si d*ominu*s *etcetera*. Et si tant*um* non indig*eat etcetera*. S*umma* vj op*er*a. Et to*tum* computa*tur* in bl*ad*is d*omi*ni tassand*is*. Et eq*ue*.

Op*er*a yemal*ia*. Et de MD lviij op*eribus* yem*alibus* p*r*ouen*ientibus* de xix Custumar*iis* in North*e* Craule quor*um* quil*ibe*t op*er*abi*t* qual*ibe*t septiman*a* int*er* festum s*anc*t*i* Mich*ael*is *et* gulam augusti ij op*er*a ex*ceptis* inde iij septim*anis* festiuis vi*delicet* natal*is* d*omi*ni Pasche *et* Pentecost*es* in quibu*s* non op*er*abu*nt* nec sup*er*ius on*er*ant*ur* in capit*e* vi*delicet* de quol*ibe*t iiij[xx] ij op*er*a *et quando* trit*urant* quil*ibe*t trit*urabit* iij b*ussellos* fr*ument*i v b*ussellos* ordei iij b*ussellos* pisar*um* vel vescar*um* vel vj b*ussellos* auen*arum* p*ro* j op*er*e *et* valet opus ob. q. S*umma* MD lviij op*er*a. D*e* quibu*s* In acquiet*anciis* iij Caruc*ariorum et* ij b*er*car*iorum* CCCC x op*er*a cuil*ibe*t iiij[xx] ij op*er*a. In acquiet*anciis* iij ferling*orum* t*er*r*e* quor*um* op*er*a relax*ata* de antiquo vt sup*ra* CC xlvj op*er*a cuil*ibe*t iiij[xx] ij op*er*a. In acquiet*anciis* ix ferling*orum* t*er*r*e* inf*ra* vend*ita* ad volunt*atem* d*omi*ni DCC xxxviij op*er*a cuil*ibet* iiij[xx] ij op*er*a. In acquiet*ancia* j ferling*i* t*er*r*e* nup*er* Joh*an*nis Sely vt sup*ra* iiij[xx] ij op*er*a. In def*ectu* op*er*um j ferling*i* t*er*r*e* nup*er* Joh*an*nis Sely q*uia* in man*ibus* d*omi*ni p*ro* def*ectu* tenent*is* iiij[xx] ij op*er*a. S*umma* que sup*ra*. Et eq*ue*.

Op*er*a facienda in com*m*uni.[1] Et sci*endum* q*uo*d om*n*es Custum*arii* in North*e* Craule portabu*n*t l*ite*ras uel br*ev*ia vsq*ue* M*er*don*am* vel Ou*er*-

[1] Possibly com*m*uni*bu*s.

ton*am* quociens neccess*e* fu*er*it. Et ecia*m* cariab*unt* j *quarter*i*um* auenar*um* vsq*ue* Woluesey p*ro* mora d*omi*ni ib*ide*m cum ij Custum*ariis* in Wodecote. debent eciam claudere *et* sustinere in co*mmun*i cu*m* auxilio omni*um* Custum*ariorum* in Suthecraule xvj p*er*tic*as* palicii circa p*ar*cum de Walth*a*m debent eciam querer*e et* cariar*e* cum equis *et* carect*is* suis fenu*m* p*ro* aueriis d*omi*ni vbicu*m*q*ue* empt*um* fu*er*it Ita quod possint ire *et* redire p*er* j diem. Et debent p*re*dict*i* Custum*arii* de Suth*e*craule in co*mmun*i invenire v homi*n*es ad colligend*um* poma in gardino de Walth*a*m et debent car*iare* lana*m et* cas*eum* d*omi*ni vsq*ue* H*a*mpton*iam* u*e*l Bitterne. Et si d*ominu*s volu*er*it aliqua*m* domu*m* edificar*e* debent querer*e* m*er*em*ium et* cariar*e* vsque Craule *etcetera*.

§§ 26. Accounts of the Farmer of the Demesne Lands and Stock and of the Collector of Rents, 29 Sept., 1503 — 28 Sept., 1504.

This document is made up of (1) a joint account of the farmer and the collector of rents and (2) the grain account of the farmer. The second is a simple statement of the grain which the farmer had received from the lord, only sixty-two quarters in all. Doubtless this represented a dwindling in grain cultivation during the period 1450–1500.

The joint account runs on pretty much like the old reeve's account of the earlier period. The reeve himself has receded into the background. He still existed and received an acquittance of 5s. which was the rental of his tenement. Whether he was identical with the collector of rents is not clear.

The chief receipts are from the fixed rents and the farm of the demesne lands and stock. The 'yield of the manor' has gone down to 38s. 10d. It consisted of pannage, agistment, pasture, and churchscot. The fact that pasture was still included is indicative of the fact that fairly early in Crawley's history the lord had fields, or rather furlongs, which he used for his own purposes, whether for tillage or pasture. All but one of these furlongs belonged to the farmer, but that does not mean that they belonged exclusively to him. Probably, as of old, they were in rotation given over, in whole or in part, to the tenants. And probably also they were in rotation used for arable and for pasture. The only clearly identified piece of permanent pasture is "le Short."

Although some of the underwood was given to the farmer, some of it was sold to the tenants for the repair of their buildings.

The lord still derived some income from the annual recognition of servile status. He permitted two men to go elsewhere, one to Abingdon, on condition that he be present at the tourn of Hocktide. In the earlier century two appearances a year were required.

The commutation of labor services was still a prominent, though not a lucrative, source of income. Twelve farthing holders of North Crawley paid 46s. in lieu of labor services. And twenty-four holders of virgates (double virgates and half virgates) of South Crawley paid 8s. to be free from the carriage of the lord's wood.

There were really two farms, or leases, one of the conies at 3s. 4d. a year for twenty-four years, and the other, the more important farm, of the demesne lands and stock, including buildings and all other things pertaining to husbandry, and including also all uncommuted services such as the carrying of manure and the washing and shearing of the sheep.

The second lease mentioned was made for thirty years, to begin apparently 29 September, 1491. It was in favor of Henry Couper, perhaps the son of John Couper who had held a twenty-one year lease beginning in 1487.[1] The amount paid was the same in both cases, but in the latter the lessee received 100 more ewes and 50 more hogasters. Whether he paid more for the lease is not known.

The farmer was apparently more active than the collector of rents, paying to the lord almost three times as much during the year. He seems to have collected the fixed rent.

William Wayte paid a fine for a farthing land in North Crawley and another for a virgate and 32 acres in addition in South Crawley. He was the lord's serf and he was inheriting the bondland possessed by his father. But in combining holdings in North and South Crawley, he was breaking up the old order of the manor. William Davy was doing the same thing, only his holding in South Crawley was smaller.

William Albroke is entered as defaulting on his rent. It is stated that he now pays in Mardon. This is a curious survival of

[1] See above §§ 23, pp. 466 ff.; also §§ 49, p. 545.

an entry found in the earliest account, for the year 1208–9, when it was said that his rent was rendered in Mardon,[1] not that he lived there. When William died, we shall probably never know. Probably it was in the twelfth century. But in the sixteenth, he was put down as living in a nearby village. This is typical of the stupid persistence of certain parts of manorial accounts which can safely be read for the later period only with the earlier well in mind.

CRAULEY[2]

Comp*ot*us Henrici Couper Firmar*ii et* Thome Dauy Coll*ectoris* re*ddi*-*tus* ib*id*em p*er* tempus p*redictu*m.

Arr*eragium* Null*um*.

Redd*itus* assis*i*. S*ed* re*spondent* de lxiiij s. vj d. de toto re*dditu* assis*o* ib*id*em ad f*estu*m Natal*is* d*omi*ni. Et de lxvij s. x d. de toto redd*itu* assis*o* ib*id*em ad f*estu*m pasche. Et de lxiiij s. vj d. de toto redd*itu* assis*o* ib*id*em ad festu*m* Natiuit*atis* S*anct*i Joh*ann*is Bapti*st*e. Et de c iiij s. j d. de toto redd*itu* Assis*o* de toto re*dditu* assis*o* ib*id*em ad f*es*-*tu*m s*anct*i Mich*ael*is arch*angel*i. Et de xx d. de incr*emento* redd*itus* iiij acr*arum* terr*e* de d*omi*nic*o* d*omi*ni in le Estfeld*e* iux*ta* le pythill*e* p*er* ann*um*. S*umma* xv li. ij s. vij d.

Annual*es* Recogn*itiones*. Et dc viij d. de Nich*ola*o Gibbys de annuali recognic*ione* sua vt possit morare [sic] ex*tra* lib*er*tat*es* d*omi*ni videl*ice*t apud Abyngdon*iam* du*m* d*omi*no placu*er*it *et* venire ad Turn*um* de hock*e* an*nuatim et* maner*e* natiuus d*omi*ni vt prius. Et de vj d. de Wil-l*elm*o Stephyns de an*nuali* recognic*ione* sua ut possit morare ex*tra* lib*er*-tat*es* d*omi*ni *et* venire ad turn*um* de hock*e* annuati*m et* maner*e* natiuus d*omi*ni ut p*r*ius. S*umma* xiiij d.

Ciminu*m*. Et de iiij d. de p*recio* j l*i*br*e* Cimini de re*dditu* Joh*ann*is Skyllynge p*ro* vna Crofta vocat*a* le how*e* nup*er* Joh*ann*is Estwey. S*umma* iiij d.

Vendic*io* op*erum*. Et de iiij s. de Joh*ann*e Mille p*ro* op*er*ib*us* j Fer-ling*i* terr*e* nup*er* Ric*ard*i Chiddene quond*a*m henrici Wodecote sic sibi relax*atis* du*m* d*omi*no placu*er*it. Et de iiij s. de Will*elm*o Couche al*ias* Stephyns p*ro* op*er*ib*us* j ferling*i* terre nat*ive* nup*er* Rog*er*i Couche nat*ivi* d*omi*ni quond*a*m Joh*ann*is Sely Jun*ioris* sic sibi relax*atis* du*m* d*omi*no placu*er*it. Et de iiij s. de Joh*ann*e plymton' p*ro* op*er*ib*us* j ferling*i* terre nat*ive* voc*ate* Bodyes londys nup*er* Ric*ard*i Sely nat*ivi* d*omi*ni sic sibi relax*atis* du*m* d*omi*no placu*er*it. Et de iiij s. de Thoma Gibbys p*ro* op*er*i-b*us* j ferling*i* terr*e* nativ*e* nup*er* Joh*ann*is Joh*ann*is Gibbys nat*ivi* quon-

[1] See above, §§ 5, p. 189.

[2] MS., P. R. O., Ecclesiastical Commission, Various, 155852.

d*a*m Joh*ann*is Sely sen*ioris* vocat*i* veynes sic sibi relax*atis* du*m* d*omi*no placu*er*it. Et de iiij s. de Will*elm*o davy p*ro* op*er*ib*us* j ferling*i* terr*e* nat*ive* nup*er* Katerine Went sic sibi relax*atis* dum d*omi*no placu*er*it. Et de iiij s. de hugone Carpynter p*ro* op*er*ib*us* j ferling*i* terr*e* nat*ive* nup*er* Will*elm*i Couche nat*ivi* d*omi*ni quond*a*m Ric*ard*i palmer sic sibi relax*atis* per annu*m* du*m* d*omi*no placu*er*it. Et de iiij s. de Joh*ann*e davy filio Rog*er*i davy p*ro* op*er*ib*us* j ferling*i* terr*e* nat*ive* nup*er* Joh*ann*is Sely filii Will*elm*i Sely nat*ivi* d*omi*ni quond*am* Thome Corbett sic sibi relax*atis* du*m* d*omi*no placu*er*it. Et de iiij s. de Joh*ann*e Aleyn' p*ro* op*er*ib*us* j ferling*i* t*er*r*e* nat*ive* nup*er* Rob*er*ti Wayte nat*ivi* d*omi*ni quond*a*m Thome Aleyn' sic sibi relax*atis* du*m* d*omi*no placu*er*it. Et de iiij s. de Will*elm*o davy p*ro* op*er*ib*us* j ferling*i* terr*e* nat*ive* nup*er* Thome davy quond*a*m Rog*er*i leigh' sic sibi relax*atis* du*m* d*omi*no placu*er*it. Et de x s. de op*er*ib*us* iij ferling*orum* terr*e* nat*ive* nup*er* Will*elm*i hudmann Rob*er*ti Gibbys *et* Will*elm*i Farnehill*e* sic eisdem relax*atis* causa inopie eor*un*dem p*ro* qual*ib*et ill*arum* iij s. iiij d. modo tenet Joh*ann*es Mille sic sibi relax*atis* du*m* d*omi*no placu*er*it. S*umma* xlvj s.

Vendic*io* Bosc*i*. Et de xlvij s. vj d. de p*recio* ix acr*arum et* di*midie* subbosci vend*itarum* in North*e*wode hoc anno p*recium* acre v s. D*e* iij Acr*is* subbosci p*ro*str*atis* in Bosco d*omi*ni p*redict*o hoc anno vlt*ra* predict*as* ix acr*as et* di*midiam* n*ihil* q*uia* liber*antur* Firmar*io* pro expen*sis* domus sue in howsebote Set r*espondent* de xvj d. de p*recio* viij lopp*es* viij arbor*um* dat' tenent*ibus* d*omi*ni ib*id*em p*ro* rep*aracione* t*enem*ent*orum* suor*um* hoc anno p*recium* le lopp*e* ij d. Et de iij s. de henrico Cooper p*ro* p*recio* xij lopp*es* xij arbor*um* delib*er*at' ad rep*aracionem* Man*er*ii ib*id*em p*recium* le lopp*e* iij d. sic sibi vend*it*' hoc Anno. S*umma* lj s. x d.

Vendic*io* Car*iagiorum* Bosci. Et de viij s. de p*recio* xxiiij^or^ Cariagi*orum* ut ex*tra* vendit*orum* p*re*cii Cariag*ii* iiij d. S*umma* viij s.

Exit*us* Man*er*ii. Et de iij s. de pannag*io* porcor*um* Custum*ariorum* ad f*estu*m s*anct*i Martini. D*e* porc*is* Agistat*is* in Northwoode n*ihil* hoc anno q*uia* null*a* pessona Set r*espondent* de xvj s. de agistam*ento* vacca*rum et* Bouic*u*lor*um* hoc anno ad t*ur*nu*m* de hocke. D*e* pastur*a* in Drakenorth*e* neq*ue* in trendell' neq*ue* in hosilden*e* neq*ue* in makefurlong*e* neq*ue* in Bash*a*m nichil q*uia* p*er*tin*et* firmar*io* cu*m* firma sua Set r*espondent* de iij s. iiij d. p*ro* pastur*a* vocat*a* le Short sic vendit*a* homag*io* ib*id*em hoc anno. D*e* auc*is* neq*ue* de Capon*ibus* nichil q*uia* p*er*tin*ent* firmar*io* Set r*espondent* de xvj s. vj d. de p*recio* iiij^xx^ xix gall*orum et* Gallin*arum* de Churs*etto* Custum*ariorum* ut ext*ra* vendit*orum* p*recium* cap*itis* ij d. Nec r*espondent* de x d. de p*recio* ij^c^ ouor*um* Gallinar*um* nichil q*uia* p*er*tin*ent* firmar*io* Nec r*espondent* de pell*ibus* lannat*is* pell*ibus* Nud*is* pell*ibus* Agnin*is* neq*ue* de pellectul*is* nichil q*uia* p*er*tin*ent* firmar*io* cu*m* firma Bidenc*ium* Nec r*espondent* de lana gross*a* fract*a* neq*ue* de lana Agnor*um* n*ichil* p*ro* consi*m*ili. S*umma* xxxviij s. x d.

Firm*a* Cunic*u*lor*um*. Et de iij s. iiij d. de firm*a* Cunic*u*lor*um* in Northe*w*ode hoc anno sic dim*issa* Joh*anni* Wykys pe*r* Will*elmu*m froste Sen*escallum* terr*arum* d*omi*ni ad term*inum* xxiiij annor*um* hoc Anno xiij^mo^. *Summa* iij s. iiij d.

Firm*a* Man*er*ii cu*m* firm*a* bidenc*ium*. Et de vj li. xiij s. iiij d. de Firma om*nium* terr*arum* d*ominical*i*um* p*ra*tor*um* *et* pastur*arum* ad husbondr*iam* p*er*tin*entium* sic dim*issa* henr*ico* Couper p*er* reu*e*rend*um* in Chr*ist*o patrem *et* d*omin*um d*omin*um petru*m* Courteney Winton*ien*-*sem* Ep*iscop*um p*er* Indent*uram* ad term*inum* xxx annor*um* hoc anno xiij^mo^ sol*uendo* ad ij anni t*er*mi*n*os principal*es* videl*ice*t ad festa pasche *et* s*anc*ti Mich*ae*lis arch*angel*i. Et de xv li. iij s. iiij d. de firma [pro] cccc xl Multon*ibus* x hurtard*is* cccc ouibu*s* m*a*tric*ibus* cc l hogg*astris* soluend*o* ad f*estu*m s*anc*ti petri q*uo*d dicit*ur* Aduinc*u*la sic dim*issa* prefato henrico p*er* di*ctu*m d*omin*um Ep*iscop*um p*er* Indentur*am* p*re*dic-t*am* pro t*er*mi*n*o p*redict*o hoc anno xij^mo^ ut sup*ra* Redd*itu* Assis*o* pannag*io* porcor*um* Custum*ariis* op*er*ibu*s* in denar*iis* extent*is* ward*is* Maritag*iis* Releu*iis* Finibu*s* h*e*riett*is* bosc*is* Escaet*is* For*isfacturis* Am*erci*a-*mentis* Turn*is* Cur*iis* p*redict*o Maner*io* ex*ceptis* *et* penit*us* d*omi*no reseruat*is*. Et p*redict*us henr*icus* firm*arius* om*n*es domos man*er*ii p*redict*i Strami*n*e Coop*er*t*as* ut in Coop*er*tur*is* necnon muros terr*eos* ear*un*dem bene *et* sufficient*er* rep*ar*abit virgulab*it* et sust*entabit* su*m*pt*ibus* suis p*ro*pr*iis* et expens*is* dur*ante* t*er*mi*n*o p*re*dicto. Et p*re*fat*us* Ep*iscop*us om*n*es domos Man*er*ii p*redict*i Tegul*is* Coop*er*t*as* *et* om*n*es Muros petrinos *et* [1] in Coop*er*tur*is* *et* in gross*o* Maerem*io* ben*e* *et* suffic*ienter* rep*ara*-b*it* *et* sustent*abit* su*m*pt*ibus* suis p*ro*pr*iis* *et* expens*is* durante t*er*mi*n*o p*redict*o. Et p*re*dictus henr*icus* firm*arius* om*n*es haias sepes *et* Fossat*a* man*er*io p*redict*o p*er*tin*entia* ben*e* *et* suffic*ienter* excurabit *et* plantabit su*m*pt*ibus* suis p*ro*pr*iis* *et* expens*is* dur*ante* t*er*mi*n*o p*redict*o *et* ea om*n*ia ac dom[os] vt p*re*dicit*ur* om*n*ibu*s* suis incu*m*bentibu*s* bene *et* sufficient*er* rep*ar*atu*m* [2] vnacu*m* toto Stauro tam viuo q*ua*m mortuo p*r*out in dorso huius libri spesificat*ur* in adeo bono quo ea recepit vel meliori modo in fine term*ini* sui dimittet *et* rep*ar*abit ve[l] p*re*c*ium* inde ad eleccio*ne*m d*omi*ni. Et p*re*dictus Firmar*ius* h*ab*ebit iij acr*as* subbosc*i* in bosco d*omi*ni ib*ide*m tempo*r*e seasenabili p*ro*st*er*nend*o* p*r*o suo haybote *et* Fyrebote Annuati*m* p*er* visionem *et* delib*erationem* Ministr*orum* d*omi*ni ib*ide*m *et* vnam togam de sect*a* valector*um* d*omi*ni vel vj s. viij d. ad eleccio*ne*m d*omi*ni durante termi*n*o p*redict*o. Et residuu*m* vero conuen-*cionis* Indentur*e* patent [sic] in Comp*ot*o de anno t*ranslationis* d*omi*ni petri Courtney nup*er* Ep*iscop*i Winton*iensis* iij^cio^. *Summa* xxj li. xvj s. viij d.

Fines *et* Maritag*ia*. Et de xiij s. iiij d. de Tuth*ingpenny* ad Turn*os* s*anc*ti Martini *et* hocke. Et de ix s. de Will*elm*o dauy nat*iv*o d*omi*ni filio

[1] Probably for ut. [2] Probably an error for reparata.

Joh*ann*is dauy Jun*ioris* nat*ivi* d*om*ini p*ro* j mes*suagio et* j ferling*o* terre nat*ive* in Craueley in Boriali p*ar*te eiusdem voc*atis* Chopyns nup*er* in tenur*a* Thome longe nat*ivi* d*om*ini *et* nup*er* Kat*er*ine Went vidue Que deuener*unt* in man*us* d*om*ini p*er* morte*m* dic*te* Kat*er*ine Went h*a*bend*is* p*er* pleg*ium* Joh*ann*is dauy Jun*ioris*. Et de iij s. iiij d. de Joh*ann*e Baker p*ro* j mes*suagio et* j ferling*o* terre nat*ive* in Crauley in p*ar*te bori*a*li eiusdem voc*atis* Newslond*es* nup*er* Thome dauy nat*ivi* d*om*ini que deuener*unt* in man*us* d*om*ini p*er* morte*m* dic*ti* Thome h*a*bend*is* p*er* pleg*ium* henrici Couper Firmar*ii* ib*i*dem. Et de v s. de Will*elm*o Wayte nat*ivo* d*om*ini fil*io et* here*de* Joh*ann*is Wayte nup*er* filio *et* here*de* Thome Wayte nat*ivi* d*om*ini pro j Tofto *et* j ferling*o* terre nat*ive* in Crauley in bori*a*li p*ar*te eiusdem ville que nup*er* fuerunt d*ic*ti Joh*ann*is p*a*tris sui Et q*ue* alicia nup*er* vxor d*ic*ti Joh*ann*is nup*er* in viduetate sua [tenuit?] p*er* pleg*ium* Joh*ann*is Mille *et* Joh*ann*is Symnes cui quidem Joh*ann*i Symnes custod*ia* predict*i* Will*elm*i Wayte committ*itur* quousqu*e* ad legittima*m* etatem suam p*er*uen*er*it. Et de v s. de eodem Will*elm*o Wayte nat*ivo* d*om*ini filio *et* here*de* Joh*ann*is Wayte nup*er* fil*ii et* here*dis* Thome Wayte nat*ivi* d*om*ini pro j mes*suagio et* j virg*ata* terre nat*ive* contin*ente* xxxij Acr*as* terre in Crauley in p*ar*te Austr*ali* eiusdem qu*e* nup*er* fuer*unt* d*ic*ti Joh*ann*is Wayte p*a*tris sui *et* qu*e* alicia nup*er* vxor d*ic*ti Joh*ann*is tenuit in viduetate sua h*a*bend*is* p*er* pleg*ium* predict*um* in forma p*re*dict*a*. Et de v s. de Will*elm*o Davy filio Joh*ann*is dauy sen*ioris* nat*ivi* d*om*ini pro j mes*suagio et* j ferling*o* terre nat*ive* in Crauley in p*ar*tè bori*a*li eiusdem qu*e* deuener*unt* in man*us* d*om*ini p*er* morte*m* dic*ti* Joh*ann*is Dauy p*a*tris sui h*a*bend*is* p*er* pleg*ium* henrici Couper· *et* Thome dauy. Et de x s. de eodem Will*elm*o davy nat*ivo* d*om*ini filio Joh*ann*is dauy sen*ioris* nat*ivi* d*om*ini p*ro* j mes*suagio et* dimidi*a* virgat*a* terre nat*ive* in Craueley in p*ar*te Austr*ali* eiusdem nup*er* dic*ti* Joh*ann*is p*a*tris sui *et* que deuener*unt* in man*us* d*om*ini p*er* mortem dic*ti* Joh*ann*is p*a*tris sui h*a*bend*is* p*er* pleg*ium* henrici Couper *et* Thome dauy. Su*mm*a l s. viij d.

Vendic*io* Stauri Null*um*.

Perquisit*a* Turn*orum et* Curiar*um*. Set r*es*pond*ent* de iij d. de perquis*itis* Turn*i* s*an*c*ti* Martini. Et de viij d. de perquis*itis* Turn*i* de hocke. Et de n*ihil* de perquis*itis* Curiar*um* p*er* balliv*um* tent*arum* int*er* dictos Turn*os*. Su*mm*a xj d. Su*mm*a tot*alis* Recepte [sum missing].

Acquiet*ancie* reddit*us*. Idem Computa[n]t in acquiet*anciis* reddit*us* j preposit*i* p*er* annum v s. De Acquiet*anciis* reddit*us* j fabri *et* iij Caru-cariorum terr' [1] annum x s. viij d. cuil*ibet* eor*um* ij s. viij d. nichil q*uia* ad Custum*ariam* firma*m* ex conuencione. De Acquietanciis reddit*us* j berc*arii* Multon*um* p*er* annu*m* j barcar*ii* ouium matric*ium* hogges-tror*um* p*er* Annu*m* viij s. cuil*ibet* illor*um* ij s. viij d. n*ichil* quia pertin*et*

---

[1] Doubtless a mistake for per.

firmar*io* cu*m* firma Bidenc*ium*. Et in acquiet*ancia* redd*itus* j heyward*i* ex conuenc*ione* fact*a* cu*m* sup*er*uis*ore* p*er* annu*m* vj s. viij d. S*umma* xj s. viij d.

Def*ec*tus Redd*itus*. Et in def*ec*tu redd*itus* [terre] Will*elm*i Stronge tract*e* in d*ominicum* p*er* annu*m* ij s. Et in def*ec*tu r*eddit*us Will*elm*i de Cur*ia* pro consi*m*ili ij s. viij d. Et in def*ec*tu redd*itus* Will*elm*i Albroke q*ui* modo rem*anet* ad Merdon*am* p*er* annu*m* v s. Et in def*ec*tu redd*itus* [terre] Will*elm*i Crouche tract*e* in d*ominicum* per Annu*m* ij s. viij d. Et in def*ec*tu Rob*er*ti Key p*ro* consi*m*ili ij s. viij d. Et in def*ec*tu redd*itus* terr*e* j porcarii p*ro* consi*m*ili ij s. viij d. Et in def*ec*tu redd*itus* terr*e* Ric*ard*i vaccarii p*ro* consi*m*ili ij s. viij d. S*umma* xx s. iiij d.

Vad*ium* Ball*iv*i. Et in vad*io* Joh*ann*is Wyly Ball*iv*i ib*id*em p*er* vnu*m* annu*m* Integr*um* cap*ientis* sec*undum* rat*am* x m*arcarum* xxvj s. viij d. residuu*m* capit in Aliis loc*is*. S*umma* xxvj s. viij d.

Custus domor*um*. Et in denar*iis* sol*utis* Ric*ard*o Colswayne p*ro* vj ᵐ Tegul*orum* ab eo empt*is* le M. ad v s. xxx s. Et sol*utis* eidem p*ro* l heptyle ab eo empt' ij s. Et sol*utis* eidem p*ro* xij Crest*is* ab eo empt*is* xij d. Et sol*utis* eidem pro xxxvj Gutter hippes iij s. Et sol*utis* p*ro* cariag*io* p*re*dict*orum* vj ᵐ. Tegul*orum* a domo d*ict*i Ric*ard*i vsq*ue* firm*am* d*omi*ni de Crauele p*ro* quol*ibe*t Carect*ato* xvj d. viij s. Et sol*utis* eidem p*ro* viij q*uar*ter*iis* Calcis vsti empt*is* q*uar*ter*ium* ad xij d. viij s. Et p*ro* cariag*io* eoru*n*dem A puteo vsq*ue* dict*am* firmam xij d. Et sol*utis* p*ro* vj ᵐ lathenayles empt*is* M. ad ix d. iiij s. vj d. Et sol*utis* p*ro* D et di*midio* v penynaile empt*is* C^na ad v d. ij s. iij d. ob. Et sol*utis* p*ro* iiij ᵐ cccc lathes empt*is* C^na ad v d. xiij s. x d. Et p*ro* cariag*io* eoru*n*dem vsq*ue* dict*am* firm*am* xij d. Et sol*utis* p*ro* iiij^or b*ussellis* de Tilepynnes le b*ussellus* ad vj d. ij s. Et sol*utis* p*ro* iiij^or Carect*atis* zabuli *et* cariag*io* eoru*n*de*m* xij d. Et sol*utis* Ric*ard*o Shirwyn' Carpentar*io* ib*id*em conduct*ori* ad t*asc*ham p*er* Ed*mundu*m Walle ad grounsellan*dum* Granariu*m* Aulam *et* coquinam ac p*ro* imposic*io*ne de Walplat*es* Syderesons xij Copul*is* de Sparr*is* Ac p*ro* dore Stothes dua noua hostia [sic] *et* ij fenestr*is* cum Stothis ad idem cu*m* dolac*io*ne Maeremi*orum* et v Sarrac*oribus* eiusdem ib*id*em occupat*is* xlvj s. viij d. Et sol*utis* Joh*ann*i pleter lathamo ib*id*em conduct*ori* ad t*asc*ham per Ed*mundu*m Walle ad de nouo facien*dum* vnam vstrinam vocat*am* j kyle ad desup*er* Siccand*um* Bras*ium* *et* j furnu*m* *et* le grounde pynnyng*e* orrii feni Granar*ii* *et* aule ib*id*em xxiij s. iiij d. Et sol*utis* Joh*ann*i helyer ib*id*em conduct*ori* ad t*asc*ham p*er* d*ictu*m Ed*mundu*m Walle p*ro* tegulac*io*ne xv ᵐ nouar*um* *et* vet*erum* tegular*um* p*re*c*ium* M. xij d. xv s. S*umma* viij li. ij s. vij d. ob.

Expen*s*e Sen*escalli*. Et in Expen*sis* Will*elm*i Froste vice Sen*escalli* Ac Nich*ola*i Morton*e* Sup*er*uis*oris* terr*arum* d*omi*nical*ium* hac vice ac alior*um* officiarior*um* d*om*ini ib*id*em exist*entium* p*ro* Turn*is* S*anct*i

Martini *et* hoc*ke* tenend*is* hoc anno ut pat*et* p*er* ij bill*as* sigillat*as* xij s. x d. S*u*mm*a* xij s. x d.

Clausur*a* copicii. Et in denar*iis* solut*is* pro f*a*ctur*a* iiij qu*a*rentena-*rum et* xxxij p*er*ticat*arum* noue haie circa copic*ium* dom*i*ni ap*ud* North-wode cap*iendo* p*ro* qual*ibet* quarentena xx d. *et* p*ro* qual*ibet* p*er*tica ob. viij s. S*u*mm*a* viij s.

Liber*a*c*io* denar*iorum*. Et in denar*iis* liberat*is* M*a*gistr*o* Roger*o* lay-borne cler*i*co Thes*au*rario de Woluesey p*r*imo die Maii p*er* man*us* Thome dauy Coll*ectoris* redd*itus* ib*i*d*em* anno *regni regis* henrici vij xviij^{uo} iiij li. vj s. viij d. vij^{mo} die Junii anno sup*r*ad*i*cto p*er* man*us* eius-*dem* collector*is* xxxvij s. iiij d. xvij die Nouembr*is* hoc Anno xix^{no} Regis pred*i*c*ti* p*er* man*us* d*i*c*ti* Coll*ectoris* vij li. xvij^{mo} die Nouembr*is* d*i*cto anno xix^{no} p*er* man*us* firm*a*r*ii* xxvj s. viij d. xxviij^{uo} die Nouembr*is* eodem Anno xix^{no} p*er* man*us* d*i*c*ti* firm*a*r*ii* ad ij vices p*er* bill*as* vij li. vj s. iiij d. Et liber*a*t*is* eidem Thes*au*rario p*er* man*us* firm*a*r*ii* p*er* man*us* Ric*a*rd*i* Bateresby sine billa xj li. xiiij s. vj d. ob. in toto ut p*a*t*et* p*er* bill*as* inde liberat*as* *et* int*er* memor*a*nd*a* huius anni rem*a*n*entis*. xxxiij li. xj s. vj d. ob. Et liber*a*uit Thes*au*rario hospicii dom*i*ni ut de precio xx multon*um* ad vsu*m* hospicii dom*i*ni apud farnehame liber*a*-tor*um* xxvj s. viij d. S*u*mm*a* xxxiiij li. xviij s. ij d. ob.

S*u*mm*a* alloc*ationum et* liber*a*c*ionum* xlvij li. iiij d. Que S*u*mm*a* coequalis est cu*m* S*u*mm*a* to*talis* R*e*c*e*pte sup*r*ad*i*cte. Et Eque

CRAUELEY

Compo*tus* pred*i*c*ti* henr*i*c*i* Firm*a*r*ii* ib*i*d*em* p*er* tempus pred*i*c*tum*.

Fr*u*m*en*tu*m*. Idem computat de xv qu*a*rter*iis* frum*en*ti de rem*a*n*enti*-*bus*. S*u*mm*a* xv qu*a*rter*ia*. Et rem*a*n*en*t xv qu*a*rter*ia* frum*en*ti in mani-*bus* d*i*c*ti* firm*a*r*ii* ad reliberand*a* in fine t*er*m*i*ni sui.

Curall*um* n*i*h*il* qu*i*a p*er*tin*e*t firm*a*r*i*o.

Ord*i*u*m*. Set r*e*s*pondet* de xxiiij qu*a*rter*iis* ordii de rem*a*n*entibus*. S*u*mm*a* xxiiij qu*a*rter*ia*. Et rem*a*n*en*t xxiiij qu*a*rter*ia* ordii in m*a*n*ibus* d*i*c*ti* firm*a*r*ii* ad *r*eliberand*a* ut sup*r*a.

Pise. Et de iij qu*a*rter*iis* pis*a*rum de rem*a*n*entibus*. S*u*mm*a* iij qu*a*r-ter*ia*. Et rem*a*n*en*t iij qu*a*rter*ia* pis*a*rum in m*a*n*ibus* d*i*c*ti* firm*a*r*ii* ad reliberand*a* ut sup*r*a.

Vesce. Et de iiij qu*a*rter*iis* vesc*a*rum de rem*a*n*entibus*. S*u*mm*a* iiij^{or} qu*a*rter*ia*. Et rem*a*n*en*t iiij qu*a*rter*ia* vesc*a*rum in m*a*n*ibus* d*i*c*ti* firm*a*r*ii* ad *r*eliberand*a* ut sup*r*a.

Auene. Et de xvj qu*a*rter*iis* Auen*a*rum de rem*a*n*entibus*. S*u*mm*a* xvj qu*a*rter*ia*. Et rem*a*n*en*t xvj qu*a*rter*ia* Auen*a*rum i n m*a*n*ibus* d*i*c*ti* fir-m*a*r*ii* ad *r*eliberand*a* ut sup*r*a.

Equi. Et de ij Equis de rem*a*n*entibus*. S*u*mm*a* ij. Et rem*a*n*en*t ij equi prec*ii* cap*itis* xiij s. iiij d. in m*a*n*ibus* d*i*c*ti* firm*a*r*ii* ut sup*r*a.

Affri. Et iij Affri de rem*anentibus*. S*umma* iij. Et rem*anent* iij Affri p*recii* cap*itis* vj s. viij d. in man*ibus* d*icti* firm*arii* ad r*eliberandos* ut sup*ra*.

Boues. Et de ix bob*us* de rem*anentibus*. S*umma* ix. Et rem*anent* ix boues p*recii* cap*itis* xj s. in man*ibus* d*icti* firm*arii* ad r*eliberandos* ut sup*ra*.

Tauri vacce et Bouett*i*. Null*um*.

Multon*es*. Set r*espondent* de cccc xl multon*ibus* de rem*anentibus*. S*umma* iiij^{c} xl. Et rem*anent* iiij^{c} xl multon*es* in man*ibus* d*icti* firm*arii* p*recii* cap*itis* xviij d. ad r*eliberandos* ut sup*ra*.

Hurtard*i*. Et de x hurtard*is* de rem*anentibus*. S*umma* x. Et rem*anent* x hurtard*i* p*recii* cap*itis* xviij d. in man*ibus* d*icti* firm*arii* ad r*eliberandos* ut sup*ra*.

Oues matric*es*. Et de cccc ouib*us* matric*ibus* de rem*anentibus*. S*umma* iiij^{c}. Et rem*anent* cccc oues matric*es* p*r*ecii cap*itis* xiiij d. in man*ibus* d*icti* firm*arii* ad r*eliberandas* ut sup*ra*.

Hogg*ast*ri. Et de cc l hogg*ast*ris de rem*anentibus*. S*umma* ij^{c} l. Et rem*anent* cc l hogg*astri* p*recii* cap*itis* xij d. in man*ibus* d*icti* firm*arii* ad r*eliberandos* ut sup*ra*.

Veller*a* lana agnin*a* lana fract*a* pell*es* nud*e* pell*es* lanut*e* pell*es* agnin*e* pellectul'. Nichil q*uia* p*er*tin*ent* firm*ario* cu*m* firma bidenc*ium*.

Sus. Set r*espondent* de vna sue de rem*anente*. S*umma* j. Et rem*anet* j sus in man*ibus* d*icti* firm*arii* p*r*ecii iiij s. in manib*us* d*icti* firm*arii* ad r*eliberandam* ut sup*ra*.

porcelli. De porcell*is* de ex*itu* d*ict*e suis n*ich*il q*uia* p*er*tin*ent* firm*ario*.

Galli et Galline. Set r*espondent* de j Gallo et v Gallin*is* de rem*anentibus*. Et de c xxv gall*is* et gallin*is* de Churs*etto* cust*umariorum* ad f*estum* S*an*ct*i* Martini. S*umma* c xxxj. De quib*us* In def*ect*u Churs*etti* terr*e* Will*elm*i Stronge tract*e* in D*ominicum* p*er* annum iiij. Et in def*ect*u Churs*etti* Will*elm*i de Cur*ia* iiij. Et in def*ect*u churs*etti* terr*e* Will*elm*i Crouche p*ro* consim*i*li iiij. Et in def*ect*u Churs*etti* Will*elm*i Knaue p*ro* consim*i*li iiij. Et in def*ect*u Churs*etti* terr*e* Will*elm*i Wilde vocat*e* packys q*uia* relax*at*' ei p*er* fine*m* iiij d. Et in def*ect*u Churs*etti* terr*e* Will*elm*i Dauy fil*ii* Joh*ann*is Dauy sen*ioris*[1] ij. Et in def*ect*u Churs*etti* terr*e* Joh*ann*is Aleyn ij. Et in def*ect*u Churs*etti* *Christ*ine longe ij q*uia* non coniungant p*ro* quol*ibe*t eor*um* ij. Et in vendic*ionibus* ut infra iiij^{xx} xix p*ro* xvj s. vj d. S*umma* c xxv. Et rem*anent* j gall*us* et v gallin*e* in man*ibus* d*icti* firmar*ii*.

Vtensilia. Et de ij Caruc*is* cu*m* iij p*a*rib*us* farrament*orum* et toto apparat*u* ferr*i* p*ro* xvj bob*us* p*recii* cap*itis* int*er* se xx s. j b*ussello* ferr*o* ligat*o* p*recii* x d. j Carect*a* ferr*o* ligat*a* cu*m* corp*or*e et Scala p*r*ecii xvj s. viij d. j Corda carect*aria* p*recii* xx d. ij Capistr*is* Coreis p*recii* int*er* se

[1] Struck through.

xviij d. *et* iiij capistr*is* de canabo nullius val*oris* j lather nullius valor*is* j vate null*ius* val*oris* p*ro* dayera j Tripode iij formis p*ro* casiis imponend*is* tribul*o* ferr*o* ligat*o* j seue vect*er*' et xij tracchis nullius val*oris*.

Et hec om*n*ia rem*anent* in man*ibus* dicti firmar*ii* ad rest*ituenda* ut sup*ra*.

Vtensilia fabr*ilia*. Et de j magno Andefeld' ferr*eo* j pykehorne ferr*eo* non ponder*atis* j p*a*re le Belowes ij forge hamores j hand hamer ij par*ibus* Tong*es* j pare pyncers j Butt*er* j par*e* de Tongys ponder*antibus* int*er* se xviij l*ibras*.

Et hec om*n*ia rem*anent* in man*ibus* Will*elm*i Craneworth' fabr*i* ad r*eliberanda* ut sup*ra*.

Op*er*a Custum*aria*. Op*er*a Custum*aria* non arent*ata* p*er*tin*ent* firm*ario* cu*m* firma sua ex*ceptis* op*e*rib*us* Cariac*ionis* bosc*i* et certa op*er*a p*r*ius vsitat*a* patent in pipa de anno t*r*anslac*ionis* d*omi*ni Petri Corteney Winton*iensis* Ep*iscop*i sec*un*do.

Car*iacio* Bosc*i* p*recii* Cariag*ii* iiij d. Et de exit*u* op*e*rib*us* cariac*ionis* bosc*i* p*roue*n*ientibus* de xxv Custum*ariis* in Craueley in p*ar*te Austral*i* q*uorum* quil*ibe*t Cariabit j Carect*atam* Bosci vsq*ue* Woluesey erga f*estu*m Natal*is* d*omi*ni n*ihi*l q*uia* eodem p*er*cipiend*o* non r*espondebit* q*uia* null*us* Bosc*us* ibi*de*m. S*umma* xxv. De quib*us* In alloc*ati*one Collect*ori* Redd*itus* ib*ide*m causa officii sui p*er* annu*m* j car*iagium* p*recii* carect*ate* iiij d. Et vend*ita* infra xxiiij p*ro* viij s.

§§ 27. The Audit of Accounts, 25 Nov.—10 Dec., 1560.

Apparently the heading reads: 'The days of the audit for one whole year ending at the feast of St. Michael the Archangel — in the second year of Elizabeth.' That is, in substance, the year of account ran from Michaelmas to Michaelmas. During this particular year the audit occurred in the period from 25 November to 10 December. It is probable that the accounts were made up in the various manors and boroughs early in November. Then an official was sent out to inspect the several rolls of the manorial officials, often consisting of one or two skins, and to check up on their tallies and other records of business. Doubtless these original rolls were then carried off by the episcopal official to the bishop's treasury at Wolvesey in Winchester, where they were copied out to form the pipe roll of the whole bishopric. Probably at least two officials were sent out, one going eastward as far as Southwark (London), the other westward as far as Taunton.

Crawley was but one manor in the bailiwick, or group of manorial estates. These bailiwicks formed convenient units for the holding of courts and the auditing of accounts. Obviously not all the manors belonging to the bishopric are mentioned. Apparently only those are specified, in which the actual auditing took place.

In the Middle Ages the accounts in Crawley were made up, first by the reeve and the sergeant, later by the reeve and the bailiff of the bailiwick. After about 1450 they were put together by the collector of rents and the farmer of the demesne. It is, of course, a question whether this present list of dates constituted the occasions on which the sergeants or bailiffs went out to the manors to help in some way with the accounts, or whether these were the days on which an official, very much like an episcopal auditor, made his rounds after the accounts had all been closed locally. The latter explanation seems to be more likely.

Dies audit*ionis*[1] p*ro* A*nno* integro finit*o* ad festu*m* s*ancti* Mich*ael*is arch*angel*i [anno[2]] sec*und*o Elizab*ethe*.

Ball*ivata* de Sutton Stok*e* Crauley	lune xxv	novembr*is*
et longwood*e*	Martis xxvj	
Ball*ivata* de Meo*n*	Mercur*ii* xxvij Jouis xxviij	nove*m*br*is*
Ball*ivata* de walth*am*	ven*er*is xxix sabat*i* xxx	nove*m*br*is*
ball*ivata* de altaclera cu*m* fernh*am* merton et Southworke	D*omi*nic*a* p*ri*mo d*e*cembr*is*	
	lun*e* 2° Martis 3°	dece*m*br*is*
Ball*ivata* de Taunton cu*m* knoill hind[on] et fontell	Mercur*ii* 4° Jouis 5°	decembr*is*
Witteney cu*m* Soke	ven*er*is 6° Sabati 7°	decembr*is*
	D*omi*nic*a* viij decembr*is*	
offic*ium* Thes*aurarii*	lun*e* 9° Mertis 10	decembr*is*

[1] MS., P. R. O., Ecclesiastical Commission, Court Rolls, 109/7, fol. 41.

[2] 1560 has been stricken out at this point.

§§ 28. An Unenrolled Account of the Farmer of the Demesne, and of the Reeve, 29 Sept., 1746—28 Sept., 1747.

The farmer of the demesne and of the stock along with the reeve were responsible for this account which is apparently the original and was probably made up on the manor for the use of the bishop. From such originals the pipe roll had been constructed and later the rent books. This account is a late, lonely, and not very creditable survivor of a long lineage.

The old forms and perhaps original entries were still persisted in. The fixed rents, issues of the manor, and churchscot were very old, some, or all of them, probably going back to the Anglo-Saxon period. The tithingpenny corrupted to (Tuth) lingered on from at least the thirteenth century, but at a reduced rate, 3s. 4d., instead of 13s. 4d. fixed in the same century. The field called "Short" or "Shirt" was a long-familiar item, as was the holding called "the How," occupied by the Auditor who, because of his office, did not pay the old-time 4d. a year, the commuted rate of a pound of cummin.

There are no perquisites of court, no heriots, and no sale of underwood. The reeve still got an abatement of rent, as did the hayward, only the latter received more. This seems to reflect the declining importance of the reeve.

The accounting in some respects is more satisfactory than in earlier accounts. The charge and discharge are more completely separated, and the "Back of the Accompt" is given. The latter relates at this time simply to churchscot and the carriage of wood. On the other hand, there appear to be errors in both the rents of assize and the abatements. The rents and customary dues (including the abatements) bring in a little more than the farm or lease of the demesne (home farm) and the stock (sheep). It is to be noted that of the many items originally included in the farm, only these two have survived.

A translation of a surrender of land occurs, for the enrolling of which surrender a fee of 1s. was paid. This enrollment would stand as witness to the title to the holding. A yardland or virgate in South Crawley was involved, the yardland still containing 32 (customary) acres.

CRAWLEY [1]

The Accompt of Anthony Henley Esq. Farmer there and of Richard Eyles Reeve there for one whole year ended at the feast of St. Michael the Archangel and in the One and Twentieth Year of the Reign of our Sovereign Lord George the Second King over Great Britain and so forth and in the 14th Year of the translation of Benjamine Lord Bishop of Winchester.

Arreares. None.

Rents of Assize. But they Accompt for iij li. iiij s. vj d. for the whole Rents of Assize there at the feast of Christmas. And For iij li. viij s. x d. for the whole rents of Assize there at the feast of Easter. And For iij li. iv s. vj d. for the whole rents of Assize there at the feast of St. John the Baptist. And For v li. iv s. j d. for the whole rents of assize there at the feast of St. Michael the Archangel. And For j s. viij d. of Henry David for an encreased Yearly Rent for four Acres of Land of the Lords Demesnes in Eastfield near the Puthill. Sum xv li. iij s. v d. [sic].

Cummin. But they do not Accompt for iiij d. for the price of a pound of Cummin for the Rent of Henry Dawley Esq. for One Croft of Bond Land called the How because it belongs to the Lords Auditor for his Fee by our Ancient Custome.

Sale of works. But they Accompt for ij li. viij s. for the Works of Several Bond tenants for Several farthing lands yearly released to them. Sum ij li. viij s. od.

Issues of the Mannor with new Rents. And For ij s. for the pannage of the Hoggs of the Customary Tenants at the feast of St. Martin Yearly. And For xvj s. for the Agisting of Cows and Heifers Yearly. And for iij s. iv d. for the pasture called the Short. And For ij d. for a New Rent of Thomas Seymour for One Acre of Land in the Middle North Field Yearly. And For ij li. v s. for the price of 90 Cocks and hens Sold this Year as appeares by the Back of this Account. Sum iij li. vj s. vj d.

Farm of the Conies. And For iij s. iiij d. for the farm of the Conies in Northwood yearly being so demised by the Lord to the Tenants. Sum iij s. iiij d.

Farm of the Demesnes. And F[or] vj li. xiij s. iiij d. for the farm of all the Demesn Lands Meadows and pastures thereunto belonging being demised by the Lord Bishop of Winton unto Henley Esq. And For xv li. iij s. iiij d. for the farm of 440 Sheep Ten Rams 400 Ewes and two Hundred Teggs paid Yearly at the feast of St. Peter the imprisoned. Sum xxj li. xvj s. viij.

[1] MS., P. R. O., Ecclesiastical Commission, Various, 159473 (one of 103 MSS.). Folded parchment. Endorsed "Crawley 1747."

New Rent. And For iiij d. of [——][1] for a new Rent. Sum iiij d.

Sale of the Carriage of Wood. And For ij li. for the price of the Carriage of 24 loades of Wood Yearly as appeares by the Back of this Acccompt. Sum ij li.

Pidgeons hold. And For j li. for the farm called the Pidgeons hold late granted by lease. Sum j li.

Fines of Land. And For iij s. iiij d. for certain Money called Tuth at the turns of Saint Martin and Hocke Yearly. And For xij d. of James Waite for haveing the Inrollment of a certain Surrender and release to him made by Ruben Sims which followeth in these words Crawley Mannor Be it remembred that on the Eighteenth day of April in the year of our Lord One Thousand Seven Hundred and Forty Seven Reuben Sims Executor of the last will and Testament of Reuben Sims his late Father Dec*eas*ed who intermarried with and Survived Joan Waite Daughter of James Waite Dec*eas*ed Came before John Cholwell Esq. steward of the Bishoprick of Winchester and Surrendred remised released and for ever quit claimed into the hands of the Lord of the Said Mannor as well the Sum of Twenty Poundes of Lawfull Money of Great Britain and all Arreares of Interest for the Same charged upon the Coppyhold Lands and Tenements herein aftermentioned in and By the Admittance of the said James Waight Dec*eas*ed Inrolled at the Turn of Hock in the Seventh Year of King William the Third to be paid to the said Joan Waite as also all the right title and Interest which the said Reuben Sims hath or can claime to One Messuage and one parcell of purpresture Land containing half an Acre on the South part of the Said Messuage and One Yard of Bondland containing xxxij Acres of Land on the South part of Crawley to the use and behoofe of the Said James Waite and his heires according to the Custome of the Said Mannor Now being in the peaceable poss*ess*ion and Seizin of the said premisses So that Neither the Said Reuben Sims nor his heires Ex*ec*-*u*tors or Orators shall or will at any time hereafter claime or Challenge any right title or Interest into or out of the same premisses but of and from all Such right title or interest Shall and will be for ever secluded and Debarred by these presents Reuben Sims All which at the request of the said James Waite are inrolled in the Court Rolls of the Said Mannor. Sum j s. paid to the Bishop

Herriotts [——][1] paid to the Bishop [——].[1]

Sale of Underwood. And For [——][1] for underwood sold this Year. Sum none.

Perquisites of Court. And For [——][1] perquisites of Court this Year. Sum [——].[1] Sum of the Charge aforesaid [——][1]

Abatement of Rent. He also the said Reeve accompts for an abate-

[1] Blank.

ment of 5s. to the Reeve Yearly and Six Shillings and Eight pence to the Heyward Yearly. Sum xj s. viij d.

Allowances of Rent. And For xv s. for an Allowance of Rent of Several pasturelands above charged under the title of Rents of assize because it is let with the Demesne Lands. Sum xv s.

Land tax. And For ij *li.* xij s. for Land tax this year. Sum ij [li.] xij [s.]

Paid to the Treasurer. And For 7 *li.* 10 s. paid to the treasurer this year. Sum [——].[1] Sum of the abatements 4 *li.* 2s. 8d. And remaines indebted the Sum of xiij [li.] ij [s.] iij [d.]

Crawley. The Back of the Accompt[2] of the Said Reeve for the said time.

Cocks and Henns. He Accompts for 125 Cocks and Henns being Churchetts due by custome at the Feast of St. Martin Yearly. Sum 125.

Abatements. He abates four for Lands heretofore belonging to William Strong And four for Lands heretofore belonging to William Cruch And four for Lands heretofore belonging to William Knave in the whole xij and to Widowers and Widows for a Moiety of their Churchetts the Number of [——].[1] Sum [——][1] and remaines [——][1] which were sold as within as [sic] Six pence each.

Carriage of Wood. And he Accompts for the Carriage of 25 Loads of Wood for 25 customary Lands on the South Part of Crawley. Sum xxv.

Abatement. And he abates for the Carriage of One Load to the Reeve Yearly for the Executing of his office. Sum j and remaines 24 which were sold as within at xx d. each.

§§ 29. Court Fines and Amercements, 29 Sept., 1236—28 Sept., 1237.

An earlier statement of fines and amercements (purchasia) for Crawley is to be found elsewhere.[3] This particular list is taken from an ordinary reeve's account, and is included here only because it includes the breech (two instances) of the assize, presumably, of bread and ale. There are relatively few occurrences of this offence in Crawley.

Here we find the payment called 'for relaxing the due,' later designated in Crawley records the 'thithingpenny' or 'cert.' The

[1] Blank. [2] The compotus super dorsum of earlier accounts.

[3] See above, §§ 5, p. 189.

whole tithing pays five shillings twice a year, at hockday and at St. Martins. The origin of the due is now not to be discovered. Because of its (apparent) universality in England, it must have been of royal origin and not of local or manorial imposition, at least originally.[1] Certainly it came to be a regular customary due —paid by the tithing in connection with its appearance at the greater hundred court. Apparently it was paid by the tenants who were members of the frankpledge group (tithing). It was paid to the lord of the manor and apparently by him to the sheriff. Whether it was at the rate of one penny per tenant, is not clear. If so, there were at this time sixty tenants in Crawley, which is probably very near the actual number. But later, the sum was increased from 5s. to 6s. 8d.,[2] which would, by the same token, indicate 80 tenants. This number is obviously too large. Possibly what had once been a *pro rata* due, came to be a fixed sum.

Other payments are for bail, contempt of court, false claim, false oath, mistake in pleading, fighting, and marriage. There are offences against pasture, thorns, plowing, the woods, forage, stakes, and, as has been said, the assize of bread and ale.

The use of only Christian names is typical of prevailing practices.

PURCH*ASIA* [3]

Id*em* r*eddunt* co*mpotum* de v s. de t*ithing*a p*ro* occ*asion*e rel*axata*. De vj d. de Nich*olao* p*ro* pastur*a*. De vj d. de Alic*ia* p*ro* si*m*ili. De vj d. de d[avi]d[o] p*ro* si*m*ili. De vj d. de Joh*anne* p*ro* si*m*ili. De vj d. de Ivone. De vj d. de osmu*nd*o p*ro* si*m*ili. De vj d. de Matill*e*. De vj d. de Rob*erto* p*ro* si*m*ili. De vj d. de Alic*ia*. De vj d. de d[avi]d[o] p*ro* si*m*ili. De vj d. de Rog*er*o p*ro* si*m*ili. De vj d. de Joh*anne* p*ro* spinis. De vj d. de Rob*erto* p*ro* pastur*a*. De vj d. de Joh*anne* p*ro* arrur*a*. De vj d. de Elia p*ro* si*m*ili. De vj d. de Will*elmo* p*ro* bosco. De xij d. de Rob*erto*. De vj d. de Alic*ia* p*ro* si*m*ili. De vj d. de Rog*ero*. De iiij s. de Iuone p*ro* si*m*ili. De vj d. de Will*elmo* p*ro* pastur*a*. De xij d. de Rog*ero*. De xij d. de Rob*erto* p*ro* si*m*ili. De vj d. de Rel*icta* fab*ri* p*ro* assis*a* fract*a*. De vj d. de Will*elmo* p*ro* si*m*ili. De v s. de ho*min*ib*us* de litleton' p*ro* bosco. De v s. de t*ithing*a p*ro* occas*ione* rel*axata*. De vj d. de Will-

[1] See W. A. Morris, *The Frankpledge System* (1910), pp. 101–102.
[2] See above, §§ 7, p. 202.
[3] Ms., P. R. O., Ecclesiastical Commission, Various, 159285, memb. 2.

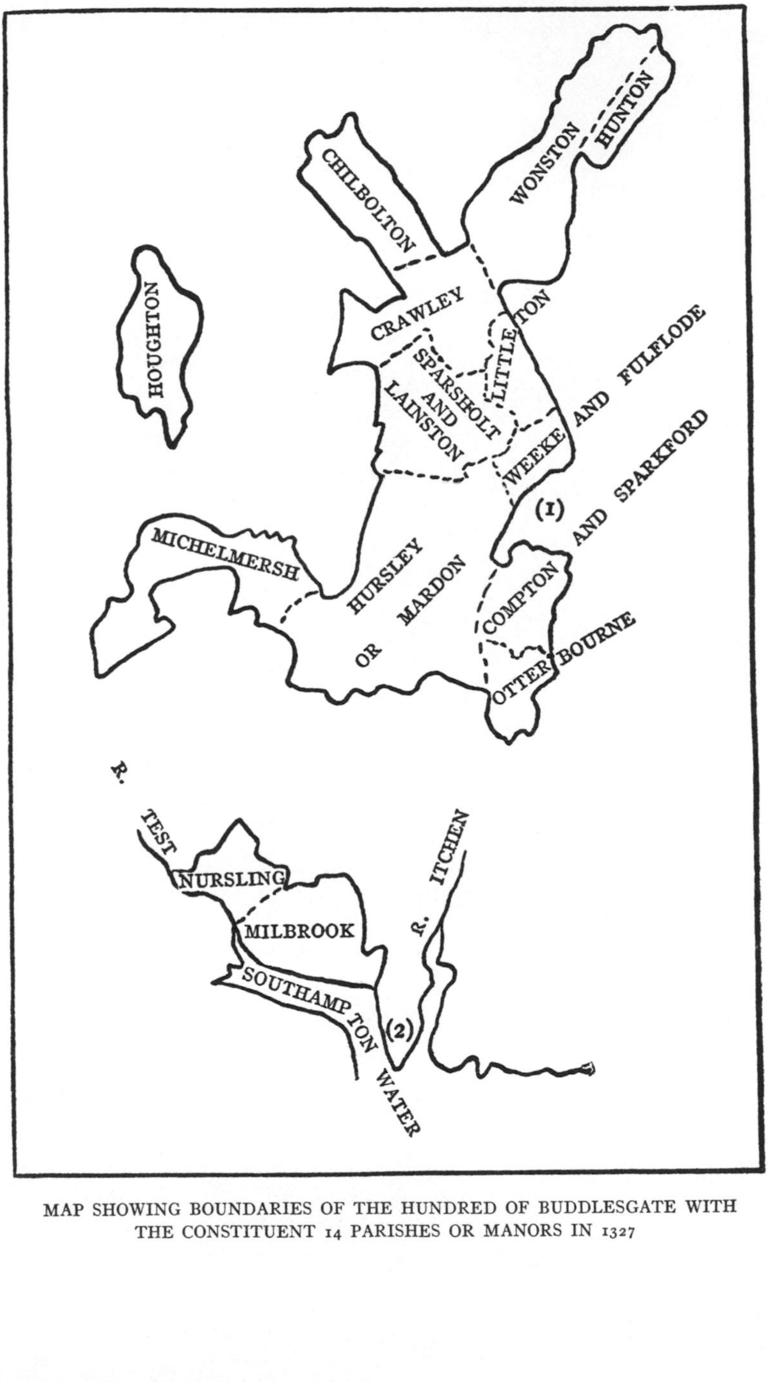

MAP SHOWING BOUNDARIES OF THE HUNDRED OF BUDDLESGATE WITH THE CONSTITUENT 14 PARISHES OR MANORS IN 1327

elmo p*ro* ass*isa* fract*a*. De vj d. de thom*a* p*ro* pleuina. De vj d. de Alic*ia* p*ro* sursis*a*. De vj d. de Will*elmo* p*ro* falso clam*eo*. De ij s. vj d. de Elia thanculf Alex*andro* thom*a* Will*elmo* p*ro* falso Jur*amento*. De vj d. de Rand*ulfo* p*ro* surs*isa*. De vj d. de Matill*a* p*ro* stultil*oquio*. De ij s. de Ingera*m* p*ro* medl*ea*. De vj d. de Iuone p*ro* virgis. De vj d. de Nich*olao* p*ro* pastur*a*. De vj d. de Rob*erto* p*ro* sim*i*li. De vj d. de Hen*rico* p*ro* furag*io*. De xij d. de Joh*anne* p*ro* bosco. De iiij s. de thanculf' p*ro* fil*ia* mar*itanda*. De iiij s. de Iuone p*ro* sorore mar*itanda*. De ij s. de Ric*ardo* p*ro* fil*ia* mar*itanda*. S*umma* liij s.

§§ 30. View of the Frankpledge in the Hundred of Buddlesgate, 11 May, 1466.

The tithingmen of the different tithings, or frankpledge groups, in the public hundred came together on Sunday, 11 May, apparently in the year 1466, and presented the failure of the members of the tithing to appear at the public court of the hundred, the breaches of the assize of ale, the presence of stray animals, and so on. The tithingman in most of the instances here printed was supposed to come five-handed (debet venire se v^to^), that is, with four companions of the tithing to make the charges. If he was short a companion, he paid 6d., once 4d., if the companion was a freeman; if a customary tenant, apparently it was 3d.

Since Crawley and Hunton constituted one tithing, we cannot tell which entries apply to each. It is likely that Richard Nevyle, Earl of Salisbury, was amerced 12d. for failure to appear as a suitor, not from Crawley but from Hunton, which he held at this time. The miller who charged excessive toll probably also belonged to Hunton, for Crawley apparently had no grist mill. John Crouche and the white wether, however, may have belonged to Crawley. At any rate, Crawley men were coming into touch with the men of other villages at the public hundred court. In the case of Crawley and Hunton, it was the whole tithing apparently, and not just the tithingman and five of his fellows, who went forth to make known the evil deeds of the members of their group.

There is a similar record for 5 William and Mary (1692–93). The tithing of Crawley and Hunton was among the seventeen tithings of the Hundred of Buddlesgate and Barton.[1]

[1] MS., P. R. O., Ecclesiastical Commission, Court Roll, 78/26.

Butlesgate Hundr*edum* cum Visu F*ra*ncii Plegii tent*um* ib*idem* die Sabb*at*i xj^{mo} die mens*is* Maii Anno sup*radict*o [1]

Decenarius de Chilbolton' ven*it* se v^{to} vt deb*er*et.
Decenarius de Brandesbury ven*it* se v^{to} vt deb*er*et.
Decenarius de Wonsyngton' ven*it* se v^{to} vt deb*er*et.
} Et p*resen*-*tant* om*n*ia bene.

Decenarius de Nutshullyng qui venir*e* deb*er*et se v^{to} non ven*it* nisi se quarto q*uia* Joh*ann*es p*ar*ker' jun*ior* qui sequi deb*er*et d*ict*am decen*am* fac*it* def*altam* i*de*o ip*s*e in mi*sericordia* (iij d.).[2] Et p*resentat* def*altam* Ten*ementis* (vj d.) terr*arum et* ten*ementorum* nup*er* Ed*ward*i Foster m*odo* Thome Hardegr*a*ue Ten*entis* (vj d.) terr*arum et* ten*ementorum* nup*er* Joh*ann*is Grenefeld*e* lib*erorum* i*de*o ip*s*i in mi*sericordia*. Mi*seri*-*cordie* xv d.[3]

Dec*enarius* de Milbroke qui venir*e* deb*er*et se v^{to} non ven*it* nisi se iiij^{to} q*uia* Joh*ann*es Tery qui sequi deb*er*et d*ict*am dec*enam* fac*it* de-f*altam* i*de*o ip*s*e in mi*sericordia*. Et p*resentat* def*altam* Ten*entium* (vj d.) terr*arum et* ten*ementorum* nup*er* Ric*ard*i Holte *et* Ric*ard*i Hunte [4] libe-*rorum* i*de*o ip*s*i in mi*sericordia*. Mi*sericordi*e vj d.[3]

Dec*enarius* de Muchelm*er*sh*e* ven*it* se v^{to} vt deb*er*et. Et p*resentat* de-f*altam* Ten*entis* [5] terr*arum et* ten*ementorum* nup*er* Ric*ard*i pisto*r*is Ten*entis* (vj d.) terr*arum et* ten*ementorum* voc*at*i Sadelers Ten*entium* terr*arum et* ten*ementorum* nup*er* Joh*ann*is Wattez [6] Joh*ann*is Canter-ton' (vj d.) *et* Joh*ann*is Em*er*y (vj d.) lib*erorum* lib*erorum*[sic] i*de*o ip*s*i in mi*sericordia*. Mi*sericordi*e xviij d.[3]

Decen*arius* de Merden*a* ven*it* se v^{to}. Et p*resentat* om*n*ia bene.

Dec*enarius* de Houghton' ven*it* se v^{to} vt deb*er*et. Et p*resentat* om*n*ia bene.

Dec*enarius* de Eldestoke cum sua de*cena* ven*it*. Et p*resentat* de-f*altam* Thome H[a]mpton [7] lib*eri* i*de*o ip*s*e in mi*sericordia*. Item p*re*-*sentat* vnu*m* multon*em* albu*m* p*recium* vj d. p*rouen*t*um* de ex*tra*hur*a* ad festu*m* pentecosten p*er* vnu*m* Annu*m* elaps*um et* Amplius *et* rem*anet* d*omi*no q*uia* sup*er*an*natus et* vend*itus* Thome Hampton' p*ro* eodem p*recio*. Ext*ra*hur*a* Rem*anet* sup*er*an*natus et* vend*itus* vj d.[3]

Dec*enarius* de Oturbo*ur*ne cum sua decena ven*it*. Et p*resentat* de-f*altam* Ten*entis* (vj d.) terr*e et* ten*ementi* nup*er* Thome Wykeh*a*m Te-*nentium* (vj d.) terr*e et* ten*ementorum* nup*er* Joh*ann*is Roger' Thome Faucon*er* (vj d.) Joh*ann*is Burgh*e* (vj d.) Rob*er*t*i* Moure (vj d.) Ten*en*-*tium* (vj d.) terr*e et* Ten*ementorum* nup*er* Rob*er*t*i* Colpas *et* Thome Sal-

[1] Extract from a MS., P. R. O., Ecclesiastical Commission, Court Rolls, 80/1.
[2] All sums in parenthesis in this account have been interlineated in the original.
[3] In the margin.
[4] postea ven*iunt* interlineated.
[5] Apparently q*uia* v*enit* is interlineated here.
[6] Postea ven*it* interlineated.
[7] postea ven*it* interlineated at this point.

man' (iiij d.) lib*erorum* id*e*o ip*s*i in mi*sericordia*. It*e*m p*resentat* q*uo*d Thom*as* Dene (vj d.) ij br*achiavit et* fr*egit* assis*am* c*e*ruis*ie* id*e*o ip*s*e in mi*sericordia*. It*e*m q*uo*d Joh*ann*es Baker' (ij d.) tab*er*nauit *et* fr*egit* as-s*isam* c*e*ruis*ie* id*e*o ip*s*e in mi*sericordia*. It*e*m p*resentat* def*altam* Wil-l*elm*i Tann*ere* [1] Thome Dene (iij d.) id*e*o ip*s*i in mi*sericordia*. Mi*seri-cordi*e iiij s. iij d.[2] It*e*m p*resentat* j bouic*u*l*um* m*aculosum*[?] p*recium* [——] [3] p*r*ouen*tum* de ex*tra*hur*a* ad f*est*um Aduinc*u*la S*anct*i Pet*ri* vlt*i-m*um elaps*um et* rem*anet* in Custod*ia* Ric*ard*i Rombold'. Ext*ra*hur*a* Rem*anens*.[2]

Decenarius de Craule *et* Hunton' cum sua decena ven*it*. Et p*resentat* def*altam* Ric*ard*i Neuyle Comit*is* Sar*um* lib*eri* (xij d.) i*de*o ip*s*e in mi-*sericordia*. It*e*m p*resentat* q*uo*d Will*elmu*s Algar' est molend*inarius et* capit tel*onium* exc*essivum* (iij d.) id*e*o ip*s*e in mi*sericordia*. It*e*m p*re-sentat* def*altam* Ric*ard*i Forder' (iij d.) id*e*o ip*s*e in mi*sericordia*. It*e*m p*resentat* q*uo*d Joh*ann*es Cruche (iij d.) j br*achiavit et* fr*egit* assi*sam* c*e*ruis*ie* id*e*o ip*s*e in mi*sericordia*. Mi*sericordi*e xxj d.[1] It*e*m p*resentat* j mult*onem* albu*m* p*recium* vj d. p[ro]uen*tum* de ext*ra*hur*a* ad festu*m* S*anct*i Mich*ael*is Arch*angel*i vlt*im*um elaps*um*. Et null*us* ven*it* ad ill*um* cal*u*mmp*niandum* id*e*o rem*anet* in cust*odia* Joh*ann*is Cruche. Ext*ra-*hura Rem*anens*.[2]

§§ 31. Presentations and Ordinances made at the Tourn of St. Martin's along with the Court, 10 Sept., 1599.

The twelve jurors were doubtless customary tenants, while the chief juror, William Edmondes, gentleman, was probably the farmer of the manorial demesnes. Walter Sands, knight, was presented as a free suitor and amerced 6d. for failure to attend the court. It is not unlikely that he was a tenant of one of the more or less separate estates such as "the Hoo" which is very old, and the Rookley House estate, possibly more recent. Richard Pitter, nineteen years and a half old, was admitted to the messuage and half virgate of bond land in South Crawley, the heriot given on the death of his father being a cow which, when sold by the supervisor of stock, brought 30s. As was the rule in Crawley, he succeeded to the holding as the youngest son; whether he was regarded as actually having reached his majority is not clear.

[1] Apparently q*uia* v*enit* are interlineated here (?).
[2] In the margin.
[3] Left blank.

There were four ordinances. (1) No copyholder or other person was to use any drag in the common fields, under the heavy penalty of 40s. If this referred to the use of a heavy harrow, it is difficult to see the point in the prohibition, unless the instrument injured the crops of others when taken from strip to strip. (2) No copyholder or other person was to keep upon the common pasture more than one young calf for each yardland in his possession. If he gave up pasture for a horse, however, he might keep two calves. The stint on tenants' rights of pasture was, of course, a common manorial restriction. On the whole, it was a rather serious limitation. (3) No copyholder possessing a yardland in South Crawley was to keep more than ten ewes apart from the common flock unless he had them on his own grounds. As we know from other sources,[1] he might have twenty-five sheep in the common flock; but here we find the prohibition that he might not have more than ten mother sheep anywhere else, except on his own grounds. Just where he was putting them or what the issue was is not clear. And (4) no copyholder was to be allowed to sublet to anyone without finding surety that the subtenant would not become a public charge. This is an eloquent testimony to the result of the much-worked leasing system. The rise of a market for land with the resulting breaking up of estates and bringing in of new tenants had not proved successful in some cases. It is noteworthy that the homage of the manor should presume to legislate on a subject which affected the agrarian policy of the manor, the lord's practices, and the lord's revenues from fines.

Here we have the two courts meeting together. One was the bishop's tourn with its jury of twelve who on this occasion found "all things well." The other was the court [baron?] with its homage, or group of tenants, who presented facts concerning suit of court, heriots, and so on, and made ordinances dealing with the cultivation of the soil. The tourn met twice a year, whilst the court [baron] might meet twice or oftener if desirable. Apparently the bishop's tourn was a kind of private hundred court, while the court baron was a private manorial court. The first was a private view of frankpledge, while the second was a private

[1] See above, § 12, pp. 44–45.

gathering of the lord's tenants. The first looked to criminal cases (in part), the latter to civil cases, in so far as such a distinction can be made. One would judge from the Crawley records that little differentiation was, in practice, made between the two courts which doubtless were held together in the hall of the manorial court in Crawley itself.

CRAWLEY *MANERIUM*[1]

Turn*us* s*ancti* Martini Cum Cur*ia* ib*ide*m tent*us* decimo die Septemb*ris* Anno regni Elizabeth*e* die gra*lia* Angl*ie* Franc*ie* et Hib*er*nie R*eg*ine fi*dei* defens*oris etcetera* Quadragesimo primo et anno trans*lationis* d*omi*ni Thome Bils*on* Winton*iensis* Ep*iscop*i Tercio.

No*min*a Jurat*orum.*

Will*el*mus Edmonds gen*erosus* Jur*atus*

Rob*er*tus Baker Launcelot*us* Waite Joh*ann*es Waite Ric*ardus* Davie Edmund*us* Symes Joh*ann*es Browninge	Jur*ati*	Ric*ard*us Beche Joh*ann*es Pitter Joh*ann*es Becham Joh*ann*es Longe Ric*ard*us Page Rob*er*tus Nashe	Jur*ati*

P*re*sentac*i*o *duode*cem[sic] p*ro* d*omi*na R*egi*na et homag*ii* Jurator*es* vi*delicet* Will*el*mus Edmonds et socii sui iurat*i* ven*iunt* et p*re*senta[n]t q*uo*d Walter*us* Sands miles est liber sectat*o*r et fecit defaltam*.* I*de*o ip*s*e in mi*sericordi*a. M*isericordia* vj d.[2]

Item p*re*senta[n]t q*uo*d Joh*ann*es Wilkins est tene*ns* Custumari*us* et fecit defalta*m* ad hunc die*m*. I*de*o ip*s*e in mi*sericordi*a. M*isericordia* iiij d.[2]

Item p*re*senta[n]t q*uo*d Rob*er*tus Pitter qui de d*omi*no tenuit s*ecun*d*um* Consuetud*inem* man*er*ii p*redicti* vn*um* mes*suagium* et di*midiam* virgat*am* terr*e* nat*ive* in avstral*i* p*ar*te de Cralley obiit Citra vlti*mam* Curia*m* Vnde accid*it* d*omi*no de heriett*o* vna vacca vendit*a* p*er* sup*er*visor*em* pro quinquaginta solidis Et q*uo*d Ric*ard*us Pitter est filius Jun*ior* et prox*imus* heres p*redicti* Rob*er*ti s*ecund*um Consuetud*inem* man*er*ii p*redicti* et est etat*is* novemdecem [sic] annoru*m* et dimid*ii* vn*ius* anni.

Hariett*us* j vacca vendit*a* p*er* sup*er*visorem pro quinquaginta solidis. Denar*ii* solut*i* Sup*er*visor*i*.[2]

Ad hanc cur*iam* ordinat*um* est modo et forma sequent*ibus* vi*delicet* That noe parson, copiholder or other shall vse anie dragge in the Com-

[1] MS., P. R. O., Ecclesiastical Commission, Court Rolls, 91/6, fol. 10.
[2] In the margin.

mon field*es* at anie tyme in the yere vppon paine that eu*er*ie p*ar*son makinge defalte shall forfaite and loose for eu*er*ie defalt*e* in that behalf*e* xl s. P*en*a posit*a*.[1]

Item ordinat*um* est modo et forma sequent*ibus* vi*delicet* that noe Copiholder of the mannor shall at anie tyme herafter weane in the Com*m*on of the mannor above one Calfe vppon A yarde Lande exsept he shall first abate Common for one horse, vppon w*hi*ch abatement it shalbe lawful to weane twoo Calfes in liewe of the same horse vppon paine of eu*er*ie p*ar*son makinge defalte in this behalf*e* to forfaite and Loose foreu*er*ie defalte xx s. Ordinac*io* Cum pena.[1]

Item ordinat*um* est modo et forma sequent*ibus* That noe Copiholder of the sowth side of Crawley shall keepe at anie tyme of the yere above Tenne ewes for a yarde lande from the Com*m*on flocke exsept he doth keepe them in his Inne ground*es* vppon paine that eu*er*ie parson makinge defalte in the behalf*e* shall forfaite and loose for eu*er*ie ewe kepte contrary to the trewe meaninge of this order vj s. viij d. Ordinac*io* Cum pena.[1]

Et vlteri*us* p*re*sentant q*uo*d o*mn*ia bene.

Ad hanc Cur*iam* ordinat*um* est modo et forma sequent*ibus* vi*delicet* That noe Copiholder of this mannor shall herafter take or receave anie vndertena*n*t exsept he shall first putt in sufficient suerties to save the parrisshion*er*s harmles*s* of all Charg*es and* Contribuc*io*ns to arise growe or be imposed vppon the parrish or anie of the parrisshion*er*s there inhabitinge by reason of anie such vndertena*n*t vppon payne to forfaite *and* loose for eu*er*ie defalte vj s. viij d. Ordinac*io* Cu*m* pena.[1]

Affur*atores* { Will*elm*us Edmond*es* / Rob*er*tus Baker } Jur*ati*

§§ 32. Presentations and Elections at the Tourn and Court, 20 March, 1601.

This time there were fourteen jurors, John Wilkins, senior, being the chief juror or tithingman. The names of three other jurors were stricken out. Apparently two of the men in question were themselves presented, one for absence, the other for failure to perform his customary services. The two affuratores were the assessors of amercements. Both the tithingman and the reeve were elected. One wonders whether the reeve had been elected from the very first.

[1] In the margin.

The duality of the court is indicated by the words Juratores and duodecem on the one hand and Curia and homagium on the other. Two classes of tenants are found. The free-suitor element had been in earlier times very scant or non-existent. At this time it is doubtful whether there were more than two or three free tenants. Of course the customary tenant predominated.

The amercement of 6s. 8d. for not coming to shear and wash the lord's sheep was a heavy one. This item is one of the interesting survivals of the old non-week-work.

CRAWLEY *MANERIUM* [1]

Turn*us* de Hock*e* Cum Curia Man*er*ii ib*ide*m tent*us* vicesimo die Martii anno regni Elizabeth*e* dei gr*ati*a Anglie Franc*ie* et Hib*er*nie Regine fidei defen*soris etcetera* Quadragesimo tercio et anno translac*ionis* d*omi*ni Thome Bilson Winton*iensis* Ep*iscop*i Tercio.

Esso*n*ia [——] [2]

No*mi*na Jur*atorum* p*ro* d*omi*na R*egi*na et homag*ii*

Joh*ann*es Wilkins sen*ior* Jur*atus*

Will*elm*us Edmond*es* Jur*atus*

Rob*er*tus Baker Jur*atus*	Ric*ard*us Beche Jur*atus*
Lancelotus Wayte Jur*atus*	Joh*ann*es Pitter Jur*atus*
Joh*ann*es Browninge Jur*atus*	Ric*ard*us page Jur*atus*
Ric*ard*us Davie sen*ior* Jur*atus*	Joh*ann*es Wayte Jur*atus*
Ric*ard*us Allen Jur*atus*	Joh*ann*es Wilkins Jun*ior* Jur*atus*
Rob*er*tus nashe Jur*atus*	Henric*us* puckenhall Jur*atus*

p*re*sentacio *duode*cem[sic] p*ro* d*omi*na R*egi*na et homag*ii*.[3]

Jurator*es* vi*delicet* Joh*ann*es Wilkins sen*ior* et socii sui iurat*i* ven*iunt* et p*re*sentant q*uo*d Walter*us* Sands miles est liber sectator et fecit defalta*m*. I*de*o ip*s*e in mi*sericordi*a. M*isericordia* vj d.[3]

Item p*re*senta[n]t q*uo*d Joh*ann*es Beacham est tene*n*s Custu*marius* et fecit defalta*m*. I*de*o ip*s*e in mi*sericordi*a. M*isericordia* vj d.[3]

Item p*re*senta[n]t quod Edmu*n*dus Symes vnus tenenciu*m* Custu*ma*rior*um* d*omi*ni man*er*ii pred*icti* non venit ad tonend*um* et Lavand*um* oves d*omi*ni sec*un*d*um* Consuetud*inem* man*er*ii p*redicti* pr*o*ut de iur*e* debet et ex antiquo Consuevit. I*de*o ip*s*e in mi*sericordi*a. M*isericordia* vj s. viij d.[3]

Et vlteri*us* p*re*sentant q*uo*d o*mn*ia bene

Affurator*es* { Johannes Wilkins sen*ior* / Lancelot*us* Wayte }

[1] MS., P. R. O., Ecclesiastical Commission, Court Rolls, 91/7, fol. memb. 50.
[2] Blank.
[3] In the margin.

Edwardus Robert*es* elect*us* est in officiu*m* decenar*ii* ib*ide*n. et Jur*a*-*tus* est

Ric*ard*us Page elect*us* est in officiu*m* p*re*posit*i* ib*ide*m et Jur*atus* est.

§§ 33. Presentations and Elections at the Tourn and Court, 19 April, 1649.

The duality of the old-time court is clearly set forth in this document. On the one hand, there is the lord's tourn or leet in which there are two presentations made by the jurors, one of cert money (the medieval tithingpenny) at the early rate of 6s. 8d., the other that "all was well." On the other hand, there is the court baron with its homage which presents two free suitors and three customary tenants for absence. The customary tenants had to pay 4d. each, the free suitors 6d. each. It is stated that the two free suitors owed suit at the public (?) hundred court. The death of a tenant is recorded, as also the election of a tithingman and a reeve. The amercements were fixed, not by two affeerers but by the whole homage.

The new lord of the inter regnum period was John Pigeon. It is tempting to say that he was responsible for the clearer differentiation of the two courts. The new lord was the proud possessor of both a private hundred court (court leet or tourn) and a court baron. And he had at the time two free suitors — often regarded as necessary for a full-fledged manor. There were also the stalwart customary-tenant families, the Godwyns, the Pitters, and the Waytes. A strange name, Edward Roseblade, crops up suddenly, as has happened frequently before, showing either the effect of a freer land policy or of marriages with persons outside the manor.

CRAWLEY MANER*IUM* [1]

Turn*us* de Hock cu*m* Curia Baron*is* Joh*ann*is Pigeon Ar*migeri* do*mi*ni man*er*ii pred*icti* ib*ide*m tent*us* decimo nono die Aprilis Anno d*omi*ni Millesimo sexcen*tesimo* quadrage*simo* Nono.

No*mina* Jur*atorum* p*ro* leta *et* homag*ii*.

Will*elm*us Godwyn Jur*atus*

[1] MS., P. R. O., Ecclesiastical Commission, Court Rolls, 99/7, fol. 8.

Rob*er*tus Pitter Will*elm*us Stevens Will*elm*us Browning Will*elm*us long*e* Nich*ol*aus Pile Rob*er*tus wilkins	Jur*ati*	Rich*ard*us Beech*e* Georgius Penton Ed*ward*us Roseblade Thomas wayte Joh*ann*es Symes Thomas Allen	Jur*ati*

Decen*nar*ius ib*id*em vi*delice*t Georgius Penton cu*m* decen*n*a s*ua* Jur*ati* ven*iunt et pr*esentant q*uo*d d*an*t d*omi*no de certo ad hunc diem vj s. viij d.

Et vlter*ius* pr*e*sentant q*uo*d o*mn*ia bene.

Presentac*io* Jur*atorum* p*ro* leta *et* homag*ii* [1]

Juratores ib*id*em vi*delicet* Will*elm*us Godwyn *et* socii s*ui* Jur*ati* ven*iunt et pr*esentant q*uo*d Christiana dawley vid*ua* et d*omi*na Lumley sunt lib*ere* sectatores *et* debent sect*am* ad hunc die*m et* fecer*unt* defalt*am*. *id*eo q*ui*libet eor*um* in mi*sericordi*a vj d.

It*em* pr*e*sentant q*uo*d Will*elm*us Brodway Petrus Barton *et* Will*elm*us Wilkin sunt ten*en*tes Custum*arii* huius man*er*ii *et* ad hunc die*m* fece*runt* defalt*am*. *id*eo q*ui*libet eor*um* in mi*sericordi*a iiij d.

Item eliger*unt* Joh*ann*em Tolfry in offic*ium* decen*nar*ii ib*id*em p*ro* A*nn*o futuro et Jur*atus*.

It*em* eliger*unt* Thoma*m* wayte in offic*ium* p*r*epos*iti* man*er*ii p*ro* hoc A*nn*o *et* Jur*atus*.

It*em* pr*e*sentant q*uo*d Will*elm*us Howchem. obit*um* tenen*tis*.[2]

Affur*amentum* [3] p*er* tot*um* homag*ium*.

§§ 34. Presentations, Orders, and an Ordinance made at the Tourn and Court, 21 March, 1663.

Three groups of suitors were amerced for failure to attend court, namely, seven inhabitants paying 3d. each, two free suitors paying 6d. each, and seven customary tenants paying 4d. each. While there were thirteen tenants named as present, there were sixteen absent and amerced. These "inhabitants" seem to bear names strange to the manor; they may have been subtenants.

A son and heir is admitted to his inheritance by a composition of 30s. This was the only fine recorded. One of the tenants was amerced 20s. for having encroached upon the king's highway.

[1] In the margin.

[2] obit*um* tenen*tis* in the margin.

[3] This is preceded by a gap with a marginal entry: vide penas *et* pr*e*sentac*ion*em Jur' cu*m* d*omi*no Man*er*ii.

Eight orders were issued to make or repair gates and hedges. One ordinance was enacted that no one within the manor should permit his horses or colts to be unfettered. Apparently this was regarded as a fresh enactment. It stands as a memorial to the legislative capacity of the community of manorial tenants.

CRAWLEY [1]

Turn*us* de Hocke cu*m* Cur*ia* Mane*r*ii ib*idem* tent*us* vicesimo primo die Marcii Anno Regni d*o*mini n*o*st*r*i Caroli Secu*n*di dei g*ra*t*ia* Angl*ie* Scoc*ie* Franc*ie* *et* Hib*er*nie R*egi*s fidei defensor*is* *etcetera* decimo quinto Annoq*ue* tran*s*l*ationis* Dom*i*ni Georgii Winton*iensis* Ep*iscop*i primo.
Esso*nie* [——] [2]
Nom*i*na Jur*atorum* p*ro* Dom*i*no Rege *et* homag*ii*.[3]

Robe*r*tus Pitter — Jur*atus*		Ric*ard*us Sheapeard	
Will*elm*us Godwin		Will*elm*us Poole	
Ric*ard*us Long		Will*elm*us Brew*n*ing	
Nich*o*la*us* Pyle	Jur*ati*	Ric*ard*us Francklin	Jur*ati*
Ambros*ius* Beeche		Georgius Penton	
Thomas Allen		Will*elm*us Monke	
Will*elm*us Harris			

Decenn*arius* ib*idem* v*idelicet* Will*elm*us Brewning *et* Socii sui Jur*ati* veni*unt* *et* p*re*sent*ant* q*uo*d dant D*omi*no de certo ad hunc diem

Itim [sic] p*re*sent*ant* q*uo*d Will*elm*us Baker Robe*r*tus Hatche Jacobus Morgan Will*elm*us Newman *et* Georgius Rawlins sunt Inh*a*bitantes infra p*re*cinct*a* huius Turni *et* debent secta*m* *et* ad hanc Cur*iam* fece*runt* def*altam*. Ideo q*ui*libet eor*um* in M*iser*icordia iij d.

Itim p*re*sent*ant* q*uo*d Will*elm*us Duns Sandys *et* Henricus Dawley Sunt liberi Sectatores huius Manerii *et* debent secta*m* *et* ad hanc Cur*iam* fece*runt* def*altam*. Ideo q*ui*libet eor*um* in misericordi*a* vj d.

Itim p*re*sent*ant* q*uo*d [——] [2] Sheppeard vid*ua* Will*elm*us Long Henricus Allen Will*elm*us Page Will*elm*us Broadway [——] [2] Stevens vid*ua* Henricus Symes Sunt tene*n*t*es* customar*ii* huius Manerii *et* debent Secta*m* *et* ad hanc Cur*iam* fece*runt* def*altam*. Ideo q*ui*libet eor*um* in mis*er*icordia iiij d.

Presentacio Jur*atorum* p*ro* Dom*i*no Rege *et* homag*ii*.[3] Fine*s* Anno: Juratores ib*idem* (v*idelicet*) Robe*r*tus Pitter *et* Socii Sui Jur*ati* veni*unt* *et* p*re*sent*ant* q*uo*d Thomas Waight qui de d*omi*no tenuit huius Manerii [——] [2] citra vlt*imam* Cur*iam* obiit *et* q*uo*d Thomas Waight est filius *et* prox*imus* heres p*re*di*cti* Thome ad om*n*ia p*re*miss*a*. Et q*uo*d Joanna

---

[1] MS., P. R. O., Ecclesiastical Commission, Court Rolls, 100/4, fol. 50.
[2] Blank.   [3] In the margin.

relict*a* p*redict*i Thome def*uncti* debet gaudere p*re*miss*a* durant*e* vid*ua*-*tate* Sua Sec*un*d*u*m consuet*udinem* Man*er*ii.[1]

Itim p*re*sent*ant* q*uo*d Rob*er*tus Baker J*unior* incrochiauit Sup*er* via*m* Regia*m* ib*ide*m. p*re*cept*um* est eidem aperire incrochiament*um* p*re*-*dictum* ante festu*m* s*anct*i Mich*ae*lis Arch*ange*li p*roximo* futur*um* sub-pen*a* xx s.[2]

Precept*um* est tenentibus de Crawley q*uem*lib*e*t ex p*ar*te Sua suffi-cient*er* facere Sepes Suas v*er*sus le Downe *et* parke ante Sextu*m* diem Maii p*roximo* futur*um* subpena *cuius*libet delinquen*tis* x s.[2]

Precept*um* est si*m*ilit*er* tenentibus ib*ide*m q*uem*lib*e*t ex p*ar*te sua Sufficient*er* facere sepes vocat*as* Bottomeway hedge ante primu*m* diem Aprilis p*roximo* futur*um* Subpen*a* *cuius*lib*e*t deliquen*tis* v s.[2]

Precpet*um* est o*mn*ibus quibus de iure Spectan*t* Sufficient*er* facere Janua*m* voc*atam* way pittle gate *et* Sepes ib*ide*m ante primu*m* diem Aprilis p*roximo* futur*um* Subpen*a* *cuius*lib*e*t delinquen*tis* v s.[2]

Precept*um* est Si*m*ilit*er* o*mn*ibus quibus de iure Spectan*t* facere *et* rep*ar*are Janua*m* voc*atam* Bakers lane gate ante primu*m* die*m* Aprilis p*roximo* futur*um* Subpen*a* *cuius*lib*e*t delinquen*tis* v s.[2]

Precept*um* est Si*m*ilit*er* o*mn*ibus quibus de iure Spectan*t* facere Sepes a Norbury pales vsq*ue* Coome ante sextu*m* diem Maii Subpen*a* *cuius*-lib*e*t deliquen*tis* v s.[2]

Precept*um* est o*mn*ibus quibus de iure Spectan*t* Sufficient*er* facere Sepes a buttes gate to delledge ante Sextu*m* diem Maii p*roximo* futu-*rum* subpen*a* *cuius*lib*e*t delinquen*tis* v s.[3]

Precept*um* est o*mn*ibus quibus de iure Spectan*t* Sufficient*er* facere Sepes apud Thornam ante decimu*m* diem Maii p*roximo* futur*um* Sub-pen*a* *cuius*libet delinquen*tis* v s.[3]

Precept*um* est omnibus quibus de iure Spectan*t* sufficient*er* facere Januas voc*atas* Millere lane gate *et* Winchester lane gate ante sextu*m* diem Maii p*roximo* futur*um* subpen*a* *cuius*lib*e*t delinquen*tis* vs.[3]

Ordinat*um* est ad hanc Cur*iam* q*uo*d nulla p*er*sona infra Man*er*iu*m* p*redictum* p*er*mittet equos Seu pullos Suos incompeditos anglicé vnfet-tered Subpen*a* v s.[4]

Will*elm*us Page elect*us* est in officiu*m* decenn*arii* de Crawley *et* Jur*atus*.[5]

Ed*ward*us Butterley elect*us* est in officiu*m* p*re*posit*i* ib*ide*m *et* Jur*atus*.[2]

Afferr*atores* { Rob*er*tus Pitter / Will*elm*us Godwin } Jur*ati*

[1] In the margin: Herr*iettus* p*er* composic*ionem* xxx s. in custodia Prepo*s*it*i* ib*ide*m.

[2] In the margin: Elect*io* prepo*s*it*i*.

[3] In the margin: pen*a* po*s*it*a*.

[4] In the margin: Ord*inatio* cu*m* pen*a*.

[5] In the margin: Elect*io* decenn*arii*.

§§ 35. Court Presentation of the Commutation of the Customary Service of Carrying Manure to the Fields, 4 April, 1690.

There is but one notable feature here. The tenants in South Crawley from at least the thirteenth century [1] had been accustomed to carrying the lord's dung from the demesne farm gate to the demesne fields. Twenty-five tenants had participated in this service, each carrying one load to the demesne fields and each receiving for his own fields one load. The reeve had been exempt from this service because of his office.

Now at last, after at least over 400 years, the service was commuted to a money payment of 24s., the reeve not paying anything by virtue of his office. Apparently the customary tenants shouldered this burden of 1s. each in lieu of the service, and probably they continued to pay it until the enclosure in 1795. Since the lord had long leased his home farm to the general farmer, the services had been due to the latter. And henceforth it is the general farmer who is to receive the money in lieu of the service. In the fifteenth century, as before, all commutation money went to the lord. This present instance is indicative of what was happening: the general farmer, who had leased the home farm, was gradually taking the place of the lord. On the whole, the general farmer seems to have driven a good bargain. He was to receive 24s. in cash and could keep the 25 loads which the tenants (including the reeve) had formerly received for their own lands.

Here we find one of the few references to the lord's steward who presided over the court and was responsible for the writing out of the court rolls. Under one name or another, he had apparently been visiting Crawley, holding courts since at least 1208 when the extant reeves' accounts begin.

CRAWLEY [2]

Turn*us* de Hocke cu*m* Curi*a* Man*er*ii p*redicti* ib*ide*m tent*us* quarto die Aprilis Anno r*e*gni D*omi*nor*um* n*ost*ror*um* Will*elm*i et Marie Regis *et* Regine Angl*ie* *etcetera* Sec*un*do, Annoq*ue* tra*nslationis* D*omi*ni Petri Winton*iensis* Ep*isco*pi Sexto.

[1] See above, §§ 11, pp. 229 ff.

[2] MS., P. R. O., Ecclesiastical Commission, Court Rolls, 104/2, fol. 51.

N*omin*a Jur*atorum* pro D*omin*is Reg*e* et Regina et Homag*ii*: [1]

Henricus Sym*m*es Jur*atus*

Nathaniel' Pyle Rob*er*tus Pitter Ambrosius Beech Georgius Penton	Jur*ati*	Will*elm*us Hacke Rich*ard*us Shepperd Joh*ann*es Cooper Joh*ann*es Tompson	Jur*ati*
Rob*er*tus Baker Jacobus Waight Will*elm*us Pitter Joh*ann*es Page iun*ior*	Jur*ati*	Michael' Batchelor Philippus Isron Joh*ann*es Wilkins Joh*ann*es Harris	Jur*ati*
Joh*ann*es Wilkins Will*elm*us Harris	Jur*ati*	Rich*ard*us Fifeild Joh*ann*es Long	Jur*ati*

21:

Decenn*arius* ib*id*em (vi*delice*t) Henricus Long cu*m* Decenn*a* sua Jur*ati* [2] ven*iunt* et p*re*sent*ant* q*uod* dant D*omi*no de Certo ad hunc diem.

It*em* p*re*sent*ant* [——] [3]

It*em* p*re*sent*ant* q*uo*d Will*elm*us Newman Elizabetha Webb vid*ua* et Joanna Houchen vid*ua* sunt Tenen*tes* Custom*arii* huius Manerii et debent secta*m et* ad hanc Cur*iam* fecer*unt* Defa*u*lt*am*. Ideo quilib*e*t eor*um* in mi*sericordi*a iiij d.

Et vlter*ius* p*re*sent*ant* q*uod* omnia bene.

Presentac*io* Jur*atorum et* homag*ii*.[1] Jurat*ores* p*redicti* p*re*sent*ant* in his Anglic*ân*is verbis seque*ntibus*, — Item wee present that whereas a Service is due from Severall of the Tenanants [sic] of the South side of this Manno*r* to be p*er*formed yearly to *the Lord* of the s*aid* Manno*r* as to his Demesnes in carrying of Dung from the Farme Gate into the Feilds belonging to the said Demesnes for four and twenty days (vi*delice*t for every day one Load) for which Service when p*er*formed the s*ai*d Tenants are to have four and twenty Loads of Dung yearly out of the Lords Gate belonging to the Demesnes for and towards the Improvement of their own Lands Now att this Court there happening a Difference betweene the Tenant to the Demesnes and the Ten*ants* obliged to p*er*forme the said Service about the doeing thereof for that there is a new Farmehouse built att a greater Distance than before where the Dung is and will be made and the Severall Tenants lookeing vpon it as more trouble to them in the performance of the Said Service

[1] In the margin.

[2] At this point it is difficult to elongate satisfactorily. Forms in other accounts have been followed here.

[3] Blank.

It is therefore agreed att this Court betweene the Tenant to the Demesnes and the other Tenants that they shall yearly pay four and twenty Shillings to the Farmer of the Demesnes for the Said four and twenty days Service and remitt their Severall Loads of Dung due to them, And the Reive of the said Mann*or* for the time being is yearly to be excused from paying his Share of the four *and* Twenty Shillings as he was from his Share of performing *the* Carting days in respect of his service in p*er*forming the Office of Reeve and soe much of the foure and twenty Shillings to be yearly abated as the Reives Share amounts to which agreement is Ordred to be entred in the Court Rolls of the said Mann*or* by *the* Steward accordingly.

§§ 36. Land Fines, 27 Feb., 1553.

The entries found in this badly written document are simply the fines, normally entered in the court rolls but here set down separately because of the growing importance of land fines. In this particular record there are fines for succeeding to a kinsman's holdings, for entering upon lands formerly held by another family, and for licence to sublet, or put out to farm, for a period of years.

One gavelland of bondland containing eleven (customary) acres, had long been held in lease without a fine, that is, apparently, as a tenancy-at-will. The gavelland is apparently simply gafol-land, or money-rent land. It is not to be inferred that the practice had been developed, of converting a customary holding with its fine for entry and with its customary rent into a simple leasehold, or tenancy-at-will.

The most interesting case is that of Randolph Davy who had escheated his land because he, a bondman, had sublet his holding without the lord's permission. He is now forced to pay a fine and a a heavy one, for having the permission to lease for five years. One wonders whether the holding was worth so much (84s.) during the period in question. In addition, it is stated that the fine for his holding is henceforth to be 5s. 4d. — for instance, when his heir succeeds to the property. Apparently he was soon manumitted, for the entry 'manumitted' is made above the original record.

Here we see clearly enough two important developments: (1) there was coming into being a brisk market for customary holdings, and (2) the lord was rising to the point of demanding a share of the income from subletting. All this came at a time when, it is ordinarily considered, only large holdings were desirable and desired. Of course, some of the subletting was to increase the holdings of those who had lands insufficient for their needs. Still, the lands were unenclosed and used chiefly for tillage, that is, apparently for the old type of agriculture.

CRAWLEY [1]

Fin*es* ib*ide*m fact*i* ad Turn*um* de hock' ib*ide*m tent*um* penultimo die februar*ii* Anno r*egni* r*egis* Edwardi sexti septi*mo*.

F*inis* Anno xiij S[tephani] ep*isco*pi [2] v s. Joh*anne*s davy frater jun*ior* *et* p*roximus* heres henr*ici* Davy p*ro* j Mes*suagio* *et* ij ferling*is* t*erre* nat*ive* in boriali p*arte* de Crawley j Mes*suagio* *et* j virg*ata* t*erre* nat*ive* in austral*i* p*arte* de Crawley q*ue* deuen*erunt* in ma*nus* d*omi*ni p*er* mort*em* p*redicti* henrici davy fr*at*ris sui h*ab*end*is*.

p*ro* j Mes*suagio* *et* [3] j gauellond t*erre* nat*ive* cont*inent*' xj acr*as* iac*entes* in [——] [4] Crawley q*ue* henr*icus* dauy diu tenuit in locag*io* absq*ue* fine h*ab*end'

p*ro* viij acr*is* t*erre* iac*entibus* in co*mmun*ibu*s* campis in boria*li* p*arte* de North crawle v*idelicet* iij acr*is* inde voc*atis* budland*es* iac*enti*-*bus* in north in campo occid*entali* ib*ide*m *et* iiij acr*is* q*uo*nd*am* fuit le droueway p*ro* ouib*us* d*omi*ni iac*entibus* in Combfurlong*e* j acr*a* inde iacente in furlong*e* ib*ide*m no*min*at' [——] [4] q*uas* will*el*m*us* wayt diu te*n*uit in locag*io* absq*ue* fine.

Thom*as* Symys p*ro* lic*entia* dimitt*endi* ad firm*am* quand*am* p*ar*cel-l*am* t*erre* voc*atam* wheatgarstons cont*inentem* xx acr*as* t*erre* nat*ive* in dec*enna* de Crawley cuicu*m*q*ue* volu*er*it a fest*o* s*anct*i Mich*ael*is Arch-*angel*i p*roximo* futur*o* post dat*um* p*re*sent*is* ad fine*m* *et* termi*num* quin-q*ue* Annor*um* p*roximo* sequen*tium* *et* plenar*ie* complend*orum* p*er* ple-*gi*um Ric*ard*i moreley. [Finis] vj s. viij d.[5]

Randolphus davy manumiss*us* p*ro* j Mes*suagio* *et* j ferling*o* t*erre* nat*ive* in p*arte* boriali de Crawley q*ue* deuenerunt in ma*nus* d*omi*ni p*er* escaet*am* eo q*uo*d dict*us* Randol*phus* nat*ivus* existens ad firm*am* dimis-s*it* dict*a* Mes*suagium* *et* ferl*ingum* t*erre* p*ro* t*ermin*o Annor*um* sine li-cenc*ia* *et* contra cons*uetudinem* Man*er*ii h*ab*end*is* ita q*uo*d finis sit im-pos*iterum* v s. iiij d. vi*delicet* antiqu*us* fin*is* ut p*atet* de[6] a*nn*o xix[no] fox *et* ult*er*ius lic*encia* est ei ad firma*m* dimitt*ere* o*mn*ia p*re*miss*a* cuicu*m*q*ue* volu*er*it a festo Annunciationis b*ea*te marie v*irgini*s p*roximo* fut*ur*o

[1] MS., P. R. O., Ecclesiastical Commission, Court Rolls, 109/5, fol. 20b.
[2] About 1543–44.
[3] j Mes*suagio* *et* struck through.
[4] Left blank. [5] In the margin. [6] Interlineated.

usq*ue* ad f*inem* t*er*m*ini* v Anno*rum* p*roximo* seq*uen*t*ium*. [Finis] iiij li. iiij s. [pro] licenc*ia* di*mittendi*.[1]

§§ 37. Land Fines, [before 1560] and [April], 1560.

The fine of £7 is unusually heavy. It had been paid apparently in 1547 and was again demanded on this occasion. Two estates were involved, made up of two virgates of bondland. Just why the fine was made so heavy is not clear, unless the son and heir took title at this time, allowing his mother her rights of possession during her life (ordinarily it was during widowhood), expecting to avoid a possible further fine later — on the death of his mother.

A cottage and farthingland in North Crawley are dealt with in an unusual fashion. The cottage itself was handed over to the daughter of the former holder. She paid 12d. as a fine and her husband 6d. to hold with her. The farthingland was made up of 23 roods (usually 22, making 11 customary acres or 5½ statutory acres). These roods, or fractions thereof, were assigned to 15 holdings in North Crawley ranging from ½ rood (⅛ acre) to 4 roods (1 acre) in amount. The former holder, or one bearing the same name, got two of the roods. The fines were 21d. per rood. From this instance we get a clear idea of the small size of holdings in North Crawley.

A small miscellaneous estate was handed on to the widow of the deceased tenant. It had been held by her husband by lease without fine for entry (in locagio absque fine). Of the 9½ acres, 4 were in one furlong, 3 in another in North Crawley, 1 in South Crawley, and 1½ in the lord's demesne. It is unusual to find a tenant holding in both North and South Crawley. Clearly the lord had some separate demesne, but it was probably still divided into small strips. The rental is put down at 5s. The holding was annexed to a messuage and farthingland in North Crawley.

This document indicates clearly the breaking up of small unit holdings to form larger ones. We must not assume, however, that it went very far. There were at least 15 holdings in North Crawley at the time. The common practice of calling an estate after the name of an earlier holder is here abundantly illustrated.

[1] In the margin.

The scribe was either very ignorant or very careless. Certainly he wrote an abominable hand and made many mistakes. The document is blurred and the edges were cut off when the folios were stitched together to form a book. A*nno* S*tephani* xxij (1555–56?) and A*nno* fox xxj (1521–22) refer to Bishops Stephen Gardiner and Richard Fox.

CRAWLEY [1]

[Ad Turnum Sancti Martini??]

F*inis* A*nno* Edwardi Sexti primo vij li. Edmu*ndus* Sim*mes* filius Thome Syms p*ro* j Tofto et j virg*ata* di*midia* t*erre* nat*ive* in Crawley in p*ar*te australi voc*atis* woodcott j Tofto et di*midia* virg*ata* t*erre* nat*ive* in Crawley voc*atis* Skinn*er*s in p*ar*te austr*ali* q*ue* deuen*erunt* in Man*us* d*omi*ni ex reddic*ione* pred*icti* Thome Syms p*at*ris s*ui* sub condic*ione* q*uo*d dionisia vx*or* pred*icti* Thome h*ab*ebit teneb*i*t et gaudeb*i*t o*mn*ia et sing*u*la premiss*a* dura*nte* vit*a* s*ua* p*er* pll*egiu*m [sic] Rob*er*t*i* ostmo*n*d. f*inis* vii li.[2]

f*inis* A*nno* S[tephani] xxij° v s. iiij d.[3] Will*elmu*s wayt*e* Jun*ior* p*ro* j Mes*suagio* et j ferling*ata* t*erre* nat*ive* in boriali p*ar*te de Crawley voc*atis* Randall q*ue* deuen*erunt* in Man*us* d*omi*ni ex redd*icione* Thome wayte de Wurthey h*abend*is p*er* pll*egiu*m will*elm*i wayte s*enioris*.

fin*is* A*nno* fox xxj° xiij s. vj d. Ric*ard*us davy*e* filius Jun*ior* et p*rox-imus* heres henrici davy p*ro* j Tofto j mes*suagio* et j ferling*ata* t*erre* nat*ive* in Crawley in parte boriali voc*atis* prestland*es* cu*m* iiij acr*is* de d*omi*nic*is* domini in le Estfild*e* iux*ta* putthill q*ue* deuen*erunt* in man*us* d*omi*ni p*er* Mortem Margerie Rel*i*cte pred*icti* henric*i* q*ue* tenuit premiss*a* durant*e* vid*uetate* sua h*ab*endis p*er* pll*egiu*m Rob*er*t*i* osmond. f*inis* xiii s. vi d.[2]

f*inis* A*nno* p*re*d*icto* xiiij d. Idem Ric*ardus* p*ro* j Tofto et j ferling*ata* t*erre* nat*ive* co*ntinente* p*er* estimac*ionem* xj acr*as* in p*ar*te boriali voc*atis* mora*ntes* q*ue* deuen*erunt* in Man*us* d*omi*ni vt sup*ra* h*abend*is. f*inis* xiiii d.[2]

f*inis* A*nno* pred*icto* ix s. Id*e*m Ric*ardus* p*ro* j M*essuagio et* j ferling*ata* t*erre* nat*ive* co*ntinente* p*er* estimac*ionem* xj acr*as* t*erre* nat*ive* in boriali p*ar*te de Crauley q*ue* deuen*erunt* in Man*us* d*omi*ni vt sup*ra* h*ab*end*is*. f*inis* ix s.[2]

f*inis* A*nno* pred*icto* ij s. vj d. Id*e*m Ric*ardus* p*ro* j Tofto et j ferling*ata* t*erre* nat*ive* in Crauley voc*atis* osmondes q*ue* deuen*erunt* in Man*us* d*omi*ni vt sup*ra* h*ab*end*is*. f*inis* ii s. vi d.[2]

[1] MS., P. R. O., Ecclesiastical Commission, Court Rolls, 109/7, fols. 39–41.
[2] In the margin.
[3] In the margin, iiij s. iiij d.

Robertus wayte pro licentia dimittendi ad firmam j messuagium et virgatam terre native in australi parte de cralley j messuagium et j virgatam dimidiam in Cralley in parte australi ac j Toftum j cottagium et quinque acras terre native in cralley in parte boriali cuicumque voluerit a festo sancti michaelis archangeli proximo futuro vsque ad finem termini vij annorum proximo sequencium et plenarie complendorum. finis v s.[1]

finis Anno xxij Stephani episcopi cum j Messuagio et j ferlingata terre et j cotagio et j ferlingata terre et officina fabrili xv s. Johanna heliar' pro j Cotagio in northcrawley quondam Willelmi plumtons et postea willelmi drew quod deuenit in manus domini ex reddicione gewing Mathew fratris sui habendo per pllegium henrici hellyer. finis xij d.[2]

finis Anno xix° fox v s. iiij d. Henricus Helliar' pro Johanna Heliar vxore sua cum terris suis predictis tenere cum prefata Johanna vxore sua per plegium Roberti osmand. finis vj d.[2]

Ad Turnum de hocke Anno domini Johannis White wintoniensis episcopi iiij°.

Thomas Stevens alias couch pro iij^bus rodis unius acre terre vt iacent in communibus campis in furlong vocat' Markefurlonge in decenna de crauley in boriali parte quamdiu iacent in manibus domini ob defectum finientis habendis Ita [quod] predicte 3 rode terre vt iacent imposterum anexentur Messuagio et ij ferlingatis terre native in north crauley vocatis chiddens sub fine et redditu predictarum ferlingatarum terre ibidem. finis v s. iij d.[2]

Gawing Mathew pro ij rodis terre ut iacent in communibus campis in north cr[aw]ley in furlonge vocat' Merkefurlong quamdiu iacent in manibus domini ob defectum finientis habendis Ita quod dicte ij rode terre imposterum anexentur messuagio et ij ferlingatis terre [in] north [Crawley] vocatis bodies et plumtons sub fine et redditu predictarum ferlingatarum terre ibidem. [Finis] iij s. vj d.[1]

Ricardus Davi senior pro j roda terre sicut iacet in communibus campis in northcraw[ley] in Markefurlong quamdiu iacet in manibus domini ob defectum finientis habenda Ita quod dicta roda terre anexetur imposterum tofto j Messuagio et j ferlingate terre in north crawley dimid' gauellond vocatis barlinges sub fine et redditu predicte ferlingate terre ibidem. finis xxj d.[1]

Georgius Nash pro j roda dimidia terre sicut iacent in communibus campis de north crauley quamdiu iacent in manibus domini ob defectum finientis habendis Ita quod predicte roda et dimidia anexentur impos-

[1] In the margin.

[2] In the margin. The iij d. appear to have been crossed out.

terum cottagio et ferlingate ipsius georgii vocatis carpenters sub fine et redditu predicte ferlingate terre ibidem. finis ij s. vij d.[1]

Willelmus Wayte pro j roda terre in communi campo in furlong vocat' Markefurlonge in north crauley quamdiu iacet in manibus domini ob defectum finientis habenda Ita quod predicta roda terre imposterum anexetur Messuagio et ferlingate terre ibidem vocatis Randels sub fine et redditu predicte ferlingate terre ibidem. finis xxj d.[1]

Willelmus be[cc]he[?] pro j roda terre in communibus campis in north crawley in furlong vocat' Markefurlong quamdiu iacet in Manibus domini ob defectum finientis habenda Ita quod predicta roda imposterum anexetur j Messuagio et ferlingate terre predicti Willelmi vocatis pilles[?] ibidem sub fine et redditu eiusdem ferlingate terre ibidem. finis xxj d.[1]

Johannes davy pro ij rodis terre sicut iacent in communibus campis de northcrauley in furlong vocat' Markefurlong quamdiu iacent in Manibus domini ob defectum finientis habendis Ita quod predicte ij rode terre anexentur imposterum Messuagio et ferlingate terre dicti Johannis vocatis [——]ns sub fine et redditu predicte ferlingate terre ibidem. finis iij s. vj d.[1]

Johannes davy [——] [2] pro j roda terre sicut iacet in communibus campis de northcrauleye in furlong vocat' Markfurlong quamdiu iacet in manibus domini ob defectum finientis habenda Ita quod predicta roda terre anexetur imposterum messuagio et ferlingate terre predicti willelmi vocatis sewalles sub fine predicte ferlingate terre et sub redditu predicte ferlingate terre videlicet. finis xxj d.[1]

Johannes davye frater henrici davi pro ij rodis terre sicut iacent in communibus campis de Northcrauley in forlong vocat' Markfurlong quamdiu iacent in Manibus domini ob defectum finientis habendis Ita quod predicte ij rode anexentur imposterum Messuagio et ij ferlingatis terre vocatis Amys ibidem sub fine et redditu predictarum ferlingatarum terre ibidem. finis iij s. vj d.[1]

Thomas Wayt pro j roda terre sicut iacet in communibus campis in northcrauley in vno furlong' vocat' Markefurlonge quamdiu iacet in manibus domini ob defectum finientis habenda Ita quod dicta roda terre imposterum anexetur Tofto et j ferlingate in north vocatis Cootes sub fine et redditu predicte ferlingate terre ibidem. finis xxj d.[1]

Ricardus davy at well pro iiij rodis terre sicut iacent in communibus campis de north crauley in vno furlong vocat' Markfurlong quamdiu iacent in Manibus domini ob defectum finientis habendis Ita quod dicte iiij rode terre anexentur imposterum Tofto et ferlingate terre vocatis Simondes in north crauley sub fine predicte ferlingate terre et sub redditu ferlingate predicte. finis vij s.[1]

[1] In the margin. [2] Obliterated.

Thomas Allen pro j roda terre sicut iacet in communibus campis de northcrauley in vn' furlong vocat' Markefurlong quamdiu iacet in Manibus domini ob defectum finientis habenda Ita quod predicta roda terre imposterum anexetur Tofto j messuagio cum croft et clauso adiacente et j ferlingate terre et dimid' gauellond vocat' gibbes in boriali fine [1] de crauley sub fine et redditu predicte ferlingate terre ibidem. finis xxj d.[2]

Robertus Wayte pro dimidia roda terre sicut iacet in communibus campis de northcralley in furlonge vocat' Markefurlong quamdiu iacet in Manibus domini ob defectum finientis habenda Ita quod dicta dimidia roda terre imposterum anexetur messuagio et virgate dimidie in australi parte et cottagio et iij acris in north vocatis Maldes in north sub fine et redditu predicte virgate terre dimidie ibidem. finis x d. ob.[2]

Willelmus Couch pro j roda terre sicut iacet in communi campo de northcrauley in furlong vocat' Markefurlong quamdiu iacet in Manibus domini ob defectum finientis habenda Ita quod dicta roda terre imposterum anexetur Messuagio et ferlingate terre predicti Willelmi in north crauley vocatis Couches sub fine et redditu predicte ferlingate terre ibidem. finis xxj d.[2]

Johannes Baker pro j roda terre sicut iacet in communibus campis de northcrauley in vn' furlong vocat' Markefurlonge quamdiu iacet in manibus domini ob defectum finientis habenda Ita quod predicta roda terre imposterum anexetur messuagio et ferlingate terre vocatis neweslandes sub fine iij s. iiij d.[3] et redditu predicte ferlingate terre ibidem. finis xxj d.[2]

Mergeria relicta willelmi Wayt pro viij acris terre iacentibus in communibus campis in diuersis furlong' in northcrauley videlicet iij acris insimull in furlong vocat' Bedlandes et iiij acris insimull iacentibus in Trendellfurlong juxta combe hedge et alia acra iacente in australi parte de crauley vocata stapleacre cum j acra dimidia terre de dominicis domini vocatis le pittell in orientali parte de crauley quas Willelmus wayte nuper maritus dicte Margerie tenuit in locagio absque fine habendis [4] tenendis sibi pro termino vite sue reuercione inde spectante rectis heredibus Willelmi Wayt nuper viri sui per finem ii[?] librarum x [s.].[2] Ita quod predicte viij acre terre [5] in communibus campis et ille acra et dimidia de dominicis domini deinceps anexentur j Messuagio et ferlingate terre native in boriali parte de crauley sub fine v s. et sub redditu predicte ferlingate v s. Et j acra in australi parte de crauley vocata Staple acre annexetur imposterum Messuagio et virgate terre native

[1] Error for parte.
[2] In the margin.
[3] Probably iii s. iiij d. is an error which the scribe failed to erase.
[4] Crossed out.
[5] A correction of vij acre terre is interlineated.

sue in Suthcrauley sub fine et redd*itu* pr*edicte* virgat*e* v*idelicet* fin*e* v s. f*inis* xl s.[1]

Gawin*us* Mathew p*ro* lic*encia* d*imittendi* ad firm*am* o*mn*es t*erras* *suas*[2] et fra[riga]biles[?] crawley cuida*m* Rob*er*to osemo*nde* a fest*o* S*anctorum* phi*lippi* et jacobi pr*oximo* futur*o* ad fine*m* te*rmini* dece*m* Annor*um*.

§§ 38. Land Fines, 13 Sept., 1571.

Two heavy fines were collected from an heir of five years of age for having his deceased father's two holdings on the occasion of the marriage of his mother. His stepfather was to be his guardian. The fine for the farthingland and pyghtell in North Crawley was 20s.; for the virgate in South Crawley 21s.

A widow and two guardians paid fines for subletting holdings: v s. for subletting for 20 years, 6s. 8d. for 10 years, and 3s. 4d. for 3 years. The holdings all differed in size as well as in the period of the lease.

It would seem that one advantage of the subletting system was that a widow might marry another tenant of the village and her husband might sublet the widow's, or her son's, tenement, if he did not care to cultivate it himself.

CRAULEY[3]

Fines ib*ide*m, fact*i* xiij die Septembr*is* Anno p*redicto* [13 Eliz.].

f*inis* Anno Eliz*abethe* Regine vj et Rob*erti* ep*iscop*i iiij xx s.

Thomas Brownynge filius jun*ior et* p*roximus* heres Rob*erti* Brownynge p*ro* j Mes*suagio et* j ferlingat*a* t*erre* nat*ive* j toft*a* et j ferlingat*a* t*erre* gabul*a*nd ac j pyghtell*e* cont*inent'* ij acr*as* t*erre* p*urprestu*re in boriali p*ar*te de Crawley q*ue* deuene*runt* in man*us* d*omi*ni eoq*uo*d Helena nup*er* vx*or* p*re*d*icti* Rob*er*ti q*ue* te*nuit* premiss*a* dur*ante* vid*uetatc* s*ua* cepit in viru*m* quend*a*m Ric*ardu*m pregneshe p*er* q*uo*d for*isfecit* stat*um* s*uum* in p*re*miss*is* h*a*bend*is* p*er* pl*egiu*m Ric*ard*i pregnesshe cui custod*ia* p*redicti* Thome cu*m* t*erris* s*uis* p*re*d*ictis* co*mm*ittit*ur* q*uo*usq*ue* p*er*uen*er*it ad s*uam* plena*m* etate*m* m*od*o etatis v Annor*um* sub condicione q*uo*d bene et suffic*ienter* rep*ar*abit et sustentab*i*t omnes *et* o*mnimo*d*is* rep*araciones* p*er*tin*entes* ad p*re*miss*a*. f*inis* xx s.[1]

[1] In the margin.
[2] o*mnes* t*erras* s*uas* have been substituted for i mes*suagium* in the manuscript.
[3] MS., P. R. O., Ecclesiastical Commission, Court Rolls, 111/1, fol. 12.

finis Anno *predicto* xxj s. Idem Thomas *pro* vno Mes*suagio* et j virgat*a terre* nat*ive* in austr*ali* p*ar*te de Crawley q*ue* deuen*erunt* in Man*us* d*omi*ni vt sup*ra* h*abe*nd*is* p*er* pl*egium* p*redictum et* custod*ia* c*ommitti*t*ur* vt sup*ra* sub condic*ione* vt sup*ra*. f*inis* xxi s.[1]

Ric*ard*us pregneesshe Gardianus p*redicti* Thome p*ro* lic*entia* d*imittendi* ad firm*am* o*mni*a et sing*u*la p*re*miss*a* cuid*a*m Joh*anni* newman*n et* assignat*is* s*uis* A fest*o* s*anct*i Mich*ael*is Arch*angel*i vsq*ue* ad fine*m* t*ermini* dece*m* Annor*um* p*roximo* sequen*tium* et plenar*ie* complend*orum*. f*inis* vj s. viij d.[1]

Joanna baker vid*ua* nup*er* vx*or* Joh*ann*is baker p*ro* licenc*ia* dimittend*i* ad firm*am* j Mes*suagium* et j ferlingat*am* t*erre* nat*ive* voc*ata* neweslond*es* in borial*i* p*ar*te de Crawley cuicu*mque* volu*er*it A fest*o* s*anct*i Mich*ael*is Arch*angel*i p*roximo* futur*o* vsq*ue* ad fine*m* t*ermini* xx Annor*um* p*roximo* sequen*tium et* plenar*ie* complend*orum*. f*inis* v s.[1]

Thomas borne gardianus Joh*ann*is Wayt p*ro* lic*entia* dimittend*i* ad firma*m* j Mes*suagium* et j virgat*am* t*erre* nat*ive* in Crawley in austr*ali* p*ar*te cont*inentem* xxxij acr*as* t*erre* nat*ive* j toft*am* et j ferlingat*am* t*erre* nat*ive* voc*atas* Cootes in borial*i* p*ar*te de Crawley cont*inentem* xj acr*as* t*erre* ac j rod*am* cuicu*mque* volu*er*it A fest*o* s*anct*i Mich*ael*is Arch*angel*i p*roximo* futur*o* vsq*ue* ad fine*m* t*ermini* triu*m* annor*um* p*roximo* sequen*tium* et plenar*ie* c*om*plend*orum*. f*inis* iij s. iiij d.[1]

§§ 39. Land Fines, 17 March, 1586.

An heiress, apparently married, paid fines for having three estates, her father and mother being still alive and their rights of possession being specifically reserved. For the farthingland in North Crawley, the fine was 4s., the same as it had been in 1578. For 7 acres in North Crawley and for purpresture land, the fine was 5s., the same as in 1546–47. And for one farthingland and a half, of gavelland, also in North Crawley, the fine was 5s., as it had been in 1546–47. Just why the parents wanted to have the matter of reversion and fine settled at this time is, of course, not stated.

An heir of seven years of age fined for three holdings, apparently on the remarriage of his mother who was to be the guardian of the boy and of his lands. The heir was to receive the lands on reaching full age. The rent of 6s. and all services were to be rendered, as also a new rent of one ewe each year. Here we have a slight

[1] In the margin.

promise of a new system of rents which, however, never materialized. If the lords had been able to impose new rents in kind, the semi-manorial system still surviving, might have attained new vigor.

The holdings of this estate were one virgate in South Crawley, a farthingland, one rood and one acre in North Crawley, and also a single acre in North Crawley.

This single acre was called prima acra, doubtless a customary acre. It was located in Lytteldowne furlong in Myddellnortthefeild. This is a complete description of the acre in question. It also is evidence of the dual nature of the common-field system in Crawley. The acre and furlong were not in middle field, but in middle north field, that is, in the middle common field of North Crawley.

CRAWLEY[1]

Fines ib*id*em fact*i* ad Turn*um* de hock xvij^{mo} die Marcii Anno Regni d[omine] Elizabethe Regine Anglie *etcetera* xxviij^{uo}

f*inis* A*nn*o Ro*berti* ep*iscop*i xviij iiij s. Elizabetha Coll*en*' p*ro* j Mes*suagio et* j ferlingat*a terre* nat*ive* cont*inente* xj acr*as* in borialli p*ar*te voc*atis* Sewells *et* ij rod*is* in markefurlonge q*ue* deven*erunt* in man*us* d*omi*ni ex redd*itione* Ric*ar*di Davy sen*ioris* p*a*tris s*ui* h*a*bendi*s* pr*e*fat*e* Elizabethe *et* heredi*bus* de corp*ore* s*uo* legittime p*ro*creat*is et* p*ro*creandi*s et* pro defect*u* talis exit*us* reman*ere* rect*is* heredi*bus* pr*e*fat*i* Ric*ar*di sub condic[i]one q*uo*d p*redictus* Ric*ar*dus h*a*bebit tenebit *et* gaudebit o*mn*ia *et* singula p*re*miss*a* dur*ante* vit*a* s*ua et* Rosa vxor p*redicti* Ric*ar*di dur*ante* vidu*etate* s*ua* p*er* pl*egi*um Ric*ar*di Davy. f*inis* iiij s.[2]

f*inis* A*nn*o S*tephani* ep*iscop*i xvj^{to} v s. Eadem Elizabethe p*ro* j Cot*agio et* vij acr*is terre* in boriali p*a*rte ac j cot*agio* et iij acr*is terre* nat*ive* in Campo de Crawley voc*ato* middelfeilde q*ue* deuen*erunt* in man*us* d*omi*ni vt supra h*a*bendi*s* vt supra sub condic*ione* p*redicta* p*er* pl*egi*um p*redictum*. f*inis* v s.[2]

F*inis* A*nn*o p*redicto* v s. Eadem Eliz*abetha* p*ro* j Mes*suagio* j ferlingat*a* di*midia* gauell*and* in borialli p*ar*te de Crawley q*ue* deuen*erunt* in man*us* d*omi*ni vt supra h*a*bendi*s* vt supra sub condic[i]one p*redicta* p*er* pl*egi*um p*redictum*. finis v s.[2]

f*inis* A*nn*o Ro*berti* ep*iscop*i sec*un*do v s. Ric*ar*dus Allen' filius Jun*ior et* p*roximus* heres Joh[ann]e Allen' p*ro* j Messuagio et j virgat*a terre* nat*ive* in austr*ali* p*ar*te de Crawley j ferlingat*a terre* nat*ive et* di*mid*'

[1] MS., P. R. O., Ecclesiastical Commission, Court Rolls, 112/4, fol. 20.
[2] In the margin.

gauillond in borialli p*ar*te ac j rod*a* t*erre* in markefurlonge *et* ; acr*a* t*erre* p*ur*p*resture* q*ue* deuen*erunt* in man*us* d*omi*ni eo q*uo*d Joh*anna* relict*a* p*re*d*icti* Joh*annis* q*ue* ten*uit* p*re*miss*a* dur*ante* vid*uetate* s*ua* cepit in vir*um* quendam Will*elmum* Baker p*er* q*uo*d for*isfecit* statu*m* s*uum* in p*re*miss*is* h*a*bend*is* p*er* pl*egium* p*re*d*ictorum* Will*elmi* *et* Joh[ann]e [c]ui custoddi*a* Ric*ardi* cu*m* t*erris* s*uis* p*re*d*ictis* co*m*mittat*ur* durant*e* minoritatem etat*is* p*re*d*icti* Ric*ard*i modo etat*is* vij Annor*um* reddend[o] inde d*omi*no o*mn*ia redd*itus* op*er*a cons*uetudines* *et* s*er*vicia ac alia on*er*a quecumq*ue* durant*e* t*ermin*o p*re*d*icto* ac annuatim j oue*m* matrice*m* in consider*atione* redd*ituum* premissorum deliber*andorum* quando p*re*fat*us* Ric*ard*us p*er*ven*er*it ad s*uam* plenam etate*m*. finis v s.[1]

f*inis* A*nn*o R*oberto* ep*iscop*i quarto xij d. Idem Ric*ard*us p*ro* j acr*a* t*erre* iac*ente* in Co*mmuni* Campo voc*ato* myddellnorthefei[l]d in lytteldowne farlonge *et* est p*ri*ma acr*a* ib*ide*m q*ue* deuen*it* in ma*nus* d*omi*ni vt supra h*a*bend*a* *et* custod*ia* co*m*mitta*tur* vt supra.

§§ 40. Land Fines in a Reeve's Account, 1610–11.

These entries, corresponding to the purchasia or perquisita of the earlier reeves' accounts, occur in an account for the year 1610–11 kept by the reeve and the farmer of the demesne.

The sum of 5s. was paid for permission to farm to a subtenant for the period of twelve years, a cottage with a garden, apparently without any arable land.

The chief case is that of Henry Pucknoll, a blacksmith, who paid two fines to the lord for leasing two holdings. One fine was 15s. for leasing a messuage and a farthingland and also a cottage and two roods of land along with a blacksmith's shop, in North Crawley. The blacksmith, or his wife, was to hold as long as either should live. The rent to be paid by them was £5 a year, payable half yearly, and with only four days' grace allowed. This rent was to be paid, not to the lord but to the tenant who was Anna Geffery, doubtless daughter of the former blacksmith, Amos Geffery. Having married Christopher Elie of Hunton, Anna had no use for the land. But reversion of the land rested in her and her heirs. She had made a pretty good bargain. There was also another holding which her father had possessed in North Crawley. It was a cottage and five acres. For leasing this, Pucknoll, the new

[1] In the margin.

blacksmith, paid a fine of 2s. to the lord. Whether any rental was due is not stated.

Clearly everybody ought to have been happy. The lord received considerable fines and, of course, the services and customs still due. The heiress received a handsome yearly rent. And the blacksmith got larger holdings which he doubtless expected to cultivate with profit, though it would have to be under the open-field system using the naked-fallow method of husbandry. The blacksmith was one of the new class of tenants, or, in this case, of subtenants, who had ambitions and capacities. Such a class was not satisfied with the old units of 5½ acres of land, common in North Crawley. The splitting up of holdings, and the recombination of the same, met the needs of this class. It might have been easy enough for a brawny blacksmith to ply his trade and also cultivate his lands of about eleven acres, but just how would he use his three houses, if there were actually three, as appears to have been the case? It would seem that the blacksmith's own proper holding was a shop, a cottage, and two roods of land. But, as is indicated in an earlier record,[1] such a man of strength had previously possessed two tenements besides his shop.

FINES TERR*ARUM*[2]

Et de xiij s. iiij d. de Tuth[ingpenny] ad Turn*um* sancti martini et hock*e* per annum. Et de v s. de Will*el*mo Davye p*ro* licenc*ia* dimittend*i* ad firma*m* vnu*m* Cotagiu*m* cum Curtelag*io* et gardin*o* in decen*na* de Crawley Cuicumq*ue* honesto et idoneo subtenent*i* volu*er*it A festo s*an*cti mich*ae*l*is* Arch*angel*i prox*imo* nunc futur*o* vsq*ue* ad finem et terminu*m* duodecem [sic] annoru*m* extunc prox*imo* sequen*tium* et plenarie complend*orum* Ita tamen q*uo*d redd*itus* op*er*a Consuetud*ines* et servic*ia* inde debit*a* et debend*a* D*omi*no p*er*solvant*ur* et fiant p*er* pl*egium* Ambrosii Davys. Et de v s. de Joh*ann*e Davye filio Jun*iore* et prox*imo* hered*e* Henrici Davye defunct*i* pro vno messuagio et vn*a* ferlingat*a* terr*e* nat*ive* vocat*is* Aymes continent*e* xj*cem* acr*as* terr*e* nat*ive* in boreal*i* parte de Crawley q*ue* deven*erunt* in manus d*omi*ni per mortem pred*icti* Henrici Davye patris sui habendis Salvo semp*er* iure malline davy vid*ue* relict*e* pred*icti* Henrici in p*re*missis dum solam et Castam se

[1] See above, §§ 37, p. 522.

[2] MS., P. R. O., Ecclesiastical Commission, Various, 159473. One of about 103 rolls.

gesserit s*ecundum* Consuetud*inem* man*er*ii pred*icti* p*er* pl*egiu*m Ric*ard*i Page. Et de xv s. de Henrico Pucknoll de Crawley in Comitatu South*amptonie* Blacksmyth et katherina vxor*e* eius pro vno messuagio et vna ferlingat*a* terr*e* nat*ive* cont*inente* vndecem acr*as* vocat*is* Plumptons vno Cotagio et vn*a* ferlingat*a* terr*e* nat*ive* cont*inente* vndecem acr*as* vocat*is* Boddies ac vn*o* Cotag*io* cu*m* officin*a* fabril*i* in North Crawley ac duabus rod*is* terr*e* sicut iacent in Co*mmun*i campo de North Crawley vocato Homefield*e* in furlong*e* vocat' markefurlonge quondam Amosi Geffery defunct*i* q*ue* deven*erunt* in manus D*omi*ni ex reddic*io*ne Christoferi Elie *et* Anne vxor*is* eius filie vnice et prox*ime* hered*is* pred*icti* Amosi Geffry dict*a* Anna Coram Sen*escal*lo sola examinat*a* existent*e* s*ecundu*m Consuetud*inem* man*er*ii pred*icti* Habend*is* prefat*is* Henrico Pucknoll et katherine vxor*i* eius pro *et* durant*e* termino vitaru*m* predictorum Henrici Pucknoll et katherine vxor*is* eius et alterius eoru*m* divcius vivent*is* s*ecundu*m Consuetud*inem* man*er*ii pred*icti* Sub Condi*c*ione tamen q*uo*d pred*icti* Henricus Pucknoll et katherina vxor eius vel assignati sui solvent sev solvi facient vel eoru*m* aliquis solvat seu solvi faciat p*r*efat*is* Christofero Elie et Anne vxor*i* eius heredib*us* vel assigna*tis* dicte Anne durant*e* termino vitaru*m* pred*ictorum* Henrici et katherine et alterius eoru*m* divcius viven*tis* an[n]uatim et quolib*e*t anno quinq*ue* libras legalis monete Anglie ad duos Anni terminos vsuales vi*delice*t ad festa Annu*n*ciacio*n*is be*a*te marie virginis et s*an*cti mich*ael*is Arch*angel*i vel infra spacium quatuor dieru*m* prox*imorum* post quodlib*e*t festu*m* festoru*m* pred*ictorum* equis porc*io*nibus Prima soluc*ione* inde incipiend*a* in festo Annu*n*ciac*i*onis be*a*te marie virginis nunc prox*imo* futur*o* vel infra quatuor dies prox*imos* post idem festu*m* Et quelib*e*t soluc*io* inde fienda apud vel in modo domo mansional*i* p*r*efat*i* Christoferi Elie situat*a* et existent*e* in Hunton in Com*itatu* South*amptonie* et post decessu*m* pred*ictorum* Henrici Pucknoll et katherine vxor*is* eius et sup*er*vivent*is* eoru*m* vel post aliquam defalta*m* fiend*am* in soluc*ione* predictaru*m* quinq*ue* libraru*m* ad aliquod festu*m* festoru*m* pred*ictorum* vel infra quatuor dies prox*imos* post aliquod eorundem festoru*m* provt sup*er*ius limitat*um* et appunct*um* est, tunc remaner*e* inde pred*icte* Anne Elie et heredibus suis s*ecundu*m Consuetud*inem* man*er*ii pred*icti* per pl*egiu*m Roberti Nashe. Et de ij s. de eisdem Henrico Pucknoll et katherina vxor*e* eius pro vno Cotagio et quinq*ue* acr*is* terr*e* nat*ive* in boreal*i* parte de Crawley in decen*na* de Crawley quondam pred*icti* Amosi Geffery que devenerunt in man*us* d*omi*ni vt supra habend*is* vt supra Sub Cond*i*cione vt supra Remaner*e* vt supra p*er* pl*egiu*m pred*ictum*. S*um*ma xl s. iiij d.

§§ 41. Surrender of Arable Land, 23 April, 1612.

Ambrose Davye went before the clerk of the bishopric and surrendered his holding of land to the lord, keeping for himself the messuage in which he lived, along with the granaries and other buildings. Ambrose Davye also possessed a cottage with a curtilage and garden actually in the possession of a kinsman for which, apparently, he paid to the lord each year 3s. and four chickens along with other rents and services.

It is interesting to note just what Ambrose surrendered. It was a farthing land of a little over eleven (customary) acres. Five acres were located in four parts of Homefield (otherwise Eastfield). Four acres were in Middlefield, two in each of two different furlongs. Two acres were in one furlong in the Westfield, where was located the parrock of land called Overhouse. Here we see the three main fields, all in North Crawley. But the important consideration is that the arable strips have been separated from the messuage or residence. In this way we see preparation made for larger holdings of land on the one hand and a class of cottage holders, ultimately landless cottage laborers, on the other hand. Even the right to pasture a cow was separated from the residence and made to go with the arable. The document does not tell us what was done with the arable so surrendered.

The Crawley surrenders here reproduced occur in a book of surrenders which includes those on the various manors of the bishopric of Winchester.

CRAWLEY *SURSUMREDDITIO*[1]

Memorand*um* quod vicesimo tercio die Aprilis anno regni d*omi*ni n*ost*ri Jacobi dei gr*ati*a Anglie Francie et hib*er*nie Regis fidei defensor*is etcetera* decimo et scocie quadragesimo quinto venit coram me Anth*oni*o Dawley Arm*iger*o Cl*er*ico Ep*iscop*atus wintoniensis Ambrosius Davye et sursum reddid*it* in manus d*omi*ni vnu*m* ferlingat*um*[2] terr*e* nat*ive* in bori*ali* parte de Crawley vocat*um* Overhowse vna cum Co*mmun*ia pastur*a* pro vna vacca tantum et non amplius in Crawley pred*ict*' quod quidem ferlingat*um* terr*e* nat*ive* iaect et bundatur provt sequitur vi*de*-

[1] MS., P. R. O., Ecclesiastical Commission, Court Rolls, 136/3, fol. 10.

[2] In the margin: f*inis* a*nno* Jacobi R*egis* nu*nc* Anglie *etcetera* primo cu*m* vno mes*suagio* ix s.

licet tres acr*e* inde iacent in quodam Campo vocato the homefield vnde vna acr*a* abuttat super quandam p*ar*okam terr*e* vocat*am* overhowse, vna alia acr*a* inde iacet in quodam furlongo vocat*o* Smalethornes, et vna alia acr*a* inde iacet in vlterior*e* parte pred*icti* Campi vocat*i* homefield anglice at the farther end of the said field. Et quatuor acr*e* de pred*icto* ferlingat*o* terr*e* nat*ive* alia parcell*a* iacent in quodam Campo vocat*o* the middlefield vnde due acr*e* iacent in quodam furlongo vocat*o* waterslade prox*imo* adiacent*e* ad quandam sepem vocat*am* Palmers Hedge anglice lyinge neerest to Palmers hedge et alie due acr*e* inde iacent in quodam furlongo vocat*o* downe furlonge, et alie due acr*e* de pred*icto* ferlingat*o* terr*e* nat*ive* alia parcell*a* iacent in quodam Campo vocat*o* the westfielde in quodam furlongo ib*id*em vocat*o* Gassen furlonge Et due al*ie* acr*e* inde vocant*ur* the roode at the vpper ende of homefield et vna p*ar*ok*a* terr*e* de pred*icto* ferlingat*o* terr*e* nat*ive* resid*uo* voca*tur* overhowse (E[x]cept*um* semper tamen et reservat*um* prefato Ambrosio Davye et heredibus suis secundu*m* Consuetud*inem* man*er*ii pred*icti* totu*m* illud messuag*ium* in quo id*e*m Ambrosius Davye modo inhabitat in Crawley pred*ict*' cu*m* horr*eis* et aliis edificii[s] sup*er*inde edificat*is* Except*um* eciam et reservat*um* vn*um* Cottag*ium* cum Curtilag*io* et gardin*o* in decen*na* de Crawley pred*ict*' nup*er* in tenur*a* Rob*er*ti Davye et modo in tenura Will*el*mi Davye filii eiusdem Roberti) ad opus et vsum Ric*ard*i Davye et heredum suoru*m* *secundum* Consuetud*inem* man*er*ii pred*icti* Habend*o* p*er* reddit*um* p*er* annu*m* iij s et duoru*m* galloru*m* et duaru*m* gallinaru*m* et p*er* omnia alia redd*itus* op*er*a Consuetud*ines* et servic*ia* inde debit*a* et consuet*a*.

sign*um* Ambrosii Λ Davye

Capto Die et anno supradict*is*
apud Civitat*em* winton*ie* coram
me Anth*onio* Dawley
In presencia Martini Yalden
John Ɨ moncke
his marke
Fra: Buckley

§§ 42. Surrenders of Holdings for the Purpose of a Mortgage, 1 July, 1613.

Ambrose Davye surrendered to the lord three copyholds in North Crawley for the use of John Wilkins who apparently had loaned him money, on condition that he or his heirs receive the lands back on the payment of (apparently) £192 on 29 September,

1619. The total acreage involved was about 37 customary acres, or about 18½ statutory acres. Attached to each of the three holdings of farthingland was a messuage or toft.

The later final concord is not at all clear. Default was to be made by the mortgagor if the loan was not repaid, but on condition that the mortgagee pay to the mortgagor £120, which may have been a part payment on the mortgage loan. From all this, we can unfortunately conclude nothing definite concerning either the value of the land or the rate of interest. All the Latin entries have been crossed through in the manuscript, while the English entry is allowed to stand as the final agreement.

Under the new conditions of freer exchange of land, three holdings had been massed together, and all three may now be lost through a mortgage. Alas for our ignorance of the cause of the mortgage!

CRAWLEY *SURSUMREDDITIONES*[1]

Memorand*um* quod primo die Julii Anno regni D*omi*ni n*ost*ri Jacobi dei gr*ati*a Anglie Francie et hib*er*nie Regis fidei defensor*is etcetera* vndecimo et Scocie quadragesimo sexto Coram Anth*oni*o Dawley Arm*iger*o Cl*er*ico totius Ep*iscop*atus Winton*iensis* venit Ambrosius Davye et sursum reddid*it* in manus d*omi*ni vn*am* toft*am* vnum mesuag*ium* et vn*am* ferlingat*am*[2] terr*e* nat*ive* in Crawley in parte boreal*i* vocata prestlande*s* cum quatuor acr*is* de D*omi*nicis D*omi*ni in le estfild iuxta puthill ad opus et vsum Joh*ann*is Wilkins Jun*ioris* et heredum suorum se*cun*dum Consuetud*inem* man*er*ii pred*icti* Sub Condicione tamen q*uo*d si pred*ictus* Ambrosius Davye heredes executores et administratores vel assignati sui solvant seu solvi faciant vel eoru*m* aliquis solvat seu solvi faciat p*refat*o Joh*ann*i Wilkins Jun*iori* executoribus vel assignatis suis integram sum*m*am Centum et octoginta et duodecem librarum bone et legalis monete Anglie in et super vicesimum nonum diem Septembris qui erit in anno D*omi*ni millesimo sexcentesimo decimo nono apud vel in modo Domo mansional*i* pred*icti* Joh*ann*is Wilkins Jun*ioris*, situat*a* in Crawley pred*ict'* in Com*itatu* South*ampt*o*nie* sine fraude avt vlterior*e* dilac*ion*e Quod tunc pred*icta* sursum reddic*io* vacua erit et nullius effectus alioquin in suo pleno robore et effectu stabit et permanebit.

Item die et anno supradict*is* coram prefat*o* Anth*oni*o Dawley venit

[1] MS., P. R. O., Ecclesiastical Commission, Court Rolls, 136/3, fol. 16.
[2] In the margin: *finis* anno Jacobi R*egis* Angl*ie etcetera* primo xiij s. iiij d.

pred*ictus* Ambrosius Davye et sursum reddid*it* in man*us* D*omi*ni vn*am* toft*am* et vn*am* ferlingat*am*[1] terr*e* nat*ive* Cont*inentem* p*er* estimac*ionem* xj[cem] acr*as* in parte boriali vocat*as* Morrant*es* ad opus et vsu*m* pred*icti* Joh*ann*is Wilkins Jun*ioris* et heredu*m* suoru*m* sec*und*u*m* consuetud*inem* man*er*ii pred*icti* sub Condic*ione* supradict*a*.

Item die et anno supradict*is* coram p*re*fat*o* Anth*oni*o Dawley venit pred*ictus* Ambrosius Davye et sursum reddid*it* in man*us* D*omi*ni vn*am* toft*am* et vn*am* ferlingat*am*[2] terr*e* nat*ive* in Crawley vocat*as* Simond*es* cu*m* p*er*tinenc*iis* et omnia et singula alia terras Co*mmun*ias et ten*emen*ta Custum*ar*ia ip*s*ius Ambrosii Davye Cum pertinen*ciis* in Crawley pred*ict*' ad opus et vsum pred*icti* Joh*ann*is Wilkins Jun*ioris* et heredu*m* suoru*m* sec*und*u*m* consuetud*inem* man*er*ii pred*icti* Sub Condic*ione* supradict*a*.

signu*m* p*re*fat*i* Ambrosii Davye

Capt*o* die et anno supradict*is* apud Civitat*em* Winton*ie* coram me Anth*oni*o Dawley.

In presencia Martini Yalden
Lancelot LW wayte
Robert X Nash
his marke
Richard Wilkins
Fra: Buckley

Memorandu*m* that vppon the xxix[th] Daie of September last the parties above named agreed to discharge thes seu*er*all surrenders *and* afterwards before me tooke newe absolute surrenders of this land 6 oct 1619[3]

signu*m* Ambrosii ▷ Davie
signu*m* Joh*ann*is ‡ Wilkins Jun*ioris*
p*resencia* Martini Yalden

Memorandu*m* it is agreed betwene the saide parties w*ith*in named that yf defalt of payment be made of the saide som of one hundred fower-score and twelve poundes before mencioned at the daie of payment before lymited and apointed wherby the said Copihold landes shall become forfeited that then the said John Wilkins the yonger his heires executors or assignes shall paie vnto the said Ambrose davye his heires executors or assignes the som*m*e of one hundred and twenty pound*es* lawfull monie of England more (over and besides the said one hundred fowerscore and twelve poundes before mencioned) for A full satisfaccion and recompence of the full worth and valewe of the Cus-

[1] In the margin: f*inis* a*nno* pred*icto* xiiij s.
[2] f*inis* a*nno* p*redicto* ij s. vj d.
[3] This additional memorandum is in another hand.

tum*ar*ie Inheritance of and in all the said Custum*ar*ie and Copihold land*es* and p*re*misses

signu*m* Λ̄ Ambrosii Davye
signu*m* I Joh*ann*is Wilki[ns] Jun*ioris*

In witnes *and* presence of
Martin Yalden
Richard Wilkins
Fra: Buckley
Robert X Nash
Lancelot LW Wayte
his marke

§§ 43. Surrender for the Purpose of a Mortgage, 7 April, 1634.

A farthing land and an additional rood in North Crawley were surrendered by Richard Pucknoll to the lord, to the use of Richard Symes who apparently has loaned to Pucknoll a sum of money for a period of two years and one day. The mortgagor surrenders the title to the mortgagee, via the lord of the manor, presumably actually keeping the use of the land in the meantime, on condition that restoration of title be made if the loan is repaid when due.

It is possible that the loan was £40 at 8 per cent for the two years. This would have amounted to the £46 8d. If the amount of land was 5¾ statutory acres, as seems to have been the case, then the mortgage was at the rate of a little under £8 an acre. Apparently the land was mortgaged while unattached to any messuage or toft. Anthony Waight had possessed it; Richard Pucknoll surrendered it; and Richard Symes, as mortgagee, was in line to receive it.

CRAWLEY[1]

Memorandu*m* q*uo*d septimo die Aprilis Anno Regni d*omi*ni n*ost*ri Caroli dei gr*ati*a Anglie Socie Francie et hib*er*nie regis fidei defensor*is* *etcetera* decimo Coram martino yalden gen*eroso* Cl*er*ico Tocius Ep*isco*-*p*atus Winton*iensis* venit Rich*ard*us Pucknoll et sursu*m* redd*idit* in man*us* d*omi*ni vna*m* ferlingat*am* terr*e* nat*ive* et vn*am* rod*am* terr*e* in boreal*i* p*ar*te de Crawley nup*er* Anthonii Waight Jun*ioris*, Ad opus et vsu*m* Rich*ard*i Symes et heredu*m* suoru*m* *secundum* cons*uetudinem* man*er*ii, Sub Condic*ione* tamen q*uo*d si p*re*dic*t*us Rich*ard*us Pucknoll

[1] MS., P. R. O., Ecclesiastical Commission, Court Rolls, 138/2, fol. 122b.

hered*es* executores vel assignat*i* sui solvant seu solvi faciant vel eoru*m* aliquis solvat seu solvi faciat p*re*fat*o* Rich*ardo* Symes executoribus vel assignat*is* suis plena*m* et integram sum*m*am quadraginta sex libraru*m* et octo solidoru*m* bone et legalis monete Anglie in et super octavu*m* diem Aprilis qui erit in anno Domini Millesimo sexcentesimo Tricesimo sexto Apud vel in modo domo mansionali Marci[ni] Symes scituat*a* et existent*e* in Sparsholt in Com*itatu* South*amptonie* Quod tunc hec p*re*sens sursu*m*redd*itio* vacua erit et null*ius* vigoris Alioquin in suo pleno robore et effectu stabit et p*er*manebit.

Capt*o* die et anno supradict*is*
Coram Martino Yalden
In p*re*sencia Anthonii Yalden
sig*num* Roberti R Gudge
hugh bud

Richard
Pucknell

§§ 44. Surrender for the Purpose of a Mortgage, 15 April, 1635.

Joint tenants, John and Richard Wilkins, surrendered to the lord for the use of William Browninge, one half-virgate in South Crawley. This land had been part of two messuages and two half-virgates.

The purpose was doubtless to facilitate the mortgage which, apparently, with the interest was to amount to £62. Repayment was £4 (interest) at the end of one year and a day, another £4 (interest) at the end of a similar period, and the balance £54 at the conclusion of the third period of a year and a day. Apparently the sum loaned was £50 and the rate 8 per cent per annum.

CRAWLEY [1]

Memorandu*m* q*uo*d decimo quinto die Aprilis Anno Regni d*omi*ni n*ost*ri Caroli dei grat*ia* Angl*ie* Scocie Francie et Hib*er*nie R*egis* fidei defensor*is* *etcetera* vndecimo Cora*m* Martino Yalden gen*ero*so Cl*er*ico Ep*iscop*atus Winton*iensis* venerunt Jo*han*nes Wilkins al*ia*s Muncke et Rich*ard*us Wilkins al*ias* Muncke et sursumreddid*unt* in man*us* d*omi*ni Man*er*ii pred*icti* dimid*iam* virgat*am* terr*e* nat*ive* in austral*i* p*ar*te de Crawley modo in occupac*i*one p*redic*ti Joh*an*nis Wilkins al*ia*s Muncke nup*er* p*ar*cell*am* duor*um* mes*suagiorum* et duar*um* dimid*iarum* virgat*arum* [2] terr*e* in Austral*i* p*ar*te de Crawley p*red*ict' Ad opus et vsu*m* Wil-

[1] MS., P. R. O., Ecclesiastical Commission, Court Rolls, 138/6, fol. 6b.

[2] In the margin: f*inis* Anno Elizab*ethe* xxxviij° cu*m* ij*bus* mes*suagiis* et dimid*iis* virgat*is* terr*e* nat*ive* xiij s. iiij d. modo p*er* divis*ionem*.

lelmi Browninge et heredu*m* suoru*m* secu*n*dum Cons*uetudinem* Ma*ner*ii Sub Condit*i*one tamen q*uo*d si p*re*d*i*cti Joh*an*nes et Rich*ard*us hered*es* executor*es* vel Assign*ati* sui solvant seu solvi faciant vel eoru*m* Aliquis solvat seu solvi faciat p*re*fato Will*el*mo executoribu*s* vel Assign*atis* suis plena*m* et integra*m* Sum*mam* sexaginta et duaru*m* libraru*m* bone et leg*a*lis monete Angl*ie* modo et forma sequ*entibus* vi*delicet* In et sup*er* decimu*m* sextu*m* diem Aprilis qui erit in Anno d*omi*ni Mill*es*imo sexcentesimo et tricesimo sexto sum*mam* quatuor libraru*m* consi*mi*lis leg*a*lis monete Angl*ie* (p*ar*cell*am* inde) Et in et sup*er* decimu*m* septimu*m* diem Aprilis qui erit in Anno d*omi*ni Mill*es*imo sexcentesimo et tricesimo septimo sum*mam* quatuor librarum consi*mi*lis monete Angl*ie* (Al*iam* p*ar*cell*am* inde) Et in et sup*er* decimu*m* octavu*m* diem Aprilis qui erit in Anno d*omi*ni Mill*es*imo sexcentesimo et tricesimo Octavo sum*mam* quinquagint*a* et quatuor libraru*m* consi*mi*lis monete Angl*ie* in plena solut*i*one p*re*d*ict*e sum*me* sexagint*a* et duaru*m* libraru*m* q*ue*lib*e*t soluc*i*o soluc*i*onis p*re*dict*e* inde fiend*a* Apud vel in modo domo mansional*i* p*re*d*i*cti Will*el*mi Browninge situat*a* et existent*e* in Crawley p*re*dict' in Com*itatu* South*amptonie* Quod tunc hec p*re*sens sursu*m*redd*itio* vacua erit et nullius vigor*is* Alioquin in suo pleno robore et eff*ec*tu stabit et p*er*maneb*it*

Signu*m*
Joh*an*nis ⌶ Wilkins al*ia*s Muncke

Capto die Et Anno supradict*is*
Cara*m* [sic] Martino Yalden
In p*re*sentia
W*illel*mi Welsterd'
John Gifford

Richard Wilkins
18 September 1638
The some due this surrender is dischargd by Consent of the p*ar*ties And Anewe taken.

1 mes*suagium* et dimidi*a* virgat*a* terr*e* nat*ive* *etcetera*.

William Browninge

§§ 45. Surrender of an Estate for the Purpose of a Mortgage, 4 Dec., 1652.

William Godwyn loaned to William Page £40 for 4 years at 6 per cent, interest being payable at the end of each year. Both of the families concerned have been prominent in Crawley in modern times, and both are represented today. The fact that Godwyn had £40 to loan is probably indicative of a prosperous agriculture, there being apparently no other source of income, such as the woolen industry so prominent in other parts.

The estate mortgaged for the loan was made up of two complete units — two messuages, two yards, and two half yardlands, plus a pittle of $1\frac{1}{2}$ acres. In all, $33\frac{1}{2}$ customary acres, or $16\frac{3}{4}$ statutory acres, were involved. The mortgage was clearly not a heavy one for an estate made up of two complete units.

It is noteworthy that this document, like many in the Commonwealth and Protectorate Period, is in English with modern dating. Doubtless William Kelsey was the steward of several manors of which Crawley was but one.

CRAWLEY [1]

The fowerth day of december in the yeare of our Lord one thowsand six hundred fifty and two Before William Kelsey Steward of the said Mannor came William Page and did surrender into the handes of the lord of the said Mannor two Messuages w*i*th two Curtelages *and* two half yardland*es* of Bondland in Crawley conteyning two and thirty acres of land [2] in the Southpart of Crawley, and one p*ar*cell of land called A Pittle conteyning one acre and a half vnto the vse and behoof of William Godwyn and his heires according to the Custome of the Mannor vppon Condic*i*on notw*i*thstanding that if the said william Page his heires Executo*rs* *and* Administrato*rs* or assignes doe pay or cause to be paid or any of them doe pay or cause to be paid vnto the said William Godwyn his Executo*rs* Administrato*rs* or assignes the full some of Forty and nyne pound*es* and twelve shilling*es* of lawfull money of England in manner *and* forme following that is to say in *and* vppon the sixt day of december w*hi*ch shalbe in the yeare of o*ur* lord God one thowsand six hundred fifty and three the som*m*e of Eight and forty shilling*es* one p*ar*cell thereof in *and* vppon the seaventh day of december which shalbe in the yeare of o*ur* lord one thowsand six hundred fifty and fower the like some of Forty and eight shilling*es* another p*ar*cell thereof, in *and* vppon the Eight day of december w*hi*ch sha*l*be in the yeare of o*ur* lord one thowsand six hundred fifty *and* fiue the like some of Forty and eight shilling*es* another p*ar*cell thereof, and in *and* vppon the Nynth day of december w*hi*ch shalbe in the yeare of o*ur* lord one thowsand six hundred fifty and six the some of Forty and two pound*es* and eight shilling*es* of lawfull money of England in full payment of the said some of Forty nyne pound*es* and twelue shilling*es*, the said seuerall payment*es* to be made att or in the nowe dwelling house of the said William Godwyn scituat*e* in Crawley in the County of South*ampton*, That then

[1] MS., P. R. O., Ecclesiastical Commission, Court Rolls, 139/11, fol. 5b.
[2] In the margin: fyne in the 4th yeare of K*ing* Charles v s. viij d.

this present surrend*er* shalbe void *and* of none effect orells shall stand remayne *and* bee in full force effect and vertue.

William paige

Taken the day *and* yeare
aforesaid before mee
Will Kelsey
In presence of Arthur Lipscumb
John Feilder

§§ 46. Surrenders for the Purpose of a Mortgage, 29 Sept., 1671.

William Broadway mortgaged his three tenements for £300 at 6 per cent for 3 years, interest being due at the end of each half year. The first tenement was made up of a messuage and a virgate of bondland in South Crawley and a "Pittle" of an acre in the east end of Crawley. John Fountain, Esq., of Middlesex made the loan which was to be paid back at the home of Henry Mildmay, Esq., of Twyford, Hampshire.

The second tenement surrendered and mortgaged was part of a granary (or barn), orchard, and yard (or curtelag*ium*) and a half virgate of bondland made up of 16 acres (according to estimate rather than actual measuring). These 16 acres lay in the 3 common fields of South Crawley: 7 acres in Eastfield, 4¼ in Homefield (Middlefield), and 4¾ acres in Westfield. Attached to this tenement was the right of common pasture for one cow and for other beasts of burden.

The third tenement was a virgate of bondland and an acre and a half of purpresture land in South Crawley.

The total holding mortgaged was 2½ virgates, plus a pittle containing 1 acre and a piece of purpresture land of 1½ acres. This seems to amount to 82½ customary acres (taking the virgate to amount to 32 customary acres) or 41 acres one rood by statutory measure. Apparently only the first tenement had a residence, the second possessing only part of a granary and part of a yard, the third being made up only of arable. All were in South Crawley. Here was a reconstructed estate which the Browning family had arranged for itself and which at this time it hypothecated.

CRAWLEY MAN*ER*IUM S*URSUMREDDITIONES*[1]

M*emorandum* q*uo*d vicesimo Nono die Septembris Anno Regni D*omi*ni n*ost*ri Caroli Sec*un*di dei gr*ati*a Angl*ie* Scoc*ie* Franc*ie et* Hib*er*nie Regis fidei defensor*is etcetera* vicesimo tercio ven*it* cora*m* me Jacobo Earle Cl*er*ico Ep*iscop*atus Winton*iensis* Will*elm*us Broadway *et* Sursu*m*redd*idit* in man*us* D*omi*ni vnu*m* mess*uagium et* vn*am* virgat*am* terr*e* nat*ive* in austral*i* p*ar*te de Crawley *et* vn*am* p*ar*cell*am* terr*e* voc*atam* a Pittle cont*inentem* vn*am* acr*am* iacen*tem* in orien*tali* fine de Crawley[2] p*redict*' ad opus *et* vsu*m* Joh*ann*is Fountaine de Lincolnes' Inne in Com*itatu* Midd*lesexie* Ar*migeri et* hered*um* Suor*um* sec*un*dum cons*uetudinem* Man*er*ii Sub condic*io*ne tamen q*uo*d Si p*redictus* Will*elm*us Broadway hered*es* executores siue Assign*ati* sui soluent seu solui facient seu eor*um* aliquis soluet seu solui faciet p*re*fat*o* Joh*ann*i Fountaine executorib*us* adm*inistratori*b*us* siue Assign*atis* suis plena*m et* integra*m* sum*mam* trecentar*um* quinquagint*a et* quatuor librar*um* leg*al*is monete Angl*ie* modo *et* forma Sequen*tibus* (vi*delice*t) novem libras vn*am* p*ar*cell*am* inde in et Sup*er* vicesimu*m* nonum diem Marcii qui erit Anno D*omi*ni 1672 novem libras al*iam* p*ar*cell*am* inde in *et* sup*er* vicesimu*m* nonu*m* diem Septembris tunc p*roximo* Sequen*tis* novem libras al*iam* p*ar*cell*am* inde in *et* Sup*er* vicesimu*m* nonu*m* diem Marcii qui erit Anno D*omi*ni 1673 novem libras al*iam* p*ar*cell*am* inde in *et* Sup*er* vicesimu*m* nonu*m* diem Septembris tunc p*roximo* Sequen*tis* novem libras al*iam* p*ar*cell*am* inde in *et* Sup*er* vicesimu*m* nonu*m* diem Marcii qui erit Anno D*omi*ni 1674 *et* plena*m* sum*mam* trecentar*um* et novem librarum resid*uum* inde in *et* Sup*er* vicesimu*m* nonum diem Septembris tunc p*roximo* Sequen*tis* in plena satisfacc*io*ne *et* soluc*io*ne p*redicte* sum*m*e trecentar*um* quinquagint*a et* quatuor librar*um* q*ue*libet soluc*io* soluc*io*num p*redictarum* fiend*a* apud vel in modo domo manc*io*nali [sic] cuiusdem Henrici Mildmay Ar*migeri* Scituat*a et* existent*e* in Twiford in Com*itatu* South*ampt*o*nie* q*uo*d tunc hac p*re*sens sursu*m*redd*itio* vacua erit *et* nullius vigoris alioquin in suo pleno robore *et* eff*ect*u stabit *et* p*er*manebit.

Idem Will*elm*us Broadway die *et* Anno sup*radictis* Sursu*m*redd*idit* vt Sup*ra* p*ar*tem horrei modo existen*tem* le threshing flower *et* p*ar*tem pomarii et atrii Siue curtelag*ii* in Crawley[3] p*ro*vt modo Sunt divis*a et* Sep*arat*a p*er* metes *et* bundas *et* di*midiam* virgat*am* terr*e* nat*ive* in austral*i* p*ar*te de Crawley p*redict*' cont*inentem* p*er* estimac*ionem* xvj^{m} acr*as* terre iacen*tes* in tribus Campis co*mmun*ibus ib*id*em vnde in Campo voc*ato* le Eastfeild quinq*ue* acr*as et* in furlonge ib*id*em apud Thornham duas acr*as et* in Campo voc*ato* le Homefeild quatuor acr*as et* quarter-

[1] MS., P. R. O., Ecclesiastical Commission, Court Rolls, 140/9., fol. 100.

[2] In the margin: f*ini*s Anno xiiij^{o} Car*oli* sec*un*di xiij s. iiij d.

[3] In the margin: f*ini*s Anno p*redicto* vj s. viij d.

ium vn*ius* acr*e*, *et* in Campo voc*ato* le westfeild quatuor acr*as* dimid*iam* *et* quarter*ium* vn*ius* acr*e* in decenn*a* de Crawley p*redict'* *et* Co*mmun*iam pastur*am* p*ro* vn*a* vacc*a* *et* p*ro* al*iis* aueriis p*er*tin*entibus* ad terr*am* p*re*-d*ictam* (nup*er* p*ar*cell*am* duor*um* mess*uagiorum* *et* di*midie* virgat*e* terre nat*ive* ad opus *et* vsu*m* vt sup*ra* Sub Sep*ar*alib*us* condic*ion*ib*us* vt sup*ra*.

Idem Will*elm*us Broadway die *et* Anno sup*radictis* sursu*m*redd*idit* vt sup*ra* vna*m* virgat*am* terr*e* nat*ive* *et* vna*m* p*ar*cell*am* terr*e* p*ur*p*res*t*ure* cont*inentem* vn*am* acr*am* di*midiam* quond*am* Will*elm*i Seeley in australi p*ar*te de Crawley [1] ad opus *et* vsu*m* vt Sup*ra* sub sep*ar*al*ibus* condi-c*ion*ib*us* vt sup*ra*.

Capt*o* die *et* Anno sup*radictis* William Broadway
coram me Jacobo Earle
In p*re*senc*ia* Robert Earle

§§ 47. Surrender of Tenements, 13 Oct., 1679.

William Browning surrendered his holdings for the use of John Godwin, who himself later (in 1686) surrendered similar lands to a mortgagee. Why William parted with his lands for the use of John is not stated. But clearly we have here two of the most prominent families, the Brownings and the Godwins, engaging in the exchange of lands in the seventeenth century.

The estate surrendered was made up of 22¼ acres, as follows: 7 acres were in Buttsfield (probably a furlong in Homefield), 9½ acres in Middlefield, 4 acres in the "feild by the north" (probably Westfield) all in North Crawley; one acre at Norwood, or Northwood, in South Crawley, and 2½ roods in the common field of North Crawley. Just which this common field of North Crawley was, is not clear. Here, as elsewhere, Markfurlong seems to have borne this special designation, but it was really a furlong, not a field made up of furlongs.

To only one bit of the estate were there any appurtenances (woods, pasture, and the like), at least as far as the document goes. The outstanding significance of the document is, as in so many other cases, that it gives evidence of the splitting up of old-time holdings.

[1] In the margin: f*ini*s Anno p*redicto* x s. iiij d.

CRAWLEY MAN*E*RIUM *SURSUMREDDITIONES* [1]

Memorand*um* q*uo*d decimo tercio die octobris Anno R*e*gni d*omi*ni n*ost*ri Car*oli* sec*un*di dei gr*ati*a nunc R*egi*s Anglie *etcetera* tricesimo primo ven*it* cora*m* me Jacobo Earle gen*eroso* cl*er*ico Ep*iscop*atus Winton*iensis* Will*elm*us Browning et sursu*m*redd*idit* in man*us* d*omi*ni Man*er*ii p*re*d*icti* vigint*i* et vn*am* acr*as* [2] terre arrab*ili*s iacen*tes* in trib*us* sep*ar*alib*us* Campis in boreal*i* p*ar*te de Crawley (vi*delice*t) septem acr*as* (siue plus sive minus) in Campo vocat*o* Butts Feild novem acr*as* et dimid*iam* (sive plus siue minus) in medio campo et in Campo vocat*o* the feild by the north quatuor acr*as* (siue plus siue minus) cum Hor-r[eis] erect[is] in et sup*er* terr*as* oliveri Poole ac etiam vn*am* acr*am* (siue minus) apud Norwood cu*m* Boscis comm*un*i pastur*a* et al*iis* appurten*an*ces [sic] eidem p*er*tin*entibus* (p*ar*cell*am* vn*ius* mess*uagii* et vn*ius* firling terr*e* nat*ive* cont*inent*' vndecem acr*as* terr*e* ac vn*um* horr*eum* cum vn' Cotes [3] terr*e* nat*ive* cont*inent*' quinq*ue* acr*as* terr*e* et dimid*iam* in boreal*i* p*ar*te de Crawley) [4] Ad opus et Vsu*m* Joh[ann]is Godwin et hered*um* suor*um* sec*un*dum Cons*uetudinem* Man*er*ii.

Id*em* Will*elm*us die et Anno sup*radictis* sursu*m*redd*idit* vt supra du*as* rod*as* [5] et dimid*iam* terr*e* iacen*tes* in co*mmun*i Campo de Crawley in boreal*i* p*ar*te in furlong*e* vocat' Marke furlonge Ad opus et vsu*m* vt supra.

William Brown[i]ng

Capt*o* die et Anno sup*radictis*
Coram me
Jacobo Earle

In p*re*senc*e* of
James knight
Thomas Lovell Ju*nior*

§§ 48. Surrender for the Purpose of a Mortgage, 2 Nov., 1686.

This is specifically called a mortgage in a marginal note. John Godwin surrendered a messuage and two farthinglands and also a cottage with eleven acres in North Crawley for the use of Abigail Rothwell, widow, of Riversden. The widow had loaned to John

[1] MS., P. R. O., Ecclesiastical Commission, Court Rolls, 140/7, fol. 19.
[2] In the margin: F*ini*s Anno xiiij° Caroli s*ecun*di vij s. modo p*er* divis*ionem* v s.
[3] Probably for Cott.
[4] This part of the parenthesis was omitted in the manuscript.
[5] In the margin: F*ini*s Anno sup*radicto* ii s. vii d.

Godwin £260 for six years at five per cent, interest being payable at the end of each year, amounting in all to £338.

Just why one holding should be called a messuage with two farthinglands (five acres and one half each), while the other is called a cottage with eleven (customary) acres, is not clear. Apparently they were at this time approximately equal, each containing a residence and yard or garden and eleven (customary) acres of arable land.

CRAWLEY MAN*ER*IUM *SURSUMREDDITIO*[1]

Memorand*um* q*uo*d vicesimo die Novembris Anno r*e*gni D*omi*ni n*ost*ri Jacobi Sec*un*di Die gr*ati*a nunc R*egi*s Angl*ie etcetera* Sec*un*do Annoq*ue* D*omi*ni 1686 ven*it* coram me Jacobo Earle gen*eroso* Cl*e*rico totius Ep*iscop*atus Winton*iensis* Joh*ann*es Godwin de Crawley *et* Sursumreddidit in man*us* D*omi*ni Man*er*ii p*redicti* vn*um* Mess*uagium et* du*as* firlingat*as* terr*e* nat*ive* vn*um* Cottag*ium* cum vndecem acr*is* terr*e* p*er* Estim*ationem* in P*ar*te Boreal*i* de Crawley[2] Ad opus *et* vsum Abigail' Rothwell de Riversden vid*ue et* hered*um* Suor*um* Sec*un*d*um* Cons*uetudinem* Man*er*ii p*re*dicti Sub Condic*i*one tamen q*uo*d Si p*redictus* Joh*ann*es Godwin heredes Executores Sive Assign*ati* Sui Solvent Seu Solvi facient vel eor*um* aliquis Solvet Seu Solvi faciet p*re*fate Abigail' Rothwell hered*ibus* sive Assign[at]is Suis plenam *et* integram Sum*m*am trecentar*um et* triginta *et* octo librar*um* legalis monete Angl*ie* modo *et* forma Sequen*tibus* (vi*delice*t) tresdecem libr*as* vnam P*ar*cellam inde in *et* Sup*er* vicesimum primum diem Novembris qui erit Anno D*omi*ni 1687 tresdecem libras al*iam* P*ar*cellam inde in *et* Sup*er* vicesimum primum diem Novembris qui erit Anno D*omi*ni 1688 tresdecem libr*as* al*iam* P*ar*cell*am* inde in *et* Sup*er* vicesimum primum diem Novembris qui erit Anno D*omi*ni 1689 tresdecem libr*as* al*iam* P*ar*cell*am* inde in *et* Sup*er* vicesimum primum diem Novembris qui erit Anno D*omi*ni 1690 tresdecem libras al*iam* P*ar*cell*am* inde in *et* Sup*er* vicesimu*m* primum diem Novembris qui erit Anno D*omi*ni 1691 *et* plena*m* Sum*m*am ducentar*um* Septuaginta *et* trium librar*um* resid*uum* inde in et Super vicesimum primum diem Novembris qui erit Anno D*omi*ni 1692 q*ue*libet Soluc*i*o Soluc*i*on*um* p*redictarum* fiend*a* apud vel in modo domo manc*i*onal*i* cuiusdam Will*el*mi Complin gen*erosi* Scituat*a et* existen*te* in Kingsgate Street p*ro*pe Civitat*em* Winton*ie* q*uod* tunc hac [sic] p*re*sens

[1] MS., P. R. O., Ecclesiastical Commission, Court Rolls, 142/2, fol. 14b.
[2] In the margin: f*ini*s Anno primo Jac*obi* Sec*un*di xx s.

Sursumredd*itio* Sit vacua *et* null*ius* vigoris alioquin in Suo pleno robore *et* effectu Stabit *et* p*er*manebit [1]

John Godwin

Capt*o* die *et* Anno sup*radictis*
cora*m* me Jacobo Earle
In p*re*senc*ia*
Wm Complin

§§ 49. Wills of Yeomen (1513, 1517, 1616, 1656, 1761, and 1815) and an Inventory of Property (1616).

These six wills were all made by members of old Crawley families. Some of the funniest of the wills have been omitted: those published here are valuable for the light thrown upon a class of yeoman farmers about whom we otherwise know very little.[2] Such wills, although used by genealogists and local historians, have not been adequately appreciated in economic and social history. This is the more surprising in view of the fact that urban wills have been used a good deal for general historical purposes.

After the body and the soul had been consigned to their proper places, the worldly goods were divided among loving and disappointed relatives. Overseers were appointed by the testators to assist or supervise the executors.

The wills deal chiefly with personal property. Bondland passed to the youngest child by custom. Leased land was devised, if the lease still had a period to run. The earlier testators had chiefly sheep to leave behind; the later ones had a good deal of hard cash. The amount of money devised by William Godwin and Thomas Pern is noteworthy. Unfortunately only the will of 1616 has an inventory attached.

[1] In the margin: 14° Octobris 1693. I*tem* John Newland husband of the Sa*i*d Abigail Ro[t]hwell did acknowledge to haue had *and* rece*ive*d full satisfacci*o*n of this mortguage *and* desire it may be crossed out of the booke witnes my hand

Jo: Newlyn

Witnes Ja: Earle.

The whole entry is accordingly crossed out.

[2] See above, § 28, p. 96, and § 32, p. 112. William Coper may not have been a yeoman farmer himself, but he belonged to a rising yeoman family.

(*a*) [A filed copy endorsed]: 1513 Johannes Cop*er* de Crawly [1]

Jh̄c.

In dei no*mine* Amen Anno d*omini* s*ecundu*m cursu*m* et computa*cion*em eccl*es*ie Anglicane Mill*esi*mo cccc xiij die vero Mensis Januarii xvij ego Joh*ann*es Cop*er* p*a*rochi*e* de Crawley Winton*iensis* Dio*cesis* compos mentis et sane memorie condo testamentu*m* meu*m* in hunc modu*m* In primis com*m*endo ani*m*am meam Deo o*mn*ipotenti b*ea*te Marie virginis ac omnib*us* s*an*ctis corpusq*ue* meu*m* sepeliend*um* in eccl*es*ia siue in Cimit*er*io ecclesie beate Marie de Crawley p*re*dict' Item lego eccl*es*ie Cath*edrali* S*ancti* Swithuni Winton*iensis* xx d. Item lego Margarete filie mee cc oues It*em* om*n*ib*us* filiolis meis v*idelicet* vnicuiq*ue* eor*um* vnu*m* Agnu*m* Item vnicuiq*ue* fam*ul*o michi famulanti vna*m* oue*m* It*em* vnicuiq*ue* puero*rum* Thome Smyth ij oues It*em* lego vx*or*i Thome Smyth xx^{ti} oues It*em* Edithe Mody ij oues It*em* Alicie Mody xx^{ti} oues It*em* lego filio Ric*ard*i Poore x oues It*em* volo q*uo*d Thomas Smyth *et* Willelmus filius meus h*ab*eant insimul om*n*es Annos et t*er*minos meos in firma mea de Somborne p*ar*ua occupando t*er*ras eiusd*em* sicut ego occupaui et in eadem feci et q*uo*d executores mei no*n* subtraha*n*t aut vendant aut aliquo modo aliene*n*t predict*os* annos meos de dict*o* Thom*a* [—] [2] vel eor*um* alt*er*o alienari ve [sic] faciant durant*e* annis et t*ermi*nis meis p*re*dict*is* in dict*a* firma et q*uo*d ip*s*i Thom*as* et Will*elmus* soluant anuos reddit*us* eiusd*em* p*er* equales Residuu*m* vero bonor*um* meor*um* non legator*um* debit*is* meis p*ri*us solut*is* do *et* lego Agneti vx*or*i mee *et* Will*el*mo filio meo quos constituo et ordino meos executores ut ip*s*i disponant ea p*ro* a*nim*e mee salute p*ro*ut eis mclius videbit*ur* Et ordino Rob*ertum* Tanner testame*n*ti mei supervisore*m* et volo ut h*ab*eat p*ro* labore suo xx^{ti} ariet' oues Et volo eciam q*uo*d Agnes vx*or* mea p*re*dicta h*ab*eat cameram suam cu*m* om*ni*b*us* inibi content*is* Ita q*uo*d filius meus Will*el*mus nullu*m* h*ab*eat introitu*m* nec cu*m* rebus in ea quouismodo se int*ro*mittat absq*ue* speciali licencia *et* p*er*missione vx*or*is mee p*re*dict*e* Hiis testib*us* Rob*er*to Tanner Ric*ard*o Pooer Joh*ann*e Mody cu*m* aliis.[3]

(*b*) [A filed copy endorsed]: 1517 Will*el*mus Cop*er* de Crawlie [4]

Will*el*m*us* Cop*er* xvij

In dei no*mine* Anno d*omini* M^{mo}ccccc^{mo}xvij^{mo} die vero mens*is* Septembris vij^{o} Ego Will*el*mus Copper Sane memorie Condo testamentu*m* meu*m* i*n* hu*n*c modu*m* in p*ri*mis Com*m*endo a*nim*am meam deo om*ni*pote*n*ti beate marie o*mn*ibu*s* Sa*n*ctis corpusq*ue* meu*m* sepeliendu*m* in

[1] MS., Winchester Probate Registry, Consistory Court.

[2] Obliterated; perhaps some small word missing.

[3] No act; endorsed "Testamenta data anno do*mi*ni M^{o} vc^{o} xiij^{o}," having apparently served as the outer cover for other wills of this same year.

[4] MS., Winchester Probate Registry, Consistory Court.

eccl*es*ia beate Marie de Crauley It*em* lego eccl*es*ie Cathedrali xx d. It*em* lego eccl*es*ie de Crauley ix oues Item lego vnicuiq*ue* iiij^{or} filior*um* meor*um* x li*bras* Item volo ut Alic*ia* vx*or* mea q*ua*ndo sibi placuerit haberet sacerdotem p*er* annu*m* scelebra*n*tem p*ro* a*nim*a mea et a*nim*a p*at*ris mei Item lego Roberto chyddyn famulo meo iiij^{or} oues Residuum vero o*mn*iu*m* bonor*um* meor*um* non legator*um* debitis meis p*ri*us solvtis do et lego Alic*ie* vx*ori* mee *et* Henrico copper quos facio meos veros Executores Item lego p*re*fato Henrico xc^{s}[1] p*ro* porcione sua Item Cons*tit*u*o* et facio Joh*ann*em Tutt sup*er*visorem hui*us* testamenti Hiis testib*us* D*omi*no Hugone Gwyn curato de crawley Waltero mowmfort cu*m* aliis.

(*c*) [Original will and inventory, endorsed]: 1616 Rich*ar*dus Beche de Crawley — 1616 — Julii [2]

In the name of god amen I Richard bech of the parish of craly beinge sike and weak in bodie but of good memore praysed be allmighty god dooe ordayn and make this my last will and testament the sixt day of Desember 1615 In man*n*er and forme foloi*n*g feurst I geue and bequeth my soull too allmighty god my Creatore and Redemer and my bodey to be bured In Cristen bureall Ite*m* I geue to my sonne Richard bech tooe beds Ite*m* I geue to my sonne Richard Bech fiue akers of wheatt wch is upon the halfe eyard land thatt I dooe Rentt of John monke Alsoe my will is thatt my sonne Richard bech shall hould the halfe eyard land thre eyre tooe begene att mikellmas next folowing Also my will is thatt my sonne Richard shall haue the Rest of the land too sow wth barle for this eyre belonging to the sayd halfe eyard land It*em* I geue to my sonne Richard four horsses with the cartt and plow and all things thervnto belonginge It*em* I geue to my sone Richard iii kene It*em* I geue to my wiff the best Cow Item I geue to my son Ambros bech iii akers of wheatt lieng . . . in the north sied all the rest of my goods . . . I geue . . . to gan my wiff whom I doe make executres of this my last will and testament and I doe appoyntt to be my ouerseers of this last will Robart modee of kingsomborn and Richard Dane wittnes hervnto . . .

Richard —|— Bech

Richard Ӡ Dane
John ʕ pitter
Willem Ɛ baker [3]

[1] Written "xcf." [2] MS., Winchester Probate Registry, Consistory Court.

[3] Proved before the Commissary of the Archbishop of Canterbury Metropolitan within the diocese of Winchester, 4 July 1616, by the widow Jane and Robert Mowdy of Kings Sumborne husbandman.

[Inventory]

febreary *the* vij 1615

An inventore of all the goods and Chattels of Richard bech of the parish of Craly in the County of South' late desesed taken In the presens of Lavnslett Wayt and Richard Davie as foloweth

Imp*rim*is his bede and his aparell	iij l. vj s. viij d.
Item one bedd furnished *and* one bedsted	xl s.
all the lennen	l s.
tooe Chests and one Coffer	xvj s.
one tabell bord and a Sied bord a forme and a Chare and a cobbard	x s.
all the bras	xx s.
all the pewter	xiij s. iiij d.
barrels Cevers and tobs	x s.
one mell to grind mault	x s.
the bacen att Roff	xv s.
tooe quarters of wotes	xxvj s. viij d.
one quarter and a hafe of wheatt	xliiij s.
Eight quarter of barle	viij li.
four horsses and harnes belonging to them	viij l.
one Cart *and* a doungpott *and* a plow *and* thre harrowes	iij l.
hey and theches	xx s.
the woodd in the barton	x s.
It*em* three Ceine and a bolloke	viij li.
three Score and nine sheppe	xx l. x s.
seuentene acers and a halve of wheatt and theches uppon the ground	xvij li. x s.
Sume lxxxij li. xj s. viij d.	

(*d*) [William Godwin, 1656] [1]

I William Godwin of Craley in the County of Southampton yeoman doe make my last will and Testament ⌈12 Aug., 1656⌉ first I commend my body to the earth, and my soule to God that gaue it . . . . Item I giue to the poore at my buryall two pounds. Item I giue to my Daughter Rebecca Ten pounds to be paid when her husband Walter Sutton shall fine the liueing at Chilbolton for his children Item I giue his two Children Twenty pounds a peice to be paid when they seuerally come to *the* age of sixteene yeares. Item I giue to my Daughter Elizabeth Two hundred pounds to be paid at the day of marriage, or at Twenty yeares of age. Item I giue my Daughter Sara two hundred pounds

[1] MS., Somerset House, Prerogative Court of Canterbury, 357 Berkley.

[payable in like manner]. Item I giue to my sonne Thomas all the Deedes, right, and title I haue at Wallup with Two hundred pounds to be paid at fourteene yeares of age. Item I giue my son*ne* John Two hundred pounds to be paid to him at the age of fourteene yeares. Item I giue to my daughter Mary Two hundred pounds to be paid at the day of marriage, or at Twenty yeares of age. All the rest of my goods, and Cattells and Chattell goods I giue to my wife, and to my sonne Willia*m* whom I make my whole, and sole Executors of this my will and Testament. In witnesse whereof I haue sett my hand and seale, the day, and yeare first aboue written. Alsoe, I doe desire my brother John Godwin, and my brother in Law William Rothwell to be my Ouerseers and for theire paines I giue them forty shillings a peice William Godwin Witnesses Nicholas Pill. Robert Pitter, William Rothwell.[1]

(*e*) [Original will endorsed] [2]

Pitter, John of Crawley Peculiar — Will 1761.

In the Name of God Amen I John Pitter of Crawley Do make this my Last Will and Testament in writing and manner following that is to say I Recommend my Soul to God Almighty and my Body to be Buryed at the discretion of my Loving Wife whom I make my Hole and Sole Executurix of all my Hole Effects as money Goods Bills Bonds Nots of hand and What Els as Long as (her Naturall Life doth Last) [2] (she lives my Wido) [3] And affter her deces my will is to dispose it as [3] follows

Item I give to my dafter [3] daughter mary page — fifty pounds
Item I give to my Son Thomas pitter — one Hundred pounds
Item I give to my daughter Elizabeth pitter — one Hundred pounds
Lastly I give to all my former Children one shilling each — And what more theare is I Leve to the discretion of my Executrix of this my Last Will and Testament

heare by Revoking all former Wills made by me

In witness I have heare vnto sett my hand and seale [4] the 31st of Oct*o*be*r* in the yare one [5] thousand Seven Hundred and fifty four

The Inter Lining wase
before the Sining

John Pitter

mary Butterley (SEAL)
John Wickham

The 16th October 1761

[1] Proved at London, 27 Oct., 1656, by Rebecca Godwin, relict, *and* William Godwin, son*ne* of joint executors.

[2] MS., Winchester Probate Registry. So far as can be judged this will was written by the testator.

[3] Struck through. [4] The seal is "blind." [5] Interlineated.

Margaret Pitter the above Named Executrix
was duly sworn before Me.

J: Freer Sur[rogate].[1]

(*f*) Notes from the will of Thomas Pern of Crawley, co. Southampton, yeoman.[2] 14 Feb. 1815.

To James Judd of Romsey, miller, and James Fitt of Headbourne Worthy, co. Southants, yeoman, £2,300 in trust that the interest be paid to my wife Elizabeth during widowhood; in the event of her remarriage £500 is to go to her for her absolute use, the remainder [3] is to be transferred to my sons Thomas, William, and John Pern at 21, and to my daughters Ann, Elizabeth, and Emma Pern at 21 or on marriage.

To my three sons £1,500 each at 21; my three daughters £1,000 each at 21 or on marriage.

My farming business is to be continued until my youngest child attain 21, my two trustees carrying on the same for the maintenance and education of my children.

My wife is to be permitted to live in my dwelling-house during widowhood and until my youngest child attain 21.

As soon as my youngest child has attained 21, my trustees are to convert into money all the farming stock, and add the same to my residuary personal estate.

All my stocks, funds, mortgages, and securities to my two trustees for the use of my 6 children as tenants in common. All lands, hereditaments, leaseholds, or premises vested in me in trust for any persons or by way of mortgage, are to go to the use of the said James Judd and James Fitt that they may make conveyances according to the said trusts.

Executors — the said two trustees.

Witnesses — John Birch George Godwin Jun*io*r
T Woodham.

Proved 22 July, 1815, by James Judd and James Fitt.

"Sub £12,500" written at the end of the probate.

§§ 50. Crawley in Arms, 1523, 1569, 1914–18.

In the charter of 909 the men of Crawley were said to be liable to serve in the army as well as to be obliged to keep in repair both

[1] There is no seal here for the Act.

[2] MS., Somerset House, Prerogative Court of Canterbury, Registered 393 Pakenham. There are no other papers with the filed will.

[3] In stated proportions.

castle and bridges.[1] During the Anglo-Norman period Crawley village apparently escaped feudal service. Since the bishop owed knights' service for his manors in general, and for the hundred of Buddlesgate in particular, however, we are led to suspect that the service for Crawley may have been attached to some more or less separate estate, such as Hunton [2] or possibly the one later called Rookley House.

In the sixteenth century a national levy or militia was developed, or revived, to strengthen the Throne against its internal feudal and dynastic enemies and against its foreign enemies on boundary or seacoast. The occasion of the muster of 1523 was the war against the Scots and on the Continent. Great efforts were made to provide money and ships, ammunition and soldiers. Whether Crawley men were sent to the North or to the Continent is unknown. Certainly they were still serfs, but perhaps even then they were possessed of the rising spirit of freedom.

Whether the list of 1523 includes Hunton as well as Crawley is not clear. Certainly there are many strange names in it, particularly the first seven. Some of the old families, however, are represented — Allen, Wayt, Stephens, Plompton, Page, and Couper. In all, 18 persons are listed, one being a woman, one assigning his equipment to two others, and one unspecified. Of the 15 others, four were archers and 11 billmen. Apparently those worth so much were expected to provide themselves with prest-money, to the extent of 10 per cent of their personal property. In respect of property, the Waights and Pages stood high. The two best endowed with worldly goods are classed as archers. The equipment of the billmen is put down as jacks (or coats-of-mail), jacks complete, or German revettes. One of the last-named belonged to the parish. How proud the parish must have been of this doughty array!

The occasion of the muster of 1569 seems to have been the Northern Rebellion. A commission was issued to a few of the notable men of the county to list the males in their jurisdiction

[1] See above, §§ 3, pp. 179, 181.

[2] About 1286 Anselm Basset held two knights' fees in Hunton. *Register of John de Pontissara, Surrey Record Society*, vol. VI (1924), p. 594.

who might be of use in war. This was done for each of the hundreds in the county, and, within the hundred, for each of the tithings. It is to be noted that in the present case the list is of the men of the tithing of Crawley and Hunton together. These two constituted a single tithing but two manors.

The commissioners of muster returned to the central government certificates containing the names of the men able to serve, together with other information concerning their equipment. A man was put down as "able" if he was between sixteen and sixty years of age, if he was strong in body, and if he had something like the necessary equipment. Just what this equipment was for Crawley, we are not told. Apart from the holders of the How and the Rookley House estate, there was no person likely to be recruited as a light horseman or a demi-lance. Crawley would more probably provide armed corselets, harquebusiers, archers, and especially billmen. The general responsibility for such a muster came to rest upon the shoulders of the lord lieutenant of the county.[1]

In the Crawley list of national militiamen we find but sixteen names. The familiar families are Davy, Stevens, Wayte, Pitter, and Alin. The last few names on the list, perhaps the last five, probably belonged to Hunton. We miss the names of Couper, Paige, and Godwin, and they do not seem to occur in another list of horsemen. The ratio of the unable to the able in the whole hundred was 140 to 184. At this ratio Crawley itself should have supplied about twenty-two instead of eleven, if we assume at least fifty families in the village at the time. This failure to rise to the local level of national service may have been due either to the chance circumstances of a small number of able-bodied adult males at the time or to the permanent poverty of North Crawley tenants. About half the villagers, living in the north part, had such small plots of land that we may infer they were too poor to provide themselves with the equipment necessary for war.

It is fitting to include here the sacrifices of Crawley in later wars. The diminution of population during the early nineteenth

[1] See Gladys S. Thompson, *Lords Lieutenants in the Sixteenth Century* (1923), pp. 85–86, *et passim*. See also MS., P. R. O., State Papers, Domestic, Elizabeth, vol. LIX, no. 63 (Nov., 1569).

century indicates the drain involved in the struggle against Napoleon, though the draw of the industrial North may also be reflected. In the war against Germany, 1914–18, Crawley played its part by housing and employing Belgian refugees, by accommodating soldiers' wives and children removed from danger zones, and by sending its youth to the front. It was not bows and arrows, nor yet jacks and pikes this time, but it was the same ruthless outside force pressing in upon the community. In the parish church of Crawley there is an honor roll. The old yeoman families are not represented, but Stevens and Cuell are long-familiar names. Two of the group had become corporals, a distinction somewhat curtailed by the levelling influence of an alphabetical order.

(*a*) CRAWLEY [1523] [1]

	John Salmon hath ij Jakk*es* assigned		
able bill*es* ij	Will*iam* Bryan		
	David Pynk		
able bilman	John (Shepd) [2] Bechamp		
	Cissile Bechamp in gud*es*	v li.	x s.
able arch*ers* ij	Thomas Bechamp		
	Will*iam* Bechamp		
able bilme*n* ij	John Alyn in gud*es*	vij li.	xiiij s.
	Thomas Wayt*e* in gud*es*	v li.	x s.
	William David in gud*es*	vj li.	xij s.
able bilman	and he hath a Jak Complet*e*		
able bilman	John Pether hath a Jak Complet*e*		
	William Stephuns in gud*es*	v li.	x s.
able bill*man*	William Plompton hath a Jak Complet*e*		
able archer	John Page in gud*es*	xiiij li.	xxviij s.
	Thom*as* [sic] David Im*er*e hath a Jakk Complet*e* and in gud*es*	vj li.	xij s.
able archer	John Wayt*e* in gud*es*	xij li.	xxiiij s.
able bilman	Harry Coup*er* hath j payar of alme*n* Revett*es* Complet*e*		
	It*em* the p*ar*ishe haue a Comyn harnez almen Revett*es* assigned		
able bilman	to John Page		

[1] MS., P. R. O., Exchequer T. R. Miscellaneous Books, no. 19, fols. 201–202. Muster for the whole shire of Southampton, certified to the Star Chamber, quindene of Easter, 14 Hen. VIII, containing full lists of names, with an account of the armor possessed by each person, and the prest money levied. 821 pp., originally in vellum covers.

[2] Erased.

(*b*) The hable menne within the hundred off Budlesgate.[1] Tythinge of Crawle *and* Hunton [1569]

Robert Pitter
Robert Alin
Wyll*iam* Roffolde
Michaell Rawlinge
Thomas Stevens
John Wayte
Henry Davy
Rabert Baker
Henry charchard
John Grigory
John Pitter
Richard Bushel
Richard Googe
Nicholas Winkorth
Rob*er*t Jeffrie
Francis Hawkins

(*c*) War Memorial, 1914–18, north aisle of Crawley church.

Pte. Arthur Bundy
Pte. Ernest Cox
Pte. William Cuell
Pte. Arthur James Elcock
Pte. William Henry Norris
Lf. Cpl. Hry. Ernest Piper
Pte. Herbert Arthur Piper
Rifm. Arthur Tom Riggs
Pte. Albert Stevens
Cpl. Arthur Geo. Weatherall
Pte. Herbert Hry. White

§§ 51. Excerpts from the Parish Registers of Crawley, 1646–1927.

The parish registers began to be kept in England in the year 1538, apparently in imitation of the Netherlands. The original order of Thomas Cromwell, issued in that year, stated that there

[1] MS., P. R. O., State Papers, Domestic, Elizabeth, vol. LIX, no. 8. Certificate by Sir Henry Seymour, Sir Adrian Ponynges, and others, Commissioners of Musters, of able men, horse, armour, and weapons, and General Musters of the whole County of Southampton, 10 Oct., 1569. The heading to one of the folios of this document gives the date 11 Elizabeth.

was to be one book for recording weddings, baptisms, and burials, which was to be kept in one coffer with two locks and two keys. One of the keys was to be kept by the parson and one by the two churchwardens. Entries were to be made once a week, on penalty of 3s. 4d. for neglect.[1] The first books, being commonly made of paper, were subject to destruction by damp and mishandling. Ignorance and indolence on the part of the parish clergyman, parish clerk, and churchwardens are responsible for the bad preservation and fragmentary condition of books which might have become an even more valuable source for the study of social history than they are. Interest in them has been so great as to lead to the publication of many.

The earliest parish register found in Crawley is a book made of paper and purchased in the year 1672. The first entries were set down either from memory or from other records. The earliest baptisms are dated 1646 and 1647, the earliest burial apparently 1665, and the first marriage 1675.

The value of the parish registers of Crawley comes from the vital statistics, genealogical data, and occupational evidence which they contain. Since they are incomplete for Crawley people and include some outsiders, their value is somewhat lessened. There are also serious gaps, for instance, in burials for the period 1678–95. It is to be hoped that the bad condition of Crawley registers is not typical of those in England generally.

The age of the buried is given beginning only at the end of the eighteenth century and then only irregularly. In the nineteenth century we note the considerable ages of people buried. There is surprisingly little evidence of smallpox, though three deaths from that disease occurred in 1808.

It is only from the parish registers that one learns about the inhabitants of the parish who were not suitors at the manorial court. It is surprising how many names occur in these registers that are not met with in the court rolls.

[1] See J. Charles Cox, *The Parish Registers of England* (1910), pp. 2–3.

VITAL STATISTICS FOR DECENNIAL YEARS

Year	Baptisms	Burials	Marriages
1680	4	[—] [1]	none entered
1690	6	5 (in 1695)	" "
1700	4	5	2
1710	3	4	none (1 in 1709)
1720	2	4	none
1730	5	10	none (2 in 1728)
1740	6	4	2
1750	6	3	1
1760	6	8	3
1770	8	none	2
1780	9	3	1
1790	8	none	none
1800	10	4	2
1810	10	5	1
1820	13	6	none (5 in 1821)
1830	8	6	4
1840	9	4	3
1850	16	6	4
1860	14	2	none
1870	11	2	2
1880	15	6	1
1890	4	6	2
1900	9	2	2
1910	8	5	3
1920	6	5	3

[1] Wanting.

[Baptisms]

Bap*tised* fortonn [1]

John Waite the sun of Thomas Waite bapti*sed* May [3?] 1649

Elizabeth Waite the daughter of Thomas Waite Bapt*ised* 14 March 1652

Thomas Waite the son of Thomas Waite bap*tised* 13 day of march 1657

[1] MS., Crawley, The Register of Crawley Bought In the yeare of Our Lord 1672. Robert Pitter *and* Richard Long Churchwardens, p. 1, col. 1. Perhaps "fortonn" was written for "forgotten."

This book is ruled for "Baptisms, Marr*iages* Burialls," three columns to the page, but the entries are made in a disorderly fashion and baptisms or births occupy the earlier pages of the book. The book is kept in an iron safe in the parish church of Crawley, in charge of the rector and the churchwardens.

Hester Scudamor Turner filia Joh*annis* Turner cler*ici* bap*tised* June 11: 1664
Joanna Turner filia Johan*nis* Turner bap*tised* 29 Aug. 1665.
Maria Turner filia John Turner cler*ici* bap*tised* 16 Apri. 1667
Walter Turner the son of John Turner Bap*tised* 15 No. 1668;
Theophilus Turner filius Johan*nis* Turner bap*tised* Decem. 7. 1671.

These [1] two children were forgotten to be register*ed* and are now set down by me who baptized them

Elizabeth Wilkins the daughter of John and Elizabeth Wilkins was baptized the 3 of March $167\frac{8}{7}$

Sarah Wilkins the daughter of John and Elizabeth Wilkins was baptized 17 of September 1679.

Sarah Godwine [2] filia Johan*n*is Godwine bapt*ised* decimo die Septembris anno Domini 1646.

Abizaele Godwine the daughter of John Godwine was baptized 8 day of June in the year 1676.

Mary Thomson filia James Thomson bapt*ised* July the 2 1674

Jane Wilkins filia Richardi Wilkins baptizata fuit 19 of October 1676

Dorothy Pitter the daughter of Rob*er*t Pitter was baptized the 5 day of March $167\frac{6}{7}$

Sarah Thomson the daughter of James Thomson baptized the first day of May 1677

Michael Batch*e*lour the son of Michael Batchelour was baptized the [8?] December 1676

John page [3] the son of John page was baptized the first day of August in year 1677.

Margery Newman the daughter of Will: Newman was baptized the 18 october 1677

Mary Penton the daughter of George Penton was baptized 12 August in year 1677

William Waite the son of James Waite was baptized December 19 1677.

[1] MS., Crawley, p. 3, col. 2.
[2] *Ibid.*, p. 6, col. 1.
[3] *Ibid.*, p. 7, col. 1. Consecutive entries begin here.

BAPTISMS SOLEMNIZED IN THE PARISH OF [CRAWLEY] IN THE COUNTY OF [SOUTHAMPTON] IN THE YEAR[1] [1827]

When Baptized	Child's Christian Name	Parents' Name Christian	Parents' Name Surname	Abode	Quality Trade or Profession	By whom the Ceremony was performed
March 4th 1827	William son of	William *and* Mary	Lawes	Crawley	Shoemaker	Samuel Best Curate
March 18th	Martha daughter of	John *and* Elizabeth	Bramble	Crawley	Labourer	"
March 22nd	John[2] son of	Thomas and Jemima	Oakes	Crawley	Labourer	"
April 15th	Emma daughter of	William *and* Martha	Hill	Crawley	Labourer	"
May 20th	William Pitt son of	Samuel *and* Charlotte Hillis	Best	Crawley	Clergyman	"
May 27th	Mary Anne daughter of	John *and* Francis	Cook	Crawley	Blacksmith	"
June 10th	William son of	George *and* Elizabeth	Heele	Crawley	Carpenter	"
July 1st	Henry son of	George *and* Anne	Brown	Crawley	Labourer	"
Sept. 24th	Charlotte daughter of	James *and* Elizabeth	Cooper	Crawley	Gentleman	"
Nov. 4th	Ann daughter of	Nicholas *and* Sarah	Hankin	Crawley	Labourer	Walter Blunt Curate
Dec. 2nd[3]	Marianne daughter of	John *and* Anne	Grunsell	Crawley	Carpenter	"
[June 27 1828	William son of	Thomas *and* Frances	Pern	Crawley	yeoman	
Dec. 4 1831	George son of	"	"	"	Farmer]	

[1] Printed headings.
[2] "Privately bap*tised*" occurs in the margin.
[3] "Named Dec. 2nd. Rec*eiv*ed into the Congregation Jany 13th 1820. W. B." is the entry in full.

BAPTISMS (*Continued*)

When Baptized	Child's Christian Name	Parents' Name Christian	Surname	Abode	Quality Trade or Profession	By whom the Ceremony was performed
1885 1st Jan.	Effie	George *and* Emily	Hawkins	Crawley	Carpenter	W. H. Castle-man Curate in charge
16th Jan.	Albert	George *and* Sarah Ann	Tongs	Crawley	Servant at the Court	" "
1st Feb.	William Ernest	Wm Francis *and* Jemima	Barrington	Wotton St. Lawrence	Gardener	" "
15th Feb.	Ellen Charlotte	James *and* Annie	Maloney	Crawley	Laborer	" "
29 March	Walter Gordon	Frederick William *and* Amy Constance	Pain	Crawley	Farmer	" "
2 Ap.	Pricilla Violet	George *and* Hannah	Bramble	Crawley	Laborer	" "
5 Ap.	Walter Thomas	Edward *and* Elizabeth	Cuell	Crawley	Gardener	" "
5 Ap.	William George	William *and* Ellen	Hall	Crawley	Carter	" "
June 7th	William Edgar	George Henry *and* Anne	Stratton	Crawley	Gardener	F. F. Madge Minor Canon of Winchester off. Minr.
July 12	Frank David	John and Louisa	Talmage	Leckford Down	Labourer	Edward M. Mee Rector
5 Oct.	Sarah Jane	Jane Stevens *and* Frederick	Freemantle	Crawley	Labourer	" "
Nov. 8th	Alfred Thomas	John *and* Ann Maria	Humphries	Sparsholt	Innkeeper	John Spittal off. Min.
Dec. 25	Rosina Caroline	Tom and Rhoda	Clift	Crawley	Carter	Edward M. Mee Rector

BAPTISMS SOLEMNIZED IN THE PARISH OF [CRAWLEY] IN THE COUNTY OF [HAMPSHIRE] IN THE YEAR ONE THOUSAND [NINE HUNDRED AND TWENTY SEVEN][1]

When Baptized	Child's Christian Name	Parents' Names Christian	Parents' Names Surname	Abode	Quality Trade or Profession	By whom the Ceremony was performed
May 29	Ronald Frank	Charles *and* Annie Elena Kate	Ricketts	Crawley	Gardener	James Deans off. min.
May 29	Basil John	Albert Thomas *and* Anna Florence	Jellett	Crawley	Motor Mechanic	James Deans
July 24	Georgina Isabel Dora	George *and* Isabel Julia Marie Louise	Philippi	Crawley Court	Gentleman	H. Purefoy Fitz Gerald
Aug. 9	Alan Herbert	Frank *and* Maud Winifred	Andrews	New Barn Farm	Farm Bailiff	P. D. Maddock off. Min.
Nov. 20[2]	William Victor	William John *and* Eleanor Kate	Taylor	Chilbolton Down	Carter	H. H. D. Bolton offg. priest

[1] The previous entry is 12 Dec., 1926. [2] Born 17 Oct. *1927*.

[Burials]

Hester Scudamor Turner[1] filia Joh*annis* Turner Sepul*ta* May 3. 166[5?].
Margeret poole[2] was buried the 4 of october 1675.
Alice Skeat was buried 11 october in the year 1675.
Margeret Allen was buried october 19 1675
Will*iam* Hacke was buried october 17 1675
Rob Wilkins was buried 3 of January 1674
Rich*ard* Wilkins was buried 26 of December 1674
Ambrose Houcke was buried in 16 Febr. 1674.
Mary Beech[3] the wife of Ambros Beech Buried November the 24 in the yeare 1675
Will*iam* Rathell was buried 19 of December 1675
Sarah page widdow was buried 12 of Aprill 1678
Richard Beech was buried the 13 of April 1678

[1] MS., Crawley, Parish Register, bk. I, p. 1, col. 3.
[2] *Ibid.*, p. 3, col. 3.
[3] *Ibid.*, p. 5, col. 3.

Christopher Archer died Feb. 2 and was buried at Hunton Feb. 4 1698 and affidavit was brought by John Pitter Feb. 10. 1698.

Will*iam* Bruning[1] of the parish of Crauley in the county of Southton maketh Oath that Anne Bruning of the parish of Crauly in the county of Southton lately deceased was not put in wrapt, or wound up, or buried in any shirt shift sheet or shroud made, or mingled with flax Hemp silke Hair Gold or sylver, or other then what is made of sheeps wool only — nor in any coffin lined or faced with any cloth stuff or any other thing whatsoever made or mingled with flax hemp silk Hair gold or sylver or any other materiall but sheepeswool only dated the 24th day of octo*ber* in the 38th year of the raign of our Sovereign lord Charls the secound king of England Scotland France and Ireland annoq*ue* D*omi*ni 1678

Sealed and prescribed by us
who were present and wittnesees
to the swearing of the above
said affidavit

Mary Barlow
Will. Bruton

I Oliver St John esq one of his majesty justices of the peace for the County of South*ampton* doe hereby certifie that the day *and* year above said the said Will*iam* Bruning came before me and made such affidavit as is above specified according to a late Act of Parliament intituled an act for burying in woollen witness my hand the day year above written

St. John.

[Burials — *continued* — 1927]

Name	Abode	When buried	Age	Ceremony by
Mary Ann Sandon	St. Paul's Hill Winchester	Jany. 21 1927	89 years	W. Irwin
Hannah Bramble	Crawley	Feb. 15 1927	79 yrs.	W. Irwin
Mary Godwin	Crawley	19 Feby 1927	75 yrs.	W. Irwin
Elisha Cox	Crawley	26 Feby 1927	86 yrs.	W. Irwin
Emily Watts	Sutton Scotney	May 11 1927	91 years	W. Irwin
Elizabeth Ann Brown	50 Kingston Hill, Kingston	27th June 1927	88	F. W. M. Cox Asst. Curate
William Burrington Salter	The Beeches, Crawley	26th July 1927	11	F. W. M. Cox Asst. Curate
Nora Joan Salter	The Beeches, Crawley	26th July 1927	7	F. W. M. Cox Asst. Curate

[1] The note of affidavit of burial in woolen is frequently omitted from the entries which follow; when it occurs, the entry is given here.

Name	Abode	When buried	Age	Ceremony by
George Waterman	Crawley	15 August 1927	83 years	P. D. Maddock off. Min.
John William Ryder	Crawley	Aug. 31 1927	73 years	W. Irwin Rector
Mary Brown	St. Paul's Hill, Winchester	Oct. 15 1927	77 yrs.	W. Irwin Rector
Charles Peter William Notley	County Hospital	16 Dec. 1927	12 Days	W. Irwin

[Marriages]

Weddings.

John Allin[1] was married to Ellin Masters 3d Jan. in year 1675
Alexander Wade[2] and Jane Airy was married in 1677 Sep. 18
John Cooper and Elizabeth Rumsey were married in 7 octo. 1678
Nath*aniel* Pile and Elizabeth Beech were married Decem. 16. 1691
Thomas Butterly and Elizabeth Newman nupti fuere May 11 1693
Will Eyer of the parish of Alton in the county of South[ton] and Sarah Herring were married at Crauly 1694 July 17
John Hanniton and Jone Buxy were married octo 31 1682
Will*iam* Butterly and Anne Long were maried 2 Novem. 1682
Will*iam* Stephens of Winto*n* and Eliza*beth* Geeds [?] were married 16 June 1681
Nich*olas* Lucas and Christian Blake of the Soke neer Winton was married 27 May 1683.

§§ 52. Excerpts and Notes from the Churchwardens' Accounts, 1766–1831.

Churchwardens were laymen chosen annually to assist the parson in the administration of church affairs. The two churchwardens were generally to be chosen by the parson and the parishioners jointly, but if there could be no agreement then the parson was to choose one, the parishioners the other. What the practice was in Crawley has not been noted. There was a church reeve as early as 1386 in England, and church masters in 1429. But in

[1] MS., Crawley, Parish Register, bk. I, p. 3. [2] *Ibid.*, p. 4.

Crawley these officials appear in the records late, their own extant accounts beginning only in 1766.[1] Presumably the earlier accounts have been lost. A parish clerk is mentioned and his salary given at two pounds a year.[2]

The contents of the accounts fall into three categories: the receipts from the rates assessed on property holders, the disbursements, and the yearly surplus of money (or deficit) with interest and investments.

Each year a rate was decided upon — 2d., 3d., and so on in the pound. Then one, two, or more rates were levied, according to the requirements of the time.

CHURCHWARDENS' TAX LEVY

Year	Rate	Total Amount £	s.	d.
1766	1 rate	2	8	7
1768	5 rates	15	10	4
1770	2 rates	4	17	2
1782	6 rates	24	15	6½
1784	1½ rates			
1798	3 d. per £	19	6	9¾
1800	2 d. per £	13	11	8¼
1830	3 d. per £	19	13	11

The changes in the contributors and contributions are indicated in the following table.

Year	No. of Contributors	Largest Contribution s.	d.	Per cent paid by the Five Largest Contributors
1766	25	13	4	56.4
1778	24	23	4	78.3
1800	13	59	11¼	82.2
1830	21	87	11	63.4

Probably two or three changes are involved in these figures, but one is unmistakable, namely, that there had been a consolidation of estates.[3] Land was always subject to the levy but houses only

[1] For earlier accounts in England, see J. Charles Cox, *Churchwardens' Accounts* (1913), pp. 15 f.

[2] For other officials in Crawley, see above, § 8, pp. 22 ff.

[3] See above, § 32, pp. 111 ff., and below, §§ 57, pp. 630 ff.

THE PARISH CHURCH

A photograph

when the occupant was able to pay. Personal property was exempt.

The money collected from the rates was used for various purposes. Much of it went for the repairing and cleaning of the church building, for the sacraments, and for equipment. The parish clerk's salary was paid out of it. Church meetings and visitations were a source of expense. Celebrating victory over the French was a popular pastime, even though much belated. In 1809, £5 were paid to Dr. Wickham of Sutton for inoculation. Similar payments had been made to him for services during 1796–98.[1] Later, in 1840, the practice of inoculation in the case of smallpox was prohibited by statute.

Expenditures for the relief of the poor are frequently found. Travellers passing through were given a mite to help them along. A poorhouse was supported, apparently in Crawley itself, and a house of industry, presumably outside the parish. Contributions were made to the county hospital. Relief seems to have been given to people in their own houses. Their houses were glazed and otherwise repaired. In 1809 and 1811 "poor chimneys," to the number of thirty-eight, were swept. If there were two chimneys to a house, there must have been about nineteen poor families receiving indoor relief.

The extent of poverty in Crawley in the period in question can be guessed at but not carefully estimated. We might compare churchwardens' accounts, overseers' books, and the decennial censuses.[2] There seem to have been three categories of inhabitants. There were the very well-to-do who paid the poor rates. There were those too poor to contribute to the rates, but not in need of aid themselves. And there were the needy poor. If Crawley still had (say, in 1810) about fifty houses in the village and a few more elsewhere in the parish, then the three classes of families numbered about twenty each. How much of such poverty was due to the war and how much to the new economic conditions in the village must remain a subject for speculation.

[1] See below, §§ 53, pp. 578, 584.

[2] No census returns earlier than 1841 have actually been examined.

The many entries for the payment of bounties on sparrow heads and hedgehogs is indicative of the effort of the time to bring about better agricultural conditions.[1] Whether the killing of these enemies of crops was an infant industry is nowhere stated.

[EXCERPTS FROM DISBURSEMENTS AND RATES, 1766–1769]

The Disbursement James Waight and thomas Pern for the year 1766.[2]

Bread *and* wine for three Sacraments		9 s.	3 d.
Clerks waiges	£ 2.	0 s.	0 d.
att Visitation	0.	5 s.	0 d.
fee *and* penticost notice	0.	8 s.	11½ d.
paid for this Book [3]		3 s.	0 d.
for waishing the Surplis 3 times *and* table Cloth *and* napkin *and* for mending the Surplis	0.	5.	0.
Gave to a man Burnt att Sea	0.	0.	6.
3 people with a pass	0.	1.	0.
people Burnt att Sea	0.	1.	0.
with a pass	0.	1.	0.
woman with a pass	0.	0.	6.
man *and* woman with a pass	0.	1.	0.
Saylor *and* wife with a pass	0.	1.	0.
Gave an old Soldier	0.	0.	6.
man *and* woman with a pass	0.	1.	0.
Collis's Bill is	0.	18.	5.
Blacksmiths Bill is	0.	3.	0.
	5.	0.	1½.

Recd.			
Stock in hand last year	1.	11 s.	0¾ d.
Intress money	0.	0.	8.
gathers 2 Rates	4.	17.	2.
	6.	8.	10¾
the disbursements	5.	0.	1½
	1.	8.	9¼

[1] See J. Charles Cox, *Churchwardens' Accounts* (1913), chap. xx.

[2] MS., Crawley Church safe, Church Wardens' Accounts, 1766–1831. Excerpts from pp. 1–5, notes from other parts. Copied by Miss Lilian J. Redstone.

[3] The book is of paper, with vellum covers.

Aprill the 21st 1767

James Waight and thomass pern have passed their accounts and wee do appoint John Courtney and John paige to be Churchwardens for the year Ensuing Remains Stock in hand 1. 8. 9¼

A RATE MADE FOR THE PARISH CHURCH OF CRAWLEY 1766

The Hon*ora*ble Lord Northington for manor house	0.	2.	0.
The Hon*ora*ble Lady Arundell for Rookly house	0.	2.	0.
Dito for Close *and* Garden	0.	0.	2½.
Mr. Crop for Rookly woods	0.	1.	6.
Will*iam* Pitter for Newbarn farm	0.	13.	4.
John Courtney for Rookly farm	0.	6.	3½.
Richard Eyles for his own	0.	2.	5½.
Richard Eyles for Mr. Pyles	0.	1.	8½.
Richard Eyles for Mr. Godwins	0.	1.	10.
Richard Eyles for Simes	0.	1.	8.
Richard Eyles for thompsons	0.	0.	2.
James Waight for his own	0.	1.	8.
James Waight for Pitters	0.	2.	4.
James Waight for Broadways	0.	1.	4.
James Waight for Morgens	0.	0.	8.
James Waight for Carters	0.	0.	11.
Thomas Pern	0.	3.	0.
John Paige for his own	0.	0.	5.
John Paige for pitters	0.	1.	6.
John Merrill Esq. for Crates	0.	1.	0.
Revd. Mr. Taylor for Browns *and* Coxes	0.	0.	2.
farmer feilder for hoo Close	0.	0.	3.
Mrs. Broadway for her house	0.	0.	1.
Jonathan Short	0.	0.	3.
thomas Browning for the Malt house	0.	0.	6.
Mrs. Fifield for Norwood	0.	1.	4.
	2.	8.	7.

THE DISBURSEMENT OF JOHN COURTNEY AND JOHN PAIGE FOR 1767

gave to people for fire	0.	1.	0.
gave to 7 Semen with a pas	0.	1.	0.
gave to 2 men burnt at Sea	0.	1.	0.
gave to Semen	0.	1.	0.
Bread and Wine for 3 Sacraments	0.	9.	6.
paid the Clarks waiges	2.	0.	0.
fees penticost notice	0.	8.	11¼.
Expence at Visatation	0.	5.	0.
for waishing the Surplis 3 times *and* table Cloth	0.	3.	6.
for bell Ropes	0.	14.	0.
Blacksmiths Bill	0.	8.	6.
Collis's Bill	1.	0.	6.
Bricklayers Bill	0.	5.	8.
Loomer's Bill	0.	2.	3.
	4.	1.	10¼
Recd. Stock in hand last year	1.	8.	9¼
Intress money	0.	8.	0.
gathers 2 rates	4.	17.	2.
	7.	1.	3¼
the disbursements	4.	1.	10¼
	2.	19.	5.
Aprill the 5th 1768 John Courtnay and John paige have passed their accounts and we do apoint James Waight and Richard Eyles to be Churchwardens for the year ensuing there Remains Stock in hand	2.	19.	5.

THE DISBURSMENT OF JAMES WAIGHT AND RICHARD EYLES FOR 1768

att Visitation	0.	5.	0.
fees	0.	8.	11.
Bread *and* wine for three Sacraments		10.	3.
Clarks waiges	2.	0.	0.
waishing *and* mending the Surplis *and* table Cloth	0.	4.	0.
Saylors widow	0.	0.	6.
woman with a pass	0.	0.	6.
Oile for the Bells	0.	0.	6.
Glazure's Bill	0.	0.	9.
paid for letter from Mathews	0.	0.	6.
Blacksmiths Bill	1.	1.	6.
John Gliders Bill	7.	13.	8.
Carrage of the Bell Wheels	0.	5.	0.
	£12.	11.	1½.
Recd. Stock in hand Last year	2.	19.	5.
Intress money	0.	8.	0.
Gathers five Rates	12.	2.	11.
	15.	10.	4.
Disbursement is	12.	11.	1½
	2.	19.	2½

March *the* 29 1769 James Waight *and* Richard Eyles have paseed their accounts and we Do apoint Richard Eyles and Mr. Henry Hobs Church wardens for the year Ensuing

Remains Stock in hand 2. 19. 2½.[1]

[1] The rate for 1768, is as for 1766 and 1767; except that — Revd. Mr. Hare is assessed (instead of Lady Arundell) for Rookley Ho. 2s. 0d.; and for Dog Close and part of the garden 2½d. Mr. Hobbs for Newbarn farm (instead of Wm. Pitter). Revd. Mr. Bathurst for Crofts (instead of Merrell). Mrs. Fifield for "Norwood Bargen."

DISBURSEMENTS OF RICHARD EYLES FOR *THE* YEAR 1769

Att visitation		0.	5.	0.
Fees		0.	7.	11½.
Clark's Waiges		2.	0.	0.
Bread *and* Wine for three Sacraments		0.	10.	0.
Oile for the Bells		0.	0.	6.
for Mending and washing the Cirpuls		0.	4.	0.
Collices Bill for Repairs to the Church		1.	18.	8½.
The Masons Bill		1.	3.	8.
The Blacksmiths Bill		0.	13.	6.
	£	7.	3.	3½
Stock in hand Last year		2.	19.	2½
		4.	4.	1.
Interest Money		0.	8.	0.
Remains		3.	16.	1.
April the 17th 1770				
We do agree to Gather two Rates which is		4.	17.	2.
Remains in hand		1.	4.	1.

April the 17th 1770.

Thos. Pern have past His account and is approved of and do nominate and appoint Thomas Perrin and John Page to be Church wardens for the year Ensuing.

NOTES ON DISBURSEMENTS, 1770–1831

Disbursements

By Thos. Pern, 1770 Total £5. 8. 6½.
for binding the Great Bible 14 s. 6 d.
agreed to gather 2 rates [1]
appoint Thos. Perrin and John Page chw., 2 Ap. 1771.

By Thos. Pern, 1771 Total £5. 10. 4.
Collices bill for reapaires £0. 14. 10.
collarmakers bill for to Bering strapes 8 s. 0 d.
Loomers Bill for Bear 2 s. 4 d.
agreed to gather 2 rates
appoint Richard Bayley and Richard Eyleys, 21 Ap. [1772].

[1] The rate for 1769 had been the same as for 1768.

By Richard Bailey, 1772 £10. 7. 2.
Bricklayers Bill £2. 7. 2.; for a "sirpulace"
£3. 17. 6.; a prayer book 12 s.
Agreed to gather 5 rates.
"Paid to Mr. Pickering £5 which money the
Churchwardens is to pay Interest for yearley *and* every
year after the rate of 10 d. p*er* pound."
Appoint John Picknail and John Page.

By John Pickering, 1773 £4. 13. 8½
5 bell ropes 12 s. 6 d.;
Loomer for beer for workmen 2 s.
Collect 3 rates.
"Paid to Far: Pern 5£ which Money is to be Paid
Interest for at 10 d. p*er* £ p*er* Cent p*er* annum."
Appoint Thos. Pern and James Fitt chwns.

By Thos. Pern, 1774 £4. 17. 2½.
Gather one rate.
Same churchwardens.

By Thos. Pern, 1775 £3. 12. 1½.
Gather one rate.
Appoint John Pickering and John Page chwns.

By Thos. Pern, 1776 £5. 13. 10½.
Gather 3 rates.
Appoint Ric. Bailey and John Page.

By Richd. Bailey, 1777 £4. 16. 11.
One rate.
Appoint James Fitt and Thomas Perrin.

By James Fitt, 1778 £4. 9. 10.
Gather one rate.
Appoint John Pickering and Thomas Perin.

By John Pickering, 1779 £7. 19. 5.
Mr. Caves Bill for Boards and writing
the ten commandments £1. 19.
Gathered 1½ rate.
Appoint Thos. Pern and Jn. Page.

By Thos. Pern, 1780 £9. 5. 5½.
Kimbers Bill £2. 3. 5.; Jacob Pern for Bell
ropes £1. 2.; George Travis for bell ropes £1. 1.
Gather 2½ rates.
Appoint Richd. Bailey and Thos Pern.

By Richd. Bailey, 1781 Gather 1 rate. [No appointment recorded.]	£4.	11.	2½.
By Farmer Fitt, 1782 Richard Kimber's bill repair the Tower £8. 8.; Mr. Milsom Tileing the Back Side of the Church etc. £11. 6. 1.; Far: Page for Carriage of Poles (to make Scaffold) 7 s. Gather 6 rates.	£24.	15.	6½.
By Thomas Pern, 1783 "Great Book" £4. 4.; Paid Mr. Dunford For Bond of The Register Book 6 s.; Jacob Pern for Bel ropes £1. 8.; Master Cooks old Bill last year £1. Gather 2½ rates.	£10.	9.	11½.

Attached to this page with sealing-wax is a slip of paper:

"I promise to Indemnify the Churchwardens *and* Overseer of the Poor of the Parish of Crawley from any Expense they may from time to time be at Relieving Sarah Shepherd, or her child Charlatte Shepherd, in Pursuance of a sum of money Lodged in my hands for said Purpose as witness my hand this *2nd* day of November 1776

Wm. Bant"

By John Pickering, 1784 Gather 1½ rates. Appoint Jas. Fitt and Jn. Pickering.	£5.	13.	6.

Disbursements continue thus, but note the following entries:

1789 — repairing the seats, etc.	£2.	16.	9.
1796 — Sparrow heads 13 s. 1 d.			
1797 — Paid for Sparrow Heads 17 s. 5½ d.; for Ringing Beating Duch fleet Oct. 11, 10 s. 6 d.; for old Sparrow Heads 1 s. 5 d.; for Dozen old Sparrow Heads 2 s.; Elton glazing 4 windows	£4.	3.	9.

ABOUT THIS TIME DISBURSEMENTS INCREASED. TOTALS ARE AS FOLLOWS:

		£	s.	d.	
Thos. Pern,	1792.[1]	6.	17.	11.	
G. Godwin,	1793.	9.	3.	3½.	
[blank],	1794.	[blank.]			
Wm. Pern,	1795.	6.	5.	5½.	
" "	1796.	5.	16.	11½.	
[Geo. Godwin]	1797.	11.	0.	5.	
		+21.	12.	11½.	
	1798.	22.	18.	1.	
	1799.	15.	12.	9.	
	1800.	19.	2.	2½.	
	1801. } 1802. }	46.	14.	6.	
(Besides,	1803. }	45.	12.	1. }	, repair of church, etc.)
	1803. }	7.	0.	1. }	
	1804.	14.	9.	2.	
	1805.	19.	6.	1½.	
	1806.	12.	13.	10¼.	
G. Godwin,	1807.	14.	15.	9.	
"	1808.	35.	3.	10½.	
"	1809.	20.	6.	11½.	
"	1810.	29.	16.	0.	
"	1811.	10.	14.	7½.	
"	1812.	21.	1.	10½.[2]	

[1] That is, Easter 1792 to Easter 1793.

[2] And the like down to 1831, when the book ends, G. Godwin being nearly always churchwarden.

FOLLOWING IS AN EXCERPT OF THE DISBURSEMENTS FOR A TYPICAL YEAR, 1798–99.

		£	s.	d.
	Boock in debt Easter 1798	1.	1.	$6\frac{1}{4}$
May 27,	Paid for Sackratement Wine		5.	3.
	" " young Sparrow Heads	1.	0.	0.
	Gave to a man in Distress	0.	1.	0.
Sept. 18,	Paid at Visitation	0.	14.	$6\frac{1}{2}$.
	Expenses at Do.	0.	5.	0.
Oct. 3,	Gave for Ringing *et*c for Beating french fleet	0.	7.	6.
7,	Paid for Sackratement Wine	0.	5.	3.
20,	Paid Diddams *and* Day Cleaning Chirchyard *et*c.	0.	12.	10.
Nov. 10,	Paid on a count Victory	0.	2.	0.
Dec. 25,	Paid for Sackretement Wine	0.	5.	3.
	Paid for old Sparrow Heads, 38 Dozen *and* 5	0.	19.	$2\frac{1}{2}$.
March 23,	Paid for Sackratement Wine	0.	5.	3.
	Paid Holdaway Bill	3.	1.	7.
	" Clarks Waiges	2.	0.	0.
	" Bill to Do.	1.	3.	1.
	" Glazers Bill	0.	15.	2.
	" Mr. Luckes' Bill	9.	14.	$8\frac{1}{4}$.
		22.	18.	1.
	Rate at 3 d Pound	19.	6.	$9\frac{11}{24}$.
	Book in Dett	3.	11.	$4\frac{11}{24}$.

FURTHER NOTES ON DISBURSEMENTS, 1799–1831

			£	s.	d.
1800,	May 29,	on account of young sparrows in somer.	1.	0.	0.
	Aug. 9,	subscribed to Hospital.	2.	12.	6.
1805,	Nov. 13,	Paid for Nelson Victory.	0.	15.	0.
		1 pound of candles at church.	0.	1.	0.
1806,	Feb.	8 dozen old sparrow head.	0.	4.	0.
	May 12,	6 Heag Hoggs.	0.	2.	0.
	Sept. 16,	to Northwood Briff for fire.	0.	2.	6.
1807,	May 2,	Paid the money in hand with 42 Pounds odd shillings Recd. at			

			£	s.	d.
		the House of Industrey make-ing togeather fifty Pounds, then Discharging a Bound Due to Mr. Henton Bailey on Craw-ley Parish for the use of the Woork House with all Intresst Due thereon.			
1809, May	16,	at a Church Meeting Held.		6.	4.
		Hegg Hogs.		15.	0.
July	28,	Paid Mr. Wickham's Bill for innocklinck.	5.	0.	0.
		Glazier's bill for Poor Houses, etc.		14.	7.
Oct.	26,	(Paid for sweeping 38 Chim-neys) [1] to Poor Book.		19.	0.
		Paid Parish Part in Bassoon.	2.	10.	0.
[1810, Oct.	4],	Michas 1810, Paid of this Book on account of Rec'ing Eighteen Pounds 4 shillings and 2 Pence at the House of Industrey to make 20 Pounds to discharge a Bond due to Tho' Young of Upsomborne £40.	1.	15.	10.
1811, Oct.	21–2,	Paid for sweeping 38 Poor Chimneys.		19.	0.
1812, Dec.	17,	Paid carriage Regester Book from London.		2.	2.
1813,		Gave Ringers on the Victory of March.			
July	4,	(News came) Wellenton over the french Armey.		16.	0.
July	30,	Paid Shepherd and Son at Poor Houses.		6.	0.
Oct.	15,	Paid to Shepherd Repering Poor Houses		6.	0.
1814,		Paid for Removel of E. Collis from Winton			
		Clark's fees Berer to Woman	1.	0.	0.
		Horse Cart Man etc.	0.	4.	0.
1814,		Pees [sic] Gave for Ringing etc. etc. for Victory.		9.	6.

[1] Struck through.

1814, Aug. 8,	Ext. on Account of Peas [sic] for Ringers and Singing etc.	3.	0.	0.
1821, Mar. 29,	Paid Post for an Order made out in Wales to Crawley Parish to Rec*eive*. Tho. Neiol in Great Distress a Servant of the late Rd. Meyler Esq. of Crawley.	0.	2.	1.
1821, May 31,	Paid Cariage for Neails Box from Hut to Sarrum.	0.	2.	0.
1822, Oct. 19,	Paid Cooper on Road 7½ Days by Order.	0.	10.	0.
1822	Paid at Visitation Diet Money etc. for New Bishop.		18.	11½.
July 8,	Paid Bill for the Bilding at Woork House to Nappe [?] Bank.	8.	16.	3.
Oct. 19,	Paid Cooper on Roads 7½ Days By order overseer.		10.	0.
1823,	Paid for sweping 14 Poor Chimleys.		4.	8.
Nov. 5,	Gave to the Ringers as Costom Dec. 31.		5.	0.
Dec. 25,	Gave Wm. Davis and His Wife on their Way to London haveing no Home nor Cash, being sent from Rookley by Mrs. Allee. (Mr. Allee ill).	0.	2.	0.
1824, Jan. 27,	Paid Carpenter and Stuff for Poor House Dore.	0.	2.	0.
1824, Mar. 25,	We do Nominate and appoint John Birch and George Godwin Churchwardens for the year Ensuing Thos Pern and Wm Wade overseers.			
1824, Mich.	Paid to County Hospital for one year.	1.	1.	0.
1826,	[Various payments to G. Hackines for glazing, belfry boarding etc.] and for gallery at church	£30.		
	[The book ends abruptly 29 Aug., 1831.]			

NOTES ON RATES, 1770–1831

1770 —

Hon. Lord Hendley for the manor ho.
(instead of Lord Northington 1769)

James Fitt	"	Rookley Farm (instead of John Courtney 1769)
Thos. Pern [1]	"	Waights (instead of Jas Waight 1769)
" "	"	Glydes (Carters) (instead of Jas Waight 1769)
" "	"	Morgans (instead of Jas Waight 1769)
Richard Eyles [1]	"	Pitters (instead of Jas Waight 1769)
" "	"	Broadways (instead of Jas Waight 1769)
" "	"	Browns and Coxes (instead of Rev. Mr. Taylor 1769)

Total £ 2. 8. 1.[2]

1776 — "Esq. Willins" for the manner house.
H. R. H. The Duke of Cumberland for Rookley House Dog Close and part of garden.
[John Pickering takes the place of Rich. Eyles] except Esq. Williams for Pitters.

Total £ 2. 8. 1.

1778 — John Williams Esq. for Great House.
1777 — Gather one rate which is £3. 19. 9.

[1778] A Rate made by the Church Wardens of Crawley for the Year 1778

	£	s.	d.
John Williams Esq. for Great House.		5.	10.
The Rev. Mr. Bathurst.		1.	6.
H. R. H. Duke of Cumberland.		6.	8.
Leod. Cropp Esq.		1.	6.
Mr. Bailey	1.	3.	4.
Mr. Perrin, His own, Waights, Glides, Morgans, Simes, Brown Coxes, Pagis and Pillers [sic].	0.	17.	2.
Mr. Pickering for Eyles, Godwin, Thomsons Pitters and Broadways.	0.	11.	6.
Mr. Fitt.	0.	9.	5.
Mrs. Fifield.	0.	2.	1.
Mr. Fielder.	0.	0.	3.
Far. Page.	0.	0.	6.
	3.	19.	9.

[1] In addition to their previous assessments.
[2] As above until 1773. No rate for 1774–75.

N. B.

1780 — Sir Willoughby Aston (for the Great House) [1]

1790 — Rookley House blank; Mr. Ballard for Rookley Woods; 1792 he pays also for Roockley House.

1794 — Richd. Meyler Esq. instead of Sir W. Aston (who was entered in 1793)

1800 — Church Rate at 2 d. in the Pound.

Rd. Meyler Esq.	1.	6.	8.
For late Terrel Esq.	0.	1.	6.
Chas. Morris Esq. Roockley Wood.	0.	4.	4.
Geo. Lovle [= Lovel] Esq. Roockley House.	0.	13.	4.
Mr. Bailey's Farm.	2.	18.	0½.
Mr. Thos. Pern's Farm.	2.	19.	11¼.
Mr. Mead's Farm.	1.	14.	8.
Mr. Godwin's Farm.	2.	3.	11.
Mr. Pickering Farm.	0.	15.	11.
Mr. Fifield's Farm.	0.	5.	9½.
Mr. Paige Farm.	0.	4.	5½.
Mr. Fitt Hoe Close.	0.	1.	0.
Mr. Allin.	0.	1.	6.
	13.	11.	8¼.

N. B. Easter 1806 — Easter 1807

T. W. Bethell Esq. House lands etc. (instead of Meyler.
New Barn Farm " " Mr. Bailey).

Easter 1830 to Easter 1831, at 3 d. in the Pound

Mr. Allee Rookley Farm	2.	12.	0.
" " " Woods	0.	4.	6.
Rd. Bright, Esq. Part of House and Land	1.	1.	9.
Cook, Widow		1.	0.
Veller, Rd. Publice House tennent Malbury		1.	6.
Fifield, Northwood Farm	0.	8.	6.
Fitt, Mr. James for Hoe Close	0.	1.	0.
Godwin, G. Senr. House	0.	1.	6.
Goodwin, G. Junr. House	0.	1.	3.
Gover, Messrs Wm. and Rd. for Copp'	0.	5.	0.
Holdeway's House	0.	1.	0.
Holdway Ro*ber*t House	0.	1.	0.

[1] Here follows a gap in the rates.

Kent, Rd. House	0.	0.	9.
Llovel, Esq. Rookley House	0.	10.	0.
Morroson, John farm	1.	3.	10½.
Nevill, Wm. House and land	0.	2.	3.
Pern, Mr. Thomas farm	3.	14.	10½.
Pern, " " for Belt	0.	14.	10½.
" " " for house cald Malt House	0.	1.	6.
Paige, Mr. Charles farm	0.	12.	1½.
Read, Mr. Geo. farm	3.	4.	3.
Wade, Mr. Wm. farm	4.	7.	11.
Willis, Wm. House Malt etc.	0.	0.	9.
	19.	13.	2.
Cook, John House			9.
	19.	13.	11.

§§ 53. Excerpts from the Overseers' Poor Books, 1776–77 and 1797–98, and Totals 1777–1835.

Overseers were legislated into existence in the year 1572[1] to look after the poor, thereby relieving the parson and the churchwardens. As the accounts of the churchwardens of Crawley show, however, the churchwardens did not give up their interest in the poor, and indeed one of the two was commonly an overseer of the poor.

In 1776–77, twenty-eight rates brought in £84 18s. 8d., at 6s. 8d. each. In 1797–98 the rate stood at 2s. a pound, providing £154 12s. 7d. The most remarkable development in the period in question was the increase in the total amount levied and spent, as is indicated in the final table. In the period 1779–99, the expenditure for poor relief more than doubled. In the period 1799–1829, it almost quadrupled. In all probability the wars of 1793–1801 and 1802–15, in celebration of the victories of which the Crawley people made so much music, played their part in giving to the parish widows and children to care for. But most of the early increase occurred before the wars and much of the later came after them. Some other forces must have been at work. The enclosure of 1795, to be sure, preceded the first of the two increases. No

[1] 14 Elizabeth, ch. 5, § 16. *Statutes of the Realm*, vol. IV (1819), p. 593.

great industrial developments, however, occurred in or near the district in which Crawley is located. We are forced to explain the situation as due primarily to the poor laws themselves, the situation being aggravated by war's losses, high prices at times, and the encroachment of the yeomen on the laborers. Of course, conditions in the County of Southampton may account for part of the increased expenditure for which Crawley itself was not to blame.

The yeomen farmers were not unwilling — so far as we know — to bear the burden. It can probably be said that they were paying their own laborers partly in wages and partly in poor rates, under the so-called Speenhamland system, particularly from 1796 onward. The five rate payers (including the rector) who contributed the largest sums actually paid over 70% of the total in 1776–77. At this time, however, there were twenty-three or twenty-four contributors in all, not very far from half of the total families living in the parish.

The overseers contributed to the county rates and to the county hospital. They gave to travelling seamen and to sick and indigent parishioners. Cash, food, rent, faggots, and nursing were supplied. The wives and children of Crawley men, living in other parishes, were provided for. Both indoor and outdoor relief were given. The house of industry was there to receive all whom the overseers would not assist in their own homes. A certain Dr. Wickham of Sutton was paid for services, apparently for inoculating the poor with smallpox so as to obviate the severer ravages of an epidemic.[1]

The whole years disbursement of James Fitt overseer of the Poor of the Parish of Crawley from Easter 1776 to Easter 1777 [2]

Is	£79	0 s.	11 d.
We do agree to Gather 28 Rates which is	84	18	8
Remains	5.	17.	9.
Interest Money	0.	3.	4.
Recd for Pentons goods	0.	12.	0.
The Book Indebted at Michaelmas	1.	1.	2½
Easter 1777 Remains in Hand with the Book	7.	14.	3½.

[1] See above, §§ 52, p. 563.

[2] MS., Crawley Church safe, Crawley Poor Book, 1776–97, p. 1. Copied by Miss Lilian J. Redstone.

We whose Names are under Written have perused the above account and we allow of the same, and we do Nominate and appoint Thomas Perrin and Richard Bailey Overseers for the Year Ensuing

[all sign] Jno Pickering
John Birch
John Paige

15 th April 1777 verified on oath before us

[sign] F. Swanton
N. St. John.

A Rate made for the Relief of the Poor of the Parrish of Crawley for the year 1777

		s.	d.
John Williams Esq. for the Great House *and* Pitters Living		10.	10.
The Revd Mr. Taylor for the Parsonage	1.	0.	10.
" " Mr. Bathurst for the Crofts	0.	1.	6.
His Royal Highness the Duke of Cumberland for Rookley House	0.	6.	8.
Leo'd. Cropp Esq. for Rookley Woods	0.	1.	6.
Mr. Bailey for New Barn Farm	1.	3.	4.
Far. Perrin His Own Weights Glides Morgans Simes's Browns Coxes and Pagises	0.	12.	2.
Far. Pickering for Eyles, Godwins, Thomsons, Pitters *and* Broadways	0.	11.	6.
Far. Fitt for Rookley Farm	0.	9.	5.
Mrs. Fifield for North Woods	0.	2.	1.
Far. Fielder for How Croft	0.	0.	3.
Far. Page for His Own	0.	0.	6.
	5.	0.	7.

5th April 1777 We confirm the above Rate and do appoint Thomas Perrin and Richard Bailey to be Overseers for the year ensuing.

[signed] F. Swanton.
N. St. John.

				s.	d.
1797		Disburst by Jno Pickering to Crawley Poor [1]		s.	d.
May	6.	To Jas. Elford		2.	0.
	13.	For confirming the Book Pd. by Far. Reade	2 s. 0 d.	10.	6.
		Do. Expences	2 s. 0.		
		New Book	6 s. 6.		

[1] MS., Crawley Church, Crawley Poor Book, 1797–1822.

May	14.	Sarah Archer	3 weeks at 3 s. 6 d.		10.	6.
	21.	Peter Head ill	4 Galln. loaves		4.	4.
		To Brown's wife from Ap. 27				
		to May 21. Pd. Ap. 27	2 s. 0 d.			
		Pd. the Midwife	5 s. 0 d.			
		Sarah Archer (Nurseing)	4 s. 0 d.			
		a neck of Mutton (Browns)	2 s. 11 d.			
		E. Russell's Bill for (Do)	6 s. 0 d.			
		Allen's Bill Do	7 s. 3½ d.			
				1.	7.	2½.
	21.	Wido. Shepard		0.	10.	0.
		Gaiger		0.	4.	0.
		Redding		0.	8.	
		Collis		0.	8.	0.
		Carter's Daughter		0.	8.	0.
		Fifield			6.	0.
		Dear			8.	0.
		Tarrant			8.	0.
		Dench			5.	0.
		Brown		1.	16.	0.
		To Eliz. Russell for Archer's child			3.	0.
June	8.	Gave Two seamen			1.	0.
June	18.	Shepard			10.	
		Gaiger			4.	
		Redding			8.	
		Collis			8.	
		Carter			8.	
		Fifield			6.	
		Dear			8.	
		Tarrant			8.	
		Dench			5.	
		Brown		1.	16.	
		Charles Archer's Child			12.	
July	1.	To Elford			1.	
	16.	Shepard			10.	
		Gaiger			4.	
		Redding			8.	
		Collis			8.	
		Fifield			6.	
		Dear			8.	
		Tarrant			8.	
		Dench			5.	

			£	s.	d.
July	16.	Brown	1.	16.	
		Archer's child		12.	
	25.	To Caseley		2.	
		To Mr. Simmons County Rates	7.	1.	8.
Aug.	13.	Shepard [and the rest exactly as of 16 July]			
		To Eliz. Russell for James Caseley (ill) from July 2. to Augt. 13. 6 weeks	2.	14.	
Sept.	10.	Shepard [and the rest down to Archer's child] Caseley 4 weeks at 6 s.	1.	4.	
	27.	To Lueza Bungy *and* Co. (in Distress)			
		Expences at Allens 1 s. 3 d. gave them 3 s.		4.	8.
Oct.	8.	To Ann Carter from Ap. 23 to Oct. 8 24 weeks	1.	4.	
		Shepard [down to Archer's child, as before]			
		Caseley 1 week 6 s. 1 week 7 s. 6 d. *and* 2 weeks at 9 s.	1.	11.	6.
	15.	To Jas. Caseley		9.	
		a letter from Portsmouth			4.
	24.	To Mr. Simmons County Rates Midsumr. Sessions £3. 10. 10.; Michs. Sessions £7. 1. 8.	10.	12.	6.
Nov.	1.	To Sarah Ward		2.	6.
	2.	To Mrs. Steel for a Year's house Rent for Caseley	2.	0.	0.
		To a Sailor in distress			6.
Nov.	5.	Shepard [down to Archer's child, as before]			
Nov.	17.	To Sarah Ward		2.	6.
	19.	To Ann Carter		2.	0.
	21.	Allen's Bill		19.	4.
Dec.	3.	Sheapard [exactly as of 16 July, except that Dench has 4 s. only, down to Archer's Child]			
		To Wido. Lambourn for 14 weeks at 1 s. 6 d. per week	1.	1.	
	9.	To a sailor's wife in distress			6.
		To Hannah Shepard nursing Dame Shepard		4.	

Dec.	9.	To Jno. Carey		5.	
	31.	Wido. Shepard		10.	
		Do. Gaiger		4.	
		Redding		8.	
		Dear		8.	
		Collis 8 s. 0. } Do. (ill) 2.s. 2. }		10.	2.
		Archer's child		12.	
		Brown	1.	16.	
		Ann Carter 6 weeks		10.	11.
		Jno. Carey		6.	
		Wido. Dench		4.	
		Do. Lambourn		6.	
		Fifield		6.	
1798					
Jan.	16.	To Mr. Birch for a year's house Rent for Jno. Burrough to Michas.	2.	0.	
Jan.	16.	To Bennett felling 3 score Tithe Wood (Rookley Copse)	0.	9.	0.
	22.	To Jas. Elford		4.	0.
		To Jas. Allen's Bill for Dinner *the* Jany. 11 on Acct. of settleing for the Poor to be admitted to *the* house of Industry	1.	14.	6.
	28.	To Jas. Elford		2.	
		Wido. Shepard		10.	
		Gaiger		4.	
		Reading		8.	
		Tarrant		8.	
		Dear		8.	
		Collis		8.	
		Charles Archer's child		12.	
		Brown	1.	16.	
		Ann Carter		5.	6.
		Jno. Carey		8.	
		Wido. Dench		4.	
		Do. Fifield		6.	
		Do. Lambourn		6.	
Feb.	3.	Pd. Mrs. Browning for 300 Faggots for the Poor at 15 s. per Hundred		2.	5.
		Jno. Pickering for Carriage of Do.		2.	
	4.	To Jas. El[f]ord		2.	
		To a sailor in Distress	0.	0.	6.

			£	s.	d.
1798					
Feb.	25.	Wido. Shepard [down to Lambourn, as of 28 Jan., except that Ann Carter has 8 s. 10 d.]			
March	2.	To Jas. Elford		2.	
	6.	Peter Head		1.	
	13.	To Elford		2.	
	17.	To Jas. Elford		2.	
		A letter from Willm. Maiden		0.	4.
		(To Peter Head) 1½ days make faggots Rookley Coppice		2.	3.
	23.	Jas Elford		2.	
	25.	Wido. Shepard [down to Lambourn, as of 28 Jan., except that Brown has £1. 12. for 3 weeks at 9 s. and 1 week at 5 s.; Ann Carter has 7 s. 3 d.]			
		Peter Head		3.	10.
	28.	Jas. Elford		2.	0.
Ap.	3	To Do.		2.	0.
[—]		To Do.		2.	0.
		For Carriage of Wood for Burgess June 1797 } 7 s. 6 d.; Do. March 1st. 1798 7 s. 6.d.		15.	0.
		To the Overseer of Twyford 52 weeks pay for Tuffin's wife *and* child to Ap. 8. 1798 at 3 s. per week	7.	16.	0.
1798		Disburst			
		To the Overseers of St. Swithin for 9 weeks pay for Wm. Maiden's Wife *and* Child from Ap. 1 to June 3, 1797	1.	7.	
		To Do. from June 3 to Septr. 9 14 weeks at 3 s. per week	2.	2.	
		Paid to Wm. Maiden 14 weeks from Septr. 16 to Decr. 24. 1797	2.	2.	
		For Carriage of 3 Load Faggots from Rookley Copse	1.	2.	6.
April	12.	Charles Simse's Bill		4.	6.
		Far: Pern's Bill for house Rent	12.	10.	
		1 year's Rent for Jno. Carey	1.	11.	6.
		Half a Year's for Richd. Burgess	0.	15.	9.
		G. Godwin (Senr) Bill	4.	0.	0.

April 12.	Jas. Holdaway Bill		1.	6.	8.
	Doctr. Wickham (Sutton) Bills		1.	8.	10.
	G. Cook Bill			4.	2.
	Eliz: Kent Bill			8.	0.
	Far: Godwin for Wards house Rent		2.	0.	0.
	To Do. Pd. to County Hospital		1.	1.	0.
	Mr. Wickham's Bill for two Years				
	to Easter 1797 — 8. 3. 6.	}	14.	14.	0.
	To Do. to Easter 1798 — 6. 10. 6.				
	Do. Jas. Allen's Bills		1.	2.	7.
Ap. 18.	To Jas. Elford			2.	0.
	Total		£165.	15.	7½.

Recd. with the Book	£29. 6. 7½.
Collect Rates at 2 s. in the pound	£154. 12. 7.
	£183. 19. 2½.
Disburst	£165. 15. 7½.
Remains in hand	£ 18. 3. 7.

We do nominate and appoint Thos. Pern and Richd. Bailey Overseers for the Year Ensuing May 5th 1798

Verified on oath before

F. W. Swanton.

TABLE COMPILED TO SHOW TOTAL EXPENDITURE

	£	s.	d.
1776–77 [1]	79	0	11
1777–78	80	13	3½
1779–80	115	2	0
1789–90	149	16	5¼
1797–98	165	15	7½
1799–1800	127	13	5
1809–10	290	5	5¾
1819–20	439	18	1
1829–30	463	10	5
1834–35	352	4	5 [2]

[1] The year runs from Easter to Easter.
[2] The last complete year shown in this form.

§§ 54. Excerpts from the Originals of Court Presentments, 1697–1858.

These court presentments are taken from the original records, separate sheets of paper turned in by the officials twice a year. The two sessions were at Hocktide in the spring and St. Martin's in the autumn. The lord's tourn and the customary court or court baron had met from the beginning of the manorial accounts. They still had some vigor in the period in question as a court for agricultural matters, at least up to enclosure in 1795. Apparently it was as a customary court or court baron rather than as a tourn or leet that the court transacted most of its business, even though the tourn forms were retained.

The court, considered as a single entity, was made up of a jury and affeerers, at which the reeve and tithingman were elected. It is clear that the suitors wanted certain results, even though the amercements went into the coffers of the lord. That they took their duties of a combined legislative body and court of first instance rather lightly at times is indicated by the entry directing Farmer John Pitter to provide beer at the next court under heavy penalty. And how significant that a West Saxon joke should turn on drinking!

Among the many things done by the court were the following: the registration of mortgages and wills, the keeping of the stocks and whipping posts in good condition, making clear the customs and laws of inheritance, keeping the highways open and clean, recording the death of a copyholder and the incoming of his heir, and, of course, most prominently the regulation of the routine of agriculture.

These regulations deal with the erection and repair of hedges, fences, and gates, with plowing, pasturing, right of common, and the duty of going a-bounding around the common fields. The tenants had sheep, cows, horses, pigs, and ducks. They were limited as to the number of animals they could keep on the common pasture. Their "owne ground," however, was available for additional stock.

From these presentments we learn that there were in Crawley common arable fields, common pasture at Northwood Park, and such individual plots as had been set aside for exclusive use and possession.

There were apparently two kinds of common fields, the corn fields and the summer fields. The former were probably planted to wheat, barley, and oats, while the latter were left fallow. It was stated in a presentment for 1744 that no one was to plow before July first in the summer fields "except what is more than one years Lea or that ground wich the fold have ben ouer." The meaning of the word "lea," sometimes very difficult, seems here to be fallow pasture. Doubtless some tenants were anxious to plow their share of the fallow, by way of preparation for their winter-grain crop, as early as might be. The others apparently resented the loss of their fallow pasture. It would seem that we have here in Crawley the old rotation of a winter grain, a spring grain, and fallow. Pasture in Crawley was apparently found in four places: on the stubble of corn fields after August first, the fallow pasture, the common permanent pasture, and such bits of separate pastures as may have been set aside for the purpose. The prohibition against putting infected horses upon the commons of the manor was accompanied by a heavy fine, but at best the enforcement must have been difficult because of the fact that a disease commonly got a start before discovery.

If "the Tenant of Crawley Farm" refers to the farmer of the demesne, then we have an interesting bit of conflict (in 1793) just before the enclosure. This "Tenant" was declared by the homage of the manor to have no right to the road that ran across their cowdown to any of his "Commonfields." They and he were using the common fields jointly; but he was not to trespass on their cow pasture. The antagonism may have been brewing over the subject of enclosure. The tenants could win in the parliament of Crawley, but the farmer of the demesne (some of the more successful copyholders and the lord of the manor) could win in the parliament of the nation. In this connection, it was the latter victory that was decisive: the tenants lost their cowdown.

A clear distinction was made between borough English which applied to bondland and primogeniture which governed purpresture land. It is evident that lord and tenants had alike accepted these customs and perpetuated them. A distinction was made between freeholders who paid 6d. when absent from court, copyholders who paid 4d., and mere inhabitants who were mulcted only 3d. Whether Henry Simes and Edward Bellenger were inhabitants only, and therefore had no right to pasture a horse on the common, except by special purchase of the right from their neighbors who possessed it, is not made clear.

Here are the old families — we may call them the yeoman families of Crawley — represented in the court. The Perns are here, and the Pitters, the Godwins, the Paiges, and the Waites.

Many of the documents from which the following excerpts have been taken are very badly written. Unfortunately no second verification of the parts here printed has been practicable.

1. St. Martin's (24 Sept.), 1697 [1]

It*em* we present that the hegges and gates against the Whet feld be sofitiently Made and Mended by the fest of St. Martin on paine of five shillinges Euery defalt.[2]

2. Hock (31 March), 1699

It*em* we present that the hegges be sofiten[t]ly made and Mended Round the parcke by the sixth day of May upon paine of fiue shillings euery defalte.[3]

3. St. Martin's (19 Sept.), 1701

Imprimis wee present William Waight to be tything man for the year Ensuing.

It*em* wee present that no man shall plough in the Earsh feilds vntill the 16th day of January vpon *th*e paine of 5 shilling an aker.[3]

It*em* wee present that no man shall plough nor soe any part of Norman downe without a generall Consent of all the Commoners upon paine of 5 s. an acre.[3]

[Nine names of jury occur here.]

4. St. Martin's (21 Sept.), 1702

Impr*im*is: Wee p*re*sent William Godwin[4] to be Tythingman for the year ensueing for the Tything of Crawley.

Item Wee p*re*sent the Hedges and Gates ag*ainst* the Wheat Feilds to be out of repaire and wee order the same to be repaired before the Eleaventh day of October next on pain of 5 s. on every one concerned that shall make default.[3]

[1] MS., Millbank, Ecclesiastical Commission, 159560. Presentments, 1696–1729.
[2] pena posita written in the left-hand margin.
[3] sub pena written in the left-hand margin.
[4] Jur*atus* interlineated in a different hand.

Item Wee p*re*sent all those that have any Cattell on the Com*m*on Feilds that they drive the same out of the said Feilds (Sheep onely excepted) on or before the Feast day of St. Luke next on pain of 10 s.[1]

[Thirteen names follow as "the Jury" and the Tythingman. Freeholders to pay 6 d., copyholders 4 d., inhabitants 3 d., for failure to appear at court.]

5. St. Martin's (24 Sept.), 1703

[The jury presents the deaths, election of tythingman and also reeve, and orders concerning cattle, hedges, etc.]

6. St. Martin's (22 Sept.), 1704

Item wee p*re*sent that all those that keepe Cattell in o*u*r Com*m*ons that they rid them from the Comon before the Feast of St. Luke on pain of 5 s. eu*er*y one making default [2] (Sheepe only Excepted).

Item we p*re*sent the hedges ag*ainst* the corn-feildes to [be] out of repaire *and* order the owners to repaire the[m] before the last day of November on pain of 5 s. [each making][3] default.[2]

Item wee p*re*sent that eu*er*y one rid Norwood Copice of their Sheepe before Mich*aelm*as day on pain of 5 s. eu*er*y one making default.

Item wee p*re*sent that o*u*r pond is out of repaire and eu*er*y P*er*son that have a Yardland ought to send a laborer *and* their horses *and* Cart in ord*er* to repaire it the same to be done before St. Lukes day next upon pain of 10 s. each making default eu*er*y one to send p*ro*porcionable to their Estates.

7. St. Martin's (4 Sept.), 1705

It*em* we present Edward Broadway for not makeing his hedge against Tho. Thornam ground According to the present of the Last Court: which was vnder the penalty of ten shilling Every Default.

8. Hock (26 March), 1708 (complete)

The p*re*sentments of the Jury at the Court Leet and Law day and Court Baron of this Mannor appointed to be holden here the six *and* twentieth day of March Anno D*omi*ni 1708.

Inpr*imi*s: wee p*re*sent the death of Ambrose Beech one of the Customary Tennants of the Mann*or*.

Item wee p*re*sent William Waite to serve the office of Reeve for the Yeare ensueing.[4]

Item wee p*re*sent Edward Broadway for not repairing his hedges at Thornham whereby he has Forfeited the sum*m*e of tenn shillings.

Item wee p*re*sent that Farm*er* Pitter repair his hedges at Norman downe by the tenth day of May next upon pain of Fifty shillings.

[1] si*mi*liter in the margin.
[2] Sub pena in the margin.
[3] Manuscript torn.
[4] Jur*atus* written in the left-hand margin.

Item wee order to repair his hedges ag*ainst* the parke upon pain of x s.

Item wee p*re*sent that every one make his Fences ag*ainst* Mr. Dawlys dawne by May day next upon pain of x s. on eu*er*y one making default.

Item wee order that no[n]e Feed the Greens w*i*th his Cattle nor plough up the same before the First of August next on pain of x s.

Item wee p*re*sent and order *that* eu*er*y one Ring his *and* their hogges before the[y] putt them in the Feilds on pain of Forfeiting 5 s. each.

Item we order eu*er*y one to make his hedges *and* gates ag*ainst* the Corne Feilds by the 1st of May upon the penalty of 3 s. 4 d. eu*er*y one making default.

Item wee order eu*er*y P*er*son to Fetter their horses w*i*th Iron Fetters before they turne *them* into the parke on pain of 5 s. eu*er*y one soe offending nor put in more horses[1] thene their number and stent.

Item wee p*re*sent that none plough their sum*m*er Feild till six weeks before Mich*aelm*as upon pain of Fifty shillings.

9. St. Martin's (14 Sept.), 1709

Item wee order eu*er*y P*er*son haveing hedges ag*ainst the* Cornefeilds to repair *them* by St. Andrewes Tyde on pain of 3 s. 4 d. each making default.

Item that none Surcharge the Com*m*on with horses or Cattle on pain of 20 s.

Item wee order euery one to ring their hogs *and* pigs by the 2th instant on pain of 3 s. 4 d. making default.

Item wee order that noe p*er*son keepe above 16 ews on a Yardland on pain of 20 s. soe offending.

10. Hock (28 March), 1712

The presentments of the Juery at the Cort of Hoke.

Item we present John Waite the next reaue for this year ensuing.

Item we present that the heges about the parke be made sofishent by *the* 10 of May upon *the* penelty of £2. 0 s. 0 d.

Item we present that the heges againest the kopes next lainson down[2] upon the penelty of £1. 0 s. 0 d.

Item we present that the gates and heges all in generel against the korne feldes be made up by the furst of may upon the penelty of 2–10–0.

Item we present that no man shall plow in the sumer feeld tell a weeke before midsumer upon the penelty of 3–0–0.

[1] "into the Feilds" is interlineated.

[2] "by *the* 10 of may" is interlineated.

It*e*m we present that no man shall feed no horses nor kowes in the wast ground in the Corne feeldes tell lamas day upon the penelty of 0–10–0.

It*e*m we present that if any man put any horses into the parke with out fett*e*res he shall pay 0–5–0.

It*e*m we present that botame way hege be made very sofishent by the first day of September [1] upon the penelty of 3–10–0.

It*e*m we present that no man shall put no hoges in the feeldes without ringing upon the penelty of 1–0–0.

Item we present that the komen feelde be clered of all cattell ex[c]epet sheep by [2]

Item wee p*re*sent that Edward Broadway hath forfeited the pawne of twenty shillings layd on him at the last Cort for that he did contrary to an order of the same Cort plow up and Sowe an acre of the heather furlong to the p*re*judice of the other Tenants.[3]

Afferr*ers*	John Pitter John Godwin	Jur*ati*	Frehold*ers* — vj d. Co[p]yhold*ers* — iiij d. Inh[ab]itants — iij d.

The Names of the homage sum*m*oned to Serve at a Cort held the 28th day of March, 1712

John Pitter sen*ior*	Jur*atus*	Ed*ward*us Bellinger Will*elm*us Hacke Jacobus Thompson Henr*ic*us Long	Jur*ati*
Ed*ward*us Broadway Joh*an*nes Godwin Georgius Penton Rich*ard*us Morgan	Jur*ati*		
Joh*an*nes Page sen*ior* Joh*an*nes Waite Michael Batchelir W*illel*mus Butterly	Jur*ati*		

11. Hock (27 March), 1713

Imprimis wee present that Edward Allen a Customary Tenant of this Mannor did Surrender in Mortgage certain Copyhold lands he held of this Mann*or* to the Use *and* behoofe of John Futcher of Rumsey Clothier and his heires upon Condic*i*on to be void upon the s*aid* Edw*ard* Allens paying unto the said John Futcher the sum*me* of £172. 10 s. at the times therein appointed *and* limited for paym*ent* of the same, which said sum*me* was not paid to the s*aid* John Futcher according to the Condic*i*on in the s*ai*d surrend*er* but now remaine due. Wee doe therefore p*re*sent that the s*aid* Edward Allen hath Forfeited his

[1] "the first day of September" is interlineated.
[2] The rest of this item is inked out.
[3] In the margin: afferrd at x s.

Estate in the s*aid* p*re*mises and the s*aid* John Futcher ought to be admitted Tenant.

12. St. Martin's (19 Sept.), 1713

Item we present that Edward Broadway was prejudicale to the Com*m*en by putting one Cow more then his usuall stent.[1]

13. Hock (25 March), 1715

Item we present that farmer Pitter shall macke or cause to be made a very good and lawfull fence betwene the parck and fearmer Buxes ground by the first of may or forfete fiue pound if he refuse to doe it.

Item we present that no pearson or pearsons shall feed any of thaier Catell in the Corne feelds except it be in thaier owne ground befoere the first of aguste apon the penelty of fiue shilings.

Item we present that no man shall put any horses in to the parke without feters of Iron or forfete fiue shillinges if they doe.

Item we present that Henery Simes and Edward Bellenger haue no right or priuiledge of any hors comon in the park except thay hier thaire comons of other naibors.

Item we present that no pearson or parsons shall plow any of his or thaier land in the summer feeld before the first of June apon the penelty of ten shillings an acker.

Item we present that the stockes and wiping poste be put in repaier before easter next insuing.

Item we present that on thursday the twelfth of may euery tenant belonging to the comon feelds shall goo a bounding or forfite halfe a crown if he neglect except a lawfull cause shall hinder.

Item we present that no pearson shall go through the standing corne in time of haruest with horse and carte or wagon without cuting of a way or asking leafe of thaier naibors to go through ether at landes end or eles whare apon the penelty of thirty shillinges.

14. St. Martin's (5 Oct.), 1716

Impr*imi*s wee p*re*sent Ambros Pyle tythingman.

Item wee p*re*sent that euery P*er*son to clear the fields of all Cattle Except Sheep before St. Lukes day on pain of x s. *and* the horses to be taken by the 13th instant.

Item wee order the Gates and hedges ag*ainst* the Corn Fekdes by St. Andrewes day on pain of x s. before St. Andrewes day.

Item wee order that none shall plow out on Wheats *and* Fetiles without making a hedland on pain of iij s. iiij d. before the 11th of No*vember*.

[1] This is the fourth complaint or entry against him.

15. St. Martin's (9 Sept.), 1720

Item we present Robert Pitter to be tythingman for the year ensuing.

Itam wee present that no boody plowes in the Earsh feeld not tell the 16 day of January upon penelty of 0–5–0 Euery eaker.

We present that farmer John Pitter shall bring sum beare to the nexte corte apon the penelty of twenty shilings.

John Godwin	Robert Pitter
John Pitter Sen*ior*	William Butteley
John Sims	John × Paige
Will*iam* Waite	John ⊁ Lomer
Thamas Broadway	
Richard Morgen	

16. St. Martin's (16 Nov.), 1723

Item we present that no parson shall cut any busheses at the Cowdowne or northside sheep-downe nor farsen besides the Tenanents but what thay fetch at thaier backes apon the penelty of twenty shillings every defalte.

Item we present that no parson shall plow any of thaier grownd in the wheate earsh grownd or in that feeld before the 16 day of January on the penelty of 10 shillings *the* acker.

Item we present that it is the Custom of our maner to pay no hearyeates apon a surender and Licke wise to haue the Cut of the Norwood Coopes at five shilling an acker.

17. Hock (24 March), 1726 [1]

Item we present that no parson shall not plow any ground in the sumer feelds except laine or what the fold gooes ouer untell the first of august on the penelty 10 shilings.

Item we present that thare is no highway athirt northsid wheat feeld for cartes and wagens to go if any parson persume to go through the corne shall forfite 5 shilling.

Item we present that the tenentantes shall all go abounding the first thirsday in may on the penelty of 2 s. 6 d.

18. St. Martin's (1 Oct.), 1731 [2]

Item we present that Stephen Newman Seniour and Stephen Newman Junjour to keep the sheep of from the cowdown on the penelty of 1–0–0.

19. Hock (27 March), 1735

Item we Present the Death of the Honourable Esq. Merell since the last Corte A Coppeyholder of this maner *and* John his son next heaier.

[1] This would be 1727, new style.

[2] Here begins ms. 159561. Presentments, 1730–60.

Item we Present that the widow Hack shall macke up hur fences About hur garden by the 26 of may or forfite tenn shilings.

20. Hock (25 March), 1737

Item We Present that thare shall be no duckes Keept to goo into Meer Pond after Mayday *the* first on *the* Penelty of 10 s.

21. St. Martin's (8 Oct.), 1739

Item we present that no body shall plow but one acre and a half to a yard land and the ground that the fold goes over before the first day of Janvary upon the pena[l]ty of five shillings an acre.

Item we present that no body shall lay any Straw or Mockell in the Street upon the penalty of five Shillings every default.

22. Hock (30 March), 1744

Item we present that no body shall not plow any grownd in the fields Called the sumer fields except what is more than one years Lea or that ground wich the fold have ben ouer before the first day of July upon the penjalty of five shillings every acer.

Item we present that no body shall not feede any of the greens or Roads in the corn fields from the first day of may till the first day of august upon the penjalty of five shillings euery default.

23. Hock (29 March), 1745

Item we present that no body Shall not put any Infected horsess as Mainge faishons or glanders upon the Comons of the maner upon the penjalty of five pounds for every default.

24. St. Martin's (15 Oct.), 1750

We present that every body shall make headlands so that they may do no damage to the Corn nor to the grass at Shirt upon the penjalty of five shillings every default.

We present that no body Shall keep any ducks in the parish pond upon the penjalty of five Shillings the default.

25. St. Martin's (28 Sept.), 1754

We present the death of Edward Fae a Copyhold Tenant since the last Court *and* his youngest Daughter Mary to be his next heir which s*aid* Mary is the now Wife of Richard Goodchild.[1]

26. Hock (29 March), 1755

Item We present that all Persons having a Right to Wood in the Lords Coppice shall Carry out the Same before the twenty fourth day of June next under the penalty of five Shillings for every Load.

27. St. Martin's (29 Sept.), 1758

We present that the Rector of Crawley has no Right to a Way from the Parsonage Close into the Common field called South side Field.

[1] Rich. Goodchild makes his mark as one of fourteen. A poor laborer?

28. St. Martin's (19 Sept.), 1793[1]

Crawley Manor. The Presentment of the Jury at a Court Leet and Court Baron there held the 19th day of Sept., 1793.

We present George Godwin Jun*ior* Tithingman for the year ensuinge.

We present that no person in plowing his land in the Commonfields shall turn his plough on other persons Corn to damage the same under the penalty of five Shillings.

We present that the Rector of Crawley hath no right to a way from the parsonage Close into the Comon field called Southfield.

We present that there is no lawful road from Gaston Stile to Dellage pond but only the Church road.

We present that the Tenant of Crawley Farm hath no right to a Road across our Cowdowne to any of his Comonfields.

We present that no Sheep shall be let into Northwood Coppice to feed the same under the penalty of five pounds.

Tho. Pern	The Mark of
Geo Cooke	John + Russell
Will*iam* Godwin	Geo. Godwin Jun*ior*
Thomas Loomer	John Kent
Rich*ard* Trift	Geo. Godwin
Chars. Cimes	George Steel
	Will*iam* Pern

[After this the chief business was to present the tithingman and reeve and the death of copyholders.]

29. St. Martin's (29 Sept.), 1813

We present William Willis for a Nuisance in having broken the Head of the Pond at the Bottom of Crawley Street by which the Water is wasted to the Injury of the Inhabitants of Crawley And we order him to stop the same within one Month on the pain of Twenty pounds.

We present the Death of Joseph Bramble a Copyhold Tenant of this Manor And that his widow is intitled to the premises he held of this Manor for her Widowhood.

[Nine signatures and 3 marks.]

30. Hock (7 April), 1831

Crawley Manor.[2] The Presentments of the Jury and Homage at the Court Leet and Court Baron of the said Manor there holden the 7th day of April 1831.

Imprimis We present that the Bondland and Purpresture and other Land within the said Manor if annexed to Bondland under the same fine altho the Bondland shall be the least do descend and ought to de-

[1] From ms. 159563. Presentments, 1791–1820.

[2] From ms. 159564. Presentments, 1821–59.

scend as Tenements of the Tenure and in the nature of Burrough English not only to the youngest Son or Youngest Daughter and for default of such Issue of such customary Tenant to the youngest Brother or Youngest Sister but also for default of such Brother and Sister of such customary Tenant to the next Youngest Kinsman or Kinswoman of the whole Blood of the Customary Tenant in possession how far soever remote and that a Youngest Grandchild youngest Nephew and Youngest Niece shall succeed in the place of their Father or Mother altho such Parent shall have died before he or she shall have fined.

We also present the purpresture demesne and other Land not annexed to Bondland within the said Manor do descend and ought to descend to the eldest Son and in default of a Son to the eldest Daughter and for default of such Issue of such customary Tenant not only to the eldest brother or eldest Sister but also for Default of such Brother and Sister of such customary tenant to the next eldest Kinsman or eldest Kinswoman of the whole Blood of the Customary Tenant in possession how far soever remote and that an eldest Nephew or eldest Niece shall succeed in the place of their Father or Mother altho such Parent shall have died before he or she shall have fined.

We also present that the Widow of a Customary Tenant dying seized is to hold his Lands and Tenements for her Chaste Widowhood without fine she coming to the first Court after his Death claiming the same and paying a Penny.

We present Robert Holdaway to remain Tythingman for the year ensuing.

We present George Godwin Sen*ior* to remain Reeve and Hayward for the year ensuing.

We present a Mortgage made on the 2nd August 1824 by James Holdaway to the use of Henry Twynam of Bishop's Stoke Gentleman forfeited for nonpayment of the Principal Money and Interest.

G. Godwein Sen*ior*	W*illiam* Hill
George Read	Chas Paige
Tho. Pern	George Steele
George Godwein Jun*ior*	J*onathan* Morrison
John Cooke	W*illiam* Stillbury
Rich. Kent	his W*illiam* + Serle mark

31. (24 Aug.), 1859[1]

We also present that the husband of a Copyhold or customary tenant ought to fine for her lands and pay half the preceeding fine but that he shall hold such Land only for his Wife's Life.

[1] Such entries as those above are repeated down to the part dealing with the widow, one being added, e. g., in the last entry (24 Aug., 1859), printed here.

§§ 55. Act of Parliament for Enclosure, 1794.

The full text of the Act, in so far as it relates to Crawley, is here reproduced, partly because of its value for Crawley and partly because such private acts of Parliament are not commonly accessible in print. The Act relates to Crawley and Bishop's Sutton, both being held by the Bishop of Winchester as lord, Crawley northwest and Bishop's Sutton northeast of the City of Winchester.

Eight persons are named as petitioners for the enclosure. Almost all were large landholders: probably Richard Meyler and Thomas Pern were together possessed of over half of the manor. The purpose for the enclosure is said to have been the improvement of agriculture, so difficult in a system of scattered strips and common fields.

Besides the bishop, there were four classes concerned — the leaseholders, freeholders, customary tenants, and inhabitants. The first and third classes were the most important. The inhabitants had no land rights. Whether they were possessed of cottage rights or were just renters is not clear.

All the common lands were to be truly surveyed by the commissioners and apportioned to those possessing rights thereto. Hedges, ditches, and fences were to be provided and maintained by the recipients of allotments, except in the case of the rector.

As compensation for the loss of rights, the bishop was to receive one fiftieth of the commons, downs, and waste grounds, and one thirtieth of the common woodlands. His share was to be placed near to the mansion house of the farmer of the demesne. And as compensation for his glebe lands lying in the commons, the rector was to receive enclosed lands near to the rectory. Other tenants were to be given new holdings in proportion to their old ones,the new ones to be near to their residences. What was allotted to them must be accepted.

It is explicitly stated that there is to be no change in tenure. A copyholder was to hold by copy of the court roll and a freeholder as before. This is clear enough, but why an exception was made for leaseholders is not clear. They were to lose their leases, at least all except one. We may surmise that they were dispossessed because otherwise they and their rights would stand in the way of enclosure. Richard Bailey, the sublessee of Richard Meyler, was allowed, however, to keep his lease. He held Manor Farm, that is, the bulk of the demesne lands. It is therefore clear that Richard Meyler was not an operating, but a gentleman, farmer.

Just how the tenants actually fared in the enclosure is very difficult to discover. They were expected to give up some of their lands [1] to the lord to be added to the Manor Farm or demesne lands. This was to be done as the purchase price of freedom from surviving dues and services, which were said to be worth twelve guineas a year. Probably these included in practice the washing and shearing of the lord's sheep (actually the demesne farmer's sheep) and the carrying of wood for the lord's use. In theory they probably also included other services such as carrying letters and briefs and carting the lord's corn to market, which in fact, however, were no longer effective.

In marked contrast to the preparation for a new technique of agriculture is the retention of the old tenures. The most important tenure at the time was copyhold. The copyholder still had to pay rents, fines, heriots, dues, payments, and services, only the first three probably being of any great significance. If any copyholder wished to change his copyhold into a freehold, he had to pay a lump sum for what was called enfranchisement.

It is specifically stated that the old-time courts and their profits were to be retained by the lord. And to him was reserved the privilege of hunting, hawking, fishing, and fowling in the fields of Crawley. This right could be extinguished only by enfranchisement. Rather ironically, it is stated that to the lord still belonged the right to timber growing in the common woods. In other words, it appears, the common woods were to be the lord's woods.

After enclosure, there was to be nothing really common in Crawley.

An Act For *Dividing, Allotting, and Inclosing divers Common Fields, Common Woods, Common Downs, and other Commonable Places within*

[1] Probably the amount so lost to the tenants was one thirtieth of common woodlands and one fiftieth of the other common lands, already referred to.

the Manor and Parish of Crawley *in the County of* Southampton; *and of certain Open Common Fields, Common Meadows, Waste Lands, and other Commonable Places within the Parish of* Bishops Sutton *in the said County.*[1]

Preamble. Whereas there are within the several Parishes of *Crawley* and *Bishops Sutton* in the County of *Southampton*, certain Common Fields, Common Woods, Common Downs, Common Meadows, Waste Lands, and other Commonable Places:

And Whereas the Honourable and Right Reverend Father in God *Brownlow* Lord Bishop of *Winchester*, in Right of his Church and See of *Winchester*, is Lord of the Manor of *Crawley*, and is entitled to the Lords Right in the Soil of the said Commons and of the Waste Lands within the same Manor; and is also Proprietor of the Manor Farm there held by *Richard Meyler* Esquire, under a Lease for Lives granted by the said Lord Bishop: [and the said Lord Bishop & others are lords of the manors intended to be inclosed within the parish of Bishops Sutton]:

And Whereas *Richard Meyler*, and *Thomas Pern*, *John Pern*, *Robert Pitter*, *George Godwin* the Younger, *John Glide*, *William Waight*, *Sarah Morgan* Widow, and divers other Persons, are the Owners and Proprietors of or interested in the said Common Fields, Common Woods, Common Downs, and other Commonable Places within the said Parish of *Crawley*; . . . [names of owners, etc. in Bishop's Sutton]:

And Whereas the Lands of the respective Proprietors in the said Common Fields, Common Woods, Common Downs, Common Meadows, Waste Lands, and other Commonable Places, lie intermixed and dispersed in small Parcels within the said respective Parishes, and therefore in their present Situation are incapable of any considerable Improvement; and as it would be very advantageous to the several Persons interested therein and entitled thereto, if the said Common Fields, Common Woods, Common Downs, Common Meadows, Waste Lands, and other Commonable Places, were divided and inclosed, and specific Parts and Shares thereof allotted and set out to the several Proprietors, in Lieu of and in Proportion, as near as may be, to their several and respective Estates, Rights, Interests, and Properties therein; but as such Division and Inclosure cannot be effectually made and established without the Aid and Authority of Parliament;

May it therefore please Your MAJESTY,

That it may be Enacted, and be it Enacted by the King's Most Excellent Majesty, by and with the Advice and Consent of the Lords Spiritual and Temporal, and Commons, in this present Parliament assembled, and by the Authority of the same, That *John Tredgold* of

[1] MS., Private Acts, 34 George III, ch. 81.

Chilbolton in the said County of *Southampton* Yeoman, *Richard Eyles* of *Eastmoen* in the said County of *Southampton* Yeoman, and *Thomas King* of *Mottisfont* in the said County of *Southampton* Yeoman, shall be, and they are hereby appointed Commissioners for setting out, dividing, and allotting the Common Fields, Common Woods, Common Downs, and other Commonable Places within the said Manor and Parish of *Crawley* . . . [relates to Bishop's Sutton]: And in case any of the said Commissioners shall refuse to act, or shall die before executing the Award or Awards hereinafter mentioned, the surviving or remaining Commissioners for the separate Parishes aforesaid shall, within Twenty Days after the Refusal or Death of any such Commissioner or Commissioners, or as soon after as conveniently may be, by Writing under his or their Hand and Seal or Hands and Seals, appoint a Commissioner in the Room of every Commissioner refusing to act or dying; and such New Commissioner or Commissioners shall have the same Powers as if he or they had been originally named in this Act; and that all Acts, Matters and Things hereby directed to be done and executed by the said Commissioners for the said respective Parishes, may be done and executed by any Two of them, and the same shall be as valid and effectual as if done and executed by all the said Commissioners hereinbefore named for such respective Parishes.

Notice of Meetings. Provided always, and be it further Enacted, That the Notice shall be affixed on the principal Door of the Parish Churches of *Crawley* and *Bishops Sutton* respectively, of the Time and Place of the First Meeting of the said respective Commissioners for putting this Act in Execution, at least Eight Days before such Meeting; and also the like Notice of all their subsequent Meetings, (Meetings by Adjournment only excepted,) and that none of their Meetings be held at any greater Distance than Twelve Miles from *Crawley* and *Bishops Sutton* aforesaid respectively; and that no Person shall be capable of acting in the Execution of the Powers given by this Act as Commissioner, (except in appointing the First Meeting and administering the following Oath,) until he shall have taken and subscribed an Oath to the following Effect:

Commissioner's Oath. "I A. B. do swear, That I will faithfully and honestly, to the best of my Judgment, do and execute all Things appertaining to the Office and Duty of a Commissioner by virtue of an Act of Parliament for Dividing, Allotting, and Inclosing divers Common Fields, Common Woods, Common Downs, and other Commonable Places, in the Manor and Parish of *Crawley* in the County of *Southampton;* and . . . [relates to Bishop's Sutton]."

Which Oath it shall be lawful for any One of the said Commissioners to administer; and the said Oath so taken and subscribed by each Commissioner, shall be inrolled, with the respective Awards or Instruments hereinafter directed to be made and executed by the said respective Commissioners.

Provided always, That if at any Meeting appointed to be holden as aforesaid, it shall happen that no more than One of the said Commissioners shall attend, such Commissioner may adjourn such Meeting to such Time and Place as he shall think most convenient.

Valuation and Survey. And, for the more just and regular Division and Distribution of the said Common Fields, Common Woods, Common Downs, Common Meadows, Waste Lands, and other Commonable Places within the Manor and Parish of *Crawley* aforesaid, and Parish of *Bishops Sutton* aforesaid, hereby directed to be divided, allotted, and inclosed as aforesaid, and for the better ascertaining the same, Be it further Enacted, That as soon as conveniently may be after the passing of this Act, the said Common Fields, Common Woods, Common Downs, Common Meadows, Waste Lands, and other Commonable Places hereby directed to be divided, allotted and inclosed, shall be qualited and valued by the said Commissioners for their respective Parishes, or their Successors, or by such Person or Persons as they shall respectively, by any Writing under their Hands for that Purpose, nominate and appoint; and that a true and perfect Survey, Admeasurement, and Plan shall be made of the said Common Fields, Common Woods, Common Downs, and other Commonable Places intended to be inclosed in the said Manor and Parish of *Crawley*, by *George Barnes* of *Andover* in the said County of *Southampton*, Land Surveyor . . . [relates to Bishop's Sutton], provided the said George Barnes and . . . [another] shall, in all Things, conform to the Orders of the said Commissioners respectively, but if they shall not conform to the Orders of the said Commissioners respectively, or die before completing the same, then by such Person or Persons as the said respective Commissioners shall appoint; in which Surveys, Admeasurements, and Plans shall be described and delineated all such Particulars as may be necessary and proper for enabling the said Commissioners respectively, to execute the Trusts reposed in them by this Act; and such Surveyor and Surveyors, his or their Assistants, and also the Person or Persons (if any) who shall assist in valuing and qualitying the said Lands, shall verify on Oath, (if required by the said respective Commissioners,) the Truth, Fidelity, and Impartiality of their Proceedings; which Oath or Oaths the said Commissioners respectively and their successors, or any One of them, are and is hereby empowered to administer, and shall be to the Effect following:

"I A. B. do swear, That I will faithfully, impartially, and honestly, according to the best of my Skill and Judgment, execute and perform all such Matters and Things as, according to the Nature and Duty of my Office and Employment, ought to be done by me, for carrying into Execution an Act *for dividing, allotting, and inclosing the Common Fields, Common Woods, Common Downs, and other Commonable Places in the Manor and Parish of* Crawley *in the County of* Southampton, *and* . . . [relates to Bishop's Sutton]; and that without Favour or Affection, Prejudice or Malice to any Person or Persons "whomsoever."

"So help me GOD."

And the said Oath so taken and subscribed shall be inrolled with the Award or Instrument hereinafter directed to be made by the said Commissioners.

Power to enter to value and survey. And be it further Enacted, That the said Commissioners for their respective Parishes, and their Successors, and every or any of them, and all Persons appointed or to be appointed to make such Valuations and Surveys respectively as aforesaid, their Assistants and Servants, may, and they are hereby empowered and authorized, from Time to Time, as often as shall be necessary for the Purposes aforesaid, to enter into and upon the Premises directed and intended by this Act to be valued and surveyed respectively as aforesaid, every or any Part or Parts thereof, without any Hindrance or Molestation whatsoever.

Commissioners to determine Differences. And be it further Enacted, That if any Difference or Dispute shall arise between the Proprietors or Persons interested in the said intended Divisions and Allotments, or any of them, touching or concerning their respective Shares, Rights, or Properties of or in the said Common Fields, Common Woods, Common Downs, Common Meadows, Waste Lands, and other Commonable Places, or any of them, or any Part thereof, it shall and may be lawful to and for the said Commissioners respectively, and their Successors, and they are hereby authorized, to examine Witnesses upon Oath, (which Oath they or any One of them are or is hereby empowered to administer,) and thereupon, or upon a View, Evidence, or other Satisfaction, to hear and finally determine the same; and such Determination or Determinations shall be binding and conclusive to the Parties and all other Persons interested therein.

Not to extend to Titles. Provided always, That nothing herein contained shall authorize the said Commissioners, or either of them, in their respective Parishes, to determine any Difference or Dispute which shall arise touching the Title of any Person or Persons in or to any Part of the Lands to be allotted by virtue of this Act, for which the Parties may commence and prosecute such Suits and Remedies as they shall be advised and think proper; but no such Difference or Dispute shall impede or delay the said respective Commissioners, or any of them, in the Execution of the Powers vested in them by this Act; but the Division and Inclosure by this Act directed to be made shall be proceeded in, notwithstanding any such Difference or Suit: And in case of any such Difference or Suit, the said Commissioners in their respective Parishes shall set out the Land which shall be allotted in lieu of such disputed or litigated Property, so that it may be distinguished from any other Lands, and may be had and taken by the Person or Persons who, upon the Determination of such Difference or Suit, shall become entitled to the same.

Roads. And be it further Enacted, That the said Commissioners shall, in their respective Parishes, and they are hereby severally required, by Stakes, or other proper Marks, to set out or appoint convenient Public and Private Roads and Ways, and also such Ditches, Mounds, Fences, Common Drains, and Common Sewers, Watercourses, Banks, Bridges, Gates, and Stiles, in, through, and over or by the Sides of the said New Inclosures or Allotments to be made by virtue of this Act, in such Directions and Situations as the said respective Commissioners, so setting out and appointing the same, shall think proper; provided all new Public Carriage Roads, which shall be set out and appointed by the said Commissioners respectively as aforesaid, shall be and remain Forty Feet Broad at the least between the Ditches, except Bridle Roads and Footways; and that it shall not be lawful for any Person to erect any Gate across any of the said Roads, or to plant any Trees in or near the Hedges on the Sides of any of the said Roads, at a less Distance from each other than Fifty Yards; and the said respective Commissioners, after they shall have ascertained the said Public and Bridle Roads and Footways, and caused the same to be marked and staked out, shall give, or cause to be given, Six Days Notice at least, to be affixed on the principal Doors of the several Parish Churches of *Crawley* and *Bishops Sutton* aforesaid, and inserted in the *Salisbury and Winchester Journal*, and *Hampshire Chronicle*, (if such Papers are then circulated,) of the Day or Days by them appointed to receive any Objections that may be made to any Public and Bridle Roads and Footways so set out or omitted to be set out and ascertained in pursuance of this Act; and the said Objections, and the Names of the Persons making the same, Together with the Resolutions of the said several Commissioners thereupon, shall be entered in the Minutes of the Proceedings of the said several Commissioners, in Books to be kept for that Purpose, and such Resolutions shall be binding and conclusive to all Parties concerned; and such Public Bridle Roads shall, at all Times for ever thereafter, be repaired and amended by and at the Expence of the Inhabitants and Occupiers of Land in the said Parishes respectively, in like Manner as the Public Roads in the said Parishes are or ought by Law to be repaired; and that all Private Roads and Footways to be set out by the said Commissioners in pursuance of this Act, shall be of such Breadth, and be made and repaired at the Expence of such of the said Proprietors, and in such Manner as the said respective Commissioners shall in that Behalf order, direct, and appoint; and that it shall not be lawful for any Person, after the said Public and Bridle Roads and Footways shall be so set out, and after the hearing and determining of Objections (if any shall be made) to the Public and Bridle Roads and Footways so to be set out as aforesaid, to use or claim the Use of any other Roads or Ways in, to, through, or over the Fields, Woods, Downs, and Grounds hereby intended to be divided and inclosed, or any Part thereof, either on Foot or with Horses, Cattle, Carts, or Carriages; and that all former Roads and Ways, or so much of them as shall not be set out and appointed as aforesaid, shall be deemed Part of the Lands and Grounds to be divided and inclosed by virtue of this Act, and shall be allotted and divided accordingly as Part thereof; and the Herbage growing and renewing in and upon the Roads and Ways so to be set out or appointed as aforesaid, shall be and for ever remain to and for the Use and Benefit of such of the Proprietors respectively, whose Allotments or Lands shall be next or adjoining to the said Roads and Ways, in such Manner and in such Shares or Proportions as the said Commissioners shall, by their respective Awards, direct or appoint.

Turnpike Roads not to be altered. Provided always, That nothing herein contained shall authorize or empower the said Commissioners, or any of them, to alter, divert, or turn any Turnpike Road or Roads leading through the said Parishes respectively, or any Part of them.

Commissioners to appoint Surveyors for forming, etc., Public Carriage Roads. And be it further Enacted, That the said Commissioners for the said respective Parishes may, and they are hereby authorized and required, within Three Calendar Months next after the passing of this Act, to appoint One or more Surveyor or Surveyors in each of the said Parishes of *Crawley* and *Bishops Sutton*, (with such Salary as to them shall seem proper and requisite to be paid to such Surveyor or Surveyors,) for the first forming and putting into good and sufficient Repair the Public Carriage Roads in, upon, and over any Part of the said Lands and Grounds; and the Expence of such Salary, and of such first forming and repairing, which shall be incurred over and above the Statute Duty, shall be raised and paid in the same Manner as the Costs and Charges of surveying, admeasuring, dividing, and allotting the said Lands and Grounds, and of the Awards, are hereinafter directed to be raised and paid, to the Intent that the Inhabitants of the said Parishes of *Crawley* and *Bishops Sutton* (not being Proprietors or Owners of such

Lands and Grounds) may not be charged or burthened with any Part of the Costs of first forming, making, and repairing such Public Highways, (other than the Statute Duty, a Proportion whereof the said Surveyor or Surveyors, so to be appointed as aforesaid, is and are hereby authorized and required to call out and employ on such Public Highways so to be set out and appointed,) until the same Roads shall, by the said Surveyor and Surveyors respectively, so to be appointed as aforesaid, be certified before the Justices of the Peace for the said County of *Southampton*, at their General Quarter Sessions, to be completely formed and made good; and that such Public Highways shall, from the delivering such Certificate or Certificates to the said Justices, and the severally allowing and confirming the same by them, be repaired and kept in Repair in such Manner as the Public Highways in the several Parishes aforesaid are by Law required and directed to be kept in Repair; which Certificate or Certificates the said Surveyor and Surveyors respectively, so to be appointed as aforesaid, shall, and he or they is or are hereby authorized and required, within Two Years from the signing the respective Awards or Instruments hereinafter mentioned, to deliver to the said Justices, at their Quarter Sessions, or give sufficient Reason to the Satisfaction of the said Justices for a further Allowance of Time, (not exceeding One other Year,) which such Justices are hereby empowered to allow, for delivering the same, under the Penalty of Ten Pounds, to be raised and levied by Distress and Sale of the Goods and Chattels of such Surveyor or Surveyors making Default as aforesaid.

Soil of the Public Roads Vested in the Lord of the Manor. And be it further Enacted, That the Right of the Soil of all the Public Roads so to be set out or appointed as aforesaid, which shall be directed by the said Commissioners to be laned or fenced off, shall be, and the same is hereby vested in the said several Lords of the said respective Manors of *Crawley*, *Bishops Sutton*, *Ropley*, and *Sutton Westcourt*, otherwise *Westercourt*, aforesaid.

Allotment to the Lord as Owner of the Soil. And be it further Enacted, That the said Commissioners appointed for the said Manor and Parish of *Crawley*, shall ascertain the Value of One Fiftieth Part, Quantity, Quality, and Situation considered, of all the said Commons, Downs, and Waste Grounds in *Crawley*, and also of One Thirtieth Part of the said Common Wood Lands in *Crawley* aforesaid, hereby directed to be divided, allotted, and inclosed; and shall and do set out and allot unto the said Lord Bishop, and his Successors, Lords of the said Manor of *Crawley*, (exclusive of all other Allotments to the said Lord Bishop for and in respect of his, or his Lessees, Common Rights or other Property,) such Parcel or Parcels of Land, (Quantity, Quality, and Situation considered,) as shall in the Judgment of the said Commissioners be equal in Value to One Fiftieth Part of the said Commons, Downs, and Waste Grounds, and also One Thirtieth Part of the said Common Wood Lands hereby intended to be inclosed, after setting out the Public Highways, in lieu of and as a Compensation for the Right and Interest of the said Lord Bishop and his Successors in and to the Soil of the said Commons, Common Woods, Downs, and Waste Grounds in *Crawley* aforesaid, and so as the same be put and placed as near to the Mansion House now occupied by the said *Richard Meyler*, as Lessee under the said Lord Bishop, as conveniently may be; which Allotment when so made, the said Lord Bishop and his Successors shall have Power to lease for Three Lives.

Allotment to the Rector, etc. And be it further Enacted, That the said Commissioners appointed for the said Manor and Parish of *Crawley* (after they shall have set out and allotted to the said Lord Bishop such certain Parts and Parcels as aforesaid, in respect of his Right of Soil) shall, and they are hereby authorized and required to set out and allot unto and for the Reverend *Matthew Woodford* and his Successors, Rectors of *Crawley* aforesaid, so much and such Parts of the said Common Fields and Grounds hereby directed to be divided, allotted, and inclosed as aforesaid, as (Quantity, Quality, and Situation considered) shall, in the Judgment of the said Commissioners, be deemed a full Equivalent and adequate Compensation for all the Glebe Lands lying within or Parcel of the said Common Fields and Commons within the said Parish of *Crawley;* and that such Allotment and Allotments to be made to the said *Matthew Woodford* and his Successors as aforesaid, in lieu of the Glebe and other Rectorial Lands there, shall be laid as near as conveniently may be to the Rectorial House and Buildings of the said *Matthew Woodford* in *Crawley* aforesaid; and that the Expence of inclosing, hedging, ditching, and Ring-fencing the Allotment or Allotments to be made to the Rector of *Crawley* aforesaid, shall be paid and defrayed by and out of the Monies directed to be raised for defraying the Expenses of obtaining and passing this Act, and putting the same in Execution; and after the making of the said Inclosures, and Hedges, Ditches and Fences, to the Allotment or Allotments of the said Rector, all such Hedges, Ditches, and Fences shall for ever thereafter be kept in Repair by the Owner or Owners of the adjoining Allotment or Allotments, in such Shares and Proportions as the said Commissioners by their General Award shall direct: And in case the Hedges, Ditches, and Fences shall not from Time to Time be properly maintained and kept in Repair, it shall and may be lawful to and for the said Rector, and his Successors, to appeal to any One Justice of the Peace of the said County, who is hereby authorized and empowered to hear and determine the same, whose Determination therein shall be final and conclusive.

General Allotments to be made in Crawley. And be it further Enacted, That the said Commissioners for the said Manor and Parish of *Crawley*, and their Successors, shall set out, divide, assign, allot, and award all the Residue and Remainder of the said Common Fields, Common Woods, Common Downs, and other Commonable Places so intended to be divided, allotted, and inclosed as aforesaid in the said Parish, unto and amongst the several Owners, Proprietors, and Lessees thereof, and other Persons who, at the Time of making such Division and Allotment as aforesaid, shall be entitled to and interested in the same, in Proportion to their respective Shares, Rights, and Properties therein at the Time of making their Award hereinafter directed to be made, having due Regard to the Quality, Situation, and Convenience, as well as the Quantity, of the Lands to be allotted as aforesaid; which said Allotments so to be made by virtue of this Act shall be laid as near and contiguous to the respective Estates of the several Persons entitled to the same as conveniently may be, and shall be in full Bar of and Compensation for their several Rights and Interests in and upon the said Common Fields, Common Woods, Common Downs, and other Commonable Places; but the Powers so vested in the said Commissioners, of setting out, allotting, and awarding the said Common Fields, Common Woods, Common Downs, and other Commonable Places in the said Parish of *Crawley*, shall not extend to, or take Effect in, or upon, any Part of the said Manor Farm, so held by the said *Richard Meyler*, except in a certain Field called *Hook*, and a certain Piece of Land called *Hundred Acres*, Parcel of the said Manor Farm, of which Eighty Acres, lying on the South Side thereof, may be allotted and given in lieu of Lands to be allotted to the said Manor Farm; and also except such Quantity of Land, lying on the South Side of certain Fields called *Winyard*, *Hamshill*, and *Crofte's Furlong*, as the said Commissioners shall judge expedient and think proper to be allotted in lieu of and be a full Recompence and Satisfaction for the Lands intended to be allotted out of the Common Fields, Common Woods, Common Downs, and other Commonable Places to the said Manor Farm of *Crawley* aforesaid. . . . [relates to Bishop's Sutton].

Allotments to be fenced. And be it further Enacted, That the said several Allotments, or such and so many, and such Part and Parts of them as the said Commissioners in their respective Parishes shall think fit so to order, shall be Ring-fenced by the Owners thereof, excepting the Warden and Scholars, Clerks of *Winchester* College, [and another] who are exempted from all Expences whatever, either with or without Quicksets, or sufficient Stake Hedges, within such Time, and in such

Manner and Proportions, as the said Commissioners for their respective Parishes shall, by their Award, direct and appoint; and if any Person shall neglect or refuse to make such Fences, according to the Directions of the said Commissioners, then it shall be lawful for any Person interested in the Lands next adjoining to such Unfenced Lands, to exhibit a Complaint in Writing against the Person who ought to have fenced the same, before any Justice of the Peace for the said County of *Southampton*, who shall inquire into the Nature of the Complaint, and examine Witnesses upon Oath, (which Oath such Justice is hereby empowered to administer,) and shall and may, if he shall see Cause, direct the Person exhibiting such Complaint, to make such Fences, and when the same shall be so made, such Justice shall ascertain the Expence thereof, and by Warrant under his Hand and Seal, directed to any Person whomsoever, cause the said Expence to be levied by Distress and Sale of the Goods and Chattels of the Person so neglecting or refusing as aforesaid, rendering the Overplus (if any) to the Owner of such Goods and Chattels, after deducting the Costs and Charges of such Distress and Sale.

Provided always, That it shall be lawful for any of the said Owners, after their Allotments shall have been staked out, and before the signing of the said Award or Awards, with the Consent of the said Commissioners in Writing, to Ring-fence their Allotments, or any Parts thereof, in such Manner as the said Commissioners in their respective Parishes shall think proper.

Allotments to be accepted. And be it further Enacted, That all and every Person and Persons to whom any Allotment or Allotments shall be made by virtue or in pursuance of this Act, shall, and they are hereby required to accept the same, within Three Calendar Months next after the Date and Execution of the Award of the said Commissioners for the Parish in which the same shall be situate, and also, at his, her, or their own respective Costs and Charges, to mark, ascertain, and perpetuate the several and respective Boundaries thereof, within such Time and in such Manner as the said Commissioners respectively shall in and by their said Award order or direct; and in case any Person or Persons entitled to such Allotment or Allotments shall neglect or refuse to accept, inclose, and fence in the same as aforesaid, within the several and respective Times before-mentioned, then the said Commissioners shall cause such Allotment or Allotments to be inclosed, hedged, ditched, or fenced as they shall think proper; and the Expences thereof, in case the Person or Persons entitled to such Allotment or Allotments shall refuse or neglect to pay the same on Demand, shall be levied and raised by the said Commissioners in Manner hereinafter mentioned with respect to the Expences of making the said several Inclosures.

Allotments to be accepted by Guardians etc. Provided also, And be it further Enacted, That the respective Husbands, Guardians, Trustees, or Committees, or Persons acting as Guardians or Trustees or Attornies of or for any Person or Persons being under Coverture, Minors, beyond the Seas, or Lunatics, or otherwise incapable by Law to accept such Allotments so to be made as aforesaid, shall be, and they are hereby enabled and required to accept thereof, for the Use of such Person or Persons so incapacitated as aforesaid.

Non-acceptance not to bar Infants. Provided nevertheless, That the Non-claim or Non-acceptance of any Guardian, Husband, Trustee, Committee, or Attorney, shall not exclude or in anywise prejudice any Person or Persons under any such Disability or Incapacity, who shall accept such Allotments within Six Calendar Months after such Disability or Incapacity shall be removed, nor of any Person or Persons who shall be entitled as Heir or in Remainder or Reversion after the Death of any Person dying under such Disability or Incapacity, who shall claim within Six Calendar Months next after his, her, or their Right, Title, or Interest shall have, or shall be known to him, her, or them to have, descended or accrued.

Commissioners to direct the Course of Husbandry. And be it further Enacted, That in the mean Time and until such Divisions and Allotments shall be made as aforesaid, all the Pasture, Tillage, and other Lands lying in the said Common Fields hereby directed to be divided, inclosed, and allotted as aforesaid, shall be cropped and sown by the respective Owners or Occupiers thereof, with such Sort of Corn, Grain, Turnips, or Grass Seeds, and in such Proportions, and shall be kept, ordered, and continued in such Course of Husbandry, as the said Commissioners for their respective Parishes, and their Successors, shall, by any Writing or Writings under their Hands in that Behalf, order or appoint, any Usage or Custom to the contrary thereof notwithstanding.

Commissioners may extinguish Right of Common. And be it further Enacted, That the said Commissioners for the said respective Parishes, and their Successors, may at any Time or Times, by Notice in Writing to be affixed on the principal Door of the Parish Churches of *Crawley* and *Bishops Sutton* aforesaid, as the Case may require, extinguish all or any Parts of the Rights of Common in, over, and upon the said Lands to be inclosed in such Parishes, or either of them, and that from thenceforth all such Rights of Common shall cease and be for ever extinguished.

Power to make exchanges. And, for the more convenient situation and Disposition of the several Farms, Lands, and Estates within the said Manor and Parish of *Crawley*, and Parish of *Bishops Sutton* aforesaid, Be it further Enacted, That it shall be lawful to and for all or any of the Owners or Proprietors of any Messuages, Lands, Tenements, or Hereditaments, New Allotments, or Old Inclosures, within the said Parish of *Crawley*, and Parish of *Bishops Sutton* aforesaid, being Tenants in Tail, or for Life, or by Copy of Court Roll, or for a Term of Years determinable on Lives, or for any Term of Years at a small Annual Quit Rent, and also for Husbands, Guardians, Trustees, Committees, or Attornies acting for and on Behalf of any such Owners or Proprietors respectively, who are under Coverture, Minors, Lunatics, or beyond Seas, or under any other legal Disability, and also for all Bodies Politic and Corporate, being such Owners or Proprietors, to exchange all or any of their said Messuages, Buildings, Lands, Tenements, or other Hereditaments, New Allotments, or Old Inclosures, within the same Parishes, so that all such Exchanges be made by and with the Consent and Approbation of the said Commissioners for the respective Parishes of *Crawley* and *Bishops Sutton* aforesaid, and their Successors, and be ascertained, specified, and declared in their said Award or Instrument, or in some other Deed or Instrument under their Hands and Seals, to be inrolled in like Manner as the said Award; and all such Exchanges so to be made shall be good, valid, and effectual in Law, to all Intents and Purposes whatsoever, notwithstanding the Interest of the Persons exchanging, in the Lands or Estates to be respectively exchanged as aforesaid, may be of a Nature different from each other, and notwithstanding the Want of sufficient Title in the exchanging Parties, or any Will, Settlement, or Limitation affecting the Premises so to be exchanged: Provided always, That no such Exchange shall be made by or on the Behalf of any Owner or Proprietor holding by Copy of Court Roll, Lease or Leases for One or more Life or Lives, of any of the Messuages, Buildings, Lands, Tenements, and Hereditaments comprised in such Leases or Copies respectively, without the Consent in Writing of the Person or Persons, Bodies Politic or Corporate, under whom the same Premises shall be so held for the Time being; and that the Charges attending such Exchanges shall be paid at the joint Expences of the Parties concerned therein; and that no Exchange shall be made of any of the Messuages, Lands, Tenements, and Hereditaments to the said Manor Farm of *Crawley* other than is before mentioned, or by the Rector of *Crawley*, or by the Vicar of *Bishops Sutton*, or their Successors, by virtue of this Act, without the Consent and Approbation of the Lord Bishop of *Winchester* for the Time being.

Allotments and Exchanges to be to the same Uses as former Estates were held for. And be it further Enacted, That all and singular the Lands and other the Premises which shall be so respectively allotted or exchanged under or by virtue of this Act, shall, immediately after the making such Allotments and Exchanges, be, remain, and enure, and the several Persons to whom the same shall be allotted or given in exchange as aforesaid, shall from thenceforth stand and be seised thereof and interested therein, to, for, and upon such and the same Estates, Uses, Trusts, and Purposes, and under and subject to the same Wills, Settlements, Limitations, Powers, Remainders, Charges, and Incumbrances, and shall be of such and the same Tenures, and held by such and the same Rents, Heriots, and other Services as the several and respective Messuages, Lands, Tenements, Old Inclosures, New Allotments, and other Hereditaments, in lieu or in respect whereof such Allotments and Exchanges shall be respectively made as aforesaid, now are, or might, would, or ought to have been held for, subject or liable to have been charged with or affected by, in case the same had remained unallotted, uninclosed, and unexchanged, or this Act had not been made.

Liberty to take away Trees. And be it further Enacted, That in case any Lands or Grounds whereon any Trees, Thorns, Hedges, Bushes, or Shrubs shall, at the Time of making such Allotments, be standing, growing, or being, shall be allotted to any Person or Persons other than such as was or were the Proprietor or Proprietors, Owner or Owners thereof at or immediately before such Allotments were made, then it shall and may be lawful for such former Owners or Proprietors respectively, at any seasonable Time or Times to be appointed by the said Commissioners respectively after such Allotments shall be made, to enter upon the Lands and Grounds upon which such Trees, Thorns, Hedges, Bushes, or Shrubs shall be standing, to cut down and carry away the same.

Provided nevertheless, That no Hedges or Trees shall be cut down, unless the Owners thereof shall first have Licence under the Hands of the said Commissioners so to do; and in case the said respective Commissioners shall think it proper that any such Trees, Thorns, Hedges, Bushes, or Shrubs shall be left standing and remaining on any such Allotment or Allotments, that then they shall order and direct the same accordingly; and the Person or Persons to whom such Allotment or Allotments shall be made, on which such Trees, Thorns, Hedges, Bushes, or Shrubs shall be standing or being, shall pay for the same as the said Commissioners acting for their respective Parishes shall direct, and in Default of such Payment, the same to be recovered in like Manner as the Costs and Expences of making the said Awards and Allotments are hereby directed to be recovered; and if upon making such Allotment or Allotments, the said respective Commissioners shall think it convenient to order any Person or Persons to whom such Allotments shall be made, to make a greater or less Proportion of the Fences and

Boundaries of the same than his, her, or their due and proportionable Part of such Fences, then the said Commissioners respectively may regulate and equalize the Proportion of the Expence of making the same, by ordering and directing the Person or Persons who shall make a less Part of such Fences and Boundaries than his, her, or their just Share and Proportion, to pay unto the Person or Persons who shall make a greater Part of such Fences and Boundaries, so much Money as in the Judgment of the said Commissioners respectively shall be a Satisfaction and Compensation to such Person or Persons making more than a just and due Proportion of such Fences against his, her, or their Allotment or Allotments respectively, the same Money to be recovered in like Manner as the Costs and Expences of obtaining this Act and carrying the same into Execution are hereby directed to be recovered.

Allotment to be made for Services to be done by the Copyhold Tenants of Crawley. And whereas there are certain Dues and Services to be paid, done, and performed by the respective Copyhold Tenants of the said Manor and Parish of *Crawley*, to the Manor Farm aforesaid, so held by the said *Richard Meyler*, which may be estimated at the Rate of Twelve Pounds and Twelve Shillings *per Annum*, or thereabouts, on an Average, to be taken of the said Dues and Services (exclusive of the Quit Rents and other Customary Payments due and payable to the said Lord Bishop, Lord of the said Manor, by the said Copyhold Tenants): And whereas it is proposed, that the said Dues and Services shall be annulled, and in lieu thereof, a certain Allotment of the said Common Fields to be made and appropriated to and for the Uses of the Owner of the said Manor Farm: Be it Enacted therefore, That the Amount of the Value of the said Dues and Services shall be valued and ascertained by the said Commissioners acting for the said Manor and Parish of *Crawley*, and in lieu thereof, a certain Proportion or Allotment of the said Common Fields, Downs, or other Commonable Places within the said Manor and Parish of *Crawley*, shall be made and appropriated to the said Manor Farm, and be held and enjoyed therewith, so that the Estates liable to pay and perform the said Dues and Services shall be entirely free and discharged from the same; and the said Allotments shall, in lieu thereof, be held and enjoyed by the respective Owner or Occupiers of the said Farm, and such Allotment shall be held and enjoyed by the said *Richard Meyler* or his Lessee, as appendant or appurtenant to the same, and be put and placed, as near as Conveniency will admit, to the said Mansion House of the said *Richard Meyler*, being Part of the said Manor Farm.

Power to Commissioners to divert Old Roads in Crawley. And be it further Enacted, That in case it shall appear to the said Commissioners of the said Parish of *Crawley*, from the Certificate of the Rector and

Churchwardens of the Said Parish, that there are any Public Highways, Bridle Roads, or Footways in, through, over, or on the Sides of any of the Old Inclosed Lands within the said Parish of *Crawley*, which may be diverted and turned, without Inconvenience to the Public, into any other Public Highways, Bridle Roads, or Footways, or be diverted and turned, so as to make the same more convenient to the Public, and the said Commissioners shall approve of the same; that then and in such Case it shall be lawful for the said Commissioners and their Successors, in and by their said Award, to be made as hereinafter is directed, to order and direct such Public Highways, Bridle Roads, and Footways to be altered and turned in such Manner as the said Commissioners shall (agreeable to the Intent and Meaning of such Certificate) think proper and reasonable.

Award. And be it further Enacted, That the said Commissioners for the Manor and Parish of *Crawley* shall, as soon as conveniently may be after they shall have completed and finished the Allotments and Exchanges of the said Common Fields, Common Woods, Common Downs, and other Commonable Places in the Manor and Parish of *Crawley* aforesaid, hereby directed and intended to be divided, allotted or exchanged as aforesaid, pursuant to the Purport and Directions of this Act, form and draw up, or cause to be formed and drawn up, an Award or Instrument in Writing, for describing and comprising the same; and the said Commissioners for the said Parish of *Bishops Sutton* . . . [relates to Bishop's Sutton]; and which said Awards or Instruments shall severally express the Quantity in Statute Measure of Acres, Roads, and Perches, contained in the said Common Fields, Common Woods, Common Downs, Common Meadows, Waste Lands, and other Commonable Places, and the Quantity of each and every Part and Parcel thereof, assigned, or allotted, or given in Exchange to and for each of the Proprietors, and the Situation, Abuttals, and Boundaries of the same respectively, and shall also contain proper Orders and Directions for fencing and mounding the said several Allotments, and for keeping the said Mounds and Fences in Repair, and also a Description of the Roads, Ways, and Footpaths to be set out and appointed by the said Commissioners respectively, in, over, and through the said Premises, and shall likewise express and contain such other Orders, Regulations, and Determinations as the said Commissioners shall think proper and necessary to be inserted therein, conformable to the Tenor and Purport of this Act; and which said respective Awards or Instruments, with Plans of the same to be annexed thereto, shall be fairly ingrossed or written on Parchment, and signed and sealed by the said respective Commissioners, and shall, within Twelve Calendar Months next after the same shall be so signed and sealed as aforesaid, be severally inrolled among the Court Rolls of the Lord Bishop of *Winchester* in the several Manors of *Crawley* and *Bishops Sutton* aforesaid, and be deposited in the Office of the Clerk of the Peace of the County of *Southampton;* and the said Clerk of the Peace, or his Deputy, is hereby required to receive and keep the same among the Records of the said County, for which he shall demand or receive no greater Fee than Six Shillings and Eight Pence; and the said Awards, or any Copy thereof, or of any Part thereof, signed by the said Clerk of the Peace, or his Deputy, or by the said Commissioners respectively, purporting the Truth of such Copy, shall be admitted and allowed as Evidence in all Courts whatsoever; and the said Clerk of the Peace, or his Deputy, shall be entitled to receive, for every such Copy made at his Office, the Sum of Two Pence *per* Sheet, reckoning Seventy-two Words to each Sheet; and the said Clerk of the Peace, or his Deputy, shall permit and suffer any Person or Persons whomsoever, at any seasonable Time or Times, to inspect and peruse the said Awards, paying for every such Inspection and Perusal One Shilling and no more; and the said Awards or Instruments, so executed as aforesaid, shall be binding and conclusive upon all Parties interested in the said Inclosures.

Proprietors dying not to Impede the Execution of this Act. And be it further Enacted, That if any of the Proprietors or Persons interested in the said several intended Divisions and Inclosures shall happen to die before the making of the Allotments, or the Execution of the said respective Awards, the Powers and Authorities in this Act contained shall not be determined or suspended; but the Share or Shares in the Premises of the Party or Parties respectively so dying shall be allotted to the Person or Persons who shall, at the Time of making the Allotments, appear to the said respective Commissioners to be in the Possession of or entitled to the same; and such Person or Persons shall be liable to the Charges and Expences and other the Conditions of this Act as aforesaid; and the said Commissioners in their respective Parishes, and their Successors, shall and may proceed to execute the Powers and Authorities given to them by this Act, in such Manner as they might have done in case no such Death had happened.

No former Estate to be affected. Provided always, and be it further Enacted, That nothing in this Act contained shall be deemed, adjudged, or taken to revoke, make void, alter, or annul any Will or Settlement, or to prejudice any Person having or claiming any Jointure, Dower, Portion, Debt, or Incumbrance out of, upon, or affecting any of the Lands intended to be inclosed as aforesaid, or the Lands, Tenements, or Hereditaments which shall be exchanged in pursuance of this Act, or any Part thereof respectively, but the several Lands, Tenements, and Hereditaments so to be inclosed or exchanged shall, from and immediately after the making such Allotments or Exchanges, be, remain, and endure to the several Persons to whom the same shall be allotted or given in Exchange as aforesaid; and such persons shall from thenceforth stand and be seised thereof to such and the same Uses, and subject to such and the same Wills, Settlements, Limitations, Remainders, Charges, and Incumbrances as the several Lands, Tenements, or Hereditaments in lieu whereof such Allotments or Exchanges shall be made, now are, or would have been subject or liable to be charged with or affected by, in case the same had remained uninclosed or unexchanged, or this Act had not been made.

Leases to be void in Crawley, except New Barn Farm. And be it further Enacted, That all and every Lease and Leases now subsisting at Rack Rent of all or any Part of the Lands, Tenements, or Hereditaments to be inclosed or exchanged in pursuance of this Act within the said Parish and Manor of *Crawley*, and all other Agreements for any Time or Term therein, shall, immediately upon such Allotments or Exchanges being made, cease, determine, and be utterly void, and the respective Lessees or Tenants thereof shall have and receive of the respective Owners and Proprietors of such Lands, Tenements, or Hereditaments, such Satisfaction as the said respective Commissioners shall ascertain as reasonable to be paid to such Lessee or Lessees, Tenant or Tenants, on Account thereof, as an Equivalent for the same, save and except one Lease or Agreement made to *Richard Bailey* to hold the Manor Farm of *Crawley* aforesaid, as Tenant to the said *Richard Meyler;* but the said *Richard Bailey* shall be at liberty, and is hereby authorized and empowered to hold and enjoy such Lands and Grounds as shall be allotted in lieu of his former Holding, for and during such Time or Term of Years as he then had in such former Holding then to come and unexpired, with the full Benefit and Advantage attending the same, under the same Yearly Rents, Covenants, Conditions, and Agreements, as are expressly mentioned and contained in the said Lease. . . . [Relates to Bishop's Sutton.]

Expences of the Act. And be it further Enacted, That all the Charges and Expences incident to and attending the obtaining and passing this Act, and of the surveying, admeasuring, planning, valuing, dividing, and allotting of the Lands and Grounds hereby intended to be divided and allotted as aforesaid, and all other Expences of carrying this Act into Execution, (except in such Cases as are otherwise hereby provided,) shall be borne and paid by all and every the Owners and Proprietors of Lands and Grounds hereby directed to be divided and inclosed, to whom Allotments shall respectively be made as aforesaid, in such Proportions, and at such Time or Times, and to such Person or Persons, as the said Commissioners acting both for the Parishes of

Crawley and *Bishops Sutton* shall, by Writing under their Hands, order and direct: and in case any Person shall refuse or neglect to pay his or her Proportion of such Charges and Expences, according to such Directions of the said Commissioners, then the said Commissioners shall and may, and they are hereby authorized, by Warrant under their Hands and Seals directed to any Person or Persons, to cause the same to be levied by Distress and Sale of the Goods and Chattels of the Person neglecting or refusing to pay as aforesaid, rendering the Overplus (if any) to the Owners of such Goods and Chattels, after deducting the Costs and Charges of making such Distress and Sale; and in case no sufficient Distress can be had or taken as aforesaid, it shall and may be lawful to and for the said Commissioners, by Writing under their Hands and Seals, to authorize any Person to enter into and upon the Land to be allotted to the Person refusing to pay as aforesaid, and to have and receive the Rents and Profits thereof, until thereby his or her Proportion of the said Costs and Charges, and also the Costs and Charges attending such Entry upon and Receipt of the said Rents and Profits, shall be fully paid: Provided always, That nothing herein contained shall extend to charge the said Lord Bishop or *Matthew Woodford*, or their Successors, with any Part of the said Costs, Charges, or Expences for or in respect of their said respective Allotments, Part of the said Common Fields, Common Woods, Common Downs, and Waste Grounds so to be made to the said Lord Bishop and *Matthew Woodford* respectively by virtue of this Act; but the Share and Proportion of the said Expences in respect to the said Manor Farm so held by Lease of the said Lord Bishop, shall be paid and borne by the said *Richard Meyler;* and in respect of the other Lands and Grounds so to be inclosed by virtue of this Act, the same shall be charged upon, borne and defrayed by the respective Owners and Proprietors of such Lands as herein is mentioned and directed. . . . [Relates to Bishop's Sutton.]

Proprietors advancing to be repaid with Interest. And be it further Enacted, That if any of the Owners or Proprietors of Lands, or any other Person or Persons interested in the said Lands and Grounds hereby intended to be divided and inclosed as aforesaid, shall advance any Sum or Sums of Money for the Purpose of defraying the Expences of obtaining and passing this Act, or of carrying the same into Execution, every such Owner and Proprietor shall be repaid the same, with Interest after the Rate of Five Pounds *per Centum per Annum*, out of the First Monies that shall be raised for defraying the Expences by virtue of this Act: Provided always, That every Owner or Proprietor who shall attend any Meeting to be held in pursuance of this Act, shall bear and pay his or her own Expence at such Meeting.

Power of borrowing Money. And be it further Enacted, That it shall be lawful to and for the several Owners and Proprietors of the

Lands and Grounds to be allotted and divided as aforesaid, in the said respective Parishes of *Crawley* and *Bishops Sutton*, and to and for the Husbands, Guardians, Trustees, Committees, or Executors in Trust of any of the Owners and Proprietors of the said Allotments, being Femes Covert, Minors, Lunatics, or under any other Disability, and Attornies lawfully constituted for and on the Behalf of Persons beyond the Seas, and for any of the said Owners and Proprietors, being Tenants in Tail or for Life or Lives, or for any Term or Terms of Years at small Rents, or upon any other Contingency, and also to and for the Trustees of any Poor Lands, School Lands, or Charity Lands, (other than and except the Rector of *Crawley* and the Vicar of *Bishops Sutton*,) to whom any Allotments shall be made in pursuance of this Act, and to and for every of them respectively for the Time being, to charge the said Allotments with such Sum and Sums of Money as the said Commissioners shall, by their said Award, or any other Writing under their Hands and Seals, adjudge necessary to pay and defray the respective Charges and Expences incident to and attending the obtaining this Act, and carrying the same into execution, and of making Interior or Sub-division Ditches, Mounds, and Fences within the said Allotments, so that such Money do not exceed Twenty Shillings an Acre; the same to be paid to such Person or Persons, and to be applied in such Manner, as the said Commissioners respectively shall direct; and for securing the Repayment of such Money, with Interest, to grant, mortgage, or demise the Lands so to be charged unto the Person or Persons who shall advance such Money, his or her Executors, so as in every such Grant, Mortgage, or Demise, to be made by any Persons, being Tenants in Tail, or for Life or Lives only, or for any Term or Terms of Years at small Rents, or upon other Contingency as aforesaid, there be contained a Proviso or Condition to discharge and pay One Twentieth Part of the Principal Money Yearly, and likewise to pay and keep down the Interest of the Money to be thereby secured during his or her Life or other Estate in the Premises, so that no Person afterwards becoming entitled to the Premises shall be liable to pay any larger Arrear of Interest than for One Year preceding the Time that the Title to such Possession shall accrue and commence; and every Charge, Grant, Mortgage, and Demise to be made as aforesaid, shall be valid and effectual in the Law, notwithstanding any Want of Title, or any Settlement, Will, Trust, Limitation, or Incumbrance affecting such Lands, or any Part thereof, then in being, or capable of taking Effect to the contrary.

Rector of Crawley and Vicar of Sutton may lease their Allotments. And be it further Enacted, That it shall and may be lawful to and for the said Rector of *Crawley* and the said Vicar of *Bishops Sutton*, and their Successors, by and with the Consent and Approbation of the Lord Bishop of *Winchester* for the Time being, by any Writing or Writings under his Hand and Seal, to lease or demise all or any Part or Parts of the Allotment and Allotments to be set out to and for the said Rector and Vicar respectively, or their Successors, Rectors and Vicars as aforesaid, to any Person or Persons, for any Term or Terms not exceeding Twenty-one Years, to commence from the Date of the said Award or Awards respectively, at the best and most improved Rent or Rents, and without taking any Fine or Fines for the same, and so as no such Lease or Leases be made without Impeachment of Waste, and so as the Lessee or Lessees to whom such Lease and Leases shall be made, shall be obliged Yearly and every Year to spend, spread, and consume in an husbandlike Manner, upon the Premises so to be demised respectively, all the Manure arising from the Produce thereof respectively, and so as there be contained, in every such Lease and Leases, Clauses of Re-entry on Non-payment of the Rent and Rents to be therein or thereby respectively reserved, and so as the respective Lessee and Lessees do execute Counterparts of every such Lease and Leases, which, under these Restrictions, shall be good, valid, and effectual, to all Intents and Purposes, any Law or Usage to the contrary notwithstanding.

Commissioners to account. And be it further Enacted, That the said Commissioners respectively, and their Successors, shall, and they are hereby required to enter an Account or Accounts of all Monies which shall be raised or assessed upon the Parties interested in the said Common Fields, Common Woods, Common Downs, Common Meadows, Waste Lands, and other Commonable Places, and of all the Charges, Expences, and Disbursements which shall accrue or be made or paid by the said Commissioners respectively by virtue of this Act, in Books; which Account or Accounts, with the Bills and Vouchers concerning the same, shall be produced by the said Commissioners respectively to the Owners and Proprietors of the Lands and Grounds in the respective Parishes aforesaid, hereby intended to be divided and allotted, at a Meeting to be appointed for the Execution of the said Award, if thereunto required by the said Owners and Proprietors, or any One of them; and which Books of Accounts shall be signed by the said Commissioners respectively, and shall be deposited in the Chests of the several Parish Churches of *Crawley* and *Bishops Sutton* aforesaid.

Fees to be paid to Commissioners. And, for preventing Disputes which may arise touching the Compensation that the said Commissioners shall or ought to have for their going to and from their Meetings, and Attendance upon the Division of the Lands and Grounds hereby intended to be divided, allotted, and inclosed, and for executing the Powers vested in them in and by this Act, and for all such other Journies and Attendance as they may be obliged to make either before or after their signing and executing the said Award in, about, or concerning the Matters contained in this Act, or any Thing to be done by them in pursuance thereof, or of the Trusts hereby in them reposed, Be it further Enacted by the Authority aforesaid, That the said Commissioners shall respectively be paid the Sum of One Pound Eleven Shillings and Six Pence a piece for each Day they shall respectively travel or attend for the Purposes aforesaid, for their Trouble and Expences in such their Journies and Attendance.

Method of recovering Penalties. And be it further Enacted, That all Penalties and Forfeitures by this Act imposed, shall be levied and recovered by Distress and Sale of the Offender's Goods and Chattels, by Warrant under the Hand and Seal of any Justice of the Peace acting within the said County, which Warrant such Justice is hereby empowered to grant, upon the Confession of the Party or Parties, or upon the Information of any credible Witness upon Oath; and the Penalties and Forfeitures when recovered, if not hereinbefore directed to be otherwise applied, shall be paid in Manner following (that is to say); One Moiety thereof to the Informer, and the other Moiety thereof to the Overseers of the Poor of the said respective Parishes, for the Use of such poor Persons of the said Parish and Parishes as shall not at that Time receive Parish Alms, to be distributed to the said poor Persons in such Manner as such Justice shall direct or appoint; and in case sufficient Distress shall not be found, or such Penalties and Forfeitures shall not be paid forthwith, it shall and may be lawful to and for such Justice, and he is hereby authorized and required, by Warrant under his Hand and Seal, to cause the Offender or Offenders to be committed to either of the Houses of Correction for the said County of *Southampton*, there to remain without Bail or Mainprize, for any Time not exceeding One Calendar Month nor less than Fourteen Days, unless such Penalties and Forfeitures, and all reasonable Charges attending the same, shall be sooner paid.

Appeal. Provided always, and be it further Enacted, That if any Person or Persons shall think him, her, or themselves aggrieved by any Thing done in pursuance of this Act, then and in every such Case (except in such Cases where the Orders and Determinations of the said Commissioners are directed to be final and conclusive) he, she, or they may appeal to any General Quarter Sessions of the Peace, which shall be held in and for the said County of *Southampton*, within Four Calendar Months next after the Cause of Complaint shall have arisen, such Appellant or Appellants first giving Fourteen Days Notice at the least in Writing, of his, her, or their Intention to bring such Appeal, and of the Matter thereof, to the said Commissioners, or some of them; and the Justices, in the said General Quarter Sessions, are hereby required to hear the Matter of every such Appeal, and to make full Order therein, and award such Costs as to them in their Discretion shall seem reasonable, and by their Order or Warrant, to levy the Costs so awarded by Distress and Sale of the Goods and Chattels of the Party or Parties, Person or Persons, liable to pay the same, rendering the Overplus (if any) to the Owner or Owners of such Goods and Chattels, after deducting the reasonable Charges of such Distress and Sale; which Determination or Order of the said Justices shall be final and conclusive to all Parties and Persons therein concerned.

No Appeal against the Roads after the First Sessions. Provided also, That no Appeal shall lie against any Act of the said Commissioners, touching their setting out and ascertaining, or omitting to set out or ascertain, any Public Road or Roads, unless the same shall have been objected to by the Person or Persons making such Appeal, at the Day appointed by the said Commissioners respectively to receive Objections thereto, and unless the same be made at the First General Quarter Sessions of the Peace, to be held as aforesaid, next after such Day and Determination of the said Commissioners, and Fourteen Days Notice to be given to One or more of the said Proprietors interested therein, and to the said Commissioners, of such Appeal being intended to be brought.

Tenure of Allotments. And be it further Enacted, That the Lands which shall be allotted by virtue of this Act, in lieu or in respect of any Lands, Messuages, or Tenements lying within the said Parishes of *Crawley* and *Bishops Sutton*, which before such Division were Copyhold, shall, from and ever after the Execution of the said Awards or Instruments, be deemed to be Copyhold, and within the said Manor and Parish of *Crawley* and Parish of *Bishops Sutton* respectively, as the Case may happen to be; and shall be held for the same Estates, Terms of Years and Interests, and subject to and under the same Provisoes, Conditions, and Agreements as the said Messuages, Tenements, and Lands in lieu of which the same were so allotted as aforesaid, were respectively holden, and shall be held at and under the same Yearly and other Rents, Fines, Heriots, Dues, Payments, and Services as the other Copyholds within the said Manors and Parishes respectively are or shall be subject and liable to; and all Copies of Court Roll, by which the said Copyhold Estate or Estates is or are held, shall be deemed and construed to be valid and binding on the respective Parties to all Intents and Purposes, any Thing in this Act contained to the contrary notwithstanding; and that the Lands which shall be allotted by virtue of this Act, in lieu or in respect of any Lands, Messuages, or Tenements lying within the said respective Parishes, which are Freehold, shall, from and after the Execution of the said Awards or Instruments, be deemed Freehold within the said Manor and Parish of *Crawley* and Parish of *Bishops Sutton*, as the Case may happen to be, though the same were before Copyhold; but all such Right of Common as belongs to such Freehold, Copyhold, and Leasehold Premises, or any of them, in, over, and upon the said Lands and Grounds intended to be divided and inclosed, shall be nevertheless utterly extinguished and destroyed, as hereinbefore is declared.

No Fine to be taken on First Admission to Copyhold Allotments, nor Copyhold Rents increased. Provided always, and be it further Enacted, That no Person to whom any Copyhold Lands, Parcel of the Lands or Grounds which shall be allotted and inclosed or exchanged by virtue of this Act, shall, on account of such First Allotment or setting out in Exchange, pay any Fine for the same to the Lord or Lords of the said respective Manors; and that the Copyhold Rents, Fines, and Lords Rents or Customs, Chief Rents or Quit Rents, and other Dues, now or heretofore payable yearly by the Copyholders to such Lord or Lords, shall never hereafter be increased in respect of the new allotted Estates to be made from the said Lands and Grounds by virtue of this Act; yet, nevertheless, the Fines and Heriots to become due to the Lord or Lords upon every future Death, Exchange of Lives, or Alienation, shall be paid to the Lord or Lords in respect of such Copyhold Estates to be allotted to any Person or Persons by virtue of this Act, according to the Customs of the respective Manors.

For pleading this Act in an Action of Trespass. And be it further Enacted, That in case any Action of Trespass or Replevin shall be brought on account of any Distress or Replevin that shall be made by virtue of this Act, it shall be sufficient for the Defendant or Defendants to set forth generally in his, her, or their Plea, Avowry, or Justification, that the Rent for which such Distress was made, became due by virtue of this Act, which shall entitle such Defendant or Defendants to give in Evidence all Matters necessary to make out his, her, or their Title thereto, without specially pleading the same.

Saving of Rights to Lords of Manors. Provided always, and be it further Enacted, That nothing in this Act contained shall prejudice, lessen, or defeat the Benefit, Right, Title, or Interest of the Lord or Lords of the said respective Manors, Seignories, or Royalties wherein the said Common Fields, Common Woods, Common Downs, Common Meadows, Waste Lands, and other Commonable Places hereby directed to be divided, allotted, and inclosed, or any Part thereof, are or is lying and being, (other than such Rights of Soil and Common Rights, Dues, and Services as are intended to be barred and extinguished by this Act,) but such Lord and Lords respectively for the Time being, shall and may, from Time to Time and at all Times hereafter, hold and enjoy all Rents, Services, Courts, Perquisites, and Profits of Courts, and all other Royalties and Privileges to the said respective Manors belonging or appertaining, as fully and beneficially as if this Act had not been made.

Saving the Right of the Bishop of Winchester, [and of another] . . . to the Liberty of hunting. Provided always, and be it further Enacted, That nothing herein contained shall prejudice or take away any Right claimed by the said Lord Bishop as Lord of the said Manors of *Crawley* and *Bishops Sutton* aforesaid, or his Successors . . . [relates to Bishop's Sutton] in or to the Privilege or Liberty of hunting, hawking, fishing, and fowling, in upon and over the Common Fields, Common Woods, Common Downs, Common Meadows, Waste Lands, and other Commonable Places hereby intended to be divided and inclosed, but that they shall respectively have and enjoy such and the like Privilege and Liberty of hunting, hawking, fishing, and fowling at all seasonable Times, in, upon, and over the said Common Fields, Common Woods, Common Downs, Common Meadows, Waste Lands, and other Commonable Places, after the same shall be inclosed, as they would have been entitled to in case this Act had not been made; or of the said Lord Bishop's Right to the Timber growing or hereafter to grow on the Common Woods within the said Manor of *Crawley;* but that the said Lord Bishop and his Successors, Lords of the said Manor, shall hold, use, and exercise such Rights therein, and with the Privileges thereto belonging, as have been heretofore accustomed to be used and enjoyed over the same; and the said Persons to whom the said Allotments shall be made of the said Common Woods in *Crawley* aforesaid respectively, shall, and they are hereby required to do the utmost in their Power to preserve the Timber growing or hereafter to grow within the same, and shall and will permit the said Lord Bishop and his Successors, Lords of the said Manor of *Crawley*, to exercise the Right of marking or setting out certain Standards therein, as is provided by the several Statutes now in being for the Preservation and Growth of Timber, and to have the Privilege of entering in and upon the said Common Woods, and of cutting, carting, and carrying away the said Timber, at all seasonable Times in the Year, the Lord of the said Manor and his Servants doing no wilful Damage therein.

General Savings. Saving always to the King's Most Excellent Majesty, his Heirs and Successors, and to all and every Person or Persons, Bodies Politic and Corporate, his, her, and their Heirs, Executors, and Administrators, all such Estate, Right, Title, and Interest, (other than those meant and intended to be barred and destroyed by this Act,) which they, every or any of them, had and enjoyed of, in, to, or out of the said Common Fields, Common Woods, Common Downs, Common Meadows, Waste Lands, and other Commonable Places hereby intended to be divided, allotted, and inclosed, before the passing this Act, or could or might have had and enjoyed in case this Act had not been made.

§§ 56. Part of the Enclosure Award of 18 March, 1795, setting forth Allotments and Exchanges of Allotments, attested 15 Aug., 1827.

The enclosure award has not been found, but part of it, "the extract of award," as it is called, is here reproduced — that listing the allotments given to Thomas Pern and the Reverend Matthew Woodford. Thomas Pern was a customary tenant holding fifteen and three quarters yardlands, ostensibly 252 (statutory) acres, and possessing rights in common fields, woods, and downs. These accumulations of small bits he gave up — it seems incredible — apparently in return for almost 752 (statutory) acres in eight different plots. The largest of these plots contained 330 acres apparently embracing the field called Shirt which had so long maintained its identity.

Eleven persons are mentioned as recipients of allotments and six are said to have signed the award. The Perns, Morgans, and Paiges, old customary tenant families, were among those who signed away much of what remained of the old order of village agriculture. Richard Meyler and the Reverend Matthew Woodford, the other two signers, were, of course, newcomers.

Rookley Farm is clearly recognized as a separate entity. A number of holdings are called ancient enclosures. These referred to the enclosures made at different times before 1795 and looked back to as ancient in that year. Just how many fields were ancient enclosures in 1795 cannot now be determined. At least seven seem to be referred to here. It is not unlikely that some of these go back to the Middle Ages, perhaps to the thirteenth century, more particularly the plots belonging to Manor Farm, such as Hookfield and Hundred Acres. The last named is said to contain forty-seven (statutory) acres and one rood, or ninety-four (customary) acres and one half. This was sufficiently near to 100 acres to justify the appellation.

The exchanges of allotments apparently occurred at the time of the award or soon thereafter, for the greater convenience of those concerned. The whole document, here printed, seems to have been drawn up primarily to settle the extent and identity of the estate of Thomas Pern on the occasion of its transfer to Alexander Baring, Lord Ashburton.[1] Apparently also the extract of award was first made in 1795. The present document was a copy made in 1827. It was compared at that time with the original award of 1795, doubtless to make sure of the descriptions of plots.

Allotments to Thomas Pern
18th March 1795 [2]

By Award of this date the Commissioners [3] appointed for carrying into execution an Act of Parliament made and passsed in the thirty fourth year of the Reign of his late Majesty King George the Third intitled "An Act for dividing allotting and inclosing divers Common fields Common Woods Common Downs and other Commonable Places within the Manor and Parish of Crawley in the County of Southampton" did allot Award and Confirm unto Thomas Pern as Copyhold Tenant in respect of fifteen Yard Lands and three Quarters and all other his — Rights and Interests in over and upon the Common Fields Common Woods Common Downs and other Commonable Places within the Manor and Parish of Crawley aforesaid The Eight following Plots or Parcels of Land (that is to say) One Plot [4] or Parcel situate in Thornham containing One Hundred and Nine Acres three Roods and eight Perches bounded on the West by Rookley Farm on the North East by the public Carriage Road and Driftway hereinafter described leading from Winchester aforesaid to Stockbridge aforesaid and on the South by the Parish of Sparsholt. One Other Plot [5] or parcel situate in Homefield, Littlefield, Westfield, Peach-hill, Shirt, and containing three hundred and thirty Acres bounded on part of the South by the public Carriage Road hereinbefore described leading from

[1] See MS., Millbank, Ecclesiastical Commission, 153108, fols. 25–31 (29 March, 1828).

[2] MS. at Crawley Court, copied by J. O. Robertson, Esq., of Crawley. This should be compared with MS., Millbank, Ecclesiastical Commission, 153108, fols. 25–31 (29 March, 1828).

[3] John Tredgold, Richard Eyles, and Thomas King.

[4] 1st Allotment. Nos. 32, 33, *and* 34 on the Plan constitute this allotment.

[5] 2nd Allotment. Nos. 31, 30, *and* 36 constitute this allotment.

Crawley to Kingsomborne aforesaid, On part of the West and the remaining part of the South by Land hereinafter awarded as a Pond or Watering Place for Sheep for the use of the said Thomas Pern and others, On the South West by the said Public Carriage Road and Driftway leading from Winchester aforesaid to Stockbridge aforesaid, On the North West by Rookley Farm, On part of the North and the remaining part of the West by Lands belonging to Little Somborne, On other part of the North on part of the South East on part of the North East and other part of the North other parts of the North East and North by Lands in the Parish of Leckford, On other part of the North by Lands in the Parish of Chilbolton, On other part of the North East by the next Awarded Allotment, On other part of the South East and other part of the North East by an Allotment hereinbefore awarded to the said Lord Bishop in lieu of right of Soil, On the remaining part of the North by the Public Carriage Road and Driftway hereinbefore described leading from Southampton aforesaid to Crawley aforesaid, On other part of the North East by the first Allotment hereinbefore awarded to the said Matthew Woodford as Rector aforesaid, On other part of the South East other part of the North East the remaining part of the South East and other part of the North East by an Allotment herein-after awarded to the said John Birch and Martha his Wife and on the remaining part of the North East by the first Allotment hereinafter awarded to the said William Waight. ONE OTHER [1] Plot or Parcel situate in Middlefield and Homefield containing One Hundred and Thirty Acres and four Perches, Bounded on part of the South and part of the West by ancient Inclosures of the said Richard Meyler On other part of the West and the remaining part of the South by an Allotment hereinbefore Awarded to the said Lord Bishop and Richard Meyler Lessee as aforesaid in lieu of Customary dues and Services, On the South West by the last Awarded Allotment On other part of the West part of the North and the remaining parts of the West and North by Lands of the Parish of Chilbolton, And on the North East and East by the Public Carriage Road and Driftway thereinbefore described leading from Crawley to Testcombe Bridge aforesaid. ONE OTHER [2] Plot or parcel situate in the Middlefield containing twenty five Acres three Roods and Seven Perches bounded on part of the South West by the public Carriage Road and Driftway leading from Crawley to Testcombe Bridge aforesaid, On the North by Lands in the Parish of Chilbolton, On the North East by the Manor Farm of Crawley aforesaid, On part of the South East by an ancient Inclosure belonging to the

[1] 3rd Allotment. Nos. 9, 12, 29, about two thirds of 10–11, 8, *and* 7, and some adjoining Nos. constitute this allotment.

[2] 4th Allotment. The description of this allotment suits No. 51 on this Plan.

said Manor Farm called Hookfield and Exchanged to the said Thomas Pern as hereinafter mentioned, And on the remaining parts of the South West and South East by the Second Allotment hereinbefore awarded to the said Matthew Woodford as Rector aforesaid and exchanged to the said Thomas Pern as hereinafter mentioned. ONE OTHER [1] Plot or Parcel situate in Homefield North of the Village of Crawley aforesaid containing Eighteen Acres three Roods and thirty six Perches bounded on part of the South by ancient Inclosures of the said Village of Crawley, On part of the West and the remaining part of the South by an Allotment hereinafter Awarded to the said Nicholas Hankin, On the remaining part of the West by the public Carriage Road and Driftway hereinbefore described leading from Crawley to Testcombe Bridge aforesaid, On part of the North East by part of an ancient Inclosure belonging to the Manor Farm of Crawley aforesaid called Hundred Acres and exchanged to the said Thomas Pern as hereinafter mentioned, On other part of the North East by other part of the said ancient Inclosure belonging to the said Manor Farm called Hundred Acres and exchanged to the said Sarah Morgan as hereinafter mentioned, and on the East by the First Allotment hereinafter awarded to the said Sarah Morgan. ONE OTHER [2] Plot or Parcel situate in Norwood Coppice containing fifty Acres Two Roods and thirty eight Perches bounded on the South West by the Parish of Sparsholt, On part of the North and on the West by the Second Allotment hereinafter awarded to the said Robert Pitter, On other part of the North by the ancient Inclosures of the said George Godwin and Charles Paige respectively, On part of the East and the remaining part of the North by the Third Allotment hereinafter awarded to the said Charles Paige On the remaining part of the East by ancient Inclosures of the said George Godwin and Charles Paige respectively, On the South East and the remaining part of the East by the Third Allotment hereinafter awarded to the said John Pern and on the South by the Third Allotment hereinafter awarded to the said John Glide. ONE OTHER [3] Plot or Parcel situate on Ball Down containing One Acre two Roods and twenty six Perches bounded on the North East by the Public Carriage Road and Driftway hereinbefore described leading from Crawley to Littleton aforesaid, On the South East by the end of an ancient Road or Lane called Croftes Lane and on the remaining parts thereof by the Second Allotment hereinafter awarded to the said John Pern which said last described Allotment is exchanged to the said John Pern as hereinafter is

[1] 5th Allotment. No. 48 on the Plan constitutes this allotment.

[2] 6th Allotment. This allotment is sold to Mr. Gover.

[3] 7th Allotment. This allotment is an exchange by the award to John Pern (see the end of this extract).

mentioned. AND ONE OTHER [1] Plot or Parcel situate on the said Cowdown and Gore containing Eighty four Acres three Roods and twenty five Perches exclusive of all Roads and Ways through and over the same bounded on the South East by Lands belonging to the said Manor Farm On the South West by the fifth Allotment hereinafter awarded to the said John Pern and exchanged to the said Richard Meyler as hereinafter mentioned On the North West by Barton Stacey Cowdown and on the North East by the Second Allotment hereinbefore awarded to the said Richard Meyler which said last described Allotment is exchanged to the said Richard Meyler as hereinafter is mentioned. THE FENCES for Inclosing the first described Allotment against the public Roads bounding the same for inclosing the Second described Allotment against the said public Roads bounding the same and against the said Plot or Parcel of Land to be awarded as a Pond or Watering Place for Sheep against the said Allotment to the said Matthew Woodford, Rector as aforesaid and against the said first Allotment of the said William Waight For inclosing the third described Allotment against the said Public Road bounding the same. For inclosing the fourth described Allotment against the said Public Road bounding the same. For inclosing the fifth described Allotment against the said Public Road bounding the same against part of an ancient Inclosure of the said Manor Farm called Hundred Acres exchanged to the said Sarah Morgan as hereinafter mentioned and against the said first Allotment to the said Sarah Morgan and for inclosing the seventh described Allotment against the said Public Road bounding the same to be made and for ever thereafter to be maintained and repaired by and at the expence of the said Thomas Pern and the future owners and occupiers of the said several respective Allotments for the time being.

Allotments to Mr. Woodford The Rector

THE SAID Commissioners also Allotted and Awarded and Confirmed unto the Reverend Matthew Woodford and his Successors Rectors of Crawley aforesaid for and in respect of his Glebe Lands the two following Plots or Parcels of Land that is to say One Plot [2] or Parcel situate in Homefield containing six acres three Roods and thirteen Perches bounded on part of the North by the Public Carriage Road and Driftway hereinbefore described leading from Southampton aforesaid to Crawley on the East and other part of the North by a Garden of the said Richard Meyler, On the remaining part of the North by a Garden

[1] 8th Allotment. This allotment is an exchange by the award to Richard Meyler as the Lessee of the Manor Farm.

[2] 1st Allotment retained by Woodford.

and Home Close of the said Matthew Woodford, On the North East by an ancient Inclosure of the said Thomas Pern and exchanged to the said Matthew Woodford as hereinafter mentioned On the South East by an Allotment hereinafter awarded to John Birch, And on the West by the second Allotment hereinafter awarded to the said Thomas Pern. AND ONE OTHER [1] Plot or Parcel situate in Middlefield containing two Acres two Roods and twenty perches bounded on the West by the public Carriage Road and Driftway hereinbefore described leading from Crawley aforesaid to Testcombe Bridge aforesaid, On the North and East by the fourth Allotment hereinafter awarded to the said Thomas Pern, And on the South by an ancient Inclosure of the said Richard Meyler called Hookfield (exchanged as hereinafter mentioned) which said Allotment is exchanged to the said Thomas Pern as hereinafter is mentioned. THE FENCES for Inclosing this Allotment against the said public Carriage Road and Driftway bounding the same to be made by the said Rector and the future Owners and Occupiers of the said Allotment for the time being.

Exchanges

AND for the more convenient situation and disposition of the several Farms Lands and Estates within the said Manor and Parish of Crawley the several following Exchanges and Tenements have been made by the several Proprietors thereof respectively and whose consent thereto is testified by their being parties to and sealing and executing these Presents and by and with the consent and approbation of the said Commissioners and by virtue of the Powers and Authority granted in the said Act for such purpose (that is to say) the said Matthew Woodford Rector of Crawley aforesaid by and with the consent and approbation of the said Lord Bishop of Winchester testified as aforesaid HATH given and granted and by these Presents DOTH give and grant unto the said Thomas Pern ALL THAT the second Allotment [2] hereinbefore Awarded to the said Mathew Woodford as Rector aforesaid containing two Acres Two Roods and twenty Perches IN EXCHANGE for part of an ancient Inclosure in the Village of Crawley aforesaid containing [—] [3] bounded on the South East by an Inclosure belonging to the said Thomas Pern, On the South West by the first Allotment hereinbefore Awarded to the said Matthew Woodford as Rector aforesaid and on the remaining parts thereof by an ancient Inclosure belonging to the said Matthew Woodford. AND the said Thomas Pern HATH given and granted and by these Presents DOTH give and grant unto the said Mat-

[1] 2nd Allotment. This allotment was exchanged by the award to Thomas Pern and constitutes some part of the allotments of the estate as it now is.

[2] Exchanges by Woodford. This 2nd allotment exchanged to Thomas Pern for part of an ancient Inclosure.

[3] [Left blank on manuscript.]

thew Woodford and his Successors Rectors aforesaid All That Part of an ancient Inclosure situate in the Village of Crawley aforesaid containing [—] [1] In Exchange for all the second Allotment hereinbefore awarded to the said Matthew Woodford containing two Acres two Roods and twenty Perches.

And the said Richard Meyler as Lessee aforesaid by and with the Consent and Approbation of the said Lord Bishop testified as aforesaid Hath given and granted and by these Presents Doth give and grant unto the said Thomas Pern All That ancient Inclosure called Hookfield [2] together with a small part of an ancient Inclosure called Hundred Acres containing Forty seven Acres and one Rood bounded on part of the South West by the public Carriage Road hereinbefore described leading from Crawley to Testcombe Bridge aforesaid, On part of the North West by the second Allotment hereinbefore awarded to the said Matthew Woodford as aforesaid. Exchanged to the said Thomas Pern as hereinbefore is mentioned, On the remaining part of the North West by the fourth Allotment hereinbefore awarded to the said Thomas Pern, On the North East by Lands belonging to the said Manor Farm, On the South East by part of the said Inclosure called Hundred Acres exchanged to Sarah Morgan as hereinbefore mentioned and on the remaining part of the South West by the fifth Allotment hereinbefore awarded to the said Thomas Pern. Also part of the said ancient Inclosure called Winyard field,[3] And Also part of an ancient Inclosure called Bottomfield containing together forty three Acres three Roods and four Perches bounded on part of the West by the public Carriage Road as hereinbefore described leading from Crawley to Littleton aforesaid. On part of the North and on the remaining part of the West by ancient Inclosures belonging to the said Thomas Pern and John Birch and Martha his Wife respectively On the remaining part of the North by ancient Inclosures belonging to the said Manor Farm, Thomas Pern and others, On the East by other part of the said ancient Inclosure called Bottomfield belonging to the said Manor Farm, And on the South by part of the said ancient Inclosure called Winyard Field exchanged to the said Charles Paige as hereinbefore mentioned. In Exchange for all that the Eighth Allotment hereinbefore awarded to the said Thomas Pern containing Eighty four acres three Roods and twenty five Perches. And the Said Thomas Pern hath given and granted and by these Presents Doth give and grant unto the said

[1] [Left blank on manuscript.]

[2] Exchanges by Richard Meyler as Lessee of the Manor Farm. This first piece of land was together with the two next mentioned pieces exchanged to Thomas Pern for his said 8th Allotment, and it constitutes Nos. 49 *and* 50 on the Plan.

[3] These other two pieces constitute Nos. 76 and probably part of 77 on the Plan.

Richard Meyler as Lessee aforesaid ALL THAT the said eighth Allotment hereinbefore awarded to the said Thomas Pern containing Eighty four acres four Roods and twenty five Perches IN EXCHANGE for All that ancient Inclosure called Hookfield together with a small part of the said ancient Inclosure called Hundred Acres containing forty seven acres and one Rood. Also for part of the said ancient Inclosure called Winyard Field And also for part of the said ancient Inclosure called Bottomfield containing together forty three acres three Roods and four Perches hereinbefore described.

THE SAID John Pern HATH given and granted and by these PRESENTS DOTH give and grant unto the said Thomas Pern ALL THAT ancient Inclosure called Penton's Picked Piddle [1] containing One Acre two Roods and twenty six Perches bounded on the North by an ancient Road or Lane leading from Crawley to Sutton Scotney aforesaid, On the East by ancient Inclosures belonging to the said Thomas Pern On the South by an ancient Inclosure belonging to the said John Birch and Martha his Wife, And on the West by ancient Inclosures Belonging to the said Thomas Pern, Charles Paige, and others. IN EXCHANGE for ALL THAT the Seventh Allotment hereinbefore awarded to the said Thomas Pern containing one Acre two Roods and twenty six Perches AND the said Thomas Pern HATH given and granted and by these Presents DOTH give and grant unto the said John Pern ALL THAT the said Seventh Allotment hereinbefore Awarded to the said Thomas Pern containing One Acre two Roods and twenty six Perches IN EXCHANGE for ALL that ancient Inclosure called Penton's Picked Piddle containing One Acre two Roods and twenty six Perches hereinbefore described, ALL which Exchanges hereinbefore ascertained set forth and declared are made and are hereby declared to be made by and with the consent and approbation of the said Commissioners Partys hereto:—

Examined the extract of award on this
and the 6 preceeding sheets with the
award itself,[2] with which is entirely agreed
at the office of Jas. Lampard Esq.
Solicitor and Steward of Crawley Manor at
Winchester the 15th Day of August 1827

(Sgnd) Jno Marshall
10, Liverpool Street,
Broad Street Bldngs
London

[1] Exchange by John Pern. This piece of land was exchanged to Thomas Pern for his said 7th Allotment and constitutes part of No. 78 on the Plan.

[2] Parties signing award being the Commissioners Lord Bishop, viz. Rector M. Woodford, Richard Meyler, Thomas Pern, John Pern, Sarah Morgan, and Charles Paige.

§§ 57. Owners and Occupiers of Tenements owing Tithes or exempt therefrom in the Parish of Crawley, about 1837.

Manor Farm, or roughly the demesne, was in the hands of Richard Bright, a descendant of the Meylers. His holding may be analysed as follows:

	Acres	Roods	Perches
Owned and occupied	167	2	15
Owned and rented out	879	3	24
Rented from Lord Ashburton	11	1	7
	1,058	3	6

The part owned and occupied was made up of the mansion house, pastures, and woodlands. The holding owned and rented out was the largest single unit in the parish. It was leased by William Wade who was himself an owner — of over six acres of pasture and arable and possessing a house and garden. Probably he was a customary tenant. In all, he seems to have cultivated 886½ acres. Judging from the location of his holdings, we would conclude that he was living apart from the village, apparently at New Barn Farm with his fields in the district of the Warren. How we would like to know the system of cultivation that he followed!

The second holding belonged to Lord Ashburton (Alexander Baring) who had married a Philadelphia heiress and who had been created baron in 1835. His country residence was not at Crawley but at Northington, Hants, which he had purchased in 1817 and which is still the family seat. It seems that Ashburton had purchased the old Pern holding, awarded to Thomas Pern at the enclosure in 1795. It is noteworthy that nearly 696 acres of his estate of 744½ acres were rented out to Thomas Pern. This holding was largely north and northwest of the village.

Thomas Pern, yeoman, about 36 years of age,[1] occupied the largest amount of land in the Parish of Crawley.

	Acres	Roods	Perches
Rented from Lord Ashburton[2]	695	3	24
Rented from the lord bishop	13	0	8
Owned and occupied	570	2	20
Total	1,279	2	12

[1] See below, §§ 58, p. 651.

[2] Really somewhat more than this: Robert Waight and Thomas Pern jointly leased a little over three acres from Ashburton in addition to the amounts above.

In addition, Gentleman Pern, as he was sometimes called, owned six tenements (houses and gardens) and one garden. Whether he cultivated all his land as one unit or as two or more, is not stated. Certainly he had at least two sets of farm buildings in the village itself. The cultivation was overwhelmingly arable. But whether this was for the production of the usual grains or also partly for fodder for animals, is not clear. Probably it was a scientific rotation which included grain for man and grain, green crops, and roots for sheep and cattle.

The third big agricultural unit was Rookley Farm, lying to the extreme west of the village, with its separate homestead. It did not include Rookley House, the rival of Crawley Court as a dwelling. The number of acres was nearly 698. Ownership was vested in three persons whose names are apparently strange to Crawley, as indeed is the case with the occupier, Lawrence Turton Allee, called yeoman in the Census of 1841.[1]

The fourth holding in size was Robert Waight's scattered fields, south and west of the village, amounting to a little over 164½ acres which he owned and occupied, and three acres which he leased jointly with Thomas Pern. Two of his tenements, made up apparently of houses and gardens, he let to people of the village.

Thomas Page had seventy acres of his own and leased forty from the bishop. They were south on the Littleton boundary, apparently with the homestead at or near where Littleton House stands to-day. Apparently the Pages had lived the longest in Crawley of any of the families so far mentioned.

South by west of the village were the holdings of Robert Fifield, 69½ acres of which he owned and nearly 3½ of which he leased from the bishop.

These six farms, if we may call them such, amounted to over 3,000 acres. The five farmers of the village itself were both owners and renters.

There were apparently ten cottagers who owned their cottages and gardens, only two of them possessing any extra land. One of these two was a widow and of a yeoman family; the other had left

[1] See below, §§ 58, p. 652.

Crawley by 1841 (not being in the census of that year). The number of cottages, not owned by the occupiers was as follows:

1. With extra land	1
2. Without extra land	14
Occupied by	
Single families	5
Two adults	7
Three "	1
Four "	1

It is probable that many of the cottages were tied to the estates of the larger cultivators; that is, were occupied by the laborers of the owner. Pern had six and Waight two such cottages. In all, there were at least thirty-seven probable laborers whom we can count in this tithe list, with more in the background.

How many of the cottages were owned by mortgagees and rented to Crawley laborers is, of course, not indicated. One cottage, owned by Edward Twynam, was probably the same as was forfeited in 1831 to Henry Twynam of Bishopstoke, gentleman, for non-payment of a mortgage.[1] At the time of the present survey this was but one of three tenements held by the same person and probably rack rented to the villagers.

The old village had not entirely disappeared when there were five staunch cultivators who owned some of their lands and leased more, and ten cottagers who owned their own homes and gardens. Doubtless in all cases ownership meant simply customary tenure — subject to a small rental, fine for admission, and the payment of a heriot.

The bishop of Winchester as lord was the recipient of all customary rents and other such dues. But the bishop also possessed lands to the extent of fifty-seven acres which he leased to three farmers in varying amounts, as we have seen.

Besides the occupants of Crawley Court and Rookley House, and besides the tenant farmers and agricultural laborers and other servants, there were two carpenters, one blacksmith, and, of course, the one rector.

[1] See above, §§ 54, p. 595.

The use of the lands surveyed is indicated by the following official summary.

Meadow or pasture	420	acres
Woods	257	"
Arable	2,803	"
Glebe (not in hands of rector)	10	"
Total acreage of Crawley	3,500	"
Acres paying tithes	3,490	"

The present document came into existence in connection with the commutation of tithes provided for by an act of parliament passed in 1836.[1] These tithes had long been paid to the rector of the parish. They had been paid in kind by the several tenants. From the standpoint of the rector, this was unsatisfactory because of the variations in the amounts received and the prices which the products fetched, and because of the trouble of housing the goods and selling them. From the standpoint of the tithe-payers, the old system of paying in kind discouraged improvement because the tithe, or tenth of produce, being levied on gross production, took no account of cost of improvement.

In order to make the tithe independent of the mere matter of yield per acre, it was commuted to a money charge. Roughly stated, the parish was reckoned as responsible for the average tithe paid over a period of seven years ending with Christmas, 1835. This sum was then divided into three equal parts, one for wheat, one for barley, and the third for oats. The price of a bushel of each was then divided into the sum for each. This gave a certain number of bushels which was to remain constant. For Crawley the figures fixed on 15 April, 1837, were as follows:

Grain	Price per bushel s.	d.	No. of Bushels
Wheat	7	0¼	625.70623
Barley	3	11½	1,111.57895
Oats	2	9	1,610.00000
Total			3,347.28518

Thus it was estimated that Crawley lands (fixed at 3,490 acres) owing the tithe were to pay the value of 3,347 bushels of grain each

[1] 6 and 7 William IV, chap. 71.

year. In order, in subsequent years, to determine the amount of rent charge due, it was necessary simply to multiply the numbers of bushels indicated above by the current prices of the three grains and to add the total. On the whole, this system favored the tithe payers and injured the clergy. By 1901 the £100 of 1837 had sunk to £66 15s. 9¾d. Into the new arrangement came, not the uncertainties of local weather but of world prices. At the same time, such improvements in agricultural technique as were made by Pern or Wade or the others went wholly to the improver and not to the rector.

To help bring about the new system of rent charges in money, instead of tithes in kind, the whole parish was surveyed about 1837.[1] The survey maps and the descriptions which accompany them are among the most valuable sources for a study of the agricultural and social history, not only of Crawley but of Great Britain.

[1] This is the date on the manuscript, apparently written by a later hand. The articles of agreement for the commutation were executed at Crawley 15 April, 1837. The map is dated 7 Sept., 1839. The actual survey, therefore, took place between these two dates.

Landowner[1]	Occupiers	Plan No.	Lands and Premises	Culti-vation	Statute Measure a.	r.	p.	Payable to Rector £	s.	d.
Lord Ashburton	Himself	44	Plantation	W.[2]	2	0	37			
		45	"	"	4	3	26			
		46	"	"	7	3	10			
		47	"	"	3	2	38			
		120	" (Formerly part of Dogkennel)	"	1	0	0			
		124	Plantation	"	10	3	12			
		129	Part of the Belt Plantation	"	8	3	16			
					39	1	19			
	Reverend Philip Jacob	58	The Old Garden	P. etc.	1	1	22	0	10	0
	Thomas Pern	38	Shirt	A.	39	2	38	6	15	1
		39	Little Thornham	P. D.	2	0	14	0	1	2
		40	Thornham	A.	17	0	16	3	3	3
		41	Great Thornham	"	90	2	18	19	9	6
		48	Mainstone	"	62	1	7	13	7	9
		49	Peach Hill	"	57	2	0	11	10	0
		50	Butts Field	"	39	1	0	9	12	3
		52	Little Field	"	46	2	11	12	16	0
		53	Home Field	"	20	3	9	5	8	1
		54	West Field	"	43	3	16	12	19	1
		89	Stables Barns & Yards	—	0	2	5	—	—	—
		90	Paddock	P.	1	0	11	0	6	5
		97	Tenements Barns & Yards	—		1	16	—	—	—
		98	Paddock	P.		2	23	0	3	9
		121	Kennel Close	"	5	1	0	0	19	9
		122	Private Road	R.	0	0	25	—	—	—
		123	Plot	P.	1	2	0	0	4	6
		125	Kennel Close	A.	5	1	21	1	9	6
		126	Bush Field	"	3	3	37	0	19	6

[1] Ms., Ministry of Agriculture and Fisheries, Southampton, 7006 Crawley.

[2] Abbreviations: A., arable; W., wood; P., pasture; P. D., pasture down; R., road; F., furze.

Landowner	Occupiers	Plan No.	Lands and Premises	Culti-vation	Statute Measure a.	r.	p.	Payable to Rector £	s.	d.
		127	Bottom Field	A.	20	3	34	6	1	6
		128	Arable Field	"	7	1	14	1	16	0
		130	Middle Field	"	70	3	22	14	3	7
		132	Upper Hook	"	28	1	27	4	16	6
		133	Hook Field	"	33	2	24	8	1	10
		134	Part of Hundred Acres	"	13	2	16	3	14	8
		135	Home Field	"	18	3	36	6	7	1
		144	Home Pasture	P.	4	0	11	1	4	5
		147	Homestead	—	0	3	26	0	3	0
		154	Paddock	P.	1	1	20	0	8	8
		155	Garden	—	0	0	13			
		224	The Pightle	A.	6	0	14	1	15	2
		225	Bottom Field	"	41	0	8	11	18	0
		226	Crooked Pightle	"	9	3	12	3	2	10
					695	3	24	162	18	10
	Richard Bright	106	Plantation — formerly part of the Pleasure Ground	W.	4	2	13			
		107	Orchard — formerly part of the Kitchen Garden	P. etc.	2	1	3	0	12	6
		108	Plantation — formerly part of the Pleasure Ground	W.	2	2	19			
					9	1	35	0	12	6
Lord Ashburton and his lessee Robert Waight	Robert Waight and Thomas Pern	43	Hut Green	P.	3	0	33	0	2	4
William Allen	James Ventham, James Hewell, John Newman	157	Tenements and Garden	"	0	0	35	—	—	—
Richard Bright	Himself	105	Mansion House Offices and Pleasure Ground		9	2	14	0	3	6
		109	Plantation and Road	W.	1	0	13	0	0	2

Landowner	Occupiers	Plan No.	Lands and Premises	Cultivation	a.	r.	p.	£	s.	d.
		110 and 111	Orchard and Garden	P. etc.	2	2	18	0	15	4
		112	Plantation	W.	1	3	15			
		113	Part of the Belt Plantation	"	3	2	27	0	1	3
		114	Plantation	"	0	3	37			
		115	Bush Field	P.	3	3	9	0	14	2
		116	Gravel Heap Field	"	6	3	4	1	5	0
		117	Plantation	W.	3	0	39	0	0	7
		118	Kennel Pasture	P.	5	2	37	1	3	1
		119	Plantation — formerly part of the Dogkennel	W.	0	1	6			
		174	Plantation	"	4	2	0	0	3	10
		175	"	"	8	1	37			
		180	Keepers House etc. — part of the Warren	P.	11	0	14	1	4	4
		181	Part of the Warren	W.	13	1	10	0	11	7
		182	" " " "	"	22	3	27	1	0	10
		183	Plantation	"	7	3	15			
		184	New Road	W.	2	3	10			
		185	Plantation	"	3	1	30			
		186	"	"	3	3	0			
		193	"	"	0	0	10			
		195	"	"	2	2	29	0	11	3
		204	"	"	6	3	15			
		206	"	"	4	2	1			
		207	"	"	0	1	28			
		211	"	"	4	3	30			
		212	Road	—	0	1	33			
		267	Allotment in North Wood	W.	29	3	27	0	17	8
					167	2	15	8	12	7

Landowner	Occupiers	Plan No.	Lands and Premises	Cultivation	Statute Measure s.	r.	p.	Payable to Rector £	s.	d.
	Sarah Sundon Mary Burrough Ann Brown	102	Tenements	—	0	0	4	—	—	—
	Himself	103	Timber Yard and Sheds	—	0	0	31	—	—	—
		136	Arable Plot	A.	1	2	21	0	11	6
					1	3	12	0	11	6
	George Hawkins	137	House Carpenters Shop and Garden	—	0	1	16	0	4	0
		138	Paddock	P.	0	1	18			
					0	2	34	0	4	0
	William Wade	171	House Penfolds	A.	9	1	7	2	10	2
		172	Hundred Acres	"	62	3	38	18	9	6
		173	Brockleys	"	52	1	5	13	12	0
		176	Longlands	"	51	2	28	14	19	10
		177	Fair Lot	"	27	0	0	5	15	3
		178	Cow Down	P.	28	3	23	2	9	2
		179	Great Cow Down	D.	178	3	16	11	10	9
		187	Part of Silvers Hill	A.	47	1	29	7	18	6
		188	" " " "	"	11	1	3	1	17	7
		189	" " " "	"	45	2	35	7	13	0
		190	" " " "	"	18	2	36	3	8	0
		191	" " " "	"	33	0	13	6	13	0
		192	" " " "	"	28	3	0	5	4	6
		196	The Penfolds & Droveway	P.	31	2	21	2	7	0
		197	Paddock	"	2	2	17	0	7	8
		198	Homestead	—	2	0	32	0	5	6
		199	Hog Close	P.	2	1	1	0	6	6
		200	Bottom Close	A.	13	2	19	4	1	9
		201	Great Mead	"	26	0	31	7	3	2

Landowner	Occupiers	Plan No.	Lands and Premises	Cultivation	Statute Measure a.	r.	p.	Payable to Rector £	s.	d.
		202	Part of Winter Hill	A.	37	2	17	9	17	6
		203	" " " "	"	40	0	8	10	13	3
		205	Norman Maiden Down	P. D.	14	3	15	0	17	6
		208	Part of Norman Down	A.	34	0	38	7	9	9
		209	" " " "	"	40	1	2	7	6	6
		210	Part of Winter Hill	"	37	2	32	7	19	4
					879	0	26	160	16	8
John Bramble, Sen. / John Bramble, Jun.	Themselves	148	Tenements and Garden	—	0	0	34	—	—	—
Sir Frederick Hutchinson / Hervey Bathurst Bart	James Fitt	277	Ball Down Field	A.	8	1	2	2	7	1
		278	Coppice Row in d°.	W.	3	1	18	0	3	2
					11	2	20	2	10	3
Henry Cordery	George Lovell	1	Rookley Mansion House Offices Yards Gardens and Pleasure Grounds	—	7	1	22	0	5	0
		2	Dog Kennel Close	P.	3	0	38			
					10	2	20	0	5	0
Charles Cook	John Cook and Robert Holdaway	100	Tenements and Garden	—	0	0	23	—	—	—
	Himself	101	House Smith's Shop and Garden	—	0	0	21	—	—	—
William Dancaster	John Morrison	227	Pasture Close	P.	2	3	11	0	14	6
		228	Road leading to Pasture Close	"	0	0	13	—	—	—
					2	3	24	0	14	6
Robert Fifield	Himself	279	Backet and Launceston Close	A.	22	0	0	5	12	4
		280, 281, 282	Coppice Rows in Backet and Launceston Close	W.	0	2	20	—	—	—
		283	Yew Tree Close	A.	9	2	29	2	9	6

Landowner	Occupiers	Plan No.	Lands and Premises	Cultivation	Statute Measure a.	r.	p.	Payable to Rector £	s.	d.
		284	Coppice	W.	5	1	37	0	5	1
		285	"	"	2	3	11	0	2	8
		286	Barn Close	A.	5	0	30	1	11	1
		287	Long Close	"	23	0	14	6	11	7
		288	Coppice Row in Long Close	W.	0	3	2	—	—	—
					69	2	23	16	12	3
Bishop of Winchester & Robert Fifield his Lessee	Robert Fifield	266	Grubbed Ground	A.	3	1	23	0	13	3
Ann Godwin	George Godwin	99	Paddock and Garden	P. etc.	0	1	21	—	—	—
	Herself	141	House and Garden	—	0	0	18	—	—	—
George Godwin	Himself	142, 143	House Garden and Paddock	P.	0	1	35	—	—	—
	John Grunsell	150	Cottage and Garden	—	0	0	28	—	—	—
William Gover	Himself	271	Orchard	P.	1	0	38	0	5	10
		272	Brick Yard Kilns etc.	—	2	1	31	—	—	—
		273	Cottages and Gardens	—	0	1	15	—	—	—
				Carried forward	4	0	4	0	5	10
		274	Coppice	W.	42	2	7	1	5	0
		274	Grubbed Ground	A.	3	3	21	0	17	5
		276	Plantation	W.	0	1	6	—	—	—
					50	2	38	2	8	3
David Heron	Himself	139	Cottage and Garden	—	0	0	13	—	—	—
William Hills	Himself and William Samdom	145	Cottage and Garden	—	0	0	23	—	—	—
Reverend Philip Jacob	Himself	62	Part of Paddock	P.	0	0	37	0	1	4
	John Hills	85	Cottage Garden and School House	—	0	0	22	—	—	—

Landowner	Occupiers	Plan No.	Lands and Premises	Cultivation	Statute Measure a.	r.	p.	Payable to Rector £	s.	d.
Richard Kent	Himself	161	Cottage and Garden	—	0	0	24	—	—	—
Charles Morris, Charles Harrison, and Rowland Henry Lenthall	Lawrence Turton Allee	3	Homestead	—	1	3	37	0	7	0
		4	Cowleaze	P.	3	1	16	0	14	8
		5	"	"	17	3	29	3	5	1
		6	"	"	6	3	29	1	5	1
		7	"	A.	24	1	32	5	17	9
		8	Home Field	"	45	3	35	11	17	8
		9	Coppice Row in Home Field	W.	0	3	32	—	—	—
		10	Shepherd's field	A.	44	0	18	11	18	6
		11	Long field	"	49	3	34	12	0	8
		12	Devils Row	W.	0	3	26	—	—	—
		13	Dibdels field	A.	52	2	17	12	13	5
		14	Dibdels Coppice	W.	1	2	39	0	1	2
		15	Halls Parlor	"	2	3	26	0	2	0
		16	Little Field	A.	30	0	36	5	18	9
		17	Coppice	W.	0	0	34	—	—	—
		18a	North Field	A.	39	3	28	8	8	8
		18b	Coppice Row in North Field	W.	1	0	18	0	0	7
		19	Rood	—	0	1	22	—	—	—
		20a	Hawkers Field	A.	25	1	37	6	10	3
		20b	Coppice Row in Hawkers Field	W.	0	3	2	—	—	—
		21	Heath field and Spleck field	A.	24	3	35	4	3	3
		22	Little Heath field	"	7	2	1	1	7	2
		23	Bakelands and North Dibdels field	"	72	3	27	12	3	9
		24	Spleck Coppice	W.	7	3	6	0	6	6
		25	Road	—	0	0	15	—	—	—
		26	Spleck Coppice	W.	1	2	20	0	1	2
		27	" "	"	7	2	12	0	5	3
		28	Strip by Turnpike Rood	P. D.	0	1	30	0	0	2

Landowner	Occupiers	Plan No.	Lands and Premises	Culti-vation	Statute Measure a.	r.	p.	Payable to Rector £	s.	d.
		29	Bushy Coppice	W.	12	3	26	0	7	6
		30	Down	P. & F.	6	1	7	0	2	4
		31	Coppice	W.	1	0	16	0	0	11
		32	"	"	0	2	21			
		33	Rough Hill	R. P.	13	1	11	0	4	9
		34	Whiteberry Coppice	W.	22	3	9	0	8	3
		35	Dibsdell Coppice	"	24	0	3	0	19	7
		36	Windmill Hill and Cow Down	A. & D.	141	3	18	18	18	9
					697	3	4	120	10	7
Thomas Page	William Willis	75	Beer House Outbuildings Garden Orchard	—	0	2	7	—	—	—
	Himself	213	Home Close	A.	3	2	29	0	16	3
		214	Orchard	P.	1	3	10	0	4	8
		215	Homestead	—	0	1	36	0	1	6
		216	North Croft	A.	7	3	3	1	10	5
		220	Vineyard Field	"	20	2	8	5	1	0
		221	Peaked Pightle	"	3	0	12	0	15	1
		256	Coppice	W.	1	2	12	0	0	6
		260	The Drove	R.	0	3	21	—	—	—
		261	Pond Close	A.	7	3	15	1	16	7
		262	Long Croft	"	19	2	32	4	7	0
		263	Coppice	W.	3	0	27	0	1	3
					70	2	5	14	14	3
Bishop of Winchester and Thomas Page his lessee Thomas Page		257	West Field and Pigeon Hole	A.	14	0	28	3	4	1
		258	Ten Acres	"	10	2	22	2	13	9
		259	Dell Field	"	6	3	36	1	9	1
		264	Leven Acres	"	7	2	6	1	11	4

Landowner	Occupiers	Plan No.	Lands and Premises	Culti-vation	Statute Measure a.	r.	p.	Payable to Rector £	s.	d.
		265	Inner Piece	A.	1	1	12	0	4	6
					40	2	24	9	2	9
Thomas Pern	Himself	70	Part of Home Field	A.	9	2	23	3	0	6
		73	Thorns	R. & P.	0	0	36	0	0	3
		78	Homestead and Part of Garden	—	0	1	25	—	—	—
		82	Part of Home Paddock	P.	1	0	17	0	6	6
		83a	Farm Buildings and Yard	—	0	2	16	—	—	—
		84	Part of Paddock and Plantation	P. etc.	0	3	27	0	5	5
		170	Part of Way Pightle	A.	2	2	31	0	15	4
		229	Part of Warren Pightle	A.	2	2	2	0	14	3
		231	Long Pightle	"	2	2	5	0	14	4
		232	Burrow Pightle	"	2	0	21	0	12	1
		233	Millers Lane Pightle	P.	1	3	10	0	4	2
		236	Stand Pightle Field	A.	34	3	25	9	19	0
		237	Long Field	"	47	0	16	11	7	0
		241	Part of Plantation field	"	38	2	7	8	14	4
		242	Sourlands	"	20	3	7	4	8	0
		246	Great Down	"	43	0	27	9	15	0
		247	Middle Down	"	26	1	30	5	19	6
		248	Part of Park field	"	5	1	22	1	4	3
		253	Part of Crawley Park	P.	36	0	12	2	2	6
		254	Coppice	W.	18	3	36	0	7	0
					295	3	35	60	9	5
		71	Part of Home Field	A.	6	0	5	1	17	11
		76	Homestead and part of garden	—	1	0	3	0	3	0
		77	Part of Home Paddock	P.	0	1	0 }			
		86	Part of Paddock	"	0	1	0 }	0	3	0
		169	Part of Way Pightle	A.	2	2	0	0	14	3

Landowner	Occupiers	Plan No.	Lands and Premises	Cultivation	Statute Measure a.	r.	p.	Payable to Rector £	s.	d.
		217	Ham Hill	A.	45	2	23	7	12	7
		218	Upper Vineyard Field	"	54	2	8	10	0	10
		219	Vineyard Field	"	28	0	7	7	11	9
		230	Part of Warren Pightle	"	2	0	0	0	11	6
		238	Small part of Long Field	"	0	0	8	0	0	3
		239	Plantation	W.	0	2	5	—	—	—
		240	Part of Plantation Field	A.	15	1	23	3	5	0
		249	Part of Park Field	"	22	0	1	4	13	0
		251	Peaked Down	"	24	2	31	5	4	4
		252	Part of Crawley Park	P.	14	1	17	0	17	0
		270	Coppice	W.	10	2	12	0	5	10
					227	3	23	43	0	3
		153	Paddock	P.	0	3	15	0	5	0
		167	Arable Field	A.	12	2	36	4	3	8
		168	" "	"	33	0	39	9	19	2
					46	3	10	14	7	10
	Thomas Brown, William Hatcher, Thomas Serle, Isaac Newman	74	Garden	A.	0	0	38	—	—	—
	John Summerly, William Heron	81	Tenements and Garden	—	0	0	16	—	—	—
	Joseph Elliot, Robert Burrough, Thomas Brown	83b	Tenements and Garden	—	0	0	32	—	—	—
	George Harrington, William Tongs	151, 152	Tenements and Garden	—	0	1	15	—	—	—
	John Judd, Christopher Pitter	159	Tenements and Garden	—	0	0	30	—	—	—
	George Brown, James Shepperd	160	Tenements and Garden	—	0	0	18	—	—	—

Landowner	Occupiers	Plan No.	Lands and Premises	Culti-vation	Statute Measure a.	r.	p.	Payable to Rector £	s.	d.
	Sarah Lawes, Thomas Serle Thomas Oake, William Hatcher	234	Tenements and Garden	—	0	0	35	—	—	—
Bishop of Winchester & his Lessee Thomas Pern	Thos. Pern	255	Grubbed Ground	A.	13	0	8	2	19	0
The Churchwardens and Overseers	Themselves	156	Garden	—	0	0	10	—	—	—
George Steele	Himself and William Tongs	158	Tenements and Garden	—	0	0	30	—	—	—
Richard Turton	Himself	146	Cottage and Garden	—	0	0	26	—	—	—
Edward Twynam	William Millberry	79 80	Public House and Garden	—	0	1	8	—	—	—
	John Morrison	93	House Carpenters Shop Yard and Garden	—	0	1	20	—	—	—
	James Hendy	149	House Outbuildings Yard and Garden	—	0	1	26	—	—	—
William Wade	Himself	162	House and Garden	—	0	0	29			
		163	Paddock	P.	0	0	26	0	9	6
		164	"	"	0	2	12			
		165	"	"	0	2	32			
		166	Arable Field	A.	4	3	37	1	15	4
					6	2	16	2	4	10
Robert Waight	Harry Cuel, William Sandon	88	Tenements and Garden	—	0	0	24	—	—	—
	Stephen Ewens Sophia Weston	140	Tenements and Garden	—	0	0	29	—	—	—
	Himself (R. Waight)	65	Part of Home Close	A.	1	3	8	0	6	4
		66	Part of Home Close	"	8	0	5	2	8	6
		67	Middle Field	"	25	3	25	6	12	2

Landowner	Occupiers	Plan No.	Lands and Premises	Culti-vation	Statute Measure a.	r.	p.	Payable to Rector £	s.	d.
		68	Hut Field	A.	24	0	15	5	11	2
		69	Path Field	"	29	3	20	7	13	6
		87	Paddock	P.	0	2	0	0	3	0
		94	Homestead	—	1	0	30	0	3	0
		95	Paddock	P.	0	2	9 }	0	6	0
		96	"	"	0	1	38 }			
		222	Lower Pightle	A.	3	0	1	0	17	10
		223	Higher Pightle	"	2	2	37	0	16	0
		244	Morns Field	"	30	1	24	6	8	3
		245	Morns Down Field	"	25	2	15	3	0	3
		269	Coppice	W.	10	2	3	0	5	10
					164	2	30	34	11	10
Ralph John Thomas Williamson	Himself	91	House Stables and Garden	—	0	1	5 }	0	6	0
		92	Paddock	P.	0	2	28 }			
					0	3	33	0	6	0
Reverend Philip Jacob (Glebe)	Himself	55	Pasture Field	P.	2	3	17			
		56	" "	"	2	3	16			
		57	" "	"	1	0	7			
		59	Parsonage House Offices Pleasure grounds etc.	—	1	3	29			
		60	Barn and Yard	—	0	0	29			
		61	Roadway	—	0	0	10			
		63	Part of Paddock	P.	0	2	8			
		64	Plantation	W.	0	0	17			
		104	Church and Church Yard		0	1	34			
					10	0	7	2	10	0
			Roads		27	0	18			

SUMMARY

Landowner	Occupiers	Statute Measure			Payable to Rector		
		a.	r.	p.	£	s.	d.
Lord Ashburton	Himself	39	1	19	—	—	—
	Reverend Philip Jacob	1	1	22	0	10	0
	Thomas Pern	695	3	24	162	18	10
	Richard Bright	9	1	35	0	12	6
Lord Ashburton and his Lessee Robert Waight	Thomas Pern & Robert Waight	3	0	33	0	2	4
William Allen	James Ventham, James Kevell, John Newman	0	0	35	—	—	—
Richard Bright	Himself	167	2	15	8	12	7
	Sarah Sandom & others	0	0	4	—	—	—
	Himself	1	3	12	0	11	6
	George Hawkins	0	2	34	—	4	0
	William Wade	879	0	26	160	16	8
John Bramble, Senr., John Bramble, Junr.	Themselves	0	0	34	—	—	—
Sir Frederick Hutchinson Hervey Bathurst, Bart	James Fitt	11	2	20	2	10	3
Henry Cordery	George Lovell	10	2	20	0	5	0
Charles Cook	John Cook and Robert Holdaway	0	0	23	—	—	—
	Himself	0	0	21	—	—	—
William Dancaster	John Morrison	2	3	24	0	14	6
Robert Fifield	Himself	69	2	23	16	12	3
The Bishop of Winchester and Robert Fifield his Lessee	Robert Fifield	3	1	23	0	13	3
Ann Godwin	George Godwin	0	1	21	—	—	—
	Herself	0	0	18	—	—	—

Landowner	Occupiers	Statute Measure			Payable to Rector		
		a.	r.	p.	£	s.	d.
George Godwin	Himself	0	1	35	—	—	—
	John Grunsell	0	0	28			
William Gover	Himself	50	2	38	2	8	3
David Heron	Himself	0	0	13	—	—	—
William Hills	Himself and William Sandom	0	0	23	—	—	—
Reverend Philip Jacob	Himself	0	0	37	0	1	4
	John Hills	0	0	22	—	—	—
Richard Kent	Himself	0	0	24	—	—	—
Charles Morris, Charles Harrison, and Rowland Henry Lenthall	Lawrence Turton Allee	697	3	4	120	10	7
Thomas Page	William Willis	0	2	7	—	—	—
	Himself	70	2	5	14	14	3
The Bishop of Winchester and his Lessee Thomas Page	Thomas Page	40	2	24	9	2	9
Thomas Pern	Himself	295	3	35	60	9	5
		227	3	23	43	0	3
		46	3	10	14	7	10
	Thomas Brown, William Hatcher, Thomas Serle and Isaac Newman	0	0	38	—	—	—
	John Summerly and William Heron	0	0	16	—	—	—
	Joseph Elliot, Robert Burrough and Thomas Brown	0	0	32	—	—	—
	George Harrington and William Tongs	0	1	15	—	—	—
	John Judd, Christopher Pitter	0	0	30	—	—	—
	George Brown, James Shepherd	0	0	18	—	—	—
	Thomas Serle, Thomas Oak, William Hatcher, Sarah Lawes	0	0	35	—	—	—
Bishop of Winchester and his Lessee Thomas Pern		13	0	8	2	19	0

Landowner	Occupiers	Statute Measure			Payable to Rector		
		a.	r.	p.	£	s.	d.
The Churchwardens and Overseers	Themselves	0	0	10	—	—	—
George Steele	Himself and William Tongs	0	0	30	—	—	—
Richard Turton	Himself	0	0	26	—	—	—
Edward Twynam	William Millberry	0	1	8			
	John Morrison	0	1	20			
	James Hendy	0	1	26			
William Wade	Himself	6	2	16	2	4	10
Robert Waight	Harry Cuel and William Sandom	0	0	24	—	—	—
	Stephen Ewens and Sophia Weston	0	0	29	—	—	—
	Himself	164	2	30	34	11	10
Ralph John Thomas Williamson	Himself	—	3	33	0	6	0
Reverend Philip Jacob Glebe	Himself	10	0	7	2	10	0
	Roads	27	0	18	—	—	—
		3556	0	3	662	10	0

(Signed)

Charles Osborn

§§ 58. Census of the Civil Parish of Crawley, 1841.

The total population in the year 1841 was found to be 372, the same as in 1831, and only 48 more than in 1801. It is noteworthy that while the ages were in all cases set down, being required, the occupations were in many cases omitted, being optional with the individual.

Table of Occupations

Unspecified (chiefly women and children)		236
Lodgers (later erased)		4
Specified		132
Agricultural laborers	68	
Female servants	14	
Male servants	9	
Carpenters	8	
Yeomen	5	
Independent	3	
Housekeepers	3	
Others	22	

How largely agricultural the parish was, is indicated by the following rough analysis.

Classes of Occupations

Agriculture	76
Housework	26
Industry	21
Trade	3
Public service	3
Ind[ependent]	3
	132

In the 81 inhabited houses, lived 98 families, and, as has been said, 372 persons. All of the people were born in the county, except 15. Two households had one servant each, five had two, one three, and two four. All of the yeomen had servants, one having four, another three, one two, and the others one each.

It is notable that the steward came from Scotland, though he bore an old-time Crawley name. At the present (1928), the estate manager is also a Scotsman. This same estate agent has checked off the houses which he thinks were probably located in the Village of Crawley itself. The number of houses is 58 and the inhabitants 290. This may be a considerable underestimate, the number of houses probably being about 69.

ENUMERATOR'S SCHEDULE FOR THE PARISH OF CRAWLEY, BUDDLESGATE LIBERTY, CO. HANTS.[1] DATED 12 JUNE, 1841.

Abbreviations

Line thus | = head of the household
Line thus / = end of the names of each family
Lines thus // = end of the names of the inmates in each house
15 yrs. = persons aged 15 yrs. and under 20
20 yrs. = " " 20 " " " 25
25 yrs. = " " 25 " " " 30
30 yrs. = " " 30 " " " 35
and so on up to the greatest ages.
f. s. = female servant
m. s. = male servant
yeom. = yeoman
ag. lab. = agricultural labourer
[× placed by Mr. J. O. Robertson in 1928 opposite houses probably located in Crawley Village]

	Names of each person who abode therein the preceding night	Age & Sex		Profession, Trade Employment or of Independent means	Where born. Whether in the same co.
		Males	Females		
|	Jn. Sumner	24		Clergyman	y. [i. e. yes]
×	Rebecca Sawyer		45	f. s.	y.
//	Hen. Reeves	20		m. s.	y.
|	Thos. Pern	40		yeom.	y.
	Francis "		40		y.
×	Ann "		15		y.
	Thos. "	15			y.
/	Edw. "	4			y.
	June Bourough		15	f. s.	y.
//	Sarah Noyce		15	f. s.	y.
|	Jac. Courtney	30		yeom.	y.
×	Eliz. "		25		y.
	Eliz. "		8 mos.		y.
/	Hannah Brown		58	f. s.	y.
	Eliz. Bye		20	f. s.	y.
	Ann Newman		20	f. s.	y.
//	Wm. Herly	20		m. s.	y.
|	David Waite	50		steward	(Scotland)
×	Eliz. "		25		y.
	Joseph "	3			y.
/	Catherine "		1		y.
	Fanny Harris		20	f. s.	y.
	Jane Laws		13		y.
//	Geo. Holdway	18		m. s.	y.

[1] MS., P. R. O., Census 1841, bundle 403.

Names of each person who abode therein the preceding night	Age & Sex		Profession, Trade Employment or of Independent means	Where born. Whether in the same co.
	Males	Females		
| // Jn. Newman	76		ag. lab.	y.
| Lawr. Allee	63		yeom.	y.
Sarah "		50		y.
Wm. "	25			y.
Sarah "		22		y.
Chas. "	21			y.
/ Eliz. "		19		y.
Geo. Hendley	17		m. s.	y.
Mary Knight		17	f. s.	y.
// Phebe Kerby		41	f. s.	y.
| Geo. Sotheby	4			n.
× Georgina "		6		n.
/ Sarah Lane		55	ind.	y.
Sarah Blake		24	f. s.	y.
Martha Ladd		21	f. s.	y.
Bridger Millroy	20		m. s.	y.
Geo. Wilshire	14			y.
// Jas. Maton	64		m. s.	y.
| Thos. Paige	25		yeom.	y.
× Hannah "		25		y.
Thos. "	3			y.
Francis "		2		y.
/ Eliz. "		5 mos.		y.
Olive Butcher		20	f. s.	y.
Hen. Pottle	15		ag. lab.	y.
// Jn. Vince	15		ag. lab.	y.
| Eliz. Gover		45	ind.	y.
× Saml. "	9			y.
Jane "		8		y.
Maria "		6		y.
Mary "		20		y.
// Wm. "	20			y.
| Robt. Waight	40		yeom.	y.
/ Francis "		35		n.
// Joseph Henly	25		m. s.	y.
| Geo. Godwin	67		tailor	y.
× Geo. "	30		tailor & grocer	y.
Sophia "		28		y.
Lewis "	4			y.
/ Mary "		2		y.
// Geo. Bennett	30		ag. lab.	y.
| Wm. Tongs	30		ag. lab.	y.
× Fanny "		33		y.
Jn. "	11			y.
Eliz. "		8		y.
Chas. "	5			y.
// Wm. "	2			y.

Names of each person who abode therein the preceding night	Age & Sex		Profession, Trade Employment or of Independent means	Where born. Whether in the same co.
	Males	Females		
| Jn. Hill	27		grocer	y.
× Eliz. "		34		y.
/ Esther "		4		y.
// Geo. Steele	23		carpenter	y.
| Hen. Kewel	55		ag. lab.	y.
× Hannah "		55		y.
Jas. "	21		ag. lab.	y.
Chas. "	18		ag. lab.	y.
// Thos. "	14			y.
| Geo. Grace	26		bricklayer	y.
× Louisa "		32		y.
Walter "	5			y.
// Chas. "	1			y.
[Sic] Thos. Webb	22		journeyman	y.
Wm. Farly	21		labourer	y.
Hannah Pritchet		15	f. s.	y.
Martha Miles		14	f. s.	y.
Eliz. Bone		64	(lodger) [1]	y.
// Pheabe Milbury		3	(do.) [1]	y.
| Martha Hill		47		y.
× Thos. "	15		ag. lab.	y.
Emma "		15		y.
Walter "	12			y.
Ellen "		10		y.
Joseph "	7			y.
// Emely "		3		y.
| Wm. Tibble	30		gardener	y.
× Jane "		40		y.
// Emely Hering		8	(lodger) [1]	y.
| Saml. Hawkins	20		carpenter	y.
× Jane "		25		y.
/ Mary "		1		y.
John. Bennett	20		policeman	y.
Thos. Dukey	20		carpenter	y.
Wm. Willis	24		malster	y.
// Ann "		25	(lodger) [1]	y.
| Geo. Harrington	68			y.
/ Honour "		64		y.
Ann Hanaford		32		y.
Jn. "	28			n.
Albert Archer	9			n.
Ann Hanaford		9		n.
Anna "		2		n.
// Jn. "	6 mos.			n.
| Geo. Hawkins	60		carpenter	y.
× / Sarah "		55		y.
Eliz. Andrew		13		y.

[1] Erased, with the same ink with which the return has been checked.

Names of each person who abode therein the preceding night	Age & Sex		Profession, Trade Employment or of Independent means	Where born. Whether in the same co.
	Males	Females		
Jas. Green	25		carpenter	n.
Harriet "		30		y.
// Chas. Vince	15		ap.	y.
| Jn. Bramble	42		ag. lab.	y.
× Eliz. "		45		y.
Eliz. "		21		y.
// Martha "		14		y.
| Jn. Gruncell	34		carpenter	y.
× Ann "		33		y.
Mary "		14		y.
Ellen "		11		y.
Geo. "	9			y.
// Sarah "		2		y.
| Geo. Steele	45		carpenter	y.
× Betsey "		45		y.
Sarah "		25		y.
Ric. "	20		ag. lab.	y.
Wm. "	14			y.
Ed. "	11			y.
Chas. "	7			y.
// Mary "		5		y.
| Wm. Willis	75		malster	y.
× Ann "		60		y.
Ann "		25		y.
Louisa "		20		y.
/ Mary "		15		y.
Benj. Hobbs	45		ag. lab.	y.
// Jas. Seaward	65		ag. lab.	y.
| Wm. Tongs	55		ag. lab.	y.
Sarah "		20		y.
/ Eliza "		18		y.
// Wm. Surby	13			y
| Geo. Brown	35		ag. lab.	y
× Ann "		33		y.
Hen. "	14			y.
Ed. "	9			y.
Charlotte"		6		y.
// Eliz. "		4		y.
× | Ruth Turton		68	housekeeper	y.
Thos. Harris	18		m.s.	y.
Damis Tookway	15		m.s.	(Foreign parts)
Sarah Russell		13		y.
// Thos. Day	13			y.
× | Geo. Kewell	26		ag. lab.	y.
Eliz. "		23		y.
Jane "		3		y.
/ Fred^{k}. "	1			y.

Names of each person who abode therein the preceding night	Age & Sex Males	Females	Profession, Trade Employment or of Independent means	Where born. Whether in the same co.
// Jn. Tongs	24		ag. lab.	y.
| Thos. Brown	58		ag. lab.	y.
× Wm. "	28		ag. lab.	y.
Eliz. "		24		y.
Ann "		28		y.
Wm. "	3			y.
// Loyd "	2			y.
| Thos. Tibble	25		ag. lab.	y.
Sarah "		23		y.
// Mary "		7 mos.		y.
| Jn. Bourough	34		ag. lab.	y.
× Mary "		37		y.
Francis "		13		y.
Geo. "	10			y.
// Allis "		5		y.
| Ric. Turton	66		ag. lab.	y.
× Kittey "		63		y.
Jas. "	37		ag. lab.	y.
Chas. "	35		ag. lab.	y.
Sarah "		27		y.
Jane "		13		y.
Eliz. "		11		y.
Wm. "	9			y.
Ellen "		7		y.
Hen. "	3			y.
// Mary "		2		y.
| Thos. Kellow	60		game keeper	y.
Sarah "		55		y.
Louisa "		35		y.
// Albert "	4			y.
| Step. Ewins	70		ag. lab.	y.
× Pheby "		60		y.
Wm. "	25		ag. lab.	y.
Jn. "	21		ag. lab.	y.
// Eliz. "		20		y
| Wm. Henly	55		ag. lab.	y.
× Ann "		50		y.
Ann "		20		y.
Meria "		15		y.
// Chas. "	13			y.
| Joseph Ellott	60		ag. lab.	y.
/ Sophia Weston		45	housekeeper	y.
Jas. Harris	15			y.
// Mercia "		12		y.
× | Chas. Barter	34		ag. lab.	y.
Betty "		30		y.
Wm. "	8			y.

Names of each person who abode therein the preceding night	Age & Sex		Profession, Trade Employment or of Independent means	Where born. Whether in the same co.
	Males	Females		
Ellen Barter		6		y.
Henry "	3			y.
⁄⁄ Albert "	14			y.
| Wm. Hern	65		ag. lab.	y.
× Step. "	27			y.
Frances "		29		y.
Mary "		7		y.
Eliz. "		6		y.
Thos. "	3			y.
⁄⁄ Sarah "		1		y.
| Robt. Bourough	40		ag. lab.	y.
Sarah "		43		y.
⁄⁄ Mary "		8		y.
| Isaac Newman	30		ag. lab.	y.
× Sally "		23		y.
Geo. "	6			y.
Eliz. "		3		y.
⁄⁄ Wm. "	1			y.
| Wm. Kewell	30		ag. lab.	y.
× Amelia "		25		y.
Mary "		4		y.
Edwin "	2			y.
⁄⁄ Sarah "		4 mos.		y.
| Hen. Weston	30		ag. lab.	y.
× Ann "		27		y.
Jn. "	2			y.
⁄⁄ Eliz. "		4 mos.		y.
| Chas. Bramble	56		ag. lab.	y.
× Ann "		21		y.
⁄⁄ Jn. "	1			y.
| Wm. Barter	38		ag. lab.	y.
× Mary "		43		y.
Geo. "	11			y.
⁄⁄ Ann "		8		y.
| Wm. Ward	27		ag. lab.	y.
Sarah "		23		y.
Eliz. "		3		y.
⁄⁄ Ann "		1		y.
| Chas. Martin	55		brickburner	y.
× ⁄ Mary "		45		n.
Percey Gill	25		brickmaker	n.
Jane Martin		15		y.
Wm. "	15		brickmaker	y.
⁄⁄ Jas. Sandom	25		carter	y.
| Wm. Bramble	30		ag. lab.	y.
× Hanna "		30		y.
Geo. Bramble	6			y.

<table>
<tr><th rowspan="2"></th><th rowspan="2">Names of each person who abode therein the preceding night</th><th colspan="2">Age & Sex</th><th rowspan="2">Profession, Trade Employment or of Independent means</th><th rowspan="2">Where born. Whether in the same co.</th></tr>
<tr><th>Males</th><th>Females</th></tr>
<tr><td></td><td>Edwin Bramble</td><td>3</td><td></td><td></td><td>y.</td></tr>
<tr><td>//</td><td>Jn. “</td><td>9 mths.</td><td></td><td></td><td>y.</td></tr>
<tr><td>|</td><td>Jn. Cook</td><td>59</td><td></td><td>smith</td><td>y.</td></tr>
<tr><td>×</td><td>Francis “</td><td></td><td>40</td><td></td><td>y.</td></tr>
<tr><td></td><td>Eliz. “</td><td></td><td>80</td><td></td><td>y.</td></tr>
<tr><td></td><td>Mary “</td><td></td><td>14</td><td></td><td>y.</td></tr>
<tr><td></td><td>Frances “</td><td></td><td>11</td><td></td><td>y.</td></tr>
<tr><td>//</td><td>Chas. “</td><td>8</td><td></td><td></td><td>y.</td></tr>
<tr><td>|</td><td>Wm. Kimber</td><td>25</td><td></td><td>ag. lab.</td><td>y.</td></tr>
<tr><td>×</td><td>Charlotte “</td><td></td><td>30</td><td></td><td>y</td></tr>
<tr><td></td><td>Hen. “</td><td>5</td><td></td><td></td><td>y.</td></tr>
<tr><td></td><td>Eliz. “</td><td></td><td>3</td><td></td><td>y.</td></tr>
<tr><td>/</td><td>Mary “</td><td></td><td>7 mos.</td><td></td><td>y.</td></tr>
<tr><td></td><td>Joseph Sandom</td><td>25</td><td></td><td>ag. lab.</td><td>y.</td></tr>
<tr><td>//</td><td>Wm. Miles</td><td>25</td><td></td><td>ag. lab.</td><td>y.</td></tr>
<tr><td>× | //</td><td>Sarah Barter</td><td></td><td>65</td><td></td><td>y.</td></tr>
<tr><td>|</td><td>Sarah Laws</td><td></td><td>46</td><td></td><td>y.</td></tr>
<tr><td>×</td><td>Thos. “</td><td>14</td><td></td><td></td><td>y.</td></tr>
<tr><td></td><td>Arthur “</td><td>11</td><td></td><td></td><td>y.</td></tr>
<tr><td>/</td><td>Hannah “</td><td></td><td>9</td><td></td><td>y.</td></tr>
<tr><td></td><td>Charlotte Benett</td><td></td><td>30</td><td></td><td>y.</td></tr>
<tr><td></td><td>Emma “</td><td></td><td>7</td><td></td><td>y.</td></tr>
<tr><td>//</td><td>Chas. “</td><td>2</td><td></td><td></td><td>y.</td></tr>
<tr><td>|</td><td>Chas. Cook</td><td>69</td><td></td><td>smith</td><td>y.</td></tr>
<tr><td>/</td><td>Thos. “</td><td>74</td><td></td><td></td><td>y.</td></tr>
<tr><td>//</td><td>Jane Hern</td><td></td><td>7</td><td></td><td>y.</td></tr>
<tr><td>|</td><td>Geo. Nicklas</td><td>23</td><td></td><td>ag. lab.</td><td>y.</td></tr>
<tr><td>//</td><td>Sophia “</td><td></td><td>22</td><td></td><td>y.</td></tr>
<tr><td>|</td><td>Wm. Hatcher</td><td>39</td><td></td><td></td><td>y.</td></tr>
<tr><td>//</td><td>Eliz. “</td><td></td><td>17</td><td></td><td>y.</td></tr>
<tr><td>× |</td><td>Ann Godwin</td><td></td><td>75</td><td></td><td>y.</td></tr>
<tr><td></td><td>Geo. “</td><td>54</td><td></td><td></td><td>y.[1]</td></tr>
<tr><td></td><td>Sarah “</td><td></td><td>44</td><td></td><td></td></tr>
<tr><td>/</td><td>Hanna “</td><td></td><td>10</td><td></td><td></td></tr>
<tr><td>//</td><td>Robt. Spring</td><td>40</td><td></td><td></td><td>n.</td></tr>
<tr><td>|</td><td>Hen. Browning</td><td>41</td><td></td><td>ag. lab.</td><td></td></tr>
<tr><td>×</td><td>Hanna “</td><td></td><td>39</td><td></td><td></td></tr>
<tr><td></td><td>Hanna “</td><td></td><td>10</td><td></td><td></td></tr>
<tr><td></td><td>Hen. “</td><td>10</td><td></td><td></td><td></td></tr>
<tr><td></td><td>Sarah “</td><td></td><td>8</td><td></td><td></td></tr>
<tr><td>//</td><td>Chas. “</td><td>5</td><td></td><td></td><td></td></tr>
<tr><td>|</td><td>Eliz. Kent</td><td></td><td>33</td><td>shoemaker</td><td></td></tr>
<tr><td></td><td>Jn. “</td><td>2</td><td></td><td></td><td></td></tr>
<tr><td></td><td>Agnes “</td><td></td><td>4 mos.</td><td></td><td></td></tr>
<tr><td>//</td><td>Keria Kennett</td><td></td><td>13</td><td></td><td></td></tr>
<tr><td>|</td><td>Christopher Pitter</td><td>59</td><td></td><td>ag. lab.</td><td></td></tr>
<tr><td>×</td><td>Harriet “</td><td></td><td>20</td><td></td><td></td></tr>
</table>

[1] Born in the same county, unless otherwise stated.

<table>
<tr><th rowspan="2">Names of each person who abode therein the preceding night</th><th colspan="2">Age & Sex</th><th rowspan="2">Profession, Trade Employment or of Independent means</th><th rowspan="2">Where born. Whether in the same co.</th></tr>
<tr><th>Males</th><th>Females</th></tr>
<tr><td>// Eliz. Pitter</td><td></td><td>15</td><td></td><td></td></tr>
<tr><td>| Jas. Sheppard</td><td>55</td><td></td><td>ag. lab.</td><td></td></tr>
<tr><td>// Mary "</td><td></td><td>40</td><td></td><td></td></tr>
<tr><td>× | Jn. Bramble</td><td>65</td><td></td><td>ag. lab.</td><td></td></tr>
<tr><td>// Mary "</td><td></td><td>57</td><td></td><td></td></tr>
<tr><td>| Jn. Tudd</td><td>52</td><td></td><td>ag. lab.</td><td></td></tr>
<tr><td>Eliz. "</td><td></td><td>51</td><td></td><td></td></tr>
<tr><td>// Jas. "</td><td>24</td><td></td><td>ag. lab.</td><td></td></tr>
<tr><td>| Wm. Tibble</td><td>60</td><td></td><td>ag. lab.</td><td></td></tr>
<tr><td>Mary "</td><td></td><td>55</td><td></td><td></td></tr>
<tr><td>// Eliz. "</td><td></td><td>16</td><td></td><td></td></tr>
<tr><td>| Chas. Ewins</td><td>33</td><td></td><td>ag. lab.</td><td></td></tr>
<tr><td>× / Sarah "</td><td></td><td>39</td><td></td><td></td></tr>
<tr><td>// Ann Witcher</td><td></td><td>14</td><td></td><td></td></tr>
<tr><td>| Robt. Pain</td><td>60</td><td></td><td>ag. lab.</td><td></td></tr>
<tr><td>× Ann "</td><td></td><td>59</td><td></td><td></td></tr>
<tr><td>// Jn. "</td><td>29</td><td></td><td>ag. lab.</td><td></td></tr>
<tr><td>× | Wm. Sandom</td><td>70</td><td></td><td></td><td></td></tr>
<tr><td>// Jane "</td><td></td><td>75</td><td></td><td></td></tr>
<tr><td>| Robt. Holdway</td><td>49</td><td></td><td>carpenter</td><td></td></tr>
<tr><td>// Sally "</td><td></td><td>49</td><td></td><td></td></tr>
<tr><td>| David Vince</td><td>86</td><td></td><td></td><td></td></tr>
<tr><td>Temperance Vince</td><td></td><td>19</td><td></td><td></td></tr>
<tr><td>// Mary "</td><td></td><td>8</td><td></td><td></td></tr>
<tr><td>| Joseph King</td><td>30</td><td></td><td>shoemaker</td><td></td></tr>
<tr><td>Sophia "</td><td></td><td>30</td><td></td><td></td></tr>
<tr><td>// Eliz. "</td><td></td><td>3 mths.</td><td></td><td></td></tr>
<tr><td>| Hen. Oakes</td><td>44</td><td></td><td>ag. lab.</td><td></td></tr>
<tr><td>/ Olive "</td><td></td><td>25</td><td></td><td></td></tr>
<tr><td>// Ric. Hankin</td><td>21</td><td></td><td>ag. lab.</td><td></td></tr>
<tr><td>× |// Jas. Kewell</td><td>60</td><td></td><td>ag. lab.</td><td></td></tr>
<tr><td>/ Sarah Sheppard</td><td></td><td>57</td><td>housekeeper</td><td></td></tr>
<tr><td>| Mary Bourough</td><td></td><td>70</td><td></td><td></td></tr>
<tr><td>× // Wm. "</td><td>12</td><td></td><td></td><td></td></tr>
<tr><td>| Wm. Sandom</td><td>51</td><td></td><td>ag. lab.</td><td></td></tr>
<tr><td>× Eliz. "</td><td></td><td>48</td><td></td><td></td></tr>
<tr><td>// Jas. "</td><td>23</td><td></td><td></td><td></td></tr>
<tr><td>| Jn. Somersby</td><td>60</td><td></td><td>ag. lab.</td><td></td></tr>
<tr><td>Betty "</td><td></td><td>63</td><td></td><td></td></tr>
<tr><td>// Geo. "</td><td>32</td><td></td><td>ag. lab.</td><td></td></tr>
<tr><td>| Hen. Ewins</td><td>29</td><td></td><td>ag. lab.</td><td></td></tr>
<tr><td>× Sarah "</td><td></td><td>21</td><td></td><td></td></tr>
<tr><td>// Sarah "</td><td></td><td>1</td><td></td><td></td></tr>
<tr><td>× //| Eliz. Paige</td><td></td><td>60</td><td>ind.</td><td></td></tr>
<tr><td>× | Jas. Ventham</td><td>61</td><td></td><td>ag. lab.</td><td></td></tr>
<tr><td>// Rachel "</td><td></td><td>59</td><td></td><td></td></tr>
<tr><td>// | Ann Pain</td><td></td><td>30</td><td></td><td></td></tr>
</table>

	Names of each person who abode therein the preceding night	Age & Sex		Profession, Trade Employment or of Independent means	Where born. Whether in the same co.
		Males	Females		
|	Charlotte Kimber		65		
/	Thos. "	10			
//	Thos. Wareham	17			n.
× |	Susan Brown		90		
//	Sally Samdom		79		
|	Saml. Glass	50		ag. lab.	
×	Mary "		35		
	Harriot "		9		
	Geo. "	7			
/	Charles "	4			
	Wm. Parker	22		ag. lab.	
	Fred^k. Bramble	18		ag. lab.	
	Wm. Godwin	16		ag. lab.	
//	Jas. Phillis	19		ag. lab.	
|	Thos. Serle	45		ag. lab.	
×	David "	17		ag. lab.	
	Hen. "	15			
	Mary "		13		
//	Wm. "	11			

| Rookley House [uninhabited]

81 Inhabited houses.	Males	187
1 Uninhabited house.	Females	185
98 Families	Total	372

§§ 59. Census of the Civil Parish of Crawley, 1851.

Clearly the census of 1851 was the most precise and definite taken up to date. The changes from 1841 are notable. Population increased from 372 to 402. Inhabited houses diminished from 81 to 79 (or 80). The number born outside of the county increased from 15 to 38. Of these 38, 16 were Irish and 5 of the Irish were trampers sleeping in stables. There were 2 grocers in 1851, in 1841 only one. And in 1851 there was a curate as well as a rector.

TABLE SHOWING FARMERS AND THEIR HOLDINGS

Thomas Pern	1,280 acres	40 laborers
Jacob H. Courtney (Manor Farm)	900 "	[28][1] "
William Allee (Rookley Farm)	679 "	22 "
Henry Reeves (Rookley House)	400 "	12 "
Robert Waight	176 "	8[2] "
Thomas Paige	124 "	5 "
	3,559 "	115[3] "

It is surprising to note that of the 3,607 acres in the parish, 3,559 were in the possession of these 6 farmers. Apparently only 48 acres remained outside their clutches, unless some of the six holdings in question extended beyond the parish boundaries.[4] All the farms were pretty much the same in amount in 1851 as in 1837. Robert Fifield with 73 acres in 1837 was supplanted by Henry Reeves with 400 acres in 1851.

The school was a new element in the census. Out of a total of 170 children (up to and including 16 years), 88 (ranging from 2 to 13 years) attended school. Children between 9 and 16 were laboring to the number of 24 — 10 plowboys, 5 farm servants, 2 shepherd boys, 2 laborers, and 1 groom, and 4 female house servants.

Crawley Parish was growing. Outsiders were coming in. Agriculture was dominant, and in the control of 6 farmers. On these farmers the rest of the people depended for a living. Big farms paid their occupiers. The presence of the school and four dressmakers with an apprentice seems to indicate a somewhat higher plane of living. And yet the 6 paupers are not reassuring.

[1] Estimated at one laborer to 32 acres.
[2] Four men and four boys.
[3] Includes children employed.
[4] Since 51 acres were in roads and under water, there were only 3556 left for fields and other plots.

CRAWLEY PARISH, BUDDLESGATE LIBERTY, HANTS

CRAWLEY PARISH, BUDDLESGATE LIBERTY, HANTS.[1] DATED 7 AP., 1851

ABBREVIATIONS

Line drawn right across the page separates one household from another.
Line commencing in column 2 separates one family from another within the same house.

hd. = head	sch. = scholar	u. = unmarried
d. = daughter	w. = wife	wid. = widow
s. = servant	grdd. = granddaughter	widr. = widower
mar. = married		

	Name and surname of each person who abode in the house on the night of 30th Mar. 1851	Relation to head of the family	Condition	Age: Male	Age: Female	Rank, profession, or occupation	Where born
1	David Waite	hd.	mar.	65		land agent	Scotland
	Eliz. "	w.	mar.		39	do. wife	Hursley Hants.
	Joseph W. Waite	son	u.	13		sch.	Crawley "
	Catherine E. "	d.	u.		11	"	" "
	Agnes H. "	d.	u.		9	"	" "
	Thos. "	son	u.	7		"	" "
	Rosabella "	d.	u.		3	"	" "
	Mary A. Thatcher	s.	u.		22	house s.	Kingsclere "
	Chas. Gaiger	lab.	u.	18		lab.	Barton Stacey Hants.
2	Geo. Bourough	hd.	widr.	39		ag. lab.	Crawley Hants.
	Wm. "	son	u.	6		sch.	" "
	Mary "	Mother	wid.		83	pauper on the receipt of parish relief	Hursley "
3	Geo. Hawkins	hd.	mar.	71		carpenter, master employing 2 men	Sutton Scotney
	Sarah "	w.	mar.		70	do. wife	East Stratton
	Eliz. Way	grdd.	mar.		22		Crawley

[1] MS., P. R. O., Census 1851, bundle 1673.

4	Chas. Rogers	hd.	mar.	26		police constable	Hordle Hants.
	Frances "	w.	mar.		27	do. wife	Newton Ringwood Hants.
	Alfred H. "	son		1			Crawley "
	Zippy A. "	d.			4 mths.		" "
	Martha Bunting	s.	u.		16	house s.	Lower Wallop "
5	Saml. Hawkins	hd.	mar.	31		carpenter	Crawley Hants.
	June "	w.	mar.		36		Rhyde Isle of Wight
	Mary "	d.			11	sch.	Barton Stacey Hants.
	Emily "	d.			8	"	Crawley "
	Ellen "	d.			6	"	" "
	Alfred "	son		3			" "
	Harriet "	d.			1		" "
6	Chas. Cooper	Hd.	mar.	37		common carrier	Kingsombourne Hants.
	Eliz. "	w.	mar.		25	carrier's wife	Crawley "
	Eliz. "	d.			4		" "
7	Wm. Tongs	Hd.		40		labourer	Week Hants.
	Eliz. H. "	d.	u.		18		Crawley "
	Chas. "	son		15		ploughboy	" "
	Wm. "	son		11		"	" "
8	Phebe Ewins	Hd.	wid.		70	pauper on parish relief	Sparsholt Hants.
	Wm. "	son	u.	27		ag. lab.	Crawley "
	Wm. "	grdson.		8		sch.	" "
9	Geo. Godwin	Househdr.	mar.	64		lab.	Crawley Hants.
	Sarah "	w.	mar.		54		Up Sunbourn Hants.
	Robt. Spring	lodger	u.	51		lab.	Nosall, Stafford
	Chas. M. Vince	lodger	u.	24		carpenter	Winchester Hants.

	Name and surname of each person who abode in the house on the night of 30th Mar. 1851	Relation to head of the family	Condition	Age: Male	Age: Female	Rank, profession, or occupation	Where born
10	Geo. Godwin	Hd.	mar.	40		grocer	Crawley Hants.
	Sophia "	wife	mar.		38	grocer's wife	Kingsombourne Hants.
	Lewis R. "	son		14		sch.	Crawley "
	Mary S. "	d.			12	"	" "
	Emily R. "	d.			10	"	" "
	Geo. R. "	son		3			" "
	Geo. "	father	widr.	76		sub post master	Winchester "
11	Hen. Serle	Hd.	Mar.	25		ag. lab.	Crawley Hants.
	Jane "	w.	Mar.		23	ag. lab's. wife	" "
	Emma "	d.			3		" "
	Arthur "	son.		1 mth.			" "
12	Martha Hill	Hd.	wid.		57	{ in receipt of relief { occasionally employed	Dinton Wilts.
	Walt. "	son	u.	21		ag. lab.	Crawley "
	Joseph Bramble	lodger	u.	36		ag. lab.	" "
13	Jas. Sandom	Hd.	mar.	33		ag. lab.	Crawley Hants.
	Eliz. "	w.	mar.		31	ag. lab's. wife	Wonston
	Geo. "	son		7		ag. lab's. son at home	Crawley Hants.
	Wm. "	son		4		" " " "	" "
	Hen. "	son		1		" " " "	" "
	Wm. "	father	widr.	62		ag. lab.	" "
14	Chas. Turton	Hd.	mar.	46		lab.	Crawley Hants.
	Sarah "	w.	mar.		41	do's. wife	Bristol, Glos.
	Mary A. "	d.			13	" d.	Crawley Hants.

	Robt. Turton	son		10			Crawley Hants.
	Eliza "	d.			under 11 mths.		" "
	Jas. "	brother	u.	47		lab.	" "
15	Hen. Cory Eade	part occupier	u.	24		curate of Crawley	Redruth Cornwall
16	Hen. Pottle	part occupier	mar.	26		domestic s.	Farley Hants.
	Martha "	w.	mar.		24	servant-wife	Crawley "
	Hen. "	son		under 6 mths.			" "
	Emily Hill	s.			13	house servant	" "
17	Jn. Bramble	Hd.	mar.	53		ag. lab.	Crawley Hants.
	Eliz. "	w.	mar.		55	lab's. wife	Sparsholt
18	Fredk. Bramble	Hd.	u.	29		ag. lab.	Crawley
	3 houses uninhabited						
19	Jn. Gruncell	Hd.	mar.	44		carpenter	Kingsombourne Hants.
	Ann "	w.	mar.		43		Crawley
	Ellen "	d.	u.		21		"
	Sarah "	d.	u.		12	scholar	"
	Emma "	d.	u.		9	"	"
	Jn. "	son	u.	6		"	"
	Alfred "	grdson.		7 mths.			"
	William Tibble	lodger	widr.	70		ag. lab.	"
20	Robt. Payne	Hd.	mar.	68		lab.	Crawley Hants.
	Ann "	w.	mar.		69	do's. wife	Fareham
	John "	son	u.	39		son at home	Crawley

	Name and surname of each person who abode in the house on the night of 30th Mar. 1851	Relation to head of the family	Condition	Age: Male	Age: Female	Rank, profession, or occupation	Where born
21	Ellen Barter	occupier	u.	17		labourer	Crawley Hants.
22	Geo. Cuell	Hd.	mar.	37		lab.	Crawley
	Betsy "	w.	mar.		33		"
	Emily "	d.			12	sch.	"
	Fredk. "	son		10		"	"
	Sabina "	d.			8	"	"
	Agnes "	d.			6	"	"
	Jas. "	son		4		"	"
	Mary "	d.			3	"	"
	Eliz. "	d.			under 7 mths.	labourer's d.	"
23	Jn. Newman	Hd.	widr.	about 86		pauper on receipt of parish relief formerly lab.	Ashley Hants.
	Wm. Mansbridge	Husband son's wife	mar.	42		lab.	Kingsombourne
	Sally "	son's wife	mar.		32		"
	Geo. Newman	grdson.	u.	15		ploughboy	Crawley
	Eliz. "	grdd.	u.		13		"
	Hen. "	grdson.		9		ploughboy	"
	Wm. Mansbridge	Husband's son son's wife		8		sch.	Kingsombourne
	Chas. Newman	grdson.		7		ploughboy	Crawley
	Phebe "	grdd.			3	sch.	"
	Betsey "	grdd.			1		"
24	Wm. Bramble	hd.	mar.	43		lab.	Crawley
	Anna "	w.	mar.		43		Overton

	Jn. Bramble	son		10		lab.	Crawley
	Chas. "	son		8		sch.	"
	Eliz. "	d.			5	"	"
	Harriet "	d.			2	"	"
25	Chas. Weston	hd.	mar.	38		lab.	Crawley
	Harriet "	w.	mar.		32		Barton Stacey
	Jn. "	son		9		ploughboy	" "
	Mary Ann "	d.			7	sch.	Crawley
	Martha "	d.			5	"	"
	Tom "	son		3		"	"
26	Ric. Steele	hd.		31		lab.	Crawley
	Ann "	w.			31		Stockbridge
	Betsey "	d.			5	sch.	Crawley
	Mary "	d.			3	"	"
	Edward "	son		under 4 mths.			"
27	Wm. Willis	Hd.	mar.	33		lab.	Crawley[1] Hants.
	Ann "	w.	mar.		35	dressmaker	"
	Hen. "	son		7		sch.	"
	Alfred "	son		5		"	"
	Esther "	d.			3	"	"
	Alice "	d.			2	"	"
	Hubert "	son		8 mths.			"
28	Wm. Freemantle	hd.	mar.	43		blacksmith	Alresford Hants.
	Sarah "	w.	mar.		36	blacksmith's wife	Barton Stacey
	Emily "	d.			11	sch.	" "
	Ann "	d.			8	"	" "
	Harriet "	d.			6	"	C.

[1] Hereafter written C.

No.	Name and surname of each person who abode in the house on the night of 30th Mar. 1851	Relation to head of the family	Condition	Age: Male	Age: Female	Rank, profession, or occupation	Where born
	Fred[k]. Freemantle	son		4		sch.	C.
	Jn. "	son		2		"	"
	An infant	son		under 1 mth.		blacksmith's son	"
	Jane Gruncell	wife's sister	mar.		27	lab's. wife	Barton Stacey.
29	Jas. Ventham	hd.	mar.	68		lab.	Ashley Hants.
	Rachel "	w.	mar.		66	lab's. wife	Warneford
30	Geo. Steele	hd.	mar.	56		carpenter wheelwright	C.
	Betsey "	w.	mar.		56		Kingsombourne
	Chas. "	son	u.	17		farm lab.	C.
31	Eliz. Hill	hd.	mar.		48	schoolmistress	Long parish Hants.
	Esther "	d.			13	sch.	C.
32	Wm. Brown	hd.	mar.	35		lab.	C.
	Mary A. "	w.	mar.		37	occasionally employed	Longstock
	Wm. "	son		13		ploughboy	C.
	Mary A. "	d.			9	sch.	"
	Esther "	d.			7	"	"
	Louisa "	d.			5	"	"
	Rhoda "	d.			2	"	"
	Ellen "	d.			under 5 mths.	lab's. d.	"
33	Hen. Browning	hd.	mar.	52		ag. lab.	Littleton, Hants.
	Hannah "	w.	mar.		48		Headbourne Worthy
	Hen. "	son	u.	20		ag. lab.	" "

	Chas. Browning	son		14		ag. lab.	C.
	Emma "	d			9	sch.	"
	Wm. "	son		7		"	"
	Sarah "	grdd.			2	"	Winchester
34	Jas. Sheppard	hd.	mar.	60		ag. lab.	C.
	Mary "	w.	mar.		51	ag. lab's. wife	Stockbridge
35	Eliz. Judd	hd.	wid.		63	lab's. widow in receipt of parochial relief	C.
36	Christopher Pitter	hd.	widr.	67		lab.	C.
	Harriet "	d.	u.		30	occasionally employed as laundress	"
37	Hen. Ewens	hd.	mar.	about 38		gamekeeper	C.
	Sarah "	w.	mar.		30		"
	Sarah "	d.			10	sch.	"
	Eliz. "	d.			8	"	"
	Chas. "	son		4		"	"
	Geo. "	son		1			"
38	Eliz. Kent	hd.	wid.		41	shop keeper	Bramdean Hants.
	Agnes "	d.			10	sch.	C.
39	Hen. Oakes	hd.	mar.	56		lab.	Clatford Hants.
	Olave "	w.	mar.		37		Wonston.
40	Thos. Serle	hd.	widr.	58		lab.	C.
	Dav. "	son	mar.	28		"	"
	Anna "	son's wife	mar.		33		Chilbolton

	Name and surname of each person who abode in the house on the night of 30th Mar. 1851	Relation to head of the family	Condition	Age: Male	Age: Female	Rank, profession, or occupation	Where born
	Eliz. Serle	grdd.			10	sch.	Chilbolton
	Jas. "	grdson.		1		lab's. son	C.
41	Wm. Hatcher	hd.	widr.	51		lab.	Fairley Wilts.[1]
42	Sarah Laws	hd.	wid.		56	shoemaker's wid. in receipt of parish relief	Mitchelmersh
	Thos. "	son	u.	23		domestic s.	"
	Arthur "	son	u.	20		lab.	C.
43	Wm. Willis	hd.	mar.	88		malster	Newbury Berks.
	Ann "	w.	mar.		70	malster's wife	Kingsclere Hants.
	Mary A. "	d.	u.		27		C.
	Benj. Hobbs	lodger	u.	55		ag. lab.	Candover.
44	Thos. Pern	hd.	widr.	52		farmer (of 1280 ac. employing 40 labourers)	C.
	Ann E. "	d.	u.		27	farmer's d.	"
	S. Pain	visitor	u.		27	farmer's d.	Broughton
	Charlotte Brown	House s.	u.		17	house s.	C.
	Denis Collins			61		Irish trampers, slept in stable; vagrants	Ireland
	Margaret "				51		"
	Pat[k]. Sheen			28			"
	Mary "				26		"
	Margaret "				1		"
45	Chas. Ewins	hd.	mar.	44		grocer	C.
	Sarah "	w.	mar.		50	grocer's wife	Titcomb Wilts.

[1] Altered from Houghton, Hants.

	Jn. Ewins	lodger	u.	30		ag. lab.	C.
	Sarah Judd	s.	u.		17	house s.	Kingsombourne
46	Geo. Grace	hd.	mar.	35		builder & publican	Braishfield Hants.
	Louisa "	w.	mar.		43	builder's wife	Saint Cross
	Walt. "	son	u.	15		at home	Littleton
	Sarah "	d.	u.		12	sch.	C.
	Chas. "	son	u.	10		"	Littleton
	Alf. "	son		7		"	C.
	Thos. "	son		4		"	"
	Matilda"	d.			2	"	"
	Jas. Filpot	s.	u.	31		builder's lab.	Braishfield
47	Geo. Grigg	hd.	mar.	38		shoemaker	Litchfield Hants.
	Susanna "	w.	mar.		45	shoemaker's wife	Barton Stacey
48	Joseph Hendly	hd.	mar.	34		lab.	C.
	Mary Ann "	w.	mar.		30	occasionally working at farmer's work	Barton Stacey
	Geo. Paice	son of M. A. Hen^y: before marriage		7		sch.	" "
	Harriet Hendly				3		C.
	Martha "				7 mths.		"
49	Steph. Hern	hd.	mar.	37		lab.	C.
	Fanny "	w.	mar.		40	occasionally a servant.	Kingsombourne
	Eliz. "	d.	u.		15	" employed in fields	C.
	Thos. "	son		13		plough boy	"
	Sarah "	d.			10	sch.	"
	Wm. "	son		9		shepherds boy	"
	Charlotte "	d.			4	sch.	"
	Geo. "	son		under 8 mths.			"

Name and surname of each person who abode in the house on the night of 30th Mar. 1851	Relation to head of the family	Condition	Age: Male	Age: Female	Rank, profession, or occupation	Where born
50 Thos. Cuell	hd.	mar.	24		ag. lab.	C.
Jane "	w.	mar.		21		Sutton
Martha "	d.			1		C.
Chas. Alderman	lodger	u.	27		ag. lab.	Andover
Jn. Shephard	"	u.	24		" "	Frelton Wilts.
Hen. Scarlett	"	u.	19		" "	Bullington Hants.
Jas. Hobbs	"	u.	18		" "	Headbourne Worthy
Fredk. Hobbs	"	u.	17		" "	" "
51 Robt. Bourough	hd.	mar.	53		lab.	C.
Sarah "	w.	mar.		54	laundress	Littleton
Wm. "	son	u.	22		domestic s.	C.
Mary Ann "	d.	u.		17	dressmaker's apprentice	"
52 Thos. Brown	hd.	mar.	68		lab.	C.
Hannah "	w.	mar.		67		Andover
Betsey "	d.	u.		33		C.
Lloyd "	grdson.		12		ploughboy	"
Ellen "	grdd.			6	sch.	"
Rosanna "	grdd.			2	"	"
53 Geo. Henley	hd.	mar.	28		lab.	C.
Betsey "	w.	mar.		28		"
Mary "	d.			2	sch.	"
54 Jn. Tongs	hd.	mar.	35		lab.	C.
Louisa "	w.	mar.		48		Sparsholt
Albert "	son		13		groom	C.

	Jn. Tongs	son		5		sch.	C.
	Geo. "	son		2			"
55	Wm. Tibble	hd.	mar.	41		gardener	Northington Hants.
	Jane "	w.	mar.		52		"
	Ann Russell	visitor	u.		17	dressmaker	"
	Eliza Thompson	Niece			10	sch. at home.	"
56	Thos. Weston	hd.	mar.	39		lab.	C.
	Mary Ann "	w.	mar.		23		Barton Stacey
	Sabina Elliott	Mother in law	wid.		71		" "
57	Hen. Ings	hd.	mar.	28		blacksmith	Sparsholt Hants.
	Eliza "	w.	mar.		27		C.
	Sarah W. Ings	d.			5	sch.	Alton
	Hen. J. "	son		2		"	Long parish
	Wm. Gregory	lodger	u.	24		lab.	Odiham.
58	Wm. Cuell	hd.	mar.	39		lab.	C.
	Amelia "	w.	mar.		35		Sparsholt
	Edwin "	son		12		sch.	C.
	Eliz. "	d.			4	"	"
	Lewis "	son		1			"
59	Geo. Lansley	hd.	mar.	31		bricklayer	Abbots Ann Hants.
	Ann "	w.	mar.		30		Leatherhead Surr.
60	Anne Coulson	hd.	mar.		38	husband abroad	Chigwell Essex
	Wm. "	son		7		sch.	Hursley Hants.
	Jas. G. "	son		4			"

	Name and surname of each person who abode in the house on the night of 30th Mar. 1851	Relation to head of the family	Condition	Age: Male	Age: Female	Rank, profession, or occupation	Where born
	Eliz. Stace	Mother	wid.		73		Chigwell Essex
	Mary Blake	s.			13	house s.	Farleigh Hants.
61	Robt. Waight	hd.	mar.	50		yeom. (176 ac. employing 4 men, 4 boys, 6 women, 2 girls)	Alresford Hants.
	Frances "	w.	mar.		46		East Marden, Sussex
	Mary Steele	s.	u.		15	house s.	C.
	Bartholomew Farasey	s.	mar.	37		farm lab.	Ireland
	Catharine "	s.	mar.		35	farm s.	"
	Mathew "	s.		13		shepherd	"
	Jn. "	s.		11 mths.			Spetsbury Dorsetshire
	Thos. Hagity	s.	mar.	34		farm lab.	Ireland
	Catharine "	s.	mar.		26	farm s.	"
	Robt. "	s.		5			"
	Ellen "				4		"
	Margaret "				1		Bath. Somersetshire
	Johanna Cunningham	s.	wid.		35	farm s.	Ireland
	Jn. "	s.		14		shepherd	"
	Margaret "	s.			12	farm s.	"
	Ellen Sauntry	s.	u.		35	" "	"
62	Wm. Parker	hd.	mar.		32	farm lab.	Stockbridge Hants.
	Maria "	w.	mar.		25		C.
63	Ann Hendly	hd.	wid.		64	lab's wife, occasionally employed	C.
	Chas. "	son	u.	23		lab.	"
	Andrew Winkworth	grdson.		6		sch.	Headbourne Worthy

64	Thos. Tibble	hd.	mar.	38		ag. lab.	C.
	Sarah "	w.	mar.		33		"
	Mary Ann "	d.			10	sch.	"
	Eliz. "	d.			4	"	"
	An infant	d.			under 1 mth.		"
65	Geo. Brown	hd.	mar.	45		ag. lab.	C.
	Ann "	w.	mar.		44	laundress	Littleton
	Edw. "	son	u.	18		ag. lab.	C.
	Chas. "	son		8		sch.	"
	Walt. "	son		1			"
66	Wm. Barter	hd.	mar.	48		woodman	C.
	Mary "	w.	mar.		53		Wallop. Hants.
	Geo. "	son	u.	21		woodman	C.
	Wm. "	nephew	u.	19		ag. lab.	"
	Jas. Ealey	fath in law	widr.	about 78		formerly lab. in receipt of parochial relief	Dunford Wilts.
67	Fanny Cook	hd.	wid.		50	retailer of beer	C.
	Chas. "	son	u.	18		shoemaker	"
	Jn. Somerbee	lodger	widr.	70		(ag. lab.) working on the road.	Burghclere Hants.
68	Chas. Cuell	hd.	mar.	26		farm lab.	C.
	Sarah "	w.	mar.		25		Mitchelmersh
	Hen. "	son		4		sch.	C.
	Jane Elizth. Cuell	d.			3	"	"
	Thos. "	son		1			"

Name and surname of each person who abode in the house on the night of 30th Mar. 1851	Relation to head of the family	Condition	Age: Male	Age: Female	Rank, profession, or occupation	Where born
69 Jas. Mathew Davis	hd.	u.	23		blacksmith	Carshalton Surrey
Emily "	sister	u.		18		Barton Stacey Hants.
Sophia Sarah "	visitor	u.		25	milliner dressmaker	Carshalton Surrey
70 Phil. Jacob	hd.	mar.	47		Rector of Crawley with Hunton Chapel	Reath Glam.
Anna Sophia Jacob	w.	mar.		44	Clergyman's wife	Teston Kent.
Edith " "	d.			14	sch. at home	C.
Gertd. Louisa "	d.			13	" " "	"
Isabel Margt. "	d.			10	" " "	"
Edgar "	son		6		" " "	"
Ernest Hen. "	son		23 mths.			"
Eliza Herring	s.	wid.		43	nurse	Penton Hants.
Emily Eliza Herring	s.	u.		18	nursery maid	Winchester
Clarinda Bramble	s.	u.		48	house s.	C.
71 Thos. Kellow [1]	hd.	widr.	75		lab.	Winterbourne Stoke, Wilts.
72 Geo. Bennett	house holder	mar.	45		lab.	East Cholderton Hants.
Charlotte "	w.	mar.		41		Chilbolton
Emma "	d.	u.		17		C.
Jas. "	son		8		sch.	"
Jn. "	son		5		"	"
Edmund "	son		3			"
73 Wm. Parker [2]	hd.	mar.	about 38		lab.	Laverstock Hants.
Hannah "	w.	mar.		40		Great Stanmore Middx.

[1] New Road, Warren House.

[2] New Barn Farm.

74	Hen. Weston [1]	hd.	mar.	42		lab.	C.
	Maria "	w.	mar.		37		Stoke Charity Hants.
	Jn. "	son		11		ploughboy	C.
	Eliz. "	d.			10	sch.	"
	Geo. "	son		4		"	"
	Mary "	d.			3	"	"
75	Jacob H. Courtney [1]	hd.	mar.	39		farmer 900 ac.	Barton Stacey Hants.
	Eliz. "	w.			37	farmer's wife	C.
	Eliz. "	d.			10		"
	Harriet "	d.			8		"
	Maria Balding	governess	u.		21		Newbury Berks.
	Jane Burn	s.	u.		20	house s.	Longstock Hants.
	Maria Perren	s.	u.		24	" "	Overton
	Jn. Hill	s.	mar.	36		farm s.	C.
	Jn. Levi	s.	u.	16		" "	Long parish
	Jas. Spencer	s.		18		" "	Bishop Sutton
	Geo. Bramble	s.		16		" "	C.
	Ed. Bramble	s.		14		" "	"
	Nic. Earwaker	s.		19		" "	Bramdean
	Chas. Steele	s.		16		" "	C.
76	Thos. Paige [2]	hd.	mar.	38		farmer of 124 ac. employing 5 labourers	C.
	Hannah "	w.	mar.		37		Wallop.
	Jn. Thos. "	son		13			C.
	Mary "	d.			11	sch.	"
	Sarah "	d.			7	"	"
	Chas. "	son		5		"	"
	Ann "	d.			4		"

[1] New Barn Farm.

[2] Crofts Farm.

	Name and surname of each person who abode in the house on the night of 30th Mar. 1851	Relation to head of the family	Condition	Age: Male	Age: Female	Rank, profession, or occupation	Where born
	Wm. Paige	son		1			C.
	Chas. Butler	s.		13		farm s.	Littleton
	Mary Harmwood	s.			34	house s.	Wallop.
77	Wm. Tongs[1]	hd.	widr.	65		carter	Week
	Charlotte "	d.	u.		28	dressmaker	C.
	Ellen "	grdd.			3		"
78	Robt. Holdaway	hd.	mar.	59		carpenter	Mitcheldever
	Sally "	w.	mar.		59		Kingsclere
	Eliz. Hayes	grdd.			8	farmer's d.	Itchen Abbas.
79	Fredk. Wake[2]	hd.	widr.	41		lab.	Sparsholt Hants.
	Mary "	d.			9		" "
	Jas. "	son		7			" "
80	Jn. Miles	hd.	mar.	69		farm lab.	Lower Clatford
	Jane "	d.	u.		19	domestic s. at home	Littleton
81	Joseph Sandom	hd.	mar.	36		farm labourer	Littleton
	Dinah "	w.	mar.		33		Wonston
	Lloyd "	son		6		child at home	C.
	Sarah "	d.			4	" " "	"
	Ernest "	son		5 mths.		" " "	"
82	Jas. Cockman[3]	hd.	mar.	44		brick & lime burner	[blank]
	Sarah "	w.	mar.		45	burner's wife	[blank]

[1] Crofts Cottage. [2] Norwood Cottage. [3] Norwood Brickkiln.

83	Sarah Alleee [1]	hd.	wid.		65	annuitant	Whitchurch Hants.
	Wm. "	son	u.	37		farmer of 679 ac., employing 22 men	C.
	Sarah "	d.	u.		35		"
	Thos. "	son	u.	33		banker	"
	Jane Hayter	s.	u.		55	house s.	Wallop.
	S. May	s.	u.		17	" "	Littlesombourne
	Jane Freemantle	s.	u.		11	" "	C.
	Jas. Lane	s.	u.	14		" "	Upsombourne
84	Hen. Reeves [2]	hd.	mar.	50		farmer 400 ac. employing 12 labourers	Bossington Hants.
	Sarah "	w.	mar.		30		Andover
	Sarah Kersley	visitor	u.		20		Litchfield
	Anne Butcher	s.	u.		21	house s.	Wonston
	Wm. Clarke	s.	u.	22		general s.	Kingsombourne

No. of houses inhabited = 79.
" " " uninhabited = 3.
" " males = 203.
" " females = 200.
total = 403.
Persons not enumerated as inmates of any dwelling house = 5.

[1] Rookley Farm.

[2] Rookley House.

§§ 60. Summaries of the Censuses of the Civil Parish of Crawley, 1871–1921.

All the material in this section, here printed in the form received, was supplied by the census officials. The returns for each household could not be legally divulged: only the summaries are available for use. Unfortunately, some of the categories changed from decade to decade. The existence of a boy's academy in the parish is a disturbing factor. Twice the academy's inhabitants were listed and once not. The decline in the population of the village has been obscured by the inclusion of the academy in 1901 and 1921.

In the following table an attempt is made to present the chief changes in occupations and other conditions in the period 1841–1921. Because the census inquiries were not uniform at the different times, the figures particularly for 1841 and 1851[1] are not always comparable or reliable.

OCCUPATIONS AND CONDITIONS IN THE CIVIL PARISH OF CRAWLEY[1]

SUMMARY FROM CENSUS DATA, 1841–1921

	1841	1851	1871	1881	1891	1901	1911	1921
						[502]		[563]
Total population	372	403	411	455	410	363	481	412
Children under 15	123	164	150	168	147	109	127	103
Farmers	5	6	8	7	6	5	1	4
Agricultural laborers	68	74[2]	57	56	67[3]	32	37	50
Shepherds			8	12	11	3	4	4
Dom. servants (indoor)	17[4]	28	37	43	16	24	34	36
Dom. servants (outdoor)	9[5]	11[6]	12	21	21	29	37	23
Trainer and grooms (racing stables)		1	15	20	18			
Builders	8	8	9	21		21	10	13
Living on means and retired			5	5	3	10	6	8
Receiving public support		6	8	3	9			

[1] The academy on the borders of the parish is omitted, except for the figures in brackets.
[2] Agricultural laborers, laborers, plowboys, shepherd's boy.
[3] Probably includes some that should be listed under Dom. servants (indoor).
[4] Female servants — 14, housekeepers — 3.
[5] Male servants.
[6] Farm servants, 1 gardener, 2 woodmen.

Perhaps the chief changes registered in this table are the following: the diminution in the number of children, the decline of

[1] See above, §§ 58, pp. 650 ff. and §§ 59, pp. 659 ff.

the yeoman class, the diminution in the number of shepherds, the rise and fall of the racing stables, the increase in the number of unoccupied persons residing in Crawley, the increase in servants, and the decline of pauperism.

1871 CENSUS

Civil Parish of Crawley (Hants) — Hunton Civil Parish excluded

Population 411 (206 males and 205 females)
Children under 15 years of age — 77 males and 73 females
Persons born within the Civil Parish — 109 males and 81 females
" " outside " " " — 97 " " 124 "
(none outside England and Wales)

Occupations (Some Persons Occupied under 15 Years of Age)

	Males	Females
Farmers	8	—
Agricultural labourers (so described)	57	—
Shepherds	8	—
Indoor domestic servants	—	37
Outdoor " "	12	—
Trainer and grooms (racing stables)	15	—
Building trade	9	—
All others occupied	28	13
Living on means and retired	1	4
Supported by Union	3	5

1881 CENSUS

Crawley Civil Parish — Hunton Civil Parish excluded

Population 455	Males 233	Females 222
Children under 15 years of age 168	77	91
Born within the Civil Parish	116	92
Born outside the Civil Parish	117	130

Includes one each in Ireland and Sicily.
Includes two in Scotland and one in U. S. A.

Occupations (One Person Occupied under 15 Years of Age — an agricultural labourer)

	Males	Females
Farmers	6	1
Agricultural labourers	56	—
Shepherds	12	—
Indoor domestic servants	5	38
Outdoor " "	21	—

	Males	Females
Trainer and grooms (racing stables)	20	—
Building trade	21	—
All others occupied	24	15
Living on means and retired	4	1
Supported by Union	2	1

1891 CENSUS

Civil Parish of Crawley (Hants) — Hunton Civil Parish excluded

	Males	Females
Population 410	219	191
Children under 15 years of age	71	76
Persons born within the Civil Parish	108	78
" " outside " " "	111	113

Including 4 males and 2 females born in Ireland, 1 female born in Switzerland, and 1 female born in Brazil.

Occupations (Some Persons Occupied under 15 Years of Age)

	Males	Females
Farmers	5	1
Farmers' sons	3	—
Agricultural labourers	67	—
Shepherds	11	—
Indoor domestic servants	2	14
Outside " "	21	—
Trainer and grooms (racing stables)	18	—
All others occupied	18	—
Living on means and retired	2	1
Supported by Union	4	5

1901 CENSUS

Civil Parish of Crawley (Hants) — Hunton Civil Parish excluded

Population 502 (304 males and 198 females; of these 120 males and 19 females were enumerated in Eastman's Royal Naval Academy). The figures below are exclusive of persons enumerated in the Naval Academy, the figures for which are given separately.

	Males	Females
Children under 15 years of age	55	54
Persons born within the Civil Parish	62	50
" " outside " " "	122	129
Including Scotland	5	2
Ireland	—	1
India	1	1
Germany	1	—

Occupations (Some Persons Occupied under 15 Years of Age)

	Males	Females
Farmers	5	—
Farmers' sons	1	—
Agricultural labourers	32	—
Shepherds	3	—
Indoor domestic servants	1	23
Outdoor " "	29	—
Carpenters and joiners	11	—
Bricklayers	10	—
All others occupied	30	12
Living on means and retired	8	2

Eastman's Royal Naval Academy

Persons 139 (120 males and 19 females)
Children under 15 years of age — 77 males and 2 females
Persons born within the Civil Parish — 1 female only

Persons born outside the Civil Parish —	120 males	18 females
England and Wales	93	16
Scotland	3	—
Ireland	11	1
India	8	—
Ceylon	1	—
Canada	1	—
South Africa	1	—
Brazil	1	—
Germany	1	—
Greece	—	1

Occupations	Males	Females
School teachers	4	1
Indoor domestic servants	1	15

1911 CENSUS

Civil Parish of Crawley (Hants)

Population 481 (263 males and 218 females)
Children under 15 years of age — 67 males 60 females

Persons born within the Civil Parish	134 males	80 females
" " outside " " "	129 "	138 "
Including Canada	1	1
Scotland	4	8
Germany	1	2
Ireland	1	1
India	—	2
France	1	—

OCCUPATIONS (SOME PERSONS OCCUPIED UNDER 15 YEARS OF AGE)

	Males	Females
Farmers	1	—
Agricultural labourers	37	—
Shepherds	4	—
General labourers (poultry farm)	3	—
Indoor domestic servants	5	29
Outdoor " "	37	—
Carpenters and joiners	6	—
Bricklayers and their labourers	4	—
All others occupied	32	9
Living on means and retired	5	1

Eastman's School, Northwood Park, was on holiday at the date of the Census.

1921 CENSUS

CIVIL PARISH OF CRAWLEY (HANTS)

Population 563 (342 males and 221 females; of these 133 males and 18 females were connected with Clayesmore School, Northwood Park).

The figures below are exclusive of persons connected with the School, the figures for which are given separately.

Children under 15 years of age	63 males	40 females
Persons born within the Civil Parish	57	36
" " outside " " "	152	167
England and Wales	141	156
Scotland	7	6
Greece	2	—
Portugal	1	—
Sweden	1	—
Germany	—	2
Egypt	—	1
India	—	1
Australia	—	1

OCCUPATIONS (SOME PERSONS OCCUPIED UNDER 15 YEARS OF AGE)

	Males	Females
Farmers	4	—
Agricultural labourers	50	—
Shepherds	4	—
Indoor domestic servants	7	29
Outdoor " "	23	—
Market gardeners and nurserymen	7	—
Carpenters and joiners	8	—
Builders and their labourers	5	—
Other occupations	32	6
Living on means and retired	8	—

The greater part of the occupied population was connected with Crawley Court and the Estate.

CLAYESMORE SCHOOL, NORTHWOOD PARK

Persons 151 (133 males 18 females)
Children under 15 years of age — 70 males — females
Persons born within the Civil Parish — none

		Males	Females
Persons born outside the Civil Parish		133	18
	England and Wales	90	16
	Scotland	6	2
	Ireland	6	—
	Canada	2	—
	Switzerland	1	—
	India	2	—
	China	2	—
	Holland	1	—
	Ceylon	2	—
	Ecuador	1	—
	Montenegro	1	—
	Egypt	2	—
	Roumania	4	—
	Brazil	6	—
	Spain	1	—
	Turkey	1	—
	Russsia	1	—
	South Africa	2	—
	Portugal	1	—
	Italy	1	—

Occupations		
School teachers	11	—
Indoor domestic servants	1	17
Sick nurse	—	1
Other occupations	3	—

§§ 61. Private Census of Crawley Village, Sept., 1927, by J. O. Robertson, Esq.

This is a survey of the village, not the parish. It was made by the estate agent in Crawley.

There were 67 houses and bothies in which dwelt 187 members of families, 28 servants, and 7 lodgers. The total population was 222. There were 61 children absent, all but 4 living nearby. Of the 61, there were 32 who were engaged in rural pursuits and 29 living in towns. It would seem that Crawley's agriculture did not require all the agricultural labor that the village produced.

Though the population was smaller than at any other time in the Modern Period, the people were probably better off in houses, furniture, and equipment than ever before. There were 43 of the households that had at least one bicycle each, 16 one radio, and 13 one automobile.

Of the heads of the households, 31 were concerned with agriculture and 4 with personal service, both groups being connected with the Court. Besides, there were 7 house-builders (or repairers), 5 public servants, 5 retired or disabled, and 7 widows. Of the 55 heads who were active and not widows, about 37 householders served Crawley Court directly and exclusively. Probably only about 10 were tolerably independent of the Court, the remaining 8 being only occasionally and partly independent.

In the Census of 1851 the chief people in the village were six tenant farmers, some of them obviously prosperous. In 1927 there was one towering estate and predominating Court. At the bottom of the social ladder were the laborers and servants, with a few artisans. In between were the estate agent, the agricultural expert, a tutor, a clergyman, and a retired admiral.

Occupier	Name of house	No. in family	Servants	Occupation of head	Occupation of others	Years in Crawley	Cycle	Auto	Radio	Lodgers	Absent children: How many	Absent children: Where	Absent children: Rural	Absent children: Urban
Philippi	Crawley Court	3	14	landowner		26		yes	yes					
"	Garden Cottage	1		gardener		3	yes							
"	" Bothy	2		gardener		4	yes							
"	Stable "	4		groom-valet		20	yes	yes	yes					
						25								
Ryder		2		widow		14	yes				2	1 near 1 abroad		2
Davis	Sunnyside	2		retired blacksmith		60	yes	yes			1	near		1
Graves		2		chauffeur		8		yes	yes					
E. J. Brown		3		gardener	1 gardener	40	yes							
Short		2		carpenter		20	yes							
Woolford	Post Office	3		postmaster		24	yes		yes					
Clark		2		farm laborer		10	yes				1	near	1	
Clark		1		auto hire		10		yes						
Booth		3		motor driver (farm)		26			yes					
Godwin	Shop and Bakery	1		master baker		40	yes							
Steele	Ivy Cottage	4		electrician		35		yes	yes					
Cox		5		garden laborer	1 garden laborer	40	yes				1	near		1
Johnston	White House	1	2	widow		2		yes	yes					
Twiton		2		garden laborer		60	yes				1	near		1
Coldicott		5		butler		1		yes						
E. Booth		3		garden carter		50					6	near	5	1
Stock	Police Cottage	2		policeman		1	yes							
Mrs. Piper	Orchard Cottage	1		widow		70					4	near	2	2
Green	" "	2		widow	farm laborer	20	yes			2	4	near	4	

Occupier	Name of house	No. in family	Servants	Occupation of head	Occupation of others	Years in Crawley	Cycle	Auto	Radio	Lodgers	Absent children: How many	Where	Rural	Urban
Williams	Orchard Cottage	1		dairymaid		8	yes							
C. Booth	" "	3		builder's laborer		28	yes							
Rutt		3		farm laborer	farm laborer	63	yes		yes		6	near	4	2
Rolfe		3		farm laborer		8	yes							
Martin		3		farm laborer		40	yes			2				
Brewer		4		gamekeeper	1 farm laborer 1 keeper	30	yes			1	2	near		2
C. Steele		5		farm laborer	farm laborer	60	yes							
H. Green		3		farm laborer		25								
Judd		3		baker	1 garden laborer	25	yes				1	near	1	
Wibberley	Pond House	4		farm manager	assistant farm manager	5		yes	yes		1	near		1
White		2		shepherd		4	yes							
Brown		2		widow		50					3	near	1	2
Wayman		1		pensioned laborer		60					2	near	2	
Rev. Irwin	Rectory	2	2	clergyman		5		yes	yes		1	near		1
Kelly	Paige's	3		farm laborer	1 gardener	50	yes							
Pledge	Manor House	2	3	tutor		26					1	abroad		1
Thick		3		carpenter	1 electrician	24	yes		yes					
Horne		3		shepherd		60	yes				3	near	3	
Sellex	Fox and Hounds	1	1	innkeeper		55	yes			1				
Kimber		4		roadman	1 pensioner	12	yes							
Green		2		farm laborer		23								
Shepherd		3		gardener		15	yes							
Salter		3		gamekeeper		2	yes							

Occupier	Name of house	No. in family	Servants	Occupation of head	Occupation of others	Years in Crawley	Cycle	Auto	Radio	Lodgers	Absent children			
											How many	Where	Rural	Urban
Hall		2		farm laborer		25				1	3	near	3	
Jellett		3		farm laborer		20	yes							
Wilson	Oak House	1		painter		24								
Bailey	" "	3		bricklayer		20	yes							
Douglas	" "	2		shopkeeper	1 carpenter	24	yes							
Gaiger	" "	4		farm laborer		35	yes							
Stevens	" "	5		widow	2 farm boys	30	yes							
Fish	School House	2		schoolmistress	motor engineer	15		yes	yes					
Kenton		4		disabled soldier		20	yes							
Lay		5		farm laborer	2 farm laborers	20	yes							
Cuell		5		widow	2 farm laborers	50	yes				3	near	3	
Robertson		2	1	estate agent		26		yes	yes		1	Glasgow		1
	Court Laundry	3		laundresses		*ca.* 5	yes							
Broadway	Red House	2	1	estate carpenter retired		60	yes		yes		4	1 Scotland 3 near	2	2
Piper		4		cowman		25	yes							
Hall		4		farm laborer		25								
Cuell		1		engineer		60			yes		3	near		3
Browning	Dower House	2	4	retired admiral		4		yes	yes		1	near		1
Willis	Dower Cottage	6		chauffeur		8	yes				2	near	1	1
Phillips	" "	2		gardener		1								
Riggs		3		estate carpenter	apprentice carpenter	25	yes				4	near		4
Total		184	28				43	13	16	7	61		32	29

NOTES [of Mr. Robertson]

Column 3 indicates the number in family living in the house.

Column 4 indicates the number of servants in addition.

Column 11 indicates the number of lodgers.

Thus the total of the three columns (222) gives the population of the village. Absent children are not included in the population.

Many of the householders are the children of other householders.

The most striking feature of the list is the number of small families.

The number of lodgers is smaller than is the case in most villages. This is accounted for by the fact that provision is made for single men who have their own accommodation in bothies and are included as householders. Also a number of men employed in the village live in neighbouring villages.

The number of people working allotments is so small that I have not specified them. The reason is that Mr. Philippi enlarged the garden of anyone who wanted it and consequently most of the people have as much ground close to their cottages as they can conveniently work.

19 September 1927

§§ 62. Present Agricultural Methods, September, 1928, by Professor Thomas Wibberley.

During the late war Professor Wibberley played a prominent part in Irish agriculture. It was logical that he should be called to Crawley after the war to increase the yield and decrease the yearly deficit. His work was at first successful (1922–25), but subsequently (1926–28) the progress in the face of uncontrollable difficulties was uneven. It seems that he has somewhat turned his interests from farm management to the production of high-quality seeds. His account of experiences in Crawley is here printed in his own words.

Not until the spring of 1917 did those who were directing the destinies of the war realize that the plough furrows, in a war essentially a trench war, were of parallel importance. Then followed a panicky food production campaign. Farmers were exhorted to cultivate every available acre, but circumstances were decidedly unfavourable to the adoption of such advice. In the first instance, the men necessary for the cultivation of the land had long joined the fighting forces. In the case of Crawley, the present Squire of the Manor, George Philippi, at the outbreak of the war enlisted in a Cavalry Regiment. Long before the Conscription Act of 1916 had been passed, almost every available farm labourer from Crawley was already enrolled in the County or

Hampshire Regiment. When food became the vital factor of the hour, with a zeal tempered more by patriotism than foresight, the owner of the Crawley Estate sent word from the Front to plough every available acre, regardless of cost. Those in charge of the Estate, with even less thought than its owner, carried out the latter's instructions literally. Steam and tractor ploughs (some of them absolutely useless for the purpose) were at once brought in, but instead of being utilized for food production on land already in cultivation, the area of which was already considerable, these implements were set to plough hundreds of acres of useless barren down land. This land — as aërial photographs show — had last been under cultivation when England had a Celtic population. Attempts were made to replace the absent labour by introducing land girls — mostly town bred and therefore useless. The net result was that the land got fearfully foul with weeds. Artificial fertilizers not being procurable, the increased cultivated area resulted in an all-round decrease in crops and stock.

For two or three years after the war, conditions were not very favourable for any scheme of land reclamation. Agricultural requirements, seed, manures, feeding stuffs, implements, and labour were only procurable at prices far above their economic value.

Apart from the latter factors, it is extremely doubtful whether, given every facility, the three bailiffs, under whose direction the farms were worked, could ever have brought the land back to a proper state of cultivation. Their methods were purely empirical and they were completely lacking in scientific knowledge and organizing capacity.

This serves to focus attention on one of the many weak features of the English agricultural system of education. We have many well-equipped agricultural colleges and experimental stations. The whole attention of these institutions seems to be directed to purely scientific work.

On the other hand, the average practical farmer and bailiff is devoid of all scientific knowledge. Between the scientific and practical worker there exists a very wide gap which little or no effort has been made to bridge.

As far as the agricultural labourer is concerned, no attempt whatever is made to give his early education an agricultural bias. The children in the village school at Crawley receive precisely the same education as the children living in the heart of London. Their little heads are crammed with such facts as that Manchester is famed for its cotton industry, Sheffield for the manufacture of steel, and Liverpool for its shipping. They have to memorize such features as the width of the Ganges and the height of the Himalaya, though they may never have to swim the former nor climb the latter. Did one wish to devise a system of education, with the specific object of enticing rural labour to industrial centres, one could not improve upon the existing system.

Not only was the land of Crawley in a foul unproductive condition, but the implements and buildings were in a very dilapidated state. It would probably have been more economical at the outset to have scrapped all the implements and replaced them with new ones; but, at the time the writer took over the management of the farms (June, 1922), many new implements were unprocurable. Due to the unsettled state of the coal and iron industries in the post-war years, and due also to the general disorganization, implement manufacturers, who during the war had been manufacturing munitions, had scarcely recommenced the making of agricultural implements.

There is an old English agricultural saw: "One year's seeding is seven years' weeding." It certainly proved to be the case as regards Crawley. As already stated, the writer took on the management of the lands in June, 1922. Not until the present autumn, 1928, could one say that the land had reached a fairly clean state of husbandry. In practically every year the accounts show that the actual cost of cleaning the land, cultivating and sowing, has been from £2,000 to £3,000 more per annum than the estimated value of the crops in the soil at the time of the annual valuation. The cost of repairing buildings and machinery has varied from £500 to £1,000 per annum, whilst in 1928, now that the land is clean, the actual expenditure on labour is 40% lower than in 1922, though the area under crops is far greater than in that year.

As to the actual method of cultivation and management a brief description may be of interest. For some years the whole tendency of British agriculture had been to change from arable to pastoral farming. Such arable as still exists is more or less confined to the light, easily worked land, of which Crawley is typical.

The present arable rotations commonly consist of slight modifications of the old Norfolk rotation. These rotations are entirely unsuitable for present-day conditions. In the first place, from 80 to 90% of the crops must be sown in a very brief period in spring time, and harvested in an equally brief period in autumn. The result is that the rotations do not provide an even distribution of labour throughout the year. Another drawback is that great harvesting risks have to be faced, and it has often happened that through bad weather at harvest time the corn is either totally destroyed or much depreciated in value, through wet weather. Also, under the Norfolk rotation and its modifications, a goodly proportion of the land is left idle during the late autumn, winter, and early spring months.

To overcome these and other difficulties, the writer some thirty years ago devised a system of intensive arable farming known as "continuous cropping." This system is planned to (1) give a more even distribution of labour throughout the year; (2) to reduce harvesting risks by growing a large area of fodder and forage crops, which thrive best under wet weather conditions; (3) to provide a great amount of work for tractors, by planning to have a large amount of land cultivated and sown in the summer and early autumn when wet weather conditions help — instead of hinder — tractor work and when the days are longer; (4) to reduce the labour of saving crops and manuring the land by folding sheep who consume the crops on the land; (5) to reduce the expenditure for feeding stuffs by growing albuminous farm crops, e. g. vetch silage, vetch hay, and sainfoin; (6) to increase the available soil nitrogen by growing legumes; and (7) to breed new types of forage crops and seed cereals, the latter suitable for light-land farming.

As compared with live-stock farming on pasturage, forage cropping has many advantages. In the first place, under a forage cropping system more than double the amount of animal products can be obtained from the land, as compared with the output from similar land under grass, more employment is found on the land, and one is not so much at the mercy of the season. For instance, in a dry summer the hay crop is invariably short and pastures are bare. In such a season it is comparatively easy to increase the forage cropping area and more liberally to manure the crops, thereby providing an abundance of winter keep.

As an example of a typical continuous cropping rotation carried out at Crawley, we may give the following:

1st year Autumn sown wheat, with which is sown in spring time yellow trefoil and rye grass

2nd year Trefoil folded off from April to mid-June, followed by 3 sowings as follows:

		Fed off
A	1/3rd sown mid-May, rape kale	Jan., Feb., March
B	1/3rd sown end of May, marrow kale	Nov. and Dec.
C	1/3rd sown June "Hardy Greens"	Oct. and Nov.

3rd year C and ½B sown Jan. "Quite Content" oats
½B and A sown spring barley

4th year	A	Giant Star rye and rye grass sown in autumn of 3rd year	consumed April
	½B	Trifolium early red sown in spring of 3rd year	" May
	½B	Trifolium late red sown in autumn of 3rd year	" June
	½C	Vetches sown autumn of 3rd year	" July
	½C	Vetches sown Feb. and March of 4th year	" August

5th year Autumn sown wheat with rotation grasses and clover sown in spring

6th year (1) Rotation grasses cut for hay June
(2) Rotation aftermath September

7th year Rotation grasses — first crop consumed May — aftermath cut for hay late July

8th year Rotation grass ley broken for wheat as in first year

A study of the rotation will show that continuous green feed is provided all the year round, and that prior to the sowing of a cereal crop a forage crop is consumed on the land. The necessity

(*a*) RAPE-KALE — A NEW FORAGE CROP, BRED BY CROSSING GIANT RAPE AND CURLY KALE, PROFESSOR WIBBERLEY IN THE FOREGROUND

A photograph, taken about 1926 and reproduced with the permission of *Country Life*, England

(*b*) TWIN CITY TRACTOR TURNING IN VETCH STUBBLE AFTER FOLDING WITH SHEEP

A photograph, taken about 1926 and reproduced with the permission of *Country Life*, England

for using carted farmyard manure is done away with; expensive crops, such as swedes and mangolds, requiring hand labour for hoeing are practically dispensed with.

As often happens, we get a surplus of such forage crops as trefoil, vetches, and trifolium. These can be converted into hay or into ensilage on a stacking plan devised by the writer. The reader may not be familiar with some of the crops mentioned. Rape kale (Brassica Wibberleii) is a hybrid plant produced by the writer by crossing the common curly kale and giant rape. It is sufficiently hardy to stand the severest winter and is also absolutely immune to finger and toe disease and mildew — two of the greatest pests of the Brassicas in these countries.

Marrow kale (Brassica Wibberleii 2) is a further cross of rape kale and marrow stem kale. This grows more quickly than rape kale and does not contain the thick central stalk of the marrow stem parent, which stalk was found in practice to tear the wool off the sheep, and necessitated a great amount of labour to clear off the land after the crop had been folded off and before ploughing for the succeeding crop.

The "Quite Content" oat is a new hybrid bred by the writer by crossing "Svalof Victory" with "Grey Winter" oat. It is very hardy and suitable for sowing in January, and in consequence immune from the attack of frit-fly. It is also very resistant to drought, and very productive, yielding 10 qrs. per acre and indeed often 30 cwt.

As to the wheats, these are all pure line strains, some being merely selected, others, like "Yeoman's Master," being new hybrids. In these parts, until recent years, wheats were always grown on heavy land. These strains have been developed so as to be productive and drought resistant, and therefore suitable for lighter soils. They have come very much into favour in recent years, so much so that probably 75% of the wheat area in southwestern England is now sown with seed raised at Crawley.

In competition with wheats from all over England, these wheats obtained first prize in every class, and also the special prize for the best wheat on exhibition at the competition held at the Birmingham Show in December, 1927.

In order to give an insight into the increased output from the soil, the following table is reproduced from an article of H. G. Robinson, B. Sc., Vice-Principal of one of our leading agricultural colleges. The article appeared in *Country Life*, August 7th, 1926.

	1922			1923			1924			1925		
	£	s.	d.	£	s.	d.	£	s.	d.	£	s.	d.
Corn Sales......	1,692	3	2	573	8	6	1,282	1	7	7,857	11	11
Sheep Sales......	3,375	0	11½	2,270	16	11	2,705	4	1	4,051	11	9
Wool Sales......	298	5	6	215	16	6	280	4	11	559	8	8
Dairy Sales......	858	16	1½	895	18	2	929	17	9	1,162	6	6
Totals........	£6,224	5	9	£3,956	0	1	£5,197	8	4	£13,630	18	10

	£	s.	d.	£	s.	d.	£	s.	d.	£	s.	d.
Labour.........	5,749	18	10½	5,266	18	0	4,811	14	10	5,360	18	8
Fertilizers.......	1,624	9	3	869	10	3	967	10	9	1,395	14	1
Feeding Stuffs...	1,559	14	1	1,322	9	11	1,372	8	8	1,601	8	0
Hire of machinery, and coal......	1,212	13	3	730	7	4	1,389	13	0	1,648	13	7
Totals........	£10,146	15	5½	£8,189	5	6	£8,541	7	3	£10,006	14	4

Later returns are not given because conditions were abnormal. In 1926 mildew attacked corn crops throughout the British Isles, reducing the average yields by 40%. A similar disaster has probably not occurred for sixty years. Prices for sheep also slumped terribly in the same year. We have had a record harvest in the present year (1928). Sheep, milk, and wool have also advanced in prices, returning to the 1925 level, and the output for 1928 will probably exceed that of 1925.

It is necessary in providing the above figures to refer to the very low state of fertility to which the land had fallen by 1922 and to remind the reader that such a large increase in output and decrease in expenditure would not be possible under average conditions.

It will be easily understood that to carry out such a complicated rotation of cropping, as outlined above, on an area of over 2,000 acres, calls for a considerable amount of organization. Personal supervision is impossible, and written instructions giving details of cropping, manuring, and sequence of feeding would necessitate a very large amount of written material which in the end would only confuse the minds of the men with whom one has to deal. As far as possible, the actual management has been departmentalized, but this soon reaches its limits in actual farming practice. Nevertheless, it is necessary for the actual farm manager, the two foremen, the head shepherd, and the motor lorry driver to know exactly how the land is to be cropped during at least one year.

In order to dispense with written details, the writer devised a coloured map scheme of cropping. A distinct separate colour is used for each crop. In the top left corner of each field, a small rectangular insertion is made, indicating the second crop to be sown; and in the bottom right corner, a triangular insertion is put to indicate the third crop. A field coloured green indicates a field of wheat for the current year. A yellow rectangular insertion, placed as stated above, means yellow trefoil is to be sown amongst the growing wheat, whilst a blue triangle in the bottom right corner indicates that rape kale is to follow the yellow trefoil.

By this system the shepherd can see at a glance, month by month, what kind of food will be available for the flock. If, for instance, he has been feeding his animals on astringent food like clover aftermath and if the next change is to hardy greens, he will commence to feed his flock a little astringent food like cotton cake to counteract the laxative tendencies of the green food. Again, say there is danger of the supply of rape kale being exhausted before rye is ready, he can automatically supplement his food supply by the use of hay or ensilage.

As regards the motor lorry driver, part of his duty is to transport implements from one part of the farm to another. He knows the sequence of cropping and the different implements required for each crop. By the time the horses and tractors assemble to commence tillage or harvesting operations, all the implements should be already in the field. This prevents an enormous amount of loss of time. The manager and foreman can also lay their plans to mix fertilizers for each particular field, work which is done in wet wintry weather, when work out of doors is not possible.

The farming scheme is also arranged so that fields of wheat, oats, barley, and rotation aftermath adjoin. In harvest weather, it is often possible to cut and also to stack wheat, when oats or barley are not fit. If the weather is very good, the man in charge of a harvesting gang will take advantage of the good weather conditions to harvest the barley. Less favourable weather will be devoted to oat harvesting, whilst in dampish weather the wheat harvest will be attended to. If the weather is too wet for cereal cutting or carting, conditions are usually admirable for ploughing and sowing the rotation grass aftermath with wheat. Accordingly all horses, tractors, and men proceed with such work.

As to the future of the system, it would seem that with suitable modification, it may yet prove the salvation of arable farming in these parts. Fortunately, the gentleman farmer type in recent years has adopted the system, and since this class has been largely responsible for the introduction of every new method in our agricultural practice, one may expect that history may again repeat itself.

§§ 63. Social Conditions in Crawley in the Twentieth Century, by F. W. Pledge, M.A.

The author of this all-too-brief description of recent conditions in Crawley has made a careful study of the general history of the village, published privately in 1907, and has lived through the period here described. He is of those who exist more or less apart from, but not socially unconnected with, Crawley Court. The rector has been the forerunner, if not the nucleus, of this group. This group does not cultivate the soil nor derive an income from the land. To them Crawley Village is a good place in which to live. Like the teachers in the parish school, the writer of this section is a cultural link with the outside world. He prepares young men for Cambridge and for Oxford. In his square brick house, modestly set back from the village street behind a stretch of green sward, reading and studying must be congenial pursuits. A stone's throw away is the ancient pond, and in the rear are the broad fields of the village. What he has observed during his stay in Crawley is best told in his own well-chosen words.

"To the left lies the dilapidated and unattractive village of Crawley." Thus summarily a *Guide to Hampshire* dismissed

Crawley in 1900. Nor was the curt description unwarranted. For, apart from the general effects of agricultural depression, the Crawley Court Estate and the farm properties throughout the parish had been in the market for many years. In consequence there was rapid material deterioration. Many of the cottages were ruinous and derelict. The population was aged and impoverished. Sickness was prevalent and seasonal unemployment common.

Happily, the property passed into the hands of a new owner,[1] a warm-hearted philanthropist, whose hobby was building. Soon Crawley was transformed into a model village. New houses were built, while old ones were reconstructed, adorned and improved. Crawley, resurrected and rendered architecturally attractive, became the goal of the curious visitor. Sickness diminished to an astonishing degree and increased prosperity was visibly revealed in the healthier, better-clothed, children of the labourer.

Nor did the reforms end here. A store was opened, supplying goods to the villagers at absolutely wholesale prices. A bath-house was established and well patronized. A club was instituted, containing a comfortable reading and entertainment hall and a billiard room with three tables. The languishing cricket and football clubs were lavishly supported and a Saturday half-holiday inaugurated even for agricultural labourers. This, since become general, was then entirely novel in rural districts.

Other changes in social conditions have been due to legislation and administrative progress, and so are common to the whole country. The Education Act of 1902 threw the maintenance of the School on the public rates. Hitherto it had been largely dependent on intermittent and uncertain voluntary contributions, with the result that the salaries of the underpaid teachers were often in arrears while the School was understaffed and ill-equipped. All that is now a thing of the past. The buildings have been renovated and more than doubled in size and adequately furnished with all necessary apparatus.

A change too has appeared in the attitude of parents towards education. A new generation has arisen, the first of free and com-

[1] Otto Ernst Philippi, of Crawley Court, 1900–15.

pulsory primary education. A quarter of a century ago mothers and fathers were only too anxious to withdraw their children from school as soon as they were qualified to leave, often as early as twelve years of age, or to gain temporary release of them on any plausible pretext. Whereas now, when children must remain at school until the end of the term, in which they become fourteen years of age, the parents are eager to keep them there and to take advantage of all possible extensions and continuations. In fact, there has grown up generally a belief that "Education is a good thing."

The subject of education inevitably calls to mind the modern problem of Birth Control. Its exercise is obvious even in this comparatively remote village. A generation ago ninety to one hundred children attended the school. Now the village contributes only half that number. The falling-off is greater than at first sight appears. For in the meantime the age limit of enforced attendance has been appreciably raised. Formerly families of eight were frequent, and those of ten, or more, not uncommon. But among the younger generation the one-child family is only too prevalent, while a family of five is almost phenomenal. Disputes may rage as to whether Birth Restriction is a blessing or a curse, a virtue or a sin, a gospel to be propagated or a practice to be denounced, but all the while economic pressure or the increasing pursuit of pleasure silently assert themselves.

A generation ago there was an almost entire lack of recreation or relief from the monotony of daily toil. The sole relaxation for the wives was to be found in the monthly Mothers' Meeting organized and presided over by the Rector's wife. It is not without interest that the first of these now general institutions was founded in this village a little more than a century ago. Crawley, therefore, is the parent of the Mothers' Meeting. This must not be confounded with the Women's Institute, which is mainly a post-war creation, with no specifically religious or sectarian character and widespread throughout the kingdom. Its object is partly social, to unite all classes of the female population and produce a sense of community; partly educative, by means of frequent lectures and instruction in various handicrafts. In theory it is founded on a purely democratic and egalitarian basis. But in practice, so far as the election of local officers is concerned, the ancient principle of "all the best places for all the best people" seems to hold good.

Whereas at the beginning of the twentieth century many, if not most, of the adult inhabitants had rarely been further than Winchester, and, within the writer's recollection, there were women who had not been beyond the limits of the village for four or five years on end, now, thanks to the generoisty of Mr. and Mrs. Philippi, men, women and children, have at least one annual outing to Bournemouth, Southsea, or London. Contact with the outer world is maintained too by "wireless," of which there are many installations in the village. Moreover, to judge by the sounds issuing from various cottages, many of the housewives appear to do their daily work to the music of the ubiquitous gramophone. In the winter season Whist Drives and Dances are frequent and well attended.

The chief revolution, however, is in the matter of communications. Thirty years ago there was but one post a day and newspapers were already twenty-four hours old when they arrived. For long there have been two deliveries and despatches daily, while newspapers are regularly delivered each morning and even on Sundays. Before the war there was a carrier once or twice a week, taking two hours at least to reach Winchester. There are now five or six well-patronized motor-bus services daily. The small children from the outlying parts of the parish are conveyed to and from school by bus. "Joy-riding" is frequent, and the villagers are constantly "off to the pictures."

But the improvement of communications has been no unmixed benefit. Not only has the tranquil repose of the countryside vanished to be replaced by the continual drone of aëroplanes by day and night from the neighbouring air camp, the discordant clatter of motor cars and the strident pulsation of mechanical bicycles, but the roads have become increasingly dangerous as is testified by numerous and serious accidents to our people on the neighbouring highways.

In short, the once peaceful village has become a miniature of the world at large. It has come out of its isolation. Its speech conforms to the universal jargon: the ancient Doric has disappeared. It feels and thinks readily with the urban masses. It may not create opinion but it quickly responds to opinion formed elsewhere. It is characterized by the prevailing restlessness of modern life. It is easily bored. The placid yokel is no more.

INDEX

Numbers in italics indicate references of unusual importance. A continuous reference is indicated by hyphenated page numbers. Not all irregular spellings are set forth. Only the chief families are listed. A few stray villages and towns occurring only once are omitted.